THE SURVIVORS OF ISRAEL

The Survivors of Israel

A Reconsideration of the Theology
of Pre-Christian Judaism

Mark Adam Elliott

WILLIAM B. EERDMANS PUBLISHING COMPANY
GRAND RAPIDS, MICHIGAN / CAMBRIDGE, U.K.

© 2000 Wm. B. Eerdmans Publishing Co.
255 Jefferson Ave. S.E., Grand Rapids, Michigan 49503 /
P.O. Box 163, Cambridge CB3 9PU U.K.
All rights reserved

Printed in the United States of America

05 04 03 02 01 00   7 6 5 4 3 2 1

Library of Congress Cataloging-in-Publication Data

Elliott, Mark Adam, 1956-
The survivors of Israel: a reconsideration of the theology of pre-Christian Judaism /
Mark Adam Elliott.
p.   cm.
Includes bibliographical references.
ISBN 0-8028-4483-9 (paper: alk. paper)
1. Judaism — History — Post-exilic period, 586 B.C.–210 A.D. — Historiography.
2. Apocryphal books (Old Testament) — Criticism, interpretation, etc.   I. Title.
BM176.E44 2000
296'.09'014 — dc21

00-22100

To four giving parents —
Edgar† and Joy Elliott
James and Joan Koning

Contents

CONTENTS

Contents

Acknowledgments

Citations from the Bible are taken from the RSV, copyright by the Division of Christian Education of the National Council of the Churches of Christ in the United States of America, 1946, 1952; from the Apocrypha are taken from The New English Bible with the Apocrypha (New York: Oxford University Press, 1976); from the Pseudepigrapha are taken from *OTP*, vols. 1 and 2; from the major DSS are taken from A. Dupont-Sommer (*The Essene Writings from Qumran*, trans. G. Vermes [London: Basil Blackwell, 1961]); from recently published fragments of the DSS are taken from R. H. Eisenman and M. Wise (*The Dead Sea Scrolls Uncovered* [Longmead, Shaftesbury: Element, 1992]) or from F. García Martínez (*The Dead Sea Scrolls Translated: The Qumran Texts in English,* trans. W. G. E. Watson [Leiden: E. J. Brill, 1994]); from Josephus are taken from the relevant volumes in the Loeb Classical Library (Cambridge: Harvard University Press, various dates). *Citations from any of these sources, especially the Pseudepigrapha and DSS, frequently appear in an edited form without comment, or the translation is wholly that of the author,* wherever it is considered necessary to provide a clearer or more literal rendering of the original.

Abbreviations

1 En.	*1* (Ethiopic) *Enoch*
1QH	Qumran Hymn Scroll
1QM	Qumran War Scroll
1QpHab	Qumran Habakkuk Commentary
1QS	Qumran Community Rule
1QSa	Additions to the Community Rule
1QSb	Qumran Book of Blessings
2 Bar.	*2* (Syriac Apocalypse of) *Baruch*
4 Ezra	Fourth (Apocalypse of) Ezra
4QpHos	Qumran Hosea Commentary
4QpIs	Qumran Isaiah Commentary
4QpNah	Qumran Nahum Commentary
11QT	Qumran Temple Scroll
AB	Anchor Bible
AMWNE	*Apocalypticism in the Mediterranean World and the Near East* = Hellholm [1983]
Ant.	*Antiquities of the Jews* (Josephus)
AOT	*The Apocryphal Old Testament* = Sparks [1984]
APOT	*Apocrypha and Pseudepigrapha of the Old Testament* = Charles [1913a]
Aram.	Aramaic
Asc. Is.	*Ascension of Isaiah*
Ass. Mos.	*Assumption of Moses*
b.	Babylonian Talmud
BA	*Biblical Archaeologist*
BAGD	W. Bauer, W. F. Arndt, F. W. Gingrich, and F. W. Danker, *A Greek-English Lexicon of the New Testament* (Chicago: University of Chicago, 1979)

BAR	*Biblical Archaeology Review*
BJRL	*Bulletin of the John Rylands Library*
BR	*Biblical Research*
BZ	*Biblische Zeitschrift*
CBQ	*Catholic Biblical Quarterly*
CBQ(MS)	Catholic Biblical Quarterly (Monograph Series)
CCWJCW	Cambridge Commentaries on Writings of the Jewish and Christian World: 200 B.C. to A.D. 200
CD	Damascus Document
CDG	*Concise Dictionary of Geʿez* = Leslau [1989]
CRINT	Compendium Rerum Iudaicarum ad Novum Testamentum
DJD	*Discoveries in the (Judaean) Desert of Jordan*
DSS	Dead Sea Scrolls
ET	English translation
Eth.	Ethiopic
ExT	*Expository Times*
FRLANT	Forschungen zur Religion und Literatur des Alten und Neuen Testaments
Gk.	Greek
GCA	"Glossarium" in *Chrestomathia Aethiopica* (= Dillman [1866])
G-G	*A Syriac-English Glossary* = Goshen-Gottstein [1970]
Heb.	Hebrew
HUCA	*Hebrew Union College Annual*
HTR	*Harvard Theological Review*
IDB	*Interpreter's Dictionary of the Bible*
IDBS	*Interpreter's Dictionary of the Bible*, supplementary vol.
j.	Jerusalem Talmud
JBL	*Journal of Biblical Literature*
JBL(MS)	Journal of Biblical Literature (Monograph Series)
JETS	*Journal of the Evangelical Theological Society*
JJS	*Journal of Jewish Studies*
JQR	*Jewish Quarterly Review*
JQRNSMS	Jewish Quarterly Review New Series Monograph Series
JSJ	*Journal for the Study of Judaism*
JSNT	*Journal for the Study of the New Testament*
JSNT(SS)	Journal for the Study of the New Testament (Supplement Series)
JSOT	*Journal for the Study of the Old Testament*
JSOT(SS)	Journal for the Study of the Old Testament (Supplement Series)
JSP(SS)	Journal for the Study of the Pseudepigrapha (Supplement Series)
JSS	*Journal of Semitic Studies*
JTC	*Journal for Theology and the Church*
JTS	*Journal of Theological Studies*
Jub.	*Jubilees*
Lat.	Latin

LSI	H. G. Liddell, *An Intermediate Greek-English Lexicon, Founded upon the Seventh Edition of Liddell and Scott's Greek-English Lexicon* (Oxford: Clarendon, 1889)
LXX	Septuagint (cited according to Rahlfs [1979])
MS(S)	manuscript(s)
MT	Masoretic Text
NEB	New English Bible
Neotest.	*Neotestamentica*
NIV	New International Version
NovT	*Novum Testamentum*
NovT(S)	Novum Testamentum (Supplements)
NTS	*New Testament Studies*
OTP	*Old Testament Pseudepigrapha* = Charlesworth [1983/85]
Pss. Sol.	*Psalms of Solomon*
PVTG	*Pseudepigrapha Veteris Testamenti Graece*
RB	*Revue Biblique*
RQ	*Revue de Qumran*
RSV	Revised Standard Version
SBL	Society of Biblical Literature
SBLMS	Society of Biblical Literature Monograph Series
SCS	SBL Septuagint and Cognate Studies
SH	*Scripta Hierosolymitana*
Sib. Or.	*Sibylline Oracles*
SJT	*Scottish Journal of Theology*
SNTSMS	Society of New Testament Studies Monograph Series
SNTSU	*Studien zum Neuen Testament in seiner Umwelt*
ST	*Studia Theologica*
SUNT	Studien zur Umwelt des Neuen Testaments
SVTP	Studia in Veteris Testamenti Pseudepigrapha
Syr.	Syriac
TAsh.	*Testament of Asher*
TBen.	*Testament of Benjamin*
TDan	*Testament of Dan*
TGad	*Testament of Gad*
TIss.	*Testament of Issachar*
TJos.	*Testament of Joseph*
TJud.	*Testament of Judah*
TLevi	*Testament of Levi*
TNaph.	*Testament of Naphtali*
TReub.	*Testament of Reuben*
TSim.	*Testament of Simeon*
TZeb.	*Testament of Zebulun*
TDNT	*Theological Dictionary of the New Testament*
TSK	*Theologische Studien und Kritiken*

ABBREVIATIONS

VT	*Vetus Testamentum*
VT(S)	Vetus Testamentum (Supplements)
VTS	*Vetus Testamentum Syriace. The Old Testament in Syriac according to the Peshiṭta Version*
WUNT	Wissenschaftliche Untersuchungen zum Neuen Testament
ZNW	*Zeitschrift für die neutestamentlichen Wissenschaft*
ZTK	*Zeitschrift für Theologie und Kirche*

CHAPTER ONE

Why Another Book on Judaism?

It is probably true that there is greater interest today in the study of ancient Judaism than ever before in history. There are several reasons for this, the greatest being that the study of Judaism among Jews themselves has reached a climax in the last few decades. This has been augmented by increasing interest in the teachings of Judaism on the part of non-Jews. From the Christian perspective in particular, interest in the Jewish background of the New Testament has peaked, with most of the focus of late being on the relationship of Jesus to Judaism, while a critical consideration of the relation between Paul and Judaism has been undertaken for a somewhat longer period. And, of course, publication of the Dead Sea Scrolls has renewed the interest of both Jews and Christians in the subject — and in an unprecedented way has raised the attention of the entire world. A clear indication of the combined and cumulative impact of these factors is that, while many departments in the humanities are disappearing from modern universities due to economic restraints and shifting priorities, the creation of entirely new departments for the study of Judaism is a not-unheard-of occurrence.

So, what purpose could there be in yet another book about ancient Judaism, where it might seem sufficient, and certainly more economic (especially for the purposes of comparative study), to use the ample and up-to-date resources provided by others? Good purpose indeed if, as seems to be the case, previous work on Judaism has lacked vital insight in a fundamentally important area, if this in turn has presented a serious hindrance to comparative analysis, and if, as a consequence of both facts, a reevaluation of the evidence is deemed critical. The purpose of this book is not to render obsolete celebrated works from the past or to contradict more recent studies (although if its main

1

arguments and observations are sustained, it probably has the potential to do so) so much as to redress one particularly critical failure in the past study of Judaism. The reader is invited to reconsider important evidence with an open mind, to carefully weigh that evidence (not merely to weigh libraries of books created by previous scholarship), to reach a conclusion, and to contemplate the implications. This is a challenge to alter long-held and foundational ideas about a subject of critical importance in these days.

SOME NECESSARY REMARKS ON METHOD AND APPROACH

"Judaism" is far too broad a topic for any single book, so certain limitations have been placed on this book's focus, approach, and purpose. Experience would suggest that such limits, however necessary for the sake of space, can cause certain misunderstandings or methodological difficulties in the study of Judaism — limitation can be judged as deficiency. In order to avoid such misunderstandings and to further explicate the concerns of this book, more will be said about each of these areas of limitation.

Focus

Only a select portion of the field of study has been chosen for discussion, even if, as is sometimes necessary, other aspects are discussed along the way, and even if, as is *always* necessary, the entire field of study is constantly kept in view. This book is interested in Judaism as a critical element — arguably the *most* critical element — in the study of the origins of the New Testament. With this purpose in mind (which will be discussed more fully below) I have deliberately focused on one group of writings — namely, the so-called Pseudepigrapha, including (or, should we say, along with) the Dead Sea Scrolls, as well as that particular *"movement"* within Second Temple Judaism that these writings represent. It is unfortunate that the word "Pseudepigrapha" frequently evokes notions of a very enigmatic kind of Judaism, much unlike the rather more straightforward "rabbinic" Judaism, which is represented by the Mishnah and Talmuds (although, when it comes right down to it, a verdict of "straightforward" would be rather difficult to defend for this latter group of writings as well!). The Pseudepigrapha contain visions and strange teachings and revelations, many of which are written in some kind of cipher or code. A full and logical theology of these writings has been judged unattainable — their interest seems to be more on mystical experience than on sober and consistent instruction. The term "apocalyptic writings," which has commonly been used in reference to these books, has for many become synonymous with eclectic dreaming and descriptions of heavenly trivia (to repeat: much unlike the rabbinic writings as popularly conceived). The Dead Sea Scrolls, in practical terms at least, have received a more sympathetic reception, but this is somewhat of a double standard inasmuch as the Pseudepigrapha are also found among the scrolls, and the scrolls have much in common with these other eclectic writings.

So why choose *this* literature? Why, in other words, if *clarifying* the message of the New Testament is so important, has such a *concealing* and *enigmatic* literature been chosen to attain this end? Historically speaking, scholarship has seemed to concur with the problem thus stated. For it is certainly true that, even given the recent resurgence of interest in the Pseudepigrapha, studies of the background of the New Testament that focus on rabbinic Judaism still outnumber those that focus on the Pseudepigrapha by a large factor. But to be discouraged from the latter choice by the apparent mysteriousness of the literature is actually quite tragic and completely unnecessary. In fact, as this book will show, there are many positive reasons for choosing these writings. It may even seem a bit surprising, to one accustomed to conventional treatments of the subject, just how consistent, practical, and historically relevant are the topics dealt with in these books. It will also become evident (though it is not the specific concern of this volume) that the concerns of the literature are of critical importance to the illumination of the message of the New Testament.

Beyond these important practical reasons for reexamining the Pseudepigrapha and the scrolls there is also a more technical aspect, namely, the argument from chronology. It has for some time been suspected that the rabbinic literature, while very important for Judaism historically, has a relatively late provenance and context when compared to this other Jewish literature, perhaps in many respects too late — and thus too historically and ideologically distant — for satisfactory comparison with the New Testament. The Mishnah only began to be "codified" (systematically arranged and recorded) around the beginning of the third century of the Christian era, and much talmudic teaching received its final form only in the following centuries (as late as the ninth century). It is thus in marked contrast to the Pseudepigrapha and the Dead Sea Scrolls, which can all be dated to what is rightly called the formative period of Christianity, the "late Second Temple period" — approximately 200 B.C. to A.D. 100. If these writings are not contemporary with the New Testament *per se*, they are at least chronologically antecedent, unlike the rabbinic writings.

The question of chronology also serves as a reminder that the rabbinic literature (in spite of the modern perception created by the dominance of rabbinic views in treatments of Jewish and Christian history) was not formed in a vacuum and, further, did not necessarily represent universally accepted beliefs in Judaism at any time in history. It may be that the deposits of tradition in the Mishnah and Talmud formed the view of the majority, or of "official" circles, at some time or another. This is, however, obviously far from saying that it necessarily helps us to arrive at a suitable background by which to explain or evaluate the theology of the New Testament. The Talmud was the product, so we are coming to realize, of a particular — however popular — viewpoint in Judaism. It is evident that, by the time the rabbinic traditions were codified, historical events (notably the destruction of Jerusalem in A.D. 70) had already exercised a profound effect on the shape of rabbinic teaching, effectively distinguishing it from the Judaism that went before. To this should be added the fact that the Talmud also exhibits a distinct tone of reactionism toward other religious expressions including, significantly enough, the very type of Judaism that this book focuses on, as well as Jewish Christianity, which in many respects is similar to this Judaism. The point is that a literature that reacts against the milieu in which the New Testament arose can hardly provide a balanced, let alone sympathetic, portrait of the Judaism with which the New Testament had so many features in common. The rabbinic literature is not the timeless and universal summary of Jewish belief that it was once taken to be, and it does not adequately reflect the time period in which the New Testament arose. Hence the quite deliberate and, we think, entirely justified focus of the present book on the Pseudepigrapha and the Dead Sea Scrolls.

Approach

This book seeks to establish what might be termed a "systematic theology" of the Judaism represented by the Pseudepigrapha and the scrolls.

According to recent methodological orthodoxy (as well as experience and common sense), any systematic treatment of such a vast and diverse literature is in serious danger of misrepresenting it by forcing it into too neat compartments, of thus overlooking the particular concerns of each separate writing in its individuality, and of carelessly tossing all the documents into a common theological pool, treating them as if they had a single author and were written at the same time. It is accordingly widely considered preferable these days to study one writing at a time, independently of others. In fact, reaction against systematic treatments of Judaism seems to have reached a climax, so that it is even beginning to sound a little platitudinous to point out (as is so often done) that the highly subjective systematizing approach employed in the earliest years of study of the Pseudepigrapha was inspired by little more than a curious interest in these writings as "splendid examples of Jewish apocalyptic," valued only

4

for the light they might cast on parallel phenomena in the Bible. And it can hardly be denied that in initial attempts to treat these writings there was little of what could be called sympathetic study of the books for their own sake. The literature was disrespectfully strip-mined for the benefit of other interests, while little notice was taken of the independent beauty and value of the stones or the variety of color running through the layers of rock. As can be expected from such a degrading approach, lack of concern for the independent integrity of these writings ultimately led to stereotypical and often careless systematization and to a monolithic view of "apocalyptic" origins and doctrine. Critical studies on the separate books were not wanting in the earlier stages of scholarship, but these efforts were overshadowed by the often subconscious presuppositions placed like an umbrella over the whole field of study. So ingrained were ideas about apocalyptic theology in the early days that when criticisms of the approach finally arrived (notably Koch's famous and pioneering *Ratlos vor* ["Perplexed About"] *der Apokalyptik* in 1970),[1] even they betrayed a reluctance characteristic of attacks on long-nurtured sacred tradition, and initially their criticisms failed to generate a widespread repentance. It is a remarkable fact that even recent scholars most sensitive to the issues reveal (to an eye accustomed to look for the telltale signs) a subtle respect for, and even a quiet assimilation to, the orthodoxy of traditional apocalyptic scholarship.

But it is also true that, despite the rather cautious reaction by such initial reevaluations as Koch's, more recent treatments are at least characterized by a much more valid and individualizing approach than their predecessors. More concern than ever before is now being shown for the contingent nature of each work in its particular context, more care in allowing each work to announce its own emphases and concerns, more willingness to recognize a fundamental diversification of origins and viewpoints even within one document. Most important, much less attention is being paid to the quite artificial list of doctrines (such as eschatology or messianology) on the basis of which, in the past, these works were characterized and evaluated. The overbearing concern for theological context is slowly but surely being replaced by an interest in the individual messages of the writings. One can only welcome such advances in methodology and, given that they have been so desperately slow and painful in coming, deem quite unforgivable any return to the superficial systematizing approaches of earlier decades. The critique undertaken by Koch must continue, for in some ways it has been anything but thorough enough!

But — and this amounts to a significant qualification — more recent individualizing approaches have other serious shortcomings, suggesting that the pendulum has swung a little too far the other way. To put it succinctly, these ap-

---

1. ET *The Rediscovery of Apocalyptic,* 1972.

proaches have proven to be ineffective in unraveling the twisted suppositions provided by earlier systematizing approaches and have also been of limited value in solving the *religio-historical* question for which this literature still possesses significant import — namely: *What is the overall significance of these writings for the history of Judaism and Christianity?* Such contingencies seem to demand that the next stage in scholarship adopt a methodology that allows us once again to step back somewhat, in order to take a look at the larger picture.

This book attempts that step back — with an important difference from earlier systematic approaches, in that it everywhere acknowledges the real benefits of the more synchronic approaches that have arisen lately, without which any attempt to go forward would be quite misdirected. The type of critical analysis that has characterized Pseudepigrapha scholarship is accordingly everywhere assumed by the present treatment and is frequently alluded to in the footnotes where lack of space in the text precludes doing it full justice there. So it needs to be stated unequivocally that it is a matter of bringing one approach to bear on another, not of giving up on valid recent advances.

But it will still be widely agreed that addressing the above-mentioned religio-historical concern is hardly itself a sufficient justification for adopting a systematic approach, especially since it was those same concerns (and just such an approach) that in the past seriously distorted the investigation of the literature. So what is it about this approach that will help in an understanding of the Pseudepigrapha and Qumran *for their own sake?* As we see it, there are historical, sociological, and literary justifications for the approach, and a few words can be said about each. There are good reasons for this approach, first of all, from the point of view of history or, at least, the history of ideas. It is in the nature of the case probable that there were vital contacts among these writings and among their authors of the sort that would allow the investigation of one writing to naturally throw considerable light on the understanding of another. While the monolithic view of "apocalyptic" is hopefully now gone forever, this should not be taken to mean that Jewish writers of the period lacked all interaction, that there was not a certain interplay and borrowing of ideas, or that there was not a basic and reasonably intact system of belief shared by these authors.[2] One should still be open to discovering these important connections, especially when they also help to illuminate the documents in their individuality. This is especially important to acknowledge and emphasize now, when it is becoming clear from the multiplicity of detailed studies that there is a distinct danger of "losing sight of the forest for the trees." The present study, in contrast to this trend, also serves to demonstrate how substantive shortcomings in the individ-

---

2. This is a recent and valid emphasis in scholarship, balancing the overreaction against the notion of a "normative" Judaism. See ch. 2 for details.

ualizing studies can be adequately compensated for or even overcome by the investigation of the larger context of the writings (a fresh look at the whole "forest").

Another justification for this approach comes from recent advances in the sociological study of Judaism. Unfortunately the application of the science of sociological analysis to the fields of biblical and theological research has not always been carried out sagaciously or sensitively, with the result that in some quarters (especially in those possessing special interest in the material under investigation) sociological inquiry is treated with suspicion and general disrespect (no one appreciates being told that there are sociological forces — apparently beyond their control — that explain their actions and opinions). While much of the sociological type of inquiry undertaken in this book will prove to critique and even contradict sociological approaches advanced so far (see ch. 5), it is nevertheless important to acknowledge that the influences of social factors in the Second Temple period have been more or less proven to possess real (only some would say predominating) significance for the formation and explication of Jewish theology. These social perspectives — and this is our point in the present context — have tended to focus attention on relationships and contexts in such a way as to grant prominence once again to the "larger picture." This is largely due to the fact that attention to social factors has encouraged an investigation of the connections among writings, among their authors, and among the societies to which the authors belonged. This is in contrast to individualizing analyses that, no doubt largely due to self-imposed limitations on the scope of such studies themselves, have been unable to incorporate much of this important evidence. This is tragic, inasmuch as certain insights from this science possess undeniable relevance to the subject. Partly in reaction to this lack, vitally important assumptions about social continuity — fundamental to which is the existence of social movements in Second Temple Judaism — have merited a not insignificant role in the present treatment.[3] While sociological study has not always been unqualifiedly helpful for understanding Judaism or Christianity, in other words, this does not mean that a careful and proper sociological methodology (which is cognizant of its limitations as well as its real potential) cannot also help undo the mistakes of the past.[4]

3. A movement is usually defined as a social entity based not on any perceived structural unity, but on a common purpose, goal, or perspective born out of a common social situation; see *Dictionary of Sociology,* 1944, 286; *Modern Dictionary of Sociology,* 1969, 390.

4. The basic problem, in our view, is that sociological inquiry has been tendentious and philosophically oriented — often using data only to prove theories already held as true, or using data already colored by conclusions. Instead it should be used as one tool among others in a carefully controlled research environment that is cognizant of influential factors that are not sociologically analyzed.

This kind of inquiry is not limited to understanding the social contingencies of the groups or communities that form a part of a larger movement. There is also a very practical advantage relating to the treatment of the texts themselves that comes from treating them as a kind of social collectivity, inasmuch as — according to the social theorists at least — a kind of social continuity manifests itself in various ways at the textual level.[5] A linguist aware of such factors would put it this way: because texts are socially related in continuous and discontinuous ways, a continuum is established among related texts and the ideas and expressions they contain. A group of texts closely related by underlying social connections has been called a "community of texts."[6] This terminology should not be taken to mean that texts form hard-and-fast canons, as a great deal of fluidity in the boundaries of such social relationships is a natural result of overlap and discontinuity, but it nevertheless properly emphasizes the vitally important need to recognize a social interrelatedness without which the proper study of these writings has been severely impeded in the past.[7] It will become obvious as we proceed how this study has taken advantage of social theory applied to the relationship of texts.

There are more than a few other implications for a sociological approach stemming from the inherent social aspects of language and literature. One very important implication is on the *formal* plane — something very important for the study of "apocalyptic" literature, inasmuch as *forms* (such as revelations, journeys, blessings and woes, judgment oracles, etc.) are exactly what most people think of when they think of "the apocalyptic literature." It seems undeniable that there belongs to all literary forms that arise in a given social milieu something that is commonly called their *literary function* or, more specifically, their *socioliterary function*. By "socioliterary function" is meant that texts not only *say* something, they also *do* something.[8] Not only do religious authors in-

---

5. The kinds of continuity we focus on — the linguistic and the ideological — are particularly emphasized in the so-called "sociology of knowledge" as promoted by Karl Mannheim (e.g., *Essays on the Sociology of Knowledge*, 1952). For the employment of the principles of this school to our literature, see S. B. Reid, *Enoch and Daniel*, 1989, 2, 16-17.

6. The expression has been taken from J. Neusner (*Wrong Ways and Right Ways in the Study of Formative Judaism*, 1988, esp. 44-55), who employs it to emphasize the taxonomic (relationships built on traits) rather than genealogical (relationships based on origins) connection such works have with one another.

7. Cf. G. Vermes ("Jewish Literature and New Testament Exegesis," 1982, esp. 372-75), who has called for a new understanding of Jewish literature that takes into consideration these kinds of social relationships and places all Jewish literature on a developmental continuum.

8. This is related to and dependent on, but not the same as, what is called illocution, i.e., the unexpressed message of a writing, "what it really says when it says what it says." Cf. Reid, 1989, 17. Cf. also G. Theissen (*The First Followers of Jesus*, 1978), who speaks rather

tend to express theological teachings or propositions by writing, in other words, but consistently (if unconsciously) there would appear to be some *purpose* for their writing in the first place, and this purpose forms an essential part of the communication. Much more can be learned about a writer from determination of this purpose than from attention to the surface meaning of the text alone. Attention to the function of a text is an entirely appropriate, and highly practical, method for discovering information about the writer and the writing.

Sociologists of religion differ on the precise functions to be attributed to any given form, but it is widely agreed (and is common sense) that certain functions come into play in religious settings more than others: these include functions that can be said to be directed *inwardly* to the community itself — a writing (or part of a writing) might encourage, validate, warn, console, define, identify, or even excite; and they include other functions directed *outside* the community — they might define or identify (either the community or those outside), validate (the writer's community), argue, justify, explain, appeal, reconcile, discomfort, warn, revile, condemn, or even infuriate. It can be seen from these lists and is also widely agreed that one of the most important driving forces in the existence of religious communities is their claim to *legitimacy*, which, in turn, lends such typical functions to the literature of a group as "validation," "definition," "identification," "confirmation," "consolation," and "vindication" — terms that will be further defined as we proceed and that we will use often.[9] An important rule of thumb is that *similar forms tend to possess similar functions in similar social contexts:* "Each genre . . . arises in and is appropriate for use in a particular situation."[10] It should also be noted that opposing societies might (consciously or otherwise) break with convention and employ similar forms *differently* to attain their specific goals;[11] and forms can even become "dead" through repeated use until the original purpose and function is largely lost. Accordingly, the function of each text must be determined by a closer examination of the social context of the individual writing, and although determining this can sometimes become a complex matter, it is a task that is neglected at great cost.

---

more generally about kinds of responses to social factors and the functions of each of these responses.

9. Max Weber recognized the importance of legitimization in social dynamics; this continues to be maintained by many sociologists today; cf. M. Hill, *A Sociology of Religion*, 1973, 141-47; Reid, 1989, 22; J. J. Collins, *The Apocalyptic Imagination*, 1984, 32.

10. G. M. Tucker as cited by Reid (1989, 1).

11. As Reid (1989, 1) explains: "In the context of social and political rhetoric writers and speakers use genres that obfuscate social bounds in such a way as to be persuasive to a given audience. Thereby different social settings may stand behind various examples of one genre depending on the rhetorical task of the authors."

While it is sometimes tragically overlooked in form analyses today, the earliest form critics realized the social contingency involved in their discipline.[12] Again it hardly needs to be pointed out how important this is for the literature at hand since one of the most widely recognized characteristics of these writings is the employment of certain *typical* and *shared* "apocalyptic" *forms*.[13] But this observation does not only apply to the conventional and easily recognizable forms such as journeys of the cosmos or judgment oracles; less "literary" presentations also lend themselves to formal comparison and social analysis. For example, seemingly straightforward presentations of doctrine — eschatology, pneumatology, messianology — are particularly important examples of catechetical treatises evidencing social functions not easily determinable apart from the larger social context. Thus texts are only rarely intended simply to provide *information*. Since knowing about the beliefs of a group includes their attitudes toward others and toward themselves (social attitudes), it is therefore logical that one pay attention not only to what the text says, but also to what the author hoped to accomplish by saying it and why the author used a particular *form* to get the message across.

What applies so obviously to forms applies also to individual words. It is widely acknowledged that language and terminology (lexicography) are to a degree predetermined by the common linguistic, semantic, and lexicographic presuppositions of the society.[14] Obviously, the more socially isolated a group, the more specialized will their terminology become, and the more the members of that group will depend on their distinct terminology. Given the highly symbolical language of the works to be studied here, certain words appear to function (in the sociolinguistic sense) as evocative "symbols" whose meanings are to an *extreme* degree socially contingent.[15] More will be said about these in-

---

12. Reid points out how scholars like Hasslberger and Collins have lost sight of the importance of social factors originally resident in Hermann Gunkel's form-critical approach (1989, 2, 9-11).

13. For an application of the social *Sitz im Leben* to "apocalyptic" genres, see Lars Hartman, "Survey of the Problem of Apocalyptic Genre," 1983, esp. 332-35.

14. Societies possess what linguists call "presupposition pools" (for discussion see P. Cotterell and M. Turner, *Linguistics and Biblical Interpretation,* 1989, 90-94, 100-101). This term is closely related to (although in no way identical with) the term "symbolic universe" employed by sociologists. Both terms refer to the storehouse of ideas and assumptions held by a society, which are implied through the use of language even if not clearly evident to those outside the society. The latter term is used this way, e.g., by P. Hanson (*The Dawn of Apocalyptic: The Historical and Sociological Roots of Jewish Apocalyptic Eschatology,* 1979, 423-44), who defines apocalypticism "as the system of concepts and symbols in which an apocalyptic movement codifies its identity and gives expression to its interpretation of reality. Such a system may be called a symbolic universe" (432).

15. That some words function as "religious symbols" that go well beyond their sim-

stances as they arise. The point to be made here is that it is only by grouping writings of a similar social milieu that one can adequately determine the social context and solve the various questions of literary function — and thus arrive at the all-important levels of meaning intended by the author. Here then is another justification for treating these writings together.

One final justification for this kind of systematic approach — perhaps better referred to as a resignation to trends rather than a justification with any independent rationale — relates to the recent surge of attempts by both Jewish and Christian scholars to redefine Judaism from a holistic perspective. This tendency takes the form of a reaction to past generalizations about the subject and by necessity steps back somewhat from detailed analysis to define the major facets common to all of Judaism. One naturally thinks primarily, but not exclusively, of the work of E. P. Sanders,[16] who, in contrast to the more prevailing trend of the day, works systematically in order to discover what he calls "essences" in Jewish literature and eventually the "essence" of Judaism *generaliter.* While Sanders has been accused of casting his net too widely and assuming uniformity among various kinds of Judaism too fundamentally different to be grouped together,[17] his approach nevertheless demonstrates methodological presuppositions similar to those adopted here, including the idea that a basic structure of thought is likely to be widely held among Jews of similar inclination. The final phrase in that summary — "among Jews of similar inclination" — however, will receive more emphasis in this treatment than we feel Sanders gave to it. That is why we would prefer to apply this kind of generalizing historicism, which is good as far as it goes, to a *single chronologically and ideologically circumscribed movement in Judaism* rather than to *the entire Jewish world over lengthy periods of time.* (It is just such a chronological and ideologi-

---

ple lexicographical definitions is nothing new. P. Ricoeur's well-known definition and treatment of religious symbols (*The Symbolism of Evil,* 1967) outlines some of the psychological aspects, including the ability of these symbols to evoke a wide range of significance only indirectly related to the literal meaning of the terms (14-18): "symbols give rise to thought" (19). While Ricoeur deals primarily with the symbolism of abstract religious concepts like sin and guilt, he also includes examples like sky, water, moon, tree, stone, flood, and the like (14, 18). A related phenomenon is the adaptation and reemployment of biblical language, which is simply a specific instance of the use of language in its social contingencies. Collins (1984, 14) speaks of the way allusions to biblical passages and biblical language in the apocalypses serve to "bring a passage to mind" in a general way "without claiming to interpret it in a definitive way." Thus the "communicative power of the language" is enriched (16). See esp. our treatment of terms like "seed" and "tree" below.

16. Particularly in *Paul and Palestinian Judaism,* 1977.

17. This is one of the most valid of the criticisms that has been made, among others, by J. H. Charlesworth (in the first chapter of *The Old Testament Pseudepigrapha and the New Testament,* 1985).

cal insensitivity in Sanders's approach that is being recognized as its most serious flaw.) Having stated this qualification, we repeat that the approach taken in this work does not arise in a vacuum as if it were the first to take a "step back," but it is to a point influenced and invoked by the recent scholarly context.

Purpose

Finally, the subject matter of this book is limited considerably by its *purpose*. This purpose is to offer vital *prolegomena* to the study of New Testament origins. There has been much opposition in the recent past to the idea that one can combine the study of Judaism with interests in Christianity. This is not a totally unjustified concern; indeed, it is a valid reaction to former infelicities in comparative methodology. In the past "interdisciplinary" interests have often led to what can only be called a careless confusion of two religions — specifically, the invalid and quite subconscious practice of viewing Judaism through Christian eyes to the extent that the proper understanding of both is obscured. Judaism, it is implied, is better left to be studied by people of Jewish origin since it is evident (to some at least) that a Christian (or any scholar for that matter who has inherited the faith of the New Testament through tradition or society) possesses prejudices that cannot be shed in order to attain a truly unclouded view of Judaism. This critical observation has accordingly resulted in the charge that New Testament scholars have tended to select evidence that is conducive to their own conclusions.

But a few observations must be stated by way of response to this point of view. First of all, as has already been indicated, Judaism is a broad subject that cannot easily be handled without limiting the field of study somewhat. Second, no one would deny that some understanding of Judaism is helpful, if not essential, to understanding the New Testament. Third (and as a corollary of the first two), scholars of the New Testament must make some choices about what, exactly, out of the vast world of Judaism, will be the focus of their attention. In other words, the student of the New Testament must start *somewhere*. As far as this book is concerned — and only its conclusions can justify the choice of this kind of Judaism as a background of the New Testament — that "somewhere" is a movement within late Second Temple Judaism associated with the major Pseudepigrapha from that period and with the Dead Sea Scrolls. If this seems to other scholars of Judaism to be too selective, then one must appeal that the limitations of a single monograph of reasonable size like this one simply demand that a choice be made.

Furthermore there is no need to assume, simply because students of the New Testament have certain specific concerns in mind, that they cannot *also* read Judaism accurately. It is not in fact unreasonable to assert the opposite as a possibility, especially since the scholarly world is now beginning to recognize and acknowledge that the New Testament itself belongs centrally (not peripherally) to the literary world of Second Temple Judaism. Nor is there reason to deny the possibility that students of the New Testament might have mastered the context of the specific Judaism, or aspects of Judaism, enough to offer a reasonably valid historical treatment of it. In other words, the selection of particular data from Judaism does not necessarily imply a disregard for all other kinds of Judaism or the ignorance of the fuller and all-important context of Judaism. This book, in fact, is offered as a kind of demonstration that there can be a valid and sensitive treatment of Judaism from the point of view of those who seek its relevance for New Testament study. Thus it contains at one and the same time *prolegomena* for New Testament study *and* a valid study of one kind of Judaism in its own right. It asks questions that can be asked of any kind of Judaism — questions about judgment, election, and covenant — *as well as* questions that are of interest to both Judaism *and* Christianity — questions about messianology, eschatology, and soteriology. The important point in this is that even these latter topics were of concern to Judaism as well as to Christians, and it is this that has been subtly denied of late (as if such "Christian"-sounding doctrines emerged only *after* the church had separated from Judaism!). No one would deny that a historical methodology demands that the two religions not be confused — but the conclusions and implications drawn from the assumption (namely, a necessary theological separation of the two faiths in certain areas) are, as a generalization, totally unwarranted. This book has thus been motivated by certain interests related to understanding the New Testament. But one interested only in the Jewish world can read it, because it is a book about Judaism in its own right.

A WORD ABOUT SOURCES AND CRITICAL PRESUPPOSITIONS

As already mentioned, this book limits itself for the most part to an investigation of the following two groups of writings: the Dead Sea Scrolls and those writings from the Pseudepigrapha traditionally known as "apocalyptic writings" — *1 Enoch* (including the provocative Similitudes of Enoch), *Jubilees, Psalms of Solomon,* the *Assumption (Testament) of Moses,* the *Testaments of the Twelve Patriarchs,* 4 Ezra, and 2 Baruch. Other ancient writings that add something or other to the investigation will be brought to bear on the topic, but since most of the discussion and scholarship has centered on this main group of books, it seems both easier, and more confidence-inspiring, to limit the range of texts as much as possible to those that have been exposed to the most rigorous scholarly discussion. A further reason for limiting the treatment primarily to these works is, of course, that good arguments can be made for seeing them *all* as having originated in the late Second Temple period (*more or less* between 200 B.C. and A.D. 100) — a claim that cannot be made with equal confidence for any other Jewish writings with the main exception of the Apocrypha (whose concerns are only peripheral to the movement documented herein) and cannot even be made for the relatively "new" pseudepigrapha that have recently come to the fore. Much more importantly, these writings can all be confidently treated as representing essentially *Jewish* points of view from this period. It is true, however, that both of these conclusions about the date and essentially Jewish provenance of the writings have been questioned, more in regard to some books than others. So a few comments on the dating and provenance of each of these writings will more firmly establish them as valid sources for a study of late Second Temple Judaism.

The Dead Sea Scrolls

There is scarcely a more complex question in Jewish scholarship than the dating and relative chronology of the Dead Sea Scrolls. Of the five most important[18] possibilities for dating the origins of the Qumran community itself — in the early Maccabean,[19] late Maccabean,[20] Hasmonean,[21] pre-

18. Zeitlin's medieval date and Karaite provenance should be eliminated as a serious contender. For helpful (however impassioned!) presentations of the reasons for this, see G. Vermes, "The Essenes and History," 1981, 18-31, 23; G. Vermes, *Jesus and the World of Judaism*, 1983, 102-3, 131. For similar reactions to Teicher's Christian dating, see Vermes, 1981, 23, 29. This latter association seems to be particularly untenable to us as well.

19. Associated esp. with H. H. Rowley and E. Stauffer. Rowley's theory makes the "Wicked Priest" Menelaus; Stauffer's identifies the priest as Alchimus. That the "Wicked Priest" was a high priest and not an ordinary priest is suggested by the play on words between *hakkōhēn hārāšā'* (Wicked Priest) and *hakkōhēn hārō'š* (high priest). For a similar position that dates the community to the rise of the Hasidim ca. 176 B.C., see H. J. Schonfield, *Secrets of the Dead Sea Scrolls*, 1957, 22, 36-37.

20. This Maccabean dating sees in Jonathan (160-143 B.C.) or, less frequently, Simon (143/2–135/4 B.C.) the "Wicked Priest" of the scrolls; see J. T. Milik, *Ten Years of Discovery in the Wilderness of Judaea*, 1959, 84; G. Jeremias, *Der Lehrer der Gerechtigkeit*, 1963, 36-78, esp. 75-76; J. Becker, *Das Heil Gottes*, 1964, 55; M. Hengel, *Judaism and Hellenism*, 1974, 1:224; also cf. D. E. Gowan, *Bridge between the Testaments*, 1986, 171-72; Vermes (who claims to be the originator of this theory), 1981, 25; 1983, 133. For the view that Simon was the persecutor of the *moreh ṣedeq*, see W. F. Albright and C. S. Mann, "Qumran and the Essenes," 1969, 11-25, 19, 25.

21. Usually during the reign of John Hyrcanus (134-104 B.C.) — suggested by Brownlee and supported by H. Ringgren, *The Faith of Qumran*, 1963, 37, 42; cf. also

Roman,[22] and Roman periods[23] — none seems to adequately account, on its own, for the diverse historical data met throughout the various scrolls (including the confusion over the historical identity of the "Kittim," apparent developments in eschatological expectation, as well as a score of conflicting historical "clues"). While the arguments over dating are bound to continue for decades, there are plausible arguments for placing the origin of the sect as a fairly distinct body (as opposed to a loosely organized pre-Qumran movement) as early as the late Maccabean period.[24] Works like the Hymn Scroll (1QH), the Community Rule (1QS), and the War Scroll (1QM) appear to have been penned fairly early in the history of the sect, but still sometime after the initial events of organization and consolidation, perhaps not until the early Hasmonean period. The early dating of 1QH is based on the authorship of some of its hymns, appropriately named the Founder Hymns because they are presumed to have been written by the founder of the community, the so-called Teacher of Righteousness *(moreh ṣedeq).* On the other hand, the War Scroll is very difficult to place; an equally good case can be made for either an early or a late date, although extreme dates are speculative and unsupportable and the *Sitz im Leben* of the writing (the circumstances that led to its being written) would appear to place it near the beginning of the movement, approximately concurrent with the sojourn to Damascus/Qumran.[25] Perhaps some works were penned even

---

F. García Martínez and A. S. van der Woude, "A 'Groningen' Hypothesis of Qumran Origins and Early History," 1990, 540. Hyrcanus II is usually equated, according to this view, with the "Wicked Priest," and the Pharisees with the "Seekers after Smooth Things" of the Nahum Commentary (4QpNah 2 at 2:12b). For a Zadokite/Hasmonean theory of Qumran origins, see R. Eisenman, *Maccabees, Zadokites, Christians, and Qumran,* 1983, iv, 35ff., although the relationship is ideologically rather than chronologically defined.

22. The argument, associated with Dupont-Sommer, rests largely on the identification of the Kittim as Romans and dates the beginnings of the movement to just prior to Pompey's invasion in 63 B.C. (A. Dupont-Sommer, *The Essene Writings from Qumran,* 1961, 339-57).

23. A dating after A.D. 66 is associated with Del Medico and Roth. More recently this theory has been given a lengthy defense by G. R. Driver in *The Judaean Scrolls,* 1965, passim. Like other post-Christian datings, this one falters on the paleological data, which demand an earlier dating (cf. Vermes, 1981, 23).

24. Milik (1959, 84) argues that only Jonathan fits the description of the Wicked Priest who both rebuilt Jerusalem and died in torment after captivity. The only important refutation of this theory is based on the recently published 4Q448, which seems to exhibit a very positive attitude toward Jonathan (cf. R. Eisenman and M. Wise, *The Dead Sea Scrolls Uncovered,* 1992, 273ff.). There are, however, other ways to understand this fragment within the history of the sect that allow the Jonathan theory to stand.

25. Why else would it open by reflecting on the eventuation of warfare in the desert and the "return" of the "Deportation"? Y. Yadin (*The Scroll of the War of the Sons of Light against the Sons of Darkness,* 1962, 244-46) marshals detailed military data to support a

before the establishment of the community, and the Damascus Document (CD) is a notable candidate for this, although contrary evidence can be cited that suggests that it may even be a relatively late writing among the scrolls.[26] Neither a late nor an early date would, in any event, necessarily imply any lack of continuity in its teaching with the other works, and even theories that posit that it originated with a pre-Qumran sect do not argue that its teachings differ in fundamental respects from the latter group (the arguments in favor of this are historical and circumstantial, not theological). Other scrolls and fragments of scrolls, on the other hand, definitely appear to come from a somewhat later period than the initial organizational period — the Habakkuk Commentary, for example, demands a dating in the pre-Roman period at the very earliest since it contains references to Romans as "Kittim." Thus the writings known as the Dead Sea Scrolls probably represent a full century or more of literary activity (not taking into consideration, of course, biblical or Pseudepigrapha MSS).

One way out of the impasse over the dating of the various writings, and one that is gaining in currency, is to acknowledge that the community's literary

---

date in the latter half of the first century B.C. (63 B.C. to A.D. 1) but is unconvincing since terms are difficult to restrict within precise time limits. Too much has also been made of the view that, since the dualism in the War Scroll is between *all Israel* and the Gentiles rather than between the righteous and unrighteous *within* Israel, the work, or at least its sources, must be placed early, perhaps at the beginning of the Maccabean revolt, before the sect broke away from Israel (so P. von der Osten-Sacken, *Gott und Belial*, 1969, 88; cf. also Becker, 1964, 75). This ignores the fact that the much earlier Maccabean struggle was also inter-Jewish (see ch. 6 below); the Israel versus Gentiles theme in 1QM can largely be explained as traditional and related to the restoration doctrine (see ch. 11 below); there is, moreover, an intra-Jewish division between two groups reflected in 1QM (see the treatment of 1QM 1.2-3 below). More convincing, we feel, are the linguistic arguments of Osten-Sacken (73-87), who demonstrates the relatively undeveloped nature of the terms in 1QM. There is no need to insist that the mention of Kittim implies a Roman provenance (see below and cf. Osten-Sacken, who argues for the identity of the Kittim with the Seleucids and Ptolemies, 67).

26. For the view that an early edition of CD originated within the Essene movement but from a time before the sectarians broke away from the mother group, see P. R. Davies, *The Damascus Covenant*, 1982, 2-47, 202; García Martínez and van der Woude, 1990, 538-39. M. Wise (*A Critical Study of the Temple Scroll from Qumran Cave 11*, 1990a, 139-40, 146-47, 202-3) accepts the arguments of Davies and holds that the Temple Scroll comes from the circle that produced CD. Preferable to the theory of Davies is the view that the original separation was from Jerusalem, not from (other) Essenes; CD takes its place among the works of the community on the basis of the similarity of its exegesis and distinctive terminology to that of the *pešerim* (cf. Osten-Sacken, 1969, 192-93). The mention of apostasy from the sect (CD 8.19-21; [B] 1.5–2.13), on the other hand, is not sufficient evidence for a late date, inasmuch as apostasy is already alluded to in the Founder Hymns (cf. 1QH 5.22ff.). T. Elgvin ("The Qumran Covenant Festival and the Temple Scroll," 1985, 104) similarly argues that the Temple Scroll is a pre-Qumran Essene work.

activity (whatever may be said about its historical origins) took place in *several* of the time periods listed above. This approach would allow not only for the variety of historical allusions in the different writings but also for the complex processes of collocating and editing that seem to have gone on before the scrolls reached the final form in which they were found in the caves. Some theories that build on this observation maintain that terms like "the Wicked Priest" or the "Kittim" actually allude to more than one person or group, these terms being subject to a gradual change of referent throughout the literary period; some such explanation, at least, seems to be demanded by the evidence.[27]

But this is not the only explanation offered these days for the apparent theological and chronological diversity in the scrolls. Norman Golb in his book *Who Wrote the Dead Sea Scrolls?* has summed up his reasons for offering an alternative to the usual approach, which sees in the scrolls the literary product of a single circumscribed group of sectarians belonging to the party of the Essenes. He prefers to see the caves near the Dead Sea as a repository of copies of writings authored or treasured *by many different kinds of Jews* and hidden there for safety during the months leading up to and during the siege of Jerusalem in A.D. 66-70.[28] Golb also maintains that the scrolls originally belonged to the temple library (a view earlier held by K. H. Rengstorf).[29] The reasons he gives for these conclusions are many, but can be summarized under a few basic categories: (1) since Khirbet Qumran was a fortress, it could not have housed Essenes;[30] (2) the wide variety of beliefs, attitudes, and types of writings demands a correspondingly wide provenance for the writings;[31]

27. For the view that "Wicked Priest" refers to a number of different Hasmonean priests, see García Martínez and van der Woude, 1990, 537, 538-40. Similar is the theory of Ringgren, 1963, 27-29, who points out that the title Kittim could refer to any of the Gentile enemies of Israel and may have become a "designation of all the peoples who are enemies of Israel" (29). For a full discussion, cf. Jeremias, 1963, 10-35, who discerns the Romans in the use of the word, which however is also taken up as an eschatological designation for the "remnant of the peoples," making historical allusions less than certain. Schonfield discerns two distinct periods with two Teachers of Righteousness (1957, passim).

28. N. Golb, *Who Wrote the Dead Sea Scrolls?* 1995; cf. also Golb, "Who Hid the Dead Sea Scrolls?" 1987.

29. The Copper Scroll (ostensibly a record of the hiding places of treasures possibly associated with the temple) plays an important role in this theory (Golb, 1995, 120-29).

30. Golb, 1995, 18ff., 36ff. Cf. comments in this regard on the baths (20-21), the scriptorium (27ff.), pottery (30-31, 320-21), and the cemetery (34-35). The site and manuscript collection lack evidence of normal community life, such as letters, legal documents, or literary autographs (147-48).

31. Golb, 1995, 104, 259. Besides the case of 4QMMT (see below), Golb notes the fundamental dissimilarity between documents like 1QS and 1QM (80-81); the poem in praise of King Jonathan could not have been written by the authors of the sectarian scrolls

(3) the number of scribes required to copy the scrolls (representing 400 to 500 different hands) presupposes a community much larger than could have thrived at Qumran;[32] and (4) Qumran is not unique among hiding sites in the wilderness of Judea.[33] Golb also argues that there is a determined conspiracy on the part of the official scrolls team to conceal the evidence and defend the original Essene theory, while most scholars rather blindly follow their outdated proposals.[34] The world of scholarship, according to Golb, should have been alerted to problems with the Essene theory with the announcement and publication of the controversial text 4QMMT *(Miqṣāt Maʿaśēh ha-Tôra),* which is thought to exhibit similarities to a Sadducean legal stance and exhibits stark contrasts with the stance of the other scrolls (although Golb himself takes it to be a Pharisaic document).[35]

Golb offers a very impressive challenge to almost all previous scroll scholarship, and his point of view is so consistently argued that one really must deal with his thesis before continuing to work under the usual presupposition that the scrolls represent the views of a single, sectarian community living at Qumran who copied and hid scrolls. In our view, however (and the evidence for this will be spelled out in the pages of this book), these writings are not really widely representative of Judaism, but are more or less consistently "sectarian." By "sectarian" we do not mean either that they digress in their basic theological conceptuality from the rest of Judaism or that they necessarily represent a fringe group whose ideas were limited to a small number. They are sectarian in the sense that they come from a dissenting group (or movement, large or small, made up of many similar groups) whose claims on salvation are exclusive — as we will also explain below.[36] In our view this does not preclude what is probably Golb's most persuasive finding, namely,

---

(257); only 20 of the 600 scrolls refer to a *yaḥad* (294); texts like *Songs of the Sabbath Sacrifice* are not sectarian (296-97); etc.

32. Golb, 1995, 97-98, 151ff.

33. Golb, 1995, 126-40.

34. Golb, 1995, passim, esp. 217ff., 305ff.

35. Golb, 1995, 198-209. A refutation of the Sadducean provenance has been conclusively offered, in our view, and nothing prevents the document from originating with the group, or same general movement, that produced the other writings; see below.

36. Golb comments in the course of his argument that "relatively few among the virtually six hundred noncanonical writings discovered in the caves showed characteristics comparable to the separatist tendencies reflected in the *Damascus Covenant* or in the *Manual of Discipline*" (1995, 165). The contents of the present book, carefully considered, will themselves provide an adequate refutation of this opinion, though it is not the first to argue that a certain continuity exists among these scrolls. Golb, 279-80, 330-31, himself acknowledges these arguments and does not adequately answer them in our view; cf. also H. Stegemann, "The Qumran Essenes," 1992, 98-100.

that the scrolls come from a rather larger group than could ever have lived at Qumran. Furthermore, the representative copies of the Pseudepigrapha and the Hebrew Scriptures found at Qumran reveal that there were no tight controls on authorship of the scrolls in the caves, and thus one cannot automatically suppose that the authors of any of the works necessarily came from Qumran.

Just the same, if we categorize the various kinds of writings found among the scrolls, it will nevertheless be seen that the contents of the caves harmonize well with the assumption that a particular mind-set was at work behind the collection of this particular assortment of writings. The *first* grouping of writings, copies of the Hebrew Scriptures (including the Apocrypha), although not officially "canonized" at this period, were universally respected in Judaism for their antiquity and their assumed holy character; it is not difficult to see why any Jewish group would honor them if they had no particular reasons to dispute them. The *second* group, the so-called Pseudepigrapha, many of which came from a period prior to the formation of the community itself and were widely disseminated in the Jewish world (although this latter assumption is not totally proven), themselves exhibit sectarian qualities entirely in line with what can also be demonstrated for the Dead Sea Scrolls community (as we will show). Then there is a *third* category of writings, those that seem to refer to a single well-defined community with a leader (known as the Teacher of Righteousness), the subject matter of which applies directly to the management of that community; these provide the most direct evidence of a group that defined itself as in some way separate from other groups. The existence of a *fourth* category of writings containing literature that does not easily harmonize with the mind-set of the other MSS (such as the so-called *Prayer for King Jonathan*, 4QMMT, and a cryptically written astrological text) is heavily disputed (each of the candidates for this category are themselves frequently explained as in harmony with the other writings!)[37] and would be, in any case, such a minute category that it can be explained as accidental. As can easily be seen, each of these categories of writings can be rationalized as appropriate for a sectarian community such as produced the third of the categories — indeed, one would expect all these categories (authoritative Scriptures, respected works by similarly minded authors, writings belonging particularly to the community, and an insignificant number of "accidentals") to exist among such people. *It is*, on the other hand, *extremely difficult to understand how a widely representative collec-*

---

37. The instance of the cryptically written document containing astrological teachings in reverse script (4Q186 = 4QCryptic), particularly if its teachings diverged from the sectarian calendar, can be explained as an instance of censorship, not divergence (cf. García Martínez and van der Woude, 1990, 523).

tion arbitrarily and accidentally brought together would contain only such writings as these.[38]

The provenance of the scrolls, therefore, if not a relatively small retreating community at Qumran, would nevertheless seem to be a relatively larger group of similarly minded sectarians; it is our view that these sectarians *may have* originally composed a large group of dissenting Jews living in Jerusalem (in the so-called Essene Quarter?), and so we are, to a certain extent, in concurrence with Golb's thinking. The scrolls, on the other hand, certainly cannot represent writings from an official temple library, inasmuch as they *consistently* reflect a theology of dissent (again, as we will argue throughout this book) and sustain with the most deliberate of intentions a *harsh condemnation* of the temple establishment. The propensity to hide away scrolls may itself have been a *nonconformist* practice, which would also agree with our view that many of the scrolls were hidden for the purpose of preserving knowledge of the truth for a later generation (see more below), as well as to remove precious texts from the threatening presence of the Romans. (It does not, in any event, seem like "official policy" to hide scrolls in caves — why would a library curator not send precious scrolls to Diaspora Jewish communities?)[39] Some of these nonconforming Jews *may or may not* have spent time at the Qumran site (or, alternatively, in or near Syrian Damascus, or both). Certainly some kind of trek into the wilderness appears to have been undertaken by this group for reasons other than *merely* to hide the scrolls or to escape the Romans (among other things, the soteriology discussed in ch. 12 below, the presupposed location of the warring community in the War Scroll, and the "escape from Jerusalem" theme also mentioned below, practically demand this kind of emigration). It should ac-

---

38. Thus one can continue to speak of the Qumran "library." The term "library" is used for lack of a better word and implies not a physical collection of scrolls but the sum total of works consulted by this group whether they were ever saved together in a single collection or not. This library appears — in spite of Golb's protest — to have been a "sectarian" and highly *exclusive* library where (quite unlike modern libraries) only *bona fide* works would be considered acceptable for consultation (or deposit as the case may be). That is to say, if a work made it into the Dead Sea Scroll library, one can be reasonably certain, as a rule of thumb, that it first passed the test of Qumran orthodoxy. Cf. García Martínez and van der Woude, 1990, 522-25, whose arguments counter Golb's theory (stated in Golb's "Problem of Origin and Identification of the Dead Sea Scrolls," 1980; Golb, 1987; etc.).

39. The inconsistency in how the scrolls were hidden (and the many hands that must have been involved in this process) would suggest a popular attitude toward preserving sacred and important writings, such as would attain among groups with a heightened appreciation of the value of Scripture. For its part the Copper Scroll does not seem like an official document, as Golb's thesis seems to require. It makes more sense that this scroll contains rumored locations of treasures cherished by the faithful.

cordingly be noted that when the terms "Qumran," "Dead Sea community" (or "Dead Sea Scrolls"), "community," or *"yaḥad"* are employed indiscriminately in this book in referring to this group, these are more or less traditional ascriptions that do not necessarily imply anything about provenance or history. But they do imply a more or less identifiable group, one in sympathy (and perhaps even *in continuity*) with other groups that we will also analyze.

Regardless of how one assesses the various arguments about provenance in detail, a well-established conclusion of the research to date is that the origin of all the "distinctive writings" of the Qumran community (i.e., the legislative, community writings, and commentaries or *pešerîm;* omitting earlier works like *1 Enoch* and *Jubilees* and the biblical MSS) can be placed within a reasonably limited period of literary activity extending from a century or so prior to the dawning of the Christian era up to, but not beyond, the war with Rome in A.D. 66-70, and accordingly nothing prevents the scrolls from being credibly attributed to a more or less clearly defined group, albeit one with a significantly lengthy history. Even if the scrolls were penned or edited by more than one specific group, they nonetheless preserve a more or less *common point of view,* as we have already said, which is an adequate enough reason to assign them to one and the same *general movement.*[40] This is an important observation, especially when we come to scrolls like 1QS and 1QM, which are quite evidently composite works. Since it has proven difficult to dependably reconstruct sources for either work (let alone determine the particular tendencies of the sources), one must more or less rely on the essentially unified nature of the books, which is based more on a common and pervasive point of view than on unity of authorship (although this is also not unlikely). 1QM, perhaps more than 1QS, possesses a thematic unity throughout. 1QH is also clearly composite, apparently combining two basic collections of hymns or psalms ("Founder Hymns" and "Community Hymns").[41] Even given their composite nature, therefore, these books possess only one relevant *Sitz im Leben* in the community, namely, that which led to their final redaction, and can accordingly all be treated as more or less representative of the group's thought at a significant point in their history.

40. In this respect we should note the evidence of the linguistic arguments for the relations of the writings — namely, that the several orthographic peculiarities of the Heb. are consistent throughout the various writings and thus consonant with a common origin (cf. M. Mansoor, *The Thanksgiving Hymns Translated and Annotated with an Introduction,* 1961, 11). For the place of the War Scroll among the writings of the Qumran sect on this basis, cf. Yadin, 1962, 3.

41. The Founder Hymns are generally identifiable by their "I-style." We take them to have been written by the *moreh ṣedeq.* Mansoor, 1961, 45-48, collates convincing evidence for this identification based on comparisons of what is said about the *moreh* in CD with what is expressed in personal terms in the Founder Hymns.

The fact that the beliefs promoted by all these works are relatively consistent (although not uniform) is certainly a more important consideration here than the exact dating of the individual books.

1 (Ethiopic) *Enoch*

As for the books that make up *1 Enoch* (excepting, for now, the Similitudes, chs. 37–71), there is little doubt also that these writings are to be included within the time period under consideration. While discussion of dating would take us too far afield, it is worthwhile to note a significant trend in Enochian scholarship of late toward dating the provenance of all the books that make up the corpus before 160 B.C. — with some portions or at least some of the sources or early recensions originating from a time considerably earlier. The most important evidence for theories of dating emerges from J. T. Milik's treatment of the Aramaic fragments from Qumran.[42]

What is perhaps more significant, however, in view of past emphasis on the fragmentary nature of *1 Enoch,* are arguments that suggest a possible original *unity* for the corpus. This unity is argued on two important fronts. One argument comes from the fact that the discovery of the Aramaic manuscripts has forced back the later limits for the dating of each of the books considerably, resulting in a much narrower total time period for their production, and subsequently increasing the possibility that they originated within the confines of a circumscribed movement, and perhaps even from within a single group of pious scribes, or even from the hand of a single author. A second argument involves theories about the structure of the corpus itself, as the collection is thought by some to exhibit a biographical outline of Enoch's experiences, each book representing a single period from the patriarch's life, suggesting, at the very least, that some of the parts were written in full knowledge of the other parts.[43] While admittedly speculative, these suggestions are nevertheless representative of the trend toward reconsidering whether the books in *1 Enoch* are rather more closely related than previously thought. This would lessen the possibility that some of the books come from groups with beliefs alien to those of the other books, increasing confidence in using them to throw light on one another.

42. The case has been made by M. E. Stone ("The Book of Enoch and Judaism in the Third Century B.C.E.," 1978) that *1 Enoch* 1–36 and 72–82 originate in the third century. For the evidence offered by the Aram. fragments, see J. T. Milik, *The Books of Enoch,* 1976, 4-58, 139-339, passim. For this consensus, see also Stone, 1978, passim; J. C. VanderKam, "Studies in the Apocalypse of Weeks," 1984a, 522; I. Fröhlich, "The Symbolical Language of the Animal Apocalypse of Enoch," 1990, 629.

43. D. Dimant, "The Biography of Enoch and the Books of Enoch," 1983.

The *Testaments of the Twelve Patriarchs*

More serious than arguments about the date of either the scrolls or the Enochian corpus are those that bear on much-disputed books like the *Testaments of the Twelve Patriarchs* and the Similitudes of Enoch (*1 Enoch* 37–71). Discussion of the provenance of the Similitudes will be left until this can be more adequately dealt with in connection with the content and concerns of the work itself. As for the *Testaments of the Twelve Patriarchs,* few present-day scholars of the *Testaments*[44] would agree with the view of R. H. Charles earlier this century that the *Testaments* were written by pro-Maccabean Pharisees and edited in two stages, first by opponents of the Hasmoneans and then by Christians.[45] The strongest challenge has come from the widely acclaimed expert on the criticism of the *Testaments,* Marinus de Jonge.[46] In contrast to Charles, de Jonge holds that the *Testaments* were written in their present form in Greek, that they are essentially Christian, although drawing from Jewish (Hebrew) sources, that they are a late second-century work, that the complex matter of sources cannot be resolved by literary criticism or passages assigned to various stages of editing (as Charles and others have attempted to do), and that the Christian "interpolations" cannot be isolated and excised, as they are too intimately woven into the text. De Jonge has essentially given up the possibility of locating, with any degree of certainty, anything uniquely Jewish in the *Testaments.*

The truth would seem to lie somewhere between these two extremes. The Christian additions, while providing intense difficulty for textual criticism, do not seem to be as hopelessly intermingled with the original Jewish portions in our Greek edition as de Jonge suggests — they continue to be identified by scholars, and theories of interpolation are still being successfully proffered.[47]

44. For a discussion and bibliography of the recent important works, see W. H. Hollander and M. de Jonge, *The Testaments of the Twelve Patriarchs,* 1985, 1-8.

45. A position outlined in his introduction to the Greek text (R. H. Charles, *The Greek Versions of the Testaments of the Twelve Patriarchs,* 1908, ix). For the history of the study of the *Testaments,* both pre- and post-Charles to ca. 1970, see H. D. Slingerland, *The Testaments of the Twelve Patriarchs,* 1977.

46. His views in the main are reflected in Hollander and de Jonge, 1985, passim. For the following, see pp. 3, 7, 17, 27, 28-29, 37, and 85.

47. Cf. Slingerland, 1977, 104. Cf. R. A. Kugler, *From Patriarch to Priest,* 1996, 177-78: "While de Jonge's view that we can no longer isolate with confidence any sense of the original *Testament of Levi* seems too conservative, the position that goes to the opposite extreme and eliminates entire chapters because they contain hints of Christian interpolation in one or more verses is also not acceptable. We prefer a moderate approach which acknowledges that some themes that appear Christian could just as easily have emerged from a Jewish background." De Jonge himself continues to refer to "the patently Christian

While Christian passages are manifestly evident in the *Testaments,* many issues raised by other portions of the work are so patently restricted to the concerns of pre-Christian Jewish debate as could only be appropriate to an original Jewish work. The uncompromising commitment to Torah and the prohibition against intermarriage seem strange for Christians who, according to the interpolations, welcomed the Gentile mission. Large sections of the work hardly seem to have been reworked, or even retouched, in light of Christian issues and experience as one would have expected given de Jonge's theories. Some interests — such as the calendar and the priesthood — suggest matters of importance a century before the turn of the eras, and demand, at the very least, a provenance prior to A.D. 70, after which questions associated with priesthood and temple became mute. If the present *Testaments* are a complete revision, as de Jonge suggests, one wonders why these many irrelevant and, one should add, definitely *pre-Christian* concerns were not completely removed from the Jewish original(s); that they were not suggests an editorial policy that allowed much in the *Testaments* to stand as it did in the original Jewish work.

Scholars regularly take the major evidence against a *complete* Christian reworking of the *Testaments* to be the presence of a Levitical messianology that simply cannot be harmonized with the beliefs of any known Christian group of the time,[48] although, as will be argued below, this type of messianology may not actually have been intrinsic to the *Testaments.* There are, however, many Levitical references (of a "nonmessianic" type), and the editors did little to remove these from their sources even if they could have done so, given that these Levi passages are totally integrated into the warp and woof of the text. Indeed, the Levi passages appear to have been so numerous and essential to the original Jewish text that the Christian editors felt constrained to allow them to stand unaltered.[49] Again, and for whatever reason, this editorial conservatism suggests that the editors did *not* opt for a wholesale revision at all, and were pleased to allow the *Testaments* to remain an essentially *Jewish* work. It is evident that their objective (namely, to give witness to Jesus from a Jewish perspective) was felt to have been better served by this course of action than by a complete "Christianizing" of the text.

As for the view that the original language of the *Testaments* was Greek

---

elements" (*Jewish Eschatology, Early Christian Christology, and the Testaments of the Twelve Patriarchs,* 1991, 39) — betraying that he thinks they are distinguishable from the rest of the text! His notion that it is time to attend to a synchronic analysis of the text as it now stands (i.e., as "Christian Testaments" — as far as that goes; 3) should be accepted; however, data for an understanding of Judaism may nonetheless still be drawn from this text.

48. Cf. A. Hultgård, *L'eschatologie des Testaments des Douze Patriarches,* 1977, 1:75-79.

49. Cf. Hultgård, 1977, 1:79.

rather than Hebrew or Aramaic, however, de Jonge is perhaps rather more on the mark. This conclusion seems to be demanded by the presence of a number of Greek ethical terms not easily retranslatable into Hebrew.[50] Semitic parallels to the *Testaments* have been known for some time (Aramaic Levi documents found in the Cairo synagogue geniza and at Qumran, and a Hebrew testament of Naphtali also found in the geniza), and this in itself may cast serious doubt on de Jonge's findings. But it should be remembered that the relationship of these Semitic testaments to the Greek *Testaments of the Twelve Patriarchs* is not at all certain, and there are many divergences among the extant texts, which suggests that they may have been written quite independently of one another. Determining sources from internal indications is equally unsatisfactory. Speculated Levi sources or Judah sources give the impression that the present twelve testaments are amplifications of an original two or three, but it is quite likely that the Greek *Testaments* were originally written in their present twelvefold division — the continuity in subject matter and uniformity of structure within and throughout the present *Testaments* suggest a basic unity of composition rather than either a simple collation of sources or a Christian amplification of a Jewish work.[51] This document was certainly, therefore, a "Hellenistic" Jewish writing, but the fact that the *Testaments* may have been written in Greek from the beginning does not in any way preclude their usefulness as a source of *essentially Jewish* teaching, and many scholars approach the *Testaments* accordingly. Any date for their composition is possible within the Hasmonean period (mid-second century B.C.) up to A.D. 70 — although we prefer a Hasmonean date.[52]

50. Charles does offer extensive evidence of the underlying Hebrew language (cf. 1908, xxiv-xxxix), but the presence of Hellenistic ethical terminology central to the *Testaments*, which cannot be easily retranslated into Hebrew, suggests that the original language was Greek (H. C. Kee, "The Ethical Dimensions of the Testaments of the XII as a Clue to Provenance," 1977a, 259-70; Hollander and de Jonge, 1985, 28). Such terms include εὐσέβεια, σωφροσύνη, ἁπλότης, συνείδησις, etc., which are found mainly in the non-Hebrew books of the LXX.

51. H. W. Hollander (*Joseph as an Ethical Model in the Testaments of the Twelve Patriarchs*, 1981, 92-93) discerns this unity in the parenetic purpose of the writing.

52. Hultgård (1977, 1:55) places it about 100 B.C. It might be argued that the *Testaments* reflect an intense period of protest against the Hasmonean priesthood, suggesting the period following Jason and Menelaus. Significantly, Jaubert detects indications of an early and Essene-like theology in the *Testaments* (i.e, their attitude to the Temple; A. Jaubert, *La notion d'alliance dans le Judaïsme aux abords de l'ère chrétienne*, 1963, 274; cf. 277-78). Charles's date of 137-107 B.C., however, is rather feebly based on the triple attribution of prophet, priest, and king, which he believed to have been inspired by John Hyrcanus (*TLevi* 8:15; 1908, xliii).

Various Other Writings

More certain than the dates of the scrolls, *1 Enoch,* or the *Testaments* are the approximate dates of *Jubilees* (ca. 160 B.C.),[53] the *Psalms of Solomon* (shortly following Pompey's siege of Jerusalem in 63 B.C.),[54] 4 Ezra, and *2 Baruch* (within a few decades of the destruction of the temple in A.D. 70, perhaps as late as A.D. 100-120). The *Assumption of Moses* has its own historical problems, but there is little doubt that the work in its present form comes from about the turn of the era. A relatively lucid reference to Herod and his sons places the present edition, at least, in the period A.D. 7 to 30, and probably close to the beginning of that period.[55] The writing is so replete with references to the Maccabean and Hasmonean periods, on the other hand, that it has been reasoned that what we have in the *Assumption of Moses* is a much earlier writing that has been worked over and supplemented.[56]

53. Charles's view was that the book was written "between the year of the accession of Hyrcanus to the high-priesthood in 135 and his breach with the Pharisees some years before his death in 105 B.C." (*APOT,* 2:1). More widely accepted is the view of J. C. VanderKam (*Textual and Historical Studies in the Book of Jubilees,* 1977, 208-85), who assigns *Jubilees* to the period immediately following Judas Maccabeus, or to 161-152 B.C. (283-84). He discerns in passages like 34:2-9 (the battle of Jacob and his sons against seven Amorite kings, elaborating on Gen. 48:22) a cryptic reference to Judas's battles against Nicanor in 161 B.C. (218-19, 228). VanderKam resorts to some emendation to arrive at this date, which may leave some room for doubt, but his study remains valuable for the way it benefits from paleographic evidence based on the *Jubilees* MSS at Qumran, which all but establishes a pre–100 B.C. date for the book (216).

54. The view is summarized by J. O'Dell, "The Religious Background of the Psalms of Solomon," 1961, 241-42.

55. The deposition of Herod's son Archelaus in A.D. 6 apparently suggested to the writer the short reign for Herod's sons predicted in 6:7; since this prediction failed, as Philip and Antipas went on to rule for longer periods than even Herod, this narrows down the date for the extant work to soon after A.D. 7 (cf. W. J. Ferrar, *The Assumption of Moses,* 1917, 9).

56. For discussion of both sides of the issue, see G. W. E. Nickelsburg, ed., *Studies on the Testament of Moses,* 1973, 5-6, and the articles in the same volume by J. J. Collins (15-32, 38-43) and Nickelsburg (33-37).

CHAPTER TWO

Conventional Nationalistic Views of Election in Judaism

For several decades now scholars have been proclaiming the death and burial of the idea of a "normative Judaism." George Foot Moore's use of this term typified, and brought to a kind of climax, the dominance of rabbinic theology in systematic studies of Judaism up to his time.[1] But it also precipitated a barrage of attacks from scholars aware of real *diversity* within Second Temple Judaism.[2] As a result of continuing reaction, scholarship today possesses a sensitivity to the subject that only decades of repeated and harsh denials can produce. When during the height of reaction in the 1970s E. P. Sanders suggested that there could be found an "essence" common to all Judaism of the period,[3] J. H. Charlesworth charged him with attempting to revive the notion of normative Judaism.[4] Given the recent emphasis on the diversity of Second Temple Judaism, however, any recovery of the idea of normative Judaism seems unlikely.

But long- and well-established conceptions do not die as easily as all that. While the *language* of a universalizing or synthesizing of Second Temple Judaism has certainly been disparaged, this is not to say that the *critique* of the idea

---

1. G. F. Moore, *Judaism in the First Centuries of the Christian Era*, 1927, 1:125-32.

2. For rejections of the idea of a normative Judaism, cf., *inter alia*, D. S. Russell, *The Method and Message of Jewish Apocalyptic, 200 B.C.–A.D. 100*, 1964, 22; P. Sigal, *Judaism*, 1988, 1, 38-40.

3. Cf. E. P. Sanders, "Patterns of Religion in Paul and Rabbinic Judaism," 1973; E. P. Sanders, *Paul and Palestinian Judaism*, 1977, 9-10.

4. Cf. J. H. Charlesworth, *The Old Testament Pseudepigrapha and the New Testament*, 1985, 19-21, 47ff.

of a normative Judaism has been much more than superficial. In the following pages evidence will be cited for the continuing existence of what might be called a "conventional" or "standard" view of Judaism, a kind of lingering influence of the above-mentioned universalizing trend, and one that has not been seriously challenged in spite of the recent emphasis on diversity in Judaism. A quotation from Joseph Bonsirven, whose comments on the unity of Judaism are quite representative of scholars past and present, will illustrate the tremendous momentum of this conventional view even before Moore's time: "The Jews of Palestine were divided into various sects: Pharisees, Sadducees, Essenes, popular and apocalyptic groups. But in spite of differences, some superficial and others profound and essential, these sects were united by a common fund of beliefs and practices derived directly from the Bible and from revered and universally accepted traditions."[5]

Scholars like Bonsirven are specific about which beliefs united Judaism in this way. There was, first of all, Judaism's distinctive *view of divinity,* particularly God's unity and uniqueness. It is hardly surprising that this should be considered a chief doctrine of Judaism, although certain Jewish-Gnostic groups, Jewish Christian teachings, and more "orthodox" Jewish writings appear to differ in certain respects about the meaning of "unity," which has recently given rise to some new theories about the nature of Israel's belief in God in the Second Temple period. Another belief universally acknowledged to have been embraced in Second Temple Judaism regards the preeminent *place of law.* Again, it is hardly surprising that this would be considered the general belief of Judaism, although the Qumran writings, certain pseudepigrapha such as *Jubilees,* as well as the New Testament, have all been demonstrated to hold somewhat nonconformist understandings of the place of law in their belief systems. Some doubt, therefore, might exist that these "pillars" of Judaism are actually as stable as they have traditionally been held to be, and conventional views of Judaism are accordingly undergoing some reevaluation even in these vitally important areas.

The concern of this book, however, is to call a third "pillar" belief to the bench. This is the doctrine, widely assumed to belong *universally* to Judaism, of the *irrevocable national election of Israel.* In this view Israel is the people of God, different from all peoples, and as such the *focus* of God's redemptive work; the individual Israelite is secure in the knowledge that redemption is assured for the individual member of the nation. For a classical statement of this belief, closely associated with the other two elements of the "conventional view" of Judaism mentioned above, we can look to the father of modern studies of rabbinics, Solomon Schechter, a Jewish scholar who has exercised an incalculable influence on all subsequent discussions of Judaism. He

5. J. Bonsirven, *Palestinian Judaism in the Time of Jesus Christ,* 1964, vi.

speaks of these three pillars as enduring and vital essentials of Israel's faith that have never been successfully challenged: "Whenever any influence, no matter by whom advanced or by whatever power maintained, developed a tendency that was contrary to a *strict monotheism,* or denied *the binding character of the Torah,* or aimed to destroy *the unity and character and calling of Israel,* although it may have gained currency for a time, the Synagogue finally succeeded in eliminating it as noxious to its very existence."[6] Schechter's summary is in substance frequently repeated. A few representative quotations from other scholars will demonstrate how ingrained and unanimous this view has become. A similar understanding is found, for example, in the systematic treatment of Jewish theology by K. Köhler, who states that the doctrines of God, revelation, and Israel form part of the "essence" of Judaism.[7] Köhler is especially worth noting for the way he stresses the fundamental role of the doctrine of Israel in Judaism:

> Judaism . . . combines two widely differing elements, and when they are brought out separately, the aspect of the whole is not taken sufficiently into account. Religion and race form an inseparable whole in Judaism. The Jewish people stand in the same relation to Judaism as the *body* to the *soul.*

> The central point of Jewish theology and the key to an understanding of the nature of Judaism is the doctrine, "God chose Israel as His people."[8]

In work after work this view about Judaism is never seriously challenged. It is repeated by Bonsirven: "If God is one of the poles around which Jewish thought turns, Israel is the other,"[9] and more recently by P. Sigal, who is in other ways an outspoken exponent of diversity in Judaism: "Despite significant changes in the course of the evolution of Judaism, its primary doctrines recall the pristine theology of the ancient religion of Israel. These doctrines are monotheism, creation, covenant, election, revelation, and redemption."[10]

These few examples (representative of a limitless number of similar expressions)[11] are enough to demonstrate that there is acknowledged in virtually all systematic studies of Judaism a clearly circumscribed canon of belief

6. S. Schechter, *Some Aspects of Rabbinic Theology,* 1909, xvii-xviii, emphasis added.

7. K. Köhler, *Jewish Theology,* 1928, 15.

8. Köhler, 1928, 7, 323.

9. Bonsirven, 1964, 42.

10. Sigal, 1988, 1.

11. Cf. also, e.g., I. M. Zeitlin, *Jesus and the Judaism of His Time,* 1988, 8, who mentions "ethical monotheism" and the Law as two unifying religious beliefs in Judaism. A. Marmorstein, "The Unity of God in Rabbinic Literature," 1950, 72, calls the unity of God "the chief religious doctrine the Jews taught mankind."

that, in spite of any diversity in Judaism, could be viewed as the "bare essentials" of Judaism. This canon of belief quite regularly includes the idea of God, the centrality of law, and — especially important for our purposes — the irrevocable election of the nation Israel.[12] The influence of this conventional view, in turn, on studies of the New Testament is proportionately strong since, as could only be expected, the view finds its way into all comparative studies of Judaism and Christianity that depend on these Jewish theologies. James Dunn is a well-respected current scholar who, according to his own profession, is thoroughly aware of the dangers of the above-mentioned "normative" approaches. As is characteristic of Dunn, all his statements about Judaism are well considered. But as a New Testament scholar who merely consults experts in the associated, but quite separate, field of Jewish studies (as he should), he naturally admits established prejudices into his views of Judaism. In his important contribution to the question of Jewish-Christian relations at the turn of the eras, he speaks of "a common and unifying core for second Temple Judaism, a fourfold foundation on which all these more diverse forms of Judaism built, a *common heritage* which they all interpreted their own ways" — *including monotheism, election, covenant/law, and land/Temple.* "These then can be fairly described as the *four pillars* [emphasis added] on which the Judaism(s) of Jesus' time was/(were) built, *the axiomatic convictions round which the more diverse interpretations and practices of the different groups within Judaism revolved* [emphasis in original]." As for the election of Israel specifically: "If anything this is even more deeply rooted (than monotheism) already in the pre-exilic period. . . . As with the other pillars of Second Temple Judaism these convictions were re-established in the post-exilic period. . . . The same emphases come through consistently in the Jewish writings which stretch down to our period. . . ." Citing a single passage each from *Jubilees* and *Psalms of Solomon*, Dunn concludes: "It is probably unnecessary to document the point in more detail, since the thought of Israel as *God's* inheritance can be traced through many strands of Jewish literature. So too in the Dead Sea Scrolls and rabbinic traditions the conviction that Israel is God's elect, chosen, God's vineyard is absolutely axiomatic."[13] While Dunn in fact does seem to retract this generalization at one point,[14] these statements nevertheless provide particularly clear evidence of just how well established are the conventional views — notably the nationalistic under-

---

12. These three pillar beliefs continue to characterize systematization in the modern Jewish context; cf., e.g., M. Asheri, *Living Jewish*, 1980, 32-35.

13. J. D. G. Dunn, *The Partings of the Ways between Christianity and Judaism and Their Significance for the Character of Christianity*, 1991, 18-35.

14. Cf. Dunn, 1991, 105-7, 301 n. 37.

standing of election theology in Judaism — in even recent and relatively well-informed comparative studies of Judaism and Christianity.[15]

While it would seem either bold or stupid to question *any* of these pillar beliefs, perhaps some attention to the context in which the conventional view was formed will facilitate at least an objective critique of it. The fact that the origins of this view were in a very narrow and monolithic understanding of Judaism has already been alluded to. The early foundational studies were based largely, if not exclusively, on rabbinic (talmudic) Judaism, a set of circumstances that has, not insignificantly, provided grounds for the recent critique of "normative Judaism." But, beyond that, studies of Judaism have regularly been plagued with other flaws. Primary among these is the frequent practice of ignoring proper historical methodology; to be specific, drawing on *modern* Jewish belief for purposes of systematizing *ancient* doctrine. Thus it has not been rare, especially in the early and formative days of pioneering scholars, to resort to modern Jewish systematizations when lack of early data precluded complete analysis.[16] In fact, there has been a prevailing tendency *throughout* the history of scholarship to treat Judaism as timeless and, therefore, as largely *unconditioned by development*. Schechter himself is to be noted for the way he declared differences between early rabbinic Judaism and later tradition to be negligible and any and all external influences and developments to have been effectively obliterated by the "power of Judaism."[17] In a similar vein he can speak of a "Catholic Israel," the "unity of the synagogue," and the "religious consciousness of Israel," a timeless stabilizing influence that supposedly dominated in medieval writings and in first-century Judaism and is even evident in contemporary "living testimony" — to which appeal can also be made![18] For Köhler, also, systematic considerations clearly predominate over historical considerations. A recognition of the need to distinguish between early sources and later doctrine is simply not to be found in his work. Köhler's goal was rather to provide a comprehensive view of Judaism through its entire period, which is evident

---

15. This has, of course, been widely evident among many influential New Testament scholars, of whom we need mention only the notable example of Rudolf Bultmann (*Primitive Christianity in Its Primitive Setting*, 1956, 94-97, 101; *Theology of the New Testament*, 1952, 1:46-47; *Jesus and the Word*, 1935, 45). Bultmann bases the arguments for his comparative approach on this fundamentally nationalistic understanding of Judaism, thus eventually being compelled to adopt an existential overview in order to avoid the implications of a narrow particularism and to grant universal significance to Jewish history.

16. Jacob Jocz's study on election in Judaism is an unfortunate recent example of this absence of historical methodology. His *Theology of Election*, 1958, seems particularly to reflect modern concerns of church and synagogue.

17. Schechter, 1909, xvi-xvii.

18. Schechter, 1909, viii-xviii.

when he comments on his labors: "I have attempted to cover the whole field of Jewish belief, including also such subjects as no longer form part of the religious consciousness of the modern Jew."[19] He consequently draws little distinction between ancient and modern views in his strictly systematic presentation.

While other scholars from the past century — what might be termed the formative period of Jewish studies — were certainly more historically conscious than this, they nevertheless still failed to transcend the already constraining authority of the conventional view of Judaism. C. G. Montefiore represented an emerging consciousness of the need to compare (if not outrightly contrast) first-century Judaism with that found in later rabbinic tradition.[20] He is renowned for the important distinction between "Hellenistic" and "rabbinic" Judaism of the first century;[21] not only did he recognize diversity in Judaism, unlike many of his predecessors, he clearly recognized the historical problems inherent in reading back into the early centuries the rabbinic traditions of a later time. But Montefiore's work represented another trend, and that was to marginalize *non*rabbinic Judaism as cold, harsh, and inferior. In the end, he also recognized only one mainstream kind of Judaism, a Judaism that, for all his historical caution, he believed remained consistent and uniform throughout the entire period of the first to sixth centuries. Once again, therefore, the Judaism of later centuries took on a normative if not universal authority, and the standard view was further established and strengthened through this process. The historical weaknesses of these early systematizing approaches are perhaps understandable, in view of the fact that these represent pioneering attempts to do what had not been done before — to present Judaism as a system of beliefs or doctrines. But the resulting effect was to cast a die that would not be easily broken. The intention of these scholars to be general in presentation seems to have been carelessly ignored by later scholars, who uncritically repeated their views and applied them directly to the Tannaitic period and earlier times.

The above-mentioned work of George Foot Moore provides yet another example of this tendency to rely on unhistorical and generalizing studies. The criticism of this scholar — who was not only credited as being the first to coin the term "normative Judaism" but also accused of the severe overcategorization it implied — is deserved, but in a sense unfair, because Moore became a scapegoat for the already *habitual* employment of nonhistorical approaches to Judaism, and through this criticism his work eventually (if quite unintentionally) opened up a new and brighter era in Jewish studies. Moore did nothing to conceal his debt to the collective tradition of the rabbis for his reconstruction of

---

19. Köhler, 1928, ix.
20. C. G. Montefiore, *Judaism and St. Paul,* 1914, 17-18, 66-68.
21. Montefiore, 1914, 94, 114, etc.

earlier Judaism. Employing an argument similar to Schechter's "power of Judaism," he also justified a unifying approach on the basis of an invisible or mystic authority resident in tradition:

> [Judaism] may properly claim to be represented by the teachers and the writings which it has always regarded as in the line of its catholic tradition, all the more because the resulting consensus is authoritative, and is embodied in a corpus of tradition possessing not only universal authority but in some sense finality. Numerous other Jewish writings have come down to us from these centuries, to which neither biblical nor rabbinical authority attached.[22]

The historiological fallacy of this argument, of course, is that it assumes that earlier thought can be determined by later preferences (however authoritative) or that earlier thought is somehow safeguarded through random processes of preservation.[23] The problems that emerge from this kind of unhistorical thinking are obvious: modern Jewish tradition cannot claim to have preserved a comprehensive view of all, or even the most important, Judaisms of an earlier time, and the term "rabbinic" itself implies limitation to only one voice within a much greater diversity. Nevertheless, this methodology was widely accepted among scholars of Judaism, particularly, but not by any means exclusively, among those who focused on Tannaitic Judaism. This whole process, and this factor in particular, played a significant role in the emergence of an authoritative "conventional" view of Judaism, of which a basically nationalistic approach to election theology was an important part.

THE PREVALENCE AND PERSISTENCE OF NATIONALISTIC THEOLOGY IN TREATMENTS OF JUDAISM

The word "nationalism" conjures up a vast range of associations, from political ideology to military zealotism.[24] But nationalism is not only a political concept; it is also a *theological* concept, especially as it embraces a particular view of God's relations and intentions with respect to the nation Israel, and especially as it is reflected in the doctrine of the *election* of Israel. Straining out a nationalistic election theology from all the other kinds of "nationalism," however, is

22. Moore, 1927, 1:126.
23. For the view that the rabbinic literature alone is valid for a study of Judaism, cf. also R. T. Herford, *Judaism in the New Testament Period*, 1928, 11-12.
24. This is a chief subject of S. G. F. Brandon's *Jesus and the Zealots*, 1967, and is widely reflected also in W. R. Farmer, *Maccabees, Zealots, and Josephus*, 1956.

never a straightforward task, as a variety of related concepts are often juxtaposed and intertwined. A nationalistic theology could (and apparently did) consist, at one and the same time, of the hope that God would save Israel (theological ideals) by means of a national campaign (military ideals) that would result in political independence (political ideals). Regardless of its possible complexities, however, the important feature of a basically nationalistic theology, in the sense intended here, is that its *chief focus* is the life and ideals of the *nation*, in contrast to a theology that focuses on any other group or on the individual. It can be easily demonstrated how this basically nationalistic approach characterizes not only earlier, systematic studies but all recent and specialized studies of Second Temple Judaism as well, both those that deal with rabbinic literature and those that deal with the "apocalyptic" writings.

Rabbinic Studies

It is not surprising that one finds this conventional view reflected in works on rabbinic theology, since it was largely because of these writings that the view became established in the first place. One notable example, because of the extremity of its position, is the treatment of rabbinic Judaism by the German scholar Ferdinand Weber, whose arrangement and commentary on the talmudic material just prior to the turn of the century is known for its portrayal of a very harsh form of Jewish nationalism. Weber sustained his view by means of an equally strict view of Jewish legalism. So strict was this legalism believed to be that Weber was eventually constrained to deny to Judaism a doctrine of salvation of any sort![25]

While it is perhaps not surprising that Weber saw Judaism as nationalistic and particularistic, it is rather more surprising that his successors in the field, both Jewish and Gentile, and even those who have accepted a considerably more sympathetic view of Judaism, nevertheless retain a similarly thoroughgoing view of the nationalistic doctrine of Israel. Differing from Weber's rather negative and exclusive understanding of nationalism (stressing election as *restricted* to the nation Israel — namely, particularism), however, Jewish scholars tend to emphasize more positive and inclusive aspects (stressing the certainty of election, or election as the possession of *every* Israelite). But even for Jewish scholars the basic nationalistic perspective is in many ways equally dominating.

25. F. Weber, *Jüdische Theologie auf Grund des Talmud und verwandter Schriften gemeinfaßlich dargestellt*, 1897; repr. 1975, 46-79. Cf. E. P. Sanders, 1977, 37-38, for a valid critique of Weber. This denial of a soteriology naturally leaves quite a tension between election and law not resolved in Weber's work. For more on this tension see below.

We might note again the important and respected, but in many ways typical, example of Solomon Schechter, who goes so far as to refer to the rabbinic doctrine of election as "unconditional" — even the sin of Israel cannot destroy the relationship between God and his people; according to one tradition, when the prophet Elijah questioned this relationship, he was removed from his post; statements of the prophets against Israel are interpreted not as putting this relationship into question but as proving God's continuing faithfulness in spite of Israel's sin. Schechter mentions the one exception to this view among the rabbis: "The only opponent to the view of the majority regarding the paternal relation is R. Judah [ben Ilai], who limits it to the time when Israel acts as children should act." By mentioning such an exception, however, Schechter brings into sharper focus this presupposition regarding the rabbis' certainty about election.[26] The centrality of the idea of the national election is evident also in the other important doctrines of Judaism: thus God is the God *of Israel*,[27] the Law is the privileged possession of Israel,[28] and the like. These correlations are well illustrated in a synagogue prayer quoted by Schechter: "Thou hast chosen us from all people; thou hast loved us and taken pleasure in us, and hast exalted us above all tongues; thou hast sanctified us *by thy commandments* and brought us near unto thy service; O our King, *thou hast called us by thy great and holy name.*"[29]

Other scholars, like Travers Herford, also show a distinct awareness of the importance of the doctrine of national election in rabbinic literature: "Those outside the community of Israel, the Gentiles of every race, could only become effectively children of God by joining the community, or at least by sharing in the revelation made to Israel."[30] W. D. Davies perpetuates this basically nationalistic understanding: "The religion of the Torah was essentially a national religion. To accept the Torah meant not merely initiation into a religion, as did, for example, the acceptance of Mithraism, but incorporation into a nation."[31] Bonsirven is another good example of the view of the importance of national election: "For Jewish theologians that election had an eternal importance." He cites *Sifra* on Num. 5:3 as proof of the irrevocability of this election: "God always dwells among the Israelites, even when they sin

---

26. Schechter, 1909, 51-54. This view is repeated by B. W. Helfgott in *The Doctrine of Election in Tannaitic Literature*, 1954, 120-21.

27. For examples of a presentation of the rabbinic doctrine of God in a very nationalistic framework, see Herford, 1928, 17; Marmorstein, 1950, 83-84.

28. E.g., Köhler, 1928, 354-66, who dedicates a chapter to the Law in the context of the election of Israel.

29. Schechter, 1909, 57-58.

30. Herford, 1928, 158.

31. W. D. Davies, *Paul and Rabbinic Judaism*, 1955, 58-62; the citation is from p. 67.

and are unworthy." National theology is central and essential to Judaism, says Bonsirven: "These two nouns, nation and religion, ought to be written as one — nation-religion — since they stand for one substance, made of two elements. In this lies the special character and originality of Israel."[32] More recently, in an anthology of early rabbinic theology, Hyam Maccoby includes the doctrine of Israel among the four main ideas of early rabbinic literature, adding that "the Covenant was a personal bond between God and every Israelite."[33] In fact, most summaries of talmudic teaching mention this nationalistic election theology,[34] and where they do not, silence must be interpreted to reflect acquiescence to the view.

While both the exclusive and inclusive aspects of nationalistic election theology come out in these treatments of rabbinic Judaism, it is the "inclusive" view of the national election that is, in our view, most open to criticism. (In fact, however, the exclusive and inclusive aspects are merely two sides of the same coin: in both cases election is defined by distinctly *national* considerations.) As a particularly clear representation of this inclusive aspect, we might cite Montefiore: "Rabbinic Judaism was convinced . . . that for every decent Israelite there was a place in the future world, in 'the life to come.'"[35] To this statement could be compared the following by Moore: "'A lot in the World to come' . . . is ultimately assured to every Israelite on the ground of the original election of the people by the free grace of God."[36] While scholars of rabbinic thought sometimes also offer points of view that would seem to conflict with this generalizing statement, a direct challenge to this conventional understanding of things has not yet been ventured, as we will soon see.

Studies of the Jewish Pseudepigrapha (Apocalyptic Writings)

Should it be admitted that such a national election theology does in fact characterize the rabbinic writings, it is still rather surprising to note that this same generalization has long been brought to many nonrabbinic writings as well, particularly the Pseudepigrapha ("Apocalyptic Literature"). Again with respect to these writings the conventional view of Judaism, with its nationalistic election theology as a basic working assumption, has remained basically unchallenged. It is on occasion noted that these writings originate in a strict, "sectar-

32. Bonsirven, 1964, 42-51; the citations are from pp. 43, 49, and 97.
33. H. Maccoby, *Early Rabbinic Writings,* 1988, 46.
34. Cf. also, e.g., Helfgott, 1954, 120; R. A. Stewart, *Rabbinic Theology,* 1961, 146; E. E. Urbach, *The Sages,* 1975, 525-41.
35. Montefiore, 1914, 44.
36. Moore, 1927, 2:95, quoted with approval by E. P. Sanders, 1977, 147.

ian" or legalistic school of Judaism,[37] or that they contained the religious aspirations of the "pious,"[38] but this does not prevent them from being characterized as promoting an especially intense nationalism.

Certainly the most serious example of this tendency, by virtue of its continuing influence today, is to be found in the many important works of one of the preeminent scholars of intertestamental Judaism, R. H. Charles. In his introductory works, in his translation and commentary on individual writings, and in his collection (*Apocrypha and Pseudepigrapha of the Old Testament*, vol. 2) — still considered among the standard treatments in the English world — Charles revealed his commitment to the view of the "apocalyptic writings" as worthy (and therefore patriotically *nationalistic*) examples of mainstream Judaism.[39] Charles largely saw these writings as written by Pharisaic Jews[40] and accordingly containing the normal Pharisaic nationalistic perspective, a perspective that guides the pietistic authors in their portrayal of the *superiority of Judaism over the nations.*[41] In Charles's view the Gentile "sinners" are implicitly and derogatorily compared and contrasted, throughout these works, with the "righteous" Jewish people. The central message of the writings, which Charles understood largely as *eschatological* presentations, is that the dominance of God over all history will be proven at the End and will be exhibited in and through the eventual *triumph* of the nation Israel over all her foes. Given such a premise for the apocalyptic writings as a whole, one can easily see the extent to which this strong eschatological tendency in Charles's work in promoting the nationalistic understanding as well. In fact, a kind of marriage between nationalism and eschatology is everywhere evident, and this is regularly and repeatedly confirmed in other studies of Jewish "apocalyptic" and eschatology.[42] *These two ideas — nationalism and eschatology — are intimately linked in the common view that history and escha-*

---

37. As, e.g., in Charles's description of *Jubilees* as written "from the standpoint of strictest Judaism" (*APOT*, 2:11 n. 1). Cf. J. Bloch, *On the Apocalyptic in Judaism*, 1952, 130.

38. As in P. Volz, *Die Eschatologie der jüdischen Gemeinde*, 1934; cited in Bloch, 1952, 58.

39. R. H. Charles: "these apocalyptic writings . . . represented the advance of the higher theology in Judaism, which culminated in Christianity" (*APOT*, 2:163; *The Book of Enoch or 1 Enoch*, 1912, ix).

40. Regarding *Jubilees*, cf. *APOT*, 2:8; on *1 Enoch*, cf. *APOT*, 2:164; on *Psalms of Solomon*, cf. *APOT*, 2:630; on *2 Baruch*, cf. *APOT*, 2:478, and R. H. Charles, *The Apocalypse of Baruch translated from the Syriac*, 1896, viii.

41. For *Jubilees* as an apology for Israel, see Charles, *APOT*, 2:8; Charles, *The Book of Jubilees or Little Genesis, Translated from the Editor's Ethiopic Text*, 1902, xiv; similarly for *2 Baruch*, see Charles, 1896, viii.

42. Cf., e.g., Volz, 1934, passim, esp. 9, 27-28, 30-32.

tology serve to vindicate Israel from her enemies and oppressors — that is, they serve her fundamentally national goals.[43]

Charles's basic position represented fairly well the view of many of his contemporaries regarding the essentially nationalistic orientation of these works, and in turn influenced them. S. H. Hooke (the source, in turn, for no less a scholar than W. O. E. Oesterley) virtually equates apocalypticism with (exclusive) nationalism: "In the main the apocalyptic vision was nationalistic, and only occasionally do we find gleams of an ideal order of society in which distinction of nationality will disappear."[44] William Fairweather summarizes the origins of the apocalyptic writings this way: "They are the most important literary expression of the revived national sentiment which built up the Hasmonean State, and finally led to the disastrous conflict with Rome."[45]

Thus the view (even in this last extreme form!) was common to many of the pioneering scholars in this field, who revealed little inclination to subject their presuppositions to any test. But it was clearly Charles's own massive works of scholarship in particular that were and still are most responsible for the standard view (at least in the English-speaking world), and his basic positions on a whole score of matters have long been and certainly still remain the norm for many. Accordingly his influence can be seen in another more recent example of the general capitulation to conventional views of Judaism, D. S. Russell's *Method and Message of Jewish Apocalyptic.* This represents another standard work in the English-speaking world, and one of no little authority in its attempt to systematize apocalyptic theology and make it more accessible to modern students — which it does with much success. While Russell's work will certainly remain valuable for its many valid insights, it unfortunately repeats uncritically the view of Charles regarding the fundamental nationalism of the apocalyptic writings, which is contained in an eschatological framework. For Russell the apocalyptic writers "shared with one another a common purpose, acknowledged a common heritage and expressed a common hope in the ultimate triumph of God's kingdom in which the Jewish people would have a glorious part."[46] The absence of significant qualification in such a statement is certainly representative of a general inability or unwillingness to question the nationalistic view of Judaism or to recognize any inconsistencies in adopting such a view as far as these writings are concerned.

Mention should be made of one other, even more recent systematic study

43. Cf., e.g., Volz, 1934, 89-90.
44. S. H. Hooke, as cited in W. O. E. Oesterley, ed., *Judaism and Christianity,* 1969, 1:268.
45. W. Fairweather, *The Background of the Gospels,* 1926, 220.
46. Russell, 1964, 17, 27-29.

of apocalyptic literature that has at least the potential to displace Russell as the new standard work in the English-speaking world (although, unfortunately, it has never received the attention it deserves) — namely, Christopher Rowland's *Open Heaven* (1982).[47] Rowland's is actually a very perceptive treatment based on the importance of revelation in these works, and he appears in many respects to be more sympathetic to the world of apocalyptic than Russell.[48] Rowland perceives that some of the apocalyptic writings limit their message to a special group.[49] Although this is not a totally novel observation, in association with his views of the esoteric revelatory tradition of these works, it composes at least a potential and implicit challenge to conventional views about apocalyptic election theology. Unfortunately, however — and this remains the greatest omission of this and all other treatments of this corpus — Rowland is not sensitive to the potential implications of the elitist nature of revelation for the attitudes of these authors toward the national salvation. If we may be allowed to anticipate somewhat, this is perhaps because Rowland does not consider whether *part* of that elitist revelation *included* truth about essential matters like the covenant and salvation.[50]

These few representative, but important, examples from works on rabbinic theology and on the Pseudepigrapha show how persistently the conventional view of national election theology has been sustained by scholars. Judaism has unanimously been seen as nationalistic in its theology: for all its differences in detail, its *focus is chiefly upon the nation Israel, its life and its ideals. No serious attempt has been made to refute this basic assumption.* This is partly because in the history of scholarship various attempts to define "normative" Judaism have encouraged this characterization. The doctrine of national election has been considered a sign of what was "normative" or "official," while any Judaism that denied the national election, and in this way appeared sectarian, could in no way be considered "mainstream." It is no surprise, then, given the way discussions about Judaism have centered upon the identity of "official" Judaism, that Judaism has repeatedly been presented as nationalistic. Even those who have outrightly rejected the unqualified importance of the rabbinic writings for an analysis of Second Temple Judaism, or who go further and adopt the

47. C. Rowland, *The Open Heaven: A Study of Apocalyptic in Judaism and Early Christianity* (London: SPCK, 1982).

48. Although in fairness to his predecessor in the field, Russell has actually made great strides in the same direction with works like *From Early Judaism to Early Church*, 1986, and *The Old Testament Pseudepigrapha*, 1987; somewhat more conventional is his *Prophecy and the Apocalyptic Dream*, 1994.

49. Cf. Rowland, 1982, 131, 145.

50. Rowland limits his concern to what we might call matters of interest to "theological science" — eschatology, cosmology, creation, and history.

pseudepigraphical writings or the Dead Sea Scrolls as the norm, unquestionably accept many of the standard beliefs about Judaism forged during the period when the idea of normative Judaism first emerged and before the movement of these other writings into prominence.[51]

LATENT TENSIONS IN THE
CONVENTIONAL VIEW OF NATIONAL ELECTION

It is apparent that conventional views of the national election theology of Judaism have escaped direct challenge in major works on Judaism. This is consistent both with the momentum this standard view gained early on in the systematization of Jewish belief, as well as with the gradually increasing authority it has enjoyed in the long run. But it would be an incomplete survey of the field of scholarship that did not mention *contrary* voices, however feeble they may be; and there are even some indications recently that the conventional nationalistic approach may be in some jeopardy. Given the renewed interest in the intertestamental period and literature represented by names like Baumgarten, Beckwith, Charlesworth, Collins, Hartman, Hultgård, Nickelsburg, Stone, and VanderKam, it would seem that a revolution in Jewish studies based on some fresh and revealing approaches to the literature is looming on the horizon. So far, however, these glimmerings of a new direction have not inspired any direct confrontations with traditional views, but strong challenges would appear to be imminent and have in some respects already begun.

For some time scholarship has been aware of certain *tensions* latent in the nationalistic classification of Judaism. Among others there might be mentioned (1) the tension that naturally exists in the dialectic between law and election in Judaism; (2) a similar tension created by the dialectic between universalism and nationalism; (3) the problems created by the existence of a "remnant" theology in some schools of Jewish thought; and (4) the exclusivist doctrines of the Dead Sea sect (which obviously only became evident following the discovery of the scrolls). Scholarly discussion of each of these possessed the potential to lead to a thorough revision of the conventional view; it is useful to note in each case, however, how and why such tensions were not considered serious enough to place traditional views in doubt.

---

51. Thus Charles, who was most notable for opposing the view of the normative authority of rabbinic Judaism (see *Religious Development between the Old and the New Testaments,* 1914, 35 and passim), is actually himself for this reason a prime offender. For criticism of the tendency, see J. J. Collins, *The Apocalyptic Imagination,* 1984, 11-12.

Law and Election — The Pharisee Question

There is, first of all, the obvious tension between the ideas of law, on the one hand, and election, on the other. It is widely agreed among scholars that during the Second Temple period, due to various religious and historical factors, direct appeal to the written Mosaic Torah gained an ever increasing importance within the religion of Judaism, eventually displacing all other Israelite institutions — including Temple and priesthood — as the chief authority in the Jewish world. Bereft of its ancient social institutions and scattered over the known world, Judaism necessarily became established as a religion of the Book and a people of the Book. The heightened role of Torah has been variously interpreted by scholars, but it is commonly held that, because of such developments, Judaism became fundamentally *legalistic*. "Legalistic" might imply little more than that Judaism became "law-oriented," but some (particularly non-Jewish) scholars, on the basis of their systematization of rabbinic doctrine, and perhaps equally on the basis of the negative view of legalism in the New Testament, have viewed all of Judaism as a legalistic system in which the *individual* is to be judged in the afterlife according to *a scale of merits*. While scholarship on the whole has now backed off from this fundamentally negative appraisal,[52] it has nevertheless resulted in a highly individualistic view of Jewish religion.[53]

Inasmuch as all truly individualistic systems will eventually tend toward a downplaying of national ideas,[54] this individualism might seem to place all election doctrines in jeopardy, and yet such considerations of the role of the Law in Judaism — even in their most extreme forms — have failed to result in any challenge to the conventional view, which continued to be presented as a chief dogma.[55] Some scholars, moreover, were aware of the contradiction created by the juxtaposition of the traditional national theology and a highly individualistic approach to the Law. In order to resolve the resulting tension, various rationalizations have been attempted, such as the rather artificial dialectic posited between obedience to the Law as an "individual" concern and the election of Israel as a "corporate" matter. Others offered even more philosophical solutions, maintaining that the legal doctrine in Judaism was what dominated, and the idea of elec-

---

52. Notably E. P. Sanders, 1977, 33-59. While other scholars have not engaged in the strong rhetoric of Sanders, most are willing to accept that the legalistic view of Judaism is at best an incomplete view.

53. The trend toward individualism is related to increased attention to law, as noted by Herford, 1928, 20-21, 41. For the development of the idea of individual divine retribution in the eschatology of Israel, see R. H. Charles, *Eschatology,* 1913, 64ff.

54. M. A. Seifrid, *Justification by Faith,* 1992, 133-34, notes that a concern for behavior combined with individualism "brings a concomitant form of universalism."

55. See esp. Fairweather, 1926, 19ff.

tion was brought forward only out of the necessities of a growing nationalism.[56] As a good example of these various rationalizations, one could cite Herford, who opts for a rather different solution than either of the above. He distinguishes between the doctrine of merits, which he considers a strictly *psychological* matter, and the quite independent status of the individual:

> The doing of an act of service to God does make a difference to the character of the man who has done it — adds something to his character that was not there before. That "something added" is the "merit" acquired by doing the act. . . . a change had been effected in his moral being. . . . Merit being taken to be a psychological fact, and not a boastful assertion of personal excellence. . . .[57]

No matter what solution to the problem is adopted, it is to be noted that some scholars at least recognized the problem and rather unconvincingly tried to explain it away;[58] conventional views of national election, however, remained unchallenged. Not that this discussion was without important consequences, however, for it at least served to bring into relief the problem of the relationship in Judaism among such major doctrines as election, law, covenant, sin, and soteriology. Problems will always remain in attempting to define these doctrines and their relationships to each other — partly because there is a certain amount of ambiguity and overlap inherent in the terminology, partly also because the ideas were probably never consciously harmonized in the literature of Judaism. But whether such doctrines can be expected to have been consciously systematized in the ancient Jewish world or not, contradiction and general lack of logic continue to be common rules in more recent studies of law and election. For example, in his treatment of the election in Judaism, Helfgott reveals a glaring contradiction: "the ultimate reward of a conscientious observance of Torah will be the participation in the world to come which *awaits every Israelite.*"[59] Helfgott does not explain how the "ultimate reward" can be the possession of a conscientious observer of Torah and, at the same time, of *every* Israelite. Perhaps he assumes that every Israelite *was automatically* a conscientious observer of Torah. This he does not say, but if this is the logic behind his statement, he fails to explain whether this was his own view or the view of Judaism itself; he simply accepts the idea of national election, with which he juxta-

---

56. For evidence of awareness of the tension, see Volz, 1934, 67; S. Mowinckel, *He That Cometh,* 1956, 271. Charles, 1914, 112-13, attempts a synthesis.

57. Herford, 1924, 132-34.

58. N. A. Dahl surprisingly denies any contradiction between the idea of a church and the strong nationalism of Judaism (*Das Volk Gottes,* 1962, 65, 82, etc.).

59. Helfgott, 1954, 128, emphasis added.

poses seemingly contradictory statements about individual merit. All this illustrates how the conventional nationalistic view can only be sustained in the face of real tensions with other ideas that may have been emerging within the Jewish world.

The preeminent example of this tension between law and election, and a notoriously thorny question, concerns the self-understanding of the Pharisees and their relationship to the rest of Israel. According to some scholars, the Pharisees regarded themselves as the "true Israel," that is, those who exclusively obey the Law and deserve to inherit the kingdom of heaven. But a clear consensus on this issue has so far been precluded by unsettled questions about the sources to be used for Pharisaic theology. If one equates Pharisaic teaching with the rabbinic doctrine found in the Talmud, as has often been done,[60] then questions about Pharisaic election theology would overlap with the theology of the rabbis; but this is far from certain. The confusion created by this uncertainty about sources is already reflected in the most important early studies. For Emil Schürer, Pharisaic religion was not only the predecessor of rabbinism but was, in fundamentals at least, the religion embraced by all of Judaism;[61] the Pharisees, after all, had the respect of the masses; the only thing that distinguished them from other Jews was their "greater strictness and consistency."[62] And yet, without acknowledging any contradiction with such statements, Schürer proceeds to maintain also that Pharisaic *halakah* was essential and that personal salvation depended on belief in resurrection; the Pharisees were an *ecclesiola in ecclesia;* their self-designations (both *pᵉrûšîm* and *ḥᵃbērîm*) implied the social ostracism of the masses.[63] The appropriate term for such a group is a "sect."[64] They were "brothers of the Covenant, who represented the true community of Israel. Whereas in the Old Testament every Israelite is a *ḥaver* of the other, the Pharisees recognized as *ḥaver* proper only the strict observer of the Torah."[65] The juxtaposition of such contradictory statements cannot help but produce equally contradictory conclusions, such as are evident in the following con-

---

60. For this "pan-Pharisaism," see Herford, 1924, who treats the rabbinic writings under the heading "Pharisaism," as if the two were identical. E. Schürer, *The History of the Jewish People in the Age of Jesus Christ,* 1973, 1979, provides a less obvious, but nevertheless comparable, example and adequately demonstrates how this confusion of sources results in real contradictions involving the exclusiveness of the Pharisees, on the one hand, and their nationalism, on the other (see further below). A more recent example is H. Jagersma, *A History of Israel from Alexander the Great to Bar Kochba,* 1985, 71-72.

61. Schürer, 1973, 1:389-91, 395.

62. Schürer, 1973, 1:389.

63. Schürer, 1973, 1:390-91, 396-98.

64. Αἵρεσις, used of them in the NT and Josephus; Schürer, 1973, 1:400.

65. Schürer, 1973, 1:399.

cluding statement about Pharisaism: "It was the legitimate and *typical* representative of post-exilic Judaism. It merely drew the conclusions from its principles that the only true Israel are those who punctiliously observe the Torah, and since the Pharisees alone do this, they are the *only true Israel.*"[66] Schürer does not tell us how the Pharisees could enjoy public popularity when they held such exclusive claims, but even concludes that "This great authority which the Pharisees exercised was but the counterpart of the exclusive position which they adopted."[67]

Another important study, that by Joachim Jeremias,[68] is rather more circumspect in its employment of sources than Schürer. Rather than taking all talmudic theology as representative of Pharisaic belief, Jeremias confines himself to those passages that make more or less direct reference to Jerusalem "*ḥabū-rōt*," which he equates with the Pharisaic "closed societies." This term, along with the talmudic expression "holy community of Jerusalem," refers to the Pharisees as the "saved remnant," the "separated," in a manner similar to the way Christians are called "the saints." They are the true Israel in contrast to the *'am ha-areṣ* ("the people of the land," a derogatory term meaning "the unreligious"). Similarities to the Qumran community are unmistakable, and Jeremias even entertains possible relationships with them.[69] Like Schürer, therefore, Jeremias cites considerable evidence for the exclusivity of the Pharisees. Also like Schürer, he incorporates evidence for the popularity of the Pharisees. But unlike Schürer, he *does* note the contradiction implied in this evidence: that this exclusive, and religiously self-superior, group could be so popular among the very masses they rejected is surprising. Jeremias accordingly attempts to explain the harmony between the two groups by their common opposition to the priestly aristocracy.[70]

These assessments of Pharisaic teaching by two important scholars provide indications of how at least one Jewish group of this period might be interpreted as an important *exception* to a strictly nationalistic election theology. But the same scholars also appear reluctant to draw such a conclusion unqualifiedly. In fairness to these fine treatments, the problem comes down to the stubborn inconsistencies in the sources. Some scholars have attempted to deal with these by suggesting that in an earlier period the Pharisees were exclusive while later on, when they became popularly accepted and more politically involved, they tended to be more inclusive and compromising.[71] What is significant in all

---

66. Schürer, 1973, 1:400, emphasis added.
67. Schürer, 1973, 1:402.
68. J. Jeremias, *Jerusalem in the Time of Jesus*, 1969.
69. Jeremias, 1969, 247-49, 251, 259-62, 266.
70. Jeremias, 1969, 262-67.
71. Cf. M. Simon, *Jewish Sects in the Time of Jesus*, 1967, 10.

this discussion is that there has not yet arisen out of the debates about law and election, or the more specific case of the Pharisees, a significant challenge or even a renewed discussion of the conventional view of election in Judaism. And many scholars have made it clear in fact that the Pharisees, for all their exclusive beliefs, were thoroughly nationalistic in their intentions.[72]

Universalism and Nationalism — Wilhelm Bousset

Another instance of scholarly discussion at an earlier time that might have led to a challenge of the conventional view of national election theology involved the relationship between universalism and nationalism in Jewish teaching. Since it has long been recognized that universalism was central to Hellenistic ideology, it is only natural that scholars of Judaism would look for signs of emerging universalism in contemporary Judaism as well. The discussion, however, was not motivated solely out of historical concerns; dogmatic and apologetic considerations also played their part. When it seemed that the narrow "particularism" of Judaism was being compared unfavorably with the "universalism" of the gospel, a new attempt was undertaken to reveal a comparable universalism (however incipient) for Judaism.[73]

The distinguished scholar Wilhelm Bousset[74] provides a well-known example of the examination of this aspect in the emerging Judaism of the Hellenistic era *(späthellenistische Judentum)*. Along with a growing universalism, this Judaism also exhibited a distinct individualism and internalism — characteristics that set it apart from the nationalistic religion of an earlier time. According to Bousset's interpretation of history, universalism so heavily influenced Judaism at this time that even the Maccabean nationalist revival could not prevent its growth, but actually proved to further it![75] In contrast to the ancient national "cult" form of religion, an emerging Jewish "Church" resulted from the nonnationalistic, universalistic tendency. With the growing individualism (especially with regard to rewards after death) and the internalizing of religion evident in the period, individual and sectarian concerns began to prevail over na-

---

72. Cf. L. Baeck, *The Pharisees and Other Essays*, 1947, 8-12; S. W. Baron, *A Social and Religious History of the Jews*, 1952, 1:225; W. Förster, *Palestinian Judaism in New Testament Times*, 1964, 66; I. M. Zeitlin, *Jesus and the Judaism of His Time*, 1988, 15-16; L. Finkelstein, *The Pharisees*, 1946, 1:74; E. P. Sanders, 1977, 156.

73. A tendency evident, e.g., in Köhler, 1928, e.g., 8, and Helfgott, 1954, 37-39, 120-21. Cf. also W. Schmithals, *The Apocalyptic Movement*, 1975, passim, who does not write out of this polemical concern but does repeat the sentiments.

74. D. W. Bousset, *Die Religion des Judentums im Späthellenistischen Zeitalter*, 1926.

75. Bousset, 1926, 1-2, 53-86.

tional concerns: "The cleavage that is evident among the individual members of the nation, between the saints and the godless, is almost as great as that which separates the members of God's people from the foreign nations."[76] According to Bousset, however, Pharisaism/rabbinism fully resisted these developments. *Nationalism* was never entirely overcome in Judaism, and *became particularly acute* among the zealots *and the authors of the Pseudepigrapha*.[77] A major premise in Bousset's work is that the Judaism of this time was characterized as a wrestling over, and an eventual consolidation of, two streams of thought: universalism and particularism.[78] Since the tendency toward universalism and individualization was never carried out fully to the elimination of nationalism, universal tendencies were everywhere tempered by older, nationalistic views: ideas of individual judgment were still bound by nationalistic, this-worldly thought,[79] and hopes for the kingdom of God remained centered around Israel. While nationalism still survived in Judaism, only Christianity carried on to conclusion the universalistic tendencies of this period.[80]

Bousset's work naturally became influential in the many treatments of the subject that followed.[81] It is obvious from such discussions, however, that the idea of universalism was not about to be liberated from the basically nationalistic framework of Judaism in which these scholars worked.[82] Had this been the case, these discussions may well have led to a challenge of conventional views — for it is also obvious (as these studies make clear) that universalism implies not only the sovereignty of God over all the nations but over the individual as well, an implicit challenge to national election.[83]

---

76. "Die Kluft, die sich zwischen den einzelnen Gliedern des Volkes, den Frommen und den Gottlosen, auftut, wird beinahe ebenso breit, wie diejenige, die zwischen dem Angehörigen des eigenen Volkes und dem fremder Völker klafft" (Bousset, 1926, 291; cf. 54, 57, 290).

77. Bousset, 1926, 59, 86-96.

78. Bousset, 1926, 3, 53, 59, 89, etc.

79. Bousset, 1926, 4, 55-56, 292-93, 298-99, 301.

80. Cf. Bousset, 1926, 215-17, who in this way evidences an overbearing interest in dogmatic questions.

81. Thus many works demonstrate a similar understanding of, or at least deny that any contradiction exists between, nationalism and universalism; cf. Bonsirven, 1964, 73-78; Dahl, 1962, 88; Schechter, 1909, 62-64; Charles, 1914, 54-55; Köhler, 1928, 8-9, 13-14, 326; Fairweather, 1926, 30; Moore, 1927, 219-28; W. D. Davies, 1955, 58-62, 78-85, 321-22; Russell, 1964, 268.

82. Cf. Fairweather's lengthy treatment of individualism, where he evidences an awareness of the conflict between the beliefs (1926, 30-38) but argues that individualism does not "overshadow the idea of a national glory" (291). See also n. 81 above.

83. Cf. Russell, 1964, 268.

Remnant Theology — The Pre-Qumran Evidence

Still another potential challenge to a nationalistic election theology was the recognition of a "remnant theology" among some groups, that is, the view that not all Israel is saved but that God's purposes for the nation are being carried out by a relatively small number, a *remnant*. It is remarkable, however, that even where it is admitted that some groups possessed this kind of "remnant theology," the implications of such a fact are rarely explored, or are largely ignored, in favor of other theories. W. D. Davies, for example, argues that while there was an individual "remnant" doctrine among the prophets, this stream of thought was overshadowed by a prevailing nationalism, which eventually became the dominant belief in the Judaism of Paul's day.[84] Not all scholars shrugged off the issue quite so easily as Davies, however. A significant example of this is Jeremias's important and symbolic article on the notion of a remnant in Judaism and in the preaching of Jesus, released soon after the initial discoveries of the Dead Sea Scrolls but too soon to make any significant use of the discoveries.[85] In this article Jeremias nevertheless anticipates the theology of the Dead Sea Scrolls somewhat by making it clear how prevalent was the idea of a remnant in Judaism, especially among groups now known to have held many similar beliefs to those of the scrolls community. He points not only to the Pharisees as exponents of a remnant theology, but also to "Baptist groups," the Essenes, the Therapeutae, the Damascus Document, and John the Baptist.[86] Jeremias emphasizes the prevalence of this view in his summary statement: "thus we gain an impression to what a critical degree the religious thought of the ancient world of Jesus was stamped with the idea of a remnant, and how the whole religious history of Judaism was defined by attempts to establish within the national body a voluntary assembly of the holy remnant."[87]

With such a clear exposition of the remnant doctrine among various groups in Judaism, one might think that this would lead, on the one hand, to a revision (or, at least, a qualification) of the notion that Judaism was *universally* national in its election theology and, on the other hand, to the view that this remnant theology presented a valid *alternative Judaism* against which to place, for

---

84. W. D. Davies, 1955, 78-85, 321-22; cf. also Sigal, 1988, 39; Dahl, 1962, 83, 132-33.

85. J. Jeremias, "Der Gedanke des 'Heiligen Restes' im Spätjudentum und in der Verkündung Jesu," 1949.

86. Jeremias, 1949, 184-91.

87. ". . . so werden wir einen Eindruck davon haben, in wie entscheidenden Ausmaße das religiöse Denken der Umwelt Jesu vom Restgedanken geprägt wurde und wie die ganze Religionsgeschichte des Spätjudentums von den Versuchen bestimmt ist, innerhalb der Volkskirche die Freiwilligkeitskirche des heiligen Restes zu errichten" (Jeremias, 1949, 191).

example, the Jesus movement. Neither of these things resulted from the type of evidence summarized in Jeremias's article. In spite of the prevalence of the view in Judaism, Jeremias himself denied remnant ideas to Jesus' preaching, and opted instead for Jesus as a universalist teacher.[88] By all appearances, it was only his low estimate of remnant theology that prevented him from attributing it to Jesus; he thus helped perpetuate the majority view that Jesus was opposed to all remnant ideas.[89] In a paradoxical way, therefore, Jeremias's work symbolized a new victory for the conventional view of Judaism, as it implied the lower value, or at least lesser influence, of all views outside the standard one. His work is indeed symbolic of the trend, not only in Jewish studies but also in studies of the historical Jesus, *to find in vestiges of remnant theology an inferior form of Judaism,* which is therefore largely disqualified as a suitable background for the New Testament.

The Nature of "Sect" — The Dead Sea Scrolls

Finally, the most notable recent challenge to the conventional nationalistic view of Judaism is that which followed from the discovery of the Dead Sea Scrolls. Emphasis was given to the exclusive election theology of the Qumran community by a score of scholars soon after the publication of the first scrolls. Among them Kurt Schubert is particularly worthy of note for the importance he attributed to the idea of the remnant at Qumran.[90] While Schubert takes a typical es-

---

88. Jeremias, 1949, 193.

89. So, e.g., Dahl, 1962, 85, 128-30 (but cf. 145-48); L. Goppelt, *Jesus, Paul, and Judaism,* 1964, 30, 52; G. Vermes, *Jesus and the World of Judaism,* 1983, 3-57; G. Lohfink, *Jesus and Community,* 1984, esp. 25, 43-44; E. P. Sanders, *Jesus and Judaism,* 1985, esp. 28-37. The view forms the basis of many form- and redaction-critical approaches to the Gospels that date the most colorful encounters between Judaism and Jesus to later Christian-Jewish debate. (Martin Albertz and Rudolf Bultmann coined the term *Streitgespräche* to speak of the controversy-form evolved through the reaction of the early Christian community to the Jewish synagogue.) See esp. J. Hultgren, *Jesus and His Adversaries,* 1979, esp. 39, 162-64, 197-98; D. R. A. Hare, *The Theme of Jewish Persecution of Christians in Matthew's Gospel,* 1967, esp. 125-28, 147-48; J. L. Martyn, *History and Theology in the Fourth Gospel,* 1968; S. Sandmel, *Anti-Semitism in the New Testament?* 1978, passim; R. Maddox, *The Purpose of Luke-Acts,* 1982, esp. 45-46, 54, 183-84; S. H. Brooks, *Matthew's Community,* 1987; J. T. Sanders, *The Jews in Luke-Acts,* 1987, esp. 20, 23, 49-50, 54, 63. For an overview, see K. H. Schelkle, *Israel im Neuen Testament,* 1985, esp. 13-20, 26-32, 40-42, 59, and for a summary of the earlier foundational contributions of Wolfgang Trilling, M. J. Fiedler, and Ulrich Wilckens, see J. Rohde, *Rediscovering the Teaching of the Evangelists,* 1968, 74-91, 202-17.

90. K. Schubert, *The Dead Sea Community,* 1959. Cf. also M. Hengel, *Judaism and Hellenism,* 1974, 1:223; J. T. Milik, *Ten Years of Discovery in the Wilderness of Judaea,* 1959, 113ff.; J. Becker, *Das Heil Gottes,* 1964, 60-64; Jagersma, 1985, 78.

chatological view of the origin of these sectarian writings, he also recognizes the importance of another factor in the origin of this group and in the formation of its theology — its dissatisfaction with the ruling establishment.[91] The social attitudes that resulted from this dissatisfaction form the backdrop for the teaching of the community, which admonished a separation between the righteous and wicked in Israel: only members of the community were considered to be in the covenant of God; they were the elect remnant; all others were apostates and could expect eternal judgment; the promises to Israel would therefore be inherited by the community alone. This "community theology," according to Schubert, became an essential element in the outlook of Qumran.[92]

While hardly a clearer exposition of a remnant doctrine is available than this, in significant points Schubert's work is merely representative of majority opinions regarding this exclusive sect. It is quite remarkable, therefore, given the unanimity regarding such basic aspects of Qumran thought, that these observations have not led in any significant way to a reconsideration of conventional views of Judaism; nor has much thought been given to the possibility that the theology of the sect may have been rather more popular and representative in some aspects than hitherto realized. Instead the Qumran example is viewed as an *exception* and is quietly relegated to an unimportant fringe of "sectarian" Judaism that had little to compare with other forms of Judaism and little relevance to the origins of Christianity.[93] Thus, even when Schubert turns to the New Testament, this important "ecclesiastical" element discerned by him at Qumran fails to influence heavily his view of Christian origins. He does not include election or covenantal theology among "the most important identities, similarities, and differences between the teachings of the Qumrân community and those of the NT."[94] In other words, the remnant theology of Qumran fails to rank as a significant aspect

91. Schubert, 1959, 36; cf. 31, 36-41.

92. Schubert, 1959, 61, 80-83, 85-88.

93. Cf., however, voices in the wilderness such as Förster, who traces the growth of a restricted election in Judaism due to increased attention to the fulfillment of legal obligations, and points to CD 2.7–8.11; 15.10; and 1QH 14.18, 21 as signs of a rather more widespread remnant theology (1964, 7, 62), and E. H. Merrill, *Qumran and Predestination,* 1975, 8, 17-18, who posits as a common factor between Christianity and Qumran the view that established Judaism stands under the judgment of God, whereas only the individual group composes the elect.

94. Schubert, 1959, 122. Schubert does compare the election theology of Qumran and Christianity in dealing with Luke 2:14 (136-37), and he compares the community theology of Qumran in dealing with things like the "poor in Spirit" saying (137-39) and communal living (147-51) in Acts. He also compares the new covenant idea (150) in both. These passing references, however, hardly give the impression that he considered this comparison very significant.

of comparison between Jesus and Judaism.[95] This conclusion no longer seems surprising — it is on the whole entirely symptomatic of comparative studies up to the present time.

In spite of the tremendous importance of the Qumran finds, therefore, in many respects the scrolls have not altered *basic attitudes* about Judaism. Again, while many comparisons have been drawn between Christianity and the Qumran sect, little indication is given that both might reflect a *rather more widespread movement in Judaism.* At best the findings have produced a renewed emphasis on the role of the kind of "sectarianism" that Schubert and others have spoken of. The words of Matthew Black on the matter offer such an assessment: "What emerges with ever-increasing clarity from the evidence is the strength of the link between the primitive Church in the New Testament period and its sectarian Jewish background."[96] It might be noted that "sectarian" is a word that is largely employed in discussions of the sociology of religion. As used by Troeltsch and later by such students of sects as Bryan Wilson, the term "sect" (Ger. *Sekte*) carried with it a highly *exclusive* sense, such as would be applicable to a group that considered itself a remnant. This kind of sect is characterized by volunteer membership, a certain exclusivism and elitism associated with claims of enlightenment, and a hostility to the establishment from which it has made a clear break.[97] As regards Judaism, therefore, nothing would suggest an *anti*national stance more than the word "sect," and accordingly, if Schubert's analysis is to be accepted, the term would be entirely applicable to the Qumran community.[98]

95. Schubert even finds evidence of the opposite view, when he says of John the Baptist: "unlike the Qumrân people, John was not a founder of a sect. Whereas the Qumrân Essenes withdrew from the rest of Israel, which they regarded as a *massa damnata,* John addressed himself to the whole of Israel" (1959, 129). This view, which Schubert shares with a multitude of previous scholars, is not to be denied for what it affirms, but it raises some questions: Did the Qumran community not "address" the rest of Israel? Did John's openness to Israel demand or imply no exclusiveness on his part whatsoever? What about those who were not baptized? Are they part of Israel? The disregard of such questions is common, but they would appear to be of extreme importance to any consideration of John and Judaism.

96. M. Black, *The Scrolls and Christian Origins,* 1961, 88.

97. Cf. *A New Dictionary of the Social Sciences,* 1979, 169-70; *Encyclopedia of Sociology,* 1981, 248; *The International Encyclopedia of Sociology,* 1984, 345; S. J. D. Cohen, "The Significance of Yavneh," 1984, 29-30; J. Blenkinsopp, "Interpretation and the Tendency to Sectarianism," 1988, 1-2; M. Smith, "The Dead Sea Sect in Relation to Ancient Judaism," 1960, 358.

98. P. R. Davies, "Who Can Join the 'Damascus Covenant'?" 1995, 134-35, understands this perfectly with regard to the CD community: "I define 'sect' in terms of *social behaviour,* not 'deviant' beliefs . . . [the community] separated from their surrounding so-

In contrast to this strongly exclusive sense of the word, however, many sociological approaches to religion have begun to employ the term "sect" in reference to differences among *denominations* in the Christian church. This rather diluted use of the term, a use that has seemingly also been adopted by scholars of Judaism, means that the original sense used by Troeltsch has been lost[99] and confusion has ensued.[100] While in its aspect of exclusivism the word "sect" may be an entirely appropriate social description of the Qumran community, the word is not commonly used in this way by scholars of Judaism. The term has been adopted not so much to designate Jewish groups who have claimed independent status as to describe some (relatively minor) *deviations from the official religion;*[101] frequently, therefore, the term comes to imply little more than the differences that would normally exist among "fraternities." Marcel Simon, in his work on Jewish "sects" in the time of Jesus, is indicative of this trend. He settles on a definition of "sect" that goes little further than differences in praxis and certain "ritual, scriptural, [and] doctrinal" matters.[102] The only real lines to be drawn by scholars are between "official Judaism," on the one hand, and "peripheral or marginal Judaism," on the other: "a study of Jewish sects around the beginning of the Christian era must be within the framework of official Judaism vis-à-vis marginal Judaism."[103] And Matthew Black can be quoted again as he clarifies his meaning of sectarianism:

> Deviation from this official [Pharisaic] religion, centering on the Temple and Torah of Jerusalem, was "sectarianism." . . . Jewish sectarianism in its pre-Christian forms can only be usefully defined, or, indeed, defined at all, as non-Pharisaic religious movements related to the Judaism of the Second Temple.

---

ciety and regarded themselves as an *alternative* to it, not merely a *part* of it. . . . It is axiomatic that they did not regard any outsiders as belonging to the true 'Israel'" (134).

99. It should be recalled that the word was originally used by Troeltsch as a *contrast* to the idea of "Church" *(Kirche)*, not to speak of one church over against another.

100. Cf. J. Blenkinsopp, "A Jewish Sect of the Persian Period," 1990, 5-6.

101. This view has most recently been expressed by Lawrence Schiffman: "For our purposes, a sect can be defined as a religious ideology that may develop the characteristics of a political party in order to defend its way of life. The way the term is generally used in the study of ancient Judaism differs from its usual usage in religious studies, wherein 'sect' commonly denotes a group that has somehow split from a mainstream movement. Thus, in the Second Temple period, we refer to all Jewish groups as sects, regardless of size or importance" *(Reclaiming the Dead Sea Scrolls*, 1994, 72-73).

102. Simon, 1967, 6-12, who also notes this disparity in the use of the word when applied to Judaism (6), but prefers to understand "sect" as equivalent to Gk. *hairesis* ("option"; 9).

103. Simon, 1967, 15, cf. 9.

The actual situation in Judaism in the first century B.C. appears, in fact, to have been one of a widespread and dangerously proliferating and fissiparous heteropraxis, a kind of baptizing nonconformity, with many splinter groups, extending from Judea to Samaria and beyond into the Diaspora itself.[104]

In line with trends in scholarship of Judaism generally, this *innocuous* adoption of the term "sectarian" once more reveals a subconscious tendency to endorse conventional views of election. The view that "sectarian" theology and practices were carried out in the interest of *all* Israel (i.e., not only for the benefit of the sect) is an argument that seems to have been adopted by many scholars who accept that these groups were all basically nationalistic.[105] In the process, evidence for a significant abnormality in Jewish belief is *defused* by a subtle shift in terminology: scholars now employ the word "sectarian" in a *relational* sense to *contrast* the *abnormal* with "normative" Judaism — all of which demonstrates the latter's continuing dominance in modern analyses.[106] A sect is anything that appears to be outside orthodoxy (or orthopraxy) *from the point of view of the dominant or major group.* Sectarianism, as a term used in relation to Qumran or as a backdrop for Christianity, implies no more than that there existed certain unofficial groups who differed from mainstream Judaism largely in practice, but were not significantly different from other kinds of Judaism in their self-understanding. For reasons like this even the discoveries of the Dead Sea Scrolls have failed to produce any real challenge to the national election theology traditionally accepted by scholars as applying to all of Judaism.

THE PRESENT STATE OF THE QUESTION

It is against this background of discussion that the most recent important contribution to the whole question, that by E. P. Sanders, can best be evaluated. Here is a scholar who has shown real acquaintance with the issues, particularly the question of law and election in Judaism, and who has attempted to deal with each of three major groups of writings — the rabbinic writings, the Dead Sea Scrolls, and the Pseudepigrapha (though perhaps playing down the importance of the latter two categories).[107] In *Paul and Palestinian Judaism* (1977)

---

104. Black, 1961, 6, 8; cf. also Simon, 1967, 12.
105. Most explicitly by E. P. Sanders, 1977, 249-50, 66-68.
106. The danger appears to have been noted by W. O. McCready, "The Sectarian Status of Qumran," 1983, 183.
107. In *Paul and Palestinian Judaism* (1977), E. P. Sanders allows only a few pages to

Sanders takes exception to those scholars *(ut supra)* who hold that Judaism was a legalistic religion based on merit and reward.[108] His own analysis leads him to the conclusion that law did not function in Judaism in a *legalistic* way (i.e., where sins are weighed in the balance against merits) so much as in a *nomistic* way (i.e., law is a safeguard or system of maintaining those already in the covenant, salvation itself being based on God's prevenient grace)[109] — hence Sanders's well-known term "covenantal nomism." By means of this distinction between legalism and nomism Sanders effectively subjugates all legal statements in Judaism under the terms of the election.[110] The election is the only real way of "getting in" the covenant; keeping the law is merely a way of maintaining that election or of "staying in" the covenant. By elevating the importance of the national election, this also allows that the major concern of Judaism was not with a *reduction* of Judaism through the strict application of a principle of merits, as previously thought, but with the salvation (specifically the eschatological *restoration*) of *all* Israel.[111] According to Sanders, all of Judaism could well have embraced the truth contained in the Mishnaic tractate Sanhedrin 10.1, which Sanders quotes as a kind of *locus classicus* of the national election doctrine: "All Israel has a share in the world to come."[112] There is no question of a remnant, among either the Pharisees or the Essenes;[113] even the Qumran self-appellation "remnant" never refers to the Dead Sea community in its "historical existence."[114] Sanders explains that this community was not exclusive at all; its real motivation was the salvation of all Israel, which would

---

the major Pseudepigrapha (and at most just seven pages to *Jubilees*), and in *Judaism* (1992) he offers a rationale for relegating these writings to a minor place in his analysis (7-9).

108. Cf. E. P. Sanders, 1977, esp. 33-59.

109. Cf. E. P. Sanders, 1977, 75; E. P. Sanders, 1992, 277-78. Many Christian theologians, however, would find Sanders's (not so much Judaism's) understanding of grace deficient. The Jewish belief that God's grace is known in creation and in the sustaining of life is not entirely comparable with a soteriology based on grace, and this observation has nothing to do with "anger that [Sanders] dare call a non-Christian religion a religion of grace" (1992, 525 n. 56). The exodus provides a better paradigm of God's grace (cf. 1992, 526), but Sanders must assume that all Jews acknowledged the continuing efficacy of that event, a presupposition we find unsupportable (see below).

110. To use E. P. Sanders's words, the election is the "way into" the religion; obedience to the law is the "way to stay in" (1977, 180).

111. Cf. E. P. Sanders, 1985, 96.

112. E. P. Sanders allows only *exceptions* to this view on the part of certain individuals who "renounce it by renouncing God and his covenant" (1977, 147). This is true even of the Pseudepigrapha (408).

113. E. P. Sanders, 1977, 147ff., 268ff.; E. P. Sanders, 1985, 96-104.

114. E. P. Sanders, 1977, 250-55, 268 n. 79. We will directly challenge this conclusion below.

eventually become possible through the covenant received proleptically by the Dead Sea sect.[115]

Sanders has developed[116] these views in a very helpful systematic (even somewhat encyclopedic) treatment of Judaism entitled *Judaism: Practice and Belief, 63 BCE–66 CE* (1992), a book that will certainly prove to be an important addition to any resource library on the subject. This work aims to understand the Judaism and piety of the common people, in contrast to past approaches, which have assumed the dominating influence of groups like the Pharisees. As a natural development of his "common denominator" approach in *Paul and Palestinian Judaism*, where he posits a more or less universal pattern of religion,[117] Sanders here attempts to uncover evidence for a common piety or practice as well as a common doctrine. The impression is often given, and not infrequently stated, that the vast majority of Jews (and notably the priests)[118] lived faithfully according to the Law and evidenced a virtuous piety.

> Some scholars suppose that the common people were "in general lukewarm about religion," but few generalizations could be less true. . . . There doubtless were exceptions to this general loyalty . . . but the adherence of most Jews to the national religion cannot be doubted.

> Even the Pharisees thought that ordinary people kept many of the purity laws.

> However they interpreted the law, Jews were zealous in keeping it. . . .

> Mostly, I like the ordinary people. They worked at their jobs, they believed the Bible, they carried out the small routines and celebrations of the religion: they prayed every day, thanked God for his blessings, and on the sabbath went to the synagogue, asked teachers questions, and listened respectfully. What could be better?[119]

---

115. E. P. Sanders, 1977, 266-68.

116. Note the familiar-sounding confession of the unity-of-Judaism school: "Belief that their God was the only true God, that he had chosen them and had given them his law, and that they were required to obey it are basic to Jewish theology, and they are found in all the sources" (E. P. Sanders, 1992, 241; for covenantal nomism, cf. 262, where one finds this statement: "Jewish theology begins with the election").

117. Here E. P. Sanders refers to "normal" or "common" Judaism as "what the priests and the people agreed upon," and he adds the bold statement — given the reaction against "normative Judaism" — that "'normal' Judaism was, to a limited degree, also 'normative': it established a standard by which loyalty to Israel and to the God of Israel was measured" (1992, 47).

118. E. P. Sanders, 1992, 182-88.

119. E. P. Sanders, 1992, 144-45, 229, 494; cf. also 20-21, 29. Simply because "'most

The implication would seem to be that this kind of Judaism was not fallen or apostate, nor was it worthy of the invectives aimed at it by popular understandings of rabbinic or Pharisaic Judaism. The people evidenced knowledge of and respect for the covenant. The evidence offered for this position is impressive as far as it goes, and it would be difficult to deny the genuine piety that existed in both Palestine and Diaspora Judaism. More significant for Sanders is the fact that these findings support his earlier contention that the Jewish world of this time was more or less homogeneously observant of the basic tenets of Judaism.[120]

While Sanders has his critics, some of them quite thorough and persuasive in their critique,[121] his views on covenantal nomism have enjoyed more or less continued acceptance,[122] and anyone would have to admit that this scholar has articulated an impressive and convincing defense of the nationalistic election doctrine.[123] Perhaps not surprisingly his work has been received as if it were the first to attempt this, but it can clearly be seen from the survey above that Sanders is merely emphasizing what has long been held as a more quiet presupposition. (There is, in our mind at least, no question of any major "breakthrough" as would seem to be suggested by the impressive reception his books have received!) While Sanders's work is in many other respects innovative — for example, in its stress on the foundational quality of God's grace — and undeniably of great value to scholarship,[124] as concerns the election theology of Judaism little real advance has been made over what has already been as-

people' . . . considered themselves loyal to God, the Bible and Israel" (29), however, does not mean that others felt the general level of piety or observance was sufficient.

120. E. P. Sanders does reveal a few cracks in the foundation in this book, however (in contrast to the dogmatic insistence of his prior work), such as when he compares other groups with the Pharisees: "The other pietists strike me as being less attractive than the Pharisees. The surviving literature depicts them as not having much of a programme for all Israel, and as being too ready to cultivate hatred of others: learn *our* secrets or God will destroy you" (1992, 494). Are such sentiments really as peripheral as Sanders implies?

121. For major points of disagreement see Charlesworth, 1985, passim; Seifrid, 1992, 46-62. E. P. Sanders's suggestion (1992, 263) that "no one who has discussed this argument [about the 'theological common denominator' in Judaism delineated in *Paul and Palestinian Judaism*] has challenged it" smacks of academic denial.

122. As noted by Seifrid, 1992, 56. Cf. Dunn, 1991, 23-25, but contrast 105-7, 301 n. 37. For his influence on scholarship see Dunn, 14, and Seifrid, 47.

123. While Sanders's real concern is to define the purpose of law, he nevertheless incorporates a strict nationalistic view of election to do this. This is recognized by B. W. Longenecker, *Eschatology and the Covenant*, 1991, 34, who prefers the term "ethnocentric covenantalism" to Sanders's "covenantal nomism" in acknowledgment of this important aspect.

124. Especially in the way his work has drawn attention to the "Lutheran" prejudices against Judaism harbored by some Protestant scholars; cf. Dunn, 1991, 14.

sumed; in fact, the subtle authority of traditional conventional views of Judaism can be perceived throughout his books. It is rather the clarity and creativity of his presentation that are outstanding. The result of his attempts is a coherent and logical argument for a conventional nationalistic view of Judaism that attempts to anticipate and meet all potential challenges. For this one can be grateful in that by its careful argumentation Sanders's work has taken the position to its logical (and, we think, impossible) conclusion and has simultaneously cleared the path for a more reasoned *reconsideration* of the whole nationalistic foundation on which he and scores of others have built. It is far from a sound foundation. The remainder of this book will explore why the conventional nationalistic approach, as it has surfaced in so many works on Judaism, actually represents the *failure of scholarship to deal adequately with some significant aspects and tendencies of Second Temple Judaism.*

CHAPTER THREE

The Judgment-of-Israel Theme

Almost two centuries before Jesus made his appearance in Palestine[1] a pietistic group of Jews, composed in all probability of representatives from every level of Jewish society (priests, scribes, as well as laymen), withdrew from Jerusalem to the wilderness for the express purpose of studying the Torah (1QS 8.14; 9.19-20)[2] — but also, perhaps even more importantly (judging from the chief subject matter of their literature), in order to reflect on the current political and religious situation in Israel. Their unrestrained dissatisfaction with this situation is a familiar theme for readers of the now famous Qumran scrolls. Familiar also is the shocking assessment this sect placed on the rest of their countryfolk, who did not share their deep feelings of discontent but seemed to do much to provoke those feelings. While the sect reserved the most damning imprecations for its immediate

1. Depending on one's view of the historical origins of the "sect." Evidence from the scrolls themselves seems to suggest continuing literary activity from the early Maccabean period right through to the early pre-Roman or even Roman times (i.e., ca. 160-60 B.C.). These limits are confirmed by paleographic considerations. There appears to be no simple solution to the question of exact dating, however.

2. The theory of Norman Golb that a retreat to the Dead Sea is not intended here (see ch. 1 above) depends on interpreting these two passages as containing a metaphorical exegesis of Isa. 40:3. It should be pointed out, however, that it is rather more difficult to interpret the second of the passages in this way, separated as it is from the original citation by little more than a column. Could the reader be trusted to sustain the metaphorical understanding when so much material intervened between the references to going out into the desert? We will encounter other instances of exegesis in the scrolls where the presence of some metaphorical features does not necessarily imply a consistent metaphorical approach. The call to the wilderness would appear to be a case where one detail in a passage was interpreted literally, even if other details demanded a metaphorical interpretation.

opponents — probably some or all of the official establishment in Jerusalem — the Qumranites seemed to be generally at odds with, and outspokenly critical of, every kind of Jewish faith but their own. It is this reclusive and isolated posture of the group that makes the scrolls a suggestive (if, from the point of view of past treatments of the subject, somewhat unorthodox) starting point for a reconsideration of the Jewish teaching about *election*. To begin with, a close look at a few representative texts will reveal the intense belief of this group that Israel was beyond salvation and in most serious danger of judgment.

AT QUMRAN

"They Have Not Sought" — 1QS 5.10-13

The first passage from the Dead Sea Scrolls comes from the section of the so-called Manual of Discipline that deals with admission of candidates into the community (1QS 5.10-13; cf. 5.7-24).[3] The passage begins with an exhortation to the candidate to *separate* himself from "men of iniquity who walk in the way of unrighteousness," for the "men of iniquity" are not "reckoned [i.e., by God][4] in His [God's] Covenant." This requirement of separation would appear at first glance to be a rather standard criterion for prospective members of a religious order or movement, and could easily be interpreted as promoting the exclusion of *Gentiles* from a strict Jewish society. There is good reason to suspect, however, that the expression "men of iniquity who . . . are not reckoned in God's Covenant" conceals a kind of religious irony, and that its reference is to those who in fact *believe* themselves to be participants in the covenant. It becomes even clearer in the words that follow that the exclusion of Israelites, not Gentiles, is the point being made by this passage, as the language used to speak of those who are excluded is drawn from biblical passages addressed to *Israel*. One might note, for example, the charge that the "men of iniquity" have not "sought" God concerning his precepts so that they might know the important "hidden matters" *(ha-nistārōt)*,[5] with the result that they have sinned "high-handedly." The term used for "sought" *(dāraš;* l. 11) is used in the Hebrew

---

3. A. R. C. Leaney, *The Rule of Qumran and Its Meaning,* 1966, 170, places the section within 5.7–7.25, which he calls *"halakah."* But this section, like the one that follows (ll. 20-24), is not itself *halakah,* but contains further instructions on entrance into the community and is at best an introduction to the *halakah,* calling the reader to return to the law of Moses.

4. חשב is in the hoph.

5. On the significance of the *nistārōt,* see further below.

Scriptures for, among other things, the seeking of revelation.[6] Perhaps of greater significance here, it is the word with which Israel is warned to seek God in times of apostasy.[7] It is rarely used of Gentiles.[8] Sinning with a "high hand" is another biblical expression used primarily with regard to Israel.[9] Israel has come to "guilt" over such matters. Only Israelites, moreover, could be said to come under the "curses of the Covenant."[10]

All these facts make it clear that these are expressions of judgment directed against some *within* Israel. These apostate members of Israel, over against whom the community is defined in this passage, are to be judged harshly. Because of their breach of the covenant,[11] the "wrath" *(ap)* and "vengeance" *(nāqām)* of God will be released (l. 12) — terms that are used in the Hebrew Scriptures of the judgment of both Israel and the nations.[12] The "judgment" involves an "eternal destruction" (l. 13); it will "leave no remnant" *(le'ên šerît)*, a typical expression for complete destruction.[13] Whatever future hope the author of this passage held out for Israel, therefore, it is clear that the Israelites referred to in this passage could only expect judgment.[14] Since the

---

6. Cf., e.g., Gen. 25:22 — particularly seeking for mysteries; cf. Dan. 2:27. This is not the only place in the scrolls where it is stated that the enemies of the sect do not know the laws or precepts (e.g., CD 2.6; CD[B] 1.5-14). Another significant use of *drš* in the Scriptures is for searching the Lord; cf. Zeph. 1:6; 1QS 1.1-2.

7. Cf. Deut. 4:29; Isa. 9:13. The Chronicler in particular evaluates history in terms of Israel's "seeking God"; cf. 1 Chron. 22:19; 28:9; 2 Chron. 25:15; 31:21. In the context of "mysteries," cf. Dan. 9:3.

8. It is difficult, e.g., to see how Isa. 11:10 could relate to the passage under investigation.

9. Cf. P. Wernberg-Møller, *The Manual of Discipline*, 1957, 96 n. 46; Leaney, 1966, 172; Num. 15:30. Without knowledge of the Law one cannot, of course, sin "high-handedly." The expression implies knowing what is right but deliberately sinning against it. Also cf. CD 8.8; 10.3.

10. Cf. also 1QS 2.6-18.

11. It is a peculiarity of the covenantal language and beliefs of Qumran that little distinction is drawn between a breach of the Mosaic covenant known to all Israel and a failure to acknowledge the unique covenant of the *yaḥad*. Here it is the former; cf. Leaney, 1966, 172.

12. While the majority refer to the Gentiles, these terms are also used of Israel; cf. 2 Kings 13:3; 2 Sam. 6:7; Jer. 11:20; 15:15; 20:12; 25:37; 44:6. The "vengeance for the covenant" in Lev. 26:25 may be the source of the idea here. Cf. 1QS 1.11.

13. Cf. l. 13. With respect to Israel this same expression is used in Jer. 11:23. Cf. also 1QS 2.13; 4.14; CD 2.6-7; 1QM 1.6. We find evidence elsewhere in the scrolls that this judgment of Israelites was thought to be an eternal matter (cf. 1QS 2.15, 17; 4.12-13).

14. Cf. also 1QS 4.12-14; CD 2.5-6. Fire is a regular element in this judgment (e.g., 1QS 4.13; CD 2.5). The place of judgment is called the "Pit," and the enemies of the sect are called "men of the Pit"; cf. 1QS 4.12-13; 9.22; 10.19; CD 6.15; 13.13-14; 14.2.

Qumranites are exhorted to actively *separate* themselves from such a lot (the flight to the *very* exclusive desert offers a revealing commentary on the importance of this!), the impression is given that *all* Israel, *with the exception of* the separatists, will experience this judgment. While it is widely acknowledged by students of Qumran that this was the attitude of the sect toward outsiders, one begins to see in this passage *why* they felt this way about other Israelites: other Israelites have not sought God properly.

Visitation on "All Who Despise" — CD 7.9–8.2

Another passage, this time from the Damascus Document, is notoriously difficult, but can easily be seen to betray much the same perspective (CD 7.9–8.2).[15] In light of 8.1-2, which seems to allude to apostates from the community itself, the whole passage might be interpreted as referring to the sect's own fallen members (cf. also 1QS 2.11-18); on the other hand, there is much in the preceding column that speaks of the judgment of Israelites completely unattached to the community.[16] It is also possible to interpret parts of the passage as looking back to the events surrounding the Babylonian captivity, in which case it would refer to apostates who broke away from the "remnant" that remained faithful during the exile. All things considered, one should probably see this entire section as addressing the matter of apostasy of past members (who were perhaps part of an earlier reform movement rather than of the Qumran sect itself),[17] a subject, however, that affords the author an opportunity to enlarge on apostasy as a more general theme. The relationship in the passage between apostates from the *yahad*[18] and other Israelite apostates therefore remains somewhat obscure. It may be that *two* different separations or rifts in the his-

15. Preferring MS A (CD 7.9–8.2) here over MS B (CD[B] 1.5-14, referred to as CD 19.5-14 by some scholars) against, e.g., M. A. Knibb, *The Qumran Community*, 1987, 58. While the literary and source-critical considerations are complex, it seems to us that the more difficult argumentation of MS A speaks for its authenticity, while the content of MS B reflects a later stage of the group's history than that spoken of in MS A. The Isa. 7:17 citation, which appears in A but not in B, also seems essential as a source for the thought of the passage. For an alternative solution that speaks for the originality of both readings, see S. A. White, "A Comparison of the 'A' and 'B' Manuscripts of the Damascus Document," 1987; cf. J. J. Collins, *The Scepter and the Star*, 1995, 81-82. The Qumran discoveries also confirm the authenticity of A (cf. P. R. Davies, *The Damascus Covenant*, 1982, 48-49).

16. Cf. 7.9-12, 16-18, 21.

17. Especially since the latter half of CD (from 6.11b onward) tends to reflect on laws specifically for the community.

18. *Yahad* is the name the Qumran community gave itself; it means something like "togetherness" or "the Unity."

tory of the community are required to explain the difficulties — and this solution has been offered. It is in any case clear that the writer envisaged a terrible fate for those outside the limits of his own group, whatever the circumstances of their apostasy may have been.

This complex passage begins with a reference to a future divine visitation ("when God visits the earth" — a stock expression for judgment)[19] and to the resultant punishment of "those who despise."[20] The writer then proceeds to quote Isa. 7:17, which he apparently regards as applicable to this visitation: "There shall come upon thee and thy people, and upon thy father's house, days such as have not come since the day when Ephraim departed from Judah" (7.11-12). The "day when Ephraim departed from Judah," according to the next lines, refers not to the division of the kingdoms in Solomon's time but to the beginnings of the desert life of the sect, when the community (code-named "Ephraim") separated from the rest of Israel (code-named "Judah")[21] and ventured to the "land of the north," that is, probably "Damascus"[22] (cf. 7.14-15, 19). The point being made by the exegesis is that there will be correspondences between this recent division in Israel and what will occur at the future judgment. It is reasonably clear what this correspondence is thought to be: as there was a *division* between the righteous sect (Ephraim) and the apostate Jews (Judah) in the recent past, so there will be an even more decisive *division* effected by divine judgment at the end of days. Judgment, in other words, will *divide Israel,* demonstrating who are the righteous and who are the apostates. Perhaps it is also implied that this division has already begun to take place through the emergence of the *yaḥad.*[23]

The mention of the escape to the "north" in the exegesis of Isa. 7:17 inspires another citation (Amos 5:26-27 in 7.14-15), followed by an interpreta-

---

19. Knibb, 1987, 58.

20. By analogy with other passages where this expression is found, we might (cautiously) add (with A. Dupont-Sommer, *The Essene Writings from Qumran,* 1961, 133 n. 3) the implied object "the commandments." It may be, however, that what they despise are the teachings of the *yaḥad,* specifically the latter's interpretation of the prophets (cf. l. 18).

21. For the application of these titles to the group and the rest of Israel, cf. Dupont-Sommer, 1961, 133 n. 3; Knibb, 1987, 59.

22. "Damascus" here almost certainly being the Judean home of the community (Qumran), a kind of code name that reflects the consciousness of being in exile from Jerusalem (cf. C. Milikowsky, "Again: *Damascus* in Damascus Document and in Rabbinic Literature," 1982). Damascus also has eschatological associations, though a more literal reference to Syrian Damascus is not out of the question (cf. B. Z. Wacholder, "Ezekiel and Ezekielianism as Progenitors of Essenianism," 1992, 195). For Golb's theories on this matter, see ch. 1 above.

23. A somewhat different approach is offered by Knibb, 1987, 59, whose solutions to the problems of the text, however, are too complex and subtle for our liking.

tion that applies the passage to the historical experiences of the community (7.15-19).[24] In the interpretation the author reveals what he sees to be the sin of the guilty party: they have despised the prophetic writings (7.18). In contrast to these people, however, the "Seeker of the Law," by which is meant the leader of the *yaḥad*,[25] acknowledges the Law and, by implication, the correct interpretation of the prophets. The theme of Israel's judgment comes through loud and clear. Judgment is pronounced on "*all* who fell back" (l. 13, speaking thus of apostates in Israel and fallen members alike).[26] Although Israel may have escaped "the first visitation,"[27] at the visitation *par excellence* the "sons of Seth" (Israel)[28] will be judged at the hand of God's representative, the "Prince of all the Congregation";[29] the judgment will involve "recompense of the wicked" and "destruction by the hand of Belial" (7.9; 7.20–8.2).

As in 1QS 5.10-13, therefore, here the harsh judgment that the sect expects for Israel *extra iustos* is clearly seen. It is not simply a matter of differentiation from a certain *specific* group of opponents (although ll. 12-14 and 18-19 would lead us to believe that some specific opponents are also in mind)[30] but from *all* those in Israel outside the group. This is made clear by the way the

---

24. Since this only partially serves the interests of the context (judgment in 7.9-13 and perseverance in 8.1-2), it would seem that this interpretation of Amos 5:26-27 enjoyed an independent existence, probably rooted in the very beginnings of the community. For further discussion of the difficulties in understanding the passage, see ch. 8 below.

25. Probably the *moreh ṣedeq*, the so-called Teacher of Righteousness or Right (Legitimate) Teacher (Dupont-Sommer, 1961, 134 n. 4).

26. Knibb, 1987, 56, renders כל הנסוגים "all the apostates." For "those who remain" (הנשארית; cf. 1.10 and 13) as an equivalent to "Jews outside the movement," see Knibb, 60.

27. Dupont-Sommer, 1961, 135 n. 1, holds that this First Visitation was the storming of Jerusalem by Pompey in 63 B.C., but this requires quite a late date for CD. We may be forced to think here instead of the Antiochian invasion and defilement of the Temple, or even of the Babylonian captivity (cf. H. Ringgren, *The Faith of Qumran*, 1963, 153; Knibb, 1987, 59). Apparently the author viewed the survivors of the exile as the righteous who concluded a kind of new covenant at that time (perhaps alluded to in CD 8.1). But many who were saved at that "First Visitation" then fell — and it is this fact that inspired the lengthy invective against apostates in this passage. The author seems to have viewed the exile and First Visitation as a relatively ineffective chastisement.

28. Knibb, 1987, 63. The expression was suggested to the author by the closing words of Num. 24:17, which he also cites in 7.19-20.

29. Cf. 7.9, 20-21; 8.2. Conceivably the *moreh ṣedeq* is meant, who is referred to as the "Star" in l. 18, although the shifting nature of the referents throughout the passage would warn against too hastily equating the Star of ll. 18-19 with the Sceptre of ll. 19-20.

30. For a good treatment of the complex problems associated with an identification of these several groups of opponents, see G. Jeremias, *Der Lehrer der Gerechtigkeit*, 1963, 79-126.

whole people outside the sect are also *implicated* in the wrongdoing of the sect's more specific opponents and are effectively bunched together with these opponents in regard to their unrighteous status. Accordingly *these opponents represent* in a concentrated sort of way *the problem with Israel as a whole*. This is suggested by generalizing references such as: *"all those who despise"* (l. 9); "There shall come upon thee *and thy people*" (l. 10; Isa. 7:17); "the books of the prophets whose words *Israel* has despised" (ll. 17-18); and "*all* the sons of Seth" (l. 21; Num. 24:17).

This association between the opponents and all Israel comes out in other scroll passages as well. A good example comes in a passage that appears to be an invective against the group of opponents *in particular* (CD 4.12–6.1) but also contains clear statements of Israel's judgment *as a whole*. Here we read that "Belial shall be unleashed against *Israel*" (4.13), "by which he ensnared *Israel*" (4.16); "whoever escapes this is caught by that, and whoever escapes that one is caught by this" (4.18-19; cf. Ezek. 13:10 — an allusion to the *universal nature of apostasy* during the exile); "*for this is a people without understanding*" (5.16; cf. Isa. 27:11); "they are *a nation void of counsel*, for there is no understanding among them" (5.17); and the like. Other lines draw a parallel between the present time and the first time of apostasy (the exile), when Israel was "led astray" and turned "away from following God" (5.20–6.2). A similar example is found in 1QH 4.5ff., where the writer dwells on the false teaching of his hypocritical opponents but also draws out the important implications of these teachers for *all* Israel. He complains to God that these prophets have led "Thy people" astray through words of flattery (4.7); they have kept "Thy people" from drinking from the sources of knowledge, misleading them in regard to their feasts (4.11-12); "with barbarian lips and in a foreign tongue do they speak to Thy people" (4.16); "but Thou wilt put their fear upon Thy people together with destruction for all the peoples of the lands, to cut off at the time of Judgment all who transgress Thy word" (4.26-27); and the like. The leaders are thus responsible for misleading the people, and the implication is that they draw Israel down *with them* into their error. In passages like these the opponents are *representative* of Israel primarily as their (false) teachers and deceivers. Significantly, it is nowhere implied that the guilt of Israel's common people is alleviated by the special guilt of its leaders. All are guilty.

Going back to CD 7.9–8.2, therefore, it is apparent now that this passage testifies to a fundamental division in Israel over, among other things, Scripture and its interpretation. This division is so serious as to lead to the "departure" of "Ephraim" from "Judah" (7.12ff.), also referred to as the "separation" (l. 12) and "escape" (l. 14) of the former. The actions and attitudes of the two parties are offered to the readers as examples respectively of "those who fell back" and those who "hold firm" (7.13; 8.1-2). While the sect is like Ephraim, which departed from Judah and are saved because they "held firm," the "others," *all* those who fell into apostasy, come under God's judgment.[31]

The Righteous and the Wicked — 1QH 15.15-19

In the hymns of Qumran we again see this judgment-of-Israel theme expressed. In 1QH 15.15-19 "the just man" *(ṣadîq)*, who has been "established from his mother's womb for the time of good-will,"[32] is contrasted with "the wicked" *(reša'îm* — a word rarely used of *Gentiles* in the Hebrew Scriptures) who have been created "for the time of God's wrath"[33] and have been "set apart from their mother's womb for the day of slaughter."[34] The writer finds support for this harsh double predestination in the Scriptures,[35] and he significantly draws from passages that allude to the sin of *Israel*. Thus the "day of slaughter" is clearly an echoing of the similar expression in Jer. 12:3,[36] which is used in the context of sin "in the land" (cf. v. 4); and the phrase "walked in the way which is not good" (l. 18) borrows the exact expression from Isa. 65:2, which also refers to God's rebellious people.[37] The wicked are described in this passage as those who have despised the covenant.[38] Their apostasy[39] is clearly seen in their rejec-

31. Adopting the language of 7.13-14, 21; 8.1-2; as well as (B) 1.10, 13.

32. למועד רצון, "time of favor" or "appointed time of grace" (S. Holm-Nielsen, *Hodayot*, 1960, 227), are other acceptable translations; cf. Isa. 49:8; 61:2; Hos. 9:5; Ps. 102:14; 1QS 3.10, 18, etc. The reference is to the doctrine of restoration.

33. ל[קץ חר]ונכה. For this reconstruction, cf. E. Lohse, ed., *Die Texte aus Qumran*, 1971, 166; Dupont-Sommer, 1961, 246. Holm-Nielsen, 1960, 231, suggests קץ רצונ[כה], "the time of thy choosing," but some expression of impending doom, providing a parallel to "day of slaughter" (and an antithesis to "time of goodwill" in l. 15) is required.

34. יום הרגה. The dualistic formulation, which divides between the righteous and wicked, is particularly clear in the literary structure of the passage as diagrammatically presented by Holm-Nielsen, 1960, 230. Here is an example where the parallelism is so precise as to be a reliable guide to reconstruction of the small lacunae in the passage.

35. Cf. also 4.38; CD 2.7-10.

36. Cf. M. Mansoor, *The Thanksgiving Hymns Translated and Annotated with an Introduction*, 1961, 184 n. 1; Holm-Nielsen, 1960, 231. Cf. also *1 En.* 94:9; 97:1; 98:10; 99:4, 15; *Jub.* 5:10; 24:28; 36:10.

37. Holm-Nielsen, 1960, 231; Mansoor, 1961, 184 n. 2. Cf. also Ps. 36:5.

38. Cf. l. 18; cf. also CD(B) 2.13-22; 1QpHab 2.3. There is wide agreement to read "Thy covenant" (בריתך; Holm-Nielsen, 1960, 231; Dupont-Sommer, 1961, 246; Lohse, 1971, 166). This forms a direct (antithetical) parallel with l. 15.

39. For probable parallels to the verbal form of מאס with ברית as an expression for apostasy, cf. 4 Ezra 7:23-24; 8:56; *Jub.* 21:4; the verb appears only in proximity with ברית here, but cf. Isa. 5:24; 30:12; Jer. 6:19; Ezek. 5:6, etc., where it appears with דבר הזה, תורה, and משפטים. Cf. Holm-Nielsen, 1960, 231. The biblical texts all explicitly refer to an apostate Israel.

tion of God's precepts.[40] As a result of their sin "great judgments" are ordained for them. Since the just are said to possess "eternal salvation" (cf. also the highly spiritualized covenantal promise of "perpetual unfailing peace"), it is to be presumed that the wicked are to experience eternal damnation. It is obvious that, for this writer, only Israelites qualify for this specific kind of condemnation, as only Israelites are related to the Law in such a way that they could be said to reject it in the terms set out in this passage. It is clear once again, therefore, that the writer holds Israel up as his particular target of criticism. They are to be judged harshly.

The occurrence in this passage of terms like "the righteous" and "the wicked," which one comes across frequently in all these writings, raises an important issue concerning the proper approach to these texts. It is becoming a common and expected procedure in the analysis of the election theology of these writings to first subject such words as these to what is called "semantic analysis" — a procedure that first establishes the linguistic significance of these important election terms before going on to generalize about election beliefs. We have deliberately avoided working in this direction, since such attempts have proven to be all but fruitless: the wide diversity of solutions produced by semantic analysis itself suggests that there do not exist enough "controls" to make this a fruitful procedure. This is so because terms like "righteous," "elect," "saints," "pious," "wicked," "sinners," and the like are such "semantically weak" terms (their social context has the potential for determining their referent entirely, overthrowing any "root sense") that to *start* by analyzing these words is clearly to start from the wrong direction. The meanings of these terms and the theology of election they imply, in other words, can only be determined by the context in which they are found — that is, by other clues as to the theology and the significance of terms of reference used by each author and community. We will, in fact, begin to see that these terms are used in predictable and fairly consistent ways *within the confines of one specific movement,* but this can only be determined by first analyzing the movement itself. That is why a thorough exegesis of passages is required here, not the application of sweeping generalizations based on presuppositions about the meaning of words like "righteous."

40. Lohse, 1971, 166, reads אמתך (Thy truth); Dupont-Sommer, 1961, 246, and Holm-Nielsen, 1960, 2, have "Thy precepts/ordinances" (משפטיך?). משפט is found in conjunction with מאס in Ezek. 5:6 in a very similar context of apostasy). In any case ולא רצו בכול אשר צויתה, "they have not delighted in all which You have commanded" (ll. 18-19), definitely points to those who possessed the Law. The emphatic "*all* (כול) which you have commanded" may imply, as elsewhere in the scrolls, that the obedience that righteousness requires involves more than traditional understandings of the contents of Torah. The contrasting phrase in l. 19, "they have chosen what you hate" (ויבחרו באשר שנאתה), appears to point to the same conclusion.

Returning then to 1QH 15, one might note that the words "the time of goodwill" in l. 15 appear to allude to the time of the restoration,[41] but it is evident that none of the wicked will participate in this blessing (theirs is "a day of slaughter"!). That the community is said to have been "raised up" from among men also suggests that its members *alone,* out of all Israel, can hope for the promises made to the righteous in this passage. Accordingly one can adopt a view like that of Sanders — that the restoration doctrine *is dominant* over the judgment theme at Qumran — only with a certain violence to the evidence. Sanders would have us interpret the judgment-of-Israel theme rhetorically, as highly contingent and temporary, quite overruled in the minds of the sectarians by their expectation of restoration. As part of the eschatological beliefs of the community, he maintains, *all* Israel will eventually be saved.[42] Granted that Sanders is trying to make logical the juxtaposition of two apparently conflicting beliefs (restoration and judgment), can one really take this view of things? Does the restoration hope necessarily make the doctrine of Israel's judgment less significant? Are the statements about this judgment only rhetorical in intent, or less important theologically than the restoration statements?

It is, of course, *methodologically* very dangerous to decide *a priori* which belief of an ancient group should be emphasized and which played down (still more dangerous, then, to apply a quite abstract theory to explain the discrepancies!). Unless such a methodology becomes absolutely necessary for lack of data, and this is certainly *not* the case here, one is on decidedly firmer ground in asking *which* of these beliefs would appear *on a sympathetic reading of the texts themselves* to be the most important. The manifestly *repeated and solemn warnings of judgment* — many more, in the case of Qumran, than sayings regarding restoration — would appear, on the basis of *both* quantity *and* sobriety of presentation, to grant to the judgment-of-Israel theme a priority *above and beyond* the restoration doctrine. It is more than a minor strain on the language of the present passage, for example, to interpret such judgment sayings as merely rhetorical or secondary in importance. A *sound* rhetorical analysis would accordingly actually suggest the priority of the judgment sayings — as is implied by the exclusivistic

---

41. The expressions are not exact, but suggestive of the same; cf. Isa. 49:8 (בְּעֵת רָצוֹן); 61:2 (שְׁנַת־רָצוֹן), the latter of which is a *locus classicus* for the restoration belief.

42. As part of this eschatological perspective, Sanders maintains, the community held up hope for the eventual salvation of all Israel at the final restoration, even though presently Israel is outside the covenant and the present experience of salvation (E. P. Sanders, *Paul and Palestinian Judaism,* 1977, 247-52, 254, etc.). Sanders takes this preoccupation with the salvation of all Israel as the foundation of eschatology in Judaism as a whole: "Judaism was not primarily a religion of individual salvation. An abiding concern was that God should maintain his covenant with the Jewish *people* and that the *nation* be preserved" (E. P. Sanders, *Judaism,* 1992, 279).

tone of l. 17 in this passage, and especially by the insistence that judgment is fore-ordained in l. 19[43] (would the sectarians be willing to retract their faith in determinism here?). This passage would seem, therefore, to preclude any notion of restoration that automatically embraces *all* Israel. There is no indication in the immediate context of any of these sayings that judgment would be in any way lessened through restoration, or through repentance — if this was even expected from the Israel of the author's day. Apparently the author thought that some representative group, like his own, would compose the restored Israel; the author's contemporaries were in any event considered unsalvageable. It is noteworthy that in the CD passage considered above a similar *certainty* of judgment is made abundantly clear in the *insistence* that the same division between the faithful and the apostates as was evident "when Ephraim departed from Judah" (cf. 7.12 above) would be *repeated* "when God visits the earth." The writer accordingly warns his readers to remain faithful to the end. Our treatment in ch. 11 of the eschatology of this and other groups will attempt to place restoration and judgment sayings in a proper and balanced perspective; but even here it would seem to be evident that any view of the restoration at Qumran must be seen to *accommodate, not displace,* this doctrine of judgment.

Judgment "in the Sight of the Nations" — 1QpHab 5.3-5

The importance of this doctrine of the judgment of Israel can be seen particularly clearly in the writings of Qumran known as the *pešerîm,* or commentaries on biblical books, in which the sectarians employed a type of interpretation in which they ignored (what moderns would call) the original context and meaning of a text in order to draw from (even apparently dormant) passages of Scripture predictions of their own present conflict, or a word addressing their most urgent concerns. This "*eisegetic*" methodology accordingly provided an ideal instrument through which the community could express what was foremost on its mind, and this consequently makes the *pešerîm* among our most valuable sources of direct information on the beliefs of the sect. It is significant, then, to find judgment-of-Israel motifs in these writings, most notably where the biblical prophecy on which the commentary is based does not itself explicitly deal with the theme. A striking example comes from the Habakkuk *pešer* and a small passage (1QpHab 5.3-5) that continues a theme already established in the opening words of the commentary — namely, *the relations and interactions between the elect and their oppressors* (1.1-6, on Hab. 1:1-3; although the

---

43. The expression is "you have created [Dupont-Sommer, 1961, 246: 'create'; perhaps 'establish' √ כון Hiph.] them [. . .] in order to bring great judgments against them."

opening rows of the column are mutilated, the words that survive suggest that the themes of persecution and the cry for vindication found in the text are taken up in the commentary). It would probably nôt be too far off to suggest that, in the eyes of the commentator, the significance of the entire Habakkuk prophecy lay with this division between the righteous people of Qumran and their persecutors.[44] This theme is even found in the eschatological sections of the commentary, which deal with the final battle; in these passages the righteous and the wicked confront one another and the righteous gain the clear and final victory. In the present passage the commentator draws from his text (Hab. 1:12-13a) an important word of consolation for the righteous in regard to this final battle:

> God will not destroy His people by the hand of the nations; but God will judge all the nations by the hand of His elect *(ones* בחירו *beḥîrāw)*.[45] And it is by the chastisement which the elect will dispense that all the wicked of His people will be found guilty [or will atone], because they [i.e., the elect] have kept His commandments in their distress. (ll. 3-6)

There is considerable debate concerning the translation and meaning of this passage, particularly the second half, and it merits a closer look. Two possible interpretations are offered; either (1) it is by means of the judgment of the world by the elect (or, alternatively, through the *suffering* of the elect) that all Israel, including the wicked, will be *saved;* or (2) it is through the elect, as God's instrument of judgment, that the wicked will be *punished.* In support of the first interpretation is the fact that the word אשם *(ʾāšām)* in l. 5, which has been translated "will be found guilty,"[46] can also be translated "will atone (for

---

44. 4Q177 = *4QCatena*[a] (cf. 4Q501) also refers to destruction against Israel, who persecutes the "men of the Community."

45. Linguistically speaking, there are various ways to view בחירו. M. P. Horgan, *Pesharim,* 1979, 32, treats it as a defectively written plural with the third-person-singular masculine suffix. W. H. Brownlee, *The Midrash Pesher of Habakkuk,* 1979, 86, disagrees, arguing that it is a collective singular similar to that found in 1QS 8.6-7. (He contrasts מצוותו, l. 5, where the defective plural is indicated by the lengthening of the penultimate syllable.) The collective meaning is suggested by an allusion to Isa. 42:1 [MT משפט לגוים יועיא; lit. "he will bring judgment to the nations," where the Servant in that passage seems to have been identified with the "elect ones." In either case agreement with מצוותו (l. 5; assuming as we do that the antecedent is the elect rather than the wicked; see below) requires us to understand a plural referent here: "the elect ones."

46. Horgan, 1979, 15, has: "all the wicked ones of his people will be convicted by those who have kept his commandments." In an attempt to deal with the problem of אשר ("because" in Dupont-Sommer's text above), which appears to lack an antecedent, Horgan suggests a possible scribal error and reconstructs the text in a way that changes its meaning substantially: "God will not destroy his people who have kept his commandments in their

guilt)."[47] The resulting expression has accordingly been taken to mean that the judgment of the world by the righteous will effect atonement for the wicked in Israel. Alternatively "chastisement of the elect" can be taken objectively as referring to the suffering of the elect,[48] giving the sense that this atonement is not effected by the judgment of the world so much as by the suffering of the community itself.

While the question cannot be solved on linguistic bases alone, P. Garnet has dealt extensively with atonement theology in the scrolls and offers convincing proof that the idea of atonement in the sense of vicarious suffering is absent from them.[49] Rather, as Garnet shows, by continuing to accept the punishments of exile, the suffering community is thought to atone *"for the Land"* according to the requirements of Leviticus 26 — but the scrolls *never* teach that the righteous in this way atone for the *wicked* in Israel;[50] atonement is only efficacious

---

distress" (32). As the text stands, it appears that a subtle change of antecedents has taken place between יאשמו and שמרו/אשר, but even this would not be a necessary assumption if we saw as the real antecedent of both יאשמו and שמרו/אשר not "all the wicked of his people" so much as the whole preceding line, including "the chastisement which the elect will dispense." Thus a reference to the elect remains, and Dupont-Sommer's "because" is probably quite justified.

47. I.e., as a guilt offering. But cf. Horgan, 1979, 32-33: "The meanings 'to expiate' and 'to atone' are unattested for the verb *'šm*, but these translations are imposed upon the text by authors who connect the following *'šr*-clause with 'all the wicked ones of his people,' i.e., 'they shall expiate their guilt, insofar as they keep the commandments.'" However, a credible translation of the word as "atone" may be traced back to Isa. 53:10, where it is said that the Suffering Servant "makes himself (or is made) an offering for sin (אָשָׁם)." Furthermore, as we will suggest, the atonement spoken of in this passage is not a vicarious act by those who keep the law, but an act of judgment of sinners that has an atoning effect. The verb אשם, unlike כפר, does not necessarily demand a theology of vicarious atonement. Thus Dupont-Sommer, 1961, 261, translates "will atone," although he recognizes the punishment aspect of this atonement, commenting that the wicked "will be finally judged and punished by the sect" (261 n. 3).

48. The phrase is literally "through their chastisement," but is usually translated as an objective genitive of the nations ("the chastisement inflicted on the nations") or as a subjective genitive referring to the elect ("the judgment that the elect inflict"). Brownlee, 1979, 87, opts for the latter since it corresponds to the biblical text cited in l. 1, although the translation of the Habakkuk verse is equally ambiguous. Both translations come to mean much the same thing if we equate the chastisement with judgment; if, however, we take it to refer to the suffering of the *yaḥad*, the object of the "chastisement" would be the elect and the subject would be God (understood). Our understanding of the word תוכחת in terms of Ezekiel 5, however, if sustained, would preclude such an understanding.

49. P. Garnet, *Salvation and Atonement in the Qumran Scrolls*, 1977, 39-40, 72-73, 119.

50. Garnet, 1977, 82-85. Atonement for the land implies the alleviation of the punishment of Gentile subjection, rather than atonement for Israel in the sense of Isaiah 53.

for the individual *if he joins the community*.[51] Whatever the salvific purpose of the existence of the community, in other words, it was certainly not a question of saving all Israel, especially apart from prior repentance and conformity to the community's teachings.

Whatever other good reasons there may be for accepting Garnet's analysis, it certainly eminently suits the mentality of Qumran uncovered so far.[52] The salvation of Israel, whether by vicarious suffering or some other kind of atonement, would not appear to be the issue in this passage at all. It would thus seem that, even if *'āšām* is to be given a nuance implying some kind of atonement, it is the second of the two interpretations above that applies. The meaning of the present passage can only be that the community effects "atonement for the land" (and, doubtless, for the elect) by exercising its vocation of *bringing judgment on the wicked* — not that the elect effect atonement for the wicked by judging the world (a thought that is also conspicuously, though perhaps inconsequentially, missing from the Habakkuk text!). Garnet agrees that one important means of "atonement" for Qumran is this work of punishing the guilty in Israel,[53] and one can see clearly elsewhere in the scrolls the belief that atonement is established through the *righteous vengeance* of the elect community, whose members are divinely appointed dispensers of judgment on the sinners *in Israel*.[54] We have already seen the importance of this vengeance theme in 1QS 5.10-13 above, and a similar approach to this passage would seem to be demanded by some remarkable correspondences with biblical records of similar judgments on Israel carried out by Phinehas, whom the community seems to have consciously emulated in their role of effecting this righteous vengeance.[55]

---

51. Garnet, 1977, 72.

52. Garnet sums up the atonement theology of Qumran in very appropriate terms when he states: "Gen. 18:32 could not cancel out Ezek. 14:16 in the thinking of a group which took seriously the ideal of Exod. 32:29" (1977, 111).

53. Garnet, 1977, 72-73. Rooting out sin by "cutting off" sinners was a common idea in Judaism; cf. E. E. Urbach, *The Sages*, 1975, 539. The most notable difference between the DSS and the Tannaites in this matter is that Qumran considered *most* of Israel sinful and the urgency for extrication correspondingly great.

54. Cf. 1QS 5.7; 1QH 4.26; 5.6-9; 6.18-19, 29-33; Garnet, 1977, 66-85.

55. Phinehas, the son of Eleazar and grandson of Aaron, is said in Numbers 25 to have turned away the wrath of God from Israel because of his great "zeal" (קנא; he took the life of an Israelite who had brought into his family a Midianite woman). The community probably interpreted the command of Lev. 26:25 regarding the "vengeance for the covenant" in the light of Numbers 31, thereby taking the initiative in dispensing the vengeance of God on Israel, a prerequisite to God's renewal of the covenant with them. In Num. 25:12-13 God says of Phinehas: "Behold, I give to him my covenant of people; and it shall be to him, and to his descendants after him, the covenant of a perpetual priesthood, because he was jealous (קנא) for his God, and made atonement (כפר) for the people of Is-

Far from the idea of atonement for the wicked, therefore, this passage actually states the antithesis — that the zealous judgment at the hand of the sect cleanses the land of sinners. The meaning of the first part of the passage (ll. 3-4) is now also illuminated: it is the elect, not the nations, who will be the *final* dispensers of judgment in the last days. This passage does not, as might appear on the surface of things, contrast two completely opposite *views* of judgment — the one holding that Israel will be conquered by the nations, the other that the nations will be conquered by Israel — so much as it contrasts two *agents* of judgment — the nations and the *elect* from Israel.[56] The expression is literally rendered "God will give the judgment of the nations into the hands of His elect." As Brownlee points out, the expression ביד ... נתן (*nātan ... beyad*) refers to the delegation of something. Hence *God* does not do the judging here, but *"into the power of the elect* God will give the judgment."[57] The important point for us is that this judgment "of the nations" at the hand of the righteous *will specifically include* the wicked in Israel: "all *(kōl)* the wicked of *his* people (*rišʿê ʿam*[58])" (l. 5).

As for the second part of the text, there may also be evidence in the use of the word תוכחת (*tôkēḥat*, "chastisement") itself that points specifically to the judgment *of Israel,* rather than to either the "suffering" of the elect or the judgment of the nations as such. This would especially be true if, as seems probable, this word is associated with משפט (*mišpaṭ*) in l. 4, for a likely origin for the thought of the passage can then be traced to Ezek. 5:5ff., where the plural of this word is also found (v. 15) and where the judgment of Israel "in the sight of the nations" context has similarities to 1QpHab 5.3ff. The reproach that Israel "has wickedly rebelled against my ordinances *(mišpāṭāy)* more than the nations, and

---

rael." Inasmuch as the idea of a "(covenant of a) perpetual priesthood" (כהנת עולם) was of utmost importance to the Qumranites (evident in their respect for Zadok), it is understandable that they would seek to follow the example of Phinehas in dealing out the judgment of God on Israel. In our present passage the sectarians are regarded as just as worthy as Phinehas to bring vengeance on the nation: "because they have kept his commandments (מצוות)" (l. 5) and because they have "eyes too pure to see evil" (ll. 6-7), etc. We have allowed that a similar atoning effect as in Num. 25:12-13 may be implied as well. Thus the elect community behaves righteously through this period of apostasy (הרשעה בקץ, ll. 7-8), both by living uprightly and by dispensing judgment.

56. This also complies with the basic position taken in the Qumran War Scroll, namely, that the sect will carry out the final battle against the nations as well as against Israel (1QM 1.1ff.).

57. Brownlee, 1979, 84-85.

58. Brownlee cites Del Medico's interesting theory about the ו that appears as a superscription in the text. The fact that *"His"* was later inserted above the line shows that for the original author the people who were to be judged had ceased to be God's people (cf. Brownlee, 1979, 85).

against my statutes more than the countries round about her . . ." (Ezek. 5:6) strikes a familiar note in the theology of Qumran. If the passage has been influenced by this judgment theme of Ezekiel, then one must assume that *mišpaṭ* and *tôkēḥaṭ* in 1QpHab both relate directly to the same theme: the judgment of Israel.[59] Thus the idea of the judgment of the whole world (with which the author begins his *pešer* in ll. 3-4) quickly narrows into the announcement of the judgment of the wicked *in Israel in particular* (at the hand of the elect) — a thought that concludes the passage in l. 5, carries on in ll. 9ff., and basically dominates the interests of the writer of the commentary from that point onward. In calling to mind passages like Ezekiel 5, the author has provided an interesting reflection on the theme of the judgment of Israel "in the sight of the nations."

Such passages as have been dealt with above are representative of a much larger group of texts in which one finds the idea that Israelites will be judged (e.g., CD[B] 1.5-14; 1QH 4.18-20, 26-27;[60] 6.29-33;[61] 1QM 1.2-3; 15.1; etc.).[62] Again, considering the frequency and seriousness with which this belief is expressed in these writings, it can hardly be treated as a minor or subsidiary dogma[63] or explained on rhetorical grounds.[64]

---

59. Having made this point, one must nevertheless at least allow that the choice of this word was determined by the presence of its root יכח in the Habakkuk text and that no specific meaning was consciously attached to it. But our point still stands.

60. "Thou wilt put their fear upon Thy people together with destruction for all (לכול) the peoples of the lands, to cut off at the time of Judgment all (כול) who transgress Thy word." עמכה, "Thy people" (l. 26), is clearly meant as a contrast to the sectarians. In spite of the likeness to the rabbinic עמי הארץ, the עמי הארצות of the same line probably refers to the nations of the world rather than to Israelites exclusively (cf. Mansoor, 1961, 128, n. 1; Neh. 10:30). But the parallelism between the first and last half of the line is synthetic: the Israelites *and* the Gentiles "who transgress Thy word" (l. 27) will be judged. The second "all" (כול) would then be emphatic.

61. Taking [בני] רשעה וכול בני אשמה, "sons of wickedness and all the sons of transgression," to include, if not single out, the Israelite opponents of the sect, employing typical language for the division in Israel.

62. For other expressions of judgment that appear to be directed mainly against Israel, cf. 1QS 1.10-11, 24-26; 4.12-14; 5.7; CD 1.3-4; 2.1, 5-7; 3.8-12; CD(B) 1.5b-14; 1QM 1.2-3, 6; 15.1; 1QH 4.18-20, 26-27. While some different perspectives on the judgment theme in Qumran are offered in these passages, they all tend to support our basic findings.

63. So Sanders (cf. 1977, 240).

64. Sanders explains contradictory statements about election rhetorically — when "thinking primarily of himself" the author of 1QS speaks of God's activity in electing; when "considering outsiders" the author emphasizes free will (cf. 1977, 266-67). Sanders chooses not to take the individual formulations of Qumran seriously in an attempt to buffer his view that "individual Israelites did not really come into the question unless they behaved in such a way as to exclude themselves from the covenant" (266).

THE WIDESPREAD CURRENCY OF THE THEME
IN OTHER INTERTESTAMENTAL WRITINGS

That the Qumran sectarians nourished an attitude of seclusion out of a conscious opposition to apostate Israel is something widely recognized by scholars. The comments made above only further uncover some of the various manifestations of the judgment-of-Israel theme in the scrolls, as well as exhibit the tremendous influence of this theme on such things as the interpretation of Scripture, the eschatology of the community, etc. The next question, naturally, is whether Qumran is to be treated as exceptional in this regard — or can similar statements of the same themes be detected in other writings of the intertestamental period? That such beliefs were expressed in a wide spectrum of writings should come as no surprise, as the Hebrew Scriptures themselves are replete with judgment oracles directed against Israel,[65] and it would seem highly probable that any dissident Jewish group would mimic this precedent. Confirming evidence of a trend in the period toward a critique of Israel is forthcoming from apocryphal books like Sirach and the Wisdom of Solomon, which, while reluctant to deny traditional national views of Israel's election outrightly, nevertheless witness to a growing recognition of the certainty of divine retribution against Israel, and to a fundamentally *individual* judgment.[66] But while these works represent pioneering and often impassioned attempts to deal with the issue of apostasy by authors still profoundly loyal to the national theocracy and thus quite unwilling to condemn Israel categorically, other writings come considerably closer to the attitude of the Qumranites and speak definitively of the sin and apostasy of Israel and of the certainty of Israel's judgment.

65. Notable examples include Isa. 1:2-31; 2:6–3:26; 9:2-21; 22:1-14; 28:1-4; 29:1–30:17; 48:1-6a; Jer. 1:14-16; 2:1–3:5; 4:5–6:30; 7:30–9:26; 10:17-22; 12:1-13; 13:1-12; 15:1-9; 16:1–17:4; Ezek. 4:1–7:27; 11:10-11; 12:1-28; 14:12-23; 18:30; 21:8-32; 24:1-14; Hos. 2:9-13; 4:1–5:15; 6:4-11; 7:11-13; 8:1–10:15; 13:1-3; Joel 1:1–2:11; Amos 2:6–3:15; 4:1-13; 5:1-3, 18-27; 6:1-14; 8:9-14; 9:1-10; Mic. 1:2-16; 2:3-5; 3:11-12; 6:9-16; Zeph. 1:4–2:2; Mal. 3:1-5 (cited according to English versions).

66. While Ben Sira remains in the mainstream of Jewish life (cf. Sir. 7:29-31; 45:6-26; 50:1-21), his doctrine of just and individual retribution is strong (cf. Sir. 2:8-18; 5:4-7; 7:16-17, 36; 11:4-28; 16:12-23), and he applies it specifically to Israel (cf. 16:6-10; 17:15-24). Cf. also Wis. 1:3-12; 2:1-24; 3:1-5, 10; 4:18–5:23; 6:6-8; 12:26; 16:1-6. For discussion of the developments evident in Ben Sira's thought, cf. M. Hengel, *Judaism and Hellenism*, 1974, 1:131-52.

The Enoch Collection

As evidence for Judaism of the late Second Temple period one could hardly overlook a very important corpus made up of writings associated with the ancient figure of Enoch. The five "books" that compose this corpus were brought together in the first few centuries of the Christian era at the latest and as a collection are referred to as *1 Enoch,* or "Ethiopic Enoch," since, before the discovery of the Dead Sea Scrolls, Ethiopic manuscripts represented the earliest extant copies of the writing and to this date remain the only copies we have of the work in its assembled form. The trend in the past century of scholarship had been to separate the individual books according to date and authorship and to further divide them into a multitude of smaller sources, emphasizing the complex literary history of the collection. The highly diverse nature of the various deposits of the Enoch traditions found among the Dead Sea Scrolls at first encouraged this tendency. Of late, however, there has been more of a trend toward dating all the Enochian books (with the notable exception of Book 2, the Similitudes of Enoch) fairly early, prior to 160 B.C., to about the same time as the historical origins of the Dead Sea sect; a couple of the books can be seen to have possessed precursors, if not to have themselves originated, as early as the third century B.C.[67] This early dating in turn suggests a more confined period of literary activity and accordingly also increases the likelihood of a more closely circumscribed provenance for the writings (or, better, for the *redaction* of the various earlier sources into one collection). The final edited version known to us as *1 Enoch* might then have originated within a small movement or even within a small group. The careful treatment of this question by Devorah Dimant, who discerns a kind of narrative unity throughout the corpus, adds some substance to this growing perception.[68] Thankfully, concerns about exact dating and questions of unity, if they can ever be solved, are not very significant here, in that there is little doubt that all of the books belonging to the collection called *1 Enoch* (leaving out of consideration the

---

67. For the dating of the Enoch MSS, cf. J. T. Milik, ed., *The Books of Enoch,* 1976, 4-58, 139-339 passim. Scholars who tend to date the material early include M. E. Stone ("The Book of Enoch and Judaism in the Third Century B.C.E.," 1978, 479-92), J. C. VanderKam ("Studies in the Apocalypse of Weeks," 1984, 522), and I. Fröhlich ("The Symbolical Language of the Animal Apocalypse of Enoch," 1990, 629).

68. D. Dimant ("The Biography of Enoch and the Books of Enoch," 1983, 14-29) suggests that each of the books makes its own integral contribution to a larger biographical outline based on (and greatly expanding!) the biblical account of Enoch's life (Gen. 5:21-24). Independent witness for this biographical process might be available in the form of *Jub.* 4:16-25 and 4Q227. If such an argument is sustainable, this would suggest at the very least that some of the books of *1 Enoch* were written with knowledge of the other parts. For confirming evidence, see the treatment of pseudonymity in ch. 10 below.

Similitudes for the time being) belong well within the period under consideration. But it is at least worthy of note that trends toward identifying a narrowly delimited social provenance for the corpus inspire more confidence in dealing with *1 Enoch* in its entirety and increase the probability that it contains relatively consistent attitudes and teachings.

The Sheep and Lambs Allegory in the Zoomorphic History (Chapters 83–90)

The Fourth Book of *1 Enoch* (chs. 83–90) contains in large part a vision, ostensibly received by the ancient hero Enoch, first relating the history of the world from its earliest beginnings up to the time of Enoch (chs. 85–88), followed by *ex eventu* prophecies of events up to the time of the real author (89:1–90:14), then leading finally into a "true" prophecy of future events (90:15ff.). A large part of this vision contains animal symbolism (hence, "Zoomorphic History"). It is relatively simple to date this work from the "hinge" or "fulcrum" passage where *ex eventu* prophecy becomes prophecy *per se* (approximately at 90:14-15, probably indicated by the words "and I kept seeing till"),[69] and the large majority of scholars confidently assign this work to the early stages of the Maccabean revolt (ca. 165-160 B.C.).[70] Of considerable interest are that part of the history immediately leading up to and including the real author's present (89:73–90:7), and the description of judgment in 90:26-27.

The theme of the history is betrayed by a repeating pattern that can be discerned in its presentation: periods of blessing under righteous leaders alternating with periods of national sin and waywardness.[71] A typical summary of this can be found in 89:41: "And when their eyes become dim-sighted until another sheep arose and led them, they would all return and their eyes became opened"; and 89:51: "Again I saw those sheep, how they went astray, going in diverse ways and abandoning that house of his." Some scholars choose to refer to this pattern as an S-E-R (sin-exile-return) pattern, but the emphasis does not seem to lie on the return/restoration theme (especially not of the whole nation) so much as on the significance of Israel's repeated failure, their deserved punishment, and God's faithfulness in raising up a righteous element in the nation.

---

69. R. H. Charles (*The Book of Enoch or 1 Enoch*, 1912, 209-12) finds doublets in vv. 13-15 and 16-18 and rearranges the text correspondingly. In fact, *two* military campaigns are in view — namely, an initial *unsuccessful* campaign against the horn, and what for the author would be the *final battle*, in which the horn will be overcome.

70. For the identification of the "great horn" as Judas, see Charles, 1912, 206-7; M. Black, *The Book of Enoch* or *I Enoch*, 1985, 276; Fröhlich, 1990, 631; etc.

71. Cf. S. B. Reid, *Enoch and Daniel*, 1989, 60.

The emphasis is hardly on questions regarding national salvation, in other words, so much as on the theme of the survival of a righteous or elect group in lieu of the failure of the people as a whole to remain faithful.

The purpose of this repeating pattern becomes particularly clear in 89:73ff. Here Israel (i.e., Israel *contemporary* with the real author) is viewed as caught in one of those periods of sin and crisis — namely, that resulting from the return of the exiles and their continued oppression by Gentile rulers (90:1-5). As in much of the rest of the history, the nation Israel is represented by "sheep,"[72] and the Gentile nations, in contrast, by various unclean animals and birds of prey.[73] But at this point a third group arises in the menagerie, apparently to be distinguished from both the wild animals and the "sheep." These are what are called "*white sheep*" and "*lambs*"[74] born from those white sheep (90:6).[75] Since in the Zoomorphic History the color white signifies righteousness,[76] it follows that these "white" sheep and their offspring represent the *righteous* Israelites of the author's time, clearly *differentiated* from other (undefined) "sheep." It is these *two* basic groups of sheep, living at the time of the author, that are important here: "lambs" (born from *white* sheep) and (other) "sheep."[77] There is admittedly some overlap in the use of these two terms "lambs" and "sheep" in the history: the lambs are said to *come from* "white sheep," and in vv. 29ff. they seem to retain the name "sheep" for themselves — although even here they are called "all the sheep *that had survived*" (v. 30) and "*those* sheep" (vv. 30-31), to distinguish them from "*those blinded* sheep" (v. 26; cf. also "those sheep were all snow-white," v. 32).[78]

---

72. Reid, 1989, 63-64.

73. Charles, 1912, 205; Black, 1985, 274.

74. Eth. *māḥseʿ* means "suckling kid, lamb, goat" (*CDG*, 31), but the Gk. reads μικροὶ ἄρσενες, which may mean either "small" or "a few (male) offspring" (as Black, 1985, 80, 275). That they are descended from the "white sheep" is the point of significance.

75. Charles, 1912, 171, distinguishes the two groups by the strictness of their rule of life — the white sheep are the faithful adherents of the theocracy, while the lambs are the Hasidim. We prefer the view that two generations of more or less the same group are being distinguished (cf. Black, 1985, 275).

76. Cf. Black, 1985, 257 n.; Fröhlich, 1990, 630. Already in 85:3-10 Adam, Seth, and the Sethian descendants are symbolized by "snow-white" cows. As Isaac points out (*OTP*, 1:63 n. *e*), Eth. *ḍaʿādā* ("snow white," "bright," "pure") is not generally used of a person's visible color. The metaphorical or qualitative sense of the word thus suggests purity or righteous character. What Aram. word(s) it may translate is rather more difficult to ascertain as no one word by itself serves this kind of *double entendre*, though תלג(כ) חור suggests itself (cf. its use in Dan. 7:9, a text highly valued by this community).

77. Reid, 1989, 65: "This . . . clearly reflects an internal conflict within second century Palestinian Judaism."

78. It is entirely understandable that the group would appropriate for themselves the name "sheep" — i.e., "Israel" — as throughout the passage the Lord is still "the Lord of

Nevertheless, a clear distinction is intended and for the most part sustained between two groups of sheep (and offspring), *both from Israel*. What is especially important is how these two groups are portrayed as being in *fundamental religious conflict*. This is evident, for one thing, from their respective responses to the present crisis: while the lambs are suddenly illuminated and given insight into the significance and danger of the present punishment and apparently repent (the lambs "began to open their eyes and see, and cried aloud to the sheep," v. 6), the sheep, on the other hand, remain unmoved by the lambs' urgent message: "But as for the sheep, they (the lambs) cried aloud to them, yet they (the sheep) did not listen to what they (the lambs) were telling them but became exceedingly deafened, and their eyes became exceedingly dim-sighted" (v. 7) — a classic expression of the rejection of the "prophetic voice" in Israel.

But who, exactly, is in the mind of the writer as he constructs this allegory of the sheep and the lambs? While the white sheep and their lambs are frequently identified with the *ḥasîdîm*, it is difficult to be certain of this identification.[79] Nor is it immediately clear who the recalcitrant sheep who refuse to listen to them are. A very general clue to the identity of the latter is given in 90:16, where it is said that the "sheep" are those who conspire with the Gentiles to *overcome* the "horn." Vv. 16ff. relate that God will usher in the day of reckoning as a direct result of the horn's zeal and prayer. This horn is often taken to be Judas Maccabeus, a contemporary hero of the author — although this identification can be made only tentatively.[80] The "sheep," in any event, are all those who resist the activities of the horn (with whom, in contrast, the author and his "lambs" are in sympathy) and may, even from this clue, be understood as any and all in Israel who set themselves up against the Maccabean heroes, or against the cause of the horn, whoever that may be.

That the lambs, on the other hand, are not to be *directly* equated with the followers of Judas and the Maccabees *might* be suggested by the fact that the horn is said to have "sprouted on one of those *sheep*" (*baɡeʿ*, v. 9) rather than on one of the *"lambs" (maḥaseʿ)*. While this alternation in terminology may simply repre-

---

the sheep" (90:15, 20, etc.), and the group would definitely want to continue to identify itself with Israel's Lord.

79. A possible link could be established between the "lambs" of v. 6 and the "rams" who "ran unto" the horn (Judas Maccabeus, v. 10) and who, according to 1 Macc. 2:42, eventually included the *ḥasîdîm*. But there are problems with the identification: (1) it is not clear that the text supports it (for one thing the Eth. word is different: *dābelā*, "male [of any animal]," in v. 10), and (2) it is not certain that the *ḥasîdîm* were anything but sympathetic supporters of the Maccabees — the description "ran unto him" would rather suggest the more zealous early response of their general followers, reported in 1 Macc. 2:29-30. Cf. Black, 1985, 276.

80. See further on this passage below.

sent a stylistic device (or be the result of translation choice), perhaps the original writer deliberately avoided implying that this leader belonged to the lambs *per se*. This possibility becomes more acute given that it is the opinion of many scholars that *Hasidic* groups, being pacifistic, felt decidedly uneasy toward the bloody exercises of the Maccabean warriors. In spite of this reservation, one can surmise that the lambs looked with encouragement upon the emergence of the "horn" as a worthy leader from the mass of Israelite "sheep," and perhaps even took this as an indication that more "sheep" would eventually be willing to join with them (vv. 9-11) — but the passage nevertheless sustains a certain distinction between the "lambs" and the "horn." This distinction is further confirmed by the contrast drawn between the lambs and those who become *followers* of the horn in the remainder of the passage. When the horn cries aloud to the sheep, *some* respond, and the text significantly calls these repentant ones "rams" (90:10). The introduction of yet another designation is strange, but seems to emphasize two things: (1) that not all the sheep responded and (2) that those who did respond were not all from the "lambs" (who were *already* repentant?). "Rams" is a quite respectable designation according to its use elsewhere in Second Temple literature,[81] but in contradistinction to the lambs, here it may well be used to designate a specifically *militant* group. It would appear, in any event, that the rams are the more or less direct followers of the horn, while the lambs represent the author's group *itself*. Even if the lambs were unable to accept the warring faction unqualifiedly, being somewhat pacifistic in tendency, they nevertheless welcomed them as a parallel movement to their own, perhaps as a militant wing to the larger conservative movement. Again historical records tend to confirm that both similarities and differences characterized the *ḥasîdîm* and the more direct followers of the Maccabees, since the former were willing to quickly abandon the Maccabees when their chief objectives had been attained;[82] but such commensurate evidence does not demand an identification of the Enochian group with the *ḥasîdîm*.[83] The important thing is that the offspring of the white sheep, the "lambs" (whether "rams" are to be distinguished from this group or not), compose an identifiable and socially distinct group in their own right.

More can now be said about the identity of the "sheep," who are everywhere

---

81. Reid, 1989, 63-64, points to the use of the term *dkr* (ram) for the elect community in 4QEn^{d}2, 3, 4QEn^{e}4, 3, and 1QEnGiants. Its relationship to the √ *dkr* = "remembrance" is a possible clue to this relationship.

82. Although even this view (based on 1 Macc. 2:42-44) amounts to no more than a plausible construction. Schonfield also finds significance in the fact that in 1 Macc. 7:12-13 the delegation of *ḥasîdîm* to Alcimus was independent of Maccabean authorization (*Secrets of the Dead Sea Scrolls*, 1957, 18).

83. The term *"ḥasîdîm"* may have been generic (although 1 Macc. 2:42 suggests an identifiable group).

contrasted with the "lambs" and oppose them outrightly (cf. vv. 11, 16). The sheep are noted for their uninvolved silence (v. 11), which suggests an abuse of power characterized by inactivity. Since this implies that they possessed the power to do something about the situation but did not, the group was either very large, or possessed political influence, or both. Moreover, since the passage appears to contrast a large group of sheep who ignored warnings and became deaf and blind and a relatively small righteous group consisting of "lambs," the "horn," and a number of repentant and apparently militant "rams" who resisted conformity and joined the cause of reform and protest, the only conclusion to be drawn is that the "sheep" represent Israel *en masse* (i.e., all those *outside* the collectivity of "lambs"). *In line with the symbolism of the work generally,* therefore, "sheep" *remains* a designation for *the whole population of Israelites,* not simply a specific group of opponents or the leaders of Israel. Thus v. 16 certainly intends *this* Israel when it says that "*all* the sheep of the field"[84] conspire together with the Gentiles in one final mass confrontation with the horn. That earlier in the history (90:1-4) this same group of "sheep" are abused and persecuted like helpless victims by the unclean beasts and evil shepherds would tend to confirm that the sheep are *not themselves* the leaders of Israel. The author even sympathizes with the sheep — they are presented as innocently blind and victim to the Gentile animals who prey on them. Leaders, moreover, are designated in the history by terms like "cows," "rams," and "shepherds" — never "sheep" *per se*. "Sheep" therefore evokes the idea of Israel as a totality rather than a certain part of it.[85] The distinct impression is gained that all who were not consciously aligned with the group were reckoned to be among the apostate "sheep." We are accordingly left with two groups, both of whom were contemporary with the author and both of whom, it would appear, were highly "visible" — on the one hand a righteous contingent, on the other the mass of Israelite apostates.

In spite of whatever empathy the author may have had with the plight of Israel, "those blinded sheep" are, according to 90:26, to be judged harshly. Vv. 24-27 describe a future judgment[86] in which books of judgment are opened. Stars (fallen angels), along with the seventy evil shepherds who had earlier

---

84. Literally "all the sheep . . . all of them," k^w*ello* . . . k^w*ellomu,* which is quite emphatic. For the use of "all" as a similar literary device in 1QS 5.10-13; CD 3.14, see above. Black (1985, 278) renders "sheep of the field" as "*wild* sheep." We are reminded here of the expression "sheep without a shepherd" in Mark 6:34 par.; cf. also Zech. 10:2.

85. Black (1985, 278) refers to them as "renegade Israel." Cf. the similar view of mass culpability in 1 Maccabees 1–2.

86. 90:24. *wak^{w}ennanē kona,* "and the judgment happened," certainly represents דינא יתב in Dan. 7:10, "the judgment was set" (we possess an exemplar for דין = k^w*ennanē*; cf. Aram. *1 En.* 14:4; 22:4; 91:12-15). The entire passage is reminiscent of the judgment scene of Daniel 7.

abused their power over Israel, go to the "place of condemnation"[87] filled with fire. The judgment of the sheep is not qualitatively different from that of the angels and shepherds, for the "blinded sheep" are thrown into "*another* abyss *like* it,[88] full of fire"; they are to be "judged, found guilty, and cast into this fiery abyss, and . . . burned . . . their bones also were burning."[89] "The abyss," we are told, "is to the right of that house"[90] and in full view of the righteous.[91] It is interesting to note from these details that the author appears to have modeled his language for this judgment of apostates on Isa. 66:24: "And they shall go forth and look on the dead bodies of the men that have *rebelled against me;* for their worm shall not die, *their fire shall not be quenched. . . .*" It is difficult to avoid the conclusion, given this colorful description of *Israel's* judgment, that the author was so completely at odds with the present situation in his homeland that he was unhindered by nationalistic doctrines from pronouncing on an apostate nation its judgment in the most extreme terms.[92] In this he differed little from the authors of the Qumran scrolls.

Calendar and Condemnation in the Astronomical Book (Chapters 79–82)

Another example of the judgment-of-Israel theme comes from one of the most widely studied portions of *1 Enoch,* the so-called Astronomical Book. Chs. 79–

87. *Makāna kʷennanē*, probably = פחת דין (see note above), or, better, פחת שבר, "a pit of destruction" (cf. Lam. 3:47). Cf. Charles, 1912, 213.

88. *Kama . . . kamāhu;* cf. כמו, "like," "similar," repeated for emphasis. Mention of a second abyss probably emphasizes that Israel is not without her own place of punishment. The use of the construction "like . . . like . . ." stresses the identity of the apostates with the condemned stars and shepherds, and does not imply that the judgment is qualitatively different from theirs, but that it is in fact final.

89. By emphasizing the completeness of the judgment, the author appears to anticipate any false view that unworthy Israel will receive a mitigated judgment. Charles feels that the unusual reference to the "bones" burning calls for an emendation, and he conjectures a couple on the basis of the Heb.: "I saw the sheep *themselves* burning" (1912, 213-14), an equally emphatic rendering. Such an emendation is not necessary if this passage conceals a reference to the vision of dry bones in Ezekiel 37 and subtly denies the possibility of resurrection (allowed by Ezekiel's version) for this group of apostates.

90. I.e., in view of the Temple, the reference being to the Hinnom Valley, which is immediately southwest of Jerusalem, the traditional location of the place of punishment "Gehinnom" (cf. Charles, 1912, 213; Black, 1985, 278).

91. Cf. v. 29; Charles, 1912, 213. See below for more on the "viewing of the fates" motif.

92. And for this reason the passage was apparently employed by Christian writers for anti-Jewish polemic (cf. *Barnabas* 16:5; Milik, 1976, 46).

82 are of particular interest, as they offer a kind of *commentary*[93] on the elaborate astronomical revelations in chs. 73–78. 80:1 states the purpose of these astronomical visions: everything is revealed not only so that Enoch can "see" the heavenly bodies (as well as their spiritual guides: "those that guide the stars of heaven") but also so that he can specifically see "those [heavenly bodies] who interchange their activities and their seasons and rotate their processions." The significance of these peculiar words is found in the following chapters, which refer to a time when the order of the sun, moon, and stars is to be broken by the evil activities of "sinners." "In the days of the sinners" (80:2) — which can only refer to the time of apostasy experienced by the author/redactor[94] — a series of curses and plagues will overtake the land.[95] These curses are traditionally associated with a breach of covenant and appear to refer more to a subsequent judgment (perhaps the final judgment) than to the flood in the literary context of the book. Cosmic[96] as well as natural[97] judgments are listed (80:2-8). Over-

93. Because we see the astronomical speculations as reflecting essentially religious, rather than scientific, concerns, we reject approaches that take these chapters to be additions to an original astronomical teaching that essentially change the meaning and function of that teaching (so Charles, 1912, 147-48; Black, 1985, 18-19; O. Neugebauer, "The 'Astronomical' Chapters of the Ethiopic Book of Enoch," 1985, 386-87). Cf. below.

94. Charlesworth renders the entire line: "In respect to their days, the sinners and the winter are cut short." This is an attempt to make sense out of a difficult passage, but a better reading is that of Charles (1912, 171) and Knibb (*The Ethiopic Book of Enoch*, 1978, 2:185): "in the days of the sinners [*bamaqaʿel xāṭeʾan;* cf. בימי חטאים, 'in the age of the sinners' — i.e., the time of apostasy] the years are cut short." The author thus alludes to biblical passages that appear to speak of an age of apostasy and the accompanying judgment of sinners, such as Amos 8:1-9 and 9:10, the latter of which contains the expression "sinners of my people" (חַטָּאֵי עַמִּי). Other passages containing references to the apostasy of God's people reflected in this verse include 2 Chron. 6:26; Jer. 3:3; 5:25; Hag. 1:10.

95. That these relate to covenantal judgment on Israel is clear from the reflection in the curses of the passages mentioned in n. 94 above. The whole verse is difficult to translate, while the meaning is clear enough; Charles (1912, 171) suggests "And shall *not* appear in their time," following a single Eth. MS, in place of the majority reading "[God] will . . . appear in their time" (so Isaac, *OTP,* 1:58); but even the latter, more difficult reading could refer to a visitation for the purpose of *judgment* (cf. the use of the "visitation" motif in DSS). Charles (171) also emends "shall stand still" to "shall withhold" through the alteration of one vowel in the Eth., a probable emendation if one relates the judgment to the withholding of rain, which seems appropriate to the immediate context.

96. In 80:3-7 we read of the sun standing still and the aberration of heavenly bodies, including a kind of cosmic-spiritual denigration. Here the cosmic bodies are personified and sinners are influenced and misled by these heavenly bodies, all of which leads to idolatrous worship. For language and ideas, all within a context of apostasy, cf. Joel 2:10; Amos 8:9.

97. In 80:2-3, 8 we read of years cut short, lack of growth, infertility, lethargy(?), drought, fruitlessness, evil things, plagues. "Their seeds" (v. 2) is a *double entendre* refer-

whelming evidence from second-century-B.C. Jewish sectarian groups suggests that such a combination of astronomical descriptions and judgment motifs can imply only one thing: Israel has departed from the solar calendar,[98] with the result that covenantal and even cosmic judgments are anticipated. It is especially noteworthy, therefore, that it is *not the Gentile world but Israelites* who are centered out for judgment in this passage, indeed in the entire book; only Israelites would be accused of abandoning the calendar, and only Israelites were subject to covenantal curses.

The rather harsh descriptions of the judgment of Israel compose a shocking aspect of the book. That such descriptions are not an unimportant detail, however, is suggested by the significant placing of a judgment oracle at the very conclusion of the section and of the book itself (just prior to the closing salutation): "the sinners shall die together with the sinners; and the apostate shall sink together with the apostate. But those who do right shall not die on account of the (evil) deeds of the people; it [the deluge-like judgment] will gather on account of the deeds of the evil ones."[99] The parallelism between "sinners" and "apostate" in these verses suggests that both are to be identified as one group. That Israelites are intended by the terms reveals the volatility of the issues and the contempt felt by the author (and his community) toward his own compatriots. Thus while the evidence provided by Astronomical Enoch is consider-

---

ring to both the retardation of the offspring of sinners and of the seeds they sow; cf. Isaac, *OTP*, 1:58.

98. Cf. 80:1, 6-7; 82:4-5; see more on this important topic below.

99. I.e., negligent, impious ones, *rasi'ān;* cf. רשעים, 81:8-9. Charles, followed by Knibb, prefers a family of MSS whose readings differ substantially: ". . . and those who practice righteousness will die because of the deeds of men, and will be taken away because of the deeds of the impious" (Knibb, 1978, 2:185). Such an idea might be comparable to Isa. 57:1-2, where the righteous are rescued by death from evil; cf. 2 Kings 22:20 for this use of being "gathered (to one's fathers)" (Charles, 1912, 174). But I prefer Charlesworth's text and translation because: (1) it represents the more difficult reading (containing the negative particle *'i*); (2) it is supported by the most ancient Eth. MSS, Tana[9] and Tana[9a] (fifteenth century; Knibb refers to this group as "significant" [1978, 1:425]); (3) it carries forward the flood motif of v. 8 (note the flood motif *yesaṭṭam,* "sink," literally "be flooded," "immersed"; see further below); (4) there is no occasion for a suffering-of-the-righteous motif here, while the accepted reading offers a much more appropriate vindication motif. As for the translation of "it will gather," Tana[9] alone preserves the probably original third masculine *singular* ending *e* (imperfect medio-passive *yetegābā'(e)* [without the conjunction], "it gathers"); Tana[9a] and other MSS have the *plural* ending *u,* which can be explained as part of an attempt to iron out the difficulties of the original reading. *gab'a* would suit either a gathering of people as in a harvest of souls *(convenit),* or a surrounding of water *(confluxit, collectus est);* cf. *GCA,* 270. The latter meaning clearly fits the Enochian context and the immediate presence of the flood motif quite well. There is no indication that a harvest of souls is intended here.

ably less elaborate than in the passages from the Zoomorphic History, some important similarities between the books are evident, notably the way the judgment specifically divides between the righteous and the apostate *in Israel*. In the astronomical chapters the righteous follow the proper calendar and the sinners fail to do so. As a study of the history of the period will clearly reveal (see below), most Israelites capitulated without resistance to the practice of the majority in accepting a "Gentile" calendar. It is accordingly evident that the author of the passage represented a hard-line minority position whose doctrine condemned a large part of Israel. That he expected judgment to come in the near future to all the unfaithful follows from this rather strict position.[100]

Breach of Covenant in the Book of Watchers (5:4-8)

Another passage of interest comes from the introductory section (chs. 1–5) of the Book of Watchers (*1 Enoch* 1–36). Much of the groundwork has already been done for us by Lars Hartman in his extensive and detailed study of the chapters (*Asking for a Meaning,* 1979), a study that devotes particular attention to the passage of interest here (5:4-8). Hartman seeks to determine a *Sitz im Leben* for chs. 1–5 in order to find the meaning of the passage for its original audience. This *Sitz im Leben* he takes to be a covenant renewal celebration much like that believed to have been practiced at Qumran annually during the Feast of Weeks.[101] The entire section contrasts the consistency and orderliness of creation (2:1–5:3) with the waywardness of Israel (5:4). As Hartman points out, this is a regular feature of "*rîb*-patterned" texts[102] and may well point to the use of this text during the Jewish festival period (Tishri 1-10).

These chapters, however, have obviously been given a new context and function as the introduction to the Book of Watchers. Whether one takes the view that chs. 1–5 have influenced the rest of chs. 1–36 or that they have been influenced, in turn, by their new context during the process of incorporation into the work as a whole, it is undeniable that the passage has become closely related to the rest of the book through many of its terms and concepts. Among its special features within this context we note the inordinately large amount of

100. Contrast our treatment (and see below) with the comment of Sanders (1977, 360) that the Astronomical Book "has nothing of interest for the present study."

101. L. Hartman, *Asking for a Meaning,* 1979, 111-19, etc.

102. While K. Baltzer speaks of the *"Gattung"* of *"Bundesformular"* (*The Covenant Formulary in Old Testament, Jewish, and Early Christian Writings,* 1971, passim), Hartman prefers the term *"rîb"* = "suit," "denouncement," since it is not so much that the covenant is being announced as that accusations are being brought forward regarding its having been *broken.*

space dedicated to the section on the orderliness of creation (8 verses), when compared to that given to other parts of the traditional *rîb* pattern (13½ verses total), and above all when contrasted to that allowed for the waywardness-of-Israel section (1 verse). The impressiveness of this orderliness-of-creation (or the "unchangeableness of nature") theme in the passage is accentuated by the fact that this is the sole element in the *rîb* pattern that is actually *unparalleled* in the biblical covenant texts.[103]

In order to explain this preoccupation with the order of creation, we might look to another passage in the Enochian corpus that also directs a sizeable amount of attention to the order-in-creation motif, namely, the astronomical chapters, in which the orderliness of the sun, moon, etc., is charted out in careful symmetry. Here, as we have already intimated, the symmetry of the universe is employed as a backdrop for the admonitions about the calendar in the rest of the work. This might explain why such interest is shown in the idea of divine orderliness in the present passage from the Book of Watchers as well: behind it stands the dispute over the calendar and the author's belief that Israel, in adopting a false calendar, has sinned to the point of breaking the covenant. More direct indications that the calendar dispute looms in the background of the present passage as well are to be detected in the wording of the "regularity" passage itself:

> Examine all the activities which take place in the sky and how they do not alter their ways, and examine the luminaries of heaven, how each one of them rises and sets; each one is systematic according to its respective season *and for their own festivals they appear;*[104] and they do not divert from their appointed order. . . .[105] (2:1)

The language of this passage, as will be further noted when we deal with the calendar issue more closely below, is actually very similar to that of certain passages in *1 Enoch* 72–82. While Hartman's treatment may possess a great deal of validity for the passage, therefore, we would concur with scholars who are beginning to draw more of a connection with the calendar debate, a connection that in some senses may be more fundamental than the connection with covenant renewal.[106]

103. Hartman, 1979, 87.

104. This phrase is from the superior Gk. witness (with Charles, 1912, 9).

105. Black (1985, 110 n. 2) recognizes the calendrical context of this expression.

106. We do not deny that the source of expression is the liturgy of the covenant renewal celebration, but discern a somewhat different function for the passage within the present context of calendrical debate, having been removed from its original covenantal context. Charles's standard approach (1912, 8) should be contrasted with that of Black (1985, 13; cf. also 111, 419), who recognizes calendrical speculation in the sources of the passage.

Particularly worthy of attention is that point in the chapters where the text turns from an exposition of the regularity of nature to a condemnation of the unfaithfulness of Israel. Here the apostates are directly addressed: "*But as for you,* you have *not* been longsuffering and you have not done the commandments[107] of the Lord, but you have transgressed and spoken slanderously grave and harsh words with your impure mouths against his greatness" (5:4). From Hartman's study we know that covenantal denouncements similar to this one were specifically used to call apostate Israel back to faithfulness. But there are other reasons besides the relationship of this passage to a *rîb* pattern for concluding that it is Israel that is being specifically addressed here. The language of this verse is framed in terms applicable only to Israelites: keeping the commandments is the responsibility and privilege of Israel alone; the charge of slandering "his greatness" would hardly possess import if addressed to any but Israelites; "grave [or proud] and hard [harsh] words" is an expression used of the Israelites in the Scriptures, one that particularly recalls the piety of the canonical psalms.[108] The severity of the judgment on the apostates is everywhere expressed: their lives will "perish and multiply in *eternal* execration" (v. 5; cf. v. 6); the covenantal "curse" thus apparently includes both worldly and eternal judgment (vv. 5-10), and the expressions are decisive, final, and even vindictive.[109] The "hardhearted"[110] ones "shall find no peace," that is, the peace

107. *Eth. te'ezaza,* "commandments"; Gk. ὑμεῖς . . . οὐκ . . . ἐποιήσατε κατὰ τὰς ἐντολὰς αὐτοῦ. Milik suggests ממרה (מאמר) after the exemplar 18:15 (partially reconstructed), suggesting a revelation that goes beyond the Torah.

108. Pss. 12:4; 37:11. Cf. also a covenantal passage like Deut. 29:17ff. The wording is sometimes also used of proud Gentile rulers; cf. Dan. 7:8, 11, 20; Hartman, 1979, 90.

109. Black (1985, 113) interprets the rather unusual wording of v. 5 to mean that while "the wicked will 'curse their days' in this life [which will be prematurely cut off: 'the years of your life will be cut off' (*taḥag^wlu;* Gk. ἀπολεῖται; Milik, 1976, 146 suggests [אבד] עבדן, a strong expression of lasting destruction)], in Gehenna, in contrast, their years will be *prolonged* 'under an everlasting curse.'" Thus the covenantal curse involves a loss of life in this world and a corresponding extension of years in a state of eternal damnation. The expressions for the latter are: "eternal curse" (*margam zala'lam;* cf. [. . . מין ע[ל]וט ע[בל]); cf. Milik, 146, and the following verse: ללוט עלם; Aram. also adds "years of your destruction" [אבדנכן י[נש . . .]) — this phrase may have been inadvertently dropped in Eth. Note also the parallel "forever" in the blessing of the righteous (v. 10). To "make one's name" part of a curse (v. 6) is used of apostasy in Isa. 65:15 (cf. Charles, *APOT,* 2:12), which is significant given that this passage speaks of the blessing of the *remnant* of Israel and is directed against those "who forsake the LORD" (v. 11).

110. *Yebussāna leb;* Gk. σκληροκάρδιοι; Milik partially reconstructs Aram. to read קשי לב[ן . . .]) (1976, 146). An exemplar may be found in 1:9, which appears to employ σκληρῶν for קשה, a word also found in the citation in Jude 15. The expression calls to mind Ezek. 3:7: כָּל־בֵּית יִשְׂרָאֵל חִזְקֵי־מֵצַח וּקְשֵׁי־לֵב הֵמָּה, "*all Israel* is hard-headed and obstinate of heart." For σκληροκάρδιοι used of Israel in LXX, cf. Deut. 10:16 (with refer-

promised in the covenant[111] (v. 5). In contrast to the apostates, the elect will have peace (v. 7) and life (v. 9) and will "inherit [the covenantal promise of] the land" (v. 7).[112] It is stated most emphatically that, in direct contrast to the wicked, the elect will not be judged (v. 9); they receive "life" and will not die "because of wrath or anger," a clear allusion to avoiding the covenantal punishments to fall on Israel.[113] All the blessings of the covenant will be theirs, "and peace shall increase their lives and the years of their happiness shall be multiplied forever in gladness and peace all the days of their life" (5:10).

1 Enoch 1–5 accordingly implies a very serious and widespread judgment on Israel since it condemns the official calendar employed in Jerusalem along with those who have *resigned* themselves to its use. This amounts to a clear and final proclamation of judgment on the generation of Israel living in the author's time[114] — from which the author and the rest of the righteous are exempted. It is due to the generalizing nature of such indictments brought against Israel that one must unfortunately take issue with E. P. Sanders and, in fact, with all conventional nationalistic approaches when it comes to books like *1 Enoch*. While Sanders would agree that *1 Enoch* allows for a strict segregation of the righteous and elect, on the one hand, and pagans and apostates, on the other, it is not valid to view the latter group as merely composed of "exceptions" to the general rule of salvation for all Israel, as Sanders does.[115] It would be exceedingly problematic at best to accept that this book or any other portion of *1 Enoch* investigated above sustains a view of election at all similar to such an interpretation of tractate Sanhedrin 10.1.

---

ence to v. 12): καὶ περιτεμεῖσθε τὴν σκληροκαρδίαν ὑμῶν καὶ τὸν τράχηλον ὑμῶν οὐ σκληρυνεῖτε. The Heb. has קשה only once in this passage (literally "no longer be hard" — i.e., stubborn); the repetition of the phrase in the LXX is emphatic; cf. also LXX Jer. 4:4, where the word is similarly added for emphasis to translate קשה. Hartman (1979, 90-91) relates the terminology to the *rîb*.

111. The phrase occurs repeatedly in *1 Enoch* (12:5; 13:1; 16:4 [of the Watchers]; 94:6; Gk. [MS Gb] 98:16; 99:13; 102:3; 103:8). In the Similitudes righteousness and peace are promised only to the "righteous and elect" (cf. 39:5; 60:5, 25); peace is a present as well as future experience there (cf. Black, 1985, 113-14). Cf. Isa. 47:22; 57:21.

112. *Meder,* "earth" or "land"; Gk. γῆ regularly translates ארע (cf. Heb. ארץ; Milik, 1976, 369, 405); it is reasonable to take this in the sense of the covenantal promise of inheriting "the land" (i.e., of Israel; perhaps also as in Matt. 5:5) rather than the whole earth; cf. Ps. 37:11.

113. *Bamaqšaft wa'ibama'et.* Cf. "in anger and in fury and in great wrath" for the dispersion of Israel on breaking the covenant (Deut. 29:28); and חֵמָה אַפֹּו in Isa. 42:24-25 (cf. v. 9); used of Israel also in Num. 1:53; 16:46; 18:5; Josh. 9:20; 22:20; 2 Kings 3:27; 1 Chron. 27:24; etc. Heb. קצף is frequently used of the Lord's wrath (Jer. 10:10; Zech. 7:12).

114. That the passage, with its antediluvian literary context, is actually addressed to the real author's contemporaries, is evident from 1:1-2; cf. Hartman, 1979, 16.

115. Sanders, 1977, 361.

The Mishnaic idea of the salvation of all Israel with exceptions (if in fact that really exists) is accordingly not an adequate paradigm for Second Temple Judaism as a whole, for it results in a number of serious problems, not least of which is that one must deal with the frequent statements in *1 Enoch* that *counter* this view of things.[116] Its nationalistic basis would appear — *ex hypothesi*, as well as from the facts of the case as they have become evident — to disqualify it as a valid, or even helpful, guide for defining the Judaism at hand.

Jubilees

Jubilees is another important witness for the late Second Temple period. Although placed by Charles in the latter part of the second century,[117] a date from circa 164 to 150 B.C. is more widely accepted today.[118] Like *1 Enoch, Jubilees* is ostensibly a revelation granted to a revered ancient, in this case to Moses as he receives the Law on Mount Sinai. The rationale for a second and additional revelation alongside the canonical Torah may be that it represents the narrative counterpart in the form of a prophecy ("the account of the division of all of the days of the Law and the testimony") to the legal material said to have been received by Moses on the mount. For its original readers this would serve to explain how narrative material came to be present in books written by Moses and to grant to this material an authoritative character equal to that of the legal portions. Given, however, that *Jubilees* seems in some places to stand in opposition to the public Torah and to challenge the latter's authority, it may be better to view this book as some form of "second law" and thus as a parallel, rather than as a supplementary, revelation. Whatever the exact occasion for the writing of *Jubilees,* one can hardly overlook its claim to offer additional laws or clarification of laws that do not appear in the Pentateuch, laws that were nevertheless held to be revealed to Moses privately on Sinai.

116. The abundant judgment theme in this literature throws the usefulness and validity of such a model seriously into question. For the sake of argument one might accept Sanders's "pattern of religion" for Judaism. But our objection to this approach can be put this way: *How helpful can it be to speak of a "pattern of religion" that embraces "the-salvation-of-all-with-exceptions" when the sheer number and uncompromising nature of the formulations of "exceptions" entirely distorts and obfuscates the "salvation-of-all" foundation?* Another problem with Sanders's thesis has to do with chronology and methodology. One must ask how a model taken from a much later period can be considered valid for this early period — possibly as much as four hundred years passed between the writing of these portions of *1 Enoch* and the codification of the Mishnah!

117. Between 135 and 105 B.C. (*APOT,* 2:1).

118. Cf. J. C. VanderKam, *Textual and Historical Studies in the Book of Jubilees,* 1977, 208-85.

Second Temple Judaism was replete with traditions about additional laws not recorded in the books of Moses. Besides what is represented by the oral traditions of the rabbis, there was also a sectarian tradition that was considerably more esoteric. Both types of tradition were carefully guarded from falling into the wrong hands, but the latter kind of tradition was especially marked by its claim to be suitable for the righteous alone, that is, only for those in a state worthy to receive it. Many of the pseudonymous Pseudepigrapha represent this latter kind of tradition, and *Jubilees* itself contains much that is suggestive of this kind of tradition. It closely follows Genesis and Exodus, but goes well beyond a mere retelling of the narrative. One would assume that the distinctive doctrine of its writer(s)/editor(s) is particularly reflected in these embellishments, an assumption that tends to prove sustainable.[119] Attention to a couple of texts where the judgment-of-Israel theme is evident in the midst of such embellishments will bear this out.

"An Evil Generation Which Sins in the Land" — 23:8ff.

Jub. 23:8ff. contains an important interlude or diversion from the main story line connected with the account of Abraham's death. The subject of the interlude is the general decline of longevity (cf. Ps. 90:10) associated with the flood (v. 9). Abraham, the passage teaches, was unable to escape the effects of the decline but, on account of his own righteous character (vv. 9-10), could not himself be blamed for adding to the evil tendency that brought it on.[120] The passage proceeds then to announce that all generations that "arise henceforth" will have their lives shortened on account of this act of judgment (vv. 11-13). Furthermore, "their knowledge will forsake them" (v. 11). In vv. 14ff. this prophecy is specifically applied to "an evil generation which sins in the land" (v. 14).[121] That these last verses refer to the author's Jewish contemporaries is scarcely veiled by the literary context of the chapter.[122] The author describes the sins of his generation carefully. They include "pollution and fornication and contami-

---

119. Cf. J. C. Endres, *Biblical Interpretation in the Book of Jubilees,* 1987, passim, esp. 249-50.

120. Cf. R. H. Charles, *The Book of Jubilees or Little Genesis, Translated from the Editor's Ethiopic Text,* 1902, 145.

121. The expression "this evil generation" (הַדּוֹר הָרָע הַזֶּה) is used of the Mosaic wilderness generation in Deut. 1:35; cf. Num. 32:13; Deut. 32:5.

122. Cf. Charles, 1902, 146-48; Endres, 1987, 55. The reference to those who resist the apostasy with "bow and swords and war in order to return [the apostates] to 'the way'" (v. 20) is a clear allusion to the Maccabean campaigns (cf. also G. L. Davenport, *The Eschatology of the Book of Jubilees,* 1971, 41-42).

nation and abomination," reproach of parents, and "renouncing[123] the covenant which the LORD made between them and himself so that they might be
careful and observe *all* of his commandments and his ordinances and *all* of his
law without turning aside to the right or left" (v. 16). The repeated emphasis on
"all" (*kᵂello*) of the Law is best understood as alluding to the failure of certain
Israelites to carry out certain important laws or to their failure to carry out *additional* commandments like those found in *Jubilees*.[124] Although elsewhere Israel is charged with apostasy based on more publicly recognized commandments (cf. 12:33-34), one is certainly dealing in the present passage with
additional (or, as the sectarian might insist, "clarified" or *"fully* revealed") law,
the ignorance or neglect of which is thought to imply an equally serious type of
apostasy. That this law was not for ancient times but bears directly on the
writer's contemporaries is evident when the author becomes more specific
about the sin in mind, namely, when he reveals that the Israelites have "forgotten the commandments and covenant and festivals and months and sabbaths
and jubilees and all of the judgments" (v. 19), expressions that once again point
to disputes over the calendar.[125] The theme of the judgment of Israel for abandoning the calendar is a frequent one in *Jubilees* (cf. also 1:14; 4:18-19; 6:32-38).
As part of this neglect Israel has failed to keep the covenant: the expression
"turn aside to right or left" in this context clearly alludes to breaking covenant
stipulations.[126] The important point here is again that the predictions of apostasy concern *Israel*. Only Israelites could be charged with "renouncing" the law
and covenant (not to mention abandoning the calendar and the proper performance of the feasts associated with it). When the passage says of these apostates
that "they will pronounce the great name but not in truth or righteousness"
(v. 21), this may point to the insincerity of the religion of the author's contemporary Israelites, or more likely to the view that uttering the divine name with
unclean lips (by reason of ritual transgression) constitutes blasphemy.

While these latter words are particularly appropriate for Israel's spokes-
men or leaders, especially the priests,[127] the author seems to implicate the

---

123. *xadigotomu* (√ *xadaga*) can mean "renounce" or "neglect."

124. The word translated "commandments," *te'zāz,* may reflect מצות, although an
exemplar exists in *1 En.* 18:15, which has מאמר; thus laws beyond the Torah may be meant;
the word translated "law," however, is the more common one for the Torah, *ḥegg.* The word
translated "ordinances" is *sherʿat* — literally "treaty," "covenant."

125. Endres, 1987, 55.

126. Cf. Deut. 5:32; 17:20; and esp. 28:14. It relates also to the "way" language of
v. 20. For more, see ch. 6 below. While Sanders (1977, 371) argues that the covenant is not
considered conditional on keeping the Jubilee laws, our treatment will thoroughly refute
this.

127. The leaders of the "evil generation" addressed in vv. 14-20, either the

greater part of Israel, rather than a few leaders, when in v. 17 he stresses both the magnitude and extent of the sin. He does this by continuing to employ the emphatic *"all/every" (kʷello)*: "For they *all* did evil and *every* mouth speaks of sin and *all* of their deeds (are) polluted and abominable. And *all* of their ways (are) contamination and pollution and corruption." The passage goes on to say that "a great plague" will come on "the deeds of that generation from the LORD," that Israel will be given over "to the sword and to judgment and to captivity and pillage and destruction," that is, the covenant curses (v. 22), and that the nations will be raised against them (also a covenantal form of punishment). The deep despair of the times is expressed in words typical of wartime: "there will be no one who will gather and no one who will bury" — a stock expression for total destruction (v. 23; cf. Jer. 8:2); "there will be *none* who will be saved" (v. 24). Thus the judgment for these sins is put in largely mundane terms, including corruption of the land, infertility, destruction of cattle and fish, and the like (v. 18). It is difficult to say whether the author was thinking also of other-worldly retribution: the punishments he lists conform to the biblical covenant curses, which themselves are oriented to "this world," while the context (v. 30), on the other hand, might suggest that the punishments go beyond this world. All in all, since these words precede the "hinge" verses (vv. 26-27),[128] one is probably justified in interpreting them in light of the Seleucid period — that is, the judgment is believed to have already begun in the author's time. It is also noteworthy that, in contrast to these evildoers and at the same time ("in those days"), there emerges "a righteous generation" — probably the community to which the author belongs — who appear as a kind of foil to the apostates, who have brought on the nation a time of great suffering and judgment.[129]

Hellenizing party under High Priest Alchimus (162 B.C.; cf. Charles, 1902, 148; VanderKam, 1977, 252-53; Endres, 1987, 55-56) or the Hasmoneans (Davenport, 1971, 43-45, who suggests that the verse was interpolated about 152 B.C.). The references may be more general, however, reflecting conventional eschatological language drawn from the Hebrew Scriptures.

128. Cf. Endres, 1987, 59; perhaps the hinge begins with v. 25; cf. VanderKam, 1977, 254; Charles, 1902, 148.

129.   And in those days, children will begin to search the law,
    and to search the commandments
        [*te'zāz*; cf. מצות, which may suggest additional commandments;
        see notes above]
    and to return to the way of righteousness. (v. 26)

The meaning of this passage depends on the identity of the "children" *(daqiq)* who "begin to search the law" (v. 26). *Daqiq* is used throughout this passage for Israel. But the children of vv. 26ff. are distinct from the apostate "children" of Israel in v. 25. (Wintermute's indefinite, anarthrous "children" in v. 26 [*OTP*, 2:101] accurately reflects

Rooting Out Sinners — 30:13-23

The narration of the Dinah/Shechem incident in *Jub.* 30:13-23 is another example of this author's practice of embellishing and interpreting the biblical accounts[130] to address the situation of his *contemporaries.* Here the story of the foreigner Shechem, "the son of Hamor the Hivite," and of his "taking" Dinah (cf. Genesis 34) serves as little more than an opportunity for, or illustration of, a lengthy exhortation strictly prohibiting intermarriage with foreigners (an issue not explicitly mentioned in the biblical narrative).[131] That this exhortation is directed to the Israel of the author's time (ca. 165-160 B.C.) is suggested by the words of v. 10, "there is no limit of days for this law," and by the tone of vv. 21-23, which begin with "I have commanded you to speak to the children of Israel that they might not commit sin or transgress the ordinances or break the covenant which was ordained for them . . . ," a warning that contemporizes words that in the biblical account were addressed to Moses regarding Israel's *future* apostasy.[132]

The author makes clear what he sees to be serious implications of the sin of intermarriage for his contemporaries: it will *not be forgiven* (v. 14); the normal means of atonement will *not* be effective (v. 16); only complete excommunication ("rooting out") will be effective in bringing relief (v. 10). It is also worthy of note that this sin is said to bring judgment, not only on the guilty parties, but on *all* Israel (v. 15). This further repetition of "all" (k^well-; cf. the Heb. cognate $kāl$; we have seen it already in connection with *Jub.* 23:14-25 and *1 En.* 90:16, and it is implied in "leaving no remnant" in 1QS 5.10-13) again gives the impression that this was a conventional expression for the *all-inclusiveness* of

---

the change of referent here; the Ethiopic language does not possess the article.) Here the former are qualified, and contrasted with the others, as "children . . . [who] begin to search the law, and . . . the commandments and to return to the way of righteousness." These righteous "children" represent the community of the author or others like them who are righteous.

130. According to Endres (1987, 121), there are significant reductions (thirty-two verses from Gen. 33:18–34:29 are reduced to three in *Jub.* 30:1-3) as well as lengthy embellishments (30:5-17 represents amplification).

131. Cf. Endres, 1987, 120, 133-34. This reinterpretation can be contrasted with a certain openness to proselytization as implied, perhaps, by Gen. 35:1ff.

132. That this is not addressed to Gentile questions, as it might appear superficially, is noted by Endres (1987, 237), who discerns a literary device in the author's employment of anti-Gentile polemic that actually serves to highlight intra-Jewish debate (241, 3, cf. 140). The charges made here are appropriate to the period of the Hellenization of Jerusalem: the sin of intermarriage is specifically said to defile the sanctuary (a real concern during the Hellenization; vv. 13-15), and other causes of defilement may have been in mind as well ("all the ways of defilement," v. 22).

Israel's judgment. This all-inclusiveness is also expressed in terms of the *corporate* guilt of Israel, a theme that the author not only raises in the exhortation section (vv. 8-9) but is also careful to read back into the historical narrative: not only the family of Shechem (as in Gen. 34:26) but *all* the men of the city were made to pay with their lives for Dinah's rape (v. 4). This detail certainly serves to legitimize the principle of corporate judgment for Israel in the author's present as well (so v. 15).[133] The author accordingly indicates that the possibility of salvation during the present time of disobedience is at best slight. Perhaps he even implies by telling this vengeful story that only those who *actively participate against* the present unrighteousness can hope to be saved. Does this strict position suggest that the author considered himself and his party to be acting as the remnant of Ezra 9:8 (there are other echoes of Ezra 9 in the passage), who reacted with comparable zeal on the basis of Ezra's proscription of intermarriage?

Israel, in any event, will be collectively judged for their sin. The passage speaks of "vengeance against the sinners" (v. 23), and when the violent and vindictive response of Levi in judging the Shechemites is held up as a model of righteousness (vv. 18-20, 23), one is reminded of the mission of vengeance against sinners enjoined on the Qumran community. The insistence that the sinner be "rooted out . . . of all Israel" (v. 10) may imply the same. This judgment is also described as "plague upon plague and curse upon curse, and every judgment, and plague, and curse" (v. 15), that is, the curses of the covenant. Perhaps to express the certainty of this judgment, the passage introduces a concept that is repeated often in this literature — the names of the righteous and of sinners are recorded in books along with their deeds — significantly again in the style of Mal. 3:16-18. The deeds of a righteous man "will be written" and he "will be written down as a friend and a righteous one in the heavenly tablets" (v. 20); all the children of Israel who are obedient will be "written down as friends" (v. 21). In contrast, apostates "will be recorded in the heavenly tablets as enemies. And they will be blotted out of the book of life and written in the book of those who will be destroyed and with those who will be rooted out from the land" (v. 22). It is clear from these final words that the author envisaged a covenantal curse ("rooted out from the land") that nevertheless included an otherworldly judgment ("those who will be destroyed").[134] Given the author's highly pessimistic view of contemporary trends in Israel, it would appear

133. For this as a revealing distinction from the biblical account, added to emphasize corporate responsibility and the prohibition of intermarriage, see Endres, 1987, 124-25, 131.

134. *Yeteḥagʷalu* — a variation of *yetehagʷalu*, "be destroyed"; more than an earthly destruction seems to be implied here (contrast שמד in the Hebrew Scriptures), as the expression is given a personal and individual application.

that he was resigned to the severe judgment that had come, and was apparently still to come, for a significant portion of his compatriots.[135] As in the Enochian literature, therefore, the idea of Israel's judgment is not treated as a minor concern in *Jubilees*. Israel has broken the covenant (cf. also 15:33-34),[136] and the entire nation is in danger of judgment for this.

The *Psalms of Solomon*

In the writings investigated so far the judgment of Israel is mostly something anticipated for the future, but in the *Psalms of Solomon* it is unambiguously presented as having in large part already taken place. The rather unique *Sitz im Leben* of the *Psalms*, namely, the storming of Jerusalem by Pompey in 63 B.C., an event that seems to have directly inspired the writing of these psalms,[137] has made it possible for judgment themes normally reserved for the future to be viewed as realized in a closely defined historical context. Apparently, however, the author combined this perspective with an ongoing belief in a future and otherworldly judgment,[138] so that in some passages it is difficult to decide if past or future judgments are intended or if, as would seem quite likely, a connection between them is implied. In regard to this historical aspect of judgment, it is worthy of note that shortly before Jerusalem was taken under siege by Pompey the psalmist and his community escaped the city (17:16-18). The resulting sense of providential rescue, and the vindication it implied, contributed to the unique perspective of the psalmist, who from his place of refuge and retreat blamed the sacking not on the presumption of the Gentile overlords so much as on the apostasy of other Jews, particularly Jerusalemites, whose condemnation (in contrast to his own deliverance) seemed to have been confirmed by their demise. One finds throughout the *Psalms of Solomon* that the retributive judgment of Israel is attributed to the sinful actions of Jerusalemites, par-

---

135. Cf. also 1:12-14, 20-22; 4:18-19; 6:10-14, 32-38; 15:33-34.

136. Cf. Davenport, 1971, 51-52.

137. For a summary of the evidence for such a view, see J. O'Dell, "The Religious Background of the Psalms of Solomon," 1961, 241-42. That Psalm 8 in particular refers to Pompey is held by most scholars (e.g., H. E. Ryle and M. R. James, *ΨΑΛΜΟΙ ΣΟΛΟΜΩΝΤΟΣ*, 1891, 73, 81; J. Schüpphaus, *Die Psalmen Salomonis*, 1977, 45-46). We take the position that the psalms were written mostly at the same time, rather than over a lengthy period of time. They have an interconnectedness of themes, and the psalm genre seems to have been adopted rather artificially. There is no evidence that this corpus has been constituted from any sort of collection of liturgical or pedagogical hymns (following Schüpphaus, 20).

138. Cf. 14:9; 15:6, 9, 13.

ticularly for their defilement of the cultus (2:3-5; 8:11-12, 22), for their sinful lives (2:6), for ignoring the voice of the righteous (2:8), for sexual immorality (2:11-14 with 2:15-21; 8:9-10, cf. 8:14-15), for uncleanness (8:22), for not being called (17:5), for not glorifying God (17:5), and for establishing an illegitimate monarchy (17:6). This judgment is promised not exclusively for the leaders in Jerusalem (so 4:1-13) but for all the people (17:19b-20). Other expressions of judgment are reserved for Gentiles (7:2-3). A close look at a couple passages will demonstrate the use of these themes, but, once again, these are merely representative of a much larger number of passages that hold Israel responsible for its own judgment (cf. also 1:6-8; 2:1-3; 14:9; 15:6-13; etc.).

"They Surpassed the Gentiles in Sin" — 8

The eighth psalm makes it abundantly clear that its author saw the recent sacking of Jerusalem as the result of God's judgment on the sin of the people (vv. 8, 15). In this judgment the leaders are particularly blameworthy: they stole from the sanctuary of God, by which the psalmist probably means that they misappropriated temple funds (v. 11), and, what is more, they even opened the gates as an invitation to the Gentiles to take the city (vv. 16-19; 2:1; cf. Josephus, *Wars* 1.142-43). Other accusations are leveled against the priests, including Levitical impurity, particularly the failure to avoid uncleanness caused by menstrual blood (v. 12; cf. 1:6-8; 2:3). But the leaders are not guilty alone, as the people seem to be implicated in their sins, particularly the above-mentioned cultic sins, for the sacrifices from which they would normally benefit are now viewed as invalidated, "defiled" by the actions of the priestly representatives (v. 12). That the author was witness to what he thought to be widespread apostasy in Jerusalem, moreover, can be seen in his attacks on "secret" sins, notably adultery (vv. 9-10), saying that *"everyone* (ἕκαστος) committed adultery with his neighbor's wife" (v. 10); this seems to be his way of expressing the same "all" motif noticed in previous passages (cf. also 2:10-11: "everyone [Gk. πᾶς] . . . entered in [to prostitutes] in broad daylight"; 17:19-20). While these expressions are obviously not to be taken overly literally, they adequately suggest the notion of the inclusiveness of sin and guilt.

In spite of what appears to be a universal view of sin, however, the author of the eighth psalm does not take a light view of sin. Jerusalem's sin is not only pervasive but also severe: the author reaches the startling conclusion that these Israelites "surpassed [even] the gentiles" in sin (v. 13; cf. 1:8; 2:12), employing conventional language expressing the shame of the people of God acting like pagans. One passage even contains a kind of "hardening" motif (cf. Mark 4:11-12 par.; Rom. 11:25), suggesting that even before the attack on Jerusalem ("while they wandered" — i.e., in disobedience) God was active in judging the people:

> . . . God concocted for them a spirit of error,
> and gave to them a cup of undiluted wine to make them drunk. (v. 14; cf.
> LXX Isa. 19:14)

Such phrases indicate the error in thinking or belief thought to lie behind the activities of the "wandering" Israelites.[139] By sinning in such a manner they acted like their ancestors (v. 22). Accordingly, as God has always been fully justified in his judgment of the nations, he is now proven just and right in "judging Israel in discipline" (vv. 25-26).[140] The judgment of faithless Israel is therefore of one kind with the judgment of the nations. Although the expression "in discipline" (ἐν παιδείᾳ, v. 26) is used of this judgment of Israel and although the immediate context sounds much like a national cry for mercy (vv. 27-30), it is clear that this author foresees only condemnation, not hope, for the sinful element among the people from which he distinguishes himself and his community.[141] The psalms are, in fact, careful to distinguish between those who are disciplined out of anger and those who are disciplined out of love. Only the pious are said to receive discipline and rebuke in what could be called a positive sense (cf. 9:6-7; 10:1-3); the suffering of the righteous is distinguished from that of sinners by its much different purpose and outcome (cf. 13:7-12).[142] Thus "the devout of God are like innocent lambs" among those who are judged (v. 23; cf. Isa. 57:1; Matt. 10:16). The devout here cannot be Israel as a whole (whatever continued sense of solidarity with Israel the author may have cherished in this and other passages) but only the righteous community, always carefully distinguished from the apostates. As in the other writings, the righteous are instruments of judgment for Israel in this psalm. Judgment comes "by

---

139. Πνεῦμα πλανήσεως is used of the Egyptian rulers in the judgment oracle of LXX Isa. 19:14 (cf. also LXX Jer. 4:11; contrast Heb. רוח צח, literally "a hot wind"); the second phrase is ἐν τῇ πλανήσει αὐτῶν — πλάνη being a metaphor for error (*LSI*, 643).

140. ἐδικαιώσαμεν τὸ ὄνομά σου τὸ ἔντιμον εἰς αἰῶνας, "we have proven right Your Name which is honourable forever." See Ryle and James, 1891, 85, for this understanding.

141. Cf. Schüpphaus (1977, 44-47), who emphasizes the rhetorical nature of the passage. The author does not actually identify with the condemned Israelites, even if his language suggests that he does.

142. For discussion of this distinction, see Sanders (1977, 392-96), who acknowledges it but argues that it is overshadowed by God's election of all Israel. We prefer the view of R. R. Hann, "The Community of the Pious," 1988, 173: "The psalms typically portray the Romans not as the sect's enemies but as their vindicators. In the sect's view of the events of 63 B.C.E., it was the unrighteous whom the Romans punished, but the sect itself was not harmed."

the mouth of the devout" — probably alluding to the warnings that they delivered to the others before departing from Jerusalem, which were unheeded (v. 34; cf. 17:16-18). It would appear from the writer's employment of eschatological language in vv. 33-34 that the earthly judgment of Israel was considered merely a prelude to future otherworldly judgments.

"From Their Leader down to the Commonest of the People" — 17

In the seventeenth psalm the opening lines are occupied, interestingly enough, not with the sin of Jerusalemites, but with the sin of the author and his community (v. 5). This sin is not specified, although it may refer in a general way to the unsatisfactory lifestyle of the psalmist and his fellows before they were enlightened in the true way of God's leading. In any event, it is because of this sin, so the author informs us, that the kingdom has been taken from *them* (vv. 3-5), usurped by other Israelites,[143] *sinners* who did not deserve it (vv. 5-6). Who exactly are the players in this unfolding drama (which continues through v. 18) is not entirely certain.[144] That the writer is able to say that the throne was stolen from *his* community may imply that this community was of Davidic lineage, but not enough is said to confirm this. Perhaps they merely defended the Davidic claim to the throne in opposition to Hasmonean claims (cf. vv. 4, 21).

But while the psalmist expresses remorse over the failures of his own group, he reserves the strongest words of censure for his opponents, the usurpers. For their arrogant and pompous act the Israelite "sinners" are guilty of bringing judgment on themselves and on Jerusalem; their entire progeny, young children and old people included, are judged in the storming of Jerusalem (vv. 7-9, 11). Apparently unmoved even by this act of discipline, however, the "children of the covenant" continue to adopt the heathen practices intro-

143. The usurpers could only be other Israelites (cf. Wright in *OTP,* 2:665; Ryle and James, 1891, 129-30; "children of the covenant," v. 15); specifically they would seem to be the Hasmoneans (cf. Schüpphaus, 1977, 66). The view of J. Tromp ("The Sinners and the Lawless in Psalm of Solomon 17," 1993) that those who usurped the throne were "foreigners" falters on the contrast implied in v. 7: "there rose up against them [the Jewish usurpers] a man *alien to our race*" — i.e., Pompey. Tromp's view that "no distinction is made in vss. 11-20 between a sinful people and a pious 'remnant'" (344) fails to take the intensity of the polemic into account.

144. In the view of Ryle and James (1891, 127), the passage refers to the Hasmonean usurpers (vv. 5ff.), Pompey (vv. 11ff.), and the sending of Aristobulus and his family as prisoners to Rome (v. 12). The righteous group are pious priests in sympathy with a Pharisaic point of view. There is little to argue with regard to the Hasmonean identification and Pompey (cf. Schüpphaus, 1977, 66), but as for the Pharisaic composition of the group, see pp. 239-40 below.

duced by their Gentile oppressors, a charge that might allude to the establishment of a syncretistic cult in Jerusalem after the Roman invasion.[145] "*No one among them in Jerusalem acted with mercy or truth*" is a biblical expression suggesting the desperately low level of moral and social degradation to which the Jerusalemites had degenerated, though it is also related to the breach of covenant, to a loss of salvation, and to apostasy.[146] These phrases again imply the inclusiveness of judgment, perhaps meaning that all Israel is implicated in the sins of its leaders, but certainly meaning that God judges Israel corporately and, with the exception of the author's group, almost indiscriminately. At some time associated with the "judgment" of the sinners,[147] as already mentioned, the sectarians leave the scene as a unit,[148] apparently driven out by the sinners, but also by their own choice. This departure is referred to as their being "saved"[149] from evil and from the midst of the sinners (vv. 5, 16-18). Thus the division in Israel between the righteous and the wicked is that which distinguishes the "saved," who form an "assembly" (συναγωγάς) and are delivered together from God's judgment. The righteous accordingly appear as a visible and clearly defined group in this passage; the boundaries between the righteous and wicked in Israel are clear to the author.

This portion of the psalm concludes, not surprisingly, with more words of judgment in the form of a pithy judgment oracle (vv. 18-20a). Natural and

145. Cf. vv. 14-15: "So he [Pompey] did in Jerusalem all the things / that gentiles do for their gods in their cities. / And the children of the covenant (living) among the gentile rabble / adopted these practices." Ryle and James take the superfluous ὅσα (καὶ πάντα, ὅσα ἐποίησεν . . .) as a corruption of ὅσια, implicating the Jews in the worship of pagan gods: "all the sacred rites performed he in Jerusalem," commenting that "the Jews *outdid* and *surpassed* the heathen in the outrageous excesses of idolatry" (1891, 134-35). Even without the emendation the phrase may imply a syncretistic cult.

146. "Mercy" and "truth" are related to the keeping of covenant in Ps. 25:10; they are the manifestation of salvation (יְשׁוּעָת) in Ps. 98:3; they are instruments by which evil is kept back in Prov. 16:6; and they are mentioned as qualities of the Davidic throne in Isa. 16:5 (cf. the same theme in our psalm). Perhaps most like our own passage, however, is the theme of apostasy as found in Hos. 4:1: "There is no אֱמֶת or חֶסֶד, / and no knowledge of God in the land."

147. Schüpphaus (1977, 69) places this after the bloodbath of vv. 11-12 rather than before. While this may be correct, the passage shows little concern for chronology, and certainty is not possible. According to 17:5, the departure was occasioned not so much by the judgment of Jerusalem (actual or anticipated) as by the provocations of the "sinners" themselves (cf. Hann, 1988, 174), so that this may have occurred at almost any time before the event.

148. The term "assemblies (συναγωγάς; Syr. kᵉnušta᾽) of the devout (ὁσίων)" implies a well-defined group; cf. συναγωγὴ Ασιδαίων in 1 Macc. 2:42.

149. Σωθῆναι ψυχὰς αὐτῶν ἀπὸ κακοῦ . . . σεσωσμένη ἐξ αὐτῶν; Syr. √ pdq; cf. פדה id. פדע; "deliver, redeem, set free"; possibly מלט, "escape," pass. "be rescued."

cosmic judgments appear to be combined in the oracle, granting a kind of theological and cosmological "behind the scenes" view of the recent events: "the heavens withheld rain . . . springs were stopped . . . ," and the like. These judgments, particularly the scattering of exiles (v. 18) and the withholding of rain (vv. 18b-19a), implicitly interpret the storming of Jerusalem in terms of covenantal curses. The oracle also sets out the *grounds* for this judgment, by which further insight is given into the universality of the psalmist's condemnation, as well as into the strictly exclusive nature of his soteriology. The psalmist explains that

> . . . there was no one among them
>   who practiced righteousness or justice:
> From their leader down to the commonest of the people,[150]
> they were involved with every kind of sin:
>   the king was a criminal;
>   the judge was disobedient;
>   the people[151] were sinners. (vv. 19b-20)

These verses accordingly compose a fitting summary of this author's message. Their highly poetic style systematically implicates the whole of the people, placing the author's indictment of Jerusalem and its priestly leadership in the wider context of the failure and judgment of *all* the people, that is, all who by participation in the fallen cult or even by more quiet submission to the status quo fall far short of the author's standards for the righteous behavior of the covenant people.[152]

150. Ryle and James see in the strange construction ἀπὸ ἄρχοντος αὐτῶν καὶ λαοῦ ἐλαχίστου ἐν πάσῃ ἁμαρτίᾳ "a very probable instance of a Hebrew idiom imperfectly understood; 'from their prince to the very least of the people'" (1891, 137). These scholars accordingly emend the text by inserting ἕως. As λαοῦ is not represented in Syr., J. L. Trafton (*The Syriac Version of the Psalms of Solomon*, 1985, 169 n. 65) argues that it is not found in the original. Schüpphaus (1977, 70 n. 326) suggests an original Heb. עד rather than עם. These incidentals make little difference to the import of the passage.

151. Gk. λαός; here also found in Syr. ('m'; cf. עם), the collective singular generally used for Israel in Syr. as in Heb.

152. Sanders's treatment of this passage (1977, 406) is quite arbitrary. He differentiates between "sinners" and the "wicked" when he remarks that "apparently all Israel, including many who have sinned, will be gathered together, with only the 'wicked,' who have sinned in such a way as to renounce the covenant, excluded." No justification is offered for this differentiation.

The Fourth Book of Ezra (2 Esdras 3–14)

The Fourth Book of Ezra (referring here to the original Jewish work, namely, the central chapters of the apocryphal 2 Esdras) consists of a series of seven visions purportedly received by Ezra, the biblical figure who contributed to the rebuilding of Jerusalem in Persian days and who was celebrated in Judaism not only as the scribe *par excellence* but virtually as the founder of postexilic Judaism. Interspersed with these visions is narrative material, commentary, and interpretation largely in the form of an emotional dialogue between Ezra and his angel-guide-interpreter Uriel. While the literary context for the work is the fall of Jerusalem in 587 B.C., it is almost unanimously recognized by scholars that the *second* destruction in A.D. 70 inspired the work and that the book was written within a few decades following this event. Being in form a theodicy, the book seems to build toward a climactic message, a religious or moral conclusion regarding Israel's suffering as seen in the recent disaster.[153] The meaning of this message is a matter of dispute, however, as is the baffling question whether the bearer of that message (i.e., the authorial voice) is the righteous scribe Ezra, who struggles sympathetically over the *Unheil* of God's world, or the divine messenger Uriel, who appears to adopt quite narrow criteria of righteousness upholding the preeminence of Torah obedience.

Scholars who are particularly sensitive to the form or literary function of the work have suggested that the premise of the book is to be discerned in a combination of both voices. The voice of Uriel represents the stern attitudes of a Judaism that holds to a consistent reward-merit system and sees in the recent sacking of Jerusalem the deserved punishment of a disobedient people, and the voice of Ezra represents another side of the author, an emotional side that cannot easily accept the sudden and tragic fate that has fallen on the chosen people. Thus the theologically informed "head" of the author battles with the more merciful and sentimental (and some would argue reasonable) "heart" of the author, the final message of the book to be discerned in a synthesis of the two facets. Another option is to see not so much a synthesis of the two positions as a kind of "movement" from the author's original stance to the final conclusions, to which he wishes to draw the readers.[154] Some would see this as a movement

---

153. For a helpful description of theodicy in relation to 4 Ezra and *2 Baruch,* see T. W. Willett, *Eschatology in the Theodicies of 2 Baruch and 4 Ezra,* 1989, esp. 11-33, 65-72, 95-112, 124-25. Cf. also A. L. Thompson, *Responsibility for Evil in the Theodicy of IV Ezra,* 1977, passim.

154. We borrow the quite appropriate term "movement" from J. E. Breech, "These Fragments I Have Shored against My Ruins," 1973, 269; cf. also G. B. Sayler, *Have the Promises Failed?* 1984.

from "head to heart" — from the stern voice of the angel toward the more conciliatory and consolatory position of Ezra.[155]

A careful reconsideration of the presentation, however, might actually lead one to conclude that the movement is somewhat in the *opposite* direction.[156] In that case, what is noteworthy about the dramatic progression of 4 Ezra is not how the voice of Ezra dominates but how *Ezra reluctantly but inevitably comes to accept the stricter point of view brought by the angel Uriel:* Israel deserves judgment (often expressed in terms of the universality of sin incriminating Israel; cf. 7:46ff.); national election does not suffice to save Israel from its lawless state (first hinted at in 3:36; for the movement of Ezra *away* from a national election understanding, contrast 3:12-17 with 6:55-59; see below); only a few — Ezra and those like him — can hope to be saved (7:76-77, 104; 8:43); and God values his creation for the sake of these few alone (cf. 7:50-61; 8:2-3). While the final solution to theodicy is God's mercy to his people in the eschatological future,[157] it is also clear that mercy is for the righteous few alone. When Ezra argues against this, he is merely warned

155. As, e.g., in the idea of the movement "from distress to consolation" put forward by Breech, 1973, 269-71.

156. Cf. M. Elliott, "Romans 9–11 and Jewish Remnant Theology," 1986, 115-23. Our thesis is based on the presence of a hinge in the argument following 8:14ff., where the movement from Ezra's defense of the national election to an acceptance of the position of the angel becomes evident. For more on the passage, see the treatment below. B. W. Longenecker describes the movement in terms of Ezra's "conversion" (brought on by the recent destruction) from an "ethnocentrism" (nationalist understanding) to an "individualistic legalism" (*Eschatology and the Covenant,* 1991, 154-55). Earlier scholars who take the harsher view to be that of the author include W. Mundle ("Das religiöse Problem des IV Esrabuches," *ZAW* 47 [1929]: 222-49); C. G. Montefiore (*IV Ezra: A Study in the Development of Universalism;* London: Allen, 1929), who speaks of the internal struggle of the author, who nevertheless sides with the "orthodox doctrine"; W. O. E. Oesterley (*II Esdras,* 1933); and W. Harnisch (*Verhängnis und Verheissung der Geschichte: Untersuchungen zum Zeit- und Geschichtsverständnis im 4. Buch Esra und der syr. Baruchapokalypse;* Göttingen: Vandenhoeck & Ruprecht, 1969; cf. Thompson, 1977, 96ff.). Sanders agrees that the voice of the angel predominates, but only in the preedited version of 4 Ezra, which does not include the final two visions (1977, 409-18). While Sanders must accordingly assert the fragmentary nature of the work, arguments for its essential unity are certainly more convincing; cf. Breech, 1973, 267-68, 274; R. J. Coggins and M. A. Knibb, *The First and Second Books of Esdras,* 1979, 109; M. P. Knowles, "Moses, the Law, and the Unity of IV Ezra," 1989, 260-61, 268-74; M. E. Stone, *Features of the Eschatology of IV Ezra,* 1989, 17, 108-10, etc.; *contra* also Oesterley, xii-xix. The decisive argument for the unity of 4 Ezra is the symmetry of its seven visions; see further below and C. Rowland, *The Open Heaven,* 1982, 131. We concur with Sanders's observation that one must not allow "form to determine meaning too exclusively," that is, to the exclusion of the important content of passages like 8:14ff. (1977, 409-13), a criticism that can particularly be directed against approaches emphasizing experience (Thompson) or the movement toward consolation (Breech).

157. Cf. Willett, 1989, 64-72.

to dissociate himself from the wicked (8:47). The sin of Israel is everywhere blamed for the destruction of Jerusalem, and the theodicy does nothing to ameliorate this charge against Israel.[158]

The author, through Ezra, consistently reveals his fear that the judgment due all men will be applied to the nation Israel. The scribe's "unanswered challenge"[159] to such a suggestion only serves to cement the inevitability of this judgment, and it now becomes clear why Ezra, finally resigned to the terrible reality and fearful of *Israel's* fate, suddenly abandons his campaign for the nations (resigning to the fact that God "knows best about mankind") and takes up his plea for *Israel* — it is for "[God's] people" that Ezra is especially "grieved" (8:14-16). Thus the very purpose of the author would seem to be related to this dramatic presentation: while the reader might share the lenient sentiments of Ezra at the beginning of the book, by following the debate between Ezra and Uriel the reader will be drawn to admit, as Ezra finally does, that the rather harsher justice of God, propounded by the angel, is after all to be accepted. Again a selection of texts will demonstrate this judgment theme.

Parables Outlining the Two Ways — 4 Ezra 7:1-25

In the prayer leading up to the third vision (see esp. 6:58-59), the scribe raises the question about the apparent frustration, in the light of recent events, of Israel's hope of inheriting the promises: "If the world [or 'land']160 has indeed been created for us, why do we not possess our world [land] as an inheritance?" (6:58-59). One passage of great interest (7:1-25) records the response of the angel, which includes further objections raised by Ezra, the interlocutor (vv. 17-18). The angel's response consists of two parable-like stories (7:3-9), followed by a more explicit and direct, although to us still somewhat esoteric, interpretation of these stories (7:10-25). The first parable is about a "sea set in a wide ex-

---

158. For such reasons we cannot agree with the sociopsychological approach of P. F. Esler ("The Social Function of 4 Ezra," 1994, 108-14), when he posits that the theodicy is an attempt to eliminate cognitive dissonance experienced as a result of the destruction of Jerusalem. For this author the destruction was both deserved and expected; it did not come with the level of surprise or righteous horror required to generate serious dissonance. Adoption of the theodicy genre was largely rhetorical.

159. Thompson, 1977, 289-90.

160. Lat. *saeculum* may represent an original ארץ (cf. also 6:55). For the land of Israel as the inheritance of God's people, cf. Num. 33:54, etc. The translation "land" here would make quite a difference in one's understanding of the passage; we prefer it, while acknowledging the ambiguity resident in ארץ, an ambiguity tolerated, if not intended, by the passage and its Israel-centered worldview.

panse," which has, however, an "entrance set in a *narrow* place" like a river. In order to enter the broad sea one must first pass through the *narrow* river (7:3-5). The second is about a city on a plain whose entrance is not only "narrow" but also flanked by fire on the right and deep water on the left (cf. LXX Ps. 66:2 for this same combination of motifs). In order for a man to "inherit" that city he must pass through the dangerous narrow entrance (10:6-9). The angel then proceeds with his application of these stories, not to the world as a whole, but particularly to Israel: "so also is Israel's portion."[161] The narrow and difficult things in both illustrations are the ways of this world (v. 12), and the broad and safe things are the world to come (v. 13). The difficult state of affairs in this world is the result of Adam's sin, at which time judgment entered the world, "and so the ways[162] of this world were made *narrow* and sorrowful and toilsome; they are few and evil, full of dangers and involved in great hardships" (vv. 11-12). The moral of the story is that the "living" must pass through the narrow experience of this life in order to enter the broad experience of the world to come.[163] The theodicy, at least to this point, is merely eschatological: the promise of the future life. Ezra should not be disturbed by these things, inasmuch as he is soon to die and partake of the life to come (vv. 15-16). But Ezra typically is not satisfied with this response, for his concern is not for himself but for others. He complains to the Lord that "you have ordained in your Law that the righteous shall inherit these things, but that the impious shall perish.[164] The righteous therefore can endure difficult circumstances while hoping for easier ones; but those who have committed acts of impiety have suffered the difficult circumstances and will *not* see the easier ones" (7:17-18). In this way Ezra takes up the case for those "impious" ("who have committed impious acts") who, unlike himself, do not have the future "easier circumstances" to look forward to, even though they have already experienced difficult ones in this life. The eschatological solution offered by the angel, in other words, does not relieve the concerns of Ezra, but only intensifies hopelessness for the impious ones.

It is important to identify the "impious" referred to here in order to un-

---

161. 7:10; cf. 6:59. Lat. *pars* — i.e., their inheritance. In Ps. 16:5 the psalmist's portion (מְנָה) is the Lord; Ps. 142:5 speaks of a "portion (חֵלֶק = 'inheritance') in the land of the living"; but certainly the allusion here is to the portions (חֵלֶק) of "land" inherited by the tribes in Ezekiel 45 and 48. Cf. the "inheritance" of the city in the illustration above (v. 9), which seems also to point symbolically to this belief. That the inheritance includes heavenly rewards is also implied in the passage; on this question see M. E. Stone, *Fourth Ezra*, 1990, 192-94.

162. We prefer the witness of the Eth. "ways" over "entrances"; cf. Coggins and Knibb, 1979, 162, and notes below.

163. Cf. v. 14; Stone, 1990, 192.

164. Cf. Ps. 37:9 as well as passages like Deut. 8:1.

derstand Ezra's fears. It is to be noted not only that these people have forfeited the future blessedness, but that they have *also* experienced "difficulty" in the present life. This cannot be Gentiles, since Ezra has already argued that they "domineer . . . and devour us" (6:57). Moreover, "difficulties" seems to allude to the recent destruction of Jerusalem, among other troubles experienced by Jews at the hands of Gentiles. Thus one can only conclude that the impious are in fact the impious *in Israel:* they alone are those who suffer, as the passage says, both "now" *and* "then" (v. 18). The passage accordingly contains a distinct irony, a kind of "double divine reversal," whereby Israel's own theology of retribution (from which they *hoped* to have benefited) recoils back on a people who have not themselves fulfilled the demands of righteousness, thus disqualifying them from this hope. The ungodly in Israel are to be the recipients of a double dose of punishment, earthly as well as future. The author no doubt intends the reader to notice that the angel typically says nothing to rationalize or moderate the awful implications of Ezra's fears. (In fact, this, with other forms of "silent treatment" response, is a device that the author repeatedly uses in his narratives, apparently to draw attention to divine *dis*interest in Ezra's arguments.) Instead the angel responds indignantly to the inference that God's judgment in this case is unjust (7:19-22):[165]

> You are not a better judge than God, or wiser than the Most High! Let many perish who are now living, rather than that the law of God which is set before them be disregarded! For God strictly commanded those who came into the *land,*[166] when they came, what they should do to live, and what they should observe to avoid punishment. Nevertheless they were not obedient, and spoke against him; they devised for themselves vain thoughts. . . .

These verses are replete with covenantal language, which confirms that their primary reference is to Israel. To be noted are the covenantal language of "choosing life" in v. 21 (cf. Deut. 30:19), allusions to the doctrine of the two ways,[167] and statements to the effect that they "denied his covenants" and were

165. Coggins and Knibb (1979, 164): "Ezra's sympathy for the wicked (verses 17-18) is sharply rejected."

166. Lat. *venientibus quando venerunt* does not specify the indirect object. The entire context may suggest that the world is meant (although note the view that v. 12 refers to "ways" rather than "entrances" to the world; see next note below). However, in the immediate context of a reflection on Deuteronomy 30, "those who entered *the land of Israel*" are meant.

167. See below. Stone (1990, 195-96) points to other writings that combine sea and path motifs (*2 Bar.* 22:3; 85:10; *Testament of Job* 18:6) and suggests that the word for "entrance" (*introitus*) may well mean "way," particularly if it is a mistranslation of מבוא/מבוי, the word used in rabbinic Heb. for "way," "entrance" (198). The word commonly used for

"unfaithful to his statutes" and have not "performed his works,"[168] all of which parallel the statement that they rejected the law "set before them" (v. 20; cf. Deut. 30:15!). This last statement is usually interpreted as referring to Gentiles, but in this context it is clearly much more appropriate to the rejection of covenant and law *by Israel.*

Similar indications in the list of sins that follows suggest that Israel is in mind: vain thoughts, wicked frauds, not investigating[169] God's ways, rejecting his Law,[170] disowning his covenants, being unfaithful in legal matters, not executing his works (7:22-24). Even the charge of declaring that the Most High does not exist, while a rather unusual accusation against Israel, may in fact give us insight into the polemical attitude of the writer; a counterpart to this language is found in 8:58, which clearly refers to Jews (cf. also 7:37 and 9:10; cf. *Jub.* 23:21, cited above). This expression would then be an exaggerated, though typical, response by the righteous to a perceived denial of the truth about God on the part of fellow Israelites. The context of the entire passage also suggests that the focus throughout is on the destruction of Jerusalem and the fate of God's chosen people, for the "inheritance" of Israel in particular is the subject matter of this section (cf. 6:58-59; 7:9-10). Judgment for these Israelites is both earthly and heavenly (cf. v. 18, quoted above). They will "perish" (v. 20).[171] Those who break the covenant can expect the "punishment" ordained by the covenant (v. 21). Here, however, the covenantal blessings and woes have been spiritualized, and include eternal consequences.[172] The angel concludes his rejection of Ezra's plea with the words "empty things are for the empty, and full things for the full" (v. 25), by which he appears to refer back once again to the narrow/broad motif mentioned above.[173]

"way" in biblical Heb., notably in Deut. 28:68; 31:29, however, is דֶּרֶךְ. The possibility, however, is further enhanced by the Eth. reading of vv. 12-13 (cf. Metzger, *OTP,* 1:537 n. *b*), which has "ways" in place of "entrances" (which does not particularly fit in the context of these verses; cf. Coggins and Knibb, 1979, 162).

168. Cf. v. 24; part of the covenantal *rîb* pattern according to Hartman (1979, 86-87).

169. *Cognosco;* cf. דרש at Qumran (1QS 5.11).

170. Again, not a reference to Gentiles; the word used in the Lat. text is *neglegatur* ("neglect," "disregard," "overlook"), which seems to imply continuing neglect of a Law that has already been received.

171. A clear reference to the אָבֹד תֹּאבֵדוּן of Deut. 30:18, where the original context suggests that "perish" is defeat in war. No such restriction is necessary, however, in our present passage; cf. Stone, 1990, 200.

172. Stone, 1990, 201.

173. It is worth noting that this motif carries a *double entendre* throughout the passage. It starts with v. 14: "narrow and vain things" (*angusta et vana haec,* singular), literally "this brief (or 'narrow') and empty matter" or even "this narrow and vain way," perhaps

"I Will Speak . . . about Israel, for Whom I Am Sad" — *4 Ezra 8:14-18*

That the author is primarily concerned about Israel and its fate is something that has needed to be carefully demonstrated for the above passage, which has often been interpreted as referring primarily to Gentiles, again exhibiting the pervading influence of nationalistic understandings of Judaism. The universal or gnomic expression of that passage (which may be *partially* a by-product of translation!) is no doubt also responsible for the common opinion that the author's interest was in the universal condition of humankind, to which he responds as a particularistic and nationalistic Jew. It is admittedly true that the author at times appears to deliberately employ gnomic expressions in order to address the particular situation of the Israel of his time, making the language somewhat elusive, even cryptic. This may have been merely an inherited feature of the diatribe style he uses, and yet the presence of an element of complaint or lamentation in the passage is, in terms of form and occasion, less like a philosophical treatise and more like Jeremiah's complaint against God's judgment *on Israel* and God's answer (Jer. 12:1-13). It is possible that the device is deliberately evasive, to avoid confrontation with opponents or as a tactful measure to stimulate interest and reflection among those who might be tempted to disregard a too direct approach. This would also suggest an alluring and strategic device whereby the author first draws out censure against Gentiles and then entices his readers into self-incrimination by gradually implicating Israel in similar sins (a device found in such diverse writings as Amos 1:3–2:8 and Rom. 1:18–3:20!).

In any case the author eventually abandons this gnomic language in the progress of his presentation in order to make absolutely clear his underlying purpose, and the second passage for consideration here (8:14-18) is, in accordance with this intention, much less evasive than the first. These verses in fact form a vitally important thematic and logical "hinge" in the argument, with the author deliberately breaking free from his universal language to drive home his message, which is that all along he has been speaking not of humankind in general but of *Israel* in particular.[174] The "hinge" is evident in the language of the passage (which is a prayer), particularly in the words italicized here (vv. 14-16):

---

referring back to the "ways *(huius)* of this world." Thus an allusion may be made, not only to the difficulties of this life, but also to the shallow quality of earthly existence that the ungodly have vainly adopted. The maxim *vacua vacuis et plena plenis* also reflects this *double entendre.*

174. Cf. Willett (1989, 69), who seems to be quite alone in picking up on this.

If then you suddenly and with a light command destroy him who with so great labor was fashioned by your command, to what purpose was he made? *And now I will speak out: About all mankind* [or "every man," *omni homine*] *you know best; but I will speak about your people [populo . . . tuo]*, for whom I am grieved, and about *your inheritance*, for whom I lament, and about *Israel*, for whom I am sad, and about *the seed of Jacob*, for whom I am troubled.

A great deal of rhetorical force is gained as the author now makes explicit what he earlier only hinted at. It is as if he has been building up to his real point: "everything that is so unfortunately true for the world in which we live is true for Israel as well."

Ezra goes on to express his remorse over the fact that he has seen "the falling away [*lapsus*, apostasy] of those (literally 'us') who inhabit the land" (v. 17)[175] and because he has "heard of the imminent judgment." The terms in which this sin is put are general and implicate the larger part of Israel. The danger of judgment for this nation is also obvious in the following plea, which is based on the doctrine of the merits of righteous individuals: ". . . look not upon the sins of your people, but at those who have served you in truth. Regard not the endeavors of those who act wickedly, but the endeavors of those who have kept your covenants amid afflictions . . ." (vv. 26-27). Significantly Ezra receives a typically *qualified* response: "Some things you have spoken rightly" (8:37); but beyond this his protests are once again largely ignored. The angel even seems to employ Ezra's words against him,[176] something that once more suggests that the author agrees with the angel against Ezra. Finally (*contra* Ezra), the point is clearly made that the righteous should be commended, not sinners justified: "For indeed I [the Lord] will not concern myself about the fashioning of those who have sinned, or about their death, their judgment, or their damnation; but I will rejoice over the creation of the righteous, over their pilgrimage also, and their salvation, and their receiving their reward" (8:38-39). It is thus abundantly evident that Israel's judgment is irreversible and eternal in spite of Ezra's intercession. The angel can only condemn the unrighteous; apparently the writer expects the readers to do likewise.

Many other texts could be brought forward as evidence of this judgment-of-Israel theme in 4 Ezra (1:4-9, 24-40; 2:1-14; 7:72-74, 78-87, 102-15, 116-31;

---

175. Preferable to "earth" or "world" is a translation that takes into account the allusion to the common biblical expression for Israel as "those who inhabit the land" (a sense virtually demanded by v. 16). Stone's treatment (1990, 265-67) accordingly falters at this point.

176. Cf. Stone (1990, 283); Coggins and Knibb (1979, 206), who compare this part of Ezra's petition to the intercession of Abraham for Sodom in Gen. 18:22-33; for another example of God's denial of intercessory prayer, cf. *Jub.* 1:19ff.

7:132–8:3; 8:26-62; 9:9, 30-37; 10:10). The motif appears to have been carefully woven into the entire fabric of the writing and dominates the literary movement of the book; it would be impossible to imagine the purpose of this book being fulfilled, or its message communicated, without this central idea of the judgment of Israel.

2 Baruch (Syriac Apocalypse of Baruch)

It is not necessary to enter into the same amount of detail for *2 Baruch* as we have for its sister writing 4 Ezra, as it is widely known that there are many points of agreement between the arguments of the two works, and the general similarity seems to extend to their literary "movement" as well. There is even the same subtle shift from a concern for the nations to a concern for (the few saved in) Israel.[177] *2 Baruch* also puts particular emphasis on the blame incurred by Israelites for the destruction of Jerusalem (1:4-5; 10:18; 62:4-5; 67:6-7; 77:2-10; 79:2; 82:2; 84:2-7). Employing a similar theodicy as 4 Ezra, this book asserts directly (5:2) and implicitly through its argumentation the right of God to judge. When Baruch appeals to the righteousness of some of God's people as merit to be weighed against the sin of the nation (14:5-7), he receives the same qualified and partial response as Ezra did (15:1), and the function of the Law to bring judgment on those who disobey and reward to the righteous is reaffirmed (15:6-8). There is a concerted attempt throughout to show that God's judgment is impartial, which in this context implies that God does not show favoritism to Israel if its people sin.[178] Judgment is based strictly on individual merit (41:1–42:8).

An appropriate summary of the judgment-of-Israel theme in *2 Baruch* can be found in a short verse that, like 4 Ezra, particularizes and applies to Israel a very strict, originally gnomic, argument about the terrible consequences of Adam's fall:[179] "For those *who are among your own,* you rule; and those who sin, you blot out *among your own*" (54:22, cf. vv. 15ff.). The verbs in this short saying are best rendered by the present tense, a stylistic feature characteristic of general maxims or proverbs. These words might be taken as just that sort of general statement were it not, however, for the twice-repeated

177. Cf. Willett, 1989, 89, 96, 98.
178. Cf. 13:8-10; 44:4; 48:26-29, esp. in light of 48:19-24; Willett, 1989, 105.
179. Against Charles's treatment of vv. 16-18 as an interpolation, originally part of Baruch's address to his people (*The Apocalypse of Baruch translated from the Syriac,* 1896, 94), cf. P. Bogaert, *Apocalypse de Baruch,* 1969, 2:104. It is true that v. 19 follows well on v. 15, and while the oracle does fit its context, it is perhaps best to understand it as parenthetical.

"among your own [people]."[180] Its message is clear: sinners will be utterly removed from the covenant people.[181]

APOSTASY IN ISRAEL

It has now been determined that the communities responsible for these writings expected a judgment that would affect Israel in particular. But one more potential protest to this reasoning still exists, best expressed by Sanders in his view that the breach of covenant was an *exceptional* occurrence. Sanders does agree that the sort of transgression spoken of in these writings is not that done by an individual, but "the kind of transgression which puts the sinners in fundamental opposition to God and his chosen people."[182] But can the assertion that this refers only to certain *exceptional* cases be sustained from the evidence?

On the contrary, direct evidence can be found that these authors considered Israel to be caught in a time of *widespread* apostasy, from which its people must repent to be saved from judgment. For example, in the seventh week of the Apocalypse of Weeks (the "week" in which the author lived), "an apostate generation[183] shall arise; its deeds shall be many, and *all* of them criminal" (93:9). The word translated "generation" here is a generalizing term used of Israel, indicated by its placement in antithetical parallelism with "the elect ones of righteousness" (= the writer's community) in the following verse. Israel is an apostate generation. Similarly, in the Book of Admonitions Enoch advises his offspring (94:1) to hold fast his words: "For I do know that *sinners will counsel the people to*

---

180. *L'ylyn gyr dbdylk 'nwn 'nt mdbrt. wl'ylyn dḥṭyn 'ṭ' 'nt mn dylk*, lit. "For those who are among your own you lead (*mdbrt*, infinitive), but sinners you blot out ('ṭ', participle) from your own (people)."

181. "Blot out," 'ṭ'. Cf. מחה, as in Pss. 69:28; 109:13, which both refer to obliteration of a name from the book of life (a covenantal motif, see below). Psalm 109 also alludes here to having one's "seed" cut off. Alternatively, although perhaps less likely, the word may reflect כרת, as in Gen. 17:14; Exod. 12:15, 19; 30:33, 38; Lev. 7:20-21, etc., where the verb is used of being "cut off" from the covenant people. In either case an allusion is being made to the covenant. It could hardly represent its cognate עטה (which in Jer. 43:12 is, however, used of Nebuchadnezzar's destruction of Egypt), which always retains the sense of "cover." The words "from your own" here seem to suggest removal.

182. Sanders, 1977, 361.

183. *Tewledd 'elut*. Black: "perverse generation" (1985, 86). The original expression has almost certainly been taken from the suggestive Deut. 32:30: דור תהפכת, "generation of perversity." Isaac's translation of Eth. *'elut* as "apostate" (it can also be rendered "perverse," "corrupt," "rebellious," "heretical") is nevertheless quite appropriate.

perform evil craft; and *every place* will welcome it . . ." (94:5).[184] While such statements may represent overgeneralizations of the extent of unfaithfulness, they at least make clear that the state of apostasy was felt to be widespread among the "people."[185] It is hardly a case of exceptions here. *1 En.* 102:5, according to the best reading, even appears to speak of a kind of *dispensation of sin:* "Be not sad because your souls have gone down into Sheol in sorrow . . . indeed, the time you happened to be in existence was a time of sinners."[186] *1 En.* 108:2-3 seems to be speaking of a similar time when it exhorts the readers to "wait patiently in all the days until (the time of) those who work evil is completed, and the power of the wicked ones is ended. . . . Wait patiently until sin passes away. . . ."

Jubilees is not without similar indications that its author believed himself to be living in an era of apostasy in Israel. In 1:7-14, which narrates the revelation to Moses about the upcoming times of exile, there seems to be a veiled allusion to the author's own time. This is especially evident in the saying that "many will be destroyed and seized and will fall into the hand of the enemy because they have forsaken my ordinances and my commandments and *the feasts of my covenant and my sabbaths.* . . . And they will forget all my laws and all of my commandments and all of my judgments, and they will err concerning new moons, sabbaths, festivals, jubilees, and ordinances" (1:10, 14; for this "predictive perspective" on the future time of disobedience, cf. Deuteronomy 28; 30:1-10). The references to the calendar as a major issue for the writer confirm that his own generation is in view here, whom he compares to the apostate generation of the exile. The relevance for the writer's contemporaries of the account of Dinah's defilement in *Jubilees* 30 has already been noted, as has the way this comparison ex-

---

184. A good rendering of the preferred Tana[9] MS has been supplied by Isaac here. Knibb's translation of recension B (1978, 2:227) — "sinners will tempt men to debase wisdom, and no place will be found for it" — amounts to much the same thing since it predicts, using stock wisdom expressions, a time when wisdom will not be embraced by Israel. Black accepts the similar reading "sinners will tempt men to entreat wisdom evilly (margin: 'do harm to the wise'), / And no place will be found for her (i.e., wisdom)" (1985, 87, cf. 296; cf. Charles, 1912, 234-35; Isaac, *OTP*, 1:75 n. *d*).

185. The word *sab'* can refer to people in general, but is a natural word to use in place of Heb./Aram. עַם, "the (Israelite) people," as a technical term in this verse. The extent of the apostasy is also indicated by the familiar and emphatic *kʷāllu (makān)*, "every (place)."

186. Isaac (*OTP*, 1:83, cf. n. *u*) follows the very important Gk. MS G[p] in his translation "the days that you lived were days of sinners." The Eth. MSS are difficult and evidently corrupt. Probably in an attempt to smooth over difficulties, or otherwise influenced by 108:2-3, the Eth. adds: "But wait patiently for the day on which is the judgment of sinners, and for the day of cursing and punishment" (Black, 1985, 96; following Charles, 1912, 255, who already emended *konkemu ḥāṭe'ān*, "you became sinners," to *kʷennanē ḥāṭe'ān*, "the judgment of sinners"). In any event the Eth. matches the Gk. in sense.

tends to a correlation between the corporate guilt of Shechem and the present corporate guilt of Israel. The prohibition of intermarriage following the story announces that "it is a reproach to Israel. . . . And Israel will not be cleansed from this defilement. . . . For there will be plague upon plague and curse upon curse, and every judgment, and plague, and curse will come. . . . *all of the people* will be judged *together*[187] on account of all of the defilement and the profaning of this one" (30:13-15). There is no atonement for such sin (30:16). While some serious covenantal sins may be atoned for by the death of the guilty party (41:26),[188] Israel must be warned through the example of the Shechemites that complete eradication will alone suffice in such cases (30:17). The generalizing view of Sanders that punishment of an individual for his transgression avails to "avert punishment which would otherwise fall on the entire people"[189] does not apply here. Judgment is not simply an individual or exceptional matter for the author of *Jubilees*. While this passage does not intimate that this particular sin has been committed by *all* the people individually (quite the opposite), it nevertheless evokes images of an apostasy that must be dealt with completely. The matter of the calendar, dealt with in the following chapter, also falls into this category of sins that bring judgment on the entire nation.

The Dead Sea Scrolls are not without their references to widespread apostasy. In an enigmatic passage, which nevertheless clearly refers to the contemporary events of the Qumran sect, it is reported that "the House of Peleg are those that went out of the Holy City and leaned upon God *at the time when Israel was unfaithful and defiled the Sanctuary*" (CD[B] 2.22-23). The expression "at the time when Israel was unfaithful" (perhaps "in the fulfillment [or fullness] of Israel's unfaithfulness")[190] seems to suggest that the author saw his own time as the epitome of the disobedience of Israel, in a long history of unfaithfulness, but also saw this as part of a predetermined course of events (cf. 11QT 59.9). The Hymn Scroll (1QH 4.6-22) for its part speaks of the present time as one in which teachers, spoken of as if they were false prophets,[191] fall

---

187. K^wellu ḥezb xebura is emphatic: "all the people together." Ḥezb may go back to העם (= the people, i.e., of Israel) through Gk. ὁ λαός.

188. "And the wrath and punishment he will cause to cease from Israel" alludes to the covenantal wrath against widespread apostasy referred to in Deuteronomy 28.

189. Sanders, 1977, 367.

190. בקץ מעל ישראל.

191. Cf. the language of ll. 7-8, 10-12, 15-18, and 20. "They have sought Thee out among idols" (l. 15) appears to be a standard phrase for false prophets (cf. Ezek. 14:1-5). Likewise: "for they have said of the vision of knowledge, It is not true!" (ll. 17-18; cf. Isa. 43:9; Jer. 27:16-17?). The passage borrows its language from Ezek. 14:1-5, which also addresses a situation of grave apostasy, especially among the leaders of Israel. These false prophets are referred to as "seers of error" in l. 20; l. 16 says that they inquire of God by means of "the preaching of prophets of falsehood."

into grave error, which means, among other things, that they reject the *moreh ṣedeq* and his teaching, withhold proper teaching, and break God's covenant, including, perhaps, adopting an alien calendar.[192] The sin of these false prophets is not simply their own disobedience, but that of leading the *entire people* ("Thy people") astray from the righteous teaching (ll. 6-7, 16). Those who fall away (including, by implication, those who trust the deceptive prophets) are contrasted with those who live "according to [God's] soul" and "walk in the way of [his] heart" (ll. 20-21).

Some newly published scroll fragments have confirmed that the time they were written was considered a period of apostasy in Israel. Excerpts from 4Q386-90 read:

> they will have no Deliverer, because . . . they have rejected My Laws, and their soul has scorned My teaching. Therefore I have hidden My face from [them, until] they fill up the measure of their sins. . . . I have abandoned the land because they have hardened their hearts against Me. . . .

> from the end of that generation, corresponding to the Seventh Jubilee since the desolation of the land, they will forget Law and festival, sabbath and Covenant. They will break (i.e., violate) everything, and do what is evil in My eyes. . . .

> [During] this jubilee they will break all my laws and all my precepts which I will command them . . . and they will begin to argue with one another for seventy years.[193]

While the literary context of these passages may well be God's words to Moses, thus making them appear on a superficial reading to refer to the Babylonian exile, the latter two excerpts definitely refer to a second apostasy, since this period is carefully dated in relation to "the desolation of the land" — that is, the exile proper.[194]

192. Cf. ll. 8-12, 17-19, and 23; Mansoor, 1961, 125 n. 1; Dupont-Sommer, 1961, 212 n. 1.

193. For translations cf. R. H. Eisenman and M. Wise, *The Dead Sea Scrolls Uncovered*, 1992, 60-64, 55-56; García Martínez, *Qumran and Apocalyptic*, 1992, 280-81. Similarly the words of 4Q181 2, 4, "to Israel in the seventieth week to [. . .] to love sin and to make them inherit evil," appear to allude to an age of sin, one apparently inspired by the fallen angels or the offspring of giants. 4Q182 cites Jer. 5:7 — "[Why should I have to forgive you? Your so]ns have deserted me and have sw[orn by what is not a god . . .]." For these latter texts, cf. García Martínez, 1992, 211-13. 4Q266 alludes to "the periods of wrath" and also possibly to the "entire era of evil" (based on the reconstruction of Eisenman and Wise, 1992, 218).

194. 4Q510 = *4QShir*[a] = *4QSongs of the Sage*[a] also appears to refer to a similar pe-

In a similar vein the War Scroll anticipates the existence of a massive apostate movement in Israel as part of the final events leading to the Great War. It opens with words of judgment against those who "come to the aid of the wicked of the Covenant, sons of Levi and sons of Judah and sons of Benjamin" (1QM 1.2). Here the enemies of the sect to be overcome in the final war are not only Gentiles but also those from Israel allied with Gentile mercenaries (or protectors). Thus the first event in the great final war and victory of the "sons of light" over the "sons of darkness" is to be the defeat of the sons of darkness living in Jerusalem — that is, apostate Israelites (1.2-3). The "Deportation of the sons of light" will "camp in the desert of Jerusalem," from which they will storm the city and remove power from the hands of wicked Jews.[195] The apostates are referred to here as "the violators *(marši'ê)* against the covenant," a term taken from Dan. 11:32,[196] a text that also appears to have served as a source of information regarding this time of apostasy. The entire verse from Daniel reads "He shall seduce with flattery those who violate the covenant; but the people who know their God shall stand firm and take action." The sect would obviously have understood itself to be those who "know their God" (the "wise" who shall "make many understand," Dan. 11:33); significantly these are also portrayed in Daniel as fighting against the "Kittim" (11:30).

Moving to the *Psalms of Solomon,* one can see that Pompey is blamed for forcing, or alluring, the people of Jerusalem into apostasy in a text already cited above:

> So he did in Jerusalem all the things
>> that Gentiles do for their gods in their cities.
> *And the children of the covenant living among the gentile rabble*
>> *adopted these practices.*
> *No one among them in Jerusalem* acted with mercy or truth. (17:14-15)

The flight of the "devout" from Jerusalem is certainly to be understood as a symbolic action indicating that the city was considered irrevocably apostate (cf. Mark 6:11 pars.; Acts 13:51; CD[B] 2.22-23 above; Isa. 52:2?), a motivation that becomes explicit in the judgment oracle pronounced against the entire city, leader and people alike (17:19-20).

One text makes it particularly clear that for the author of 4 Ezra as well,

---

riod when it speaks of "the era of the rule of wickedness" and "the guilty periods of those defiled by sins" as well as "the periods of the humiliation of the sons of light" and "the era of the humiliation of sin" (García Martínez, 1992, 371).

195. Dupont-Sommer, 1961, 169-70 n. 2.

196. Y. Yadin, *The Scroll of the War of the Sons of Light against the Sons of Darkness,* 1962, 26.

the large majority of Israel was considered to be in a lost condition. In a discussion of the sins of God's people, Ezra is instructed: "do not ask any more questions about *the multitude* of those who perish. For they also received freedom, but they despised the Most High, and were contemptuous of his Law, and forsook his ways. Moreover they have even trampled upon his righteous ones . . ." (8:55-57). The text obviously refers, in the first place, to Israelites.[197] The "multitude who perish" included a large segment of the Israelite population who had fallen in a great time of apostasy, which, in the author's view, occurred because God and his Law had been abandoned. It is not possible to accept, in view of such examples as these, that apostasy was considered by these authors to have been extraordinary or exceptional. Israel *extra iustos* is condemned by them as a disobedient people living in a grave time of apostasy.

It is probably safe now to say that in spite of the differences that characterize these various writings, they are all in agreement in their conviction that a large part of Israel — not by any means a small number — are in danger of judgment. This conviction is expressed in many ways, including the idea that Israel is presently living in a *time of apostasy.* While this would be in the nature of the case the view of a minority (the majority would hardly be interested in implicating itself!), it is worthy of note that *this position is held unanimously among the writings generally considered to be chief among the Pseudepigrapha, as well as in the Qumran scrolls* — writings that are important because they compose *a significant part of the extant corpus of pre-Christian Jewish writings* that have traditionally been taken (for reasons that continue to be valid) as *a significant block of evidence for a very important sector of Second Temple Judaism.* While it would not be possible in the compass of this treatment to consider the full implications of this fact, enough evidence has been presented to demand *a serious reconsideration of the literature that has for decades provided the basis for comparative studies of Judaism and Christianity,* and in particular *a reconsideration of the conventional nationalistic view of election theology* that has been an almost unquestioned presupposition in these studies.

197. This discussion centers on Israel since the passage follows after the "hinge" of 4 Ezra 8:14-18 (cf. also 6:55-59; 7:102-15; etc.). Cf. Oesterley, 1933, 100-101, 110; Coggins and Knibb, 1979, 204 on v. 30.

CHAPTER FOUR

Limits on the Community of Salvation

The previous chapter has provided compelling evidence that (contrary to the prevailing view) some Jewish groups nurtured a limited and exclusive rather than nationalistic understanding of salvation and election. The correlative opinion that Israel was living in a time of widespread apostasy because many had broken the covenant confirms that, in the view of these authors, a large portion of Israel had been effectively disqualified from the benefits of that covenant and of membership in God's chosen people. If it is valid to draw such conclusions about these beliefs from *negative* evidence based on what was viewed as the poor performance of Israel, one would expect to find evidence of a more *positive* kind as well. If some are *not* counted among God's covenant people on the basis of their sinfulness, on what basis are others to be included, if such a basis exists? This positive evidence might be termed *defining criteria for membership within the community of the saved* — that is, propositions to the effect that conformity to certain teachings or rituals was absolutely imperative for membership in the saved community. Such positive evidence is also readily available in this literature.

EXCLUSIVIST SOTERIOLOGY
IN THE DEAD SEA SCROLLS

The most unambiguous evidence for an exclusivist soteriology comes from the scrolls.[1] The limitation of the saved community is lucidly defined once again in

---

1. Cf. A. Jaubert, *La notion d'alliance dans le Judaïsme aux abords de l'ère chrétienne*, 1963, 248, for the "negative" evidence; M. Hengel, *Judaism and Hellenism*, 1974, 1:223.

that part of the section in the Manual of Discipline that deals with the entrance of candidates into the community (1QS 5.7-24; cf. our treatment of 5.10-13 above). In ll. 18-20a we read: "For *all* who are not counted in His Covenant shall be set apart, together with *all* that is theirs; and the holy shall not rely on *any* work of vanity. For they are *all* vanity who know not His Covenant, and He will destroy from the world *all* them that despise His word; *all* their deeds are defilement before Him, and their possessions *wholly* unclean." This passage, starting with l. 13, deals with separation from outsiders and their property. The lines quoted above give reasons for the separation and implicitly limit the saved community to the members of the *yaḥad*. It is worthy of note that the saved community is not so much contrasted with another *well-defined group of opponents,* but with the *whole mass of apostate Israel.* These apostates are spoken of in shocking terms reminiscent of the biblical condemnation of idolatry;[2] and the repetition of "all" (כול; repeated seven times in this short passage) reminds us of that familiar literary device used to imply the widespread nature of the apostasy, here particularly intended to drive home the point that the boundaries of the Qumran community also formed the boundaries of *God's* community. *All* who are not "reckoned" or "counted"[3] in the covenant are outside God's salvation and will be destroyed — there is no hope for them. But the inverse is also true: all who *are* counted in the covenant make up the company of the saved. In the words of Dupont-Sommer, "the sectarian spirit could hardly go further" in excluding nonmembers of the sect from salvation.[4]

Much the same thing is implied in another passage that narrates how God preserved a "remnant" (CD 3.13-20). As part of this work of preservation (CD 3.13c-17a, 19-20a),

> God established His Covenant with Israel for ever, revealing to them the hidden things (נסתרות) in which *all* (כל) Israel had strayed: His holy Sabbaths and His glorious feasts, His testimony of righteousness, and His ways of truth, and the desires of His will which man must fulfil that he may live because of them. He opened this before them, and they dug a well of abundant waters, and whoever despises these waters shall not live. . . . He built for them

---

2. Especially "vanity" (הבל); cf. 2 Kings 17:15, where the word is used of Israelites; "them that despise His word" is reminiscent of LXX Jer. 23:17, another passage directed at Israel (M. A. Knibb, *The Qumran Community,* 1987, 112).

3. נחשבו, "counted," "accounted," "reckoned." This may be an allusion to the names of the saved written in the heavenly books. For the biblical background, cf. Gen. 15:6; Ps. 32:2 (and thus also Rom. 4:3, 8-10); Job 33:10; Isa. 53:4; and Isa. 2:22, which has been cited in l. 17 and has inspired the present use.

4. A. Dupont-Sommer, *The Essene Writings from Qumran,* 1961, 84 n. 2.

a sure House in Israel such as did not exist from former times till now. They who cling to it are destined for everlasting life. . . .

This remnant (l. 13), with whom "God established His Covenant" ("with Israel" can only be taken representatively, not inclusively),[5] refers either to a remnant that remained faithful during the exilic period or, more likely, to another, later "remnant" probably to be identified with the original members of the sect ("till now").[6] This is also suggested by the mention of the *niśtārōṯ* ("the hidden things") that are said to have been revealed to them (l. 14) and that relate to those concerns of special import to the sect. In this regard the expression *"His holy Sabbaths and His glorious feasts"* (ll. 14-15) points to the calendar of the sect.[7] The words "His testimony of righteousness, and His ways of truth, and the desires of His will" (l. 15) appear to refer to things especially revealed to the community, which is further indicated by the reference in ll. 16-17 to the waters proceeding from the well — these waters probably refer not only to the Torah itself but to its authoritative interpretation and to revelations given exclusively to the community.[8] What is significant, however, is the superlative importance granted to these *niśtārōṯ*. Those who fulfill them will *live;* those who do not will *not live* (ll. 16-17) — an unmistakable allusion to the covenantal choice[9] partic-

---

5. The only way to understand this passage is to take it that "Israel" is representatively preserved through this covenant. The passage does not sustain any unconditional national election. The "remnant" is the only remaining Israel by which the promises made to the fathers can be salvaged (cf. Knibb, 1987, 34, for the designation "true Israel"). Similarly the forgiveness of those who defiled themselves (ll. 17-18) is not to be taken as forgiveness of Israelites who have placed themselves outside the covenant community. It refers, in its context, to the group who came out from sinful Israel (i.e., to the community), who received the truth, presumptuously held it to be their private possession (l. 18), and then later repented of this presumption as part of their salvation (ll. 18-19). In one sense Sanders is correct when he maintains that the sect did not adopt for itself the name "Israel"; but it certainly does not necessarily follow from this that the present Israel would be saved (so E. P. Sanders, *Paul and Palestinian Judaism,* 1977, 247-48).

6. While "remnant" (l. 13) may refer to that of the exile (cf. ll. 10-11), it is clear that the writer considers the conditions for membership in the remnant (cf. ll. 14-17) to be equally binding for his time. Thus the community is alluded to here as the continuation of this "remnant"; cf. Knibb, 1987, 32-33; M. O. Wise, "The Covenant of Temple Scroll XXIX,3-10," 1989, 49-60, here 58-59.

7. Knibb, 1987, 34.

8. I.e., the "hidden things"; cf. 1QS 5.11. For the well as an equivalent to law, cf. 6.4, although Knibb (1987, 35) would argue that this refers to the *interpretation* of the law. Perhaps the well is intended to represent the Law (cf. 6.4) and the waters the teachings of the sect.

9. Contrast "the desires of His will which man must fulfil that he may live because of them" (וחיה בהם) and "whoever despises these waters shall not live" (לא יחיה, l. 17). "Life"

ularly reminiscent of passages like Deut. 30:19. Here, however, our author has gone well beyond the idea of earthly recompense implied in the Deuteronomic covenant and has granted spiritual and timeless significance to the concept of "life": "those who cling to [the sure *House,* the righteous community, its priesthood, and its teachings][10] are destined for *eternal* life." Presumably, therefore, "*eternal* death" for all but the members of the sect is implied by the words "shall not live" (l. 17). The word "all" (כל) is employed here again in order to establish firmly the *exclusive* limits of the saved community.

EXCLUSIVIST SOTERIOLOGY
IN THE PSEUDEPIGRAPHA

A more transparent exposition of a soteriology that is fundamentally exclusivist could hardly be imagined than what we have seen in the Community Rule and the Damascus Document. What was at stake for the authors of both texts was the eternal destiny of the individual, something that is clearly not based on national election so much as on the individual choice whether to react positively or negatively to the teachings of the *yaḥad.* Evidence for an exclusivist soteriology in writings not directly associated with the Qumran sect may not seem as unambiguous. This probably owes not so much to differences in theology (the Pseudepigrapha, after all, were present in the Qumran library and were evidently highly revered by the sectarians, and they had their own Pseudepigrapha-like documents). It is probably due to the much less systematic, less propositional, and more emotional and revelatory ("apocalyptic") character of this literature. The Pseudepigrapha are narrative and literary works; several of the most important of the scrolls (especially 1QS and CD) are didactic and liturgical and tend to spell things out somewhat more clearly. Rather than dealing with separate texts as has been done to this point, therefore, a preferable approach will be to summarize the evidence for exclusivity according to themes: first, under the category of "revelational criteria," in which will be examined the importance of revelation and wisdom concepts, and then under the rubric "legal criteria," in which will be investigated certain laws, along with their function

---

here is a covenantal expression; cf. the important place of חיה√ in covenantal contexts, e.g., Deut. 4:1; 30:16, 19. For the expression אשר יעשה האדאם, cf. Lev. 18:5; Ezek. 20:11, 13, 21 (Knibb, 1987, 34).

10. The antecedent of the pronoun here is the "House" of l. 19, which may refer to the *yaḥad* (Dupont-Sommer, 1961, 126 n. 4) through metonymous association with the righteous lineage of priests established for them by God; for a similar figurative use of "house," cf. 1 Sam. 2:35; Knibb, 1987, 35.

and significance. In this analysis texts from Qumran will be woven into the discussion both for comparative purposes and to flesh out the treatment of that group.

The Revelational Criteria

As is well known, establishing *religious authority* was one of the dominating concerns in Second Temple Judaism. This involved defining, or redefining, *who* or *what* was to provide the authoritative standard or rule for conduct and belief for members of God's people at a time when the established offices and instruments of religious authority were breaking down. This breakdown came about as the result of certain social and political influences that were making themselves felt and creating substantial changes in the way things were done in Judea.[11] Foremost among these changes was the gradual diminution of the influence of the priestly class, which represented the traditional locus of authority in the nation as both teachers of law and guardians of the cult.[12] Among the more obvious reasons for the priests' waning influence were the repeated interruptions of the temple ritual by foreign invasion, and the disruptions and reorganizations of political systems in Palestine under Gentile rule. Perhaps equally disruptive was the open evidence of the liberalization and degeneration of the priests (a major theme in the Pseudepigrapha), which tended to make them somewhat unpopular in some quarters. Another factor in their loss of influence was the increasing recognition and democratization of a *written* canon of "law, prophets, and writings," which offered Jews the option of a comparatively objective if not totally unambiguous authority, whereas human authorities tended to be subjective and variable.[13] Another factor was the amassing and preservation of authoritative *oral* teaching (such as we find codified in the Talmuds), itself perhaps as much a response to the loss of a "living" authority in Jerusalem. And then there were the new *personal* authorities that tended to displace the traditional priestly office: the emerging role of the rabbinate, an office whose authority increased critically after the destruction of the Temple, is a well-

---

11. M. E. Stone, "Three Transformations in Judaism," 1985, 219-23; J. Blenkinsopp, "Interpretation and the Tendency to Sectarianism," 1988, 1-26.

12. Cf. E. Schürer, *The History of the Jewish People in the Age of Jesus Christ (175 B.C.–A.D. 135)*, 1973, 1:138-39; Stone, 1985, 219-22; S. Talmon, "The Emergence of Jewish Sectarianism," in *King, Cult, and Calendar in Ancient Judaism*, 1986, 165-201, here 177, 179-80. E. P. Sanders dissents from this view (*Judaism*, 1992, 173-78), but, while his protest that the Pharisees did not become the main ruling party in Jerusalem is valid, he tends to ignore other factors at work that we mention below.

13. Stone, 1985, 219-20.

known example; and we are also aware of a certain number of messianic figures and prophets who possessed their own more esoteric traditions. All these authorities claimed to possess the authentic interpretation of Scripture,[14] and the debate over revelation and interpretation that ensued from their mutually exclusive claims naturally led to conflict and resulted in the crisis over religious authority that played such a formative role in the Judaism of this period.

In the specific groups responsible for our literature, one can see that authority manifested in various ways. At Qumran the heightening of the authority of the Hebrew Scriptures was accompanied by what is referred to as the "radicalization of Torah obedience," an intense attempt to fulfill every jot and tittle of the Law. Essential to this goal was the probable claim of the sect that they alone possessed the *true* Scriptures and the only true *interpretations* of those Scriptures. At Qumran, and indeed among all these groups, there may have been a number of personal authorities such as the *moreh ṣedeq* and prophetlike figures who, in the name of patron saints like Enoch and Ezra, claimed a capacity for receiving revelation on behalf of the communities who gathered around them (see further in ch. 10 below). Then there were the claims of each of these groups to possess "wisdom," either a proverbial kind of wisdom that distinguished the sect by their greater experience and insight into life, or a wisdom that was more of a spontaneous gift.

Regardless of the exact instrument in place, many of these authorities functioned "revelationally": the *moreh ṣedeq* was an inspired exegete, charismatic teacher, and lawgiver; Enoch, Moses, Ezra, and others, perhaps through the agency of mediators or prophets, also revealed additional laws and teachings. Even the authoritative exegetical procedures that took place at the Qumran "sessions" and probably resulted in what has been termed the *pešer* literature did not involve a merely mechanical or objective method of interpretation but depended on the personal inspiration of various individuals who distanced themselves from the false interpretations of the "unilluminated." Additional laws, sectarian teaching, exegetical enabling, the possession of true Scriptures, and even "wisdom" involved "things revealed." The authority for these groups was largely resident, therefore, in various processes of *revelation*.[15] This will become more evident as we proceed, but for now it is enough to point out how this rather straightforward observation contradicts conventional views

14. Stone, 1985, 222-23.
15. Cf. C. Rowland (*The Open Heaven,* 1982), who perceptively summarizes the "apocalyptic writings" according to their attention to revelation, an aspect that also dominates in Collins's categorization of the literary forms of apocalyptic (see Collins's "The Jewish Apocalypses," 1979a, for a succinct presentation of this approach) and in Reid's approach, which employs the anthropological model of manticism (*Enoch and Daniel,* 1989, 22-23).

of Judaism as involving a static and basically conservative process of *preserving* tradition. Ironically, it may again have been the relatively subjective character of this type of authority based on revelation that itself led to the demise of these revelational groups as they eventually gave way to the security of a more institutional Judaism based on collective tradition, that is, the rabbinate. In any event revelation was an important aspect of the constitution of these groups. Our concern centers on the *significance* of this revelation rather than its content: Was it given to all Israel or only to the righteous? And did it possess a soteriological importance — that is, was it considered essential for salvation?

The "Other Law" and the Heavenly Tablets

That alternative legal writings or legal systems could have been accepted by our groups as equal and even superior to the law of Moses seems unthinkable to one accustomed to viewing the Torah as the universal standard in Judaism, but that this seems to actually have been at least to a degree the case[16] is a significant indication of the importance of revelation in our period. *1 En.* 81:6 might well be the earliest[17] text we possess that speaks of the revelation to the patriarchs of "another law"[18] distinct from the publicly recognized Torah. This law

16. B. Z. Wacholder ("Ezekiel and Ezekielianism as Progenitors of Essenianism," 1992, 192) discerns a possible source for the critique of the Mosaic law in Ezek. 20:25-26. Cf. also J. C. VanderKam, "Biblical Interpretation in 1 Enoch and Jubilees," 1993, 117. J. H. Charlesworth ("In the Crucible," 1993, 25) suggests, however, that the Pseudepigrapha were not "anti-canonical" since they regularly quote the Bible. Perhaps, then, the term "*super*-canonical should be used, as books like *Jubilees* represent higher revelation and imply that the canonical Scriptures contain *part* of the truth."

17. While B. Z. Wacholder (*The Dawn of Qumran,* 1983, 60) argues that *Jubilees'* references are primary, the expressions in *1 Enoch* being "imitations" of the Jubileean formula, his arguments for the relative dating of the two writings are not widely accepted.

18. Reading *'esma te'zāza kā'eba* with the superior Tana[9] MS; cf. Isaac, *OTP,* 1:59. M. Black (*The Book of Enoch* or *I Enoch,* 1985, 253), however, has "until you again shall give them your last charges," taking *'azzaza* as referring to a testament (cf. R. H. Charles, *The Book of Enoch* or *1 Enoch,* 1912, 173, who translates "till thou givest thy [last] commands," pointing to Heb. צָוָה). The text we have accepted suits the context of the entire verse better and is the more difficult reading, so difficult in fact that it appears to have been omitted for this reason in another MS (the evidence for *tanāzaza* over *te'ezāza* is poorer still, consisting of one dependent MS). Also in favor of our reading is that Black's reading leaves the significance of *kā'eba* (again) unexplained. Last testaments are generally given on a single occasion, and Black's reasoning that it refers to the *second* elevation of Enoch, who has already given last charges to his family before his *first* disappearance, is unconvincing. It is important to note, furthermore, that testaments do not generally require a full year to present, as implied by v. 6, nor do they require the extended teaching and writing implied

is said to have been written in "the tablets of heaven" (v. 1), and accordingly one of its salient features is its preexistence.[19] All indications suggest that the heavenly tablets were believed to contain much more than laws *per se*. A list of the sins of those who persecuted the righteous, for example, seems to be implied in the Enoch passage:

> Blessed is the man who dies righteous and upright,
> against whom no *record of oppression has been written,*
> and who received no judgment on that day. (v. 4)

As we will see from other passages, there was actually a wide variety of contents in the heavenly records — besides a list of laws,[20] they contained a list of deeds both good and bad[21] and a list of names of the righteous and unrighteous,[22] as well as revelations of the future.[23] While in theory these heavenly writings may have been believed to contain an exhaustive, encyclopedic knowledge, it is perhaps not surprising that it is specifically those matters of greatest interest and importance to the elect community that receive emphasis.[24] Thus, practically speaking at least, the contents of the tablets might be best characterized as knowledge for the elect. In this regard, a common thread runs through all the relevant texts and is quite in evidence in the Enoch passage above (cf. v. 4), namely, the revelation of the *blessing promised to the righteous* juxtaposed with *warnings of the condemnation of sinners. Such knowledge defines and confirms the elect in their righteous status.* More will be said about this function below.

What is perhaps even more important here is that this law, and the heavenly tablets as a whole, contained essential truths *of a saving kind.* This would seem to be indicated by the references to blessing and condemnation in the pas-

---

by the same verse. Charles's conjecture that *kāʿeba* reflects a dittography involving עַד, "until," and עוֹד, "again" (173), is certainly more reasonable but equally unnecessary. Few follow Knibb (*The Ethiopic Book of Enoch,* 1978, 1:269, 2:187) in his reading "until you have regained your strength" (reading *teʾēzzaza,* "become strong"). This would suit the presence of *kāʿeba* more, but nothing in the context suggests this meaning (so Charles, 173-74).

19. Cf. Stone, 1985, 228. Perhaps the notion that Wisdom dwelled with God before creation (cf. Proverbs 8) has inspired this belief; or cf. Exod. 32:32-33, where it is implied that God keeps books in heaven.

20. Particularly regarding the calendar: 1QS 10.1-8; 1QH 1.24.

21. *1 En.* 81:1-3; 90:41(?); 97:2, 6-7; 98:6-8; 1QS 10.11; *Asc. Is.* 9:19-23.

22. *1 En.* 108:3; *Jub.* 30:19-20; 1QM 12.2; 4 Ezra 6:20; 14:35; *2 Bar.* 23:1–24:1; 75:6; *1 En.* 47:3-4.

23. Cf. *4QAges of Creation* (= 4Q180-81).

24. Cf. predictions of future: *1 En.* 93:1, 3; vindication of the elect: 103:1-3; 108:10; judgment: 108:7; traditional teaching: *Jub.* 46:15; condemnation of Watchers: *1 En.* 14:1ff., 7; condemnation of the seventy shepherds: *1 En.* 89:70-71; mysteries: 106:19.

sage, as well as by the division implied between the righteous and the wicked on the basis of the instruction in righteousness: "For the upright shall announce righteousness to the upright; and the righteous ones shall rejoice with the righteous ones and congratulate each other. But the sinners shall die together with the sinners; and the apostate shall sink together with the apostate" (vv. 7-8). That Enoch is instructed not only to write down the contents and teach them to his children[25] but also to issue a "warning" against ignoring these tablets (v. 6) is a strong indication that the law contained in them was held by the author to be *binding* on Israel. The gift of another law given to Enoch is also associated with "wisdom" (82:2). It is for the "generations that are discerning." "All the wise ones shall give praise, and wisdom shall dwell upon your consciousness. . . ." Wisdom, in turn, is associated with righteousness: "Blessed are the righteous ones; blessed are those who walk in the street of righteousness and have no sin like the sinners . . ." (v. 4). Wisdom in *1 Enoch* would appear to be more or less equivalent to the idea of the special illumination of the righteous,[26] and this is confirmed by the fact that it is consistently related to the contents of the special law. Since the passage describes the unilluminated sinners as those who have failed to observe the proper (i.e., sectarian) calendar,[27] it is obvious that the heavenly tablets feature "sectarian" laws (i.e., laws that the group, however, would have considered normative). The heavenly law here is thus not simply to be equated with the public Mosaic law. It is also clear from all these aspects of the passage how essential the idea of revelation of the heavenly teachings is to the *definition* of the elect. This revelation contains saving knowledge, and it is implied that *only those who possess it are righteous.*

Nowhere is the teaching about the heavenly writings and about "another law" so pronounced as in *Jubilees*,[28] according to which this law was revealed to all the patriarchs — not only to Moses, but also to those who preceded him by many generations. Parts or all of this law was revealed to Noah as well as Enoch (*Jub.* 7:38), and to Abraham and his progeny (21:10) among others. In 33:10-17, a typical interpretive rehearsal of a biblical narrative, in this case the affair of Reuben with Abraham's concubine Bilhah, we read that "it is written and ordered in the heavenly tablets that a man should not lie with his father's wife, and he should not uncover his father's robe because that is defilement" (v. 10;

---

25. The rationale for chs. 83ff., according to Black, 1985, 253. These verses also provide an appropriate introduction to chs. 91–104 (or even 91–108; cf. also Charles, 1912, 173).

26. So E. J. Schnabel, *Law and Wisdom from Ben Sira to Paul*, 1985, 104.

27. Cf. Charles, 1912, 175.

28. Cf. 1:1, 26; 6:21-22; Wacholder, 1983, 46, 60, 62; J. Becker, *Das Heil Gottes*, 1964, 22-23. We might note that by "twofold and two natures" 6:21 seems to imply that the law of the latter days is *qualitatively* distinct from the former law.

cf. Lev. 20:11; Deut. 22:30). The penalty for this sin is death for both parties involved (vv. 10, 12-13; cf. Lev. 20:11). The emphasis on this sin of defilement in this passage was doubtlessly aimed at the author's contemporaries, who were believed to be rendered especially culpable by sins of this type.[29] The author, however, aware that Reuben continued to live after committing this sin, knew that this created problems for his view that the law in the heavenly tablets was in force in the time of the patriarchs,[30] since it implied that Reuben was not executed as the law specified. This accordingly weakened the author's presentation of the antiquity of the law and the corresponding condemnation of incest. The problem is addressed by the author this way:

> And let them not say, "Reuben had life and forgiveness after he lay with his father's concubine and while she had a husband and while her husband, Jacob, his father was alive." *For the ordinance and judgment and law had not been revealed till then* as completed for everyone, *but in your days it is . . . an eternal law for everlasting generations. And this law has no consummation of days.* And also *there is no forgiveness* for it but only that both of them should be uprooted from the midst of the people. On the day when they have done this they shall be killed. (vv. 15-17)

The argument implies that while the patriarchs for the most part practiced the law written on the heavenly tablets, it was only at the time of Moses ("in your days") that it became fully known and binding on all Israel.[31] Obviously this would appear to be somewhat of a contradiction or compromise of the view, promoted elsewhere in *Jubilees,* that the content of the heavenly tablets was known and revered in the patriarchal age. The author's intent nevertheless was to *uphold,* in the face of contrary evidence, the *antiquity* of the heavenly law. His apology also implicitly sustains the high status of the tablets as the prototypical model on which the Mosaic law was founded, for the law of Moses is seen merely to reflect what was already written there. The ultimate purpose of the passage, of course, is to condemn the practice of some Jews who have departed from the public Torah on this matter, but in doing so the passage expresses the inviolable nature of this law *specifically on the basis of its presence in the heavenly tablets.*

While in passages like these the heavenly tablets could be cited in such a way as to confirm and heighten the importance of certain laws already present in the public Torah, their authority apparently went well beyond this. In the sections that follow we will discuss laws of the heavenly tablets that are *not*

29. J. C. Endres, *Biblical Interpretation in the Book of Jubilees,* 1987, 169-70.
30. Cf. Endres, 1987, 232.
31. Endres, 1987, 170, 232-33.

found in the public Torah, suggesting that the public Torah was an *incomplete* revelation; thus it is implied that even *deficiencies* in the written Torah could be made up by appeal to the heavenly books. It was accordingly not enough that laws are found (as the author of *Jubilees* might put it) in the "open" or "public" Torah — that is, the written law of Moses contained in the Pentateuch. Even *Jubilees* 33 does not appeal to *that* public corpus of laws *per se*, although it could have done so, but conspicuously and exclusively to the *heavenly tablets*. It is not much of a step to the implication that it is *this* law that is binding on Israel, even for those who do not acknowledge its origin and authority. This law of *Jubilees* is "for everyone" (v. 16); ignorance of the laws of *Jubilees* would apparently not have been considered an excuse.[32] The exclusive nature of this law is also apparent. *Jubilees* is addressed to "those who search out the Law," in contrast to those who "will not hear" and "will even kill the witnesses" and "persecute *those who search out the Law*, and . . . neglect everything and begin to do evil in my sight" (1:12). As with the author of Astronomical Enoch, so with the writer of *Jubilees*, the "other law" written above in the heavenly tablets is not only binding, but is further an instrument of differentiation among Israelites — between the righteous and the wicked, between the saved and the judged.[33] The epithet "those who search out the Law" recalls similar language used of the exiles to Damascus (1QS 8.14-15; 9.19-20, among others; cf. Isa. 40:3); the binding nature of the Law as the possession of the righteous community is thus as conspicuous in *Jubilees* as in the scrolls. If there is a difference between the two, this would lie in their respective methods of exegesis: the specific objective of searching out the Law in *Jubilees* would seem to be to arrive at the contents of the heavenly tablets, whereas at Qumran it would be to discover *niśtārōt* apparently latent in the public Torah.

Given that the bulk of the content of *Jubilees* attempts to make this law known and to expose the transgressions of the sinners, obedience to the heavenly tablets would hardly seem to be a minor concern; moreover, there is little indication that the author thought the faithfulness of God would cover for the disobedient (*contra* Sanders).[34] It would seem rather that the laws contained on the heavenly tablets were considered *binding* for salvation — that the nonobservant are referred to as those who "neglect everything" appears to place not only the outright disobedient but even the "casually neglectful" at risk (making invalid any distinction between the two cases as maintained by Sanders). It is to be granted that *Jubilees* is addressing a situation of *apostasy*, as noted in the previous chapter, and not the conditions that exist when Israel is

32. M. Testuz, *Les idées religieuses du Livre des Jubilés*, 1960, 102.

33. Becker, 1964, 22.

34. Sanders, 1977, 371.

generally obedient to the covenant (if in fact the author ever felt that Israel was obedient! — see below). The author of *Jubilees* accordingly felt no hesitation in denying to the lax members of Israel the usual means of atonement, and without atonement the instrument for the preservation of the covenant relationship is removed.[35]

As with Astronomical Enoch, the scrolls, and *Jubilees,* other sections of the Enochian corpus are basically in accord with this view of things. As already noted, the ideas of wisdom and revelation are associated with the elect who follow the instructions of the heavenly tablets in the Book of Heavenly Luminaries. It is quite evident in the Zoomorphic History as well that the existence of an elect group is tied up with a revelation that has been given to them. According to the author of the Zoomorphic History, Israel's problem throughout history has been in the area of comprehension of God's ways:

> Then, behold lambs were born from those snow-white sheep; and they began to *open their eyes and see,* and cried aloud to the sheep [i.e., so that they might also open their eyes]. But as for the sheep, they cried aloud to them, yet they did not listen to what they were telling them but became *exceedingly deafened,* and their *eyes became exceedingly dim-sighted.* . . . Then I kept seeing till one great horn sprouted on one of those sheep, and he *opened their eyes;* and they *had vision in them and their eyes were opened.* (90:6-7, 9)

As already mentioned in connection with this passage, it is certain that the author intends us to conclude that not all Israel responded and were enlightened. While v. 10 refers to those that did respond as "rams," v. 16 predicts that the "sheep" (= apostate Israel) would eventually conspire against their leader, the "horn." The righteous lambs, therefore, are implicitly defined in this book as

---

35. Sanders (1977, 376-78) does address the concern that in some places in *Jubilees* the atonement is not considered efficacious. His solution is that when the two doctrines come into conflict the doctrine of Israel's election prevails over the denial of atonement, appealing to the example of Judah in 41:23-27. But this example is more the exception that proves the rule. If anything the exceptional nature of the forgiveness granted the great patriarch implies that it is not universally applicable to present-day apostates — they have much less reason to be forgiven than the patriarch! Sanders also ignores 41:27, which implies that, if it had not been for the righteousness of David's sons, his seed would certainly have been "uprooted." While Sanders's distinction between legalism (acquiring salvation by obedience) and covenantal nomism (maintaining salvation by obedience and rites of atonement) is an important theoretical distinction, there is no practical difference as regards exclusivity or inclusivity between committing sins of apostasy and losing the covenant (as in *Jubilees*) and failing to acquire the covenant by works (as in legalistic systems). Regardless of such distinctions, however valid in themselves, the fundamentally exclusive nature of the soteriology of *Jubilees* is not altered by Sanders's arguments.

the *"enlightened";* unfortunately, however, we have no way of knowing the content of their proclamation from this passing reference.

Book 5 of *1 Enoch* relates a similar situation using a rather different approach. Here we find extensive admonitions that implicitly contrast the righteous and the wicked. One of the chief differentiating qualities between the two groups is their wisdom or lack of it. Frequently such things as the importance of knowledge, or the danger of a lack of illumination, are expressed in strong language: "For this reason, they are devoid of knowledge and wisdom, so they shall perish thereby together with their goods and together with all their glory and honor" (98:3);

> Woe unto you, fools, for you shall perish
> through your folly!
> You do not listen to the wise, and you shall not receive good things. (98:9)

One particular passage is especially revealing and suggests an important example of how this disagreement over revelation and authority in Judaism manifested itself. It is worth quoting in its entirety:

> And now I know this mystery: For they shall alter the just verdict and *many sinners* will take it to heart; they will speak evil words and lie, and they will invent fictitious stories and write out my Scriptures on the basis of their own words [Gk. "in their own name"]. And would that they had written down *all* the words truthfully on the basis of their own speech, and neither alter nor take away from my words, *all* of which I testify to them from the beginning! Again know another mystery!: that to the righteous and the wise shall be given the Scriptures of joy, for truth and great wisdom. So to them shall be given the Scriptures; and they shall believe[36] them and be glad in them; and *all* the righteous ones who learn from them *all* the ways of truth shall rejoice. (104:10-13)

The speaker here is Enoch, who addresses his righteous offspring ("my children," 94:1). But what can be meant by "my Scriptures" (Eth. "my books"; Gk. "the Writings"), which the sinners apparently tamper with? Charles suggested that the passage refers to books containing Enoch's words only, and to the improper translation of these books into the vernacular of the sinners (Greek and Aramaic); when this action is rectified, according to Charles, the words of Enoch *will* become known to the righteous.[37] This leaves the rather difficult question why

---

36. *Wayetefěšhu,* a variation of *tafaṣeḥ* or perhaps, less likely, of *tafaššeḥa,* "rejoice in" (cf. Ps. 118:24).

37. Charles tampers rather too much with the language of this passage when he translates: "But *when* they write down truthfully all my words in their languages. . . . *Then,*

the unrighteous who mistranslated Enoch's words (i.e., nonsectarians?) would have been interested enough in Enoch's books to translate them in the first place. It would seem rather that they would have rejected them outright. A reference to translating Enoch's words also seems a little anachronistic here. As the above translation suggests, the passage has also been understood to refer to the "Scriptures"[38] — that is, the public canon. While this would explain the interest in these books by nonsectarians, it is also implied in the passage that there is something *missing* in the Scriptures of the apostates that is only given to "the righteous and the wise" (vv. 11-12), and it would seem natural that the missing portion would include the revelation given to the community by Enoch (cf. the summary of the heavenly records in "books" suitable for handing on to his descendants: 81:1– 82:6). It is not otherwise clear whether the "Scriptures" mentioned in the passage would have included books like *Jubilees* (which claims in some way to be a necessary addition to other Scripture), or what relationship may have existed between these Scriptures and the heavenly tablets themselves.

The problems would be greatly reduced if the word "Scriptures" could be taken to refer to *the total* corpus of written revelation — that is, *all* that the sectarians considered to be the "Scriptures." There would appear to be little justification, in other words, for taking this to refer to the sectarian writings only, on the one hand, or the public canon of Hebrew Scriptures only, on the other. These Scriptures would have included the publicly acknowledged books, to which were added a collection of sectarian writings, a combination that also formed the corpus of Scriptures of other groups (cf. 4 Ezra 14:37-48; *Ass. Mos.* 1:16-18). Thus when the passage says that some will "alter the just verdict [probably 'the true account (of things)'[39]]" and "will [presumably in its place] speak evil words and lie, and . . . will invent fictitious stories and write out my Scriptures on the basis of their own words" (v. 10), it would appear not only that the sectarian writings are omitted but that the *common fund* of writings has also been tampered with — thus both sins of commission and omission are involved (cf. "alter" *and* "take

I know another mystery, that books shall be given to the righteous" (1912, 261-62). This connects the thoughts rather too closely, as if the second is made conditional on the first. We take it that two separate statements are introduced by *meštira* in vv. 10 and 12.

38. The word translated "Scriptures" in this passage is literally "books" (*masāheft* = *maṣāheft*). The Gk. τὰς γραφάς has suggested the translation "Scriptures" to Isaac (*OTP,* 1:85), but the technical sense is not required even by this translation.

39. *nagara reteʿ*. Isaac (*OTP,* 1:85 n. *x*) suggests as an equivalent "word of truth," but the expression might be taken to represent the common משפט צדק, "just judgments," in the sense of legal interpretation, in this case pointing to *haggadah* rather than *halakah*. The "(evil) words," *nagar* (lit. "matter," "thing," "speech"; perhaps here: *"account"*), that the opponents speak, in view of the parallel "fictitious stories," may also imply a false narrative of the events.

away from," v. 11). This would point to, among other things, a serious disagreement over portions (or perhaps the text?) of Scripture common to both groups. It is at least clear that the *chief* sin spoken of here is the *omission of the Enochian teachings from the total collection of the Scriptures.* When it is said that the Scriptures will be given back to the righteous as a gift in the latter days (v. 12), it would seem to mean that the total corpus would be reinstated, the Enochian books as well as other sectarian teachings along with, perhaps, a more faithful edition of the common Scriptures. The author of *1 Enoch* and his community would appear to have claimed that this gift had already been given the righteous in their days (to which the future tense of v. 12, as in vv. 10-11, no doubt refers). As for the apostate contemporaries of the righteous, all who did not acknowledge the revelation given to the community, they were left with a severely truncated edition of Holy Writ. This lack is emphasized through the repetition of "many" and "all" (*kʷello* occurs four times in this short passage), words that also tend to enhance the generalizing condemnation of Israel for their treatment of Scripture; they highlight the extent of this error as well as the importance placed on *every word* communicated by Enoch: "*many* sinners will take it to heart" for they fail to consider "*all* the words . . . *all* of which [Enoch] testify to them from the beginning" (v. 11). The possession of these books accordingly serves to divide and define those who are righteous from the sinners. The "righteous" will be given the books and will "*believe* them and rejoice in them." The books contain "the ways of truth" — a possible allusion to covenantal thought, implying that keeping the covenant is possible only through obedience to these writings. Again, the possession of the revelation is equated with "wisdom" (v. 12).

In a similar vein *1 En.* 108:6 complains of "those who alter *all* the things which the Lord has done through the mouth of the prophets, *all* of which have to be fulfilled." What is notable here is that the author goes on to further qualify what he means: "For some of these things were *written and sealed above in heaven* so that the angels may read them and know that which is about to befall the sinners . . ." (v. 7). This verse is replete with problems to be addressed later, but it is obvious that *some* of the revelation binding on Israel — namely, what ought to have been understood and obeyed by "those who alter" — could be found only on heavenly tablets.[40] Whatever might be the relationship, or overlap, that exists between this distinctive revelation to the group and the teachings of the prophets accessible to all Israelites, it is certainly not a matter of proper exegesis of and obe-

---

40. The antecedent of "some of them" is unclear; cf. Black, 1985, 324. It might refer to the spirits of the sinners, or the prophets. However, the context makes it quite clear that the type of knowledge retained involves written documents. Cf. this expression with that used of heavenly tablets in *1 En.* 47:3. The association of the tablets with angels in 103:2 furthermore suggests that heavenly tablets are in mind here.

dience to the prophets *simpliciter*. The opponents of the Enochian sect have in some way corrupted (literally "changed," v. 6; cf. 104:10!) the word of the Lord, which is only to be found on the heavenly tablets. Ignoring this special revelation has serious consequences indeed (judgment by fire, vv. 5-6).

Modes of Revelation at Qumran

No little attention has been paid by scholars to the soteriology of Qumran, in which *revelation* takes a central place.[41] While it is never actually said in so many words, the impression is gained that saving knowledge includes virtually all the teachings of the community.[42] This is implied, if nowhere else, in the fact that to become a member of the community of salvation the initiate had to undergo a lengthy term of probation involving a thorough and detailed study and internalization of the group's knowledge.[43]

The teaching of the community seems to have included more than simply the true *interpretation* of the *existing* Torah — although Qumran's apparently unique hermeneutical methods alone would probably have been enough to set them apart from much of Judaism.[44] It is apparent also that the community respected the idea of "heavenly tablets" and the additional laws found on them. Ben Zion Wacholder has demonstrated that CD 5.1-6 refers to a second "sealed" Torah that was deliberately hidden by Moses in anticipation of the coming apostasy of Israel in order to preserve the true law.[45] We know from references in the Temple Scroll and from other writings that the Qumran sect assumed the existence of a second law to be revealed at the end of days,[46] and we

41. Cf. H. Ringgren, *The Faith of Qumran*, 1963, 112-13; H.-W. Kuhn, *Enderwartung und gegenwärtiges Heil*, 1966, 31; M. Mansoor, *The Thanksgiving Hymns Translated and Annotated with an Introduction*, 1961, 68; 1QH 12.22-23; 14.18-19. Sanders (1977, 259-60) presents a lucid exposition of the role of revelation in Qumran ("knowledge is the means and sign of election," 259), but he seems to ignore its implications.

42. Ringgren, 1963, 117.

43. Cf. 1QS 1.7-18; 5.7-11, 20-24 (esp. ll. 20-21, 24); 6.13-23 (esp. l. 14); 9.10-11; 1QSa 1.4-8.

44. G. Jeremias, *Der Lehrer der Gerechtigkeit*, 1963, 102; Becker, 1964, 60-64.

45. Cf. Deut. 31:26; Wacholder, 1983, xiii-xiv; Wacholder, "The 'Sealed'" Torah versus the 'Revealed' Torah," 1986, 351-63, who points to combined exegesis of Jer. 32:11-14 and Deut. 31:24-30 (cf. v. 9) as the source for this belief.

46. Wacholder identifies this law with the Temple Scroll (what he prefers to call the "Torah Scroll"; 1983, 7-12, 21, and passim; cf. also 4Q171 4.7-9; 4Q177 1.12-16; and 4Q174 1.1-13, 92-94). Not all scholars take this to be the purpose of 11QTemple; cf. M. O. Wise, *A Critical Study of the Temple Scroll from Qumran Cave 11*, 1990a, 31-32, 161ff., for various theories.

can deduce the importance of this law from the preservation of *Jubilees* in the community's library, their adherence to the calendar revealed in the tablets,[47] and the occasional reference in the scrolls to other writings promoting sectarian laws. Wacholder's evaluation of the purpose of this second law (whether or not, as he maintains, part of that law can be found in the Temple Scroll itself) as in part a remedy to the present experience of apostasy in Israel is apposite:

> The scroll responds to a central question: Why has God turned away from Israel? The answer seems to be that, as foreseen by God, the experience of Sinai was of but a fleeting duration. In spite of all the efforts of Moses, the forty years of wandering in the wilderness proved of no avail, since soon after the entry into Canaan, the people failed to observe the Law as they had promised to do in the covenant. But rather than destroy them or treat Israel like any pagan nation, God had entrusted to Moses a second Torah giving Israel another chance. Whereas the first Torah was, on account of Israel's violation, ephemeral, the second would last eternally. . . . Only if Israel will renew the covenant, then construct a new sanctuary and inaugurate a new rite, will God come down from heaven to dwell forever in Israel's midst.[48]

But the Qumranites went further than simply adhering to special revelatory traditions encompassed in a "second Torah." Their revelation was also "living," coming as it did primarily through *inspired exegesis*, which seems to have been experienced during special study "sessions."[49] This type of exegesis composed a "living" authority because it was essentially *non*traditional, being based strictly on a charismatic reading of the Scriptures, and because it also probably involved authentically new revelational content.[50] It is widely familiar, of course, from the much studied *pešer* methodology.[51] Lawrence Schiffman is probably quite correct in highlighting the important distinction be-

---

47. Wacholder, 1983, 35-38.

48. Wacholder, 1983, 31.

49. Cf. L. H. Schiffman, *Sectarian Law in the Dead Sea Scrolls*, 1983, xi and passim; M. P. Horgan, *Pesharim*, 1979, 3; C. Milikowsky, "Law at Qumran," 1986, 241.

50. So, e.g., 1QpHab 2.1-3. We cannot completely agree with K. G. Kuhn ("Die in Palästina gefundenen hebräischen Texte und das Neue Testament," 1950, 207) that what was "new" about the revelation was actually already revealed in the Scriptures and in other Jewish tradition — except, perhaps, in the form of a "mystery." We do concur fully, however, with his insistence that the sect considered this revelation to be in continuity with what went before. The Temple Scroll, for one, apparently contained entirely new festivals and enlarged significantly on ones only alluded to in Scripture; cf. Y. Yadin, *The Temple Scroll*, 1985, 89-95.

51. For descriptions of the genre, see Horgan, 1979, 250-51; J. J. Collins, "Prophecy and Fulfillment in the Qumran Scrolls," 1987, 272-73; G. J. Brooke, "Qumran Pesher," 1981; I. Fröhlich, "Le genre littéraire des *pesharim* de Qumrân," 1986.

tween two categories of law at Qumran, *nigleh* (public or revealed law) and *nistar* (hidden law), and to relate the *pešer* in part to the discovery of the latter kind of law.[52] Even though members of the sect alone knew the *nistārōt*, all Israelites were nevertheless considered responsible for seeking them out and obeying them, as Schiffman has also pointed out; again, ignorance of the laws was no excuse.[53]

It is hardly surprising that the scrolls equate the acceptance of the revelation — whether traditional sectarian law or more recently discovered *nistārōt* — with entry into the saved community. Nowhere is this more clearly presented than in 1QS 2.25–3.12, where some of the requisites for entry into the *yaḥad* are established. The passage refers to the one who "scorns [cf. Lev. 26:43] to enter the ways of God" and who will therefore "not pass into His Community of truth" (2.25-26). The reason for this exclusion is given, and it continues to be related to the community's knowledge: "his soul has loathed the teachings of Knowledge, he has not established (within him) the ordinances of righteousness[54] . . . his understanding . . . shall not be brought into the Council of the *yaḥad*" (2.25–3.2) — that is to say, he will never be a member of the saved community because he has not acquired the "saving knowledge."[55] The unconverted one remains in a state of uncleanness "as long as he scorns the ordinances of God and allows not himself to be taught by the Community of [God's] Council" (3.5-6), and his unrepentant state precludes effective participation in the community's atonement rituals (3.4-5).[56] As a result of his uncleanness, he is to be excommunicated from the *yaḥad*: not only his "possessions" but particularly his "understanding and powers [of decision?]"[57] (3.2) shall not be admitted into the community. The reference to

---

52. Schiffman, 1983, 15.

53. Schiffman, 1983, 15.

54. The rougher translation of P. Wernberg-Møller (*The Manual of Discipline*, 1957, 24), "his soul has abhorred *instructions of knowledge of righteous judgments*," may better preserve the idea here of the *corpus* of *mišpatim* revealed to the sect, which, as they believed, composed the authoritative clarification of Torah. The phrase דעת משפטי צדק might be compared, as he suggests, to the phrase "knowledge of righteous judgments" in *Pss. Sol.* 2:12; 5:1; 8:8.

55. A. R. C. Leaney, *The Rule of Qumran and Its Meaning*, 1966, 137-38.

56. The clauses יזכה נכפורים, "be purified [in the sense of acquittal or justification; cf. Job 15:14; 25:4; Ps. 51:6; Mic. 6:11] by atonement rituals," יטהר במי נדה, "be cleansed by (the) 'water of impurity,'", etc., clearly indicate that a reference is being made to some purification ritual.

57. The meaning of the noun כוח, "power," is elusive in this context. We might translate it "influences," or "abilities" (in the sense of gifts or talents; perhaps "spiritual gifts," cf. Isa. 40:31; Mic. 3:8; Zech. 4:6); it is also an appropriate expression for effectiveness in battle, perhaps alluding to the sect's preparation for the final battle (cf. Judg. 16:5). On the other

"understanding" seems to imply that the unworthy one will not be allowed into the sessions in which the *yaḥad* carries on its exegetical processes,[58] illustrating once more the supreme importance of the event of receiving revelation. Since the unrighteous is cut off from the source of teaching, he is cut off from the source of life.

By contrast, it is only by the "Spirit of true counsel"[59] that one's sins can hope to be atoned for *"when he beholds the light of life"* — a clause that suggests enlightenment (3.6-7). *"In [God's] truth"* and "by his soul's humility towards *all the precepts* of God" shall he be cleansed (3.7-9); "and he shall establish his steps to walk perfectly in *all the ways of God,* according to [God's] command concerning His regular feasts; and he shall step aside neither to right nor to left, and shall make no single step from *all* [God's] words" (3.9-11). The repeated "all" (כול) in this passage implies that the *omission of any of* these important revelations was thought to divide the righteous from the unrighteous, and to keep the unrepentant from salvation. The allusion to the calendrical order[60] makes it apparent that it is the distinctive "sectarian" teaching that is being elevated to the status of *essential teaching.*

We can learn more about the historical process that led to this attitude from the first column of CD, which introduces the *moreh ṣedeq,* whom God raised up to teach a group of "blind men" who had been groping and seeking their way for twenty years (1.9-12; cf. 2.11-13). To this group God revealed "the hidden things in which all Israel had strayed" (CD 3.14). By knowing all the regulations that Israel had disobeyed and for which the people were now experiencing the wrath of God, the sectarians would be able to avoid wrath, escape the present "exile," and begin to deal with the grave situation of apostasy in their own lives. The so-called Founder Hymns provide further insight into this relationship between the *moreh* and the revelation that he possessed. In one

---

hand, the idea might be that the unworthy will not be allowed to vote in the council. The context supports this latter interpretation.

58. Wernberg-Møller, 1957, 24.

59. Wernberg-Møller (1957, 61) prefers "Spirit of true *council*" — i.e., the Spirit of the community — comparing it to "Holy Spirit of the Community, in His truth" in the following line. Since the stubborn one is excluded from the *yaḥad,* he cannot access this teaching because it is given only by the Spirit of the community. This translation for עצה, however, makes the following phrase ("concerning the ways of man") senseless, although in either case the significance of the exclusion would be the same.

60. Cf. Dupont-Sommer, 1961, 77 n. 2, and the discussion below of the calendar. Other passages similarly associate entry into the covenant with the reception of teaching and knowledge (CD 2.2-6, 11-13; 3.12-13; 6.14–7.6; 15.6-10; [B] 2.27-34; 1QM 10.9-11; 13.8-9). Even "conversion to the Law of Moses" involves more than the public writings in CD 15.6-10, since ll. 10-11 proceed to lay out the circumstances for revealing the other "ordinances" to the initiate (cf. l. 13).

such hymn, 1QH 2.8-19, the "Teacher of Righteousness" or "Teacher of Right Teaching" (for these are certainly the best ways to render this title)[61] refers to himself as "the foundation of *truth and understanding* for them whose way is straight" and "an *interpreter of Knowledge* concerning the marvellous *Mysteries*" on behalf of the "elect of righteousness." While to the elect the *moreh* was "healing," "prudence," and "firm inclination,"[62] he was a stumbling block for outsiders — "a snare for sinners," "an object of shame and mockery for traitors," "an object of slander upon the lips of the violent" (ll. 8, 9-11; cf. also 1QH 4.23-29). That the central issue involved in the dispute was who possessed the authoritative teaching is manifest in the terms used of the *moreh*'s opponents: they are "interpreters of straying," those "who seek smooth things," "men of deceit." They even prefer the teachings of "a people without understanding" and obey the "uncircumcision of the lips" (i.e., Gentile teachings, ll. 14-16, 18) rather than listen to the *moreh*. These blind enemies do not realize that he alone can "establish the teaching" (l. 17) and that it is in his heart alone that God has "set understanding" (l. 18).[63] In contrast to these the righteous "love instruction" and "see true things"; they are "the understanding" (ll. 15, 18). From 1QS 11.3-

61. Whether *moreh ṣedeq* should be translated "Righteous Teacher" (genitive of quality; cf. Becker, 1964, 174-76; J. T. Milik, *Ten Years of Discovery in the Wilderness of Judaea*, 1959, 126) or the more familiar "Teacher of Righteousness" (objective genitive; Jeremias, 1963, 315) enters into play here. While the idea of "legitimate" teacher, in contrast to the contemporary illegitimate Jewish teachers, would certainly be appropriate to the claims of legitimization in our groups, "Teacher of Righteousness" appears to have most in its favor: (1) צדק never takes on the meaning of "legitimate" in the scrolls and always implies a relationship with God (as it does in all but secular uses in the Hebrew Scriptures; Jeremias, 308, 312-15); (2) J. A. Ziesler (*The Meaning of Righteousness in Paul*, 1972, 92; cf. also Jeremias, 312-14, for other linguistic examples) has pointed to parallel expressions like CD 6.11 (יורה הצדק, "he who teaches righteousness") that suggest that the *moreh ṣedeq* is especially the teacher of the *true and eternal covenant*, i.e., "covenant-teacher" (cf. Joel 2:23; Hos. 10:12). In 1QpHab 1.1-2 and 6.12-18 the function of the Teacher is to teach the new covenant and give inspired interpretation of the Law and the prophets. He is contrasted with the מטיף הכזב (the Preacher of Lies).

62. Terms further relevant to his role as revealer. For the view that "healing" refers to "enlightenment," cf. S. Holm-Nielsen, *Hodayot*, 1960, 34. For the expression "prudence for the simple (לפתיים)" Holm-Nielsen points to Ezek. 45:20, where the word is parallel to שגה, "transgressor through ignorance"; "the word indicates those who without insight are in danger of ending in ungodliness, but who through ערמה [here in its positive sense, as in Prov. 1:4] can be brought to their senses" (34).

63. It is possible to interpret the "man" of l. 17, who is said to have been persecuted by the opponents, as the community (cf. Holm-Nielsen, 1960, 36-37). It is accordingly the *yaḥad* who "might open the fountain of knowledge to all the understanding," but in this case our point about the community being the locus of saving knowledge would still be sustained.

7, which seems to preserve the words of the *moreh,* we learn that this revelation of the mysteries "enlightens" the righteous (ll. 3, 5). His teaching is part of the "everlasting possession" promised to Israel (l. 7). Knowledge and prudence are "hidden," on the other hand, from all other men (l. 6; also 1QH 7.32-33; 13.13-14; etc.).

In such a way revealed knowledge effectively divides Israel into two camps: the saved and the unsaved. CD 3.17, 20, a text we have already encountered, provides a good summary of this belief: "whoever despises these waters [a metaphor for the teaching] shall not live . . . [but] they who cling to it are destined for everlasting life." Hardly a more unambiguous statement of the centrality of revelation in the self-definition of the saved community can be imagined. It is accordingly undeniable that for this group a certain kind of knowledge or "enlightenment" formed the practical limits on the saved community,[64] and this is also clearly expressed in the adoption of the self-designation "sons of light" for the sect and the use of "sons of darkness" for all who remain unenlightened.[65] It may be true, therefore, that while some groups took the attitude of later rabbis who directly polemicized against any such "dynamic" view of revelation,[66] one is faced here with the bold claim to possess novel revelation (cf. 1QS 9.13-14).[67] This is a significant observation when one considers that rabbinic perspectives and priorities tend to have influenced modern characterizations of Judaism as conservative and static in regard to things revealed. The groups we have investigated offer a significant challenge to this one-sided view.

64. Cf. Schiffman, 1983, 7; Mansoor, 1961, 65-74. For the relationship of this idea to gnostic thought, cf. M. Burrows, *More Light on the Dead Sea Scrolls,* 1958, 256; Ringgren, 1963, 120; Mansoor, 1961, 66, 72-74.

65. Cf. J. J. Enz, "Origin of the Dualism Expressed by 'Sons of Light' and 'Sons of Darkness,'" 1976, 15-16.

66. J. Jervell, "Die offenbarte und die verborgene Tora," 1971, 92-93. For the view that prophecy had ceased, cf. *b. Yoma* 9b. The dichotomy "revelatory" versus "traditional" is itself somewhat artificial. It is widely recognized that rabbinic exegesis was also revelatory in the sense that it involved innovative and authoritative judgments on the meaning of the text, just as the revelation embraced by our groups was also traditional in the sense of being in continuity with earlier teaching. The use of the word "dynamic" here suggests that the difference had to do more with the *articulation* of each respective theology of revelation than with substantive differences in revelation itself. Rabbinic exegesis claimed to have been transmitted from sage to sage by word of mouth, while the revelation of our groups was more mystically revealed through prophetic kinds of processes.

67. While it is often pointed out that לעת ובעת can be rendered "from time to time," the parallel לפי העתים, "throughout time," in the same passage suggests that revelation distinctively appropriate to each age is intended by the expression.

Revelation and Faith

It is appropriate to deal next with what appears to be a development of the revelatory approach of our groups — namely, the demand for *faith* in the revelation. The matter of "believing" the books or the revelation has already been brought to our attention with regard to *1 En.* 104:12 and the Qumran scrolls. It should be noted, however, that the object of faith is not necessarily limited to written documents. In the case of the Teacher of Righteousness at Qumran, faith at least partly implies believing in the authority given to an individual. Even here, however, it can be argued that it is more the *teaching* than the *person* of the *moreh* that is in mind when it is said of his followers that they will be saved "by their works and by their faith in the *moreh ṣedeq*" (1QpHab 2.14).[68] Beyond such incidental references the notion of faith in *1 Enoch* and the scrolls remains conspicuously undeveloped. This is not true in later books like 4 Ezra, however, where faith has become a much more important, and even somewhat independent, motif. While the reference to "treasure of works" in passages like 4 Ezra 7:76-77 has led many scholars to hold up this book as a stark example of "righteousness through works of the law" (as if 4 Ezra only required perfection in the written Torah),[69] it is clearly not as simple as that. Only a few verses later we read of "the reward laid up for those who have *trusted the covenants* [note the significant plural] of the Most High" (7:83). Elsewhere in this book faith is mentioned alongside works: 13:23 speaks of those "who have *works and have faith* in the Almighty"; and 9:7-8 is even more deliberate in its mention of the two together:

> It shall be that everyone who will be saved [i.e., in the end] and will be able to escape *on account of his works, or on account of the faith by which he has believed,* will survive the dangers that have been predicted, and will see my salvation in my land and within my borders. . . . Then those who have now *abused my ways* shall be amazed, and those who have *rejected them with contempt* shall dwell in torments.

It is no wonder that Stone commented that faith and works "are used almost indiscriminately in the book."[70] But there may be a good reason for this combination of faith and works other than a simple failure to distinguish the two[71] or an attempt to grant equal importance to both.[72] It is true that in 13:23 faith is

---

68. Cf. Jeremias, 1963, 142-45.

69. Cf. Schnabel, 1985, 143, 145.

70. So M. E. Stone (*Fourth Ezra,* 1990, 269) draws a connection between "treasures of faith" (6:5) and "treasure of works" (7:77).

71. So Stone, 1990, 269.

72. R. J. Coggins and M. A. Knibb, *The First and Second Books of Esdras,* 1979, 182. This is to view "faith" as just one more work in a legalistic approach to salvation.

placed in God who delivers; but in the other cases it is difficult to avoid the conclusion that the faith spoken of has more to do with the acceptance of a way of life, or perhaps accepting the program for salvation advanced by 4 Ezra. This hunch receives confirmation when we compare the above-mentioned 9:7-8 with v. 9, where we see that those who have faith are contrasted, not with those who have unbelief, but with those who "abused my ways" and "rejected them with contempt." Similarly in 7:76-77 Ezra's "treasure of works" is contrasted with the attitude of "those who have shown scorn." Faith here, then, is *acceptance of the ways of God,* and one naturally thinks of the essentials regarded by the author (and his community) as necessary for salvation.

What would this "way" involve? That this "way" was treated contemptuously suggests that it involved aspects or beliefs *not* universally held by the Jewish world, and there is evidence in the book that faith is centered in a particular kind of revelation similar to that promoted by *1 Enoch, Jubilees,* and the scrolls, a revelation that goes beyond the public Torah. This evidence comes at the close of the book (14:37-48), where the account is told of how Ezra received dictation, by means of a truly miraculous revelation, of the contents of ninety-four books — twenty-four public books and seventy deemed suitable "for the wise among your people" only (cf. vv. 6, 26).[73] The significant thing here is not the reproduction of the twenty-four public books, for common tradition held that the historical Ezra was responsible for collating the books belonging to the Hebrew canon. What is remarkable is the interest and care shown for the *sectarian* books, which are actually set at a relatively *higher* value than the canonical books — "for in *them* is the spring of understanding, the fountain of wisdom, and the river of knowledge" (vv. 45-47). For the author of 4 Ezra *these* Scriptures were the important ones.[74] The reason for their importance is given in v. 22, where Ezra seeks to have the books revealed to him "that men may be able *to find the path,* and that those who wish to live in the last days *may live.*" It is widely assumed that the traditions of Ezra's restoration of the Scriptures that lie behind this passage originally served to explain how the holy writings survived the Babylonian captivity intact. While this may be true, that in this present context the holy writings include a number of secret books argues that the tradition of the plenary inspiration of the Scriptures was particularly brought to bear on the case of the *additional* books espoused by the writer.[75] It is these books that possess *saving value.*[76] They and the way of life promoted by them

---

73. While these esoteric books have frequently been equated with the "apocalyptic books" (an equally indefinite corpus! cf. Coggins and Knibb, 1979, 282), there is no way to determine the extent of the collection in the mind of the author of 4 Ezra.

74. Coggins and Knibb, 1979, 282-83; Stone, 1990, 442.

75. W. O. E. Oesterley, *II Esdras,* 1933, 164; Coggins and Knibb, 1979, 272.

76. Stone, 1990, 439, cf. 442.

have been treated contemptuously, but the author holds them up as showing the saving way.

Accordingly it is simply not enough to speak of salvation in 4 Ezra as proceeding from works of the Mosaic law alone, or even from some combination of works with faith in God. Clearly the intention — not totally unlike writings already investigated — is to promote adherence to a special revelation. Although there are no heavenly or mystic visions in 4 Ezra, and despite an apparent disclaimer (in the mouth of the modest Ezra!) against such knowledge (4:23), the author nevertheless speculates on a whole range of matters including eschatology, secret knowledge made known to Abraham and Moses, and, of course, the secret writings themselves.[77]

While faith is a concept frequently found in 2 Baruch as well, no unambiguous definition of the content of that faith is given, but it would not seem to consist only in faith in the Law. Those who will avoid the fiery judgment in 44:14-15 not only have "preserved the truth of the Law" but also have "insight," and 51:7 speaks not only of "those who have been saved by their works, whose hope has been in the law," but also of those "who have put their trust in understanding, and their confidence [lit. faith][78] in wisdom." Both passages exhibit close similarities to those from 4 Ezra and similarly suggest that at the very least a distinctive interpretation of the Law is involved, if not an entirely novel teaching.[79] In another instance (42:2) it is even more evident that faith is in some special revelation embraced by the community. This verse calls the saved "those who have believed," and again (as with 4 Ezra 7:76-77; 9:7-8 above) the only indication of the object of this faith comes with the contrast made in that verse with "those who have despised." One might conclude, on this basis, that the ob-

---

77. Stone, 1990, 26-27.

78. hymnwt'; cf. אמ(ו)נה. The quotation is that of R. H. Charles as revised by L. H. Burlington in Sparks, AOT, 870.

79. Another hint of this comes in 46:3-6 where, in an address of Baruch to his people, the community expresses its anxiety that Baruch's departure will result in the "light" of interpretation being extinguished: "For where shall we again investigate (ybḥ', "seek," "inquire of"; G-G 9 compares בעה) the Law, or who will distinguish between death and life for us?" The second question implies that keeping the covenant ("distinguishing between death and life") actually depends on interpretation, a step that the rabbinic teachers, e.g., do not appear to have taken (contra R. H. Charles, The Apocalypse of Baruch translated from the Syriac, 1896, 73). Hints exist in this passage that the author's community possessed specially endowed teachers (perhaps the author himself) that the readers are admonished to respect: "prepare your heart so that you obey the Law, and be subject to those who are wise and understanding with fear. And prepare your soul that you shall not depart from them [i.e., the teachers]" (v. 5), for salvation from "torment" depends on this (v. 6). In spite of some talmudic-sounding phrases, it would appear that the exegetical practices and attitudes toward law in 2 Baruch are more "sectarian" than rabbinic.

ject of faith is not only the written Torah of Moses (the public books), as scholars like Charles have assumed, but the group's own teaching as well.[80] It is specifically this teaching that has been treated contemptuously and that is so highly valued in this book (see also 54:5, 21; 57:2; 59:2; 83:8). This is further confirmed by texts in *2 Baruch* that reveal the esoteric nature of the knowledge embraced by the author: 48:3 explicitly proclaims that God does "not reveal his secrets [or 'mysteries']" [81] . . . to many";[82] rather: "You show your mighty works to those who do not know. You pull down the enclosure for those who have no experience and enlighten the darknesses, and reveal the secrets to those who are spotless, to those who subjected themselves to you and your Law in faith" (54:5). The idea of revelation (or wisdom) as a gift to pure and humble people is hardly foreign to these writings. The important thing here is that the word "secrets" suggests more than the traditional written Torah. While faith in this verse seems to be equated with "subjection" to God and the Law, the relationship is, grammatically speaking, indirect and somewhat ambiguous; faith may equally apply to the "secrets" mentioned in the same verse.

That the author embraced special knowledge above and beyond the Torah can also be seen from 59:4-11, where it is said that God showed Moses "many warnings *together with the ways of the Law and the end of time, as also to you.*" Our author significantly claims that these things were revealed, not only to Moses, but also to "you," which would seem to mean, in the first case Baruch, in the second case the "real" author's community. By "warnings" the author probably intends to allude to the types of warnings given by Moses to the children of Israel in Deut. 28:15-16. As for the "end of time," the kinds of revelations the author has in mind are specifically listed in the following verses and reveal many points of contact with revelations we see elsewhere in this literature: a description of the new Temple, the measurements of the cosmos, revelations of nature, the "times," etc. — things that elsewhere are specifically said to have been revealed to Moses (*Jub.* 1:4ff.; 50:1ff.; *Ass. Mos.* 1:16-18). It is therefore apparent that the community that produced *2 Baruch* acknowledged the binding quality of another revelation and law given to Moses other than the normative Torah held by all Israel. It is interesting, in this regard, that 57:2 ap-

---

80. Charles's view (1896, 39, 95) is that faith in *2 Baruch* is in the Law or the "Talmud." Cf. also Klijn, *OTP,* 1:633. Schnabel (1985, 157) is more correct in pointing out that while the teaching of *2 Baruch* is closely associated with the written Torah (cf. the role of scribes in making the law known; 3:6; 77:13-15; 84:9; etc.), it includes interpretation of the law; "law" itself goes well beyond the publicly recognized commandments, and "wisdom" includes sectarian knowledge (158).

81. *r'zyk;* cf. רזי.

82. The expression is *sgy*". An interesting play on the words שגיא and סיג (dross) may have been intended in the original.

pears to allude to the belief, expressed so emphatically in *Jubilees,* that this "un-written law" had already been revealed to Abraham and his sons.[83] It is adher-ence to *this* revelation that set the community of the wise apart from those who "despise" this law (cf. 42:4). Hence, once again, revelation and faith in that reve-lation distinguishes the righteous from those who are destined for judgment.[84]

Special Revelation in the Psalms of Solomon

Determining whether the *Psalms of Solomon* possess an exclusivist soteriology similar to that of these other works is rather more problematic, due to the noto-rious difficulties involved in establishing the teaching of these psalms. These difficulties seem partly to have resulted from the quite unsystematic poetic form adopted by their author (or authors), in which the intent to stir the emo-tions of the reader is often put before a concern for clear expression of a mes-sage. One might note, however, that the same kind of uncompromising ani-mosity between the community and its opponents that we find in the other works comes to tangible expression in the psalms as well, and indications exist that the psalmist's group took a fairly strict stand toward legal matters, and this may have driven a wedge between them and their fellow Jews.

For further indication of what it meant to be a member of the author's community, one can turn to *Pss. Sol.* 14:1-4:

> The Lord is faithful to those who truly love him,
>> to those who endure his discipline,
> To those who live in the righteousness of his commandments,
>> in the Law, which he has commanded for our life.
> The Lord's devout shall live by it forever;
>> the Lord's paradise, the trees of life, are his devout ones.
> Their planting is firmly rooted forever;
>> they shall not be uprooted as long as the heavens shall last,
> For Israel is the portion and inheritance of God.

This psalm is clearly modeled on the first canonical psalm and, on the surface at least, seems to refer to loyalty to the traditional Books of Moses — "the Law, which he has commanded for our life." On the other hand, these verses depart from Psalm 1 in enlarging on what it *means,* precisely, to be a faithful follower

83. Which would not seem to refer, for the above-mentioned reasons, to the "oral Law" (*contra* Oesterley, cited in R. H. Charles and W. O. E. Oesterley, *The Apocalypse of Baruch,* 1917, xxiv).

84. Also cf. 54:13-14, 16, 21; 83:8; the opposite of faith is denial in 59:2.

of Torah. The faithful are referred to as "those who *truly* love [God]" (cf. also 6:6; 10:3) and "who endure his discipline," the "Lord's devout," his "paradise," and "the trees of life," words the writer uses elsewhere for his own community. The tree motif is, of course, drawn from Ps. 1:4, but in the historical context of Pompey's siege of Jerusalem an almost triumphant nuance is granted to it by the addition of the words "firmly rooted . . . shall not be uprooted" — an especially pointed addition when it is recalled that the community of the *Psalms of Solomon* had recently flaunted their potential for survival in being spared the worst of the ill effects of the siege and in escaping from Jerusalem (see esp. 17:14-18). Those same events, in their analysis, had providentially effected a separation between the righteous and sinners (cf. also 2:33-35; 12:6; 15:3-9). Balanced with this sectarian attitude is the confession that only God's mercy brought salvation to the writer's community.[85] There are other indications in the language and ideas of the psalms that a particular group, not all Israel, has become the subject of this "reinterpretation" of the first canonical psalm. This is most notable in statements that implicitly contrast the "righteous" with the "sinners," implying that a significant division exists between the two (3:3-8 — cf. 3:9-12; 4:1, 23 — cf. 4:24-25; 14:1-5 — cf. 14:6-10). This division is sometimes based on piety or spirituality (piety, trust, and acts of repentance, 3:3-8; fear of God, innocence, 4:23; love of God, 4:25; 6:6; 10:3; 14:1; persistent and humble trust in the midst of adversity, 5:8-18; righteous living and repentance, 9:5-7; etc.). To be noted once again is the motif of how the "pious" are disciplined and rebuked but not judged (9:6-7; 10:1-3; 13:6-12).

But we also possess in the *Psalms of Solomon* more concrete indications of an exclusivist soteriology, particularly in passages that suggest revelational criteria very similar to those of the other groups, notably Qumran. There is evidence, for example, that the standard understanding of the Law is not felt to be enough. The righteous are characterized as "those who know your righteous judgments" (5:1), seemingly the same expression used in the scrolls for authoritative interpretations of the Law.[86] The psalmist accordingly refers, by using this expression, to the group that has been granted insight into crucially important revelations. That special revelations were cherished by the community seems also to be implied in the charge that the Jerusalemites would not "listen," even though obedience would have preserved them from the recent calamity (they "sinned once again *by not listening*," 2:8). This expression can mean that they failed to heed warnings of

---

85. Cf., e.g., 13:1-4, 12; 16:5; 18:1-2. The idea of protection, and the words of v. 5, "Israel is the portion and inheritance of God," seem both to be inspired by Deut. 32:9ff., except that here the title "Israel" seems to be limited to the psalmist's group.

86. ἐπισταμένων τὰ κρίματά σου τὰ δίκαια (cf. דעת משפטי צדך, 1QS 3.1). *Pss. Sol.* 2:12; 8:8.

impending doom on Jerusalem rather than that they refused to listen to the group's teachings about righteousness, but there is no reason to doubt that both are in mind. From such hardened minds, from "young and old and their children — the whole group of them,"[87] God "turned away his face" — God hiding his face being a common biblical expression for complete desertion by God.

Still further evidence that this is a group that cherished dogmatic interpretations divinely revealed to them is to be discerned in the notion of "confessing God's name." That this expression is employed in 15:2 as a metaphor for true obedience is obvious from the parallelism: "For who, O God, is strong except he who *confesses you in truth;* / and what person is powerful except he who *confesses your name?*" "Confesses you in truth" appears to be explicatory for "confesses your name." The enemies of the sect are obviously those who confess the name of God falsely or unworthily and are therefore hypocrites;[88] but the words "in truth" also evoke notions of valid teaching as opposed to false teaching, and we are reminded again of how the Jerusalemites would not *listen* to the righteous. It would seem, therefore, that the group could be said to be "confessionally oriented" as much as they were Torah oriented, although little indication is given of the content of their confession.

Admittedly these allusions to an exclusive revelation are few in number (again, one could hardly expect more systematic treatment given the emotive style of the psalms), yet they are enough to suggest once again the idea of a special revelation to the community that had the effect of setting them off from the rest of Israel. While it may be that the partisan spirit was not as radical or as forcefully articulated as it was at Qumran,[89] the tone of these psalms is nevertheless strong enough to indicate that this division was more well defined and of greater consequence than what would normally exist among "fraternities."

The emphasis on revelation in all these writings offers compelling testimony of an exclusive orientation since they regularly imply and sometimes make quite explicit that adherence to the content of the revelation is essential for living righteously and avoiding judgment. Words of Moses recorded in the publicly recognized Torah (Deut. 29:29) may have partly provided the impetus for such a belief: "The secret things *(ha-nistārōt)* belong to the LORD our God; but the things that are revealed *(wᵉha-niglōt)* belong to us and to our children forever, that we may do *all (kāl)* the words of this law." Here, "secret things" and "things revealed" recall the division between *nistārōt* and *niglōt* made at

---

87. Εἰς ἅπαξ has been taken to mean "once again," "all at once," or "once for all" (Wright, *OTP,* 2:652 n. *j*). Our translation allows that the expression may well reflect an underlying יחד (cf. H. E. Ryle and M. R. James, *ΨΑΛΜΟΙ ΣΟΛΟΜΩΝΤΟΣ,* 1891, 14).

88. Cf. ὑποκρινομένων . . . ὑπεκρίνοντο, 4:20-22, etc.

89. Cf. Sanders, 1977, 405.

Qumran. The "all" in this passage may also have been taken to imply that not only knowing the *niglōt,* but discovering the *nistārōt* as well, was *necessary* in order to fulfill the Law completely (cf. esp. *1 En.* 104:10-13, which especially seems to allude to this passage and its context). A few lines further on (Deut. 30:11-14) are more words that may have been taken as suggestive of the existence of "additional" revelation: "this commandment . . . is not in heaven, that you should say, 'Who will go up for us to heaven, and bring it to us, that we may hear it and do it?' Neither is it beyond the sea, that you should say, 'Who will go over the sea for us, and bring it to us, that we may hear it and do it?' But the word is very near you; it is in your mouth and in your heart, so that you can do it." While such passages were probably originally designed for quite opposite purposes — namely, to promote the *nonenigmatic* nature of revelation (the commandment is *simple!*) — and may actually have been intended to *discourage* speculation and the accumulation of laws and revelation, there exists evidence from a later period (notably the treatment of the passage by Paul in Rom. 10:6-8) that the verses in fact *had* been interpreted as an invitation to search the heavens and earth for *further* revelation.[90] It is to be admitted, moreover, that even a sensible reading of this passage might have taken it as an invitation to search *within oneself* ("in your heart") for the full exposition and revelation of the Law that was only partially written in the public Torah — and this might have been the understanding held by some of our groups. Whatever the origins for the idea, one would appear to be justified in viewing the revelation in question as "saving revelation." Whether knowledge of the teachings was thought in itself to procure salvation (as in later Gnostic thought) or whether revelation served only as an instrument making salvation *possible* for those who obeyed, perhaps by *preventing* nonredeemable transgression, has not yet been determined (see further below). It is enough to note here only that these teachings were not considered "optional" by those who embraced them.

Legal Criteria

The role of teaching or revelation for defining the true people of God is exemplified particularly well when it comes to certain legal matters. Thus the idea of legal criteria for membership in the saved community is in some respects merely another category of revelatory criteria. Some laws are unique in that they are presented as matters of revelation given to the righteous; it is usually these same laws that the group believes Israel has overlooked, though they are

---

90. Cf. M. A. Elliott, "Romans 9–11 and Jewish Remnant Theology," 1986, 192-93, 192 n. 25, for this and rabbinic texts.

of utmost urgency. A preeminent example of this type of legal material concerns the liturgical calendar. Because of the importance of the calendar issue as an illustration of the serious potential for division created by conflicting legislation, we will give it considerable attention here.

The Calendar

The subject of the calendar in Judaism is complex. While it is widely acknowledged that certain sectarian groups rejected the calendar employed by the official cult in Jerusalem, debate has arisen over the exact identity of the calendar they favored: Was this sectarian calendar a relatively recent innovation,[91] or did it possess (as is claimed by this literature) a precedent in ancient Jewish liturgical practice?[92] And, if the latter, what occasioned the loss of its influence and its eventual revival?[93] Was this calendar ever actually used in either the sectarian or official cult, or did it exist only in theory?[94] Are several different calendars represented by the various writings, or is there something common to them all?[95] Perhaps the only conclusion on which scholars generally agree is that the sectarian calendar(s) is (are) to be *contrasted* with the calendar used at the same time in Jerusalem.[96] The sectarian groups were, therefore, at least unanimous in their *dissent*

91. R. T. Beckwith, "The Earliest Enoch Literature and Its Calendar," 1981, 379-80, 399-400; J. M. Baumgarten, "The Calendars of the Book of Jubilees and the Temple Scroll," 1987a, 76.

92. A. Jaubert, *The Date of the Last Supper,* 1965, 38-45; S. Zeitlin, *The Rise and Fall of the Judaean State,* 1968-69, 1:30; Talmon, 1986, 113-39; J. Morgenstern, "The Calendar of the Book of Jubilees, Its Origin and Its Character," 1955, 37-54.

93. For theories, see Morgenstern, 1955, 74-75; Jaubert, 1965, 45-46; Leaney, 1966, 21-25; Zeitlin, 1968-69, 1:30; Beckwith, 1981, 385; J. C. VanderKam, "2 Maccabees 6,7a and Calendrical Change in Jerusalem," 1981 (= 1984, 97-102); P. R. Davies, "Calendrical Change and Qumran Origins," 1983, 83-84.

94. Cf. Morgenstern (1955, 64), who posits that the calendar was basically theoretical, used only for festivals and sabbaths; or J. van Goudoever ("Celebration of Torah," 1988, 461-62), who feels that only Qumran put this calendar into effect. B. E. Thiering (*The Gospels and Qumran,* 1981, 25-53) traces what she thinks to be evidence, largely resident in what she calls "Pesher-Language," for the use of this calendar in both Judaism and Christianity.

95. Those who maintain that a basic solar calendar was more or less shared by all the groups include Jaubert (1965, 17-21), S. Talmon ("The Calendar Reckoning of the Sect from the Judaean Desert," 1965), VanderKam (1981, 55), and van Goudoever (1988, 461). Those who distinguish between various kinds of calendars used by the sects include J. Obermann ("Calendaric Elements in the Dead Sea Scrolls," 1956, 294), Wacholder (1983, 54-59), and Baumgarten (1987a, 73-75).

96. Morgenstern, 1955, 74-75; Jaubert, 1965, 52; Beckwith, 1981, 384. This is espe-

from and *protest* against the calendar used in Jerusalem. This would suggest, *a priori* at least, that some measure of agreement also existed among these groups as to the basic constitution and arrangement of the *proper* calendar, but this is far from certain. We cannot hope to solve the many problems raised by the calendar question, and we do not intend to try. We wish only to clarify the extent to which the calendar was an issue for the groups involved and the extent to which the issue served to divide them from the rest of Judaism. In what way was the calendar believed to define and limit the saved community?

Of all these writings, *Jubilees* most unambiguously defends a 364-day solar calendar — though even here there is some difference of opinion over its exact constitution.[97] More significant and quite beyond question, however, is the singular importance granted to the issue in *Jubilees*. Submission to this calendar was considered by the author to be essential if the feasts and holy days were to be celebrated faithfully. This becomes particularly clear in the sixth chapter:

> For I know and henceforth I shall make you know . . . lest they forget the feasts of the covenant and walk in the feasts of the gentiles, after their errors and after their ignorance. And there will be those who will examine the moon diligently because it will corrupt the times and it will advance from year to year ten days. Therefore, the years will come to them as they corrupt and make a day of testimony a reproach and a profane day a festival, and they will mix up everything, a holy day profaned and a profane for a holy day . . . after you have died your sons will be corrupted so that they will not make a year only three hundred and sixty-four days. (vv. 35-38)

The repeated use of the word "corrupt"[98] in this passage (especially "your sons will be corrupted") sounds forceful and generalizing, as does the expression "they will mix up everything," implying that the calendrical error of the apostates is merely part of the pervading lapse of obedience in Israel. The passage also associates the eating of blood (v. 38) with calendrical error, suggesting the relevance of both for maintaining the covenant. More will be said below about the importance of the calendar for keeping the covenant, but it is clear enough from this passage that sin against the 364-day solar calendar of *Jubilees* was felt to implicate Israel in serious corruption.

---

cially evident with regard to Qumran. 1QpHab 11.6-8 speaks of a time when the Wicked Priest, the archenemy of the sect, sought to destroy the *moreh* and his community on the day of their Passover. This story is hardly comprehensible if it does not imply the use of a calendar by the sect at variance with that in Jerusalem (cf. Jeremias, 1963, 53-57).

97. Cf. Baumgarten, 1987a, 77. The theory of J. T. Rook ("A Twenty-eight-Day Month Tradition in the Book of Jubilees," 1981) seems particularly indefensible.

98. *Yāmāsenu* √ *māsana*, "decay," "be corrupt, rotten, ruined" (*CDG*, 35).

145

When we come to the various sections of *1 Enoch,* we are on less certain ground than with *Jubilees* as regards the identity of the calendar. But as to the importance of the matter there is again little reason for doubt. Some have suggested that the strongly polemical aspects of the presentation found in *Jubilees* are missing in *1 Enoch,*[99] concluding that *1 Enoch,* while upholding the sectarian calendar, must have originated from a time before the calendar had become a major issue in Judaism. Other scholars, however, have held that any allusion to the calendar intimates strong difference of opinion, and we have already noted how the polemic emerges rather more strongly in *1 Enoch* than might be perceived by modern readers insulated by time from the tensions surrounding calendrical debate. Moreover, it requires little interpretive dexterity to discern behind the intricate descriptions of the heavenly bodies in the Astronomical Book a more than casual concern for the use of the proper calendar to ensure the correct observance of the feasts and sabbaths — which is acknowledged by all recent scholars. The motivations for these extensive and detailed cosmographies are, in view of the debate, obvious enough; since an apology for a calendar is being made by these authors, they are naturally concerned to demonstrate its authority as exhibited clearly in nature.[100] This cosmic and revelatory type of defense of the "sectarian" calendar may also have implied a deliberate repudiation of other means of calendar determination, particularly that used by the Jerusalem authorities, who claimed to be empowered to decide vital calendrical matters but who no doubt did so on grounds that were considered quite unsatisfactory to our writers.[101]

Calendar polemic thus constitutes the general background of this presentation, and it is in line with this debate that the more immediate purpose of the author/compiler of the Astronomical Book becomes apparent in 80:6-8:

> Many of the chiefs of the stars shall make errors in respect to the orders[102]
> given to them; they shall change their courses and functions and not appear

99. VanderKam, 1981, 57, for whom reference to the moon points to a purely scientific interest (1984, 91).

100. The purpose of the visions — what amounts to an apology for the revelatory authority of the calendar — is established in 82:7: "True is the matter of the exact computation of that which has been recorded; for Uriel . . . has revealed to me and breathed over me concerning the luminaries, the months, the festivals, the years, and the days."

101. Their claim may have been based on traditions believed to go back to Moses, or on lunar observation; cf. Obermann, 1956, 291-93. While these authorities were empowered to delay the feasts to avoid conflict with the sabbath, our groups probably argued that human decision had no part to play in this important matter and that the calendar was preordained. Cf., again, 1QpHab 11.6-8.

102. The important word is *te'zaz,* "commandment," "decree," "ordinance," which is frequently employed in these discussions. Black (1985, 253) renders the whole phrase

during the seasons which have been prescribed for them. All the orders of the stars shall harden against the sinners and the conscience of those that dwell upon the earth. They (the stars) shall err against them (the sinners); and modify all their courses. Then they (the sinners) shall err and take them (the stars) to be gods. And evil things shall be multiplied upon them; and plagues shall come upon them, so as to destroy all.

This passage does not directly argue against the lunar calendar so much as it predicts certain incongruities that will occur between the movements of the heavenly bodies, on the one hand, and the order prescribed for them by the sectarian calendar, on the other. It may be that these incongruities are ultimately to be blamed on the errant behavior of sinners. Alternatively, a more deterministic view of things may lie behind the passage, which would then imply that the *proper* order of the heavenly bodies has first been *concealed* from the sinners, with the tragic result that they misread the heavenly signs and, only because of this, both they and the heavenly bodies became errant. Whichever approach one follows, it is nevertheless implied that sinners have *disobeyed the calendar*. It would appear in fact that the chief sin according to this book is disregard for the calendar. This can be seen, for example, in 82:5, where the particular reason for culpability is failure to recognize the four intercalary days:[103] "On this account there are people that err; they count them in the computation of the year; for the people make error and do not recognize them accurately; for they belong to the reckoning of the year."

It is not important whether the calendar of Astronomical Enoch is to be viewed as identical to that of *Jubilees,* for it is the intensity of the debate that is of concern here. Thus it is of little instance that some scholars of late have gathered contrary evidence, either from internal indications in the Astronomical Book itself or from fragments of a similar astronomical work found at Qumran, to the effect that the Enochian writings actually reflect a tolerance, concession, or even sanction of the use of a lunar calendar.[104] Moreover, whatever genuine differences exist among the various calendars, these attempts have

---

"shall stray from the commandments," taking *te'zaz* as predicate; Knibb (*AOT,* 270) takes *te'zaz* (Gk. ἐντολή) as a modifier of "stars" (Gk. τῶν ἀστέρων): "heads of the stars in command." The word is generally used of the laws (in the sense of principles) determining the courses of the heavenly luminaries, but which the stars are somehow able to disobey. We accordingly accept Isaac's translation.

103. Cf., e.g., Charles, 1912, 175. In spite of these textual difficulties, it is obvious that these four days are necessary to maintain the accuracy of a solar calendar.

104. Some have interpreted those sections in the Astronomical Book (along with others in the 4QEnastr MSS at Qumran) that give long descriptions of the courses of the moon (cf. *1 En.* 73:1–74:17) as indicating a certain tolerance, and even sanction, of the use of the lunar calendar (cf. Wacholder, 1983, 36-38; Baumgarten, 1987a, 75-77).

not been successful in overturning the majority view that in all these cases we are dealing with the defense of a basic solar calendar of some kind.[105] Besides the fact that in each case the polemic seems to demand a calendar widely divergent from the establishment calendar (which was lunar), the fragmentary condition of the Aramaic fragments from Qumran (4QEnastr) makes them difficult to assess, and the data they provide can also be made to produce a 364-day calendar similar to, if not identical with, that approved by *Jubilees*.[106] Milik, who argues for an identity between the calendar of the Qumran fragments of *1 Enoch* and that of the Ethiopic version, nevertheless posits that the author of the fragments did not present a calendar quite in the form of *1 Enoch* 72–75 consisting of twelve months of 30 days and four intercalary days. He comes to this conclusion largely because none of the extant fragments corresponds to those chapters from Ethiopic *Enoch*. Milik assumes that the author must have been attempting rather to fit the *lunar* arrangement into a 364-day period by the addition of an intercalary month every three years. He offers quite convincing proof for this from 4QEnastr[a] and 4QEnastr[b] 3.1-2, 5-6 (= *1 En.* 72:25-27), where the lunar calendar appears to be synchronized with the solar calendar.[107] That a more or less direct allusion to the four intercalary days (in the guise of the "chiefs of thousands"; cf. *1 En.* 82:12) finds its way into one fragment (4QEnastr[b] 28, ll. 2-3) confirms, at least, that the author was concerned to pre-

---

105. Charles, we believe, properly recognized that the moon is merely introduced to show the *distinctions* between the sun and moon (1912, 158). Everywhere in the Astronomical Book the superlative brightness and consistency of the light of the sun, as well as its dependability, are emphasized (73:2-3, 5-8; 73:1; 74:16-17) and contrasted with the irregular and inconsistent character of the moon (74:11, 14, 16; 79:3-5); cf. *Jub.* 6:36-37.

106. The purpose of the astronomical visions in 4QEnastr is not as clear as for the Eth. version, mainly because the condition of the MSS prevents us from making confident judgments; for the same reason, however, we may not easily conclude that the purpose of the two editions was essentially *different*. Thus when some scholars deny that the relatively early 4QEnastr MSS (J. T. Milik, ed., *The Books of Enoch*, 1976, 273, dates the *a* MS as early as the end of the third century B.C. for reasons of chirography and orthography) imply anything about the solar calendar, the argument is from silence. The portions that have been salvaged largely focus on the movements of the moon, the winds, and the stars and correspond primarily to *1* (Eth.) *Enoch* 73-74, 76, 78, 82, chapters that also speak of the variance in the amounts of light put out by the moon and describe the winds and stars — all of which is comparable to the similar chapters from the Eth. version. Milik (5) estimates that we possess only 30 percent of the total text represented by the fragments of the Astronomical Book. Furthermore, if the original "sectarian" context of 4QEnastr was largely the same as Astronomical Enoch — and the burden of proof clearly lies on those who would deny this — then it is much safer to assume that the MS represented by 4QEnastr originally possessed similar commitments to the solar calendar (this is also the conclusion of Milik [7]).

107. Milik, 1976, 274, 283.

sent a 364-day solar calendar, since intercalary days would otherwise have little relevance to the discussion.[108] The result is that at most one can only speak of *coordination,* not *concession,* when it comes to the relationship of the calendar espoused by works like 4QEnastr to the lunar calendar of the establishment, as Milik has also attempted to argue.[109] As for practical reasons that the author would attempt to synchronize the official lunar calendar to his own solar calendar, these are obvious enough, for this would facilitate the comfortable use of a solar calendar in an environment that was felt to be hopelessly entrenched in its use of a lunar calendar. This would naturally suit an early stage of calendrical debate from a time before the polemic had advanced to the point represented by the Astronomical Book.

Milik's theory would certainly explain why nothing corresponding to the direct and polemical charge against the lunar calendar in *1 Enoch* 72 and 80 has been found among the fragments. If the Aramaic Astronomical Enoch is as early as Milik suggests, there would be plenty of opportunity, especially considering the radical abridgment represented by the Ethiopic version, for the developing situation to invite more direct polemic in later editions. But while Milik's theory may accurately portray the facts, it should be remembered that it is only one theory to explain the preoccupation with the movements of the moon in the fragments. It may rather be, as was also true with Ethiopic *Enoch,* that the careful tracking of the moon's journeys merely served as a counteroffensive against the use of the lunar calendar by demonstrating in detail how the moon "falls behind" the sun and is therefore inferior to it. Indeed, there is positive evidence for this. One of the fragments does preserve a derogatory reference to the moon "falling behind" the sun (4QEnastr[b] 26, l. 3).[110] Regardless of whether Milik's theory can be accepted, however, one still observes that in all the manuscripts the central importance of the sun in calendrical reckoning is vigorously defended at all costs against capitulation to the dominant lunar calendar.

It is rather unfortunate that the preoccupation of scholars with the calendar issue in the Astronomical Book has tended to distract from the importance of this issue in other sections of the Enochian corpus, particularly in the Book of Watchers (*1 Enoch* 1–36). We have already drawn attention to indications of a calendar theme in chs. 1–5,[111] namely, the way these chapters dwell excessively

---

108. Cf. Milik, 1976, 296 n. The arithmetic for this equation is quite simple: the addition of a 30-day lunar month every three years effectively synchronizes a 354-day lunar arrangement with the 364-day solar calendar ($364 \times 3 = 354 \times 3 + 30$).

109. Milik, 1976, 274-96.

110. Note the emphatic expression מחסר מן דבר, "being diminished (or found wanting) because it follows behind."

111. Cf. also Beckwith, 1981, 389, 94, 401, who mentions the important role of the calendar in chs. 6–36 but does not explicitly mention it in regard to chs. 1–5 (although it is

on the order-in-creation theme[112] and the way the interpretive section (see esp. 2:1) explicitly condemns Israel for abandoning the calendar. There is also a significantly close relationship in terms of subject matter and language between these chapters and the Astronomical Book. In the latter the description of nature's orderliness is not limited to that of the sun and moon but extends also to that of winds, mountains, and rivers (chs. 76–77); in the Book of Watchers the descriptions of seasons, trees, etc. (chs. 3–5), also accompany the descriptions of the heavenly luminaries (ch. 2), which are all taken together as examples of steadfastness in doing the will of God. The theme of *order in creation* is also extended throughout the latter part of the Book of Watchers (chs. 17–36),[113] where Enoch goes on heavenly journeys and personally witnesses the order of the entire cosmos. In a manner similar to 80:6-8, which was cited above, this book also points out the transgressions of the stars and their resulting judgment: "they are the ones which have *transgressed the commandments of God from the beginning of their rising* because they *did not arrive punctually*" (18:15; cf. also 21:1-6; 33:2-4). The startling coincidence of terminology and many other literary parallels also point to a common fund of ideas, if not to a direct relationship of sources, for chs. 1–5 and the Astronomical Book,[114] and one can conclude that both are rooted in the same calendar debate.

---

perhaps implied, 401). Since, however, the latter chapters build on the same themes as the earlier ones (cf. L. Hartman, *Asking for a Meaning*, 1979, 143-44, who argues this through appeal to the structure of both), it is not surprising that the calendar is introduced so dramatically in chs. 1–5 as well.

112. For the relation of the cosmological theme to the calendar, see Beckwith, 1981, 401.

113. While Hartman does not pick up on the calendrical connection, he does argue that chs. 1–5 need to be interpreted in close connection with chs. 6–36 (1979, 143-44). If, as he suggests, the latter chapters are an enlargement on the earlier ones, then we can perhaps see how the fall of the Watchers in chs. 6ff. serves to explain the sin that led, among other things, to the corruption of the calendar in chs. 1–5.

114. A comparison should especially be made between the language and expression of 2:1; 5:4; and 72:1-3. Further similarities are evident in 72:35-36; 74:1-2, 17; 79:1-2; 80:6-7. Many of these similarities are evident only in the Eth., which would presumably suggest similarity in underlying editions. On general language common to both, cf. "luminaries [lit. 'lights'] (of heaven)," *berhānāt samāy*, 2:1; 72:1, 2; 75:2, 3; "(they) do not [or 'shall'] change their ways," *yemāyeṭu fenāqatihomu*, 2:1; 80:6 (cf. "[and] they do not divert [i.e., 'do not disobey'] from their appointed order," *waʾiyetʿāddawu ʾemtezazamu reʾyeqa*, 2:1 — repeated for emphasis and to serve the covenantal *rîb* pattern); "(according to its) season," *babazamanu*, 2:1; 72:1; 79:2. Frequent references can be found in both passages to "law," "commandment," "order," all of which stem from *teʾzāz* (2:1; 5:4; 72:2, 35; 74:1 [twice]; 79:2; 80:6; the verb in 72:36; 80:6); "systematic"/"rules" or "orders," *šeruʿ/šerʿāta* (2:1; 79:1 [twice]). Other terms are similar in meaning — e.g., words expressing going and coming, moving and settling, or rising and setting (*mashrā* in 72:1; *yegabeʾ wayewaḍeʾ* in 72:35;

As was already pointed out, there is also an important relationship between the calendar presentation in the Book of Watchers and the form of a covenantal *rîb* in which it is clothed. The reason for this would seem to be that calendrical sin is being put forward as the chief item in the list of transgressions against the covenant. This may even be implied in the imprecations in the introductory section of the Book of Watchers:

> But as for you, you have not been longsuffering and you have not done the commandments [*te'zaz;* perhaps not insignificantly the same word used in both 18:15 and 80:6-8 for the commands given to the stars] of the Lord, but you have transgressed and spoken slanderously grave and harsh words with your impure mouths against his greatness. . . . you shall curse your days, and the years of your life shall perish and multiply in eternal execration; and there will not be any mercy unto you. . . . (5:4-5)

In any event, one can determine from the contents of the book that it is largely sin against the calendar that has elicited this condemnation with its warnings of "eternal execration" and language invoking the curses of the covenant.

The writings of Qumran offer further proof that the calendar was a major issue for division. The importance of the calendar is symbolized by the fact that even entrance into the community is made dependent on agreement to properly maintain the times appointed for worship (cf. CD 3.14-15; 6.18-19;[115] 1QS

'egezi'ena wakamaz yewaḍe' wayewe' in 72:36; *wamegbā'u saba yegabe' ka'eneta* in 72:35; *yešareq waya'areb* in 2:1. Some terms are suggestive of order in creation, such as "positions" (*manbara* in 74:1, 2, 17 [twice]; 75:2), "procession" (*wabamuḍā'u* in 79:2), "course" (*mexqaru* in 72:35), "system" or "course" (*meḥqaro* twice in 74:1); "their ranks . . . authorities" (*ḥezabihomu . . . šelṭānomu* in 72:1; cf. "order," "way," "systematic" above). The use of the *baba-* preposition, "according to/in respect of (a certain defined category of order)" (*babazamanu* in 2:1 and *babaḥezabihomu . . . babašelṭānomu . . . wababazamanomu . . . babasememu* in 72:1), evidences a striking stylistic parallel between the passages (according to Dillmann, *Gloss,* 210 possibly = κατά); it probably reflects a relatively emphatic construction like עַל, פִּי, or כְּפִי, common formulations in the MT with respect to commandments, as here: cf. Gen. 45:21; Num. 3:16; 1 Chron. 12:23; etc. Finally, the notion of not doing commandments in one passage (5:4) finds parallels in human erring (75:2) and erring by the stars (80:6).

115. שבתות קדשו ומועדי כבודו, "his holy Sabbaths and his glorious times (lit. 'appointed times of glory')" (3.14-15), is probably to be understood as referring to the timing for the feasts, inasmuch as sabbaths and feasts are frequently treated together. The same can be said of CD 6.18-19, where in the context המועדות must refer to the festivals. The language of the passage could refer to the seventh, or sabbath, week of jubilees and thus to epochs or dispensations ("times") of the world, but how Israel could be said to have "strayed" with regard to these leaves an insurmountable problem. מועד is certainly best translated "times." "Feasts" (Dupont-Sommer, 1961, 126), while not a literal rendering, ac-

1.7-15; 3.9-10[116]) — a criterion that would be inexplicable if it did not infer a break with the conventional or official calendar in use at the time. The Temple Scroll devotes no less than sixteen columns to "the restatement of the sacrificial calendar," and although doubts have been expressed about the type of calendar espoused by the author of this scroll, there is certainly enough evidence to point to a solar calendar.[117] Nevertheless, there is again some difference of opinion among scholars over the Qumran calendar. A definitive identification of this calendar with the other sectarian calendars will perhaps never be possible with the sometimes ambiguous evidence available from the scrolls. Baumgarten, who has in other respects been the advocate of the preeminence of the solar calendar among the sects, points to a very fragmented text (4Q503, so-called Daily Prayers) that he says identifies the days of the month, and the blessing of each day, with the phases of the moon.[118] On the other hand, M. Baillet (in the original publication of the fragments)[119] was able to argue that the lunar calendar was deliberately synchronized on a three-year basis with the solar calendar in this text for practical or apologetic purposes, since the first day of the first month of the lunar calendar is made to correspond with the first day of the first month of the solar calendar every three years. This suggests a de-

---

curately represents the thought of the author, who had in mind here the annual and weekly celebrations of the cult rather than any lengthy period or dispensation.

116. While the phrase הנגלות למועדי תעודותם (1.9) has been rendered "the revelations concerning their regular feasts" by Dupont-Sommer (1961, 73), others have argued that the subject here is not the times for feasts but the times set aside for the distinctive exegetical exercises of the *yaḥad* (Wernberg-Møller, 1957, 47; Leaney, 1966, 120). However, there is little other indication in the context that times set aside for receiving revelation are in mind here, and ll. 13-15 virtually demand an interpretation referring to the times set by the calendar, מועדיהם being the word employed for the feasts (and such times as are set by the liturgical calendar) in CD 3.14 and 6.18-19 (cf. also Knibb, 1987, 82). The references in l. 14 to "anticipating" and "delaying" the times moreover suggest a tampering with the calendar.

117. Wacholder, 1983, 13, but for his views on this calendar, cf. 55. Yadin furthermore concludes from the twenty-six, rather than the official twenty-four, courses *(mišmarot)* of priests prescribed in the War Scroll that the sect accepted the fifty-two-week calendar of *Jubilees* and *1 Enoch* (as each course was active for two weeks per year; cf. Y. Yadin, *The Scroll of the War of the Sons of Light against the Sons of Darkness,* 1962, 204-6). For doubts, see Wise (1990a, 11), whose tracing of the history of interpretation nevertheless reveals that most scholars have independently vindicated Yadin's identification for a variety of reasons. M. Barker ("The Temple Measurements and the Solar Calendar," 1989, 63-64) adds important evidence to this consensus, employing trigonometry to determine that the gatehouses of the new temple serve to predict solstices and equinoxes and thus to establish the solar calendar.

118. J. M. Baumgarten, "4Q503 (Daily Prayers) and the Lunar Calendar," 1986.

119. *DJD,* 7:104ff.

liberate synchronization, much as Milik suggested for 4QEnastr. Perhaps this was simply for the purpose of bringing long-established liturgical practice into line with the demands of the solar calendar, which would have been especially desirable during a process of liturgical reform. And it should be noted that when all is said and done the actual dates arrived at for feasts and Sabbaths are those demanded by the solar, not the lunar, calendar. All things considered, the value of such fragments as these as evidence for the Qumran calendar is minimal. The text of 4Q503 is extremely fragmented, and some of the most important passages have required radical reconstruction.[120] Moreover, the description of the phases of the moon, from what can be recovered of it, is very close to the style of *1 Enoch* 73–75 and 78–79 and could again serve the purpose of illustrating the inferiority of the moon — although admittedly again hardly enough of the text remains to determine this.

Thus again it would seem to be more a matter of *coordination* than *concession* when it comes to this group's posture toward the lunar calendar. The solar calendar is once again implicitly promoted by this procedure, and the practice hardly need be taken as a compromise of the group's fundamental commitment to that calendar.[121] That the blessings are relegated to lunar days does not imply respect for the lunar calendar itself. The blessings may merely have been adopted from an earlier lunar liturgy with the purpose of transferring them unaltered to the solar calendar. It seems unlikely that traditional liturgical material would all be abandoned simply because it had been earlier associated with an apostate calendar; an adjustment of the material to fit the calendar authorized by the Qumranites would seem a likely and appropriate procedure, especially during the earlier period of their attempts at liturgical reform. Such an approach to the question has been taken by Eisenman and Wise in their publication of two other texts that, like 4Q503, also attempt a harmonization of the lunar and solar calendars in relation to the *mišmarot* (cf. 4Q320 and 4Q321). Their comments are worth quoting in full:

> Although the authors of the Qumran calendrical texts disdained the lunisolar calendar, a number of their writings synchronize the two versions. . . . The reasons for this synchronization are not entirely clear, but two suggestions may be somewhere close to the mark. First, these authors considered all time holy and its measurement ordained by God. It was probably thought necessary that someone keep a proper record of its passing. Since the opponents of the authors could not be relied upon to do so — following, as they did, an illicit system — the Qumran authors took the responsibility. In order to dis-

120. Cf. *DJD*, vol. 7, plates 35, 37, 39, 41, 43, 45, and 47.
121. Cf. the comments of Eisenman and Wise on two similar fragments (4Q320 and 4Q321; *The Dead Sea Scrolls Uncovered*, 1992, 106-19, esp. 106-8).

charge this responsibility, it would be as necessary to be able to point out errors as to know the correct answers. Thus, they tracked time by the system of their opponents as well as by their own. Second, the authors of these texts certainly expected that at some time they would be in power in Jerusalem. At that time, of course, they would impose the solar calendar, but in order to know where they were in the year, they would have to know both the false lunisolar date and the real solar date. In fact, there is some evidence that at certain points in the Second Temple period the solar calendar actually was imposed, at least for short periods.[122]

Accordingly these authors take the Cave 4 fragments as basic confirmation that the calendar at Qumran "is purely solar."

That these texts attempt to synchronize the lunar and solar calendars thus confirms the importance of the solar calendar — even if such texts lack the polemic of *Jubilees*. The fact that the community library preserved copies of *Jubilees* (and *Enoch*) could also be taken as evidence that it is the common commitment to a solar calendar that motivated all the calendrical passages we have dealt with here.[123] Accordingly, whatever one should decide about the exact identification and definition of the calendar(s) at Qumran, it is nevertheless unmistakable that, for all the authors concerned, the matter of the proper calendar was of extreme consequence. If we follow VanderKam's reconstruction of the events associated with the earliest calendrical crisis in Jerusalem,[124] it may even be that this crisis was largely responsible for the original exile of the community — though this may be making too much of the evidence.[125]

Calendar, Covenant, and Order in Creation

The importance of the issue for all these groups can be further illuminated by a consideration of some possible *origins* for the sectarian calendar. It has been suggested that one can discern these origins in the Hebrew Scriptures,[126] and J. Obermann has demonstrated the large debt of the calendrical debate to bibli-

122. Eisenman and Wise, 1992, 107-8; cf. 106-19.
123. Confirming evidence is supplied by 4Q252, which attempts to rationalize several inconsistencies in stories from Genesis. The Noah story contains a detailed defense of the 364-day year (364 days being explicitly mentioned in this regard in 2.3). 4QMMT also unambiguously insists on the use of the solar calendar (cf. H. Stegemann, "The Qumran Essenes," 1992, 1:83-166, 120, 123-24).
124. VanderKam, 1981, passim; cf. Beckwith, 1981, passim.
125. Cf. Davies, 1983, passim.
126. Cf. our treatment of CD 7.9–8.2. According to 1 Kings 12, the calendar was a major issue in the division of "Ephraim and Judah" at the time of Jeroboam I.

cal terminology.[127] One passage often cited by scholars in regard to the calendar is Gen. 1:16, which says of the fourth day of creation: "And God made the two great lights, *the greater light to rule the day*, and the lesser light to rule the night." A connection between this verse and the importance of the sun in determining the calendar was apparently seen by the author of *Jubilees*: "And the LORD set the sun as a great sign upon the earth for days, sabbaths, months, feast days, years, sabbaths of years, jubilees . . ." (2:9). It is noteworthy that the moon is nowhere mentioned in this midrashic expansion.

In *Jubilees* the 364-day calendar also seems to be grounded in the biblical account of the flood.[128] At first this seems surprising; however, it would have been quite natural for our authors to connect the giving of the calendar with the events of the flood, particularly in the context of the extensive angel theodicy associated with the flood traditions, where the granting of knowledge of the solar and lunar calendars is presented as the work of good and evil angels respectively.[129] Since the author of *Jubilees* considered the covenant with Noah the first and most important of all the covenants,[130] this would also provide a clue why the same author considered the calendar as still having serious implications for keeping the covenants among his contemporaries. Evidence for the association of the flood, the angels, the calendar, and the covenant can be found in at least one place in the Qumran scrolls as well, in a passage which implies that the "original" sin of the angels was disobeying the calendar.[131] It is highly likely also that the account of the fall of the Watchers in *1 Enoch* 6–16 is partially intended to develop the calendrical/covenantal presentation of the introductory chapters (chs. 1–5), introducing the fall as it does in order to explain the breach of covenant and accompanying failure to observe the calendar. In chs. 7–8, which teach that sin against the calendar was first propagated at the time of Noah at the fall of the Watcher-angels, it is also said that the Watchers were "[taking] wives unto themselves" and teaching various forbidden arts, with the result that "the earth brought an accusation against the oppressors" (7:1-6), apparently a ref-

---

127. Obermann, 1956, 285-90, who comments that the sect apparently went so far as to purposefully avoid rabbinic calendrical terms that did not have the Scriptures as their source (290); cf. Charles, 1912, 147; O. Neugebauer, "The 'Astronomical' Chapters of the Ethiopic Book of Enoch," 1985, 386-87.

128. Cf. *Jub.* 6:17-38; Genesis 7–8; VanderKam, 1981, 53 n. 4.

129. Beckwith, 1981, 390.

130. Endres, 1987, 226-27.

131. Cf. Talmon, 1965, 165. CD 2.18 connects the fall of the Watchers with a great trespass. The passage goes on to include Noah's sons in this sin (3.1), along with most of Israel from that time on (cf. 3.4-12). We know from 3.13ff. that this sin was abandoning the calendar, since the reference to the sin is carried right through to that passage.

erence to the covenantal cosmic witness theme.[132] What is significant, however, is what resulted from this cosmic reaction, including such things as the learning of astrology, the knowledge of "signs" (obviously heavenly manifestations), and "the seeing of the stars" (8:3). The list ends with "and Asder'el taught the course of the moon as well as the deception of man" (8:3) — which would seem to allude to the introduction of the lunar calendar. Baumgarten finds problems of synchronization in the flood accounts that seem to cast doubt on the legend as the origin of the solar calendar, but these are not insurmountable.[133]

On the whole, however, while it is clear why these authors would associate the calendar with the flood as the *occasion* for its introduction, there is nothing to suggest that flood traditions were themselves first responsible for generating the idea of a solar calendar *per se*. Nor does this connection explain why the calendar issue became so critically important. In *Jubilees* the calendar is also believed to have been revealed to Enoch (4:17-18), Abraham (17:28-30), Jacob (36:29), Levi (30:19-20), and Moses (cf. 6:32; 50:1-5), but none of these connections serves to illuminate the origins and significance of the calendar debate any better. With the exception of Gen. 1:16, which certainly seems to have been a singularly significant contributor to the belief (in regard to the choice of a solar calendar if nothing else), it would seem that attempts to relate the calendar to Scripture are only partially satisfactory, leaving open the possibility that other factors played a part.

Perhaps a better indication of where to look for the origins of the calendar debate comes with the frequent concern found in the calendar passages for the *order of creation*.[134] This order-in-creation theme appears to have been entrenched in the structure of Hebrew covenantal theology at an early time.[135] It is also evident in Judaism in its early association with wisdom concepts.[136] Rabbinic tradition, especially its legal teachings, regularly expressed a desire to order the universe of things.[137] The tendency was apparently as widespread in the

132. There may be a reference also to the blood of righteous Abel calling for vindication from the ground (Gen. 4:10; cf. also *1 En.* 8:4). However, the reference to "accusation" suggests a covenantal witness motif.

133. Cf. Baumgarten, 1987a, 76. Gen. 7:11; 8:3-4 numbers the days of the flood at 150, which would be 152 days (including the intercalary days) according to the calendar of *Jubilees*. Van Goudoever, 1988, 462-67, however, shows how the arithmetic may have been understood. Cf. also Morgenstern, 1955, 36.

134. Cf. Leaney, 1966, 21-26, 79-89.

135. Leaney, 1966, 26; Stone, 1985, 229. For the connection of order in nature with ancient covenant formulations, see Hartman, 1979, 69, 87.

136. Cf. P. Ackroyd, *Israel under Babylon and Persia*, 1970, 316-18; Schnabel, 1985, 18-19, 28-43, 112, 178-80, 225, etc.

137. Cf. J. Neusner, *Wrong Ways and Right Ways in the Study of Formative Judaism,*

Hellenistic world[138] as in Semitic thought, apparently belonging universally to the psychology of religion.[139] The relationship between the orderliness of nature (and perhaps even the calendar) and the regulations of the Law may have been inspired by passages like Psalm 19, which implicitly draws a similar connection (vv. 1-6: "The heavens are telling the glory of God . . ."; vv. 7-13: "The law of the LORD is perfect . . .").[140] It is not difficult to see, especially considering the detail with which the calendar passages outline the cosmic order, that the use of the proper calendar was thought to be one very important extension of belief in the order in creation.[141]

This connection between calendar and order of creation is particularly significant since it would also explain the similarly close connection between the calendar and the order in creation motif that is such a vital part of many covenantal passages in these writings. Perhaps this association originally took its cue from the Deuteronomic covenantal motif of the cosmic witness: "I call *heaven* [i.e., the heavenly bodies] *and earth* to witness against you this day, that I have set before you life and death, blessing and curse."[142] Perhaps the connection was also discerned in a passage such as Jer. 33:20-21, which may have been employed in support of the calendar-covenant relationship. The association of the covenant feasts and the calendar, moreover, may have been another important reason why in *Jubilees* the calendar is closely associated with Noah, the recipient of the first divine covenant, which was to serve as the paradigm for all covenants to come.[143] The calendar consequently appears as a necessary presupposition for the existence and order of all the covenants in *Jubilees*.

The order-in-creation/calendar relationship appears to be particularly influential in the covenantal traditions represented in *1 Enoch* 1–5. Here the theme of orderliness in the creation, and especially orderliness among the luminaries,

---

1988, 77-78; H. Basser, "The Development of the Pharisaic Idea of Law as a Sacred Cosmos," 1985, 115.

138. Cf. Jaubert, 1963, 197.

139. Cf. N. Cohn, *Cosmos, Chaos, and the World to Come,* 1993, though we cannot as easily accept his views about the formative function of Zoroastrian eschatology in attitudes toward order and chaos. Cohn implies that the need for order relates to the calendar, but does not go into detail (179-81).

140. Jaubert, 1963, 197.

141. Cf. Ringgren, 1963, 55-57; Leaney, 1966, 21. D. W. Suter (*Tradition and Composition in the Parables of Enoch,* 1979, 76-77) explains that the angel lists found in our literature, which are largely ornamental in nature, are similarly born out of the predisposition to order nature.

142. Deut. 30:19; cf. also Deut. 4:26; 31:28; 32:1; Isa. 1:2.

143. Cf. Morgenstern, 1955, 56-57. *Jubilees* places the origins of all the biblical covenants on the Festival of First Fruits/Weeks (the fifteenth day of the third month), which is also adopted as the authorized date for the celebration of covenant renewal.

virtually replaces the cosmic witness theme of Deut. 30:19 in the covenant formulary pattern outlined by Hartman,[144] confirming the early connection between covenantal witness and order in creation (and the calendar) alluded to above. For our purposes it is important only to emphasize that when *1 Enoch* employs for its calendrical teaching certain terms also appropriate to the order-in-creation motif,[145] it probably reveals an *early and fundamental association between the covenant formulary and concern for maintenance of the proper calendar.*[146] All this helps explain why calendar and covenant are often closely associated in these writings and, more importantly here, why sin against the calendar could be considered as *nothing less than a breach of the covenant.*

It is particularly noteworthy, therefore, that the Qumran *yaḥad* appears to have applied this covenantal association of order in creation and the maintenance of the solar calendar to their own distinctive requisites for joining the covenant community. In the opening of the Community Rule it is stated that the "volunteers" who wish to enter the "Covenant of Grace" must "behave perfectly before [God] according to all the revelations concerning their regular feasts . . ." (1QS 1.7-9). The condition of keeping the calendar is put even more emphatically in lines that follow: "they shall make no single step from all the words of God concerning their times, they shall not anticipate their times, *nor delay them* for any of their feasts [lit. 'appointed times']" (1QS 1.13-15). These words have been interpreted as a critique of the "official" rabbinic practice of legislating a short delay for the feasts (of a day or two) when necessary to avoid conflicts with sabbath sacrifices.[147] While the words "anticipate" and "delay" need not carry any such technical meaning, the passage nevertheless makes clear the superiority of the calendar of the *yaḥad* over all "corruptions." That the solar calendar possessed a built-in fail-safe mechanism against such conflicts (always placing the feasts on Wednesdays, never on sabbaths) would certainly have composed one of the obvious claims for its superiority. But certainly more pressing than such practical considerations, as far as this group was concerned, was the importance of the calendar for the keeping of covenant.[148]

Because the calendar was a matter of covenant, therefore, it was considered vitally important. But beyond this there was perhaps another reason, related to it, that the calendar was felt to be essential, a reason that also makes special sense out of the above-mentioned concern not to "delay" the feasts. This had to do with the proper *timing* of the feasts and sacrifices and the implica-

---

144. Hartman, 1979, 69, 87, and passim.
145. Note esp. "examine the luminaries of heaven," 2:1; cf. Deut. 29:1.
146. Cf. Schnabel, 1985, 179.
147. Cf. Dupont-Sommer, 1961, 73 n. 2; VanderKam, 1981, 53.
148. Cf. also CD 6.11, 17-20.

tions of this timing.[149] In *Jub.* 6:35 there is a "prophecy" about how as a result of the calendrical mix-up the sacred "feasts of the covenant" will become mundane, stripped of their sacred significance, for the people are apt to "forget the feasts of the covenant and walk in the feasts of the gentiles, after their errors and after their ignorance." V. 37 of the same passage makes it even more clear that calendrical irregularity was felt to lead to a kind of "secularization" of the feast. It speaks of a future Israel who errs in respect to the calendar, "as they corrupt and make a day of testimony a reproach *and a profane day a festival,* and they will mix up everything, *a holy day as profaned and a profane one for a holy day,* because they will set awry the months and sabbaths and feasts and jubilees." This passage states that the substitution of one day for another, whenever a feast is involved, renders a holy day profane and a profane day holy. The validity of the feasts, therefore, seems to depend directly on their correct timing, so that failure to celebrate the proper feast on the proper day disqualifies them as feasts, and, by deduction, makes the covenant renewal implied in their celebration totally *ineffective.*[150] The result is that *those who do not properly celebrate the feasts on their proper days simply miss out on the covenant.* This is also obvious when *Jubilees,* in dealing with the matter of the feast of Passover, insists on the celebration taking place on the proper day and when it states further that those who do not celebrate it accordingly will be "uprooted" from Israel (49:9). A plague will come to kill and smite on the year in which it is not properly observed (49:15). This can only mean that the Jerusalem priests and all who follow their system of sacrifice, who do not know the calendar revealed to the righteous and do not seek to follow it — which includes most of Israel — simply cannot maintain the covenant. So serious was this timing considered to be that *Jubilees* terms it an "eternal decree" (49:8), an expression particularly appropriate for laws felt to have been *abandoned* by Israel.

Like *Jubilees,* the Qumran scrolls equate the use of the wrong calendar with the confusion of the sacred and the profane. CD 6.11-20 lists various obligations accepted by those who enter the covenant (l. 11), among which are "to

149. Leaney, 1966, 89: "this correspondence [between the calendar and the structure of the universe] is very important: to alter it in any particular would throw the entire pattern of the devout and worshiping life into disharmony with the Creator."

150. As van Goudoever (1988, 466) puts it: "The right *way* and the right *day* belong to each other!" The rabbis clearly understood this. Talmon cites R. Abraham ibn Ezra: "Know that if the time-calculation of Samuel [a competing Amora] is true, our entire intercalation system is wrong and all our festive days and fasts are false, Heaven forfend" (1965, 181 n. 41). It is interesting to note in one covenantal formulary passage a repeated emphasis on "this (the same) day" (Deut. 27:9, 10, 11). It may be that this repeated reference was interpreted to mean that the covenant could only be renewed on the "same day" *each year.*

distinguish between the unclean and the clean, and to make known the distinction between *sacred and profane,* and to observe the Sabbath day according to its exact tenor, and the feasts,[151] and the Day of Fasting . . . *to set holy things apart* [i.e., to distinguish or discern days or the nature of something] according to their exact tenor . . ." (ll. 17-20). The mistiming of the feasts is clearly what makes the sacrifices of the Jerusalem Temple "vain" and therefore useless (ll. 12, 14) and why the sectarians are accordingly forbidden from taking part in them.[152] The importance of timing can be further illustrated by the observations of Jaubert, who cites certain passages from the scrolls as implying a vitally important and ongoing attempt to synchronize the heavenly and earthly worship in "perfect unison."[153] If Israel fails to synchronize its cult with the angels' heavenly cult, then how can its rituals ever be considered effective?

The idea of the correct day for each feast, therefore, as with the idea of the proper calendar generally, is no doubt a function of the covenantal demand for order in creation, an order that clearly cannot be served if the feast occurs on the wrong day. In other words, if God has established a certain order through his covenants, one must assume that he has also arranged the timing for rites that *maintain* the covenant. The insistence of *Jubilees* on the proper scheduling of the Feast of Weeks, which is given as the annual occasion for the renewal of the covenant, confirms this.[154] The importance of the exact timing of the date of this feast is everywhere made clear, as several crucial events through Israel's history are said to have occurred on this same date, the fifteenth of the third month.[155] This correspondence of dates can hardly be considered accidental; such concern for timing reveals the intention of the author to make absolutely clear his position regarding the calendar and the feasts and to make clear the tragic consequences of ignoring this timing. This lining up of dates merges with *Jubilees'* fixation with reconnecting contemporary practice with its beginnings, carrying calculations right back in order to even reestablish the rotation of the week on the foundation of the very first week (i.e., to be certain the "Wednesday" of every week is the same "Wednesday" as the first week; cf. Gen. 1:1–2:3, especially the events of the "fourth day" of 1:16, as noted above). Thus the proclivity of these groups to order history according to a predetermined scheme belongs to the tendency to follow the order of God in all things chronological, so that historical determinism and calendrical order would seem to be related.[156] Such considerations help us to understand

151. The natural meaning of המועדות; cf. CD 3.14-15.

152. Talmon, 1965, 165-66; cf. also 4QpHos 2.15-17 on 2:13.

153. Cf. 1QS 10.1-11; 1QH 12.4-10; Jaubert, 1963, 196.

154. Leaney, 1966, 101.

155. Cf. 6:19; 14:14-20; 22:1-7; 29:7; 44:5.

156. We find them linked in *Jub.* 4:17-19. Implications for the apparent interest in astrology at Qumran are obvious.

how and why these groups put such emphasis on a seemingly unreasonable demand to follow a certain calendar exactly.

For such groups as these, then, the theological as well as the historical importance of calendar legislation is obvious. While VanderKam may have overstated his case, he is nevertheless certainly correct to call the calendrical dispute one of the "more significant factors" that caused the Qumran community to leave Jerusalem, and correct also (in principle if not in extent) to conclude that "in this respect the Essenes resembled many other Jewish dissident movements from the time of Jeroboam I to the Middle Ages."[157] Even if some of the (earlier?) writings preserved in the Qumran library lack the strong polemic of other later calendrical passages, there is no doubt that this sect also eventually adopted a full apologetic for the solar calendar and did so with vindictive overtones; for them the calendar was a matter of revelation based on the fact that they (i.e., they *alone*) possessed the Spirit of God.[158] While most scholars would admit that the *historical* importance of this issue cannot be overemphasized,[159] the *social* implications of the calendar issue must also be recognized. This matter was at the center of the practical, as well as theological, life of each of these communities. *Control of the calendar implied control of the cultic life of a community, and rejection of the "official" calendar implied a challenge to the established authority.*[160] The sectarian calendar would have caused special annoyance to the Jerusalem authorities inasmuch as the centralized cult depended on a semblance of unity if it was ever to embody the doctrine of Israel as the elect people organized around worship of the one true God.[161] Divisions over the time and place of worship would hit directly at the heart of the religio-social structure of Judaism. S. Talmon argues that:

> No barrier appears to be more substantial and fraught with heavier consequences than differences in calendar calculation. An alteration of any one of the dates that regulate the course of the year inevitably produces a break-up of communal life, impairing the coordination between the behaviour of man and his fellow, and abolishes that synchronization of habits and activities which is the foundation of a properly functioning social order. Whoever celebrates his own Sabbath, and does not observe the festivals of the year at the same time as the community in which he lives, removes himself from his fel-

---

157. VanderKam, 1981, 52; cf. F. García Martínez and A. S. van der Woude, "A 'Groningen' Hypothesis of Qumran Origins and Early History," 1990, 538.

158. So Obermann, 1956, 290.

159. This should be contrasted with Sanders's low estimate of the importance of the Astrological Book: "This section has nothing of interest for the present study" (1977, 360)!

160. Cf. VanderKam, 1981, 53; Talmon, 1965, 181.

161. For evidence of this, cf. again 1QpHab 11.6-8.

lows and ceases to be a member of the social body to which he hitherto belonged.[162]

One can accordingly see how the calendrical debate contained the seeds of the downfall of traditional nationalistic theology, prompting the conclusion: "they" are not part of Israel — "we" are.[163]

The calendar is accordingly a particularly well-documented example of an issue that was put into the service of *limiting and defining the people of God*. The effects of this issue were widely felt for centuries, in the later history of nonconformist movements both in Judaism and in Christian circles influenced by Judaism.[164] A tragic fact of the division that resulted from this issue is that many calendars may actually have been competing for prominence (although, for our period, the differences among them have often been exaggerated, their unifying property certainly being their solar basis, making the calendars little more than *variations* of one another).[165] But the somewhat multifarious condition of the antiestablishment calendar may actually highlight the importance of the matter: groups were willing to tolerate diversity and confusion for the sake of getting the matter right. The intensity, diversity, and prominence of the issue, not to mention the persistence of debate, would further suggest that such concerns were not limited to a few pious scribes on the fringe of the Jewish world, but may have involved a wide spectrum of the Jewish populace. The possibility that the movement was not homogeneous, in other words, suggests that it may have been quite popular and widespread.

Additional Legal Restrictions on the Saved Community

The calendar was not the only cause of division at this time, and it will be worth briefly mentioning a few other issues related to the special *halakah* of these

162. Talmon, 1965, 163-64, who is probably also justified in the view that the sect's opposition to the Jerusalem cult was not directed against the sacrifices *in principle* (so the general view) but against the dates on which the festivals were celebrated (165). We might add that the perceived uncleanness of the priests due to their apostate state and the impure and unlawful administration of the cult also played a role in this.

163. For the soteriological implications of the calendar debate, see Talmon, 1965, 182.

164. Cf. *Pss. Sol.* 18:10-12?; *TNaph.* 3:2-5; 5:1-5; *2 Bar.* 48:9-10?; *1 En.* 41:3-9; 69:20. Calendar issues continue to be a source of division even today — namely, in the continuing controversy between Eastern and Western Christianity over the dating of Easter.

165. J. C. VanderKam (*Textual and Historical Studies in the Book of Jubilees*, 1977, 271) insists that they are all the same solar calendar. We can certainly agree with his sentiment that "it is difficult to avoid the conclusion that one distinctive theological tradition nurtured the authors of these works" (277).

communities that possessed implications similar to that of the calendar. We will deal primarily with the evidence provided by the Qumran scrolls and *Jubilees* since legal teachings are expressed in some detail in these writings, although this material appears, in turn, to be representative of a much wider sectarian *halakic* "movement" in open disagreement with more "compromising" teachings.[166]

Laws Related to Purification-Atonement at Qumran

It has already been shown how acknowledgment of the Qumran revelation was considered an essential criterion for belonging to the covenant people. An important part of this revelation was a corpus of laws, including a type of "second" law. In many cases this involved nothing more than clarification, interpretation, and application of laws already found in the public Torah, a practice that, judging from the Mishnah, seems to have been common in Judaism. But not all Qumran laws can be classified as clarifications, for some appear to have been derived *independently* of what one might call straightforward Torah interpretation — even if this new legislation, as seems always to have been the case, was later read back into the Scriptures. Accordingly an important distinction between these two types of laws appears to have been expressed at Qumran by the terms *niglōt* (publicly revealed laws) and *nistārōt* (secret laws), as noted above. It was also noted that the sect maintained that only full compliance with the *nistārōt* would guarantee salvation. Important questions that remain are (1) whether fulfilling these laws was considered to be within the grasp of nonadherents, and (2) whether even adherents of the community would be able to fulfill the laws while remaining *separate* from the community. That is, did these laws effectively divide Israel based on full membership in the sect?

Since it has already been established that membership in the *covenant of the community* was considered absolutely essential for salvation (see esp. 1QS 5.7-20), the answer to the first question is obviously no. As for the second question, Lawrence Schiffman, a member of the scrolls translation team, investigated the role and practice of Qumran law and concluded that while only *adherence* to the *yaḥad* was required for membership, *living within* the actual physical community became a practical necessity for keeping its laws and teachings. While it is true that certain allowances were set out for members living outside the physical

166. Talmon (1965, 190-91) cites *Shoḥer Tov on* Ps. 119:20 to illustrate the widespread critique of rabbinic religion by the sects: "The insolent have made great jest of me . . . again and again they say to me: You do not circumcise, and you do not keep the Sabbaths or read the Torah." The critique does not imply that the rabbis failed to practice these basics so much as that their attention to the oral law led to a compromise of the written law (perhaps especially as it was understood by the "insolent").

bounds of the *yaḥad*, it is obvious that this must have been an uncomfortable and difficult situation and that both regular physical contact with the group and continuous separation from nonsectarians were essential for belonging to this community of salvation. In contrast to the regular residents of the *yaḥad*, "Others, who were less capable of devoting themselves so extensively to the sect, dwelt elsewhere, but may have come once or several times for periods of study at this center. Only those who came to the headquarters could progress beyond the initial stages of the novitiate and enter full-fledged membership in the sect. Of these, many remained permanently at Qumran."[167]

A prime example of where deliberate association with the community seems to have been viewed as absolutely essential (whether this involved taking up residence, or making frequent pilgrimages, as Schiffman suggests) is with the *system of purification-atonement*. The two concerns — purification and atonement — were virtually equated by the sect, being related to one another in a way foreign to the Torah, where they are more or less separate issues, atonement generally applying to moral types of transgressions and purification to cultic matters, though even in the Scriptures this distinction is not consistently sustained. The original view of things, in any event, appears to have allowed that cultic impurity could occur in the normal processes of life, quite accidentally, without necessarily involving any moral sin, and requiring only purification to put things right. Atonement, on the other hand, was required for noncultic transgressions. At Qumran, in contrast, where these ideas were gradually being spiritualized, these two matters of impurity and (noncultic) transgression were merged; purity was no longer considered merely a cultic matter — all kinds of *sin* (what we call moral transgressions, but including any kind of noncultic disobedience) also led to impurity.[168] The corollary of this is that the state of purity was equated with the state of salvation and impurity with an unredeemed condition. This strict stance is reflected in the fact that entry into the covenant, without which salvation was not possible, is also spoken of as entering into and maintaining a *pure state* (see again 1QS 5.7-20). Thus the purity regulations (including both *laws for remaining pure* and *rites of cleansing* — i.e., reestablishing the pure state) take on an extreme urgency and even possess soteriological implications.

This integration of purification and atonement necessarily granted to the physical bounds of the *yaḥad*-community an unprecedented and critical importance since the community now acquired the status of a holy place or of some kind of sacred space. All and every contact with the outside world implied impurity; purity, on the other hand, was only possible within the *yaḥad* and

---

167. Schiffman, 1983, 15.
168. Wacholder, 1983, 12; for a similar spiritualization, cf. Titus 3:5.

through its rites. Both ideas are carefully expressed in 1QS 5.13-20, but more of the *theory* behind this attitude can be found in 1QS 2.25–3.12, which states that whoever fails to enter the "ways of God" — that is, the ways promoted by the community[169] — will be considered beyond atonement and consequently impure: "he shall not be absolved by atonement, nor purified by lustral waters, nor sanctified [even] by [every manner of] seas and rivers, nor cleansed by all the waters of washing. Unclean, unclean shall he be . . ." (3.4-5). There is little doubt that the ablutions alluded to in this passage are those practiced under the careful scrutiny of the community, but even if that is not the case, it remains that adherence to the teachings of the *yaḥad* (notably the stipulations for the performance of atonement rituals) *alone* rendered efficacious any and all rites, whether they were practiced inside or outside the confines of the community. It is also clearly implied in the passage that the price of failure to comply with this view of atonement was exclusion not merely from the fraternity or from some ideal state of purity (such as that special purity which seems to have originally belonged only to the priests in the Hebrew Scriptures) but from the hope of life and salvation itself: "he shall not be counted among upright men . . . he shall not be justified . . ." (3.1, 3).[170] The counterpart of this theology is that purification is assured to the one who *is* in the community and accepts its teaching:

> For by the Spirit of true counsel concerning the ways of man [available only in the community] shall all his sins be atoned. . . . By the Holy Spirit of the *Community* . . . shall he be cleansed of all his sins . . . shall his iniquity be atoned . . . shall his flesh be cleansed when sprinkled with lustral water . . . it will obtain for him the Covenant of the eternal *Community.* (3.6-12)

The juxtaposition of purification and atonement language in this passage offers a profound example of the joining of the two ideas in Qumran thought. In the context of a group who no longer accepted the purification and atonement rites of the Jerusalem Temple, such a theology could only have possessed drastic implications for the boundaries of the saved community. It is accordingly not surprising that this view of purification and atonement made its mark on the complete range of *halakah* found in the scrolls.[171] In no other area as

169. Cf. "the teachings of Knowledge," "the ordinances of righteousness" (3.1).
170. Cf. Burrows, 1958, 295.
171. Schiffman: "the basis of the complex system of the sectarian novitiate and entry of new members into the sect was the concept that *those outside of the sect were ritually impure while the new member became less and less impure through the initiation process* until he was permitted contact with the victuals of the sect. . . . At the root of the matter is the idea that *ritual impurity* and subsequent purification *are the function not of physical phenomena, but of sin and atonement*" (1983, 216, emphasis added).

this is it so evident how, by legal means, the *yaḥaḏ* effectively transferred the inside versus outside dichotomy from its traditional application to Israel vis-à-vis Gentiles, to that of the community vis-à-vis *all* outsiders, *including other Israelites*. The impurity of Israel necessarily placed them in danger of judgment because their separation from the covenant community also effectively separated them from the only viable means of atonement.

The Special Laws *of* Jubilees

The exaggerated importance of specific laws is especially notable in the book of *Jubilees*. Its teachings often contain an implicit critique of practices current in Jerusalem, especially those related to the cult. If it is valid to draw parallels with *Jubilees'* attitude toward the calendar, and it will become evident that it is, abhorrence with these other cultic practices would likewise seem to imply that Judaism had been abandoned to a condition of gross and irreparable lostness, and that all who sought to benefit from the apostate cult were necessarily also implicated in the sin and impropriety of the priests. The special nature of law in *Jubilees* stems, like that of Qumran, from its authoritative revelatory source, in particular, the "heavenly tablets." Whether or not *Jubilees* was itself considered *equivalent* to the heavenly law as it was revealed to Moses,[172] or only a witness to it, one thing is abundantly clear throughout the writing: the source of *everything* considered worthy as law in Israel is already to be found in an unambiguous and pristine form in the "heavenly tablets."[173] All other Jewish law therefore must be conformed to it. This makes the public Torah (the Pentateuch), in one sense, a second-class law — both ambiguous and derivative. It is only when one recognizes this that one can see how the law of *Jubilees* presupposes a strictly segregated elitism on the part of the author and those like him who have acknowledged the existence and superlative importance of the tablets. And while it is never put in such blunt terms, such a position is tantamount to saying that keeping *Jubilees'* law in conformity to the tablets is itself the requisite for membership in the saved community. This distinction is maintained *even if* that law *also* exists in the public Torah — an important clarification since, except for the notable example of calendar law, *Jubilees* is actually almost free of distinctly "new" law.[174] It is rather more in the area of *interpretation* and *appli-*

172. Testuz, 1960, 101.

173. A good expression of this belief comes to the fore in regard to the feast of *Shabuot* in 6:19. Testuz, 1960, 101.

174. Testuz (1960, 107-16) mentions as truly innovative laws only the limits on species of wood for the altar (which, judging from 4Q214, was not unique to *Jubilees*), the prohibition against nudity, the prohibition against giving daughters in marriage before their proper age, and several applications of the blood laws.

cation of law that *Jubilees* makes its actual contribution since laws appear to be much more strictly interpreted and applied in *Jubilees* than in other Jewish traditions. But this strictness in no way lessens the importance of following the Jubilaean law. This can be seen in the way its interpretation is given the garb of an authoritative and essentially independent revelation.

It can be demonstrated how essential this strict maintenance of law is by consideration of select examples that evidence a strong legal elitism. Most important in this regard are laws that are specifically said to involve the breach of the covenant in some way, either by outright apostasy or by sinning in such a way as to make atonement unattainable, namely, *laws about eating blood and regarding intermarriage* and, probably, *laws regarding astrological practice.* Although the covenant is not explicitly mentioned in connection with this third kind of law, the sense of alarm surrounding astrological sins in *Jubilees,* and their probable association with idolatry, implies much the same thing. One could also include other laws emphasized in *Jubilees* such as those regarding circumcision, the second tithe, and the sabbath, and various purification laws,[175] but none of these shows the radical nature of *Jubilees'* laws, since much of Judaism (but apparently not all!) would have concurred with these laws. We will accordingly give our attention to the three laws mentioned above that the community especially claimed to obey or, as we should say, claimed to obey in a way that Israel did not.

Blood Laws   It seems that the author of *Jubilees* introduces the subject of blood into his narrative wherever possible, even in narratives where no mention of or allusion to blood is to be found in the parallel in Genesis and Exodus. While *Jubilees* most frequently mentions laws against *eating* blood, various other issues bearing on the treatment of blood are raised as well, such as the disposal of blood during sacrifices and the shedding of human blood. The author regularly cites laws for each of these cases that are *more stringent* than those found in the canon of Hebrew Scriptures. These more stringent laws may have been considered clarifications of the Torah or even applications to various cases rather than *new* laws *per se,* but it again is the exclusiveness of the claim to keep these laws in ways other Jews do not that is implied. Passages like 6:6-22, 38 and 7:27-33 give extensive embellishments and commentaries on biblical passages to illustrate these laws carefully, suggesting that the author felt it necessary to emphasize certain aspects or applications *not being followed* by his

---

175. For discussion of these, see Testuz, 1960, 108; VanderKam, 1977, 242-43; Wacholder, 1983, 50-53; J. M. Baumgarten, "The Laws of 'Orlah and First Fruits in the Light of Jubilees, the Qumran Writings, and Targum Ps. Jonathan," 1987; Endres, 1987, 3, 166.

Jewish contemporaries. It is evident, in any event, that something in the situation of the author has evoked a serious concern about the mishandling of blood.

The first passage incorporates laws about blood into the covenants with Noah and Moses. While the biblical version of the story does mention blood commandments in association with Noah (Gen. 9:4-6; cf. Acts 15:29), the account of the giving of this law is greatly enlarged in *Jubilees,* appearing as the very basis of Noah's covenant (6:6-16); moreover, the sprinkling of blood associated only with the Mosaic covenant in the public Torah is also characteristically retrojected into this first "blood" covenant in Jubilees (6:11-14, a detail already contained on the heavenly tablets, v. 18). The strict warning to the Israelite descendants of Moses against eating blood alerts us to the fact that this was an important issue in the *author's* time: "so that you might keep it always," "all of the days of the earth," "command the children of Israel not to eat blood," "there is no limit of days for this law because it is forever," "they shall keep it for their generations." The punishment for disobedience is death: "the man who eats the blood . . . shall be uprooted, he and his seed from the earth" (6:12-14; cf. Lev. 7:27). In spite of this warning Moses' sons will forget this law along with the calendar: they will "be corrupted . . . and they will eat all of the blood with all flesh" (6:38).

The second passage contains the warning of Noah to his sons to keep this important commandment. It rather enigmatically associates murder with the eating of blood (cf. also 6:7-8; Gen. 9:4-6): "For I see, and behold, the demons have begun to mislead you and your children. And now I fear for your sakes that after I die, you will pour out the blood of men upon the earth. And you will be blotted out from the surface of the earth. For all who eat the blood of man and all who eat the blood of any flesh will be blotted out, all of them, from the earth" (7:27-28). The greatest imaginable punishment is envisioned for this sin (7:29). Blood must not even be *seen* on them (7:30: inferred from Lev. 17:13 and Ezek. 24:7?). Only the death of the guilty parties brings a cleansing for the land (7:33).

In both of these passages the laws about blood are rehearsed for the benefit of the future descendants of Noah and Moses (cf. 6:12-13; 7:27-28, 31, 33); this would tend to confirm that it is the contemporaries of the author who are addressed. Such allusions to eating blood probably reflect laxity in cultic purity, particularly dietary laws, which is known to have prevailed during the Hellenistic period. Eating blood is rendered more serious because, as it would seem, not only were the common people ignoring the blood commandments (cf. Lev. 17:10-14) but the priests were evidently involved in such sin as well, resulting in very serious ritual transgression. Since priests were accused in *Jubilees* of other blood transgressions — namely, intercourse with women during menstruation and failure to spill out blood on the ground properly — this would also imply that they are the chief objects of critique here. In contrast to the lackadaisical attitude of the Hellenized priests, any touching of blood represented an abomination for the author of *Jubilees*. This reflects either a kind of taboo that classified blood as one of the most detestable things or, more likely, an extreme regard for holiness that placed blood under a continual ban because of its inherent sacredness. Either way, such attitudes would have the effect of separating those who held to the Jubilaean interpretation of blood laws from those of less stringent observance.

What is noteworthy is that for the author of *Jubilees* not only those who have eaten the blood but those who partake of the unclean sacrifices that have been polluted by contact with blood lose their source of atonement. As with what we have seen with regard to the improper appropriation of the calendar and times for the celebration of the feasts, sacrifices improperly performed due to ritual uncleanness were considered *disqualified* sacrifices. Thus the author points out that, while Noah, Abraham, and the patriarchs kept the feast of *Shabuot,* their sons, including the children of Israel up until the time of Moses, "corrupted it . . . *and they ate blood*" (6:18). The feast was corrupted through the ignorance of blood laws in the past, just as the ignorance and neglect of the author's contemporaries now corrupt *their* feasts. This is a serious state for all Israel, even for the Jubilaean community, who, although they may have taken steps to withdraw from involvement in the sacrifices, nevertheless also clearly forfeited the benefit of proper cultic atonement along with the rest of the people. The sobering implications of this rather strict view of the disqualification of the effectiveness of the cult due to blood transgression come unambiguously to the fore in the startling consequences (covenantal curses) that are said to follow from blood sins: the "land" will continue to bear the sin of eating blood; only righteous vengeance on sinners will return blessing and salvation "to the land" (6:7-8, 12; 7:27-29, 32-33). Given this requisite for cleansing the land, it certainly seemed to the writer that Israel would *never* be redeemed from this widespread pollution: "For the land will *not* be cleansed of the blood which is poured out upon it, because by the blood of one who poured it out [i.e., that one alone] will the land be cleansed in all of its generations."

Thus for the author of *Jubilees* it is evident that *even partaking in the national cult constituted guilty involvement in unclean ritual.* This restriction therefore effectively defined the true righteous as those who refused to eat blood and who separated themselves from the defilement that such blood transgressions brought "on the Land."

Exogamy Another issue alluded to by *Jubilees* is intermarriage with Gentiles (exogamy). From the polemical tone with which this matter is raised, it would also seem to involve a reaction to the contemporary situation. We have already

169

seen this to be the point of the Dinah/Shechem narrative (30:5-23), which threatened covenantal judgment for this sin: "plague upon plague and curse upon curse, and every judgment, and plague, and curse will come," not only for the one who commits exogamy (including *giving* one's daughter to a Gentile), but (as may be implied) for the one who tolerates the sin: "all of the people will be judged together on account of all of the defilement and the profaning of this one" (30:15). There will be no atonement for this (30:16). Such a serious indictment again relates to the idea that all serious sins against the covenant bring defilement "upon the land," that is, against the entire people and against any hope of restoration — something also forewarned in the Deuteronomic covenantal formulation. Only severe vindictive punishment on the sinners can secure atonement. But it is really vengeance against his *own contemporaries* that is on the mind of the author when he associates the sin of intermarriage with the vengeance of Levi against the Shechemites in this passage. That Levi totally annihilated the men of Shechem for their sin is emphasized, and the warning of a similar fate is extended to present-day Israel: "Proclaim this testimony *to Israel:* 'See how it was for the Shechemites and their sons, how they were given into the hand of the two children of Jacob and they killed them painfully'" (30:17). The author thus implies that the Israel of his own day — the whole people — have broken the covenant through this sin even if exogamy was actually committed only by some.

A similar warning against intermarriage is implied by the much embellished account in *Jub.* 25:1-10, in which Rebekah gives Jacob instructions about choosing a wife. Her displeasure at the thought of Jacob taking a wife from the daughters of Canaan, as Esau did, is expressed (vv. 1-3), as is Jacob's repeated and emphatic assurances that he will never fall to temptation and make such a mistake (vv. 4-10). Both parts of the account include extensive embellishments — the former may have been suggested by *Abraham's* word to Jacob (Gen. 28:1-2, although this would be quite a distinct parallel);[176] the latter, Jacob's response, has been created virtually *ex nihilo.*[177] Two things are notable here. The first is the distastefulness of the thought of intermarriage with Gentiles and the association of it with "fornication" and "lust" — "all of their deeds are fornication and lust" (25:1). Jacob promises to avoid all this because Abraham has given him "many commands regarding lust and fornication" (25:7). The second

176. Endres cites Josephus (*Ant.* 1.265) for evidence that Jews of the time acknowledged Isaac's nonchalance regarding the marriage of Esau to Gentiles, pointing out that *Jubilees'* attitude was really much different (1987, 76). This may be why the author placed the exhortation in Rebekah's mouth rather than Isaac's. For parallels from later Jewish texts for Rebekah sending Jacob to Mesopotamia to find a wife, and for the blessing of Jacob (vv. 11ff.), see Endres, 80-81.

177. Cf. Gen. 27:46–28:5; Endres, 1987, 75.

notable thing is that the successful propagation of the elect seed of Abraham is said to depend on purity of marriage: Jacob is promised, *only on the condition of following Abraham's orders*, that "the Most High God will bless you, and your children will be a righteous generation and a holy seed" (25:3).

No doubt a most serious warning to the author's own contemporaries is intended in both of these lines of reasoning. It is moreover evident from the sheer amount of embellishment in these accounts that exogamy was a serious concern to the author and that these passages contain veiled warnings to his contemporaries.[178] This concern can be easily understood against the background of Hellenization, which was highly predisposed toward intermarriage at the time when *Jubilees* was written. The blurring of racial distinctiveness became something of an ideology in itself as the synthesis of different peoples furthered the political objectives of Alexander and his successors. Jews who wished to be part of the "New World" promised by Hellenism readily complied with the trend. Contemporary accounts also indicate that this became an issue even for the high priesthood and that the relatively strict Pharisees in at least one instance took a surprisingly liberal stance in regard to it, indulging the high priest in his marriage to a foreign woman.[179] But the ideological pressures would have made themselves felt in the total population of Judea, not merely the priests and wealthy classes. It is therefore apparent that when *Jubilees* stood against the trend (perhaps in deference to the conservative reforms of Ezra as recorded in Ezra 9), it stood against an increasingly popular practice in Palestine.[180] In spite of its currency, however, the author left little doubt about what he thought would be the implications of this serious sin, which he viewed as nothing less than sin against the covenant.

Astrology The writer of *Jubilees* appears to have adopted a similarly strict attitude toward astrological practice as well.[181] 8:3-4 and 11:8 illustrate the writer's

178. Endres, 1987, 76.

179. For discussion and texts see Testuz, 1960, 114.

180. For the theory that intermarriage had been a widespread practice even from postexilic times, see Morton Smith, *Palestinian Parties and Politics That Shaped the Old Testament*, 1971, 16-17.

181. For an interesting discussion of Judaism's relationship to astrological lore, which reveals a certain ambiguity toward it on the part of the rabbis, see J. H. Charlesworth, "Jewish Astrology in the Talmud, Pseudepigrapha, the Dead Sea Scrolls, and Early Palestinian Synagogues" (1977), which also contradicts the unsupported contention that astrology was a sectarian concern. The evidence of a single and highly enigmatic fragment (4Q186 = 4QCryptic) is hardly grounds to think that the Qumranites viewed astrological science positively, even given that sect's developed determinism. The document's reverse order of script probably implies that its contents were dangerous or at best doubtful (*contra* Milik, 1959, 15, who asserts, with no corroborating evidence or discussion, that

negative attitude toward astrological revelations (cf. also 12:16-18). The first tells of how Cainan, the great-grandson of Noah by Shem, discovered writings on stone that recorded astrological teachings engraved by his antediluvian ancestors. This teaching is said to have originated with the Watchers, which would have immediately communicated to the reader the fundamentally evil nature of astrological knowledge (and may further have suggested a relationship between this knowledge and the promotion of the invalid lunar calendar, since both involve astronomical observations). In a similar vein 11:8 tells of Serug, who lived in Ur of the Chaldees and taught his son Nahor (Abraham's grandfather) "the researches of the Chaldeans in order to practice divination and astrology according to the signs of heaven." It is significant that this practice is offered by the writer of *Jubilees* as a particularly damning example of the universal "sin and transgression" of the antediluvian times (11:6). It is even said to have issued in the terrible judgment of the earth at the hand of Prince Mastema (11:10-13).

The historical context for these sayings is difficult to establish from the sources at hand, although it is well within possibility that Israelites were practicing a type of astrology at this time.[182] We do know that synagogue floors were decorated with astrological symbols, including the zodiac,[183] though the function of these pictures is not clear. They may have served merely as symbols borrowed for ornamental purposes in order to illustrate more traditional Hebrew themes such as creation; so the widespread use of such decoration is not particularly surprising.[184] Nevertheless, it would also be quite in harmony with the sectarian mind-set to have *misinterpreted* these worthy intentions, or to have deliberately chosen to interpret them as illustrations of the widespread trend toward assimilation. Symbols used in a liturgical environment can obviously become easy targets for accusations of assimilation; synagogue decorations, when removed from their intended context, could be viewed simply as

---

enigmatic forms of writing were intended to preserve particularly important secrets; cf. also Charlesworth, 191-92). It is probable (cf. G. R. Driver, *The Judaean Scrolls*, 1965, 335ff.) that 4Q186 contains calendrical teaching that was perhaps felt to be in danger of misappropriation or of being employed for astrological purposes if it fell into the wrong hands.

182. Cf. Charlesworth, 1977, 185-88.

183. For photographs and description of a mosaic zodiac in a recently excavated third–fourth-century-A.D. synagogue in Hammath Tiberias on the Sea of Galilee (the earliest example known to date), see H. Shanks, "Synagogue Excavation Reveals Stunning Mosaic of Zodiac and Torah Ark," 1984.

184. According to Charlesworth (1977, 193), "no less than four out of the nine known synagogue mosaics place the zodiac in a prominent position." This scholar assumes that the symbols were borrowed in order to dignify traditional Hebrew images (195).

idolatrous compromise.[185] And how much more likely is a reaction to have ensued if there had actually been no misinterpretation of the motivations at all! It is curious, in this regard, that in the synagogue at Hammath Tiberias, in the most prominent location on the floor, a mosaic zodiac displays Helios, the Greek god of the sun, surrounded by a pantheon of other gods! This instance, for one, would seem to take things quite beyond mere ornamentation and would appear to represent, at best, a curious assimilation of Greek folklore or mythology within the Hebrew cult, perhaps in the name of "science." In any event one can easily see how the possession of astrological figures could be taken as outright idolatry[186] by more sensitive Israelites. This is one practice from which the writer of *Jubilees* definitely wanted to disassociate himself.

Considering the strong polemic that *Jubilees* brings to bear on these three areas or types of laws, it is certainly possible to conclude that any one of them could have inspired a real segregation of the Jubilaean community from the rest of Israel. Transgressions against these laws of *Jubilees* involved much more than normal kinds of offenses that could be repaired through the provisions of the cult; they implied rather an irreparable breach of the covenant. While it is not frequently held by scholars that the Jubilaean community had *physically* separated by the time *Jubilees* was written, it is entirely likely, due to these scruples about blood, exogamy, and astrological compromises, that such a separation was at least under consideration. The community, after all, was deeply fearful of the impending judgment coming on Israel because of such sins. One can conclude, therefore, that these concerns functioned similarly to the calendrical teachings of the community. Testuz summarizes:

> To disobey these laws is not to commit a mere misdemeanor, but a sin. "He has committed an impious act" (30:10) is said of the one who marries a daughter of a foreigner, he has "defiled" Israel, he has done a thing "abominable before the Lord" (30:11). Those who contravene these commandments are guilty of sin, of impiety, of uncleanness, of profanation; they have broken the covenant (30:21), or have despised it (21:4).[187]

The group that implicitly *defined* itself as composed of those who carefully heeded the laws of the heavenly tablets, therefore, also implicitly *limited* itself to

---

185. Cf. Charlesworth (1977, 197-200), who also argues for their ornamental function. Shanks (1984, 43-44) expresses bewilderment at the phenomenon, but likewise concludes that some kind of assimilation had taken place.

186. It is notable in this regard that *Targum Pseudo-Jonathan on* Lev. 26:1 (cited by Charlesworth, 1977, 196) permits floor mosaics under the condition that they are not worshiped.

187. Testuz, 1960, 118. Author's translation.

those who obeyed these laws. This is a further indication, therefore, of the essentially exclusive soteriology of the members of this "saved community."

Knowledge Polemic and "Defining Laws"

The view of revelation held by these communities, and in particular their treatment of special laws, well illustrates the importance of the social functions of knowledge for understanding these groups. The accumulation and synthesis of knowledge are not at all an academic exercise in the modern critical sense, where knowledge is valued for its own sake (at least ideally). *Knowledge serves polemical ends.* These groups accordingly do not place a high emphasis on sharing the common heritage of knowledge given to all Israel as if they were seeking a universal law or a better understanding of the traditions for their own sake. *Nor is such tradition the ultimate authority,* at least in practice, *but is subject to the needs of the moment.* For the same reason it is not particularly important — surprisingly, for all the emphasis on revelation — that the delineation of knowledge should exhibit absolute consistency. In fact, outright conflicting attitudes toward knowledge itself can be discerned. In a few passages in *1 Enoch* (cf. 16:3; 69:8-11), for example, the Watchers are blamed for introducing science — which amounts to a demonization of science, making science "evil"; but in *Jubilees* (4:17) Enoch is praised for introducing the very same sorts of knowledge! One can only conclude that *any* knowledge in the hands of the elect is better than *any* knowledge in the hands of the wicked; that is, a polemical intent is at work.[188] It is not, therefore, so much a matter of "what knowledge?" but of "who possess this knowledge?"

These observations about the social function of knowledge hold true in an especially revealing way when it comes to the special laws of these communities, the laws held up to be the most important or pressing. These laws should be viewed as *"defining laws."* Laws associated with the calendar, intermarriage, etc., as with the requirement of accepting the special revelation of the community generally, *serve effectively to identify,* or point out, *the elect.*[189] This is largely the

---

188. It may be that the two types of passages functioned differently in differing circumstances. Suter (1979, 84) speaks of the "inversion" of the myth as a reaction to the angelology of other groups, but there is no other evidence for such specific polemic between *1 Enoch* and *Jubilees*.

189. In line with the dominance of the eschatological perspective, these laws have commonly been treated as provisional, as a kind of "interim ethic" (e.g., J. O'Dell, "The Religious Background of the Psalms of Solomon," 1961, 256; Talmon, 1986, 222-23; Milik, 1959, 114). A preferable way to view them is in terms of the struggle over the authoritative interpretation of the law in Judaism at the time. Cf. W. Schmithals, *The Apocalyptic Movement,* 1975, 47-48; R. R. Hann, "The Community of the Pious," 1988, 177: "they regulate

case because these laws are able to be visibly confirmed or corroborated by confession or otherwise: those who practice what is required can easily be seen to do so, and the common commitment of "faithful" individuals leads to their being identified together as a group of "the righteous"; those who do not observe these laws, on the other hand, are also immediately visible, and their offense to the righteous quickly establishes them as "the wicked." The question of soteriology, accordingly, is virtually reduced to whether one *belongs to the saved* (i.e., the proper, or right) *community* (or "confession"). While these groups would obviously not have admitted the paramount importance of a limited number of "identity issues" (their claim would be to fulfill the *entire* law of Moses or the entire pristine law written on heavenly tablets), it can be easily seen how these laws could, in practice, be exalted in their function to the order of "defining laws."

This observation is certainly important for classifying and coming to grips with the notoriously difficult text 4QMMT (= *Miqṣat Ma'asēh ha-Tôrah,* "Some Works of Torah"). Ever since the initial reports about the contents of this scroll, and through the long and tedious period of debate while scholars and others awaited its official publication, this scroll was rumored to contain decisive evidence bearing on the identity of the Qumran community, and claims were made that its contents would, potentially at least, overturn the findings of decades of scrolls research. Its editor, Lawrence Schiffman, was the promulgator of the view that the laws in this text demanded a *Sadducean* provenance and that the other Dead Sea Scrolls and the community they represent were Sadducean rather than Essene, as usually maintained.[190] This was argued

---

their behaviour largely in terms of avoiding the practices thought to be characteristic of outsiders." Perhaps Dunn states it most clearly when he speaks of the process by which groups who are otherwise very similar tend to strengthen their sense of distinctiveness by emphasizing certain issues: "In this process it will be *the points of distinctiveness,* the matters on which they disagree, which inevitably will become the chief differentiation and boundary markers between the rival groups. This will mean that features of their respective profiles, which otherwise may not have been very important in relation to other features in that profile, assume a much larger importance, precisely because they are the points of differentiation, the boundary markers. We have already seen this in relation to Second Temple Judaism as a whole, in terms of self-differentiation of Jew over against Gentile, by reference to circumcision, Sabbath and food laws in particular. When it comes to differentiation *within* Judaism, *the boundary markers were bound to be precisely those points of disagreement over halakah,* over covenantal nomism: how to live as a devout and faithful Jew. Hence the exaggerated emphasis on calendar, on legitimate priesthood, and on ritual purity" (*The Partings of the Ways between Christianity and Judaism and Their Significance for the Character of Christianity,* 1991, 105-6, emphasis in original).

190. In particular a "continuing" or nonconforming Sadduceeism. Cf. L. H. Schiffman ("4QMMT — Basic Sectarian Text," 1991, 81-83; *Reclaiming the Dead Sea Scrolls,* 1994, passim, esp. 71-95).

primarily on the basis of the supposedly Sadducean flavor of the legal material in the text, though similar arguments of a few previous scholars (such as Solomon Schechter and Robert Eisenman) helped establish a basis for the Sadducean claim. Well before the publication of MMT, however, arguments had already been proffered in reaction to this theory, and these arguments have tended to hold conviction well after the scroll's official release, in spite of occasional continuing support for the Sadducean view.[191]

What is truly interesting about this text, however, is not specifically the types of laws contained in it (though we might note that it appears to deliberately insist on and consistently apply the solar calendar and warns of the consequences of intermarriage), but the zeal and sense of purpose with which these laws are defended. The text itself is a letter written, as it seems, to a high-ranking religious official in Jerusalem, and its purpose would seem to be to disassociate the Qumran community from the sins of Jerusalem and to give one final warning to the authorities about the price of their disobedience. The closing impassioned, and quite tactful, plea reveals what is otherwise evident from repeated phrases in the letter,[192] and from its imperative tone, that the most important feature of the letter is its fervent polemic.

> . . . we have separated ourselves from the multitude of the people . . . and from being involved with these matters and from participating with [them] in these things. And you [know that no] treachery or deceit or evil can be found in our hand . . . we have [written] to you so that you may study the book of Moses and the books of the Prophets and the writings of David. . . . And it is written that [you will stray] from the path (of the Torah) and that calamity will meet [you]. And it is written "and it shall come to pass, when all

191. For these arguments, cf. P. R. Davies ("Sadducees in the Dead Sea Scrolls?" 1991, 85-94), who pointed out, among other things, that of the five cases offered by Schiffman for comparison, "only one offers ambiguous confirmation" and two others are only possibilities (92); J. C. VanderKam ("The Qumran Residents," 1991, 105-8), who additionally points out that Sadducees and Essenes may have agreed with one another on various matters of *halakah* (as they both may have been "joined by their common resistance to Pharisees," 108) and that the scrolls teach "thoroughly non-Sadducaean doctrines as the existence of multitudes of angels and the all-controlling power of fate" (107); cf. also R. H. Eisenman, "A Response to Schiffman on MMT," 1991, 95-104; J. M. Baumgarten, "Some Remarks on the Qumran Law and the Identification of the Community," 1991, 115-17; Stegemann, 1992, 1:83-166, 106-7. Schiffman tried rather unsuccessfully (we think) to respond to some of these arguments, among other things by arguing that a fundamental shift to a more apocalyptic kind of Sadduceeism took place in their history under the influence of the Teacher of Righteousness (1994, 95).

192. E.g., "These are some of our rulings"; "the priest[s] should take care concerning this practice so as not to cause the people to bear punishment"; "we are of the opinion."

these things [be]fall you," at the end of days, the blessings and the curses . . . "and you will return unto Him with all your heart and with all your soul." . . . Think of the kings of Israel and contemplate their deeds: whoever among them feared [the To]rah was delivered from troubles; and these were the seekers of Torah whose transgressions were [for]given. Think of David, who was a man of righteous deeds and who was delivered from many troubles and was forgiven. We have sent you some of the precepts of the Torah according to our decision, for your welfare and the welfare of your people. For we see that you have wisdom and knowledge of the Torah. Consider all these things and ask Him that He strengthen your will and remove from you the plans of evil and the device of Belial so that you may rejoice at the end of time, finding that some of our practices are correct. And this will be counted as a virtuous deed of yours, since you will be doing what is righteous and good in His eyes, for your own welfare and for the welfare of Israel.[193]

While the letter was thus obviously written to urge repentance on the ruling establishment in Jerusalem, this attempt would appear to be somewhat perfunctory and there is little reason to believe the writers expected much in the way of results. It was more likely written to justify the group's condemnation of the establishment and perhaps also the physical separation of the group from Jerusalem — this group was not going to participate in apostasy or stay around while others were swallowed up by judgment. In fact, the element of judgment in the choice of laws is quite conspicuous. The laws center on Jerusalem (which it calls "the camp" since it has apparently adopted a "tabernacle ideology"), and the warning being offered to the guilty priests throughout the text is that the temple city will be judged severely for breaking laws set out for the city and the cult. This is not an arbitrary selection of laws, therefore, but the most serious ones and the ones most fiercely championed by the sect in the face of practices in Jerusalem. Beyond that one gains the impression that these laws are cited, not just because of their relationship to the cult in Jerusalem or their inherent seriousness, but because they were the laws that the Qumran community considered most important. Many of them are laws, or interpretations of laws, that we have already seen to be in direct contradiction to common interpretations in Judaism. The words of Sussman, recorded by P. Muchowski before the official publication of the scroll, are still appropriate:

4QMMT is a collection of the halakhot by virtue [of which] the members of the community regarded themselves to be different from the rest of Israel. Disagreements over halakhic questions were the main reason for their separation. It is an extremely significant fact that the sect's members themselves

193. *DJD*, 10:45-62.

present the motives for their alienation: . . . "We have separated ourselves from the majority of the people [*mrwb h'm*] from intermingling in these matters and from participating with them in these matters."[194]

By the time the letter was written these matters were beginning to harden into reasons for division, so that the significance of these laws does not lie with the actual debate over legislation, as if two parties were involved in legal haggling (as seems to be assumed in the Essene-Sadducee debate). The defining quality these laws had assumed means that there was no more haggling. They were more than questions of preference. They were identity issues. Compliance marked off the righteous from the condemned. What is special and important about this particular document is that in it we catch a glimpse of the function of defining laws in action as they are being articulated in a real-life situation of polemic. 4QMMT accordingly amounts to a transparent presentation of *defining laws,* although the sect no doubt promoted their universal and timeless validity.

DIVINE MERCY TOWARD ISRAEL?

Many issues relative to the judgment-of-Israel theme and the exclusivist soteriology of these Jewish writings have been considered. It has been determined that some of these groups emphasized specific *halakah,* naturally suggesting that these groups were essentially *legalistic* — that is, Torah centered, with salvation depending on obedience. As E. P. Sanders has pointed out, however, it may not be as simple as all that. He has argued that for these groups salvation does not *ultimately* depend on the merits of the individual, but on God's mercy. Since the object of God's mercy is his covenant people Israel, all Israel will eventually be saved. But the question whether salvation is by mercy or merit is admittedly not a simple one to answer for these writings. It has been suggested that the mercy-merit dialectic was rather too abstract for the Jewish theologians of this time, and even a legalistic-sounding work like 4 Ezra can be found to announce that God can be merciful "to those who have no store of good works" (8:36). The question is further complicated with groups like Qumran where the predestination of the members of the saved community is so strongly asserted (cf. 1QS 3–4) as to remove the question altogether from the ethical to the cosmic level, making merits theoretically unimportant while at

194. P. Muchowski, "Introductory Remarks on 4QMMT by Professor Sussman," 1991, 69-73, 72.

the same time qualifying severely the subjects of God's mercy. We are, in any event, not interested in unraveling this particular dialectic, as Sanders attempted to do. But it is important to note, in response to Sanders, that mercy and merit need not be seen as mutually exclusive categories. Mercy need not imply unconditional, complete, and unilateral forgiveness of sins (as is frequently recognized by theologians); it may also be seen in some way as the incentive or initiative for a life of following the law that permits, effects, or sustains obedience to the commandments.[195] More importantly here, the subjects or recipients of this mercy may be *limited* or *restricted* in some way. In this regard, the particular concern raised by Sanders that merits attention has to do with his view that God's mercy implies the salvation of *all* Israel. This question obviously possesses important implications for an investigation of nationalistic theology, but a concise review of some of the data relevant to the question will be enough to reveal that mercy is in fact *significantly qualified* in these writings.

Thus while the Book of Watchers opens with a description of a future judgment that includes, interestingly enough, the judgment of the righteous, it also significantly *contrasts* the mercy *extended* to the righteous with that *denied* to the wicked. To the righteous, God "will grant peace. He will preserve the elect, and kindness shall be upon them . . ." (1:8); to the wicked on the other hand: "you shall curse your days, and the years of your life shall perish and multiply in eternal execration; and *there will not be any mercy unto you*" (*1 En.* 5:5). Again in 27:3-4 the "righteous" are referred to when it says that "in the days of their judgment, they shall bless him for the mercy which he had bestowed upon *them.*"[196] This quite deliberate contrast between the blessed and the cursed suggests that the righteous have been shown mercy in an *exclusive* way. Unlike the others, they have no fear of judgment. It is also to be noted in these passages that the reference is to mercy *in the judgment,* rather than in enlightening or saving the righteous *in the present.* The significance of this should not be missed, for it suggests that the critical occasion for reflection on God's *ḥesed* was not nationalistic hopes for the present, so much as the notion (or fear) that Israel, even the righteous in Israel, would be subjected to the final judgment. While this need not imply an insecurity about salvation on the part of the writer and his community — the Enochian sectarians seemed very confident about God's mercy as far as *they* were concerned — the belief that not even the righteous would escape the future judgment would surely have pro-

195. Cf. Becker's views on the Hymn Scroll (1964, 70). Becker acknowledges the soteriological significance of the revelation brought by the *moreh,* which could be termed a kind of "revelatory nomism" (66).

196. Black understands the righteous as the antecedent of "their" as well as "them" in this sentence (1985, 174). The pronouns can be interpreted otherwise; cf. Charles, 1912, 56.

vided a more stimulating context for these reflections on mercy than a nationalistic covenantal theology (in which case, why would there be a mention of the judgment of Israel at all?).

When one comes to God's mercy in *Jubilees,* things are a little more complicated. As pointed out above, an occasional mention of God's care for Israel can be found in this writing. For example, *Jub.* 1:19-21 has Moses praying:

> O Lord, my God, do not abandon your people and your inheritance to walk in the error of their heart. And do not deliver them into the hand of their enemy, the gentiles, lest they rule over them and cause them to sin against you. O Lord, let your *mercy* be lifted up upon your people, and create for them an upright spirit. And do not let the spirit of Beliar rule over them to accuse them before you and ensnare them from every path of righteousness so that they might be destroyed from before your face. But they are your people and your inheritance, whom you saved by your great might from the hand of the Egyptians. Create a pure heart and a holy spirit for them. And do not let them be ensnared by their sin henceforth and forever.

This is a very nationalistic-sounding passage apparently drawing the line between Israel and the nations, not between some in Israel and others in Israel. In considering this passage, however, we must remember its form: it is a prayer. As a prayer it is contingent, optative, hopeful. It may indeed be what Moses prayed (and reflects what *Jubilees* would have thought was said during Moses' time of intercession for Israel on the mountain as reported in Exod. 32:30ff.; Deut. 9:26), but it is not necessarily implied that Moses was assured of *receiving* what he asked for. In fact, the prayer as reported by the author of *Jubilees* appears to deliberately and conspicuously outline and emphasize the *sin* of Israel, much more than any sincere intercession would do. The constant and repeated reminder of Israel's sin in the passage, in other words, hardly adds up to a good case for Israel's forgiveness. The prayer would accordingly seem to serve a rather negative rhetorical purpose as a kind of backhanded intercession.[197] Such adaptation of the prayer form would be entirely in line with *Jubilees'* practice (not alone in this literature) of employing various literary devices in order to address the problems within Israel. (We have already seen, in this regard, how apparently anti-Gentile language is used in *Jubilees* as a foil against Jewish practice.)[198] The irony of this passage is also similar to what is seen in other discourses that tactfully argue the preeminence of Israel from one side of the

---

197. The employment of the wording of Ps. 51:10-11 is superficial (the expressions actually vary in a considerable and significant way), hardly implying the same positive faith as expressed in the psalm.

198. Cf. Endres, 1987, 243.

mouth, all the while implying its unworthiness from the other side (see below for more examples).[199]

This may seem an unjustified approach to what will prove to be a vitally important passage in our treatment, but other scholars have drawn similar conclusions about this passage,[200] and one must not forget the striking parallels in 4 Ezra where the great sage Ezra prayed and was repeatedly disappointed. These writers were aware that, even when it came to the patriarchs, God was not bound by human petition (as with Abraham's intercession for Sodom in Gen. 18:22ff.). God does respond in *Jubilees* 1 with the promise that Israel *will be* restored (vv. 15-18, 23-25), but this promise is for the distant future only (i.e., the real author's own future).[201] This restoration comes only after the *present time of apostasy* (vv. 12-14, 22-23) and *is contingent on repentance* (vv. 15, 22-23). Furthermore, this understanding of the prayer is confirmed by the facts of Israel's history as they are represented by *Jubilees.* The entire record and message of *Jubilees* is that Israel *was not* spared from the dominance of Beliar,[202] from sins of apostasy, from calendrical and other errors, and from destruction (as in ch. 1 itself: vv. 19-20). As we will see below (see esp. ch. 8), other writings adopt a similarly negative perspective on Israel's history based on these words from Deuteronomy. In sum, this prayer of Moses must be read in light of the similar concession Moses makes in Deuteronomy that Israel *will* in fact break the covenant and suffer the consequences,[203] a concession repeated in substance here in *Jubilees:* the words of God that Moses is commanded to "write" will merely bear

199. Perhaps the author also intends to contrast the potential of Israel's future with the actual outcome.

200. G. I. Davenport: "The response in Jub. i, 22-25 rejects the grounds of Moses' plea. . . . these words introduce an indictment of Israel, not an oracle of the future. God knows *their contrariness . . . and their stubbornness*" (*The Eschatology of the Book of Jubilees,* 1971, 26-27, emphasis in original).

201. The structure of the passage demonstrates this. The prophecy speaks of apostasy in the Promised Land (vv. 7-11), followed by the murder of prophets and the Babylonian captivity (vv. 12-13). It is only after the apostasy related to the calendar (v. 14), however, that God's "afterward" is promised (v. 15), and even then only on the condition of repentance. The pattern is repeated in the verses that follow (vv. 22-25) — God will restore Israel on the condition of repentance, which has obviously not yet happened in the author's own time.

202. The prayer of Abraham expresses the desire that he would be saved from the "hands of evil spirits," but *Jubilees* understands Abraham's own deliverance from the spirits to be exceptional: many of his progeny fell to these spirits (cf. 1:19-21). Likewise, protection from Mastema must be invoked for the "seed of Jacob" (19:28), although not all of his seed was spared either.

203. Notably chs. 28–30; cf. also Ps. 106:41. According to Charles, the language of these verses also suggests 2 Kings 21:14; 2 Chron. 6:38; Deut. 10:16, all which assume the condition of exile.

witness against Israel for this apostasy.[204] *Jubilees* has Moses praying for Israel because this is one of the things Exodus tells us he did on the mountain in response to Israel's sin; but considering this highly emotive literary context and the unique historical context in which *Jubilees* places this account, one must be careful not to take such an exceptional passage as representing the complete thought of its writer.

The thought of *Jubilees* is better represented in the rather more direct statement that God will show "mercy" not to everyone but "to hundreds and thousands, *to all who love him*" (23:31). This expression prevents the conclusion that God's mercy has become completely absent in Israel.[205] The reference to "hundreds and thousands," on the other hand, may allude to the "thousands" of Jer. 32:18 to whom God shows mercy, a passage that significantly limits and makes conditional this mercy. The words "all who love him" does nothing to extend this number, but merely specifies the objects of God's mercy. While recognizing the great importance of God's help in enabling and protecting the righteous, therefore, by all appearances mercy in *Jubilees* remains a limited act of God on behalf of some faithful Israelites.[206] Perhaps this mercy was felt to be manifested in the gift of illumination necessary for knowing the exact definition of times, seasons, feasts, and calendar, as well as the strength to obey the laws of *Jubilees* (cf. 23:36).

The Qumran scrolls are considerably more instructive when it comes to God's mercy *(ḥeseḏ)* and the object of this mercy, which is the *particular* people of God who compose the covenant community. The Rule states that God "extends His gracious mercy *towards us* for ever and ever" (1QS 2.1). The "us" in this line are those who have sinned (1.24-26) but have now been enlightened with the "understanding of life" and "everlasting Knowledge" (2.2-3) — in other words, those who have repented and have joined (or, as far as this text is concerned, are now joining) the *yaḥaḏ*. The manifestation of this mercy, therefore, is enlightenment. As we discovered above, this enlightenment involves recognizing the importance of certain ritual and calendrical laws and, perhaps, finding the strength to obey them. It certainly also includes the acceptance of the *pešer* revelation. That God has granted the strength to turn from the error of apostasy and follow the Qumran understanding comes out clearly in the Hymn Scroll.[207] The psalmist himself, perhaps the founder of the community, relates his experience of this mercy (1QH 4.35-37; cf. 1QS 11.13-15). The present and future salvation of the members of the community also depend on God's initiative (and predestination

---

204. Davenport, 1971, 4.
205. As apparently Davenport, 1971, 45.
206. Davenport, 1971, 77.
207. Cf. 1QH 6.9; 18.19-20; etc.; 1QS 2.2-3; Mansoor, 1961, 53, 9.

— 1QH 5.5-6; 9.29ff.; 15.14-16). Mercy is experienced by them daily (6.9; 9.34). It is also apparent that it is the *special* election of the novitiates that has been predetermined (15:14-16); it is the "sons of truth" who are kept by God (9:33, 35); it is the "remnant" who will be judged mercifully (6.8-9); only the one who keeps the covenant (i.e., of the community) is "established . . . from his mother's womb" (15.15). While there is no mention of mercy in relation to restoration in the scrolls, there is otherwise nothing new or different from what has been noted above except that the *exclusive and limited* object of this mercy is particularly accentuated in these writings. Mercy is not the possession of Israel; it is, rather, the unique possession of the *yaḥaḏ*.

The same themes are largely repeated in *Psalms of Solomon*. Mercy is upon those who have understanding, implying that understanding or knowledge is one fundamental manifestation of mercy.[208] The objects of this mercy are variously designated as those "who fear the Lord" (2:33; 13:12; 15:13), "the righteous" (2:35; 9:7), "those who persistently call upon him" (2:36; 6:1-6; 9:6), "his devout" (2:36; 13:12), "all those who love [God]" (4:25; 6:6), "the poor" (5:2), and the like. There are also statements in the psalms to the effect that God's mercy is toward Israel, as in 7:8-10 and 9:8-11, though the latter is a prayer and may again indicate more of a wish than a statement of fact; thus Ryle and James ask whether the prayer for mercy is "a statement or a wish" and conclude that "the latter seems most probable."[209] It also appears to be future looking: "May the mercy of the Lord be upon the house of Israel *forever*." Similar prayers appear at the end of each of Psalms 9–12 and appear to be "wishes," since it is regarded as evident that in recent events God's mercy *has* been at least temporarily suspended. It would seem also to be implied in such passages that this mercy is now being experienced only by those under discipline (7:9) or that mercy is part of a prayer directed toward the *restoration* of Israel (7:10; 8:27-28). Repentance is in any case essential (9:6-7). In sum, it seems that the group represented by the psalms felt no inconsistency in believing in their special election, even though God has likewise held out his hand of mercy to Israel historically and will again do so (perhaps with better results) at the restoration. In each case "the 'Israel' which is the object of such mercy is always a people which turns to God in repentance."[210]

One passage implies that God's mercy *overlooks the sin of the pious* (9:7). Here is a concrete indication that, accompanied with repentance, God's mercy overcomes sin:

---

208. Cf. 2:33; 16:1-5. According to 16:1-5, mercy would appear to be coexistent with understanding, not the result of it.

209. Ryle and James, 1891, 94.

210. M. A. Seifrid, *Justification by Faith*, 1992, 130-31, cf. 127-28.

And whose sins will he forgive except those who have sinned?
You bless the righteous, and do not accuse them for what they sinned.
And your goodness is upon those that sin, when they repent.

This can be taken together with other statements, like that of 15:13, which says that the righteous "shall live by their God's mercy," and the highly personal hymn of 16:1-5, which relates the story of the psalmist's experience of merciful "jabbing," which brought him to repentance. These three passages together imply a conception of mercy that borders on the Pauline conception of grace in its three aspects: clemency for sins committed, infusion of spiritual strength, and stimulation to conversion. Substantial differences must not be overlooked either: mercy in the *Psalms of Solomon* is not as thoroughgoing or absolute as in Paul, and statements about this mercy must also be juxtaposed with other statements about merit (e.g., 14:1-2). Mercy, in other words, like the theology of the psalms generally, is still fundamentally legalistic.[211] But much more important even than these comparisons is that, as with Paul, *mercy is neither universal nor national in its orientation.* This is revealed most distinctly in those statements about mercy that take on a special nuance in view of the fact that the author had recently witnessed a very concrete example of God's mercy in delivering his community from the ill effects of Jerusalem's siege in 63 B.C. It is probably safe to assume that such cataclysmic circumstances helped to bring belief in God's mercy to the fore, as can be seen in 13:1-4 (cf. vv. 6-12). This is another indication that those who escaped — the author's company — have been shown mercy in a way not experienced by others.[212]

211. In 14:1-2 the expressions "who *live in* the righteousness of his commandments" or "in his law" (τοῖς πορευομένοις ἐν δικαιοσύνη προσταγμάτων . . . ἐν νόμῳ . . . ἐν αὐτῷ) seem to indicate a rather legalistic understanding of the purpose of God's law, closely associated here with the covenantal life motif (indicated by the expression "commanded for our life [εἰς ζωὴν ἡμῶν]" that follows; cf. ζήσονται ἐν αὐτῷ, "who live by (or in) [the Law]," v. 3; cf. Deut. 30:19-20) — the implication being that one fulfills God's commandments in order to find life. The employment of the "ἐν" motif here also forms an interesting contrast with Paul's own mystic soteriology and may similarly indicate, to use Seifrid's words, the limits of the "sphere of operation of God's mercy" (1992, 61).

212. Seifrid accordingly responds to Sanders's preoccupation with the Tannaitic material: "The problem of determining the significance of God's covenantal 'mercy' is sharpened when one moves from the relatively irenic Tannaitic materials to the more combative writings such as the Psalms of Solomon. Here a clear distinction emerges between the righteous and wicked within Israel. An appeal to God's strict justice can be directed against 'sinners,' while a plea is made for God's mercy upon the 'pious.' The question arises as to whether notions of unmerited favor are qualified by the restrictions placed upon the sphere of operation of God's mercy" (1992, 61). He also concludes that "Divine promises for salvation no longer apply to the whole of Israel, but to the 'pious' alone" (131).

There is little said about the subject of mercy in the other writings. The role that God's mercy plays in the theodicy of 4 Ezra[213] and how this mercy is extended, in the end, only to the righteous, have already been noted. There is clearly a "special election" emerging in this book based neither on works (as a justifying principle)[214] nor on unconditional grace, but on mercy shown to the chosen few. It is probably true, however, that with all of these writings, including 4 Ezra, the matter of mercy and merit has not been systematically addressed or rationalized by their authors in a way we might wish.[215] Based on some significant differences between, say, *1 Enoch* and 4 Ezra, however, it is probably safe to say that the whole concern was going through a process of development or a stage of growing awareness in the period, through which one does at least begin to get a clearer picture of the role of mercy in these writings. It is nevertheless evident throughout the period that mercy was not considered by adherents to this movement to be extended to all Israel, but is repeatedly and emphatically applied to the righteous alone. Statements to the effect that God is merciful to Israel may imply that the righteous have inherited this mercy or that mercy will be experienced by Israel contingent on repentance. Even when added together, such sayings cannot overturn the otherwise limited understanding of mercy projected by these works. One accordingly cannot accept the implications given to the aspect of mercy by Sanders; these particular writings do not recognize the idea of mercy on *all* Israel with the judgment of a few wicked exceptions; rather, mercy applies to a limited group set apart from the rest of Israel. While these authors do not overlook the mercy once extended to the nation Israel or deny the possibility of mercy to a repentant people in the future, the righteous alone are the manifest recipients of God's mercy in the present.

We have now considered a selection of writings deliberately chosen because they offer startling and clear-cut exceptions to conventional nationalistic views of Second Temple Judaism. While some schools of thought in Judaism no doubt sustained a strong theological nationalism, our conclusion for these groups, at least, is that there is very little evidence of this. It would appear, in fact, that these same groups *rejected with express purpose* nationalistic senti-

---

213. T. W. Willett, *Eschatology in the Theodicies of 2 Baruch and 4 Ezra*, 1989, 68-71.
214. Cf. Willett, 1989, 70.
215. We could hardly expect a fully developed "Lutheran" view of grace. The evidence rather points to ambiguity. Sanders's suggestion that the authors of some of these works held that the righteous were saved by mercy and the wicked were judged according to deserts might provide a solution to *our* questions — but compared to the unsystematic presentations of these writers, such solutions sound very "Lutheran" themselves!

ments and commitments. This has been *negatively* demonstrated through references to a belief in an unmitigated judgment of what must have been a majority of Israelites and by reference to the (in the eyes of these writers) inexcusable apostasy of that majority (ch. 3). It has been *positively* demonstrated by reference to the clear boundaries placed by these groups upon the saved community which by necessity excluded much of Israel and, in way of confirmation, by reference to the exceptional quality of the mercy which God is said to extend to the righteous in Israel (ch. 4).

Given these data, what can we say has happened to Israel's doctrine of national election, or to the idea of the national covenant, among such groups? While attempts to answer these questions from a *theological* perspective are forthcoming, it remains first to come up with an *historical* explanation for the baffling statements that we have seen — that is, an explanation for how, and under what circumstances, any self-respecting Israelite group could possibly formulate what in every sense appears to be a doctrine of "special election."

CHAPTER FIVE

Reform and Dissent — The Sociohistorical Context

Since certain features of these writings evince a judgment-of-Israel theme and an exclusive view of salvation, this tends to place in doubt conventional nationalistic views of election, at least as pertains to *this type* of Judaism, and one might conclude on this basis that much of the study of Judaism has been based on false assumptions. The danger, however, of considering such features in isolation from their historical context is that they might be wrongly interpreted or, more likely still, be given undue emphasis. Their real importance can only be determined by attention to the historical and sociological context in which they were written. Another way of saying this is that there is a kind of circularity involved in exegeting historical texts: the texts throw light on the background, which throws light on the texts, which shed still more light on the background, and so on. It is this background, or context, that the present chapter intends to clarify. Doing this will also help to answer important questions like: What led the authors of these texts to this position? If a strongly nationalistic sentiment existed in Judaism, how is it that some Israelites arrived at such an exclusivist soteriology? What reasons would one part of Judaism have for pronouncing judgment upon another?

Several different approaches have been taken to the question of sociohistorical backgrounds for these writings. These can best be discussed under four broad categories: (1) *classical sociological approaches*, (2) approaches that emphasize *Hellenism as an historical catalyst*, (3) approaches from the point of view of *intra-Jewish social conflict*, which take as their starting point the existence of a Jewish "reform party," and (4) more recent sociological theories, particularly those that employ *"displacement theories."*

187

Classical Sociological Approaches

Max Weber's designation of the Jewish people as a "pariah" people (*Pariavolk*, "outcasts") is now a famous socioreligious description and the usual starting point for most sociological studies of Judaism.[1] Weber further defined "pariah people" as "guest" people, those without a homeland of their own, surrounded by foreigners, and segregated from others by their particularistic (i.e., exclusivistic) law and cult.[2] Tracing developments through the exilic period that led to this social condition and concentrating on the formative roles played by prophecy, traditional ritualism, and the priestly oriented Torah, Weber concluded that these developments encouraged an exclusivist Israelite ethic that, in turn, eventually culminated in the birth of a "confessional association" *(konfessionelle Glaubensgemeinschaft)*, an inward-looking state of existence provoked by the confinements of a foreign (Babylonian) context. During this period a "dualism of in-group and out-group morality" developed on the basis of certain laws like sabbath and dietary regulations and helped to cut Israel off from her Gentile neighbors even while its people were forced to live among Gentiles. This process was furthered by Ezra's absolute prohibition of intermarriage, which sealed the absolute segregation of the people and guaranteed it for the future.[3] One might say that Israel had become an island unto itself, and this, for Weber, was the most important and creative social factor in the Jewish experience in exile and throughout postexilic history as well.

Weber's results, not to mention his methodology, have been repeatedly questioned.[4] One of the most revealing critiques by a scholar studying this particular period of Jewish history comes from S. Talmon, who raised issues with certain aspects of Weber's typology.[5] Weber assumed that all significant sociological relationships could be described within the above-mentioned pattern: "in-group" (Israel) versus "out-group" (Gentile nations).[6] In fairness to Weber, he was limited in his analysis of Judaism to Jewish documents known prior to the discovery of the Dead Sea Scrolls, and he relied heavily on secondary sources for his understanding of Judaism. Partly as a result of this limited knowledge (which naturally included the acceptance of a nationalistic understanding inherited from scholars of Judaism), Weber did not even consider that

1. M. Weber, *Ancient Judaism*, 1952, 51, 336, 363, 417, etc.

2. Cf. Weber, 1952, 51, 417.

3. Weber, 1952, 336-54.

4. Cf., e.g., A. Momigliano, "A Note on Max Weber's Definition of Judaism as a Pariah-Religion," 1987, 231-37.

5. S. Talmon, *King, Cult, and Calendar in Ancient Judaism,* 1986, 165-201. For a summary of challenges to Weber from various fronts, cf. 166-69.

6. Weber, 1952, 343ff.; Talmon, 1986, 185-86.

a third type of relationship was involved.[7] This relationship Talmon calls the "in*ner*-group" relationship, to be distinguished from the "*in*-group" relationship.[8] This third "inner-group" typology takes into consideration the divisions *within* Israel that were in evidence from the early postexilic period on.[9]

More recent sociologists who adopt standard sociological approaches have now at least acknowledged that important problem not sufficiently addressed by their forerunner — the problem of sectarianism in Judaism.[10] As is well known, a large percentage of these sociologists have embraced the basic tenets of Marxist socioeconomic theory and have applied them to the sects in Judaism.[11] In line with this perspective it is commonly maintained that with the repeated loss of land and cult experienced by the Jews the condition of the very poor in Israel became especially vulnerable and even intolerable, resulting in angry responses of separation and protest. Besides the fact that much of this kind of sociological characterization based on economic models has been rejected as oversimplified, the notion that separation and protest were especially characteristic of the *poor* is itself a supposition not confirmed by the data.[12] Evidence from the scrolls, for example, suggests that some of the members of the

---

7. Talmon, 1986, 172-73, also blames the generally "unsatisfactory *Stand der Forschung* in the history of the Second Temple period in Weber's days, especially with reference to the last two centuries B.C.E. and the first century C.E." (171).

8. Talmon, 1986, 185-86.

9. Talmon, 1986, 176-87.

10. "In this context, the issue of 'in-group vs. out-group morality' does not apply to the separation of Jews from non-Jews, but rather pertains to the internal diversification which had manifested itself distinctly already in Judaism of the days of the Return, intensified at the height of the Second Temple Period and reached its apex in the first century of the Christian era" (Talmon, 1986, 200). While Weber did treat the Pharisees and the later rabbis (repeating, however, the commonly accepted belief by scholars of Weber's era that after A.D. 70, "all Judaism became Pharisaic"; cf. 1952, 391), this did not allow him the insights into a well-documented separatist group from the Second Temple period such as the Dead Sea Scrolls now provide. Weber understood the Pharisees and rabbis as "brotherhoods," a "community of like-minded persons" (386-87), a characterization still perpetuated by many recent studies of sectarianism. Talmon suggests that the new evidence from Qumran must "prompt a reevaluation of Weber's describing the Pharisees' stance as Sektenreligiosität" (174).

11. Cf. S. W. Baron, *A Social and Religious History of the Jews,* 1952, 1:262-85, 2:3-61; H. Jagersma, *A History of Israel from Alexander the Great to Bar Kochba,* 1985, 2, 22-27, 57-58, 65, 92-94; R. T. Herford, *Judaism in the New Testament Period,* 1928, 59-60; W. W. Buehler, *The Pre-Herodian Civil War and Social Debate,* 1974; for summary, cf. 68-69. For political factors, cf. Buehler; S. J. D. Cohen, "The Political and Social History of the Jews in the Greco-Roman Antiquity," 1986, 34-48.

12. Cf. M. Smith, *Palestinian Parties and Politics That Shaped the Old Testament,* 1971, 79-80; S. B. Reid, *Enoch and Daniel,* 1989, 34 n. 69.

Qumran community were people of means,[13] and scholars have pointed to other disparities in the evidence.[14] It would also seem logical that the economically depressed would be too constrained by their situation to react effectively in ways that these sociologists have suggested. But beyond these very good reasons for doubt, such approaches, like Weber's, also still tend to relegate the greatest importance to the one plane of social relationships — Jews versus Gentiles — and relatively little to Jews versus other Jews. In fact, all these socioeconomic approaches generally focus on the dualism of Jew versus Gentile because blame for economic disadvantage and therefore all the protest and reaction are naturally assumed to be directed against the Gentile rulers of Israel, particularly the Seleucids, and not against others in Israel — who on the whole are felt also to have been relatively poor and powerless (another misleading presupposition). Sectarianism was therefore fundamentally the reaction of *all* Judaism against the Seleucids, not of individual groups against other groups or against the Jews' own leaders. The social categorization "sect," in other words, was applied to *all* of Judaism; or, as it was occasionally articulated: "all Judaism was in form sectarian," a position not far from Weber. This view, it might be added, was dependent upon the common but now known to be largely mistaken equation of the Pharisaic "sect" with "official" or mainstream Judaism; the vast majority of Jews, it was implicitly believed, were "Pharisaic"; thus Judaism itself was sectarian in character — again, compare Weber.

More recently, however, largely because of the discovery of the Dead Sea Scrolls, more careful attention to the Pseudepigrapha, and generally improved historical methodology as well, it has become quite evident that some — indeed most — Jews belonged to no *single* party or sect (least of all the Pharisees!). "Pan-Pharisaism," as it has come to be called, has needed to be reevaluated. As a result more recent (and more adequate) characterizations of

---

13. The reference in 4QpHab 12.10 to הון אביונים (lit. "the wealth of the poor") has suggested to some that terminology of poverty was not strictly literal (cf., e.g., H. Ringgren, *The Faith of Qumran,* 1963, 143), and it is likely on other grounds that the Qumranite theology of humility and poverty was primarily ideological. In any event, as Reid points out, it would be "simplistic to propose that social protest is the sole provenance of those who are economically deprived" (1989, 34 n. 69). In the case of Qumran, at least, it would seem that poverty was *not* the primary motivation for protest.

14. W. Schmithals, *The Apocalyptic Movement,* 1975, 142-45, e.g., finds little evidence of economic depravity in the apocalyptic writings; rather, their authors were from among "people of more than a little culture and education" (144). T. W. Willett, *Eschatology in the Theodicies of 2 Baruch and 4 Ezra,* 1989, 44, points to the upper-class provenance of the "apocalypses" as indicated by their association with wisdom, their learned style, and their esoterism. Note that Josephus (*Ant.* 13.284) suggests that the Seleucid period was a time of unprecedented prosperity for the people in Jerusalem, the countryside, and the Diaspora.

sectarianism recognize that Judaism accommodated a *multiplicity* of societies or *sub*societies existing together (often in conflict) within the larger Israelite society and within the still larger Ptolemaic or Seleucid society. With such new advances in understanding, older social theories that implied a *uniformity* of social experience for all of Judaism began to seem less relevant. And since the problem of the existence of independent sects remained particularly problematic for these theories, a more realistic and less simplistic view of the inner-pluralism of Jewish society was needed.

Hellenism as an Historical Catalyst

Turning away somewhat from sociological description, scholars began to fill this need with more historically based theories. To be precise, some scholars proposed that developments and events in Palestine were partly or largely a function of the *influx of "Hellenism"* (the politics, language, culture, and lifestyle of advancing Greek ideology and society). Weber himself, it should be noted, recognized the formative influence of Hellenism on Judaism, particularly on growing sectarianism (i.e., for him, Pharisaism).[15] More recently, however, Hellenism has been seen to have a more material, less subtle, influence than previously realized, an influence that eventually led to both positive and negative reactions within the Jewish world — and strong reactions at that![16] At first Greek thought moved into Judea gradually, however, and relationships between Jews and Greeks in the early period, notably those with Alexander himself, were quite cordial.[17] This is an important fact indeed — it signified that many aspects of Hellenism would be able to infiltrate the Hebrew world virtually unopposed so that, before long, the two societies and two lifestyles would become to a high degree intertwined. But it also assured that *reaction,* which also seemed to have built up only very gradually at first, would assume an even more noncompromising and explosive form during the periods of crisis and conflict that were to come. It is in this crisis and conflict between Judaism and Hellenism that this second group of scholars comprehend the origins of social upheaval and of sectarian debate in Judea.

It is unanimously agreed that foremost among the historical factors that led to the "crisis" that eventually climaxed in Judaism's bloody resistance

---

15. Weber, 1952, 385.

16. Cf. M. Hengel, *Judaism and Hellenism,* 1974, vol. 1, passim; esp. conclusions, 310-14; Smith, 1971, 57-81.

17. For the evidence that Alexander was welcomed by the residents of Palestine, including Jews, cf. Gafni, CRINT, II/2, 3-4.

against its Gentile overlords were tendencies toward syncretism between the Jewish cult — reverenced for its purity — and other more "heathen" forms of worship. In other words, it was only when Hellenism began to have *obvious* religious implications that many Jews reacted. A potent legal expression of this syncretism is the well-known edict of Antiochus IV "Epiphanes," which was accompanied by the ritual defilement of the temple on 15 Kislev 167 B.C. and effectively eradicated the distinctly Jewish aspects of the cult.[18] The cause, and exact significance, of this event are widely debated. Antiochus's "campaign against Judaism" has been interpreted, on the one hand, as an expression of a mad ruler's rigorous personal *Hellenizing program* (Antiochus assuming the weight of the "blame"); but, from a completely opposite point of view, it has also been viewed as only the *result of the Jews' resistance to Hellenism*, which in turn enraged the ruler and further hardened him in his intentions (Jews assuming the weight of the "blame"). While it has commonly been supposed that Antiochus was an oppressive and even demented ruler, theories about his actions based on merely psychological explanations have become the subject of scrutiny and controversy of late, and there is a growing tendency to reject them as oversimplistic. The rather more philosophical or ideological explanation that Antiochus IV coerced the Jews to abandon their religion in the interest of his program to eradicate Judaism and instill a universal form of religion out of his commitment to Hellenization has also been thrown into doubt for various reasons. The policy of "Hellenization," for one thing, normally favored a measure of religious autonomy and embraced freedom and variety. Antiochus, with the possible exception of his action in 167 B.C., is generally portrayed in the sources as following this policy and otherwise exhibits no propensity for eradicating the religions of his subjects in favor of his own ideologies.

Whatever the exact motivations at work, the proscription of traditional Jewish practice (including such central facets as sabbath and circumcision) and the order to initiate a program of daily sacrifice to foreign gods were very real and became centrally important factors in the subsequent reaction. So if psychological or ideological motivations fail to explain Antiochus's actions, some other explanation is required, and one solution has been offered by what might be called Jewish conspiracy theories. Such theories maintain that the events of persecution were catalyzed by a Hellenizing party *within* Judaism,[19] an understanding that is strongly encouraged by the writer of 1 Maccabees (esp. 1:11-15). This writer lays blame squarely on the shoulders of some

---

18. For the event and its implications, cf., e.g., E. Schürer, *The History of the Jewish People in the Age of Jesus Christ (175 B.C.–A.D. 135)*, 1973, 1:147-56; S. Zeitlin, *The Rise and Fall of the Judaean State*, 1968, 77-78.

19. Cf. V. Tcherikover, *Hellenistic Civilization and the Jews*, 1961, 89, 117-34.

of his own people, particularly those who were captivated by the Hellenistic ideal and appeared willing to betray traditional Jewish ways to implement it. It has even been suggested by some that such a Jewish "reform party" *actively conspired* with Antiochus in a joint objective of eradicating traditional Judaism, and it was in the name of this common cause that both parties agreed to establish a pagan altar in the Jerusalem Temple. Elias Bickermann is noted for adopting a quite radical position with regard to the involvement of these Jewish "Hellenizers." Responding to clues from 1 and 2 Maccabees that imply the existence of a very *active* reform movement, Bickermann supposed that these reformers not only supported Hellenization in principle, but even promoted civil persecution against the traditionalists in order to speed up the process of Hellenization.[20] He justifies these conclusions with the following type of reasoning:

> It will hardly have mattered to Epiphanes, a man who attended the lectures of the Epicureans, whether the people of Jerusalem, like those in Hierapolis, abstained from pork, or following the Greek taste, preferred that particular food. The reformers, however, who had emerged from Judaism, naturally considered every iota of the law as no less significant than did the orthodox. And, like all religious reformers, they surpassed the traditional believers in intolerance, by arranging a bloody persecution against the "backward."[21]

The persecuting campaign of Antiochus, in line with this, was at the instigation and even the invitation of certain Jews who were committed to ridding the people of outmoded vestiges of their traditional religion, which these reformers saw as obstructing the progress of the Hellenistic ideal. Bickermann points out, furthermore, that the reform movement was no elite movement since the majority of people were by this time involved with Greek ways.[22]

Bickermann's thesis has been received with enthusiasm — it was given significant support, for example, in the detailed scholarly work of Martin Hengel,[23] and most scholars now accept the historical fact of the two-party theory, or at least the existence of a Hellenizing reform group. But Bickermann's thesis was not persuasive enough to settle the issue altogether. Two types of responses are worth noting. There are those, first of all, who have questioned the source and derivation of Bickermann's understanding and have virtually re-

---

20. E. Bickermann, *The God of the Maccabees*, 1979, 1.

21. Bickermann, 1979, 89-90.

22. The "many"; cf. 1 Macc. 1:43, 52; 2:16, 23; 6:21; although the wealthy leaders of the group were presumably among the most active in the persecution (Bickermann, 1979, 90).

23. Hengel, 1974, 1:267-309.

turned to the older position. Roger Beckwith, for example, denies that there was ever anything so concrete as a well-defined "reform party" in Judaism that sought the Hellenization of the people,[24] and Fergus Millar argues that Antiochus's military endeavors do cohere with the view that he was attempting to eradicate the practice of Jewish law on programmatic grounds.[25] A second type of response to Bickermann comes from those who take issue with the degree of *direct* involvement by the reform party in the actual religious persecutions. Among them, Victor Tcherikover presents Antiochus's motives as political rather than strictly religious — although the former necessarily involved the latter.[26] He explains that as a result of a certain visit of Antiochus to Jerusalem (for the purpose of plundering the Temple treasury) the Jerusalemites began to incline away from the now politically weak Seleucids, of whom Antiochus was a member, in favor of the Ptolemies (who had originally acquired the Egyptian portion of Alexander's kingdom and had earlier ruled in Palestine). Then, on rumors of Antiochus's death, the city reverted to more traditional ways altogether and halted attempts to make Jerusalem a Greek polis. It was this more than anything that provoked Antiochus to take desperate actions. Thus Tcherikover concludes that "it was not the revolt which came as a response to the persecution, but the persecution which came as a response to the revolt."[27] This attempt by Tcherikover to reverse the usual order of cause and effect is not, however, without its problems. Tcherikover assumes a Syrian presence in the Temple area and changes in the Temple cult an entire year prior to the well-known decree forbidding Jewish worship, which involve inferences based on a doubtful interpretation of the sources.[28] It is also questionable whether one can disregard the evidence of 1 Maccabees, which suggests that the *main thrust* of Jewish rebellion came about as a *response* to the Antiochene persecution and not previous to that persecution. The more or less established reliability of 1 Maccabees is accordingly a damaging crux for this theory.[29]

24. Cf. R. Beckwith, "The Pre-History and Relationships of the Pharisees, Sadducees and Essenes," 1982, 3-46, 41.

25. F. Millar, "The Background to the Maccabean Revolution," 1978, 1-21.

26. Tcherikover, 1961, passim. Cf. also D. E. Gowan, *Bridge between the Testaments,* 1986, 77-80. For a slightly different approach from a political perspective, cf. B. Reicke, *The New Testament Era,* 1968, 52, 54-57.

27. Tcherikover, 1961, 191.

28. There is no indication in *Ant.* 12.246-47 that the opposition was to cultic reform, or that the event necessarily led to it, but was probably political, based in pro-Ptolemaic sentiments.

29. Tcherikover's point that the counterreform movement already had taken root by the time of the formal persecution is well taken. But can we go so far as to effectively transfer the blame for the campaign from the Hellenizers to the ḥaśidim, as he does (cf. 1961, 198-203)? According to 1 Maccabees, the *initial* campaigns of Mattathias were

The notion that political influences were at play, however, is a point well taken, and it is perhaps not surprising that many scholars have chosen a compromise position between two extremes, reasoning that, on the one hand, the evidence for intra-Jewish debate is compelling but, on the other hand, there is also little doubt that Antiochus's character and motivations — particularly his political motivations — played a significant role.[30] Otto Plöger attempts to combine the various factors playing into Antiochus's attitude, while also sustaining the theory about the involvement of the Hellenizing Jews:

> we are probably justified in assuming that the relation of Antiochus to the Jewish community was determined in the first instance, at any rate, by political considerations. The fact that in the course of time other motives of a financial and ideological nature assumed prominence should certainly not be denied or underestimated; but action of this nature would have been inconceivable without encouragement from the Jewish side. In fact, in view of the plans of Hyrcanus it is conceivable that the circles which had enlisted in support of the Seleucids in Jerusalem, especially the Tobiad family, were concerned to dispel the hesitations of the new ruler and, by means of a "Hellenistic" statement of belief, to present him with the spectacle of a politically reliable Jerusalem.[31]

However the various motivations are combined in terms of detail, it would seem that Antiochus, still hurting from the military humiliation recently experienced at the hand of the Romans in Egypt, was partly compelled by political ambition and pride to take action against the Jewish community. On the other hand, it must be accepted as probable that not even an enraged ruler would have acted in an unpopular fashion. It is much more likely that there was a strong presence in Jerusalem of those in favor with Antiochus. These people realized that their welfare could only be enhanced by a still more favorable political alignment, and to this end they provided the king with guarantees that they would reform the cult and faith of Israel in order to discourage traditional — and anti-Seleucid — sentiments. Although these same people would scarcely have envisioned the horrible events that followed, they may have assured Antiochus that firm measures taken by the secular authority against the traditional religion would, in the long run, also promote their common objectives. Such an understanding coheres well with the fact that the Hellenized (as

---

fought, *not* against the Seleucids, but against his own renegade Israelites, implying that the counterrebellion arose in *response* to the edict of Antiochus (cf. Bickermann, 1979, 90).

30. Cf. Zeitlin, 1968, 1:77-78; O. Plöger, *Theocracy and Eschatology,* 1968, 2; Gafni, CRINT, II/2, 7-8; etc.

31. Plöger, 1968, 6.

opposed to traditional) Jews probably had the upper hand in Jerusalem at the time, enjoyed the support of the populace, and generally appeared (to Antiochus if to no one else) to be in control of things.[32] It is true that the superior position of the reformers may have been more the result of political domination than of popular approval *per se*. It is also true that the large majority of the people probably remained uncommitted or even silently opposed to the view of the Hellenizers (which is suggested by the popularity of the Maccabean movement, at least among the population outside Jerusalem).[33] But it would also be consistent with human nature, and the rather utilitarian outlook of average people, for this majority to remain inactive and uninterested. There are many instances in the history of every people in which the lack of political will by the people ensures that the will of those with ambitions, however misdirected, wins the day. The review of the history of late Second Temple Judaism outlined below will generally bear this out in that case as well.

To whatever extent the reform movement is to be seen as *actively* cooperating with the actions of the king (as opposed to more passive compliance), all versions of this approach are at least similar in their opinion that Antiochus offered political support to one faction of Israelites, who are regularly referred to as the "Hellenizers" or "the reform party," and that this support was to the disadvantage of another faction, which one might call the "conservatives" or "traditionalists." Much of what went on in Jerusalem can accordingly be explained as a result of interaction between two types of Judaism: an establishment Judaism that was very progressive and may even have encouraged a thoroughgoing Hellenistic reform in Jerusalem and a traditional, conservative Judaism that would eventually resist the changes to be brought onto the cult and the people and provoke the events about to unfold in the Maccabean revolt. It should be noted that not all of this latter group would resort to military and political counterreform or even allow themselves to be identified with the Maccabees and their type of response; others chose physical and ideological separation.[34] Thus a new explanation for the conflicts that raged in Judaism has been formulated in terms of two basic groups within the Jewish community whose differences came to a head during the reform attempts of Antiochus. While earlier sociological studies credited the actions of the reform largely to motivations *outside* Judaism, concern for the meaning of historical events shifted attention to motivations *within* the nation. In this respect, therefore, historical inquiry has done scholarship a service that sociological inquiry by itself could not manage.

32. Cf. Schürer, 1973, 1:145.
33. Millar, 1978, 12.
34. This diversity of reaction was recognized by Schürer (1973, 1:145-48) and the editors of the volume (1:153 n. 37); cf. also Gowan, 1986, 80.

Recent Approaches, Including Displacement Theories

With this willingness now to recognize the existence and involvement of *various groups within Judaism,* renewed attempts have been made by scholars to bring sociological analysis to bear on the question. Typically these attempts apply "displacement" theories to particular groups, or "subsocieties," within Israel at various periods in history. The main feature of these groups is that they have been ousted from some privileged position, or if not originally socially prominent, have at least separated themselves from the security and acceptability of mainstream life in Judaism in some way.[35] The most significant advance of these approaches over older sociological treatments, therefore, comes with their recognition of the complex social structure *within* Judaism.[36] Paul Hanson, in his study of apocalyptic groups, led the way in this new approach.[37] While Hanson claimed that his study was not about apocalypticism as a sociological phenomenon but about "apocalyptic eschatology," which is a "religious *perspective,*"[38] his work in many ways resembled earlier sociological approaches, but with important differences: his study emphasized the *intra*-Jewish nature of the conflict and put less emphasis on the direct influence of Hellenism.

> What did the visionaries of the sixth century and the Zadokites of the second have in common? Not party affiliation, but a common status in the community. Our study indicated that that status was one of *disenfranchisement and alienation* from the institutional structures of the community which made peers of disciples of Second Isaiah, defrocked Levitical priests, and likely other minorities within the community which remain anonymous to us.[39]

Hanson accordingly adopted a sociopsychological approach to the question of the origins of apocalyptic eschatology. He arrived at his conclusions by noting that the chief difference between the "apocalyptist" and the "prophet" was that the apocalyptist did not relate his prophecy to the historical context, to the daily life of the nation, as did the prophet. Thus apocalyptic eschatology is a

---

35. Gowan (1986, 357), R. R. Hann ("The Community of the Pious," 1988, 173), J. Blenkinsopp ("A Jewish Sect of the Persian Period," 1990, 9-10, 18-19), and D. W. Suter (*Tradition and Composition in the Parables of Enoch,* 1979, 69, cf. 164) apply this theory to various periods in Israelite history.

36. M. Weber had already spoken of the formation of pietistic movements in Judaism resulting from the political displacement of the intellectual proletariat (*The Sociology of Religion,* 1963, 125-26), but the discussion was typically contained within the context of Jewish-Gentile relationships.

37. P. D. Hanson, *The Dawn of Apocalyptic,* 1979, passim.

38. Hanson, 1979, 431, emphasis in original.

39. Hanson, 1979, 409, emphasis added.

truncated form of prophecy, prophecy without earthly implications and applications, and accordingly possessing its own distinct "symbolic universe."[40] Only a displaced group outside the mainstream of life would ignore the established institutions and political life of the nation the way this literature does. Hanson accordingly concluded that the apocalyptic perspective had its origins within a persecuted minority of the disfranchised, alienated, or displaced members of Israel and that it reflected a kind of antipathy between establishment and sectarian Judaism in the context of which an antiestablishment apocalyptic mind-set could take root. Hanson's treatment of examples of emerging apocalyptic from the Hebrew Scriptures (Isaiah 55–66, Zechariah 9–14, etc.) suggests that this religious perspective was manifested at a relatively early time, and that the establishment/sectarian controversy possessed a correspondingly lengthy history. Hanson also effectively depoliticized apocalypticism: it is not to be associated with any one party in Judaism but is characteristic of many groups across a wide spectrum of time. Along with his attempt to root the movement in antiestablishment protest, this is perhaps the strongest contribution of his work.[41]

Another recent sociological treatment, that of S. B. Reid,[42] subjects individual portions of Daniel and *1 Enoch* to investigation according to the sociological models of sectarianism provided by Bryan Wilson, categorizing each writing and portion of writing according to its "focus of identity" ("mass," "community," or "communion," terms first introduced by George Gurvitch). This approach, not unlike other displacement theories, works on the hypothesis that "social change is the by-product of the encounter of two cultures, usually of unequal power and status," what Reid calls the "diffusion theory." His conclusions are interesting: Daniel originated among a group forming what the typology terms a "community" — those who primarily define themselves over

40. We must differ with Hanson somewhat: these groups did not promote an ahistorical stance, as is often assumed for them. However, they do not relate their concerns to the state of the established institutions, as did the canonical prophets, and for this reason Hanson's view is fully justifiable.

41. Drawbacks to Hanson's study include his overconfidence in a form-critical and typological methodology that he employs to date writings with exactitude and to set them into precise sociological settings (for criticism of Hanson's "syllable counting" methodology as oversimplistic, cf. J. Blenkinsopp, "Interpretation and the Tendency to Sectarianism," 1988, 13). The exclusion of all perspectives except the eschatological one raises the question whether Hanson has not also, by this self-limitation, excluded other important data essential for discerning the *Sitz im Leben* of the material. One might also wish he had given more attention to some of the instances of *intertestamental* "apocalyptic" in order to establish and confirm a parallel between their sociological context and that of the canonical examples.

42. Reid, 1989, passim.

against the larger social entity, in this case the Hellenistic world. *1 Enoch* (in its several portions), on the other hand, comes from a "communion" — those who primarily define themselves over against their more immediate social context, in this case the *rest of Judaism*. Thus while Hanson rooted "apocalyptic" writings in intra-Jewish conflict between establishment circles and displaced groups in a general way, Reid demonstrated how this comes to bear on one of these writings in particular: the group responsible for *1 Enoch* has clearly defined itself, not over against the Gentile or Hellenistic world, but over against the rest of Judaism.

Not all recent attempts based on displacement theories have been as helpful as those by Hanson or Reid. One possible reason for their failure is that sociologists frequently try to import foreign typologies for their investigation of ancient Jewish groups. Few sociological approaches, in fact, bring to Judaism typologies and models that have been developed for the specific purpose of categorizing *Judaism*. Much more common is the application of typologies and models originally developed for the purpose of categorizing Christianity. A good example of this is what is known as the "millenarian" model, which, although it is applied to the study of Judaism, at several points betrays a much more obvious relevance to later Christian and Christian-like groups, particularly groups stressing the need for conversion. A millenarian movement, as described by S. R. Isenberg,[43] emerges in a time of social unrest and offers the promise of decisive social change. According to D. J. Tidball,[44] there are four prerequisites for the movement to arise: (1) there must be a desire for change created by a stressful situation, usually resulting from social injustice; (2) there must be a "new interpretation of life"; (3) there must be a "prophet" who grants authority to this interpretation; and (4) there must be a promise of "heaven on earth," a paradisiacal fortune to be enjoyed by members of the movement (hence "millenarianism" from the Millennium, the thousand-year motif of Rev. 20:2, 4, 6-7). These prerequisites reveal that this model is not very well suited for social analysis of Jewish groups, which may lack several of these characteristics, but is much better suited for modern movements that exhibit most or all of them.

A variation of the millenarian typology that claims to derive its typology directly from Judaism is G. Theissen's model based on what he calls "Jewish renewal movements." While derived from Judaism, it is again to an analysis of the movement that formed around Jesus that the model is applied most rigorously in Theissen's treatment.[45] Renewal movements, according to Theissen, are products of socioeconomic, socioecological, sociopolitical, and sociocultural

---

43. R. S. Isenberg, "Millenarianism in Greco-Roman Palestine," 1974, 26-46.
44. D. J. Tidball, *An Introduction to the Sociology of the New Testament,* 1983, 28ff.
45. G. Theissen, *The First Followers of Jesus,* 1978, passim.

factors. They take root in the hinterland of Judea, where there is more independence of mind and where, on the other hand, people are more subject to external influences. This geographical factor is accompanied by a corresponding identity crisis: Who are the real people of God? Why is God punishing them with poverty and the tyrannical rule of Gentiles? And how should they react to this?[46] These questions can be plausibly credited to the minds of Second Temple Jews, but Theissen's typology is rather more difficult to apply when he defines a renewal movement in more detail as structured around three groups of individuals who play an essential "role" in the movement: (1) "wandering charismatics," who are typified by homelessness and by a lack of family and possessions and depend on the support of others, (2) "their sympathizers in the local communities," and (3) "the bearer of revelation," to which Theissen likens wandering Cynic philosophers, and although he admits that parallels for these last figures may be difficult to find in Judaism, notes that "the hospitality of Essene groups is very similar to the hospitality of local Christian communities towards their wandering preachers."[47]

Besides the difficulty that may be involved in making these criteria fit the Jewish groups we are investigating, it is obvious that once again the overriding concern in the comparison is to investigate early Christianity (the primitive Jesus movement). The "renewal movement" is a paradigm better suited to the latter (and entirely suited to Stoic conventions!) rather than to any known groups in Judaism. It is in fact difficult to determine whether Theissen actually has in mind any *concrete* instances of renewal movements *in Judaism*. He describes them as if they did exist, and in some ways the model calls to mind the Maccabean and Zealot movements, but only superficially. Obviously there will always be problems with any attempt to establish a model by which to analyze Jewish communities on the basis of typologies better suited to Christian groups. When it comes to the crucial role of the charismatic or wandering prophet in Theissen's model, for example, one fails to find consistent correlations with the Jewish groups known to us. Even the Dead Sea sect, which eventually became quite dependent on their "Teacher of Righteousness," traced their origins back to a time prior to the appearance of that Teacher when they were "like men who groping seek their way for twenty years" (CD 1.9-10). Besides the fact that it was the group, not their leader, who was "wandering," it is hard to believe that the sect enjoyed no organizational structure or social identity before the Teacher arrived (most theories of Qumran origins suggest quite the opposite!). And it is not at all clear — indeed, it is intrinsically doubtful —

46. For similarities, cf. Tidball, 1983, 48.
47. Theissen, 1978, 22.

that the groups responsible for *Jubilees, Psalms of Solomon,* the Temple Scroll, 4 Ezra, or *2 Baruch* took root in "the hinterland of Judaea."

Other important difficulties arise with such typologies, as one would expect from any attempt to investigate complex social movements by employing imported models, however valid they may be in other contexts. Beyond the difficulties of making such a model fit, however, perhaps the most significant issue raised by displacement theories, whether of Hanson, Reid, or millenarian typologists, is that they focus primarily on what might be called the *leadership versus membership* dichotomy. They all attempt to highlight the encounter between those presently in a place of power and either those who have been displaced from power or those who otherwise no longer benefit from the structures (religious and otherwise) controlled by the leadership elite.[48] While this approach focuses on intra-Jewish relationships and is for this reason a significant advance on the older sociological approaches, it nevertheless still makes the unwarranted assumption that political factors are determinative and that the crucial encounter is between the power-holding classes, on the one hand, and the "displaced," on the other. While this approach may adequately explain the "we/they" mentality in our writings, is it always the case that the Jewish *leadership* plays the role of the despised "they" in the dichotomy? Does there exist in this literature any evidence that the group *over against which* the sectarians *defined* themselves were in *every* case those possessing political and economic power?

One may well want to answer "not necessarily." Michael Stone points out that among the anti-assimilationists addressed by Ben Sira, for example, were members of the wealthy classes, and thus "to simply contrast pietistic opponents of Hellenism and rich, priestly or aristocratic assimilationists is surely to over-simplify."[49] Conversely, references to the sins of the rich and powerful are limited to a few of these writings only and may merely reflect the "ideology of poverty" of the groups.[50] Some displacement theories focus on divisions over the priesthood, the locus of power in Judaism, yet for all the interest in priestly affairs displayed in these writings the members of these groups (notably Qumran) were by no means composed entirely or even mostly of priests, disenfranchised, or otherwise.[51] Some writings that focus on the priesthood seem to do so only because of the inherent importance of the office, not because of the

48. As a good example, cf. Isenberg's "loss of redemptive media" (1974, 26-46).

49. M. E. Stone, "The Book of Enoch and Judaism in the Third Century B.C.E.," 1978, 481.

50. Schmithals, 1975, 144-45, rightly speaks of poverty as more of a correlation than a cause of the apocalyptic understanding of existence.

51. Note J. J. Collins's comments on *Ass. Mos.* 4:8 ("The Date and Provenance of the Testament of Moses," in Nickelsburg, 1973).

concerns of special interest groups composed of priests.[52] If one adds to these considerations the fact that during the lengthy period covered by these writings (third century B.C. to second century A.D.) one witnesses a *wide* spectrum of political situations, including periods of political and national rebuilding (Ezra and Nehemiah), of oppressive subjugation (Ptolemies and Seleucids, Romans), of national revival (Maccabees), of military campaign and expansion followed by disintegration (Hasmoneans), of military destruction (the second Jewish war), and of consolidation (the Tannaites), it becomes obviously futile to try to apply with consistent or dependable results any single typology based on political considerations.[53] If there is any common link among writings that otherwise assume such vastly disparate historical and political contexts, in other words, it will have to be one that transcends somewhat the various political and sociological ups and downs experienced by the nation over this lengthy period of time.

HOW DOES ONE ACCOUNT FOR THE EXCLUSIVIST ATTITUDE TOWARD ISRAEL?

In order to determine what unifying thread traverses these variegated textures of history, it would naturally be helpful to seek the historical roots of the exclusivist attitude that characterizes these writings by returning to the period in which the issues first emerged. In this regard it is oversimplistic to assume, as many scholars do, that the period of most intense Hellenization and the period of critical debate began only with Antiochus IV Epiphanes. Martin Hengel and others have shown that Hellenistic influence on Judaism was felt well before the events associated with the reign of Antiochus and that reaction to Hellenism may have started even as early as the third century.[54] Indeed, one can go further

---

52. This is manifestly true for books like *Jubilees* (cf. J. C. Endres, *Biblical Interpretation in the Book of Jubilees,* 1987, 248) and the *Testaments* (Endres, 238-47, esp. 246). Nothing in the *Testaments* would be unexpected from the pen of a lay-pietist who acknowledged the unparalleled importance of both the cultic and teaching office of the priests. This would explain the harsh critique of the Levites found in this and other works (which may be a carryover from the Hebrew Scriptures; cf. A. Hultgård, *L'eschatologie des Testaments des Douze Patriarches,* 1977, 1:92-93). More will be said about the role of Levi in these works below.

53. Nickelsburg points out how models can too easily become dies that shape our understanding of the literature (cf. "Social Aspects of Palestinian Jewish Apocalypticism," 1983a, 641-54), and Collins agrees that one cannot speak of a *single* social setting for these writings (*The Apocalyptic Imagination,* 1984, 29).

54. Some scholars now trace the origins of the major sectarian movements into the

back than that, as memories of the eighth- to sixth-century experiences of exile are still alive and surprisingly influential in the literature of this much later period, being reflected in the entire ethos of the Jewish community. This preoccupation, especially with the Judean captivity, suggests that it may contain some of the seeds of the later debate, and some scholars are now realizing that it is only in the wake of the captivity that a proper analysis of late Second Temple Judaism can begin.[55] This is, of course, never an easy task, given the relative obscurity of the events, and a survey of this "prehistory" can at best proceed rather anecdotally because of the scanty existing data for this period.

In the Wake of Captivity

The tendency to respond to religious differences with protest and division is evident even in the preexilic and exilic communities. Recently scholars have become more aware of the tendency, even in these early periods, away from national and toward more sectarian forms of religious expression.[56] Some Israelites were demonstrably dissatisfied with a national identity or, at least, with what was felt to be an unsuccessful attempt by Israel to live up to her faith. Accusations of impiety and breach of covenant can be found. Individualism also increasingly eclipsed the corporate and national approach to religion. There are indications that even before the exile some division existed within the nation: the preexilic prophets spoke of a wide diffusion of apostasy, the earliest chapters of Isaiah being a good example of prophecy addressed to a remnant community that held itself alone to preserve the true faith of Israel.[57] Scholars like Morton Smith and, more recently, Margaret Barker have traced the sociological origins of the much later divisions that existed in Israel from these preexilic years.[58] It is quite probable that the most significant developments to-

third century B.C. and even well before that; cf. Plöger, 1968, passim; Smith, 1971, passim, 29; L. H. Schiffman, "Jewish Sectarianism in Second Temple Times," 1981, 1-46, 4; Beckwith, 1982, 3-46; Talmon, 1986, 176-86; M. E. Stone, "Enoch, Aramaic Levi and Sectarian Origins," 1988, 159-70, esp. 164, 170; Blenkinsopp, 1990, 6-7 (cf. n. 6), cf. 8-20.

55. Cf. Blenkinsopp, 1988, 25.

56. Scholars who root Jewish sectarianism in the exilic period include M. Smith, "The Dead Sea Sect in Relation to Ancient Judaism," 1960, 350ff.; Talmon, 1986, 169ff.; and Blenkinsopp, 1988, 3ff.

57. Smith, 1971, 45-46; Blenkinsopp, 1990, 11-14. Mowinckel called the Isaian circle "a quite definable body, with a more or less fixed organization . . . a 'sect' . . . a religious fellowship" (*He That Cometh*, 1956, 251-52).

58. Smith speaks of the syncretism of the popular cult and the offense this created for the "Yahweh-alone" party throughout the history of Israel (1960, 350). From a rather different perspective, Barker accepts that the maintainers of the royal cult and theology,

ward segregation of groups of Israelites, however, are to be associated with the exile itself, which radically altered both the history and thought of Israelites. While the distinction drawn by previous generations of scholars between preexilic national "Israel" and postexilic ecclesiastical "Judaism" has no doubt been subjected to exaggeration, there certainly would seem to be some truth to the idea that the loss of land, cult, and self-government at the dispersion had serious systemic consequences. The exile had the effect of placing in doubt that sense of security that belonging to the nation had previously brought with it. The resulting increase in the role of introspection in spirituality, the heightened importance of some aspects of the law brought about by life in a pagan context, and ensuing expressions of individualism in worship and piety all contributed to the sense of change. Perhaps most importantly here, this event served to dissolve national coherence and led to a kind of fragmentation of the people into different groups.[59]

These tendencies toward fragmentation took concrete form in the emergence out of the experience of exile of three distinct and competing groups: (1) those that were allowed to remain in Judea ("dwellers"), (2) the exiles to Babylon who later returned to populate Palestine ("returnees"), and (3) those who stayed on in Babylon ("settlers"). The postexilic writings record not only the exclusivist claims of the returnees to compose the holy remnant of Israel but also the conservative counterclaims of the dwellers.[60] The claims of the Babylonian settlers to represent the continuing Israel are also well known, especially from later records. Moreover, even within these basic divisions fissures developed, such as that which divided the returnees who joined in the restoration attempts of Ezra and Nehemiah. This division came about as a result of the reforms initiated by Ezra directed against the religious assimilation of Israel

---

with their more polytheistic understanding, represent the originators of true Yahweh worship, the Deuteronomistic monotheistic reformers being the innovators (*The Older Testament*, 1987, esp. 18-19, 26-29, 68-69, and passim; *The Great Angel*, 1992, esp. 12-113). While Barker takes *1 Enoch* to be an example of the development of the earlier theology, the strongly Deuteronomistic expression in the covenantal thought of *1 Enoch* (cf. ch. 6 below) would seem to militate against this conclusion.

59. Cf. Gowan, 1986, 9, 14-15; Talmon, 1986, 177ff.; Smith, 1960, 351-52.

60. The influence of the former group is discussed by Smith (1971, 83). Regarding the latter group, cf. Gowan, 1986, 30-33; Talmon, 1986, 182-89; 2 Kings 24:14; 25:12, 21; 2 Chron. 36:20-21; Ezra 4:1-3; 6:19-22; Jeremiah 24; Ezek. 11:14-21; Hag. 2:10-14; Zech. 7:14. In Hag. 1:12-14 the "people of the land" are called "all the remnant of the people." 1 and 2 Chronicles largely concern themselves with defining the true Israel (cf. the early chapters of 1 Chronicles). These books promote the tribes of Judah and Benjamin out of which they see the true line of Israel preserved, draw attention to the royal line of David, and center the cult in Jerusalem (cf. P. R. Ackroyd, *Israel under Babylon and Persia*, 1970, 297-300).

during the period of the exile, especially against the corruption of the priest-hood.[61]

Ezra's policies took concrete form over one particular issue, the proscription of intermarriage with Gentiles. The importance of this issue for the returnees is evidenced in the apparent willingness of some Jews (not by any means without exceptions) to abolish all previous nuptial bonds with foreign wives (Ezra 10:3-5). No doubt this prohibition of exogamy had numerous social and political implications for the new community, as scholars have pointed out; but the records insist (and no reason has been supplied to doubt the accuracy of the reports) that *religious* motivations were paramount. Ezra and his followers were reacting against what they considered a long period of spiritual barrenness resulting in (and further aggravated by) the exile and against the apostasy of many of God's people, who had demonstrated in various ways their abandonment of "the traditions of the fathers." It was understandably hoped that by such radical measures the distinctiveness of Israel's faith might survive, and there is reason to believe that it was somewhat successful in this goal. Here, then, is an example of where "sectarian" measures no doubt also eventually served more "national" ends.[62] But national goals were not without cost, for this period is regarded as one in which concerns for purity of religion that had formerly separated the people of God *from the nations* were now being directed *inwardly* upon the nation itself — resulting in divisions *within Israel*.[63] Strict religious criteria for membership in the true remnant of exiles (the *gôlâ*) were now being rigorously applied.[64] This is accordingly the first recorded instance of the elevation of religious issues to the place of *dividing and defining* (and

---

61. Cf. Reicke, 1968, 21; Ezra 9:14–10:44; Neh. 13:1-9; *Ant.* 11.297-303.

62. The practice had apparently been widely adopted by Israel well before Ezra's time, not only by the priesthood but also by the common folk; cf. Smith, 1971, 16-17, 86-87; Beckwith, 1982, 21. Smith calls "No intermarriage with Gentiles!" the "battle cry of the separatist party" (174; for its relationship to purity concerns, cf. 179-80). For a particularly extreme example of revulsion toward exogamy, cf. *Pseudo-Philo* 9:5, which polemicizes that the reason Tamar planned to have sexual relations with her father-in-law was to avoid sexual contact with Gentiles! The elders in Jerusalem at the time of Manasses are reported to have blamed the first exile on sins of intermarriage (*Ant.* 11.308).

63. Cf., e.g., Talmon, 1986, 189; Talmon, "The Emergence of Jewish Sectarianism in the Early Second Temple Period," 1987, 587-616, 300.

64. E.g., we read in Ezra 10:8 how the failure of any to convene at Jerusalem was to result in the confiscation of property and excommunication from "the congregation of the exiles." Hence Smith can refer to the "sectarian character of Nehemiah's reforms" (1960, 353-55). According to Blenkinsopp, the *bene haggolah* "developed specific norms for membership which included the prohibition of exogamy, strict observance of Sabbath and support of the temple and its personnel." It also allowed for excommunication and raised the import of certain laws to the level of "qualification for membership" (1988, 5).

thus totally preoccupying) *issues*.[65] Intermarriage effectively marked off those whom Ezra considered the true people of God from those who were not, a measure deliberately taken in spite of the risks this kind of systematic excommunication presented to an already minuscule remnant of returnees. Although Ezra's vigorous reform apparently possessed real influence at first, its effects appear not to have been very far-reaching or permanent, as a period of relapse soon followed. This period was characterized by the continued assimilation of the priesthood and the revival of exogamy.[66] Josephus reports political intrigue over the office of high priest at this time, and his account suggests that the compromises were widely known and condemned (*Ant.* 11.297-301). The book of Malachi witnesses to similar problems when it opens with words condemning the degenerate state of the priests, who are blamed for the widespread corruption (1:6-14) and for the resulting curse by the Lord on the cult (2:1-9). Paradoxically, but not uncharacteristically, however, it would be the failure of the reform itself that would eventually lead to even greater incentive to segregation. As an example of the tensions involved and of the kind of oscillation between reform and relapse that took place, one might appeal to a particularly significant and well-known early instance of exogamy among the priesthood involving the late-fourth-century-B.C. marriage of the high priest Jaddua's brother Manasses to a Samaritan princess, the daughter of Sanballat.[67] This marriage created such offense for traditional minds because Manasses, although not high priest himself, seems to have been closely identified with his brother's priesthood, either because he joined him in making the sacrifices or for other more theological reasons, perhaps related to some undisclosed belief about the sanctity of their relationship as co-members of a priestly family.[68] In any event Josephus comments on how this marriage upset the elders in Jerusalem to such a point that Manasses even contemplated divorcing his wife to quell the tensions, although Sanballat urged his son-in-law to avoid this desperate action even in the face of strong opposition (*Ant.* 11.312). These apparently conserva-

---

65. Blenkinsopp speaks of "a pragmatic rather than a theoretical basis for self-definition" and "the ongoing attempt to define what is or is not compatible with or necessary for membership in the community" (1988, 5); cf. also Ackroyd, who refers to the importance of the issue for defining and protecting the community (1970, 183). Cf. our description of "defining laws" above.

66. Cf. Beckwith, 1982, 21-22; Smith, 1971, 122-25.

67. Cf. Beckwith, 1982, 21; *Ant.* 11.302-12.

68. Josephus reports that the elders of Jerusalem resented the fact that "the brother of the high priest Jaddus was sharing the high priesthood while married to a foreigner" (*Ant.* 11.306). The meaning of this is unclear; perhaps the implication is that a high priest is able to be defiled by the actions of his own family, or perhaps Manasses actually took part in the sacrifices.

tive sentiments expressed by the Jerusalem priests were not unanimous or prevailing, however, as the historian's observations also imply that the practice of exogamy was actually widespread both within and outside the priesthood, to the point that two "sides" were emerging in the debate: "as many priests and Israelites were involved in such marriages, great was the confusion which seized the people of Jerusalem. For all these deserted to Manasses, and Sanaballetes supplied them with money and with land for cultivation and assigned them places wherein to dwell, in every way seeking to win favour for his son-in-law" (*Ant.* 11.312). It can be assumed from this passage, particularly from Sanballat's offer of support for those who "deserted to Manasses," that a group of assimilated priests and laymen were beginning to assume an identity of their own — what might well become, if tensions continued to make it politically advantageous to organize themselves further, a *party* with an independent and corporate consciousness. That this group constituted the forerunners of the later "Hellenistic reform movement" would be a logical deduction from the historical evidence.

But the important point to be drawn out here is that while the assimilationists appear as the victims of circumstance in Josephus's eyes, it takes little imagination to envision how upsetting the trend would have been to the traditional conservatives, the continuing promoters of the Ezra/Nehemiah reforms. The negative influence of the priesthood would have been rightly feared by them, in that the example of the priests no doubt possessed a strong and immediate effect on the laity as well.[69] The worst fears of the traditionalists, in fact, were about to be realized. While in this story Ezra's reforms apparently still held just enough force among the people to require the assimilationists to flee, things would not always go the way of the conservatives, who would themselves soon be the ones to take flight. Indeed, the series of events that followed nearly led to the naming of Manasses as high priest (*Ant.* 11.313-29), and this can be taken as a token of things to come. So while concrete evidence of this unfavorable change for the conservatives was yet to become openly evident, this relatively early story nevertheless reveals that conflict over issues like exogamy, which had for some time divided priesthood and people, now began to give birth to well-defined partylike groups consolidated around the two sides of the issues. These groups were about to enter into more open conflict.

---

69. The practice of intermarriage was not restricted to the elite, as Josephus suggests here, and was certainly widespread. As Beckwith (1982, 21) rightly comments: "Examples set in such quarters cannot have failed to find imitators in the nation at large, and to have outraged the supporters of Ezra's policy of separation."

The Early Hellenistic Period — The Oniads and Tobiads

Many excellent studies have been devoted to the question of the influence of Hellenism on Second Temple Judaism,[70] and little needs to be added to that discussion here. A somewhat less considered aspect of the whole question, however, is what might be called the subjective involvement of Israelites with the phenomenon of increasing Hellenization, in particular the growing awareness and response by pietistic Jews to Hellenistic ways, and the resulting division among groups of Jews over issues associated with the new Greek way of life. It has long been recognized, of course, that divisions existed on the political level, related to the often arbitrary discharge of power by the Greeks. The records of political life in Palestine disclose an exercise in advantage-seeking in which successive Jewish leaders attempted to secure harmony with Alexander's successors (the *Epigoni*). But this division was not merely political; Hellenism possessed religious as well as political implications since by far the greatest advantage in the process of securing power fell to the pro-Hellenists in Jerusalem, the same assimilationist faction in Israel already seen to be emerging in the earlier period. This process favored the progressive wing, no doubt because this group was the most receptive to Greek ways, including Greek political practices and ethics. But although the records reflect the assimilation of this more powerful section of Jewish society, acquiescence was far from universal. In fact, individuals and groups of Jews responded in a whole spectrum of ways to the new influences, from deliberate assimilation to unconscious acceptance to caution to bloody resistance. But while differences of reaction that separated one response from the next were not always clear, there nevertheless eventually emerged a quite visible dichotomy between those who were to the greatest degree influenced by Hellenism and those who were candidly intolerant of it. Out of this polarization arose two groups of people who were more or less clearly identifiable on either side of most issues: the *traditionalists* and the *Hellenists*.

A premium illustration, and important instance, of this division in Jewish society is the well-documented history of the perpetually feuding Oniad and Tobiad families. While the Oniads had for some time occupied the office of high priest by dictate of tradition, the Tobiads constantly opposed the Oniads, and repeatedly attempted to purchase the high priesthood to offset the traditional method of inheritance and thereby oust the Oniads. When the Tobiad Joseph was eventually granted tax-farming privileges normally reserved for the high priest, the history of the two families reached a significant turning point. And when the Tobiads finally managed to place their own Menelaus in the of-

70. Especially those by Hengel (1974; *Jews, Greeks, and Barbarians,* 1980) and Momigliano (*Alien Wisdom,* 1975).

fice of high priest, the confrontation between the two families climaxed. Beyond the interest in these two aristocratic families for their own sake, however, what is also important about their history is that in many ways the Oniads and Tobiads embodied the conflict that was raging between the traditional conservatives and the reforming Hellenists also on the rather more modest stage of *popular* belief and custom. Indeed, in some respects these two families actually generated the conflict felt at lower levels of society. Others found themselves drawn into their battle, and their high visibility causes the histories of these two clans to bear witness to issues that divided *all* Israel.[71]

It would be going a little too far in this characterization to say that the Oniads and Tobiads represented consistent and exact antitheses — Oniads the conservatives and Tobiads the innovators. (And it would be especially unwise to overgeneralize in this case since the two families were even related by marriage.) Some of the Oniads, for example, exhibited very progressive attitudes and created real offense for the more pious members of society. An obvious instance of this is Jason, the Oniad and brother of conservative Zadokite high priest Onias III, whose love for the Hellenistic lifestyle probably directly contributed to his installation as high priest by King Antiochus. That the Oniads fairly consistently remained the object of conservative hopes, however, and that the Tobiads represented the will of the reformers and other less active tolerators of Hellenism, nevertheless stands as a more or less valid rule of thumb, despite incidental evidences of positive social interaction between the families. Divisions over religious concerns also retained strong political overtones, and any politicization of the issues necessarily involved the two families, conservatives tending more or less consistently to support the Oniads. What is important and can be clearly seen, however, is that purely political interests were not the only, or even the main, considerations at work. This is doubtless why there was even less political consistency than ideological consistency evident within (and between) these two families, although this is rarely pointed out.[72]

The earliest known mention of the Tobiad name is in references to the Ammonite Tobias as an enemy and conspirator against Nehemiah and his policies (Neh. 2:10; 4:7; 6; 13:4-9). Many scholars feel that the influential businessman of the mid–third century of the same name mentioned by Zenon (in the so-called Zenon papyri)[73] was descended from this Tobias; this later Tobias is

---

71. Cf. Jagersma, 1985, 30.

72. Even the Tobiad family was itself split in their political loyalties for a time (cf. Gowan, 1986, 66, for details), as were the Oniads (Onias II, e.g., once changed his loyalties), and both families found themselves in support of the same party at various times, usually for reasons of convenience (as when the Ptolemies supported the Tobiads' rival Hyrcanus, and the family joined the Oniads in support of the Seleucids, an occurrence summarized by S. Zeitlin, *The Rise and Fall of the Judaean State*, 1969, 1:69).

also mentioned by Josephus, who refers to him as the brother-in-law of the high priest (*Ant.* 12.160). There are uncertainties that prevent the positive identification of these earlier references with the Tobiads from the Hellenistic period, but even if the association cannot be confidently sustained, it is at least true that the adversarial relationship between the earlier Tobiad and the conservative Nehemiah paralleled subsequent frictions between the Tobiad family and the conservative priesthood in the third century.

The history of these later Tobiads begins about 250 B.C. with another ill-fated marriage, this time between the sister of High Priest Onias II and an Ammonite prince. This marriage, like that of Manasses to Sanballat's daughter mentioned above, would have been considered quite illegal since it involved the high priest and was doubtless treated with horror by the upholders of tradition,[74] even though the union was typical of a now widely accepted practice (and, depending on one's interpretation, of course, may not have been specifically outlawed in the Bible). It was from this union, in any event, that the influential wing of the Palestinian Tobiad family descended, and, no doubt partly due to the circumstances of their origins, they continued from that point on to represent the liberal option in Jerusalem. They were an international breed, steeped in Greek ways, influential in political circles, and born wealthy. This contrasted with the relatively weak economic situation of the people of Judea, and the presence of this family must have overwhelmingly impressed the Jewish population, among whom examples of wealth and influence were scarce. The attractiveness of the strong personality of the Tobiad Joseph, for example, would have been compelling — many Jews would have been proud of his world-class achievements, ambitions, and real power.[75] Added to this new challenge to the traditional and, by every comparison, weak authority of the Oniads was the promise of economic advantage to be gained from the Tobiad goal of making Jerusalem into a Hellenistic city.[76] And since the Ptolemies would clearly have preferred to deal with Jews sympathetic with their own wishes,[77] influence and acceptance in the Ptolemaic court would have fallen upon the Tobiads naturally. It was just this political influence that would eventually be felt, for better or worse, by everyone in Jerusalem.

While one can speak of pro-Oniad and pro-Tobiad factions in Judea as well as pro-Seleucid and pro-Ptolemaic factions, which might give to the whole

73. Reicke, 1968, 46-47; Gowan, 1986, 63.

74. Beckwith (1982, 34) feels this union may in fact have been the event that sparked the emergence of the proto-Essene movement.

75. Tcherikover, 1961, 133-34. Josephus eulogizes Joseph and other Tobiads (*Ant.* 12.160, 190-219).

76. Zeitlin, 1968, 1:79.

77. Reicke, 1968, 47.

affair the look of mere political debate, it can again be seen that ideological concerns never lay far behind the political alliances. An example of the preeminent importance of religious issues is discernible in the story of Onias II, who as high priest suddenly and resolutely refused to pay the annual tax to the Ptolemies (*Ant.* 12.158-85). This seems to have been partly an act of defiance following a conversion of loyalties to the Seleucids,[78] and it was positively received and even encouraged by conservatives. Certainly it was not a *practical* measure by any stretch of the imagination, for it scandalized the Ptolemaic court and put Jerusalem in grave danger. The significance of the act should accordingly be seen in the religious point it made,[79] for the refusal was paramountly a challenge to the secular authority, whose aspirations promised to eventually erase the political and, more importantly, religious freedom of Israel. This aspect of the repudiation becomes evident only when some time later the Tobiad Joseph sought to preserve the peace by paying the tax (and coincidentally bought for himself tax-farming rights). It has been justifiably argued that an attitude of voluntary submission was communicated to the authorities in this act, which eventually, through Antiochus IV, would prove destructive to the welfare of Judaism.[80] Politics, in other words, constantly mirrored not only individual interests but also matters of conscience vis-à-vis Hellenism and the "new world order" that it promoted. Thus Zeitlin concludes in regard to the affair:

> This was the fundamental conflict between the High Priest Onias and the sons of Joseph. It did not revolve merely about the question of who should be the high priest or who should control the city market. The conflict had far wider implications. It had its roots in the perilous choice of policy that the Judaeans had to make. Onias and his associates sought to perpetuate Judaean life in accordance with the laws of the Pentateuch and the ideals of the prophets. This faction wanted their life to be centered around the Temple and was opposed to foreign cultural interests. . . . The sons of Joseph, Simon and his brothers, although they were priests and descendants of the High Priest Simon I, lost interest in Judaism.[81]

To what extent the common people were aware of the ideological aspects of these political actions is a matter of debate. Perhaps in cases like this one religious implications had become obscured by a political veneer. The populace

---

78. Gowan, 1986, 66. Contrast Zeitlin, 1969, 1:61-62.
79. Zeitlin, 1969, 1:63.
80. Reicke, 1968, 48, 51.
81. Zeitlin, 1968, 1:78-79. "The roots of the conflict were not only social and economic, but also ideological and religious" (73).

were divided between pro-Ptolemaic and pro-Seleucid supporters, and it may have been a complete secret to the commoner that behind the political alignment of Tobiads with the Ptolemies could be found progressive ideological beliefs, perhaps even motivations, and that the Ptolemies conveniently served the Tobiad ambitions. Perhaps the average Jew little cared to make such theoretical distinctions. Whether consciously or otherwise, however, the populace supported the Tobiads along with their radical ideology and the family was establishing a solid place of respect among the people. We read that Joseph's above-mentioned action in paying the taxes was welcomed by the people, who thanked him for saving the nation (*Ant.* 12.165). He had become their *prostatēs,* their "champion."[82]

The conservative traditionalists would have been overwhelmed by this support so thoughtlessly given to the Tobiads. It now seemed that the champions of Hellenization and assimilation were joined by a massive following, providing tragic evidence to the pious conservatives that the traditional way of life was being threatened at every level. That the Tobiad family enjoyed a term of office in Jerusalem for the better part of a century, during which they seem not to have been seriously or publicly opposed, implies that they had the support of the majority of the populace throughout the period.[83] The general ignorance of the spiritual implications of the political state of things would have been especially frustrating to those with conservative sensitivities, for the populace had forgotten the many evils committed by this family against the Jewish religion: that they were friends of the Samaritans;[84] that Joseph purchased the tax-farming rights from the king, thus acknowledging the rights of the secular authority in these vital areas;[85] that this same Tobiad committed unlawful acts in marrying his niece;[86] and that others from this family even built rival temples and promoted syncretistic cults within them.[87] The common people lacked the insight and discernment to resist Greek ways and the will to counter the ever-increasing Greek temperament of their politics — so, at least, it would have appeared to those faithful to the tradi-

---

82. *Ant.* 12.167. The growing popularity of the Tobiads can be seen from *Ant.* 12.239, which states that by the time of Hyrcanus the majority of the populace supported the Tobiads.

83. Beckwith, 1982, 33-34; Smith, 1971, 27; Zeitlin, 1969, 1:67.

84. *Ant.* 11.174; 12.168. Joseph borrowed tribute money from them.

85. *Ant.* 12.175-79. The secular authorities also promised him troops to carry out the program of tribute (cf. 180).

86. *Ant.* 12.186-89. This was a second marriage, under very unusual circumstances. Josephus tells how Joseph lusted after his brother's daughter, whom he assumed was a foreign [!] dancing girl, and sought to make her his bride. Needless to say, this would have been viewed as scandalous for someone seeking the office of high priest.

87. *Ant.* 12.228-36; 13.62-63; cf. Smith, 1971, 92-93, 96ff.

tional way of life. Resignation, by these same nonconformists, to the view that the general populace were irretrievably lost to Hellenization finds its context in the crisis brought on by progression and secularism. It it is not surprising, given the strict position of some of these groups, that some assigned to the whole lot the status of apostates. These pious activists, who generally supported the Oniads and whatever conservative policy furthered their goals and eventually formed the core of the anti-Hellenistic movement in Judaism, were becoming an enormously outnumbered minority. Such people as these qualify as authors of some of the more ancient portions of the books of Enoch.

The Maccabean Period

Attitudes adopted during the early years of the Tobiad dynasty in the Ptolemaic period (roughly corresponding to the third century B.C.) would appear to have continued during the Seleucid era (into the second century B.C.). Just as the Oniad-Tobiad controversy was a central feature of the social life of the early Hellenistic period, later years were similarly characterized by controversy between Hellenists and traditionalists. There seems little reason to doubt Ben Sirach's observations from about this time (about 180 B.C.), who criticized what he saw as a highly compromised lifestyle in Jerusalem, in the process providing insight into the emerging divisions and antagonisms between old and new lifestyles in Jerusalem.[88] The bitterness of this scribe toward the Hellenized upper class seems to have been his consuming fire; but his demeanor was still mostly polite, and, being strongly nationalistic, he did not appear to be willing to give up on the leaders and the nobility, despite their sinful attitudes. Others would be much less tolerant, as we will see.

Questions about the existence and role of a Hellenizing party in Judaism during these years have already been raised. Scholars almost unanimously acknowledge the existence of such a group, however well organized or defined,[89] but there is considerable controversy, as has been mentioned, about the extent of what could be called the "official" role and influence of this "Hellenizing party." One must ask, however, just how important it is to answer such a question — politically framed as it is. In other words, it is important to consider not only what was happening among the official circles (and it is those circles that are understandably given the most attention in the historical documents) but also among the "common people," that is, the uneducated and even the poor. Sociologists have rightly criticized the predisposition of scholars to limit their

88. Cf. Tcherikover, 1961, 150-51.
89. Recently Beckwith, 1982, 43; Gowan, 1986, 73-80.

consideration to the role of the politically astute, the established, and the upper classes in their historical investigations, inasmuch as this has perpetuated a "sociology of the powerful." Of equal or greater importance, in their minds, is how the *general populace* reacted to the goings-on in the society. Unfortunately, however, scholars of Second Temple Judaism have not frequently adopted this agenda,[90] which is especially unfortunate since the authors of our writings seemed to have interacted with several levels of society, and in any event hardly restricted themselves to what might be viewed as "official" concerns. Beckwith, realizing the importance of this issue, reasons that the Hasidim defined themselves as the "pious" in contrast not only to the leading Hellenizers, but to "all the negligent, the 'people(s) of the land' whose non-observance of the Law always troubled the Pharisees so greatly, and of whom the Hellenizers were just conspicuous examples."[91] The implications of this are hardly unimportant. It is one thing when there prevails among the whole populace a mood of revolt against the ruling minority (the upper echelons of society seem much less intimidating when the majority join in common cause against them), but it is much more serious for the few persistent conservatives when they lack the support, not only of the ruling powerful, but of the majority of common people as well. The existence of a group of leaders organized in a "Hellenistic reform party," in other words, would not have been as frustrating to the pious as the general and widespread passivity of the people. The conservatives would have reasoned that, even if the power structure could be overthrown (as it eventually was by the Maccabees), the people should not be counted on to capitalize on the moment — change would be entirely lost on them. The important matter in all this, therefore, is the extent to which the people of Israel were perceived to have become comfortable with Hellenistic ways, particularly those ways that radically challenged traditional authority and lifestyle. One may begin to get a feel for this by subjecting the sources to questions like: To what extent did the Jewish population participate in the Hellenization of Judaism? How would this participation have been perceived by conservatives?

One can begin to answer such questions by considering the period of the first hellenophile high priest, Jason, who replaced his exiled brother Onias III. This appointment, at the instigation of Antiochus IV, gave those of a traditional mind-set plenty of reasons to take offense. To begin with, the secular, rather than traditional, mechanisms at play in the appointment were highly irregular for the Jewish world. Jason had, for all intents and purposes, *purchased* from

90. Although E. P. Sanders (cf. *Paul and Palestinian Judaism,* 1977, and esp. *Judaism,* 1992, passim) must be given due credit for his emphasis on the faith of the common people.

91. Beckwith, 1982, 40-41.

Antiochus the privilege of having the high priesthood transferred to him.[92] This style of appointment obviously represented the culmination of a long process toward the secularization of the office, and it would prove to be just one of many similar irregularities in the future,[93] but at this stage would certainly have been viewed as unwelcome progress by some. Tradition also required the eldest of brothers, which Jason was not, to be made high priest. In view of the sacredness ascribed to these "details" of priestly order and purity, the appointment of Jason naturally created outrage for traditional priests and supporters of the traditional priestly lineage. The appointment was supported, on the other hand, by the sons of Joseph even though Jason was an Oniad, apparently because he accepted the progressive ideals of the Tobiads, but also because this appointment represented the dissolution of the traditional method for naming high priests according to a predetermined succession — a favorable development for the Tobiads, who always seemed to entertain hopes of eventually having the office themselves.[94] Jason was also startlingly Greek in mind-set, especially when compared to his pious predecessor. The Greek name Jason itself, which he had chosen to replace his traditional Hebrew name,[95] aptly illustrates the preferences of this ambitious graecized Jew. It is accordingly not surprising that Jason is referred to in the sources as the leader of a pro-Greek faction.[96] There is good reason to believe that this faction was not confined to a few of the wealthiest families, but had in fact acquired the sympathies of a large number of Jews. Even a contradictory figure like Antiochus would not likely have replaced a conservative high priest with a Greek sympathizer against the express wishes of the general populace. The whole action, furthermore, seems to have been met with general acquiescence. There was apparently opportunity to protest this appointment, since it was a while later when Menelaus took over Jason's office and the people, in preference for Jason, sought to prevent this (*Ant.* 12.237ff.). But there is certainly no record of any disturbance on Jason's accession. One can

92. Cf. Schürer, 1973, 1:148; Gowan, 1986, 74-75; *Ant.* 12.239; 2 Macc. 4:7. The Tobiads may have had a role in influencing the decision of Antiochus; cf. Tcherikover, 1961, 157-59.

93. Earlier Bagoas, general of Artaxerxes, had attempted unsuccessfully to appoint the high priest (*Ant.* 11.297-99). While Alexander granted Sanballat's request to appoint Manasses high priest, the intervention of High Priest Jaddus prevented this (*Ant.* 11.313-39). In the time of Ptolemy Philadelphus, the ruler gave High Priest Eleazar a purple robe (πορφύραν; *Ant.* 12.117), which, while not implying recognition of royalty (cf. *Ant.* 11.35), reveals a more secular perspective in the understanding of the office.

94. Cf. Zeitlin, 1968, 1:81.

95. Josephus reports that this Jesus ('Ιησοῦς; cf. Heb. name *Jeshua/Joshua*) had changed his name to the fully graecized "Jason" ('Ιάσονα; *Ant.* 12.239).

96. Jason was backed by a group of Hellenists (1 Macc. 4:14; cf. 1:11). Cf. also 2 Macc. 4:9, where these are given the name "Antiochenes."

safely conjecture, therefore, that traditionalists felt helpless to protest and remained silent and dumbfounded at the turn of events, and at the widespread disinterest in the affair.

Other concrete evidence tends to confirm this insight into the progressive nature of Jason's character. It was during his time in office that the *gymnasium* and *ephebium* were introduced into Jerusalem (2 Macc. 4:9, 12). The *gymnasium* was essential as an institution not only for the social and cultural reason that it facilitated the much-enjoyed Greek games, but also for the political reason that its establishment was a virtual requisite if the city was to be incorporated as a Greek polis[97] — something eagerly desired by more progressive Jerusalemites. Endeavor to attain the status of polis and thus to receive the privileges of friendship with the king and citizenship in the empire appears to have advanced unimpeded by traditional restrictions. Even the priests appear not only indifferent but positively responsive to the idea and, apparently not perceiving any danger or contradiction in their involvement, eagerly enrolled in the Greek games themselves. This fact is polemically related in the following quotation from 2 Maccabees, which coincidentally makes clear that not all Jews were unalarmed by the developments. The revulsion expressed by this author was probably not untypical of certain segments of the conservative Jewish population:

> Hellenism reached a high point with the introduction of foreign customs through the boundless wickedness of the impious Jason, no true high priest. As a result, the priests no longer had any enthusiasm from their duties at the altar, but despised the temple and neglected the sacrifices; and in defiance of the law they eagerly contributed to the expenses of the wrestling-school whenever the opening gong called them. They placed no value on their hereditary dignities, but cared above everything for Hellenic honours. (4:13-15)[98]

97. Tcherikover, 1961, 163. R. Doran ("Jason's Gymnasium," 1990, 99-109) disputes Tcherikover's claim that in building the *gymnasium* "Jason was changing the constitution of Jerusalem by redefining admittance to the citizen body through ephebic training" (103) on the basis that only birth, not ephebic training, was necessary for citizenship in the polis in the second century B.C. Whatever the case may be about citizenship, the important thing is that many young Jerusalemites, notably the priests, were entering the *ephebium*, and that the *ephebium* both facilitated the creation of a Greek polis and reflected the determined policy to do so. Doran also doubts (with little reason, we think) that nudity and *epispasm* were practiced (106-8), but Doran's point that the real issue may have surrounded the system of education in the *ephebia* is well taken: "Education at an ephebia was not necessarily a prerequisite for citizenship . . . but it would have had a profound impact on the power relationships within that body" (108).

98. It is interesting that vv. 16-17 view the events about to occur as a vindictive, earthly judgment on sin against the law.

This quotation suggests that the assimilation of Israel's youth was widespread. Thus the mention of the priests does not appear to refer to an exceptional instance of the involvement of priests in Hellenistic customs. It serves more as an extreme example of widespread youthful zeal for the new way of life. The point is that if not even the priests possessed scruples about this kind of activity, the average layperson would obviously not act with any more reserve. In any event the *ephebium* dictated both attitude and fashion, and it is unimaginable, especially in view of the example of the priests, that youthful pressure would *not* have led to widespread conformity.[99] It was, of course, not participation in the *ephebium* itself that would have caused the most offense. The problem lay with the resulting compromises. *Epispasm* — the surgical concealment of circumcision — will have been encouraged by this new relationship with the gymnasium since it served to obliterate an embarrassing mark of differentiation among the athletes. But an act that seemed natural in view of the modernizing trends of the time would have possessed ultimate significance for those sensitive to the issue and would have been viewed as *voluntary* abandonment of the traditional way of life — nothing less than the removal of the sign of the covenant! While it may be true that not every Jerusalemite sought to register as a citizen of the new polis, nevertheless the city had already been effectively transformed from a Jerusalem to an Antioch, and this fact would necessarily influence to a high degree the circumstances of every one of its inhabitants.[100] While the actions of Jason might, therefore, be termed political and ideological rather than religious, the implications for the life of the citizens and the predicament this caused for the nonconformists were thoroughly religious and would have proven intolerable to the conservative mind.

The appointment of Jason's successor Menelaus seems to have been met with much less favor among Jerusalemites. This may be partly due to the circumstances that surrounded his accession: although he was a cousin of Jason, he deceitfully ousted Jason by outbidding him in tribute to the king.[101] But it more likely had to do with the fact that, since he was a Tobiad, Menelaus's appointment also now meant that the office fell to someone from outside the customary line of priests (being an Oniad on the maternal side only, his paternal ancestry being Benjaminite).[102] Menelaus had several other strikes against him as well: apparently he helped himself to temple funds and once even helped Antiochus plunder

---

99. Reicke, 1968, 53: "Now, to the horror of traditionalists, fashionable students turned up everywhere in the characteristic uniform of the Attic ephebi: a broad-rimmed hat . . . a short riding cloak . . . and bare legs."

100. Cf. Tcherikover, 1961, 165.

101. Cf. 2 Macc. 4:23-25; Schürer, 1973, 1:149.

102. For evidence, cf. Schürer, 1973, 1:149.

the Temple.[103] The information Josephus supplies regarding Menelaus is somewhat muddled and unreliable,[104] but one can take it as reasonably certain that Jason revolted against Menelaus much as Josephus describes and that this had the effect of dividing the people, the Tobiads taking the side of Menelaus[105] "while the majority of the people supported Jason" (*Ant.* 12.239). This shows the deep admiration the people felt toward Jason but also demonstrates that even the most fickle Jerusalemites were not about to tolerate this recent innovation of having a non-Oniad as high priest. This illustrates the rather interesting fact that while the Hellenization brought by Jason was met with some tolerance, this particular ritual/genealogical offense was considered too heinous to be ignored. Surprisingly, in spite of what might be viewed as a conservative reaction, the actual result of the rebellion, according to Josephus, was an even more thoroughgoing liberalization and the abandonment of traditional values: "Menelaus and the Tobiads withdrew, and going to Antiochus informed him that they wished to abandon their country's laws and the way of life prescribed by these *(tēn kat' autous politeian)* and to follow the king's laws and adopt the Greek way of life *(tēn hellēnikēn politeian echein)*" (*Ant.* 12.240). Menelaus accordingly represented the more extreme Greek sympathies in Jerusalem, and his eventual confirmation in the office of high priest implied, in general terms, the direction in which things were moving, at least for the time being.

With the storming of the Temple in 167 B.C., however, those pietistic types who had all along hesitated to regard the changes brought about by the appointments of Jason and Menelaus as progress were left with only the bitter vindication of their conservative sensibilities. The motivations and historical influences working on Antiochus when he stormed Jerusalem and the Temple have already been considered. It seems best to acknowledge the inherent probability that Antiochus did have some strong personal motivations and that these were as likely to be political as ideological — the violent reform was intended to secure loyalty to his person and to gain the upper hand of influence in Judea,[106]

---

103. 1 Macc. 1:20-24; 2 Macc. 5:15-16; *Ant.* 12.248-50. For discussion of Menelaus's deeds, cf. Jagersma, 1985, 47.

104. Josephus attributes the building of a gymnasium and the concealing of circumcision to his time in office (*Ant.* 12.241), but this seems already to have happened in Jason's time; cf. 2 Macc. 4:9. Perhaps the practices were furthered in the time of Menelaus, who is described by Josephus as "giving up whatever other national customs they had" and imitating "the practices of foreign nations" (*Ant.* 12.241).

105. Tcherikover assumes that even Jason proved too traditional for the Tobiads, and this is why they supported the new appointment (1961, 170-71).

106. Political motivations seem to be assumed by Josephus's account in *Wars* 1.31-33, where he describes rival claims in Jerusalem while disputes over the suzerainty of Syria went on between Antiochus IV and Ptolemy VI.

rather than to secure commitment to Hellenization itself (as suggested by the fact that he had already provided legal protection for the preservation of Judaism). It is difficult, in any event, to believe that this ruler possessed a personal program of abolition or reform of the Jewish ancestral laws. He was more likely motivated by his political ambitions than by ideological ambitions.

Consistent with these personal political motivations, a full appreciation of the king's actions is possible only if one assumes that Antiochus was trying to do what was generally considered sound political practice in the ancient world — namely, granting legislation pleasing to the general populace (and coincidentally favorable to the ruler's aims) in order to win the hearts and the loyalty of his subjects. The growing interest in the Greek way of life, as outlined above, the gradual (if passive) acceptance of it by the populace, and the presence of more *active* Hellenizers (even if still a relative minority), add up to an emerging *consensus* among the people *in favor of* the new way of life. Thus when *both the populace and official circles of Judaism seemed to the king to favor the Greek way of life*, it was now left only to silence the relatively small group of traditionalists who gathered around the Hebrew cult. Antiochus's action in Jerusalem was designed precisely to accomplish this since, as he saw it, or as it was explained to him, the only thing preventing these emerging Greek minds from becoming part of the *oikoumenē* (that is, the truly international community) was the residuum of traditional sympathy that gathered around the Temple and constrained the Judean people from taking the decisive steps into the new life. Antiochus does not seem to have realized the implications of his action or the true sentiments toward the Temple that somehow had survived the gradual modernization of Jerusalem; his intentions were to please all who sought the new life, whether authorities or common people, by legislating and enforcing changes that would guarantee that progress would go ahead.

It would be entirely in line with this (even granting the lack of concrete historical confirmation for this fact) that the *occasion* for Antiochus's actions was an official request by Jewish officials that Jerusalem be registered as a Greek polis. Josephus claims that the Samaritans forwarded a letter requesting a similar privilege, and although this report may have been contrived under the inspiration of anti-Samaritan sentiments, it is at least possible that such a letter, and an analogous letter representing the wishes of Jerusalem authorities, were in fact sent to the king.[107] Whether the request came by official letter or otherwise,

---

107. For the text of the letter from the Samaritans disowning Judaism and requesting their temple to be dedicated to Zeus Hellenios, cf. *Ant.* 12.257-61; cf. also 11.340-41. Smith (1971, 190) argues that another letter similar to the Samaritan one was sent to Antiochus from Jerusalem. The text of the extant Samaritan letter, however, implies an attempt to divert something that in fact *happened* to the Jews, and accordingly suggests that

however, there would appear to be no ulterior motive on the part of Josephus for the accusation that Menelaus persuaded Antiochus "to compel the Jews to abandon their fathers' religion" and that the priest thereby "compelled his nation to violate their own laws" (*Ant.* 12.384-85); such statements seem to reveal knowledge of an official request of some kind. In short, the above-mentioned political motivations of Antiochus were probably bolstered by some kind of invitation from Menelaus, all the Tobiads, or them and many others. This combination of factors as we have described them would certainly be adequate to explain the resulting events. As for the exact motivations of such hellenophiles in Jerusalem, it seems to have been their aim only to give the cult a more Hellenistic form (which, in their view, merely involved assimilating the Hebrew — and Greek — designation "Lord of Heaven" to the Greek "Zeus Olympus"), not to create offense with what could be interpreted as desecration. It is hardly necessary to go so far as to conclude that they actually *instigated persecution* against their own people. Blame for the violence and offensiveness of the reform may have to be left entirely at the feet of Antiochus's extravagant impulsiveness.

But what is important here is that the chain of events — regardless of the exact sequence and key players — would have been interpreted by the pious as the result of, and in a way the deserved judgment upon, the growing apostasy of the people. Much of this "popular apostasy" would not actually have been motivated by any particular attraction to Greek ways so much as by peer pressure and gradual assimilation. Very few, in all likelihood, would have considered themselves, or would otherwise have resembled, "hellenophiles" in any obvious or official sense. Added to this relatively innocent kind of assimilation, however, there were probably outright acts of compromise unwillingly performed through imminent fear of the royal edict[108] — many were willing to compromise simply to preserve their lives.[109] As a result, even if apostasy was *not taken*

Jerusalem had failed to make the request. Perhaps this was only because they lacked the Sidonian connection on which the Samaritans based their suit. Some have argued that this. letter is not genuine, being anti-Samaritan propaganda; but cf. Zeitlin (1968, 1:93), who argues that the Samaritans could well have had their own progressive wing, even if the action was not representative of the group as a whole.

108. As argued by Millar, 1978, 20-21. Josephus comments that "many of the Jews, some willingly, others through fear of the punishment which had been prescribed, followed the practices ordained by the king" (*Ant.* 12.255); Mattathias urges his sons to preserve the ancient customs and form of government and "not to make common cause with those who are betraying it *whether of their own will or through compulsion*" (*Ant.* 12.280). A similar capitulation of some citizens to Greek ways even before the persecution may have resulted from fear toward the Tobiad leaders and their servant Menelaus, just as it did toward Antiochus and his agents after that time.

109. Zeitlin, 1968, 1:90. The account in *Wars* that suggests that the orders to sacrifice swine and to abandon the practice of circumcision were "disobeyed by all (πάντες)," is

to be the cause of the events, it would have been seen as the eventual result. This may seem an unfair view of things, but it is more than probable, knowing the sectarian spirit, that even unwilling capitulation would have been considered by traditionalists as tantamount to apostasy. No excuses would be allowed, as can be seen from the famous example set by the zealous Mattathias, reported in 1 Macc. 2:1-24, who performed his act of vengeance not on the pagans only, but on a fellow *Israelite* in the act of idolatrous sacrifice. If this important incident can be taken as representative of how the events would have been viewed by traditionalists, it suggests that they would have regarded all apostates — whether from willful cooperation or under duress — as just that: *apostates.*

The Maccabees apparently thought that traditional values, including their understanding of the nation as the elect people, were values worth fighting for; that is why they opted for *militant reform* as opposed to retreat or passive protest. It is interesting, however, that the nationalistic uprising that resulted from the leadership of the Maccabees did not prove equally appealing to all, and it is well known that a decided reserve was expressed toward the Maccabees by those other traditionalists known as the Hasidim. The reason for this surprising disapproval of one group expressing protest by another group also expressing protest seems to have nothing to do with either the militant attitude of the one or the supposed pacifistic attitude of the other — contrary to conventional opinion — since both groups are described as willing, though reluctant, to take up arms.[110] The reason for the difference of opinion perhaps has something to do with the fact that the Maccabean movement was felt by pietistic groups like the Hasidim to be too nationalistic and thus too dependent for its success on the repentance of the whole people. Perhaps in line with this thinking, the Maccabean movement was also felt to be doomed to failure because of the changeableness of the national climate and the people's repeated failure of nerve. The incident, alluded to above, of the slaying by Mattathias of the Jew about to offer unclean sacrifice to a pagan god, illustrates that the Maccabean movement itself recognized the need to deal not only with the completely unacceptable Gentile rule but also with the compromise that had slowly infiltrated the holy nation itself. The real issue, therefore, lay with the divided loyalties of the people. That the Maccabean movement would itself eventually be opposed more strongly by Jews than by Gentiles, in the form of the same large and influential hellenophile movement that set in motion the original "reform," suggests that the Hasidim were eventually proven right on this score.

---

surely to be taken as an expression of the strength of Hebrew convictions and ideals, rather than as an accurate description of the actual course of events.

110. Besides the Hasidim, Josephus appears to refer to others who resisted Antiochus's reforms but did not elect military response (cf. the "righteous and pious"; *Ant.* 12.284).

As for this new wave of Hellenistic reformers, in the records we often read of Jewish Hellenistic conspirators who aligned with the Greeks in their attempt to overthrow the upstart Maccabean guerrilla movement. In one place Jewish hellenophiles living in Palestine are said to have held out in the citadel of Jerusalem when Judas besieged it in 163-162 B.C., eventually taking their complaint against this action to the king (*Ant.* 12.362). Probably joined by a number of their fellows from throughout Palestine, they were eventually given state protection by Demetrius; at their instigation this king sent no less than three campaigns against Judea.[111] These anti-Maccabean Hellenists probably included the most stalwart of the new generation of graecized Jews who had already had the upper hand before Mattathias came along, had survived the recent transfer of power, and now fully intended to continue in their liberal ways after the movement was quashed. The anti-Maccabean resistance, in the light of such occurrences, does not seem to have been an inferior movement by any means, and it is clear that by the time of Judas's death the Jewish Hellenists again have the upper hand.[112] The Maccabean history reports that "After the death of Judas the renegades raised their heads in every part of Israel, and all the evil-doers reappeared. In those days a terrible famine broke out, and the country went over to [the Hellenizers'] side. Bacchides chose apostates to be in control of the country" (1 Macc. 9:23-25).

Another significant fact is that (even in spite of the pro-Maccabean stance of the sources) there is no indication that the Maccabee brothers and their followers outnumbered the Greek party even at the height of their campaigns. Given that many of the more passive Israelites, for obvious reasons, would have preferred to support the party favored by the Seleucid king, it is likely that the nationalistic movement was a *minority* movement throughout the total length of its early history.[113] That the Maccabees failed to win over the sentiments of most of the common people is illustrated by the successful appointment to the high priesthood of Alchimus, another symbol of the resurgence of the Hellenistic spirit. His appointment was widely accepted by the populace[114] even though he consciously opposed Judas (*Ant.* 12.391) and eventually was responsible for the massacre of many Jews, including sixty Hasidim (*Ant.* 12.395-96, 400; 1 Macc. 7:21). This last action appears to represent little more than cowardly

111. Reicke, 1968, 59.
112. Buehler, 1974, 57-58.
113. Gowan, 1986, 85-86.
114. Josephus reports how Alchimus spoke kindly to the populace and won over many, including a force from among the "irreligious and renegades" (ἀσεβῶν καὶ πεφυγαδευμένων; *Ant.* 12.399). That Alchimus could so easily unite the people and the "renegades" suggests a certain apathy toward the Maccabean style of nationalism, if not toward all traditional values, on the part of the people generally.

and compulsive conduct and might have reflected either an official or unofficial (but now quite conventional) policy of intimidation, perpetuating the reign of terror against the pious initiated by Antiochus and the Tobiads. Thus while failing to attain the support of most of the people in their fight against paganism, the Maccabees' greatest enemy became the members of their own nation. Schürer characterizes the period as an internal struggle for Gentile support between the pro-Greek faction and the nationalists.[115] While the Maccabees sometimes gained the upper hand, this was by no means always the case.

So what is the value of the Maccabean history for our purposes? It is worth mentioning at this point that the Maccabean nationalist movement does not represent the ideological ethos of the writings we are investigating, which, it is widely thought, more adequately reflect the views of Hasidim or, we should prefer to say, *Hasidic-like* Jews. The value of the Maccabean history lies rather in the way it highlights the widespread division within the nation between those who continued to campaign for liberal reform and those who, shocked into action because of 15 Kislev 167 b.c., desired to return to the old ways. Although the Maccabean agenda was inspired by a posture of protest similar to that which is evident in the writings investigated here, it departed significantly from the fundamental *antinationalistic* attitude of those writings. The Maccabean movement, for its part, was nationalistic *from the beginning*, so much so that this commitment to a national program is partly to be blamed for the fact that those who eventually inherited the Maccabean vocation — under the rubric "Hasmoneans" — became as offensive to the pious as the syncretism that the movement originally had attempted to overthrow had been offensive. It is perhaps worth noting, in this regard, that while a good number joined the movement, in the long run the Maccabees did little to change the circumstances of the masses or to secure for them a more favorable religious environment. This may be taken once again as a kind of historical confirmation that the pietists were not entirely mistaken in their negative assessment of the movement that sought to drive back the forces of paganism but could not do so with lasting effect.

The Decline of the Hasmoneans

Following the death of Judas Maccabeus, whatever popular support was enjoyed by the sons of Mattathias diminished considerably, offering the liberal wing in Jerusalem an opportunity once again to secure its position.[116] Such

---

115. Schürer, 1973, 1:167-68.

116. For a graphic description of the unrestrained resurgence of the Hellenists, cf. *Ant.* 13.2-5.

changes in fortune conservatives would naturally blame on the leaders of the revolt and on the disintegration of traditional ideals in the Maccabean family that appears to have taken place about this time. Besides losing the support of the Hasidim, the nationalistic leaders may also have been abandoned by other conservative groups. Some of the historical references in the Qumran scrolls, for example, seem to reflect opposition toward the Maccabean Jonathan from the early years of that sect.[117] While this Jonathan, successor of Judas, possessed some of the qualities of a "zealot for the law" previously embodied in his brother and his father and even outdid all his predecessors in attaining international recognition for the legitimacy of the movement (*Ant.* 13.5-147, 174-80), there are already subtle indications in his actions that new policies were being adopted and novel directions sought and that political motives were taking precedent over religious motives.[118] Jonathan was highly involved in the politics of the empire and played by the rules of the game. As a revealing example, Alexander Balas, onetime claimant to the throne, was able to purchase Jonathan's loyalty to further his personal political ambitions (1 Macc. 10:1-20). This act, though conventional in Greek politics, set a dangerous precedent for Israel since it ignored the potential conflicts that would later place the two ideologies in irreconcilable tension. It also presaged the time when the Hasmonean dynasty would be drawn fully into political compromise and would seek to preserve the dominance of their new order at the cost of religious and national concerns.

In other ways Jonathan and his successor Simon departed from tradition and created offense, the former by his acceptance of the office of high priest from the hand of Alexander Balas (152 B.C., 1 Macc. 10:21), and the latter by accepting this position (*Ant.* 13.213; *Wars* 1.53) and perhaps also by donning the purple robe as a symbol of royal claims.[119] While the common folk appear to

117. The so-called "Prayer for King Jonathan" (4Q448) may reflect more positive sentiments (or hopes) felt toward this leader during his early years, before signs of degeneration set in, on the part of the community or, less likely, some other Jewish group. Rather than evidence of the divergence of opinion among the scrolls (or proof of their diverse origins), it may be taken as evidence of the change of reputation among the Maccabean successors.

118. Jagersma, 1985, 67.

119. 1 Macc. 10:61-62. For the interpretation of this act, cf. Reicke, 1968, 61. Earlier high priest Eleazar had received a purple robe (πορφύραν) from Ptolemy Philadelphus (cf. *Ant.* 12.117), and Jonathan a purple robe and a gold crown (note στέφανος, not διάδημα as in *Ant.* 13.113) from Alexander, but neither occasion implied any recognition of royalty (cf. *Ant.* 11.35; 13.84-85 where Josephus argues that the purple robe did not mean "king" so much as "First Friend"; πρῶτον . . . φίλων, although cf. also 84-85, which implies that Jonathan was no longer "subject to the king"). Josephus elsewhere attributes the outright claim of royalty to Aristobulus (*Ant.* 13.301; *Wars* 1.70).

have accepted such developments as a welcome sign of the growing power of their political representatives (both figures received their offices by popular acclaim and with celebration), a change in priestly line offended others who sought to honor what they acknowledged to be the only legitimate and authorized line of priests, the Zadokite priesthood.[120] Of this line the brothers were not members, being priests of the Joarib family. Perhaps because of this, many more of the traditionalists, notably the conservative priests, began to change their view of the movement initiated by the Maccabees. Popular acclaim would hardly have been considered by such traditionalists to be a valid instrument for establishing a new line of priests, especially if Zadokites were still available for the position.[121] For such reasons pious critique was probably aimed even at the righteous Simon, who was recognized by some as a kind of savior figure since he brought welcome relief to the nation.[122] Like his brother, however, Simon was also politically astute. He issued coins, an act that demonstrates growing economic security and independence, though it would have received cautious acceptance at best from those wary of breaking the commandment against graven images. Moreover, like his brother, Simon tended to give priority in his administration to political interests and was not reluctant to employ the military to the extent that he could be justifiably accused of being quite a "man of bloodshed," something inappropriate, not to mention unlawful, for priests.[123] Jonathan and Simon accordingly represent the end of a process by which the traditional hereditary method of naming the high priest was lost to more secu-

120. 1 Maccabees 14; *Ant.* 13.213; *Wars* 1.61. The words "The Jews and their priests confirmed Simon as their leader and high priest in perpetuity until a true prophet should appear" (1 Macc. 14:41) imply that the priestly supporters of Simon treated this as one of those truly unique historical occurrences where an old line of priests had come to an end and a new line needed to be confirmed. Schürer (1973, 1:193) would appear to be correct when he takes the "in perpetuity" of this verse to indicate that a new *hereditary line* was proclaimed. Such an abandonment of the traditional line would naturally have outraged Zadokites.

121. Whether they were or not is discussed by Beckwith (1982, 10-11). As for the idea of a democratic means of appointment, this would appear to have been an acceptable practice in emergencies, if we can accept the testimony of 1 Maccabees 14. One must remember, however, that the common people were probably considered by the pious to be largely apostate and ignorant of tradition, and thus unworthy or unable to make such a decision. Their authority would not be accepted in the face of the revelational authority claimed by our groups.

122. Cf. the language used in 1 Macc. 14:41-47. Simon is even credited with inspiring a "Hebrew renaissance," to borrow the term of Reicke (1968, 63). Among other things, the traditional Hebrew language was cultivated during his time.

123. Cf. Schürer, 1973, 1:174; Reicke, 1968, 63-64. The hands of this ruler would likely have been considered rendered perpetually unclean by contact (however indirect) with human blood.

lar processes: first usurpation (Jason and Menelaus), then recognition by Gentile overlords (Alchimus), then, following a period when the office was vacant, popular assent (Jonathan and Simon). It is again obvious that conservatives would have looked on the masses who consented to or were passively agreeable to the new arrangements as ignorant and apathetic rebels against God's ordained order.

The later Hasmoneans, with their dual claim to be high priests and chief governing authorities in secular matters, effectively created one new office out of what was traditionally two. These "priest-kings," as they have come to be called, also became infamous for their further debasement of the originally lofty Maccabean leadership objectives. While the initial Maccabean campaigns combined religious and political motives in a way generally acceptable to the pious mind-set (their program successfully climaxed in the rededication of the Temple in 162 B.C.), a deliberate and provocative shift in attitude was soon to become evident. Seeds of change could already be seen in Judas, who was not satisfied with restoring religious freedom but sought also to repossess the political boundaries of the golden age of the monarchy — something that was eventually accomplished under Simon's successor John Hyrcanus. "It was quite clearly no longer a matter of protecting the Jewish faith but of consolidating and extending Jewish power" — as Schürer so aptly puts it.[124] It is also not difficult to see, however, that the political kind of nationalistic hopes nurtured by these later Hasmoneans failed to provide what the people really needed, and the events of history would again eventually vindicate those who opposed them. The lofty ideals of the Maccabees were now paradoxically reversed. Outright oppression of the very people the Maccabees once sought to deliver was the policy adopted by Hyrcanus, who provided unambiguous evidence of how far things had disintegrated by his time. He held little respect for the true security of the people and ruled them harshly. The story is recorded how, when Jerusalem was besieged by Antiochus VII Sidetes, Hyrcanus forced all who were not able to fight out of the city, and they were left to starve to death.[125] Hyrcanus also plundered the tomb of David, a desperate and reprehensible means of raising funds to support a mercenary army (*Ant.* 13.249; cf. *Wars* 1.61), which itself was a significant departure from earlier practice and from cherished tradition and another reason for offense among the pious.[126] The story of Hyrcanus's

---

124. Schürer, 1973, 1:165.

125. And despite such cruel pragmatic measures, there nevertheless resulted from the battle a weighty tribute resulting in oppressive taxes. Schürer (1973, 1:203) relates the events. Josephus communicates a more positive sentiment toward the leader, and refers to the time as one of prosperity; *Wars* 1.284.

126. For this as an offense and a sign of Hellenism, cf. Schürer, 1973, 1:207; Gafni, CRINT, II/2, 14; Buehler, 1974, 58-59.

conversion from the Pharisees to the Sadducees is often repeated. Schürer's estimate of the reason for this would appear, from what we have seen, to be essentially correct: "The more his political interests came to the fore, the more those concerned with religion receded into the background. . . . in view of the distinctly worldly character of his policies, no sincere association with the Pharisees was in the long run possible."[127] There is, not surprisingly, ample evidence that Hyrcanus deliberately adopted Greek customs and therefore probably also was in sympathy with the Greek party in Jerusalem.[128]

But while a Greek posture can only be more or less implied from the facts of Hyrcanus's life, his son and successor Aristobulus unashamedly adopted and promoted Greek ways, even taking on the title "hellenophile."[129] His exercise of power was explicitly unconscionable. In order to silence all possible opposition to his rule, he unscrupulously committed his brothers to prison along with his mother, whom he allowed to die there (*Ant.* 13.302). Not only did Aristobulus inherit the high priesthood, but against his father's express wishes he sought to control all secular matters as well, going beyond even his predecessors and acting as a thoroughly secular king.[130] It is not entirely clear whether his adoption of the title "king" itself was widely felt to be offensive, but insofar as he had no claim to be a son of David and did not belong to a traditional royal line it would certainly have been one more reason for protest on the part of conservative supporters of the Davidic hope.[131] That he forcibly Judaized the northern districts of Palestine, including Galilee,[132] also suggests a significant shift from a religious to a merely militarist nationalistic program, although it is again difficult to assess how this would have been viewed by the public. It leaves one to ponder, however, whether the gap separating the Hasmonean brand of nationalism from more traditional views of theocracy had not by this time become quite unbridgeable.

The long and oppressive rule of Alexander Jannaeus — whose name suggestively combines Hebrew and Greek elements (noted in *Ant.* 13.322-23) — offered no respite for those of conservative sensibilities. Salome Alexandra, the

---

127. Schürer, 1973, 1:213; cf. Buehler, 1974, 59; *Wars* 1.67; *Ant.* 13.299.

128. As, e.g., the giving of Greek names to his sons; cf. Schürer, 1973, 1:217.

129. Φιλέλλην — "lover of Greek ways"; *Ant.* 13.318; cf. *Wars* 1.71-85; a clear indication that "the Hasmonean dynasty had officially entered in to the world of Greek culture and commerce" (Buehler, 1974, 59). Aristobulus was thus regarded as friend of the Hellenists (cf. Jagersma, 1985, 87).

130. Josephus says Aristobulus was the first to officially adopt the role of king, "the first to put a diadem (διάδημα) on his head" (*Ant.* 13.301; cf. *Wars* 1.70).

131. There are indications from Josephus that the acceptance of the title "king" was offensive to many more traditional-minded Jews (cf. *Ant.* 14.41).

132. Cf. Schürer, 1973, 1:217.

wife of Aristobulus, had on the death of her husband released the brothers he had incarcerated and married one of them, Alexander, the eldest, proclaiming him high priest. While superficially resembling the Hebrew tradition of levirate marriage, this action was clearly more politically motivated and recalled a Hellenistic practice employed by royalty for the express purpose of perpetuating or extending a dynasty.[133] It is during Alexander's term of office that our sources first speak of outright protest against the Hasmoneans by the populace,[134] but unrest must have been building for decades. The people were apparently unhappy with the high priest's unworthiness to offer sacrifices; the story of the pelting of Jannaeus with citrons by worshipers at the Feast of Booths is offered by Josephus as an illustration of this (*Ant.* 13.372). Other instances of emerging protest and of Jannaeus's lack of concern for Jewish sensitivities are well known. After being charged with being the son of a prisoner of war (and thus potentially the result of a rape by foreigners: a most compromising set of circumstances for a high priest, however unfair the charge!), Jannaeus quelled the protest by massacring six thousand Jews (*Ant.* 13.373). This incident was followed by repeated confrontations and the death of multitudes of common people (*Ant.* 13.376; *Wars* 1.91-95).

The popular protest that emerged under Jannaeus serves to illustrate that the Jewish populace would follow their leaders only so far, and hatred for the oppressive regime may have been one of the reasons the populace submitted, for a while, to the Pharisees (*Ant.* 13.400). The possibility even exists that the country now experienced some kind of conservative religious reform directed by the Pharisees,[135] but that this was very superficial is indicated by the way the people again received Jannaeus with jubilation after successful military campaigns (*Ant.* 13.395ff.). It would not be surprising if conservative traditionalists interpreted the events as a sign of the fickleness of the people; frequent changes of loyalties would only have increased their suspicions that the people were ignorant, unprincipled, and unreachable. This much, if little more, can be confidently inferred about their attitude, given that the historical sources mostly focus on the leadership and only hint at the reactions of conservative minds.

133. Cf. Reicke, 1968, 69. T. Ilan ("Queen Salamzion Alexandra and Judas Aristobulus I's Widow," 1993, 181-90) does not find evidence in the sources for this (levirate-type) marriage; instead, the very un-Hebraic practice of nominating the queen to succeed the dead king composes the instance of the "considerable Hellenistic influence on the Hasmonean court" (190).

134. Cf. Schürer, 1973, 1:222-23.

135. This might be suggested by the fact that Alexander's advisers needed to appeal to Alexandra for protection against the Pharisees (*Ant.* 13.411-15).

From Pompey to the Jewish War

While the short reign of Alexandra (76-67 B.C.) represented a temporary respite from religious and political unrest, this relative peace did not last under her sons and successors Hyrcanus II and Aristobulus II, who settled the succession by what were becoming for the Hasmoneans characteristic political manipulations. During this period the populace appears to have taken a greater role in the political life of the nation, and following an initial period with Aristobulus in power the contest between the brothers was eventually settled in favor of Hyrcanus, who was also the rightful successor by reason of seniority. He then proceeded to secure his position by outmatching Aristobulus in battle. Both aspiring leaders had their opponents, and with good reason. As an example of the degraded state of the politics, even the celebrated and righteous Onias was stoned to death when he evidenced a spirit of conciliation and hesitated to confirm Hyrcanus in his office. So irresolute and restless was the behavior of the mob who represented sentiments against the rule of these brothers (cf. *Ant.* 14.41) that the country was often ruled by anarchy.

The end of this restless period would, however, come soon, marked by the storming of Jerusalem in 63 B.C. by the Roman Pompey, who not surprisingly sought to take advantage of the weak internal situation in Judea to further his goal of expansion. Already anticipating a decisive move by Pompey, both Aristobulus and Hyrcanus sent emissaries to meet Pompey's general, Scaurus, with offers of tribute. Aristobulus won out and for a while managed to preclude war (*Wars* 1.128). Another delegation, this time sent by the Jewish people, pleaded for the dissolution of the Hasmonean dynasty altogether in favor — according to Josephus — of the traditional priestly theocracy. It is worth noting that while this might be interpreted as a conservative development, it perhaps more likely represented a rejection of the monarchist claims of the brothers for various reasons, although it may also have reflected the growing influence of the Pharisees. It would seem, in any event, that economic and political considerations were more influential than religious concerns.[136] It is moreover impossible to say whether the request reflected the views of a large number of citizens. After a time Pompey's favor shifted to Hyrcanus, and Aristobulus was forced to retreat. On his return Aristobulus prepared to go to war with Rome, but eventually surrendered to Pompey (*Wars* 1.131-40). Aristobulus's men refused to give up, however, and this was no doubt the factor that forced Pompey into his forceful subjugation of Jerusalem. Hyrcanus's party, meanwhile, opened the

---

136. We can generally agree with Buehler, therefore, that the "religious question had always been present, but in the pre-Herodian period it was over-shadowed by the power struggle" (1974, 120).

gates to Pompey, in this way claiming him as their ally, while Aristobulus's men assumed a defensive position on the Temple mount. A great massacre ensued (*Ant.* 14.58-72; *Wars* 1.143-53). Significant here is the intensity of the intra-Jewish rivalry during all these occurrences, which is reflected in reports about the civil war that raged within the city walls,[137] although the storming of Jerusalem probably had the effect of temporarily quelling this intra-Jewish violence. Politically speaking, surprisingly little change took place in Jerusalem as a result of Pompey's campaign. The city was made tributary to the Romans (*Ant.* 14.74; *Wars* 1.154), but Judea remained relatively autonomous, its secular affairs being placed under the Syrian governor Gabinius, followed by Crassus. Hyrcanus was forced to abandon the title of king but retained the priesthood,[138] which could only have rekindled the feelings of those who rejected Hasmonean sacerdotal legitimacy.

Some of the *Psalms of Solomon* (esp. 8 and 17) provide an illuminating commentary on these events from the perspective of one severely critical of Hyrcanus's action in opening the city gates to Pompey. This does not imply that their author stood in sympathy with Aristobulus; he rather seems to have belonged to a separate Davidide party (a group claiming descent from David or, at the very least, sponsoring messianic hopes) who would have rejected both Hyrcanus and Aristobulus on the basis of their non-Davidic lineage. Perhaps the author or some from his party were even among the emissaries to Pompey requesting the dissolution of the Hasmonean priesthood.[139] What is notable in these psalms is the sense of utter frustration expressed at a Judaism represented not only by those who opened the gates to Pompey but apparently also by others who took up arms at the Temple and by others still who viewed the events with passive lack of concern and became helpless victims in the massacre. As already noted, it was the condition of the people generally, as much as the vanity of the leaders, that caused sincere grief for this author. The theological evaluation of the situation spelled out in the psalms accordingly emerged from the psalmist's doctrine of divine retribution: the judgment was from God, and the

137. Cf. *Wars* 1.150, which comments that "most of the slain perished by the hands of their countrymen of the opposite faction" (cf. *Ant.* 14.70)! Josephus puts the number at twelve thousand. For the intense division over attitudes to Pompey, cf. *Ant.* 14.58-59; *Wars* 1.143.

138. Caesar confirmed Hyrcanus as ἐθνάρχης and ἀρχιερεύς; cf. Schürer, 1973, 1:272; *Ant.* 14.73.

139. The delegation may also have included some Pharisees who would have concurred with our author's critique, either because of the non-Zadokite origin of the Hasmonean priesthood or the non-Davidic origin of their claims to royalty, or both; cf. Gowan, 1986, 93. There are strong reasons, however, for doubting the Pharisaic authorship of the psalms; cf. more below.

blame belonged entirely to the sinful people Israel. The tumultuous religious and political history of Israel leading up to this event offered the psalmist some incriminating data for such a theological interpretation. In his view little had happened in the past three centuries to indicate that Israel had ever truly returned from their spiritual exile. The emergence of a Hellenizing party, the antics of Antiochus IV, the corruption of Maccabean nationalistic hopes, the Hasmonean reign of terror — all of these unfortunate periods of oppression were seen as fully merited by the impiety of the nation.

The events that followed 63 B.C. represented a turning point in Jewish political history. On one side stood the last of the Hasmoneans; on the other the emergence of the Herodian dynasty. By 47 B.C. Antipater, father of Herod ("the Great"), had been nominated procurator *(epitropos)* of Judea and proceeded to put out any nationalistic spot-fires that remained from the earlier conflagration. Early on, while still a youth acting as his father's agent, Herod himself became known for his uncompromising treatment of active nationalist movements, and this reputation was to follow him the rest of his life.[140] As governor *(stratēgos)* of Galilee Herod put down nationalistic uprisings until his harsh reactionary methods created problems with the Jewish authorities in Jerusalem, with the result that he was called before the Sanhedrin to undergo trial. The eventual result of this insult to his person was that Herod marched against Jerusalem itself, the violence of his temper restrained only by the slightly more moderate Antipater. It was during the office of the high priest and self-proclaimed king Antigonus (the last of the Hasmoneans) that Herod purchased for himself the right to be king of Judea from Octavian. But to free his new territory from Antigonus, Herod besieged Jerusalem and eventually took both temple and upper city.[141]

Herod's was a rule filled with Gentile ways and Gentile compromises. While respected for his massive efforts in building and restoring the Temple, Jerusalem, and the territory of the Jews, Herod was also a shrewd and calculating friend of the Romans. He was often opposed by the Jewish populace on the charge that he was an Idumean "half-Jew" (*Wars* 1.181; *Ant.* 14.403), but apparently also because of the force, murder, and intrigue he frequently employed to put down Jewish resistance. He levied heavy taxes, encouraged the Hellenistic games, built theaters and amphitheaters in and around Jerusalem, and, worse yet — as far as the pietists would have been concerned — financed the erection of temples to foreign gods and to Caesar. Even his reconstruction of the Jewish

140. Cf. *Wars* 1.199-202 for Antipater's own campaigns against nationalist uprisings, and 1.204ff. for the account of his sending the youthful Herod to Galilee to carry out the same; for later action of Herod in crushing the "Brigands," cf. *Ant.* 14.420-30; *Wars* 1.304-5, 309ff., 316, 431-33.

141. Cf. *Ant.* 14.465ff.; *Wars* 1.295-96, 343ff. for the war against Jerusalem and the great loss of lives.

temple possessed Hellenistic and cultural rather than religious motivations.[142] His polygamy no doubt also created offense. Herod did, however, perhaps have one thing in his favor — he finally appointed a Jew of genuine sacerdotal lineage, Hananel, to the office of high priest, acknowledging his own disqualification from the office due to birth. But this state of affairs was not long lasting, as Hasmonean priests reasserted their claims to legitimacy until Aristobulus was eventually granted the high priesthood under great pressure, Herod unlawfully dismissing Hananel and effectively undoing the one act that might otherwise have endeared him to the conservative wing.

Not surprisingly there are few indications in the records as to the response of traditional conservatives to the reign of Herod.[143] Josephus himself condemns Herod's disrespect for tradition (*Ant.* 15.267), but if Josephus took such a view of this aspect of Herod's rule it is unlikely that pious conservatives were any more sympathetic. Herod's initiatives toward the goal of the Hellenization of Jerusalem surpassed even those of Jason and Menelaus as he cleared the way for open practice of the Graeco-Roman lifestyle. Certainly, therefore, a great number of the residents of Jerusalem who were already succumbing to the gradual changes would have ventured further along the way toward modernization, either willingly or from pressure from Herod or from respect for the leader. That many did is evident from indications in Josephus that, along with resistance, Herod also had many supporters (*Wars* 1.335) and the historian himself (revealing the inconsistency of his position) occasionally comes to the king's defense (*Wars* 1.354-56). Herod's encouragement led to renewed involvement in the gymnasium, not to mention other trends toward catching up with the times, and there are signs from this period as well that such activities produced offense among conservatives, who again nurtured the view that those who carelessly capitulated were nothing short of apostates from Judaism. An example of this type of judgmental attitude toward Jerusalem's citizens might be discerned in the prognostications of a certain righteous man named Samaias, who not only predicted the harm Herod would bring on the people but (perhaps invoking Jeremiah's advice to apostate Jerusalem vis-à-vis Nebuchadnezzar) even advised on the occasion of Herod's rise to power that he be admitted into the city since "on account of [the people's] sins they would not be able to escape him" (*Ant.* 14.174-76). This suggests that not only the offenses of Herod but also the general trend toward assimilation on the part of *the people themselves* — some of which obviously resulted from his influence — produced difficulties for conservatively minded Jews like Samaias.

142. For all these things, cf. Schürer, 1973, 1:295, 304-5, 309, 311-12, 314.
143. Unless the New Testament is thought to contain these, as is likely; cf. Matt. 2:1-19; 14:1-6 pars.; 6:14-22 pars.; Acts 4:27; 12:1-23.

Following Herod's death there occurred a second nationalistic uprising marked, as with that under the Maccabees, by strong difference of opinion among the masses. Political manipulations, along with general unrest in Jerusalem, were elevated beyond precedent in this period, leading to rebellion. Herod's son Archelaus quelled the rebellion by bloody means, and Jewish reaction to this may be what in turn eventually led to a Roman invasion of the Temple area in A.D. 70. But not everyone concurred with the reactionary sentiments that eventually led to war. According to Josephus (whose comments must be treated with due caution, since he clearly had an axe to grind), the country was severely divided and even "owed its ruin to civil strife." He blames in particular one group of "Jewish tyrants who drew down upon the holy temple the unwilling hands of the Romans," by whom hc means all those who embraced a zealot ideology (*Wars* 1.10). Even given his nuanced presentation, one may nevertheless understand why tensions resulted in widespread nationalist revolt. The Herodian dynasty ruled with an iron fist and Herod's strict and unpredictable character was reflected in his offspring. Agrippa I repeated the civil practices of Herod,[144] while other Herodian kings married illegally, compromised their uniqueness as Jews, and slaughtered their countrymen. Archelaus himself took liberties in appointing and dismissing high priests and particularly scandalized the populace by an illegal marriage. The accusations against him resulted in Judea being placed under direct Roman administration — which just increased the malaise.[145] Under Roman governors completely insensitive to Jewish tradition, oppressive burdens were placed on the populace, including heavy tax increases. Jewish tax collectors — who embodied the loss of traditional Jewish sensibilities and served the hated regime — correspondingly fell into considerable disfavor. The result was further rebellion, and following that, the incidents of A.D. 70.

This period of Jewish history is regularly dealt with by historians interested in questions of historical causation. Most theories blame the destruction of Jerusalem on a series of political events[146] or on the unfortunate resurgence of eschatological expectation.[147] Such explanations may havc their

144. Particularly with regard to his ambiguously articulated negative attitude toward traditional Judaism implied in his method of governing; cf. Schürer, 1973, 1:451-52.

145. Schürer's summary is well articulated: "[The Roman officials] were, like all petty rulers, above all conscious of their own arbitrary power, and through their infringements they in the end so aggravated the people that in wild despair they plunged into a war of self-annihilation" (1973, 1:357).

146. E.g., Reicke, 1968, 256.

147. E.g., Gafni, CRINT, II/2, 25. Other theories invoke unrealistic military ambitions or theologically inspired nationalism (cf. T. A. Idinopulos, "Religious and National Factors in Israel's War with Rome," 1991, 50-63).

validity. What is perhaps not surprising, however, is that the writers of the period itself are considerably more theological in their approach than modern historians, and this may well give one good insight into how some people of the time viewed the events, especially given that these theological views seem to have been quite widespread. Josephus's political bias against the zealot nationalists of his time is well known, and yet Josephus adds a theological reason for the destruction of Jerusalem: God has judged Israel for its stubborn refusal to cooperate with the superior influences (i.e., the nations) whom God has ordained to rule over Israel. The people have only themselves to blame. Therefore, "the flames . . . owed . . . their origin and cause to God's own people" (*War* 6.251). More specifically, Josephus blamed the nationalistic ideology, which he believed resulted in the otherwise quite unnecessary storming of Jerusalem.

Josephus was clearly not alone in this judgment. The authors of 4 Ezra and *2 Baruch,* like the author(s) of *Psalms of Solomon* 8 and 17 a century and a half earlier, possessed a not dissimilar doctrine of divine retribution. Josephus, then, would actually have concurred with some conservative groups in his theological interpretation of the situation. The view that A.D. 70 was a judgment from God was probably widely current. Those of a more pacifistic attitude would particularly agree with Josephus's evaluation of exactly where to place the blame, while others would have supported the militant nationalists since the zealot movement to a certain extent at least championed the cause of a wide range of conservative groups. The authors of 4 Ezra and *2 Baruch,* for their part, seem to have been convinced that God's judgment was directed, not only against failed zealot attempts, but against *a general state of apostasy in Israel.* The whole nation seemed to be caught up in futility and hopelessness. Nationalistic attempts to save Judaism, although commendable, were disappointing, being characterized by bloodshed and infighting.[148] The repeated warmongering and senseless party strife might well have been interpreted as final proof of Israel's fundamental problem with sin. Several recent scholars agree that this was the point of view taken by many Jews who survived the event. While it is true, as Stone says, that theodicy became one type of response in postdestruction Judaism,[149] Neusner has reminded us that reflection on the destruction of the city or the Temple itself was not the only or even the major concern;[150] and scholars like Neusner,[151] Co-

148. For the history of conflict among the three zealot leaders at this time, John, Simon, and Eleazar, cf. Schürer, 1973, 1:500-503.

149. Cf. M. E. Stone, "Reactions to the Destruction of the Second Temple," 1981, 195-204.

150. Cf. J. Neusner, "Judaism in a Time of Crisis," 1972, 313-27.

151. Neusner, 1972, 316.

hen,[152] Kirschner,[153] F. J. Murphy,[154] Goldenberg,[155] and Stone himself[156] have each in their own way pointed out that many Jews blamed the destruction on the sin of Israel, just as had been done for the first destruction of Jerusalem over six centuries earlier.

THE ORIGINS AND IDENTITY OF A MOVEMENT

Our survey of the period between the first and the second destructions of the Temple has witnessed an almost endless variety of religious, social, and political influences and experiences acting on the Jewish world. While no two stages of this lengthy duration were identical by any means, a limited number of outstanding influences or factors have nevertheless been seen to have been repeatedly and consistently at work throughout the period. While these factors probably had their origins in the exile, they became especially noticeable during the late Second Temple period (200 B.C. to A.D. 100) — noticeable, that is, partly due to the relatively detailed nature of the sources for that period and partly to the infelicitous rule of the Seleucids, which so forcefully brought these factors to the fore. These influences, or factors, can be summarized as follows: (1) influences tending to move the Jewish people away from traditional understandings and practices, in particular the influx of Gentile thought and ways resulting from dominance of foreign powers — namely, Greeks and Romans; (2) the gradual acceptance of the new ideology by the priests and other Jewish leaders and a corresponding liberalization of the nobility; (3) the involvement by growing numbers of the population in the liberalizing tendencies and a corresponding downgrading of traditional ideas among the masses; and (4) the existence of relatively small groups of dissidents to the religious reform who saw in both active and passive involvement in the reform and in the liberalization of the people as a whole signs of a general failure to remain faithful to the religion of Israel — that is, a mass apostasy. Occasionally the protest of such groups resulted in active and more or less well-organized reform parties being formed, but more frequently it resulted in division and factionalism of a less-organized kind.

152. S. J. D. Cohen, *"Shekhinta ba-Galuta,"* 1982, 147-59.

153. Cf. R. Kirschner, "Apocalyptic and Rabbinic Responses to the Destruction of 70," 1985, 27-46.

154. Cf. F. J. Murphy, "2 Baruch and the Romans," 1985, 663-69, 664.

155. Cf. R. Goldenberg, "Early Rabbinic Explanations of the Destruction of Jerusalem," 1982, 517-25, esp. 517.

156. In spite of his emphasis mentioned above; Stone (1981, 196) refers to Jth. 5:17-18; 2 Macc. 5:17-20; and *Pss. Sol.* 2:1-3, 16 (197).

Even where such groups are not explicitly mentioned in the historical records, it has nevertheless become clear in this historical survey that conditions existed throughout the entire Second Temple period conducive to the emergence of a movement or movements of protest. The writings surveyed in the previous chapters of this book provide primary evidence of such movements, but certainly they are not the only records of protest to have been produced, nor do they represent the only groups who protested. Furthermore, they probably do not contain the only form of protest. Both strongly *nationalistic* reactions and the reactions of groups who rejected the nationalistic response, even to the point of becoming *non*nationalistic or even *anti*nationalistic in posture, will certainly have emerged. This paradoxical occurrence, that reactions to similar stimuli can nevertheless adopt opposite responses, is to be expected. While a strongly nationalistic view of the election of Israel would have motivated certain groups to take action appropriate to this understanding, namely, to attempt to reform the national vision, those who resigned themselves to the failure of the national model would have reacted by condemning that national vision. It is specifically this latter type of group that is of interest here and that seems to be represented by our writings.

The historical survey above accordingly offers a context in which the judgmental critique and the exclusivist attitude found in those writings can be *acknowledged* and, having been acknowledged, *understood*. While motivations naturally overlap, it has been suggested that the cause of the protest stems as much from *religious* as from strictly political or economic factors.[157] This is an important point, given the universal tendency among sociologically oriented approaches to overlook philosophical factors in favor of economic or political factors. One must remember that historically the Jewish people (unlike many other peoples) have been characterized most by their religion, not by economics or politics, and accordingly this religious factor cannot be reduced to a byproduct of one of those other factors — without, that is, completely misrepresenting things. When it comes to the traditional conservatives of the late Second Temple period, to be specific, one is dealing with *the reaction of pietists to perceived apostasy in Israel.* Central to the debate are disputes about things like the sanctity of the priesthood, the importance and interpretation of law, and religious authority. Among many peoples and religions of the world these things may have been side issues, hardly worth ideological and even physical separation and heated protest — but among Hebrews these were life-and-death issues. Economics and politics, on the other hand, did not carry complete influ-

---

157. We would thus agree with the basic approaches of scholars like Plöger (1968) and Smith (1971) that the issues were religious, while not necessarily agreeing on what they see to be the main point or points of disagreement.

ence as social factors for a people whose religion *was* their life. In more anthropological terms, worship was as strong and fundamental a drive as any other necessary comfort or primitive need. While strictly political concerns may have played a role, therefore, the attempt to approach these writings from *a priori* political theories is to overlook their main significance. They directed their message of dissent to the apostasy that they perceived *within*[158] Israel. While not going as far as we have in our conclusions, a growing number of recent approaches have recognized that during the Second Temple period a popular and widely felt dissatisfaction with the status quo on the basis of religious convictions is evident in the emergence of movements independent of the Jerusalem establishment, resulting in a sharp increase in sectarianism throughout the period. Many of the Jewish writings selected for study in this book are now being viewed as part of this general trend, quite in contrast to an earlier tendency to view them as reflecting the mainstream of Jewish thought.[159] The Qumran scrolls have played a formative role in this development, serving to draw attention to the sectarian nature of many of the teachings typical of this literature. Terms like "penitential,"[160] "reforming,"[161] or "millenarian sects"[162] have been placed on the groups that produced these writings,[163] and although the use of the word "sect" in these characterizations does not imply all that we think it should (as already pointed out), this trend nevertheless focuses attention on *intra-Jewish* conflict in a way that has not previously been done.

It is not the intention here to further catalogue each of the writings according to their specific sociological grouping. Although the terms "Hasidim" and especially "Essene" have been used extensively, it is still difficult to say, given present knowledge, whether or not these can be treated as anything more than generic terms that may or may not have corresponded to the limits of the

---

158. To restate the view of Bickermann (1979, 84), the Jewish opposition to Antiochus actually represented "a civil war, a religious struggle between reformers and orthodox. But posterity has remembered it as a war against the Seleucids" (approvingly cited by Endres, 1987, 238).

159. Cf. Gafni, CRINT, II/2, 3; J. C. Greenfield and M. E. Stone, "The Enochic Pentateuch and the Date of the Similitudes," 1977, 51-65, 56-57; Collins, 1973, 30-31; D. M. Rhoads, "The Assumption of Moses and Jewish History," 1973, 53-58; Suter, 1979, 52-72; J. D. G. Dunn, *The Partings of the Ways between Christianity and Judaism and Their Significance for the Character of Christianity*, 1991, 105-7; contrast this with Jaubert's view of Jubilees as a "confrérie" or "caste" (*La notion d'alliance dans le Judaïsme aux abords de l'ère chrétienne*, 1963, 112-15).

160. Hengel, 1974, 1:180.

161. M. A. Seifrid, *Justification by Faith*, 1992, 132; Beckwith, 1982, 7-10; cf. Endres, 1987, 237, who uses the term "restorative reform."

162. Cf. Hann, 1988, 177ff.

163. Cf. also Reid, 1989, passim, esp. 38-69, 77, 89-91, 131, 133.

movement defined herein. A wide range of theories have been expressed for Qumran, for example (including Pharisees, Sadducees, Zealots, Christians, and Karaites), but the emerging consensus regarding the scrolls is that they represent the views of a group of "Essenes" *similar to* those spoken of by Philo, Josephus, and Pliny.[164] Even if this identification could be established, a great deal still rests on the words "similar to." That the title could, in this case, be applied in a generic sense only follows from the fact that factious groups such as Qumran would unlikely have deliberately identified with other groups under a single denomination. The problem is accordingly reduced to the question whether the Qumran sectarians *and* the Essenes spoken of by the ancient historians are to be *directly equated.*[165] If they are to be equated, the ancient descriptions appear to be in considerable error in regard to some important details. For example, Josephus attributes to the Essenes an interest in astrology for deterministic purposes, but we have already concluded quite a different function for astronomical interests among these groups. But if direct identification is not justified, then the continued use of the term "Essene" is a questionable practice, especially since the scrolls exhibit absolutely no interest in, or sense of fraternity with, other similar "Essene" groups such as would allow for the application of the term to the scrolls community. That the Qumranites were "essene" (generically speaking, therefore, with a lowercase "e") may be granted as far as it goes, but one may not confidently assume that any ancient definition that went beyond the generic sense would have applied to this group. One thing is at least clear, however, and that is that there were other similar groups, indeed a whole movement, that would have been much in sympathy with many of the views and with the basic attitude of the Qumranites.

164. For discussion and critique of the Essene theory of Qumran origins, first formulated by E. L. Sukenik, and now the *opinio communis,* cf. H. Stegemann, "The Qumran Essenes," 1992, 83-166. The theory is given strong, although not completely unambiguous, archaeological support by R. de Vaux ("Qumran, Khirbet–'Ein Feshkha," 1978, 4:978-86). The resurgence of the Sadducean theory based on Schiffman's study of 4QMMT is the only recent strong challenge to the Essene view, but it appears to have lost momentum. For this approach, cf. L. H. Schiffman, "4QMMT — Basic Sectarian Text," 1991, 81-83; for valid counterarguments that, we feel, successfully oppose the idea, cf. in Kapera, ed., *Qumran Cave Four and MMT,* 1991, the articles by Davies (85-94), Eisenman (95-104), VanderKam (105-8), and Baumgarten (115-17); cf. also Stegemann, 106-7. We believe the term "Essene" is valid, but only as a generic term, and that historically speaking the Qumran community may have been a quite distinct branch of a much wider movement that included those whom Josephus and Pliny refer to as "Essenes."

165. As argued by Albright and Mann: "it is still a fact that no other remotely comparable oasis between Jericho and Masada, and north of Engedi, can be found to accommodate the Essene community than that which housed the settlement at Qumran" (1969, 12).

As for the term "Hasidim," references in 1 Maccabees give the impression that the term was associated with a known and fairly well-defined group of people. This group apparently arose in reaction to the events surrounding the rule of Antiochus IV and eventually became or at least formed a part of the Essenes.[166] Even here there is some question, however, whether the name can be taken as signifying a distinct, identifiable group or whether it is simply a synonym for "the faithful" and better taken as another generic and widely applied term for all kinds of traditional, conservative, or religiously zealous Israelites. One finds the anarthrous *sunagōgē Asidaiōn* in 1 Macc. 2:42-44, which NEB translates "a company of Hasidaeans," but this need not imply a distinct and well-defined group with any political organization or even a common origin.[167] One reads in the same passage: "all who were refugees from the troubles came to swell their numbers, and so add to their strength" (v. 43), a statement that may merely attempt to categorize a prevailing opinion and imply little more than an undefined movement binding together people of similar attitude rather than a defined group with membership requirements, records, or rituals of their own. In 2 Macc. 14:6 *Hasidaeans* are identified as followers of Judas (*hoi legomenoi tōn Ioudaiōn Asidaioi*, NEB: "Those of the Jews who are called Hasidaeans"), but this also gives little indication of the term's referent. 1 Macc. 7:12-13 might, on the other hand, identify the Hasidim with a certain specific group of "scribes," but a careful analysis of the language used does not demand such a limitation.[168] Even if the Maccabean literature used Hasidim as a proper name, however, this implies neither that the word was restricted to that use elsewhere, nor that any of the groups we are concerned with in this study was Hasidim in this specific sense. Like "Essene," this term is probably applicable to our groups only as a generic term.

There is a distinct danger, therefore, in associating any of these writings with groups known from other sources. Another common, and even more questionable, practice is to gather references from many sources, unite them

166. Cf. H. J. Schonfield, *Secrets of the Dead Sea Scrolls*, 1957, 14-15, 22.

167. As J. R. Bartlett assumes (*The First and Second Books of the Maccabees*, 1973, 40): "Here they are mentioned as an already existing party. They seem to have belonged to the scribal class, the interpreters of the law" who reacted to the suspension of their duties as lawyers.

168. It reads καὶ ἐπισυνήχθησαν . . . συναγωγὴ γραμματέων ἐκζητῆσαι δίκαια καὶ πρῶτοι οἱ Ασιδαῖοι ἦσαν ἐν υἱοῖς Ισραηλ καὶ ἐπεζήτουν παρ' αὐτῶν εἰρήνην. NEB translates: "A deputation of doctors of the law came . . . asking for justice. The Hasidaeans were in fact the first group in Israel to make overtures to them (lit. 'and they sought peace with them')." καὶ πρῶτοι κτλ, on the other hand, would appear to be open to a number of interpretations that do not all imply the precise identification that this translation does (e.g., "But the *ḥasidîm* were first and foremost among all the Israelites — including these scribes — in seeking peace with them"). The words "in fact" in NEB are interpretative.

under one rubric, and attribute all or many of the writings to this one group (such as the Pharisees).[169] The impossibility of relating the authors or editors of the *Testaments of the Twelve Patriarchs,* for example, to either Maccabeans or Pharisees has already been commented on. Whether their author might be seen as a member of the Qumran community has been considered,[170] but this connection is equally difficult to sustain. Certainly if one must draw connections, it is preferable to speak of general movements rather than of distinct groups, and in fact a new consensus seems to be emerging for many of these writings that denies that they stem from Pharisaic circles and affirms instead that they originated within the same general movement that produced the Dead Sea Scrolls.[171] This emerging consensus seems to be a most preferable option, and the nature of the Qumran library, which contained several of the Pseudepigrapha, again supports the view that many groups existed through this period that were related to Qumran by their common protest and tendency toward separation. Hultgård accordingly points to *general* ideological similarities (notably reaction to the establishment) among otherwise widely diverse writings such as the *Psalms of Solomon,* parts of *1 Enoch,* the Qumran writings, and the *Testaments.*[172]

Such a view of things is a useful way not only to relate groups and their texts with other groups and other texts, but also to understand the complex relationships within the textual history of the individual documents. Since the discovery of several parallel but nonidentical documents similar to the *Testaments of the Twelve Patriarchs* (such as Cairo Geniza *Testament of Levi* and Qumran Aramaic *Testament of Levi,* a portion of a Hebrew *Testament of Naphtali,* as well as multiple Qumran fragments), these have been used in attempts to reconstruct the source history of the *Testaments* as if they were primarily related chronologically and sequentially. But it is doubtful that it will ever be possible to reach a consensus on how these diverse texts were related

169. Cf. Reid, 1989, 14: "The problem with such a position is that it is tautological. Once the characteristics of a certain group are defined, there is the danger that one may maintain that a group has been found merely on the basis of an artificial definition."

170. This has been argued as an option by, among others, de Jonge (cf. H. D. Slingerland, *The Testaments of the Twelve Patriarchs,* 1977, 44-82). The "man . . . who renews the Law" in *TLevi* 16:3 has been considered to refer to the *moreh* of Qumran (cf. Hultgård, 1977, 1:102, 6, who otherwise concludes that only ideological, not historical, connections exist between the two communities; 130).

171. Cf. Slingerland, 1977, 44-82; Hultgård, 1977, 1:102, 106, 116-36. The discovery of a vast and complex textual tradition in the Qumran library for books like *1 Enoch* and the *Testaments* suggests that the people of the scrolls collected rather than authored these books.

172. Cf. Hultgård, 1977, 1:116-36. He refers to "un même courant du judaïsme, les milieux plus populaires dont les porte-parole sont avant tout les *ḥᵃkāmīm*" (134).

chronologically. These texts may better be used to reveal the similarities among different groups instead of being treated as sources for the history of a single textual tradition — in other words, as evidence that several related, but distinct, groups could embrace and employ similar characteristic literary conventions and traditions and write their own testamentary literature associated with the twelve patriarchs, *in order to direct a similar message to the Israel of their time* (while not denying that they may also have employed common sources). The similarities among the texts, in sum, may be ideological rather than merely, or even primarily, textual.[173] These groups need not all be described as Essene groups or directly associated with the Dead Sea sect, and some independence among them would be suggested by the *differences* in the written traditions and fragments as they are now extant; but these documents all suggest, nevertheless, a rather broad sectarian context for writings like the *Testaments of the Twelve Patriarchs,* the Dead Sea Scrolls, and the other writings as well. The important thing, therefore, is not determining the exact social provenance of each individual writing but describing the relationships, probably theological as well as social, that we have discerned to have existed among these writings. One can safely speak of a common or general movement, even if we cannot successfully relate it to other known movements.

What Should This Movement Be Called?

The question that remains is: What should this general movement be called? It has already been established that the movement is fundamentally a *protest movement* and that it expressed itself in *nonnationalistic* terms. The notion of protest certainly captures well a central attitude characterizing these groups; however, inasmuch as groups as diverse as those that produced 1 Maccabees may also be referred to as part of the general protest movement, and since there were probably other groups who like the Maccabees were apparently not explicitly antinationalistic or "separatist" in the way our groups were, it would be desirable to more closely define the specific movement at hand.

The notion of *displacement* is perhaps helpful in this definition, but only if it is understood that (1) the displacement is not so much political or economic as it is religious, and (2) the alienation is directed against the masses as

---

173. While Kugler does trace chronological relationships, he also discerns certain ideological parallels in the different texts — they were likely employed as an *alternative* or even *critique* of the present priesthood, rather than as an apology for the Levitical priesthood *per se,* and they were not necessarily written by priests (*From Patriarch to Priest,* 1996, 109, 136-37).

much as against the establishment. These groups can be described as *noncon-formist* or even *anti*conformist, since this properly conveys a distinction in their behavior and beliefs from popular or official norms ("official" referring to the point of view of an authority or establishment against which these groups were reacting). But the fact that these groups claim to represent a divinely *authorized* or *sanctioned* minority upholding long-revered tradition would tend to reverse, from their point of view, the sense of nonconformity into more of a conscious-ness of *conformity* or of some kind of *continuing* status. Moreover, it may be true, and actually seemed to be the case at times, that many facets of this "mi-nority" view enjoyed predominance in religious and even political circles. Ac-cordingly it might be best to refer to the movement, and the groups within the movement, as *purist, conservative,* or *traditionalist.* These descriptions are fre-quently used to speak of Qumran and other "apocalyptic" groups, but while they are certainly applicable, the confusion that exists over the use of such terms has already been alluded to. It is also true that other groups that cannot be said to belong to this movement — groups that oppose it, in fact — are fre-quently also conservative and traditionalist in some respects.

It might be most helpful, therefore, to refer to the more circumscribed movement in which our groups participated simply as a *"Movement of Dissent,"* in distinction to other groups belonging to the larger "Protest Movement." This rubric well expresses this movement's opposition to what was going on else-where in Israel, and while it implies departure from some other norm or stan-dard, it allows that the groups felt that *they,* not the others, were on the right track. It also contrasts the movement with other protest movements that adopted nationalistic and reforming approaches; the groups we are concerned with here opted for a clean break with nationalistic Judaism. "Dissent" is an ap-propriate term for this sense of "over-against-ness."

All that is fine for sociological definition. But these groups lived in a world that was shaped and controlled, not by our understanding of sociological categorization, but by concepts derived from their tradition. Alongside *Move-ment of Dissent,* therefore, one might try defining such groups using more "He-braic" socioreligious terminology. Keeping in mind (1) the conservative aspects of these groups, (2) their minority consciousness, and (3) their corporate con-sciousness, it would help us define the movement were we to grasp a concept from the Hebrew Scriptures (which these groups also frequently use) that actu-ally describes the movement accurately. We refer to the concept of the *remnant.* The idea of the remnant in Israel through history expressed this sense of con-tinuing, or conserving, the true Israelite religion; it expressed a minority con-sciousness; and it certainly lent itself to developments in a corporate or com-munity direction. Beyond these things it would appear that the idea of a remnant (even where the term is not used specifically) granted *theological legit-*

imation for the emergence of this movement. Most sociological categorizations fail to take into account this theological and historical aspect in attempts to define these groups. For the sake of maintaining an important connection with this distinctive theological history, therefore, the term *"Remnant Groups"* will be used to refer to the kinds of groups we find within the *"Movement of Dissent."*

A Word of Caution

In conclusion to this chapter it should be stated clearly that one cannot claim that the dissident attitudes mentioned above were necessarily shared by a *wide* circle of Judaism, or that the writings resulting from it were in any way more representative, or more "standard," than other views of Judaism. In fact, although the movement may well have enjoyed more or less "popular" approval at different times, it is precisely this *minority* aspect of their view that was distinctive and was no doubt partly determinative for their self-identity. As will now be argued in the remaining chapters, it is out of this self-consciousness as a minority that both beliefs and literary conventions were shaped. Moreover, given that many of these beliefs and formal conventions are strikingly similar to what we see in the New Testament, the point is also being made that this essentially nonnationalistic view is too *important* a voice in Judaism for scholars to go on referring to nationalistic voices as if *they* were the only significant ones, particularly, one might add, in the context of prolegomena to the study of the New Testament.

CHAPTER SIX

Dualistic Covenantal Theology

In systematic treatments of Jewish theology in the past, the notion of covenant was considered to be one among many other more or less equivalent concerns. Lately, not least due to the publication of E. P. Sanders's treatments of Judaism, appreciation for the primacy of the idea of covenant in Jewish thought has increased considerably, although it is difficult to understand why it should not always have been obvious that covenant was much more than a peripheral matter in the Jewish world. In any event it is more widely realized now that it is the *other* ideas in the theology of a Jewish group that are likely to have been peripheral. If the distinctive ideas of a Jewish writer did not affect his view of covenant, in other words, chances are that these ideas did not play a major role in his total view of things. Of course, even this very valid observation about the importance of covenant can and has been subject to excesses,[1] but the opposite mistake of tragically overlooking the important place of covenant theology, especially in the writings presently under consideration, has been much more common[2] and could with justification be called one of the more tragic blunders in the history of biblical and Jewish theology.

The problem seems to be that scholars have repeatedly failed to recognize

1. One thinks of Sanders's own reduction of Judaism to its "essence," which is conceptualized in terms of covenant. While an important and central idea, one must be careful not to discern covenantal theology where it is not intended, as cf. G. Quell, *TDNT,* 2:111.

2. Thus, e.g., even Jaubert notes but a single allusion to covenant in *1 Enoch* (60:6; *La notion d'alliance dans le Judaïsme aux abords de l'ère chrétienne,* 1963, 261-62) and suggests there is no covenantal theology at all in the *Testaments of the Twelve Patriarchs* (271-72)!

important covenantal thought, largely because many of the characteristic terms of the covenant — like "life and death" and the language of blessing and curse — have in time (through overuse in theological jargon as well as through loss of original context) undergone a considerable alteration in meaning. An outstanding example has been the tendency to overlook the covenantal significance of the word "life," which has become distanced from its important covenantal context, where it originally served to summarize the blessings promised in the covenant (cf. Deut. 30:15). While the covenantal associations of this word may be rather subdued in some texts, it is nevertheless erroneous to simply understand "life" in the Greek philosophical sense of *zōē* as either a natural or divine *force* (as we have become subconsciously accustomed to do). The word (even in eschatological expressions like "eternal life") frequently retains its more Hebraic sense, evoking both the quantitative and qualitative measure of human existence — that is, a good or bad experience of life. The relevance of this is even more pointed where either formulation or context suggests that the idea of *covenant* lies not too far in the background (granting that each case must be judged individually, of course). It is for reasons such as this that one can concur with the recent judgment that even where the term "covenant" is wanting in some texts, other terminology and formulations often betray that covenant is in view (a principle of interpretation already adopted in chs. 3 and 4 above). Thus indications of the writer's views of covenant are often forthcoming from these very kinds of passages, so that this is where much of the evidence to be used in a reconstruction of the covenant theology of Judaism must come from, especially where more direct indications are lacking.

Treatments of the theology of covenant have always shown that there was a tension or contradiction inherent in the idea of a covenant between God and Israel, the tension between covenant as *"gift"* (emphasizing that the covenant is given by God's grace) and as *"demand"* (emphasizing the requirement of obedience to the covenant by Israel).[3] As with many theological concepts in the ancient Near Eastern world, this basic inner contradiction was probably not consciously recognized or felt to be problematic. It seems that the extremes — *gift* versus *demand* — existed only hypothetically, while in practice all Jewish theologies embraced both aspects *to an extent*. These facts tend to make the many efforts to resolve the tension somewhat pointless. At the same time it is impor-

3. The contrast between the two aspects (and we quite advisably use the word "aspects" rather than "types" of covenant to avoid the implication that they are incompatible ideas) has been emphasized largely by modern theological treatments. These modern studies — apparently out of the theological inclination of nineteenth- and twentieth-century theology to locate a "higher" view of religion — have largely emphasized the idea of covenant as *gift*. But the idea of demand must be given equal attention in any balanced view of covenants in Judaism.

tant to emphasize that not all Jewish groups would have felt exactly the same about covenant, with the result that their views would even have come into conflict.[4] It will be helpful, therefore, to briefly describe the two (quite hypothetical) views of covenant, along with certain of their implications, in order to set up our own analysis of the data.

At the one extreme is the *unconditional* view of covenant, which emphasizes the aspect of gift or givenness: God has gracefully given a covenant to Israel and will remain faithful to it in spite of any disobedience or waywardness on the part of the nation. This covenant could therefore (in its most extreme form, of course) also be described as *inviolable* or undefilable, inasmuch as no sin could break it. As there could accordingly never be an occasion for another covenant to displace this covenant, it would make the covenant *permanent* and virtually irreplaceable (perhaps suggested by *'ôlām*, "forever," "eternal").[5] This leads logically to the idea of *irrevocability*. One can see how this view of covenant would breed a certain kind of conservatism or traditionalism. In order to immunize the covenant community from new ideas that threaten the security offered by such a covenant, all previous revelation would be hardened into an identifiable and limited corpus and would become the supreme object of reflection and ultimate authority. Other authorities perceived as in competition would be contradicted. (All these tendencies are recognized to have existed to a certain degree in some Jewish groups of the Second Temple period.) In short, this would result in a *static* view of covenant as every and all change would be avoided. Furthermore, *ultimate* significance would be applied to such a view of covenant. The major covenants with Abraham or Moses would naturally assume their place as the supreme covenant(s).[6] Since these covenants were made with Israel and contained promises to the entire nation, this would make the covenant *national* property and would doubtless further encourage *nationalistic thinking*.[7]

---

4. For this reason Sanders's attempt to define all Judaism uniformly under the rubric "covenantal nomism" is especially rash.

5. Although עוֹלָם need mean no more than "(for) a long time"; cf. its root, עָלַם, "hidden," thus "time without evident bounds." The idea of metaphysical eternity also occurs, however.

6. Even Paul in a similar vein argues the superiority of the former over the latter in his letter to the Galatians (cf. 3:15ff.).

7. As cf. Sanders's view of "covenantal nomism." Recognizing the nationalistic implications of Sanders's covenant theology, B. Longenecker has preferred the term "ethnocentric covenantalism" (*Eschatology and the Covenant*, 1991, 174ff.). Longenecker has been criticized by M. A. Seifrid (*Justification by Faith*, 1992, 64-65, 133-35) for adopting this term as an expression of the covenantal theology common to all Judaism, since it falsely (in Seifrid's mind) emphasizes ethnic over ethical concerns. Longenecker's goal, however, was to outline a notable *exception* to this covenantalism (which is partly also

One thus arrives at one extreme, and clearly hypothetical, view of covenant, which can be described in terms like "unconditional," "inviolable," "permanent," "irrevocable," "static," "ultimate," "national," and the like. In reaction to an earlier tendency to view the covenant as legal and conditional, more recent treatments of the subject are frequently committed to demonstrating that this unconditional view of covenant (although not in the extreme form that we have described it) was held by much of Judaism.[8] This is the interpretation given to covenant by E. P. Sanders, appealing to *b. Sanhedrin* 10.1 ("All Israel has a place in the world to come") as representative of the covenantal theology of Second Temple Judaism as a whole.

At the other extreme is the view of covenant that emphasizes *demand*. Such an approach sees covenant as *conditional* on the performance of certain basic duties or requirements. In this view the ancient idea of a treaty involving "stipulations" required by the "suzerain" (here God) is recalled (significantly since the Mosaic covenant is believed to have originally been modeled on such ancient Near Eastern treaties). Failure to perform or to meet the standard invalidates the covenant. Accordingly importance is necessarily placed on the *legal* aspects of the covenant. Since particular requirements involve the cooperation of the individual, the covenant would also tend to be interpreted *individualistically*. In its extreme form, the corporate notion of election would be entirely subjugated to the individual's acceptance or rejection of the terms of the covenant and mechanisms would be put into place by which either to judge the individual or to facilitate the continuing participation of the individual within the covenant (such as atonement rituals, feasts, and regular sacrifices). Due to the uncertainty resulting from such a conditional covenant, means of renewing the covenant, or even the possibility of instituting another covenant to take the place of one that has failed, would also become desirable if not, at times, absolutely necessary. In contrast to static notions of covenant, therefore, this would grant what could be called a more *dynamic* nature to the idea of covenant, leaving it open to change and

---

Seifrid's concern), which Longenecker finds in 4 Ezra. The entire discussion exemplifies the difficulty of employing any one term in an all-encompassing manner to describe the "center" of Judaism.

8. Foremost among these is Jaubert's treatment of covenant in Judaism (1963, esp. 27-31). Systematic theologian J. Jocz (*The Covenant*, 1968) acknowledges the two aspects of the covenant in the Hebrew Scriptures: "The unconditional aspect of the covenant . . . is as indigenous to the Old Testament as is the conditional one" (29). The "conditionless covenant" was a prophetic innovation (27). The rabbis recognized both aspects (39). But he strongly favors, in contrast to many of his former peers, a "conditionless" view of covenant (42), and he repeats this supposition throughout his work (e.g., 55-56, 57-58, 103, etc.).

improvement. While former covenants might be considered paradigmatic, no covenant would be considered sufficient in itself, including either the Abrahamic or Mosaic covenants. Many covenants are therefore possible and different ones would come into prominence from time to time. Such a view of covenant would tend to be more tolerant of *innovative revelation,* which might involve either significant advances in doctrine, or merely clarifications. It would demand a less nationalistic orientation, inasmuch as God judges individuals, and could easily lead to various cosmic and *universalistic* applications.[9] Hence, in complete contrast to the first view described above, there is — hypothetically at least — a covenantal theology that can be described using terms like "conditional," "individual," "legal," "dynamic," "renewable," "innovative," "revelatory," and perhaps even "universalistic."

As already suggested, these types are not likely ever to have existed in their extremes. Jewish groups would have synthesized and combined the aspects of both, producing a variety of final products that nevertheless would be all *well within the spectrum of possibilities of what one would expect for covenantal thought.* Thus it is hardly necessary to conclude that the options were limited or that all groups thought the same on such matters.[10]

DYNAMIC AND DUALISTIC VIEWS OF COVENANT

So what can one say about the writings from the Jewish movement of dissent from this period? Indications have already emerged in preceding chapters that the view of covenant in these writings tends to be both "dynamic" and "dualistic." This should not come as a complete surprise since there is already evidence for these tendencies in portions of the Hebrew Scriptures, especially in those strands commonly referred to under the rubric "the Deuteronomistic tradition."[11] The Enochian corpus draws out the conditional nature of the cov-

---

9. Seifrid appropriately stresses this aspect when he argues that emphasis on individual behavior "brings a concomitant form of universalism" (cf. also above). P. R. Davies likewise acknowledges that the strongest barriers were between the Damascus community and *other Israelites* — leaving open the possibility for non-Jews to join their sect ("Who Can Join the 'Damascus Covenant'?" 1995, 135ff.): "The sect is hostile to Israel but largely indifferent to the world beyond" (135).

10. Cf. Longenecker, 1991, 31-33.

11. Cf. Quell, *TDNT,* 2:122; K. Baltzer, *The Covenant Formulary in Old Testament, Jewish, and Early Christian Writings,* 1971, 34-36. S. D. Sperling ("Rethinking Covenant in Late Biblical Books," 1989, 50-73) maintains that in the late biblical period (fourth–third century B.C.), the biblical writers gave up the Deuteronomistic conditional view of cove-

enant, as seen above, and proclaims some to be in the covenant and others to be out of the covenant. Likewise *Jubilees* gives more than a passing impression that a division existed in Israel over the covenant. To this dualistic understanding of covenant, both corpora of writings added additional stipulations, including adherence to the calendar and to certain vital laws. These ideas are carried even further in the Dead Sea Scrolls, where some kind of "new" covenant is envisaged. The unifying element in all these views of covenant seems to be the need to *define the participants in the covenant* — frequently requiring a new definition of covenant, a new proof of entrance into the covenant, or even an entirely new covenant.[12] Because of the importance of covenantal thought, it will repay time to investigate these ideas in detail. While it might be equally useful to approach each writing, separately summarizing the view of each, it is perhaps more economical to approach the subject by topic. This approach is necessitated by the fact that not all the writings contain every characteristic; and in some cases only a comparison can help us understand the individual case. We will look first at the covenant under the general heading "dynamic" and then under the heading "dualistic."

DYNAMIC VIEW OF COVENANT

In order to evaluate the importance of the "dynamic" view of the covenant, we will consider such things as the multiplicity of covenants recognized by the movement, the role of innovative laws and teachings as expansions of these covenants, covenant renewal, the conditional nature of covenant, and individualistic expressions of covenant. Not all of these motifs are to be found in every one of the writings, but the presence of any one of them may signal a dynamic view of covenant.

---

nant for an unconditional view. Even if Sperling's arguments can be sustained for some writings, the intertestamental period shows a distinct return to Deuteronomistic conditional formulations. Nehemiah 8–9 and Ezra 9–10 also express the view that Israel has failed to keep the covenant and is in need of renewing it; cf. M. Smith, "The Dead Sea Sect in Relation to Ancient Judaism," 1960, 356-57.

12. Endres cites with approval the view of Morton Smith that a "characteristic pattern of sectarian groups is a proclivity for self-definition by means of binding 'themselves together by entering into a covenant to maintain their peculiar practices'" (*Biblical Interpretation in the Book of Jubilees*, 1987, 240).

Multiplicity of Covenants

It is perhaps not surprising that our writings refer to a number of different covenants, since many are also referred to in the Hebrew Scriptures. What is notable, however, is the apparent reluctance to elevate any one of these covenants to the status of "*the* (supreme, or 'one and only') covenant" — whether that be the Abrahamic covenant or the Mosaic covenant. Significantly also, the term "covenant" is rarely, if ever, equated with the Mosaic institution of the law in a generalized way, as seems to be the case elsewhere in Judaism.

Jubilees specifically mentions a number of covenants, those with Noah (6:4ff.), Abraham (14:17-20), Jacob (29:7-8), and perhaps Moses (1:1). If any one of these covenants is to be considered primary for *Jubilees,* it would be neither the Abrahamic nor the Mosaic, but the *Noachic* covenant.[13] The reason for the importance of *this* covenant in *Jubilees* is never discussed. Perhaps it has something to do with its antiquated and pristine character — it is the first "covenant" of the Bible. But ultimately even it is derived — that is, it is merely a reflection of the perfect law found in the heavenly tablets, as noted above. Significantly, while Moses is the chief character in the narrative world of *Jubilees,* a covenant *per se* is never explicitly associated with his name; he is told only to write the "divisions of the days" (1:1). This may be due to the fact that Moses' covenant is understood in *Jubilees* as little more than a *renewal* of the ancient laws and covenants (everywhere Mosaic legislation is introduced by reference to former patriarchs)[14] rather than a novel covenant possessing independent status. But another possibility must be considered, namely, that the author was also attempting to *distract* somewhat from *this* covenant in order to draw attention to *other* covenants that his group held to be comparatively more important. Perhaps the author even wished to downplay the Mosaic covenant since it was given irrevocable status by the opponents of his group (a sure indication of a more static view of covenant on their part) and perhaps also because the author did not agree with prevailing emphases and interpretations placed on that covenant. That some such motivation is at work is suggested by the fact that the author frequently draws his lessons for the future (i.e., for his *contemporaries*) from the *patriarchal stories* rather than from the Mosaic legislation; significantly the authority even for *legal* exhortations is also based, not on revelations made to Moses (which would seem to be the most direct route for appeal), but on earlier covenants.[15] It would seem, in any event,

---

13. Cf. Jaubert, 1963, 105-8; Endres, 1987, 227.

14. *Jubilees* 50 suggests that the important content of the covenant made with Moses centered on the types of laws already revealed to the patriarchs (particularly, in this case, with regard to sabbath).

15. Important instances of this practice are the exhortations surrounding the

that there were pressing issues for the author for which appeal to covenants *other* than the Mosaic better served his purposes. Knowing the context of debate going on in the Jewish world of this time helps us to see what these purposes were: *the author was attempting to reintroduce or emphasize certain aspects of past covenants that were felt to have been carelessly ignored by Israel but were still important to the author and his community.* The author is able to take this position because his view of covenant has clearly not become "static" in the sense that one covenant takes precedence in importance over all the others.[16] Although it is not discussed in the book itself, the data suggest rather a *coherent* (and perhaps developmental) view of the covenants in which each one takes an important place in an accumulating notion of covenantal revelation leading to some kind of ideal covenantal obedience (i.e., leading back to the prototypical covenant known to the heavenly tablets).[17] The first revelation of covenant was given to Noah and further revelations have come with each successive covenant, but the *only* ultimate and perfect covenant is to be found in the heavenly tablets.

Clearly the most important covenant for the Qumranites was the covenant that was confirmed with the Damascus exiles in the relatively recent past ("the New Covenant in the Land of Damascus," CD 18.21); but other covenants are named and appear to be considered of continuing validity. The Damascus Document refers to "the covenant of the Patriarchs" (CD 1.4; 6.2) and "the Covenant of the Fathers" (8.18; (B)1.31) in ways that suggest that they are still in effect in the present time. Wise argues that these covenants made with Abraham, Isaac, and Jacob were considered to be of perpetual validity for *all* Israel in contrast to the covenant made at "Damascus," which applied only to the elect, the idea of perpetuity being taken from the biblical reference to those covenants being made with Israel *leʿôlām* (forever). One of the former covenants is specifically mentioned as being renewed at the end of time (11QT 19.3-10), namely, the covenant made "with Jacob at Bethel," which would include a rebuilding of the Temple along with the reinstitution of the cultic laws.[18] In contrast to this

---

Noachic covenant in 6:17-38 (regarding the Festival of Weeks, and blood), and the Abrahamic in 16:25-32 (regarding proper circumcision).

16. This is perhaps the reason the covenant *with Moses* is not explicitly mentioned in *Jubilees,* even if the laws of Passover are thoroughly covered in ch. 49. The Feast of Weeks also takes precedence over this feast in *Jubilees.*

17. Perhaps Endres has summarized accurately when he says that "in Jubilees all of the individual covenants collapse into a single covenantal relationship, which began with Noah's covenant with God in *Jub.* 6:1-21" (1987, 227).

18. Cf. M. O. Wise ("The Covenant of Temple Scroll XXIX,3-10," 1989, 56, 59), who compares this passage with Lev. 26:9-12, which explicitly applies the terms of Jacob's covenant to all Israel as his descendants. "The covenant of the *TS* [Temple Scroll] is a reaffirmation and reapplication of the patriarchal covenant made at different times with Abraham, Isaac and Jacob" (59).

kind of emphasis on continuity, 1QH 13.11-12 speaks of *setting aside* "the former covenants,"[19] implying a more developmental notion in which the new things that have been established take precedence over the old. But this cannot be taken as more than an indication of the *relative* importance of the covenants: the other covenants — particularly the Mosaic and the Zadokite — appear to possess continuing validity. And while the evidence is somewhat ambiguous, the Qumran community seems to have especially valued a series of priestly covenants, seeking perhaps to fulfill these in some way through its own priestly organization.[20] The ancient Zadokite covenant may be what is referred to in 1QSa 1.2 as "the law of the sons of Zadok the priests and of the members of *their* Covenant *(bᵉrîṯām)*," although this may be just another reference to the Covenant of Damascus. In any event, the importance of the precedent set during the earlier "Zadokite covenant" regarding the priority of the Zadokite priestly line is one element of that covenant that is certainly regarded as having continuing validity.

19. קימי קדם. While Holm-Nielsen denies any reference to a covenant in this verse, Dupont-Sommer (*The Essene Writings from Qumran*, 1961, 242, cf. n. 3) is certainly correct in taking these words (lit. "that which you established before") as referring to the covenants. While the word קים is not used in this sense anywhere in the Bible (only used once, in Job 22:20, where it has the obviously unrelated meaning "adversary"), rabbinic literature has been cited to support the sense "that which is," "that which is determined," thus: "law," "custom," or "covenant." Confirmation that this passage refers to covenant comes from the passages upon which it was obviously patterned: Isa. 42:9 and 43:19. The Lord who does "a new thing" is the one who also "makes a way in the sea, / a path in the mighty waters, / who brings forth chariot and horse . . ." (43:16-17) — that is, provides a new exodus-like deliverance (originally in reference to a return from exile). For the word "covenant" itself in the context of the Isaiah passages, cf. Isa. 42:6; 49:8. The community could well have interpreted such language of the making of their new covenant (for the relationship of the exodus deliverance motif and the making of a covenant among our groups, particularly Qumran, cf. ch. 12 below). Another interesting suggestion is that of Mansoor, who relates this making new to the rabbinic doctrine of the periodic renewal of creation, suggesting that it was also an eschatological theme (*The Thanksgiving Hymns Translated and Annotated with an Introduction*, 1961, 178). The real question here is whether the passage is referring to creation or revelation; while the first part of the hymn would seem to be a creation liturgy, the immediate context is of God's establishing the righteous remnant, and thus the passage actually refers, as do the lines that follow, to revelation, again confirming its relation to the new covenant. Even if this connection cannot be sustained, the general idea that God has introduced new things speaks of fundamental innovation over what went before. See more on the passage below.

20. Jaubert points to the priestly covenants made with Aaron and Phinehas (cf. Sir. 45:25) and alluded to in 1QS 5.2, 9, 21; 1QSa 1.2; 1QSb 3.22-23 (1963, 146). All in all, however, these passages would seem to refer to the covenant as recently established with the Qumranites, a covenant that would however also embrace the Zadokite priesthood as established in the (earlier) Zadokite covenant.

Belief in the continuing validity of many covenants is not rare, and this is hardly surprising. To a certain degree all Judaism was bound to recognize the continuing validity of revelation made to Israel in the past. As a matter of practice, however, the remnant groups apparently made use of the idea of a plurality of covenants for the specific purpose of demonstrating the error of their opponents. That some polemical purpose was involved is evident from a later time in 4 Ezra in its awareness of and *insistence* on the multiplicity of covenants. In one place the author refers approvingly to the tribes of Jacob believing the "covenants" (dative plural *testamentis*, 3:32). In another place apostate Israel is contrasted with those who believed "your covenants" (*testamentis*, 5:29; cf. 7:24), which in this case might refer to a combination of ancient covenants with a more recent covenant, or perhaps merely to a renewed appreciation of the older covenants. In any case the notion of a series of earlier covenants that have now been carelessly set aside by Israel comes through very clearly in this passage.[21]

In sum, it would seem that the view of covenant held by these groups entailed incorporating and combining aspects of preceding covenants, perhaps with the intent not only of criticizing their opponents but also, more positively, of (re)constructing the *ideal* or *consummate* covenant out of the building blocks provided by each former covenant. The notion of an ideal covenant is particularly relevant to the invocation in *Jubilees* of the heavenly tablets (where the idea of a heavenly antitype may have been philosophically as well as polemically motivated). It may also be of value in understanding the idea of the "new" covenant at Qumran, which seems largely, if not exclusively, to have included the renewal of older covenants. The important thing to emphasize here is that none of the historical covenants with Israel was considered to have *exclusive* priority — and this can be said even with regard to the Abrahamic and Mosaic covenants. Each covenant added something to the total understanding.

Additions to Earlier Covenants

On account of the intense concern for continuing revelation and the accompanying willingness to allow for considerable *expansion* of preceding revelation, remnant groups in Judaism subjected the traditions they received to innovations, some of which we have already considered in chs. 3 and 4. On occasion these innovations directly influenced views of the covenant, and this is notably true with regard to the calendar, which was fundamental for participation in

---

21. The passage manifestly reflects on the recent sacking of Jerusalem in A.D. 70, for which it blames Israel's unbelief of the covenants: "those who opposed your promises have trodden down on those who *believed your covenants*" (5:29; cf. also 7:83; 8:27)!

the covenant in the Book of Watchers, the Book of the Heavenly Luminaries, *Jubilees*, and the Dead Sea Scrolls. In comparison with the calendar issue, some of these additions are actually quite minor but nevertheless significant for the way they illustrate the practice of adding to covenants.

Jub. 21:4-20 offers a good example of this. Here the author refers to the law as it was revealed not only to Moses but also to the patriarchs before Moses' time, and he makes the claim that the entire law was carefully practiced by the patriarchs. In this way the writer obviously seeks to appeal for certain laws to a greater authority than either himself or his community (or even Moses), that is, by appealing to Abraham and implicitly beyond Abraham to the heavenly tablets and the laws written upon them (laws that are also reflected, presumably, in the "books of [Abraham's] forefathers and in the words of Enoch and in the words of Noah," v. 10). Perhaps the search for an ancient (or even transcendent) authority involved an implicit admission that the matters the writer was about to expound were not clearly evident in the Mosaic law and thus required some other form of authentication. That authentication came by way of the author's authoritative source of revelation, the heavenly tablets. In this passage Abraham's last testament to Isaac provides opportunity for a series of clarifications on the laws of sacrifice. The method of "exposition" of these laws goes well beyond the clarifications typical of talmudic exegesis, which attempted to "make a fence around Torah." While *Jubilees* does contain clarifications here (vv. 10-12, 15-16), it also includes new laws (e.g., the limitations on wood allowed for the offering, vv. 12-14)[22] along with repeated cautions about blood (vv. 17-20), matters that in various ways transcend the biblical commandments.[23] That these laws were believed to have been earlier known and practiced by the patriarchs might suggest that the author viewed them not as *additional* or *innovative* laws at all, but as standard laws already widely known. That it is not simply a matter of laws commonly known, however, can be seen from the fact that these laws needed to be revealed *afresh* to Israel in the latter days in *Jubilees* itself since they had presumably been *forgotten* by Israel. Accordingly it is not so much a matter of definitely *new* revelation as the rediscovery of lost revelation. In either case the writer's appeal to traditions *other* than those known to most of Israel sufficiently demonstrates his openness to revelatory traditions that take him

22. R. H. Charles (*The Book of Jubilees or Little Genesis, Translated from the Editor's Ethiopic Text,* 1902, 134) comments that this passage "was written possibly to determine the meaning of עצי שטים [RSV 'acacia wood']" in Gen. 25:5, 10; but there is no particular method of determination or exegesis here — the law is simply stated. None of these stipulations is found in the Torah or Mishnaic *halakah;* cf. Charles (135).

23. Cf. Exod. 30:19-21; Lev. 17:13-14; Num. 35:33; Deut. 12:23. A similar example to this one is the occasion (33:1-17) on which the writer refers to the heavenly tablets to justify the death penalty for incest.

considerably beyond present understandings, and amounts to a claim to possess superlative revelation. The idea of having additions as well as clarifications to the law might seem contradictory for a *conservative* group responding to a breach of covenant in Israel, but it must be remembered that this writer was convinced his community's practice was legitimized through a higher revelation, the revelation of law *par excellence* in the heavenly tablets. This involves an obvious circularity in that the revelation served as both authorization for a negative attitude toward others who had abandoned tradition and at the same time a convenient "source" to legitimize the critique of opponents in terms of novel kinds of laws — a kind of eclectic circularity common to these groups. It can nevertheless be seen that a strong belief in revelation played a part in the understanding of covenant in *Jubilees*.

It is only in the Dead Sea Scrolls, however, that it becomes evident just how fluid the idea of covenant could be for some groups. Here one finds repeatedly mentioned a covenant of the community, which in some passages is referred to as the "New Covenant." Whether Qumran's New Covenant is to be understood as distinctly *new* and not simply a renewal of past covenants remains a debated question. Some emphasize the predominance of the Mosaic covenant — the new covenant is a kind of second phase or reapplication of the covenant with Moses, and its newness consists in an improved understanding.[24] But others view the new covenant as radically new, the Mosaic covenant supplying, at best, its foundation.[25] On the basis of the cumulative evidence from the scrolls, it would appear that there is definitely some new teaching involved in becoming a member of this covenant (as already determined above). When the psalmist (almost certainly the *moreh ṣedeq*) in 1QH 4.24 speaks of those "who inquired of me,[26] who gathered in *Thy Covenant* and heard me," he seems to

---

24. Jaubert (1963, 216-17, 222) refers to this covenant as a second phase of the Mosaic covenant, not a second covenant, referring to CD 3.4, 11; 7.5; 8.17-18; 12.11; 19.31; 20.17. The "knowledge" assumed in the new covenant does not surpass that of Moses and the Law (cf. CD 5.3-4): "Mais jamais la Lor n'avait été mieux connue et mieux pratiquée par une collectivité en Israël" (223). Cf. also J. Becker, *Das Heil Gottes*, 1964, 65. Some passages in the scrolls do seem to suggest this, but they hardly demand it. 1Q34 *bis* 2.5-6 says, "Thou hast chosen for Thyself a people in the time of Thy good-will, for Thou hast remembered Thy Covenant . . . and Thou hast renewed for them Thy Covenant." Remembering and renewing covenant need not, however, preclude the idea of a new covenant, as cf. below.

25. The common view is that the Qumran covenant reflects the fulfillment of the expectation expressed in Jer. 31:34 of a "new" covenant (cf. Baltzer, 1971, 97, who finds the distinctiveness of this covenant in the fact that, unlike past covenants, it will no longer need to be renewed).

26. We cannot accept the version of Holm-Nielsen (*Hodayot*, 1960, 84), "sought *by* me," referring to the examination of initiates upon their entry into the community and to

imply that the covenant was only recently made known, being revealed to the "saints" partly by means of his own teaching. Another passage (CD 3.13-15) sounds much like *Jubilees'* doctrine of the heavenly tablets when it says that "God established His Covenant [i.e., the 'New Covenant'] with Israel [= 'those who clung to the commandments of God,' l. 12] forever, *revealing to them the hidden things in which all Israel had strayed*" — among which are included the calendar, feasts, the "ways of truth," and the like. This is an important indication that the Qumranites believed that they possessed a more perfect and complete covenant, which, in spite of many similarities and associations with past covenants, constituted a significant advance over them. The covenant is frequently associated with novel revelation, and it is this association that makes the covenant distinctly "new" rather than being merely a restatement or even a renewal of the Mosaic covenant. This conclusion seems to be confirmed by a particularly revealing presentation of the significance of the New Covenant in 1QH 13.11-12 (according to Dupont-Sommer's reconstruction; see above): "Thou hast caused them to see what they had not known [by bringing to an end the] former [things] and by creating things that are new, by *setting aside the former covenants* and by [set]ting up *that which shall remain forever.*" Although this passage seems to state that only the things revealed in this New Covenant remain eternally valid, this need not preclude that some overlap with earlier covenants is intended, as pointed out above. However, a passage like this strongly suggests that the Qumran covenant possessed unique status partly due to its innovative quality, and not only to its eschatological significance, even though it was also probably understood as in some sense a final covenant, a covenant designed for the latter days.

There is little question, in any event, that this covenant was considered a real advance over prior covenants. While 1QS 9.13 is difficult to translate, it may also be interpreted in such a way as to provide a significant clue to the importance of new revelation vis-à-vis the covenant when it says of "the man of understanding" that "he shall do the will of God according to all that has been revealed *la'ēth ba'ēth.*" This latter expression has been variously interpreted: it might be taken to mean "according to each season (of the year?)," but more likely means something like "from time to time" or "for each time in its time."[27] The meaning would be, in this latter case, that a new revelation

---

the annual inspection of the members of the community. While דרש is used in the relevant passages referring to this practice, here the word certainly means to inquire of the *moreh,* in parallel with the following "heard me."

27. Accordingly Lohse (ed., *Die Texte aus Qumran,* 1971, 35) has "was offenbart ist für die jeweilige Zeit." H. Ringgren (*The Faith of Qumran,* 1963, 133): "in accordance with all which is revealed in each time." Contrast Wernberg-Møller (*The Manual of Discipline,* 1957, 35): "according to everything which has been revealed time and again"; but that this

is given appropriate to every new dispensation of time and would imply that every successive covenant, including the most recent one, contains uniquely new revelation applying to that time. That even conservative Jewish people could be open to this kind of *relativization* of the Abrahamic and Mosaic covenants alerts us to the essentially dynamic view of covenant held in these circles. This relativization also suggests the potential seriousness of the rift between these and other Jews who may have centered their understanding on the *inalterability* of a single and irrevocable covenant — notably that of Abraham or Moses.

Covenant Renewal

Another indication that these remnant groups nourished a dynamic rather than static view of covenant is their frequent insistence on the repeated and proper *renewal* of the covenant, without which it would become ineffective or dissolved.[28] In *Jubilees* the Feast of Weeks is expressly designated as the opportunity for this renewal of the covenant: "it is ordained and written in the heavenly tablets that they should observe the feast of Shebuot in this month, once per year, *in order to renew the covenant in all respects,* year by year" (6:17).[29] This is by far the most important feast in *Jubilees* inasmuch as its origins are traced to the primary covenant — the covenant of Noah — and beyond that to the

---

refers to the progressive nature of revelation is evident from the parallel phrase that follows and is translated by Wernberg-Møller: "He shall study the entire wisdom which has been found in chronological sequence" (comparing לפי העתים to κατὰ καίρους); and from l. 12: "in accordance with the rule proper to every season and the weight of every man." 8.15 provides an almost exact parallel to the expression: "according to all that is revealed, season by season (עת בעת)." According to Knibb, this refers to the revelation of the law in the study sessions of the sect (*The Qumran Community,* 1987, 135); but that "season by season" refers to the chronological nature of the revelation is suggested by the reference to the (canonical) Prophets in l. 16. Beyond these expressions referring to time, nothing indicates a reference to study sessions in either of these passages.

28. This idea is not foreign to the Hebrew Scriptures. Baltzer notes that while the biblical covenant was concluded "forever," a renewal of the covenant became necessary whenever it was (decisively) broken (cf. 1 Kings 8:33-50; Jer. 34:8-22), while a simple "reaffirmation" was acceptable on other occasions (cf. 2 Kings 22–23; Joshua 23; 1 Samuel 12; etc.; 1971, 51-82, 97). Accordingly the covenant renewal contained in 1QS 1–2 is in the nature of a true renewal celebrated on an annual basis "as long as the time of Belial's dominion lasts" — i.e., in recognition of curse being in effect during the entire period in which the community was in existence (62).

29. Cf. 5:17-19; L. Hartman, *Asking for a Meaning,* 1979, 110. Jaubert (1963, 105-6) refers to the Feast of Weeks in *Jubilees* as the ceremony of conversion for Israelites.

heavenly tablets themselves (6:4-22).[30] This association with Noah, rather than Abraham or Moses, suggests that the Jubilaean community held certain ideas about the feast and about renewal of covenant not universally held in the Jewish world. Foremost among these differences, and something we have already observed with regard to the calendar, is the paramount importance given to the exact *timing* of the feast. Just as there can be no relations between God and his people without a renewed covenant, there can be no renewed covenant without the renewal practiced *on the proper day* in conformity to the heavenly tablets. Given such beliefs, it would be interesting to speculate whether the Jubilaean community held its own celebration of the feast separate in time and place from other Jews, since it is clear that the writer and his community would have rejected the Jerusalem rites because of their improper timing. While little evidence is provided in the book, it would seem likely that rather than establishing a competing sacrificial cultus the community merely withdrew from the Temple, opted out of participation in the rites, and awaited the restoration, at which time Temple and cult would be purified and restored in line with the laws as understood in *Jubilees* (cf. ch. 11 below). There could be no proper renewal of the covenant until such a time as that.[31]

As in *Jubilees,* the Dead Sea Scrolls consider maintenance of the covenant dependent on covenant renewal, which was dependent, in turn, both on the proper date for renewal and on its precise celebration in line with the legislation of the community. Several passages from the scrolls have been identified as covenant renewal passages, some of them as verbatim records of the liturgy of renewal,[32] others as material reflecting but less directly associated with the liturgy, and others as legislation bearing on the renewal.[33] In con-

---

30. Cf. Jaubert, 1963, 105-8. 6:18 also suggests that *Shabuot* was already celebrated "in heaven" even before Noah's time, and reminds us that the *ultimate* origin of the festival, for the writer of *Jubilees,* was in the heavenly tablets. The date of its celebration seems also to have been made to correspond to the giving of the covenant with Noah (cf. Charles, 1902, 51-52); the connection of the feast with Noah was apparently suggested by Gen. 8:20-21.

31. Although we might note that Hartman thinks he *can* find evidence of a rite in *Jubilees* 6 (cf. 1979, 110-11).

32. Cf. 1QS 1.16–2.18; 5.13–6.8; 10.9–11.22; 1QSa 1.4-5. For discussion of such texts, cf. M. Weise, *Kultzeiten und kultischer Bundesschluss in der "Ordensregel" vom Toten Meer,* 1961, passim; Baltzer, 1971, 99-117, 169; Hartman, 1979, 73; T. Elgvin, "The Qumran Covenant Festival and the Temple Scroll," 1985, 103.

33. Cf. 1QS 5.7-20; 1QSb 5.21; CD 14.3-6; 1QH 14.8-22; 1Q34. For discussion of these passages as stemming from the renewal celebration, cf. Jaubert, 1963, 210ff. Elgvin also mentions 4QD[b] (1985, 103). Ringgren (1963, 211) takes the references to love and hate, to the coming near, and to the binding of oaths in 1QH 14 to allude to the covenant celebration. Baltzer sees most of the Damascus Document originating in the structure of

trast to the Jubilaean community (where we are not sure about their celebration of the feast), it would appear that the Qumranites *did* make provision for covenant renewal outside the Temple — in other words, that the celebration envisaged by the author of *Jubilees* actually took place at Qumran. It is rather more difficult compared to *Jubilees* to decide which of the covenants was thought to be renewed in these celebrations. The expression "New Covenant" made "in the land of Damascus" (CD[B] 2.12) suggests not only the first main occasion on which the distinctive covenant of the community was acknowledged and entered into but also a "fresh start," and it would be logical to assume that it was this covenant (rather than, e.g., the Mosaic covenant) that was renewed.[34] As for the purpose of the celebration, the admittedly ambiguous evidence of the scrolls at least suggests that each established member of the sect celebrated a renewal yearly and that this also served as an *entrance ceremony* for initiates. The former aspect seems to be referred to in 1QS 2.19ff. while the latter may be the *primary* reference in 1QS 1.18–2.18 — although since the two sections do not appear to refer to separate occasions, it can be assumed that the celebrations were concurrent and did not have independent significance apart from each other.[35] Several other scroll fragments have also been identified as originating with or relating to an annual cove-

---

the covenant formulary (1971, 114-17) — according to the following outline: 1.1–6.11, "antecedent history"; 6.11–7.4, "blessings and curses"; 9.1–16.20, "legal stipulations." For probable instruction relating to the renewal cf. 1QS 3.13–4.26. Cols. 5-9 also show the influence of the covenant formulary, according to Baltzer (99-106).

34. For the view that the "New Covenant" involved a somewhat independent renewal of the "Damascus Covenant" by a later group, cf. P. R. Davies (*The Damascus Covenant,* 1982, 53, 176-77, 186, etc.), who bases his view on a two-level approach to the redaction of CD. For a similar view of the redaction of CD, cf. H. J. Schonfield, *Secrets of the Dead Sea Scrolls,* 1957, 27, 126, etc. Such approaches do not influence the conclusion that it was not the Mosaic covenant *per se* that was being renewed.

35. A debate centers around whether the "entrance celebration" referred to in 1QS 1.16–2.18 is distinct from or continuous with the annual covenantal renewal referred to in 2.19ff. Weise (1961, 70) argues (against Dupont-Sommer, Cullmann, and Lohse) that the passages refer to the same event, on the basis that עבר, which appears in 1QS only in these passages (cf. 1.16 and 2.19ff. where it appears three or four times depending on reconstruction of l. 26), is common to both; that the term harks back to Deut. 29:11; and that it refers there to the renewal of the covenant. עבור בסרך is to be interpreted in the sense of the full formula in 1.16: וכול הבאים בסרך היחר יעבורו בברית (thus בסרך is not, as Dupont-Sommer, "in order," but refers to accepting the rule of the community, *as per* the common use of סרך in 1QS). Similarly Wernberg-Møller takes the latter passage as a description of how the *whole* community takes part in the aforementioned initiation ceremony (1957, 55); cf. also Knibb, 1987, 88; A. R. C. Leaney, *The Rule of Qumran and Its Meaning,* 1966, 135. The arguments of Weise and Wernberg-Møller would appear to be sustainable; the rite referred to in 1.16ff. was repeated yearly (as cf. 2.19).

nant renewal celebration.[36] This annual celebration was probably carried out, as in *Jubilees*, on the Feast of Weeks.[37] An enigmatic reference to a *daily* entering of the covenant is also found (1QS 10.10), although there is reason to interpret this verse nonliterally, perhaps as referring to daily *intentions* to fulfill covenant requirements.[38] Even if this passage is not taken into consideration, many other references to the need to periodically renew the covenant confirm the dynamic, repeated, and conditional nature of covenant in the scrolls community.

But what exactly took place during these covenant renewals? 1QS 1.16ff. seems to legislate if not actually recount the events of the ceremony.[39] The fragment 4Q266 seems to confirm what is otherwise obvious from 1QS, that the basic order is similar to what is recounted in Deuteronomy 27–29.[40] This section of Deuteronomy could itself have been originally intended as a guideline

36. For a list of these and discussion, cf. B. Nitzan, "*4QBerakhot*[a-e] *(4Q286-290),*" 1995, 487-506. *4QBerakhot* is interesting for the way it spiritualizes the blessing and curses component, aiming them at the leaders of the lot (God and Belial) rather than at the earthly or human levels, and indicating the participation of the heavenly beings in the earthly renewal. The texts are all notably dualistic. Nitzan concludes that "there was a certain degree of freedom in the formulation of the texts intended for recitation" (497).

37. Leaney, 1966, 97, 135; Hartman, 1979, 111; Elgvin, 1985, 103; Knibb, 1987, 88. It is interesting, however, that Wernberg-Møller (1957, 50) sees an allusion to Lev. 16:21 in 1QS 1.23 and takes from this that the renewal occurred on the Day of Atonement. The dating of the renewal on the Feast of Weeks, however, would seem to be confirmed by 4Q266 (cf. comments of R. H. Eisenman and M. Wise, *The Dead Sea Scrolls Uncovered*, 1992, 213, 216-17). For discussion of the feast days as occasions for renewal, cf. Hartman, 103-13.

38. Cf. Becker, 1964, 115. "I will enter the Covenant of God" stands in parallelism with "I will recite His precepts" (cf. also Leaney, 1966, 245, who takes it to refer to the recitation of the *Shema'*; or Dupont-Sommer, 1961, 98, who takes it to refer to prayer). That this is a general reference to personal responsibilities for regular and repeated worship is evident from similar expressions scattered through the passage, such as l. 13: "At the beginning of every enterprise of my hands or feet I will bless His Name" (cf. also ll. 14-15, 15-16).

39. Cf. Jaubert (1963, 212-14) and Baltzer (1971, 62, 169), who see the ritual rooted in ancient celebrations of the renewal of the covenant. A sign that the source of this passage is the renewal itself is the double amen that appears at the end of the passage, a possible sign of a liturgical provenance. It should be noted that the "amens" occur in the model passage, Deuteronomy 27, and may only reflect their presence there. A clearer indication that here is a liturgical piece actually used by the community is the way the terminology of the group is substituted appropriately for expressions in Deuteronomy 27ff. Furthermore, there appears little reason to cite the passage unless it was intended to be obeyed.

40. "The sons of Levi and [the inhabitants] of the camps are to gather together in the third month (every year) to curse those who depart to the right or [to the left from the] Torah. And this is the exact sense of the Judgements that they are to do for the entire Era [of Evil, that which was com]manded [for al]l the periods of Wrath and their journeys . . ." (citation from Eisenman and Wise, 1992, 219).

for covenant renewal celebrations, and internal features suggest its appropriateness for that use.[41] It would seem, in any event, that the scrolls community tried to replicate the experiences spoken of in the Scriptures as best they could. Accounts of new or renewed covenants in Nehemiah 8–9 and Ezra 9–10 also apparently informed their practice. Baltzer maintains that the 1QS passage reflects the typical order of covenant renewals with confession, prayer for forgiveness, and possibly some "mediation of forgiveness" such as a water rite (cf. ch. 12 below). It is also very clear from 1QS 1.18–2.18 that the ceremony included an invocation of blessings and curses in the fashion of Deuteronomy 27.[42] Beyond these basics it is difficult to know what else might have taken place during the renewal celebrations. There is some debate whether some or all of the meals of the community were "covenantal meals" since the priests were involved and there is no little concern for ritual details in passages referring to these meals; but on the whole concerns for purity would seem to adequately explain the attention given to proper order for meals.[43] A similar ambiguity pertains to the baths at Qumran: whether their chief function was ritual ablution, atonement, or initiation is not entirely clear. A relationship to covenant (either initiatory or reparative) is probable but, as with the meals, too little is known about the baths to throw any light on the covenant renewal celebration itself.[44]

41. Cf. 27:2-8: "on the day you pass over the Jordan . . . you shall . . . ," which either reveals that the passage was intended for this purpose originally, or that it merely suggested such a use later on; the repeated emphasis on "this (the same) day" in the context of the passage (cf. Deut. 27:9, 10, 11) might also have suggested a repeated annual performance on the "same day" of the year. Jaubert (1963, 212-13) takes this passage to be the source of the Qumran renewal.

42. Baltzer, 1971, 169.

43. Cf. 1QSa 2.17-22; 1QS 6.4-5. In view of the possibility, mentioned above, that the Qumranites felt it essential to renew the covenant on a *daily* basis, the covenantal significance of the meal would then become evident. But this is a matter of speculation. Jaubert (1963, 206) posits an indirect connection between the meal and the covenant renewal, appealing to texts like Gen. 26:30; 31:54; Josh. 9:14-15; and 2 Sam. 3:20-21 for possible relationships. On the other hand, the concern for partaking meals in ritual purity may be enough to explain the emphasis on order at the meal. Beyond that, Wernberg-Møller feels that the priestly role in the meal order in 1QS 6.4-5 does not necessarily imply a "sacramental" understanding, but might refer only to the precedence of the priest in all matters of food and drink (1957, 102-3). Leaney similarly reasons that the expressions in this passage are normal ones for the daily meals of the community and imply no sacramental thinking (1966, 182-84). The relationship between the present meals of the community and the eschatological meal in 1QSa 2.17-22 is also a familiar subject of controversy: the similarity of this passage with 1QS 6.4-5 suggests that the daily meal may have anticipated an eschatological or messianic meal (cf. Knibb, 1987, 154-55).

44. Cf. 1QS 3.9-11, whose proximity to the covenantal passages (cols. 1-2) might be taken to suggest a connection.

Beyond the straightforward requirement of maintaining the covenant, the language of the liturgical passages implies that the renewal of the covenant at Qumran and in the Jubilaean community (if not all covenant renewals)[45] was thought to be made necessary because of *apostasy*. The Qumranites may have felt themselves implicated in this apostasy or at least endangered by it. Therefore, the ritual was intended to secure for them an escape from the wrathful curses of the covenant by means of a renewal that (through a rationale not immediately evident; see ch. 12 below) repaired the damage to the covenant or, perhaps, restarted the covenant with a clean slate (thus perhaps "renewal" would be better called "reinstitution" — the idea of [re-]institution would also explain how initiation of new members and renewal by established members could coincide). If the covenant renewed at Qumran was the "New Covenant" given exclusively to them, this might mean that the covenanters were not so much avoiding the judgment coming on the rest of Israel as preventing their own covenant from falling into neglect, but the renewal probably implies both. In any event, recent affairs in the nation's history made it abundantly clear to the writers of the scrolls, as to the other writers of this literature, that some Israelites had broken the covenant. Renewal of the covenant was part of the attempt to deal with this situation.

Conditional and Individual Aspects of Covenant

The covenant that Israel was considered to have broken was probably the Mosaic covenant, but it may have been others, and 4 Ezra names plural "covenants" neglected by Israel. For all these remnant groups this clearly involved a tragic paradox inasmuch as the Abrahamic and Mosaic covenants were originally intended to be a symbol of God's merciful intent to "keep" Israel. That the covenant intended to symbolize Israel's security actually resulted in the nation's downfall nevertheless needed to be rationalized. This could only be done, within a covenantal framework, by asserting and holding together several related ideas: that God could not overlook sin in spite of the covenant; that he must remain an equitable judge; that covenant is conditional, not automatic; and that judgment must be based on individual deservedness. Warrant for this conditional and individual view of covenant was near at hand for our authors, primarily from Deuteronomy. It is not surprising therefore that there are many reflections of Deuteronomy's covenant chapters (notably chs. 26–31) in the writings of this movement since the ideas of covenant found there are themselves so highly individualistic and conditional.[46] It is in fact likely that these

45. As cf. Baltzer, 1971, 51-82, 97.
46. Although it should be noted that some scholars view the Deuteronomic litera-

authors justified their highly contingent idea of covenant on the basis of passages like Deut. 29:18-20:[47]

> Beware lest there be among you a man or woman or family or tribe, whose heart turns away this day from the LORD our God to go and serve the gods of those nations; lest there be among you a root bearing poisonous and bitter fruit, one who, when he hears the words of this sworn covenant, blesses himself in his heart, saying, "I shall be safe, though I walk in the stubbornness of my heart." This would lead to the sweeping away of moist and dry alike. The LORD would not pardon him, but rather the anger of the LORD and his jealousy would smoke against that man, and the curses written in this book would settle upon him, and the LORD would blot out his name from under heaven.

A passage like this could easily be used to explain the situation and sufferings of Israel: if *individual* Israelites do not live up to the stipulations, they will not live in the blessings of the covenant. This seems to be exactly the conclusion drawn from such a passage by our authors, since the conditions for living in God's blessing, the warnings against disobedience, and the certainty of God's just and impartial treatment of sinners are themes to be found throughout the writings of remnant groups, even where the covenant does not explicitly enter into the discussion.

Jubilees is a good example of the application of one of these principles, that of "impartial judgment," in the context of present apostasy. While reflecting on the destruction of Sodom and Gomorrah, the author states suggestively and unequivocally, on the basis of this example, the abiding principle of fairness by which God judges: "he burned them with fire and sulphur and he annihilated them till this day. . . . *And thus* the LORD will execute judgment like the judgment of Sodom *on places where they act according to the pollution of Sodom*" (16:5-6). While there might be a suggestion that the author was thinking of Jerusalem here, it is at least certain that the author's purpose did not relate so much to the historical judgment on Sodom as to the presumption that Israelites were immune to such punishments if they were careless enough to follow Sodom's example of behaving immorally. This is indicated by the passage's contemporization of the event and evocation of a consistent principle of equal

---

ture differently, arguing that those ideas are missing! Such an approach seems incredible to the present writer.

47. For the influence of Deuteronomy 28ff. on the thought and expression of the author of *Testament of Naphtali* 3–4, cf. Hartman, 1979, 77-78. He posits that these chapters, which deal with covenant obligations, heavily influenced the thought pattern of these authors, with the result that expressions from them constantly come to the fore.

punishment for equal transgression. In the context of a polemic against evil practices in Jerusalem, the message of *Jubilees* is that God will *not* in such cases turn his head and override his ethical standards. Those who do not meet the conditions demanded by ordering their lives according to the stipulations, as they are understood by our author, do not have a part in covenant life. It is accordingly possible to discern the overriding importance of the conditions of the covenant in many of the narratives of *Jubilees*. Endres subsumes this idea under that of "retributive justice" and refers to "numerous examples of the process of retributive justice in the lives of [the] patriarchs and matriarchs."

> Most notably, the Deuteronomistic pattern of retribution appeared as the structural motif in the apocalypse of Jubilees 23: brevity of life and future disaster both result directly from Israel's refusal to heed the stipulations of the covenant. . . . Non-observance of its stipulations spells disaster — the curses — while observance will result in blessings.[48]

Typically for the writings studied here — notably those that are for this reason commonly termed "apocalyptic" — themes such as retributive justice are frequently expressed enigmatically rather than explicitly. As we will see, this enigmatic or eclectic employment of literary devices does not merely reflect the artificial adoption of a visionary posture ("mantic," hallucinatory, or otherwise) but is often a quite conscious, albeit artistic, adaptation of themes raised by the Scriptures. In particular two motifs — the heavenly list of names (and deeds) and "no accepting of persons" — appear to have been borrowed from some (already *enigmatic*) formulations of covenant in the Hebrew Scriptures and then pressed into the service of the stark individualism of *Jubilees*. The heavenly list emphasizes individual judgment since it bears the *names* of those who sin, probably in the sense of "break the covenant" (e.g., 5:13). That names of the righteous are also said to be recorded in heaven expresses the opposite but corresponding idea: notice will be taken of those *individuals* who fulfill the covenant (an idea investigated below). The motif of "no accepting of persons" also emphasizes judgment for breaking the covenant. *Jubilees* 5 says that God "is not one who accepts persons, and he is not one who accepts gifts when he says that he will execute judgment *upon each one*" (v. 16).[49] While it is primarily the punishment of angels that forms the subject matter here, the historical lesson taken from their fate is certainly addressed to humankind and particularly, in this context, to individual Israelites (cf. v. 17). This theme of "no accepting of

---

48. Endres, 1987, 231; cf. also his comments on 235.

49. Echoes of Deut. 10:17 ("the LORD your God . . . who is not partial and takes no bribe") and 2 Chron. 19:7 ("there is no perversion of justice with the LORD our God, or partiality, or taking bribes") may be detected here, as Charles maintains (1902, 45).

persons" is reiterated in 21:4 in direct relation to the covenant (cf. 30:16): "he is the one who executes judgment with *all* who transgress his commandments *and despise his covenant.*"[50]

The Dead Sea Scrolls also frequently betray a conditional and individual view of covenant. CD(B) 1.1-2 cites Deut. 7:9: "He keeps the Covenant and Grace for a thousand generations *with those who love him and keep his commandments.*" While this quotation may seem at first to be a conventional expression of gratitude for God's protection of the pious, the author's real purpose is transparent: he cites this passage because it contains an implied corrective to the doctrine of a unilateral and inviolable covenant, as is evident in the fact that elsewhere his group repeatedly alludes to and even expounds on the subject of "loving God and keeping his commandments" as if to make it a point of emphasis — not only for the group members themselves that they might stay in the covenant, but obliquely for the benefit of those outside the group, from whom the group wishes to dissociate and distinguish themselves (see under "defining laws" below). This purpose becomes still more transparently evident in the lines that follow, where those with whom God "keeps covenant" are unequivocally defined: they are those who keep the rule of the land "which existed formerly"[51] and whose marital relations are guided by the law of the sect (ll. 2-3). Other passages in the scrolls also provide a corrective or qualification to the idea of an inviolable covenant. CD 8.14-18 and CD(B) 1.26-32 both quote Deut. 9:5 and 7:8 in combination, a combination that could well be employed in defense of the grace of God in saving *Israel* but is here applied *exclusively* to "the converts of Israel who have departed from the way of the people" (8.16; [B] 1.29). "The covenant of the fathers belongs to them alone" (8.17-18).[52] In a similar vein CD 3.12-14 reports that "among those[53] who clung to the commandments of God and survived them as a remnant, God established His Covenant with Israel for ever, revealing to them the hidden things in which all Israel had strayed." As noted earlier, this passage implies that the covenant now belongs to the remnant (Qumran) community alone.[54] One can conclude

---

50. The no-respecter-of-persons theme is reiterated elsewhere (cf., e.g., *1 En.* 63:8). Such a theme is appropriate to those outside the group who try to claim some privilege on a basis not accepted by the group itself. It may be directed at the politically astute, or at all nonsectarians who fail to enter into the salvation experienced in the community and are therefore still considered in danger of judgment because of their waywardness.

51. Is this the prototypical heavenly law, or a reference to the first law of the land — i.e., the Mosaic Torah?

52. Wise renders להם ברית האבות in 8.17-18 quite appropriately: "the covenant with the patriarchs applies (only) to them" (1989, 58).

53. כ̲מחויקים. Better than Dupont-Sommer's "because of those."

54. Cf. Wise, 1989, 57-59; Davies, 1982, 87. The "remnant" here may well be that left

from such a passage that the sect believed that the covenant could both be "established . . . with *Israel* for ever" and yet remain in some way exclusively applicable to a remnant. The mention of "Israel" in such a context would thus appear to be merely part of the conventional conceptualization of covenant — sustaining the original relation of the covenant with historical Israel[55] — and is not to be understood as alluding to the irrevocable nature of that covenant for the benefit of the entire nation.[56] References to Israel in these writings frequently can be taken as indications of this concern for continuity (see ch. 9 below), which is revealed here in the difficulty determining whether by "Israel" the writer refers primarily to the nation or to the sect.[57]

Another good example of the importance of individual thought at Qumran is the doctrine of "voluntary conversion." The decision to join the "Covenant of Grace" and the "Council of God" (1QS 1.7-9) is entirely an individual one; belonging to the elect nation *per se* does not make one a member of the true covenant people. This is why, apparently, "volunteers" *(han-nidābîm)* is used of those who have entered the community (l. 7).[58] Forms of Heb. *šûḇ*, which is appropri-

---

over from the exile (cf. Davies, 83; cf. Knibb, 1987, 32, who interprets this of the "initial members of the movement . . . presented as a faithful remnant which survived the exile"), as in CD 1.4ff., since the community viewed Israel as still in the exile of their sin. However, here, as there, the community represents the spiritual descendants of the exilic remnant, and the reference to the covenant made with the exilic remnant applies to them.

55. Cf. Davies, 1982, 80-81.

56. This is clear from the reference to the "hidden things (נסתרות) in which all Israel had strayed: His holy Sabbaths. . . ." For the sect as the "True Israel," cf. Knibb, 1987, 34; Davies, 1982, 81-84. It is unlikely that the author is attempting to argue, any more than *Jubilees* 6 does, that the calendar (the probable reference of "Sabbaths and feasts") was first abandoned during the exile, a fact that might throw doubts on viewing the primary reference of this passage to be the early postexilic remnant. It suggests rather that the passage throughout has the *yaḥad*, in the context of the contemporary problems of Israel, as its chief subject matter, simultaneously alluding to and invoking, at a different level, the historical precedents offered by the exile. This bi-level methodology is a common feature of Qumran hermeneutics.

57. Davies's comment is important: "It is axiomatic that [the CD community] did not regard any outsiders as belonging to the true 'Israel' (even though they were obliged to use the term 'Israel' for the wider society because no other term existed and because that definition still carried some historial value)" (1995, 134).

58. Cf. Dupont-Sommer, 1961, 73 n. 1. The force of the expression is lost somewhat in Wernberg-Møller's "devoted themselves" (1957, 22, 46; taking הנדבים as a Niph. verb) and in Leaney's "all who promise" (1966, 119). We should probably retain the translation "volunteers" in view of Philo's reference to the Essene notion of election, which he significantly defines *over against* that provided by ethnic status: "Their enlistment is not due to race — the word race is unsuitable where volunteers are concerned" (Eusebius, *Praeparatio Evangelica* 8.11, §2; cited by Dupont-Sommer, 73 n. 1). The only biblical refer-

ate as a *terminus technicus* for conversion (since it necessarily implies joining the community), are also used liberally, emphasizing the importance of individual repentance.[59] The covenantal theology of Qumran is thus fundamentally conditional: "you will distinguish anew between the just and the wicked, between him that has served God and him that has served Him not"; for "He will be merciful [i.e., only] to them that *love Him* and to them that *heed Him*" (CD[B] 2.20-22). It is without doubt the contingencies of the present crisis in Israel that led this group to place the entire emphasis on performance of the covenant: the concrete response of the individual to the demands of the covenant has become essential.

A negative reaction to Israel's state of affairs combined with the Deuteronomistic view of covenant adopted by the community thus naturally and necessarily resulted in a highly *exclusive* view of covenant. This exclusivity is exhibited in several ways. Membership in the new covenant involved accepting the teachings of the interpreted law of the community, as mentioned earlier, which obviously would have the effect of dividing those who responded positively to this demand from those who did not.[60] This division could only have been enhanced by the requirements of initiation and the periods of probation that followed, during which time the new member was tested with rigor as to his knowledge of the teachings of the sect. Various other acts of separation from those outside the community were encouraged and legislated as well, further heightening the sense of exclusivity. An example is the prohibitions that surrounded the so-called "purity" (*ṭāhºrah* = "purification") of the community in 1QS 5.7-22 (ll. 13-14). Debate still rages over exactly what this "purity" refers to: a bath? a drink? the food of the community? However one decides this difficult question, there would appear to be some connection between the "purity" and the covenant at Qumran bearing on either entry into or maintenance of the covenant. This is evident from the subject matter of the passage itself, which is marked off by a kind of *inclusio* formed

---

ence that may have given rise to the term is Neh. 11:2, which refers to those who volunteered to live in Jerusalem, and might offer a provocative hint as to the origins of the community. Did they at one time consider themselves the righteous remnant in Jerusalem before leaving for the wilderness?

59. Cf. 1QS 3.1: משוב חיו, "conversion of life"; CD 2.5: שבי פשע, "converted from sin," cf. 1QH 14.24; 6.5: שבי ישראל, "converts of Israel"; 15.7: כל השב מדרכו הנשחתה, "all who are converted from their corrupted way"; 16.1-2: לשוב אל תורת משה, "converted to the Law of Moses"; CD(B) 2.23-24: שבו עד אל, "converted to God"; cf. also 1QH 6.14.

60. Cf. 1QS 5.9-12, 19-20; 1QSa 1.4-5; 1QM 10.9-10. This includes, perhaps preeminently, the teachings of the *moreh* (CD[B] 2.27-34; 1QH 4.24 [here the √ דרש is used for inquiring of the *moreh* as one would of a prophet]; 5.9), those handed down by the priests (1QS 5.9, 21-22), and, notably, adherence to the sectarian calendar (1QS 1.7-9; 3.10). Davies (1982, 83ff.) holds that the covenant comprised four elements: (1) the revelation, (2) the human response, (3) divine forgiveness, and (4) making of the "sure house" (cf. CD 3.13–4.12).

by ll. 11 and 18, which both contain the words "not reckoned in His Covenant." From this "purity" all outsiders and fallen members are strictly forbidden (l. 13). Thus the "purity" may have been a specifically covenantal ablution or perhaps a covenant meal or even a common cup of some kind. In any case it appears to have served to maintain membership in the Qumran covenant and would have stressed the exclusive character of that covenant, even if indirectly. The exclusive character of this "purity" is further suggested by the other types of separation from outsiders enforced by this passage, including abstention from common labor and all other economic transactions with outsiders (l. 14, but cf. ll. 16-17), discussion of legal matters with them (ll. 15-16), and partaking of the same food as others (l. 16): "all who are not counted in His Covenant shall be set apart" (l. 18); "they are all vanity who know not His Covenant"; God "will destroy from the world all them that despise His word" (l. 19). They are entirely unclean (l. 20). It is not surprising then that the community drew soteriological implications from this. Being in the covenant means salvation while being outside the covenant means judgment,[61] for the covenant possessed by the community is the only valid and eternal covenant.[62]

Teaching about covenant is not as clear in other writings as in *Jubilees* and some of the scrolls. The *Assumption of Moses* in its present form represents the views of a group in existence shortly after the turn of the era. There are strong indications, however, that sources for the writing go back to Maccabean times. It combines what appears to be national covenantal doctrine with rather more

---

61. Associated with this covenant is salvation from sin (1QS 3.6b-12; CD[B] 2.27-34) and eternal life (CD 7.4-6). 1QS 5.7-22 is also a good example of the other side of the issue of this exclusive covenant — all who reject it will be judged (cf. ll. 11-20). Those who have not sought the "precepts" and are therefore not "counted in His Covenant" will experience the full force of God's "Wrath" unto "Judgment," with the result that "Vengeance (will) be exercised by the curses of the Covenant, and solemn judgment be fulfilled against them unto eternal destruction, leaving no remnant" (ll. 12-13). God "will destroy from the world all them that despise His word" (l. 19). This is in complete harmony with the many other passages in the scrolls that speak of judgment for all who refuse this special covenant (cf. 1QS 2.6-10; CD 3.12b-17; 9.10; 13.14; 15.5; [B] 1.16-17; 2.25-26). This notion of judgment for those not in the covenant is further illustrated and enforced by many references to those who have fallen from the covenant and are warned of a similar fate (cf. 1QS 2.11-18; CD 8.1-2; 9.2-39; [B] 1.5-6, 13-14).

62. 1QH 13.11-12, depending on one's understanding of the passage, appears to insist on the eternal nature of this covenant and, although this has been said of covenants, institutions, and laws before this time, goes well beyond in insisting that this covenant cancels out in some way all previous covenants (see discussion above). The scrolls do not conceal the fact that this covenant has the effect of dividing Israel (1QH 15.14-21; cf. above), for it is an exclusive covenant, acting as a canon demarcating the righteous from the wicked in Israel. For similar ideas as mentioned in the above notes, cf. also CD 15.7-10, (B) 2.22-34.

individualistic statements, like *Jubilees* and the *Psalms of Solomon,* and also like the scrolls with their tension between ethnic Israel and "true" Israel. Moses prays about (4:5; 11:17) and proclaims (as in 12:12-13) the faithfulness of God to his covenant on behalf of Israel, but also insists that only "those who truly fulfill the commandments of God will flourish and will *finish* the good way, but those who sin by disregarding the commandments will deprive themselves of the good things which were declared before" (12:10-11). The writer of this work may have been more committed to national election than other writers we have seen, but, as in *Jubilees,* the prayers of Moses preserve traditional formulations and are not truly representative of the focus of thought for the author. This comes through more clearly in many other passages, though the verses already cited set out *conditions* on the national election. Particularly important in this regard is "finishing" the course, which can only mean avoiding apostasy. The writer accordingly distinguishes between the promise of God to maintain the covenant and the actions of individuals, which bring the promise to consummation. The writer is not delineating "exceptions" to the salvation of all Israel. There would be little purpose for such an abstract and detached theological concern in the midst of an emotive work like the *Assumption.* The final verses in the book (in the extant MS, 12:12-13) are typical of a sense of urgency as would suggest the viewpoint of Jews who believed themselves to be in a faithful minority. Reflecting on the paradox of the exile of the covenant people Israel, they promote the view that the tension between individual actions and covenantal promise can be worked out providentially only in that *portion* of the nation that is spared extinction: "it is not possible for the nations to drive them out or extinguish them *completely.* For God, who has foreseen all things in the world, will go forth, and his covenant which was established, and by the oath which. . . ." We are probably witness here to one common method of combining two irreconcilable aspects of the covenant — promise (gift) and demand — in terms of the salvation of a *representative* segment of God's people.

4 Ezra is entirely in agreement with this view of the conditional and individual nature of the covenant ("covenants," 7:24). No clearer statement of this exists anywhere in the literature than 4 Ezra 7:21, where, in alluding to the covenantal passage Deut. 30:19-20, the writer announces through the voice of the angel that "God strictly commanded those who came into the world, when they came, what they should do to live, and what they should observe to avoid punishment." This is far from a unilateral or unconditional view of covenant — life and death are contingent on faithful fulfillment of certain requirements placed on each individual. The writer accordingly condemns those who have disobeyed and "denied [God's] covenants" (vv. 22-24). A strongly conditional and individualistic view of covenant can be seen in 7:45-48, where the scribe argues the individual corruption of humankind: "Blessed are those who are alive

and keep your commandments! But what of those for whom I prayed? For who among the living is there that has not sinned, or who among men that has not transgressed your covenant? . . . For an evil heart has grown up in us, which has alienated us from God . . . and that not just a few of us but almost all who have been created!" This passage assumes an individual judgment, as can also be seen when the angel announces concerning the day of judgment that "no one shall ever pray for another on that day . . . for then everyone shall bear his own righteousness or unrighteousness" (7:105). Again the words of the angel in 7:127-31 are replete with conditional and individualistic covenantal language. They allude to Deut. 30:15ff. and refer to the covenant as a "contest": "This is the meaning of the contest which every man who is born on earth shall wage, that if he is defeated he shall suffer what you have said, but if he is victorious he shall receive what I have said" (vv. 127-28). Throughout 4 Ezra the originally corporate language of the initial presentation of the law by Moses to the people ("Moses, while he was alive, spoke to the *people*," v. 129) is put in starkly individual terms ("there shall not be grief at their damnation, so much as joy over those [i.e., individuals] to whom salvation is assured," v. 131). This dramatic use of language is again like that of *Jubilees,* but here the message needs to be discerned from a consideration of the entire work in its context.

The other extant Jewish theodicy from the same period, *2 Baruch,* likewise contains covenantal expressions that imply a conditional and individual basis of judgment (e.g., 19:1-3). One passage recalls Ezekiel 18 when it states that the final condition of a person determines how that person will be judged (42:1-8).[63] This passage significantly follows on, and is intended to answer, Baruch's questions about the various conditions of Israelites at his time, some of whom have "separated themselves from your statutes" and others, in contrast, who have "left behind their vanity" (41:1-6).[64] This passage reveals how

63. For the comparison of the two passages on the basis of their doctrine of retribution, cf. P. Bogaert, *Apocalypse de Baruch,* 1969, 2:77-78; cf. also Ezek. 33:12. There is some dispute as to whether it is the *final* state alone that is to be considered in this passage. Commenting on the somewhat similar statement in 42:6 that "times will inherit times . . . all will be compared according to the length of times . . . ," Klijn (*OTP,* 1:634 n. *f*) suggests that the length of time during which one was disobedient will be taken into consideration in the judgment.

64. Both of these last two passages may compare Jewish apostates, not with faithful Jews, but with proselytes (cf. R. H. Charles, *The Apocalypse of Baruch translated from the Syriac,* 1896, 66-67; Bogaert, 1969, 2:75; Klijn, *OTP,* 1:633). Notably, while the expression "who have fled under your wings" is used in the rabbinic literature for proselytes, the opposite expression, "to flee far from the wings of the Shekinah," is employed of Jewish apostates (Bogaert, 2:75; cf. Sifre Deut. 306). Charles's view (66-68), that those who have "separated themselves" (42:4) are the Pharisees, and that the apostates in 41:3 may be Christians, evidences his basic misunderstanding of the referents and of the issues.

influential the situation of perceived apostasy in Israel was on the individualistic doctrines expressed in the book. The author of this work even fashions his doctrine of the fall in accordance with his concern to emphasize the centrality and responsibility of the *individual* in matters of sin and judgment: "For, although Adam sinned first and has brought death upon all who were not in his own time, yet *each of them*[65] who has been born from him has prepared for himself the coming torment. And further, *each of them* has chosen for himself the coming glory. . . . *Adam is, therefore, not the cause, except only for himself, but each of us has become our own Adam*" (54:15, 19). There could hardly be a clearer expression of the individualistic understanding of one's eventual fate than these verses, since they may even deliberately contrast corporate (i.e., nonindividualistic) ideas associated with "belonging to Adam's race" with the individual nature of the covenant. The passage exhibits a strong covenantal "choice" motif and suggests the contrast between free will and determination (or, more properly, between *responsibility* and *inviolability*), and this may also be hinted at elsewhere in the book.[66]

It would appear at least possible that it was just such individualistic understandings of the covenant that were originally responsible for the later contrast in Judaism and Christianity between free will and predestination. That is to say, individualistic covenantal understandings may have been developed into, or at least combined with, more psychologically nuanced ideas about individual free will. Such would appear to be the case from the *Psalms of Solomon*, which presents teaching about free will in a context that suggests that the author was actually intending to reject presumption or false security (inviolability) based on national origin. He takes the lesson of Israel's exile "among every nation" (9:1-2) as the basis of the following conclusions:

65. The construction, employed thrice for emphasis, is *'nš 'nš* (pronounced *nāš nāš*), and can be rendered "person by person," or "every person." Cf. T. Nöldeke, *Compendious Syriac Grammar,* 1904, 186, §240, for what he calls "distributive repetition." A well-known example of this Semitic construction, most commonly used with numerals, can be found in Gen. 7:2, 9. The translation suggests knowledge of a Semitic original, although a similar expression formulated in translation Gk. (as cf. the literal rendering of LXX Gen. 2:7, 9) may lie behind the Syr.

66. Charles treats this passage as a discussion of predestination and free will (1896, 91-94). Man's free will to do the law is emphasized in *2 Baruch,* in contrast to *4 Ezra* where man's inability is emphasized (cf. 4 Ezra 8:1-3). Typically for Charles this overlooks some of the covenantal associations in favor of later theological conceptualizations, but the passage possibly exhibits a development toward the later doctrine. The word "inviolability" better suits the idea of a nationalistic election than "determination" or "predestination," words that evoke much later ideas essentially foreign to the idea of covenant.

> Our works are in the choosing and power of our souls,
> to do right and wrong in the works of our hands,
> and in your righteousness you oversee human beings.
> The one who does what is right saves up life for himself with the Lord,
> and the one who does what is wrong causes his own life
> to be destroyed;
> for the Lord's righteous judgments are according to the individual
> and the household. (vv. 4-5)

In this way the author correlates the power to choose right and wrong with promises of life and warnings of destruction, thus expressing the matter of free choice in typically dualistic covenantal terms. In fact, the passage is replete with covenantal language, as one familiar with biblical (especially Deuteronomic) covenantal language will notice. This highly individualistic doctrine of choice is significantly related by the *Psalms* to each person's eternal destiny, again placing matters of covenant in line with rather more developed soteriological categories.[67] Whether the doctrine of free will in Judaism (and in the New Testament) can be definitely traced back to an original connection with individual choice about the covenant, however, is an interesting question that merits more attention than can be given here.

DUALISTIC COVENANTAL FORMULATIONS

"Dualism" refers to the propensity to order the universe according to two, usually *opposite*, categories. This practice is widely thought to have been encouraged by certain worldviews and philosophies that came to expression during the Persian and Hellenistic periods, although the tendency seems to occur very naturally within the functioning of the human mind and is in evidence in many periods, especially among religious- and philosophical-thinking societies and individuals. It is therefore questionable how deliberate or conscious, or how chronologically specific, is the tendency to think dualistically. The possible types of dualism are practically unlimited. Perhaps the most common include what is called spatial, or cosmic, dualism, namely, the dividing of the universe into "seen" and "unseen" worlds, one reflecting or patterned after the other. Another is ethical dualism, which involves categorizing things as good or evil, implying a quite distinct separation of the two rather than a correspondence as in

---

67. Although earthly deliverance is a main focus in the *Psalms of Solomon*, there is enough evidence for belief in an otherworldly judgment and destiny to conclude that this is the reference here also; cf. 14:9; 15:10, 12-13, etc.

spatial dualism. All dualisms seem to have in common a basic dissatisfaction with one's existential situation and a corresponding need to fashion an "otherness" that represents a more perfect form of existence.

Such will naturally be seen to be the case, in magnified degree, with the dualism exhibited by the Jewish writers presently under consideration since they express the sentiments of a movement characterized by dissatisfaction and dissent. Debate rages over how to label this dualism, however, and a plethora of suggestions have been offered (most commonly: cosmic, temporal, ethical, anthropological, or eschatological).[68] There has been considerably more agreement in the history of research about the origin of this dualism, namely, that a strong *Persian* (or perhaps *Hellenistic*) influence is to be discerned. But even this once practically unanimous view no longer goes unchallenged, and more and more scholars are now accepting this conclusion only with caution. Some recognize that Hebrew conservatism would not be particularly open to such external influences and have suggested that the similarities in thought are due to more universal trends or, alternatively, that factors *within* Judaism account for many of the developments.[69] Some point out that the dichotomy between "good" and "evil" (including conceptual expressions of this dualism such as "light" versus "darkness"), for example, is indigenous to the Hebrew world and characterizes Hebrew thought from its earliest beginnings.[70] Others stress that evidence of Persian influence merely reflects the more or less deliberate adaptation of foreign thought forms that, nevertheless, admirably and appropriately suit the preservation of Hebrew thought. There is no question of a deterioration of "pure" Hebraic religion in any event.[71] Still other scholars complain that

68. Notable examples include W. Schmithals, *The Apocalyptic Movement*, 1975, 23-24, 49: "temporal dualism"; J. J. Enz, "Origin of the Dualism Expressed by 'Sons of Light' and 'Sons of Darkness,'" 1976, 18: "ethical." For a useful summary of other positions, cf. J. G. Gammie, "Spatial and Ethical Dualism in Jewish Wisdom and Apocalyptic Literature," 1974, 356-85, 356-59. Among types of dualisms defined by scholars, he mentions not only spatial and ethical dualisms, but also "cosmic," "temporal," "psychological," "theological," "physical," "metaphysical," "soteriological," and "ontological" dualisms! For a similar list, to which are added "philosophical," "anthropological," "cosmological," and "eschatological" dualisms, cf. J. H. Charlesworth, "A Critical Comparison of the Dualism in 1QS III,13–IV,26 and the 'Dualism' Contained in the Fourth Gospel," 1969, 389-418, 389 n. 1. The confusion that results from the use of so many terms, not to mention the artificiality of the attempt, will be obvious to the reader.

69. For this more cautious approach, cf., e.g., Mansoor, 1961, 54; Reicke, 1968, 32-33; Schmithals, 1975, 114-23; Enz, 1976, 17-18; Gowan, 1986, 50-51.

70. Cf. Ringgren, 1963, 80.

71. Reicke makes the interesting point that conservative Jews looked back with fondness to the Persian era in their struggle against the innovations of Greek culture (1968, 32-33); cf. also O. Plöger, *Theocracy and Eschatology*, 1968, 50.

the dualistic characterization has been taken too far and that what dualism there is in the writings significantly differs from the materialistic dualism of other societies.[72] Beyond these arguments there is, of course, the vexing question as to whether there even exist enough available sources from ancient times to judge confidently whether Jews borrowed from their neighbors at all in this regard, and if they did, to what extent they borrowed and to what extent this dualism was just as much at home in Hebrew thought.

This trend toward playing down foreign influences and giving due notice to the internal influences in Jewish tradition has opened up new and promising possibilities for better understanding the dualism in this literature. What is the significance, for example, of the fact that dualistic expressions in these documents suggestively manifest a *correlation with the division between the righteous and unrighteous in Israel,* for which we have already seen abundant evidence from the literature? Can much of this "dualism" be explained, or at least partially explained, by the division between the righteous and sinners in Israel? (This could be the case whether such a division actually *created* or merely *employed* this dualism.) It is at least clear that social divisions in Israel provided ideal soil in which dualistic thought could be planted, grow, and flourish.[73] The significance of the dualism of righteous and unrighteous will be dealt with in later chapters (chs. 7, 8, and 9 below). But within this same general social and historical context another possible influence on the development of dualism, and one that is of particular import when dealing with covenantal thought, is the strongly *dualistic covenantal theology*[74] which we have already seen to be firmly rooted in Hebrew tradition. As a clear example of this dualistic covenantal theology one might start by considering *1 Enoch* 1–5. This passage has already been dealt with in some detail, but it is important to draw on it again here since Hartman has demonstrated how the passage has been deliberately structured after the pattern of the traditional covenantal formulary.[75] The

72. Cf. Gowan, 1986, 50-51. With regard to 4 Ezra, cf. M. E. Stone, *Features of the Eschatology of IV Ezra,* 1989, 183, 192-93, 223-24.

73. It is suggestive, although hardly conclusive, that Zoroastrian dualism, not unlike the dualism implicit in later gnosticism, also centers on the division between two peoples (or, more abstractly, ethical dualism; cf. Mansoor, 1961, 58). Schonfield's (1957, 117) comments on this element in gnosticism are apposite: "The common cause of the Saints against the Evildoers inevitably created something approaching a theological Dualism of a Zoroastrian type, with the inimical spirit Beliar credited with somewhat greater power and authority than was warranted by a strict Monotheism and reflecting the venerable traditions of the Cosmic Drama."

74. The term "covenantal dualism" is adopted for clarity. Cf. Jaubert's "schéma binaire" to speak of covenantal history (1963, 219).

75. In the form he calls the "*rîb*-pattern," that is, a "suit" against those who are in danger of breaking, or already have broken, the covenant; Hartman, 1979, esp. ch. 3.

formulaic language of these chapters also reflects a particularly dualistic view of covenant, as can be easily seen by placing the concluding summary of the passage in parallel columns. It is to be noted how the contrast between the fates of the righteous and the sinners according to the covenant is colorfully represented in this summary:

<table>
<tr><td>

1 Enoch 5:5-6, 7b

Oh, you hard-hearted, may you not find peace! Therefore, you shall curse your days, and the years of your life shall perish and multiply in eternal execration; and there will not be any mercy unto you. In those days, you shall make your names an eternal execration unto all the righteous; and the sinners shall curse you continually — you together with the sinners.[76]

</td><td>

1 Enoch 5:7a, 8-10

</td></tr>
<tr><td>

To you, the wicked ones, on the contrary, there will be a curse.

</td><td>

But to the elect there shall be light, joy, and peace, and they shall inherit the earth.

And then wisdom shall be given to the elect. And they shall all live and not return again to sin. . . . And they shall not be judged[77] all the days of their lives; nor die through plague or wrath, but they shall complete the number of the days of their life. And peace shall increase their lives and the years of their happiness shall be multiplied forever in gladness and peace all the days of their life.

</td></tr>
</table>

Enoch speaks here, from his perspective, of the distant future, but the chief reference is to the time of the actual author and to judgment of his contemporar-

---

76. M. Black (*The Book of Enoch* or *I Enoch*, 1985, 27), following Charles (*The Book of Enoch or 1 Enoch*, 1912, 12), has "and by you shall all who curse curse, and all sinners and ungodly shall curse by you." Charles points to similarities in the idiom of Ps. 102:8, "those who deride me use my name for a curse," but more importantly, Isa. 65:15-16, which is notable for its context; Isaiah 65 contains a seething critique of Israel's rebelliousness.

77. Gk. MSS support both "they shall not sin (ἁμάρτωσιν)" and "they shall not be judged (κριθήσονται)."

ies, which he expects to follow immediately the time when he writes.[78] This is just one of an endless number of similar dualistic passages in the literature that contrast the righteous and sinners and their respective fates. This particular passage has been cited here to illustrate that this dualistic thought may well be rooted, or at least partly rooted, in the understanding of *covenant.*

Scriptural Dualistic Covenantal Formulations

Various expressions of this "covenantal dualism" can be found in this literature, including those that implicitly root this dualism in the biblical formulations of covenant — what might be called "scriptural dualistic covenantal formulations." In the sermon that makes up the bulk of Deuteronomy, Moses is portrayed as rehearsing, for the benefit of those about to enter the land, the circumstances surrounding God's giving of the covenant, along with a summary or recapitulation of many of the individual laws. In the concluding chapters of the sermon (27–30), Moses emphasizes to his listeners the *conditions* that apply for a successful fulfillment of covenantal obligations "in the land" and the blessings or curses that will accompany obedience or disobedience of the covenant obligations. It is in these chapters that we find some of the most *disjunctive* (we should not yet say *dualistic*) expressions of covenant[79] in all of the Bible. This view of covenant is communicated both by straightforward propositional statements in the narrative and by several recurring motifs that serve to emphasize the nature of the covenant as *dividing* those positively related to the covenant from those who reject it and are rejected by it. Among these motifs are what might be called the *covenantal choice* motif, the *life-and-death* motif, and the *two-ways* motif.[80] Intrinsic to all three is the demand made by God on Israel, and notably upon individuals within Israel,[81] to choose between obedience or disobedience to the covenant.

It is this dichotomy of choice and result (blessing or curse) inherent in the Deuteronomistic covenant that is developed in a later period into a fuller *dualistic* covenantal theology — "dualistic" because this view of the covenant is

78. Cf. Hartman, 1979, 16.

79. Cf. also Lev. 26:3-45; Deut. 11:13-32. These dichotomous covenantal formulations seem also to have influenced the prophets: cf., e.g., Isa. 28:5-22; 59:1-20; Jer. 16:10-15, who also spiritualized the ideas somewhat.

80. The third of these is more well developed *outside* of Deuteronomy; nevertheless, the notion of God's "way" is also found in the context of Deuteronomy 27–30; cf. Deut. 5:33; 9:12, 16; 11:28; 13:5; 31:29; etc.

81. This portion of Deuteronomy is highly individualized. Note in 27:15ff. how the curses are directed at "the man who. . . ."

employed, as we will see, to evaluate and categorize the universe, the physical world as well as people, and because the division is more sharply intensified than the earlier "disjunctive" expressions.

Remnant groups were attracted to the covenantal theology of Deuteronomy 27ff. for obvious reasons, largely because of the connection drawn in those chapters between Israel's sins and Israel's misfortunes. Our authors and their communities believed this connection between apostasy and punishment was witnessed in Israel's past just as they were now seeing it in effect in the present time. The words of Moses to the people of Israel — "See, I have set before you this day *life and good, death and evil. . . .* I have set before you *life and death, blessing and curse;* therefore *choose life . . .*" (Deut. 30:15, 19) — are subtly reapplied in *1 En.* 94:3-4 in an exhortation to "the righteous": "Now to you, those righteous ones, I say: Do not walk in the evil way, or in the way of death! Do not draw near to them lest you be destroyed! But seek for yourselves and choose righteousness and the elect life![82] Walk in the way of peace so that you will have life and be worthy!" Here the covenant of Deuteronomy is made even more unambiguously dualistic and individualistic by being applied to the situation of the writer and specifically to the division existing between his community and the rest of Israel. The readers ("the righteous") are warned not to draw near "to them," apparently those who do not follow the way recommended by this community.[83] What may originally have been a corporate warning to all Israel, therefore, is now interpreted as an *individual* choice between two ways, pointing to the possibility (indeed the inevitability) of a split created by the dualistic nature of the covenant.

In this passage the three above-mentioned dualistic covenantal motifs are combined: choosing, life and death, and the two ways. Similar combinations can be found throughout many of the writings. Choosing is combined with the life-death dualism in *Pss. Sol.* 9:4-5.[84] *TLevi* 19:1 contains a similar metaphor for choice applied to the strongly individual piety of the *Testaments:* "And now,

---

82. While the *Tana* MSS do support the reading "a life of *goodness*" (= ἀγαθωσύνη = טבותא, according to Black, 1985, 296), "an elect life" remains both the more difficult reading and coheres excellently with the intention of this passage, which is to recall Deut. 30:19-20. The author would then be picking up the "choose"/"elect" theme here, although it is to be admitted that the "good" theme is also present in the Deuteronomy passage (cf. 30:15).

83. Something confirmed by the words that follow, which refer to holding fast "my words" (v. 5; i.e., the traditions of Enoch).

84. Cf. also *Pss. Sol.* 14:2. Seifrid significantly bases the view of covenant in the *Psalms* in the basic dualism "between 'pious' and 'sinner.' Concomitantly, the concept of a divine covenant with all of Israel is reinterpreted. . . . The covenant is now seen to apply to a limited group within the nation, who maintained fidelity to *Torah* in an age of impiety" (1992, 132).

my children, you have heard everything. *Choose for yourselves light or darkness, the Law of the Lord or the works of Beliar.*"[85] *Ass. Mos.* 12:10-11 picks up the important idea of following the "way" of God: "those who truly fulfill the commandments of God will flourish and will finish *the good way*, but those who sin by disregarding the commandments will deprive themselves of the 'good.'"[86] The concept of turning aside to the right or left is also closely associated with the concept of choice and with the two ways at Qumran.[87] The converts to the covenant are warned to "not depart from His precepts of truth to walk either to right or to left" (1QS 1.15),[88] which entails acceptance of the distinctively new revelation at Qumran, including the authorized calendar (1QS 3.10).[89] While each of these cases of life/light versus death/darkness and the two-ways motif reveals a dependence on biblical disjunctive covenantal expressions, it is notable that in their present contexts their original application to Israel has been both strongly individualized and contemporized. They are now employed to emphasize the contrast between righteous and unrighteous individuals and groups presently existing within Israel.

4 Ezra and the Syriac *Apocalypse of Baruch* follow the others in this respect, except that in these works covenantal dualistic expressions become major themes. When the angel announces unequivocally to Ezra that "God strictly commanded those who came into the world, when they came, what they should do to live, and what they should observe to avoid punishment" (7:21), this harks directly back to similar expressions in Deuteronomy (e.g., Deut. 30:11ff., 15ff.), which lends authority to the author's unwavering insistence on the judgment of those who "disregard" the Law (7:20). Somewhat later Ezra adopts the terminology we have been observing and complains that the evil *yēṣer* has "grown up in us, has alienated us from God, and has

85. "Levi's final exhortation is a summons to make a basic choice," according to Hollander and de Jonge (*The Testaments of the Twelve Patriarchs*, 1985, 183), who also place it within the covenant formulary and refer to LXX Josh. 24:14-22; Deut. 26:17; 30:15, 19. The Gk. reads here ἕλεσθε οὖν ἑαυτοῖς ἢ τὸ σκότος ἢ τὸ φῶς. The verb is also found in Josh. 24:15, referring to the choice facing the Israelites.

86. In parallel with "good way," "the 'good'" also refers to the "good way" or "good things" or perhaps "rewards of the good way."

87. Cf. 1QS 1.15; Deut. 28:14; 5:32; cf. 17:11, 20; *Jub.* 23:16.

88. For the expression "right or left" in this passage, Wernberg-Møller points to Deut. 17:20; 28:14 (1957, 49).

89. Along with the "neither to right nor to left" motif, this passage also contains the expression "ways of God." For this latter expression Wernberg-Møller compares Deut. 10:12, 16; 11:22; 13:6 (1957, 64). In a similar vein (if we can accept the reconstruction of Dupont-Sommer), 1QH 9.17-18 contrasts those who are in the covenant and those who are outside according to the dichotomy of "life and death"; cf. Dupont-Sommer (1961, 232).

brought us into corruption and *the ways of death,* and has shown us the *paths of perdition* and removed us far from *life*" (7:48). So important is this dualistic understanding of covenant in 4 Ezra that the author is able to refer to the covenantal choice in stark terms as the "*contest* which every man who is born on earth shall wage" (7:127), an expression that again alludes to Deut. 30:15ff. ("Every man" may be biblical language for "every Israelite," or it may evidence the emergence of a philosophical dualism in 4 Ezra in which the entire universe — not simply Israel — is thought to be divided according to the covenant.)[90] The words that follow continue the dualistic covenantal language: "For this is the *way* of which *Moses,* while he was alive [i.e., before his death in Deuteronomy 34], spoke to the people, saying, '*Choose for yourself life, that you may live!*' But they did not believe him, or the prophets after him, or even myself [God] who have spoken to them" (vv. 129-30). Thus a major theme in 4 Ezra is that breach of the covenant is not exceptional but widespread.[91] Similar expressions that all hark back to this important passage from Deuteronomy and emphasize the universal failure of humankind to obey the covenant can be found in *2 Baruch* as well.[92]

Scriptural dualistic expressions of covenantal theology were accordingly very important to the remnant movement; but their influence seems to have continued well beyond both the period and the movement itself to later groups and movements, perhaps even generating a number of motifs whose relationship to the above expressions is not entirely clear but nevertheless seems certain. It may even be, for example, that there is some connection between the idea of "two ways" as formulated in the writings we are examining and the doctrine of "pairs" known to the rabbis and later Gnostic groups.[93] That there is some literary connection between the idea of "two ways" and that of "pairs" seems to be implied by certain sayings in the *Testaments of the Twelve Patriarchs* that are also dependent on dualistic covenantal ideas and that tie the two ways

90. This might well give insight into the gnomic, or universalizing, language of 4 Ezra, which we have already noted.

91. Cf. 7:20, 48: "not just a few of us but almost all who have been created!"

92. Cf. 19:1-3; 84:2 (cf. 45:1-2; 46:3).

93. Although it is arguable that rabbinic thought eventually abandoned the strongly dualistic idea of covenant. Hagigah 15 relates the creation of "counterparts" with a dualism of the godly and ungodly: "For everything the Holy One, praise be to him, created he also made a counterpart . . . he created the godly and the ungodly, he created paradise and hell. Everybody has two portions, one in paradise and one in hell. The godly man who has made himself deserving, receives his and his neighbour's portion in paradise; the godless man who has made himself guilty, receives his and his neighbour's portion in hell" (quoted in K. Schubert, *The Dead Sea Community,* 1959, 70). Gammie (1974, 375-76) relates the doctrine of pairs in Sir. 36:15; 42:24-25 and in the *Testaments of the Twelve Patriarchs* to the division between two peoples (cf. ch. 6 below).

and the pairs together.[94] *TNaph.* 8:7, for example, announces that "the commandments of the Lord are *double*," which is significant since the passage possesses other reminiscences of a covenantal formulary.[95] *TAsh.* 1:1-9 offers a more complete and elaborate version of the doctrine of the two ways in terms of "twos" or "pairs":[96] "God has granted *two ways* to the sons of men, two mind-sets, . . . two models, and two goals. Accordingly, everything is in *pairs*, the one over against the other. *The two ways are good and evil . . ."* (vv. 1-5). The passage goes on to discuss the two "dispositions" (cf. the two *yēṣerîm*) in the soul — which itself may be related to another kind of dualism in the literature, that of the two worlds of spirits, since the passage proceeds to relate this dualism to the struggle with sin and Beliar (see ch. 9 below). The idea of "pairs" seems to perpetuate the notion, inherent in the "two ways" as well, that there is choice or decision involved in everything,[97] especially the covenant. This theme of decision is manifested and summarized in the important term *monoprosōpōs* (single-mindedness), which is used of the righteous in the *Testaments* and serves as a contrast to the "two faces" *(diprosōpos)* of the opponents, or "hypocrites,"[98] who apparently have trouble deciding whether to follow the way of God or not.

The Witness Motif

Thanks to the groundbreaking work of V. Korosec, E. Bickermann, G. Mendenhall, D. J. McCarthy, J. Peterson, W. F. Albright, and K. Baltzer, to name a few, it is now well known to all students of the Hebrew Scriptures that the so-called "covenant formulary" or *pattern* of the covenant found in the ancient world, which came to be reflected in the Hebrew Scriptures and in later Judaism as well, contains several components that are consistently represented in covenant texts. These components are generally delineated as (1) titulature, (2) historical prologue, (3) major and minor stipulations, (4) witnesses, (5) document clause, and (6) curses and blessings. One component of the covenant formulary that receives much attention in our literature and is developed

94. For the many sayings in the *Testaments* paralleled in the Deuteronomistic covenant code, cf. A. Hultgård, *L'eschatologie des Testaments des Douze Patriarches,* 1977, 1:236-38.

95. Hollander and de Jonge take this to be a passage announcing blessing and curse (1985, 318).

96. Cf. Kee, *OTP,* 1:816-17 n. 1.

97. Cf. Hollander and de Jonge, 1985, 338.

98. Cf. Hollander and de Jonge, 1985, 339; for the relation of this latter word to ὑποκριταί, cf. 340.

in sometimes remarkable directions (often lifted from its original context in the covenant formulary) is that of the *covenantal witnesses (against Israel)*.[99] One reads in Deut. 30:19 (cf. also 4:26; 31:29): "I call heaven and earth to *witness against you* this day, that I have set before you life and death, blessing and curse; therefore choose life, that you and your descendants may live. . . ." It is obvious that the possibilities for applying this part of the covenantal formulary to an Israel perceived to be apostate are endless, and the groups we are studying did not hesitate to spell out the implications of the witness clause in polemic against their opponents.

The reference to "heaven and earth" as witnesses in the Deuteronomy passage is intriguing to say the least, no less since students of ancient treaties have demonstrated that heaven and earth have assumed here the witnessing role originally assumed by the pagan gods of other ancient Near Eastern treaties. These scholars conclude that the original purpose of the creation-as-witness motif in the Hebrew covenant was to deliberately supplant the role played by the witnessing god in other treaties — since the "one God" of the Hebrews could not appeal to someone greater or to other gods.[100] If this is the case, such original purposes would appear, quite understandably, to have escaped the writers of the late Second Temple period. The concept of heaven and earth as witnesses is applied instead to the view, related to calendar propaganda, that the heavenly luminaries fulfill their mandate to witness by altering their courses, leading to calendrical irregularities (which, in turn, lead to still further confusion in the order of the heavenlies, which again leads to more calendrical disobedience, and so on).

This application of the witness motif to the calendar has been noted above, but the witness motif was applied to the situation of apostasy in other ways as well. Specifically, creation was portrayed as the *instrument, indicator,* and *recipient* of the curse. In the Book of Heavenly Luminaries, for example, when Israel sins in such a way as to break the covenant (here again mostly through calendar disobedience), the cosmos becomes the *instrument* of reward or judgment, an idea that seems to be related to the idea of the curses of the covenant as much as to the witness motif itself:

99. For the relationship of the "witness" motif to the covenantal formulary (and *rîb* pattern), cf. Baltzer, 1971, 10 and passim. Hartman (1979, 29) cites, not only the conventional covenantal texts such as Deut. 4:26; 30:19; and 31:28, but also the farewell song of Moses in Deuteronomy 32 (and traditions stemming from it), which seems to contain an implicit, if enigmatic, witness motif ("Give ear, O heavens, and I will speak; / and let the earth hear the words of my mouth").

100. Although, as Baltzer explains, ancient Hittite treaties also invoked mountains, rivers, springs, the Great Sea, heaven and earth, wind and clouds. These may actually have been divinized in non-Hebrew culture (1971, 14).

Through four of the openings blow out winds of blessing and through eight of
them blow out winds of pestilence — when they are sent in order to destroy the
whole earth, the water upon her, all those who dwell upon her, and all those
which exist in the waters and the dry land. . . . Thus the twelve openings of the
four heavenly directions are completed; all their orders, all their evil effects, and
all their beneficial effects have I revealed to you. (*1 En.* 76:4, 14)

Accordingly the motif of the witness of heaven and earth is frequently combined
with the idea of the curse of the covenant, confirming that these ideas went hand
in hand: "And now, do know that your deeds shall be *investigated* — from the sun,
from the moon, and from the stars — for heaven by the angels, on account of
your sins which were committed upon the earth. . . . Every cloud, mist, dew, and
rain shall *witness against you;* for they shall all be *withheld from you,* from descending for you; and they shall not give heed, because of your sins" (100:10-11).
Here the sun, moon, and stars seem to be agents of angels who bring judgment,
along with clouds, mist, dew, and rain, with the result that the much-needed rain is
withheld (a specific curse of the covenant), ideas that are in turn associated with
the creation as *witness* ("investigated," "witness against you"). The passage is followed by a sarcastic invitation to the sinners to offer reverence to the heavenly
bodies, which, one might speculate, alludes to actual incidents of worship of the
heavenly bodies in the Gentile (if not also the Jewish) world. It is warned, however, that this ill-advised action will likewise backfire onto the sinners (vv. 12-13).

Another interesting and related application of the cosmic witness motif
and the effects of disobedience on nature is found in the chapter that immediately follows these sayings. Here heaven and earth are put forth as witnesses to
the providence and might of God. Sinners do not fear God, even though his
strength can be seen in the sometimes destructive forces of the rain, seas, and
drought (101:1-9). "But you, sinners, who are upon the earth, fear him not! Did
he not make *the heaven and the earth* and all that is in them? . . . Do not the sailors of the ships fear the sea? Yet the sinners do not fear the Most High" (vv. 7-9).
Here the cosmic witness motif appears to have been brought down to the very
practical level of a daily witness to God's sovereignty and therefore a warning
for humankind (indeed, for Israel) to fear him and at all costs to avoid the
curses of the covenant. Another text, this time from the Similitudes, expresses
this conviction in clear tones:

In those days, my eyes saw the mysteries of lightnings, and of lights, and their
judgments;[101] they flash lights for a blessing or a curse, according to the will
of the Lord of the Spirits. . . . He showed me whether the sound of the thun-

---

101. Black, 1985, 225: "ordinances," *kʷennanēhomu;* perhaps from משפטיהם or
חקותיהם.

der is for peace and blessing or for a curse, according to the word of the Lord of the Spirits. After that, all the mysteries of the lights and lightnings were shown to me that they glow with light for blessing and for contentment.[102] (*1 En.* 59:1-3)

This speculation about the purpose of thunder and lightning sustains the close connection between breach of the covenant and the active and continual responses of the cosmos in curse and judgment. Many years later the writer of *Psalms of Solomon* 17 is still aware of this connection between sin, the cosmic order, and judgment. Hence the cosmic character of this terse judgment oracle, directed at widespread apostasy in Jerusalem:

> For the heavens withheld rain from falling on the earth.
> Springs were stopped,
>> from the perennial springs far underground
>> to those in the high mountains.
> For there was no one among them
>> who practiced righteousness or justice. (vv. 18b-19)

While this passage might be interpreted as an exaggeration or metaphor based on the circumstances of the siege of 63 B.C., it nevertheless strongly suggests that the psalmist interpreted an actual drought and other natural calamities accompanying the siege as unambiguous symptoms of covenantal curse.[103] One need only compare the words of v. 18b, "the heavens withheld rain from falling on the earth," with Deut. 11:16-17, "Take heed lest . . . he shut up the heavens, so that there be no rain," or 1 Kings 8:35, "When heaven is shut up and there is no rain because they have sinned against thee," for clear evidence that the breach of covenant was felt to have cosmic implications associated with the curses of the covenant. The theme of judgment on apostasy, and similar theological reflection on the event, are also evident in *Pss. Sol.* 2:9a, which poetically states that "the heavens were weighed down, / and the earth despised them, / for no one on the earth had done what they did."

This idea of the witness of heaven and earth against apostates from the covenant is exhibited in other ways in the Book of Heavenly Luminaries as well. As mentioned earlier, neglect of the calendar was believed to have thrown the cosmic order into confusion, suggesting that creation acts as an *indicator* or *symptom* of the situation of apostasy: "In respect to their days, the sinners and

---

102. Probably better read "curse," from a confusion of שָׂבְעָה, "plenty," "contentment," with שְׁבוּעָה, "curse"; cf. Black, 1985, 225.

103. Cf. H. E. Ryle and M. R. James, *ΨΑΛΜΟΙ ΣΟΛΟΜΩΝΤΟΣ*, 1891, 136, although the reference to Josephus, *Antiquities,* is mistaken.

the winter are cut short. . . . The moon shall alter its order, and will not be seen according to its normal cycles" (*1 En.* 80:2, 4). Again the idea of heaven and earth witnessing is also interpreted to mean that the curse of the covenant fell directly on the weather, fields, and produce. That is, the negative reaction of heaven and earth to a breach of covenant was partly felt by creation directly as a *recipient* of the punishment.[104]

These texts accordingly show that creation is not just a passive or symbolic witness but is directly involved in the experience of curse as *instrument*, *indicator*, and even *recipient* of the curse. The witnesses are regularly personified in order to accommodate these developments. It is also noteworthy that not only *"heaven and earth"* act as witnesses against apostate Israel in the literature of Second Temple Judaism but a similar role is played by angels and a variety of other phenomena. A good example of this comes in the midst of a lengthy consolation passage in *1 Enoch* 104, which contains a number of small judgment oracles whose apparent function is to console the righteous with the announcement of retribution against the "sinners." In one of these Enoch warns the sinners that, while they may feel that they are presently escaping judgment, "light and darkness as well as day and night witness [literally 'see'] all your sins" (v. 8). Since the passage suggestively mentions "light and darkness" and "day and night" together as the instruments of the witness, the calendar debate might be discerned in the background of the passage, although the passage does not refer to the calendar explicitly.

Regardless of the specific form or agency of the witness, the importance of the covenantal witness motif in this literature must not be overlooked, for much of the formal character of what is frequently termed the "apocalyptic genre" derives from its intense preoccupation with the cosmos. This preoccupation should accordingly not be viewed as merely the convention of the "apocalyptic" form making its impression on the literature, or as some kind of "scientific interest" in the cosmos, as has often been suggested. It bears important testimony to a vital connection between covenant and cosmology, which reflects the influence of the witness motif and of the dualistic covenant on the distinctive character of this literature.

Not all instances of the witness motif utilize this personification or are framed in cosmological terms. The witness of heaven and earth appears as little more than part of the linguistic decor of the covenantal curse in the *Assumption of Moses*. The experience of the captivity is put forward as the fulfillment of Moses' warnings, and "witnesses" remain an uninterpreted element in the warning (unless, as is possible, "dryness" of existence in exile alludes to the withholding of rain).

---

104. For a possible source of the idea, cf. Deut. 28:15-35.

Then, considering themselves like a lioness in a *dusty plain, hungry and parched,* the two tribes will call upon the ten tribes, and shall declare loudly, "Just and holy is the Lord. For just as you sinned, likewise we, with our little ones, have now been led out with you." . . . "Is this not that which was made known to us in prophecies by Moses . . . when he solemnly called *heaven and earth as witnesses against us* that we should not transgress God's commandments . . . ? These things which have come upon us since that time are according to his admonition declared to us at that time." (3:4-5, 11-13; cf. Deut. 30:19)

The implication that Judah is just as guilty as the northern tribes is noteworthy here, as it indicates that the writer probably considered his contemporary Israelites to be still in exile when he wrote — the exile being understood as the epitome of the covenant curse. This is confirmed by the fact that while the passage alludes to the suffering of the Babylonian exiles, the chapters that follow indicate that the author's *own time* is primarily in mind as Israel continues to experience exile.[105]

The witness motif is left unembellished in 4 Ezra as well, where heaven and earth are called on as witnesses, this time in defense of the justice of God: "Call, O call heaven and earth to witness, for I left out evil and created good, because I live, says the Lord."[106] That there may be more than rhetorical force in these words is possible but not obvious in this passage, where little personification is evident.[107] This is not the case elsewhere in 4 Ezra, where the witnesses in 7:94 assume the active role of testifying after death on behalf of "those who have died and kept the ways of the Most High" during their lives (cf. 7:88). It is significant in this case that while the witnesses condemn the sinners, they testify to and vindicate the righteous. One might have expected such a double function for the heavenly witnesses within the strongly dualistic perspective of 4 Ezra.

---

105. We can tell that at least the ten tribes are still in exile: ch. 5 refers to the Hasmonean period, and ch. 6 to the times of the Herods, as part of this exile (cf. Priest, *OTP,* 1:929-30 nn. 5a and 6b).

106. 4 Ezra 2:14; cf. Deut. 30:19; cf. also *2 Bar.* 19:1-2; 84:2.

107. The personification of the witnesses is more evident in similar passages in *2 Baruch* like 19:1-2, which explains the choice of witnesses by appealing to their permanence: "Therefore he appointed a covenant for them at that time and said, 'Behold, I appoint for you life and death,' and he called heaven and earth as a witness against them. For he knew that his [Moses'] time was short, but that heaven and earth will stay forever." For allusion to Deut. 30:19 in this passage, cf. Bogaert, 1969, 2:46; Charles, 1896, 33.

The Heavenly Tablet Motif and the Covenant

Another important motif in these writings is the list of names of the righteous and wicked written on the heavenly tablets. As noted earlier, the heavenly tablets possessed many functions, depending on the needs or beliefs of the particular writer. They composed a storehouse of knowledge and contained the contents of the perfect law, various secrets regarding God's plan for the righteous, the names of good and evil persons, and a list of their respective deeds. The possible origins for this belief in heavenly records are several,[108] but to be noted here are important biblical instances of this motif where it is associated with the Mosaic covenant. We have already seen this motif alluded to in Deut. 29:20, where in a covenantal context the stubborn one who turns away from the Lord to serve the gods of the nations is warned that the Lord will "blot out his name from under heaven." Similarly in the account of the spelling out of the particulars of the covenant to Moses on the mountain following Israel's sin of worshiping the golden calf (Exodus 24–34), we find a prayer of Moses containing the words: "But now, if thou wilt forgive their sin — and if not, blot me, I pray thee, out of thy book which thou hast written" (32:32). The context of this saying might imply that there exists a record of one's fidelity to the covenant. Significantly in this regard Moses' plea appears to be denied, or at least modified, as the divine voice responds with conditions that remind us of the similarly worded response in 4 Ezra: "Whoever has sinned against me, *him* will I blot out of my book" (Exod. 32:33). These conditions could be and probably were taken as an indication of the radically individual nature of the covenant. It is in any event evident that the idea of heavenly records of names was associated with the covenant from an early time, as a kind of way of keeping straight those individuals who kept the covenant and those who did not. The term "book of the living" (e.g., Ps. 69:28), which is frequently repeated in the writings of the remnant groups, also suggests this covenantal context by its allusion to the life motif. Another indication that the keeping of records of names and deeds has to do with covenant is that the motif is frequently combined with heavenly witnesses. This combination is implied in the verse immediately preceding the covenantal witness motif of *1 En.* 104:8 (mentioned directly above), where there is startling invective against sinners who appear to be confident that they will avoid judgment for their sins:[109] "Now, you sinners, even if you say, 'All our

108. Cf. Exod. 17:14; 32:32-33; Pss. 40:7; 56:8; 69:28; 139:16; Isa. 29:11-12; 34:16; Dan. 7:10; 12:1-4; Mal. 3:16; cf. also Rev. 20:12; *Asc. Is.* 9:19-23 (in this Christian portion of the work, the existence of books is proof that "the deeds of *the children of Israel* were written there"); for a related idea, cf. Ezra 4:15.

109. I.e., on the basis of being Israelites. This is formidable proof that such passages are not addressed to Gentiles.

sins shall not be investigated or *written down*,' nevertheless, all your sins are being *written down* every day. . . . light and darkness as well as day and night witness all your sins" (104:7-8). This writer was conscious of the way the lives of all Israelites were carefully documented according to a system established by the covenant. Here the witnesses are once again personified; they are not only witnesses, but apparently also recorders, of what they see, and in this respect appear to act more like angels. Appeal to records in a covenantal context served as a reminder that the covenant is far from unilateral or unconditional — records must be kept of the individual performance of the covenant. The idea of God keeping books is therefore a convenient motif in *1 Enoch,* where it functions to make clear God's commitment to judging *within* Israel between those who keep his covenant and those who do not.

It is in *Jubilees,* however, that this motif is fully exploited and where it exhibits unmistakably the dualistic basis of covenantal thought. The heavenly tablets are, of course, important for the writer of *Jubilees,* and the list of names and deeds of the righteous and wicked is a correspondingly important component of those tablets. Here the names of the righteous are closely associated with their deeds, and both are connected with the motif of witness ("testimony"). The eulogy for Levi in 30:19, for example, proclaims that "a blessing and righteousness will be *written as a testimony for him in the heavenly tablets* before the God of all." What is true for Levi is true for all who act righteously: "And we will remember for a thousand generations the righteousness which a man did during his life in all of the times of the year. . . . And *he* will be *written down* as a friend and a righteous one in the heavenly tablets" (v. 20).[110] The same passage also refers to "the book of those who will be destroyed," completing the dualism.[111]

The concept of heavenly records undergoes considerable elaboration in *Jubilees,* and a clear parenetic intention is exhibited by some passages. A good instance of this is the following verses, 30:21-22, which generalize the moral taken from the example of Levi and apply it to all Israel (certainly the Israel of the author's day):

I have commanded you to speak to the children of Israel that they might not commit sin or transgress the ordinances or *break the covenant* which was ordained for them so that they might do it and *be written down as friends.* But if they *transgress* [the covenant] and act in all the ways of defilement, they will be *recorded in the heavenly tablets as enemies.* And they will be *blotted out of*

---

110. On "friend," cf. 19:9; Isa. 41:8; 2 Chron. 20:7; LXX Dan. 3:35. The designation φίλοι θεοῦ is applied to the faithful in Philo and Wis. 7:27 (Charles, 1902, 126).

111. Lat. *libro perditionum,* v. 22.

> *the book of life and written in the book of those who will be destroyed and with those who will be rooted out of the land.*[112]

This passage reveals how the idea of the heavenly records was closely related to, and indeed dependent on, belief in a dualistic covenant. Not only are books kept for the righteous, but also for the unrighteous. As regards this latter group, one reads elsewhere in *Jubilees* that those who follow Esau's example of unbrotherliness will "be wiped out from the book of the discipline of mankind, and he will not be written in The Book of Life for he is written in the one which will be destroyed . . ." (36:10; cf. 19:9). More will be said below about how the Jacob-Esau typology illuminates the division that was thought to exist in contemporary Israel.

In 4 Ezra as well the books play an important role in the final judgment (6:20; 14:35). In 4 Ezra, however, the few enigmatic references to the keeping of books in the Hebrew Scriptures are developed into a full doctrine embracing and reflecting the dualistic nature of the author's covenantal theology. This can be seen from the succinct reference in 14:35, which states that "after death the judgment will come, when we shall live again; *and then the names of the righteous will become manifest, and the deeds of the ungodly will be disclosed.*" A division between the righteous and wicked has occurred and is expressed in the dichotomy "names of righteous"/"deeds of ungodly." The parallelism suggests that the division could be described in a number of ways, as either a dualism of deeds or a dualism of status (being in or out of the book of life). This particular example also gives us a clue to the *function* of this motif within the theology of the protest movement. The book of life or the heavenly record of good and evil persons or deeds serves to *define and console* the afflicted righteous by marking them off from the apostates in Israel. Thus the righteous take comfort not only because their names are preserved in the book of life, but also because the names of their opponents are *not*. More direct evidence for this function is conveniently provided in *1 Enoch* 108, where it is explicitly stated that the book of life serves as a symbol of assurance and comfort for the righteous in the coming age:

> You who have observed the law[113] shall wait patiently in all the days until the time of those who work evil is completed, and the power of the wicked ones

112. "Rooted out of the land" is, of course, another covenantal motif.

113. The word for "law" is actually not found in this verse; Isaac has taken the word from v. 1, which is actually the term *šer'āt;* in this context it probably refers to the "covenant" (cf. the usual word for law, *ḥegg*), although the term refers elsewhere to the "order" assigned to nature (cf. *1 En.* 78:10; 79:2). Even if we choose to translate "law," this nevertheless suggests the association between covenant and the record of names discerned elsewhere.

is ended. As for you, wait patiently until sin passes away, for the names of the *sinners shall be blotted out from the Book of Life and the books of the Holy One;* their seeds shall be destroyed forever and their spirits shall perish and die. . . . And I have *recounted in the books*[114] *all their [the righteous'] blessings.* He has caused them to be recompensed, for they were all found loving God more than the fire of their eternal souls. . . . (vv. 2-3, 10)

Given these functions of defining and consoling, it is not surprising to find an occasional strong tone of vindictiveness in the use of the motif, and this comes out clearly in a powerful courtroom drama in the Similitudes of Enoch, a scene based on Daniel 7 (esp. v. 10). During the judgment, "*the books of the living ones were open* before him. . . . The hearts of the holy ones are filled with joy, because the *number of the righteous* [most MSS 'righteousness']*[115]* has been offered, the prayers of the righteous ones have been heard, and the blood of the righteous has been admitted before the Lord of the Spirits" (*1 En.* 47:3-4). The idea of the full number of the righteous is directly associated in this passage with the "books of the living" and may suggest a suitable provenance for what has conventionally — but quite wrongly — been taken as a deterministic teaching. In this passage the "number" of the righteous follows naturally from the idea of a set number of names listed in the book of the living and may actually have little to do with an abstract determinism *per se.*

Blessings, Curses, Woes, and Related Forms

Another provocative motif that illustrates the strongly dualistic understanding of covenant in these writings is that of the blessing and the curse that consistently formed an integral part of the covenantal formulary and annual renewals of the covenant.[116] The words of Moses, "Behold, I set before you this day a

114. It is not being claimed that these books are necessarily identical with the "Book of Life" in v. 3, especially if (as according to Black, 1985, 324) Enoch is the speaker in v. 10; they would then refer to the books of Enoch. It may have been held, on the other hand, that Enoch himself was responsible for writing the books mentioned in vv. 2-3, implying some kind of relationship between the two kinds of books. But if God is the speaker in v. 10, as assumed by most scholars, then the same books are referred to in both places. The confusion has likely been caused by interpolation or minor displacement, or, more likely, by translation. Black (1985, 325) and Isaac (*OTP,* 2:89 n. *f2*) suggest an interpolation of vv. 10-12 into the original, as v. 13 reverts back to the third person (as in v. 9).

115. For the preference of the reading "the righteous" over "righteousness," alluding to the idea of the predetermined number (i.e., the "fill") of good and bad souls, cf. Black, 1985, 210.

116. Cf. above; and esp. 4Q266. For origins of the blessing and curse in the

blessing and a curse" (Deut. 11:26), and perhaps also the charge to Israel to repeat similar blessings on Mount Gerizim and curses on Mount Ebal (Deut. 27:11ff.) exercised an incalculable influence on Jewish belief and expression, especially among remnant groups where the individualistic and dualistic natures of the covenant were emphasized. This influence was of two kinds — liturgical and literary: the repeating of blessings and curses is evident as a liturgical convention within the covenant renewal celebration at Qumran (1QS 1.16–2.18; cf. also 1QM 13.1-6),[117] and one also witnesses the emergence of a multifarious literary form[118] in these writings — blessings, beatitudes, and benedictions, on the one hand, and curses, woes, and imprecations, on the other.[119] Passages containing these forms or subforms compose a not inconsiderable proportion

---

covenantal formulary, particularly that form of it termed the *rîb* pattern, cf. Hartman, 1979, esp. ch. 3; for their relation to a renewal celebration, cf. Hartman, 74-75. That the covenanters associated the ideas of blessing and curse with the covenant is implied by CD 1.17, which refers to "the curses of His Covenant." For a more general introduction to the "blessing," cf. C. Westermann, *Der Segen in der Bibel und im Handeln der Kirche*, 1968, who alludes to the conditional and dualistic nature of the idea.

117. Cf. also the words of "the Sage" (identical with the *moreh?*) in 4Q510-511, who appears to have played a special role in the covenantal renewal as one entitled "to announce: Peace to all men of the covenant and to shout with a terrifying voice: Woe on all those who break it" (4Q511 3.1-4; translation by F. García Martínez, *The Dead Sea Scrolls Translated*, 1994, 371-76, *in loc.*).

118. In order to speak of a distinct "form," it is understood that three requirements come into play: (1) the literary structure defining the form has become conventional or traditional; (2) the structural elements are important, if not essential, to the message or content; and (3) a consistent purpose in employing the form is evident; that purpose can be ritual as well as more strictly literary, depending on its *Sitz im Leben*. These things seem to apply to the form under consideration. For an analysis of the woe form, cf. R. A. Coughenour, "The Woe-Oracles in Ethiopic Enoch," 1978, 192-97, esp. 193-94.

119. Many other passages demonstrate a relationship to this motif of blessing and curse, while not always showing as well-defined a literary structure as the examples we give below. Cf., e.g., *1 En.* 5:5-7; 58:2-4; 80:2, 8; 91:5-9; *Jub.* 20:5-10; 30:15; 1QS 1.3-5, 9-10; 1.16–2.18; 9.21-22; CD 1.17-18, 20; 1QM 13.1-6; *Pss. Sol.* 4:14-25; 6:1-6; 10:1; 14:1-10; 17:18-19; *TLevi* 4:6; *TIss.* 5:4; *2 Bar.* 52:2; etc. For the view that the many subforms are all related to the covenantal *rîb*, cf. Hartman, 1979, 79-80. Contrast the treatment of the Matthean beatitudes by K. Koch (*The Growth of the Biblical Tradition*, 1969, 7-8, 17-29), who traces these to the biblical "wisdom blessing" and bypasses their covenantal origins. It should be noted that while there is certainly a difference between the origins of the blessing/curse formulations, which go back to covenantal thought, and the "woes," which appear to be more of a prophetic form (cf. Isa. 5:8-22; Ezek. 24:6, 9; Hab. 2:6-19; Numbers 24; cf. הוי or אוי), there is probably little difference in our writings in terms of their function. Some of the scriptural woes are significantly directed against Israel (cf., e.g., Isa. 30:1), while others are directed against the nations (cf., e.g., Num. 21:29; Isa. 10:5; Jer. 23:1).

of these writings.[120] The so-called Book of Admonitions (*1 Enoch* 94–104), for example, is almost entirely in the form of blessings and woes. It would therefore be quite tragic if attempts to characterize such sections with labels like "apocalyptic" (as is often done) were to overlook the precise nature and function of this important literary element or fail to recognize the social contingencies so crucial to understanding it. So much the more since this form exemplifies particularly clearly the tremendous influence of the perceived apostasy in Israel on the literature of this movement.

The Book of Admonitions demonstrates this intense consciousness of apostasy and of the division within Israel. The blessings and curses/woes appear to define the righteous vis-à-vis their enemies and all others who do not hold to their teachings. For example,

> **To Sinners:**[121]
> Judgment will catch up with you, sinners.
>
> **To Righteous:**
> You righteous ones, fear not the sinners!
> For the Lord will again deliver them into your hands,
> so that you may carry out against them anything that you desire.
>
> **To Sinners:**
> Woe unto you who pronounce anathemas so that they may be neutralized!
> Salutary remedy is far from you, on account of your sins.[122]
> Woe unto you who reward evil to your neighbors!
> For you shall be rewarded in accordance with your deeds.
> Woe unto you, witnesses of falsehood!
> And unto those who prepare oppression!
> For you shall perish soon.
> Woe unto you, sinners, for you persecute the righteous![123]
> For you shall be handed over and be persecuted through oppression.
> Its yoke shall be heavy upon you.
>
> **To Righteous:**
> Be hopeful, you righteous ones, for the sinners shall soon perish
> from before your presence.

120. Coughenour (1978, 192) finds thirty-two instances of woe oracles in *1 Enoch* alone.

121. The subtitles have been added for convenience.

122. The reference here appears to be to the practice of pronouncing anathemas in order to undo spells; cf. Black, 1985, 297.

123. Contrary to the way we have presented the following lines, Black (1985, 298) takes them as referring to the righteous.

You shall be given authority upon them, such as you may wish.
In the day of the tribulation of the sinners,
your children shall be raised high up and be made openly visible
      like eagles,
higher than the vultures will your dwelling place be. . . .[124]
But you, who have experienced pain, fear not,
for there shall be a healing medicine for you,
a bright light shall enlighten you,
and a voice of rest you shall hear from heaven.

To Sinners:
Woe unto you, you sinners!
For your money makes you appear like the righteous,[125]
but your hearts do reprimand you like real sinners. . . .
Woe unto you who eat the best bread!
And drink wine in large bowls,
trampling upon the weak people with your might. . . .
Woe unto you, O powerful people!
You who coerce the righteous with your power,
the day of your destruction is coming!
In those days, at the time of your condemnation,
many and good days shall come for the righteous ones.

To Righteous:
Be confident, you righteous ones!
For the sinners are due for a shame. (95:2b–97:1b)

To Sinners:
Woe unto you, fools, for you shall perish
through your folly!
You do not listen to the wise, and you shall not receive good things.
And now do know that you are ready for the day
of destruction. . . .
Woe unto you obstinate of heart, who do evil and devour blood! . . .[126]
Woe unto you who love unrighteousness!

---

124. This might allude to those Jews who, during the Maccabean resistance, took shelter in the rocks (cf. Black, 1985, 298); but the expression is too general to decide this.

125. The reference here is to the belief that prosperity is the reward of righteousness (Black, 1985, 298-99).

126. The expression "obstinate of heart" (Gk. σκληροτράχηλοι τῇ καρδίᾳ) goes back to קשי ערף (RSV "stiff-necked"), an expression for the stubborn refusal by Israel to obey the covenant; cf. Exod. 32:9; 33:3, 5; 34:9; "devour blood" reminds us of the critique of the priesthood in our writings; cf. Black, 1985, 302.

Why do you have hopes for good things for yourselves?
Do know that you shall be given over into the hands of the righteous ones,
and they shall cut off your necks and slay you, and they shall not
      have compassion upon you.
Woe unto you who rejoice in the suffering of the righteous ones!
For no grave shall be dug for you.
Woe unto you who would set at nought the words of the righteous ones!
For you shall have no hope of life.
Woe unto you who write down false words and words of wickedness![127]
For they write down their lies so that they may commit wicked acts,[128]
and they cause others to commit wicked acts.[129]
They shall have no peace, but shall die quickly.
Woe unto you who cause wickedness![130]
Who glorify and honor false words,
you are lost, and you have no life of good things;
woe unto you who alter the words of truth
and pervert the eternal law!
They reckon themselves not guilty of sin,
they shall be trampled on upon the earth.

To Righteous:
In those days, be ready, you righteous ones, to raise up your prayers as a memorial, and place them as a testimony before the angels; and they shall bring the sins of the sinners for a memorial before the Most High. (98:9–99:3)

The decree [judgment] is with the righteous ones. (100:10)

I now swear to you, righteous ones, by the glory of the Great One and by the glory of his kingdom. . . . For I know this mystery; I have read the tablets of heaven and have seen the holy writings, and I have understood the writing in them; and they are inscribed concerning you. For all good things, and joy and honor are prepared for and written down for the souls of those who died in righteousness. Many and good things shall be given to you — the offshoot of your labors. (103:1-3)

---

127. Black: "lying words and words of heresy" (1985, 92); Eth[tana] *nagara ḥassat;* Gk. πλάνης = טעו, "apostasy," or perhaps, "idolatry"; Black, 303.

128. Black suggests that יכדבון, "they deceive," was read as יכבון, "they write" (1985, 303); but that corruption of the Scriptures may be in mind is suggested by 99:2.

129. Black: "so that men apostatize and cause others to fall away"; *yārasseʿewwo labāʿed* from √ *rasʿa,* "to apostatize"; Gk. πολλοὺς ἀποπλανήσουσιν! (1985, 92, 303).

130. Black: "who cause apostasies" (1985, 92); Gk. πλανήματα.

To Sinners:
Woe unto you sinners who are dead! (103:5)

To Righteous:
I swear unto you that in heaven the angels will remember you for good before the glory of the Great One; and your names shall be written before the glory of the Great One. Be hopeful, because formerly you have pined away through evil and toil. But now you shall shine like the lights of heaven, and you shall be seen; and the windows of heaven shall be opened for you. Your cry shall be heard. (104:1-2)

The woes in the passage are particularly appropriate for leaders and the rich, although the economic and political allusions should be seen as a by-product of the highly particularist standpoint of the author rather than as determining factors in the social constitution of this group. It is clear, in any event, that religious concerns preoccupied the mind of the author, rather than purely political or economic concerns. This concern for religious apostasy is sometimes concealed by translations of the Admonitions, and corrections of this tendency have been offered in the footnotes here.

The *functions* of the blessings-and-woes form (and related subforms) are accordingly not difficult to detect and are indeed correctly recognized by scholars. The most obvious feature of the blessings and curses, as noted above, is how they highlight the dualism of the groups, drawing implicit contrasts between the righteous and their enemies and thereby implicitly *defining* one group over against another.[131] While they *warn* (absent) sinners,[132] they simul-

---

131. According to Hartman, for Qumran "the coupling of blessing and curse as well as their context underline the dualism of the sect and its demand for *Entscheidung*" (1979, 73). Coughenour places the provenance of the woe form in the wisdom tradition. The function of this he appears to partly relate to such things as the "task of penetrating the order of the world" (1978, 197), the maintenance of the social order (194), and setting forth the "Two Ways" (195) — all traditional characteristics of wisdom literature. The last of the three in particular suits the *Sitz im Leben* of the writings as we have uncovered it, and explains why the form would be adopted here. In this regard it is interesting how 4Q525 presents a blessing based on the possession of wisdom (somewhat personified), followed by curses against those aligned with evil spirits. "Choose" and "way" metaphors are also in evidence in the curse section of this writing.

132. Cf. Hartman on the function of *1 En.* 5:5-10 (1979, 38). Cf. also J. A. Loader ("The Model of the Priestly Blessing in 1QS," 1983, 11-17), who views the function of blessings/curses in 1QS 2.2-9 somewhat differently according to its rather unique *Sitz im Leben* as part of the ceremony of admission to the community — namely, "as a warning to the new members. Thus the focal point of our text — its scopus — is a stern warning in terms of the central doctrine at Qumran [i.e., dualism]" (16-17). It is not clear that the curses in this passage were intended solely for the ears of the initiates. A preferable view is

taneously *console* the members of the group (who are present).[133] The idea of the *vindication* of the righteous comes out very clearly also. Since our groups appear to have been conscious of the need for a precedent to justify their separate existence within Israel — thus to grant *legitimation* to their movement — it can be seen just how ideal, for this purpose, would have been the tradition of Moses' (and Israel's) blessing of the righteous who remained in the covenant and cursing of those who were excluded. This legitimation would be deeply experienced: "the curse of the potential apostate is a way of protecting the group from being defiled, which at the same time is presented as a kind of sacral sanction."[134] Blessings, curses, woes, and the like were, therefore, a powerfully important instrument of *definition, validation,* and *consolation* and serve as further documentation of the fundamentally dualistic view of covenant held by those within the movement.

Revelations of the Cosmos

Accounts of journeys through the cosmos are another of those elements so common in these writings that, not surprisingly, attempts have been made to categorize apocalyptic literature according to the employment of this important form.[135] It is questionable whether the "journey" itself is really the vital characteristic of the form, however; *visions* of the cosmos that make *no* explicit mention of a journey contain many of the same elements, and the narrative framework on occasion confuses journeys with visions. The journeys and visions should accordingly be treated as a single form characterized largely by content, that is, their often detailed and always esoteric descriptions of heavenly and earthly places — while the *method of viewing* the places should not be con-

---

to see them as directed outwardly, even if they were not heard beyond the wall of the community. Loader's observation that the curses are considerably more developed than the blessings (13, 16) alerts us to the fact that these communities were alluding to the behavior of contemporaries.

133. Hartman, 1979, 63; cf. his statement: "we may reckon with the phenomenon which is not rare in modern times either, viz., that in a community accusations are hurled against people who are not present, and that this not only sharpens an opposition against those not present and bolsters up a longing for revenge on them, but also serves to strengthen the morale of the group's own ranks" (137). Cf. also Koch on the Matthean beatitudes (1969, 8). For the view that the original idea of blessing implied the "result" of salvation *(Heil)* rather than the "act" of salvation *(Rettung)*, cf. Westermann, 1968, 9-22. This points to the appropriateness of the blessing as a confirmation of salvation, and thus as a means of consolation for the righteous.

134. Hartman, 1979, 73.

135. As in the classification of Collins (cf. esp. "Introduction," 1979, 1-19).

sidered essential to the form. Hence it is preferable to refer to these under the general category of *revelations of the cosmos.*[136]

Any categorization of the form is complicated, however, by the apparently diverse *functions* of the revelations. We have, in this regard, already demonstrated that some of the revelations of the cosmos serve calendrical interests. One of these revelations, *1 Enoch* 2ff., is neither a journey nor a vision but a word of exhortation to "examine all the activities which take place in the sky," and the function of this passage, as already argued, is to impress on the reader an urgency to conform to the solar calendar. A similar calendrical purpose attaches to the Book of Heavenly Luminaries, which is referred to as a vision (72:1; cf. 74:1) but is also presented as an "itinerary" (72:1) and a list of commandments (72:2). But not all, or even most, of the revelations of the cosmos possess this calendrical function. A second group exhibits a quite different purpose, while both types occur, for example, in the Book of Watchers. Our interest here is in those revelations of the cosmos whose functions are *not* related to the calendar. These form a subcategory of *revelations of the cosmos* and might be called *revelations of places of punishment and reward*[137] since this composes their chief subject matter.

Revelations of the cosmos have attracted considerable scholarly attention. Two detailed studies appeared in the early 1980s on the *Jewish* journeys alone (many more on parallel non-Jewish phenomena can be found), by Martha Himmelfarb (*Tours of Hell*, 1983) and Mary Dean-Otting (*Heavenly Journeys*, 1984).[138] Both have their limits — one concerns itself exclusively with *late* revelations of hell,[139] and the other centers on the heavens and is limited almost ex-

---

136. Although this title has its own limited applicability, for visions/journeys of the *earth* are also found (although these may not be on the earth at all; cf. the enigmatic view of the four points of the compass in *1 Enoch* 28–36, which do not appear to relate to "real" places). It would appear, however, as explained below, that this aspect nevertheless serves the same general purpose of the revelations, since the earth is one *part* of the cosmos.

137. This is preferable to "revelations of heaven and hell," since the place of punishment is not in every case "hell," or even "hades" or "sheol" (cf. R. Bauckham, "Early Jewish Visions of Hell," 1990, 355-85; for summary, cf. 375). In the Book of Watchers, e.g., the places of reward and punishment are described as "an empty place" (*1 En.* 21:1) and "another place" (22:1), respectively; they are pictured as being at the "extremities of the earth" (Bauckham, 365).

138. For interaction with these approaches, and critique, cf. M. Dean-Otting, *Heavenly Journeys*, 1984, 20-27. She separates the Jewish journeys from Hellenistic counterparts as quite distinctive, being built on biblical models (30-31).

139. Cf. M. Himmelfarb (*Tours of Hell*, 1983, 37), who dismisses our literature as unimportant for her purposes, which are to trace a development in modes of punishment (on *1 Enoch*, cf. 52). For critique of her narrow definition, cf. Bauckham, 1990, 357; for summary of his own position, cf. 375-76.

clusively to what are better called *throne-room visions*.[140] Neither, therefore, is based on a comprehensive analysis of revelations of the cosmos, leaving some uncertainty whether the authors have truly grasped the purpose of types of the form that they have not considered (what methodological rationale is there for a noncontextual approach to the "hell" half of the tour that ignores the "heaven" half, as in Himmelfarb's study?). What is even more unfortunate for us is that they do not deal in any extensive way with the texts under consideration here.[141] As such these two studies can be of only partial relevance to the present analysis, and there would appear to be room still for a novel approach, one that makes up for some of their deficiencies. The present treatment is, of course, even more limited by space, and can only be representative in its approach; it only aims to place some new questions and new perspectives on the table.

Turning first to the Book of Watchers, what may be taken as two separate but closely related examples of these revelations can be found: chs. 12–16 and chs. 17–36. While chs. 12–16 are frequently taken to be from the hands of a later redactor,[142] both of these two groups of chapters are closely related in subject matter.[143] Thus, during the first revelation, Enoch is instructed to make known to the fallen Watchers the certainty of their torment;[144] then chs. 17ff. complete

140. What Dean-Otting refers to as "the motif of heavenly ascent." Thus she gives rather extensive treatment to *1 Enoch* 14 (1984, 39-58), and superficial treatment to chs. 17ff. (64-67). We would agree with her statement that "the Biblical throne visions influenced the heavenly ascent texts in a major way. . . . Thus we can see that the heavenly journey motif is firmly rooted in Biblical Judaism and not to be explained as a development resulting from foreign influence" (58).

141. Himmelfarb relegates texts like the Book of Watchers and the Book of Heavenly Luminaries ("tour apocalypses") to the "pre-history" of the tradition (1983, 2-3). Dean-Otting touches on some of the books we are interested in (*1 Enoch* 14; 71; *TLevi* 2:6–3:8; 4 Ezra 7:75-101), but gives preference to those containing heavenly throne visions.

142. Black restates the long-standing view that chs. 17–36 represent "a new section of the book . . . dealing with the extra-terrestrial journeys of Enoch" (1985, 155). Chs. 17–24 also contain duplicate accounts of the same journey visions, according to this author, consisting of 17:1–19:3 and 21:1–25:7, separated by ch. 20 on the seven archangels (16; cf. also Charles, 1912, 38; Bauckham, 1990, 358).

143. Hartman has provided a good case for the necessary association of the various parts of the book (particularly the introduction to the book, chs. 1–5, vis-à-vis chs. 6–36; 1979, 143-44).

144. 12:3-4; cf. v. 5: "neither will there be peace unto them nor the forgiveness of sin." Even if "forgiveness of sins" here is an Eth. expansion (cf. Black, 1985, 143; contrast 16:3), it is entirely appropriate for the practice of this author, which is to allude to the condition of humans through reference to the Watchers; cf. pp. 427-32 below. In spite of Enoch's intercession for the fallen angels (ch. 13), they are told that they "will have no peace" (16:3), yet another significant example of the unanswered-petition theme in our

this plot as they relate Enoch's mission as a bearer of the bad news given in chs. 12–16, perhaps adding a description of the Watchers' torment to confirm the existence of the place of their punishment. If this connection is essential, the two sections should be treated together, though we should still recognize that diverse sources or traditions may have been combined or that redaction may be responsible for the final form of the two-part vision.

The first part of the journey[145] begins as Enoch is beckoned by some kind of cosmic forces (14:8),[146] which then lead the patriarch into the heavenly throne room or temple, where the Lord instructs Enoch and communicates the negative response to the Watchers' petitions (14:9–16:3). That this part of the journey is actually more of an "ascent" or a throne-room vision might seem to disqualify it as a journey,[147] but the passage serves admirably as an introduction to the much more detailed and apparently more important journey in chs. 17ff.[148] Here Enoch begins his cosmic journey proper through the earth and

---

writings, which always seem to lead to the same conclusion: despite the sincere regrets and compassion of the righteous, God *must* judge wickedness.

145. The literary context for the revelations is not clear — Enoch may have received the vision during his earthly life or after his translation; i.e., when he "walked with God and was not" (cf. Gen. 5:24). The words of 12:1, "Before these things Enoch was hidden, and no one of the children of the people knew by what he was hidden and where he was," might point to his translation. Alternatively the revelation was experienced as a dream earlier on during Enoch's earthly life. This is the view of Dimant ("The Biography of Enoch and the Books of Enoch," 1983), and seems also to be indicated by certain other expressions in the preceding visions: "I saw *in my sleep* what I now speak with my tongue" (14:2). *Jub.* 4:21 appears to suggest that *before* "he was taken from among men" (i.e., Enoch's translation; cf. v. 23), Enoch was "with the angels of God six jubilees of years. And they showed him everything which is on earth and in the heavens, the dominion of the sun." While the last phrase appears to allude to *calendrical* visions, it may nevertheless reflect a more general tradition of revelations received *during Enoch's life*. Parallels of this verse can be detected in *1 En.* 12:2: "And his dwelling place as well as his activities were with the Watchers and the holy ones," which suggests that the experience mentioned in 12:1 occurred during Enoch's lifetime. Black compares also 4Q226 (1985, 142). Perhaps then *1 En.* 81:5-6 refers to an interval between *two* translations to paradise (cf. Black, 142), which would throw considerable light on these references.

146. "I saw the clouds: And they were calling me in a vision; and the fogs were calling me; and the course of the stars and the lightnings were rushing me and causing me to desire; and in the vision, the winds were causing me to fly and rushing me high up into heaven."

147. While the heavenly journeys are frequently treated as ascents to see *God*, many texts do not dwell on the vision of God's throne, as some later literature does (such as the later *merkabah* speculations; cf. Ezek. 1:1; cf. Dean-Otting, 1984, 262, for consideration of these); their interest is more on what they see on the way there and back — i.e., the places of reward and punishment.

148. Cf. the guarded comments of Dean-Otting, 1984, 64.

the "heavens,"[149] including a visit to the place where the fallen angels ("stars") will be judged (18:11–19:3). It is probably to give reality to the vision and thus further legitimate it that the benevolent angels are *named* — a typical feature of this form (20:1-6).[150] Then follows a more detailed journey through the place of punishment, a place for the "spirits of the souls of the dead" waiting for judgment (21:1-10; 22:1-7),[151] a description of the method and places of judgment of humans (22:8-14),[152] and a view of the place of reward (24:1–25:7). An enigmatic interlude, the description of a "burning fire" and "the luminaries of heaven," appears to allude to the consistency and order of the sun and stars and possibly beyond that to the calendar,[153] although the "burning fire" may refer back to the throne-room vision of ch. 14, confirming a significant literary connection with those earlier chapters.

This terse description of the contents of the revelation is enough to reveal what one repeatedly finds to be true with regard to these visions and journeys; namely, that they regularly juxtapose and even place in parallel descriptions of *judgment* of the unrighteous and descriptions of *reward* for the righteous. That part of the description of judgment relates to the fallen *Watchers* does not de-

149. The origin of the idea of *many* "heavens" may not imply Persian/Zoroastrian origins at all. Dean-Otting speculates that the Hebrew word שמים, being a plural, may have been taken to imply this (1984, 275). The expression "heaven of the heavens" or "the highest heaven" (cf. Deut. 10:14) is particularly provocative.

150. For this function of "angel lists," cf. D. W. Suter, *Tradition and Composition in the Parables of Enoch,* 1979, passim.

151. Bauckham points out that ch. 22 (in its entirety) does not portray a place of punishment (as is evident also from the presence of the righteous there), but a place of detention "where they await their punishment at the day of judgment." The actual place of punishment, in the valley of Hinnom, is not described until 26:3–27:4, although there also the punishment itself is not actually described (1990, 359).

152. Debate rages over whether to see four (cf. v. 2) or three compartments (cf. v. 9) for the deceased. We can concur with Black, who sees four places, even within vv. 9ff. (where "three" refers to the places for the unrighteous only, omitting reference to the place for the righteous). These compartments are for: (1) the righteous; (2) the sinners and oppressors of the righteous; (3) those who have suffered violent deaths and await judgment; and (4) "a class who are not completely debased, but whose sin was that they consorted with the sinners" (1985, 17). This seems to confirm that *all* but the righteous were placed in categories separate from the righteous, including not only the enemies of the sect but even those who "consorted with the sinners" (through passive compliance?). This passage shows how concerns for judgment in this passage center on Israel.

153. Cf. "it did not diminish its speed night and day," 23:2. That calendar and cosmology are combined here with the description of the underworld is evident already in 18:15: "And the stars which roll over upon the fire, they are the ones which have transgressed the commandments of God from the beginning of their rising because they did not arrive punctually." Black suggests a possible "astronomical source" for this section (1985, 15), which might indicate an interest in the calendar.

tract from this basic pattern, as the Watchers frequently function as symbols (or leaders) of the unrighteous in the Enochian literature.[154] It is this dual feature of judgment and reward that suggests that the *primary concern* of these revelations of the cosmos is *to reveal the respective ultimate destinies of the elect and the damned* and thus to define the elect and the apostate by outlining their respective fates,[155] the lengthy and detailed descriptions of the places of reward and torment adding revelational authority to the message that Israel is divided according to eternal destinies.[156] The sinners need to be warned lest they share the fate of the Gentiles; the righteous need to remain faithful. Thus a related function would be to admonish and console the righteous. These journeys hardly seem to be theological or didactically motivated, as is usually assumed; the form is too emotionally charged for that. That the purpose of these revelations of the cosmos is to emphasize the certainty of judgment for sinners and to contrast the fates of the righteous and wicked is strongly suggested by the present passage. This can be seen, for example, in words that emphasize the recompense of the righteous by building up phrase after phrase describing their bliss.

"This is for the righteous and the pious. And the elect will be presented with its fruit for life. . . .[157]

"Then they shall be glad and rejoice in gladness,
and they shall enter into the holy place;
its fragrance shall penetrate their bones,
long life will they live on earth,
such as your fathers lived in their days."

154. Cf. pp. 427-32 below. This makes the expressions of 12:3-4 ("neither will there be peace unto them nor the forgiveness of sin") and 16:3 ("no peace") particularly applicable to the human counterparts of these fallen angels, and helps to reveal the true concern of these verses.

155. As detected for some journeys by Bauckham (1990, 384). Contrast Dean-Otting, who takes the function of these texts to be didactic (1984, 6).

156. In this regard it might be significant to note that Himmelfarb considers the presence of the explanatory and interrogatory clauses opening with demonstratives ("this/these is/are . . ."; "who/what is this/these?") to compose a central distinguishing formal feature of related tours of hell (cf. 1983, 45ff.). They are missing from the Graeco-Roman parallels, and appear to reflect the influence of passages like Ezekiel 40–48; Gen. 41:26; and Zechariah 1–8 (48, 58), making them distinctly Jewish. We might ask whether the inclusion of such demonstratives points to the classification/definition function of the tours investigated here, since this literary feature serves so well to highlight details the author wishes to make emphatic. Such demonstratives are found in our passage in 18:14, 15; 21:6, 10; 22:3, 7, 9; 23:4; 25:3, 4; 27:2; 32:6.

157. Probably a description of the tree of life, although this is not stated explicitly (cf. Black, 1985, 171).

> At that moment, I [Enoch] blessed the God of Glory, the Eternal King, for he
> has prepared such things for the righteous people, as he had created them
> and given it to them. (25:5-7)

Following this comes a tour of the "center of the earth" and the new Jerusalem
(ch. 26), apparently intended to facilitate the vision of the Valley Gehinnom
(the traditional place of punishment *for Israelites,* ch. 27). With respect to this
last apparition Uriel explains:

> This accursed valley is for those accursed forever; here will gather together all
> those accursed ones, those who speak with their mouth unbecoming words
> against the Lord and utter hard words concerning his glory. Here shall they
> be gathered together, and here shall be their judgment, in the last days. There
> will be upon them the spectacle of the righteous judgment, in the presence of
> the righteous forever. The merciful will bless the Lord of Glory, the Eternal
> King, all the day. In the days of the judgment of the accursed, the merciful
> shall bless him for the mercy which he had bestowed upon them. (27:2-4)

It is abundantly clear from such a lengthy commentary on these journeys that
their purpose is to lay fully before the imagination of the reader, in the form of
an authoritative revelation, the respective fates of the righteous and unrighteous,[158] in this way serving the strict dualism of the writing. But more than
that, the passage serves to "rub it in" by portraying the righteous *viewing* with
pleasure the torments of sinners (cf. "the spectacle of the righteous judgment,
in the presence of the righteous forever"), while the righteous experience eternal glory.[159] Following these sections the journey finishes relatively quickly, the
author being concerned only to mention, for sake of completeness perhaps, the
east, north, west, and south regions. However, an additional reason for viewing

---

158. Cf. Black: "The verse [v. 3] is important for the theology of the author: the last
great judgment is to take place in Jerusalem and to become a spectacle for the righteous
and the pious for all time" (1985, 174). Those visions that serve calendrical propaganda, by
contrast, only mention the places of reward and punishment *incidentally.* Cf. the role of
1 En. 77:4 and the incidental mention of "the garden of righteousness" within the
calendrical polemic found there.

159. It is interesting, in this respect, how this feature has influenced the emergence
of the δόξα theme in our literature. Dean-Otting explains how this "glory" is transferred
from deity to God's righteous when they are in the presence of God's glory: "A link is
forged between the descriptions of Deity enthroned found in our heavenly journey texts,
and the shining, often glorious countenances of those resurrected. . . . By means of this
'transfer' Deity is brought closer to mankind, indeed the δόξα θεοῦ is shed upon the righteous" (1984, 282-83; cf. Dan. 12:2). We cannot agree unqualifiedly with her supposition
that this has to do with closing the gap in the transcendence of deity; it would seem to relate more to the theme of the reward of the righteous — namely, a share in the δόξα θεοῦ.

these places is apparently to describe the origins of good and evil — that is, the *source of blessing and curse* — in mountains, deserts, wildernesses, trees, seeds, streams, and especially the winds (chs. 28–36, esp. 34:2-3).[160] Thus we have what amounts to another judgment motif, this time related directly to the blessings and curses of the covenant.

The Book of Watchers is one of those instances of a visionary revelation combined with a journey proper. This mixture is even more conspicuous in a revelation to Enoch, described in ch. 108, that possesses aspects of both journey and vision. Regardless of this variability in formal features, however, the focus of interest in this chapter still remains on the place of punishment, of which it is said that

> into it shall be taken the spirits of sinners, blasphemers, those who do evil, and those who alter all the things which the Lord has done through the mouth of the prophets, all of which have to be fulfilled. For some of these things were written and sealed above in heaven so that the angels may read them and know that which is about to befall the sinners, the spirits of the *apostates*,[161] as well as those who defiled their bodies, revenged themselves on God, and worked together with evil people.[162] (vv. 6-7)

These expressions are all appropriate to Jewish apostates — particularly the expression "alter all the things which the Lord has done through the . . . prophets."[163] The reference to punishments being recorded in heaven not only recalls the heavenly lists of names and deeds but illustrates and enhances the message that these punishments are intended to be *fully viewed* — both as a warning

---

160. These elements may also have been fairly conventional for revelations of the cosmos. Similar descriptions appear also in the calendrical Book of Heavenly Luminaries (cf. 72:1; 74:2; 78:10; 79:2, 6; 80:1; 82:7).

161. Following certain Eth. MSS (which read *teḥutān,* "humble ones," rather than *ṣeḥutān,* "apostates"), Black prefers to render this difficult passage, "that which will happen to sinners, and to the spirits of the *humble,* and to those who afflict their bodies [i.e., the *righteous*] and will receive their reward from God, and to those who are abused by evil men" (1985, 101; cf. Charles, 1912, 271). This, however, complicates the expression, and rejects the important *Tana* MSS that have "apostates." In any event, the change of subject to the righteous takes place somewhere in the passage, whether at this verse or at v. 8 where Isaac has placed it.

162. This final phrase is significant for its reference to collaboration or, perhaps, persecution. Charles follows those MSS that read: "those who have been put to shame by wicked men" (1912, 271).

163. In this respect vv. 7-8 allude to the existence of additional revelation that is not acknowledged by the sinners. For our view (cf. also Charles, 1912, 270) that this refers to the words of the prophets, cf. treatment of this passage above.

and a guarantee of the coming judgment on sinners. Another focus of interest in this passage is the vindication of the righteous:

> Those who love God . . . he has caused them to be recompensed, for they were all found loving God more than the fire of their eternal souls; and while they were being trodden upon by evil people, experiencing abuse and insult by them, they continued blessing us. . . .[164] I shall bring them out into the bright light, those who have loved my holy name, and seat them each one by one upon the throne of his honor; and they shall be resplendent[165] for ages that cannot be numbered. . . . He will give faith . . . to the faithful ones in the resting place. (vv. 8-13)

Together these two focuses of interest — punishment and recompense — permeate the entire report of the revelation, again suggesting the dominance of this dualism in these revelations of the cosmos. The book significantly ends with still another reference to the two fates: "Then they [the faithful] shall *see* those who were born in darkness being taken into darkness, while the righteous ones shall be resplendent. The sinners shall cry aloud, and they shall *see* the righteous ones being resplendent; they shall go to the place which was prescribed for them concerning the days and the seasons" (vv. 14-15).[166] This passage again emphasizes the contrast by having the righteous "view" the fate of the damned and, as an added feature this time, the damned viewing the blessing of the righteous (note the repeated and emphatic use of "see" for both groups). This not only increases the sense of suffering communicated by the passage but offers an insight into the apparently vindictive attitude of its author. Since rewards and punishments are still a future expectation in *1 Enoch*, the sense of imminence created by the convention is a very effective and moving tool. By viewing the future the author brings his eschatological warning

164. This reading (following Eth. A) has "us" — i.e., the angels (cf. v. 5)? Other MSS contain perhaps the more difficult reading "me" — Enoch? This latter reading would cohere with the emphasis in this chapter on the special revelation possessed by this community, which centered on Enoch's revelations.

165. The light imagery here reminds us of the בני אור of Qumran; some Eth. MSS even support the reading "generation of light" in v. 10.

166. The significance of this last phrase evades. It may refer to the endlessness of the existence in the place of blessing (i.e., "the days and the seasons *forever*"). Alternatively it could be an allusion to the calendar, and to the perfect order of things reflected in the "luminaries," which become more or less equivalent here to the place of reward. *1 Enoch* 23–24 also seem to identify (although it is "another place," 23:1; 24:1) the place of luminaries in the west with the place of blessing. Much of the speculation of this writing appears to be influenced by calendrical and order-of-nature motifs. *Jub.* 2:2 also enigmatically relates the creation of the "abysses" with the creation of "evening and night" and "dawn and daylight."

into the present. That many of these texts take the form of "journeys" or "tours" is itself a device that helps evoke the sensation of "viewing," in turn granting a sense of imminence to the punishments.

One can get some added illumination on this mutual "viewing" of punishment and reward from a later passage, 4 Ezra 7:75-99. No lengthy vision of or journey through the cosmos is to be found in 4 Ezra, but the respective fates of the righteous and wicked are carefully contrasted in this passage and the function of the "viewing" motif becomes evident. Earlier, in vv. 37-38, following the resurrection, the nations (which clearly includes Israel in this case) are instructed to "*Look* now, and understand whom you have denied, whom you have not served, whose commandments you have despised! *Look* on this side and on that; *here are delight and rest, and there are fire and torments!*" Stone's comments on these passages in 4 Ezra are apposite: "This sort of sight is analogous to the concept of *recompense through seeing the fate of the other group* which seems to lie behind the pointing out of paradise and Gehenna in 7:38."[167] 7:83-84 makes this motivation quite explicit when it carefully lays out seven ways the unrighteous will suffer torment, among which are that "they shall *see* the reward laid up for those who have trusted the covenants of the Most High" and "shall *consider* the torment laid up for themselves in the last days." Predictably the righteous are vindicated by the same vision: "because they see the perplexity in which the souls of the ungodly wander, and the punishment that waits them" (v. 93). Similarly when *2 Baruch* contrasts the fates of the righteous and wicked, these purposes are again quite explicit. The experience of *viewing* the divine reversal of fates is identified and virtually *equated* with the experience of transformation in paradise in 51:5-6: "When they . . . see that those over whom they are exalted now will then be more exalted and glorified than they, then both these and those will be changed, these into the splendor of angels and those into startling visions and horrible shapes; and they will waste away even more. For *they will first see* and then they will go away to be tormented." One can only conclude that the purpose of such texts is to console and vindicate the righteous and warn the unrighteous by giving to both a preview of the rewards as well as the torments experienced by the others (cf. also vv. 85-86). While there are formal differences between these passages from 4 Ezra and *2 Baruch* and the revelations of the cosmos "proper" like those in *1 Enoch*, the value of the later texts for throwing light on the function of the earlier ones is nevertheless obvious.

One can see from these examples of revelations of the places of punishment and reward to what extent this literature is preoccupied with legitimizing the segregated existence of the authors' communities. And many other exam-

---

167. Stone, 1989, 205, emphasis added.

ples of journeys or visions of the cosmos that outline the respective fates of the righteous and wicked in dramatic terms could be cited.[168] Such passages warn their opponents and console the members of their own communities, often using extraordinarily vivid metaphors and suggestive literary devices. By such means these texts also enthusiastically promote a distinction of the righteous and unrighteous. This evidence composes an implicit but very strong proof, from a theological as well as sociological perspective, of the fundamentally exclusive nature of these groups, and especially the exclusive nature of their covenantal theology. Those who are under the blessings of the covenant will share an eternal fate in line with those blessings, and those under the curse a destiny quite consistent with the covenantal curse.

It is apparent, in this regard, that the detailed descriptions of places of reward and punishment were at least partly formed in the minds of these writers by extending the descriptions of covenantal blessing and curse and converting them into eternal states. Knowing this, we might conclude that descriptions of heaven and hell are not so much a matter of mystic knowledge or of borrowing from the folklore of neighboring peoples as an extension of covenantal language that would be entirely expected in Jewish society. In this regard the message of *1 Enoch* 28–36, which describe the origins of the blessing and curse in the context of a revelation of the cosmos, is particularly revealing. Accordingly these revelations of the cosmos do not represent just literary convention, nor do they exhibit a preoccupation with cosmic science, as often thought. They are essentially one more application of a prevailing covenantal dualism. As in the case of the witness motif, *covenant and cosmology* are again seen to be interconnected concerns. Revelations of places of punishment and reward offer an opportunity to legitimize the beliefs and claims of the group by appealing to revelational authority, while at the same time proclaiming their message with both shocking frankness and literary effectiveness. One can surmise that few forms would have made more of an impression on the reader or carried more authority than these detailed and evocative revelations.

Knowing a group's basic attitudes toward and beliefs about the covenant

---

168. Cf. Similitudes of Enoch chs. 37ff., 60–62 (cf. esp. 62:13: "The righteous and elect ones shall be saved on that day; and from thenceforth they shall never *see* the faces of the sinners and the oppressors . . ."); *2 Bar.* 59:4-11; *TLevi* 2:6–3:8. Later texts reflecting the formal conventions and possessing related functions include *3 Baruch* 3:5-8; 8:5; 9:7?; 12:8–13:4; cf. 10:5–12:7; 14:2–15:4, and the (probably superior) Slavonic version of 16:4 where, at the end of the book, Baruch is told to stand and see both the "resting place of the righteous" and "the torture of the impious"; *2 Enoch*, esp. chs. 1–38; *Asc. Is.* 7:8–10:6; *Testament of Abraham* (recension A) 10–14. Cf. also *Liber Antiquitatum Biblicarum* 23:6, as well as other works cited by Bauckham (1990, 367-69), such as *Transitus Mariae* and the Gk. version of *3 Baruch* 16:4-8.

or covenants is obviously an important step toward understanding other aspects of their theology such as those that will form the subject matter of the remainder of this book. This chapter began with two *hypothetical extremes* by which to understand and evaluate this subject. While the trend of late has been to view Judaism as embracing an essentially unilateral, irrevocable, and nationalistic understanding of covenant, the evidence uncovered herein has suggested the opposite: these groups leaned heavily toward a conditional and individual, as well as dynamic and dualistic, view of covenant. The present treatment was not intended to prove that these groups embraced the latter type of understanding exclusively or in its extreme form as it was described at the beginning of this chapter. One must be willing to acknowledge that examples might be found that suggest *aspects* of another view of covenant. The conclusion nevertheless stands that *by far the dominant view of covenant among these groups was the conditional, individual, dynamic, and dualistic view of covenant* as revealed in scriptural dualistic covenantal formulations, the witness motif, blessings and curses, and the revelations of the cosmos (notably the viewing-of-fates motif).

CHAPTER SEVEN

Soteriological Dualism

The variety of expressions of a dualistic covenantal theology examined in the previous chapter — such as blessings and curses and related forms, and revelations of places of punishment and reward — served to emphasize the distinction between those in the covenant and those outside the covenant. The revelations of places of punishment and reward, for instance, functioned within the context of perceived apostasy to *define* the two groups according to their respective fates, and thereby to *warn* the sinners and to *console* the righteous.

Given the preponderance of this division between the righteous and the wicked in these writings, some scholars have argued that *ethical dualism* is among the most important and creative of the dualisms in our literature.[1] While other attempts to explain the emergence of dualistic thought still persist,[2] this newer position tends to be adopted by scholars who are especially sensitive to the sociological influences at work. Talmon, for example, suggests that this kind of dualism characterized all the sects of the Second Temple period, particularly

---

1. J. G. Gammie, "Spatial and Ethical Dualism in Jewish Wisdom and Apocalyptic Literature," 1974, 357, 368-69, 372-85; O. Plöger, *Theocracy and Eschatology,* 1968, 48; cf. following notes.

2. E.g., P. von der Osten-Sacken, *Gott und Belial,* 1969, passim, esp. 110-15, 166-68. Even Osten-Sacken, however, recognized the importance of ethical dualism. He traced what he thought was a line of development in the scrolls from the early eschatological dualistic holy-war imagery of 1QM ("Kampfdualismus," inspired largely by the book of Daniel; cf. 28-29, 33-34, 88, etc.) through various mutations brought on by, among other things, an ethical dualistic emphasis (110-11, 114-15, 166-68, etc.). Osten-Sacken has been criticized for failing to demonstrate that the *earliest* dualism was eschatological by J. L. Duhaime ("Dualistic Reworking in the Scrolls from Qumran," 1987, 32-56, 36).

Qumran,[3] and Reid recently expressed a similar opinion in his sociological study of Daniel and *1 Enoch*.[4] Other scholars have come close to drawing this conclusion from the importance of social influences, particularly divisions, that existed in Israel and of the influence of these divisions on various kinds of dualisms. Thus Gowan acknowledges that not only Antiochus's anti-Jewish actions, but also "the bitterness caused by the division between the Hellenizers and the *Hasidim,* led to a hardening of attitudes which in apocalyptic literature is usually called dualism."[5] Plöger, for his part, attributes the eschatological dualism of the early canonical apocalyptic writings to the divisions that existed in Israel when they were written.[6] And Hengel finds with respect to Qumran that "the foundations of an individual *soteriology* and *ecclesiology* are to be seen against the background of a dualism of salvation history and anthropology."[7] Also of interest is Becker's investigation of Qumran soteriology. Becker discerns in the soteriology of the scrolls certain developments of ideas already found in the Hebrew Scriptures. For example, the biblical idea of the two "spheres of salvation" *(Heilssphären)* has become spiritualized and applied to two groups of people — the righteous and the unrighteous — at Qumran and elsewhere.[8] On the basis of our investigation of covenantal thought, we might add to this growing consensus about the influence and importance of division in Israel on dualism the further observation that it was only when this division was coupled with the kind of *covenantal dualism* that we have investigated that both together had a profound effect on the beliefs and literature of the movement and were probably largely responsible for generating the pervading dualistic character of these writings. Thus we are describing not one focus or source when it comes to dualistic origins, but two, the various dualistic themes rotating elliptically, so to speak, around two focuses: ethical and covenantal dualism.

Whether "ethical dualism" is an entirely appropriate expression for this phenomenon, however, is another question. One might better argue, given the nature of the dualism at this point in time, for the more focused term

3. S. Talmon, *King, Cult, and Calendar in Ancient Judaism,* 1986, 186-200.

4. S. B. Reid, *Enoch and Daniel,* 1989, passim; cf. 67-68, 83.

5. Cf. D. E. Gowan, *Bridge between the Testaments,* 1986, 86. Gowan does not develop this idea, however, and reverts to a discussion of the cosmic aspects of dualism only.

6. Plöger, 1968, 108-12.

7. M. Hengel, *Judaism and Hellenism,* 1974, 1:224. We would prefer to speak of soteriological rather than anthropological dualism because the doctrine of God's electing will (which was given too much emphasis by earlier scholars) is balanced at Qumran (for example) by the doctrine of free choice (recognized by more recent scholars). Cf. M. A. Seifrid (*Justification by Faith,* 1992, 132), whose comments on dualism tend to focus on this division in various ways.

8. J. Becker, *Das Heil Gottes,* 1964, 13-15, 78-79; for other writings, cf. 29-30, 66-68, 90, 109-14, 183, 144-48, 165.

"soteriological dualism,"[9] since "ethical dualism" is more applicable to a general and philosophically abstract dichotomy between good and evil (which these groups did not appear to embrace) than to a dualism distinguishing two groups of people. Our consideration of the exclusive soteriology of the movement suggested that the issue of ethics or behavior was not so much at the forefront of thought as were questions of judgment and salvation. And in contrast to much past scholarship of Judaism that emphasized nationalistic doctrines and coincidentally tended to minimize the need for a soteriology, there is little question that our dissenting movement relied heavily on what could be called their soteriological beliefs (see further below, ch. 12). The more appropriate term "soteriological dualism" would also serve to distinguish, not only between the saved and the unsaved, but also between two opposing and mutually exclusive views regarding salvation.[10] Its use, in short, avoids the implication suggested by "ethical dualism" that the groups were divided strictly according to ethical criteria and the attribution to our groups of a highly abstract and philosophical view of the nature of good and evil in the cosmos.[11]

It will be best to start with the writings found at Qumran, which provide abundant examples of the lengths to which Jewish remnant groups would go in the development and application of soteriological dualism to the situation of Israel and to their own situation as well. Students of Qumran have long recognized the multitude and variety of language employed for the righteous and unrighteous in the scrolls — which goes well beyond merely the standard terms like "righteous," "elect," "sinners," "wicked," and the like. Some passages from the scrolls are virtual inventories of sectarian terms used to define and contrast the sect with nonsectarians. Frequently these passages are extremely important due to their position in the documents or for other reasons such as their authorship. The following three examples are representative and are taken from the opening lines of the Community Rule, a Founder Hymn, and a major doctrinal (perhaps revelatory) discourse from the Damascus Document (the significant phrases are italicized in all three texts).

9. Cf. J. J. Enz, "Origin of the Dualism Expressed by 'Sons of Light' and 'Sons of Darkness,'" 1976, 18; contrast Gammie, 1974, 357-58.

10. J. H. Charlesworth ("A Critical Comparison of the Dualism in 1QS III,13–IV,26 and the 'Dualism' Contained in the Fourth Gospel," 1969, 389 n. 1) defines "soteriological dualism" as "the division of mankind caused by faith (acceptance) or disbelief (rejection) in a saviour." This represents a very *Christianized* definition, and one can make the term more applicable here by replacing the words "a saviour" with "a saving revelation," "a way of salvation," or the like.

11. We have, in this regard, already implied that foreign ideological influences may not have been as strong as traditional Hebraic ones, and it is becoming a valid assumption that Jewish thought is much more likely to operate on concrete and functional levels rather than on abstract or ontological ones.

The opening lines of 1QS amount to a summary of the whole Rule. The significance of the passage hardly needs to be argued. The presence of a love-hate dualism in this passage exemplifies the deep consciousness of the soteriological dualism that reverberates within every aspect of the writing that follows:

> . . . the rule of the Community; to seek God with [all their heart] and [all their soul] [and] to do what is good and right before Him, as He commanded by the hand of Moses and all His servants the Prophets; and *to love all that He has chosen and hate all that He has despised;*[12] and to depart from all evil and cling to all good works; . . . *that they may love all the sons of light,* each according to his lot[13] in the *Council of God;* and *that they may hate all the sons of darkness,* each according to his fault in the Vengeance of God.[14]

And so the scroll continues. Ringgren compares the contents of this scroll, its teaching on the two ways, its cultic directions, and its rule for congregational discipline with similar features in the *Didache* and the *Epistle of Barnabas* — both of which are also strongly dualistic works. Does this suggest that some later expressions of Christian soteriological dualism or "Christian exclusivism," as it is sometimes called, are rooted in Jewish thought?[15] The priority, in terms of conceptual composition of this passage, in any event, certainly belongs to soteriological dualism, not to cosmic dualism, as some have thought.[16]

In 1QH 2.8-18 the psalmist, almost certainly the *moreh ṣedeq,* reflects on his work as the founding member of the community. The division within Israel again provides the significant terminology.[17]

---

12. The object of love/hate — "all" — would appear to include both people (cf. ll. 9-11) and things (cf. ll. 4-7; cf. P. Wernberg-Møller, *The Manual of Discipline,* 1957, 45).

13. As elsewhere, גורל, "lot," retains its basic association with two groups of people, combining, however, the aspect of predetermination; cf. Wernberg-Møller (1957, 47) *contra* A. Dupont-Sommer (*The Essene Writings from Qumran,* 1961, 73 n. 2), who takes it to refer merely to "destiny."

14. The phrase could mean "in the Day of Vengeance" (A. R. C. Leaney, *The Rule of Qumran and Its Meaning,* 1966, 121) or "at the time of God's vengeance" (Wernberg-Møller, 1957, 22), the idea then being that the group's attitude toward others reflects their beliefs about the basis of God's judgment of them at the End; on the other hand, the expression as used in Num. 31:3 and Jer. 50:5 is not eschatological, and may refer to the sect taking physical action against apostates (1QS 1.1-5, 9-11; cf. 9.16).

15. The common use of a similar catechetical genre may also point to some important ideological similarities between the groups who produced these various writings. Cf. H. Ringgren, *The Faith of Qumran,* 1963, 3.

16. Cf. M. A. Knibb, *The Qumran Community,* 1987, 80.

17. Curiously Holm-Nielsen finds nothing particularly significant about the psalm: "everything in the psalm can be explained from Old Testament models. It does not contain any conscious theology. . . . The psalm may be said, therefore, to be derivative poetry based

And I have been a snare for *sinners,* but healing for *all those that are converted from sin,*[18] prudence for *the simple* and the firm inclination of *all those whose heart is troubled.* And Thou hast made of me an object of shame and mockery for *traitors,* but the foundation of truth and understanding for *them whose way is straight.* And I was exposed to the affronts of the *wicked,* an object of slander upon the lips of the *violent;*[19] the *mockers* gnashed their teeth. And I was ridiculed in the songs of *sinners* and the assembly of the *wicked* raged against me and roared like the storms upon the seas when their billows rage throwing up mud and slime. But Thou hast made of me a banner for the *elect of righteousness* and an interpreter of Knowledge concerning the marvellous Mysteries, to test [*the men*] *of truth* and to try *them that love instruction.* And I was a man of dispute for the *interpreters of straying,* [but a man of pea]ce for *all who see true things;* and I became a spirit of jealousy to *all who seek smooth things.* And *all the men of deceit* roared against me like the clamour of the roaring of great waters, and ruses of Belial were all their thoughts; and they cast down toward the Pit the life of the man by whose mouth Thou hast established the teaching and within whose heart Thou hast set understanding that he might open the fountain of Knowledge to *all the understanding.*

CD(B) 2.16-21 uses similar terminology to express the idea that the division in Israel is to become the basis of judgment. Much of the language of the passage is derived from Mal. 3:16-18 — appropriately enough, since Malachi is one of the strictest, in terms of requirements for membership in the true people of God, among all the books in the Hebrew Scriptures.

God's Anger will be kindled against *Israel. . . .* But *those who are converted from the sin of Jacob, who have kept the Covenant of God,* they will then speak one with another to justify *each man his brother* by supporting their steps in the way of God. And *God will heed their words* and will hear, and *a reminder will be written [before Him]* of them that *fear God* and of *them that revere His Name,* until Salvation and Justice are revealed to *them that fear God.* And you will distinguish anew between the *just and the wicked,* between *him that has served God* and *him that has served Him not.*

---

on O.T. models" (*Hodayot,* 1960, 39). Preferable is the view of Knibb: "Two features stand out in this material. The first is the frequent use of traditional imagery derived from the psalms of lament. The second is the use of terms for the opponents and followers of the psalmist that are sectarian in character" (1987, 166).

18. Holm-Nielsen: "פשע does not seem to indicate moral sins, but rather the ungodly world, so that the expression becomes a technical term for those who have turned away from sin and taken refuge in the covenant" (1960, 34).

19. Knibb renders the word "ruthless"; "those who act ruthlessly against the covenant" is a technical term for opponents in various scrolls (1987, 167).

These three passages demonstrate a deep consciousness of the rift within Israel. This consciousness permeates all the vocabulary of Qumran. While such dualistic terminology is frequently commented on (and hardly needs further comment here), there are other less-studied motifs that are also extremely interesting for the study of both Judaism and Christianity. Among these are a group of agricultural metaphors that, for various reasons, provide significant insight into the soteriological dualism of these groups. These will form the subject matter of the remainder of this chapter.

SEED THEOLOGY

One very provocative concept in these writings is the *zera*, "seed." The celebrated place in Jewish thought and literature enjoyed by this word no doubt partly stems from its suggestive presence in the divine address to the serpent in Eden ("I will put enmity between you and the woman, / *and between your seed and her seed*," Gen. 3:15) or from the promise spoken to Abraham ("*in your seed* shall all the nations of the earth be blessed," Gen. 22:18). "Seed" is not only an important symbol but also a conveniently adaptable symbol, since it serves equally well as an agricultural or genealogical (and therefore anthropological) metaphor.[20] Indeed, these two uses are regularly combined.[21]

In the writings we are studying the seed becomes a metaphor for the *origins* of good and evil people, but the usage is also broadened and applied more generally to all kinds of good and evil things — for example, the "seed of life,"[22] seed as a kind of spiritual material[23] or a kind of influence,[24] and perhaps even

20. The word was also widely used for male semen, which use was certainly related to the other sense: "seed" = descendants.

21. So in an enigmatic *1 En.* 80:2-3 we read about the failure of crops for the sinners. The relationship of "seed" to the crops, or alternatively to the offspring of the sinners, appears to be deliberately ambiguous. Isaac, who also notes the presence of a *"double entendre"* here (*OTP*, 1:58 n. *f*), translates: "In respect to their days, the sinners and the winter are cut short. *Their* seed(s) shall lag behind in their lands and in their fertile fields, and in all *their* activities upon the earth."

22. *1 En.* 67:2 (cf. v. 3, however, where this "seed of life" seems to be related to Noah's descendants: "I shall strengthen *your seed*"); cf. also *2 Bar.* 57:1-2.

23. *1 En.* 39:1; cf. *2 Bar.* 70:2, where the adopted reading is "the harvest of the seed (*[d]zr'why*, lit. '[of] his seeds') of the evil ones and the good ones," and where, in the context of judgment, the seeds may refer to the offspring, as well as more generally to the results of the spiritual influence, of good and evil angels (or even humans).

24. *2 Bar.* 42:4-5. Here also the "seed" may refer merely to human offspring; cf. P. Bogaert, *Apocalypse de Baruch*, 1969, 2:75-76.

the two *yĕṣerîm*.[25] It would seem, however, that these derived meanings all more or less relate back to the application of the seed motif to the existence of two groups of people. The variety in usage, therefore, owes less to a process where differing *sources* for the seed motif were brought together and synthesized, as happened in many other biblical motifs in Judaism, and more to a consistent overriding *central theme* to which many applications have been more or less related. All of the above-mentioned applications of the motif will prove to tolerate if not actually invite interpretations relating them to the definition of two peoples, the righteous and the unrighteous. Since it possessed this property, we can see that the word "seed" functioned as an *evocative* or *suggestive symbol*. In spite of the diversity of usages brought on by a wide variety of applications and contexts, in other words, the word served as a *clue* that what the author was really speaking about was good and evil *associated with a people* — the "good" seed versus the "bad" seed. In such cases the exact referent of the word is less important than the overall effect that its presence evoked in its readers as it called attention to the division within Israel.[26]

The idea of the *zeraʿ* lent itself well to such a theology of division since it was already used in similar contexts and for similar purposes in the late books (and editions) of the Hebrew Scriptures.[27] Its appropriateness as an *anthropological* motif is also obvious inasmuch as in Hebrew thought the human "seed" was viewed as a substantial element in the makeup of humankind from creation. It has been argued that each person in Hebrew society was considered, in essence, little more than a mature seed (or subsequent growth from a seed, as the case may be), not unlike what was perceived to have been the case in the plant world. These ideas about the seed's ultimate origins, and each individual as a seed, may have suggested the more generic classification of humankind as "seed," a use we find frequently in the literature under investigation. Perhaps

25. 4 Ezra 4:30; 8:6; although see discussion on pp. 374-75 below.

26. For presuppositions regarding the use of the word as a symbol in a social context, cf. ch. 1. Perhaps the most consistent semantic element in all of these uses is the idea of God as the source of the good seed. Σπέρμα was also employed in the Greek world for the "divine seed" and for spiritual offspring; cf. S. Schulz, *TDNT*, 7:536-37; cf. also 1 John 3:9. We cannot agree with G. Quell in the same *TDNT* article (538-41), that the word always carries with it the idea of the growth of organisms, being alive, vitality, force of life, etc. These secondary meanings are quite abstract and hardly evident in many instances.

27. Cf., e.g., Jer. 2:21; 31:27; Isa. 57:4; where the idea of good and bad seed is applied to groups of people. Mal. 2:15 appears to apply the term "God's seed" to the righteous who shun mixed marriages. Cf. also זֶרַע הַקֹּדֶשׁ in Ezra 9:2; זֶרַע צַדִּיקִם in Prov. 11:21. The LXX (cf. also Rom. 9:29) has σπέρμα for שָׂרִיד כִּמְעַט in Isa. 1:9, as also in some MSS of Isa. 6:13 (in place of the more literal λεῖμμα, "remnant"). Gen. 3:15 is also highly suggestive for this use.

more importantly, however, the seed concept could be removed from the ana-
tomical sphere altogether and *spiritualized,* especially where the "seed" inherited by each person was also believed to have communicated to that person his
or her moral characteristics.

The general outline of the seed theology in these writings is clear (although it does need to be reconstructed somewhat), and it goes something
like this: at creation humankind received its "seed" from God, but the fall of
the evil Watchers resulted in a new race with a new seed, whereupon the mass
of creation became "evil seed"; although the world was cleansed of sin in the
time of Noah (cf. *1 En.* 83:3-10; 84:5-6), the evil seed soon cropped up again
in Noah's sons. As can be seen from this summary, the seed does not need to
be viewed as a permanent fixture in the individual: an evil seed can be
"planted" in the heart of any person, and can, in turn, be replaced with the
good seed. This latter experience is preeminently that of Abraham, through
whom the good seed was allowed to propagate once again. The new seed
given to Abraham, however, continued to be evidenced in only *some* of Abraham's sons. It is this qualification that *only some received the good seed* that
forms the focus of the teaching, while it also reveals just how spiritualized
was the seed concept.[28] It is not all of Abraham's sons (the physical seed of
Abraham) but only the spiritual seed of Abraham that perpetuates the good
seed. Thus we are told that the seed of the wicked will experience curse (*1 En.*
80:2-3), judgment (*1 En.* 108:3; *Jub.* 16:7-9; 36:9-11), and obliteration (*1 En.*
80:2-3; 84:6; *Jub.* 16:7-9; 35:14). The individual possessing good seed, in contrast, will experience blessing and salvation.

This seed theology, as can be seen from the texts cited above, is primarily
found in the Enochian corpus, though it was also adopted by later writers. A
helpful example of this theology comes in the first dream-vision, in which
Enoch receives a terrifying vision of judgment, which he relates to his grandfather Mahalalel. (This vision contains a double reference — it alludes to both
the deluge and a future judgment: see further below.) In response to the dream
Mahalalel advises Enoch to "pray to the Lord of glory . . . so that a remnant
shall remain upon the earth and that the whole earth shall not be blotted out"
(*1 En.* 83:8; see further chs. 83–84). This view of Noah's experience as the preservation of a "remnant" is brought into direct relation to the seed theology of
the author. The actual prayer of Enoch is related in the verses that follow: "Do
not destroy, O my Lord, the flesh that has angered you from upon the earth, but

---

28. In the final chapters of *1 Enoch* the seed of the wicked one is virtually equated
with the spirit of that person, granting it a definite role in the psychological or anthropological makeup of the person; cf. the interesting expression "their seeds shall be destroyed
forever and their spirits shall perish and die" (108:3).

sustain the flesh of righteousness and uprightness as a *plant of eternal seed . . .*" (84:6). We can take it from this and similar passages that this theology is concerned with the sustaining or preserving of a righteous seed through all of the contingencies of history, particularly through all the judgments of God. Following this passage the book goes on to enlarge on the theme of the perpetuation of righteous and wicked seed in the so-called Zoomorphic History (or Animal Apocalypse), which traces the history of Israel in terms of good and evil offspring (white sheep and various other animals; e.g., *1 En.* 85:8-10). Although it is implicitly a history of the preservation of the righteous seed, however, the word "seed" itself is not used. It would seem that in the Zoomorphic History the function of the good seed has been assumed by the color white, which compares closely to the seed in its role of symbolizing the "pure substance" that guarantees the perpetuation of the righteous.

The Similitudes of Enoch also preserve what must be very early tradition about the holy seed in the same literary context as seen above in chs. 83–84. Here a kind of reversal of the consequences of the fallen Watchers takes place, as 39:1 suggests that a *new seed* will be planted in the hearts of the people who survive a future judgment: "And it shall come to pass in those days that the children of the elect and the holy ones will descend from the high heaven and *their seed* will become one with the children of the people. . . ." In place of the (wicked) "sons of God" impregnating the daughters of men, this time a more positively perceived conception is envisioned. This involves a highly spiritualized version of seed theology where "seed" seems to be equated with spirit. Whether the seed is originally that of the "elect" (= humans?) or "holy ones" (= angels?) is not entirely clear, but it is evident that this seed will be given to all the righteous "in those days." The Similitudes also trace this "righteous seed" (a spiritual substance or an anthropological principle?) back to Enoch, who seems to have been preserved for the very purpose of producing a righteous generation during the author's own time: "[God] has preserved *your righteous seed* for kingship and great glory; and *from your seed* will emerge a fountain of the righteous and holy ones without number forever" (65:12). The following words to Noah, which explain the purpose of his preservation in the flood, are certainly also significant for this seed theology: "I shall place my hands upon it [the ark] and protect it, and *the seed of life* [!] shall arise from it; and a substitute (generation) will come so that the earth will not remain empty. I shall strengthen *your seed* before me forever and ever as well as *the seeds of those who dwell with you*" (67:2-3). The origin of this idea of the preservation of Noah's seed, already witnessed in *1 Enoch* 83–84, appears to have something to do with the words *lᵉhâyyôt zeraʿ*, "preserve (keep alive) seed," in Gen. 7:3, a verse that is certainly in mind in this passage. If Noah's experiences as related in the Similitudes and elsewhere are to be taken as paradigmatic for the author's own generation —

317

and what other reason would there be for such embellishments? — that would make the flood a type of a future judgment and the seed of Noah a type of the surviving righteous who continue to represent the faithful people of God (in all likelihood, the writer's community).[29]

The fate of the righteous seed is an outstanding feature of *Jubilees* as well, a work that also assumes the shared seed theology mentioned above. Thus *Jub.* 4:7 is careful to repeat the words of Adam to Eve, "The LORD has raised up *another seed* for us upon the earth in place of Abel because Cain killed him" (Gen. 4:25).[30] It is worth noting in this respect that in *Jubilees,* as in Genesis, it is from this "seed" that the righteous line of Enosh, Enoch, and Noah is specifically said to descend (Gen. 5:6-31; *Jub.* 4:11ff.). In contrast to Genesis the account in *Jubilees* appears to be quite embellished, however, adding the names of wives and the circumstances of their marriage to the patriarchs, perhaps revealing the more detailed tradition that had developed around the antediluvian genealogy of Genesis (an extremely important tradition for *Jubilees*). *Jubilees* retains another important motif related to this concern, namely, *the naming of the righteous line of antediluvian patriarchs,* a motif that is associated in turn with the idea of the *perpetuation of the righteous seed — that is, the seed of Seth.* A reference to the righteous seed of Seth is made in a passage that delineates the righteous line of antediluvian patriarchs. It comes in the narratives about Jacob, of whom it is said: "and in his seed my [Abraham's] name will be blessed *and the names of my fathers Shem and Noah, and Enoch, and Mahalalel, and Enos, and Seth, and Adam*" (19:24).[31] It is worthy to note that a similar appreciation and

29. M. Black (*The Book of Enoch* or *I Enoch,* 1985, 241) prefers to see a wordplay in v. 3: "I will establish your offspring before me for ever and ever, and I will spread abroad (taking *zarawa* as equivalent to √ זרה piel) those who dwell with you" (i.e., the animals). It is clear, however, that the "seeds of those who dwell with you" is to be understood, according to Gen. 7:3, of the *animals* that are with Noah, and thus the notion of "seed" is appropriate.

30. Eth. *zar'* = Heb. זרע.

31. Only the most righteous are named here: Jared and Kenan are omitted. Cf. also v. 27 of the passage, which singles out Adam, Enoch, Noah, and Shem, who are also the significant figures throughout this literature. The mention of Shem alludes to his importance as the origin of the righteous seed. Cf. also 22:12-13, which mentions the seed of Seth and the names of Noah and Adam. The expression "all the seed of Seth" in those verses seems to come from Num. 24:17 (where, however, as Charles, *The Book of Jubilees or Little Genesis, Translated from the Editor's Ethiopic Text,* 1902, 139, points out, כל בני־שת may originally have meant "all the sons of *confusion*"). In the context we have been uncovering for the Sethite motif, it would seem strange that the expression would refer to all mankind (as cf. Charles, 1902, 139); it might better be taken as equivalent to the "righteous seed," "some of your sons," "your seed," and "holy people" in the same verses. *1 En.* 37:1 also preserves this order in the line of righteousness going from Adam to Enoch.

respect for the "seed of Seth" is evident in Sethian Gnosticism, pointing to a possible point of contact between these writings and later Gnostic traditions, although it *might* be argued that the mention of Seth does not particularly stand out from the other names in the list in *Jub.* 19:24. Furthermore, one cannot easily detect in *Jubilees* the full-blown anthropological dualism of the Gnostic writings (humankind's fate dualistically predetermined by the possession or lack of the seed of Seth *as a biological principle*). Nevertheless, the idea of the seed of Seth (and that of the entire antediluvian righteous ancestry) would appear to be presented here as a highly spiritualized concept. Thus, while there were many "sons" of Adam, Seth, and so on, it is *only through Jacob* that the righteous seed is perpetuated, thus encapsulating the idea of a kind of spiritual inheritance of righteousness.[32]

In another prayer of Abraham we see a vital connection drawn between the rule of spirits over humankind and the possession of this righteous seed, which tends to confirm the spiritualization of the idea.

> Save me from the hands of evil spirits
> which rule over the thought of the heart of man,
> and do not let them lead me astray from following you, O my God;
> but establish me and *my seed* forever,
> and let us not go astray henceforth and forever. (*Jub.* 12:20; cf. *1 En.* 108:3)

This passage implies a dualism of seeds in Abraham's offspring only in an indirect way as it expresses the potentiality that the seed would be influenced by evil. It also follows from this prayer, and from the contingencies that it anticipates, that the promise of God to give Abraham righteous seed does not apply automatically to all of Israel, in spite of God's affirmative answer to Abraham's prayer: "And I shall be God for you and your son and for the son of your son and for *all of your seed*" (v. 24). The seed concept, in fact, would appear to be employed here precisely to *qualify* "sons" who, in this case, are equivalent to the "righteous sons" of Abraham, since the potentiality of some of the seed being misled is sustained throughout the passage, and indeed its *inevitability* is adequately portrayed in the events of Israel's history as related by *Jubilees* as a whole, as observed earlier.[33]

---

32. J. C. VanderKam ("The Granddaughters and Grandsons of Noah," 1994a, 457-61) shows how the *Genesis Apocryphon* (1QapGn) from Qumran goes to some trouble to list and match the number of granddaughters and grandsons of Noah so that marriages could be confined to the immediate family of Shem and the line of Shem remain uncontaminated after the flood.

33. The inevitability of apostasy is held out, e.g., in the opening passages of the book, in which God's promise to Israel is mentioned (*Jub.* 1:7-25). For similar ideas about

Further qualification and definition of the idea of the righteous seed is implied in the insistence that *only one* of Isaac's seed will continue to flourish. Such statements in *Jubilees* are likely to be paradigmatic and evidence the *principle* of the *selectivity* of seed, a process that in *Jubilees* includes the continual redefinition and *reduction of the righteous seed*. For example, 16:16-18, by means of various embellishments, emphasizes that while Abraham and Isaac had *many* sons, only a select line would be chosen:

> And we [angels] blessed him [Abraham] and we announced to him . . . that he would not die until he begot six more sons and he would see them before he died. And [better: "but"] through Isaac a name and seed would be named for him. And all of the seed of his sons would become nations. And they would be counted with the nations. But from the sons of Isaac one would become a holy seed and he would not be counted among the nations because he would become the portion of the Most High and all his seed would fall into that which God will rule so that he might become a people to the LORD, a possession from all people, and so that he might become a kingdom of priests and a holy people.[34]

Here the promise is that Jacob specifically would arise as a "holy seed," which cannot refer to all of Jacob's descendants. That the writer intended such a qualification on this seed is evident in the similar characterization of Abraham's righteous seed as "a righteous planting" and a "holy seed" (v. 26) — terms that effectively define the people of God as the members of the author's community.[35] Moreover, this is the only conclusion to be drawn from the fact that the truly righteous "seed" are identified as obeying the correct order for the feasts:

> And we eternally blessed him *and his seed who are after him* in every generation of the earth[36] because he observed this feast in its appointed time according to the testimony of the heavenly tablets. Therefore it is ordained in the heavenly tablets concerning Israel that they will be observers of the feast

---

Israel's seed being influenced by apostasy, cf. 4Q388 where we read about a "son of Belial" who "will cause the multitude to be defiled (and) there will be no seed left" (although "seed" might refer to the failure of crops here), and 4Q390 where we read that the apostates "will pollute their seed."

34. Contrast the much shorter version in Gen. 25:1-2.

35. Cf. the use of "righteous planting" in 36:6 (cf. also 1:16; 21:24); for the application of this terminology to the author's community, see below.

36. The significance of the words "his seed who are *after him* in every generation of the earth" may be more than temporal. The idea of "after" may itself imply an ideological as well as a genealogical connection.

of booths seven days with joy in the seventh month. . . . And there is no limit of days for this. . . . (vv. 28-30)[37]

The mention of Jacob's "seed" is particularly conspicuous in Abraham's blessing of Jacob (19:15-24), which is also a lengthy embellishment of Gen. 25:28 — "Isaac loved Esau . . . but Rebekah loved Jacob." That the author is not simply repeating the biblical account but is deliberately promoting a doctrine of the reduction/selection of the *spiritual* seed is again indicated by the prayer for protection of the seed against Mastema: "And may the spirit of Mastema not rule over you or *over your seed* in order to remove you from following the LORD who is your God" (v. 28). The implication here is accordingly clear: all who follow the spirit of Mastema — the opponents of the order prescribed in *Jubilees* — are disqualified from the "seed" of Abraham. Their "seed" will not be saved anymore than that of Esau, who forsook God — "both he and his sons" — apparently by seeking Gentile wives (35:14).[38] It is not accidental, therefore, that Abraham refers to the progeny of Isaac as "your seed and the *remnant of your seed*" (21:25).

Similarly in another important passage Abraham blesses Jacob with words that refer, in a qualified manner, to *"some"* of Isaac's sons:

> May the God of all . . . *elect* you and your seed *so that you become* a people for him who always belong to his inheritance *according to his will.* . . .

> *May* the LORD give you *righteous seed*,
> and may he sanctify *some of your sons* in the midst of all the earth. . . .
> Be strong before men;
> and rule over all *the seed of Seth*;
> *then* may your ways be righteous, and the ways of your sons,
> in order to be a holy people.
> May the Most High God give you all the blessings
> with which he blessed me,
> and with which he blessed Noah and Adam;
> may they rest upon *the holy head*[39] *of your seed* throughout

---

37. Further definition of the seed is implied in the banishment of Ishmael (i.e., since Hagar was not an acceptable spouse for Abraham; 17:4-7). The account is similar to that of Gen. 21:9-21 with the apparently significant omission in *Jubilees* of the second of the promises to Ishmael that he would become a "great nation."

38. In this respect it is interesting how 30:10 states that one's seed is given to *Moloch* as a result of intermarriage.

39. Charles takes Gen. 49:26 and Num. 6:9 to be the source of this expression. While the context of the latter passage throws little light on its use here, it is notable how Gen. 49:26 (which also contains a reference to Jacob within the blessing of Joseph) might be

> each generation and forever. . . .
> And may he *renew* his covenant with you,
> *so that* you might be a people for him, belonging
> to his inheritance forever. (*Jub.* 22:10, 11, 12-13, 15)

This passage is replete with dualistic terminology, in the midst of which one finds several references to the "seed." The significance of some of the terms is not entirely clear, but the highly qualified and conditional tone of these promises is obvious, being correctly emphasized in translation through the employment of conditional clauses ("may he/you . . . then/so that," etc.). Other references to the propagation of the righteous seed are similarly qualified. We read, for example, that Isaac's seed will be blessed because Abraham was obedient to the covenant (24:11; likewise Isaac, 36:6). *If* Jacob respects the prohibition of marrying Gentiles, the Most High will bless him "and [his] children will be a righteous generation and a holy seed" (25:3; contrast Gen. 28:1-4, where the blessing is offered unilaterally). In the same passage it is said that righteousness will be "revealed" to the seed of Jacob (25:15). These qualifications demonstrate that the matter of belonging to the holy seed was entirely *conditional*.

The principle of selectivity and reduction that one finds in *Jubilees* is certainly also responsible for the interest shown by the book in the wives of the patriarchs. Their roles not only help to explain *why* only some of their husbands were chosen, but establish the vital importance of the proper *combination* of patriarch and matriarch for the earliest processes of this selection. That all these devices are intended to exhort and warn the present generation of Israelites is obvious. The seed theology of this writing is summarized in the maxim: "May the LORD Most High bless the man who does righteousness, *him and his seed forever*" (36:16). A statement like this in the form of a petition has the effect of individualizing and contemporizing the election process already seen to be at work in the patriarchal history. Such sayings also reveal the heart of the message of *Jubilees*.

It is worth mentioning here that another of the exceptional themes of *Ju-*

---

taken to signify a reduction in the seed; cf. RSV: "The blessings of your father / . . . / may they be on the head of Joseph, / *and on the brow of him who was separate from his brothers.*" The allusion in the last phrase is obviously to the righteous attitude of Joseph, although our author may not have interpreted the expression in terms of the synthetic parallelism intended by Genesis, so much as taken it as a separate reference to those particularly righteous individuals from among Jacob's descendants. (Note that the expression in MT, נְזִיר אֶחָיו, may have played a similar role in an early Nazarite ideology.) The Eth. rendering "holy head" is therefore not only awkward but misleading. Apparently the author intended to say something like "may [the blessings of Abraham] rest upon the head of those of [Jacob's] seed who separate themselves," which is an exact parallel to the expression "sanctify some of your sons" in v. 11.

bilees is the distinct preference for the figure of Jacob over his brother Esau. In comparison to Genesis, *Jubilees* provides an exaggerated and embellished view of the enmity between Jacob and Esau. It has been suggested (anticipating a closer look at this in a later chapter) that the purpose of the Jacob-Esau motif is to emphasize the destruction of brotherly interrelations that characterized *the time of the writer.* What is more important here, however, is the implication this kind of typology possessed for the theology of the seed. This theology is frequently intermingled with the Jacob-Esau theme; in fact, the majority of the references to the "seed" in *Jubilees* are found in those sections recounting Jacob's taking of the blessing from Esau. The purpose of this would appear to be to outline the contingencies, as well as the forces of providence, involved in the process of defining the true seed.[40] While good things are spoken about Jacob's seed, warnings about the judgment and removal of the seed are made in regard to Esau.[41] The closely related themes of brotherly relations and the reduction of the holy seed are suggestively combined and seem to be applied to the writer's generation in the announcement that the "seed" of him who harms his brother will be judged (*Jub.* 36:6, 9-11).[42] It is from this example of Jacob and Esau, in other words, that a general maxim is drawn that the Lord will bless "the man who does righteousness, him and his seed forever" (36:16). Jacob and Esau appear in this way as paradigms of the righteous and unrighteous seed in the author's time.

Similar to this Jacob-Esau theme, and not limited to the book of *Jubilees* this time, is the portrayal of the patriarchs Levi and Judah. Some remnant groups apparently considered themselves the true spiritual offspring of those two preeminent tribes (again anticipating forthcoming discussion), just as others thought of themselves as the true offspring of Jacob. In this connection it is worth noting the special blessing in *Jub.* 31:5-20, 31-32 of the seed of Levi and Judah, who are appointed to "bless all of the *seed of the beloved*" (v. 15). The blessing —

> Whoever blesses you will be blessed,
> and all who hate you and afflict you and curse you
> will be uprooted and destroyed from the earth and they shall be cursed
> (v. 20)

---

40. Cf. ch. 26; 27:19-27. The latter passage, which contains only occasional elaborations, is an almost exact replica of Gen. 28:10-22; reasons for this uncharacteristic adherence to the text are not clear, although it is interesting how the Genesis passage itself centers on the idea of Jacob's "seed"; the author may have wished to preserve this emphasis for the sake of his own seed theology.

41. Cf. esp. 35:14; cf. also words regarding Ishmael's seed in 17:4-7.

42. Cf. the account of Esau's unprovoked attack in ch. 37.

— is apparently directed, through this literary device, to the righteous in Israel living at the time of the author.

The *Testaments of the Twelve Patriarchs* (in their present recensions as well as their sources) dwell on the Levi and Judah theme even more consistently, and probably with similar motivations. Here again the "seed" of Levi (or Judah) is associated with great blessing in the future (*TLevi* 4:3). In *TLevi* 15:4, however, it appears that even the descendants of Levi will be in danger of obliteration because of their sin. One way to explain this apparently contradictory preference for Levi's seed *alongside warnings* against his tribe is to view the association with these patriarchs as spiritual or paradigmatic rather than genealogical. Thus it is the seed of the *true* followers of Levi, not his natural descendants, who will be blessed. *TLevi* 15:4 also implies the reduction of Levi's seed to a still smaller seed to be spared from among his descendants (in this sense not differently from the other tribes), so that again there is no question of inviolable privilege based on natural ancestry.[43]

The idea of the propagation of a righteous seed is also found in the Dead Sea Scrolls. In a fairly lengthy consideration of Israel's history, the author of the Damascus Document summarizes: "And in all these times [God] raised up for Himself men named with a name, in order to leave survivors upon the earth and to fill the face of the world with their *posterity (mizzar'ām)*" (2.11-12). That this posterity consists of the remnant made up of the Qumran community is the only conclusion to be drawn from a passage in the War Scroll: "Thou madest a Covenant with our fathers and hast established it *with their seed* for everlasting ages. And a reminder of Thy Grace is in the midst of us in all Thy glorious testimonies, to succour the remnant and the survivors of Thy Covenant" (13.7-8). "A reminder of Thy Grace" is an enigmatic phrase perhaps referring to the revelation granted to the community, or to the individual "testimony" of its members, who relate their experience of God's graciousness in delivering them or in delivering their ancestors (cf. "all Thy glorious testimonies"), and both suggestions have been offered. In using this particular lan-

---

43. If righteous Lot's seed can be removed (God "will not leave seed of man for him on the earth in the day of judgment," *Jub.* 16:9), this becomes a paradigm for any who sin that they might also have their seed "removed" and "uprooted." The biblical precedent for the removal of the seed of sinners is abundant, but the removal of Lot's seed is not mentioned in the account of Genesis; its presence here reflects a principle that, in its individualistic theology, is applied to all who sin. Other passages that mention a "seed" in the *Testaments* apparently refer to a messianic person (*TReub.* 6:12; *TLevi* 4:3?). *TSim.* 6:5 associates the glorification of Seth (or Shem, depending on the MS) with the manifestation of a messianic personage. The divinity of this figure may suggest a Christian addition, while his relationship to Seth (or Shem) raises the problem of what kind of Christian group would produce such a saying.

guage of memorial, and given the immediate context, however, it would seem rather to point to the covenant renewal celebrations. In any case it is this special possession of the community ("in the midst *of us*") that sustains the members of the *yaḥaḏ*, who compose the "remnant and survivors *of Thy Covenant*," the "seed" that bears the torch of covenant faithfulness first given to the fathers. In this way the idea of the seed promised to the patriarchs is emancipated from strictly genealogical application. The writer has no qualms about alluding to his own group as that "seed" first promised to Abraham.[44]

Seed theology also provides a valuable point of contact for understanding the *Psalms of Solomon*. These psalms typically advance no assurances regarding the purity of Israel's seed. In one place the pedigree of the Jerusalemites themselves is placed in question; speaking of Pompey's attack on the "inhabitants of Jerusalem," *Psalms of Solomon* 8 relates that "[Pompey] led away their sons and daughters, *those profanely spawned (ha egennēsan)*. / They acted according to their uncleanness, *just as their ancestors*" (vv. 20-22a, probably referring to the priests who ignored the Levitical ceremonial laws).[45] A similar message is to be gleaned from the messianic *Psalms of Solomon* 17, which states unequivocally that it was specifically to David's seed that the promise was made (vv. 4-6; contrast: "those to whom you did not promise," v. 5). That is why in the destruction of Jerusalem certain other "seed" *(sperma)* were "uprooted" (vv. 7, 9). God "hunted down their descendants *(sperma)*, and did not let even one of them go" (v. 9). While one cannot argue that only the direct descendants of David were considered to form the limits of God's people, it would appear that only those who have aligned themselves with David's promise receive the blessing promised to him (see further below). The author does not seek to redefine the righteous seed by taking away the promise to Abraham (and Jacob, 18:3); nevertheless the passage shows that the author does not acknowledge any inviolable privilege based strictly on ancestry. This is true even in a passage that appears otherwise to promote a traditional view of Israel's election (18:3-5). Even here the promise to the "seed of Abraham" is restricted to those who respond positively in repentance to the experience of Israel's judgment. The passage states that "your love is for the seed of Abraham, an Israelite," but this must be taken in association with what follows,

> Your discipline for us is as for a firstborn son, an only child,
> *to divert the perceptive person from unintentional sins* [lit. "from ignorance

---

44. For other "seed" sayings in the scrolls, cf. 4Q386, "there will be no seed left," in reference either to the exile or to a future time of apostasy; and 4Q390, which similarly says of Israel, "they will pollute their seed."

45. Cf. H. E. Ryle and M. R. James, *ΨΑΛΜΟΙ ΣΟΛΟΜΩΝΤΟΣ*, 1891, 85.

in incomprehension"].

May God *cleanse Israel for the day of mercy*. . . . (18:3-5a)[46]

These psalms accordingly exhibit a strong consciousness of seed theology, differently expressed but in substance not unlike what has been seen so far.

4 Ezra provides a particularly interesting instance of the development of seed theology. In continuity with other seed traditions investigated above, 4 Ezra 3:11 states that all the righteous have descended from Noah,[47] but in other regards the seed motif is developed in this book in a variety of novel directions. In several passages the "seed" becomes almost equivalent to the later rabbinic idea of *yeṣerim,* although it is still markedly different from this later idea and is at best suggestive of rather than truly parallel to it (cf. 3:20-27; 4:30; 8:6).[48] Perhaps the chief advance over the earlier form of the seed motif, however, is that 4 Ezra typically focuses more on the rationalization of the division in Israel than on its historical roots in the patriarchal era. It is accordingly upon this more philosophical concern that 4 Ezra brings the seed motif to bear, which tends to spiritualize the motif considerably. One example of this kind of spiritualization, and one that is of considerable relevance to the New Testament, is found in a kind of "seed parable" not unlike some of the seed parables of the Gospels.[49] "For just as the farmer sows many seeds upon the ground and plants a multitude of seedlings, and yet not all that have been sown will come up[50] in due season, and not all that were

---

46. Wright, *OTP,* 2:669 n. *d;* cf. n. *e,* comments that the phraseology mimics Prov. 13:1; 21:28 ("he who hears"), and is directed at "one who is sensitive to the learning experience of punishment."

47. "Dereliquisiti autem ex his unum, Noe cum domo sua; ex eo iustos omnes" may, in the light of passages like *1 En.* 84:5-6, etc., have originally contained a reference to Noah's seed (cf. Metzger, *OTP,* 1:528); in any event, the idea of all the righteous descending from Noah is present.

48. Cf. M. E. Stone, who traces the ideas of the evil heart and the evil *yeṣer* back to Gen. 6:5 (*Fourth Ezra,* 1990, 63 n. 18). But in passages like 4:30 and 8:6, the "seed" (which may or may not be *equated* with "heart"/inclination) is more closely associated with a kind of wisdom than with a psychological property such as is true of the later *yeṣerim* speculation, and it retains agricultural associations (note: "grain," "fruit," "cultivation," etc.; 4:30-32); somewhat closer to the idea of the *yeṣerim* than either the "evil seed" or "evil heart" may be the "evil root" of 3:22. On the other hand, if the heart and root motifs are all related to Deut. 29:18, as is probable, they might be taken as equivalents. There certainly does not seem to be careful systematization of the various motifs and concepts. For a suggestive association between *yeṣer* and apostasy, cf. Deut. 31:21, which certainly seems to have played a role in the formation of the *yeṣer* doctrine in 4 Ezra.

49. For the comparison, cf. R. J. Coggins and M. A. Knibb, *The First and Second Books of Esdras,* 1979, 206.

50. The Lat. renders the expression by *salvabuntur,* under the influence of the interpretation. Eth. and Syr. have "live" (Metzger, *OTP,* 1:543).

planted will take root; so all those who have been sown in the world will not be saved" (8:41). Here the author adopts an agricultural metaphor, but it can be easily seen from the interpretation (which is signaled by the word "so," Lat. *sic*) that the agricultural sense is only background for the "moral" of the parable: *as only some seeds actually germinate, so only some people will be saved.*[51]

Given the evocative presence of the seed motif in this parable, however, the question remains whether the entire significance of the parable has been appreciated simply because this basic surface meaning/correspondence has been intercepted. In light of the discussion of seed theology above, one would want to consider whether the word "seed" in this parable has not taken on some more *symbolic* value — that is, whether it evokes associations well beyond the agricultural level of meaning and contains *independent* significance *for the interpretation.* This in fact *is* suggested by the interpretation, which, perhaps surprisingly, carries on a level of meaning for seed beyond the agricultural realm — cf. "those who have been *sown* in the world." The sowing metaphor obviously not only functions as the "prop" for the parable but communicates the idea of God planting seeds of the righteous and the unrighteous in the world. Here the presence of the word "seed" effectively implies an entire seed theology. Not only is a comparison intended, therefore, on the first level of interpretation (i.e., not all seeds come up and not all people are saved), but the appearance of the word "seed" in the parable also conjures up, on a second level, a number of associations already held with respect to the word "seed": it is God who has planted good *and* evil seed in this world, and those who partake of the good seed will be saved and those who partake of the evil seed will not. The parable therefore goes from a statement of fact about the fewness of the saved to a suggestive allusion to the process and the conditions of election: one must contain the good seed — which perhaps in this context implies the teaching of the community. The implications for this second meaning therefore transcend those of the surface meaning considerably, for a relatively sterile point of fact ("few will be saved") now becomes a subtle claim on the part of the author and his community to hold saving truth. When the *entire* parable is read with this level of meaning in mind, the parable not only makes perfect sense but its significance is considerably heightened.

2 Baruch also seems to spiritualize the seed motif considerably. *2 Bar.* 42:4-5 implies that impure seed can result from "mingling with foreigners ("who mingled themselves with the seed of the mingled nations"; v. 4),[52] a sug-

---

51. Cf. Stone, 1990, 283-84.

52. *w'thltw czr" d'mm' dhbykyn.* Kljin's translation (*OTP*, 1:634) as given here is more literal than Argyle's (*AOT*, 862), who has "mingled with foreigners of mixed descent."

gestive allusion to the sin of apostates that involved either their intermarriage with Gentiles or sharing of a more general kind in pagan ungodliness.[53] The latter understanding is perhaps most supportable, for if intermarriage is intended by the "mingling," it is rather more difficult to understand the parallel phrase that follows: "who mingled with the seed of the people who have separated themselves" (v. 5), as this is a rather unique expression for "pure" marriage practices. Since the passage further suggests that this mingling can be repented of, perhaps the seed refers to a spiritual influence of some kind; it could conceivably refer to false teaching, or ritual impurity.[54] 2 Baruch again seems to be moving in the direction of a spiritual application of the seed motif when the "promise of life" granted to Abraham and his sons can be said to be "planted" in 57:1-2, suggesting that the good seed is a kind of "principle of life" planted within the righteous.[55] By analogy the evil seed would be a negative influence of some kind. One also encounters what amounts to a mixture of agricultural and genealogical metaphors in the description in 70:2 of the final judgment as "the time [when] the world has ripened and the harvest of the seed of the evil ones and the good ones has come." These "seeds" might refer to the human followers of evil angels and good angels (or spirits), or perhaps to the spirits or souls of the righteous and unrighteous. In sum, the ambiguous use of the term "seed" in 2 Baruch again points to its function as more of a suggestive *symbol* than a technical term with a consistent referent.

53. "Seed" might mean no more than "descendants," perhaps "race," in the verse (cf. Bogaert, 1969, 2:75-76, who translates "La race des peuples mélanges" and suggests that Syr. ʾr" might render Gk. διασπορά as *per* Sinaiticus MS of Syr. Gospels Jn. 7:35). It is not clear, however, that intermarriage with the diaspora would create offense, and in any event, the description of these people in v. 5 suggests pagans; it is better to compare the expression to הָעֶרֶב in Jer. 25:20, 24, "foreigners" (= ἐθνῶν συμμίκτων; *Pss. Sol.* 17:15) as Charles does (1897, 67); cf. also Neh. 13:3.

54. It is curious that *1 En.* 89:75 offers almost an exact parallel: "the sheep . . . got mixed among the wild beasts" (cf. R. H. Charles: "Israel sinned still further in mingling among the heathen nations" [*The Book of Enoch or 1 Enoch*, 1912, 204]; lit., according to Isaac, *OTP,* 1:69 n. g5: "they were joined together with them"). This phrase appears to assume a mixture of ideas and religion rather than intermarriage, although that too may have been intended. The emendation of our present passage by Charles, which equates the separated people with *Israel* (pl. ʾmmʾ, "of the peoples," to sg. ʾmʾ, "of the people [Israel]"; *The Apocalypse of Baruch translated from the Syriac,* 1896, 68; for rejection of this emendation as improbable, cf. Bogaert, 1969, 2:77), overlooks entirely the context of the passage (chs. 41–42), which teaches judgment on the basis of an individual's final state in a way similar to Ezekiel 18. The "separated people" are the righteous.

55. Schulz in fact (*TDNT,* 7:537, 543) centers seed terminology in this idea of creative element, or origin of life.

PLANT METAPHORS

Similar in function to the seed motif are a variety of other agricultural motifs that abound in these writings. One frequently reads of trees, forests, branches, vines, plants, and a variety of plant parts that serve as chief symbols in prayers, discourses, visions, and parables. It would seem at first glance quite impossible to discern a common link between such diverse images, drawn as they are from a wide variety of biblical sources and subject to the adaptation and application of the individual and often diverse purposes of the authors. In point of fact, however, these various images all seem to be related to one another and to reflect similar ideas. The unifying factor in their use may be explained by their origins. (1) The proximity of these images to the *zera'*-thematic in some texts suggests a relationship to seed ideas,[56] and it is even possible that these images "grew" out of seed theology or, at least, alongside of it. (2) An alternative explanation for their common function could be that all of these motifs are variations of a basic plant-thematic derived from a common expression found in these writings as well as in the Hebrew Scriptures — the dual expression "to be planted/uprooted." The Bible uses this metaphor for being established safely and securely "in the land" (to be "uprooted" implies curse, judgment, and removal from the land), and "being planted" is therefore also associated with covenant.[57] In the writings of our movement the expression is frequently removed from the context of a physical land,[58] but it is still regularly associated with a highly conditional view of covenant — for example: "Remember that once Moses called heaven and earth to witness against you and said, 'If you trespass the law, you shall be dispersed. And if you shall keep it, you shall be planted'" (*2 Bar.* 84:2).[59] So it would seem that this biblical usage could have been partly

---

56. *1 En.* 84:6 is suggestive of this. Isaac renders the expression "sustain the flesh of righteousness and uprightness as a *plant of eternal seed.*" Black discerns in the Eth. *takla zar'* an Aram. figure of speech, "as a seed-bearing plant," reflecting the similar expression in Gen. 1:11 (1985, 257). Either way the ideas of seed and plant are closely related in this verse. Cf. also 4 Ezra 4:28-32, 39, which contains a number of harvest metaphors; the reference to fruitfulness in 3:20 appears to be associated with the tree of life (cf. also 8:6; Stone, 1990, 73, 266; cf. also "root" in v. 22).

57. As can be discerned in texts like Exod. 15:17; 2 Sam. 7:10; 1 Chron. 17:9; Pss. 1:3; 44:2; 80:8-15; 92:3; Isa. 5:7; Jer. 2:21; 11:17 (cf. vv. 1ff.); 12:2; 17:8; 24:6; 31:28; 32:41; 42:10; 45:4; Ezek. 17:22-23; Amos 9:15; etc.

58. Cf. B. Halpern-Amaru (*Rewriting the Bible*, 1994, passim), who reconsiders what four Jewish writers of the period (including the authors of *Jubilees* and *Testament of Moses*) have done with doctrine of the land, since the literal fulfillment seemed remote.

59. Cf. Deut. 4:26; 27:3; 28:36-37; 30:15-16, 19-20; etc. For a similar association with the land, cf. 4Q374 2, 2, 5. The relation of this text to the community is uncertain, however (for text and analysis, cf. C. A. Newsom, "4Q374," 1992, 40-52, esp. 42).

determinative in shaping the plant imagery in this literature and may have helped to give the various images a certain uniformity. (3) Since these motifs are all basically to be understood against the same soteriological dualism as noted above, the association drawn in the Bible between plant motifs and various people — in particular, God's people[60] — would also have helped to link together the motifs. (4) The suggestion has also been made that the idea of "planting" evokes the notion of the blessings of Eden, and thus it would not be surprising if these images were found particularly useful by groups promoting *restoration*.[61] Agricultural motifs, whatever their exact origin, were obviously both authoritative and serviceable agents for the message of these groups.

Plant of Righteousness

A frequently used designation in these writings is "plant of righteousness." S. Fujita argued that this and various other plant metaphors have a long-standing usage in Judaism as metaphors for the righteous *within* Israel,[62] and there seems to be little doubt of this for passages like *1 En.* 10:16, which proclaims that a "plant of righteousness and truth will appear forever" at the end of days. (The association of the plant with "the righteous ones" in the following verse suggests that the righteous people of God are in mind, rather than a messiah, for example.) The "plant of righteousness" is accordingly a corporate metaphor and, in the context of the Book of Watchers, certainly refers to the author's community or, perhaps, to the righteous in Israel generally. The description that follows in vv. 18-19 continues the plant motif — with little division between what precedes and what follows — but the motif itself rather surprisingly shifts from the anthropological back to the agricultural nuance of the term to express the harvest bounty of the restoration age: "in those days the whole earth will be worked in righteousness, all of her *planted with trees,* and will find blessing. And they shall plant pleasant trees upon her. . . ." This combination of anthropological and agricultural metaphors, as noted above about

60. Cf., e.g., Ps. 1:3-4; Isa. 65:22; and notes below.

61. Cf. 1QH 6.16 and 8.10-12, which clearly allude to Eden (cf. Dupont-Sommer, 1961, 227 n. 2; M. Mansoor, *The Thanksgiving Hymns Translated and Annotated with an Introduction,* 1961, 151, 154). On the identity of the Eden plantation with Qumran in 1QH 8.12, cf. H. Ringgren ("The Branch and the Plantation in the *Hodayot,*" 1961, 3-9, 6; but contrast Holm-Nielsen, 1960, 148, who denies that Genesis 2 was the principal source). Cf. also *Pss. Sol.* 14:3-4; Isa. 17:11; 35:7; 41:19, which refer to various trees planted in the desert in a restoration context.

62. Cf. S. Fujita, "The Metaphor of Plant in Jewish Literature of the Intertestamental Period," 1976, 30-45, esp. 36-37. Cf. Isa. 5:7; Reid, 1989, 48.

the seed motif, again witnesses to the fluidity and interchangeableness of the symbolism of the literature.[63]

Elsewhere in *1 Enoch* the plant is similarly used to speak of the righteous. The opening of the Apocalypse of Weeks makes the identification clear in its tripartite parallelism: "And Enoch said, 'Concerning the children of righteousness, concerning the elect ones of the world,[64] and concerning *the plant of truth*, I will speak these things'" (93:2). The book's other usages vary little from this basic significance, except in some instances the plant seems to refer not only to the righteous people during the author's time but also to the plant of righteousness in its *historical existence from the time of the exile* and even before the exile. The Apocalypse of Weeks is accordingly able to speak of righteous individuals such as Abraham and Jacob in similar terms as "the plant of the righteous judgment" and "the eternal plant of righteousness" (93:5).[65] But the most revealing use of this expression comes when the author uses "plant" to speak of his own generation. At the end of the time of apostasy "there shall be elected the elect ones of righteousness *from the eternal plant of righteousness*, to whom shall be given sevenfold instruction concerning all his flock" (93:10). The use of the word "eternal" to modify "plant of righteousness" here suggests that the idea of the plant is understood historically, as encompassing the righteous people in its present manifestation along with the plant of righteousness in its historical existence. The consistent usage of the expression elsewhere in *1 Enoch* to refer to the righteous part of Israel precludes taking it as an expression for the national or ethnic Israel in contrast to the elect, as some have done.[66] The term is rather deliberately expanded here to include the whole line of the righteous through history, from whom also descend the elect contemporary with the author. Much the same use recurs in the Zoomorphic History. Enoch's prayer "that a remnant shall remain upon the earth" (83:8) includes the words: "Do now destroy, O my Lord, the flesh that has angered you from upon the earth, but sustain the flesh of righteousness and uprightness *as a plant of eternal seed* (or *eternal seed-bearing plant*)" (84:6). While one may surmise that the expression here refers to Noah and his progeny, many hints in the passage imply that the message is directed at the real author's time, as previously noted. In any event, it is clear

---

63. Cf. also *Jub.* 7:34-37. As Reid (1989, 48) suggests, the plant-of-righteousness motif would seem to have implied hopes for the restoration from its earliest use in the period of the exile — this would explain the interaction between the plant metaphor and the idea of blessing of the natural world during the restoration.

64. *xeruyāna 'alam*. Better: "eternal elect."

65. Black points out, however, that these expressions include both Abraham and his seed (1985, 290).

66. Cf. Black, 1985, 291.

that the "plant" here refers to a righteous people or, perhaps more inclusively, to the entire line of righteousness that extends throughout history. The association of the plant with the "seed" is also worth noting.[67]

Jubilees uses the motif in a similar way, and establishes an even more deliberate parallel with seed imagery. Thus in 16:26 the "righteous planting for eternal generations" is paralleled with "a holy seed" that will come from Abraham. That this communicates the idea of a reduction of Abraham's seed to the righteous community has been established above.[68] It is instructive how Isaac is also promised a "righteous plant in all the earth throughout all the generations of the earth" (21:24), remembering that the Isaac and Jacob/Esau themes probably serve as historical paradigms of God's reduction and definition of the elect seed. While again the plant is not all Israel but the righteous within Israel, the emphasis here does appear to be on a restoration of that seed to its fullness (on which, cf. ch. 11). But the entirely conditional nature of the election of this plant is nevertheless sustained in the words of Noah to his sons: "do justice and righteousness *so that* you might be *planted in righteousness* on the surface of the whole earth" (7:34). Once again this language typically tails off into a strictly agricultural metaphor (cf. vv. 35-38). While 1:16, on a superficial reading, might seem to speak of the entire restored nation as a "righteous plant," the election theology of *Jubilees* is not so straightforward as the first chapter would suggest on its own, as noted above; it must be interpreted within its literary context.

In the scrolls the plant would seem in most cases to refer to the community. 1QS 8.5 proclaims that "the Council of the Community shall be established in truth as an everlasting planting" and goes on to speak of the community using a plethora of election terms ("House," "Company," "witnesses," "chosen," and various other building metaphors; cf. ll. 5-8).[69] The "house" imagery in the verse has long been recognized as "(New) Temple" imagery applied to the community.[70] The passage also draws on the "stone" imagery of Isa. 28:16; 26:1; and Ps. 118:22, which is applied to the *yaḥad,* providing evidence of the use of stone motifs prior to the New Testament that may actually refer to the saved community rather than

---

67. For the authenticating function of these motifs in a polemical setting, cf. Fujita, 1976, 44.

68. Cf. also Fujita, 1976, 39; for the relationship of seed and plant ideas in *Jubilees,* cf. 36.

69. For the use of מטעת עולם (ל) as a designation for the community, cf. Dupont-Sommer, 1961, 91 n. 2. Wernberg-Møller points to a similar association of plant and house motifs in Ecclus. 3:9, where נטע is rendered by οἶκος, and the corresponding verb by προσανοικοδομεῖν, the root נטע "apparently conveying to the grandson of the author the idea of housebuilding" (1957, 124).

70. Cf. Leaney, 1966, 216; Wernberg-Møller, 1957, 124-27.

a messiah.[71] That all of the stone and building images in the passage may be related to the community as the "New Temple" is suggested by the repetition of the phrase "Company/Dwelling of infinite holiness for Aaron" (ll. 5-6, 8-9), which evokes images of Temple and priestly cult. The passage seems to reflect the view that the sectarian cult was intended, by means of a spiritual kind of worship, to take the place of the apostate priesthood and cult in Jerusalem,[72] although this interpretation is far from unanimous. The association of worship imagery and corporate imagery is also found in 1QS 11.8 where the "eternal planting" seems to designate the earthly manifestation of the "assembly" or "lot of the Saints," whose membership is both earthly and heavenly (cf. "Sons of Heaven" in the same line). Thus in each of these cases the terminology clearly refers to the Qumran community as the righteous "planting" in Israel.

It is possible that a backward-looking, or historical, nuance similar to that found in *1 Enoch* and *Jubilees* is sometimes implied in the use of the terminology at Qumran, but this is nowhere clearly found. The fact that the expression is employed in the so-called Founder Hymns (1QH 6.15; 8.6, 9-10, 20) suggests that the motif belonged to the community's parlance during its earliest organizational period and that it may have been applied as a term for the righteous in Israel before the founding of the *yaḥad*. On the other hand, there is no clear indication in these hymns that the term referred to any such group. The only place where this might be the case is in a notoriously problematical passage, CD 1.4-7, where one reads of the "root of planting" that God caused to spring from "Israel and Aaron" (l. 7). If the expression does not actually refer to the sect — the language is inexact and the references shift inconspicuously — it may offer the single instance at Qumran where "planting" terminology refers to the prehistory of the community. There is no doubt that a reference to the exilic period is intended in the first part of the passage, but it is unclear at what point the subject matter shifts to the community contemporary with the author. The solution to the interpretation of the passage rests with the significance of the 390 years (ll. 5-6) and with the force of the participial prefix *l*[e] in the same lines — "in the time of wrath, three hundred and ninety years [*after?* or *during which?*] [God] had delivered them into the hand of Nebuchadnezzar king of Babylon, He visited them, and caused a *root of planting* to spring from Israel and Aaron."[73] In neither case would the reading necessarily imply a very distant

71. One can concur with Leaney: "Ps. 118.22, often and very aptly quoted in the NT ... as a symbol of the rejected Messiah, seems to have been originally that of a rejected and restored Israel" (1966, 219). Implications for this use of the motif in the New Testament have yet to be fully explored.

72. As cf. Leaney, 1966, 216, 219.

73. For discussion of these problems and the significance of the preposition, cf. G. Jeremias, *Der Lehrer der Gerechtigkeit*, 1963, 153-62.

time past. If one accepts the first option (l^e = "after"), this would date the visitation and the root of planting 390 years following the return from exile and, depending on the perceived date of that return, would result in a date somewhere between the middle of the second century and the late first century. The second option (l^e = "during which") might imply that the root of planting emerged at an unspecified time during the exile, perhaps early on, and this would then refer to those who remained righteous throughout that time of testing. But this is a very large and unspecified period of time: it could refer to the people who supported Joshua and Zerubbabel, those associated with Ezra and Nehemiah, or the Enochian groups already in existence during the third century B.C. If the author thought Israel was *still* in exile (which, judging from other texts, is a position the community seems to have held), the "root of planting" could have emerged very recently, perhaps again pointing to the origins of the community itself in the relatively recent past. All of this type of argumentation implies, of course, that the 390 years is to be taken literally, while it has also been argued that 390 years is either not an exact figure or is to be taken figuratively.[74] Given the intense concern for chronological arithmetic at Qumran, however, it is difficult to avoid the conclusion that the 390 years mentioned in ll. 5-6 was intended literally, although this would still leave unsolved the problems mentioned above. While a solution may be quite unattainable, it is worth noting that the expression "from Aaron and Israel" might itself best be taken as an allusion to the present community since it is used consistently this way elsewhere (cf. more below). When this expression is found within the fuller title "root of planting from Aaron and Israel," this would especially seem to point to the *yaḥad.* Even should "planting" be taken to refer to the exilic community, and the context of ll. 5-8 perhaps favors this, the word "root" might still be taken as a qualification, pointing again to the present community.

74. The basic positions are that 390 years (1) refers literally to the period *following* 586 B.C. and leading up to the period of the founding of the community itself (which would then be ca. 196 B.C., minus the 20 years mentioned in l. 10 = 176 B.C.; cf., e.g., H. J. Schonfield, *Secrets of the Dead Sea Scrolls,* 1957, 22); (2) is an error for the 490 years, which would equal the seventy weeks of years given in Daniel as the length of the captivity (although concern for accurate dating would seem to preclude this, and theories exist, moreover, that allow for the "missing" 100 years to be accounted for); or (3) is nonliteral or deliberately symbolic, referring either to the time leading to the return from captivity (under Nehemiah and, later, Zerubbabel) or to the actual period of incapacitation itself (cf. Knibb, 1987, 21; G. Jeremias, 1963, 158-62, who nevertheless takes the words that follow in ll. 7ff. in reference to the immediate prehistory of the sect). P. R. Davies (*The Damascus Covenant: An Interpretation of the "Damascus Document,"* 1982, 65) attempts to untangle the difficulties through a theory of secondary editing — the "remnant" of l. 4 was equivalent to the "root" of l. 7 in the original discourse, but through editing these terms have become distinct, the latter now referring to the new community.

The plant(ing) motif is featured most conspicuously in the earlier works of our period, although it is hardly insignificant for the understanding of the *Psalms of Solomon* that it is found in that book as well. *Pss. Sol.* 14:4-5 employs the expression within a hymn proclaiming the faithfulness of God to "those who truly love him," "the Lord's devout," etc. The passage says,

> . . . the trees of life . . . are his devout ones.
> *Their planting is firmly rooted* forever;
>   they shall not be uprooted as long as the heavens shall last.[75]

The first canonical psalm seems to provide one of the sources of the metaphor here, and the mention of "trees of life" and "(up)rooted" suggests other plant motifs that will be investigated below. Other examples of this usage from a later time include *1 En.* 62:8[76] and *2 Bar.* 57:2, where one witnesses a more or less consistent use of plant motifs in the service of corporate thought, defining the elect as the faithful plant(ing) of God. Given the covenantal associations of this motif, it is apparent that these communities employed it as a self-assertion of their status as the righteous who have inherited the promises of the fathers.[77]

Various Tree Motifs (Including Root, Branch, and Forest)

Tree motifs are another example of plant-related imagery that can provide helpful insight into the concerns of remnant groups. With these tree motifs one witnesses a somewhat unconventional use of terminology already familiar from the Hebrew Scriptures,[78] and in some cases the essence of the message of these groups can be discerned exactly from this unconventional, or interpretative, aspect. There appear to have been two main applications of tree imagery current in Judaism. The first involved the development of the tree-

75. This extolling of the righteous, however, ends in v. 5 with the words "For *Israel* is the portion and inheritance of God." The question, again, is whether the many references to the "devout" in this passage should be allowed to influence how we define "Israel" in this case, or the other way around. For reasons already mentioned we have decided firmly on the side of the former option. Cf. likewise Fujita, 1976, 31.

76. Black translates "And the congregation of the elect and holy shall be *sown*, / And all the elect shall stand before him on that day" (1985, 60), but comments that Eth. for "sown" represents a translation variant of נצר, "to plant" (236).

77. Cf. Fujita, 1976, 44.

78. For tree metaphors, cf. esp. Gen. 2:9, 16-17; Judg. 9:7-49; Pss. 1:3; 92:12-14; Prov. 3:18; 11:30; 13:12; Isa. 17:11; 35:7; 41:19; 44:3; 60:21; Jer. 17:5-8; Ezek. 20:47; 31:1-18; Dan. 4:4-27; Zech. 4:1-14.

of-life motif.[79] The second, a usage already developed in the Psalms and prophetic literature, employed the tree motif for nations and at times especially for Israel or the righteous.[80] These two usages could be combined,[81] and when this happens in our literature it evokes images of the restoration of Eden, similar to that mentioned above in connection with the planting motif (cf. 1QH 16–17; 8.11-12; *Pss. Sol.* 14:3-4). E. R. Goodenough has shown that in ancient Jewish and pagan art the branch or leaf could represent the entire tree, demonstrating the potential for interrelationship between the various symbols. The tree could be an olive, oak, pine, or fig tree with no apparent alteration of significance,[82] and examples can be cited of the image of the forest being used along similar lines.

The application of the tree motif to Israel and to the righteous in the biblical tradition obviously invited a similar application in the writings of our movement. That tree and plant motifs were sometimes combined is clear from 1QH 6.14-19, where they are juxtaposed and even intermingled:

79. According to E. R. Goodenough (*Jewish Symbols in the Greco-Roman Period*, vol. 7, *Pagan Symbols in Judaism,* 1958, 1:87-134), this followed an ancient convention found throughout the Gentile world where the tree symbolized a whole list of positive life forces: power, blessing, victory, immortality, relationship to divinity, nourishment, fertility, and salvation. The "tree of life" represented the source of life and was a particularly important motif in Judaism and Christianity (cf. Rev. 22:2, 14, etc.). It is worth noting that in some instances of pagan art the tree of life is an image of sustenance where, like the parable of the mustard seed in the Gospels, the birds flock for protection (cf. Goodenough, 1:96). For the vision of the tree of life in the context of a cosmic revelation, cf. *1 En.* 32:1-6.

80. For the tree as a symbol of nations or kingdoms, on the basis of Daniel 4, 7–8, cf. 4Q547, 552-53. This use is unfortunately given less prominence by Goodenough, doubtless because he was investigating art forms that related to individual interpretation (e.g., sarcophagi) rather than the literary deposits of ancient Israel; however, he appears to overlook this second usage with regard to temple and synagogue decor, an unfortunate thing in our estimate. This symbolism would appear to be the motivation for the use of the palm branch on Hasmonean and Herodian coins, as well as those memorializing the First and Second Jewish Wars. Goodenough (1958, 1:88-89) rejects the geopolitical association of the palm tree as a "symbol of Judaea" and prefers to relegate to it strictly religious significances. Goodenough allows, however, that the branch symbolizes the victory of the Jewish nation (cf. 121). Jewish mystic texts equate the fruit of the tree by the water with the "saints"; Israel comes from the tree in Zohar Shemoth 2, 2a (ET 3,3); Philo, *On Sobriety,* 65-66, reflects the tradition that identifies the tree with Israel, which begins at the root, Shem (cf. Goodenough, 1:130-34). For biblical and intertestamental texts that relate the tree to Israel, cf. G. Jeremias, 1963, 256.

81. The tree used in this national sense would then refer to the triumph or vindication of the nation, or the nation as a source of blessing or spiritual life, a particularly appropriate motif in our writings. Goodenough (1958, 1:125) does hint at this relationship but does not go into it at length.

82. Goodenough, 1958, 1:87.

And Thou hast sent out a sprouting as a flower that shall bloom for ever,[83] that the Shoot *(nēṣer)* may grow into the branches of the eternal planting. And its shade shall spread over all [the earth and] its [top] reach up to the heavens and its roots go down to the Abyss. And all the rivers of Eden [shall water] its [bou]ghs and it shall become a mighty forest, [and the glory of] its forest shall spread over the world without end, as far as Sheol [for ever]. (ll. 14-17)

The plant in this passage slowly takes on the form of a tree, and then a forest; eventually the description tails off into a combination of tree, light, fountain, and fire motifs (ll. 18-19). Particularly suggestive is the fact that this tree, not unlike the mustard tree of the Gospel parable, grows to such a size that it covers not only the world but the entire cosmos. Jaubert relates this image of "l'arbre cosmique" to the fact that the *yaḥaḍ* considered itself to be in communion with the angels who dwelt in heaven — an idea that would seem to be foreign to Jesus' parable.[84]

Contrary to many interpretations of this passage, a purely messianic interpretation of the psalm would appear to be precluded by the fact that the opening motif of the "Shoot" *(nēṣer,* l. 15), which, for its part, is a transparent messianic motif[85] (perhaps referring to the Teacher of Righteousness),[86] does

83. This part of the line is a reconstruction; Holm-Nielsen suggests שורשם, "their root," and בציץ השדה [ע]ד, "the flowers of the field (forever)" (1960, 115), agreeing on the use of plant motifs.

84. A. Jaubert, *La notion d'alliance dans le Judaïsme aux abords de l'ère chrétienne,* 1963, 192. An interesting cosmic tree motif also occurs in 4Q547 in reference to Babylon (reflecting Daniel 4, 7–8; cf. R. H. Eisenman and M. Wise, *The Dead Sea Scrolls Uncovered,* 1992, 72-73, who also suggest Ezekiel 17, 31 and Zech. 11:2 as a background).

85. For the messianic interpretation, cf. Dupont-Sommer, 1961, 219 n. 2. Arguing against this understanding is Holm-Nielsen (1960, 115), but נצר/*nēṣer* is too obviously suggestive of the messiah to explain it otherwise (for the parallel motif, צמח as unambiguous reference to a messiah, cf. 4Q285).

86. While there is not enough compelling evidence to suggest that the psalmist himself is meant by the "Shoot," there is a possibility in 7.10, 19 that the Teacher and the "branch" (עפים, lit. "foliage") are equated. One problem with this, however, is the allusive change of pronoun in l. 10: "has appointed *him*" (נתתו; read נְתַתַּנִי, "has appointed me," by E. Lohse, ed., *Die Texte aus Qumran,* 1971, 138). A further problem exists with the use of עפים rather than נצר in that verse, which is too distant from 6.15 to suggest, with Dupont-Sommer (1961, 222 n. 5), that the pronoun refers back to the נצר. There is also an important, although subtle, difference between the Teacher being appointed as a branch (as a community founder?) and the "Shoot" *growing* into branches (expressing the historical evolution of the community?). Rather the Teacher is one of the branches, perhaps a main one, who along with the community will grow into the tree of cosmic proportions. This reflects a deliberate interrelationship that is established in the scrolls between the Teacher and the community; cf. 1QH 10.15-16 (depending, once again, on its reconstruction).

not dominate in the balance of the passage. The passage does appear to allude to the belief that at the coming of the messiah the messianic community will experience a period of growth until it reaches universal proportions,[87] but this does not change the fact that these several motifs — "sprouting," "flower," "bloom," "branches," "(eternal) planting,"[88] "shade," "roots," "boughs," "forest" — all refer in one way or another to the *community,* whether in their present, future, or perhaps heavenly manifestations. This is especially clear, not only from the appropriateness of such terms as corporate metaphors, but also from the context where the psalmist had just referred in the immediately preceding verses to the "men of Thy council" and "a common lot with the Angels of the Face . . ." (ll. 13-14).

This type of imagery is further developed in the colorful trees-by-the-water psalm (1QH 8.5ff.) in which the psalmist seems to refer to himself as a kind of spring that waters the garden,[89] while the community itself is referred to as "a planting of cypress and elm mingled with box," and "trees of life" who shall "send out a Shoot for the everlasting planting."[90] That the "Shoot" *(nēṣer)* is not the messiah but merely another expression for the community — perhaps in its character as a growing community — may be indicated by the way the "trees of life" are said to "take root *before* they send it [the Shoot] out" (l. 7),[91] but such an understanding would be out of harmony with the use of the term in 6.15ff.

87. Cf. Dupont-Sommer, 1961, 219 n. 2.

88. Cf. l. 15 and the parallel to this passage, 8.6, for the expression "eternal planting."

89. Cf. l. 5; perhaps also referred to as a fountain of life in l. 13. The expressions allude more to teaching than to the Teacher, although the personal remarks in ll. 14-16, 21-36 suggest that the psalmist not only thanks God for the tree of life in which he flourishes (as Holm-Nielsen, 1960, 142ff.), but in some sense takes credit for being the *source* of its life (as Dupont-Sommer, 1961, 225 n. 2).

90. Here Dupont-Sommer (1961, 226 nn. 2-5) assumes that all of this language refers to the community. Cf. also G. Jeremias, 1963, 256; Fujita, 1976, 40; *contra* Holm-Nielsen (1960, 148-49), whose arguments against this are weak. He takes "trees of life" symbolically for "new life in the covenant" (although no precedent is given for this use of the tree motif) and argues that the understanding of the expression that takes it to refer to the saints is complicated by the mention of the נצר, which would thus point to *another* congregation. No such problem would exist, however, if the נצר were taken to be the messiah (a conclusion hardly avoidable in our opinion), but Holm-Nielsen finds this interpretation too allegorical (149). Holm-Nielsen presupposes the absense of messianic teaching in the Hymns, and this has apparently led him to this position; but even given this, it is remarkable that he feels able to deny the kind of "allegorization" that he wishes to avoid here (is "tree of life" = "new life in the covenant" any less allegorical?).

91. Ringgren (1961, 6) and Dupont-Sommer (1961, 226 n. 3) favor this interpretation. A distinction could accordingly be drawn between the "trees of life," the historical remnant, and the Shoot, the community itself.

above. It is more likely that this psalm refers to the community's role in *preparation* for the messiah, just as the earlier psalm alluded to the *results* of his coming. Thus, with the exception of this Shoot that is "sent out," the motifs in the passage can again be understood corporately as referring to the community, especially in its act of seeking the teaching symbolized by the stream/water motif.[92] As with the hymn investigated above, however, caution would be well advised before trying to draw detailed and consistent associations between the images and their references. It is enough to acknowledge that the accumulation of plant images together suggests general truths about the origins and life of the righteous community.

An added feature of this hymn is the identification of other kinds of trees — "trees by the waters" — alongside the "trees of life." While the "trees of life" find water, the other "trees by the waters . . . shall direct no root to the stream," an antithetical image again expressing the soteriological dualism that is constantly working in the background of Qumran thought. Whether a circumscribed group of opponents or Judaism as a whole is in mind here is not immediately clear. If the image is derived from Ezek. 31:14, as it would seem, it could have been applied to the entire nation, in this case pointing to a complacent and unfaithful Israel.[93] The very fact that these "trees by the waters" are unable to benefit from the waters also strongly suggests that the expression is an all-encompassing term for "unilluminated" Israel, out of the midst of which the community as the "trees of life," who have embraced the teachings of the *moreh*, are distinguished.[94] That Israel outside the *yaḥad* is referred to here is again confirmed by l. 6: "Trees of life *are hidden among* all the trees by the waters in a mysterious realm."[95] The "mysterious/secret" place (cf. also ll. 10-11) might allude to the special revelation given to the

---

92. For water as a metaphor for right teaching in Judaism, cf. G. Jeremias, 1963, 256. Fujita implies that water comes from the "fountain of mystery" (1976, 41), according to his rendering of ll. 6-7. In any event, the water is the revelatory teaching of the community, either the interpreted Law, the instruction offered by the *moreh ṣedeq*, or other sources of revelation (Fujita apparently equates it with teaching of the *moreh*, as well as with the Law, 43-44). The connection with teaching, specifically "knowledge," may be sustained also by an allusion to the "tree of life" — cf. "tree of the knowledge of good and evil" (Gen. 2:9, 17).

93. Cf. Ringgren, 1961, 3; Dupont-Sommer, 1961, 226 n. 2.

94. G. Jeremias (1963, 260-61), following Dupont-Sommer (1961, 226 nn. 2ff.), detects references to a variety of groups here: the "trees by the waters" are orthodox Judaism, the "trees of life" the Hasidim, the "Shoot" the Essenes. This is to specify too closely the referents of the last two terms, which are merely extensions of the tree metaphor to refer to the initiative of the trees of life in seeking out the *moreh*'s teaching.

95. Holm-Nielsen: "trees of life at the secret wellspring, which hide themselves among all the trees by the water" (1960, 142).

community[96] or to the separateness of the sect or to their communion with the heavenly realm of angels, and in any case, "all the trees" would refer to the — by every comparison — much larger nation of apostate trees (since the trees of life are able to be hid among them). The fact that the writer appears to have picked up the dualism from the canonical Psalm 1 tends to confirm that this is an application of the tree metaphor to the Jewish community as a whole, since this psalm itself can be interpreted to refer to conflict between two groups of opponents within Israel: the righteous and the wicked (whether or not that was the original import of the language of the psalm is another question). The mixture of good and evil trees reminds one of the wheat and tares parable in the Gospel (Matt. 13:24-30), and the hiddenness of the trees of life among the trees by the water recalls the parable of the leaven hid in the flour (Matt. 13:33 par.). The parables of growth, particularly that of the mustard seed (Matt. 13:31-32), also find a comparison in the words of ll. 8-9 (cf. again Ezek. 31:13): "And in the Shoot,[97] near by, all the beasts of the thicket shall graze, and its stock shall be a grazing place for all that pass by, and all the winged birds shall use its branches."

Tree imagery continues to make its influence felt in later writings, those of the first century B.C. and well beyond. A very similar use of plant — particularly tree — motifs is found in *Pss. Sol.* 14:3-4, a passage again inspired by the first canonical psalm. Here the idea of the writer's community as trees is again combined (as in 1QH 8 above) with the "tree of life" motif from Genesis 2–3.

---

96. As Holm-Nielsen (1960, 149-50, 151), who compares Isa. 8:16: "Bind up the testimony, seal the teaching *among my disciples*"; and Ringgren (1961, 6), who also identifies that which causes growth and remains hidden in l. 10 as revelation. For a slightly different sense Holm-Nielsen translates the hiph. as qal: "the shoot of holiness groweth up into a planting of truth, by hiding and sealing up its secret, so that it is not known or recognized" (142, 151). He finds a reference in 8.12 to "those who stand outside the covenant, and who, therefore, cannot take advantage from the community's communion with God" (152; *contra* Dupont-Sommer, 1961, 227, who takes it to refer to the sufferings of the Teacher, comparing Isa. 53:2).

97. נצר. The use of the word here obviously complicates, but does not preclude, a messianic understanding for the term in the preceding lines. What we have here is probably a typical (and not entirely unconscious) confusion between messiah and community, the "Shoot" being a versatile motif for both (here perhaps more for the community than for the messiah). We do not need to see, as Dupont-Sommer, a reference to a suffering-messiah motif in the passage and have followed Holm-Nielsen in his translation: "a dwelling place (i.e., a place to graze) unto all who pass" (1960, 142, 150-51; contrast Dupont-Sommer: "trod underfoot by all that pass by," 1961, 226), since the more positive translation of Holm-Nielsen conforms much better to the positive expressions that encompass it.

The Lord's devout shall live by it[98] forever;
  the Lord's paradise, the trees of life, are his devout ones.
Their planting is firmly rooted forever;
  they shall not be uprooted as long as the heavens shall last.

Given the corporate and dualistic context we have uncovered for this collection of psalms, the use of metaphors like "trees of life," "the Lord's paradise" (= Eden),[99] "devout (ones)," and "planting" (which shall not be *"uprooted"*) — all of which stand in parallelism with one another — tends to confirm that the author of this psalm envisaged his own community as composing in an exclusive way the people of God.

Adaptations of the Tree and Vine Allegory

In 4 Ezra 5:23 and 9:21 the two images of a tree and vine are combined. This combination is already found in Ezek. 17:1-24, which provided some of the imagery for the passages from the Qumran hymns above. It is very instructive for a proper understanding of 4 Ezra to note how this author handles these images. In the Ezekelian "parable" (*māšāl*, Ezek. 17:2) the nobility of Judah is compared to the topmost part of the cedar of Lebanon that is carried off into exile to a foreign land by a great eagle (Babylon; cf. vv. 4, 13). One of the Jewish royal nobility, Zedekiah (cf. 2 Kings 24:17), however, is spared by the eagle and is planted like a "seed" in "fertile soil" and by "abundant waters." This seed grows into a "low spreading" vine (vv. 5-6), but soon sends out roots toward *another* great eagle (i.e., Egypt; v. 7). At this point the vision is interrupted with a warning against appealing to Egypt for protection: the vine is to be pulled out, cut off, and allowed to wither (vv. 9-10). Thus in the parable we see the punishment God brings upon the "Judah-cedar," as well as that which comes upon the spared "vine" of Zedekiah for his guilt in breaking the covenant of the Lord by seeking the protection and favor of Egypt (vv. 18-19). But while both the captives and Zedekiah (the tree and the vine) are eventually judged in the parable, this does not mean total obliteration. According to vv. 22-24, God will take a "tender twig" from a "sprig from the lofty top of the cedar" (as v. 22 can best be understood) and will "plant it upon a high and lofty mountain . . . that it may bring forth boughs and bear fruit, and become a noble cedar; and under it will dwell all kinds of beasts; in the shade of its

---

98. Apparently, the Law. This coheres with the idea of the trees of life being fed by the waters of revelation at Qumran, and seems to have been inspired by Ps. 1:2-3 or possibly Prov. 3:18.

99. Goodenough notes a restored-Eden motif in the passage (1958, 1:127).

branches birds of every sort will nest. And all the trees of the field shall know that I the LORD bring low the high tree, and make high the low tree, dry up the green tree, and make the dry tree flourish." This tender twig would appear to refer to a new line of royalty that God will raise up, one not yet evident to Ezekiel's contemporaries. One might call this Ezekiel's "messianic" (or, at least, predeterministic) resolution of the problem of the historical failure of Judah to live up to divine expectations: God will provide a new and worthy royal line.

This is not at all the function or significance of the symbolism in 4 Ezra, however, as the parable has been exploited for this author's purposes in quite novel circumstances. The images of the tree and vine are not only removed from the original historical context but are blended in a way they were not in Ezekiel. In 5:23 Ezra says, "O sovereign Lord, from every forest of the earth and from all its trees you have chosen one vine," and augments this with a whole list of similar comparisons,[100] all of which are intended to establish the general comparison of the "one" nation Israel versus the "many" nations of the world (v. 28). It is not difficult to detect the very nationalistic perspective typically brought to the discussion to this point by Ezra.[101] As has frequently been seen in this book, however, the nationalistic sentiments of Ezra are discouraged by the angel, this time through a subtle *adaptation* of the tree and vine motifs. When the motif reappears in 9:21, God announces through the angel that in fact God has saved, not the *whole* vine, but merely "*one grape* out of a cluster, and *one plant* out of a great forest." That this application of the vine and tree images is intended to emphasize the limitations set on God's salvation is evident in the words that immediately follow: "So let the multitude perish which has been born in vain, but let *my grape and my plant* be saved, because with much labor I have perfected them" (v. 22).[102] For the meaning of this statement one might recall another that sounds very much like it: "Let many perish who are now living, rather than that the law of God which is set before them be disregarded!" (4 Ezra 7:20), words determined earlier to contain a reference to the majority in Israel who disregarded God's

---

100. Namely, "from all the lands of the world you have chosen for yourself one region, and from all the flowers of the world you have chosen for yourself one lily, and from all the depths of the sea you have filled for yourself one river. . . ."

101. For the vine as a motif for Israel (frequently an Israel in rebellion), cf. also Ps. 80:8-16; Isa. 5:7; Jer. 2:21; Hos. 10:1; 14:7. According to Stone (1990, 127), all the various images presented in the verse can be taken as symbols for Israel.

102. For agricultural motifs used to express the idea that only a very few will be saved, cf. Isa. 17:6; cf. also Amos 3:12 (Stone, 1990, 300). Stone appropriately comments: "the language that originally described Israel is probably used to refer to the eschatological survivors, an idea found repeatedly in 4 Ezra" (300).

law,[103] and we are back to the same point made earlier: 4 Ezra is not concerned with the nations, but with Israel.

It is thus noteworthy how through this subtle *adaptation* of the tree and vine metaphors the author employs conventional terminology and alludes to conventional beliefs through the voice of the scribe Ezra, but then adjusts and corrects the conventional understanding to make it correspond to the *angel's* teaching, which is in line with the stricter or "sectarian" understanding of plant motifs as referring to the faithful people of God in the midst of unfaithfulness. By means of this process the interpretation ignores the original intention of the vine and tree motif in Ezekiel, which points to a coming royal line (although, in fairness to 4 Ezra, it is evident how the theme of the preservation from judgment could easily have been read into the original parable by later readers; cf. Ezek. 17:22-24). In short, the *adaptation* or *nonconventional usage of conventional language* helps emphasize the remnant theology of 4 Ezra.

There is a remarkably similar, although probably independent, "adaptation" based on Ezekiel 17–18 in *2 Baruch* where the forest and vine terminology is applied even more explicitly to the situation of the "messianic community" (as it has not inappropriately been called). In the vision of 36:1–43:3 one reads how the seer witnessed a forest and "over against it [the forest] a vine arose, and from under it a fountain ran peacefully" (36:2-3). This fountain became a veritable flood and submerged the forest (36:4). Although one cedar was seen to survive the initial deluge, it also was "cast down" (36:5-6). All that remained, therefore, was a vine and a fountain (36:6). The vine was then seen to chastise the cedar: "Are you not that cedar which remained of the forest of wickedness? Because of you, wickedness remained and has been done during all these years, but never goodness . . ." (36:7-8). Judgment is pronounced: "Therefore, O cedar, follow the forest which has departed before you and become ashes with it . . ." (36:10-11). The vision concludes with the prosperity of the vine and the continued judgment of the cedar (37:1).

The interpretation that follows (39:2–43:3) makes clear how all these images are to be interpreted. The forest represents the nations (divided into various periods in 39:3-6), and the one cedar that is spared for awhile is the mightiest of the nations so far (Rome). It is said of this nation that "all who are polluted with unrighteousness will flee to it like the evil beasts flee and creep into the forest" (39:6). Perhaps there is in these words another allusion to those in Ezekiel's time who appealed to the power of Egypt for their protection, the message for the contemporaries of *2 Baruch* being that Israelites who have

---

103. It is noteworthy also that Stone finds in this verse an allusion to the covenantal witness motif, thus strengthening the view that Israelites in particular are being chastised here for their disobedience (1990, 200).

compromised themselves and have become polluted through their contact with the Gentiles will fall with them. After this time the messiah and the messianic community will arise: "at that time the dominion of my Anointed One *which is like the fountain and the vine,* will be revealed" (39:7). The messianic community of the author is thus represented as the vine that will prosper after the judgment, and perhaps the fountain is to be understood once again as the source of saving knowledge (revelation), something that appears to be evident from statements like "under it [the vine] a fountain ran peacefully" (36:3) and "that vine arrived with the fountain in peace and in great tranquillity" (36:6). But what makes this vision truly a challenge to the nationalistic application of the vine and the fountain to all Israel is the postscript attached to it.[104] Baruch asks: "For whom and for how many will these things be? Or who will be worthy to live in that time? . . . For behold, I see many of your people who separated themselves from your statutes and who have cast away from them the yoke of your Law. Further, I have seen others who left behind their vanity and who have fled under your wings" (41:1, 3-4). The answer is not surprising: "The good that was mentioned before will be *to those who have believed,* and the opposite of these things will be *to those who have despised*" (42:2).[105] Baruch is then typically consoled and instructed to speak to his "people" (43:2). Thus the vine, the righteous community referred to as "the remnant[106] of my people who will be found in the place that I have chosen" (40:2), alone survives and flourishes as the writer of *2 Baruch* applies the lessons of Ezekiel 17, in a somewhat altered form, to the situation of his own community.

SOME IMPORTANT IMPLICATIONS OF SOTERIOLOGICAL DUALISM

Neither 4 Ezra nor *2 Baruch* adopts the message of Ezekiel 17 unaltered. In fact, their reapplication and adaptation of these motifs reveals the powerful influence of the theology of the remnant (which is about the only consistent aspect

104. *2 Bar.* 41:1–43:3. Because of the relevance of this passage here, we cannot agree with Charles (1896, 66) that chs. 41–42 have been displaced from after ch. 30.

105. Interestingly enough, there follows this passage a clarification based on the highly individualistic teaching regarding the "final state" of the repentant and unrepentant, a teaching clearly based on the lesson of Ezekiel 18, the chapter that follows Ezekiel's forest-vine parable. It is apparent, therefore, that the entire presentation is modeled on these chapters from that book.

106. ṣr'h d'my. The phraseology is familiar and bears the semi-technical translation "the *remnant* of my people" rather than "the *rest* of my people."

of the reapplication in both cases) and offers compelling evidence that these agricultural motifs have been brought into the service of a pervasive soteriological dualism. In fact, all of the various motifs investigated in this chapter both individually and collectively witness to the central importance of soteriological dualism among these groups — there are two camps: "righteous" and "sinners"; "sons of light" and "sons of darkness"; "lot of God" and "lot of Belial"; the "few" and the "many"; etc. *These two camps divide not only Israelites from Gentiles, but Israelites from other Israelites.* This is certainly the most distinctive, and as a formative influence the most important, belief of these groups. And as the following chapters will show, the deep consciousness of this *soteriological dualism* — born of the real-life experiences of these groups — *dominates not only the motifs and symbols, but the theological thought and formal conventions of this literature* as well. It accordingly will become clear how the distinguishing literary features of the writings usually characterized as "apocalyptic" can be in large part credited to the influence of what might be called a corporately based soteriological dualism.

These groups possessed plenty of precedent for this kind of thinking and writing. Biblical texts like Isaiah 24–27 and Zechariah 12–14, which are not surprisingly held to be among the earliest examples of the "apocalyptic" mind-set, notably also possess a strong soteriological dualism.[107] These texts contain references to the judgment of Israel (Zech. 12:1ff.; 14:1ff., 12-14), the remnant that survives (Isa. 24:6, 13; Zech. 13:7-9; 14:16), a great destruction/preservation event probably modeled on the flood (Isa. 24:18-20; cf. ch. 12 below), and they appear to make reference to a defined number of the "righteous" as well (Isa. 26:7).

The existence of this corporately directed soteriological dualism raises questions relevant to New Testament study that can only be answered in a provisional way within the confines of the space available here — namely: Do the groups within this movement experience aspects of corporate life usually attributed only to Christianity? That is to say, have these groups already developed a "corporate soteriology"? And is there evidence in their belief for things like "corporate personality," "corporate mysticism," or "corporate solidarity," as this concept is variously called?[108] While there is little evidence that these

107. This has not gone totally unnoticed. Plöger (1968, 59-67, 88-94) notes the influence upon these texts of a division within Israel between eschatological and noneschatological groups. W. Schmithals (*The Apocalyptic Movement*, 1975, 132) similarly posits that apocalyptic thought begins with the declarations of the prophets that Israelites cannot rely on past saving events because they have broken the covenant.

108. For discussion see A. R. Johnson, *The One and the Many in the Israelite Conception of God*, 1961; A. R. Johnson, *Sacral Kingship in Ancient Israel*, 1955, 1ff. For this idea as applied to Paul, cf. *inter alia*, N. T. Wright, "The Messiah and the People of God," 1980, 1-11.

groups conceptualized their group consciousness of salvation in terms of a corporate mysticism such as one finds so frequently expressed in the writings of Paul (cf. the "in Christ" and "body of Christ" motifs), it is beyond doubt that *soteriological dualism was operative not only on the individual but also on the corporate level*. Regardless of whether one goes so far as to name this aspect of thought "corporate personality" or "corporate mysticism," it is certainly true that *identity with the company of the saved, its knowledge and its practices,* was virtually equivalent to salvation itself. This phenomenon might be better called *corporate identity*[109] — a term with the distinct advantage of noting and emphasizing the importance of *belonging* that is manifested through such things as believing in the group's revelation, accepting the messianic personages favored by the group, and suffering with the group, while not necessarily implying anthropological or psychological theories or ontological categories implied by the above terms as used by scholars with regard to biblical thought.[110] Corporate identity, in other words, need imply no more than that *these kinds of social relationships imply shared beliefs, shared priorities, shared experiences, and* insofar as they also imply a shared soteriology, *a common salvation*. This would then be a significant step toward corporate categories of thought such as one finds in Paul and is, of course, also highly significant for a sociological definition of these groups.

Corporate Identity in Shared Experiences

Corporate identity is evident in these writings in various allusions to the importance of community. Nowhere is a communal consciousness more evident than in the sectarian writings found at Qumran.[111] This is seen, for example, in the

---

109. Cf. Hans Mol's term for the decisive society as a "focus of identity."

110. The idea of corporate personality was originally investigated by H. Wheeler Robinson (cf. esp. *Corporate Personality in Ancient Israel*, 1980, passim), who gave to the terminology of corporate thought strong pyschological nuances. His investigations take their cue from the instinctive psychological element believed by some earlier anthropologists (namely, J. Pedersen) to have existed extensively among the peoples of the ancient world. For more recent approaches that stress the legal, exegetical, literary, and social approaches to the question, rather than the psychological, cf. J. R. Porter, "The Legal Aspects of the Concept of 'Corporate Personality' in the Old Testament," 1965, 361-80; J. W. Rogerson, "The Hebrew Conception of Corporate Personality," 1970, 1-16, 15; Robinson, 29-30, 38; Johnson, 1955, 8ff. Another possibly promising approach for understanding this corporate thought is the *Heilssphären* discussed by J. Becker.

111. Jaubert lists the implications of the communion of the *yaḥad:* (1) community of goods, (2) mutual responsibility, (3) correction, (4) exclusion, excommunication, (5) love/hate and vengeance ideas (1963, 184-89).

way the community thought of itself as united with the saints and angels in heaven forming one great cosmic "union" of those who belong to God, a view perhaps also found elsewhere in our literature (cf. *Jub.* 31:14 and *TLevi* 4:2). It is also indicated by the linguistic breadth of the term *yaḥaḍ*, their favorite word for "community," and one expressing the idea of "unity" or "togetherness."[112] In the Founder Hymns of 1QH the *moreh* repeatedly insists that the salvation he has brought to light is for the benefit of his community, and, as already noted, he employs a number of motifs to express the essence and importance of this "participation in a divine fellowship"[113] (cf. 1QH 7.29-30; 11.9-14). The scroll writers were also well aware of the view that others in Israel were not believed to share in this corporeity, and so they could express their view of the community in a negative way also, that the rest of Israel would be judged according to their relationship to that community — namely, according to their treatment of it and their acceptance or nonacceptance of its revelation. It is almost as if the center of salvation had become the *yaḥaḍ* itself, leading to the conclusion that soteriology was to a point *defined* in terms of corporate *identity*.[114]

There are scores of references in the literature to the shared social conditions of these groups and to the common attitudes that resulted from these conditions, notably the theology of suffering[115] and the ideology of humility and poverty,[116] which were both at least partly created by those common cir-

---

112. Ringgren, 1963, 202. It is inconceivable that this term did not have a biblical source. Its significance is partly no doubt derived from Ps. 133:1, where the word refers to *brotherliness;* from Ezra 4:3, where it refers to *exclusiveness;* and/or from texts like Mic. 2:12 and Hos. 1:11 (a slightly different form of the word), where it either alludes to the *remnant* or serves as a *"gathering motif"* related to the idea of the restoration/reunion of Israel and Judah. It is accordingly a rich and variegated term.

113. Cf. Mansoor, 1961, 64, who uses the term.

114. Jaubert refers to the existence of the community as itself a "living criteria" ("le critère vivant") as regards a person's fate in judgment (1963, 248).

115. Texts expressing this identity through common suffering include: *1 En.* 95:2, 4-7; 96:4-5; 100:7; 103:9-15, and passim; *1 En.* 108:8-10; *Jub.* 1:12; 36:1-11; 1QH 3.6-12; 9.23-26; 1QM 1.11-12; 15.1; 17.1; *Pss. Sol.* 13:7-12; *2 Bar.* 52:5-7; 70:3-5; 78:5-6; 83:8-23. This suffering is often inflicted by the group's opponents. We can cite, as a major study of the relationships between persecution, vindication, and the origins of the doctrine of resurrection, G. W. E. Nickelsburg, *Resurrection, Immortality, and Eternal Life in Intertestamental Judaism,* 1972; cf. also L. Ruppert, *Die leidende Gerechte,* 1972. This latter book is particularly disappointing, however, due to its largely nationalistic presuppositions, producing a considerably distorted view of the idea of the suffering of the righteous, at least as it bears on the works we are mainly considering.

116. For combined ideologies of humility and poverty that accompany this ideology of suffering, cf. *1 En.* 108:8-9; 1QH 5.20-22; *2 Bar.* 48:19-20. For expressions of unworthiness on the part of the righteous, cf. 1QH 1.21-27; 3.19-25; 4.29–5.4; 5.5-6; 17.18-19; 18.25-28; etc.

cumstances. The humility theme is particularly strong in the *Testaments*, where it is expressed through various motifs: the "simplicity" motif (cf. *haplotēs*);[117] the "good man" and the "good mind" (cf. *TIss.* 3:1–5:5); the theology of *imitatio Dei*;[118] and the insistence on love *(agapē)* for the righteous. The righteous man, exemplified by Joseph, is simple *(haplous)*; he endures *(hupomonē/ hupomenein)* and will be exalted/rewarded by God *(hupsoun)*.[119] There are parallels to these important ideas at Qumran, for example in the idea of the virtues of the "simple-minded,"[120] and we have seen that these groups, for all their claims to righteousness, still confessed their sins/sinfulness (cf. esp. *Psalms of Solomon* and DSS). While these attitudes seem to contradict the confidence shown elsewhere that the group alone composed the righteous in Israel, Gammie has an interesting theory about how acknowledgment of sinfulness and confession of guilt is associated with ethical dualism (practically what we have called soteriological dualism) as a corrective on the self-righteousness that can occur: "even where the concept [i.e., ethical dualism] is fully accepted, writers recognize and in a variety of ways combat its inherent weakness of fostering self-righteousness: by commending humility (Sirach), by confession of guilt (Daniel), and by acknowledgement of the inevitable sinfulness of man in contrast to the surpassing purity of God (Thanksgiving Scroll, 4 Ezra)."[121] Gammie's solution sounds somewhat anachronistic (and rather too Pauline), but one cannot discount the possibility that Paul (and the Gospel writers, for their part) were aware of Jewish precedent for bearing one's righteousness with humility.

The ideology of poverty is certainly another indication of this corporate identity.[122] "Poor" *('ebyônîm)* was a self-designation for the community at Qumran, and while this no doubt reflected the existential situation of many members of the community, the poverty has been understood as not only real but ideological.[123] The two aspects are not mutually exclusive: both would have been *created* by, and certainly *presupposed*, a strong religious stance.[124] Part of the reason for alluding to the group as poor and oppressed was no doubt to

117. For the importance of this virtue in *Testament of Issachar*, cf. H. W. Hollander and M. de Jonge, *The Testaments of the Twelve Patriarchs*, 1985, 38.

118. Hollander and de Jonge, 1985, 43, apply this phrase to the teachings of *TBen.*

119. Cf. H. W. Hollander, *Joseph as an Ethical Model in the Testaments of the Twelve Patriarchs*, 1981, 48.

120. For פתאים at Qumran, cf. 1QH 2.9 (cf. Prov. 1:4; 8:5).

121. Gammie, 1974, 384.

122. Cf. CD(B) 1.7-14; 1QH 2.32-35; 5.20-22; 10.3-12; 1QM 11.7-9, 13; 13.14; *Pss. Sol.* 5:2, 11; 10:6; 15:1; etc.

123. Cf. G. Jeremias, 1963, 141.

124. Cf. Ringgren, 1963, 141.

present the community as the fulfillment of Scripture (esp. the comparable ideology of poverty and persecution in the Psalms), and not merely to reflect the situation of its members. 4QpHab 12.10 even refers rather contradictorily to the "wealth of the poor" *(hôn 'ebyônîm)*. Although one should not take too much from this short reference, it is clear that possessions were not themselves considered evil.[125] Nothing, on the other hand, would pull the righteous together into a strong unit more than a poverty that shared a common source and cause.

These groups frequently shared a common sense of destiny as well. Besides believing themselves to represent the locus of restoration in the present and/or future (cf. ch. 11), they tolerated common fates of persecution and believed themselves to be providentially led by God. A suggestive indication of their corporate identity and sense of common destiny is the recurring "escape from Jerusalem" motif already noted in the writings of several of these groups.

The Edificatory and Consolatory Nature of This Literature

Corporate consciousness can be seen above all in the nature of this literature as *edificatory*. It can be argued that all of it is written to benefit the addressed community. This edificatory purpose is expressed in a spectrum of ways, ranging from general encouragement at one end of the spectrum to legal imperative at the other. In the middle one can discern various shades and types of consolation, some of which lean toward the "imperative" (encouragement to act faithfully) and others toward the "indicative" (statements of theological fact intended to encourage). As for how legal imperative serves this edificatory purpose, the social and corporate implications of legal material in its function as "defining laws" have already been discussed above. Laws serve to define and confirm "who are the righteous" and grant consolation in this manner. The "letter of consolation," on the other hand, is an excellent example of a formal convention employed to build up the community without specific reference to legal requirements. Alternatively referred to as the "community epistle," this form is appropriately adopted by 4 Ezra and *2 Baruch* and is particularly well suited to demonstrate the consciousness of the groups as being the *Israel within Israel*. Only the righteous community receives the letters and gains insight into God's plan for them. Not unlike the New Testament epistles, letters (referred to in *1 En.* 1:2; 94:1-5; 1QH 1.34ff.; and outlined in *2 Bar.* 77:12, 17-26; 78:3–86:1; 81:1; 82:1; 85:4, 6) contain words of exhortation and are deliberately and specifically addressed to the "saints."

125. Cf. Ringgren, 1963, 143.

The origin of this formal convention seems to be the letter of Jeremiah to the exilic community, and it is adopted here, perhaps, on behalf of the present remnant "in exile." These can be termed "letters of consolation" in line with their most obvious function. Their presence in this literature also affords good cause for a comparative study with the New Testament epistles, which are similarly addressed to *whole communities.*

But much more prevalent than either legal material or forms like letters of consolation are the many extensive and detailed exhortation sections. Here again the *Testaments of the Twelve Patriarchs* provide obvious examples of how apparently general *exhortations* functioned to define and identify the community as the true members of Israel. The *Testaments* are in large part composed of exhortations,[126] and each contains at least some words of exhortation, often of great length. These exhortations are regularly inspired by, and follow on the description of, some activity or attribute of the respective patriarch and center on a single moral theme implied in that activity or attribute — for example, envy (Simeon), simplicity (Issachar), hatred (Gad), single-mindedness (Asher), chastity (Joseph). The purpose or function of these exhortations, however, has not been adequately addressed by scholars. Hollander and de Jonge insist that the exhortations are of a "general nature," an attempt to spread a universal or gnomic piety, and are not a clue to the meaning of the *Testaments* in either their Jewish or Christian form.[127] However, to refer to the *Testaments* as "exhortatory writings" and then to grant little distinctive value to the exhortation sections obviously fails to deal adequately with the question of their function for the writer(s) and first readers. While these exhortations have been taken by these scholars in a general gnomic sense as instruction for *Gentiles,* they clearly pertain to Israel. An issue like intermarriage, for example, possessed little relevance for the world outside of Judaism. Combined with the thoroughly dualistic theology of the *Testaments,* the issues dealt with in the exhortations suggest that some more definite and immediate function is intended, even if it is not immediately evident on the surface of the text. Again it is worth considering whether such exhortations, like legal material in general, functioned to define the true people of God by setting out certain "defining issues." Do the morals promoted

---

126. For the importance of the exhortation sections in all of the *Testaments,* cf. Hollander and de Jonge (1985, 32), who take these to be the "center" of the testaments: "the Testaments have to be regarded as a collection of exhortatory writings."

127. Cf. Hollander and de Jonge, 1985, 32, 43-44, 84: "The exhortatory sections which form the core of the book . . . contain little or nothing that is distinctively Jewish or Christian: they are clearly meant to express what is naturally and universally good, and to warn against what all men, Jews and non-Jews, Christians and non-Christians should abhor" (84).

in the *Testaments,* in other words, characterize the attitudes and actions of the *true* people of God (as opposed to the others)?

In fact, all of the main issues raised in the exhortations can be shown to function in exactly this way. These exhortations can be categorized into three groups: those centered on (1) sexual immorality, (2) brotherly relations, and (3) a pure, simple, and honest lifestyle. It is notable that there is not a single testament that does not clearly fit into these three categories with respect to its exhortation section.

1. *Exhortations related to sexual immorality.* This type is numerous and dominant in the testaments of Reuben (cf. *porneia;* 1:6-10; 3:9–6:4), Judah (cf. chs. 13–15, 17–18), and Naphtali (cf. chs. 2–3), as well as in the important *Testament of Joseph.* In contrast to his brothers, Joseph possesses chastity (*sōphrosunē*). Other incidental sayings on the theme can be found throughout the *Testaments* (e.g., *TSim.* 5:3; *TIss.* 2:1-4; 7:2-7). The presence of this group of exhortations is hardly surprising. The pious in Israel obviously felt particularly sensitive to sexual sins, which offend both socially and religiously (cultically). The dawning of Hellenistic ideals brought to Judaism abundant compromise in this area, and these issues accordingly took their place in the *Testaments* as predominant defining issues.

2. *Exhortations related to brotherly relations.* Obviously the story of Joseph's relations with his brothers serves particularly well as a backdrop for exhortations related to brotherly relations, just as the same paradigm suits the exhortations regarding sexual issues mentioned above.[128] But, again, these exhortations have a more profound function than providing detached biblical exegesis. Considerations of the need for brotherly kindness are natural for a group struggling with intra-Jewish conflict, especially when being persecuted or shut out of the mainstream of Jewish life because of this conflict and the treatment they receive from their brothers. Themes related to brotherly relations can be found in the testaments of Simeon (on jealousy; cf. 2:6–4:9), Zebulon (on brotherly compassion; cf. 1:4–5:4), Dan (on anger and deception, 1:3–5:3; 6:8), and Gad (on hatred, 1:4–7:7). In contrast to the unkind attitudes of the brothers, Joseph honors (*etimōn, TJos.* 10:6) them and endures (*hupomonē,* 17:1) their abuse. The sins of anger and hatred in Dan and Gad are colorfully depicted as directed against Joseph, thus relating them directly to the matter of *brotherly* relations. Behind such sayings one can detect the same conflict among these communities as expressed through the ideologies of suffering, poverty, and humility noted above. It would be wise to take into account the

---

128. Hollander and de Jonge appropriately comment on Joseph's important role in the *Testaments:* "Often the patriarch's attitude toward Joseph is the main biographical item in a testament, illustrating particular vices" (1985, 33).

fact that the kind of persecution implied in these exhortations to brotherly kindness is hardly an issue among individuals (in spite of the fact that the paradigm centered on the individual Joseph), but is easily imaginable as taking place between groups. The authors of the *Testaments* were accordingly commenting on the unfair treatment the righteous community received at the hands of those who professed to be their brothers but, by their attitudes, revealed they were not *true* brothers.

3. *Exhortations related to a pure, simple, and honest lifestyle.* These exhortations, which also promote the theme of humility and the ideology of poverty outlined above, are relevant to the actual situation of the writer's community as a minority and also provide evidence that these exhortations served much more than gnomic interests. These types of exhortations can be found in the testaments of Judah (on possessions; 19:1-4), Issachar (on the "simple" lifestyle = *haplotēs;* 3:1–5:5), Asher (on single-mindedness; cf. 1:3–6:5; cf. also *TIss.* 3:5), and Benjamin (on pure-mindedness; 3:1–6:7; 8:1-3). The presence of these three emphases suggests a combined concern for horizontal and vertical relationships. There is no reason to believe that this group of exhortations made up some kind of "monastic rule," but even if they were intended for a group in relative seclusion, the emphasis was not on solitary piety so much as on group relations. The message of such exhortations for the opponents of the writer's community, who perhaps unjustly lived in relative luxury while the pietist group suffered disadvantage, is abundantly evident.

It is perhaps not insignificant that the "two greatest commandments" (to love God and one's neighbor) are evident in the *Testaments* in the context of such exhortations.[129] These commandments are conspicuously general, and thus function more to define true obedience than to provide real guidelines for behavior. In fact, they suit well a group who had internalized obedience and defined salvation more as belonging to the elect group than as obeying outward laws. This raises the question whether Jesus and Paul deliberately chose this generalizing summary of the law because these commandments both retained a defining function — that is, the truly righteous act on the basis of love — while at the same time they did not emphasize or particularize legal requirements. In any event, the suggestion that these commands functioned already in Judaism as defining laws or issues is quite in conflict with the approach of de Jonge, for whom this type of exhortation functioned as an apology for the Christian understanding of the law, and for the relative importance of the two love commands. For this scholar the patriarchs served as models of "exemplary servants of God. They obeyed the essentials of God's law summed up by Jesus Christ, the new lawgiver, in the two great commandments of love towards God and one's

---

129. For the evidence for the two love commands, cf. Hollander, 1981, 7.

neighbour."[130] Besides the fact that such exhortations — unless created *entirely* by Christian hands — must previously have served some function in a Jewish milieu (indeed, they would have been common in that environment), this theory falters on the obvious fact that most of the twelve patriarchs in this work *failed miserably* to live in love with their brother Joseph and were thus hardly worthy examples! The function of the love commands would seem rather to be associated with the feelings of the group in protest against their oppressive brethren who, like Joseph's brothers, did not live up to the calling to love. There is therefore little reason to doubt that the abstract piety of the *Testaments* — including exhortations to sexual purity, attention to the important corporate bonds between brethren, and admonition toward a pure and simple lifestyle — served to address the question of differences between the author's group and the rest of Israel and, implicitly at least, to define the elect according to their behavior. It is accordingly significant that in some places it is implied that only by heeding the words of the patriarchs spoken in the testaments will the "sons" find salvation; the fate of these sons delineated in the future sections is in fact often related (positively or otherwise) to these exhortations.[131] If nothing else, this suggests the kind of soteriological dualism and corporate consciousness witnessed elsewhere in these writings.

National Identity or Emerging Ecclesiology?

One might ask, in conclusion, what relevance this notion of corporate identity had for the attitude of these groups toward the national election. It is obviously true that this corporate identity, which focused on *only a portion* of Israel, represented a profound reaction to the idea of a national identity that focused on the ethnic Israel. This reaction probably did not emerge all at once, and one sees in these writings only the beginnings of the development of a separate corporate existence outside of Israel in which only some Israelites take part — a separate existence such as that which fully materialized in Christian theology of a much later period. Even with these groups, however, some distance has been gained in the process, a process that *began with reaction/protest to perceived apostasy and a move away from one corporate identity* (ethnic or national Israel) and *ended with the establishment of another entirely new corporate identity* (the

---

130. M. de Jonge, *Jewish Eschatology, Early Christian Christology, and the Testaments of the Twelve Patriarchs*, 1991, 167.

131. Hollander and de Jonge point in this respect to *TDan* 6:9; *TNaph.* 8:2; *TGad* 8:1; *TBen.* 10:5 (1985, 51). They comment: "There is undoubtedly a *clear and intrinsic connection* between the exhortations and the predictions of the future" (51).

group of righteous). This new identity at this stage possessed several ties with the older identity but had nevertheless in substance abandoned it, being characterized by an essentially disparate notion of "belonging." After all, if a national group in the dispersive form in which "Israel" existed at this time could possess a consciousness of belonging, how much more could a reconstituted Israel-within-Israel who had formulated theological and circumstantial rationale for forming a new corporate identity gain a sense of belonging that did *not* include others from Israel! One should not be surprised, in other words, that such a separatistic and dissenting corporate identity existed within Israel during this tumultuous time, in spite of many recent denials of the possibility.

Other processes are evident. On the soteriological level one also witnesses a move away from a national "soteriology" (better: covenantal nationalism), an increased attention to individual categories, and, finally, the emergence of a soteriology based on a renewed (but entirely redirected) experience of corporate consciousness. This last stage of the development is the important one, inasmuch as soteriology is no longer centered on the nation, nor has it become entirely individual, but through an emerging "corporate identity" stimulated by shared experiences of crisis has become *ipso facto* a *corporate soteriology* focused on a remnant of Israelites. As becomes quite explicit in the case of Qumran and is perhaps implied in the other works, requirements for membership were adopted and self-designations that implied exclusive claims on membership in God's people were preferred.[132] To employ the term "ecclesiology" for this resultant self-consciousness might involve anachronism (being itself a Greek term, and too fully loaded with accumulated semantic content), but the growing and relatively well-defined structural characteristics of these groups and their already strong self-understanding as the people of God *within* Israel certainly establish them as the predecessors of the kind of ecclesiology later developed within the Christian church. In the light of Qumran, the ecclesiology even of Matthew's Gospel is hardly to be considered as novel (or anachronistic, as the case may be) as previously thought. But to pursue a comparison would take us too far afield — our purposes have been served by drawing attention to the significance of *soteriological dualism,* a term that describes the important structure of thought that emerged from the various stimulations offered by the environment of late Second Temple Judaism and that proved to become a dominating theological ingredient in these writings.

132. These terms are found in close association with limited membership at Qumran, and include *yaḥad* (unity, togetherness, community); *ʿedah* ("congregation" — ancient term for Israel's cult community); *ʿeśah* ("council," "counsel," perhaps "community"); and occasionally *qāhāl* ("assembly" — used of Israel in the Hebrew Scriptures).

CHAPTER EIGHT

A New Approach to Apocalyptic Forms

We observed in the previous chapter how agricultural motifs served to explicate and legitimize the dualistic soteriology of remnant groups, seemingly in direct contradiction of more nationalistic understandings. An investigation of blessings and woes-related forms and revelations of the cosmos (places of reward and punishment) in a previous chapter and a summary look at exhortations in the last chapter suggested that rather consistent functions were granted, not only to motifs, but to many of the *literary forms* employed by these authors as well. That some of these forms were employed repeatedly suggests that they possessed considerable importance for these groups. Two other representative examples of forms that recur with some regularity and relate particularly well to the explication of soteriological dualism are to be investigated here: "historical rehearsals" and "testaments." Other forms, while equally representative, tend to vary in message and in the nature of their precise function in a way that these do not. For example, because of their variety, the many visions in these writings cannot easily be investigated under a single formal category. The vision form was apparently used with a less restricted purpose, in order to communicate a whole range of information, and many other apparently independent forms in this literature are really only subforms of that larger category. A study of these visions belongs more properly under a consideration of revelation, and the reader is referred to ch. 4 for the motivation for employing the vision format.

HISTORICAL REHEARSALS — LEGACY
OF ISRAEL'S PAST PERFORMANCE

Of no little importance to this literature is its philosophy of history. This may seem like a natural enough statement except for the fact that some approaches to this literature in the past have asserted, without careful consideration of the facts as we see them, that apocalyptic represents the total rejection of history.[1] Granted that the visionary form may give the impression that the emphasis has shifted entirely off history and onto the eternal heavenly stage, and while it is true that, in the view of these authors, history has failed to produce an abundant harvest of righteousness, several considerations militate against a too negative conclusion about the role of history in these writings. To begin with, it is hasty to assume that apocalypticists did not expect salvation to take place within the natural realm. Simply because the authors of these works were frequently transported into the heavenly world should not be allowed (as it often is) to obscure the fact that they were soon afterward returned to the earthly world to witness God *fulfill* the plan revealed to them in the vision. As will be seen in ch. 12, these groups regularly expected a transformation within history not totally out of line with other Jewish views of restoration. Traditional views that the restoration would be brought about *within* history through the agency of a messiah, or even through military means, are not lacking. A new temple is frequently seen to arise, along with a new but nevertheless quite "earthy" form of worship that includes sacrifices. The righteous exercise power, and others bow to them in reverence in this new world (whereas there would presumably be no one *but* the righteous in a world outside of history!). All these events are guided by the determining will of God as revealed in visions, and although the final age may be thought to last forever, there is no reason to believe that history comes to an end. It seems that the prophetic and often very critical view of the course of history that one finds in these writings has been confused, by some scholars at least, with a strict kind of determinism that does away with historical processes altogether. But this is not found here — while Israel has certainly failed in the realm of history, this is not enough reason to assume a philosophical and existential view that places the blame entirely on history or envisions its termination.

The philosophy of history of these works is often colorfully portrayed by various rehearsals or "recitals" of Israel's past. Thanks largely to the work of Baltzer, one can connect these forms with what was probably their original *Sitz*

---

1. Cf. esp. W. Schmithal's highly existential approach to apocalyptic theology, which views it primarily as the profanation of history (cf. *The Apocalyptic Movement*, 1975, 79-82): "God has written off history" (82).

im Leben, namely, the second main part of the covenantal formulary, the so-called antecedent history.[2] While many of the historical rehearsals have been separated from the other parts of the covenant formulary and have even become rather artificially fused with future "apocalyptic timetables," it would nevertheless appear that some relationship to this original covenantal context is frequently sustained even in new contexts. Regretfully the appended future-looking timetables (such as one finds in the Apocalypse of Weeks and the Zoomorphic History) have often received undue emphasis while the historical rehearsals to which they are attached, and which are often significantly larger in size, have attracted little interest. At times the purpose of these historical rehearsals has even been minimized or entirely subjugated in importance to the timetables. Consider, for example, the comment by Collins: "The claim that the whole course of history was revealed to Enoch before the flood is a literary device, which serves various purposes. It conveys a sense of determinism, since the course of history was foreknown even then. Most importantly, *it inspires confidence in the eschatological predictions with which these revelations typically end*."[3] This commonly accepted opinion that the rehearsal is merely the handmaid of the more important future revelations is invalid for three reasons: (1) the opinion is based on the false characterization of this literature as primarily concerned with eschatology; (2) this view implies that the (by comparison much larger) historical sections are largely expendable; (3) the historical portions of these periodizations can be shown to possess, not only independent significance, but also a quite consistent function within the context of these writings. Unlike what is usually imagined to be the case, the purpose of the historical rehearsals is not dominated by the literary device of *vaticinia ex eventu* (cf. ch. 11) — that is, they are not added merely to create the illusion that the author is an ancient author viewing things from the perspective of ancient times — and accordingly the future sections are not shorter merely because of the (real) author's limited perspective or sudden lack of knowledge vis-à-vis the *vaticinia ex eventu* (i.e., due to that author's chronological position posterior to the *hinge* in the *vaticinia ex eventu*). The future sections are shorter because they are also less important, and this is proven by the way they consist of stock phrases and beliefs that suggest they do not contain the heart of the author's message at all. All these facts in turn suggest that it is actually the future, not the historical, section that has been added to complete the sense of a total view of history revealed to the ancient worthy and to create an illusion that distracts at-

2. Cf. K. Baltzer, *The Covenant Formulary in Old Testament, Jewish, and Early Christian Writings,* 1971, 10.
3. J. J. Collins, "Prophecy and Fulfillment in the Qumran Scrolls," 1987, 272, emphasis added.

tention from the real author. It should be noted that the addition of a future section conceals the hinge, or present time of the real author, just as much as the addition of the historical section would have done. In short, these writings take history very seriously and have a very serious message to convey *about* history.[4]

This message can partly be seen through the subtle changes in content and function that, through repeated use, the *antecedent history* portion of the covenant formulary has undergone. The original role of this portion in the ancient treaty, one still evident in the covenants in the Scriptures, was to establish past precedents in the relationship between a suzerain and his vassal, and by this means to effectively define the parameters for a future relationship. The original emphasis in these rehearsals was on the might, or in some cases the benevolence, of the suzerain and on his subsequent right to exercise control over the vassal. In the early Hebrew covenants this translated into a list of Yahweh's saving acts in which he was shown to be *ṣadîq* (just).[5] Significantly, however, the antecedent history eventually became more of a confession of Israel's sins in later works (cf. Nehemiah 9–10), and this aspect eventually dominated.[6] A further development took place in the Second Temple period as the confession of Israel's sins evolved into more of an imprecation against Israel for her many sins, and it is to this development that the present texts relate best.[7] The function of these kinds of pas-

---

4. Similarly an appeal to fourfold Persian (Zoroastrian) models to explain the purpose of the historical periodization tends to distract from the important function of the historical rehearsals. I. Fröhlich ("The Symbolical Language of the Animal Apocalypse of Enoch," 1990, 630-31) sought to analyze the Zoomorphic History according to a supposed fourfold presentation of history, but this is a fruitless exercise given that there is no explicit fourfold presentation to be found there! Her structuring of the passage is quite artificial; the symbols do not shift in a consistent enough way to make identification of four separate units possible. She posits that the four periods reflect the Danielic scheme (Daniel 2, 7–8) just as the seventy periods reflect Jeremiah 25/Daniel 9 (633-34). She is closer when she notes that the Zoomorphic History no longer deals with the nations but only with Israel (635).

5. Cf. Baltzer, 1971, 46; cf. Nehemiah 9–10.

6. Baltzer comments on how this area is developed in Ezra 9–10 (1971, 48). Following the exile "historical retrospect turns increasingly into a review of the history of Israel's sins" (92). Such a development may be at least partly explained by Hartman's *rîb* pattern, and the fact that some of the texts functioned as "suits" or "denouncements" against Israel, rather than strictly renewals (cf. L. Hartman, *Asking for a Meaning*, 1979, esp. ch. 3). The imprecation would, in that case, have a rather more lengthy history than suggested by Baltzer's treatment.

7. This is particularly clear in the "antecedent history" section of CD 1.1–6.11, where "disobedience or obedience to the commandments of God is gauged in each case, *with distinct stress on apostasy and its consequences*" (Baltzer, 1971, 114, emphasis added). In the *Testaments of the Twelve Patriarchs* as well, "the fundamental difference lies in the

sages to define and warn and legitimize division (another clear expression of the soteriological dualism of these writings) is accomplished by a survey of the history of Israel's (*not* the entire world's) *failure to keep covenant*. Biblical prototypes for this view of history of failure might have been found in the Psalms (cf. Pss. 78, 106), but it certainly takes on a heightened importance and plays a central role, for obvious reasons, in the literature of dissent.

History Repeats Itself in *1 Enoch*
(Zoomorphic History and Apocalypse of Weeks)

The Zoomorphic History (*1 En.* 85:1–90:42) offers perhaps the preeminent example of an historical presentation where the failure-of-Israel theme prevails. While this presentation includes both an historical (*1 En.* 83:1–90:14) and an eschatological section (90:15-42) and both work together to communicate the message of the writer, the historical rehearsal section certainly possesses independent importance and the future section would seem to be tacked onto it rather than the other way around. The animal symbolism, as mentioned above, serves to outline the respective righteousness of the participants in the historical drama: God's people are clean animals such as sheep, rams, and cows, while Gentiles are unclean beasts (cf. 89:10); only patriarchs (e.g., Seth, Moses) and angels are symbolized by human figures; white, furthermore, is the color of righteousness in this drama,[8] notably that of the righteous patriarchs and, of course, of the author's own righteous community as well. The drama exhibits a unique pattern as history proceeds through alternating periods of good and bad or, more specifically, periods of peace and righteousness interspersed with periods of sin and apostasy.[9] This alternating pattern is in fact a typical feature

---

differing interpretations of history.... 'Example' replaces 'antecedent history'" (146), with the result that eschatological sections are not merely future predictions but also reflect the curse for breaking the covenant (154).

8. Or "purity"; cf. M. Black, *The Book of Enoch* or *I Enoch*, 1985, 257. The color code is well represented in 85:3 and is broken only once, in 89:9, where the colors allude to the three races that descended from Noah's sons.

9. A. Jaubert rightly calls this a "rythme périodique de rupture et de conversion" (*La notion d'alliance dans le Judaïsme aux abords de l'ère chrétienne*, 1963, 219). S. B. Reid (*Enoch and Daniel*, 1989, 60) refers to these alternating periods under the rubrics danger (86:1-6; 88:1-4; 89:5-8) and redemption (87:1-4; 89:1, 9). A. B. Kolenkow ("The Assumption of Moses as a Testament," 1973, 71-74) calls this alternation *"Doppelschema."* Fröhlich understands the dichotomy less chronologically: "Each period is in fact a dichotomic system. The dichotomy is indicated by the contrast of the colours white-black and by the contrast of oxen–wild animals, sheep–wild animals, sheep-shepherds. These contrasts point to the contrast of elect-sinner and the contrast Israel-peoples" (1990, 632).

of these historical rehearsals, in this case represented by the alternating birth of dark and white animals (cf., e.g., 89:9, 11, 12) as well as in later periods by the way hopes for restoration are constantly being frustrated by periods in which the sheep go astray (cf., e.g., 89:32, 51, 54, 74). Not to be missed in this schematization is the fact that Israel is blamed throughout for the unfortunate events of its own history;[10] the "killing of the prophets" theme, evident in vivid form in 89:51-54,[11] drives home this point. An S-E-R pattern, sometimes held to compose the underlying structure of the history, in actuality surfaces only once — namely, during the exile, when it would be virtually impossible to omit the factor of "return." Elsewhere the return motif is significantly lacking, and there is little mention of hope, mercy, or grace extended to those who have gone astray. Nor is any remorse expressed over their judgment (cf. 89:55-58).[12] While the return from exile may have occasioned some reason for rejoicing, this is considerably mitigated by the fact that the postexilic community is blamed for having polluted the sanctuary.[13] Thus even this glimmer of the S-E-R pattern proves to amount to nothing.

The Apocalypse of Weeks is another example of a periodization of history that includes both past (weeks 1-7; *1 En.* 93:3-10) and future portions (weeks 8-10; 91:12-17).[14] The writer's present, the hinge of the passage, is represented by

10. Observed by Reid, 1989, 60.

11. The reference in 89:51 to the prophets sent to the ten tribes appears to be to the massacre of the prophets by Ahab and Jezebel (1 Kings 18:4; cf. 19:2ff.). On the other hand, the invective clearly also includes Judah and Jerusalem, and it is not at all clear in this passage that only the historical ten tribes are chastised; in 89:54 the "sheep" are specifically from the southern kingdom; the writer does not write from a "Judah perspective." Language of apostasy permeates these verses; cf. 'emk^{w}ellu sehtu, (Gk.) πανταχόθεν ἐπλανήθησαν, "they went away completely" (v. 54; Black: "they fell away entirely," suggesting כול תעו; 1985, 270); "diverse ways" (v. 51) seems to be a mistranslation of "in the ways of error" (cf. Ps. 19:13; Black, 269). The passage includes a description of the abandonment of the Temple, the surrendering of Jerusalem to the enemies, and general apostasy (cf. 2 Kings 16:1-2; 16:7-8).

12. Although vv. 61-64 of this passage, which deal with the excesses of the seventy shepherds, reveal a moderate amount of regret. As with Ezra and Baruch in the writings that bear their names, Enoch shows regret throughout ch. 89 but God does not.

13. A reference to a lack of piety on the part of the returnees is made in 89:73 (cf. Malachi 1–2; Ezra 9–10; *Ass. Mos.* 4:8); it seems the author saw his own generation as a continuation of this unacceptable postexilic condition. The return from exile is even described as another "dispersion" in 89:75.

14. The problems associated with the present inversion in the Eth. text (the last three weeks *precede* the first seven weeks in all Eth. MSS) seem now to have been finally resolved by discovery of the Aram. fragment 4QEn^g, which confirms that the Eth. has undergone displacement and that the weeks should be rearranged, as Charles and others already had done, into logical order (cf. J. T. Milik, ed., *The Books of Enoch*, 1976, 48). J. C.

the significant *seventh* week (93:9), which contrasts the "apostate generation" that shall arise, apparently at the week's beginning, with the "elect ones of righteousness from the eternal plant of righteousness" that shall be elected "at its completion."[15] This basic dichotomy is also characteristic of the weeks both prior to and following the seventh week. Thus while "judgment and righteousness" prospered in the first week,[16] the second was one of "great and evil things" (93:3-4). While one man (Noah) is saved during that second week, yet shall injustice take over once again with even greater force (93:4). Thankfully during the third week a man "shall be elected as the plant of the righteous judgment, and after him one shall emerge as the eternal plant of righteousness" (93:5);[17] the fourth and fifth weeks shall contain positive occurrences as well, including the giving of the law and the building of the Temple (93:6-7). But the sixth week is a period of apostasy for those in the "kingdom": "all of them [shall] be blindfolded, and the hearts of them all shall forget wisdom" (93:7-8). Within this sixth week the ascension of Elijah takes place, but also the destruction of the first Temple and the dispersion (93:8).[18] Following this comes the seventh week, which picks up the division between the righteous and unrighteous in the author's own time. It is noteworthy that the basic dichotomy between the righteous and unrighteous continues in the

---

VanderKam, "Studies in the Apocalypse of Weeks," 1984a, 512, concludes on the basis of the same MS that 91:11-16 had been displaced from its original position in ch. 93, rather than the other way around. He also demonstrates (contradicting Dexinger quite convincingly) that the Aramaic fragments point to an original order quite like the present Eth. (cf. Milik, 246-47), only with the Apocalypse of Weeks in its original position (513-18). The editorial changes in the Eth. can accordingly be explained as an attempt to accommodate a misplaced leaf of the original.

15. This seventh week (93:9-10) originally included part of 91:11, now displaced in the Eth. version (cf. 1QEn.^{g} 1, iv; Milik, 1976, 265-66). This verse (in Aram.) further describes the role of the righteous in "rooting out the foundations of violence" (i.e., executing judgment).

16. The rendering of the expression in 93:3 in a positive sense (Isaac: "judgment and righteousness continued to endure") is contested by Black, who follows Dillmann in his translation "judgment and righteousness *was delayed*," since "mankind's degeneration began with the watchers in the days of Jared, Enoch's father," and not *following* the birth of Enoch (A. Dillmann, *Chrestomathia Aethiopica*, 1866, 289). In this case the first event mentioned is one of sin rather than of righteousness.

17. Referring to Abraham and Isaac, or Abraham and Jacob? Alternatively it refers to Abraham and all righteous descendants. Black suggests "his posterity" for "after him"; cf. אכר, "after," with אכרה, "posterity" (1985, 290). We saw earlier how it is the (spiritual) children of Abraham who compose the "plant of righteousness" in association with the patriarch.

18. The verse speaks of "the whole clan of the chosen root" being dispersed. This suggests that all Israel went into exile; Black, however, renders: "the whole people *and the captains of the host*," following 2 Kings 25:26 (1985, 291).

eighth to tenth weeks, the author's future, although in these weeks God also acts to establish righteousness through judgment and salvation (cf. ch. 12 below). The eighth week is a "week of righteousness" in which the "oppressors, and sinners shall be delivered into the hands of the righteous" and the righteous shall be vindicated (91:12). In the ninth week comes a preliminary judgment in which the world is converted to righteousness (91:14); in the tenth comes the great and final judgment (91:15), followed by the cosmic re-creation (91:16), and "many weeks without number forever" (91:17). This outlining of the fates of righteous and sinners in the future portion reveals that the concern of these predictions is closely associated with the pattern of the historical rehearsal. The purpose of both sections, therefore, is not primarily to focus on determinism, or on the future outcome itself, but on the division within Israel. The author's terse narrative highlights the polarity between the righteous and unrighteous and the respective fortunes and calamities of the nation that have resulted from the presence of both elements throughout Israel's history. The future section was apparently added to reveal that God will soon act to resolve the downward spiral of Israel's history. It is significant, in this regard, that ch. 107 (if one can assume that it belonged originally to the same work) offers a view of history not unlike that presented here, one that is explicitly said to be based on the heavenly tablets: "Then I beheld the writing upon them [the heavenly tablets, cf. 106:19] that one generation shall be more wicked than the other,[19] until a generation of righteous ones shall arise" (107:1).

Jubilees — History of Rebellion against the Covenant

In contrast to the relatively terse and systematic periodizations of the Zoomorphic History and the Apocalypse of Weeks, the entire book of Jubilees is composed of historical recital. That this recital is integral to the author's purpose is evident already in the opening of the book, where Moses is told to write a record of the "division of all the days of the Law and the testimony" (1:4). The word "testimony" should be taken in the sense of covenantal witness: the record is going to contain an assessment of Israel's performance vis-à-vis the covenant.

Similar to the other treatments, Jubilees evinces a philosophy of history based on Israel's repeated failure. The first chapter serves as the introduction to

---

19. Black reads: "And I beheld written in them that generation after generation shall wrong them" — this final "them" referring to the descendants of Noah. "The reading יבאש בהון 'shall wrong them,' referring back to the descendants of Noah (the Remnant) of 106.18, is supported by the reading ἐπ' αὐτοῦς = עליהון (Enᶜ5 ii 29) at the end of the verse" (1985, 323). Thus this is essentially a history of the remnant, the "seed of Noah."

this history: the promise of God to be faithful to Israel is recorded (vv. 15-18, 22-25), but equal space is allotted to predictions of apostasy (vv. 7-14, 19-22). We have already indicated (cf. ch. 4) how these two themes work together to implicate Israel: "In light of their rebellion the account will bear witness against them"[20] (cf. 1:8-9). The formal convention already employed in Deuteronomy 31–32, with its similar future-looking perspective and prophecies of apostasy, provides the author with an opportunity to chastise his contemporary Israelites.[21] Thus *Jub.* 1:22 can be considered a summary of the philosophy of history of this book: "I know their contrariness and their thoughts and their stubbornness. And they will not obey until they acknowledge *their sin and the sins of their fathers*" (cf. Deut. 31:27; Lev. 26:40; Neh. 9:22). To the author of *Jubilees* the history of the "fathers" is a history of sin. This is true, for example, of the period of the wilderness: "for I know their rebelliousness and their stubbornness before I cause them to enter the land which I swore to their fathers" (1:7; cf. again Deut. 31:27). Much the same is said about the settlement period as well:

> and they will turn to strange gods, to those who cannot save them from any of their affliction. And this testimony will be heard as testimony against them, for they will forget all of my commandments . . . and they will walk after the gentiles and after their defilement and shame. And they will serve their gods . . . because they have forsaken my ordinances and my commandments and the feasts of my covenant and my sabbaths and my sacred place. . . . And they will make for themselves high places. . . . And each of them will worship his own idol so as to go astray. And they will sacrifice their children to the demons and to every work of the error of their heart. (1:8-11)[22]

The history of apostasy continues during the period of the prophets, as can be seen from the following *killing-of-the-prophets* formula:[23]

> And I shall send to them witnesses so that I might witness to them, but they will not hear. And they will even kill the witnesses. And they will persecute

---

20. G. L. Davenport, *The Eschatology of the Book of Jubilees*, 1971, 22.

21. This is also the observation of D. J. Harrington, "Interpreting Israel's History," 1973, 61-62 — on which see more below: "Moses is instructed to view both the past and the future history of Israel; this is precisely the concern of Deut 31–32. . . . The idea is that future generations will be able to look into the book and see how righteous God is and how stubborn his people has been." Cf. also Davenport, 1971, 22, 26-27.

22. For language of the passage, cf. Deut. 31:19-20, 26; 2 Kings 7:15; Ezra 9:10-11; 2 Kings 17:2; Exod. 23:33; Deut. 7:16; Josh. 23:13; etc.

23. For the rejection-of-the-prophets theme, cf. 2 Chron. 24:19; 36:15-16; Jer. 25:4; Neh. 9:26.

those who search out the Law, and they will neglect everything and begin to do evil in my sight. . . .[24] And they will forget[25] all of my laws and all of my commandments and all of my judgments, and they will err concerning new moons, sabbaths, festivals, jubilees, and ordinances. (1:12-14)

This leads up to the period of the exile (cf. 1:13), after which God promises to make them return — although, significantly, only a "righteous plant" is actually mentioned as returning and being assured that God will not forsake them (1:16-18). Even these verses promise a more complete restoration in the future, however, as it appears that even apostate Israel will, in some measure at least, repent and return to God (1:22-25; cf. below, ch. 12); it is to this that 50:5 refers when it summarizes the history presented in *Jubilees* as a history of apostasy: "And *jubilees will pass until Israel is purified from all the sin of fornication, and defilement, and uncleanness, and sin and error.* And they will dwell in confidence in all the land. And then it will not have any Satan or any evil one. And the land will be purified from that time and forever." This reference in the closing portion of the book harks back to the opening chapter, providing a kind of *inclusio* (cf. 1:22) that demonstrates that the history-of-failure motif composes a major theme in the material that comes in between.

Thus *Jubilees* can in its entirety be referred to as a "historical recital" in the tradition of other histories of failure. Its negative interpretation on the history outlined in prophetic form in Deuteronomy (which could otherwise have been treated much more positively if the inclination to do so had prevailed) is not entirely unique among the writings of the movement of dissent. An MS from Cave 1 (1Q22 = 1QDM = 1Q*Words of Moses*) also recalls the address to Moses in Deuteronomy and betrays a similarly negative interpretation of them which is quite conspicuous:

[Take] the heavens and the [earth as witnesses] for they will not love what I have commanded them, they and their so[ns, all the] days [they live upon the ea]rth. [However] I announce that they will desert me and ch[oose the sins of the na]tions, their abominations and their disreputable acts [and will serve] their gods, who for them will be a trap and a snare. They will [violate all the] holy [assemblies], the sabbath of the covenant, [the festivals] which today I

---

24. Cf. 2 Kings 21:15. The single MS Charles prefers here gives an interesting reading for "they will neglect everything and begin to do evil," namely, "they will abrogate *and change* everything so as to work evil" (reading *yewēltu* instead of the majority *yewētnu*, "begin [to work evil]"). A reference to the abandonment of the calendar during the exile is possibly forthcoming from this reading, something that would tend to be confirmed by the words that follow.

25. For "forget," cf. Deut. 4:28; 28:36, 64 (Charles, *The Book of Jubilees or Little Genesis, Translated from the Editor's Ethiopic Text,* 1902, 5).

command [to be kept. This is why] I will strike them with a great [blow] in the midst of the land. . . . And when all the curses happen to them and strike them until they die and until they are destroyed, *then they will know that the truth has been carried out on them.*[26]

Predictions of Deuteronomy Fulfilled (but Never Resolved) in a History of Pollution — *Assumption of Moses*

Not unlike *Jubilees,* the entire *Assumption of Moses* is in the form of an historical rehearsal written *ex eventu* with characteristic attention devoted to the author's present (or near present; cf. 7:2–9:7). A single verse, the final one, represents a true future prediction (10:1). This agenda is much like the other historical treatments investigated above; the book even brings to mind the opening words of *Jubilees* when it claims to be "the prophecy which was made by Moses in the book of Deuteronomy" — namely, concerning the future failure of Israel to keep covenant (1:5). While it clearly possesses some of the features of a "testament" (cf. esp. 1:15-16), the book is better described as an historical rehearsal presented *ex eventu* with a very terse future prediction appended. In form it diverges considerably from the testament genre, even though recent commentators on the book prefer to designate it the *Testament of Moses,*[27] a name that has all but displaced the older title *Assumption of Moses* (although there is also little advantage to this older and more familiar rubric since the "assumption" is only alluded to in the text as we have it).[28] The work, furthermore, does not show any real dependency on testamentary models but reflects in detailed fashion the contents of Deuteronomy 31–34.[29] The reason for the choice of form is apparently that the biblical passage on which it is modeled invites, in imitation of Moses, a "prediction" of the future of Israel, partic-

26. 1Q22 1.5-11; cf. 2.4, 9-10. The text is cited from F. García Martínez, *The Dead Sea Scrolls Translated,* 1994, 276-77.

27. Cf. J. J. Collins, "The Date and Provenance of the Testament of Moses," 1973, 15 n. 1; for discussion of the title, cf. G. W. E. Nickelsburg, ed., *Studies on the Testament of Moses,* 1973, 5. For an approach that presents this book as a testament, cf. Kolenkow, 1973, 71-74.

28. This title is actually borrowed from patristic writings that referred to this, or possibly a similar writing, as Ἀνάληψις Μωυσέως. The work, available in one Lat. MS only, does not contain such words in its extant form, but since it ends abruptly in the middle of a sentence, it makes good sense that the original text may well have continued with a more extensive reference to, or even an account of, the assumption proper. Cf. W. J. Ferrar (*The Assumption of Moses,* 1917, 5-6), who insightfully assigns this classification: "our 'Assumption' is mainly [Moses'] prophecy of the vicissitudes of the chosen people."

29. Noted by Harrington, 1973, 59-68.

ularly its future apostasy,[30] and this is exactly the element in the *ex eventu* history that the author wishes to emphasize. Similar to *Jubilees,* this book presents a repeating pattern of sin and judgment, while God's mercy in delivering Israel from the exile is also evident (cf. 4:1-6). Some have sought to recover an S-E-R pattern in the *Assumption,* but the "R(eturn)" portion is again significantly muted; it seems as if the author was interested largely in drawing out the future references to apostasy in Deuteronomy 31–32 and downplaying the promises to Israel in chs. 33–34.[31]

More distinctive of this book is the way history is delineated in terms of the actions of the *tribes* rather than the whole nation, in a manner not totally unlike the *Testaments of the Twelve Patriarchs.* During the settlement period the "two holy tribes will be settled" in Judea while "the ten tribes will establish for themselves their own kingdom with its own ordinances" (2:4-5). But in spite of this basic division between two and ten tribes, the tribes apparently respond quite individually and differently to the opportunity: some will "offer sacrifices in the chosen place," others will "build the walls," while others "will violate the covenant of the Lord and defile the oath which the Lord made with them. They will offer their sons to foreign gods and they will set up idols in the Temple that they may worship them. Even in the house of the Lord they will perpetrate idolatry and carve images of all sorts of animals" (2:7-9).[32] The "two holy tribes" centered out for interest are, of course, the southern tribes Judah and Benjamin. But they receive less than unqualified acclamation as they are implicated as partners in sin with those that separated, as 3:5 seems to suggest: during the exile, "the two tribes will call upon the ten tribes, and shall declare loudly, 'Just and holy is the Lord. For just as you sinned, likewise we, with our little ones, have now been led out with you.'" After this time, when God restores their exiled condition, the reluctant and partial obedience of the nation becomes evident again and is once more related by the author in terms of the divided interests of the tribes. In 4:7-9 there can be detected an attempt to combine a theology of the remnant (note: "some parts") with more conventional historical themes (i.e., the two and ten tribes): "*some parts* of the tribes will arise and

---

30. Cf. Nickelsburg (1973, 60-61, 63), who also hesitates to refer to it as a testament for this reason (8, 10).

31. Harrington notes that *Jubilees* concentrates on Deuteronomy 31–32 at the expense of chs. 33–34 (1973, 61-62). The return from exile is seen as a "partial vindication" only (64), and the "eschatological vindication" will be experienced only by the "faithful remnant" (64-65). The pattern Harrington suggests is: apostasy, punishment, partial vindication, apostasy, punishment, and eschatological vindication (65). This obviously entails a significant nuancing of the S-E-R paradigm.

32. Perhaps this is related to the similar accusation of idolatry by *Jubilees* mentioned above. The sin is the decoration of the Temple with animal symbols.

come to their appointed place, and they will strongly build its walls. Now, the two tribes will remain steadfast in their former faith. . . . But the ten tribes will grow and spread out among the nations. . . ." But this return from exile will prove to be ineffective.[33] Ch. 5 is worth repeating in its entirety because it demonstrates how the author felt that the nation was *still* caught in the darkness of manifold sin following the return:

> And when the times of exposure come near and punishment arises through kings who sharing their crimes yet punish them, then *they themselves will be divided as to the truth.* Consequently the word was fulfilled that they will avoid justice and approach iniquity; and they will pollute the house of their worship with the customs of the nations; and they will play the harlot after foreign gods. For they will not follow the truth of God, but certain of them will pollute the high altar by [. . .] the offerings which they place before the Lord. They are not priests at all, but slaves, yea sons of slaves. For those who are the leaders, their teachers, in those times will become admirers of avaricious persons, accepting polluted offerings, and they will sell justice by accepting bribes. Therefore, their city and the full extent of their dwelling places will be filled with crimes and iniquities. For they will have in their midst judges who will act with impiety toward the Lord and will judge just as they please.

In spite of the presence of a remnant in this period (v. 2), things get worse, not better, when a "powerful king" arises over them (probably Herod, who is said to reign for thirty-four years in 6:6), along with a line of wicked priests who "perform great impiety in the Holy of Holies" (6:1-2). Once again, following the reign of this king and his descendants, things fail to improve under the hand of "a powerful king of the West who will subdue them" (6:9). With this reference the narrative, as far as *past* history is concerned, comes abruptly to an end. So while the historical rehearsal in the *Assumption of Moses* is not as detailed as in *Jubilees* (it is, after all, considerably shorter), or as colorful as the Zoomorphic History (it has, after all, adopted a more benign form of presentation), the purpose and perspective of this rehearsal is evident throughout: *Israel's history is a history of sin and apostasy.*

Little resolution of this problem of the failure of Israel in history comes in the passages that end the book. Following the statement about the powerful king of the West is a description of the time proximate to that of the author, which is evident from a clear "hinge" verse: "When this has taken place, the

---

33. Hence, as with the other historical rehearsals in *ex eventu* form, an S-E-R (sin-exile-return) pattern is hardly to be discerned here, *contra* J. J. Collins, "Testaments," 1984a, 325-55, 330.

times will quickly come to an end" (7:1). Then follows a detailed description of the severe time of oppression apparently experienced by the author or his near contemporaries (7:3-10). While possessing many of the features of what are commonly called "messianic travail" passages, which are generally treated as essentially eschatological, this passage, like many others similarly denotated, actually reflects the sufferings of the author's time.[34] The *Assumption* proceeds to say more about "this end" (8:1–10:1), but even this material appears to be more *ex eventu* than genuinely future.

The book, in the form we have it, comes to an end with a man from the tribe of Levi — enigmatically referred to as "Taxo" — who will come to encourage the faithful to remain faithful. While Mowinckel understood Taxo to be a lawgiver and messianic forerunner,[35] others since have interpreted the name as a pseudonym for one of the Maccabees,[36] or as a fictional or ideal figure who serves as a representative of the righteous.[37] In any event Taxo, although not a "messiah" *per se* (as will be defined in ch. 10 below), is nevertheless a significant figure in the hopes of the author (or editor, if the reference was added later). But even with the help of Taxo, whoever he is, it will take the intervention of

34. Either the time of the author himself (as in the case of an early edition of the *Assumption*) or his near contemporary fellow-righteous (as would be required for the later edition). Nickelsburg and Collins argue about the significance of this section, which speaks about a time of distress before the End, as it applies to dating the work (cf. Nickelsburg, 1973, 20-21, 34-35). Nickelsburg argues that it represents the experiences of the author from the Hasmonean period while Collins argues that it is a "stereotyped description of the future eschatological woes" based on the Antiochene persecution. While we agree with both scholars that the description was influenced by the Antiochene persecution, we cannot agree with Collins that it was eschatological in the sense of future (i.e., for our author; as cf. the example of Mark 13:14, which, according to this theory, was modeled on Dan. 9:27).

35. The name τάξων, "orderer," he sees to be the Gk. translation of Heb. *mehoqeq* of Gen. 49:10, used in CD of the "Lawgiver" (S. Mowinckel, *He That Cometh*, 1956, 300-301; cf. also Collins, 1973, 22-23).

36. Ferrar, 1917, 34: "the name TAXO transliterated into Hebrew as TAXOC by the use of a common cipher becomes Eleazar. . . . With his story is here amalgamated that of the widow's seven sons . . . and his 'cave' corresponds to that of the Chasids" (34 n. 1); cf. 1 Macc. 1:53; 2:31; 2 Macc. 6:18-19; ch. 7; 4 Macc. 5:3. Is it significant that 2 Macc. 6:18 also refers to Eleazar as a teacher of the law?

37. Ferrar (1917, 34) referred to him as "the Ideal Patriot." Collins believes Taxo is an ideal figure intended as an antitype to Mattathias in the strongly anti-Hasmonean *Assumption of Moses*, and as a pacifistic, pious, and perfect Jew, again in contrast to Mattathias and to the ideology of violent revolution (1973, 30). Nickelsburg (1973, 36), on the other hand, sees Taxo as a composite of the Maccabean heroes — even the martyrs of 1 Maccabees 2 and 2 Maccabees 7 are partly fictional characters modeled on the story of Taxo! His death effects a change in circumstances for Israel (36-37).

God's kingdom (tersely predicted in one final[?] verse; 10:1) to set things right. How this is to come about — whether the coming is to be a "cataclysmic" event or a long process, and by what agency — was perhaps once spelled out in the verses that originally followed, but the contingencies of textual transmission (was the page removed because history proved that things worked out differently?) have denied us answers to such questions.

Testaments of the Twelve Patriarchs — Testament as Literary Context for Scathing Historical Critique

A quite similar view of history is forthcoming from the *Testaments of the Twelve Patriarchs,* where the historical rehearsal/recital form has been absorbed into another larger (testament) form. Each separate testament contains a prediction of the tribe's future, but these "future" sections, being *vaticinia ex eventu,* actually consist of words that more adequately suit the *history* of the tribe up to the time of the real author. Only at the point where the author's present comes into view do these "future" passages evolve into more strictly eschatological portions.[38] One must accordingly distinguish between historical and eschatological sections, even though both are presented in a future format.[39] Some of the historical sections adopt the formal characteristics of an historical rehearsal more than others, some of them being quite short and unstructured, but even in these the familiar philosophy of history is evident. As with the *Assumption of Moses,* these are tribal histories; they are also histories of failure (or apostasy),[40] for each testament contains, as a regular part of the contents, a prediction *ex eventu* of the *sins* of the particular tribe.[41] This emphasis on the history of individual tribes may result from the formal structure of the work as a whole, containing as it does a collection of individual testaments of the tribal patriarchs,

38. Cf. the description of A. Hultgård, *L'eschatologie des Testaments des Douze Patriarches,* 1977, 1:85.

39. The failure to distinguish has tragic implications for interpretation. The eschatological portions also include the highest instance of christological and restoration passages and may have been later appended to the historical sections, as they would appear to contain the clearest Christian additions. The failure to distinguish between the two types of sections in the past has at times led to a theory of Christian origins for both, and thus for the work as a whole.

40. Hultgård points to the use of the word βδέλυγμα for this abandonment of the pure religion of Yahweh, a word that in the LXX translates תועבה and שקוץ (1977, 1:87).

41. Cf., e.g., *TReub.* 6:5; *TSim.* 5:4; *TLevi* 10:2-3; 14:1–16:5; 17:8-11; *TJud.* 17:1–23:5; *TIss.* 6:1-4; *TZeb.* 9:1-5; *TDan* 5:4-6; 7:3; *TNaph.* 4:1-5; 5:1–7:1; *TGad* 8:2; *TAsh.* 7:2; *Testament of Joseph* 19; *TBen.* 9:1. For the apostasy motif as applied to the tribes in both the historical and present context, cf. Hultgård, 1977, 1:85.

but it hardly explains the overriding emphasis on the *sins* of the tribe. Even the tribes of Levi and Judah, to which are ascribed preeminent honor, are "predicted" to fail. Hultgård has suggested that the reference to the individual tribes testifies to a tendency during this time to speak of Israel commemoratively in terms of twelve tribes; thus each tribe could be taken to represent the experiences of *all Israel*.[42] The disappointment expressed with regard to each tribe would then suggest the tremendous influence of the failure-of-Israel theme on the mind of the author who adopted this form to express his message colorfully and emphatically.

Attempts to see in the *Testaments* an S-E-R pattern,[43] while valid to a point, tend to miss the main purpose of the histories. The prevailing idea in an S-E-R pattern, as it is most frequently expressed by biblical scholars, is the unilateral and almost deterministic divine intention to return the people of Israel to blessing even if they have previously sinned (although, in fact, biblical S-E-R patterns are notably *conditional*). But this raises the question with regard to the *Testaments* as to how such a trenchant and relentless *critique* of Israel is to be harmonized with the prospect of their eventual salvation, which is not clearly mentioned, nor is it applied to the majority of Israel. Furthermore, there are problems in this approach with the way the individual testaments are structured; as in the *Assumption of Moses*, the "R" (Return) portion of these supposed instances of the pattern are conspicuously lacking, as can be seen by the data supplied by Hollander and de Jonge, themselves strong supporters of the S-E-R approach.[44] The result is that apostasy and judgment sections appear with much greater frequency, and are considerably larger, than the promise sections, which are better relegated to the category of restoration passages (on which cf. ch. 11).[45] At best one could refer to a truncated or muted use of the

42. Hultgård, 1977, 1:51, 86. As an example of this he points to *TZeb.* 9:5, which speaks of all Israel but is addressed only to the sons of Zebulon (cf. n. 7).

43. Most thoroughly argued by Hultgård (1977, 82-203, esp. 191-99), although he refrains from citing the evidence for this approach. His treatment gives the impression that the pattern is applied relatively uniformly in the *Testaments*, which even de Jonge has admitted is clearly not the case.

44. Cf. H. W. Hollander and M. de Jonge, *The Testaments of the Twelve Patriarchs*, 1985, 39-41, 53-56. The table on 53-54 reveals that out of fourteen supposed instances of this pattern, all but five of the "R" components either "contain only hints" or are clear Christian portions. Even these five quickly dissipate: *TJud.* 23:5 and *TZeb.* 9:7 are textually uncertain and therefore probably late Christian additions; *TIss.* 6:4 limits itself to the return from exile, as does *TNaph.* 4:3 (which also refers in v. 4 to *renewed* acts of apostasy following the return from exile!); *TDan* 5:9, on the other hand, refers to the exodus. It should be noted that none of these refers clearly to a *restoration* for the real author's future.

45. Where these are found they are heavily imbued with Christian language, as Hollander and de Jonge observe (1985, 56; cf. M. de Jonge, "The Future of Israel in the Testa-

S-E-R pattern from Deuteronomy, and on any considered judgment the composition of the *Testaments* is better understood apart from this pattern, as the biblical "testament" model contains all the elements necessary to understand the formal origins of the *Testaments of the Twelve Patriarchs*. The future-oriented historical rehearsals in the *Testaments* — although evidencing some independence from the testament form and possessing a suggestive similarity to other rehearsals — merely represent an embellished element of the original testament form. The historical rehearsal element of the testament form is particularly suited to the purpose of our groups, since their "predictions" supplied a suitable literary context for the negative review of Israel's history.

The *Testament of Levi* provides a good example of a fairly lengthy prediction of failure. While the exhortation section is very small in this testament (ch. 13 only), the predictions of the future, and the accounts of apostasy and judgment, are lengthy and appear to be very important[46] — probably because the failure of the priesthood in Israel was considered one of the most regrettable of the recent developments in the author's time. For all of the hopes attached to this tribe, its failure is colorfully depicted, covering several chapters (14:1–18:1).

> And now, my children, I know from the writings of Enoch that in the end-time you will act impiously against the Lord, setting your hands to every evil deed; because of you, your brothers will be humiliated[47] and among all the nations you shall become the occasion for scorn. (14:1)

> You will bring down a curse on our nation, because you want to destroy the light of the Law which was granted to you for the enlightenment of every

---

ments of the Twelve Patriarchs," 1986, reprinted in de Jonge, *Jewish Eschatology, Early Christian Christology, and the Testaments of the Twelve Patriarchs*, 1991, 164-79, 173). This begs the question how the R portion of an S-E-R pattern can be so patently Christian. Why would Christians feel compelled to propagate an S-E-R pattern? We cannot agree that all instances of a theology of return or restoration are Christian creations — they are a natural element in the presentation. It is possible, however, that the return sections have been greatly enlarged by Christian embellishment and accordingly now appear to contain a more developed restoration doctrine than originally. Whatever argument one pursues, the notion of an S-E-R pattern dissolves.

46. Cf. Hollander and de Jonge, 1985, 129.

47. The use of this word, αἰσχυνθήσονται, lays blame for the exile on this tribe, since the word is used in several exile passages in the LXX (cf. Hollander and de Jonge, 1985, 169; Ezra 9:7; Isa. 29:22; Jer. 2:26; cf. Hos. 10:6; etc.). Another indication that Levi is blamed for the exile comes from the word against Levi's sons, who are warned that "for seventy weeks" (i.e., ten jubilees; cf. 17:2) they shall "wander astray and profane the priesthood and defile the sacrificial altars" (16:1).

man, teaching commandments which are opposed to God's just ordinances. (14:4)[48]

You take gentile women for your wives and your sexual relations will become like Sodom and Gomorrah. (14:6)

For a more conventional example of an historical recital, formally speaking, we must turn to ch. 17, which presents a narrative depicting the history of the priesthood in seven jubilees ("in each jubilee there shall be a priesthood," 17:2). This sevenfold scheme is in many ways similar to the Apocalypse of Weeks, which plots rises and falls through the first seven weeks, except that this history also depicts a consistent and progressive downward trend over the total length of the history.[49] In the first jubilee the priesthood is established — "the first person to be anointed to the priesthood will be great . . . and his priesthood shall be fully satisfactory to the Lord . . ." (v. 2); in the second jubilee the priesthood shall likewise be glorious (v. 3); but in the third and fourth weeks the priests shall suffer (vv. 4-5) "and all Israel shall hate each one his neighbor"; and then "the fifth shall be overcome by darkness; likewise the sixth and the seventh" (vv. 6-7). Typically, however, our author reserves the worst experiences of darkness for his own period:[50] "In the seventh there shall be pollution such as I am unable to declare in the presence of human beings, because only the ones who do these things understand such matters. . . . In the seventh week there will come priests: idolaters, adulterers, money lovers, arrogant, lawless, voluptuaries, pederasts, those who practice bestiality" (vv. 8, 11). Then begins the eschatological prediction of the vengeance that will come upon them from the Lord, and an announcement of a *new* priest who shall be raised up to replace the fallen priesthood (18:1-2).[51]

48. While the Gentiles may be alluded to in the words "every man," nothing in this portion compels us to believe (with Hollander and de Jonge, 1985, 170) that such sin-sections are essentially Christian, or that the sin is thought to be committed against Jesus Christ. The reference to intermarriage in v. 6, if it is at all associated with what we read in v. 4, practically demands a Jewish context.

49. Cf. Kee (*OTP,* 1:794 n), who refers to "the progressive debasement of the priesthood" in this seven-stage history. Cf. also Hollander and de Jonge (1985, 175), who refer to "the gradual decline of the levitical priesthood." Other testaments reveal this negative historicism as well. *TIss.* 1:11 advises: "Treachery and human trickery are increasing, and treachery is spreading over the earth."

50. Indicated by the number seven and the fact that a decisive end is predicted for the priesthood after this time (cf. 18:1). Also, the fact that the exile is depicted during the fifth week would seem to require that the seventh refers to the author's present. It appears to be this same period that *TDan* 6:6 refers to as "Israel's period of lawlessness."

51. The idea of an end to the present priesthood may have been deduced from Isa. 22:15-19 (as later interpreted by Eusebius, e.g.; cf. Hollander and de Jonge, 1985, 179).

Although not containing a formal rehearsal *per se,* Judah's testament offers similar ideas in a typically enigmatic form. In this testament the role of Judah's tribe is described using an unusual metaphor: "You [Judah] shall be like a sea to them" (21:6) — "to *them*" (αὐτοῖς)[52] apparently referring back to "the sons of Israel" *(huion Israēl)* in the previous verse. The whole of Israel's fate, it would thus seem, is tied up with that of Judah, the tribe of kings.[53] The comparison of the sons of Judah with a sea continues: "as in it [the sea] the just and the unjust are tempest-tossed, some are taken captive, some become rich, so also every kind of man shall be in you: Some shall be exposed to danger, some taken captive, some shall grow rich by looting" (21:6). This appears to refer to the way the fortunes of individual Israelites, like the peoples of the rest of the world, tend to rise and fall with their kings: some become rich, others are taken captive, etc.[54] The prospects of some in Israel appear very grave indeed when their rulers, the sons of Judah, do not act on behalf of the best interests of all

52. For the preference of this reading over less difficult variants ἐπ' αὐτῆς, αὐτόν, or ἐν αὐτοῖς, cf. M. de Jonge, ed., *The Testaments of the Twelve Patriarchs,* 1978, 74; Hollander and de Jonge, 1985, 221 n. 63.

53. Depending on the reading adopted here, the reference would seem to be specifically to the kings of Judah. Following Hollander and de Jonge, we might wish to preface the sentence with the words "But you will be king in Jacob" (1985, 222-23), in which case "you" in "you shall be to them like the sea" refers to the kings from Judah, and the whole expression composes a metaphor for the disobedience of Israel's kings.

54. Hollander and de Jonge (1985, 221) take the final words of v. 6 to refer to the influence of the nations *upon* Israel, rendering part of v. 6: "so also every race of men (will be tossed) on you." The problem is how to incorporate the words ἐν σοί in the expression οὕτως καὶ ἐν σοὶ πᾶν γένος ἀνθρώπων. Kee (*OTP,* 1:800), whose rendering we have already edited, has: "so shall it be in every race of mankind," apparently ignoring the words altogether! It is actually not a difficult phrase to translate. The "in you" corresponds to the "in it [the sea]" from above, thus completing the comparison: "as in it . . . thus also in you. . . ." Literally, therefore, the translation would be: "as in it . . . so also in you every race (γένος) of man." This does leave a problem as to the meaning of "every race of man" being in Judah! De Jonge (in *OTP,* 548, this time) actually adopts the reading: "so also shall every race of men be in you." While this is certainly a possible reading, it leaves open the question of the meaning of γένος. This can only be solved if we take the word to mean "type" or "kind" (a meaning accepted by *LSI* — hence our translation: "so also every kind of man shall be in you"), which makes perfect sense with what follows: "Some shall be exposed to danger, some taken captive, some shall grow rich by looting," which delineates the list of "kinds of men." The plural ἀνθρώπων, rather than the generic singular that would have been used in the case of "every race of man," also favors this reading. In the *Testaments* γένος is regularly used as "race" or "generation" (cf. *TReub.* 3:5; *TSim.* 7:2; etc.); here is another good example of the more qualitative use of the word, as we discovered for 1QS 3–4 above. The meaning "as is true with all other races of men" — i.e., among the Gentile nations — fits the context but is less easy to arrive at in translation without positing an omission.

their citizens but are accused instead of adopting the despotic measures typical of worldly kings:

> Those who rule shall be like sea monsters,
> swallowing up human beings like fish.
> Free sons and daughters they shall enslave;
> houses, fields, flocks, goods they shall seize.
> With the flesh of many persons they shall wickedly
> gorge crows and cranes.
> *They shall make progress in evil; they shall*
> *be exalted in avarice.*
> Like a whirlwind shall be the *false prophets:*
> *They shall harass the righteous.* (21:7-9)

Perhaps not surprisingly, this abuse of power by the kings of Israel is specifically directed against the righteous in Israel. Thus the passage suggests that some *Israelites* will be taken captive while others will become rich — one's fate entirely depending, as can be imagined, on one's association with the power holders in Israel. Thus we have a classic protest against the establishment by those most persecuted by it. This is evident in the mention of false prophets and those who harass the "righteous" in the final lines of the oracle. As a result Israel will be thrown into complete turmoil because of the chaotic situation of this tribe: "The Lord will instigate among them factions set against each other and conflicts will persist in Israel" (22:1).[55] In this way the author, through the clever use of a sea metaphor, blames the misfortunes of Israel — apparently extending into his own time — on the unjust and vacillating (cf. 21:6) policies of her rulers (a theme also familiar from the histories of the biblical books Kings and Chronicles). The result is the kind of disagreement and factionalism ("factions set against each other and conflicts in Israel") that, as the author may have been implying, has given rise to the very kinds of protest groups we are studying.

Israel's History Reveals the "Evil Heart" in 4 Ezra

Some passages in 4 Ezra stand out as similar in many respects to this type of historical rehearsal, starting with the scribe's prayer recounting the history of

---

55. Hollander and de Jonge notice the general reference here: "if a particular period is meant, it is that of the kings after Solomon" (1985, 223). Such a general reference is more suggestive of the author's present. This passage may well reflect upon the experience of the Hasmoneans and the exploits of Pompey as Hultgård maintains, particularly the references to those who rule (21:7) and the "rule . . . terminated by men of alien race" (22:2).

the world at the beginning of the book (3:4-27).[56] Here a pattern or cycle of good and evil in history, especially Israel's history, can be discerned. God created Adam, but he transgressed (vv. 4-7). From Adam there sprang the nations, but these followed their own will (vv. 7-8). Noah was saved through the flood, and while a few were saved with him, his ancestors were even "more ungodly" (vv. 9-12). God chose Abraham and the rest of the patriarchs and Moses, but Israel still possessed an "evil heart" and sinned (vv. 13-22). God raised up David, "but the inhabitants of the city transgressed, in everything doing as Adam and all his descendants had done, for they also had the evil heart" (vv. 23-27). The author concludes: "Thus the disease became permanent; the law was in the people's heart along with the evil root, but what was good departed, and the evil remained" (3:22). This pessimistic view of things anticipates the author's reflections on the repeated apostasy of God's people that follow later in this book. This focus on the "evil heart" paradoxically also provides the author with an instrument of defense of people's actions who, because they are hindered by the "evil heart," are simply unable to do what is right.[57] As we have already seen, this latter line of argumentation is largely rhetorical and the tension between good and evil is resolved only for the righteous in Israel.

So, although the author uses this historical rehearsal for his own literary purposes, he nevertheless accepts the basic premise of the other rehearsals that present the history of Israel as one of failure. Like the *Testaments*, 4 Ezra advances the view that history is characterized by a gradual moral degeneration, which is accompanied by other signs of a general diminution (cf. 5:50-55).[58] He repeats the belief that the fathers failed to keep the law (9:32), and that they are followed in this disobedience by the present-day Israel: "our fathers . . . received the Law of life, which they did not keep, *which you also have transgressed after them*. Then land was given to you for a possession in the land of Zion; but you and your fathers committed iniquity and did not keep the ways which the Most High commanded you" (14:29-31).

---

56. While relating this passage to the theodicy of the book, Stone notes the function of this opening historical recital as "*an indictment of Israel, supporting the charge made against Israel* by God or his representative" (*Fourth Ezra*, 1990, 61). It is notable that this passage does not take on any real function as part of the theodicy until vv. 28ff., which suggests that it may have possessed an independent life before being incorporated into 4 Ezra. Its character as an "indictment to Israel" is still quite appropriate to its present context.

57. T. W. Willett, *Eschatology in the Theodicies of 2 Baruch and 4 Ezra*, 1989, 58.

58. For ancient parallels to the idea of the diminution/degeneration of the generations, cf. Stone, 1990, 153. J. M. Myers suggests that the existence of giants in the early period (cf. Gen. 6:3-4; Num. 13:33; Amos 2:9) was the source for this belief (*I and II Esdras*, 1974, 195).

Israel's History Portrayed in a Meteorological Metaphor in *2 Baruch*

One of the most vivid and interesting — not to mention lengthy — historical recitals is found in a vision in *2 Baruch*. It consists of two parts, the "vision" proper (53:1-11) and a lengthy interpretation that follows on a prayer of Baruch (56:1–74:4). The contents of the vision are typically unusual, but its overall purpose and message is easily discernible. In the vision a rain cloud pours down black and white waters in alternating fashion. This happens no less than twelve times — six times each for black and white — followed by another (thirteenth) pouring down of "much darker" waters for a while. The vision concludes with observations of lightning and of twelve rivers (53:8-11), which are not interpreted and do not appear to be essential to understanding the vision.[59] In the interpretation of the vision the seer is told that the cloud represents history ("the length of the world which the Mighty One has created," 56:3). The alternating black and white waters obviously stand for events or periods of relative sin and curse, on the one hand,[60] and righteousness and blessing, on the other[61] — the same alternating view of history encountered in previous examples. As with the Zoomorphic History, white and black symbolize good and evil in the processes of history.[62] The author's philosophy of history is typically pessimistic as well, for he comments during the vision that "the black [waters] were always more [plentiful] than the bright [waters]" (53:6). This is not what might be called an international view of history, as it seems on a superficial reading, but is rather distinctively *biblical* history. The black waters are intended to reveal the failure of *Israel's* history to produce a consistently righteous people in spite of God's repeated provision of blessing (white waters).[63]

59. Charles understands this period of the messianic era, and queries whether the twelve rivers symbolize the Gentile nations that submit to the messiah, or the twelve tribes of Israel (*The Apocalypse of Baruch translated from the Syriac*, 1896, 89).

60. Cf., e.g., 56:5, etc. These include the transgression of Adam and its results (56:5-16); the sins of the nations after the flood (58:1-2); the works of the Amorites that polluted Israel in the days of the judges (60:1-2); the perversion of Jeroboam and the kings, followed by the Assyrian captivity (62:1-8); the wickedness of the days of Manasseh when the glory of the Most High removed itself from the sanctuary (64:1–65:2); and the Babylonian captivity (67:1-9). Israel is implicated in this history (cf. 60:2-4; 66:3-5; etc.).

61. Cf., e.g., 57:1, etc. These include the coming of the three patriarchs "and of those who are like them" (57:1-3); Moses and Joshua "and all those who are like these" (59:1-12); David and Solomon and the golden age in which the inhabitants of the land did not sin (61:1-8); the rule of Hezekiah (63:1-11); the reforms of Josiah (66:1-8); and the predicted rebuilding of Jerusalem (68:1-8).

62. Cf. Jaubert, 1963, 219.

63. J. G. Gammie compares the ethical dualism of *2 Baruch* with that of the War

This alternating view of Israel's history is confirmed in the words of explanation: "the Most High made a division at the beginning for only he knows what will happen in the future. For with regard to the evils of the coming impieties which occurred before him, he saw six kinds. And of the good works of the righteous which would be accomplished before him, he foresaw six kinds, with the exclusion of that which he should accomplish himself at the end of the world" (69:2-4). The fact that this summary mentions "the righteous" (in Israel) and implies that the white waters concern them also implies that the black waters have the wicked as their subject matter (i.e., especially the wicked in Israel). One witnesses soteriological dualism as much at work here as in previous examples.

The final black waters "which are blacker than all those preceding" (69:1) refer to the present trials experienced by the author and his community, and are accordingly presented by means of a "future" revelation granted to Baruch (70:1ff.). As in some of the previous rehearsals, the author's own time of distress demands the most attention and the lengthiest treatment (cf. 70:3–71:2). This part of the passage is frequently cited as an instance of "birth pangs of the messiah" or "messianic travail" passages, but it takes on its colorful and dramatic character only because it largely describes the *present* period of intense suffering experienced by the author and his community. Again the designation is somewhat misleading. Following this period judgment typically comes at the hands of God's "Servant, the Anointed One" (70:9), and restoration is symbolized by still more "bright waters which come at the end after these black ones" (72:1; cf. 72:1–74:4). Accordingly the author's view of history is not *hopelessly* pessimistic. He places his trust in God's intervention at the end of time, and the coming of eternal white waters: "For that time is the end of that which is corruptible and the beginning of that which is incorruptible" (74:2). Here is an example where it is difficult to maintain, with Schmithals et al., that "apocalyptic" thinkers abandoned history altogether. As God had intervened in "bright" periods, so will he intervene in the messianic age. This age does appear to be qualitatively different from what proceeded it, but this hardly suggests a rejection of the processes of history or the negation of historical experience in the eschatological age. History is deliberately narrated with the specific purpose of revealing the failure of Israel to remain faithful to God and the covenants. This negativeness should not be mistaken as negation.

Scroll in this regard ("Spatial and Ethical Dualism in Jewish Wisdom and Apocalyptic Literature," 1974, 383).

The "Sins of the Fathers" in the Dead Sea Scrolls

Not all of these writings express their philosophy of history in such colorful terms as the Zoomorphic History, the Apocalypse of Weeks, *Jubilees,* the *Assumption of Moses,* or the vision of the black and white waters in *2 Baruch,* but a similar perspective is nevertheless evident in other ways. There is no formal "historical rehearsal" in the Dead Sea Scrolls (1Q22 cited above is not a rehearsal *per se*), but a similar appreciation of history can certainly be discerned there. Allusions in the scrolls suggest that, as in *Jubilees,* the *yaḥad* also possessed a theology of the "sins of the fathers." This exact expression is found in 1QS 1.25-26 in a liturgical context, and in a somewhat different context in CD(B) 2.29 is found the confession: "we have been wicked, we and our fathers, by walking against the commands of the Covenant" (cf. also 4Q266 and 4Q390). The first citation would suggest that the confession of the sins of Israel/the fathers was elemental to the regular cultic rituals of the sect, which is no surprise given that confession of the sins of the fathers also composed a common element in the order for covenantal renewal as part and parcel of the suppliant's own confession of sin.

But it is perhaps even more significant that the concept of the sins of the fathers had infiltrated the nonliturgical parlance of the group as well, as would be suggested by the use in the second passage above.[64] Nonliturgical examples can

---

64. A comparison of the above-mentioned liturgical passage (1QS 1.24–2.1) and the more or less spontaneous confession in a hortatory or didactic passage (CD[B] 2.28-30; P. Wernberg-Møller, *The Manual of Discipline,* 1957, 51, is one who denies a ceremonial character to the passage from CD) suggests that the basic structure and lexicography of the confession remained intact, but there is no question of direct literary relationships.

1QS 1.24–2.1	CD(B) 2.28-30
נעוינו [פשענו חט]אנו <u>הרשענו</u>	כי אנו <u>רשענו</u> גם אנחנו גם
אני [<u>ואב]ותינו</u> מלפנינו <u>בלכתנו</u>	<u>אבותינו בלכתנו</u> קרי בחקי הברית
[קרי בחוקי] <u>אמת וצד</u>[ק]	<u>צדק ואמת משפטיך</u> בנו
<u>משפטו</u> בנו ובאבות[ענו]	

We have been sinful, we have rebelled, we have sinned, *we have been wicked,* we and *our fathers* before us, *by going against* the precepts of truth. And *just* is God who has fulfilled His *judgment* against us and against our fathers.

Truly, *we have been wicked,* we and *our fathers, by walking against* the commands of the Covenant; *justice* and *truth* are Thy *judgments* towards us.

The differences in wording suggest that the sin-of-the-fathers motif had not been hardened into a consistent confession and that such language had a life outside liturgical contexts; or, to view it another way, the liturgical language of confession had thoroughly invaded the nonliturgical language of the community. For discussion, cf. A. R. C. Leaney, *The Rule of Qumran and Its Meaning,* 1966, 128-29.

also be found in the Hymn Scroll. The psalmist in 1QH 4.34 "remembers" *(zākar)* not only his own sins but "the unfaithfulness of my fathers." In the Hebrew Scriptures *zākar* is used of thinking about one's own sins (Gen. 41:9; Ezek. 21:29; Pss. 25:7; 79:8; etc.) and of urging God to remember his mercy (e.g., Ps. 25:6),[65] so the word hardly demands a liturgical context although it was frequently used in such contexts. Holm-Nielsen, on the other hand, assumes a liturgical context for the Qumran expression "the unfaithfulness of my fathers" even in the Hymns;[66] but this last hymn, which has a clearly personal tone, would seem to offer an example of where language otherwise used in formal liturgy had infused the language of personal devotion. In another hymn the author reflects on the deeds of God in history ("the works of Thy mighty Right Hand . . ."), which stand in sharp contrast to "the sins of the fathers" (1QH 17.17-18).[67] This form of the sins-of-the-fathers motif, coming as it does in the midst of historical recital, again suggests more than simple conformity to liturgical confession and that the failure-of-Israel thematic was internalized and treated with some importance in the theological thought and language of the community. Holm-Nielsen also did not have the benefit of Cave 4 MSS, in particular one fragment in which this connection between the sins of the fathers and historical recital is made entirely clear apart from a liturgical context. This recently published fragment was apparently part of an historical-prophetic document based on the words of Moses in Deuteronomy, and it dwells, among other things, on the apostasy of the priesthood and a time of rebellion and contains the words (of God to Moses): "And I will speak to them and send them Commandments, and they will understand to what extent they have wandered astray, they *and their forefathers.*"[68] All indications are that this sins-of-the-fathers motif was born out of an intensely negative philosophy of his

65. Cf. S. Holm-Nielsen, *Hodayot,* 1960, 86.

66. Holm-Nielsen, 1960, 86.

67. There is some question as to how to render פשעי ראשונים in this passage. A. Dupont-Sommer (*The Essene Writings from Qumran,* 1961, 250) has "sins of the fathers," while E. Lohse (ed., *Die Texte aus Qumran,* 1971, 171) has the more literal "der Sünden der Früheren." Holm-Nielsen (1960, 246) and M. Mansoor (*The Thanksgiving Hymns Translated and Annotated with an Introduction,* 1961, 189) agree on "my previous sins." The context of confession, however (although not by any means necessarily the initiation ceremony; as Holm-Nielsen, 146), would suggest a confession of the sins of the author's predecessors. "My previous sins" also would normally require the article on the modifying adjective.

68. For text and translation of 4Q390 = 4QpsMoses^c = 4QPseudo-Moses Apocalypse^c, cf. R. H. Eisenman and M. Wise, *The Dead Sea Scrolls Uncovered,* 1992, 55-56; F. García Martínez, *Qumran and Apocalyptic,* 1992, 280-81. This fragment is related by the editors to a series of others that together make up parts of a single text (cf. 4Q387a, 388, 389). Eisenman and Wise (60-64) speculate that some of these same fragments belonged to a "Second Ezekiel" text (4Q386-89), but the particular text we cite from is more appropriately assigned to Moses.

tory, therefore, rather than liturgical conformity. There is nothing unusual about this in itself, as the motif is used in nonliturgical contexts in the Scriptures, frequently in spontaneous confessions similar to those of the Hymn Scroll (cf. Ezra 9:7; Jer. 3:25; Dan. 9:6, 16).

Significant also is the conspicuous tendency in the confession of the community to shift the focus from the sins of the individual members of the *yaḥad* to others outside the sect, to humankind generally and Israel specifically. This might be taken as evidence of an ingrained preponderance to self-righteousness had not the writer and the community, occasionally at least, included themselves among those who have sinned and need forgiveness. But the concentration on the "fallenness of human nature" and the "emptiness of the human situation" in the scrolls, themes well recognized by students of Qumran,[69] might provide examples of how the sect has distanced itself somewhat from the sins of others and distanced itself from the *responsibility* for sin (to which cf. the clear parallel in Rom. 7:7ff., esp. v. 17). This would in some cases also explain the importance placed on the sins of the fathers, which tends to project the blame for Israel's condition onto its sinful past. One passage even suggests that, contrary to conventional formulations, the community preferred to "recount" the sins of the fathers rather than "confess" them, as if again to distance the righteous community from the sins of Israel's past.[70]

Ben Zion Wacholder's theory about the nature and role of the "second Torah" at Qumran may also reveal something of the distinctive view of history held by the community. Wacholder believes that the sect held a relatively negative view of the patriarchs (usually held in high regard by other Jewish groups) because of the absence of the "sealed Torah" in the period *prior to* Zadok; this is why David is held in a *negative* light in CD 5.1-6, a passage that clearly places the blame for David's actions on the fact that he did not possess this true and higher law.[71] Thus the history of the true Israel really does not begin until this law is made known to Zadok and is transferred to his Zadokite followers (the

---

69. J. Becker, *Das Heil Gottes,* 1964, 138-39, who refers to the "Nichtigkeit und Sünderverfallenheit (des Menschen)."

70. Wernberg-Møller finds it significant that in 1QS 1.23 the "*htwdh* [i.e., 'confess'] of the biblical passage has been replaced by *msprym* [i.e., 'recount'/'enumerate'], the oral confession being the concern of the whole community, and not only that of the priest(s), acting on behalf of the laity" (1957, 50). The subtle change of wording may also serve to replace the "vicarious" confession with an act of *disassociation;* it would appear to be a matter of *disowning Israel's past* as much as one's own. Confessions like these are typically related to the covenantal renewal (cf. Baltzer, 1971, 62, 84, 97, etc.; Wernberg-Møller, 50; cf. M. Weise, *Kultzeiten und kultischer Bundesschluss in der "Ordensregel" vom Toten Meer,* 1961, 79-80).

71. Cf. B. Z. Wacholder, "The 'Sealed' Torah versus the 'Revealed' Torah," 1986, 364-65.

community and their spiritual predecessors). Thus salvation history is alone manifested in these righteous "spiritual descendants" of Zadok.[72] If Wach-older's argument could be sustained, this would place considerable importance for the understanding of the community on the sectarians' radical approach to sacred history with its view of the failure, not only of Israel, but even of Israel's chief heroes. This view naturally contrasts sharply with the "elitist" view of the *yaḥad*'s own role in that history.

There is also evidence in the scrolls that the Qumran community shared with the other literature a view of Israel's history as a series of periods of apostasy into each of which a few righteous figures, or a small remnant, makes its appear-ance. Jaubert refers to this as a "rythme périodique" in which the chief role in each time belonged to a remnant. She offers several examples from CD 5. After the infidelity of Jacob, Moses and Aaron come (CD 5.18; cf. 3.8); after the infidel-ity of the desert come Eleazar and Joshua (CD 5.3-4); after the infidelity of the time of the judges comes the high priest Zadok (CD 5.4-5).[73] This philosophy of history finds explicit expression in one passage in relation to the exile: "For be-cause of the unfaithfulness of those who abandoned Him He hid His face from Is-rael and its Sanctuary and delivered them up to the sword. But remembering the Covenant of the Patriarchs, He left a remnant to Israel and did not deliver them to destruction" (CD 1.3-5). It was according to this pattern of preservation of a rem-nant in history, apparently, that God was thought also to preserve the author's own remnant community (ll. 5ff.). As discussed earlier, the "remnant" here al-ludes to the surviving postexilic community, or perhaps to the immediate spiri-tual ancestors of the community, but the term equally applies to the sect that viewed this earlier community as its prototype (see more, ch. 12).

These groups accordingly give evidence of a philosophy of history having little in common with the S-E-R periodization frequently held to dominate their view of divine history. Employing elaborate literary creations or motifs like the "sins of the fathers,"[74] these groups communicate their understanding

---

72. Cf. Wacholder's statements that "The new Moses, Zadok, to whom the eschato-logical Torah *was* revealed, functionally replaces David in a redeemed Israel" (1986, 365); "Taken as a whole, our passage presents in capsule form a revolutionary revision of Israel's past from Moses to David, and which leads through Jeremiah to the immediate future" (366).

73. Cf. Jaubert, 1963, 218-19.

74. The *Psalms of Solomon* make passing reference to a belief in the sins of the fa-thers, but this is nevertheless enough to demonstrate that the particular view of Israel's history held by this author and his group was, in essentials, the same as the others.

> They acted according to their uncleanness, *just as their ancestors;*
> they defiled Jerusalem and the things that had been consecrated
> to the name of God. (*Pss. Sol.* 8:22)

of the history of an Israel that, along with mankind generally, fails to meet God's just requirements and has done so with regularity. *The history of Israel is a history of failure.*[75] But there is more, for in each period God also raised up a righteous figure or group of people who keep the covenant. Thus two groups are always present throughout Israel's history: those who keep and those who fail to keep covenant.[76] This was not an abstract theological concept; in the words of Morton Smith, "it reflected the experience of a repeatedly disappointed minority."[77] A similarly dualistic view of history is also found in the Hebrew Scriptures, so it was not an entirely novel innovation.[78]

TESTAMENTS — FINAL WORDS OF REVERED PARTRIARCHS

Testaments — records of the last words of celebrated figures to their children before they die — appear in a variety of contexts in writings both within and outside of the protest movement, being well suited for expressing any number of concerns. They vary in both their formal characteristics and in their contents, with the rather unfortunate result that a genre definition on the basis of either criterion is difficult, if not impossible.[79] Perhaps the most that can be

75. Similar expressions of the failure-of-Israel theme are found in *Asc. Is.* 2:3-6 and *Sib. Or.* 1:1-3, 73ff., 87-103, 104ff., 287, 307-8. Interesting is the fact that the Christian portion of *Ascension of Isaiah* (3:21-31) relates the history of the church according to the same pattern of apostasy!

76. This is what Jaubert, in reference to Qumran, calls "un schéma binaire de l'histoire de l'Alliance" (1963, 219).

77. M. Smith, *Palestinian Parties and Politics That Shaped the Old Testament,* 1971, 52.

78. Smith, 1971, 15. There are subtle differences, however, between the two historical dualisms. Whereas in the Scriptures the emphasis is frequently on the *times* of good or evil brought on by the actions of the nation (an emphasis also maintained in our writings), here the emphasis is also more personal — namely, the consistent presence of a *witness* to righteousness, culminating in a "plant of righteousness" or of some kind of righteous remnant in the author's day.

79. For a concise history of the attempt, cf. H. W. Hollander, *Joseph as an Ethical Model in the Testaments of the Twelve Patriarchs,* 1981, 1-6. Cf. also Hollander and de Jonge, 1985, 29-33; Collins, 1984a, 325-26, who is willing to characterize the form according to its narrative framework but not according to its contents. We should perhaps agree that the form is discernible by the presence of a farewell discourse; however, little beyond that gives consistency to the form. The testament of Abraham in *Jub.* 21:1-26, e.g., is somewhat similar in contents and appears to share much the same social function as the *Testaments of the Twelve Patriarchs,* but scarcely shows any close resemblance in form beyond

said about the form of Jewish testaments is that they generally share three components with their biblical prototype — the gathering of the offspring of the patriarch to hear his last words, the patriarch's prophecy of his sons' or grandsons' future, and the account of the patriarch's death[80] — in other words, the basic elements of the narrative framework. Some records of "final words" lack even these basics, however, and may be better categorized with other literary forms, as noted above in regard to the *Assumption (Testament) of Moses,* which is better termed an historical rehearsal in the form of *ex eventu* prophecy.[81] Because of the fluidity in the definition of testament, therefore, only a single example of the form will be considered here, namely, the collection of testaments referred to as the *Testaments of the Twelve Patriarchs.* If this testament collection is not representative of all other testaments, it is at least an eminently suitable example of the kinds of things that can be done with this highly suggestive literary form.

The contents of these testaments exhibit a fairly consistent pattern, however, with some alternation in the order thereof.[82] One finds in each: (1) the *introduction,* stating the occasion for the testament; (2) an *interpretative or midrashic historical narrative,* usually outlining some feature of the patriarch's life, normally consisting of an enlargement on some comment made in Scripture about him, and usually derived from the canonical testament of Jacob in Genesis 49; (3) a *parenetic section* containing a word of exhortation

---

the basic narrative framework (last words and report of death); it is much shorter and omits some of the other features essential to the *Testaments.* Hollander and de Jonge accordingly conclude that "The Testaments [of the Twelve Patriarchs], in many ways, stand by themselves" (33).

80. Cf. Hollander, 1981, 1.

81. Collins includes this work in his consideration of testaments, along with the *Testament of Job* and the *Testaments of the Twelve Patriarchs,* but likewise admits that these and others vary considerably in their use of the testament form: the *Testament of Moses* "consists almost entirely of prediction," and the *Testament of Job* "is predominantly retrospective and is a re-telling of the life of Job" (cf. 1984a, 326). The *Testament of Abraham,* as Collins points out (326), can hardly be called a testament since it contains no farewell discourse at all. Anita Kolenkow ("What Is the Role of Testament in the Testament of Abraham?" 1974, 182-84) points out that the word "testament" is not appropriate to this work since it contains no actual testament, and since tradition otherwise ascribed no testament to this patriarch. Many of the formal aspects of a testament are lacking in the *Testament of Solomon* and the *Testament of Adam* as well (Collins, 327). For still other testaments, cf. *1 En.* 81:5-6; 82:1; *Jub.* 21:1-26.

82. Hollander (1981, 1) divides the testament form into three parts, the middle part (the farewell speech) also being divided into three. His analysis comes closest to ours. Collins (1984a, 325) similarly suggests a three-part pattern of content for these testaments: (1) historical retrospective, (2) ethical exhortation, (3) prediction of the future. For further discussion, cf. Hollander and de Jonge, 1985, 29-33.

appropriately based on the experiences of the patriarch;[83] (4) *prophecy about the future* that generally centers on the future sins of the tribe and its eventual fate — often compared to or contrasted with the fates of the tribes of Levi and Judah — or the emergence of a leader from these tribes, or other words of exhortation relative to Levi and Judah, and which consists, as already noted, of *ex eventu* as well as truly predictive prophecy; and (5) the account of the patriarch's *burial*. For obvious reasons an approach to the *Testaments* that sees their composition modeled on passages like Genesis 49 is preferable to one that sees them, with scholars like Hultgård, composed according to an S-E-R pattern.[84]

The Function of Testaments

The function of these testaments can be determined from things like their *distinctive subject matter, functional characteristics,* and *literary context.* We can deal with each one in turn. As for their distinctive subject matter, if one views the first, second, and fifth components above as purely formal or conventional, this leaves the third and fourth components as opportunity for the author to present his distinctive message. The third component frequently dwells on matters of sexual behavior or brotherly relationships. The fourth contains the historical rehearsal or another form of the failure-of-Israel theme cast in a future, predictive framework (see above). The message of these sections accordingly centers on two main subject areas: *ethics* and the *"future" of Israel.* This fairly consistent content of the testaments provides insight into the role the form played in this movement and the purpose of the author in employing it.

One can understand something of this purpose by observing other, more functionally related, characteristics as well. Testaments clearly depend on the aura of authority that they bring with them. The form is useful as a medium of revelation, possessing important biblical precedents.[85] The modern problem with the "pseudonymity" of the testaments apparently did not arise in the ancient world. Perhaps it would have been accepted that, since many such testaments were recorded and preserved in the biblical records, the existence of other testaments not found there would have been considered possible, even

---

83. "The illustrations for the admonitions are taken from the patriarch's own experience. The experiences of the fathers (especially those of Joseph) have a normative function for their sons: they make clear what one should do or should avoid" (Hollander and de Jonge, 1985, 32).

84. Hultgård, 1977, 1:191ff.

85. Cf. Genesis 49; Deuteronomy 33; Joshua 23–24; 1 Samuel 12; 1 Kings 2:1-9; 1 Chronicles 28–29.

likely — their authors would no doubt have hoped, in any event, for their immediate recognition and reception *as authentic.*[86]

Testaments were also entirely appropriate as authoritative instruments
for revelation because of their literary context or putative situation of delivery,
being spoken during the most solemn time of life — not *anyone's* life, moreover, but a *patriarch's* life.[87] As deathbed words they would have been considered a kind of eleventh-hour wisdom to the patriarch's beloved sons, spoken
when the speaker was particularly solemn and penitent, able to view his world
and life in retrospect and with unsurpassed objectivity and integrity. The patriarch was near to his fate and in an appropriate attitude of repentance, which
suggests an appropriate time for prophetic inspiration. Anything said by the
patriarch at this time would certainly be treated as important, truthful, and inspired. To reject these words, on the other hand, would be to despise the grave
of holy dead men. God's people would surely be hesitant to disobey the final
words of their fathers. Thus the testament form was chosen because of its overall effectiveness as a medium of revelation.

Hollander has worked extensively on the function of the *Testaments* and
assumes, with a growing number of scholars, that the parenetic sections were
the most significant to the authors.[88] He accordingly plays down the future (eschatological) sections which, he says, have received too much attention in the
past and are in any event patently *Christian.*[89] Thus each testament functions as
moral exhortation, or as an apology for an ethical — i.e., properly "Jewish" —
lifestyle. The figure of Joseph in particular demonstrates this, as he is held up as
an example *par excellence* of the "good man" and the pious lifestyle.[90] But surely

---

86. That the *Testaments* were intended to be taken seriously as the *actual* words of
the patriarch (rather than as merely literary creations) is evident in the way they appeal to
other authoritative writings — e.g., *1 Enoch* and the heavenly tablets (for passages and discussion, cf. Hultgård, 1977, 1:83-84). It is clear in any event that the pseudepigraphic style
of the work would *not* have been considered a hindrance to acceptance; testaments appear
to have been promoted as genuine accounts of the patriarch's last words or, as argued below, genuine (and therefore, in the eyes of the seer, legitimate) *prophetic* records *in the
name of* the patriarch.

87. As Collins remarks: "Every tradition-oriented society has attached great importance to the last words of famous men" (1984a, 325). Kolenkow (1973, 71) cites *Genesis
Rabbah* 62 regarding the last words of the righteous: "In order to allow the righteous to die
in peace, he is allowed to have disclosures of the other world during life."

88. Hollander, 1981, esp. 6-7.

89. Hollander, 1981, 7.

90. Joseph represents "the ideal of moral behaviour" (Hollander, 1981, 62). The
brothers are "bad examples" (50). "Not only in his own farewell-discourse is Joseph put
forward as a good example for his sons, but his brothers too refer to him on their death-
beds, exhorting their sons to be like Joseph. He was the one who kept himself free from

the chief problem with such an approach is that it too easily dispenses with the problem created by the relationship between the future references (which are not all eschatological, as pointed out earlier) and the parenetic sections, overly emphasizing the latter at the expense of other elements. One might ask: Why so much and so detailed *(ex eventu)* prophecy in the *Testaments?* This approach leaves unanswered some other important questions as well: Where is a suitable context to be found for such hortatory/apologetic literature?[91] Does the theory adequately take into account that the polemic of the *Testaments* is *not* directed at Gentiles or Christians but at Jews (members of the tribes of Jacob)? Is a very general edificatory or ethical purpose such as suggested by Hollander urgent or emotive enough, socially speaking, to draw out such a colorful and at times polemical tone as in the *Testaments?*[92]

A preferable approach to the *Testaments* would take into account the background of apostasy and protest. Their message, as understood from this perspective, would be discerned in a *combination* of ethical and "future" aspects. Testaments offer an ideal opportunity to subtly "predict" *ex eventu* the *situation of apostasy* in which the nation finds itself. Their effectiveness, on the other hand, comes from their emotive character: testaments "demand" a hearing from those who may not wish to hear (i.e., "apostates"). The end result is that "future" Israel is warned against things like sexual immorality, and Israel's priests, against liberalization.[93]

---

adultery, who never stopped loving his brothers, who was full of mercy, compassion and forgivingness, who humiliated himself. He was a righteous man tried by God and rewarded and exalted afterwards" (65). He was the "good man" (ὁ ἀγαθὸς ἀνήρ), a Hellenistic-Jewish ideal (65-66, 92) fundamental to which is the keeping of the law (67, 91).

91. Hollander suggests a (Christian) "school" in comparison with Jewish Hellenistic philosophical schools (1981, 96). While this is possible for the immediate context of the writing, it hardly explains the wider context of debate the *Testaments* address. It is not valid, in any event, to assume that such schools embraced the abstract concept of learning for the sake of learning itself (*diatribe,* e.g., was notably polemical). In the present case the authors appear to deal with polemical concerns in the Jewish community, eliminating the possibility that the *Testaments* were simply an objective collection of traditions presenting a moral lifestyle. There is no evidence in the *Testaments* that their message was directed at an antinomian Christianity — the insistence on a messiah from Levi and Judah would seem to preclude a Christian messianology for either the writer or recipients.

92. The fact that they borrow the language of Wisdom (Hollander, 1981, 64) is hardly an answer to the question about their social function. Nor does the fact that their parenesis centers on piety and the relationship to the neighbor, rather than the Torah, imply that a Christian ethic is being promoted. It should be remembered that the ethic of Qumran was also pietistic and relationship oriented, but hardly to be taken as Christian for this reason. Cf. H. Ringgren, *The Faith of Qumran,* 1963, 135-36. To the concept of *haplotēs* (ἀπλότης) in the *Testaments* can be compared *tom* (תם) and *yošer* (ישר) in the scrolls.

93. Interestingly the investigation of R. A. Kugler, *From Patriarch to Priest,* 1996, of

A prime example of how the testament form condemns the sexual sinful-ness of Israel comes with the *Testament of Joseph*. This testament typically ex-pands on incidents from Joseph's life, highlighting his reputation for brotherly faithfulness, piety, and moral propriety in staving off the advances of Potiphar's wife (*TJos.* 2:1–9:5). The testament then turns this example into a condemna-tion of Israel's sexually immoral actions, partly by using lengthy exhortation (10:1–11:7; 18:1-4), partly by allowing the historical facts to "speak for them-selves."[94] Joseph's brothers naturally receive relatively less laudable attention and are remembered more for their sin than for their righteousness. The story of Joseph's treatment by his brothers thus serves as the foundation tale for ex-hortation and reproof; for this reason it is often the individual patriarch's treat-ment *of Joseph,* and his own contrasting sins, that establish a basis for ethical critique in each individual testament.[95]

The "Good Man" Joseph as a Foil for the Unrighteous

Each testament repeats the same basic pattern: experience of a patriarch (espe-cially vis-à-vis Joseph), exhortation based on that experience, and future pre-dictions regarding Jacob's offspring — that is, *Israel.* If, as in most cases other than the *Testament of Joseph,* a patriarch is remembered for some sin or nega-tive behavior, this in turn becomes the basis for warnings about Israel's *future* apostasy. The exhortation sections and future predictions are accordingly very

---

the various *sources* for the *Testaments* also reveals a pervasive dualism in the precursors of the *Testaments*. He suggests that the purpose of the antecedent *Testament of Levi* docu-ments was similarly that of critiquing the priesthood, while the ethical material offers a paradigm for the righteous: "Levi and any who follow his example are destined to be God's favored cultic servants, for they never turn away from faithful service. . . . *Aramaic Levi* is perhaps in part a protest document aimed at expressing dissatisfaction with the priest-hood of the author's day, and at offering an alternative" (109); "Throughout the book the author's dualism appears over and over again; there are forces that seek purity and righ-teousness, and wisdom and learning, while there are others that promote impurity and in-iquity, and foolishness and ignorance" (136); "On one hand there are priests who do not realize the ideal evinced by Levi with his passion for purity and attachment to the roles of scribe and sage. . . . On the other hand there are priests who accept the norms established in Levi. . . . *Aramaic Levi* is a rejection of the former kind of priest, and a plea for accep-tance of the latter type" (136-37); etc.

94. This is significant in view of the fact that Joseph is the earliest example of the re-jection of the righteous by Israel found in the tradition, a point expressed by Stephen in Acts 7. For the relevance of this story to historical divisions within Israel, cf. Smith, 1971, 47.

95. Hollander and de Jonge, 1985, 33.

closely interrelated, the latter often growing out of the former. Thus the failures of the patriarchs are seen not only to presage, but also to typify, the later failures of Israel, who sin as they do.[96] One can see how, in this typological presentation, "the good man" (ho agathos anēr) Joseph virtually becomes a paradigm for the righteous group, and the brothers paradigms for the rest of Israel. Joseph thus serves not *simply* as an *example* of a righteous life, although this cannot be denied altogether (this theory would explain his own righteous ways but does not explain the concentration on sin or brotherly relations in the parenesis, nor does it explain the future component); Joseph rather serves *primarily as a springboard* to draw attention to the future sins of Israel in their time of apostasy. Thus Joseph should not be viewed as the center of attention in the *Testaments* to the exclusion of the other brothers, who are equally important in the presentation. Rather, the life of Joseph is here treated as a source for *haggadah* that provides opportunity to center in on (1) sexual morality, (2) brotherly relations, and (3) pride, all three of which possess obvious relevance in respect to Israel's "future" behavior. These three are also what might be viewed as socially relevant concerns for a relatively small group estranged from the rest of Israel who have been offended by what they see as the sin, hatred, and social distinctions promoted by their opponents. Thus Joseph in his role as *agathos anēr* becomes a foil for the unrighteous. Thus there is a kind of soteriological dualism expressed in the use of the term "the good man" itself.[97]

Along with this effective, but subtle, literary function of the testament form, more explicit statements condemning the sin of Israel also tend to confirm this approach. The *Testament of Levi* offers a particularly important example of this in centering out the priesthood for criticism. It speaks of how the sons of Levi will act impiously, transgress and even destroy the Law, plunder the Temple, commit adultery and intermarry (10:2-3;[98] 14:1–16:5).[99] Among some of their other sins are pride and persecuting the righteous — standard com-

96. Baltzer, who views the testaments as another example of the preservation of the covenant formulary, also notes developments in the function of the "example" section — i.e., no longer strictly "antecedent history," so much as a new interpretation of history reflecting the author's view of the past sins and apostasy of Israel. This interpretation in turn influences the eschatological (future) sections, which expose the working out of the curse on the sinful people (1971, 146, 154).

97. It should be emphasized in this regard, as Hollander also notes, that the term comes largely from wisdom literature where "the 'good man' is the righteous, God-fearing man, *the counterpart of the sinner or the wicked man*" (1981, 67, emphasis added). Cf. Prov. 13:22; Eccles. 2:26.

98. The apparent reference to the veil of the Temple may evidence tampering by Christian editors; however, τὸ ἔνδυμα seems to conceal another more original judgment metaphor (cf. Kee, *OTP*, 1:792 n. 10b; also cf. Hultgård, 1977, 1:95).

99. Hultgård interprets 14:5-6 in reference to cultic prostitution (1977, 1:98-99).

plaints leveled at an apostate priesthood. The priests are not the only ones to be openly criticized, however, preventing the conclusion that a priestly controversy of some kind has generated such indictments. Judah's tribe is also said to transgress; their sins include "love of money" and "sexual promiscuity," things that lead to dullness in hearing God's word (*TJud.* 17:1–23:5 passim). The *Testament of Dan* mentions intermarriage as part of his tribe's abandonment of the Lord (5:4-6). The patriarch Benjamin predicts that his sons *"will perish, with few exceptions,"* because of their sexual promiscuity (*TBen* 9:1).

Other passages that do not mention any specific sin nevertheless just as clearly reveal the function of the *Testaments* as warnings against what is seen as the apostate behavior of the Israel of the late Second Temple period. Thus Judah gives an *ex eventu* account in typical testamentary form of the factions that will exist among his descendants (*TJud.* 21:6–22:3). The *Testament of Issachar* "predicts" that "in the last times" the sons of Issachar will apostatize (6:1-4; see above). Referring again to "the last days," Zebulon tells how his descendants "will be divided" (*TZeb.* 9:1-5).[100] The strife of Zebulon's descendants contrasts sharply with the exemplary behavior of their tribal ancestor, who is held up by his testament as a particularly righteous individual worthy of emulation: "I shall be glad in the midst of my tribe — as many as keep the Law of the Lord and the commandments of Zebulon, their father. But the Lord shall bring down fire on the impious and will destroy them to all generations" (*TZeb.* 10:2-3). Dan similarly refers to "Israel's period of lawlessness" (*TDan* 6:6), prophesying that his sons "would go astray from God's law, that they would be estranged from their inheritance, from the race of Israel, and from their patrimony" (7:3). The author revealingly interjects the words: "and that is what occurred."

Although the literary context of the *Testaments* points to the period of the exile as the primary reference of some of these prophetic words of warning, there are indications (similar to those of other writings investigated above) that one must go beyond the literary context to discover the real message of the *Testaments*. There is little doubt in this regard that the author has primarily in mind his *contemporary* situation. As if in acknowledgment of this double significance, the *Testament of Naphtali* announces not one but *two* captivities for Naphtali's sons: *after returning from exile* they will stray from the Lord and live according to the way of Gentiles, committing the lawlessness of Sodom, and will "neglect the Lord and act impiously" (4:1-5). The sons of Gad are similarly warned that *"at the end"* they will *"depart"*[101] from

---

100. The primary reference being to the years of the divided monarchy (cf. Hollander and de Jonge, 1985, 272).

101. The verb ἀπόστασθαι, "desert," is elsewhere used with ἀπὸ κυρίου in the *Testa-*

Levi and Judah and will "live in all manner of wickedness and evildoing and corruption in the sight of the Lord" (*TGad* 8:2; cf. also *TSim.* 5:4). Presumably the *Testament of Asher* also addresses the latter days when it says that this tribe will be found "heeding not God's Law but human commandments, being corrupted by evil" (7:5). In a passage from the *Testament of Benjamin* whose significance is clouded somewhat by its Christian additions, Benjamin mentions the inevitability of Israel's judgment. This judgment is significantly related to a lack of brotherly love on the part of Israel, something they will be judged for by the Gentile Midianites, who, in contrast to this, "loved their brothers" — "for the Lord first judges Israel for the wrong she has committed and then he shall do the same for all the nations. Then he shall judge Israel by the chosen gentiles as he tested Esau by the Midianites who loved their brothers" (10:8-10).[102] The prognosis of this patriarch is particularly bleak inasmuch as he even predicts that eventually the "kingdom of the Lord" will be taken away from this tribe altogether (9:1; for another prime example of the sin of lack of brotherly love, cf. *TJud.* 21:1–22:3).

The "Good Man" Joseph as a Paradigm of Righteousness

It is accordingly not difficult to discern the function of the testamentary form in these passages in condemning present-day Israel by means of the *combination of ethical and future material*. But this combination also offers the opportunity for the author to *define who he does think belongs to the righteous community*. It is in the exhortation part of the testaments, particularly where exhortation is based on the more *worthy* examples of some of the sons of Jacob, that the author outlines criteria for a righteous existence. The moral examples of Levi, Judah, and Joseph in particular are given the most attention throughout the *Testaments,* reflecting the belief that these patriarchs came closest to meeting God's righteous requirements in their attitudes and actions. Thus even Benjamin advises his tribe to "pattern your life after the good and pious man Joseph" (*TBen.* 3:2); and Simeon implies that such an *imitatio* of Joseph is es-

---

ments (cf. Hollander and de Jonge, 1985, 336), suggesting that deserting Levi and Judah is tantamount to deserting the Lord. The fact that this happens "at the end" also precludes seeing a reference to the divided kingdoms in the time of Solomon here.

102. Hollander and de Jonge include the words: "for the unrighteousness done to him, because they did not believe that God appeared in the flesh as a deliverer" (1985, 438). Kee's omission rightly reflects the limits of the Christian interpolation, although the idea of Israel being judged by Gentiles in v. 10 is also somewhat suspect. The entire section was not interpolated, however, as indicated by the allusion to Levi and Judah as the "brothers" Benjamin should have loved.

sential to receive the covenant "blessings" (*TSim.* 4:5).[103] Issachar is also held up as an example of perfect righteousness (*TIss.* 7:1-17). The important thing is that these statements hardly constitute general encouragement to seek a higher lifestyle or piety; the matters at hand are obviously felt to entail grave covenantal consequences[104] (as will be witnessed again in the investigation of the pneumatology of the *Testaments* in the following chapter). To this feature one can compare the relationships between exhortation and "defining laws" discussed earlier.

A similar paradigmatic purpose would seem to be involved in recalling the sinful acts of the patriarchs as *negative* examples, and in the exhortations to avoid the grief and judgment that result from their sins. A good example of this is the long warning in *Testament of Judah* 11–17 against committing the sin of lust after the example of the patriarch, a sin that is partly blamed on wine. Likewise Reuben has advice for his "brothers and sons":

> See here, I call the God of heaven to bear witness to you this day, so that you will not behave yourselves in the ignorant ways of youth and sexual promiscuity in which I indulged myself and defiled the marriage bed of my father, Jacob. But I tell you he struck me with a severe wound in my loins for seven months, and if my father, Jacob, had not prayed to the Lord in my behalf, the Lord would have destroyed me. (*TReub.* 1:6-8)

The prayer of Reuben's righteous father appears here as the explanation for Reuben's continued life, a curious but no doubt necessary rationalization typical for this literature, the implication again being that most Israelites would certainly not fare so well should they commit sexual sins.

In conclusion, one can discern a double function for the testament form in the *Testaments of the Twelve Patriarchs*: to warn Israel regarding their apostasy, on the one hand, and to establish a standard of righteous behavior, on the other. The parenesis found in them is accordingly not directed to Gentiles or to Christians but to apostate Jews and, in a way, as a safeguard to the righteous. This double function may even be explicitly alluded to in the opening of the *Testament of Levi*, which describes this testament as an account of "the things

---

103. The verse reads, "Guard yourselves therefore, my children, from all jealousy and envy. Live in the integrity of your heart, so that God might give you grace and glory and blessing upon your heads, just as you have observed in Joseph."

104. In this regard it may be that the calendar continued in this period to be another of these dividing issues. The *Testament of Naphtali* possesses a typical order-in-nature passage that implies that failure to keep the calendar is tantamount to adhering to "wandering spirits" (3:2-5), and associates this sin with the captivity (4:1). In an enigmatic passage Levi and Judah are portrayed as grabbing the sun and moon (5:1-5), perhaps also alluding to the fact that those who followed their example would maintain the proper calendar.

that he decreed to his sons concerning *all they were to do* [function of defining the righteous community?],[105] and the things *that would happen to them until the day of judgment* [function to warn Israel of apostasy and judgment]" (*TLevi* 1:1). The employment of the testament form is, in any event, a good example of the adaptation of biblical formal models to explicate an exclusivistic posture, while simultaneously condemning apostates. Thus together with historical rehearsals, testaments provide evidence of the soteriological dualism that played such a formative role in the creation of the unique literary forms characteristic of this movement.

---

105. The words πάντα ἃ ποιήσουσι can, of course, be translated as a simple future "all that they would do." If so, the emphasis would be on the future deeds of the sons of Levi and their punishment ("all that would happen to them until the day of judgment"). Hollander and de Jonge translate it this way, commenting that "clearly their evil deeds are envisaged." The expression is comparable with *TLevi* 10:2; *TJud.* 18:1; *TZeb.* 9:5; *TNaph.* 4:1. The idea of receiving instruction for behavior is not, however, foreign to the idea of this or the other testaments.

CHAPTER NINE

The Dualistic Trajectory
of Pneumatology

The soteriological dualism that issued from the situation of perceived apostasy in Israel did not merely influence literary motifs and forms, it dominated the entire theology of these groups. A particularly important case of this, which will also serve as one example among many of the results of the influences more widely at work, comes in *pneumatology*: the teachings about the spiritual world. While the word itself has been restricted to teachings about spirits and demons, it is best to include under the concept a fairly wide range of beliefs, including the doctrines of spirits, angels, and even good and bad dispositions or *yĕṣerîm* — since our groups do not appear to have distinguished between these phenomena the way moderns are accustomed to do.[1] It is frequently recognized that far-reaching developments in pneumatological thought took place in the

---

1. As will be seen frequently below. On the confusion of terminology, cf. G. Johnson, "'Spirit' and 'Holy Spirit' in the Qumran Literature," 1960, 27-42, esp. 30; J. Pryke, "'Spirit' and 'Flesh' in the Qumran Documents and Some New Testament Texts," 1965, 361-80, esp. 350. For the development of the idea of *yĕṣerîm* into an individualistic doctrine, cf. R. E. Murphy, "*Yēṣer* in the Qumran Literature," 1958, 334-44. Passages that employ "spirit" and "angel" interchangeably include 1QH 1.7-12; 13.2; 15.13-14 (for other scroll passages, cf. Y. Yadin, *The Scroll of the War of the Sons of Light against the Sons of Darkness*, 1962, 231-32); *Jub.* 15:31; cf. Num. 27:16; Ps. 104:4 (M. Treves, "The Two Spirits of the Rule of the Community," 1961, 449-52, mistakenly maintains that in the Scriptures spirits and angels are never equated). The failure by modern scholars to sufficiently recognize this interchangeability of terminology results in a quite artificial separation of angelology and pneumatology.

393

Second Temple period (especially when compared with the embryonic pneumatology of earlier portions of the Hebrew canon). It has often been held that a chief development at this time concerned the increased importance of angels, thought to reflect an increasing transcendent view of the divine — that is, angels compensated for God's distance by acting as divine agents. But in the light of the already impressive angelology of the Genesis narratives, the book of Daniel, and Zechariah 9–14, it is doubtful that psychological factors can be principally credited for the attention given to angels in this period. Given the increased concern with revelation among these groups, this development may relate more to the function of angels as *mediators of revelation* than to any supposed increase in transcendence. Angels are a *bona fide* instrument of God's revelation in the Scriptures, and the long lists of angel names along with their specific areas of operation and authority, such as one finds in these writings, can be seen to relate primarily to the need to legitimize this revelation.[2] Angels were not only instruments of revelation but a vital item in the list of things revealed as well.[3] Just the same, it cannot be doubted that real developments associated with this concern with revelation did take place and that these developments eventually resulted in an entirely new frame of reference and an accompanying new terminology, both of which are already seen emerging in the earliest writings of the movement: *1 Enoch, Jubilees,* and the scrolls. Later writings such as the *Testaments of the Twelve Patriarchs,* 4 Ezra, and *2 Baruch* also depend on and reflect much the same basic pneumatological stance as the early writings of the period.

Influences from Persia, Babylonia, and Greece on these developments may be admitted, particularly with respect to the implicit cosmic dualism that runs through this pneumatology.[4] But since other more endemic factors were also involved, it is quite legitimate to view this as a genuine and largely independent development within Judaism, one entirely relevant to the traditions of Jewish groups.[5] Chief among these factors was, without doubt, the continued

2. Cf. D. W. Suter, who detects a sectarian provenance for the angel lists (*Tradition and Composition in the Parables of Enoch,* 1979, 75-76).

3. Yadin: "every sect and group boasted of knowing the ultimate secrets of this doctrine" (1962, 229).

4. Cf., e.g., K. G. Kuhn, "New Light on Temptation, Sin, and Flesh in the New Testament," 1957, 94-113, 98-99; A. Dupont-Sommer, *The Essene Writings from Qumran,* 1961, 77-82, for Persian and gnostic influence; H. Ringgren, *The Faith of Qumran,* 1963, 80; J. Becker, *Das Heil Gottes,* 1964, 96-103; P. von der Osten-Sacken, *Gott und Belial,* 1969, 139-41; J. H. Charlesworth, "A Critical Comparison of the Dualism in 1QS III,13–IV,26 and the 'Dualism' Contained in the Fourth Gospel," 1969, 400-401; E. Schweizer, *The Holy Spirit,* 1980, 34. Denied by Treves, 1961, 450.

5. Cf. A. E. Sekki, *The Meaning of* RUAH *at Qumran,* 1989, 63-67; P. Wernberg-

prophetic influence in Israel. While in some quarters of Judaism the end of prophecy and of unmediated spiritual experience generally was being proclaimed (cf. 1 Macc. 4:44, 46; 9:27; 14:41), scholars are beginning to recognize that this generalization cannot be applied equally to all types of Judaism in the Second Temple period;[6] the ongoing pneumatic experiences that are evident within our movement would, for one thing, have played a leading role in sustaining a lively interest in the spiritual world (cf. more below).[7] But most important of all, developments in pneumatology during this period were reflections of the historical and sociological context, a context rooted in the division that existed in Israel. The undeniability (as some saw it) of Israel's apostasy must have provided a perplexing dilemma for faithful Jews; the eventuality that God's own people would be caught in mass disobedience could only have created difficulties for those who also believed and cherished the divine promise to preserve and protect the holy nation. This tension between promise (or hope) and reality necessarily gave rise to various attempts at a national theodicy that attempted to explain the inexplicable presence of evil within Israel and its most severe consequence, divine rejection. Many of these attempts, as it turns out, were framed in pneumatological terms.[8]

The emerging pneumatology is foremostly distinguishable by its belief in the two camps of spiritual beings as represented in the dichotomies *God* versus *Satan, angels* versus *demons, good spirits* versus *evil spirits,* etc. This belief is not always presented in terms of a clear dualism, as in many instances only one of the groups of angels or spirits is mentioned. It is evident, however, even in such

---

Møller, "A Reconsideration of the Two Spirits in the Rule of the Community (1QSerek III,13–IV,26)," 1961, 413-41, esp. 416-18, 428, 441; M. Barker, *The Older Testament,* 1987, 19.

6. G. Johnson, 1960, 37; Schweizer, 1980, 30-31. That the rabbis granted authority to oral law and seemed thereby to hold an implicit doctrine of continuing revelation also causes problems for the view; a paradox recognized by G. T. Montague, *The Holy Spirit,* 1976, 114-15.

7. Another factor that no doubt encouraged such speculation was the expectation of the coming of the Spirit upon Israel that would mark the beginning of the restoration and would separate those possessing the Spirit from those without; cf. Isa. 61:1; Ezek. 11:19-20; 36:25-27; 37:1-14; 39:28-29; Zech. 12:10; Montague, 1976, 45ff.; Schweizer, 1980, 26-27. G. Johnson (1960, 29) also points to Exod. 10:1; Amos 3:6; Isa. 19:14; 1 Sam. 16:15; 19:9; 1 Kings 19:21-23.

8. For pneumatology as an attempt to solve the problem of evil, cf. Charlesworth, 1969, 393-94; J. C. VanderKam, *Textual and Historical Studies in the Book of Jubilees,* 1977, 264. For introductory summaries of the development of the doctrine of the Spirit through the periods of the Hebrew Bible and Second Temple Judaism, cf. Montague, 1976, passim; Schweizer, 1980, passim. These studies reveal that this period of development resulted in a division of the spiritual world into two separate camps.

cases, that both sides are presupposed. Neither does this dichotomy imply an *absolute* dualism that makes God and Satan out to be equal in power or effects. This observation has dogmatic implications, and the essential distinction of God and Satan are for this reason sometimes rigorously defended.[9] But dualism's failure to override monotheism has itself quite justifiably been taken as an indication of the essential Jewishness of this belief. Indeed, much of this "pneumatological dualism" can already be found — albeit in an incipient form — in the Hebrew Scriptures.[10]

As important as these questions of development are, we leave them behind, for the pertinent concern here regards the *function* of this kind of dualistic pneumatology in this particular period and among these remnant groups. It is naturally worth considering, and has often been assumed, that this pneumatology functioned as a solution to the question of evil in the world — that is, particularly the actions and attitudes of *Gentiles*.[11] It has yet to be seriously considered, on the other hand, whether pneumatology reflected yet another response to perceived apostasy *within Israel*.[12]

JUBILEES — ISRAEL ABANDONED TO EVIL SPIRITS

The pneumatology of *Jubilees* is quite complex, but nevertheless lends itself to some systematization. A good starting point is 15:31-32, which distinguishes between God's choice of Israel and the nations and tells how, "over all of them he caused spirits to rule so that they might *lead them astray* from following him. But over Israel he did not cause any angel or spirit to rule because he alone is their ruler and he will protect them and he will seek for them at the hand of his angels and at the hand of his spirits and at the hand of all of his authorities so that he might guard them and bless them. . . ." It was God's intention when call-

9. "Orthodoxy remains safe," as Milik put it with regard to Qumran (*Ten Years of Discovery in the Wilderness of Judaea*, 1959, 118).

10. M. A. Knibb (*The Qumran Community*, 1987, 95-96) points to teaching about God's Spirit (Judg. 14:6; 1 Sam. 10:10), about independent spirits (2 Kings 19:7; Num. 27:16), and about evil or lying spirits (1 Sam. 16:14-16; 1 Kings 22:21-23).

11. A typically nationalistic view of the matter is provided by Volz with regard to the demonology of the *Testaments* (*Die Eschatologie der jüdischen Gemeinde*, 1934, 32).

12. The beginnings of the association of the Spirit with the judgment of Israel corresponded, according to Montague (1976, 35-36), with the book of Micah (cf. 3:8): "What is clearly unique about Micah's message . . . is that this power and authority, this prophetic spirit of Yahweh, is given him not to mouth automatic salvation but on the contrary to expose the sin of Israel. . . . for the first time in our sources there is a clear relationship of the spirit of the Lord to the ethical life of Israel" (36). Cf. also Isa. 4:4ff.; 27:4ff.

ing Israel to distinguish them from the nations by his own *unmediated* guidance, and to inflict the nations, in contrast, with spirits who would mislead them. This idea is already found in the biblical covenant passage Deuteronomy 27–32 (cf. 32:8), from which in fact the entire *Jubilees* passage derives the substance of its teaching.[13] But what is notable is that the present passage is not intended, as it might appear to this point, to *dignify* Israel by referring to its privileged status, for the following verses reveal that this promise to Israel has attached to it *conditions,* one of which is circumcision. It is precisely this condition, furthermore, that Israel will fail to carry out:

> And now I shall announce to you that the *sons of Israel will deny this ordinance* and they *will not circumcise* their sons *according to all of this law* because some of the flesh of their circumcision they will leave in the circumcision of their sons. And all of the *sons of Beliar* will leave their sons without circumcising just as they were born. And great wrath from the LORD will be upon the sons of Israel because *they have left his covenant* and have turned aside from his words. . . . they have made themselves like the gentiles. . . . there is therefore for them no forgiveness . . . from all of the sins of this eternal error. (vv. 33-34)

The movement of the entire passage accordingly serves not to dignify but to *condemn* Israel. Through failure to *properly* circumcise their sons, Israel will disqualify themselves from the spiritual privileges granted by God and will, presumably, come under the influence of misleading spirits *along with* the Gentiles. This appears to be confirmed by the telling reference in the passage to "all the sons of Beliar" who leave their sons uncircumcised, a reference, clearly, to Israelites inasmuch as the following line speaks in parallel fashion of the apostasy of the "sons of Israel" from the covenant ("they have *left* his covenant," v. 34).

The type of circumcision referred to here is *not any* circumcision, but one carried out under exact rules and timing. The author quite deliberately refers not only to Jews who fail to circumcise their sons, or do not complete the task satisfactorily (out of respect for Greek preferences?), but also to those careless about performing the rite on the *eighth day* without exception (v. 25). If an al-

---

13. Cf. v. 33 with Deut. 28:15ff., etc. R. H. Charles (*The Book of Jubilees or Little Genesis, Translated from the Editor's Ethiopic Text,* 1902, 112) points to the covenantal passage Deut. 32:8-9, especially the LXX version, for the idea expressed here that God alone will be Israel's Ruler; cf. also Sir. 17:17; Dan. 10:13, 20-21. In another group of texts, on the other hand, the idea that God assigned to Israel their own spirit or angel can, perhaps equally significantly, also be found. Dan. 12:1 has Michael ruling over Israel, and in *1 Enoch* 89 Israel is placed under seventy shepherds, perhaps angels, for a limited time.

lusion to the calendar or to calendrical debate is to be discerned here, this requirement could itself have disqualified many Jews.[14] Whatever the exact issues (the fact that they are veiled in this passage might suggest that they were widely known), it is typically the Jubilaean sect's *own* understanding and interpretation of the laws of circumcision that are held to be binding on Israel, since they are believed to represent the only legitimate teaching. The author obviously feels that it is only by *this* circumcision that Israel can retain her spiritual privilege and be protected from the onslaught of foreign spirits (cf. vv. 25-30, 33-34). If the polemic against those who leave "*some* of the flesh of their circumcision" (v. 33) refers to the practice of cutting away less flesh than was normal — a style apparently adopted and preferred during the Hellenistic period in order to help conceal the marks of circumcision — then the group may be taking offense at what it saw to be an epidemic of malpractice.

The shocking thing is that those who compromise in this or any other[15] way appear to be completely abandoned to Beliar. This passage accordingly draws a suggestive connection between one's approach to circumcision and one's "pneumatological condition." Perhaps the words of v. 27, "*Because* the nature of all of the angels of the presence and all of the angels of sanctification was thus from the day of their creation," explain why improper circumcision has spiritual implications — namely, because even the angels are circumcised or, as the passage may be better understood, "spiritually circumcised" or "circumcised in heart" (angels were probably widely believed to be asexual beings; cf. Mark 12:25 pars.). One cannot hold fellowship with angels — a carefully guarded privilege of the righteous community — in an uncircumcised condition. This is not the only example in Judaism of the practice of angels being cited as justification for an interpretation of the law, nor is it the only example of a warning not to appear unworthy in the presence of the angels by acting in an immodest or unholy way (the reasoning is cited rather hypothetically by Paul in 1 Cor. 11:10). This association between pneumatology and circumcision probably composes a specific case of a more general rule that acts of apostasy of *any* kind possessed grave *spiritual* implications (hence forgiveness is absolutely denied, v. 34). Given the strict and eclectic nature of Jubilaean law, our author no doubt believed a large group of Israelites had failed to properly circumcise their sons. The conclusion? Israel would seem to have been abandoned to evil spirits.

Other passages in *Jubilees* also warn of the imminent danger of Israel being led away by evil spirits. The author appears to be aware of how severe this

---

14. Cf. Charles, 1902, 110; Wintermute, *OTP,* 2:87.
15. The inclusive expression "*all* of this law" (v. 33) and the plural "*sins* of this eternal error" (v. 34) would suggest that diverse kinds of omissions are in mind here.

position is, and how potentially volatile would be a direct confrontation with other Israelites over the matter. This is apparently why he handles the issue tactfully, even enigmatically, and why he frequently employs literary devices like paradigm and even a certain amount of irony to get this point across. So when 7:27; 10:1-14; 11:1-6 refer to the way the demons will lead the sons of Noah astray, the author seems to be hinting that Israel will similarly be lured out of her pure and pristine state by these demons. And likewise, when protection from Beliar or Mastema is invoked for the seed of Jacob, it is because this author considered the good seed that was intended to dwell in the Israel of his day, the contemporary "seed of Jacob," in real danger of evil influence. The rhetorical function of this motif of invoking protection from Beliar/Mastema is again evident in the prayer of Moses for Israel, a prayer that implies that when Israel is caught in apostasy she comes under the influence of evil demons: "do not let the spirit of Beliar rule over them to accuse them before you and ensnare them from every path of righteousness so that they might be destroyed from before your face" (1:20). The same idea is repeated in Noah's prayer that God would not allow the evil Watchers and their offspring spirits to "cause corruption among the sons of your servant" (10:5) and in Abraham's blessing of Jacob: "may the spirit of Mastema not rule over you or over your seed" (19:28). Since the condition necessary for staying in the covenant was that Israel remain faithful to the laws "concerning new moons, sabbaths, festivals, jubilees, and ordinances" (cf. 1:14), it is not difficult to see why our author considered such prayers to have been — as regards most of Israel — unheeded, and why he viewed the present apostate Israel *en masse* to be under the influence of "demons" (cf. 1:11).

For *Jubilees*, in short, *those who do not follow the Jubilaean law are given over to demons.* At times *Jubilees* states this same truth somewhat antithetically, perhaps under the impress of determinism: *those who do not follow the Jubilaean law prove themselves to have been abandoned to demons* — hence the transparently rhetorical motif of the invocation of protection. VanderKam, who does not apply this observation to the division within Israel specifically, has nevertheless picked up on the idea:

> The two theses that God is good and that he has predetermined every occurrence inevitably involve predestinarian systems in the vexing problem of how to explain the unquestionable existence of evil. But the Qumran sectarian literature and Jub. attempted to deal with this difficulty by positing — to use later theological language — a permissive will of God. Once man has chosen the way of disobedience, the Lord permits evil spirits to mislead him continually. . . . The evil spirits and their victims form one camp; the obedient angels and the elect constitute the other. All rational creatures belong in these

two camps. . . . The consequence for the human race is that it is polarized into two camps.[16]

Thus the pneumatology of *Jubilees* functions to define the two camps that make up Israel (and indeed the world), and in this way contributes to the strongly dualistic perspective of the book.

THE DEAD SEA SCROLLS — DUALISTIC PNEUMATOLOGY DEFINES THE METAPHYSICAL UNIVERSE

The doctrine of spirits in *Jubilees* quite clearly functioned to accentuate the division in Israel and in part to explain it in metaphysical terms. This pneumatology accordingly composed a kind of theodicy that attempted as much to explain the presence of apostasy in Israel as to explain sin in the world. The pneumatology of the scrolls surpasses in complexity that of *Jubilees*,[17] which is perhaps not surprising since the documentation is so much greater there, although the pneumatologies of the two are remarkably similar in most important aspects. One major difference is that pneumatological dualism in the scrolls pervades all theological thought, dominates the definition of the group vis-à-vis Israel, and indeed explains the entire cosmos, to an extent that it did not in *Jubilees*.

The Two-Spirits Passage

1QS 3.13–4.26 is the lengthiest treatment of the subject in all of the scrolls and has been discussed exhaustively.[18] The passage states that people possess a *variety*

---

16. VanderKam, 1977, 264, 7.

17. For the various uses of *rûaḥ* in Qumran, cf. A. A. Anderson, "The Use of 'Ruaḥ' in 1QS, 1QH and 1QM," 1962, 293-303. Montague (1976, 117ff.) sums up the confusion in the meaning of spirit at Qumran: "it is not always easy to determine to what extent the gift is thought to be the breath or power of God himself, to what extent the holy angel, and to what extent a disposition put into the faithful" (123). Apparently many theological streams and views of spirit have been brought together in the complex pneumatology of Qumran.

18. Cf., e.g., K. G. Kuhn, 1957, 97-101; Wernberg-Møller, 1961, 413-41; Treves, 1961, 449-52; Anderson, 1962, 298-301; H. G. May, "Cosmological Reference in the Qumran Doctrine of the Two Spirits and in Old Testament Imagery," 1963, 1-14; J. Licht, "An Analysis of the Treatise on the Two Spirits in DSD," 1965, 88-99, 88-90; Osten-Sacken, 1969, 116-89; J. L. Duhaime, "L'instruction sur les deux esprits et les interpolations dualistes à Qumrân (1QS III,13–IV,26)," 1977, 566-94; Sekki, 1989, passim.

of spirits,[19] although a basic division also exists between "*two* [basic] Spirits" (3.18) who have been appointed to everyone by God, the spirits of "truth" and "perversity."[20] These two chief spirits may have been equated and were certainly at least associated respectively with the "Prince of light" and the "Angel of darkness" mentioned a little further on in 3.20-21.[21] When it is stated that the Prince of Light and the Angel of Darkness each possess their own "sons" — the "sons of righteousness" and the "sons of perversity" (3.20-21) — one recognizes the same soteriological dualism as with *Jubilees,* where the world is divided between these two spirits: "In these walk the generations of *all* the sons of men" (4.15). This is the first hint that this passage does not deal so much with spirits, as would appear on the surface, as with *people.* Thus when the passage goes on to describe the two spirits and their effects, it is actually the fates (judgment, "visitation") of the two groups of *people* (who "walk in [each] spirit," 4.2-14) that are featured.

As somewhat of a contrast to these statements about the world being divided according to two spirits, we are also told in this passage that the "sons of righteousness" may at times *also* be led astray by the Angel of Darkness (3.21-22), and there is in fact a hint of the doctrine of a "mixture" of spirits in each individual.[22] There is accordingly little consistency in this passage over

19. לכול מיני רוחותם; 3.14. Various spirits are mentioned in 1QH, but these are clearly divisible into good (1.32; 3.22-23; 14.13; 16.9) and bad (1.21-22; 3.21; 6.23; 7.5; 13.15-16). Two distinct spirits of good and evil are referred to in 1QH 14.11.

20. 3.15-19; 3.25–4.1. Sekki, with the majority of scholars, understands "all the spirits" of l. 14 anthropologically (1989, 194-95) while, in contrast to the majority, he takes the "two Spirits" of l. 18 in the same sense and only "the Prince of light" and "Angel of darkness" in ll. 20-21 as cosmic beings (196-200). The fact that the spirits are said to be allotted לו, "for (each person)," rather than בו, "in (each one)," suggests for Charlesworth (1969, 398) that cosmic forces rather than inner dispositions are referred to. It is doubtful, however, whether the prepositional prefix implies so much; inner dispositions, no less than cosmic beings, could be said to be allotted "for" someone.

21. Equated: Anderson (1962, 298-99); Charlesworth (1969, 391). Associated: Sekki (1989, 198-200).

22. Cf. 4.15-16: "They walk in their two ways . . . according to the share of each [spirit?], according to whether he has much or little," and 4.24: "according to each man's share of Truth and Righteousness, so does he hate Perversity." The first passage does not necessarily imply this, however; it can easily be read to imply that *only* the "generation" of light (and their "host") shares in the good spirit and only the "generation" of perversity (and their "host") shares in the evil spirit. The latter passage, on the other hand, need imply no more than that these two groups share the *qualities* (i.e., not the spirits) of truth and righteousness. Such relative statements as these nevertheless suggest that the spirits are not given in *equal measure* to all, as Wernberg-Møller suggests (1961, 433); cf. Anderson, 1962, 300. The phrase "in equal parts" (3.16; 4.25) apparently refers to the total distribution in the world, not to the individual's share in the spirits, as the above-quoted verses would contradict this latter notion altogether.

whether only *one* spirit is assigned to each individual or *both* spirits are apportioned in some relative measure to each person. One would naturally want to allow such an inconsistency in a teaching that is perhaps partly based on experience and the apologetic needs of the moment, and partly on systematic doctrine. One would probably also need to appeal to the influence of experience and apologetic rhetoric to explain another apparent inconsistency in the passage — whether the dualism implied in it is fundamentally cosmological or anthropological (i.e., psychological), whether, in other words, two cosmic beings (namely, angelic beings) are referred to in the spirit language of the passage or inner "dispositions" in humans are referred to throughout.[23] If one accepts that cosmic dualism is intrinsic to the thought of the passage, a correlative problem arises as to how such predestinarian thought can possibly be harmonized with the remainder of the Qumran pneumatology (largely that of 1QH, which is substantially noncosmic). Source criticism and various theories of alteration, development, and textual insertion, such as those suggested by P. von der Osten-Sacken and J. L. Duhaime, have been employed in order to explain this contradiction.[24] A. E. Sekki, on the other hand, has thoroughly examined the passage in the light of the entire field of previous scholarship and has fallen decisively on the side of dispositions rather than cosmic beings.[25] In this way he argues for the essential unity of the passage based on

23. Cosmological: K. G. Kuhn, "Die in Palästina gefundenen hebräischen Texte und das Neue Testament," 1950, 199-200; K. G. Kuhn, 1957, 98-99; May, 1963, 1-14; Charlesworth, 1969, 398, 402. Anthropological/psychological: Becker, 1964, 84-89, who sees both aspects of the passage combining to present a consistent anthropology, its "dualistisch-prädestinatianischen Geisterlehre" serving to help clarify the "anthropologischen Situation" (84); cf. also Wernberg-Møller, 1961, 419ff.; in contrast to his earlier willingness to see cosmic dualism in the passage, cf. *The Manual of Discipline*, 1957, 67; Treves, 1961, 449-52; and Sekki, 1989, passim. For a valuable treatment of the history of interpretation of Qumran pneumatology that brings this divisive issue out clearly, cf. Sekki, 1-69.

24. Cf. Osten-Sacken (1969, 17-27, 116-89), who is followed by Duhaime (1977, 24, 240, 567). For an analysis of the problem, cf. again Sekki, 1989, 50.

25. This scholar approaches the texts linguistically and determines that "in the nonbiblical, Hebrew sectarian writings every contextually unambiguous use of *ruaḥ* as an angel or demon is syntactically masculine, whereas every contextually unambiguous use of *ruaḥ* as the spirit of man (with one exception) is feminine" (Sekki, 1989, 5; cf. 185-87). All important instances of *rûaḥ* in the passage (with the exception of 4.6; 4.23; and also 4.21a, which refers to God's Spirit; but not 4.21b!; cf. 207-11) are accordingly to be understood as dispositions (cf. 200ff.), while 3.20-21 do not employ *rûaḥ* and do refer to cosmic spiritual beings. The one interesting (and in our view damaging!) exception is רוחי אמת ועול (spirits of truth and perversity) in 4.23, which Sekki takes to be angels and demons in contrast to the use of the similar expression רוחות האמת והעול (spirits of truth and perversity) in 3.18-19, which he takes to be dispositions! He does this on the basis of a subtle semantic distinction: the latter employs the fem. pl., while the former uses the masc. pl. We

psychological categories, alleging that more traditional statements of cosmic dualism have been inserted by the author of the passage, resulting in some discontinuity in thought. Granted the persuasive arguments for this conclusion, however, Sekki himself notes that the psychological dualism implied in the passage is *everywhere related to* the existence of two spiritual beings in the *cosmos;*[26] there exist, moreover, compelling arguments for a cosmic interpretation of some of the expressions that Sekki sees to be psychological.[27]

Such attempts to approach the passage as a coherent source of teaching about the spirits have led only to desperation and frustration, as Sekki's treatment of the history of interpretation, along with his own attempt at a solution, have revealed. It is doubtful that a rigid consistency of logic should be sought for ideas presented in the passage. Nor does it really help to investigate the literary and source history of the passage in hopes of unraveling the difficulties (as Osten-Sacken and Duhaime have attempted to do), as what to do with the text as we *presently* have it is still a problem.[28] It is probably better to resign to a synthetic approach: since the role of the cosmic spirits can be more or less explained by the psychological influence they exert on the "sons of men," one should probably accept, as do most scholars, that the writer(s) found no real difficulty with a *combination* of what appear to us as somewhat contradictory pneumatologies.[29] While it is possible, therefore, to posit a kind of loose logic for the passage, it would also appear that careful distinctions between the various meanings of *rûaḥ* (spirit) were not made by the Qumranians, just as entire categories of spiritual existence (from angels to dispositions) were probably not carefully separated and consciously defined, so much as subconsciously related under the influence of experience and an overriding dualistic mind-set.

---

might ask whether this is enough of a difference to demand a change of meaning for the phrase within such a short compass!

26. Sekki, 1989, 198-99, 204, 215-16. Sekki posits that the cosmic pneumatology was the more traditional of the two, and that it was included by the author in his more innovative psychological treatment (199-200).

27. Particularly impressive is the comparison by Charlesworth (1969, 399) of the language of 3.19 referring to the origin of the spirits in a "spring/fountain of light/darkness" (ממקור חושך/במעון אור) to words in the document published by Allegro that appear to speak of opposing cosmic beings ("spirits") as dwelling in a "house of light/well of darkness" (בבור החושך/בבית האור). On the other hand, such water images as "fountain" refer to the source of revelation in the scrolls, and that may be all that is intended here. As May (1963, 2-4) points out in criticism of Wernberg-Møller, the doctrine of two ruling spirits is well documented elsewhere in the scrolls (cf. esp. CD 5.18; 1QM 13.2-12 where both are mentioned together), and it is not possible to purge our passage of cosmic dualism altogether.

28. Cf. the comments of Wernberg-Møller, 1961, 417.

29. Charlesworth, 1969, 395; Anderson, 1962, 299; Becker, 1964, 84; et al.

Whether one views the passage as dominated by a psychological or a cosmic perspective, by the idea of a mixture of spirits or by cosmic predeterminism, it is evident that such distinctions are not essential to understanding the message and purpose of the original author/compiler.

This lack of consistency in *content* opens up the question whether the passage was intended to teach doctrines at all, or whether other concerns lent a more *purposeful* (and, perhaps, more emotive than logical) coherence to the passage. One alternative is to suppose that the author was a terribly inconsistent thinker, teacher, or writer/compiler; but the passage is not void of all logical progression and demonstrates a measure of literary dexterity.[30] We are left to conclude that while on the surface the passage appears to present teaching about objective realities (cf. 3.13), its real significance once again lies in the fact that it functioned (perhaps quite unconsciously) as a statement of opposition to the enemies of the sect. It makes sense that socially motivated utterances and writings aimed against opponents, unlike more sober-minded didactic treatises, would emerge spontaneously rather than systematically and reflect present sources of friction between two groups of people. All these things — spontaneity of treatment, social friction, and attention to groups of people in conflict — are evident in this passage.[31] It is accordingly significant, as alluded to above, that one can, by even casually reading through the discourse, justifiably conclude that the most outstanding feature is not the strict dualism between two spirits, but the dualism *between two groups of people.*

This dualism is already apparent in the opening words of the passage: "And He allotted *unto man* two Spirits" (3.18). It is also abundantly evident in the lists of circumstances of the saved and unsaved *(Heils- und Unheilskataloge)*[32] that are found in the midst of the passage. These lists define two peoples by alluding to the dualism implicit in the covenant:

> And as for the Visitation *of all who walk* in this [good] Spirit,
> > it consists of healing and abundance of bliss,
> > > with length of days and fruitfulness,
> > and all blessings without end,
> > and eternal joy in perpetual life,
> > and the glorious crown and garment of honour in everlasting light.
> >> (4.6-8)

---

30. Cf., e.g., the intricate parallelism and the careful ordering of the passage cited below (4.6-8, 11-14). The entire passage (3.13–4.26) is marked by repeated expressions and allusions that suggest an editorial unity.

31. Cf. the apposite comments of Pryke (1965, 350-51).

32. Literary rubrics adopted by Osten-Sacken (1969, 158-63).

And as for the Visitation *of all who walk* in this [evil] Spirit,
  it consists of an abundance of blows administered by all the Angels
    of destruction in the everlasting Pit by the furious wrath
      of the God of vengeance,
    of unending dread and shame without end,
    and of the disgrace of destruction by the fire of the regions
      of darkness.
And all their times from age to age
    are in most sorrowful chagrin and bitterest misfortune,
    in calamities of darkness till they are destroyed
    with none of them surviving or escaping. (4.11-14)

While it may be difficult to judge social motivations behind this or any other passage, this passage's preoccupation with blessing and recompense again suggests that the issue is not spirits so much as groups of people in conflict.[33] The importance of this division between two peoples is evidenced by the prominence of the "walk" motif in the twice-repeated opening statement of the two contrasting halves of the passage: "as for the Visitation of *all who walk* in *this* Spirit . . . as for the Visitation of *all who walk* in *this* Spirit . . ." (4.6, 11). From a literary perspective the prominent position and repetition of the statement serve to highlight it in both cases, since the phrases that follow modify and are semantically subordinate to it.[34] The identification of two groups is made abundantly clear also by the fact that the underlying "two ways" doctrine is a common method of alluding to the dualistic covenant, as noted earlier.[35] Similar conclusions could be drawn for the function of the lists of virtues and vices *(Tugend- und Lasterkataloge)* in 4.3-6, 9-11, which illustrate and define these groups by spelling out the characteristics of living in the respective spirits. It is not, in other words, merely a matter of belonging to one or the other spirit, but also of belonging to one or the other *community* (i.e., group of people).[36]

Wherever spirits are mentioned in the two-ways passage, they are associated with a group of people: the "sons of men" possess various spirits (3.13-

33. *Contra* Wernberg-Møller, 1961, 424, 430ff.

34. We have indented Dupont-Sommer's text above in order to portray the semantic structure of the passage. The subordinate expressions are indented more than the prominent ones.

35. The two separate introductory formulations (3.18 as the heading for 3.18-25 and 4.2 as the heading for 4.2-18) read, respectively, "He allotted unto man two Spirits that he should *walk* (הלך) in them until the time of His Visitation" and "these are the *ways* (דרך) of these (Spirits) in the world." The entire passage 3.13–4.26 contrasts the two groups according to their "walk" (3.20-21; 4.6, 11, 12, 15, 18, 24) and according to the two "ways" (4.17, 19, 22).

36. Clearly recognized by Ringgren, 1963, 71-72.

14); God allotted *"unto man"* two Spirits (3.18); the Prince of Light and the Angel of Darkness rule over their own "sons" (3.20-21); the Spirit of Truth produces good fruit in the "sons of truth," while the Spirit of Perversity produces evil in his followers (4.2-14); these same spirits cause men to walk in truth or perversity (4.23-24); God has "divided these Spirits *among the sons of men,*" and their possession of these spirits will determine their fate in judgment (4.26). It would accordingly be justifiable to identify 4.15 as a kind of thesis statement for the entire presentation: "In these two Spirits walk the generations (תולדיהן *tôlᵉdôt*) of all the sons of men, and into their two divisions (מפלגות *miplaggêhen*) all their hosts are divided from age to age." The word "generations" (also found in the introductory words of 3.13) seems to hark back to Genesis 1, where it implies little more than "genealogy," but is here adapted as a suitable word to designate the two basic *kinds* of people and to allude to their respective *qualities* of existence down through the ages.[37] Thus what is stated in 3.13 as a title: "concerning the *generations* of all the sons of men," is recapitulated in 4.15: "In these two Spirits walk the *generations* of all the sons of men." The *inclusio* formed by these two statements indicates the subject matter of the whole: "(regarding) the (two) generations

37. Both 3.13 and 4.15 contain the expression תולדות כול בני איש. The translation of תולדות is difficult, and has accordingly been subjected to the prejudices of translators; but there is no precedent in Qumran for translating it "origins" with Wernberg-Møller (cf. May, 1963, 2, 2 n. 8; Duhaime, 1977, 568; *contra* Charlesworth, 1969, 397, who critiques the purely psychological connotation given the word in Wernberg-Møller's interpretation) or "Quelle" (in the sense of "Bereich"; Osten-Sacken, 1969, 146-48). Other uses in Qumran (CD 4.5; 1QM 3.14; 5.1) carry the meaning "lineage, generations." Stemming from √ ילד, "bring forth," the word may well imply the quality of the begetting rather than merely the temporal aspect (cf. Ger. *Geburt, Geboren, Nachkommen(schaft)* in contrast to *Generation, Menschenalter*). To this we can compare a variety of uses of דור in the Hebrew Scriptures where the word takes on a negative nuance (cf., e.g., Deut. 32:5; Pss. 78:8; 95:10; Jer. 7:29; for the contrasting positive nuance, cf., e.g., Pss. 14:5; 24:6; 112:2) and a score of uses of γενεά in the Gospels where the same negative sense seems to be intended (e.g., Mark 8:12, 38; 9:19 pars.). It is entirely appropriate therefore in the context of this discussion about two groups of people to retain the translation "generations" with emphasis on the qualitative aspect of the begetting. Accordingly we can agree with Leaney (1966, 146-47, commenting on its use in 3.13) when he suggests that the word refers to "a description of character" or "the men typical of (the) age." "*Generations* of all the sons of men" accordingly refers qualitatively to the *two* kinds of human offspring — the righteous and the wicked. Cf. *1 En.* 93:9-10 for another possible example of this usage (where "an apostate generation" is antithetically parallel to "the elect ones of righteousness"). The double use of תולדות in 3.19 is rather harder to decide, but the sense could be: "The generations of (the sons of) truth *live in* (or *find sustenance in*) a spring of light, and the generations of (the sons of) darkness *come from* (or *are nurtured from*) a fountain of darkness."

(or types) of men."[38] That the division is thought to bisect Israel and not merely mankind as a whole, is implied by the identification in the passage of the "just" or "the perfect of way" as those whom God has "chosen . . . for an everlasting Covenant" (l. 22) — that is, members of the covenant in contrast to all others. In 4.9-11 the list of distinguishing qualities of the unrighteous (*Lasterkatalog*) points unmistakably toward Israel. "Slackness in the service of righteousness," "impiety," "great hypocrisy,"[39] "the ways of defilement in the service of impurity,"[40] "blindness of eye and hardness of ear, stiffness of neck and heaviness of heart causing a man to walk in all the ways of darkness"[41] are all vices particularly appropriate to Israelites with whom the community was closely related in its preretreat experience — not to Gentiles. Thus one can see how the doctrine of the spirits might have functioned within the context of intra-Jewish debate to legitimize and explain the division felt to exist *within Israel*, not to outline a doctrine of predestination[42] or to speculate on the metaphysical workings of the spiritual world.[43] The old dualism between Israel and the nations, in other words, has been effectively replaced with a new spirit-dualism between those of the good and those of the bad spirits *within* Israel, while not abandoning the reference to other nations also.[44] It is therefore not entirely surprising, as confirmation of this, that an underlying

38. Wernberg-Møller contends that מפלגיהן cannot refer to two groups of people (1961, 431-32), and he is probably justified in this as far as it goes. The suffix of this word "*their* divisions" may refer either to תולדות in the present line or to the רוחות last mentioned in 4.9 (in the sg.; represented by אלה in our line). In the case of the former, however, "their hosts" (masc. pl.) would then have to refer to groups of people that are given as an inheritance (נחל; to whom?); but the hosts would rather appear to be spirits who are given to men as a possession as in 3.18; צבאות is also a more appropriate word for angels than for men (as in צבא השמים, "hosts of heaven"). Thus the "divisions" are two groups of angels into which all the "hosts" of angels are divided. Immediately after this, however, the subject reverts to the two groups of men who "walk" (יתהלכו) in the "two ways" of the respective spirits.

39. חנף would appear to refer to religious sin: "profanity," "impiety," "pollution," "rebellion," rather than more general "wickedness," as Dupont-Sommer, 1961, 80.

40. Knibb (1987, 100) understands this as "illegitimate worship." The terms are reminiscent of a reversal of true cultic piety in Israel.

41. These words appear to allude to the group's frustration in trying to get a hearing for their teaching among other Israelites; cf. Isa. 6:9-10.

42. Wernberg-Møller, 1961, 421; Treves, 1961, 451. One must not go so far as to deny a predestinarian teaching in Qumran altogether, as pointed out by May (1963, 6).

43. J. G. Gammie ("Spatial and Ethical Dualism in Jewish Wisdom and Apocalyptic Literature," 1974, 381) contests Charlesworth's view that the doctrine of the two spirits represents a modified cosmic dualism.

44. Observed by A. Jaubert, *La notion d'alliance dans le Judaïsme aux abords de l'ère chrétienne*, 1963, 132.

ethical dualism is discerned by the literary critical scholars Osten-Sacken and Duhaime in *both* the sources for the passage and in the final redaction.[45]

An Elitist Pneumatology

In the heat of such inner-Israelite debate, it is obvious why laying out the spiritual claims of the community was felt to be more important than consistency in thought, which is frequently abandoned in favor of the polemic. This same lack of consistency generally characterizes other presentations of pneumatological teaching in the scrolls as well. While in some places one witnesses the influence upon *each* individual of varied spirits or dispositions (psychologically oriented pneumatology; cf. esp. 1QH), other parts of the scrolls acknowledge (or at least imply) that men fall into one of two camps, that belonging to God or that belonging to Belial (cosmic pneumatology; cf. esp. 1QM). Certainly the two views can be synthesized by saying that while all men are influenced by various kinds of (natural?) spirits, nevertheless they are considered to be *owned* by one or the other of the cosmic spirits[46] — even if the synthesis can be sustained only with a certain violence to logic. The result, in any event, is an emotive, rather than logical, presentation.

This quite astonishing elitism in the sect's pneumatology is accordingly the element that gives a purposeful coherence to the passages and gives evidence, once again, of a prevailing soteriological dualism. To put it in starkly sociological terms: *the important thing* (and arguably the only *consistent* thing) *in the case of either basic kind of pneumatology, is that the righteous come out on top and the unrighteous are condemned.* This is true for both kinds of sayings. (1) That the doctrine of the "mixture" of spirits is ultimately brought into service of a soteriological dualism can be seen from the fact that the spirits (or dispositions) create *characteristic ethical qualities and actions* in their subjects and

---

45. Osten-Sacken believes this ethical dualism to have originated in the eschatological dualism of Daniel and holy-war traditions (although contrast J. L. Duhaime, "Dualistic Reworking in the Scrolls from Qumran," 1987, 36-38, regarding this supposition). Duhaime's view (cf. 1987, 55-56; Duhaime, 1977, 574-94) is that the literary sources are all basically ethical in content, and that the final product functioned as a missionary tract, as an exhortation to follow the way of truth; he notes legitimizing and warning functions for the passage. The literary history of the passage accordingly traces the social history of the growing tension between the sect and its opponents. Cf. also K. G. Kuhn, 1950, 206. These sociologically sensitive approaches exhibit an important contrast to the more abstract philosophical appeals to predestination, or to eschatological or cosmic dualism (cf. Licht, 1965, 89; Charlesworth, 1969, 394, 402).

46. Cf. Anderson, 1962, 301; Leaney, 1966, 155; even Sekki, 1989, 216-17.

that the righteous possess more good features than the unrighteous (as cf. the *Tugend-* and *Lasterkataloge*).[47] The righteous cannot lose even in circumstances of testing — they are *ultimately triumphant* despite whatever influence evil spirits have over them.[48] (2) As for the cosmic pneumatology, it is even clearer that the issue is *belonging* to one Spirit or another. Both of these pneumatologies imply a kind of elitism in spiritual matters that one would expect from a group that divided Israel into two camps. Even if the righteous are influenced by evil spirits, ultimately they *belong* to the Angel of Truth. This claim takes precedence over inner logic. People are either "in" or they are "out," irrespective of their varied life experiences. Both of these teachings are therefore synthesized (forcibly or otherwise) in favor of the righteous. The passage contained in 1QS 3.13–4.26 may well be unique among the writings of Qumran for many reasons — particularly its combination of ideas with a fairly strict cosmic dualism.[49] However, the *fundamental association of pneumatological teaching with soteriological dualism* is equally evident in various other passages from the scrolls as well, confirming an ongoing, inherent, and essential relationship between the two dualisms.[50]

Four categories of this thought, with representative texts, are worthy of mention here.

1. Primary among such texts are numerous references to the fact that while the *righteous possess God's Spirit and side with the holy angels/spirits*, the *unrighteous*

47. Anderson speaks of "the extent of the influence of the respective spirits" by which they are divided into two groups (1962, 301). Wernberg-Møller's contention that the idea of a mixture of spirits excludes the possibility of the division of human beings into two groups (1961, 420) is in any event untenable.

48. Something that is clearly expressed in the conclusion to the mixture-of-spirits passage: "*but* [i.e., in spite of testing at the hand of the Angel of Darkness] the God of Israel and His Angel of truth succour all the sons of light" (3.24-25).

49. It is noteworthy that Zoroastrian texts, which have been claimed to stand behind this cosmic dualism, also exhibit the other kind of dualism of which we have been speaking. Yasna 30:3-4 (quoted by Ringgren, 1963, 78) speaks of the "the two primal-spirits" between whom "the wise choose aright, but not so do the foolish." The passage continues: "When these two spirits came together, they created the first Life and Non-Life and ordained that finally the Worst would fall to the share of the followers of falsehood, but the Best Mind to the followers of right."

50. A good example of another lengthy passage that does this is 1QH 15.13ff., where we read: "I know that the inclination of every spirit is in Thy hand . . . before ever creating him. . . . Thou alone hast [created] the just . . . whereas Thou hast created the wicked [for the time of] Thy [wr]ath" (ll. 13, 14-15, 17). Ringgren (1963, 75) also refers to a damaged passage from the Habakkuk Commentary (14.11) that suggests the same relationship between pneumatological and soteriological dualism: "for according to the command of the eternal spirits [. . .] good and wicked [. . .] their reward (or work)."

belong to the party of Belial. The association of spiritual blessing with the community — whether the Holy Spirit of God (an expression that can certainly be used within proper limits)[51] or the good spirit (disposition) within man — is abundantly evident where the Spirit, or good spirits, are gifts given to the righteous, the source of their wisdom and righteousness, and evidence of their status. The following language should be considered instances of this:

    a. "the spirit of the righteous (רוח צדיק)" (1QH 16.10).

The phrase as used in the Hymn Scroll may imply individual thought, given the individual nature of the psalm within which it is found. However, given the corporate nature of the term *ṣadîq* elsewhere in the scrolls, a corporate nuance for the phrase should not be too quickly abandoned. The fact that the line says God has "allotted" this spirit would seem to tie it into the deterministic teaching of cols. 1QS 3–4, which refer to two groups.

    b. "in accordance with the [ever]lasting Spirits . . . between goodness and ungodliness . . . [sea]led their reward" (1QH 14.11-12).

The passage is perhaps too fragmented to learn very much from; however, it contains a strong soteriological dualism: the dichotomy "goodness and ungodliness," the association with vindication in the words "sealed their reward," along with the context of the passage[52] suggest this. This passage, not unlike 1QS 3.13–4.26, would appear to define the members of the two groups according to their spirits.[53] It may very well demonstrate that the authors of 1QH and

---

51. The key is simply to avoid reading the expression in terms of later trinitarian theology. Given that the community certainly alluded to the Spirit of God in the Hebrew Scriptures as a Unique Being in at least some of its uses of רוח (ה)קדוש, the title "Holy Spirit" (as opposed to the less distinctive "spirit of holiness") remains valid in these cases (*contra* M. Mansoor, *The Thanksgiving Hymns Translated and Annotated with an Introduction,* 1961, 76; cf., similarly, Anderson, 1962, 301). The Qumranites were certainly on their way toward distinguishing this Spirit from all other spirits, terminologically as well as theologically, and we should perhaps view this as an intermediate step toward the more developed pneumatology. G. Johnson, e.g., finds references to the Spirit at Qumran as "creative, sustaining, illuminating, and renewing at the final judgment" (1960, 38ff.) — attributes appropriate to the Unique Spirit of God — but qualifies: "the Spirit like the hand, the mercy, the wisdom, and the law of God might be personified; but there is no real *hypostasis,* no clear theology of the Spirit of God" (41). For texts that employ "holy Spirit," cf. Pryke, 1965, 345 n. 3.

52. A reference to "all that Thou lovest" and "all that Thou hatest," reminiscent of 1QS 3–4, appears to be contained in the quite fragmented ll. 10-11.

53. Dupont-Sommer (1961, 244 n. 2) takes these to be the two (cosmic) Spirits of

1QS both knew of the teaching of the two spirits, and the interpretation of these lines ultimately would depend on one's view of the two-spirits passage.

c. "And He made known *to them* His Holy Spirit by the hand of His Anointed" (CD 2.12).

This statement belongs with the teaching that in every age God has raised up "survivors" (l. 11) to whom he has "made known . . . His Holy Spirit" by the prophets and, probably as well, other anointed leaders. That the *yaḥad* identified with this historical remnant is clear; accordingly the implication is that they alone "know" the Spirit in the present age. From the allusion to the prophets it would appear that the emphasis is on the Spirit as Revealer (or perhaps on the "spirit of prophecy").

2. It is certainly justifiable to say that for Qumran the Spirit is preeminently *the Spirit of the community,* and this exact expression ([ד]רוח היח *rûaḥ hay-yāḥad*) occurs in 4Q477[54] while the equally provocative term "the Holy Spirit of the Community" is found in 1QS 3.7.[55] The important title implies a sign or validation of the election of the *yaḥad*. Many other passages imply a similar direct relationship between the Spirit and the community. Some notable examples include:

a. "[the scorner (cf. 2.25)] allows not himself to be taught by the Community of His Council (עצתו). For by the Spirit of true counsel (עצת) concerning the ways of man shall all his sins be atoned" (1QS 3.6-7).

Here the author of 1QS implicitly associates the community with the Spirit. As the *yaḥad* ʿaṣat teaches, so the *rûaḥ* ʿaṣat atones by teaching (i.e., the "counsel" concerns "the ways of man"). The language is not exact but suggestive. The

---

good and evil in 1QS 3-4. Sekki (1989, 129-31), for similar reasons, takes them to be human dispositions.

54. The context is not well preserved, making the exact reference indeterminable. It is uncertain whether סיד implies that someone misled the sectarians or rejected the Spirit; in the latter case, only would the distinctive Spirit of God be in mind. Montague nevertheless sees this as anticipating "the Pauline view of the church as the holy community, successor to the temple in which God's spirit dwells" (1976, 123-24).

55. (בו)רוח קדושה ליחד. This instance of the use of *rûaḥ* appears to refer to God's Unique Spirit (as cf. Sekki, 1989, 92-93), although if it does not, it nevertheless still clearly associates the positive spiritual condition with membership in the *yaḥad*. Lohse (1971, 11) supplies clarifications by way of parentheses: "Und durch den heiligen Geist (, der) der Gemeinschaft in seiner Wahrheit (gegeben ist,) wird er gereinigt von allen sein Sünden."

good spirit resident in the righteous[56] alone grants, or communicates, saving knowledge; that teaching is also found only in the community; hence, by deduction, the Spirit is only in the community.[57]

b. "the appointed times for the Institution of the Spirit of holiness (or 'Holy Spirit')" (1QS 9.3).

Pryke translates the expression *lîsôd rûaḥ qôdeš* as "institution of the holy spirit" or "association of spiritual holiness" and compares this to *hē koinōnia tou hagiou pneumatos,* "the fellowship *(koinōnia)* of the Holy Spirit," from 2 Cor. 13:13.[58] This makes *rûaḥ/pnuema* in both cases the "Spirit of the Community," with the emphasis on "belonging" and the "unity of membership" that is brought about by the Spirit. While *yśwd* usually means the foundation of a building, a building metaphor is not being employed here. The fact that building metaphors commonly refer to the community elsewhere in the scrolls, however, suggests that the expression may have originated in such a metaphor. In that case the "foundation of the Spirit" still relates to the possession of the Spirit by the *yaḥad* who compose the New Temple or spiritual building. On the other hand, Pryke suggests that the word itself could be translated much like *yśd* in Jer. 6:11; Pss. 64:3; 89:8, as an "assembly" or "community" of some kind. In either case the expression is parallel to רוח קדושה ליחד‏(בו) of 1QS 3.7 above, and is perhaps best rendered the "assembly of the Holy Spirit (or spirit of holiness)." In such passages as these the Spirit is quite obviously understood to be the *rûaḥ yaḥad.*

c. "Such are the counsels of the Spirit to the sons of truth in the world" (1QS 4.6).

"Counsels" (here in its construct form *śûdê*) could be taken to mean "secret" or "mystery" that God reveals to his prophets as in Amos 3:7, which would suit well the context of the passage. The special *relation* of this spirit to the community, as their adviser and revealer, is evident in the passage. Whether a reference to the Holy Spirit or merely inner dispositions is intended, it is clear that the spiritual influence is felt to operate corporately as well as individually.

A similar relationship between the Spirit and the community is also im-

---

56. The meaning here according to Sekki, 1989, 106-8. The closeness of this reference to v. 7, which clearly does refer to God's Spirit, however, might well be thought to cast some doubt upon his conclusions.

57. Cf. G. Johnson, 1960, 40.

58. Pryke, 1965, 346-48.

plied in several of the Founder Hymns where the *moreh* presents himself as a chosen "container" of the Spirit.[59]

3. This positive relationship of the *yaḥad* to the Holy Spirit/good spirits is paralleled by the conviction that the community was also in *good standing with the angels*, who not only succored them in the present but would also be agents for their deliverance in the future. The idea is adequately communicated in the following expressions:

a. "Dominion over all the sons of righteousness is in the hand of the Prince of light" (1QS 3.20).

This Prince of Light may or may not be directly identified with the Spirit of Truth in the same passage. "Prince," however, would appear to be a more appropriate title for an angelic being (cf. Dan. 10:20-21). These words would then imply that the *yaḥad* submitted itself to a kind of guardian angel. It may be, on the other hand, that we have here a typical example of the identification of angels and spirits.

The War Scroll reinforces this close association between angels and the community to an unprecedented degree.[60] It is replete with assurances to the readers that God's holy angels will come to the help of the community during the all-important final battle:

b. "the King of Glory is with us accompanied by the saints"[61] (1QM 12.8).
c. "The pow[ers] of the host of angels are among our numbered men" (1QM 12.8).

59. More certainly here than in 1QS a reference to the possession of God's Unique Spirit. Cf. "Thou . . . hast poured out Thy holy Spirit within me" (1QH 7.6-7); "the Spirit that Thou hast put in me" (1QH 12.11-12); "the Spirit which Thou hast put in me" (1QH 13.19); "[I have] entered . . . Thy holy [Spi]rit" (1QH 14.13; text restored); "thou hast favoured me . . . with the Spirit of Knowledge" (1QH 14.25); "I . . . searching [Thy] Spirit (Mansoor, 1961, 185 n. 15, restores [אמתך] רוח: 'Thy true Spirit') . . . clinging fast to [Thy] ho[ly] Spirit" (1QH 16.6-7); "[thou] hast favoured me with Thy Spirit of mercy" (1QH 16.9); "the Spirit which Thou hast put [in me]" (1QH 16.11); "cleansing me by Thy holy Spirit" (1QH 16.12; note that the psalmist implicitly associates himself in this with all "them that love Thee and . . . keep [Thy] com[mandme]nts," l. 13).

60. While one also sees this kind of teaching throughout the scrolls, and in various places in the Enochian literature as well (e.g., *1 Enoch* 43 and 104), nowhere do we find such a preoccupation with the idea as in this scroll. For texts and discussion, cf. H.-W. Kuhn, *Enderwartung und gegenwärtiges Heil*, 1966, 66-70; and Osten-Sacken (1969, 222-32), who traces the idea back to holy-war theology.

61. By which, apparently, are meant the angels or perhaps the deceased redeemed.

d. "the Valiant of Battle is in our congregation" (1QM 12.9).
e. "the host of his spirits[62] accompany our steps" (1QM 12.9).
f. "the King of Glory is with us and the host of His spirits accompany our steps" (1QM 19.1).
g. "Thou didst appoint the Prince of Light in former times to bring us help" (1QM 13.10).

The Hebrew Scriptures know of the protection of angels in times of battle. But in these texts the *yahad* itself conspicuously becomes the benefactor of this protection *in place of Israel*.[63]

h. "For the multitude of the saints in heaven . . . and the hosts of angels in Thy holy realm. . . . And the elect of the holy people hast Thou set for Thyself upon the earth . . . ranked according to their Thousands and their Myriads together with Thy saints and angels" (1QM 12.1-4).

Not only do the angels succor the saints in the time of battle, they fight alongside them and appear to form part of one and the same "camp." In this text this relationship does not go beyond military alliance, but is surely related to speculations and associations drawn between the present righteous remnant of Israel and the Israel of the wilderness who lived in the "camp" that surrounded the tabernacle (4Q477 contains the provocative term "camps of the Many," which suggests that the community accepted this identification). This idea, or complex of ideas, is especially developed in the text entitled *Angelic Liturgy*, alternatively named *Songs of the Sabbath Sacrifice (11QShir Shabb or "Sabbath Shirot")*. In this text every office on earth has a counterpart in heaven — angels even function there as priests function on earth, teaching and perhaps even offering sacrifices.[64] The present passage portrays the saints on earth as reflecting the very strict order of the company of angels in heaven in "their Thousands and their Myriads,"[65] and suggests

---

62. The spirits here and in the next citation are angels, according to Sekki, 1989, 163-64.

63. Cf. Exod. 23:20; 33:2; 2 Kings 19:35; 2 Chron. 32:21; Yadin, 1962, 237, 237 n. 2, who fails to pick up on the distinction between Israel and the community.

64. Interesting are the comments of M. J. Davidson on this text: "the *Sabbath Shirot* enabled the worshipping community to experience the validation of its claim to be a holy temple with a legitimate priesthood, whose service was parallel to that of the heavenly angels with whom they were closely associated. . . . as the Qumran worshippers praised God together with the angels, they would have been reassured in their belief that they were the legitimate and holy priesthood. . . . This would have been despite the contradictory evidence of their exclusion from the Jerusalem temple" (*Angels at Qumran*, 1992, 237).

65. Cf. Yadin, 1962, 241.

something that is also rather more clearly put forward in *Sabbath Shirot*, namely, that the sect considered itself to be in communion with, and perhaps even *organically united* with, the angels as part of a unified company of heaven. The passage implies that three groups belong to this camp: the elect on earth, the saints (who have died) in heaven, and the angels.[66]

i. "Thou hast cleansed the perverse spirit from great sin that he might watch with the army of the Saints and enter into communion with the congregation of the Sons of Heaven. And Thou hast cast an everlasting lot for man (in company) with the Spirits of Knowledge (גורל עולם עם רוחות דעת)" (1QH 3.21-23).

Perhaps the union of angels and men in one camp as in *(h)* above is what is intimated by the use of the term גורל (*gôral,* "lot") here and elsewhere in the scrolls — a term that may carry the ideas of "predestination" and "possession/inheritance" along with "communion" or "togetherness."[67] The use of *gôral* in this text occurs in a revealing enough context, but even here its meaning is somewhat ambiguous. The idea of lot as "designated inheritance (i.e., by lot)" seems to be combined with the idea of lot as membership in a group. Both ideas are traditional and may for that reason have been brought together. The "army of the Saints" appears to refer to the righteous.[68] The "congregation of the Sons of Heaven," on the other hand, are the angels.[69] God has ordained forever the fate of the righteous to be *with* the "Spirits of Knowledge."[70] It is unclear what connection, if any, exists between these spirits of "knowledge" and the Spirit of

---

66. For this communion with the angels, cf. Yadin, 1962, 241; Jaubert, 1963, 189-92; Ringgren, 1963, 127-32.

67. While some passages may well imply predestination (cf. 1QH 3.22-23, where, however, the idea of predestination may well give way to the biblical idea of lot as inheritance), "shared possession" probably supplies the sense of the word for most passages (cf. esp. 1QS 11.7-8, where the idea of community also exists). K. G. Kuhn draws a connection between the use of גורל at Qumran and the New Testament use of κληρονομία (1950, 200). Eph. 1:18 (τῆς κληρονομίας . . . ἐν τοῖς ἁγίοις) is a good example of the use of this word to indicate membership in the people of God. Thus Yadin relates the use of this term to the communion of men and angels (1962, 241). 1QH 11.11-12 most clearly brings out the idea of togetherness or communion; cf. also 1QH 3.21-23.

68. *Contra* Mansoor, 1961, 117 n. 5.

69. Cf. *1 En.* 6:2; Mansoor, 1961, 117 n. 6; this communion with the angels takes place in the present; cf. Holm-Nielsen, 1960, 68.

70. Sekki employs linguistic patterns to determine that the reference in this last expression is also to angels (1989, 159-60), demonstrating again the blurring of distinctions between angels and spirits:

Truth in 1QS 3.18-19. This entire group of heavenly and earthly saints seems also to have been referred to as "the everlasting assembly" (l. 21).[71]

j. "For Thou hast caused [them] to enter Thy [glo]rious [Covenant] with all the men of Thy council and into a common lot with the Angels of the Face; and none shall treat with insolence the sons [...]" (1QH 6.12-13).

Ringgren translates ll. 12-13: "Thou hast caused [...] to come into Thy [...] to all men of Thy counsel and in the lot of association with the angels of the Presence, *and there is no mediator*," thus stressing the importance of the direct, unmediated fellowship of the angels with the elect.[72] Alternatively the expression makes the point that the community required no interpreter to explain the meaning of the Scriptures.[73] The association of the community with the *mal'akâ pānîm* (Angels of the Presence) in either case demonstrates the exalted status of the members of the sect and the significance they gave to this idea of communion with the angels.[74] The word *gôral* accordingly implies the community or communion that the elect on earth have with the angels, while the idea of "possession" or "inheritance" remains in the background of thought.

4. The negative side of this association of pneumatology with soteriological dualism is the *attribution of the inspiration of the opponents to Belial or demons.* The idea that Israel could harden itself against the Spirit of God was previously known in Israelite tradition (cf., e.g., Zech. 7:12), but this notion was carried to extremes in the scrolls.

a. "I have abandoned the land because they have hardened their hearts against Me . . . I have removed its inhabitants and abandoned the land *into the hands of the Angels of Mastemoth*" (4Q389).[75]

---

71. סוד עולם; although Holm-Nielsen (1960, 67-68) follows Sjöberg in restricting this to the earthly community.

72. The word מלץ, usually translated "scoffer" (Dupont-Sommer, "insolence"), Ringgren relates to Job 33:23, where it has the meaning "interpreter, intercessor, mediator" (1963, 86-87).

73. Mansoor, 1961, 143 n. 2.

74. Another interpretation is offered by Holm-Nielsen: "the phrase is used of the highest ranking angels, who do not have to use a mediator, but may speak directly to God" (1960, 114).

75. For text and translation of this and the following excerpts from Cave 4, cf. R. H. Eisenman and M. Wise, *The Dead Sea Scrolls Uncovered*, 1992, 56, 60-64. Mastemoth (from משטמה = either "destruction" or "hatred") is a variation of Satan; cf. Hos. 9:7-8.

While the present time is described as "the dominion of Belial" in the opening section of the Community Rule,[76] this fragment appears to be even more explicit about the negative spiritual state of apostate Israel, since it frames its indictments in terms of the removal of God's Spirit from the Temple in Ezekiel's visions.[77] This no doubt offered a biblical justification for the sect's view that the Israel of the present day did not possess the Spirit of God, since they were still unrecovered from the apostasy of the exile. Another Cave 4 MS, which has been associated with 4Q389 (but appears to be addressed to Moses rather than Ezekiel), similarly claims that "the Angels of Mastemoth will rule over them"; "the rule of Belial will be upon them" during the period of apostasy; and "Seventy years from the day when they broke the [Law and the] Covenant, I will give them [into the power of the An]gels of Mastemoth, who will rule them, and they will neither know nor understand that I am angry at them because of their rebellion, [because they aban]doned Me and did what was evil in My eyes, and because they chose what displeases Me . . ." (4Q390 1, 11; 2, 1.4-8).

Compare also:

b. "All dominion over the sons of perversity is in the hand of the Angel of darkness" (1QS 3.20-21).[78]
c. "Belial like a counsellor is with their heart" (1QH 6.21).[79]
d. "a congregation of Belial" (1QH 2.22).
e. "the army of Belial . . . shall come to the aid of the wicked of the Covenant" (1QM 1.1-2).
f. "the schemes are of Belial which they conceive" (1QH 4.13-14).
g. "Belial . . . and all the spirits of his lot" (1QM 13.2).
h. "the spirits of [Belial's] lot" (1QM 13.4).
i. "all the spirits of [Belial's] lot are angels of destruction" (1QM 13.11-12).

These expressions, along with the other examples listed above, contrast the state of the righteous with the rest of Israel: while the saints belong to God,

---

76. I.e., dominion of Belial *over Israel;* 1QS 1.18, 24. Here the word translated "dominion" seems to allude to the influence of Belial over the apostates; it appears here in conjunction with the description of a people.

77. The official editors appear to assume that the words are addressed by God to Moses since they assign this series of fragments to "pseudo-Moses." But Eisenman and Wise have perhaps picked up on the proper context by assigning them to Ezekiel.

78. Cf. "the Angels of Mas[t]emoth will rule over them" (the apostate Israel; Eisenman and Wise, 1992, 54). A blessing is pronounced upon the possessors of wisdom in 4Q525, while those who are aligned with evil spirits are cursed.

79. The passage continues: "[and in accord]ance with the scheme of ungodliness they defile themselves with transgression," showing also that sin is inspired by Belial.

outsiders belong to Belial; while the community is counseled by the spirit of holiness, the opponents are inspired by their "counselor" Belial; while angels help the righteous in the final battle, the wicked are accompanied by "the army of Belial"; while the righteous belong to the "lot" of God, all others belong to Belial's "lot." This illuminates the fundamental dualism between the righteous and wicked based on their pneumatological condition — namely, their respective relationships with the good/bad spirits/angels. While, as we have seen, this pneumatological dualism is usually expressed either positively or negatively only, a recently published Cave 4 MS actually combines the two in a lucid presentation of the division of the world into two camps according to their pneumatological condition. Following a denunciation of human sin, it is written:

> According to the powerful deeds of God and in line with their evil, according to the foundation of their impurity, he delivered the sons of the heavens and the earth to a wicked community until the end. In accordance with God's compassion and in accordance with his goodness and the wonder of his glory he approaches some from among the sons of the world [. . .] so that they can be considered with him [in the community of] the gods like a holy congregation in the position of eternal life and in the lot of his holy ones [. . .] . . . each man according to the lot assigned to him . . . for eternal life.[80]

The numerous parallels in thought and language with the other Qumran scrolls, particularly the distinctively "sectarian" scrolls like 1QS, help identify this text closely with those other scrolls. The soteriological and pneumatological dualism of this passage is obvious and quite reminiscent of the two-spirits passage from the Community Rule. Here again the idea of the righteous forming a union of angels and men in one camp or "unity" is found, as is the mirror opposite: the wicked are relegated, along with fallen angels, to a kind of "wicked community."

Other aspects of the teaching of spirits in the scrolls also reflect this context of division, including the idea of "spiritual conversion" to the group as the means of salvation. It is apparent that some of these authors thought of a kind of spiritual "transfer" from the realms of darkness to the realms of light that occurred at conversion, the time of entry into the yaḥad. There has been considerable debate over whether the Spirit of God is believed to be given at conversion or whether the human spirit is merely cleansed and renewed at that time. Much of the discussion centers on passages like 1QS 3.7-12 and 1QH 3.21; 4.31;

---

80. 4Q181 (= *4QAges of Creation*) 1, 2-5. The purpose of this text is not at all clear. Perhaps it belongs to a general or systematic treatment of sin and salvation. The "delivered" motif recalls the similar language in Romans 1.

11.12-13.[81] While the references in the Hymn Scroll seem to refer to a natural, "created" spirit in humans, 1QS 3.7ff. seems to present the "holy Spirit" as a gift at conversion. CD 16.4-5, which may be even more substantial evidence of a "transfer" of realms, states that "on the day on which a man undertakes to be converted to the Law of Moses, the Angel of Hostility will depart from him. . . ." The passage suggests an experience of deliverance from the negative spiritual forces and would seem to imply entry upon a new positive spiritual experience of some kind. The scrolls do not offer enough evidence to decide whether the *rûaḥ* is thought to enter into humans, or only influence them from without, although attempts have been made to decide the question.[82] However one decides about this and similar questions, however, the important thing is that Qumran pneumatology is not characterized by conformity to current teaching or by careful systemization of thought, so much as it has been radically shaped by the influences of the current division in Israel — resulting in a kind of cosmic-pneumatological "Israel-theodicy."

TESTAMENTS OF THE TWELVE PATRIARCHS — CHOOSING BETWEEN GOD AND BELIAR

Among the first things one notices in the *Testaments* is the frequent reference to spirits. Conspicuous also, however, is the almost one-sided attention to the *neg-*

---

81. For the view that the Spirit is given at conversion, cf. K. G. Kuhn, 1950, 201; E. Sjöberg, "Neuschöpfung in den Toten-Meer-Rollen," 1955, 131-37; *contra:* E. Sjöberg, "Wiedergeburt und Neuschöpfung im palästinischen Judentum," 1950, 44-85, 78-81; J. Schreiner, "Geistbegabung in der Gemeinde von Qumran," 1965, 161-80, esp. 166ff. Interestingly Sjöberg changed his mind between his 1950 and 1955 articles, originally discerning in 1QH 4.29-33 a cleansing of the natural, created spirit in man ("Dieser Geist wird beim Eintritt in die Sekte gereinigt, nicht geschaffen," 79), but later, on the basis of 1QH 11.10-13, preferring the view of Kuhn that "es handelt sich also um die Neuschöpfung beim Eintritt in die Sekte, nicht um die ursprüngliche Schöpfung des Menschen" (1955, 133)! Schreiner denies these conclusions and, like Sjöberg in the 1950 article, is willing only to allow that a restoration of the human spirit is experienced on entering the community; the gift of the Holy Spirit, in the sense of Ezek. 36:24-29, however, remains a strictly eschatological hope (175-77). Sekki (1989, 89), on the other hand, suggests that *rûaḥ* in 1QS 4.6 refers to the "eschatological" Spirit active in the community in the present.

82. Pryke (1965, 346) views the spirit at Qumran as referring to "the supernatural part of man's nature as a gift from God, given or withdrawn at His desire" in line with the similar teaching of the Hebrew Bible. It does have the advantage of harmonizing sayings that appear to be in conflict, particularly teachings about a holy spirit that contrast with those of the two created spirits; on the other hand, it does not explain references to an apparently independent and unique "holy Spirit" in the scrolls.

ative side of the spiritual world composed of Beliar and his hosts; this does not necessarily imply an abandonment of dualism but would seem rather to suggest, as confirmed by other internal indications, that the work is preoccupied with the problem of evil, notably apostasy.

In other ways the pneumatology of the *Testaments* is similar to what we have already seen. The question raised by the Qumran texts about the metaphysical makeup of the spiritual world applies equally to the *Testaments,* which exhibit a comparable level of ambiguity: spirit apparently refers to both natural forces (anthropological or psychological) and cosmic entities. Thus some passages speak of the spirits in very natural ways, as spirits of deceit, spirits of sleep, spirits of error, etc., which blind their subjects so that they cannot understand the law.[83] On the other hand, the personal and independent nature as well as the cosmological origin of these spirits is often alluded to. So while at times the spirits appear to be merely metaphors for human frailty, they are also frequently personified and appear to work through the respective weakness as quite independent beings. Thus the "Prince of Error" *employs* the jealousy of Simeon against Joseph (*TSim.* 2:7). One also reads that a powerful angel accompanied Judah everywhere (*TJud.* 3:10), while the same patriarch was blinded by the "prince of error" (*TJud.* 19:4). As with the scrolls, the ambiguity is not resolved in texts like *TJud.* 16:1, which says that wine contains "four evil spirits" — are these to be understood as metaphysical or natural phenomena?[84] On still other occasions the apparently natural spirits are confused with and related to Beliar in a way that suggests again that little distinction is drawn between inner dispositions and cosmic influences.[85] One might assume that this paradox is created through the careless joining of sources, except that this lack of pneumatological homogeneity is evident even within the compass of small

83. Cf. esp. *TReub.* 2:1–3:9. For other anthropological/psychological applications of the language, cf. *TSim.* 4:7-9; *TDan* 1:8-9; 2:1, 4; 3:1; for a clear presentation of the spirits as dispositions, cf. *TJud.* 20:1-5.

84. Other passages are equally ambiguous. In *TZeb.* 9:7 the spirits would appear to be personal, inasmuch as LXX Gen. 3:13 uses the same verb for the deceiving of Adam and Eve; cf. H. W. Hollander and M. de Jonge, *The Testaments of the Twelve Patriarchs,* 1985, 273, who discern the influence of Christian teaching in the passage; but only the words "God in human form" are suspect — the reference to "Jerusalem (whom God will choose)" in v. 8 betrays the fact that the passage is Jewish, the idea of the messiah being secondary.

85. Cf. the expression "the spirits of error and of Beliar" in *TLevi* 3:3; for Beliar, cf. also *TReub.* 4:7, 11. It is interesting also that God is said to "dwell" (κατοικέω) in the compassionate one (*TZeb.* 8:1; *TBen.* 6:4; *TDan* 5:1?; *TJos.* 10:2-3?; *TNaph.* 8:3?; if the idea is present in this final passage, this would demonstrate the authenticity of words generally taken to be secondary). This might indicate the essential personal nature of the pneumatology of the *Testaments* as well.

passages. For example, *TDan* 3:1-2 speaks quite naturally of anger: "Anger is evil, my children, for it becomes the motivating force of the soul itself. That force has strange effects on the body of the angry man; it dominates his soul, and provides the body with a peculiar power so that it can accomplish every lawless act." On the other hand, anger almost assumes an independent existence even in this passage, and a few verses later appears to be closely tied in with the realm of spiritual beings: "Anger and falsehood together are a double-edged evil, and work together to perturb the reason. And when the soul is continually perturbed, the Lord withdraws from it and Beliar rules it" (4:7); and in the following verse: "Avoid wrath, / and hate lying, / in order that the Lord may dwell among you, / and Beliar may flee from you" (5:1). Similarly with *TAsh.* 1:8 — "if the mind is disposed toward evil, all of its deeds are wicked; driving out the good, it accepts the evil and is overmastered by Beliar." The *Testaments* seem to view the natural spirits as instruments through which the cosmic spirits work and, perhaps in combination with this, consider resignation to those evil inclinations as having grave spiritual implications, even leading to possession by Beliar. It is certain, in any event, that the function of this pneumatology does not relate to scientific or metaphysical interests, nor was the primary desire to present a carefully worded didactic treatise on spiritual things, but was largely emotive and polemical.

These texts demonstrate that the pneumatology of the *Testaments* is also quite ethically oriented, as one would expect in discourses that center on lifestyle and law. It is here, however, that the fundamental dualism of the work is especially evident. The spiritual world favors the righteous: the "spirits of error have no power over" the men of integrity (*TIss.* 4:4); if the readers, like Issachar, are ethically upright, "no act of human evil will have power over you" (*TIss.* 7:7); and godly living will keep one from Beliar (*TBen.* 3:2-3). The dualism comes to expression quite clearly in some passages, as in *TNaph.* 8:4, 6, where it is stated that the devil will flee from the good, on the one hand, but will inhabit him who does not do good, on the other. Likewise *TAsh.* 6:4: "For the ultimate end of human beings displays their righteousness, since they are made known to the angels of the Lord and of Beliar."[86] The *Testaments* recognize the power

---

86. According to this translation of Kee (*OTP*, 1:818), the passage might be understood to refer to a kind of preknowledge on the part of the good and evil angels. Those who will live righteously in their life are foreseen and protected by God's angels; those who will not are similarly known ahead of time and are ruled over by the angels of Beliar. In such a case it would be interesting to compare the kind of rationalizing going on in the mind of the author of 1QS 3.13–4.26 (cf. also *TJud.* 20:1: "two spirits await an opportunity with humanity: the spirit of truth and the spirit of error"). On the other hand, Hollander and de Jonge render *TAsh.* 6:4, "For the ends of men show their righteousness, *when they recognize* the angels of the Lord and of Satan" (1985, 356). Either translation (active or pas-

of free will (cf. esp. *TLevi* 19:1-4), and there are also evidences of a doctrine of spiritual conversion where, when turning to the Lord, one experiences a transfer from the powers of evil to good. To the evidence of *TDan* 5:1 mentioned above can be added *TSim.* 3:5, which simply states that "if anyone flees to the Lord for refuge, the evil spirit will quickly depart from him, and his mind will be eased." While this passage may well refer to resisting the inner temptation to give in to the (natural) spirits in humankind rather than to conversion *per se,* it is evident here again that repeated decisions for evil involve lasting spiritual implications: thus sexual immorality "separates from God and leads men to Beliar" (*TSim.* 5:3); when Beliar rules the Lord withdraws (*TDan* 4:7); but through godly living the Lord will "dwell among you, / and Beliar . . . flee from you" (*TDan* 5:1). In *TAsh.* 6:5 "enter[ing] eternal life" is equated with coming to know the "angel of peace," which apparently occurs after a transfer from the dominion (whether realm or merely influence) of the "evil spirits."[87]

This idea of a transfer of dominions provides insight into the function of pneumatology in the *Testaments* since, as was the case for the scrolls, it implies the removal of the national election as the basis for soteriological claims. In this regard we might note that some passages speak directly of how the spirits have misled those in Israel, not simply the nations. Israel is not kept unconditionally safe from the powers of the enemy. As with the scrolls, even the righteous Israelites are at times bound to be influenced by both camps of spirits. It is prognosticated of the sons of Issachar in particular that they will "ally themselves with Beliar" (*TIss.* 6:1),[88] while the readers of this testament are also promised that a way of repentance is open to them so that "every spirit of Beliar will flee from you" (7:7). As for the priesthood, *TLevi* 9:9 announces that the "spirit of

---

sive) of γνωρίζοντες is possible, although the absence of a preposition indicating an indirect object (such as εἰς or πρός) perhaps argues against Kee's translation. The active translation might be preferred in light of v. 5: "For when the evil soul departs, it is harassed by the evil spirit which it served . . ." (although both approaches could be made to cohere with the ideas of this verse). In this case we have an idea similar to the eschatological viewing of fates mentioned above, but v. 5 nevertheless still refers to the experience of the two spirits/angels during one's lifetime. The dualism is in any event quite explicit: "Satan/Beliar operates through his spirits, also called τὰ πνεύματα τῆς πλάνης" (cf. v. 2; Hollander and de Jonge, 356, who also note the dualism in this verse; 183). The expression "angel . . . of Beliar" is only found here; this is parallel to τὸ πονηρὸν πνεῦμα in v. 5. The dualism is completed by juxtaposition of such expressions with the "angels of the Lord" in v. 4.

87. Hollander and de Jonge (1985, 117) cite *TIss.* 7:7; *TDan* 5:1; *TNaph.* 8:4; *TBen.* 5:2 as parallels to the idea of Beliar/the devil departing from the faithful.

88. The word for "ally," (προσ-)κολλᾶσθαι, used three times in the passage, is the one generally used for cleaving *to God* (LXX Deut. 11:22; Josh. 23:8; 4 Kgdms. 18:6; Ps. 72:28; Hollander and de Jonge, 1985, 248). This not only increases the sense of shock at the apostasy of Issachar's sons, but also reveals the dualism of the author.

promiscuity" will be its downfall. Apparently the failure of the priesthood in the author's time was felt to follow from a demonically inspired liberalism summed up by the use of the word "promiscuity."[89] That it is *Jewish opponents* of the group who come under particular scrutiny and blame in the *Testaments* is evident in the indictment of the "two-faced" hypocrites who serve Beliar (*TAsh.* 3:1-2)[90] and "imitate the spirits of error and join in the struggle against mankind" (6:2). Such words are manifestly directed at those from Israel who, instead of being part of the solution for mankind, are revealed to be part of the problem.[91]

Significantly the rule of good and evil spirits is also related to the dualistic and individualistic view of covenant expressed in *TLevi* 19:1-4: "Choose for yourselves light or darkness, the *Law of the Lord or the works of Beliar*."[92] Two (groups of) spirits rule over the world, and it is a matter of decision and orientation toward the Law (as understood by the group) as to which spirit(s) will have dominion in an individual's life. This dualistic and individualistic doctrine of the two spirits, or groups of spirits, is in direct contrast to a nationalis-

89. πορνεία. For the word, commonly used in the *Testaments*, cf. *TReub.* 1:6; 3:3; 4:6-8, 11; 5:3, 5; 6:1, 4; *TSim.* 5:3, 4; *TLevi* 9:9; *TJud.* (title); 12:2; 13:3; 14:2-3; 15:2; 18:2; *TDan* 5:6; *TJos.* 3:8; *TBen.* 8:2; 9:1; 10:10 (M. de Jonge, ed., *The Testaments of the Twelve Patriarchs*, 1978, 242).

90. διπρόσωποι. The word is found in 2:2-3, 5, 7-8; 4:1, 3-4; 6:2; *TDan* 4:7. The word ὑπόκρισις is used but once in the *Testaments* (*TBen.* 6:5), although the idea is found repeatedly.

91. This reference to *Israel* in the doctrine of the spirits is confirmed by the insistence in *Testament of Naphtali* 3 that failure to keep the calendar (suggested in the order-in-nature passage in vv. 2-5; in this regard Hollander and de Jonge note the similarities of this passage to *1 Enoch* 2–5; [1985, 306]) is tantamount to adherence to "wandering spirits" (v. 3); from such a sin *captivity* will result (cf. 3:5; 4:1-2). The reference to captivity implies, even if the calendar association cannot be sustained, that Israel is chiefly in mind here.

92. The views of Hollander and de Jonge about this verse can hardly be sustained when they remark that "The dualistic elements in the exhortation stress the importance of making fundamental decisions and choosing between good and evil, God and Beliar. They do not divide mankind into two categories: a small group of those who observe the law rigidly and thus correctly, and a much larger group who do not take the commandments seriously" (1985, 47). This position produces problems for their treatment (cf. 47-50), and reasons for the denial are never given. The similarity between the doctrine of the *Testaments* and that of the other writings we have been investigating rather suggests the opposite. That the groups are not divided on the basis of individual commandments does not preclude that this dualism is evident in the pneumatology itself. The writer certainly believed that the world was divided between those who followed God and those who followed Beliar — this was based on obedience to the content of the exhortations, no matter how abstract.

tic understanding: these two spirits "await an opportunity with humanity" (*TJud.* 20:1-5). Which spiritual realm will own the individual — whether that individual belongs to Israel *or not* — comes down to a matter of choice. If one assumes a similar sectarian context for the *Testaments* as for *Jubilees* and the scrolls, therefore, it would appear from this analysis of the pneumatology of the *Testaments* that it functions in a similar way as for the other groups, as a manifestation of a deeply ingrained soteriological dualism that divides, not only the whole world, but Israel in particular.

THE ALL-IMPORTANT FLOOD PARADIGM

A great deal of interest is shown in the figure of Noah and in the circumstances surrounding the flood, particularly in *1 Enoch* and *Jubilees,* as well as in a number of smaller scroll fragments from Qumran, including *Genesis Apocryphon.*[93] While this might be thought only natural, since Noah belongs to the period of history covered by these writings, it hardly explains the repeated and lengthy attention given to this figure, or to the evidence the writings provide for a well-developed tradition centered on the flood. In *Jubilees* stories associated with Noah receive proportionately greater space than other parts of Israel's early history, and among all the covenants the Noachic one is primary. The concentration on events surrounding the Deluge in the Enochian writings makes clear the vital importance of the motif for this corpus as well. Noah appears to have held a similar degree of respect as his great-grandfather Enoch in these books. It is even possible that Enoch's importance was partly derivative of Noah's inasmuch as the flood forms the all-important context for Enoch's revelations. Any explanation of the theology of these books must therefore account for the emphasis on Noah and the flood found in them.

The fact that the Noachic tradition goes well beyond what is mentioned in the much terser biblical account has given rise to theories of multiple or par-

---

93. A considerably fragmented text that, because of the poor state of preservation, can be of little assistance in either this or following sections dealing with Noah or the flood. The beginning and end of the text have been lost, and it is speculated that the original full text composed a complete reworking or midrash of Genesis; cf. J. A. Fitzmyer, *The Genesis Apocryphon of Qumran Cave I,* 1971, 3, 6-7. However, the story of Noah and the flood and the events following on the flood receive more than proportional treatment (cols. 2-17 of twenty-two columns presently extant), and if the work continued at that rate, much more than a single scroll would be required. The text is reminiscent of both Qumran exegesis and the theological concerns of *Jubilees* and *1 Enoch* (Fitzmyer, 10-11, 16).

allel traditions, and even to the suggestion that the account in the Book of Watchers antedates the Genesis version.[94] As for the original sources for the story, these may be quite ancient, as parallels for the flood from the ancient Near East are well known.[95] Charles first sought to identify the more immediate sources of the Enochian flood accounts in the lost "Book of Noah" mentioned in *Jub.* 10:13-14 and 21:10 — although scholars have expressed doubt that such a source can be successfully identified in the present works, not to mention whether it even dealt with the same subject matter we find in either *1 Enoch* or *Jubilees*.[96] It is also important to keep in mind the possible intricacies of the process of transmission so as not to hastily assume, as scholars have readily done, that Noah stories in these writings were simply embellishments of a single source (namely, Genesis).

That said, however, questions of sources and relative chronologies of the traditions are not as important as the functions of the accounts as they appear in these books. Given the theme of the righteousness of Noah, which frequently recurs in these stories, this function might be taken to be didactic or parenetic (i.e., intended to teach or influence behavior).[97] In determining an even more important function, however, it is helpful to consider more closely, not only the context in which the stories about Noah and the flood were cherished and pre-

94. Cf. J. T. Milik, ed., *The Books of Enoch*, 1976, 30-31, arguing that the Genesis account is abridged. The chief arguments against this are noted by M. Black, *The Book of Enoch or 1 Enoch*, 1985, 124-25: (1) the apparent change of "sons of God" in Genesis to "children of heaven" in *1 Enoch* to avoid offense (the opposite is hardly conceivable) and (2) other fragments (4Q180-81) cite Gen. 6:1 verbatim. For discussion of this suggestion as it relates to the Enoch traditions in Gen. 5:21-24, cf. J. C. VanderKam, *Enoch and the Growth of an Apocalyptic Tradition*, 1984, esp. 28-33.

95. For a useful analysis of these, cf. L. R. Bailey, *Noah*, 1989, 11-27, esp. chart, 14-16; VanderKam, 1984, 33-51, as it relates to Enoch.

96. One ancient Gk. MS of *Testament of Levi* also refers to "the book of Noah." For description and discussion of the possible contents of the book and of scholarship related to its identification in *1 Enoch* and elsewhere, cf. F. García Martínez, "4QMessAr and the Books of Noah," in García Martínez, *Qumran and Apocalyptic*, 1992, 1-44, 25-27, 39, 43-44. The book of Noah is not found in the ancient catalogues, but its existence seems not to be in doubt. In García Martínez's view, the document contained much of the same material as the Watcher theodicy and considerably more as well. For denial of the book of Noah as a source of the Similitudes, cf. Suter, 1979, 32.

97. Noah is the first person in the Bible to be called "righteous." This detail is picked up by the author of Ezek. 14:14 and by Philo; cf. J. P. Lewis, *A Study of the Interpretation of Noah and the Flood in Jewish and Christian Literature*, 1968, 7, 9, 15-16, 90, etc. Lewis accordingly interprets the function of these texts parenetically (15-16); it is noteworthy, however, that even Lewis discerns several passages (mostly from our writings) in which the moral interest is *not* paramount (cf. 24ff.). For more on the importance of Noah's righteousness, cf. ch. 10 below.

served, but even more importantly, other traditions *for which* the story of Noah in turn served as the context or framework. In *1 Enoch* and *Jubilees*, at least, these other traditions include the story of the fall of the Watchers and the subsequent release of evil spirits. Since this story functions as an account of the origins of evil spiritual beings, it is evident that Noah tradition itself was largely preserved because of its relevance for the pneumatology of these groups. In other words, while the significance of the story of Noah in these writings cannot be exhausted in terms of this pneumatological purpose (cf. ch. 12 below), this purpose is at least strongly intimated by the original function of the Noachic tradition as a primitive *theodicy*.[98]

This theodicy, in fact, is thought by some to be more primitive, and was certainly at times more prevalent, than the theodicy of the fall of Adam, which is the more familiar explanation for evil among the biblical faiths. So while it is true that the story of the fall takes over the center stage of theodicy in later periods, in these works the blame is placed squarely on angels who fell into rebellion against God. This preference for a Noah-flood-angel theodicy perhaps reflects the particular concern of the authors for Israelites, since the Adamic theodicy is distinctly universalistic and would therefore be unsuited for the authors' purposes.[99] Primarily, however, it suited the spiritualizing tendencies of a theology that was moving toward a distinctly pneumatological explanation for sin. Whatever the exact origins of this explanation for evil, it is apparent that the idea of retrograde angels became associated with the story of the flood at some time during the development of the traditions. The mysterious ante- and postdiluvian contexts, only hinted at in the Bible, invited metaphysical speculation (in Hebraic as well as other Semitic flood traditions), and it is obvious from our writings that an important clue was taken from the enigmatic mention at the beginning of the biblical Noah story (Gen. 6:2) of how "the sons of God" had relations with "the daughters of men." This passage could have been interpreted (or was originally *written*) to imply that angels through intercourse

98. For the view that the pneumatology of *Jubilees* serves as a theodicy, cf., e.g., VanderKam, 1977, 264.

99. Cf. M. Barker, *The Great Angel,* 1992, passim, for the antiquity of the theodicy. Oesterley (in R. H. Charles and W. O. E. Oesterley, *The Apocalypse of Baruch,* 1917, xxviii) cites Tennant, who reverses the usual direction of the development. For him the individualism of the period rendered unsuitable the more ancient understanding of the relationship between Adam and sin. This development is attested in the contradictory statements about Adam's sin in *2 Baruch*. One could agree, in either event, that the angelic theodicy certainly does reflect a more individualized approach to the question of sin than the Adamic. The highly personal forces of fallen beings also explain, in a way the historically related Adam theodicy could not, how sin (apostasy) could have such an intense and recurring influence on certain Israelites who once again seemed to have fallen into its power.

with humans raised spiritual offspring and subsequently changed the course of history.[100]

The basic contents of this angel theodicy are in *1 En.* 6:1–16:3, where the tradition appears to have been preserved in a detailed and typical form (cf. also *1 En.* 15:8–16:4; 86:1-6; 88:1-3; 90:20-24; 106; *Jub.* 5:6, 10; 7:27; 10:1-14; 11:1-6). Here is told how the angels (referred to in the Ethiopic of *1 Enoch* as "Watchers") involved themselves in a heinous sin, taking wives for themselves from among the "daughters of men" (cf. Gen. 6:2), thereby committing an unpardonable form of adultery (the relevance of this account to the issue of exogamy is transparently obvious).[101] The Watcher-angels were subsequently cast out of heaven as an initial punishment (cf. Isa. 24:17-23). Meanwhile the female humans gave birth to the giant offspring of this union (cf. the *nepalim* of Gen. 6:4). It is the eventual death of these giants that, in turn, produced the race of demons — the spirits of the dead giants. (One can also see, from a story like this, how spirits had become so closely identified with angels.) The flood was the occasion for the judgment of both humans as well as these demons. In other accounts the detail is included that only *nine-tenths* of the demons were bound and punished at this time while *one-tenth* of them were granted freedom (cf. *Jub.* 10:7-11).[102] The demons that remained continued to influence Noah's sons, eventually gaining the upper hand in spite of being warned of their certain judgment.

It would seem *unlikely* from what has been ascertained about these writings so far that the flood-Watcher-Noah account functioned merely as theodicy[103] — that is to say, that the tradition was related for relatively undetached, didactic purposes, to teach *about* the origins of evil. What is the

---

100. The referents are, of course, not obvious from the Heb. While a variety of interpretations of the expression "sons of God" are possible, Codex Alexandrinus, for one, translates בני־האלהים with ἄγγελοι τοῦ θεοῦ (υἱοὶ τοῦ θεοῦ in v. 4); other Gk. versions tend to translate literally, while the Targum of Onkelos replaces it with רברבים, "great men" or "princes" (Targum of Pseudo-Jonathan, בני רברביא; cf. Lewis, 1968, 86, 90ff.).

101. Cf. Lewis, 1968, 18, 20-21.

102. In this way, apparently, the present existence of evil can be harmonized with the justice of God in judging the others. While in *Jubilees* it is the continued influence of a tenth of the fallen angels that explains the presence of evil in the world, in *1 Enoch* this role is taken by the spirits of the giants who were the offspring of the Watchers. This judgment of nine-tenths of the demons at the time of the flood becomes a paradigm for the last judgment, to the point that it is difficult to determine the exact reference of the judgment sayings that accompany the Noah story.

103. C. Rowland (*The Open Heaven*, 1982, 93) suggests that this story no longer functions as a theodicy, as it did originally, but serves only to introduce the figure of Enoch. We would concur that this theodicy has been removed from its original context and has been given a new function, but this function is not *totally* unrelated to theodicy, becoming an Israel theodicy.

evidence that suggests that these passages could relate to the soteriological and pneumatological dualism of the groups? The internal evidence is perhaps somewhat ambiguous; cumulatively, however, a strong case can be made.

1. *The story is typological.* Certain aspects of the angel theodicy, even in its earliest forms, would have suggested a relationship between the fall of angels and the division of mankind into two groups based on their pneumatological condition. The fact that the demons were formed from the union of *both* angelic and human parents (*1 En.* 15:8–16:2), for example, probably suggested certain anthropological implications — namely, that the demons would continue to create further "spiritual offspring" in humans and thus spread their evil influence.[104] The account in Genesis 6 may itself have been taken to indicate similar spiritual implications of the fall when the divine voice is said to announce: "*My Spirit (rûḥî) shall not abide in man forever*" (v. 3). This may have been taken to mean that humans could very well *lose* God's *rûaḥ* and be infested with evil spirits instead.[105] It probably suggested to the author that his sinful contemporaries, like the offspring of the Watchers, had been born of an evil, rather than a good, begetting.

2. *The fallen Watchers are joined by sinners.* Stronger indications of this relationship to soteriological dualism are forthcoming from *1 En.* 10:14, which states (according to a probable rendering) that "those who collaborated with them [the giant offspring of the Watchers and the resulting demons] will be *bound together with them* from henceforth unto the end of all generations." Although these "collaborators" are not identified, the judgment pronounced in the passage seems to include all those humans influenced by the demons.[106] The pas-

---

104. Suter relates this ultimate mixed marriage to the doctrine of *mamzerim:* "The mixture of two realms, the heavenly and earthly, which are originally good in and of themselves, produces evil results" (1979, 86). We are witness (once again) to some complex interconnection between such things as the law against intermarriage *(mamzerim),* order-of-creation doctrine, the calendar, and the good and evil spirits.

105. In this regard it is interesting to note also the words of Gen. 8:1, רע האדאם יצר לב — perhaps, "the inclination (note: *yeṣer*) of the heart of man is evil." That this was taken to imply that the evil inclination was introduced into the heart as a direct result of the fall is a real possibility and provides evidence that the Noah event was given pneumatological significance.

106. Cf. Black, 1985, 138. This reference to the human "collaborators" may give a clue to understanding the following verse as well. Black notices the difficulty with the judgment pronounced on the "sons of the watchers" in that verse (v. 15), "since the destruction of the giants has already been described at v. 9 (and was the duty of Gabriel, not Michael)" (139). Are we to see in these "sons," not the giants, but the *human* "offspring"? This would accord well with the subject of vv. 14 and 16.

sage would then set up a contrast between these humans and others who will be saved, stating that all "injustice" is to be removed from the earth and that the righteous alone will "escape." The phrase "you will have no peace," used of the Watchers in 16:3, is used elsewhere in this book for sinful Israel, also suggesting the correspondence between their respective fates.[107]

3. *The Watchers teach Israel how to sin.* In the same Book of Watchers one reads how the giant offspring of the Watchers taught "the people" war, vain personal ornamentation, various sciences, incantations, astrology, and the lunar calendar,[108] with the result that "there were many wicked ones (or: 'there was much wickedness') and they committed adultery and erred, and all their conduct became corrupt" (*1 En.* 8:1-4).[109] This passage implies not only that sin results from the activity of demonic beings, but also the way this has come about. The Watchers have imparted a false wisdom, the same false wisdom referred to a little later when God pronounces the judgment of the Watchers and informs them that they do not have "all the mysteries" but only "the rejected mysteries" (16:3).[110] Since the knowledge that led to sin includes *war, personal ornamentation, astrology, and the activities of the moon,* it is certainly justifiable to see here also an allusion to the present sin of the Israelites who have tragically accepted for themselves the "rejected mysteries," teachings that have their roots in demonic inspiration. It would appear from this false-knowledge motif that *the*

---

107. Cf. 5:5; 12:5; 13:1; 94:6; Gk. 98:16; 99:13; 102:3; 103:8. Barker gives considerable attention to the correspondence, particularly in the Book of Watchers, between the fallen angels and the priests (the chief sin being intermarriage) and between the giants and rulers: "we may regard the dispute over priestly purity as one in which the angel mythology was not only deemed relevant, but was of sufficient status to be presented as the *basis* for criticizing the religious establishment of the time" (1987, 64-65).

108. As we understand "the course of the moon as well as the deception of man" in *1 En.* 8:3. The Gk. apparently substitutes the general astronomical terms ἀστρολογία, ἀστεροσκοπία, and ἀεροσκοπία for the unfamiliar Aram. נחשא, which Black translates "auguries" ("omens," "divinations"; 1985, 128); thus "the auguries of lightning . . . of the stars . . . of fire-balls . . . of earth . . . of the sun . . . of the moon." But (א)נחש can mean "to observe signs" as well as "practice divination." It is to be noted that all of these terms are related to an astronomical context, which would seem an unusual limitation for references to magical practices.

109. We take this statement to refer back to "the people" of v. 1 rather than giants, as it would appear that this is also the subject intended in v. 4: "And they cried and their voice reached unto heaven."

110. Isaac in *OTP*, 1:22, is probably justified in correcting the sg. "mystery" to the pl. "mysteries," since it is difficult to understand what the singular would refer to. This approach is preferable to the emendation suggested by Black: "there was no secret that was *not* revealed to you; and *unspeakable* secrets *you know*" (1985, 35, 155).

condition of fallen Israel was being explained as the result of the inspiration of evil demons, something following from, and reminiscent of, the fall of the angels itself.

4. *Evil spirits continue to mislead Israel.* Jubilees outlines in some detail how the sin of the Watchers led Noah's sons astray (10:1-14), indicating that the continuing influence of evil spirits, even on *Noah's* descendants, is an important matter to the author.[111] When Mastema is said to have misled the sons of Noah, we read a statement that sounds in many ways like Qumran doctrine: "And he [Mastema] sent other spirits to those who were set under his hand to practice all error and sin and all transgression, to destroy, to cause to perish and to pour out blood upon the earth" (11:5). Expressions like "all error and sin and all transgression" and "pour out blood upon the earth" suggest that the sins of Israelites are in the back of this author's mind as he writes.[112]

5. *A remnant will alone escape future judgment.* That the Noachic theodicy ultimately functions as an expression of the soteriological dualism of these groups is equally evident in statements to the effect that out of the ensuing judgment a righteous remnant will be saved. In one passage God addresses the angels about Noah, the coming judgment on the Watchers, and the blessing of the righteous:

> And now instruct him in order that he may flee, and his seed will be preserved for all generations. . . . Destroy injustice from the face of the earth. And every iniquitous deed will end, and the plant of righteousness and truth will appear forever and he will plant joy. And then all the righteous ones will escape; and become the living ones until they multiply and become tens of hundreds; and all the days of their youth and the years of their retirement they will complete in peace. And in those days the whole earth will be worked in righteousness. . . . (*1 En.* 10:3, 16-18)

It is interesting that what begins as a description of judgment at "the Deluge" (10:2) tails off, as can be seen from the last words of the quotation above, into a description of a future judgment.[113] This would suggest that the judgment of

---

111. While Charles (1902, 78) finds evidence of the Book of Noah here, García Martínez suggests that the passage is too much like the rest of *Jubilees* to allow this (1992, 36-38). If so, this would help to confirm that the author is expressing his own views here rather than merely drawing on his source.

112. References here to "fornication" and "impurity" probably also possess this combined parenetic and polemical intent; cf. Lewis, 1968, 20.

113. This happens almost imperceptibly, with only two significant indicators being given that a shift in time reference is intended. The first is a period of strife followed by "seventy generations" when the Watchers are bound beneath the earth (v. 12). Only fol-

the Watchers at the Deluge is intended as a paradigm for this future judgment, or that the judgment *commenced* at the flood is believed to be *completed* in the future judgment — probably *both*. Through this basic correspondence the author warns his contemporary readers that those who continue to sin after the example and teaching of the Watchers can expect to be punished as they will be. The present-day Israel is thereby itself implicated and warned of the coming judgment when only the "righteous ones will escape" (v. 17).[114]

6. *Calendar references betray the interests of the author*. Evidence that the Watcher theodicy actually concerns the sin of Israel can also be found in allusions to the calendar. In *1 En.* 18:15-16 we read: "And the stars which roll over upon the fire, they are the ones which have transgressed the commandments of God from the beginning of their rising because they did not arrive punctually. And he was wroth with them and bound them until the time of the completion of their sin[115] in the year of mystery." If these allusions to the judgment of the stars are not clear enough to implicate Israel in covenantal sin, the following dialogue — where the question of "which sin" is discussed in length for emphasis — makes things unmistakable. The question-answer style of this passage indicates that an important revelation is about to be made which the reader is expected to take as foundational to the message of the whole.

> At that moment I [Enoch] said, "For which sin are they bound, and for what reason were they cast in here." Then one of the holy angels, Uriel, who was with me, guiding me, spoke to me and said to me, "Enoch, for what reason are you asking and for what reason do you question and exhibit eagerness?

---

lowing this initial period of confinement, we are told, will their judgment come ("until the day of their judgment and of their consummation, until the eternal judgment is concluded," v. 12). The second indication is the presence of significant time-indicating phrases: "in those days" (v. 13) and "at the time when" (v. 14). The juxtaposition of "present" and "future" may be due to the combination of sources; García Martínez agrees with those scholars who discern the Book of Noah as a source for 10:1-3 (1992, 29), to which, then, could have been added material leading up to the eschatological references. Cf. Milik (1976, 248), who takes the "seventy generations" to refer to the time stretching from the days of Enoch and Noah until the end of time.

114. While the references to "all the righteous" may in one sense refer to the immediate descendants of Noah (cf. Black, 1985, 139, who refers them to Noah and his family), it is questionable, given the eschatological language here, that this exhausts the reference entirely.

115. It may be better to read "punishment (for their sin)" here with Black (1985, 160; taking ἁμαρτία = (ה)אטח in the sense of "consequences for sins"). It is no doubt true also, however, that our author anticipated the restoration of the created order, particularly that of the errant heavenly bodies, and this may be what is meant here.

These are among the stars of heaven *which have transgressed the commandments of the Lord* [i.e., cf. calendrical irregularities mentioned above in 18:15] and are bound in this place until the completion of ten million years, according to the number of their sins." (21:4-6)

Through this literary device the reader is now led to ask whether a transgressing Israel could ever hope to escape if even starlike beings were not granted immunity from punishment. The answer is obvious: punishment for angels and apostates who transgress or ignore the calendar will be one and the same.

The use of "stars" as a symbol for angels (cf. Isa. 14:13) in this passage may itself imply a connection between the fall of the angels and the calendar. In the Book of Heavenly Luminaries this becomes even more apparent when the aberrant activities of the heavenly bodies is explained as the activity of personal authoritative beings (cf. "chiefs of the stars," "leaders," "captains over thousands," stars as "gods," etc.; *1 En.* 80:6-7; 82:8-20). These fallen angel-stars accordingly lead Israel into the serious sin of disobedience against the calendar, which has covenantal implications. In the Zoomorphic History it is the *dark-colored* animals who are specifically said to have had intercourse with the angels, who are again symbolized as stars (86:2-4; cf. 88:1-3). Throughout the rest of the history, therefore, when the righteous are characterized as white and the unrighteous as *dark* or colored, we are perhaps to see the tainting influence of the Watchers perpetuated in their dark offspring. The resulting evil influence could be felt even among the Israelite sheep who are contrasted with the "snow-white sheep" (the saints, 90:6).

In conclusion, it would appear from the available evidence that pneumatological expressions in this literature were at least partly developed in order to serve the soteriological dualism of these groups. The presentations should hardly be considered merely didactic in purpose: the authors have little interest in establishing the metaphysical composition of the spirit world. In fact, their presentations are notably functional, occupied almost entirely with the differing effects of the spirits upon (two groups of) people. Even the theodicy that records the origin of evil spirits is applied directly to the existence of two kinds of people. By means of the lists of sins predicated to the Watchers and to the spiritual offspring of the evil Watchers, part of Israel is implicated in this theodicy. These developments set the belief in spiritual beings on a distinctly dualistic trajectory that is conspicuously carried on in the writings of the New Testament. Of particular interest in this regard is the fact that in these writings possession of God's Spirit or the good spirit has become a confirming sign of election, defining the saved over against the unsaved.

CHAPTER TEN

The Messiah-for-the-Elect

The early development of messianological belief is an enigmatic area within the study of ancient Judaism, and there exists much controversy, even over such a basic question as how one should define "messiah."[1] Most studies get around this problem by talking about messianology as involving a process of development leading from loose terminological associations and indefinite beliefs at an early stage to more hardened concepts later on. This seems to be a valid approach, and accordingly our working hypothesis will be that messianology was in various stages of development at this time and that it is precarious to speak of a single idea of a "messiah" (whether Davidic or otherwise) as if all these groups meant the same thing by it, or even to assume that they thought of any

---

1. Some justify narrowing the use of the term so as to refer exclusively to a royal figure (e.g., S. Mowinckel, *He That Cometh,* 1956, 168) or to a secular warrior figure (e.g., R. B. Laurin, "The Problem of Two Messiahs in the Qumran Scrolls," 1963, 39-52, 40-42, 48). By far the more common approach of late, however, has been to admit an ambiguity and wide range of meaning for the term. To insist with many of these scholars that all original references were nontitular and are to be translated "anointed" (as if this foundational sense everywhere dominates over the titular sense) seems, however, to take things too far. M. de Jonge ("The Role of Intermediaries in God's Final Intervention in the Future according to the Qumran Scrolls," 1969; reprinted in M. de Jonge, *Jewish Eschatology, Early Christian Christology, and the Testaments of the Twelve Patriarchs,* 1991, 28-47, 28-29) attempts to get around the problem by preferring the term "intermediaries" over "messiah" for the special figures in our literature. In many cases, however, this probably does injustice to the biblical connection and developments of the term that eventually led to the titular use of משיח and the distinctive ideas associated with the title. While certainly not originally containing the semantic content of later Christian use, the word "messiah" in many cases still best communicates the ideas involved.

433

hard-and-fast concept when they employed the term "messiah" or other messianic designations or descriptions.

But the purpose of this chapter is not primarily to fit the evidence into existing developmental schemes or to invent a new one, although the present investigation may have implications for this task. We are more interested in the significance various personages had for the authors of our writings and their communities in the *individual cases* where they are mentioned. We wish moreover to describe and categorize this significance for each case, and have thus opted for a synchronic approach to the subject, rather than the more usual diachronic approach that attempts to draw lines of continuity and to define relationships.

APPROACH AND PRESUPPOSITIONS

One approaching the messianology of these particular writings is immediately confronted with the differentiation made by some scholars between the so-called "traditional-earthly messiah" and the "apocalyptic-transcendental messiah."[2] This conventional differentiation, however, will not only distract from our main objective but is overcategorizing and indeed categorically false. Since a growing number of scholars deny the validity of this approach, we scarcely need to defend our abandonment of it except to say that some of our "apocalyptic" works contain very mundane ideas of the messiah (frequently a mixture of concepts is found)[3] while ideas related to a future earthly king can become quite miraculous and transcendent in rabbinic sources as well. Accompanying this outmoded approach also is the view that messianology is among the *essential* aspects of apocalyptic writings.[4] Actually messianic themes in these writings receive less attention than many other subjects; in some places references to a messianic person are merely incidental to the topic under discussion. Furthermore, there is very little of what could be termed systematic treatment of this subject. Even contradictory ideas appear to be grouped together, as if the authors were drawing upon a

2. For the distinction, cf. Mowinckel, 1956, 281; P. G. R. de Villiers, "The Messiah and Messiahs in Jewish Apocalyptic," 1978, 75-110, esp. 82; L. Schiffman, "The Concept of the Messiah in Second Temple and Rabbinic Literature," 1987, 235-46.

3. Cf. the ram with the great horn and the white cow of *1 Enoch* 90, or the Davidic-type messiah of *Psalms of Solomon* who possesses transcendental qualities (cf. 17:35); Schiffman, 1987, 236.

4. Mowinckel (1956, 342), e.g., called the sayings about the messiah "the heartbeat of apocalyptic."

storehouse of conventional beliefs in order to add fullness to descriptions whose main emphasis was upon other concerns — as we will indeed discover to be the case. Perhaps surprisingly, some of the later talmudic (particularly amoraic) writings actually contain a more systematic and certainly more consistent treatment of the messiah.[5] Recognizing the superficiality of such outworn attitudes hopefully clears the way for an approach which allows that *other matters* took precedence over messianological speculation in these writings and that these matters, in turn, significantly *influenced* messianic beliefs in profound ways.

Certainly a more valid generalization than any mentioned above is that these writings describe more what the messianic figures *do* than who they *are*; in modern parlance, messianology is primarily functional rather than ontological.[6] One must accordingly be cautious of categorizations based strictly on *ontological* questions and concerns (such as preexistence, relation to divinity, etc.) — an approach that often still dominates — and seek instead to concentrate on the *role* of the individual. This will hopefully bring us closer to understanding the significance and function of these figures for our authors and their communities, because we will be attempting to understand these figures in *their* way and not *ours*.

It would appear that many types of roles are assigned to various personages in our literature. Among them are figures recognized for their role as *progenitors,* the "fathers" who bear importance primarily because of their significance as the highly respected ancestors of God's people. To this category belong, for example, those figures who constitute and perpetuate the holy "seed" mentioned in an earlier chapter. Another group consists of *paradigmatic* figures whose role goes beyond that of the progenitors in possessing qualities or actions that are *exemplary* or *normative* for the life of the group addressed by the literature. These figures appear in parenetic passages where their example encourages the reader to some positive action, or they serve as paradigms of the superlative righteousness of the group vis-à-vis the outsiders who do not exhibit a similar righteous standard. A third group consists of *mystical* or *revelatory* figures who possess either preexistence or heavenly existence and are able

5. Cf. D. E. Gowan, *Bridge between the Testaments,* 1986, 394; Schiffman, 1987, 241-44, who finds the emphasis among the Amoraim rather surprising.

6. For the functional approach as applied to the Qumran messianic belief, cf. de Jonge, 1991, 34, 40. For studies of early Christology that recognize that, especially for the most ancient Jewish and Christian messianological conceptions, a functional approach is more appropriate than ontological categories, cf. O. Cullmann, *The Christology of the New Testament,* 1963, 3-4; R. H. Fuller, *The Foundations of New Testament Christology,* 1965, 247-48; and R. N. Longenecker, *The Christology of Early Jewish Christianity,* 1970, 63-64, 154-56.

from their exalted position in the spiritual sphere to offer authoritative teaching and advice to those to whom they reveal themselves.

We will consider a few examples of each of these before focusing on a fourth group we *cautiously* refer to as *messianic* figures. It seems best to include in this category those personages who possess *both eschatological* (in the sense of fulfilling the final purposes of God; see next chapter) and *redemptive* roles (as instruments of salvation).[7] This is by necessity a somewhat modern definition that nevertheless provides a useful heuristic categorization and serves to complete the spectrum of roles in evidence in late Second Temple Judaism. It is also appropriate to the actual attitude of our writers toward important personages in their belief systems, since a superlative place was reserved for figures who come in the future to save their people. For these we reserve the title "messiah(s)." Any good analysis must recognize various categories, even if not exactly these four, but it must be kept in mind that a single personage regularly belongs to more than one of these groupings.

It has frequently been suggested by biblical scholars that the seeds of messianological belief in the Hebrew Scriptures, and the ancient Near Eastern and more distinctively Hebrew ideas out of which messianic belief emerged, were at least at first entirely noneschatological and national, formed within the context of ancient royal theology and centered (in Israel's case) upon a worthy king descended from David.[8] These hopes eventually became future-oriented in postexilic Judaism but, according to some scholars, did not lose their national orientation until Christianity took the decisive step from a messianism based on national hopes to one directed toward the salvation of an elect community.[9] Accordingly the starting point of many studies of messianology and Christology in the New Testament period is the assumption that Judaism awaited this Davidic messiah and that Jesus was the first to challenge this militant and nationalistic image. It is again with such predominating conventional views in mind that we take up the question of messianology, and in line with our investigation to this point, consider the possibility that some kinds of Judaism had already embraced aspects of an *a*-nationalistic messianology well before the Christian era.

7. Since the discovery of the scrolls, it is really no longer valid to speak of messiahs merely as "*eschatological* figures" (cf., e.g., Mowinckel, 1956, 3). There were many eschatological figures at Qumran who did not fit the special redemptive role of messiah (the person called the *moreh ṣedeq*, although possessing eschatological significance, was probably not a "messiah" in this sense).

8. Cf., e.g., Mowinckel, 1956, passim; S. Talmon, "Types of Messianic Expectation at the Turn of the Era," in Talmon, *King, Cult, and Calendar in Ancient Judaism*, 1986, 202-24, 205.

9. Expressed clearly by Talmon (1986, 213) but assumed by many.

THE MESSIANIC CONTEXT: PROGENITORS, PARADIGMS, AND MYSTICAL AND REVELATORY FIGURES

We will consider the many diverse roles of personages in this literature before investigating various instances of "messiah" (i.e., eschatological deliverance) figures. Not only is this necessary to establish a valid *context* for this study, but it is also essential for making clear how the appearance of "messiah" figures relates to the very complex and diverse interest in traditional figures in Judaism. Among the more important of these types of figures were *progenitors, paradigms,* and *mystical/revelatory figures.*

Antediluvian Heroes — Seth, Enoch, and Noah

Featured among those personages we call *progenitors* stands Seth, who has already been described in connection with the seed theology of these groups in that he appears as the progenitor of the race of all righteous "seed."[10] Standing second in the lists of patriarchs and the first to have brothers (and sisters), Seth takes his place as the first to be divinely selected as the righteous seed. It is possible that Genesis might itself allude to this idea of divine selection in the words of Eve given in explanation for the naming of Seth: "God has appointed *(šāth)* for me another child *(zera')* instead of Abel, for Cain slew him." The idea of Seth being "appointed" or "raised up" as a "seed" is certainly suggestive. Books like *Jubilees,* at least, seem to have given this significance to the Genesis passage (cf. 4:7).

Even being second in the line of ten antediluvian patriarchs, however, was apparently not given the same importance as was granted to Enoch and Noah, who respectively assume the distinguished seventh and tenth positions in the lists, these numbers implying for our authors a certain importance within the antediluvian chronology.[11] Like Seth, they are also significantly represented as perpetuators of the righteous "seed." Thus in *1 Enoch* 83–84 Noah is the "righteous seed" who in answer to Enoch's prayer (cf. 84:6) is saved from the destruction of the earth. The remainder of the Zoomorphic History is accordingly preoccupied with the idea of the preservation of the seed in Noah's descendants, which it portrays using the symbols of dark- and white-colored animals.

---

10. This notion may be related to the parallel idea in Judaism that ancestors were believed to contain all their descendants within their bodies.

11. The fact that Enoch and Noah were embraced by the same communities is not surprising, given their common historical origins. Cf. D. S. Russell, *The Old Testament Pseudepigrapha,* 1987, 27.

Likewise Noah is instructed in the Book of Watchers to hide himself and "flee" so that "his seed will be preserved for all generations" (*1 En.* 10:3).

This interest in the seed indicates that these figures were not merely progenitors, but paradigms. The many allusions to Noah and his kin as the "righteous remnant" would appear to be deliberate extensions of this paradigmatic significance. In the introduction to the Zoomorphic History (*1 Enoch* 83–84) Enoch is instructed to pray that a "remnant" (identified with the "plant of eternal *seed*" mentioned above, 84:6) may be saved from the coming destruction of the earth, and perhaps behind this idea of a "remnant" lies a reference to the military idea of complete (or virtually complete) annihilation, an idea indigenous to ancient Near Eastern warfare. To this idea our writer, perhaps in continuity with the thoughts of the author of the corresponding portion of Genesis, has added his belief in the promise of the Creator to preserve a small representation of his creation in order to make possible the continuation of the species — that is, so it would not be totally annihilated. Presumably in this book the remnant is directly identified with Noah and his family, but it is noteworthy that even among Noah's descendants a continuing sifting of this remnant goes on, so that the reducing effects of the salvation of the seed is again evident, something that is clear from the symbolism of 89:9ff., which traces the "dark" history of Noah's descendants. One might say this is the beginning of the working out of the paradigmatic significance of the Noah remnant, which will only be fully realized in the remnant of the latter days.

Likewise the Book of Watchers gives to the remnant idea a paradigmatic significance. The theme of the flood is of course pervasive in this book, and Enoch refers directly to the preservation of the "seed," as noted above. A few verses following that reference, he states that a "plant of righteousness and truth will appear . . . and [it] will plant joy forever. And then all the *righteous ones will escape* [another remnant term]" (10:16). In a similar way in Book 5, Enoch announces the coming of a righteous seed who will survive the judgment. During the "first consummation," he reports, "a certain man (Noah) shall be saved" (93:4). Here it is evident, in fact, how narrowly the race escaped complete annihilation, as it now becomes represented by a solitary righteous man and his family. But it is the words "*first* consummation" that point unmistakably to the paradigmatic significance of this remnant theology, since presumably much the same kind of remnant will be preserved through the implied *second* consummation.

Similar ideas appear in a portion of the so-called Book of Noah (*1 Enoch* 106–7, more likely a book of *Enoch*, as the latter speaks in the first person in 106:8, 13, 19), where Enoch previews the whole course of events to come, telling of both "destruction" and the salvation of a "remnant" (cf. also the remnant terminology "shall be left," 106:16-18). Noah, Enoch is told, "shall be the *rem-*

nant for you; and he and his sons shall be saved from the destruction which shall come upon the earth" (106:18). The reader is then referred to the "still greater oppression" that will follow this act of salvation (106:19), which again hints that the experiences of the remnant Noah are going to be repeated to a certain degree during the events of the (real) author's day.

The identification of Noah as a personification of the remnant idea is accordingly evident throughout the Enochian corpus (some MSS of the final chapters of *1 Enoch* go so far as to connect the etymology of the name "Noah" directly with the preservation of a remnant).[12] That the purpose of this identification was to serve paradigmatic interests is undeniable. That such a significance was shared among a sector of Judaism, and for a long period of time, is evident in the much later 4 Ezra, whose author has come to immortalize Noah as "the progenitor *of all the righteous who survived* the Flood."[13] That Judaism at large may actually have shared this view is suggested by Ben Sira, who proclaims:

> Noah was found perfect and righteous,
> and thus he made amends in the time of retribution;
> therefore a remnant survived on the earth *(egenēthē kataleimma tē gē)*,
> when the flood came. (Ecclus. 44:17)

A similar tradition is alluded to in 1 Peter where reference seems to be to the fallen Watchers who disobeyed "when God's patience waited in the days of Noah, during the building of the ark, in which a few, that is, eight persons, were saved through water" (3:20). The "few" motif deliberately harks back to the remnant idea associated in this tradition with the salvation of Noah. This passage from 1 Peter has long been recognized for its reliance on Jewish teaching. Now we can see clearly what kind of teaching this would be.

Given this important and complex tradition, therefore, the term "progenitor" hardly exhausts the significance of these two figures. Besides providing a paradigm for the surviving remnant, Enoch was a *paradigmatic* or exemplary figure for the Enochian communities for other reasons too. For one thing he

---

12. *1 En.* 106:18 reads: "call his name Noah, for he shall be the remnant for you." Black (1985, 322): "That the original here was נֹיחַ = ἀνάπαυσις (as Milik proposes) is borne out by the explanation of the etymology in G^b ἐφ᾽ οὗ ἂν καταπαύσητε καὶ υἱοὶ αὐτοῦ.... G^b = Eth. ὑμῶν (ὑμῖν) κατάλειμμα introduces a second etymology of the name 'Noah,' based on another sense of the word נוח"; cf. Sir. 44:17. Things are further complicated by 107:3 ("he will comfort the earth"; Black: "he will rejoice the earth"), which offers yet "another interpretation of נוח but in this case again along the lines of the Biblical exegesis of Gen. 5.29, perhaps from ינַיהֲנוּ" (M. Black, *The Book of Enoch* or *I Enoch,* 1985, 323).

13. Described here also as the one who was "left" in the flood (3:11). Cf. Russell, 1987, 37.

was renowned for his righteousness[14] and apparently also for his wisdom.[15] It is certainly not insignificant that Enoch had also experienced in his life many of the struggles that the readers of his writings were now experiencing. Furthermore, as great-grandparent of Noah, he was in a good position to see not only God's judgment but also his ability to deliver the righteous, and accordingly could be a great encouragement to the readers.[16] These readers may even have believed that they would one day experience a translation to heaven similar to Enoch's.[17] For such reasons, some kind of identity[18] was no doubt felt between the "patron" Enoch and his community. Much the same can be said for Noah, who was the righteous man *par excellence*. He is actually the first in the Hebrew Scriptures to be called "righteous" (Gen. 6:9), a fact also noted in Ezekiel (14:14, 20; cf. also Sir. 44:17). Described in Gen. 6:9 as "blameless," he, like Enoch, "walked with God."[19] Noah's experience of the flood naturally placed him in a unique position to understand the trials of the righteous and to offer consolation inasmuch as he, if anyone, had direct experience of the deliverance of God from trouble, as is perhaps again best evident in the citation from Sir. 44:17 above. It was Noah's righteousness that made possible the preservation of a remnant in his time.

Enoch and Noah seem to have been important not only as progenitors and paradigms, but also for their role as *revelatory figures*. Since they lived in the time before the flood, which had taken on paradigmatic significance for some of our authors, they are presented as possessing great insight into matters of judgment, insight they used to teach their future righteous offspring how to prepare for and avoid the judgment in the latter days. The earlier-mentioned *double entendre* in the introduction to the Zoomorphic History, in which the

14. Sir. 44:16, e.g., refers to him as "an example of repentance to future generations," and the Watchers address him in *1 En.* 12:4 as "scribe of righteousness" (cf. also *Jub.* 10:17). He is accordingly referred to as "the Righteous One" in the Similitudes of Enoch, and is lavished with expressions that imply a reputation for righteousness (cf. *1 En.* 38:2; 46:3; 53:6; etc.).

15. Russell (1987, 25) suggests that antediluvian heroes were generally considered men of outstanding wisdom (outside of Judaism as well); this kind of tradition may also have influenced the place of Enoch as the wise man *par excellence*.

16. Cf. A. Hultgård, *L'eschatologie des Testaments des Douze Patriarches,* 1977, 1:83.

17. Cf. L. Hartman, *Asking for a Meaning,* 1979, 127.

18. Hartman, 1979, 127.

19. Both Enoch and Noah are therefore important as spiritual examples of walking with God, a notion that may have been associated with the covenantal idea of walking in the (right) way, etc. The association of these two due to their righteousness is clear in *Jub.* 10:17, which describes Noah's life as "more excellent than any of the sons of men except Enoch"! His righteousness significantly included a decisive rejection of all of the teachings of the Watchers (cf. *1 En.* 65:6ff.).

first judgment is intended to prefigure a yet-to-come future judgment, is suggestive in this regard. In this role of revelatory figure, Enoch had uniquely revealed to him such things as the depth of the sin of humanity, God's purpose in judging the world, and the role of the angels. This would have possessed incalculable importance and interest for the real writer's community, who needed to know, and to express, how and why God was active in judgment *in their time* as well. They accordingly looked to Enoch, the witness of the first deluge, for insight into the meaning of the expected second deluge.

Other kinds of revelation received by Enoch through direct experience are equally important. His calendrical teaching demanded special respect since he lived at a time of great sin when calendrical irregularities were believed to affect, and be affected by, the spiritual aberrations of the Watchers; he even acted as mediator on the Watchers' behalf. Enoch was also particularly well suited to receive revelation because of his preexistence and his *continued* existence in heavenly places. The tradition that Enoch "walked with God; and he was not, for God took him" (Gen. 5:24) suggests all of these elements: his righteousness, his advantageous position for receiving revelation, and his eternal existence.[20] Tradition holds (probably on the basis of this verse) that Enoch never died, and he accordingly may have been thought to live on in the heavenlies for the very purpose of being able to communicate his traditions to those who could enter into fellowship with him or otherwise become privy to the mystical tradition associated with his name.[21]

Some of the Qumran fragments (4Q535 and 536) confirm a similar role for Noah, associating him with great wisdom and proclaiming that "he will reveal Mysteries like the Highest Angels" and "he will know the Secrets of mankind. His Understanding will spread to all peoples, and he will know the Secrets of all living things."[22] *Jubilees* is also certainly aware of the element of warning transmitted along with traditions about Noah. Noah and his children were left

---

20. Cf. Russell, 1987, 37.

21. His continued life made him an excellent candidate for watching over the whole history of revelation, guarding the sacred writings, and delivering them to his people (cf. also *2 Enoch* 35; for Enoch as a receiver of revelation against the Near Eastern background, cf. Russell, 1987, 39).

22. 4Q535 1.8; 4Q536 1.8-9. Cf. also 4Q535 1.5, 9; 2.11. 4Q536 also mentions the enigmatic "Three Books" that will be learned by Noah (1.5; perhaps the "heavenly tablets"), and 4Q535 says that "One will write the words of God in a book that does not wear out" (2.12). These books seem to be the source for Noah's revelations and may point to the origins of the view that Noah knew the calendar, feast days, and other laws as mentioned in *Jubilees* 6. The fact that these texts, like *1 Enoch* 108, posit a perfect birth for Noah seems to reflect the "righteous" motif alluded to above (cf. R. H. Eisenman and M. Wise, *The Dead Sea Scrolls Uncovered*, 1992, 33; 36-37 for text). 4Q536 1.10 refers to Noah as "the Elect of God," suggesting the identity of this figure with his "elect" community.

as a remnant, it says (7:25-26), but Noah's children would be misled by demons (7:26-27). It is incumbent, therefore, upon the future generation to avoid such a fate: "And now, my children, hear and do justice and righteousness *so that you might be planted in righteousness*" (7:34).

Patriarchs — Abraham and Jacob

Another fitting candidate for the role of progenitor is Abraham. What is perhaps most significant, however, is that Abraham is *not* given the kind of attention that an Enoch, a Noah, or even an Isaac or Jacob is given in some of our writings.[23] Given his prominence in Genesis and Judaism generally, this disinterest is conspicuous and may have something to do with the downplaying of national ideas (since Abraham was unanimously claimed as the "father" of the nation) as well as with a desire to emphasize the conditional nature of the covenant made to him. This conditional aspect is more adequately exhibited by his progeny,[24] and this would itself explain the shift of interest to *Jacob*, particularly in *Jubilees*, where he assumes the role of progenitor *par excellence.* Jacob also embodies the notion of selectivity in the choice of the seed, as already noted. On the other hand, Endres explains this preoccupation with Jacob as reflecting the need to reestablish an important feeling of identity in the time of Antiochus IV by focusing on and insisting upon certain commands of the Jubilaean covenant like forbiddance of intermarriage and separation from Gentiles. The place of Jacob as the first recipient of the covenant thus served to help focus attention upon this covenant.[25] It is difficult to see how the very specific requirements of the *Jubilaean* covenant could be served, however, by reference to Jacob, whose sons conspicuously also fail to separate themselves from Gentiles; and Jacob could hardly be thought of as more significant vis-à-vis the covenant than Abraham! Endres is perhaps closer to the truth when he suggests that Jacob's "central significance results more from God's choice of him than from his demonstrated covenantal fidelity" and that the "author's use of the Jacob tradition probably points to a specific inner-Jewish debate over election and the covenant" (cf. Rom. 9:6-13).[26] This would appear to be the reason why

---

23. We have not included the so-called *Testament of Abraham* in our review since it is somewhat later and fraught with difficulties for interpretation, although the work may well have affinities with our movement. It does not, however, necessarily imply any special attention to Abraham in the movement as a whole.

24. For a conditional formulation of the promise to Abraham, cf. *Jub.* 12:20.

25. J. C. Endres, *Biblical Interpretation in the Book of Jubilees,* 1987, 229-31.

26. Endres, 1987, 230, 229.

so much emphasis is placed on the preservation of the righteous by means of imitating Jacob's righteousness in *Jub.* 25:1-22.

It is evident that Jacob, like many of the other progenitor figures in this movement, functioned to grant *identity* to the group that claimed to be his legitimate descendants. These groups composed the seed who continued to follow in the footsteps of Jacob, or the true seed of Seth, or the remnant first addressed by Enoch and embodied in Noah and his kin. But Jacob's role also went well beyond progenitor to that of a kind of *paradigm* of the righteous, just as Esau, in turn, seems to have symbolized for the author of *Jubilees* the unworthy Israelites (a paradigmatic role already alluded to). *Jubilees* demonstrates this primarily through extended elaborations on the brotherly relations between Jacob and Esau, particularly as these embellished sections portray the *persecution* of Jacob by Esau, the *derogation* of the latter's character, the brokenness in *brotherly relations* between the two, and the important *confirmation* of Jacob over Esau intended by the Rebekah-embellishments. Rebekah speaks to her husband Isaac about their sons: "One request I beg of you. Make Esau swear that he will not harm Jacob and will not *pursue* him hostilely because you know Esau's inclination, *that it has been evil since his youth*" (35:9). This passage indicates that Jacob and Esau no longer tolerate one another (as they do in Genesis); an element of *persecution*[27] has entered the picture. This strongly suggests that the Jubilaean community had been persecuted by others who are now represented or symbolized in the story by Esau. Other passages suggest much the same thing. Isaac responds to the request of Rebekah with words that predict the inevitable actions of Esau and ultimate triumph of Jacob when he is persecuted by his brother:

> And you say to me that I should make him swear that he will not kill his brother, Jacob. If he swears he will not abide by his oath, and he will not do goodness, but only evil. But if he wishes to kill Jacob, his brother, he will be given into the hand of Jacob. And he will not escape from his hand because he will fall into his hand. And you should not fear on account of Jacob because the protector of Jacob is greater and mightier and more honored and praised than the protector of Esau. (35:15-17)

Recall that Isaac never *explicitly expressed* his changed loyalties from Esau to Jacob in the Genesis narrative. Does this not allow that Isaac never actually ratified the change of status between the two? What does this accordingly say about the *official* status of Jacob? To make up for the silence in the biblical account, *Jubilees* provides an elaborate answer from the mouth of Rebekah, who takes Isaac's place as spokesperson in this part of the history. Typically, words not recorded in Genesis are placed on her lips, and because of the lengthy addi-

---

27. 'iyesdedo √ sadada, "pursue," "persecute."

tions she actually gains a much more central position here than she had in the original narrative. All of this is for the purpose of making clear the validity of Jacob's assumption of the role as the righteous progenitor (cf. 25:1-3, 11-23; 26:1–27:18; 35:1-27). Rebekah is thus being called upon to make up what was felt to be a serious deficiency in the biblical account. And Isaac, for his part, is not without his own speeches, not found in the biblical account, which are created to make abundantly clear his change of mind as well: "I know and see the deeds of Jacob, who is with us, that with all his heart he is honoring us. And I first loved Esau more than Jacob because he was born first, but now I love Jacob more than Esau because he has increasingly made his deeds evil. And he has no righteousness because all of his ways are injustice and violence" (35:13). As a result of this view of Jacob and Esau, the righteous seed is now proclaimed to be resident solely in Jacob. Of Esau Isaac proclaims: "And neither he nor his seed is to be saved for they will be destroyed from the earth, and they will be uprooted from under the heaven since he has forsaken the God of Abraham and he has gone after his wives and after their defilement and after their errors, he and his sons" (35:14).

It is probably true that few Jews would have challenged the priority of Jacob over Esau merely on the basis of Isaac's silence. Other motivations must have been behind the lengthy embellishments, and these would seem to relate to the typology at work here and the inner-Jewish conflict in which the Jubilaean community was embroiled. Some passages appear to reflect the situation of persecution that the Jubilaean community found itself faced with. Rebekah pleads with Esau: "I ask of you on the day when I die . . . that you and Jacob [will] love one another, and that one will not seek evil for his brother, but only love him" (35:20). These words suggest that Jacob and Esau are mutually responsible to care for one another. However, it is clear that Esau alone is to be blamed for the strife between them — when goaded by his sons (37:1-13), he eventually arranges a confrontation with his brother that ends in his own subjugation (37:14–38:14). His promise to abide by his mother's words is therefore patently deceitful, and the real guilt of Esau, who should have treated his own flesh with more respect, becomes manifest. "And Jacob, my brother, I shall love more than all flesh. And I have no brother in all the earth except him alone. And this is not a great thing for me if I love him because he is my brother and together we were sown in your belly and together we came forth from your womb. And if I do not love my brother, whom shall I love?" (35:22). The situation of the writer of *Jubilees* can also be discerned in the testament of Isaac in which he exhorts both brothers to pursue righteousness:

> And among yourselves, my sons, be loving of your brothers as a man loves himself, with each man seeking for his brother what is good for him, and act-

ing together on the earth, and loving each other as themselves. . . . And now I will make you swear by the great oath . . . that each one will love his brother with compassion and righteousness and no one will desire evil for his brother from now *and forever* all the days of your lives so that you will prosper in all your deeds *and not be destroyed.* And if either of you seeks evil against his brother, know that hereafter each one who seeks evil against his brother will *fall into his hands and be uprooted from the land of the living and his seed will be destroyed from under heaven.* . . . I have been speaking and exhorting you, my sons, according to the judgment which will come upon the man who desires to harm his brother. (36:4-11)

Such words (note especially those placed in italics) suggest strongly that the opponents of the Jubilaean group were being warned that they would be judged for their unfair treatment of the righteous. As only Israel abides in the "land of the living" (if the reference here is to the physical Palestine), this would confirm that a division in Israel is envisaged. Remnant theology (employing seed and plant motifs) has accordingly been read into the account of Jacob and Esau in order to express the point that those who are obedient will continue to represent the righteous seed, while those who disobey (i.e., particularly the injunction to live peacefully with their brothers) will be uprooted. The emphasis on the expression "against his brother" implies once again that physical descent is no guarantee of preservation as this righteous seed. This provides an implicit warning to Israel not to rely on their physical origins alone.

That this story is a paradigm for the situation in Israel during the writer's generation is suggested by other indications as well, particularly the contrasts drawn between the respective characters of Jacob and Esau, and the way Esau's character is denigrated. The words of Isaac cited earlier suggest that Esau's problem is with his "heart" — that is, his psychological composition. While Jacob honors his parents "with all his heart," all the ways of Esau are "injustice and violence" (35:13). This theme is enlarged upon during the confrontation between the brothers. Esau admits that the contention reflects deep emotions in himself that will not easily be denied. They are like primitive instincts from which he is powerless to escape, while Jacob continues to exhibit a strong sense of honor:

> Mankind and beasts of the field have no righteous oath which they have
>   surely sworn forever.
> But daily they seek evil, one against the other, and each one seeks to kill
>   his enemy and adversary.
> And you will hate me and my sons forever.
> And so there is no observing of fraternity with you. . . .[28]

---

28. V. 19b is not found in Eth., but it suits the context well (as cf. Wintermute, *OTP,*

Hear these words of mine which I will speak to you.
If a boar changes his hide and his bristles and makes them soft as wool,
and if he brings forth horns upon his head like the horns of a stag or
    sheep;
then I will observe fraternity with you. . . .
And if the wolves make peace with lambs so as not to eat them or assault
    them,
and if their hearts are set upon them to do good,
then peace will be in my heart for you.
And if the lion becomes a friend of the ox,
and if he is bound with him in a single yoke,
and he plows with him and makes peace with him,
then I will make peace with you.
And if the raven becomes white like the Raza bird,
then know that I will love you and I will make peace with you. (37:18-23)

Accordingly the persecution motif, the exhortations to brotherly kindness, the presentation of the seed motif, and the anthropology/psychology of
these passages indicate, individually and in concert, that the Jacob/Esau story
has been all but stripped of its conventional and biblical function as explaining
the historical discord between Israel and Edom (although this connection is
mentioned rather incidentally in 38:14) in order to be employed as a paradigm
for the present tensions between the righteous and the unrighteous *within* Israel. This is especially clear from the length of treatment allowed to the story,
from its repeated emphasis on brotherly relations,[29] and from the way the criteria for division and exclusion are stated (in the above verse): intermarriage, ritual defilement by Gentile ways, and the acceptance of false teaching — typically
divisive and notably *Jewish* issues. One is bound, therefore, to conclude that the
community identifies with Jacob and his experiences while the rest of Israel is
implicated in the portrait of Esau and his sinful ways, particularly in his willingness to take Gentile wives.[30] The paradigmatic role of Jacob and Esau is ac-

---

2:126 n. *h*); in this passage Jacob disavows the charge that he would act in the way Esau implies in vv. 18-19, again demonstrating the relative righteousness of Jacob, and his admira-
ble sense of honor.

29. Strangely G. L. Davenport (*The Eschatology of the Book of Jubilees,* 1971, 67) appears to invert the order of significance: "The function of the command for brotherly love
at one time must have referred to fellow Israelites. It was added to the Jacob-Esau narrative
as an attack upon the Edomites"!

30. Other writings also seem to reflect this paradigmatic role of Jacob and Esau. Inasmuch as Jacob is associated with light and Esau with darkness in Judaism, J. J. Enz ("Origin of the Dualism Expressed by 'Sons of Light' and 'Sons of Darkness,'" 1976, 16-17) suggests that the Jacob/Esau dichotomy may partly be responsible for the terms "sons of light"

cordingly so developed that it is almost as if those within the community *were* Jacob; those outside (notably other Jews) *were* Esau.

Levi and Judah

When it comes to paradigmatic figures, one must also consider as possible examples the patriarchs Levi and Judah in the *Testaments of the Twelve Patriarchs,* who, because of their importance to our discussion of messianology, will receive some detailed attention here. The exact significance of Levi and Judah in our writings is much discussed,[31] but a consensus as to this significance is lacking. (1) The older view that relates the priestly and royal tribes to the adoption of priestly and royal functions by the Hasmoneans possesses real problems: Levi and Judah appear together only in *1 Enoch* and *Jubilees,* which are *pre*-Hasmonean books, and in the *Testaments,* which appears, if anything, to be *anti*-Hasmonean! Levi and Judah are also mentioned *separately,* which does not suggest a *combination* of functions in a single individual. (2) Problems exist, on the other hand, with relating Levi simply to an apology for the priesthood, as some try to do, since the issue surrounding the priesthood at this time was not its validity or importance but the identity of its true *representatives.* (It should be noted that the focus on Levi, rather than Aaron or Zadok, is necessitated by the literary context of *Jubilees* and the *Testaments,* where it would be anachronistic to refer to the later priests.) (3) To treat all references to these figures as implying two messiahs also presents problems. One can point to many references in the *Testaments* to Levi and Judah that cannot be called strictly "messianic," for they are either primarily *historical* — referring back to the historical personages Levi and Judah — or, more often, refer to their descendants.[32]

---

and "sons of darkness" at Qumran. A continuing association with Jacob may be evident in references to the "house of Jacob" (cf., e.g., *Pss. Sol.* 7:10). The figure Joseph in *Jubilees* and the *Testaments of the Twelve Patriarchs* probably offers an example of a paradigmatic-identity figure similar to that of Jacob. In the *Testaments* Joseph's brothers, who persecute him wildly, would seem to function as paradigms of the rest of Israel who mistreat the righteous community.

31. Alongside the literature cited below in relation to the "messiahs of Aaron and Israel" at Qumran, cf. esp. G. R. Beasley-Murray, "The Two Messiahs in the Testaments of the Twelve Patriarchs," 1946, 1-12; R. E. Brown, "The Teacher of Righteousness and the Messiah(s)," 1969, 37-44; Laurin, 1963, 43-45; F. F. Bruce, "Recent Contributions to the Understanding of Hebrews," 1969, 260-64; T. L. Donaldson, "Levitical Messianology in Late Judaism," 1981, 196-97; A. J. B. Higgins, "The Priestly Messiah," 1967, 210-36; K. G. Kuhn, "The Two Messiahs of Aaron and Israel," 1957a, 54-55; de Villiers, 1978, 75-76.

32. For a discussion of this kind of passage, cf. H. W. Hollander and M. de Jonge, *The Testaments of the Twelve Patriarchs,* 1985, 57.

Among these theories, the messianic approach to the figure of Levi still frequently carries the weight of opinion, thus exhibiting how persistent is the assumption — made early on in the study of the *Testaments* — that messianological belief was among the more dominant beliefs in this literature. This prejudice, however, is certainly better shed in favor of a fresh reevaluation of the *Testaments* that attempts to discern the emphases and message of the original author(s). The messianic approach, furthermore, really fails to explain the preoccupation with Levi and Judah: it does not, for example, explain why the entire tribe in each case was considered dominant or important (as in *TJud.* 21:1-5). The two tribes hardly need to have been granted such priority simply for the messiahs to have originated from them. Nor is it a matter of the relative purity or righteousness of these tribes, since, as we have seen, they are not spared the harsh criticism meted out to the other tribes. Perhaps the clinching evidence against the messianological approach comes from a number of Levi passages in which there appears a single messiah from the tribe of *Judah* (cf. *TDan* 5:10; *TNaph.* 4:5; 8:2-3; *TGad* 8:1; *TBen.* 11:2), which would be especially surprising if the emphasis on the tribe of Levi was related to belief in a priestly messiah. All of these facts suggest that the importance of Levi and Judah goes well beyond the matter of the origins of two messiahs.

The suggestion of Hultgård that the two figures in the *Testaments* are actually paradigmatic — that Levi represents the ideal priest, and that this figure was (perhaps later?) combined with traditions about Judah[33] — is accordingly worth serious consideration. This thesis builds on his earlier view of the *Testaments* as containing "l'ideologie de 'Lévi et Judah,'" an ideology that developed partly in reaction to the Hasmoneans.[34] This approach is confirmed by Endres, who views the Levitical emphasis in *Jubilees* from much the same perspective.[35] The group that created the *Testaments* took the examples of these patriarchs as in some way normative for their own community. This appears to be a valid approach to at least one of the well-known "messianic" passages, *TJud.* 21:1–22:3, which does not mention a messianic kind of figure at all until 22:3 (and then again in 24:1ff.). The historical nature of the first part of the passage is obvious; there is no reference here to a future redeemer or messianic figure:

33. Cf. A. Hultgård, "The Ideal 'Levite,' the Davidic Messiah, and the Saviour Priest in the Testaments of the Twelve Patriarchs," 1980, 93-110; building on Hultgård's earlier treatment of the subject (*L'eschatologie des Testaments des Douze Patriarches*, 1977, 1:15-81); for related views, cf. H. D. Slingerland, *The Testaments of the Twelve Patriarchs*, 1977, 77.

34. Hultgård, 1977, 1:59, 62, 75, 93, etc.

35. Endres refers to the "Levitical ideology" of *Jubilees* (1987, 238-39), and calls Levi the "ideal priest" (242).

And now, children, love Levi so that you may endure. Do not be arrogant toward him or you will be wholly destroyed. To me God has given the kingship and to him, the priesthood; and he has subjected the kingship to the priesthood.[36] To me he gave earthly matters and to Levi, heavenly matters. As heaven is superior to the earth, so is God's priesthood superior to the kingdom on earth, unless through sin it falls away from the Lord and is dominated by the earthly kingdom. For the Lord chose him over you to draw near to him, to eat at his table to present as offerings the costly things of the sons of Israel. (*TJud.* 21:1-5)

The words expressing the preeminence of Levi over Judah might reflect the abandonment of royal theocratic ideals in favor of a priestly organization in Israel at this time. This does not necessarily imply that the group was heavily dominated by priests, as this could have been a common sentiment at the time. But what is more significant and, coincidentally, quite suggestive of the context of debate is that these words seem to imply *a fallen priesthood in Jerusalem* that has become subjected "through sin" *(di' hamartias)* to earthly authorities. This tends to be confirmed by the following passage, which we have already seen to refer to the author's contemporaries, the apostates of Israel. The passage is important again here because, in association with what has gone before, it implies a contrast between two groups — those who honor Levi (and Judah) on the one hand, and those who ignore God's order and are accordingly thrust into conflict and confusion, and eventually judgment, on the other: "The Lord will instigate among them *factions* set against each other and conflicts will persist in Israel. My rule shall be terminated by men of alien race, until the salvation of Israel comes, until the coming of the God of righteousness, so that Jacob may enjoy tranquility and peace, as well as all the nations" (*TJud.* 22:1-2; cf. 21:6-9). The patriarch not only enjoins upon his sons obedience to Levi, therefore, but also tells of a time when the God-given order for the nation, with Levi at the head over Judah, will be ignored, bringing chaos (cf. 21:6-9). It is only following this that prophecies of the coming prince from Judah occur (22:3; 24:1ff.). Thus the tendency of scholars to treat the interest in Levi and Judah as reflective of the messianology of the *Testaments* can only indirectly be the case. The exhortations to honor Levi and Judah in the above passages would suit better their role as patrons of the *Testaments* community, figureheads representing the cor-

---

36. To this superiority of the priesthood over the royal prerogatives, cf. the Aramaic Testament of Levi from Qumran (= 1Q21 = 1QAramaic Levi = 1QTLevi ar; cf. also 4Q214, 540, and 541): "the sovereignty of the priesthood will be greater than the sovereignty of [the kingship]" (F. García Martínez, *Qumran and Apocalyptic,* 1992, 266). This spells out rather more clearly that a comparison of relative powers of these offices, and not the priority of a Levitical messiah, is being contemplated in such texts.

porate identity of the group who *believed themselves alone to emulate the ideals expressed by these figures.*

The paradigmatic function for Levi might well be brought to the fore in what is a well-known but enigmatic passage, *TLevi* 8:11-19, where all three offices of prophet, priest, and king — among others (cf. v. 17) — are ascribed to Levi's sons. Hollander and de Jonge typically attribute this triple acclamation to a Christian perspective,[37] but this is neither necessary nor likely, as Jesus was not believed to come from the tribe of Levi. Likewise, the triple ascription can hardly relate to the claims of the Hasmoneans since the issue surrounding this group of priest-kings was not their right to *rule* so much as their right to act as *high priests* (i.e., a quite different concern than that shown in this passage). And while some of the Hasmoneans were hailed as great national leaders and teachers, the office of prophet does not seem terribly appropriate for this group, especially for the later Hasmoneans. The blurring of functions in this passage would also be quite out of the ordinary if it were a case of applying to a son of Levi ruling functions normally reserved for Judah, especially since these are elsewhere in the *Testaments* quite clearly ascribed to Judah. Perhaps the solution lies instead in the fact that these references have paradigmatic rather than strictly literal significance — namely, the *spiritual* offspring of Levi-Judah will inherit all the blessings promised to the nation (including the rights to serve as prophets, priests, and kings) since they alone remain faithful to God's order. This coheres with the view expressed in *TIss.* 5:7-8 that the spiritual seed of Abraham was channeled through Jacob, then through Levi and Judah, and finally through those who are "subject" to them: "And Levi and Judah were glorified by the Lord among the sons of Jacob. The Lord made choice among them: To one he gave the priesthood and to the other, the kingship. Subject yourselves to them, and live in integrity as did your father."

This raises the question as to what this relationship between the patron and his spiritual children would be based upon. The basis could not have been only, or even primarily, genealogical, as it cannot be assumed that only Levites and Judahites were welcomed among the ranks of the *Testaments* community. The same conclusion seems to be demanded by the fact that the descendant tribes of Levi and Judah are never *categorically* honored in the *Testaments* — far from holding these tribes to be beyond reproach, the *Testaments* offer an extensive, and sometimes extremely pointed, critique of them.[38] It would appear, therefore, that the group considered themselves to be the *spiritual* descendants of Levi and Judah only, in the sense of holding to the legitimate priestly and royal prerogatives and insisting on the rights of those offices. In other words,

---

37. Hollander and de Jonge, 1985, 153.
38. Cf. esp. *TLevi* 16:1-5 (cf. chs. 14–16).

the promises extended to these tribes became the foundation on which the community was built; thus the promises were not only made to the members of those tribes but to the entire righteous community of Israel. In honoring the tribes of Levi and Judah, the community also believed itself, through this kind of identification, to have effectively inherited the mandate first given to the fathers of these tribes to be passed onto those tribes and eventually to all Israel. In one place this mandate for Israel is described as the wisdom first given to Levi to pass on to his "sons" (an allusion to the teaching role of the priests), which also has to serve as a light for Israel: "The light of knowledge you shall kindle in Jacob, and you shall be as the sun for all the seed of Israel. . . . Therefore counsel and understanding have been given to you so that you might give understanding to your sons concerning this" (*TLevi* 4:3, 5; omitting the Christian interpolation, v. 4; cf. Neh. 8:9). The *Testaments* community was accordingly composed of supporters of a legitimate priesthood and of a legitimate Davidic government in Jerusalem — not because they belonged to the Levi and Judah tribes, but because they recognized these offices to be essential to the religion and welfare of the state. It was also a highly consequential fact that *this order of things, a legitimate priesthood and a Davidic government, was presently not experienced in Jerusalem.*

Such a paradigmatic role for Levi and Judah does not completely exhaust the significance of these figures (this kind of conviction probably stood side by side with more specific messianological developments, including belief in future ideal figures from Levi and Judah; cf., e.g., *TLevi* 4:2-6; 5:2-3; 8:11-12; 18:9ff.; *TJud.* 22:3; 24:1–25:1; *TIss.* 2:5; 5:7-8), but it nevertheless would appear to point to one important and highly creative function for the figures in the *Testaments.* As for other reasons why Levi may have been considered such an important figure, it is perhaps significant, for one thing, that the origin of the Levitical ministry is associated in the Hebrew Scriptures with the role of the Levites as *avengers* against the *apostate sons of Israel* who worshiped the golden calf (Exod. 32:25-29, cf. esp. v. 29). This has obvious relevance to Qumran's self-consciousness as instruments of righteous indignation in Israel, concerning which they may have sought to follow the example of another priestly figure in Israel, Phinehas the son of Eleazar son of Aaron (Numbers 25; cf. 1 Macc. 2:24-26, 54).[39] This Phinehas is portrayed in a similar role to that of Levi in the golden calf incident. In *Jubilees* as well, Levi (along with Simeon) is portrayed in the role of avenger of the shame of Dinah in her rape by Shechem (*Jub.* 30:4;

---

39. The well-known *4QTestimonia* (= *4Q175*) has been described as a pearl-stringing of biblical "messianic" texts, although it is possible that these texts are actually cited in reference to *historical* personages (such as Levi; cf. l. 14). The writing may accordingly serve more paradigmatic purposes.

as also in Gen. 34:25). It was for *this* act, rather than the golden calf incident, according to *Jubilees,* that Levi was awarded the priesthood (30:17-20);[40] and the example of Phinehas is also reflected in the language of the passage.[41] There is accordingly a vivid connection drawn here between the Levitical theme and that of divine retribution in Israel, themes already associated in the Scriptures and further exploited by our authors (cf. also *TLevi* 5:3-4). Levi's importance in our movement certainly seems to be associated with this priestly-zeal connection and seems partly responsible for the attention granted him.

Still another reason for Levi's notoriety and importance in our movement is that the authority for *teaching* was believed to rest primarily with the priests at this time (cf. Deut. 33:10: "They shall teach Jacob thy ordinances, and Israel thy law"). In numerous passages the sons of the patriarchs are commanded to "obey" Levi and Judah (cf. *TReub.* 6:8-12; *TSim.* 7:1-2; *TIss.* 5:7-8; *TNaph.* 8:2-3; *TGad* 8:1),[42] while in one passage it is maintained that some will draw close to Levi to observe his teaching and will as a result be implicated with Levi in all kinds of sins (*TDan* 5:6-7)! The only explanation for such contradictory statements about Levi is that the community held — not unlike the Qumranites — that its own Levitical members alone composed the authentic or valid priesthood. These deliberately segregated themselves from the apostate priesthood referred to in the *Testament of Judah* above, believing themselves alone to possess the true teaching. Through all of these kinds of passages the readers are accordingly being exhorted to listen to their priests and to follow the teaching resident in the community. There is also an allusion to the notion that most of Israel has departed from the traditional teachings brought to them through the instrument of the priestly office. The fact that Judah is associated with Levi in some of these passages (*TSim.* 7:1-2; *TIss.* 5:7-8; *TNaph.* 8:2-3; *TGad* 8:1) is rather more surprising. Perhaps one is witness here to some pro-Judah editing by a later scribe, as suggested by some scholars. On the other hand, it may be that the readers are being exhorted to obey Levi's *teaching,* on the one hand, and Judah's *ruling prerogative,* on the other. None of the above passages demands more than this, and our basic conclusions about the function of these figures are not greatly influenced by such passages.

It would be helpful by way of confirmation to know whether the community of the *Testaments* ever employed "Levi and Judah" as a more or less direct self-reference. One rather difficult passage might suggest that the community, if not actually employing this phrase as a self-designation, nevertheless did be-

---

40. Cf. Endres (1987, 147), who notes that, far from being honored, Levi and Simeon are disparaged in Gen. 49:5-7 for this act of violence.

41. Cf. Endres, 1987, 150.

42. Cf. Hollander and de Jonge, 1985, 40-41.

lieve themselves to be part of a "Levi-Judah" community. The passage, which is directed toward Simeon, reads:

> For I have seen in a copy of the book of Enoch that your sons will be ruined by promiscuity, and they shall injure with a sword the sons of Levi. But they shall not be able to withstand Levi, because he shall wage the Lord's war and will triumph over all your battalions. And they will be *few in number*,[43] *distributed among Levi and Judah*, and *from you* there will be no one for leadership, just as our father predicted in his blessings. (*TSim.* 5:4-6)

This passage probably does not contain any direct historical allusions but is composed from sources found in Gen. 49:7 and the "book of Enoch." Although the identity of the latter passage is not possible from the extant Enoch material, the reference to the Levites who "wage the Lord's war" against sinful Israelites "ruined by promiscuity" suggests passages like *1 En.* 90:9ff. regarding the "great horn" Judas and his troops, although this passage by itself is probably not sufficient to explain the belief entirely (it may be that the "war" is merely part of the standard eschatological beliefs of the author, whether derived from Enochian traditions or not — the passage does not specify how much is Enoch material). The words "these forces distributed among Levi and Judah will be few in number"[44] recall Simeon's promiscuous sons, mimicking Gen. 49:7b: "I will divide them in Jacob / and scatter them in Israel." Here it is particularly notable how the pair "Jacob and Israel" has been subtly replaced by "Levi and Judah," thus suggesting that the author of the *Testaments* took "Levi and Judah" to be a designation for the righteous in Israel with which he replaced the more nationalistic term "Jacob and Israel" as found in Genesis. This is admittedly still far from understanding "Levi and Judah" as an actual self-designation employed by the community on any regular basis, but it at least suggests the possibility that it was so used.

The reduction of Simeon's number to a "few" and the state of anarchy in his tribe suggest that, in contrast to Levi and Judah, tribes like Simeon have become symbolic of the unrighteous in Israel.[45] A number of texts contrast Levi and Judah in their righteousness with the failure of the other tribes. We read, for example, that the sons of Issachar "ally themselves with Beliar" (*TIss.* 6:1).

43. We do not follow Kee's reading here, preferring the more literal rendering of καὶ ἔσονται ὀλιγοστοί.

44. Kee's translation (*OTP*, 1:786-87) leaves this somewhat ambiguous; better is that of de Jonge (*AOT*, 524), who relates it, as seems natural, with "your sons" of v. 4 and the "they" (contained in the δυνήσονται) of v. 5.

45. Hollander and de Jonge: "in the OT God makes his enemies ὀλιγοστός . . . and this is also Israel's punishment when it disobeys God" (1985, 122; cf. Lev. 26:22; Sir. 48:16; Obad. 2; Isa. 16:14; Ezek. 29:15).

The beloved of the Lord alone can hope to restore the tribe of Benjamin and "fill up what was lacking of [his] tribe" (*TBen.* 11:5)[46] — implying that even this relatively righteous tribe was fallen through sin.[47] Taken together, therefore, these passages suggest that while "Levi and Judah" represented the righteous, the other tribes cumulatively represented the unrighteous. Levi and Judah would accordingly seem to be prime examples of how some figures played the role of paradigms for the community. This will have important implications for our investigation of the messianology of the *Testaments* as well.[48]

The Enigmatic Zadok

Levi's paradigmatic role in the *Testaments* suggests a similar role for the provocative and allusive figure "Zadok," so well known to students of the scrolls. Several theories posit the identity and significance of the name Zadok as well as the significance of the community's association with this personage. While some theories find in this Zadok a contemporary leader, namely, the Saddok associated with Judah son of Hezekiah, this is quite unlikely since Judah and his revolutionary companions thrived during the first century A.D., too late for most estimates of the date of the scrolls. The more reasonable position is to discern in the use of the name an allusion to the legendary biblical priest Zadok, the son of Eleazar and grandson of Aaron, with whom are associated numerous biblical promises pertaining to his and his descendants' future roles as priests. This is by far the majority view. This Zadok received the right to administer the sacred rites in the time of David and Solomon and is also referred to along with his descendants in Ezekiel (44:15; cf. also 40:46; 43:19; 48:11), where he is acknowledged as the rightful heir of the priesthood in the restored Ezekelian Temple. Given the critique of the Jerusalem cult evidenced in the scrolls, and in view of the fact that the Zadok family ceased to hold the office in Jerusalem when

---

46. The "messianic" figure in *Testament of Benjamin* 5 was thought, according to some early Christian witnesses, to refer to Paul (cf. Hollander and de Jonge, 1985, 442-43) — hence the reading ἀφ' ἡμῶν ("from me," i.e., the patriarch Benjamin); but this reading is only found in the inferior and late sixteenth-century Ankara MS. A more ancient, well-testified, and more difficult reading has ἀφ' ὑμῶν ("from you"). One solution to the enigmatic reference is to see the community addressed here by means of ἀφ' ὑμῶν: the messiah will arise from among the readers. For MSS evidence, cf. M. de Jonge, ed., *The Testaments of the Twelve Patriarchs*, 1978, 171; for description of MS *m*, cf. xxiii.

47. Cf. also *TSim.* 5:4; *TGad* 8:2; etc.

48. Some of these observations, as we have noted, apply to *Jubilees* also. It is interesting in this regard that Davenport interprets the name Judah in *Jub.* 31:19-20 as a kind of covering term for surviving Israelites (1971, 65-66).

Menelaus took it over in 171 B.C. (one of the most likely arch-foes of the sect or their forerunners), hope for a return of the priestly line of Zadok could be expected from a protesting group like the Qumranites who were more than a little unimpressed with the current state of the priesthood.

That the priest from David and Solomon's time is alluded to in these texts from Qumran may be confirmed by an important, thoroughly discussed, and enigmatic passage, CD 3.21–4.6, which appears to cite Ezek. 44:15 with a small but significant alteration in wording. The Hebrew of the Ezekiel passage furnishes either "the priests, Levites, sons of Zadok" or "the Levitical priests, the sons of Zadok," perhaps referring to two groups ("priests and Levites — sons of Zadok"; cf. RSV) or more likely just one group ("the Levitical priests who are the sons of Zadok"; cf. NIV). The Damascus Document, however, supplies a conjunction between the latter two designations: "the priests and the Levites *and* the sons of Zadok." This has the effect of making three groups out of Ezekiel's one or two groups and invites, or at least allows for, the tripartite interpretation that follows in CD: "The priests are the converts of Israel who went out from the land of Judah; and the Levites are those who joined them. And the sons of Zadok are the chosen of Israel" (ll. 2-4). This, of course, is a creative bit of exegesis, but it leaves open the question whether the interpreter refers to three separate groups or merely gives three names to the same group, or, again, whether he refers to priests at all by these priestly titles or democratizes priestly names and applies them to the entire community composed of priests and laymen. Each option is entirely possible given the *pešer* exegetical methodology the scroll authors frequently applied, especially to the prophets. It would be difficult in any event to argue seriously that the commentator had in mind a contemporary lay leader by the name Zadok, for in that case he probably would have said so. The fact that he cites this text probably indicates that biblical Zadok texts were largely responsible for the interest his group showed in Zadok. The Zadok in that text is the ancient priest, and the commentator gives no indication that he thought it alluded to any contemporary figure.

Considering this very enigmatic text and other texts containing the name of Zadok, scholars have rightly questioned whether the idea of the descendants ("sons") of Zadok at Qumran is really intended to be understood literally as referring to a line of priests descended from Zadok. An article by W. F. Albright and C. S. Mann argued that the Qumranite "Zadokites" and the "Sadducees" (as they are referred to in modern translations of the Gospels; both titles conceivably could derive from Heb. *ṣaddoq*) differed in their understanding of what composed a true descendant of the revered priest. The Sadducees, true enough, represented more or less the actual *physical descendants* of their forerunner. The *Qumran Zadokites*, on the other hand, fully realizing the impurity and compromise that had penetrated the ranks of the official priesthood and generally rejecting the Temple establishment associated with the Sadducees, sought to hold *themselves* up as the true "sons of Zadok" — that is, as the "true Israel." "In the atmosphere of the reform movement after the exile," write Albright and Mann, "the question must have been raised as to whether simple physical descent marked a son of Zadok, or whether there were other considerations too" — a question necessitated, the authors argue, because of the problem of intermarriage that threw into considerable doubt the physical circumstances of the birth and the worthiness of the priests.[49] Parting company with this line of reasoning to a point, Beckwith nevertheless sees similar circumstances in the appropriation of the name even by the Sadducees:

> it seems improbable that the Sadducees were stressing their genealogy or even the known views of the Zadokite family in calling themselves Zadokites. More likely, they used the title in the same way as the Essenes, in the passages from the *Rule of the Community* and the *Damascus Document* cited above, with conscious reference to the way the "sons of Zadok" are described in *Ezk.* 44,15; 48,11, and as meaning those priests who were faithful to God.[50]

A similar view of the nonliteral nature of this descendancy is also maintained, in a rather more indirect way, by Wacholder.[51] Part and parcel of the relationship of the community with the historical Zadok, according to Wacholder, was their possession of the "sealed" law that was originally associated with the name of Zadok and was later entrusted to the community. With the words "sons of Zadok," therefore, the community designated themselves the maintainers of the Second (true) Torah. The term does not imply that they were all priests; it is just one reflection of the importance placed on the community's revelation and its connection to Zadok. The use of the word *ṣaddoq* (i.e., *Zadok*) is therefore deliberately evocative, suggesting both the importance of this revelation and of the community's self-understanding as keepers of the saving tradition. Wacholder explains that not only *ṣaddoq* but also (by a probable word association) *ṣedeq* (righteousness) — as in *moreh ṣedeq* — and even *ṣadiq* ("righteous," the adjective) may have contained, in the minds of the sectarians, nuances of meaning associated with the possession of the "sealed Torah." The historical Zadok was thus a kind of "first *moreh ṣedeq*"[52] and accord-

49. W. F. Albright and C. S. Mann, "Qumran and the Essenes," 1969, 17-18, 21.

50. R. T. Beckwith, "The Pre-History and Relationships of the Pharisees, Sadducees and Essenes," 1982, 12.

51. B. Z. Wacholder, "The 'Sealed' Torah versus the 'Revealed' Torah," 1986, 361-67; B. Z. Wacholder, "Ezekiel and Ezekielianism as Progenitors of Essenianism," 1992, 191, 194.

52. Wacholder, 1986, 366.

ingly: (1) the predecessor and paradigm of the community's own revered Teacher (the *moreh ṣedeq*), (2) the predecessor of some future *moreh ṣedeq* expected by the community, and (3) a kind of paradigm for *all* the "sons of ṣaddoq/ṣadiq" (i.e., the members of the community).

Whether or not there was any conscious association with Zadok in the use of some of these words (much less all of them), as Wacholder suggests, the possibility is very real that this figure, like Levi, stood less as the physical ancestor of the community and more as their paradigm or "spiritual ancestor," and it is for this reason that the *yaḥad* emulated this person and honored his name (and, if one follows Wacholder in this, his *Torah* as well). This paradigmatic significance for "sons of Zadok" provides another good reason for denying that the movement represented at Qumran was exclusively, or even primarily, a *priestly* movement. Some scholars, indeed, would go even further in their reaction to this opinion and insist that since CD 3.21ff. interprets the "sons of Zadok" as the "chosen of Israel," it is predominantly the lay members of the sect who are in mind in the former title! This, however, is a quite unwarranted conclusion drawn from a single and very enigmatic text, especially as elsewhere in the scrolls "sons of Zadok" refers explicitly to priests and even "chosen of Israel" is an appropriate designation for priests. The fact that the passage apparently originally offered a genealogical list of priest families following the example of priest lists in the postexilic writings (the passage is now missing in the MSS, but a conspicuous lacuna marks its original place in the text), also suggests that the "chosen of Israel" at least *included* the priestly portion of the community. But the point may be well taken as far as it goes, for on any reading of this passage it appears likely that all three terms used of community members in the CD text designate both lay and priestly members of the community *without discrimination,* and that it is *not* the actual chronological descendants of Zadok who are in mind so much as all the members of the community who considered themselves to be "spiritual offspring" of Zadok.

One should probably not go so far as Jaubert, however, who arrives at the startling conclusion that since matters of "spirit" were more important than "race" to the Qumranites, the sect reserved the right to elect its own priests according to their "spirit" and to ignore the historical election of the priestly line.[53] This would not only eliminate all grounds for protest against the Jerusalem priesthood based on departure from proper lineage, but would also effectively remove any rationale for honoring the name Zadok in the first place. It seems, in other words, that even if the entire community — lay and priest alike — could be termed "Zadokites," they nevertheless still held a great deal of re-

---

53. A. Jaubert, *La notion d'alliance dans le Judaïsme aux abords de l'ère chrétienne,* 1963, 152.

spect for the family of priests who went by the name, and still held strictly to traditional rules for the priesthood. We know from a number of passages elsewhere in the scrolls that the sectarians respected not only the priestly *office* but the priestly *teaching* as well, and this suggests that priests from traditional lines of priestly families were active in the community in interpreting and even adding to the law: "The decision [regarding the suitability of a candidate] shall lie with the sons of Aaron who volunteer in common to establish His Covenant and to attend to all the commandments which He has commanded . . ." (1QS 5.21-22). That the *yaḥad* had priests of their own whom they highly regarded can also be concluded from CD 14.3-6, which indicates that the community recognized the teaching and leading roles of the priests. This passage refers to the "constitution of all the camps" (a reference to a future restored Israel?) whose order is headed by priests: "Let them all be counted by name: the priests first, and the Levites second, and the sons of Israel third, and the proselytes fourth. . . . And let them be seated in this order, and in this order let them question on all matters. And the priest who is overseer of the Many. . . ."

In conclusion, the entire community thought of themselves as, in some sense, "sons of Zadok" while still recognizing that this name (and perhaps at times even the title "sons of Zadok" itself) had special application to the real priests. For the priests the title implied both the righteous character and the pure and proper genealogy of those who were not only legitimately born priests, but lived up to the name. These acted officially as priests in the community, if for no other reason than to exercise the priestly duty of teaching. The important point here, however, is that once again we see how figures carry such strong paradigmatic significance in a community as to make it quite difficult (for us at least) to divide between references to a single personage in history, references to his direct physical ancestors, and references to entire communities who carry his name!

The *Moreh Ṣedeq*

Like Enoch and Noah, other figures probably possessed a *revelatory* or even *mystical* role in certain communities, which is not surprising given the important place of revelation in these groups. Until recently scholars have tended to subdue any idea of a prophetic "living" voice in Judaism. Lately, however, the mysticism of these groups has been compared to manticism and other prophetic types of phenomena, and although these comparative models are often much too distant from Hebrew ideas of prophecy (chronologically and ideologically speaking) to be of much help in this task, the attempt at least recognizes that prophetism did assume an important and relevant place in the practice and beliefs of some quarters of Judaism. The problem, of course, is that there is virtually no documentation that relates in any detail to the process of receiving and transmitting such prophetic teaching. The most adequate source material available for the question, and even this is often too vague to be helpful, comes from the scrolls, and in particular from statements made by and about the enigmatic *moreh ṣedeq* figure. The *moreh* is the only documented example from the period of a living person who was considered to possess the kind of extraordinary revelatory gifts that are associated with him in the scrolls. In this role as *Revealer,* the *moreh* was distinguished from other teacher figures, as the claim is made that his office and calling are unparalleled and unequaled, not able to be filled by anyone else.[54] So important was his teaching, as it would appear from certain texts, that the fate of all Israelites was bound up with their acceptance or rejection of it.[55] The *moreh* must have been a character of tremendous spiritual influence and charisma, possessing a truly unique ability to "receive" revelatory knowledge combined with a strong sense of vocation to pass this revelation on to others. He was an extremely important figure for many other reasons too — some scholars even maintain that he was considered a *messiah* (although not in the way we have defined "messiah" above).[56]

What is important here is the Teacher's intimate association with his *community.* It can be said that the *moreh* could not have existed without the *yahad,* just as the *yahad* could not have existed without their Teacher.[57] He was

54. Cf. G. Jeremias, *Der Lehrer der Gerechtigkeit,* 1963, 165, 175.

55. Cf. 1QH 2.8-14; 7.12; H. Ringgren, *The Faith of Qumran,* 1963, 185-87; G. Jeremias, 1963, 141, 146, 164-66, 266; cf. Num. 11:12.

56. He was certainly considered a kind of forerunner of the messiah(s) and in some respects possibly also one of them; cf. Ringgren, 1963, 198; G. Jeremias, 1963, 307. Possible indications that the *moreh* was considered to be a messiah are the expectations for a future דורש התורה (CD 7.18?), which would seem to have been a term also used for the historical founder of the community (cf. 1QS 8.11-12; CD 6.7), and the reference in CD 6.11 to a יורה הצדק who will return "at the end of days" (for this term used of the Teacher, cf. CD 20.1, 14). We would, however, tend to agree with Jeremias (286-307, esp. 283-306), who strongly opposes the view that the *moreh* was a messiah; the יורה צדק would seem to refer to a different figure inasmuch as the historical teacher and the future messiahs are mentioned together with no particular connection being implied between them (cf. CD 19.35–20.1, 14; 283-84). The hope for such a future teacher or messiah in the garb of the "prophet like Moses" is well documented in other Jewish traditions, but the Teacher of Righteousness is never referred to in such terms. More likely the community saw some paradigmatic connection between their Teacher and his future messiah counterpart; cf. de Jonge, 1991, 38. For more on the question, cf. below.

57. J. H. Charlesworth: "[The Righteous Teacher] obtains meaning in and through his insoluble link with one specific community" ("Jesus as 'Son' and the Righteous Teacher as 'Gardener,'" 1992c, 140-75, 150).

an instrument of salvation for the community,[58] and certain texts have been interpreted as implying that he even suffered vicariously for them (although this is generally doubted).[59] Indeed, the Teacher is hardly mentioned in the scrolls *without* reference to the community, and this goes for the so-called Founder Hymns as well as the sect's other writings. A good example of a Founder Hymn in which this essential relationship is expressed is 1QH 2.6ff., a hymn we have already commented on.[60] The hymnist proclaims in dualistic fashion:

> I have been a snare for sinners, but healing for all those that are converted from sin, prudence for the simple and the firm inclination of all those whose heart is troubled. And Thou hast made of me an object of shame and mockery for traitors, but the foundation of truth and understanding for them whose way is straight. And I was exposed to the affronts of the wicked,[61] an object of slander upon the lips of the violent. . . . But Thou hast made of me a banner[62] for the elect of righteousness. (ll. 8-11, 13)

The words that follow this passage continue to present the dichotomy between the community of the righteous and the unrighteous traitors while defining the chief roles of the Teacher as founder and gatherer of the righteous community. The *moreh* had in effect become the instrument of division in Israel.[63] Other hymns fill out our understanding of the Teacher as the foundation of his community, such as the following examples:

58. "Der Heilbringer," according to G. Jeremias, 1963, 175.

59. Cf. Ringgren, 1963, 185-86; G. Jeremias, 1963, 298-307.

60. We can hardly agree with S. Holm-Nielsen (*Hodayot,* 1960, 39-40) that this psalm was not written by the *moreh* or that it was simply derived from biblical models of poetry (i.e., without any particular reference to personal experience).

61. The parallelism and context of the verse suggest that ואהיה על עון רשעים has been adequately translated by Dupont-Sommer, against views that an atonement for the wicked is intended (*contra* E. Lohse, ed., *Die Texte aus Qumran,* 1971, 117; cf. Holm-Nielsen, 1960, 35). For other translations, cf. M. Mansoor, *The Thanksgiving Hymns Translated and Annotated with an Introduction,* 1961, 106; M. A. Knibb, *The Qumran Community,* 1987, 165.

62. A. Dupont-Sommer (*The Essene Writings from Qumran,* 1961, 205 n. 3) has suggested that נס here refers to the root of Jesse in Isa. 11:10, a connection Holm-Nielsen describes as "rash" (1960, 35). The expression probably implies no more than the essential role of the *moreh* as the head *of a community,* although the messianic allusion may be significant.

63. It is no wonder that G. Jeremias sums up the contents of the hymn with these words: "Wenn man diesen Psalm mit einer Überschrift versehen wollte, dann würde man am besten den Satz aus dem vorher besprochenen Loblied wählen (7,12) . . . 'Um an mir zwischen Gerechten und Revler zu scheiden'" (1963, 195; cf. 199). The reference in 1QH 7.12 is to Mal. 3:18.

And at daybreak[64] Thou hast appeared unto me in Thy might and hast not covered with shame the face of all them that inquired of me, that gathered in Thy Covenant and heard me, that walk in the way of Thy heart and are ranked for Thee in the assembly of the Saints. (4.23-25)

And Thou hast created [me] for Thy sake to fulfil the Law, and to teach by my mouth the men of Thy council in the midst of the sons of men. . . . (6.10-11)

The *moreh ṣedeq* was the "father" of the community (1QH 7.20-21), its "Founder" in more ways than one: he not only built it, but its continued existence depended on his teaching.[65] This teaching was like a spiritual fountain upon which the "everlasting planting" depends for its life (1QH 8.4-10, 16-26).

Another set of references, not to the *moreh* but to "the Sage" — almost certainly one and the same figure — has emerged from the newly released Cave 4 fragments. One of these passages (assuming they refer to the *moreh,* but whether or not they do) shows how central a figure can become to the idea of covenantal obedience. The words quoted below are very similar to the ones from the Hymn Scroll:

You have placed on my lips a fount of praise
and in my heart the secret of the start of all human actions
and the culmination of the deeds of the perfect ones of the path,
the judgments of all the works that they do,
to vindicate the just one in your faithfulness
and pronounce the wicked guilty for his fault;
in order to announce: Peace to all men of the covenant
and to shout with a terrifying voice:
Woe on all those who break it.[66]

This strongly dualistic text shows again how this teacher had in effect become an instrument of division in Israel. He was able to exercise this function because of the special wisdom that had been revealed to him.

As for receiving the revelation, scholars search the scrolls in vain for clues that might explain exactly how the Teacher went about receiving his words of

64. The translation of Holm-Nielsen (1960, 77) is perhaps preferable: "(revealest) . . . unto a perfect light," which emphasizes the clarity of illumination rather than its occasion.

65. For the term *Gründer,* cf. G. Jeremias, 1963, 148, cf. 191-92, in reference to 4QpPs37 2.15-16.

66. 4Q511 (= *4QShir^b* = *4QSongs of the Sage^b*) 3.1-4. For text and translation, cf. García Martínez, 1992, 371-76. The "Sage" is also mentioned in 4Q510 1, 4; 4Q511 2, 1.1.

truth. It may have occurred during the "sessions" held by the *yaḥad*, during which, possibly, the *moreh* as well as others received divine understanding and utterance. It may have been more through the written word, through the exercise of writing *pešer*. On the other hand, the above texts suggest that the *moreh* was a preacher, and that his illumination or inspiration occurred when he opened his mouth and began to speak. In other words, his teaching was in some respects similar to that of the biblical prophets, on the one hand, and John the Baptist, on the other. Given such broad guidelines for comparison, however, when it comes right down to it we know less about the prophetic methodology of the Teacher described in the Qumran scrolls than we do about the act of prophecy as experienced by the great Hebrew prophets, and not much more than we know about John the Baptist (and we could wish to know much more about either of those). It would appear that a consciousness of illumination can exist in the absence of any systematic methodology for receiving inspiration; the illumination is naturally considered the important thing by the prophetic community and the act of prophecy or prophetic teaching may have been quite spontaneous. This probably explains why we know so little about what was in effect a quite subjective spiritual experience.

Pseudonymity

One can gain more insight into these matters by looking at some of the other writings, and the form of revelation featured in them. Unlike the *moreh*, most of the figures represented in these writings were not physically present (i.e., still living) with the community. How exactly these figures were thought to *reveal* depends much on what one thinks of the phenomenon called *pseudonymity*. Many suggestions for this have been offered, often rather dogmatically.[67] All of them seem to view pseudonymity as a rather deliberate falsification, usually for the purpose of promoting views that would not normally have gained a hearing

---

67. I.e., pseudonymity (1) became necessary when literary prophecy as a traditional authority had established itself and the prophetic age was considered to be over (R. H. Charles, *Eschatology*, 1913, 200; *APOT*, 2, 8; his theory has been repeated countless times); (2) illustrated and served the deterministic views of the writings (P. Volz, *Die Eschatologie der jüdischen Gemeinde*, 1934, 6); (3) validated the genuine future prophecies in the writings by means of fulfilled *ex eventu* prophecies made by the ancient figure (a widely accepted view). It is notable that these views assume the importance of a certain doctrine (the end of prophecy) or a certain highly philosophical and ideological point of view (determinism) or imply the use of a literary sleight of hand to promote a message (validation through *ex eventu* prophecy). The extent to which these kinds of *abstract* factors played a decisive role in the phenomenon must be considered debatable at best.

without the device — that is, without attaching a famous name to them. But not enough attention has been given to how *improbable* this is, inasmuch as a discovery or even suspicion of falsification would automatically override any authority the message may have wished to project, just the *opposite* of what was intended, and a very risky *mode d'operation* indeed! Far more likely is that works presented under the names of ancient worthies either contained *traditional* material whose origins were lost to antiquity or, alternatively, that the material was believed to have been transmitted in more *mystical* ways. Their primary claim to authority lies elsewhere, in other words, independent of the device of pseudonymity, at least as conventionally understood.

A couple of considerations speak *against* the idea of traditional material being preserved in this way. While no doubt traditional *ideas* are present, this approach still leaves in question the *origin* of the material in a cohesive *pseudepigraphon* — the final product must have come from *somewhere*, and it can hardly be that all of the highly diverse material loosely circulated in an oral form, and is much less likely that it was associated with one figure, be it Enoch or Ezra or someone else. (Note that the lengthy and involved form of the tradition is quite unlike the comparatively terse sayings of the rabbis that were transmitted by memory.)[68] Whatever tradition is represented, in other words, was consciously collated into reasonably coherent narrative forms and was given the stamp of the personality whose name is associated with it. If that is the case, then, in terms of final import and message, these books did *originate* with a contemporary figure or figures inasmuch as a collation of tradition still bears the character of the collator, effectively making it *his* work. Then there is that feature of these writings which we have seen repeatedly — namely, the many *addresses (or asides) to the contemporary readers of* the work. Where, in a collation of tradition, would this feature find a place? Such a feature suits rather better the presupposition that an editor or original composer was chiefly responsible for the final product.

This leaves the other option that these writings, each associated with a famous character, originated through more mystic or prophetic means that, one might speculate, involved some kind of communication with the patriarch. We mentioned above the various "corporate personality" theories associated with this literature and preferred the term "corporate identity" to avoid the various psychological and ontological implications usually associated with such theories.[69] When it comes to the messianological thought of these

---

68. Cf. B. Gerhardsson, *Memory and Manuscript*, 1961, esp. 136-43.

69. For the problems with Russell's corporate personality approach to the question of pseudonymity, cf. C. Rowland (*The Open Heaven*, 1982, 65), who questions the use of the ambiguous term for this phenomenon and warns that it is "virtually impossible to describe with any degree of certainty the psychology of the writers of the apocalypse."

groups, one finds, in fact, very little evidence of the kind of interaction between "the individual and the group" that implies any more than a functional relationship of identity, and theories that place pseudonymity within those categories have accordingly failed.[70] Nevertheless, the corporate personality approach probably does point in the right direction, since it at least allows one to view pseudepigraphy from the point of view of genuine belief and experience rather than to assume more surreptitious motives. There would seem to have been something significant and distinctive about these figures that led our groups to accept that they were still active in revealing helpful words of wisdom to them. The translated Enoch who never experienced death and presumably could have been seen to possess a kind of "continued life" was certainly in a position to be this kind of prophetic revealer. To judge from Mark 12:26-27, there circulated many other traditions about the continued life of other patriarchs.[71] They must have been considered alive for some purpose: Did our groups believe that this purpose was to make themselves known to the righteous for their encouragement?

The possibility that this is true for works like *1 Enoch* has already been suggested above. But what can one say about 4 Ezra and *2 Baruch,* for example, which appear to be highly literary, rather than revelational, in style? These works are *dramas* — and therefore perhaps not "genuine" pseudepigrapha in the sense of *1 Enoch, Jubilees,* or the *Testaments of the Twelve Patriarchs.* They seem to employ Greek rhetorical (or better: Hebrew theodicic) forms to present their group's soteriological views, perhaps merely adopting a pseudonymous authorship in rather loose conformity to other pseudepigraphic works (perhaps also in recognition of the appropriateness of figures like Ezra and Baruch to address the situation of A.D. 70). Even these latter writings, however, may not have lost their revelatory function altogether. It has already been noted, for example, how in the literary context of the books that bear their names Ezra and Baruch each address their communities, communities that seem to function as significant parallels to the later communities (those of the "real" authors), seemingly for the purpose of consoling these later groups. When these ancient scribes address people, or write letters to the exiles, in other words, it is the *contemporary* communities of the real authors who are actually being addressed. Furthermore, even though Ezra and Baruch reveal their message in the form of a drama that takes place over a lengthy period of time, it is noteworthy that it is

---

70. As well demonstrated by J. W. Rogerson, "The Hebrew Conception of Corporate Personality," 1970, 11; Rowland, 1982, 65.

71. The view that Moses did not die may have been suggested by Deut. 34:6; cf. also Luke 9:28ff. and, much less ambiguously, *Ant.* 4.326. That a number of returning/translated figures were expected is suggested by a comparison of 4 Ezra 14:9 with 6:26.

related in the first person (4 Ezra 3:1; etc.; *2 Bar.* 3:1; etc.) — it is thus Ezra's (or Baruch's) *own* story. Further evidence that one is dealing with basically the same mode of revelation in these books as in the others are some very unusual and suggestive statements like 4 Ezra 14:9 that appear to announce the ascension of Ezra (in a manner similar to Enoch and Elijah)[72] and imply a continued interaction between the saint and "those like him," including, presumably, the writer's community: "you shall be taken up from among men, and *henceforth you shall live with my Son and with those who are like you, until the times are ended.*" That this passage refers to Ezra's being "taken up" would suggest that, like Enoch and Elijah, this ancient worthy was viewed as possessing a "continuing life." It was in this state that Ezra was believed to carry out his office of Revealer to the Righteous, with whom, as indicated by the words "those who are like you,"[73] he possessed an extraordinarily special relationship.

Some have suggested that Ezra is depicted in this passage as one of many prophets who were expected to come before and signal the advent of the messiah, just as Elijah was expected to do in Malachi's prophecy, or in the fashion of a "prophet like Moses."[74] That these kinds of figures were believed to have returned at this time is evident from the example of the *moreh ṣedeq,* who appears to have been considered a "prophet like Moses"[75] and was certainly considered a forerunner of the messianic age. Another near-contemporary figure, John the Baptist, was also considered in some way to be the incarnation of the spirit of Elijah by the Christian community (cf. Matt. 11:14; the expectation that Elijah would return was evident in other Gospel pericopes as well; cf. Matt. 27:47 par.). While a prophet *"like"* Moses is admittedly not identical with the idea of an Elijah *redivivus*–type of figure (since the former only implies similarity, not

72. Cf. R. J. Coggins and M. A. Knibb, *The First and Second Books of Esdras,* 1979, 275; M. E. Stone, *Fourth Ezra,* 1990, 420. Some MSS (but not Lat.) contain a description of this ascension/translation following ch. 14. That this is what is intended by the words "taken up" *(recipieris)* is evident in 6:26, where *recepti* is related to "have not tasted death." For a similar experience by Baruch, cf. *2 Bar.* 13:3; 43:2; 46:7; 48:30; 76:2; etc.

73. The expression can hardly refer to Enoch and Elijah, who were transported before Ezra (as cf. Coggins and Knibb, 1979, 275), inasmuch as the expression is not used in this way elsewhere in 4 Ezra. It is better to take this as an expression for the people of the messiah of whom Ezra was a part (cf. W. O. E. Oesterley, *II Esdras,* 1933, 167; Stone, 1990, 420, who calls them the "companions" of the messiah). Thus we have here another statement of the intimate relationship between Ezra and his companions (as cf. esp. 8:62; referred to again in v. 13 of our passage), particularly, in this case, those saints now present in heaven (Coggins and Knibb, 275).

74. Cf., e.g., R. N. Longenecker, 1970, 33.

75. For data cf. R. N. Longenecker, 1970, 33-34 n. 28; *contra* G. Jeremias, 1963, 297-98; J. J. Collins, *The Scepter and the Star,* 1995, 113. It may be more correct to say that he was a "new Moses" or "*a* prophet like Moses" than "*the* prophet like Moses" *par excellence.*

identity, as in the latter case), there is nevertheless evidence that the various expectations were combined — for example, Moses himself was believed to have experienced a translation.[76] In other words, the same implications seem to have been drawn from time-space journeys of figures such as Enoch as were drawn from the reincorporation of the spirit of figures such as Elijah, namely, that these patriarchs were still living, serving, and revealing in the present.

D. L. Tiede has demonstrated from the *Assumption of Moses* reasons for considering Moses himself one of these kinds of revelatory figures.[77] In contrast to Greek presentations of Moses as a virtuous paradigm, philosopher, or national hero, the *Assumption* presents the patriarch in much the same way that other pseudepigraphs *(1 Enoch, 2* and *3 Baruch,* 4 Ezra, *Testament of Solomon)* present their main figures — namely, as revelatory (prophetic) figures. Thus the *Assumption* employs the term "mediator" *(arbiter)* for Moses (1:14; 3:12) in his role as intercessor on behalf of Israel, a role that did not end with his natural life (cf. 12:6).[78] Tiede points to the exalted language used by the *Assumption* to speak of the patriarch — "sacred spirit worthy of the Lord," "manifold and incomprehensible," "lord of the word," "God's chief prophet throughout all the earth," "the most perfect teacher in the world." Such things as the idea of a "prophet like Moses," the concept of Moses as an ἄνθρωπος θεοῦ *(anthrōpos theou;* cf. LXX Deut. 33:1), the fact that Moses met God face-to-face, and the wonders performed at his hand, not to mention the type of Moses-speculations that can be found in the rabbinic literature, may all have added to this image of Moses as a mystical revelatory figure who continued to live and reveal in the present.[79]

In a similar vein Michael Wise attributes the Temple Scroll to an author who wrote as a kind of second Moses:

> Following Yadin and Wacholder, many scholars have concluded that the author of the TS was perpetrating a pseudepigraphon; with this scroll, he was

76. The ancient attribution "Assumption of Moses," Ἀνάληφις Μωυσέως, to a work of our period — whether to be equated with our own *Assumption of Moses* or not (on the existence of this document, cf. G. W. E. Nickelsburg, ed., *Studies on the Testament of Moses,* 1973, 5) — confirms that traditions existed that held that Moses was translated.

77. Cf. D. L. Tiede, "The Figure of Moses in the Testament of Moses," 1973, 86-92.

78. A possible source of the idea that Moses did not die can be found in Deut. 34:6; cf. Luke 9:28ff.; *Ant.* 4.326. 2 Macc. 15:14 reveals that some also believed "Jeremiah, the prophet of God" was still active in the role of intercessor long after his death; cf. *2 Bar.* 2:2.

79. Tiede, 1973, 92: "Like Daniel and Taxo, Moses receives and transmits much more than the tablets of stone. What Joshua dutifully transcribes is basically different from what is recorded in Deuteronomy, but corresponds more closely to Moses' knowledge of the secrets of the times as mentioned in other contemporary writings" (*Jubilees,* 4 Ezra, *2 Baruch,* etc.).

claiming to have found a lost book, written by Moses, but hidden for centuries. In my view, however, the TS is not pseudepigraphic. The redactor was not claiming to have found a book written by the "old" Moses. He was much more audacious. He wrote in his own behalf as the New Moses. The reason that so much of the TS recapitulates the first Mosaic Law is simply that he believed in the verity of that revelation. From his perspective, it was only natural that, when God vouchsafed a new revelation for life in the land, much of the first revelation would remain in force.[80]

Evidence accordingly suggests that the person of Moses was viewed as living on through the "prophet like Moses" who not only carried his name but was viewed as virtually identical and equivalent to Moses himself, an embodiment of the Great Lawgiver returned to carry on an important phase of his ministry. Perhaps, further, it was Moses himself who was thought to assume the guise of the prophet/author of writings like the *Assumption of Moses* or the Temple Scroll as these authors penned, or spoke, the words found in the books. And it is not difficult to see that the same kind of thing would have been true with *Jubilees*, which in all important aspects presents us with the same kind of writing. In any event, one has moved, with this explanation, from mere identity to some kind of mystical phenomenon.

Like Moses in *Jubilees*, or *Assumption of Moses*, therefore, one may ask whether the *writer* of 4 Ezra himself was actually considered an *Ezra redivivus*, or at least one of the prophets scheduled to return in the last days. The process that would lead to this prophet consciousness is certainly a matter of speculation. Nevertheless, all of the evidence of a returning prophet expectation suggests that: (1) "pseudo"-Ezra was in fact an historical prophet who either authored 4 Ezra or was responsible for the traditions found in it; (2) this person was believed to be a prophet who could speak "in the spirit of Ezra"; (3) the messiah, who was not Ezra, was also expected soon. One can note in defense of this reconstruction that the Ezranian community certainly believed in other messianic forerunners and, of course, that Ezra would be one of them. This is evident when one combines 4 Ezra 14:9 (above) with 6:26, where the angel is reported to have said: "they [those who are saved in the end, v. 25] shall see *the men who were taken up* [cf. the expression in 14:9 above!], *who from their birth have not tasted death;* and the heart of the earth's inhabitants shall be changed and converted to a different spirit." These final words about heart-change and conversion are appropriate indications of a prophetic ministry, particularly in

---

80. M. O. Wise, *A Critical Study of the Temple Scroll from Qumran Cave 11*, 1990a, 188-89. The author of the scroll Wise takes to be the Teacher of Righteousness of the end of days, following P. R. Davies's theories concerning the redaction and interpretation of CD 6.11 (cf. 184ff.).

the role of ushering in the restoration. Since the community viewed itself as those who would survive to the end, they obviously expected to meet with and see "Ezra." This, they may have believed, has now happened through the author of the work bearing Ezra's name. Noteworthy again is how the close relationship of Ezra to the saved community implies the exclusive nature of the wisdom and revelation that can lead to salvation. In his role as revealer, therefore, Ezra identifies in a special way with his community. Much the same is probably true for Baruch in the book bearing his name.[81]

Hence pseudepigraphy, even in the case of 4 Ezra, depends on the presence of a prophetic spirit within the community. Pseudepigraphy was neither predominantly a device to gain attention nor a strictly literary convention. Ezra was not only an historical figure, but an ever-living, mystical revealer figure. Perhaps in all these books, therefore, what has been called "pseudepigraphy" actually witnesses to a mystical revelatory experience based on the ability of the patriarch to continue communicating *with* or *through* prophets. How this experience was thought to be initiated is not clear. Whether the patriarch initiated the communication, or whether the prophet was first caught up in a mystical experience in which he visited the heavenlies, is not certain, although the latter is perhaps suggested by the pervasiveness of heavenly journeys in these writings.[82] In any event, it seems likely that the authors (or at least their immediate sources) were prophets who could speak "in the name" or "in the spirit" of the patriarchs they represented, perhaps even assuming the guise of a *patriarch redivivus*,[83] perhaps also serving in this office as important forerunners of the messiah. Such an understanding of pseudepigraphy satisfies the growing recognition that this device was not intended primarily to impress or to deliberately mislead its readers, so much as it composed a sincere form of prophetic activity.[84]

81. Cf. *2 Bar.* 13:3; 43:2; 46:7; 48:30; 76:2; etc.

82. Although the tours are presented as if taken by the *patriarch* himself, they seem to conceal a parallel experience by the receiver of the revelation, who may have claimed to have taken a similar journey or to have mystically *represented* the patriarch in his journey. It is perhaps not impossible that the mystic was also believed to assume the identity of the patriarch during the revelations. While Reid's comparison of pseudonymity with African mantic categories of revelation is helpful here, the distance chronologically and geographically (not to mention ideologically) between the two societies in question leaves room for serious doubt. The proper context is that of the revelatory experiences that were part of the esoteric traditions of Judaism itself (Rowland, 1982, 65).

83. In this regard it is noteworthy that Ezra (in the form of the prophet *redivivus?*) was expected to be seen by the righteous at the end of days; cf. 4 Ezra 6:26.

84. Thus even "Pseudepigrapha" as a title for our collection is misleading insofar as it implies a deliberate attempt to falsely attribute writings to an ancient author, or otherwise implies a merely *literary* rather than prophetic convention.

In spite of much diversity, the one consistent element observed throughout the entire spectrum of belief in special figures was the *implicit but essential relationship between the figure and the righteous community. Progenitors* functioned as the origin of the righteous seed that the community represents; *paradigmatic* figures functioned to define the community in terms of its behavior and circumstances, and sometimes even as "patrons" of the community; *revealer figures* communicated to their special groups eclectic and saving knowledge, a fact that is particularly suggestive of the exclusive soteriology of these sects. The figure-community correlation would thus appear to reveal a significant component of the thought of these groups when it came to developing ideas about, and forming relationships with, the figures of past and present. That this is a valid observation when it comes to the redeeming figures we call "messiahs" is an hypothesis that will be considered in the next section.

THE MESSIAH-FOR-THE-ELECT

It is commonly held that hopes for a specially anointed ruler from the line of David were already emerging in the sixth century B.C. and perhaps earlier, and that the originally very mundane ideas associated with this person were gradually eschatologized and idealized during the period of the Second Temple. One might refer to this developing messianology as the "conventional messianology" since it is universally treated that way by scholars, and because it would seem to have a legitimate claim to the greatest antiquity. In the writings of the movement of dissent, however, interesting and surprising evidence suggests either that the Davidic messianology was not as influential as has been thought, or that it was not all that highly regarded by these groups. This can be seen in one of three ways: (1) the Davidic image of the messiah is combined with aspects from other figures; (2) a priestly messiah is juxtaposed with, and even takes precedent over, a royal messiah; or (3) Davidic aspects are missing from the messianology altogether. These hints would lead one to question the widespread assumption that Judaism *unanimously* embraced the idea of a royal figure, along with the very nationalistic aspirations associated with his coming. Was a nationalistic messianology the only option in Judaism? If Davidic messianology was the "conventional messianology," were there "unconventional" messianologies, or at least unconventional applications of this messianology, in our movement?

Messiah in the Zoomorphic History

A quite enigmatic figure that fits the basic category of messiah is the ram with the great horn in *1 En.* 90:9-16, which is thought to refer to Judas Maccabeus or possibly an unknown teacher and leader of the Enoch sect. In either case this would imply a fulfilled messianic hope. It would seem, however, that this straightforward historical identification does not completely fill the bill, for in v. 31 "that ram" appears again in company with the ascending Enoch and at a time subsequent to the judgment and the establishment of the new Temple (i.e., beyond present historical circumstances; vv. 20-29). While scholars have maintained that this ram is Elijah, there are problems with this identification,[85] and some kind of connection with the earlier "ram with the great horn" would seem to be intended. If so, we may be witness to a figure who makes multiple appearances — an historical teacher or deliverer who will also play an important part in the eschatological events. Historical figures with eschatological roles are not unknown in our writings, as we will see below, and it is significant, in this regard, that the ram with the great horn is (like Enoch) nowhere actually said to *die* in the Zoomorphic History. To further complicate things, a "snow-white cow" appears in vv. 37-39 as well, a figure who seems to be a kind of second Adam, which in turn may have been equated with the messiah.[86] It would appear, therefore, that the messiah in the History is a *composite* figure: historical personage, future ascending figure, and a kind of cosmic Adam figure (a representative of redeemed humankind?) combined. All things considered, this approach is preferable to one that sees three different figures here.

More significant for us — whether we see one or three figures — are the functions of this (these) messianic personage(s). Besides the obvious function of a conquering or delivering figure, the ram is presented, in line with the analysis of revealer figures above, as a great *illuminator*: "he opened their eyes; and they had vision in them and their eyes were opened" (v. 9). More significant still, the ram also gathers a people, a holy troop gathered for battle under the auspices of the "Lord of the sheep" and his angels: "He cried aloud to the sheep, and all the rams *saw him and ran unto him*" (v. 10; cf. vv. 13-19). This role of marshaling a people might be part of the conventional warrior-messiah role, although it seems to be given disproportionate emphasis here in relation to other traditional aspects that, in comparison, seem to be played down. Thus while the

---

85. It is based on a comparison with 89:52, which, however, refers to Elijah as a persecuted "sheep," not a ram. Cf. Black (1985, 279), who argues that the ram Judas Maccabeus of 90:9-10 may be intended; but this is not without difficulties, as it fails to explain how Judas came to be with Enoch in the high tower in 89:52.

86. Black, 1985, 280.

ram does enter into battle like a warrior-messiah (v. 13), it is actually the Lord of the sheep himself who does the smiting (v. 18). A still clearer indication that what is portrayed here is a kind of "messiah for the elect" is that the ram does not deliver *all* Israelites (in fact, they are mostly rallied *against* him) but only the other "rams" (vv. 10, 16). A similar observation holds for the second Adam of vv. 37-38. The description of this figure is not highly developed,[87] but what is said is significant: besides receiving reverence from the nations (v. 37), his only function is to serve as a kind of paradigm for his "kindred," who all become *like him* — that is, "white cows."[88] While it is somewhat difficult to determine the exact significance of these verses and the figures in them,[89] it would nevertheless appear that the messiah functions as the focus and figurehead of the righteous in the last times.[90] Whatever more traditional categories are also employed to describe them, both the great horn/ram and the snow-white cow (or the composite figure they represent) function as "messiah for the elect."

87. Cf. de Villiers, 1978, 81. The absence of traditional elements serves to emphasize his role as messiah for the elect.

88. "I went on seeing until *all their kindred* were transformed, and became snow-white cows. . . . The Lord of the sheep rejoiced over . . . all the cows" (v. 38).

89. V. 38b is notoriously difficult: "and the first among them became something (Eth. *nagar*; Gk. ῥῆμα), and that something became a great beast with huge black horns on its head." Several suggestions have been offered for *nagar*/ῥῆμα. While Charles takes the Aram. טלה, "lamb," to have been mistaken for מלה, "word," by the Gk. translators, B. Lindars doubts this and suggests that the original was אמַּר, "lamb," and that "the Christian translators took advantage of the ambiguity in the Aramaic to render it λόγος, so making the vision a prophecy pointing forward to Christ" ("A Bull, a Lamb and a Word," 1976, 483-86, 485). This otherwise brilliant solution unfortunately brings in another "lamb," which would seem to point to *two* messiah figures in vv. 37-38, an inexplicable occurrence. Black accepts A. Dillmann's conjecture that behind *nagar* = ῥῆμα lies a transcription of Heb. or Aram. (א)ראמה, "wild ox," "buffalo," possibly referring to the descendants of Ham (*Chrestomathia Aethiopica,* 1866, 280), a suggestion that is equally inexplicable (where are mentioned the other sons of Noah?). We do not seem to be near a solution for the enigma unless we take *nagar* as a more accurate translation than ῥῆμα in the existing text as "something" and as referring to the original (note: "first among them") "snow-white cow" — i.e., to the same messiah, who is now portrayed as undergoing some changes himself from a "something (indescribable?)" into a "great beast with huge black horns."

90. This would be true even if the words "I went on seeing until all their kindred were transformed" (v. 38) refer to the remainder of unconverted Israel being brought into the fold during the restoration, a restoration significantly effected by the messiah (on which cf. ch. 9). It is to be noted how this occurs only *subsequent to* Israel's judgment and the vindication of the elect, and is *subject to* the *transformation* (repentance?) of the unrighteous. The verse seems to imply that only by being converted and transformed, by becoming themselves "snow white" — i.e., by becoming *like the elect* and *like their messiah* — can these be joined to the righteous.

Messiahs at Qumran

There are many special people in Qumran's past, present, and future — "Zadok," the "Interpreter of the Law," the *moreh ṣedeq,* the "Lawgiver," etc. The relationships of these individuals to one other are at best complex and probably indeterminable. In some cases two or more appellations appear to be only different names for the same person. To what extent any were considered "messiahs," furthermore, is wrapped up with the question of what makes someone a "messiah." Since the above-mentioned figures all appear to belong to the historical past of the group, we will not consider them as messianic figures or treat them here in any detail, although it is worthy of note that each tends to sustain the vital connection we have already established between leader and *yaḥad,* since it was to these leaders that the origins, knowledge, and aspirations of this particular group are attributed.[91]

As for those figures that do fulfill messianic roles, the term "prince of the congregation" (נשיא העדה *n^esî' ha-'ēdāh*) appears in 1QSb 5.20 and twice in an important fragment (4Q285) and, in a slight variation, "prince of the *whole* congregation," in CD 7.20, 1QM 5.1, 4Q279, and 4Q376.[92] This personage would appear to be equivalent to the Davidic royal messiah, as he is expected for the future according to 1QSb 5.20, has military functions in judgment according to CD 7.20-21, and acts as a warrior-messiah in the final battle according to 1QM 5.1. The title appears to be taken from Ezek. 34:24 and 37:25,[93] which equate the prince with a Davidic ruler. As for the functions of this messiah, almost too obvious to be mentioned are the exclusive claims made for this prince by the use of the term *N^esî 'ēdah — 'ēdah* being a virtual synonym for *yaḥad* to speak of the exclusive community.[94] Thus, in line with all that has been witnessed so far, the "congregation" of which this figure is the prince is the exclusive community. The prince comes on their behalf in the final days to fulfill their aspirations or to complete their vocation of bringing judgment on the

91. J. J. Collins, "Teacher and Messiah?" 1994, 193-210, 204, also explains the relation between past, present, and future figures as related to the restorative aspect of Qumran's eschatology — i.e., to the attempt to revive and perfect the institutions of Judaism — and there may be something to this idea.

92. נשיא כ(ו)ל העדה; cf. also the "prince" of CD 5.1, which term displaces "king" in Deut. 17:17, which is cited there, and may be equivalent to "the mighty man" of 1QM 12.10.

93. J. T. Milik, *Ten Years of Discovery in the Wilderness of Judaea,* 1959, 124. Y. Yadin (*The Scroll of the War of the Sons of Light against the Sons of Darkness,* 1962, 278) reads 1QM 5.1 "[shield] of the prince," in which case we might also cf. 1 Sam. 1:21.

94. They are juxtaposed in 1QSa 2.11-21, on which see more immediately below. For יחד cf. ll. 11, 17, 18, 21; for עדה (and other derivatives) cf. ll. 11, 12, 13, 16, 21. The phrase "Congregation of the Community" (עדת היחד) in l. 21 combines the terms.

land. If behind this representation of the messiah is the "conventional" Davidic messianic model, one can nevertheless see how this sect interpreted an otherwise nationalistic model to suit its own starkly exclusive claims.

A messiah would seem to be featured in the important, and well-known, woman-in-travail passage (1QH 3.6-18). Several characters appear in this drama: a pregnant woman (ll. 7-12), her child (ll. 8-12), an "Asp" (? see below; ll. 12, 17-18), and the mother of this "Asp" (ll. 12, 18). Approaches to this passage differ on whether a messiah is to be discerned in any of these references. There are four basic interpretations (which do not all attempt to interpret every character): (1) the child is the messiah and the Asp is an anti-Christ type of figure; (2) the woman is the community, the child is the messiah, and the mother of the Asp is the opponents; (3) the woman is the *moreh ṣedeq* and the child is the community; (4) the woman is merely a metaphor for some major crisis experienced by the psalmist and/or the *yaḥad*, the other images merely serving that imagery while possessing no independent symbolic significance.[95] The first two of these are variations of a messianic approach,[96] the latter two represent nonmessianic interpretations.[97]

Part of the difficulty here is that the hymn writer is speaking metaphorically of a situation of grave distress by combining naval (ll. 6-7, 12-16) with travail (ll. 7-12) metaphors. These two metaphors are linguistically, rather than logically, interrelated through a wordplay in the Hebrew, making it difficult at best to interpret the confused referents in the passage.[98] Since these kinds of

---

95. Thus Holm-Nielsen considers most of this imagery "accidental" (1960, 62).

96. Cf., e.g., Dupont-Sommer, 1961, 208-9; more recently expressed by Knibb, 1987, 174ff.

97. For a denial of the messianic interpretation, cf. Holm-Nielsen, 1960, 61-62; Mansoor, 1961, 90-91; Ringgren, 1963, 193, 196-97; de Jonge, 1969 (see n. 1 above), in de Jonge, 1991, 42-43; J. Pryke, "Eschatology in the Dead Sea Scrolls," 1969, 44-57, 50-51; D. C. Allison, *The End of the Ages Has Come,* 1985, 9-10. Note that "corporate" understandings of the motif do not actually preclude "messianic" interpretations as our own analysis has repeatedly implied!

98. While producing a rich literary effect, this also results in terminological ambiguity (or perhaps deliberate *double entendre*). מֹשְׁבֵּר can be pointed (מִשְׁבָּרְ(ים ("waves," "breaker," "surf"; cf. 2 Sam. 22:5 where it is also used with מוּת; Jon. 2:4; Pss. 42:8; 88:8; 93:4) or מַשְׁבֵּר ("mouth of the womb"; cf. Hos. 3:13); חבלי, "bonds," can also mean "birth pangs" (cf. Mansoor, 1961, 113, who refers to it as "a skillful play on words"; Ringgren, 1963, 193). Uses of בכור (ll. 8, 10, 12) are also ambiguous (from √ בכר = "first-born," or בכור = (ב +) כור = "furnace"; cf. Isa. 48:10; but the word is also used of the female genitals in rabbinic literature; cf. Holm-Nielsen, 1960, 54-55, who accordingly translates מכור "*womb* of the pregnant one" rather than Dupont-Sommer, "crucible"; a double meaning might therefore be intended here). Holm-Nielsen suggests that ll. 8-12 are "almost impossible to translate on account of the constant double meaning of the words" (53). This lib-

distress or "danger metaphors" can stand independently of messianic passages, the designation of such passages as "*messianic* travail" or "birth pangs of the *messiah*" tends once again to ignore the possibility that they may have had a rather different provenance than messianology. This may itself cast doubt on a messianic interpretation. Having said that, this passage does in fact appear to introduce the messiah in rather cryptic terms. The woman in travail is about to bring forth her "first-born" (l. 8), "the Man of distress" (depending on one's translation; l. 9), a "man-child" (l. 9), "a Marvellous Counsellor with his might" (l. 10), "and he shall deliver men[99] from the billows because of Her who is big with him" (l. 10). It is little wonder that such expressions, particularly those that allude to suffering and to the Isaian Servant Songs, have invited parallels with New Testament thought about Jesus. However, except for the one very questionable rendering "Man of distress," this messiah is not himself portrayed as suffering.[100] Nevertheless, these kinds of references are at least suggestive of a messiah, and it seems unavoidable to conclude that some such allusion is being made here.[101]

Perhaps the most convincing and favored alternative to the messianic approach is the corporate approach implied by (3) above. There are those, first of all, like Ringgren, who insist that the messianic-sounding language that comes from the Servant Songs of Isaiah is intended by the writer to retain the same corporate significance as the songs have in their original context.[102] This would make an expression like "Marvellous Counsellor" a reference to the commu-

---

erality in use of language would seem to suggest a similar liberality in images and increase the possibility that messianic allusions (even if secondary to the main thought) are intended (*contra* Holm-Nielsen, 54).

99. We must follow Holm-Nielsen against Dupont-Sommer in his translation of גבר, which never means "everybody" but may well tolerate a collective sense here (Holm-Nielsen, 1960, 58).

100. According to Dupont-Sommer (1961, 208 n. 2), והרית גבר הצרה בחבליה can also be rendered: "And She who is big with the Man *is in* travail, in her pains." Similarly Lohse (1971, 121) has "und die mit einem Männlichen schwanger ist, leidet Pein in ihren Wehen." While it would be somewhat more natural to render *geber hētsērah* as the construct, these alternate renderings, if a little redundant, would remove the "troublesome" suffering-messiah reference. The view of Eisenman and Wise (1992, 24-25, 29) that a messiah killed by Jerusalem authorities can be found in 4Q285 is doubtful. The mention of Kittim in that passage suggests that the messiah *does* the killing, and the passage in question can be translated in such a way as to produce this sense.

101. *Contra* Holm-Nielsen (1960, 63) and Ringgren (1963, 193), who apply the Servant language to the community. The "Marvellous Counsellor" appears in l. 10, however, to be juxtaposed with the community, which would seem to preclude an equation of the two.

102. Ringgren, 1963, 196-97.

nity. The difficulty with such an approach, however, shows itself particularly clearly when one attempts to make sense out of l. 10, where the "Marvellous Counsellor" is expected (according to the translation of Dupont-Sommer) to "deliver men from the billows *because of* (note: *bᵉ*) *Her who is big with him*." This produces the rather awkward sense that the community, as the Marvellous Counsellor, will perform a redemptive work (unique to the scrolls) in honor of the *moreh* (again, a quite unique statement), who is described as a pregnant woman about to give birth (stretching the language, to say the least!). However, Dupont-Sommer has introduced purpose (or at best agency) into his translation, and one does better to follow Holm-Nielsen and translate "*in* her that is pregnant with him," giving a sense for the passage (not, however, sustained by Holm-Nielsen) of "he will deliver men . . . from *among* the pregnant one (= the community)" — that is, the messiah will deliver those in the *yaḥad*. The language is, in any event, more appropriate to the community and the messiah than to the *moreh* and the community. The language is not corporate in the way Ringgren understands it, therefore, although much of the messianic language exhibits a corporate nuance. Ringgren has apparently mistaken the *association* of messianic belief with corporate self-consciousness for an *equation* of the two. As for Ringgren's contention that even the "branch" in 1QH 8 is to be interpreted corporately, it is true, as already pointed out, that agricultural motifs are frequently used corporately, but we now know from the recently published fragment 4Q521 (quite likely also 4Q285) that צמח (*ṣemaḥ*) was definitely used as a messianic motif.[103]

Others, like Mansoor, equate the birth of the male child with the emergence of the sect, which Mansoor (rather self-contradictorily) refers to as the "messianic community."[104] This would disqualify the passage entirely as messianic teaching as it would then nowhere explicitly refer to a messiah. Again, in our view the allusions to a messiah are rather too strong (esp. cf. l. 10) to accept these arguments. It is simply impossible to avoid the messianic tone of the whole passage (as suggested by Mansoor's rubric "messianic community"). It is true that there may be a lack of clarity between the "messianic community" and the "messiah," but this may again be evidence of how intricately interwoven (and even confused) are messianic and corporate thought in the passage. Moreover, the use of symbolism appears to be deliberately suggestive rather than consistent. The reality of this inconsistency is unintentionally emphasized by Holm-Nielsen, who is in all respects opposed to messianic interpretations. He qualifies his strictly nonmessianic approach with these surprising words, and

103. Cf. Eisenman and Wise, 1992, 29.
104. The idea that birth is given to the "messianic community" here leads one to ask what makes the community "messianic" if not a "messiah."

the tentativeness in his language suggests that he regrets his attempt to be oversystematic in his approach to a very freely worded passage. While the language could be used in a strictly nonmessianic way, "On the other hand, one must not overlook the fact that the birth imagery by far exceeds the usual figurative language in these psalms. Likewise, it must be admitted that lines 9-10 more than represent the pains themselves and extend to their result, the child's birth. . . . The account of a second woman, who is pregnant with corruption or a serpent, similarly points to a more detailed concept. . . ."[105] The symbolic language is nebulous, eclectic, and — most of all — suggestive, but it is difficult to sustain a nonmessianic interpretation and it seems best to accept that the messiah is indeed featured in this passage.

If we can accept the identification of the child as the messiah, how then is the mother to be interpreted? The basic approaches mentioned above again offer two basic explanations — the mother and child represent: (1) the community and the messiah (messianic interpretation); or (2) the *moreh* and the community (nonmessianic interpretation). The fact that the passage starts out in the first person, "I was confused like the Woman about to bring forth" (l. 7), leads one to think of the *moreh* speaking here and accordingly suggests (2), the nonmessianic interpretation. But we have already determined that a messianic reference in the passage is probably intended, and can perhaps resolve the difficulty by assuming that while the passage *starts out* by comparing the *hymnist* to a woman about to give birth (ll. 7-8a), the *entire suffering community* is represented by the woman *in the remainder of the passage* (ll. 8b-12a), and it is *this* woman who is said to give birth to the messiah. Apparently, while the author began speaking of his own suffering, for which he employed a travail motif (cf. all of ll. 6-7), this reminded him, by word association, of the *community's* travail (the subject of ll. 8bff.) and, coincidental with this, of their calling to bring forth the messiah.[106] This approach involves a certain shift in meaning and inconsistency in expression in the passage, but we know from elsewhere in the Founder Hymns and even in this hymn (note the above-mentioned wordplay) that the author is capable of inexactitude in the use of terms and of a sudden shift of metaphors. Moreover, a transition from the individual to the corporate

105. Holm-Nielsen, 1960, 63.

106. We can agree with Knibb here: "the psalmist is describing his distress by means of three images: a ship of the sea, a besieged city, and a woman in labour. The last of these images is, however, developed at such great length that it seems difficult to think of mere illustration. In fact it appears that the thought of the distress accompanying childbirth leads the psalmist to describe the birth of a particular individual, the messiah, and the distress that was expected to accompany his appearance, the so-called birth-pangs of the messiah. . . . By this means the psalmist is able to link his own sufferings to those that would inaugurate the new age" (1987, 174).

is natural enough from what was concluded about the Teacher earlier, and would be facilitated here by his close identity with his community in their common suffering.

This approach is further confirmed by l. 12b, where another woman who is ready to give birth, this time to "the Asp," enters the scene. The Asp might be a metaphor for the opponents of the sect, but an indirect one at best, for "Asp" and "Perversity" (l. 18) are images respectively of Satan and the Angel of Darkness in 1QS 3.18-21, although the terms do not *necessarily* need to be translated in a personal sense there.[107] That the one who *bears* the Asp (the mother of the Asp), rather than the Asp itself, stands for the community of opponents would in any event sustain the current metaphor much better. Perhaps, then, one is to see in this Asp a kind of child of Belial or even an antimessiah, and although it would be impossible to determine such a belief from this passage alone, it seems that some such evil personification did figure into the expectation of the sect.[108] A perfectly acceptable alternative explanation is that the Asp stands for the *teachings* promoted by the sect's opponents or, perhaps, to a sort of demonic offspring created by this teaching.[109] Whatever one decides about this second child, it is nevertheless clear that the two *women* (in the latter part of the passage especially) have become metaphors for the community and its opponents, a conclusion that generally

107. The word "Asp" or "Viper," אפעה, could mean "groaning" (Holm-Nielsen, following Silberman) or "nought" (Mansoor). Thus "works of the Asp" in l. 17 could accordingly be rendered "deeds of wickedness" or "acts of nought," etc.

108. J. M. Allegro refers to the fragment of the Isaiah commentary that mentions an anti-Christ figure taking part in a battle on the plain of Jezreel (i.e., Megiddo; *The Dead Sea Scrolls*, 1964, 169-70); cf. 4Q175 (= 4QTestimonia), ll. 23-25. The idea of an anti-God figure *par excellence* may have been more current than is usually thought. Stone recognizes the idea in Isa. 14:13; Dan. 7:8, 11, 25; 11:36 (cf. also *1 En.* 9:1-2); and in 4 Ezra 11:40-43 (1990, 351-52; although we doubt this last reference; cf. below). D. Flusser ("The Hubris of the Antichrist in a Fragment from Qumran," 1988, 207-13) finds in the one who claimed to be "son of God" in 4Q426 one of these anti-Christ figures.

109. It is difficult to avoid seeing references to the world of demons in the use of this terminology, as this would certainly explain the serpent or dragon mythology that seems to lie behind it. Holm-Nielsen admits that תהומות in l. 15 contains a "personification of infernal beings" (1960, 59) and that יפתחו in l. 16 "may allude to the opening of the netherworld, so that the demons get an opportunity to ravage the earth" (59; suggesting also the possibility that this refers to an opening for the ungodly to descend into hell). "The works of the Asp" (l. 17; Holm-Nielsen, "deeds of wickedness"; Mansoor, 1961, 115, "acts of nought") are taken by Holm-Nielsen to refer to all the "spiritual creatures and accomplices of the devil," among whom would be false teachers: "the community of never-do-well, i.e., of Belial," the "circle of nought"; cf. Matt. 3:7. On the other hand, the contrast to the covenant in 1QH 2.28 suggests that "Asp" and "Vanity" allude primarily to the teachings of the opponents.

supports an identification of the man-child with the coming messiah. While this community/opponent dialectic recalls the soteriological dualism of the scrolls, the community (mother)/messiah (child) correlation fits in well with the kind of strong relationship between corporate and messianic thought earlier discerned in the "Prince" messianology.

The *yaḥad* thus sees itself as responsible (or privileged) for giving birth to the messiah.[110] It would appear from l. 8b that the hymn writer expected the messiah imminently. The reason for this is significant: *"for the children have reached as far as the billows of Death,* and She who is big with the Man of distress is in her pains."[111] That travail-like suffering is a sign of the emergence of the messiah appears to be made in ll. 10-12, an enigmatic passage where the community/woman correlation is even more fully evident: "Every womb suffers pain and terrible anguish at the time of child-bearing, and terror seizes them that conceived these children; and at the time of the bearing of her first-born every terror unfurls over the crucible of Her who is with child." In this passage the "children" (with another subtle shift of metaphor) are the community — again indicating the close identity between community (children) and messiah (firstborn child).[112] The fact that this suffering is partly stimulated by the opponents of the sect (ll. 12-13, 17) again recalls the fundamental division that existed in Israel at this time. The *yaḥad* reasoned that out of the present distresses the messiah would come as their *Deliverer* — there may not be any indication here that he would suffer *with* them. The important point is that *only out of the elect community* would the messiah come at all. This is further compelling evidence of the predominance of the idea of a messiah-for-the-elect in the scrolls.

110. If the woman in Revelation 12 symbolizes the Jewish remnant that gives birth to the messiah, as many believe, this would offer an interesting parallel (as cf. Knibb, 1987, 174; even Holm-Nielsen, 1960, 62 admits similarities). Now available also is the text from Cave 4, *4QApocryphal Lamentations A* (= 4Q179; cf. 4Q501), which speaks of all Jerusalem as a wounded, abandoned, and barren woman, and is in sense close to the vision of the disconsolate woman in 4 Ezra (9:38ff.). In these latter kinds of passages the woman is Jerusalem judged rather than, as here, a saved remnant that gives birth to the messiah. It would appear, therefore, that the woman could be a symbol *either* for Jerusalem as a whole or, perhaps, for the righteous contingent of Jerusalemites who carry on the service of the woman in giving birth to the messiah (i.e., since Jerusalem is no longer worthy to do so).

111. This plural "children" and its parallelism with "She who is big" indicate that the suffering woman in the passage is a community rather than an individual. The fact that the "children" are in existence, while the "Man of distress" is still awaited, also implies different referents.

112. This hardly "frustrates" the messianic interpretation (Holm-Nielsen, 1960, 55), since so far the language has been anything but consistent in this passage.

No discussion of Qumran messianology would be complete without a consideration of the much-discussed multiple messianism of the sect. The perennial debate over the possibility that groups like Qumran or the authors of the *Testaments of the Twelve Patriarchs* could have expected two (or more) messiahs is a familiar one, although the view is practically unanimous that the Dead Sea sect at some point in its history expected two, perhaps three, eschatological figures.[113] Discussion focuses on various references to a messiah or messiahs of "Aaron and Israel" in the scrolls. The plural "messiah*s* (or anointed ones) of Aaron and Israel" appears only in 1QS 9.11, while the singular "messiah (or anointed one) of Aaron and Israel" is found in (all extant MSS of) CD 12.23–13.1 and CD(B) 1.10-11 and "the messiah *from* Aaron and *from* Israel" is found in CD(B) 2.1. "Messiah of Israel" is found in 1QSa 2.20. Other passages similarly suggest that more than one messiah was expected for the future, although it is perhaps worth noting that they do *not* all use the words "Aaron" and "Israel" in association with these figures.[114] Theories that attempt to explain these divergencies differ widely in their approach and usually only account for part of the data. They can be summarized as follows:

1. The view that the original *multiple* messianism of the sect, represented by 1QS, has been altered or corrected in medieval copies of CD (where the singular appears) to match later, more conventional beliefs in a single messiah. Given that for years our *best* complete manuscript of CD was the rather late medieval one from the Cairo geniza, this possibility held some appeal. An obvious problem for this theory has now been created with the discovery of fragments of CD found at Qumran, which support an original *singular*.

2. The reverse view, that the original singular messianic belief represented in CD was eventually replaced by a more developed dual messianic belief found in 1QS, after priestly interests began to dominate. This theory, which attempts to explain the multiple messianism by appealing to the influence of the Hasmoneans (a priestly family who became kings), unfortunately conflicts seriously with the strongly *anti*-Hasmonean stance of the scrolls (why would this group honor a family they apparently de-

113. Cf., e.g., Allegro, 1964, 167-68; Schiffman, 1987, 239. As for the *Testaments*, however, contrast Beasley-Murray, 1946, 1-12, with de Villiers, 1978, 87.

114. A "messiah of Israel" and a priest appear together in 1QSa 2.17-22. The much discussed *Testimonies* collection (4QTest), which appears to refer to a prophet, Davidic ruler, and priest, is a terse document whose missing context makes it difficult to categorize or interpret. Whether the writing functioned similar to the New Testament "testimony" passages is still debated; cf. Milik (1959, 125), who speculates about the consoling function of the work.

spised?).[115] It is in any event likely that priestly messianic belief was inherited by the group from the beginning, being widely disseminated from a considerably earlier time.[116]

3. Theories that approach the problem by redefining, and generally playing down, the notion of "messiah" as a central or consistent belief in the scrolls. Since the word for messiah *(māšîaḥ)* would not have possessed technical sense at this time, the translation "anointed one(s)," with its much less restricted nuance, has been suggested as more appropriate.[117] This tends to remove any difficulty with variations in number or types of figures. R. B. Laurin, however, has suggested that the development toward "messiah" as a technical term can already be detected at Qumran, although only in those places that refer to a Davidic, military figure.[118] While it is no doubt valid to point out how modern treatments have overtechnicalized messianic terminology, therefore, it would be very difficult to argue against the existence of certain eschatological messianic figures who carried *superlative* importance at Qumran.[119] To think that *no* systematization of belief took place would also seem highly uncharacteristic for the sect.

4. The view that "the anointed (ones) of (or from) Aaron and Israel" refers to the community itself, not to future messiahs. The obvious advantage of such an approach is that variation between the plural and the (generic) singular in the above expressions would then be purely stylistic. This view fails, however, to take account of the obvious messianic language in these (and other) passages, or to explain how the community could come to be so designated.

115. Accordingly Collins (1995, 90-95) justifiably prefers to attribute interest in priestly messianism to *disappointment* and *criticism* of the Hasmoneans: "The plurality of messianic figures . . . implicitly rejected the combination of royal and priestly offices by the Hasmoneans" (95). It did this by spelling out the requirements for two separate offices, whereas the Hasmoneans attempted to combine them.

116. Hultgård has pointed to evidence from the Hebrew Scriptures and pre-Hasmonean writings for the attribution of royal prerogatives to the priesthood; he suggests that the Hasmoneans merely *exploited* the Levitical ideology for their own purposes (1977, 1:37-38, 43-44). M. E. Stone ("Enoch, Aramaic Levi and Sectarian Origins," 1988, 159-70) points to the antiquity of 1Q21 and 4QLevᵃ, which feature Levitical messianology and which Stone dates to the third century B.C. For possible biblical origins for priestly messianology, cf. Deut. 18:15-19 (a prophet like Moses, who was of Levitical descent); Ps. 110:4; Zechariah 3–4; Mal. 3:1-4; 4:5-6; Dan. 9:24.

117. Cf. de Jonge, 1991, 41-42.

118. Laurin, 1963, passim.

119. To the more well-known evidence can be added that provided by fragments like 4Q521 and 4Q285 that unambiguously refer to a final deliverance figure.

It is admittedly difficult to construct a solution out of the limited and varied data offered by the scrolls. It is quite likely, however, that each of these four solutions, in spite of their respective weaknesses, actually contributes something to a solution. So, as for (1) and (2), there does seem to be some development of beliefs, or at least expression, taking place. But one should also recognize the validity in positions 3 and 4. To begin with, it is probably best to acknowledge that the word *mašiaḥ* was not *fully* technicalized (as in [3] above) and that evidence for its employment as a technical term, even for a Davidic messiah, is at best ambiguous at Qumran (note that the word "Prince" was the commonly accepted term). Messianology was still being developed in terms of multiple "anointed" figures expected for the end of time. It would be difficult in fact to imagine a Qumran without an expectation of a separate teacher, ruler, priest, and/or lawgiver/scribe *par excellence,* each created in the image of his historical counterparts and each expected to come sometime soon to join and deliver the elect. Nevertheless, it is safe to say that, among many less well-defined figures, two were emerging as more distinct "messiahs": a priest and a king. (To this we should perhaps also add a third — a prophet — as in the Qumran *Testimonies,* although he would seem to be more of a precursor or forerunner of the messiahs than a messiah himself.) Perhaps even more fruitful is the recognition (*as per* [4] above) that the term "Aaron and Israel" (although, we will argue, *not* the fuller and probably derived expression "*anointed* (ones) of Aaron and Israel") likely served, at least in certain periods, as a *self-designation* for the community. We find this expression, in the form "Israel and Aaron," used in just such a way in CD 1.7.[120] Moreover, given that the messiahs of this community were probably all conceptionalized as messiahs-of-the-elect, it would cohere well with this that the name "the messiah of Aaron and Israel" (CD 12.23–13.1 and CD[B] 1.10-11) and, *notably,* "the messiah *from* Aaron and *from* Israel" (CD[B] 2.1) appropriately emerged as near synonyms for "messiah of the elect."

How, then, would this explain the many variations of the terminology in the scrolls? If, as many scholars suspect, CD was among the earliest documents at Qumran, the term "messiah of Aaron and Israel" as found there would represent one of the original instances of the adoption of the term, in this case to speak of the royal personage who arises out of the community[121] (note how the

---

120. In line with our previous treatment of CD 1, this "root of planting . . . from Israel and Aaron" refers either to the historical remnant or to the community itself; cf. above.

121. Mowinckel correctly perceived this with respect to the Damascus Document: "The expression means simply that the Messiah will come from the midst of the community itself ('those of Aaron and Israel') i.e., the community which consists of segregated priests and laymen" (1956, 289).

two passages having this designation refer to militant messiahs). In that case a *single* messiah would be referred to,[122] and clearly emphasized in this use is that the messiah is the messiah of the community — somewhat cryptically presented as the messiah from (the true) "Aaron and Israel." The plural in 1QS is not a problem now either. Two possibilities present themselves. Either the plural was introduced in recognition that *two* messiahs would emerge from the *one* community "Israel and Aaron," or "messia*s* of Aaron and Israel" represents a simplistic linguistic adaptation of the singular.[123] While a multiple messianic belief was probably held from an early time, the latter theory would mean that only at a somewhat later time (when 1QS was written or before?) was the expression "messiah of Aaron and Israel" (= "messiah *from* Aaron and Israel" as we find it in CD) adopted, through a "misreading" of the expression "Aaron and Israel," as if it were a reference to *both* the Davidic messiah and the "Priest." As we said, this would have been a strictly linguistic adaptation: from "messiah from the community" to "(one) messiah from Aaron and (one) messiah from Israel."[124] The form "messiahs from Aaron and Israel" would then have offered a kind of instant *double entendre* for the priest and king combination — they not only come *out of* the community (as in the original expression) but one specifically comes from (the priestly portion) "Aaron" and the other from (the "lay" portion) "Israel." This approach would seem to be confirmed by the fact that the expression "anointed of Aaron" is not found in the scrolls (as is its counterpart "anointed of Israel"), indicating that the expression never enjoyed an independent existence as a term for "the (eschatological) Priest" — exactly what we might expect given our developmental proposal.

It can therefore be argued that all of these kinds of messianic designations could well have originated with "Aaron and Israel" as a self-reference of the community, even if the exact process involved in the adoption and employment of each term is not obvious. This would also explain why these messiahs can

---

122. Cf. de Jonge, 1991, 41.

123. Evidence of the continuing influence of the original expression is forthcoming from the same passage where we read "the men of the Community shall set apart a House of Holiness [for Aaron] . . . and a House of Community for Israel . . ." (ll. 5-7). J. C. VanderKam ("Messianism in the Scrolls," 1994, 220-21) complains that Aaron and Israel cannot express the notion of "all Israel" (or the whole community), since the two are separately treated in these lines. On the contrary, it cannot be imagined that the author envisioned *two* different communities/"houses" in using this language; they are parallel expressions for one entity (merely emphasizing two slightly different functions), just as "Israel and Aaron" was a designation for the whole community.

124. Collins (1995, 79) refers to such a development as a "remarkable coincidence," but there is no coincidence involved; rather, the development is better attributed to the contingencies of linguistic evolution within a group that was convinced of the potential for the multiple application of language.

quite naturally be referred to without an accompanying "Israel" or "Aaron" in the scrolls — the qualifiers are not essential to the idea of the messiah, as is usually implied in studies of Qumran messianology; they rather originally belonged to, and still retain a connection with, the complex nomenclature of self-reference at Qumran.

One is thus witness to a messianology intimately related to an exclusive self-consciousness and for which the caption "messiah(s) of the elect" is appropriate. This coheres with the messianic belief exhibited by the scrolls generally, which gives evidence of two recurrent operative principles: (1) the messiah is seen as *emerging directly from* the community, and (2) messianic thought is closely interconnected with the *idea* of the elect community, to the point that it is not clear in some passages whether the *yaḥad* or the *māšîaḥ* is being referred to. A particularly important, although enigmatic, reference to a "Teacher of Righteousness" who comes at the end of days (CD 6.11; cf. 7.18-21) would seem to provide further evidence of (1),[125] as would a number of other indications elsewhere in the scrolls.[126] As for (2), the woman-in-travail passage, as the trees-by-the-water passage treated earlier, offers abundant evidence of this kind of interconnection and even confusion between the messiah and the community. The scrolls accordingly furnish a singularly distinctive example of what can be called a doctrine of the "messiah for the elect."[127]

125. Milik sees in the reference to Damascus in 7.18-21 an indication that "the Essenes expected the messiah to be born in their circles" (1959, 127).

126. The words "when God will have begotten the Messiah *among/with them*" (אתם) in 1QSa 2.11-12 are a special instance. It is implied throughout this passage that this messiah (we assume that the banquet referred to is eschatological, but our observations hold regardless) is fundamentally the messiah of the *community* (*yaḥad;* as this community is continually referred to in the passage; cf. ll. 11, 17, 18, 21, despite his being called "the Messiah of Israel" in l. 14). Along with the Priest, this messiah shall bless the bread of the banquet, following which "all the Congregation of the Community shall bless, each according to his rank." We can well imagine that all who are "out of order" with respect to this — the rest of Israel — will in no way be included in the final banquet.

127. An enigmatic passage in 4Q252 reads (according to Eisenman and Wise, 1992, 89) "until the Messiah of Righteousness, the Branch of David comes, because to him and his seed was given the Covenant of the Kingdom of His people in perpetuity, *because he kept (. . .) the Torah with the men of the Community* (היחד), because (. . .) refers to the Congregation (כנסת) of the men. . . ." It is practically impossible to tell whether this text, which is based on Gen. 49:10-11 (also messianically interpreted in 4Q252), alludes throughout to a future messiah, or also to someone else in the past, or whether the *yāḥad* named here is the community associated with the sect of the scrolls. It is at least potentially another particularly clear presentation of the messiah-for-the-elect.

The Multiple Messianism of the
Testaments of the Twelve Patriarchs

It would be worthwhile at this point to consider a phenomenon parallel to the messiahs of Aaron and Israel at Qumran — namely, that messianology associated with the names Levi and Judah in the *Testaments of the Twelve Patriarchs*.[128] It has often been felt that some relationship must exist between the two groups at the point of their multiple messianology. The only significant mention of Levi and Judah in the scrolls, however, is too ambiguous to make a confident decision on whether the sect held similar views of these particular figures as the *Testaments*,[129] and it is otherwise quite impossible to determine what the relationship between the two beliefs might be, except in a general way. A double messianism, if that is what it is, may have been common among Jewish groups otherwise unrelated. Despite this uncertainty we can nevertheless still ask whether messiahs of Levi and Judah *function* comparably to those of Aaron and Israel at Qumran. We are a long way toward this conclusion already. As we noted above, the figures of Levi and Judah in the *Testaments* serve as paradigms for the author(s) and their community who maintained a deep commitment to the ideals of a righteous government through Judah and a righteous priesthood through Levi. It is not hard to see that the Levi-Judah community exhibited the same hopes and sentiments toward the priestly and royal prerogatives as did the community that somewhat similarly referred to itself as "Israel and Aaron." In both cases this posture was no doubt partly in reaction to the perceived need for the nation to retreat from syncretistic politics and impure religion and to once again honor its divinely appointed offices.

As mentioned earlier, it would appear that most references to Levi and Judah in the *Testaments* are actually not messianic, nor do they relate to the future so much as to the *history* of the two tribes, a history relayed through a type of prophecy *ex eventu,* and an inherent part of the testament form. A minority of passages in the *Testaments,* however, point rather more unambiguously to a figure or figures with what we would call messianic status. One such, *TDan* 5:10ff., seems to refer to a single messianic figure from Judah and Levi when it states:

---

128. For our arguments against the view (cf. Hollander and de Jonge, 1985, 59-63) that the messianic and eschatological sections are entirely Christian, cf. our discussions on pp. 23-25 and 370-71n.45 above.

129. They appear together with Benjamin in 1QM 1.2, but whether the three tribes are negatively portrayed as enemies of the sect (as Dupont-Sommer's translation implies [1961, 169]) or, more positively, taken to be represented by the sect (perhaps as another designation for the sect; cf. Yadin, 1962, 257; P. R. Davies, *1QM, the War Scroll from Qumran,* 1977, 114) is a disputed point.

> And there shall arise for you from the tribe of Judah and Levi *(ek tēs phylēs Iouda kai Leui)* the Lord's salvation.
> He *(autos)* will make war against Beliar. . . . (v. 10)

Determining the exact meaning of such *translated* texts is notoriously difficult. Taking the text at face value, however, we note that the singular "he" *(autos)*, the antecedent of which is the Lord's "salvation" (a metonymic reference to the messiah), seems to refer not to two messiahs but to one. That this messiah is seen to emerge from *two tribes,* on the other hand, raises an important question. Does this refer to the matriarchal and patriarchal sides of the messiah's ancestry? The singular "tribe" *(phylēs)* is hazardous to this theory. If, however, the words "and Levi" *(kai Leui)* represent, as is sometimes believed, an addition to conform the text to other dual references in the *Testaments* (the occasional reversed order of "Judah and Levi," as here, might be taken either for or against this suggestion), the singular *might* be explained as a survival of the earlier form where Judah alone was mentioned. But if in reality there is no question of a secondary addition here (and we should note that this would imply sloppy editing to say the least), the possibility is to be noted that "(the tribe of) Judah and Levi," like "Aaron and Israel," might have served as a kind of self-designation for the community. While this passage is perhaps not enough by itself to support such a theory, this approach does make sense of the translated passage as it stands.

More evidence can be found in a quite similar passage, *TGad* 8:1: "Tell these things to your children as well, so that they will honor Judah and Levi, because from them *(ex autōn)* the Lord will raise up a Savior *(sōtēra)* for Israel." Here we have basically the same text as *TDan* 5:10, except for a more consistent agreement of language through the use of the plural "from them" *(ex autōn)*; the possibility of a later addition of "and Levi" *(kai [ton] Leui)* would, in this case, remain a satisfactory theory, but it is obviously not the only possibility. The singular "Savior" *(sōtēra)* implies that the two tribes combine in some way to produce *one* messiah. Again the possibility exists that the expression "Judah and Levi" refers to the righteous community. But is it only a possibility? Significant, in this regard, are the words that immediately follow in v. 2: "I know that at the end your children will depart from them *(apostēsontai . . . ap' autōn)* and will live in all manner of wickedness and evildoing and corruption in the sight of the Lord." The curious use of *apostasthai* (ἀπόστασθαι, "to fall away") makes this departure from Judah and Levi sound very much like a religious apostasy *from the Lord*.[130] The phrase "(depart) *from them*" *(ap' autōn)* moreover seems to combine the tribes into a unit, almost as if Judah and Levi do not refer to the messiah's ancestry at all, but to the two tribes *together* and, perhaps, to a unified

---

130. Hollander and de Jonge, 1985, 336.

body of teaching associated with those tribes. The impression created by the two verses together is that the righteous teachings as well as the messiah himself originate *in* the Levi-Judah community.

Somewhat less certain evidence comes from *TBen.* 11:2: "And in later times there shall rise up the beloved of the Lord, from the seed of Judah and Levi *(ek spermatos Iouda kai Levi)*,[131] one who does his good pleasure by his mouth. . . ." The phraseology used in the following verses (vv. 2-5) suggests that the *single* messiah referred to here is the traditional Davidic messiah with conquering attributes. Unless "and Levi" *(kai Levi)* in v. 2 is an addition, Judah and Levi are again treated as *one* entity from which the "seed" of the messiah arises. The singular form "seed" *(spermatos)* would also appear to preclude a reference to the matriarchal and patriarchal ancestries of the messiah, as even a generic singular implies a previous combination of the tribes rather than the involvement of two separate tribes, although it is difficult to say just how conclusive this linguistic argument is on its own merits.

What is clear is that all of these passages refer to a *single* messiah. It is noteworthy that other passages seem to know of only one messiah as well. *TNaph.* 4:5 speaks of "a man who effects righteousness" who is not associated with any tribe. A little later in the same testament, however, Naphtali exhorts his sons to "be in unity with Levi and Judah" (8:2),[132] but again only one messiah appears to be in mind as the verse continues: "for through *Judah* will salvation arise for Israel." We might conclude that this passage addresses the question of his *lineage:* from Judah, while the passages above address his *provenance:* from the righteous community "Levi and Judah," although this is still largely inference.

As for the "priestly messiah" in the *Testaments,* where is he? Considering the attention that this "priestly messianology" has received in the past, it is perhaps surprising that *TLevi* 18:1ff. contains the only more or less clear allusion to a future priestly ruler from Levi.[133] In this passage *all* of the future messianic

---

131. The text appears to have been tampered with at this point. De Jonge's text reads ἐκ τοῦ σπέρματός μου, which later Christian editors interpreted as a reference to the apostle Paul, who was a Benjaminite. This certainly is the more difficult reading; however, the one adopted, although representing only one MS, coheres well with the messianic views of the *Testaments* so far investigated. It can therefore be *cautiously* accepted.

132. In this regard the Hebrew Testament of Naphtali 7:6 has a suggestive parallel: "Therefore, I command you not to associate with *the sons of Joseph,* but only with Levi and Judah" (cited by Hollander and de Jonge, 1985, 316).

133. Other passages such as *TReub.* 6:7-12; *TLevi* 4:2-6; 5:2-3; *TJud.* 21:1-9 only appear to do so; no mention of a *future* Levite can be discerned — only the historical role of Levi is referred to. *TJud.* 23:1-3 mentions a messiah but offers no indication it is the Levitical messiah; he is called "my salvation." *TJud.* 17:5-6; 24:1–25:1 also allude to a traditional, not Levitical, messiah. Interestingly, though, 25:1-2 implies that in the restoration

functions appear to be attributed to Levi. Even the king from Judah is said to descend from Levi (vv. 14-15)! This figure is said to establish a new priesthood (v. 14). The passage as it stands, however, is very muddled, and is not the kind of clear presentation of Levitical messianology one might have expected from an author who composed it with the express purpose of presenting this priestly messiah. It perhaps represents a rather sloppy attempt by a later editor to combine the offices of prophet, priest, and king (see our comments on *TLevi* 8:11-19 above), along with references to the *historical* role of the Levi tribe, with the idea of a Levitical messiah. While the passage as it stands does refer to a "new priest," the verses that follow sound more like allusions to a *royal messiah*.[134] In view of the difficulties and brokenness of the logic of the passage, it would be precarious on the basis of this passage alone to conclude that there is any messiah from Levi in the *Testaments*. Thus all references to a Levitical messiah dissolve on close inspection — and some scholars accordingly refuse to see any Levitical messianology in the *Testaments* at all.[135]

That the messianology of the *Testaments* is, on closer inspection, so (surprisingly) "Davidic" can also provide a clue to why the words "and Levi" appear to be tacked on *after* "Judah" in some of these passages, resulting in the order *"Judah and Levi."* That about half of these future messianic passages have the name Judah *first*[136] certainly accords with the conclusion that the *Davidic* messiah, not a Levitical messiah, is predominantly in mind in these passages. Another corollary of the occasional prioritizing of the name Judah is that there might not be a question of *secondary addition of* "and Levi" in the *Testaments* at all, as is often thought, for if this were the case one would expect the editor to have consistently added the word "Levi" *before* "Judah" in order to more closely conform his text to the Levitical messianology of the rest of the *Testaments* (if that is indeed what he wished to do). Thus the conclusion that references to a messiah from Levi and Judah allude to the same kind of messiah-from-the-elect as in the other writings, particularly the messiah(s) from Aaron and Israel

---

Levi will be preeminent among the tribes, Judah second. A reference to a conquering Levi is found in *TSim.* 5:4-6, but this is certainly intended to allude to the Maccabees as argued above.

134. Hultgård has pointed to evidence from the Hebrew Scriptures and other pre-Hasmonean writings for an attribution of royal prerogatives to the priesthood (1977, 1:37-38, 44). This, however, does not amount to an attribution of royal prerogatives to a Levitical messiah *per se*.

135. Cf. Hollander and de Jonge, 1985, 61. A future priest is spoken of in *TLevi* 18:9ff., but he is nowhere called a "messiah," or given any of the other traditional messianological features. In that one passage alone can it be said that a *broadly* messianic view of a coming priest can be discerned.

136. Three out of six times, according to Hollander and de Jonge, 1985, 41.

at Qumran, remains a strong possibility. This (single) messiah in the *Testaments* would appear to be the traditional royal messiah.

The only alternative theory with any merit is that the messiah is to arise *through* one parent from Levi and one from Judah. The evidence presented above has suggested that this is not what is intended. But certainly the best evidence that what we have here is a messiah originating from the Judah-Levi community is that the same kind of distinctively *corporate* messianology that is evident in other writings can be found in messianic passages in the *Testaments* also. *TDan* 5:10-12 is one of these passages:

> And there shall arise *for you* from the tribe of Judah and Levi the Lord's salvation.
> He will make war against Beliar;
> he will grant the *vengeance of victory as our goal.*[137]
> And he shall take from Beliar the *captives, the souls of the saints;*
> and he shall turn the hearts of the *disobedient ones* to the Lord,
> and grant eternal peace *to those who call upon him.*
> And *the saints shall refresh themselves* in Eden;
> *the righteous shall rejoice* in the New Jerusalem. . . .

The words in italics highlight the way the messiah is intimately related to the readers of the testament — cf. the "saints," the "righteous," "those who call upon him," etc. The messiah will vindicate them by bringing vengeance on their enemies, releasing the righteous from bondage, and converting the "disobedient ones." He shall give Eden, the new Jerusalem, *to them.* To this evidence can be added *TLevi* 18:8-14, which in its present form refers to a Levitical messiah (but cf. comments above):

> For he shall give the majesty of the Lord to *those who are his sons in truth forever.* . . .
> And in his priesthood the nations shall be multiplied in knowledge on the earth, . . .
> but *Israel shall be diminished by her ignorance*
> and *darkened by her grief.*
> In his priesthood sin shall cease
> and lawless men shall rest from their evil deeds,
> and *righteous men shall find rest in him.*
> And he shall open the gates of paradise;

---

137. The emendation πέρασιν to πατράσιν, "victorious vengeance to *our fathers,*" as suggested by Hollander and de Jonge (1985, 286 n. 19), is not required to make sense of the verse. The victory here is that of the righteous, who typically appear as the instruments of vengeance.

he shall remove the sword that has threatened since Adam,
and he will grant to *the saints* to eat of the tree of life.
The spirit of holiness shall be *upon them.*
And Beliar shall be bound by him.
And he shall grant *to his children* the authority to trample on wicked spirits.
And the Lord will rejoice *in his children;*
he will be well pleased by *his beloved ones* forever. . . .
. . . all *the saints* shall be clothed in righteousness.

If this passage is not wholly a Christian addition (its ideas are not completely foreign to the kind of Jewish thought already encountered in these writings), it again witnesses to the kind of corporate messianology we have been uncovering. *The messiah has his origin in the community of the saints; he serves their needs and brings them salvation and vindication.* The rest of Israel would appear to be judged by him on behalf of the saints ("Israel shall be diminished"; "lawless men shall rest from their evil deeds"; etc.).

In view of such texts, it would appear that there is scarcely a *clearer* example of corporate messianology than that found in the *Testaments*.[138] The formulation (messiah from) "Levi and Judah" recalls the similar expression "messiah of Aaron and Israel" in its original and fundamental association with the corporate body of the righteous. If the community did not actually refer to itself as "Levi and Judah," they at least clearly felt themselves to be the only ones who held faithfully to the ideals associated with the names of those two tribes.

The Messiah in the *Psalms of Solomon*

While the *Psalms of Solomon* hardly evidence anything like a preoccupation with a messiah (in psalms like the eighth and eleventh where we might expect a messiah, God himself promises to bring deliverance), evidence of a quite "traditional" — namely, nationalistic, eschatological, and political-royal — messiah can be clearly discerned in the seventeenth and eighteenth psalms (17:4-6, 21-42; 18:5-9). It is arguable, however, that this Davidic messiah is quite pacifistic in contrast to other more militant conceptions,[139] revealing again the variety

---

138. Significantly there are signs that Christian editing elsewhere in the *Testaments* has actually *individualized* the originally corporate messianology! This can be seen in the differences between the Aram. and Gk. recensions of *TJos.* 19:11, and in the Christian additions to *TNaph.* 8:3.

139. Cf. de Jonge ("The Expectation of the Future in the Psalms of Solomon," in de Jonge, 1991, 3-27, 12), who points to Deut. 17:16-17 as one possible source of this nonmilitant messiah.

in expression of the belief and significantly qualifying our use of the word "traditional" for this messiah. References to Israel and to a national type of messiah do nevertheless seem to indicate the author's respect for more traditional ideas. The messiah is called "the son of David" (17:21); he is invoked to rule over God's servant Israel (17:21), judging the unrighteous rulers (of the nations, 17:22) and the "gentiles" who trampled Jerusalem (17:22), to rule with an "iron rod," and to "destroy the unlawful nations with the word of his mouth" (17:24); the nations "will flee from his presence; / and he will condemn sinners by the thoughts of their hearts" (17:25). He will "judge peoples and nations in the wisdom of his righteousness" (17:29).

It is certainly not insignificant, however, that references to a traditional type of messiah are joined by others that relate the coming of the messiah *to the particular situation of the community*.[140] We have noted on several occasions the exclusivistic tone of the seventeenth and eighteenth psalms in their reference to the righteous community. Psalm 17 traces the overthrow of a counterfeit Israelite monarchy in favor of that promoted by the community (vv. 3-9), lashes out at the covenantal infidelity of the ruling group and applauds their deserved judgment (vv. 14-15, 18-20), all the while contrasting this fate with the story of the escape of the righteous from Jerusalem (vv. 16-18). Psalm 18 continues by contrasting the judgment of the wicked with the beneficial discipline of the righteous (vv. 1-9) and by eulogizing the solar calendar of the sect (vv. 10-12). This dualistic polemic is not insignificantly applied to the messiah as well, not only in the hope that he will "drive out . . . the *sinners* from the *inheritance*" (17:23; a clear reference to the apostate regime) but also in the more positive function of gathering a "holy people whom he will lead in righteousness" (17:26) and by references to the righteous and spiritual nature of his rule over his people (17:26-28, 33-34, 41-42). While a traditional restoration eschatology is found in the seventeenth psalm, the writer's awareness of the less-than-ideal state of affairs in Israel leads him to insist that the messiah "will not tolerate unrighteousness even to pause among them, / and any person who knows wickedness shall not live with them" (17:27); "there will be no unrighteousness among them in his days, / for all shall be holy, / and their king shall be the Lord Messiah"[141] (17:32); "he will expose officials and drive out sinners" (17:36, 39). A consideration of how such "nationalistic" emphases can be regularly preserved in expressions of hope in a future restoration, even among

---

140. De Villiers (1978, 80) also discerns a fading of the nationalistic expectations, although he credits this to the adoption of more universal ideas in these psalms.

141. Gk. χριστός κύριος. Cf. *Pss. Sol.* 18:5, χριστοῦ αὐτοῦ; 18:7, χριστοῦ κυρίου; title, ΤΟΥ ΧΡΙΣΤΟΥ ΚΥΡΙΟΥ. De Jonge takes 17:32 to be a translator's error for what should be χριστός κυρίου, "the Anointed of the Lord" (1991b, 10, 14-15, 21 n. 25), although others have offered Ps. 110:1, the use of κύριος for pagan kings like Herod and Agrippa I and II, and the rabbinic expression "King Messiah" as parallels to the present Gk. reading.

groups otherwise dominated by a highly exclusive soteriology, will be delayed until the next chapter. It is obvious, however, even from these few references, that the messiah of these psalms is the Vindicator and Restorer of the writer's community and of its beliefs and values, and in many important features provides another example of a messiah-for-the-elect.

Enoch — Son of Man in the Similitudes (*1 Enoch* 37–71)

The books and articles that have been written on the Son of man could fill a good-sized library. Thankfully we are exempt from dealing with the most perplexing issues here — notably those bearing on the use of the Son of man terminology in the New Testament, particularly relating to the so-called circumlocutionary approach.[142] With one possible exception, discussed below, "Son of man" is not a circumlocution in the Similitudes but a messianic designation applied to an individual. The clearest evidence for the essentially Jewish nature of the work, as well as the individual attribution of the Son of man title, is the identification of "this Son of man" with Enoch in the concluding chapters. Despite protests to the contrary, the message of these chapters is essential to the messianology of the whole, and theories that the final chapters were added at a later time[143] fail to recognize the dramatic nature of the presentation, for these chapters merely complete an identification that is hinted at throughout the developing "plot," even before it is established in the rather more decisive revelatory theophany in the concluding passages of the book (note comments on the citations below).[144] The work would accordingly seem to be dominated by its intention to present the hero of the movement — no one other than Enoch — as the one who has been given the role of judging the world at the end of time, a message that would be quite incomplete without chs. 70–71.[145] No precedent exists for such an association of the messiah with

---

142. For a recent helpful survey of the major issues, see C. C. Caragounis, *The Son of Man*, 1986, 9-33.

143. Cf., e.g., Caragounis (1986, 93-94), whose theory admits that there is hidden/revealed portrayal in the Similitudes (114-15) but posits that the final identification is not made.

144. M. Casey, *The Son of Man*, 1979, 102.

145. The chief argument for the independence of these chapters seems to be the contrast in content with ch. 69 (as cf. Black, 1985, 250). However, the translation of Enoch is not only appropriate as a closing for the work, it also repeats many of the themes of the early part of the book, particularly chs. 46–48. For a recent reassessment of the question that falls heavily on the side of the authenticity of these chapters, cf. J. C. VanderKam, "Righteous One, Messiah, Chosen One, and Son of Man in 1 Enoch 37–71," 1992, 178-85.

Enoch in Christian circles,[146] although significantly this would appear to have occurred elsewhere in Enochian circles in Judaism.[147]

It is for this and several other equally compelling reasons that one really must conclude that Similitudes is a pre-Christian writing from about the turn of the eras. However, the question of dating is not as crucial as the fact that one finds here an example of *essentially Jewish* and, it should be emphasized, *"sectarian"* speculation on the Son of man thematic.[148] Our use of the term "Enoch–Son of man" for this figure is accordingly deliberate, for it both reflects the direct identification of Enoch with the Son of man and, perhaps more importantly, avoids judgments about the relationship of the Similitudes' use of Son of man terminology to the use made by the Hebrew Scriptures or the Gospels. Matters of origin or possible direction of influence are thus left out of consideration. Whether at the time the Similitudes were written there were already circulating ideas regarding an "apocalyptic son of man figure" is another important question,[149] but a solution to this is not essential to our discussion (ac-

146. Cf. G. Bampfylde, "The Similitudes of Enoch," 1984, 9-31, esp. 10. For the view that the Similitudes is not the exception to this, cf. J. C. Greenfield and M. E. Stone, "The Enochic Pentateuch and the Date of the Similitudes," 1977, 57.

147. Casey, 1979, 103-6; Black, 1985, 188-89.

148. While space precludes adequate treatment here, our chief reasons for this conclusion include: (1) discussions of historical allusions in the Similitudes have not favored a second-century-A.D. date as relegated to them by J. C. Hindley ("Towards a Date for the Similitudes of Enoch," 1968, 551-65) and, if anything, suggest a first-century-B.C. date; cf. Greenfield and Stone, 1977, 51-65, 58-60; D. W. Suter, *Tradition and Composition in the Parables of Enoch,* 1979, 24ff.; Bampfylde, 1984, 9-31, 25-26; Black, 1985, 187; Caragounis, 1986, 90-91; (2) the failure to find copies of Similitudes among the DSS is an argument from silence (cf. Greenfield and Stone, 55-57, 63) — Similitudes may have been produced by representatives of an Enoch sect not directly associated with the authors of the other Enoch books or, alternatively, the compiler of Enoch books at Qumran (or some predecessor in this process) may simply have ignored Similitudes (which, moreover, may have been written at some time subsequent to the Qumran collation); (3) there is a noticeable relationship of concerns between Similitudes and *1 Enoch,* notably the solar calendar, but many more as well; (4) these same concerns are significantly Jewish in relevance (calendar, Noachic theology, and soteriological dualism, among others); (5) there is significant evidence that the social function of the writing coheres with that of the other writings we have been investigating; and particularly (6) the function of parables as a revelatory medium that exhibits a strong element of soteriological dualism. All other arguments aside, the emerging consensus within Similitudes scholarship *strongly favors* (a return to) recognition of their pre-Christian Jewish provenance; cf. F. H. Borsch, "Further Reflections on 'the Son of Man,'" 1992, 130-44, 141; M. Black, "The Messianism of the Parables of Enoch," 1992, 145-68, 162-68; VanderKam, 1992, 169-91.

149. It is widely denied by, e.g., Casey (1979, 112). The concept was maintained by Mowinckel (1956, 351ff.), who posited that the Danielic conception must be based on earlier ideas, which are better expressed in the Similitudes than in Daniel.

tually we believe that Similitudes represents a somewhat original usage of the terminology), and so we will not directly address that matter either. We wish only to consider, in relative isolation from other concerns, this one important example of pre-Christian (or at least non-Christian) Jewish messianology for its own sake.

While our interest, therefore, is not in lines of influence and development *per se*, we assume with the large majority of scholars that the Similitudes have been heavily influenced by Daniel 7[150] — this relationship is evident in the use of the term "Son of man" (despite the unique forms in which we find the expression),[151] in the many literary relationships throughout the chapters,[152] as well as in the adoption of several incidental details from Daniel 7.[153] Whether the expression "like a Son of man" in Daniel 7 itself is to be interpreted of a "messianic" personage is not entirely relevant.[154] It has been argued, and is otherwise obvious, that the author of the Similitudes interpreted the expression messianically by employing his own hermeneutical criteria, however misguided they may seem to us. It must be remembered that Jewish exegetical procedure often ignored the linguistic restraints considered

150. Cf. Suter, 1979, 13; Casey, 1979, 99ff.; Black, 1992, 146; *contra* Mowinckel (1956, 353), who traces the ideas in *1 Enoch* to more ancient Man-speculation.

151. Casey, 1979, 103. As is frequently noted, the Ethiopic translator of the Similitudes always includes the demonstrative with the expression ("*this* 'Son of Man,'" etc.). This can be explained simply from the fact that the article is lacking in the Eth. language, the demonstrative being added to represent an original article by the translator (cf., e.g., Mowinckel, 1956, 362; Casey, 103; Black, 1985, 206; Caragounis, 1986, 106 n. 115); the demonstrative form is used in this way to translate ὁ υἱὸς τοῦ ἀνθρώπου in the Eth. versions of the Gospels (cf. Mowinckel, 362; F. H. Borsch, *The Son of Man in Myth and History*, 1967, 147). We prefer the view that the demonstrative with "Son of man" also refers back to the figure introduced originally in 46:3 or, more likely, to the vision in Daniel itself (7:13-14). In regard to the latter possibility, Black explains the demonstrative as a "self-referring pronoun" at 69:26, 29, and 71:17, rendering αὐτὸς ὁ υἱὸς ἀνθρώπου — i.e., "a familiar Semitic locution . . . referring to an important personage" (207). Casey demonstrates how the absence of the demonstrative in every case of translating "the Elect one" in the Similitudes proves that its use here was not a stylistic option used in translation — it must have been extant in the original (100; although Black, 206-7, is quick to point out that this does not apply for the Eth. translation of the Gospels). This use of the demonstrative to draw associations serves well the movement of the plot and the final revelation of Enoch as Son of man, as we will see (cf. also Caragounis, 95, 105-10).

152. Delineated by Caragounis, 1986, 101-9; cf. also Borsch, 1967, 149.

153. Cf. Casey, 1979, 110.

154. For the view that the Son of man is Israel, cf. Mowinckel, 1956, 350; Schiffman, 1987, 238; for the messianic interpretation, cf. Caragounis, 1986, 45-48, 61-81; Borsch, who relates the figure to Royal Ascension motifs (1967, passim, chiefly 135-44).

important by moderns (the rabbinic *middoth* providing clear evidence of this), and that there would therefore have been little to prevent the Similitudes' literal or concrete application of what was originally intended only as a symbol in Daniel.[155] Moreover, "Son of man" is employed with such variety elsewhere in the Hebrew Scriptures as to suggest that our writer possessed plenty of precedent to justify his own decidedly titular application. This possibility obtains even in the absence of a current Son of man theology, but is enhanced by the probability that in some quarters the phrase was already in use, if not as a full-blown messianic title, then at least as a "fixed expression" — to borrow the term of Maurice Casey.[156] Regardless of *our* linguistic distinctions, in other words, the Son of man "expression" is solicited by this writer in order to serve his particular messianic views. That this author considered "Son of man" a messianic title is not in doubt. The repeated intermingling of Son of man terminology with titles like "the Elect One," and especially "the Anointed," perhaps also "the Righteous One," provides important evidence that this terminology was being related (perhaps in novel ways) to other messianic beliefs.[157]

The notion of a Son of man as presented by Daniel would have been extremely well suited to the concerns of an exclusivistic group such as produced the Similitudes. As is commonly known, the "(one like a) Son of man" (Dan. 7:13) is closely matched up, in the Danielic vision, with "(the people of) the *saints* of the Most High" who are mentioned later in the same chapter (vv. 21-22, 25, 27). This latter phrase actually seems to serve as a rather enigmatic inter-

---

155. If, in fact, any abuse of linguistic convention has taken place at all! Cf. Black: "It is a capital error to assume that Heb. בן־אדאם or Aram. בר־(א)נשא, '*the* Son of man,' could not be used as a designation or with titular force for a particular individual, especially for one of a class 'where usage has elevated into distinctive prominence a particular individual of the class.' . . . The designation or title '*the* Son of man' to refer to the Daniel figure of 'one like a son of man,' could as well be used in Aram. or Heb. and with the same force as ὁ υἱὸς τοῦ ἀνθρώπου" (1985, 207). Collins (1995, 185) distinguishes between two types of "apocalyptic symbols," allegorical (interpreted symbol) and "mythic-realistic" (identified symbol), and suggests that in 4 Ezra the Son of man is a mythic-realistic symbol for the messiah whereas in Daniel 7 it is still an allegory. But why could this distinction not also apply in the original Daniel 7 vision?

156. Casey, 1979, 104. Cf. also Caragounis, 1986, 28; Black, 1985, 207. R. N. Longenecker (1970, 86 n. 103) points out that the wording "one *like* a Son of man" (כבר אנש) in Daniel need not have prevented a titular use of the expression, inasmuch as ὁμοίον υἱὸν ἀνθρώπου was employed as a title in Revelation, and the terminology of "likeness" can be found with christological implications elsewhere (e.g., ὁμοίωμα in Phil. 2:7 and ἀφομιόω in Heb. 7:3).

157. Black, 1985, 189; Caragounis, 1986, 95, 105-10. For the complexity of this composite messianic figure, and possible sources, cf. VanderKam, 1992, 185-91.

pretation of "one like a Son of man" in the closing interpretative section of the vision,[158] and even though an identification of the two phrases may not have been intended by the original author, an association between the Son of man and some "saints" is nevertheless *invited* by the present form of the text. It would accordingly not be surprising if interpretative adaptations of the entire Daniel vision such as one finds in the Similitudes were quite common within sectarian contexts, for the very reason of the narrowly particularistic messianology produced by this identification. The so-called Son of God text from Cave 4 may point to one other group that appreciated the identification. This text, heavily influenced by the thought of Daniel 7, transmits with a certain awkwardness, and in close proximity to one another, references both to the "people" and to the Son of man as if the author recognized but did not know how to explain the identity between the two.[159]

This would suggest that the use of the terminology by these groups did not imply some abstract "apocalyptic" seeking for a heavenly figure in contrast to a Davidic materialistic messianology, as is often suggested;[160] our movement was involved in exegesis and was merely capitalizing on what they took to be a firmly established connection between the Son of man and the "saints." Such a connection is in fact suggested in the final words of the Similitudes: "So there shall be length of days *with that Son of Man,* and *peace to the righteous ones;* his path is upright *for the righteous,* in the name of the Lord of the Spirits forever and ever" (71:17).

To further observe how the Similitudes draws upon this identification between the saints and the Son of man, one need only follow the dramatic plot from its beginning to its climactic conclusion in chs. 70–71, noting the various ways the relationships between Enoch–Son of man and the righteous are emphasized throughout. A listing of all the relevant passages follows:

158. Besides those theories that see a direct equation of the two, cf. H. W. Robinson, who described this relationship in terms of "corporate personality" (*Corporate Personality in Ancient Israel,* 1980, 29-30). Cf. also Borsch, 1967, 144; for vindication motifs related to this, cf. N. Perrin, "The Son of Man in Ancient Judaism and Primitive Christianity," 1966, 17-28; Casey, 1979, 24-25, 39-42; Caragounis, 1986, 115-19.

159. Indeed, the identity is implicitly, if awkwardly, made: "People will crush people, and nation nation, until the *people of God* arises and causes everyone to rest from the sword. *His* Kingdom will be an Eternal Kingdom, and *he* will be Righteous in all his Ways" (4Q246). While the messiah is clearly intended in the latter words of this passage, we interpret the claim to be the "son of God" in the text as representing the hubris of a Gentile king rather than as a self-designation of the messiah. Cf. the approach of Flusser (1988, 207-13) with that of Eisenman and Wise (1992, 70-71).

160. Borsch (1967, 155) argues the very opposite when he suggests that the Son of man conforms in many ways to Davidic royal messianology.

- In 37:4 we read the enigmatic statement that Enoch has been granted "the lot of eternal life," which, as with similar statements about the *moreh ṣedeq* in the scrolls, suggests that he is able to dispense the knowledge of eternal life to his group of disciples.[161]
- In 38:2-3 we read of the "Righteous One" who "shall appear before the face of the righteous, / those elect ones," a paramount example of the combination of appellatives used to express the leader/people consolidation.[162] His function is typically to "reveal light to the righteous" while judging the "sinners"/"those who deny the name of the Lord of the Spirits." The soteriological dualism implied by this contrast of terms is both evident and significant.
- In 39:6 we read further of "the Elect One of righteousness"[163] who, it is clearly implied, is in company with "the elect ones . . . without number *before him*." The "Elect One"/"elect ones" consolidation is again worthy of note.
- In 45:3-6 we read of the function of the "Elect One" to judge, and especially to vindicate, the righteous. He shall "dwell *among them*." The express purpose of this judgment role is also given: "For in peace I have looked (with favor) upon my righteous ones and given them mercy. / . . . / But sinners have come before me so that by judgment / I shall destroy them from before the face of the earth." Thus we have another clear expression of soteriological dualism related to the functions of the messiah.
- Chs. 46–47 begin the vision of the Son of man *per se*, who, by the roles described here, can be identified with the Elect One and Righteous One of the previous chapters (i.e., Enoch). Daniel 7 is given a messianic interpretation.[164] The chief function of the Son of man is to judge (46:4-

161. The same ambiguity of meaning for "the lot" exists here as at Qumran. V. 3 and the first part of v. 4 say that "wisdom" had not been "given" (√ *wahaba*) to Enoch at an earlier time, but now the "lot of eternal life" has been "given" (√ *wahaba*) to him, suggesting a parallel between "wisdom" and "lot of eternal life." Perhaps the combination of the ideas of names written in books with "everlasting life" and "the wise" in Dan. 12:2-3 has given birth to the complex idea of the "lot of eternal life" that includes the idea of the people as much as that of wisdom leading to salvation.

162. Cf. Mowinckel, 1956, 378-79.

163. The close parallels between the "elect ones" and the "Elect One" have created confusion in the MSS. We agree here with Black (1985, 197) against M. A. Knibb (*The Ethiopic Book of Enoch*, 1978, 2:126), preferring the singular reading for reasons of suitability to the context. All MSS also read *qedmēhu*, "before him," which demands a singular antecedent.

164. Although it is not stated explicitly that his mission involves delivering the righteous, this is implied throughout the whole passage. That his time of appearance is the final judgment is evident from (e.g.) the opening of the books. That the passage is based on Daniel 7, cf. Black, 1985, 206. Cf. 46:1 for strong literary parallels.

8),[165] apparently in response to the prayers of the "righteous" (ch. 47), who are also called "the faithful ones" (46:8). The whole world of angels will congregate together to join in prayers of vindication for these righteous ones (47:2) who will be avenged (vv. 3-4).[166]

- In 48:1-10 we read that the Son of man was "given a name" before creation, apparently anticipating the later identification with Enoch in chs. 70–71 and implying that this identification was predetermined.[167] Anticipatory also is the statement that "the wisdom of the Lord of Spirits *has revealed him* to the holy and righteous" (v. 7).[168] His function as the messiah-of-the-elect is thus also made explicit. Similarly: *"He will become a staff for the righteous ones in order that they may lean on him and not fall"* (v. 4). The messianic status of the Son of man as Servant of the Lord is indicated by a reference to "the light of the gentiles" (v. 4) and "He will become the hope of those who are sick in their hearts" (v. 4; cf. Isa. 61:1-2). He is referred to as "the Chosen One" who also reveals secrets to the "righteous and the holy ones" (vv. 6-7). "For *this purpose* he became the Chosen One" seems to refer to his role as messiah-of-the-elect (vv. 1-2, 4) or his role as light of the Gentiles (v. 4), or to his worthiness as an object of reverence (v. 5). The righteous "will be saved in his name and it is his good pleasure that they have life" (v. 7). The mighty, in contrast, will be unable to save themselves (v. 8). Not only will the Son of man exercise judgment, but the sinners will also be delivered "into the hands of my elect ones" (v. 9) who are agents and, typically, witnesses of this fiery judgment (of Israel in Gehenna?). The mighty "have denied the Lord of

---

165. That Israel is involved in this judgment is evident from v. 8.

166. The final *faqada* in the verse means "to wish," "desire," "seek," "consider," "require," etc.; *tafaqda* (pass.), "be necessary"; (Isaac, *OTP*, 1:35, "admitted"). Black (1985, 210) suggests a mistranslation of בקש, "seek" (originally intended to mean "require," as to "require blood of the righteous"; cf. v. 4), and thus "avenge."

167. Naming might imply only ownership or commissioning (Black, 1985, 210), but its mention here may also look forward to the announcement of the identity of the name, an identity previously held secretly (62:5-9) but now revealed to be Enoch (cf. 71:14). It is also said that "through his name they shall be saved" (50:3). Real confirmation that "name" means title or designation, rather than ownership, however, comes with 69:27, where it is said that "the name of that (Son of) Man was revealed to them," and 70:1, where the name of the Son of man (or Enoch; see below) was "raised up." Black himself recognizes the possibility that "name" has this function of identifying Enoch (cf. 250 n. 1).

168. *wakašato laqeddusān waṣādeqān ṭebabu la'egzi'a manāfest* — clearly: "And the wisdom of the Lord of Spirits has revealed him to the holy and righteous ones." This translation (also cf. Black and Knibb) is clearly superior to that of Isaac: "he (Enoch) has revealed the wisdom of the Lord of the Spirits to the righteous and holy ones."

the Spirits[169] *and his Messiah*" (v. 10), perhaps suggesting that deliberate and active identification with the Enoch-messiah has soteriological implications in this book.

- In 49:1-4 the Son of man is the possessor of wisdom. In these verses the relationship between messiah and people is spiritualized: "In him dwells the spirit of wisdom . . . and the spirit of those who have fallen asleep in righteousness" (v. 3).[170] This rather unusual expression seems to identify the people and their messiah particularly closely. If we are to accept the text as it stands, the emphasis in the first part of the verse on wisdom, insight, and understanding would seem to suggest that what the righteous share with the Son of man is a common "spirit of enlightenment" rather than some metaphysical relationship, although perhaps the latter is intended here also.[171] The messiah being called "the Elect One" again implies an association of all the Elect One references with the Son of man (v. 2). He is the judge of the "secret things" that have been made known to the righteous alone (v. 4).

- In 50:1-5 the same themes are repeated, and the mutual relationship between the elect and their messiah is again emphasized along with the vindication of the elect in contrast to the rejection of sinners. "He heaped evil upon the sinners; but the righteous ones shall be victorious . . ." (v. 2). Significantly the possibility of repentance is held out to "the others" (who seem to be Gentiles)[172] who look on and see the judgment: "through his name they shall be saved, and the Lord of the Spirits shall have mercy upon them, for his mercy is considerable" (v. 3); but it is never forgotten that "the unrepentant in his presence shall perish. . . . he will not have mercy upon them" (vv. 4-5).

- In 52:1-9 the messiah exercises his cosmic powers in transforming the world in the End. No indication of other functions can be found.

- In 53:6-7, immediately following a description of judgment, we discover

---

169. The expression is, significantly, antithetically parallel to "believ[ing] in the name of the Lord of the Spirits" (43:4; Black, 1985, 195). Scriptures that may have inspired this expression, such as Isa. 59:13 and Jer. 5:12, refer to the apostasy of *Israel*. For the view that the kings and mighty in the Similitudes are apostates, cf. Volz, 1934, 22-23.

170. The passage is an adaptation of Isa. 11:2 and a possible corruption (Black, 1985, 212-13). The new emphasis on the righteous comrades of the Son of man seems entirely appropriate — however unclear the thought may be.

171. Cf. Mowinckel, 1956, 377.

172. Black (1985, 213) takes this to be a translation of אחרים in the sense of aliens and foreigners, i.e., Gentiles. This is particularly significant in indicating that the chief object of the author's words of judgment are Israelites; when they are punished, even Gentile onlookers will repent.

that "the Righteous and Elect One will *reveal the house of his congregation*. . . . And the righteous ones shall have rest from the oppression of sinners." It is clear that the righteous in the righteous/sinners dualism compose "the house of his congregation."[173] Here a building motif is employed to restrict the "congregation" to the members of the writer's group or, as the case may be, to all others considered to compose the righteous. That they are "revealed" implies that they are vindicated by being proven righteous — that is, shown to be "in the right," to "have the right way," to be legitimate sons of God. It is revealed that these, and none other, are the true Israelites. Their revealing thus also matches that of their messiah, the Son of man. Here the limitation of the messiah's (positive) influence to the righteous Israel-within-Israel is made abundantly clear.

- In 60:10 "Son of man" is used for the only time in this book as a circumlocution for Enoch. This probably evidences no more than a freedom and inexactitude in the use of expressions typical of our writer, if it is not in fact a secondary interpretation by the translator, for "Son of man" as a title still dominates in this work. Otherwise the coincidence of phraseology would appear at best to be somewhat subconscious here; it may deliberately anticipate the identification of Enoch with Son of man in chs. 70–71.

- In 62:5-9, a passage heavily influenced by Daniel 7, "Son of man"[174] is said to have been "concealed from the beginning," but God later "revealed him to the holy and elect ones. The congregation of the holy ones shall be planted, and all the elect ones shall stand before him." When exactly this revealing is thought to have taken place is not clear, although the fact that he is here revealed to the readers of the Similitudes would suggest that he has been revealed to all the righteous (and only the righteous) throughout time, to those, that is, who have preserved and adhered to Enoch's special revelation. We also read in this passage that the rulers of the world will seek his mercy, but circumstances will deny them this mercy (vv. 9-10). These were the oppressors of the "elect ones" (v. 11). The "righteous and elect," on the other hand, will be saved and wear the "garments of glory" (vv. 13-16). Again the messiah is seen to function as the Savior specifically of the elect. This is highlighted in the moving statement of v. 14,

---

173. It is not any temple that is referred to here, unless as a metaphor itself for the righteous community. Black traces the expression back to כנסת in the sense of "assembly" (1985, 209); cf. בית הכנסת. The Qumran בית יחד or בית קדוש may be considered as parallels.

174. Black maintains that the omission of the demonstrative here definitely points to the titular use of "Son of man" (1985, 207).

that "the righteous and elect ones . . . shall eat and rest and rise *with that Son of Man* forever and ever."

- In 69:27 we read that the "name of the Man (or Son of Man)"[175] was revealed to "them."[176] That Enoch is in mind here is evident because it is said of him that "he shall never pass away or perish from before the face of the earth" — anticipating the translation (*as per* Gen. 5:24). In v. 29 the references to Daniel 7 are so strong as to indicate once again the importance of this passage to the whole drama.

This brings us to that important climax, 70:1–71:17, where Enoch is explicitly identified with "that Son of man" (note esp. 71:14).[177] How this identification is possible when the two figures are portrayed in the visionary material as having separate existences (cf. 70:1) is not made clear. Did Enoch only *become* the Son of man (which would appear to be the thrust of 48:6)? Or was he the Son of man from the beginning, who is now suddenly revealed (to himself and others) to be Son of man (which would seem to be implied by the course of argument of the

175. According to Black (1985, 207), instances of "the Man," where they occur (possibly here and at 71:14), are another indication of a titular use.

176. According to the present reading, "them" would appear to be the cosmic forces or heavenly bodies mentioned in vv. 16-25, although Black (1985, 249) suggests that vv. 26-29 have been removed from their original context and placed here (as it is difficult to imagine these natural things "believing" in v. 25). It is also possible that vv. 16-26 were inserted, or formed a natural parenthetical section, making the antecedent of "them" the "children of the people" in v. 15. Vv. 16-26 might be a parenthetical passage dealing with the enigmatic "oath." The problem with this view is that it is not certain that "children of the people" refers to the elect; it may well refer to the rest of Israel. In either case "them" would refer to the elect, in line with the use of the pronoun elsewhere in *1 Enoch*.

177. Admittedly there may be room for debate here, inasmuch as 71:14, at the point where the identification is made, employs a different phrase (in the Eth.) for "Son of man" than the other passages, and this phrase could well be circumlocutional (cf. Mowinckel, 1956, 443-44). On the other hand, several considerations militate against this or, at least, against the importance of this: (1) the relating of the Son of man with the "Antecedent of Time," and other literary expressions, indicates that Daniel 7 is still clearly in mind; (2) other messianic salutations are directed at Enoch (cf. "who are born in righteousness" with צמח צדקה of Jer. 23:5; 33:15; cf. Black, 1985, 252); (3) Enoch is granted an exalted status in line with previous similar statements directed at the Son of man; (4) there would likely have been no difference in wording in a Semitic original; (5) 62:5 and 69:27 clearly employ this expression of the messiah (and it is, all in all, the more natural of the renderings in Eth. En. for the expression used in Daniel). Cf. further reasons in Black (206-7). Slight variations in wording such as we have here (if reflecting the original) may have been intended to increase the enigma and mystery of the whole presentation, a calculated stylistic device that has the dramatic effect of putting a little mystery back into what is otherwise an abundantly clear revelation.

whole book)? In either case the identification of Enoch with the Son of man at the end of the book would not have come as a total surprise to the readers — not only because hints had been offered throughout the writing that the identification was forthcoming, but also because Enoch was eminently suited for the role as preexistent heavenly figure and quasi-divine messiah, enjoying an unending life because of his translation, participating fully in the heavenly goings-on. When in ch. 70 we are informed of the fictional time frame (literary context) of the revelation vis-à-vis the historical lifetime of Enoch, we see that it takes place immediately before Enoch's translation, a very appropriate occasion for this identification of Enoch as "Son of man." This revelation of Enoch as the Son of man fits in perfectly with the increasing drama of the plot throughout the Similitudes, which dwells on the dichotomy of the essential and original *hiddenness* of the Son of man contrasted with his *revelation to the righteous*.[178] As essentially eclectic revelation this dramatic framework is entirely suitable, just as are the ambiguities resident in the linguistic adaptability of the term "Son of man" itself. To understand the mysteries associated with his identity requires some insight: this insight is the possession of the elect alone.

To summarize and conclude, one can see how this author, through the drama of the translation of Enoch, and through reflection on his hiddenness and revelation, aims to honor this important figure. One can also see how his view of the messiah (for which he borrows the Son of man formulation) is colored entirely by his soteriological dualism. Significantly, even after the important identification has been made, the book continues to present the messiah-for-the-elect theme in emphatic form. To Enoch–Son of man it is announced:

> "Everyone that will come to exist and walk shall follow *your* path, since *righteousness never forsakes you*. Together with you shall be *their dwelling places; and together with you shall be their portion. They shall not be separated from you forever and ever and ever*." So there shall be length of days with that Son of Man,[179] and *peace to the righteous ones; his path is upright for the righteous*. . . . (71:16-17)

178. VanderKam prefers to see a "hiddenness" motif in the Similitudes rather than one of "preexistence" for Enoch–Son of man (1992, 179-82). Mowinckel: "The central theme in the Similitudes of Enoch is that this secret . . . has now already been revealed to the elect. . . . The full secret and its meaning are hidden from sinners and unknown to them. 'The great privilege of the righteous is that they have learned to know these divine secrets, and thus to know the Son of Man also'" (1956, 385, 7). For other examples of this hidden/revealed motif, cf. 4 Ezra 7:28-29; 12:32; 13:26. Was Isa. 49:2 a possible source for this view?

179. The Eth. has "that son of the offspring of the mother of the living" — i.e., the seed of Adam and Eve (and, after them, Seth), perhaps an allusion to the Son of man as *bar-Enosh* (Eve's grandson and the son of Seth; cf. Aram. בר (א)נשא).

Along with the above-quoted 71:14, this passage answers to 46:3 — "This is the Son of Man, to whom belongs righteousness, and with whom righteousness dwells." In contrast to the idea of a nationalistic messiah,[180] the Son of man/ messiah/Enoch is the possession of the righteous alone to whom he has alone been revealed, and who alone benefit from him. They receive wisdom and revelation from him, will be saved by him, will witness and join in his judging action against the unrighteous and sinners, and will dwell with him forever. As progenitor, paradigm, and revealer, Enoch became the special possession of the righteous; so also as messiah is Enoch the messiah-for-the-elect. This connection is further confirmed by the other titles used for him, including "the Righteous One" and "the Elect One," which are entirely appropriate designations for the leader of those similarly named "the righteous ones" and "the elect ones."[181]

Messiah Concepts in 4 Ezra

A variety of designations for a messiah are found in 4 Ezra, but there is no reason to think that more than one figure is intended. While earlier scholars, particularly source critics like Box,[182] attributed the various messianic presentations in this book to two rather carelessly combined sources, one favoring an earthly messianic king from David's line who would deliver Israel from the Romans and the other a transcendent apocalyptic figure who would act as cosmic judge, such an approach has recently been reevaluated. More widely accepted now are the findings of scholars like Michael Stone who have determined that Davidic messianology and Son of man messianology inspired by Daniel 7 are so intimately interwoven in the visions that it is impossible to appeal to sources, or to divide the material in any convincing or helpful manner. While several streams of traditional messianic thought may have played their part in the conglomerate of ideas in 4 Ezra, the author has clearly made them his own in order to present his own message. Once again, therefore, the redactional unity of the book is more or less sustained.[183]

Stone's thesis and article on messianology in 4 Ezra come to two other important conclusions that we can accept as axiomatic for our study: (1) there

---

180. Most scholars are willing to see the Son of man as an embodiment of the transcendent and universal, as opposed to the nationalistic, eschatology. Surprisingly, however, C. Steuernagel ("Die Strukturlinien der Entwicklung der jüdischen Eschatologie," 1950, 481) takes it to be an expression of a *national* eschatology expressed in transcendent terms.

181. Cf. Black, 1992, 150-60, esp. 160; Mowinckel, 1956, 384; CD 3.20; 1QH 10.28; 11.6.

182. Cf., more recently, Caragounis, 1986, 124-25.

183. Cf. also Coggins and Knibb, 1979, 168.

is evidence that the messianology of the author was largely traditional, and that these traditional elements do not express the interests of the author; rather what he does with these ideas, and how he enlarges on them, provides insight into his purposes; (2) messiah ideas themselves are not central to the concerns of the author — they are instruments that serve other concerns: "the Messiah was not the answer to the questions that Ezra was asking. . . . the place of the Messiah in the author's eschatological scheme cannot be doubted, yet it is misleading to see him as the exclusive center of his aspirations."[184] One of Stone's express purposes, accordingly, was to discover the "function" of the messiah "in the total eschatological scheme of the book," but he admits that "the role of the Messiah in the total eschatological thought of IV Ezra is difficult to assess."[185]

Perhaps the above quotes offer a clue to the reason for the impasse in themselves. One might ask, in this connection, why the author's messiah ideas must serve "the total eschatological thought" of the book at all. The emphasis on eschatology is understandable given the history of 4 Ezra scholarship, but in view of our findings we must ask whether this does not allow far too much influence to eschatological categories. One must search for a function for messianology that satisfies the statements made in the book itself. Stone recognizes very few consistent elements running through each of the major presentations of the messiah, but perhaps he has unknowingly struck on an important one when he observes: "The appearance of the assumed together with the Messiah is a consistent feature of IV Ezra. A similar notion is the concept of the Elect Ones seen with the Elect One in heaven or before the Lord found in the Similitudes of Enoch."[186] He repeats much the same observation in a later article:

> In general, while few features of the Messianic figure are found in all passages, most are found in a majority of them and only few are completely contradictory. The Messiah is pre-existent in all texts. Where information is provided, he is expected to take care of the righteous survivors. . . . The term "survivors" is common to all sources where the subject is raised except the vision of chapter 13.[187]

These themes we have seen to be central to the important soteriological dualism of 4 Ezra and of other books, but Stone thinks of them as little more than a

---

184. M. E. Stone, "The Concept of the Messiah in IV Ezra," 1968, 295-312, esp. 312; cf. M. E. Stone, *Features of the Eschatology of IV Ezra*, 1989, 226-27.

185. Stone, 1968, 295, 312.

186. Stone, 1989, 134.

187. Stone, 1968, 310-11; cf. also Stone, 1990, 212-13. For the final statement regarding ch. 13, however, cf. our treatment below.

peculiarity of 4 Ezra: "The particular formulation of the idea of the companions of the Messiah which was observed in IV Ezra was not paralleled elsewhere. The identification with the assumed righteous of those who are to come with the Messiah and the occurrence of these as his companions in heaven were found to be unique in this book."[188] Abundant evidence has already been presented to illustrate that ideas like the association of the messiah with his elect people, his protection and guidance of them, and their eventual vindication through his work of judgment are hardly restricted to 4 Ezra (although, granted, the idea of an *assumption* of the righteous with the messiah might be considered somewhat unique). It is only left to further illustrate how consistent this association is for the various messianic passages in 4 Ezra.

The Servant-Messiah

4 Ezra 7:26-29 mentions a time when the signs will be fulfilled, the new Jerusalem and the new land (or earth) will be revealed, and a select group, elsewhere referred to as "survivors," will be delivered from the evils of the time and "shall see my wonders" (vv. 26-27). Thus both the new land and these "wonders" (rewards or signs?) are prepared for, revealed to, and eventually rewarded to the survivors.[189] At this significant point in the revelation a messianic figure is introduced for the first time in 4 Ezra (vv. 28-29). There remain questions about the original designation here, inasmuch as a Christianizing hand is evident in the Latin text, which reads "my son Jesus" in v. 28 and "my son the messiah" in v. 29. It is to be noted, however, that such tampering has had limited effect on the passage; the duration of the messiah's death, for example, is left at seven days (v. 30), which conflicts with what was certainly universal Christian belief (the messianic era is also given as four hundred, rather than one thousand, years as in Rev. 20:3-4, although this is not quite so compelling an objection). The Syriac and Ethiopic texts have simply "my messiah" in v. 28. It is arguable that the Greek *Vorlage* actually read *pais* (παῖς), which can be rendered "servant" or "child," and Stone accordingly retains the full "my *servant* the messiah"[190] with its allusion to the Isaian Servant Songs.

What is important for our purposes is what is said about this figure: "my servant the messiah shall be revealed *with those who are with him,* and *those who remain* shall rejoice four hundred years" (v. 28). The next verse adds that, following the four hundred years, the messiah will die along with the rest of the

188. Stone, 1989, 228.
189. Stone, 1990, 214-15; for the new land, cf. 9:8; 12:34; 13:48; *2 Bar.* 29:2.
190. Stone, 1989, 75; cf. also Mowinckel, 1956, 294.

world so that "no one shall be *left*" (vv. 29-30). The presentation of the messiah is therefore significantly cloaked in remnant terminology,[191] and the important phrase "those who are with him [i.e., the messiah]" (v. 28) sounds like it might be a conventional phrase for the messiah-of-the-elect in an eschatological context.[192] In fact, the messiah possesses no other outstanding function here, not even that of traditional dispenser of judgment.[193] In light of this, there would appear to have been no other motive for including the figure, since he is in other respects quite dispensable; *he is only a messiah as he is a messiah for his people.*

The Lion-Messiah

Some of the basic features of the eagle vision in 4 Ezra (chs. 11–12) have obviously been inspired by the vision of the four beasts (= four world empires) of Daniel (7:1ff.),[194] although in details there is little resemblance between the two, as in Ezra's version a variety of other biblical and traditional motifs are each in turn allowed to dominate. Daniel's fourth beast becomes an eagle and is interpreted as Rome. A lion — not similar to the lion found in Daniel but clearly a messianic reference inspired by the presence of the Son of man in Daniel — confronts the eagle (11:37–12:1). Extensive symbolic descriptions of the historical situation are also added (11:3-35; 12:13-30), but these, like the above-mentioned details, appear to be largely traditional. The significance of the vision for the author must accordingly be sought in other, more unconventional details, and, as we have proceeded in other instances, the function of the messiah must be determined from additions to or enlargements upon traditional ideas. Dividing the essential from the traditional in this way is complicated somewhat by the fact that a very artistically minded author apparently attempted to create his own rather original symbol for the

191. Note: "everyone who has been delivered"; "those who remain"; "no one shall be left." Stone, 1990, 370.

192. Cf. 1 Thess. 3:13; 2 Thess. 2:1; etc. This connection is noted by Stone (1989, 134; 1990, 215). The context hardly suggests angels here (cf. Stone, 1990, 215 n. 54). The fact that this has parallels with "those who are like you (*sc.* Ezra)" also militates against any other interpretation for either phrase.

193. Judgment is mentioned only in vv. 31ff., which, however, is apparently carried out by the Most High only; cf. vv. 33, 37. De Villiers also notices that the messiah's function in this passage is solely that of bringing revelation and joy to the "survivors" (1978, 91; cf. also Stone, 1990, 215).

194. Casey, 1979, 123; Caragounis, 1986, 123-24; Stone, 1990, 345; 12:11-12; cf. Dan. 7:2ff. This is especially indicated by the way four beasts are alluded to but only the fourth is explained.

messiah while still following in substance the content of the Son of man vision from Daniel. This means that what one interprets as unique to the vision may have possessed only a literary function. Nevertheless, there are indications in this vision of a similar perspective on this messiah as in the passage investigated above.

The lion in the vision does one thing only: he confronts the eagle with strong words of condemnation in the name of the Most High (11:38-46), which words seem eventually to lead to the eagle's destruction (12:1). This castigation includes words of rebuke for the way the eagle has oppressively "held sway over the *world*" (11:40-41). But this is not all, for in the following verses the content of the rebuke narrows considerably — it is Rome's treatment *of the pious* that is the real concern: "you have afflicted *the meek* and injured *the peaceable;* you have hated *those who tell the truth,* and have loved liars; you have destroyed the dwellings of *those who brought forth fruit,* and have laid low the walls of those who did you no harm. And so your insolence has come up before the Most High . . ." (11:42-43). While the "meek" and "peaceable" might refer to Israel as a whole, this would be a rather uncharacteristic way to speak of the whole nation. "Those who tell the truth" and "who brought forth fruit," especially when contrasted with "liars," are more reasonably interpreted as designations for the righteous community.[195] In this passage, therefore, the author seems to be applying traditional Jewish themes in rather unconventional ways, as he implies not only a Rome versus Israel dichotomy but also one between the righteous and the rest of Israel. Apparently the author felt this was a valid interpretation of the Danielic imagery. As for the *Sitz im Leben* of this interpretation, perhaps the author was reacting to collaborations between the Israelite leaders and the Romans that had the effect of putting pressure on the righteous; perhaps he felt there was a conspiracy to silence the pious wing in Judaism; either could be a possible motivation given the history of conflict revealed in ch. 4 above.

If this approach seems doubtful on its own merits, the interpretation passage that follows the vision confirms it. It is worth quoting the entire interpretation passage as regards the lion-messiah:

> And as for the lion that you saw rousing up out of the forest and roaring and speaking to the eagle and reproving him [the eagle] for his unrighteousness, and as for all his words that you have heard, this is the Messiah whom the Most High has kept until the end of days, and who will arise from the posterity of David, and will come and speak[196] to *them* [the posterity of David]; he

---

195. De Villiers, 1978, 93-94.

196. "And who will arise from the prosperity of David, and will come and speak" is from the Syr. The various Lat. MSS attempt to deal with the difficult passage, and while none of them completely represents the Syriac, they all contain the words *ad eos* with

will denounce *them* for *their own* ungodliness and for *their own* wickedness, and will cast up before *them their* contemptuous dealings. For first he will set *them* living before his judgment seat, and when he has reproved *them*, then he will destroy *them*. But he will deliver in mercy *the remnant of my people, those who have been saved throughout my borders*, and he will make them joyful until the end comes, the day of judgment, of which I spoke to you at the beginning. (12:31-34)

Here the Davidic messiah represents the traditional element in the passage.[197] The simple fact that he judges is thus hardly to be taken as particularly significant.[198] One can better discern the author's interests by noting the focus of this important interpretation section. This is no longer upon the *eagle* whom the lion reproves, as in the vision itself, but upon *"them"* — namely, the "posterity of David" — whom the lion also reproves in this passage.[199] It says of "them" that the lion will "speak to" and "denounce" them, "cast up before them their contemptuous dealings," judge, "reprove," and finally "destroy" them. In contrast to this, moreover, the messiah will *deliver* another people, described as "the remnant of my people, those who have been saved throughout my borders," evoking once again the idea of "survivors."[200] The only other thing said about the lion-messiah in the interpretation section is that he will give his remnant-people joy (v. 34). All of this suggests once again that the idea of a messiah-for-the-elect, who is a *vindicator* of the elect and a judge of the remainder of Israel, dominates in the thought of this passage.

---

which our pl. reference begins. Should the Syr. represent an interpolation, the pl. pronouns nevertheless still require a pl. antecedent.

197. Note that knowledge of the Davidic messiah appears to be assumed. The words "this is the Messiah whom the Most High has kept until the end of days, (and who will arise from the posterity of David)" are not interpretation so much as identification; they simply evoke a traditional theme. The lion motif serves the similar purpose of referring to the traditional messiah (cf. Stone, 1990, 368).

198. *Contra* Stone (1989, 108), who takes this to be his most important function.

199. These "them" cannot be the eagle (i.e., Rome; as Coggins and Knibb, 1979, 251-52, assume; NEB similarly interprets the pronouns as "those rulers"; cf. v. 32 NEB) but only "the posterity of David" (i.e., Israel or at least Judah), which forms its logical and literary antecedent. The fact that a reference to the remnant follows these verses proves unequivocally that a dualism is being established in the passage. This dualism continues, in the form of a statement about the wisdom given to the righteous, in vv. 35ff.

200. On the "messianic woes" and "survivors" as motifs that highlight the division of the righteous from the wicked, cf. Stone, 1990, 369-70.

The Man-Messiah

The following vision of the Man from the Sea (ch. 13) is also clearly inspired by the visions of Daniel,[201] suggesting that its "man" terminology alludes to the Son of man of Dan. 7:13.[202] That this man figure is a messianic personage is evident in that the same terminology is used here as for other messianic figures in the book.[203] Distinctive elements in the vision and its interpretation include the association of the man with the Zion mountain (vv. 6-7, 35-36), and the hostile gathering of "an innumerable multitude of men" against the man and the subsequent judgment of this lot (vv. 5, 8-11, 33-38) — i.e., a messianic war. While these are rather novel aspects when compared to Daniel 7, they would nevertheless seem to represent a common stock of beliefs in the period when 4 Ezra was written. Part of the vision and interpretation relates the conventional belief in the messiah as Judge of the nations as well (vv. 11, 37-38), while the fourth beast of Daniel 7 is again interpreted as Rome. None of these things accordingly would appear to represent the main concern of this passage.

Our attention is drawn to other, more enigmatic, aspects of the vision and interpretation that better reveal the purpose the author had in developing

201. Cf. Coggins and Knibb, 1979, 256; G. K. Beale, "The Problem of the Man from the Sea in IV Ezra 13 and Its Relation to the Messianic Concept in John's Apocalypse," 1983, 182-88, 182-86. Beale's explanation of the novel elements in 4 Ezra 13 (as also in Revelation) as polemical irony (parody) is well worth considering as one explanation for the development of Daniel 7 tradition.

202. When we read "the form of a Man" (according to Eth. version) or "one like the appearance of a Man" (according to Syr. version) or simply "the Man" (according to Lat. version) in this work, we are certainly to conclude that this kind of terminology has reference back to messianic ideas, if not to the exact expression found in Dan. 7:13. The Latin may omit part of the phrase through *homoioteleuton*, rather than preserve an ancient reading. The Syr., being linguistically closest to Heb./Aram., appears to support either בן אדם or בר אנש for the original. Casey (1979, 124-25) disagrees, arguing that בר אנש or בן אדם would have appeared as υἱὸς ἀνθρώπου in Gk. and *filius hominus* in Lat. While Stone holds that variations in the terminology in 4 Ezra (*homo* in the vision and *vir* in the interpretation) represent translation style only (1968, 303), Casey again argues that this suggests the absence of a Son of man reference — *vir* witnessing to איש, a general term for man. Casey nevertheless acknowledges that the man figure of Daniel 7 has inspired the text. Stone (307) notes that "the Man" remains a symbol throughout the vision — only in the interpretation is the servant-messiah brought into the picture, which suggests that the author was not drawing on a previously established equation of Son of man and messiah (308). If so, 4 Ezra may well witness to an independent messianic interpretation of Daniel 7.

203. Cf. "this is he whom the Most High has been keeping for many ages" (v. 26) with 12:32. The words "who will himself deliver his creation" (v. 26) indicate a deliverance function for the messiah.

this man messianology. These aspects are mostly found in the interpretation section, which tends to confirm that they represent the author's own concerns.[204] A passage of particular interest in that section comments on that part of the vision in which, following scenes of judgment, Ezra sees "the same man come down from the mountain and call to him *another multitude which was peaceable.* Then many people came to him, some of whom were joyful and some sorrowful; some of them were bound, and some were bringing others as offerings" (vv. 12-13).[205] This must be an important scene to the author, as the interpretation of these words from the vision section composes the bulk of the interpretive section.[206] As for the identity of these people or peoples, we read: "as for your seeing him gather to himself another multitude that was peaceable, these are the ten tribes which were led away from their own land into captivity in the days of King Hoshea, whom Shalmaneser the king of the Assyrians led captive" (vv. 39-40). In many ways this seems to represent the standard doctrine of the gathering of the ten tribes, and scholars have accordingly explained the passage as an apology for the continued existence of the tribes in the face of their apparent disappearance.[207] The passage goes on to explain just how such a thing is possible: these (or at least some) exiles had journeyed or escaped from the place of exile to a secret uninhabited place (where, apparently, they were believed to be living still):

> he [Shalmaneser] took them across the river, and they were taken into another land. But they formed this plan for themselves, that they would leave the multitude of the nations and go to a more distant region, where mankind had never lived, that there at least they might keep their statutes *which they had not kept in their own land.* And they went in by the narrow passages of the Euphrates River. For at that time the Most High performed signs for them, and stopped the channels of the river until they had passed over. Through that region there was a long way to go, a journey of a year and a half; and that country is called Arzareth. Then they dwelt there until the last times; and now, when they are about to come again, the Most High will stop the channels of the river again, so that they may be able to pass over. Therefore you saw the multitude gathered together in peace. But (Lat. *sed et*) those who are *left of your people, who are found within my holy borders, shall be saved.* (vv. 40-48)

---

204. Cf. Stone, 1968, 310; Stone, 1990, 396, 9-10.

205. The last phrase in this citation alludes to the idea of Gentiles bringing an offering of the exiles to Jerusalem during the restoration (cf. Isa. 66:20).

206. Cf. Stone, 1990, 397.

207. Cf. Coggins and Knibb, 1979, 268.

The uninhabited land spoken of in the passage is given the cryptic name "Arzareth," which has been explained as preserving an original Heb. 'areṣ 'aḥaret, the "other land" to which Deut. 29:28 predicts the exiled children of Israel would be removed as a punishment for disobeying the covenant.[208] It was to this place, by means of a Moses-type deliverance across the dried-up Euphrates riverbed, that this "other multitude which is peaceable" ventured, and where they were able to keep the law in a way that was not possible "in their own land."

This passage reflects the author's view that (some from?) the ten tribes remained righteous in spite of their exile, and would accordingly return at some future time in order to join with other Jews in their homeland, presumably to experience the restoration.[209] By such a means the author may have attempted to explain how God would gather a righteous *multitude* when only a *few* within Jerusalem and Judea were actually deserving of this blessing. In any event, clearly the author expected the righteous within Palestine to be joined by others from outside. This is coherent with that other conviction that salvation would be possible only in a renewed holy land. But whatever motives were at work, ultimately this final Moses-like deliverance and restoration was probably inspired by passages like Isa. 11:16:

> there will be a highway from Assyria
>> for the remnant which is left of his people,
> as there was for Israel
>> when they come up from the land of Egypt.

This passage might help explain many of the individual motifs of the 4 Ezra passage as well. The remnant terminology with which the passage is replete, if at all dependent on Isa. 11:16, would seem to indicate that the author held that the returnees would be composed of only a *remnant* of the exiles. Indeed, that *not all* of the exiles were considered righteous is possibly confirmed by v. 13, which relates that "many people came to [the messiah], some of whom were *joyful*" — apparently the righteous returnees — "and some *sorrowful*" — apparently those coming for judgment, including, in all probability, *other Israelites*.[210] Corresponding statements in the interpretation clarify the matter of

---

208. Coggins and Knibb, 1979, 269; Metzger, *OTP*, 1:553 n. *k*.

209. Stone (1990, 404), who compares Isa. 11:11-13; Jer. 30:3.

210. The verse accordingly continues: "some of them were bound, and some were bringing others as offerings." The bound are Gentiles. Coggins and Knibb reluctantly find Gentiles in the "sorrowful" of v. 13 as well (1979, 261; cf. also Stone, 1990, 387); it is possible, however, to view the "sorrowful" as some of the exiles, based on the Isaian passage from which the idea of the offering of the Gentiles originated and which does not refer to

who would be saved in the end: only the "survivors" from Palestine and the *pure* from among the returning exiles.[211] Whatever traditional elements the author incorporates, in other words, he forces into his own nonnationalistic view of who are the righteous.

The summary at the end of the passage simply reads: "those who are left of your people, who are found within my holy borders, (shall be saved)" (v. 48). The words in parentheses are found in the Syriac version only, but the substance of these words is found again in v. 49. The Latin text of this verse bears its own difficulties for translators, as these manuscripts imply that *two* different groups are intended. Some have therefore assumed that the Latin reading is a corruption,[212] but it is in fact likely that two groups are actually intended in this passage and that this verse refers not to exiles so much as to the inhabitants of Palestine. In other words, after the angel has explained to Ezra about the lost tribes, this verse adds a comment about those of most immediate concern to Ezra, namely, that group of people still visible to Ezra (whom Ezra "sees") — those Jews still living in Palestine. Concerning *these* people, the angel says *only the remnant* ("those who are left") can expect to be saved. The people of the messiah accordingly include a peaceable multitude (presently unseen by Ezra) *along with* a *remnant* of Ezra's fellows (whom he can see). It is noteworthy that by assuming the restoration would include both some from Palestine and (perhaps many) more from the "other land," the author alleviates the strict doctrine of the remnant somewhat — but only somewhat. Although not many Palestinian Jews shall be saved, yet there shall be "another multitude" who will be.

A rather different explanation of the passage was offered by Mowinckel[213] and is worth considering. Referring to ancient traditions, he takes the trip to the far-off land *Arzareth* through an *underground* route[214] originally to have been a metaphor for the dwelling place of the righteous, Paradise (cf. *1 En.* 61:12) or heaven. Mowinckel suggests that the writer has reinterpreted the myth to refer to a physical location and the actual ten tribes. Perhaps, however,

---

Gentiles coming bound; this passage mentions (1) the bringing back of the exiles by the Gentiles (Isa. 66:20) and, perhaps more significantly, (2) retribution against the "men that have rebelled against [God]" (66:24). It is difficult, however, to make too close a connection between 4 Ezra and Isaiah here, and the entire verse may refer to returning Jews and Gentiles in general terms. If this is the case, then the author has treated the belief as traditional and develops it in his own exclusivistic direction, as the interpretation will go on to show.

211. V. 48. Cf. Stone (1990, 405), who points to the fundamental difference between the two cases of survivors and returnees from exile.

212. Cf. Coggins and Knibb, 1979, 269.

213. Mowinckel, 1956, 381-82.

214. Mowinckel takes the "narrow passages of the Euphrates river" to refer to the underground "Tigris-tunnel at Bylkalein" (1956, 381-82).

the writer still intended the legend to refer to the heavenly existence of the saints in continuity with this original significance. If these saints consist of those now departed, the passage would then teach a kind of final reunion of the dead remnant with the remnant still alive ("those who [remain] of your people, who are found within my holy borders") and a reunion of both with the Son of man. This theory that the ten tribes are the glorified saints is at least as worthy of consideration as the above restoration theory, perhaps more so, as it adheres with the rather strict remnant theology of the book generally that (if we have properly appreciated this aspect of 4 Ezra) seems to offer little hope for those who do not follow the soteriological program promoted by the author's community. It also alleviates the problem of believing that some real, although ethereal and hidden, geographical location exists in which the ten tribes physically dwell.[215] It is probably neither necessary nor possible, however, to decide which theory best suits the evidence. In either approach it is a matter of two groups, both of whom are considered to have remained faithful. In either theory, moreover, the number of saved in Palestine is said to be relatively few. It seems that for the author of 4 Ezra those who live in the holy land are simply not able to keep the law (cf. v. 42 above).

But the angel has these significant words for those who do meet the requirements for righteousness: "As for what you have said about *those who are left*, this is the interpretation: He who brings the peril at that time will himself protect those who fall into peril, who have works and have faith in the Almighty. Understand therefore that those who are left are more blessed than those who have died" (vv. 22-24). In spite of the enigmatic twists and turns in the account, "the peaceable multitude" (the "ten tribes") *along with* "the survivors" ("those who are left/remain") together compose a holy remnant who have maintained their faith throughout the period of the exile (or apostasy). Once again, therefore, all indications suggest that the messiah is the messiah-of-the-elect who does not function in this passage in any other *significant* capacity than to be with and deliver the survivors at the end of days:[216] "this is he whom the Most High has been keeping for many ages, who will himself deliver his creation; and *he will direct those who are left*" (v. 26); "when he destroys the multitude of the nations that are gathered together, he will defend the *people who remain*. And then he will show *them* very many wonders" (vv. 49-50). Accord-

---

215. One notable piece of evidence against the theory, however, is that *Ant.* 11.133 seems to refer to a tradition about the withdrawal of the ten tribes to a "country" in the trans-Euphrates, and this tradition seems to be intended literally.

216. Cf. De Villiers (1978, 95-96), who surprisingly takes this gathering of the remnant to be part of traditional *nationalistic* messianic ideas that the author has preserved *along with* regular features of the Son of man!

ingly the revelation of this messiah-for-the-elect is made only to Ezra and to "those who are like him":

> Just as no one can explore or know what is in the depths of the sea, so no one on earth can see my Son or *those who are with him,* except in the time of his day. . . . you alone have been enlightened about this, because you have forsaken your own ways and have applied yourself to mine, and have searched out my law; for you have devoted your life to wisdom, and called understanding your mother. Therefore I have shown you this. (vv. 52-56a)

Thus, as in the Similitudes, this man is a hidden messiah who is revealed only to the elect (cf. also 14:9).

It is now evident that the diversity of figures in this literature is much greater than is usually acknowledged in studies of messianology. They include a whole range of progenitors, paradigms, mystic or revelatory figures, as well as eschatological, redemptive "messiah" figures. Recognizing this diversity proved to be vitally important since it served to highlight what was the *common* element among them — namely, how in various ways each emphasized the relationship between the figure and a particular community or group of righteous. These figures accordingly transcend conventional nationalistic categorizations. They are *more* than merely the patriarchs of Israel's past — because their existence implied a spiritual relationship with their people — and are at the same time something *less* than national heroes — because they were believed to represent the righteous community, not all of Israel. It is apparent, therefore, that *these groups rewrote the historical records to reflect their own perspective on the significance of Israel's ancestors.*

The fact that the anticipated "messiah" was often in substance a paradigmatic figure believed to *reappear* at the end of time suggests that belief in these kinds of superlative eschatological-redemptive figures was based on a notion of association with a people similar to that of the other types of figures. This was confirmed by a closer analysis of the important passages. This tendency held true even for the "nationalistic" Davidic messiah featured in the *Psalms of Solomon,* in various guises in the Enochian literature, and as the man in 4 Ezra: even these otherwise traditional portrayals of the messiah in essentials fit the mold of the messiah-of-the-elect. The significant distinction that this study has revealed to have been operative in Second Temple Judaism, therefore, was *not* that *between a materialistic earthly messiah in contrast to a heavenly "apocalyptic" Son of man,* but between *a nationalistic view of the messiah's role in contrast to the view of the messiah in these groups as messiah-of-the-elect.* Residual indications in these writings that there also existed at this time the more conventional view of a messiah who would come to save the entire nation can be found —

but traditional elements, where they are not completely removed, are incidental rather than essential to these presentations. The implications of a messianology that stresses this exclusive aspect at the expense of the nationalistic ideal should be obvious. The very literature that is usually associated with the most fruitful developments of messianic ideas defines its messianology in very "unconventional" ways. That the messiah was *not* coming for the nation so much as for the "elect," therefore, is a central tenet that must be acknowledged whenever one consults these writings as a foundation for studies of messianology or Christology.

CHAPTER ELEVEN

Eschatology in a Dualistic Context

It must be determined, first of all, what is meant by the term "eschatology." It is customary to think (in line with the Greek linguistic roots of this word) in terms of "end," "finality," "the *last* things,"[1] etc. Unfortunately, this definition tends to perpetuate the misconception that the Jewish and Christian world believed in the *end of everything per se*. But even groups who envisaged a future and final cataclysmic event probably did not hold to the rather philosophical idea of the "end of history" as the eradication of time (as cf. the "many weeks without number forever" of *1 En.* 91:17), as an obliteration of material existence, or even as a new period so qualitatively different from what went before as to be discontinuous with history or historical existence.[2] That the concept of finality is foreign, or at best secondary, in Jewish eschatological beliefs is suggested, furthermore, by the rather broad semantic range and employment of the biblical word for "End" (*qēṣ*),[3] a breadth of meaning and usage that is also frequently carried over into the languages of translation. Partly as a result of the

---

1. Cf. R. H. Charles, *Eschatology*, 1913, 1; P. Volz, *Die Eschatologie der jüdischen Gemeinde*, 1934, 1. Cf. also G. B. Caird, *The Language and Imagery of the Bible*, 1980, 243.

2. Although one might conclude this from treatments like that of Volz (1934, 63-66, 96-97), who limits his appeal for this view to two relatively late (post-Christian!) writings — *2 Baruch* (44:9; 51:10) and 4 Ezra (7:50) — hardly making the doctrine representative of the entire period. Cf. the critique of this misconception by C. Rowland, *The Open Heaven*, 1982, 38, and J. J. Collins, "Apocalyptic Eschatology as the Transcendence of Death," 1974, 21-43, 25-27.

3. Cf. Caird (1980, 244), who points to the resultant danger "that in using the one word eschatology . . . we should overlook the fact that we may be using words such as 'last,' 'final' and 'end' in different senses."

word's indefiniteness and no doubt also of a determination not to spell out the details of the future too specifically, it is often difficult to determine at what point was this *"End"* (what might better be referred to as the *eschatological goal*). Is it the last judgment, the commencement of God's (or the messianic) kingdom, or has it already begun in some way in the author's present? It is well recognized that this blurring of End terminology is characteristic of the eschatology of the Hebrew Scriptures in their references to the Day of Yahweh and the "end of days," and there are indications that our groups merely perpetuated the inexactitudes latent in these concepts.[4]

One way out of the impasse created by this inexactitude in language and concepts is not to speak strictly in terms of *eschatology* — in the sense this word usually carries, as a systematization of final events — but in terms of *teleology* — which carries the idea of a *philosophy* about the future resolution of historical inequalities, about the betterment of the human situation, and about fulfilling the purpose of existence. Teleology implies the view that history is moving progressively and purposefully, although somewhat indeterminably, toward some future goal, which may not be the end of the world at all.[5] This indeterminacy does not imply that eschatological presentations are to be approached qualitatively or existentially;[6] it merely asserts that inexactitude is a quite ac-

4. Cf. J. Carmignac, "La notion d'eschatologie dans la bible et à Qumran," 1969, 17-31, who reviews the use of the end-of-time terminology in the MT and LXX and concludes that both Heb. 'aḥarit and Gk. eschatos imply "next" *(suivant)* rather than "last" *(dernier; 18-20)*. The expression 'aḥarit hay-yamim (end of days) never refers to the end of the world but rather to various historical events in the Scriptures. We might clarify, however, that some uses of it could easily be interpreted in a futurist sense (e.g., Ezek. 38:8, 16; Dan. 10:14; Hos. 3:5) if that is not the way they were originally intended; but his point is well taken that even these do not strictly refer to the end of the world *per se*. The terminology refers to some indeterminate future event ("un avenir indéterminé"). Carmignac goes on to show how this use of language was perpetuated in the scrolls (22-27).

5. Cf. Caird, 1980, 256-57: "The idea that things are what they are in virtue of their purpose or goal has a long and honourable record under the name of teleology," accepting the qualification that this teleology is "sensitive (as the Greek philosophers were not) to the reality and significance of historical events."

6. While traditional treatments of eschatology in our writings take eschatological sayings about time — both relational (past, present, and future) and quantitative (the time of the end, etc.) — quite literally as part of the Hebrew teleological point of view, some scholars now insist that this eschatology had a qualitative aspect (epochs are categorized according to their significance), and others insist that eschatology is to be considered existentially, or according to its linguistic function as myth in a society; cf., e.g., A. N. Wilder, "The Nature of Jewish Eschatology," 1931, 201-6; Caird, 1980, 243ff., esp. 253-71; for a kind of semi-existentialism, cf. Collins (1974, 41-43), who maintains that a real future was envisioned but argues that the eschatology was significant primarily for its effects on present experience; some scholars apply to the Gospel sayings a similar nonliteral approach to

ceptable feature of what we call eschatology, which is really concerned more with the purposes of history than with exact timing. Although teleology has generally been judged a more "Greek" than "Hebrew" idea, it is evident that what biblical scholars have customarily referred to as eschatology nevertheless carried with it strong teleological implications.

How important this consideration is can only be grasped when one recalls how central a role past scholars have viewed eschatology to have played in "apocalyptic" literature. Many of these scholars, especially since Volz,[7] have assumed that the purpose of the eschatological material in these writings was to work out the *timing* of the End — as if motivated by some urgent curiosity. More recently the tendency has been toward the realization that the works themselves do not actually exhibit this careful and systematic interest in arithmetic — they are frequently evasive and lack the mathematical detail often supposed for them. This observation will be borne out in the treatment of texts below, where any predisposition toward calculation is seen to be balanced by a reticence to provide either a *firm* date or a date in the near, verifiable future. The calculations and predictions of the future appear to possess more of a literary purpose in attempting to convince the readers of the revelational authority of the writers, which may be the very reason these same writers prefer, for obvious reasons, to veil their predictions and calculations in a safe kind of ambiguity.

More recent studies, which tend to respect the works in their individuality and avoid treating them uncritically as a collectivity, have also revealed a variety in eschatological beliefs among, and even *within,* individual writings. This confirms that no *universally accepted pattern of events* for the final days was in existence, as some early studies assumed. The many failed attempts to characterize "apocalyptic" writings according to a *current* and *common* eschatological schematization might have itself led to this conclusion, but attempts are still made to come up with one.[8] This is not to deny that eschatology had its tradi-

---

eschatological language (cf., e.g., C. F. D. Moule, *The Gospel according to Mark,* 1982, 102). In the light of the importance of the calendar outlined above, and of the implied relationship between the calendar and the periodization of history, one is tempted to take references to time rather more literally than do these theories.

7. Volz (1934, 6, 135-47), appealing to Ps. 74:9 in support! Even Volz admits that inexactitude is found in, e.g., Daniel, and that frequently the belief in the coming End is communicated in terms of the total age of the world, rather than related to current events, which often places the proposed date some distance from the author of the work concerned. Some of these works also admit no accurate knowledge of the time of the End: "Gott allein kennt das Ende der Zeiten" (146; *2 Bar.* 21:8; 69:2).

8. Cf. F. C. Burkitt, *Jewish and Christian Apocalypses,* 1914, 2; cf., more recently, J. Schreiner, "Zur Eschatologie in der Zeit zwischen den Testamenten," 1986, 32-43, esp. 35-36. Schreiner provides a typical abstract systematization, but he also characteristically draws most of the evidence from 4 Ezra and *2 Baruch;* under his category "Das Ende und

tional aspects, but rather to affirm the abundance and very great variety of traditional building material out of which our writers and their communities could construct their eschatological teachings.[9] Thus in the final analysis the "eschatological goal" of a certain writing can only be determined from internal indications.

It is accordingly imperative that one concentrate on the main features and functions of the eschatologies of each work, and avoid emphasizing dates and events or reconstructing a precise chronology (that the writings do work with dates to a point is not denied — it is however a matter of where to put the emphasis). Little emphasis, in fact, should be given to most of what, on the surface at least, appear to be the main components of eschatological passages. The fact that many of these components were traditional, and that they are often presented in a confused or unclear manner (i.e., they were not carefully systematized), provide particularly good indications that traditional elements were not essential to the author's objectives. It must be considered, therefore, whether in formulating eschatological teachings the author did not mainly seek to establish the order of *events* of the future, but possessed a more abstract *purpose* consonant with the concerns of his community. Aspects and attitudes specifically *emphasized* by each writer provide clues to these more important underlying concerns and functions.

This also raises the question once again of the relationship of these writings to their social and historical context. Previously scholars tragically discerned this context only in a circular way by reference back to eschatology. The perceived eschatological style or tone of the writings (often prejudiced by an overriding interest in the genre of Revelation and the nature of the Gospel and Pauline eschatological teachings) led to their characterization as *essentially* eschatological. We have already noted many instances in which this characterization is patently false: things like the "pseudepigraphical" posture of the author and his *ex eventu* perspective, for example, have created the impression that the teaching is future oriented, when in actual fact it frequently relates more to the (real) author's present. These writings, at least, are *not* encyclopedias of eschatology.[10] But this characterization has continued and has gone on to exercise

---

der kommende Äon," no less than ten of eleven citations in the text come from these two writings; the other comes from the (perhaps) equally late Similitudes.

9. Both of these facts have for a long time been noted by students of eschatology, including Volz himself (1934, 1).

10. As once again the influential Volz (1934, 4) seemed to assume. Volz implied that eschatological teaching was the chief purpose of pseudepigraphy, and he employed these writings as a source for constructing a cross section of the whole gamut of Jewish eschatological beliefs. Charles (1913) brought this presupposition to his treatments of the Hebrew Bible and the New Testament, as well as the Apocrypha and Pseudepigrapha. It is notewor-

significant influence on the determination of the *context* of the writings. This context usually has been taken to be the Seleucid and Roman dominations of Palestine, and accordingly the conventional view of the *function* of this eschatology was to assure the readers that (1) God would soon bring to an end the overlordship of the Gentiles (often through a messiah figure) and (2) God would place Israel back on top of world history, subjecting the nations to her. The result is a substantially nationalistic approach to eschatology, a view that has infiltrated even recent studies and has reinforced, as already noted, those sociological approaches that promote various views of disenfranchisement.

If the chief interest of these writings, on the other hand, is *not* to teach eschatology, or if the eschatological characterization referred to above is otherwise thrown into doubt, this will obviously possess serious implications for prior evaluations of the function of eschatology in this literature. In this connection one might note that the methodology of the eschatological approach has been plagued with a lack of historical confirmation, and has accordingly been severely critiqued;[11] the content of the generalization has also come under careful scrutiny of late.[12] Certainly the divergences between, and even within, the eschatologies of the books and the lack of lucid, systematic, comprehensive, or at least coherent presentations of eschatological views cast serious doubts on the traditional evaluation of the importance of this doctrine in these writings.

---

thy that Charles approached the texts as if they could tell him mostly about *individual* eschatological beliefs at the time, just as Collins (1974, 30ff.) has more recently stressed the role played by the individual's consciousness of the transcendence of death. But on the whole our works contain very little reference to the eschatology of the individual. These writings are also frequently characterized according to the prevalence of "eschatological dualism" (conceptualized in terms of the contrast between "this world" and "the world to come"), as noted earlier. A welcome exception to this tendency can be found in Rowland (1982, 38 and passim).

11. This was the chief complaint of Koch in his *Ratlos vor der Apokalyptik*. G. L. Davenport says with regard to his own analysis of eschatology in *Jubilees:* "This study of Jubilees has shown the need for a full scale reconsideration of the meaning of apocalyptic. Although the standard distinction between prophetic and apocalyptic eschatology has been followed for this study, the qualifications that have been made on numerous occasions indicated the inadequacy of categories established primarily on the basis of content analysis" (*The Eschatology of the Book of Jubilees,* 1971, 78-79).

12. Notably Rowland (1982, 1-2, 23-37): "The variety of emphases and interests which are to be found in the apocalypses should make us wary of raising particular elements to the level of a norm when their presence may have been dictated by the needs of the moment. Only a few of the apocalypses are dominated by urgent expectation of the coming of the new age and eschatology" (28). The old dichotomy between rabbinic and apocalyptic thought based on eschatology is also invalid since the literatures of the two groups exhibit many of the same basic ideas about eschatology (29-37). Cf. also M. E. Stone, "The Book of Enoch and Judaism in the Third Century B.C.E.," 1978, 488-89.

In spite of the cracks beginning to be evident in the eschatological foundation, however, the basically nationalistic approach to the writings that has been built upon it remains stubbornly intact.

Another tendency, all too well established in scholarly circles, is differentiating between a *traditional, worldly-historical, and national* eschatology embraced by most of Judaism, on the one hand, and a *transcendental, "catastrophic," and universal* eschatology that characterized the writings of our movement, on the other — a dichotomy often associated with the two types of messiahs mentioned in the previous chapter.[13] This difference in attitudes toward eschatology, and especially the adoption of an otherworldly eschatology, so it is believed, were generated by the disappointment felt over the repeated failure of Israel's hopes for domination to materialize. But such treatments have unfortunately accepted a characterization quite artificially forced upon the subject, perhaps symptomatic of the tendency of a past generation to categorize things in oversimplistic terms. The characterization is frequently admitted to be an overgeneralization even by writers who adopt it, who also acknowledge that many otherworldly and historical expressions of eschatology are found side by side in the same writings.[14] The view of scholars like Charles, Volz, and Mowinckel that the doctrine of the millennium was invented in order to reconcile the two kinds of eschatologies, the national-messianic and the otherworldly, itself reveals an awareness of a dichotomy that hardly could have ex-

13. Thus Charles speaks of a transformation of eschatological belief from an earthly to a heavenly kingdom that took place in the apocalyptic writings (1913, 179). He uses the word "catastrophic" of this eschatology (181). Volz's work is heavily dependent on this dichotomy (1934, passim; cf. 2, 63-71, where "die altjüdische nationale Eschatologie" and "die neue erweiterte Eschatologie" are compared and contrasted with the help of a chart; cf. 69). This scholar, however, admits that books like the Similitudes already reveal a fusion of the two ideas (361). Cf. also S. Mowinckel, *He That Cometh*, 1956, 261ff., esp. 267. C. Steuernagel ("Die Strukturlinien der Entwicklung der jüdischen Eschatologie," 1950, 479-80) cautiously accepts these categories but wishes to stress the interplay of the various lines and adds a third category: "individual eschatology."

14. Thus Volz refers to the "Mittelstufen" between the two positions (1934, 2), but his work reflects that there are some of these *Mittelstufen* in nearly every example of eschatology (cf. 25, 26, 30, 36, 51, etc., in regard to apocalyptic and rabbinic eschatology alike)! The confusion and inadequacy of these categories are well illustrated, e.g., by J. Pryke ("'Spirit' and 'Flesh' in the Qumran Documents and Some New Testament Texts," 1969, 46-48), who evaluates the Qumran doctrine as essentially an historical eschatology! The community viewed itself as fulfilling historical prophecy that told them to "make straight in the desert a highway for our God" (1QS 8.13-14). Cf. also Rowland, 1982, 48: "There are certainly signs in some apocalypses of a belief that this world would be replaced by a new order of existence, but hardly ever do we find this belief replacing a hope for a period of bliss in this world. When an other-worldly eschatology does appear, as, for example, in 4 Ezra 7.31ff., it is juxtaposed with a this-worldly eschatology."

isted in practice.[15] One would better speak of a number and variety of details in the expectations at this time — mostly stemming from a number of suggestive scriptural passages — which individual writers combined as best they could. While there probably did exist what might be called nationalistically oriented eschatologies in contrast to sectarian and universalistic varieties, to suggest that the former eschatology was merely associated with earthly categories of reality while the universalistic eschatology was associated primarily with transcendent thought is an invalid distinction. It remains the purpose of this chapter to determine more exactly the function of the eschatological portions, and to evaluate the implications of eschatology for the definition of the movement under consideration.

THE DIALECTIC OF RESTORATION IN THE ZOOMORPHIC HISTORY

As already noted, the eschatological section of the Zoomorphic History (*1 En.* 90:14-39) is essentially a relatively short (twenty-six-verse) addendum to a much lengthier historical rehearsal (85:3–90:13). This rather unbalanced distribution of subject material along with the unsystematic, and at times even confused, presentation of eschatological teaching in this addendum (see below) casts doubt on the view that eschatology possessed dominant importance in this writing. The purpose of the historical rehearsal is, therefore, obviously *not* solely to set the stage for eschatology, as has been thought (the *independent* importance of the historical rehearsal part of this passage has been dealt with in ch. 10). It is accordingly noteworthy also, in spite of the fact that eschatological teaching has been carefully appended to a highly symbolic historical rehearsal in this way, that the author does not use this schematization in order merely to calculate the timing of the End.[16]

As noted above on ch. 90, a *hinge* from past to present and another from present to future both occur within a short passage (90:10-16). The intervening verses elaborate on the ministry of the "great horn." Where exactly the second hinge, indicating the transfer from present to future, is to be located is unclear. The intervention of God's help is reported in v. 14, but there is nothing cata-

---

15. Cf. Volz, 1934, 71ff.

16. Charles (1913, 188) takes the fact that the end of the domain of the seventy angels was to take place within the present generation as proof that the end was at hand, but this tells us no more than we already know, namely, that the author probably expected to witness the final events.

clysmic or miraculous about this intervention, and the battles referred to may actually have occurred in history.[17] Vv. 15-16 sound a little more futuristic: God comes in "wrath" and *all* the nations of the world conspire against the horn, things that sound like decisive events in the unfolding of the future rather than historical reporting. In v. 17 the End is clearly in view as the books of judgment are opened, and in v. 18, as the Lord is said to judge with the "rod of his wrath," the earth swallows those who are judged. The rapid succession of events, from the battle of the horn to the great judgment, suggests that final events would evolve out of the battles the author was witnessing during his lifetime. Perhaps this also explains how the "historical" ram evolves into a kind of eschatological conquering messiah in this text.[18]

The eschatological section, wherever exactly it begins, opens with scenes of judgment. The opening of books of judgment (cf. vv. 14, 17, 20) is an important theme that runs through the entire passage, evincing the kind of covenantal and soteriological dualism characteristic of the Zoomorphic History as a whole. In vv. 14ff. the mention of books implies that deeds are being carefully recorded, although unfaithful Israel presumes that they are not. In vv. 20ff. the books are again opened — this time not for recording, but for carrying out the judgment. Following the initial scenes of judgment, the history continues with the renewal of the Temple (vv. 28-29), the vindication of the righteous sheep (vv. 30-32), a restoration that includes the nations (vv. 33-36), and finally the coming of the messiah (vv. 37-38), whereupon Enoch awakes and the vision ends (v. 39).

A few chapters earlier (ch. 83, the first dream vision; not part of the Zoomorphic History and perhaps not originally connected with it) Enoch has a vision of judgment similar to the descriptions of judgment in the history. The literary context here is the flood, but there are strong indications that the author is alluding to a future judgment. His descriptions of this judgment possess final and cosmic aspects beyond that of opening the floodgates or the windows

17. M. Black suggests that this verse refers to Judas's confrontations with the Syrian Lysias, and appeals to 1 Macc. 4:30-31 and 2 Macc. 11:6-7 for similar references to petition and angelic intervention before the battle (*The Book of Enoch* or *I Enoch*, 1985, 277).

18. As noted in the previous chapter. Another division of the text may be important also. In vv. 15ff. God pours out his wrath through the "sheep" in a decisive victory *on earth*, while in vv. 20-27 a judgment occurs *in heaven* against the fallen stars, the seventy shepherds who ruled over Israel, and Israel itself ("those blinded sheep," v. 26). The presentation appears, therefore, to entail a dualistic cosmology that sets events in heaven in parallel with those on earth. The fact that books are opened during both scenes (v. 17; cf. v. 20) suggests this kind of dualism. It may be, on the other hand, that the passage intends to suggest that a second and quite distinct judgment in heaven is to be experienced by those who previously took part in the earthly battle and that cosmic dualism is not a major factor here.

of heaven; water is not mentioned, and the entire physical world, rather than being flooded, is thrown into the "great abyss" (vv. 3-4). A vital correspondence between the first (flood) and second judgments is even more explicit in Enoch's prayer, where he states, in connection with the present sins of the angels, that "your wrath shall rest upon the flesh of the people until the *great day of judgment*" (84:4). It seems, therefore, that the first great judgment during the flood was preliminary, only brought to completion in the second. The passage suggestively corresponds to the description of the judgment in the Zoomorphic History where the stars (fallen angels) are judged along with the guilty shepherds and the blind sheep in one final judgment scene (90:24-25, partly based on Daniel 7). This judgment is also fiery, rather than watery (vv. 24-25), and in its center stand the fallen Israelites ("blinded sheep," vv. 26-27). Thus both scenes of judgment appear to essentially follow similar beliefs about the judgment of angels as well as humankind, and this tends to confirm that the entire Book 4 of *1 Enoch* was penned by the same author or group of authors. In any event, both passages remind the reader that apostate Israel, along with the nations who have also allowed themselves to be misled by the fallen angels, will be judged indiscriminately.

There are obviously some inconsistencies in the eschatology of the Zoomorphic History: judgment occurs against Israel (i.e., all the blind sheep) and is portrayed vividly by images of burning (vv. 26-27) — one could hardly call this a temporary chastisement of Israel; the image used is of complete obliteration[19] — yet without apparent conflict the author goes on to describe "all the sheep" happily worshiping within the restored Temple (vv. 29, 35-36). The author may have been attempting to harmonize exclusivistic claims with restoration hopes in this passage, but the two ideas are not easily juxtaposed. A closer look at the restoration section of the passage will bear this out.

> Then I saw all the sheep that had survived as well as all the animals upon the earth and the birds of heaven, falling down and worshiping those sheep, making petition to them and obeying them in every respect. . . . they set me down in the midst of those sheep prior to the occurrence of this judgment. Those sheep were all snow-white, and their wool considerable and clean. All those which have been destroyed and dispersed, and all the beasts of the field and the birds of the sky were gathered together in that house; and the Lord of the sheep rejoiced with great joy because they had all become gentle and returned to his house. I went on seeing until they had laid down that sword

---

19. This is another of those passages containing a "viewing of the fates" motif applied to Israel. It is reminiscent of Isa. 66:24 (also applied to Israel): "And they shall go forth and look on the dead bodies of the men that have rebelled against me; for their worm shall not die, their fire shall not be quenched, and they shall be an abhorrence to all flesh."

which was given to the sheep; they returned it to the house and sealed it in the presence of the Lord. All the sheep were invited to that house but it could not contain them all. The eyes of all of them were opened, and they saw the beautiful things; not a single one existed among them that could not see. (vv. 30-35)

At first sight the expression "*all* the sheep" in v. 29 would seem to refer to the righteous, inasmuch as the next verse defines these as "all the sheep *that had survived*" (v. 30).[20] If the "sheep that had *survived*" are the righteous,[21] however, who then are "those sheep" who are shown reverence *by them* in the same verse? Perhaps the former phrase refers to those who escape the present conflicts, spoken of as "rams" in v. 10; it makes more sense, however, that "all the sheep that had survived" (along with "all the sheep") refers to *other* redeemed or restored Israelites — that is, *all surviving Israelites* — and that we have here a presentation of Israel's restoration. An emendation of the passage suggested by Black might be taken to suggest that a qualified or limited restoration is in view,[22] but if sense can be made out of the expression as it stands, it would perhaps be best to understand "those sheep" as the righteous (cf. also v. 32, "*those sheep* were all snow-white") and "*all* the sheep" as Israel. This is confirmed by vv. 32-36 where the author refers to a restoration in which Israelites, including those who formerly could not "see," return *en masse* to the Lord.

Other participants in the drama would appear to be quite conventional and traditional, rather than essential to the message of the author, and their inclusion in the compass of a short passage, which was probably felt necessary for the sake of completeness, tends only to add more uncertainty and chaos to the passage. The dispersed who return in v. 33 alludes to the return of the exiles to join the righteous. They are also described as those who were "destroyed," apparently referring again to the dispersions.[23] The "beasts of the field and birds of the sky" are the Gentiles who come to Jerusalem during the restoration accompanying the returning exiles; they have "become gentle" (v. 33). The "sheep," on the other hand, who are seen laying down the "sword" that was given them and placing it in the Temple (implying that their efforts were recog-

20. It may be that "all" is not used in v. 29 in an inclusive sense but merely to indicate the location of the sheep under consideration ("they were *all in the Temple*").

21. Cf. Black, 1985, 279.

22. Black suggests a reading for the similar words "(in the midst of) those sheep" (v. 31) that, if it could be accepted, is more indicative of a *limited* restoration — "(sheep) who were without condemnation" (i.e., "all the sheep" are the righteous alone; 1985, 279). The extant reading should probably be accepted, however, if sense can be made of it, since it is not only preferable as the most difficult reading, but is uncontested in the MSS evidence.

23. Cf. 89:69; *contra* Black (1985, 279), who takes it to refer to the righteous dead.

nized by God, but that now peace had come; v. 34), might be the Maccabee-rams, or a militant Israel generally. Ethnic Israel is perhaps more unambiguously referred to in the following words: "*All the sheep* were invited to that house but it could not contain them" (v. 34).

However one sorts out these conflicting references, there is little doubt that the author is enlarging on his version of a restoration doctrine in this passage, which is surprising given the highly exclusive pattern established earlier in the history. It would seem, in fact, that the author did little to rationalize his juxtaposition of exclusivistic claims with restoration hopes. He seems merely to have brought together these two trains of thought, applying animal symbolism to explicate both, but without concern for logical consistency. The writer was apparently aware of the tensions he was creating by doing this — having Israel both condemned and saved at the End. Signs of this tension may be evident in the text itself. The phrase "all the sheep *that had survived*" (v. 30) may have been an attempt at glossing over the difficulties: Israel is judged, but there are still survivors. The enigmatic phrase "they set me down . . . *prior to . . . this judgment*" (which judgment?; v. 31) may also evidence an uneasiness, but this phrase is so difficult to interpret that emendations are frequently suggested. Perhaps, however, the phrase signifies that the author or a later editor (as the case may be) saw the events of vv. 28-39 as logically or even chronologically prior to v. 20. The words of v. 31: "prior to the occurrence of this judgment," do seem recapitulatory, as if to say that the judgment of the sheep *followed* their gathering together in the new temple. This would suggest then that the author envisaged a radical restoration involving a total miraculous return of all Israel *before* the judgment. But this is still a very problematic interpretation, and it does little to reduce the difficulties resident in the entire passage. It is difficult to avoid the conclusion that two components of eschatology that do not easily harmonize have been placed together and synthesized with limited success, resulting in a contrast between the rather pessimistic teaching of the history and the more positive eschatological conclusion.

There are, however, aspects of the passage that tend to grant continuity between this synthesis and the rest of the history. For example, certain distinctive roles continue to be sustained for "those (righteous) sheep" and "all the sheep" (Israel), respectively. The way v. 30 has Israel honoring "those (righteous) sheep" is conspicuous to say the least: "I saw all the sheep that had survived as well as all the animals upon the earth and the birds of heaven, *falling down and worshiping* those sheep, *making petition to them and obeying them in every respect.*" The righteous accordingly continue to be distinguished from the rest of Israel by their worthiness and by the respect due to them. The idea of *vindication* comes through most clearly, and the righteous in Israel never lose their special distinction entirely.

The restoration appears to be qualified in other respects as well due to the soteriological posture of the writer. In v. 35, for example, the surviving sheep from Israel are portrayed as experiencing illumination: "the eyes of all of them were opened . . . not a single one existed among them that could not see." Here only an *illuminated* Israel is represented, perhaps indicating that, in the mind of the author, repentance and identity with the saving revelation composed important requisites for the restoration of Israel. That some from Israel are seen to be converted to the way of the righteous is strongly suggested also in vv. 37-38, which announce that at the advent of the messiah ("snow-white cow") "all their kindred were *transformed,* and became snow-white cows." Whether vv. 37-38 consciously build upon the message of vv. 34-36 or represent the influence of other traditional material is impossible to say. While these passages seem to assume a *complete* restoration (cf. "not a single one . . . could not see," "all their kindred"; cf. Rom. 11:26), it is in any event clear that Israel is restored *on the condition that they now identify with the messiah-of-the-elect and with the elect themselves.* The Israel of the restoration is a "converted" Israel (a similar paradox is exhibited in Rom. 11:26, 28-32, where God's "mercy" is nevertheless predicated on the basis of obedience).

In spite of inconsistencies, therefore, the writer's main point nevertheless comes through — namely, that the righteous take center stage in the restoration. All others have only two possible fates: judgment, or some kind of miraculous or gracious preservation (which the author does not attempt to describe in any detail). This tends to *vindicate* and *legitimize* the righteous; they are on the right path: restoration comes by joining their movement.

One can summarize the eschatology of the Zoomorphic History as follows. While emphasizing judgment in his work, the author nevertheless also has *at least some* survive from outside his group, and he seems to have had a distinct *purpose* in doing this. Ideas about the restoration were too firmly rooted in the author's tradition for him to remove them altogether, so the author has qualified the teaching considerably. A doctrine of the restoration is preserved only in a form that emphasizes the importance of the righteous in that restoration. Their salvation alone is secure. That the resultant combination of judgment and restoration motifs created real difficulties is evident in the text; but by preserving the latter hope the author offered a somewhat creative dialectic that prevented the history from being utterly pessimistic.

JUDGMENT AND VINDICATION
IN THE BOOK OF WATCHERS

Besides the relatively vivid descriptions of judgment, very little detail is given in the Book of Watchers about the coming of the End. The perspective, nevertheless, is once again that of a group who believed themselves to be living in the final days. The literary context for the relevant passage (1:1–5:10) is an address to Enoch regarding the first deluge, similar to that of the first dream vision mentioned above (chs. 83–84), and like that other vision, the subject matter here is not the flood itself but a *future judgment* that the author and his readers believe to be imminent (Lars Hartman has made the case for this double meaning so carefully as to make its repetition here unnecessary).[24] The theme of the future judgment, significantly enough, is already expressed in the opening words of the book: "The blessing of Enoch: with which he blessed the elect and the righteous *who would be present on the day of tribulation at the removal of all the ungodly ones.... I look not for this generation but for the distant one that is coming.* I speak about the elect ones and concerning them" (*1 En.* 1:1-2).

The description of the future events in the Book of Watchers revolves around two central themes: (1) the divine visitation, the judgment of the ungodly, and the upheavals of the natural order that accompany these events (cf. 1:3-7, 9; cf. 5:5-6); and (2) the blessing of the righteous (cf. 1:8; cf. 5:7-10). As for the judgment, the ungodly who are judged significantly include the unrighteous from Israel who fail to keep "the commandments of the Lord" (5:4). The "elect" appear also to experience some of the negative effects of judgment (1:7), but it is specifically the wicked who live in the last days — including, as noted above, those who fail to observe the calendar and thus sin against the covenant — who are warned. It seems that the judgment of the wicked at the hand of the righteous is already thought to have begun in the author's present (5:5-6). In contrast to these scenes of judgment, one reads about the final verdict for the righteous, which is always good: "And to all the righteous he will grant peace. He will preserve the elect, and kindness shall be upon them. They shall all belong to God and they shall prosper and be blessed; and the light of God shall shine unto them" (1:8). The vindication theme is particularly clear again in ch. 5, which makes a strong appeal to dualistic ideas of the covenant: "But to the elect there shall be light, joy, and peace, and they shall inherit the earth.... And they shall not be judged all the days of their lives; nor die through plague or wrath, but they shall complete the number of the days of their life. And peace shall increase their lives and the years of their happiness shall be multiplied forever in gladness and peace all the days of their life" (5:7, 9-10). The announce-

24. L. Hartman, *Asking for a Meaning*, 1979, esp. 16.

ment of this-worldly vindication compares with the earthly understanding of judgment in this passage, but both contrast with the more cosmic scenes of 1:3ff., suggesting that the author had little problem combining what seem to us to be two diverse views of judgment and vindication. Vindication in the Book of Watchers is not only reward for the comparative righteousness of the saints, but also reparation for their suffering. Thus one reads a moving supplication offered by the angels on behalf of the oppressed that tells how the blood of the righteous implores the angels to bring their petition to God: "The earth, from her empty foundation, has brought the cry of their voice unto the gates of heaven. And now, holy ones of heaven, the souls of people are putting their case before you pleading, 'Bring our judgment before the Most High.' . . . Their groaning has ascended into heaven, but they could not get out from before the face of the oppression that is being wrought on earth" (9:2-3, 10).

Beyond these two themes of judgment and vindication there is not enough eschatological teaching in the Book of Watchers to identify any eschatological program *per se*, and there is certainly no attempt to create or allude to a timetable of events. It is nevertheless significant that the introductory portions of the book are replete with references to judgment (which must be taken as particularly applying to Israel) as well as vindication/reward passages. One can accordingly summarize the eschatology of this book as almost entirely composed of the twin elements of judgment and vindication.

A CONDITIONAL RESTORATION IN THE APOCALYPSE OF WEEKS AND THE "EPISTLE" OF ENOCH (BOOK 5)

The Apocalypse of Weeks offers another example of an historical rehearsal with a future passage appended to it. That the author shifts from historical reminiscences into vague generalities in his future descriptions reveals not only the obvious fact that he has left his *ex eventu* format and entered into future "prophecy," but suggests that he was not particularly concerned to present a systematic eschatology for its own sake. The important hinge from past/present to future within the Apocalypse occurs precisely at the point where there exists notorious textual confusion in the MSS — namely, the sixth through eighth weeks (93:10; 91:11b).[25] Fortunately this does not preclude an adequate grasp of the

---

25. For discussion on matters of text, cf. note above. The reason for the inversion of the text has never been solved, and the possibility, for example, that the MS originally ended after the significant seventh week, and that weeks eight to ten were later added to complete the prophecy, has never been completely ruled out.

future references, and by following the numerical order of weeks one through ten we can come up with enough clues to reconstruct the events. We note, first of all, that week six refers to the apostasy ("blindness") of Israel at the time of the exile (93:8). Significantly another "apostate generation" arises at the beginning of the seventh week (93:9), while at its end "shall be elected the elect ones of righteousness from the eternal plant of righteousness, to whom shall be given sevenfold instruction concerning all his flock" (93:10). This unambiguously refers to the author's generation.[26] Thus the hinge occurs just prior to the eighth week.[27]

One is again compelled to ask, given the systematic order of this presentation, whether the significance of the Apocalypse of Weeks lies with the desire to calculate the date of the End. It would certainly appear, given that the author lived in the important seventh week, that his community expected the final events of the eighth week to *begin* shortly, perhaps within one generation. But the real significance of the system adopted here largely depends on how one interprets "weeks." If these "weeks" are of unequal length (as seems most likely),[28] then it is hardly a question of exact calculation, as this would preclude any reader from determining the timing intended by the author. Even if a constant numerical value has been assigned for each week, however, the implication would be much the same. The length of each of the "weeks" in that case, including the seventh week, would probably be 490 years.[29] The problem, however, is that no clear indication is given as to *when* in history the seventh week *began*. The somewhat indefinite mention of how an "apostate generation" will arise (93:9) is hardly enough to determine this. It is accordingly impossible to ascertain the beginning of the eighth week with any exactitude, if such a thing were even thought possible by the author; presumably many years in the seventh week could still be thought to remain.[30] But even if one assumes that the eighth

26. That week seven is the author's own generation is widely acknowledged (by Charles, 1913, 189 et al.).

27. R. H. Charles, *The Book of Enoch or 1 Enoch*, 1912, 293; Black, 1985, 292.

28. Cf. D. S. Russell, *The Method and Message of Jewish Apocalyptic, 200 B.C.–A.D. 100*, 1964, 227.

29. Each "week" would then be composed of the "seventy weeks of years" derived from Dan. 9:2. This is evident in that the period of the exile from the end of the sixth to the (present) seventh week, however it is calculated, requires several hundred years. Each of these subweeks may also have possessed significance for the author, and indications of this exist in the text (cf. the "seventh during the first week" in 93:3, and "the tenth week in the seventh part" in 91:15).

30. On the other hand, we note that the community is said to have arisen at the "completion" of this week (93:10) — the fact that the captivity occurs at the *end* of the sixth week (93:8) also suggests that the author writes near the *end* of the seventh week, 490 years later, but this cannot be established as certain.

week is to begin shortly (91:12),[31] this week does not represent the End *per se*, but rather the continuation of an earthly purgation of sinners at the hand of the righteous. Only at the "completion" of this week (91:13), *at the very least* 490 years following the advent of the righteous community, do events take place, such as the rebuilding of the Temple, that are suggestive of the "final" final events — which are themselves still not *completely* final, as the ninth week contains other warnings of *earthly*(?) judgments (91:14) before the (final, final) *final* judgment at the end of the *tenth* week in 91:15!

This throws doubt on the view that the systematization of history and the future in terms of "weeks" is to any degree intended as a calculating device. Otherwise these great lengths of time would hardly be relevant to the readers, who could not be thought to survive the remaining weeks seven to ten (at this rate the rebuilding of the Temple in the ninth week would not begin for perhaps another 500 years, while the last great judgment may not have been expected for up to 1000 years!). One is accordingly compelled to see in the "weeks" ten periods of *indeterminate* length and, given that weeks eight and nine are yet to come, acknowledge that a significant length of time must pass *before* the End actually takes place. It would seem in fact that the dawning of the End is presented as occurring gradually through several periods. A sense of imminence, should it be discerned here, has nothing to do with the End, but can be explained as merely reflecting the realization that the process has begun, or perhaps reflects an anticipation of the important next stage (notably, the vindication of the saints, a topic which could well be imagined to have invited this sense of urgency; 91:12). While the function of eschatology in the Apocalypse is clearly not to establish a timetable of events, therefore, the eschatological sections beginning in the eighth week evidence some other familiar themes, such as the *judgment of Israel* and the *vindication of the saints*. A "sword" will be given to the righteous with which they will bring judgment upon the sinners,[32] which clearly includes Israelites.[33] Then at the "completion" of that eighth week the righteous "shall acquire great things through their righteousness" (91:13).

Other passages in the book (although not part of the Apocalypse but probably belonging with it from an early stage of redaction) likewise contrast the fates of the righteous and the wicked, and imply that vindication comes in lieu of the suffering of the former:

31. The Eth. text says "the second eighth week," which suggests either that the text was tampered with to postpone the events at a later time or that this is a *seven-* or *seventy-* year week, rather than a week of years, as cf. the similar confusion in 93:3.

32. Assuming that 91:10-11 was originally part of the seventh week, rather than the eighth, as it would appear from the order of the Eth. text.

33. Probably indicated by words like "roots of oppression," "blasphemers," "those who design oppression" in 91:11 and "oppressors" and "sinners" in 91:12.

> Woe unto you, O powerful people!
> You who coerce the righteous with your power,
> the day of your destruction is coming!
> In those days, at the time of your condemnation,
> many and good days shall come for the righteous ones. (96:8)

Much the same vindictive kind of attitude is expressed later on in a lengthy theodicy (102:6–104:13). This passage ironically exposes the error of sinners[34] who feel their oppressive behavior during their life has left them in no worse position than the righteous whom they have persecuted. On the authority of the heavenly tablets this error is contradicted (103:1-3), and the ultimate vindication of the righteous is revealed. This hope for vindication then assumes the form of a "divine reversal": the righteous complain that they had "hoped to be the head and have become the tail," a reference to the covenantal promise of Deut. 28:13, 44,[35] alluding to the fact that in God's order of things the saints should have possessed authority in Israel, but they did not; the passage then offers the assurance that things will eventually be put right.[36] While some doubt exists with the original placement of ch. 108 in the book, it nevertheless exhibits a similar theme of vindication: "And I have recounted in the books all their blessings. He has caused them to be recompensed, for they were all found loving God more than the fire of their eternal souls; and while they were being trodden upon by evil people, experiencing abuse and insult by them, they continued blessing us"[37] (v. 10).

Along with themes of judgment and vindication, hopes of restoration occasionally are expressed in this book, but as in the Zoomorphic History, they appear to be inserted rather arbitrarily and somewhat ambiguously into accounts of judgment. These mostly occur in the Apocalypse of Weeks. Following the first and apparently provisional judgment of the ninth week, one reads that "all people shall direct their sight to the path of uprightness" (91:14), which suggests an anticipation of the coming restoration only. In that case, only after the judgment of the tenth week will the restoration itself begin, when there

---

34. That the opponents in this writing are other Israelites, rather than the Seleucids (suggested as a possibility by Black, 1985, 315), is indicated in 98:11-15 and 104:10-13 (both treated earlier).

35. God's promise in v. 13 is that if Israel obeys, it shall be the head and not the tail; in v. 44 the result of disobedience is a curse in which even a sojourner becomes the head and Israel the tail. Our writers seemed to have individualized this, although the motif also suggestively reflects the situation of Israel that has allowed the views of a few pagans (mere sojourners) to take preeminence over sacred Jewish tradition.

36. Cf. *Jub.* 1:16, which promises that in the restoration, when Israel seeks God "with all [their] heart and with all [their] soul . . . they will be the head and not the tail."

37. I.e., the holy angels, and with them, God.

"shall be a time of goodness and righteousness, and sin shall no more be heard of forever" (91:17). Whether or not the author attempted to harmonize, or was even conscious of the contradiction between his doctrines of judgment and restoration, is impossible to say. What is notable is that these references to a restoration merit little space compared to lengthy descriptions of judgment that will be carried out upon the wicked by the righteous (cf. most of 93:11b-14). While the relative importance of doctrines should not be ascertained on the basis of volume of treatment alone, this nevertheless suggests that the restoration doctrine is at best conventional and incidental to the eschatology of the book. While Israel is clearly judged in the seventh, eighth (note: "oppressors"), and probably also ninth weeks (note: "sinners"), the restoration receives only passing mention in the tenth.

Whether or not Israelites *outside* the circle of the righteous are to be included in this restoration is not stated and cannot be easily concluded from this passage alone. The presence of restoration language would seem to demand this, although we might note that, according to the order of events presented, by the time the restoration takes place both Israelite sinners and the nations have *already been judged* in the earlier weeks. Presumably, then, only the righteous remain to enjoy the blessing, while plenty of opportunity for repentance is provided for. The description of this as a time of "goodness and righteousness" when "sin shall no more be heard of forever" (91:17) also suggests that only the righteous have survived to reach this blessed and eternal period. Participation in the restoration would appear, in any event, to be conditional upon righteousness, as in the following verses Enoch promises to show his children "the ways of righteousness and the ways of wickedness" (v. 18) so that they might know how to attain to that time of "righteousness," "for all those who walk in the ways of injustice shall perish" (v. 19). From what one can learn of the restoration in this passage, therefore, the idea of restoration as the salvation *of all Israel* is scarcely evident, if at all. The ideas of judgment and vindication seem to have been more pressing upon our author than any hope for restoration. This is confirmed by one other interesting reference to the restoration that occurs in the final (addended?) chapters: "Then I beheld the writing upon them [the heavenly tablets] that one generation shall be more wicked than the other, until a generation of righteous ones shall arise, wickedness shall perish, sin shall disappear from upon the earth, and every good thing shall come upon her" (107:1). Apparently the author of this passage viewed the restoration as directly linked to the arising of a righteous community, a point of view in agreement with 93:10 and 91:12.

One more eschatological passage in this book merits attention — namely, the opening section of the book (91:5-11a). Whether or not this eschatological section comes from the same original source as the Apocalypse is debatable. In

contrast to the ten-weeks apocalypse, this passage simply states, in a quite succinct and general fashion, that a time of great apostasy is coming (vv. 5-7a), and
that this will be followed by the final judgment of fire (vv. 7b-9) and a general
resurrection (v. 10). Also in contrast to the Apocalypse, God, not the righteous,
will be solely responsible for judgment (cf. v. 7b). No mention of resurrection
occurs in the Apocalypse of Weeks, but is found here. There is absolutely no
temporal frame of reference offered in this passage, in contrast to the Apocalypse.

These differences are substantial, but may not be enough to posit two different traditions, sources, or authors. The differences perhaps lie with the form
of presentation only. Whatever its relationship to the remainder of the work,
this introduction adds little to what we have already seen. Predictions of apostasy (vv. 5-7) are proffered from Enoch's perspective, and it is obvious that the
time of great apostasy is not some future "messianic travail"; these words are
not strictly eschatological at all but refer to the circumstances in which the
writer and his community find themselves in the author's present.[38] Since the
judgment seems to follow the apostasy without a break between the two, however, it would appear that the End is believed to be imminent. On the other
hand, the earthly judgments of vv. 7-8 may be merely preliminary to the fiery
"eternal" judgments of vv. 9-10, as noted above with regard to the Apocalypse
of Weeks. The basic components of this eschatology — apostasy of Israel[39] followed by judgment — generally cohere with eschatological presentations elsewhere in the Enoch literature.

RESTORATION AS CONVERSION IN *JUBILEES*

Charles believed he could distinguish between the eschatology of apocalyptic
works that had a Pharisaic tendency and the eschatology of *Jubilees,* which evidenced a more Sadducean outlook. While the former presented the coming of
the End in terms of sudden, cataclysmic occurrences, *Jubilees* was satisfied to

---

38. The Eth. *kā'ebata,* "twofold," refers to a second apostasy after the flood, and is
translated "for a second time" by Black (1985, 281; *contra* Charles's "in a twofold degree").
The idea of "messianic travail" is not really appropriate for such passages (*contra*, e.g.,
Mowinckel, 1956, 295), as their chief function is to define the present, not the future.

39. The typical sins for which Israel is responsible include: "oppression" (i.e., on the
righteous community), "injustice," "blasphemy," and "uncleanliness" (ritual sin) in 91:7;
the judgment upon them is a covenantal curse ("plague," 91:7). More explicit is the statement that "all that which is (common) with the heathen shall be surrendered" (91:9), in
which the judgment-of-Israel theme comes again to the fore.

introduce the future in terms of a more gradual unfolding of the kingdom.[40] Besides the fact that scholars have largely abandoned the Pharisaic-versus-Sadducean dialectic as a solution to the social history of Judaism, there is the question whether the authors of these books would even have been conscious of the subtle implication sometimes taken from (otherwise vague) allusions to future events. *1 Enoch* dealt with future events with inexactitude — three to four ages or "weeks" are scheduled by the Apocalypse of Weeks for the unfolding of the future events (which amounts to a "gradually unfolding" eschatology if there ever was one). *Jubilees* would appear to represent a similar example of how eschatological beliefs were presented in general terms, and despite its schematizing of history according to jubilees of years, there is no indication that the author employed this format in order to compose a timetable of future events *per se*. He seems satisfied to advance the notion that sacred history unfolds in a distinct order, an interest we have already argued relates more to his presentation of calendar and covenant and less to any abstract determinism.

Recently Wacholder has detected what he thinks is a precise date for the eschaton in *Jubilees*, based on his study of 49:22–50:5 and a few parallel texts.[41] The following words of the Lord to Moses, which also serve to sum up the contents of *Jubilees*, are particularly important to his theory: "I also related to you the sabbaths of the land on Mount Sinai. And the years of jubilee in the sabbaths of years I related to you. But *its year* I have not related to you until you enter into the land which you will possess" (50:2). Perhaps, as Wacholder suggests, the enigmatic "its year" in this verse refers to the year on which End will come (which is cryptically revealed further down the passage).[42] But this seems to de-

---

40. Cf. Charles, 1912, 236. This view Charles formulated largely on the basis of 23:26-28 and 50:5, which evidence "a gradual transformation" (R. H. Charles, *The Book of Jubilees or Little Genesis, Translated from the Editor's Ethiopic Text,* 1902, 149, 258). 50:5 reads: "And jubilees will pass until Israel is purified from all the sin of fornication, and defilement, and uncleanness, and sin and error." This verse, notably the references to "jubilees," reminds us of "weeks" yet to pass in the Apocalypse of Weeks. *Jubilees* itself may simply be indicating an interval between the exodus of v. 4 and the restoration of v. 5. No "gradual transformation" would then be intended. The view is perhaps more clearly presented in 23:26-28, but if so the view is so incidental as to hardly support an entire theory of origins.

41. B. Z. Wacholder, "The Date of the Eschaton in the Book of Jubilees," 1985, 87-101. Davenport (1971, 69-70) follows Testuz in a similar theory.

42. Wacholder, 1985, 93. The "sabbaths of the land" and "the years of jubilee in the sabbaths of years" refer to the sabbath-year laws and law of jubilee in Lev. 25:1ff. Davenport, on the other hand, while also maintaining that the passage intends to calculate the date of the End, holds v. 2b to be an addition! "Vs. 2b is an intrusion into the angel's command to Moses. . . . it says that the angel did not tell Moses the precise year in which Israel would enter the Promised Land. Whoever inserted the clause must have intended it to discourage the reader from using the calendar for precisely the kind of speculation for which

mand again the unwarranted assumption that the timing of the End was so important to this author and his community that a terse and enigmatic reference to "its year" would automatically evoke the idea of the End. One might ask where a parallel or precedent can be found for addressing the question of the "year" of the End? A much simpler interpretation,[43] one that fits at least equally well into the context, is to take "its year" as a reference to the establishment of the *jubilee* year. That is, in order to establish the exact timing of the rotation of years and thus the fixing of the calendar, a reference point, the jubilee year, must itself be known. The verse then merely implies that further revelation to Israel, at a time subsequent to their entry into the Promised Land, is necessary so they can properly submit to the authorized calendar.[44]

Mention should be made of Davenport's exhaustive and insightful study *The Eschatology of the Book of Jubilees* (1971). Davenport employs a source analysis to conclude that eschatology has been allowed far too much influence in past studies of *Jubilees*.[45] The history of scholarship has produced a great deal of confusion over the exact order of events in *Jubilees*, a fact that suggests that the work is not intended to teach eschatological doctrine at all. Moreover, Davenport blames scholars for making

> no distinction between the major function of a passage and the subservient function of various elements in the passage. . . . As a result, they sometimes assign too much significance to details which have been passed along in a

---

[the original author] intended it to be used" (1971, 70). This seems like a rather convenient emendation for the sake of an unnecessary theory.

43. In order to arrive at a date for the End, Wacholder makes a critical, but very complex, assumption that there exists a direct correspondence between the 2,410-year time interval of 50:4 (he arrives at 2,410 by summing the time between Adam and Moses as forty-nine jubilees plus one week of years plus two years) and the unspecified time interval between the entry into the Promised Land and the eschaton itself in 50:5 (i.e., another 2,450 years = 2,410 + 40 years), and that this correspondence is both *intended* and *implied;* cf. Wacholder, 1985, 95. But no such correspondence is demanded or suggested by the latter verse. In fact, the number of "jubilees" is conspicuously *not* specified (v. 5), and the numbers are nowhere repeated for the later time period. Wacholder seems to be convinced that eschatology is the key to these writings. But this theory has many problems, of which this correspondence is one of the greatest.

44. This fixing of the calendar may have been viewed as irrelevant to Moses before he entered the Promised Land, either because the cult had not been properly established or because the calendar could not have been properly followed outside the land. In either event, it would have been felt natural to have remedied the problem through a further revelation; this is the exact point of v. 2, a reference Wacholder (1985, 93) finds enigmatic!

45. Cf. Davenport, 1971, 1. According to Davenport's source analysis, this is partly because the whole work is read in the light of the single source reflected in 1:4b-26 that is eschatologically oriented (14).

unit as incidental teaching. . . . If a block of material is intended for the purpose of teaching eschatological doctrine, we should expect more detail than if it is used for some other purpose.[46]

The details of the End are not important to the authors; the passages themselves are not meant to teach eschatology at all, but function to warn Israelites to live by the law, not to live as Gentiles; the eschatology of *Jubilees* correspondingly contains the important message that Israelites will not escape the judgment.[47] Davenport concludes: "Judah is the remnant in whom the promises to the ancestors will find fulfillment. In her triumph, Israel will be triumphant."[48] While one might not entirely agree with the methodology or result of Davenport's source analysis, this assessment of the place of eschatology in the message of *Jubilees* is at least impressive.

As with *1 Enoch,* the eschatology of *Jubilees* conceals a strong judgment motif and alludes to a time of restoration. Recall from our previous discussion that several of the judgment oracles in this book explicitly center out Israelites for judgment. Other passages are not so direct, but imply or allude to this judgment-of-Israel theme (such as the vivid prediction of fiery judgment for "the man who desires to harm his brother," *Jub.* 36:11). It is when one comes to the restoration element in the eschatology of *Jubilees* that the importance of this doctrine for the author becomes evident as well. While Wacholder's attempt to calculate the date of the End on the basis of 50:2 may not have been successful, this passage does address eschatological questions (in v. 5). Here one reads of an extended time of apostasy ("jubilees will pass until Israel is purified from all the sin of fornication, and defilement, and uncleanness, and sin and error") followed by a time of blessing, probably the restoration ("and they will dwell in confidence in all the land").[49] The relatively superficial treatment given to es-

---

46. Davenport, 1971, 1, 5, cf. 306.

47. Davenport, 1971, 51-54, 73-74. "Not all Israelites, but only those faithful to the Torah, will enjoy the new day" (52).

48. Davenport, 1971, 72. This is the message of Davenport's chief source document, "A"; the minor additions do not radically affect the message of the whole. "The message of the present edition of Jubilees is the message of R$_2$. . . . God . . . has called into existence a small group of faithful people . . . the faithful will eventually emerge triumphant" (77-78).

49. Wacholder sees the first period of apostasy corresponding to the time of restoration: "the sabbatical years which the land keeps will correspond to the number of years in which the observance has been neglected since the time of Creation" (1985, 95). It is unlikely, however, that the expression "the land will keep its sabbaths" (50:3-4) implies that one group of sabbaths would somehow atone for those that were missed. Wacholder (95) appeals to an enigmatic interpretation of Lev. 26:34 to sustain this, believing also that CD 1:1-10 establishes at forty years the period remaining before the consummation (97-99). The whole theory is tenuous.

chatology in this verse seems to indicate that the subject was not very important to the author and that other issues were at the forefront of thought. On the
other hand, 50:5 appears to summarize 1:7-18, 22-25 where the matter of Israel's restoration is first advanced, and the resulting *inclusio* formed by the material between these verses (which are significantly located near the beginning
and the end of the book) suggests that the idea may have been of some importance to the author.[50] The significance of 50:5, in other words, is bound up with
that of 1:7ff. with its expression of hope for restoration.

We have already mentioned the obtrusiveness of the restoration doctrine
in this first chapter of *Jubilees*. In an extensive analysis of the pertinent verses
we suggested that Moses' prayer for Israel (1:19-21) exhibits a traditional hope
for Israel's promised blessing, while also implying, however, that the history of
the nation as narrated in the book (cf. 1:7-14, 22) casts significant doubt on Israel's deservedness of that blessing. Restoration in this passage, as Davenport
has also argued, is entirely conditional on the response of the individual Israelite.[51] Implicit *conditions* on Israel's blessedness, including obedience to the
book now being written by Moses (i.e., *Jubilees*), are established early on in the
writing (cf. 1:5-6). It would appear that *the basic condition for the salvation of
the nation is accepting the foundational beliefs of the righteous community.* The
words: "And thus it will be, when all of these things happen to them, that they
will know that I have been more righteous than they in all their judgments and
deeds. And they will know that I have truly been with them," are apparently *not*
to be taken as a promise of unilateral mercy, as we have seen, so much as a justification for God's judgment of the unfaithful nation.[52] Accordingly, when it is
said that God will be "with" Israel (1:6), that they will be gathered from the nations (1:15), that they will be a blessing (1:16), that the Temple will be built in
their midst (1:17), that God will not forsake them (1:18), that they will be purified (1:22-23), that they will be called "sons" (1:25), these statements can only
be held in tension with other statements in the very *same* passages which suggest that, from the time when the promises were first made to Abraham until
the final restoration, Israel would *not* be deserving of God, and furthermore

50. The resulting *inclusio* also tends to cast doubt on Davenport's source analysis,
which attributes this part of the first chapter to a later editor.

51. Davenport, 1971, 26-27.

52. It is curious in this regard how Charles points to Ezra 9:9 ("Yet our God has not
forsaken us in our bondage") as a parallel to v. 5, without, however, noting that the context
of the verse in Ezra implies that God has saved only a remnant who are now able to rejoice
in his mercy! The verse that follows in *Jubilees* (v. 6; cited here) is also formulaic, reflecting
Deut. 30:1, and is highly conditional. Our author, furthermore, does not continue to cite
Deut. 30:2, which refers to the anticipated return from exile, a fact that may have some significance.

that *repentance* from their unfaithful state is absolutely indispensable for an experience of this restoration. Thus times of great apostasy are predicted (1:7-14, 22) from which Israel must *repent* ("return"; "when they seek me," 1:15; "return to me," 1:23). Furthermore, Israel must be cleansed, in a kind of act of spiritual conversion ("I shall cut off the foreskin of their heart . . . and I shall create for them a holy spirit, and I shall *purify* them," 1:23). They must *begin* to obey "my commandments" (1:24). It is accordingly only in such a "converted" condition, itself a gift of the restoring God, that the promise comes that "I shall not forsake them, and I shall not be alienated from them" (1:18).[53] It would accordingly be amiss to summarize the restoration theology of *Jubilees* as the unilateral action of God that overlooks the nation's sin. God is with them only when *they are with God.* There is no indication given, therefore, that the author thought this promise applied to all individual Israelites automatically while living in a state of apostasy — in fact, every indication is that restoration was *conditional* upon repentance. Israel will first conform to the righteousness demanded of God (i.e., demanded by the community) and *then* they will be restored. Given these qualifications, it is quite difficult to decide whether the author of *Jubilees* envisaged *ethnic* Israel, or only *representative* Israel, as being saved in the restoration.[54] The author merely expresses *both* his view of the special election of his community *and* his doctrine of restoration — this latter doctrine once more qualified through the influence of "sectarian" ideas. Restoration is thus treated as a *traditional* doctrine that, however, must give place to the immediate and more *essential* concerns of the writer's exclusive soteriology.

It is possible, therefore, that tradition alone is responsible for this author's ostensible concern for Israel, although we have already seen how exclusive claims could be held together with quite sincere hopes for restoration as two legitimate and important aspects of a single point of view. VanderKam suggests that *Jubilees* evinces this tension because the Jubilaean community (in contrast to the Qumranites) had not yet left Jerusalem. Thus *Jubilees'* concern is still for the entire nation of Israel.[55] However, it is questionable whether this tension can be taken as a dependable indicator of the provenance of the book. There is no indication, to cite a parallel example, that the concern for the nation lessened among the Qumranites when they journeyed into exile. Along with a re-

---

53. If much of this refers to the exile and the return from exile, vv. 20-23 in particular reflect the perspective of the "real" author and suggest a continued "stubbornness" even after the return, as argued above.

54. The ambiguity is evident in Davenport's summary of the doctrine. Contrast: "In the victory of Judah [a designation for the righteous], the destiny of Israel will be realized" with: "The battered and bruised faithful nation then will be restored to health in a renewal as wide as the creation itself" (1971, 78).

55. J. C. VanderKam, *Textual and Historical Studies in the Book of Jubilees*, 1977, 281.

spect for traditional views, the author's special concern for the doctrine may also be partly due, as already suggested, to the literary context of *Jubilees*. The author desired to portray Moses as Israel's intercessor *par excellence,* but in doing so he also drew definite limits: there would be no *automatic* restoration.

Other indications exist that *Jubilees* expected a rather limited restoration. One eschatological passage in particular (23:26-28, 30-31) appears to mention only the righteous community in connection with the blessings of the future. The limited application of this passage to the elect has already been demonstrated.

> And in those days, *children* will begin to search the law,
> and to search the commandments
> and to return to the way of righteousness.
> And the days will begin to increase and grow longer
> among those sons of men, generation by generation,
> and year by year, until
> their days approach a thousand years,
> and to a greater number of years than days. . . .
> And then the LORD will heal *his servants,*
> and they will rise up and see great peace.
> And they will drive out their enemies,
> and *the righteous ones* will see and give praise,
> and rejoice forever and ever with joy; . . .
> and they will know that the LORD is an executor of judgment;
> but he will show mercy to hundreds and thousands,
> to *all who love him.*

This passage would appear to maintain that the righteous are, at least *at present,* the only benefactors of God's salvation since the "searching out of the law and the commandments" is portrayed as occurring among these "children."[56] The author seems to view the restoration as already partly realized among these righteous ones.[57] He also seems to envisage a definite *growth* in numbers after this point (the rather modest "hundreds and thousands" perhaps invokes the belief that the restoration will reflect the ideal period of Israel's history when the tribes were divided into thousands, hundreds, etc.), but this restoration still

---

56. This does not mean that we can identify more exactly the people whom the author saw as forming this restoration, or the signs that the restoration was beginning to take place, nor to assume, with scholars like Davenport (1971, 43-44), that the success of the Maccabees was felt to bring this about, especially since the author knows of the excesses of the Hasmoneans that could hardly have been viewed as representative of the restoration (vv. 20-21).

57. Cf. Davenport, 1971, 27-28.

applies only to those "who love [the Lord]." This passage is somewhat ambiguous, therefore, and hardly provides enough evidence to conclude whether our writer successfully harmonized views about the eventual salvation of Israel with other notions about the limits of the saved community. The passage is replete with the language of vindication (vv. 27-28, 30), suggesting, at least, that the righteous and their ("true") teaching was thought to provide the essential *focus* of God's work of restoration. This is also indicated in the way the passage opens with scenes of repentance *before* moving to scenes of growth and renewal (note the "and *then* . . ." of v. 30). In fact, the consistent element in all the eschatological passages examined so far has been the expectation (if not the demand) that Israel *convert* to the way already held by the Jubilaean group. For *Jubilees,* therefore, *God's work of restoration is God's work of converting Israel to the community who possessed the heavenly tablets.* This is just what one would expect from the rather strict position toward covenant obedience embraced by the author of *Jubilees.*[58]

INSTRUMENTS OF RESTORATION:
THE COMMUNITY OF THE DEAD SEA SCROLLS

Several expressions are employed for future times and events at Qumran: "the appointed time" (*qēṣ neḥ*e*rāṣāh,* 1QS 4.25), "the new creation" (*ᶜsôṯ ḥ*e*ḏāšāh,* 1QS 4.25), "the last time" (*qēṣ (hā)'aḥ*e*rôn,* 1QS 4.16-17; 1QpHab. 7.7), "the end of days" (*'aḥ*e*rîṯ hay-yāmîm,* 1QpHab 2.5-6; 9.6), and — somewhat more distinctive to Qumran — "the (second) visitation" (*happ*e*qûḏāh,* 1QS 3.18; 4.6, 11; CD 7.21; cf. 8.3).[59] It is not clear that these designations refer to equal, or even related, periods of time. Some clearly allude to events occurring well before the End, occasionally even to the present experiences of the *yaḥaḏ.*[60]

---

58. In *Jub.* 32:19 the Lord promises Jacob that his "seed" will rule over all the nations, and that "all of the earth will be gathered together and they will inherit it forever." In view of the "seed" theology of this writing, the seed here may be limited to the "righteous seed" or include ethnic Israel in the restoration; but the saying is traditional and ambiguous.

59. A somewhat similar expression is used in Wis. 3:7; Luke 19:44; cf. H. Ringgren, *The Faith of Qumran,* 1963, 153.

60. Carmignac (1969, 22-27) determines that the expression "end of days" (אחרית הימים) at Qumran, in line with the scriptural use, never refers to the end of the world, but to the end of a (historical) period. Most frequently it refers to the end of the "dominion of Belial" (23-25); elsewhere it refers to a time of blessedness (25-26). The term indicates in a general way "what will be" *(suite)* rather than the "end" *(fin)*: "Selon la mentalité de

This variety of terms probably reflects something frequently observed about the eschatology of the scrolls; namely, that the various teachings are fundamentally disparate and the terms often inexact, making it very difficult to formulate any unified or even coherent eschatological scheme for the sect[61] or even to classify that eschatology too precisely. J. Pryke, who has investigated Qumran eschatology, accordingly questions whether a monolithic view of "apocalyptic" (i.e., transcendental, cataclysmic) eschatology can be assumed for Qumran at all. In contrast to the usual nonhistorical conception of this eschatology, he concludes:

> the sect thought that evil in the present age would increase until the community, under the inspired guidance of one of their "Orthodox Teachers," lived the sufficient life of purity essential for God to cause to be born a Messiah who would conquer the forces of evil in the forty years' war. . . . The immediate outcome of the struggle would be victory against the Romans and the orthodox Jewish leaders, with a long period of peace and prosperity. . . .

There is little consistency in the details of Qumran eschatology:

> One of the Hymns reflects the cruder eschatology in the idea of total destruction of the universe by fire, but the resurrection from the dead after a final judgment by the Son of Man is nowhere to be found in the texts. The Angelic Liturgy, a mystical prayer cycle, and the Hymns, are ethereal and Greek in their approach to the worlds to come, while the Zadokite Documents and the War of the Sons of Light and the Sons of Darkness are preoccupied with this world, with the founding of the community and its struggles for survival. . . . there is no one continuous pattern of uniform doctrine, for the Qumran documents which cover a similar period of over two hundred years oscillate between a this worldly Messianic hope and a near gnostic attitude to the future life.[62]

Pryke is not alone in recognizing this variety in eschatological doctrine at Qumran. Others have even attempted to explain it: some attribute it to the independence of the individual documents; others maintain either that the conflicting doctrines were carelessly allowed to stand juxtaposed or else were successfully synthesized (in the minds of the writers, if not in our minds); others suggest that we are witness to a development or reformulation of the doctrines

---

l'Ancien Testament et selon la mentalité de Qumrân, on assigne globalement à 'la suite des jours' les événements que l'on prévoit ou que l'on prédit pour un avenir indéterminé" (26).

61. As cf., e.g., Schreiner, 1986, 42.

62. Pryke, 1969, 45-57; citations taken from 56-57.

that took place gradually and imperceptibly; while still others try to discern some underlying structure for eschatological belief that is not evident on the surface of the texts. Norman Golb, of course, attributes this kind of theological diversity to the fact that the literature found in the caves near the Dead Sea represents the writings of many different Jewish groups of the time; the diversity in eschatological teaching at Qumran, however, is probably quite comparable to what we see in the other writings and does not, therefore, necessarily demand that several groups are represented. Whatever the cause for the diversity, Philip Davies also draws attention to the variety of belief and concludes (quite justifiably from our perspective) that this group can hardly be understood as "apocalyptic," if by the use of that word it is implied that the group was "sustained by intense eschatological expectation."[63] Davies suggestively hints instead that Qumran eschatology is characterized by an emerging ethical and spiritual (cosmic) dualism.[64] In any event, the fact that the community or communities represented by the scrolls apparently made no conscious attempt to synthesize their eschatological teaching strongly suggests that the coming of the End was *not* the most important doctrine at Qumran, nor that it played the formative role often attributed to it.

A kind of "realized eschatology" was apparently also in effect. The sect believed it was already living in the eschaton (cf. CD 1.12),[65] and that the eschatological salvation was, in a certain measure at least, already present. But what does this mean? The Damascus Document (col. 1) gives the impression that the community thought of itself as the continuing remnant of returnees from the Babylonian exile, most of whom became unfaithful (CD 7.20–8.2). This could mean that the sect considered themselves *later* returnees, to be distinguished from those who returned at the time of Zerubbabel, Ezra, and Nehemiah, or that they discounted this earlier return as entirely ineffective or incomplete, or at best conditional on the faithfulness of the returnees.[66] In any event, the eschatological beliefs of the group seem to have been rooted in the very "historical" *Sitz im Leben* of the return from exile and were, therefore, at least partly *past*-oriented. This is a

---

63. P. R. Davies, "Eschatology at Qumran," 1985, 39-55, 42. In support of this view Davies observes that the most popular theories regarding the origins of the community (i.e., either a priestly battle or a division in the Essene party) do not lend themselves to the view that eschatology was a formative concern (53-54). Thus he confronts the "pan-eschatological" approach to Jewish sectarian history: "there is actually no evidence, within or without the Qumran texts, to suggest that the Ḥasidim, or the pre-Qumran Essenes, were eschatologically highly motivated themselves" (54).

64. P. R. Davies, 1985, 47, 50-52.

65. Schreiner, 1986, 42; S. Talmon, *King, Cult, and Calendar in Ancient Judaism*, 1986, 220.

66. Cf. Talmon, 1986, 214-15.

preferable historical and ideological background against which to understand the Qumran self-consciousness than the superficial "apocalyptic" label that tends to imply a totally future and *a*historical orientation.

Was this view of the group as *legitimate returnees,* however, also responsible for the view that the eschaton was *"now"?* Talmon's explanation that the "restoration" the sectarians experienced was still only a kind of "prototypical *Urzeit* on which they modeled their vision of the future ideal aeon for whose realization they yearned" is helpful. They were merely the *first* generation of the "New Israel" to return from the exile.[67] If this perception is correct, and if the community was not only conscious of the significance of contemporary happenings but also able to envision yet future events modeled on their own experiences — that is, if they possessed an already/not-yet dialectic in their eschatology[68] — this should caution against too hastily attributing to this group a rigid identification of their period with the final events themselves. All evidence would suggest that the covenanters still expected *future* events to unfold — the End may have been some time distant.

Some have proposed that while the Qumran *yaḥad* originally possessed an immediate expectation of the final events, circumstances led them to adopt a theory of delay, and to modify, or at least clarify, their ideas about the future. 1QpHab 7.6-14 has been said to suggest such a change in perspective,[69] and the need to explain the delay may be why certain passages appear to betray initial attempts at "calculation." In Talmon's view this delay had the effect of transforming a gradual view of eschatological transformation into a cataclysmic expectation with apocalyptic features. The in-between time became an interim phase in which repentance and purification were made possible and a kind of interim ethic was instituted. This "delay" he differentiates from that of the early Christian church where the "now" was as legitimately eschatological as the "not yet." At Qumran, in contrast, an unbridgeable gap remained between the "now" and the "then," based on a failure of their hopes

---

67. Talmon, 1986, 214-15. 1QH 3.36, which we have analyzed above, is a possible indication of how the present and future were held together at Qumran.

68. For a close analysis of the relationship between present and future salvation as revealed in the Community Hymns, cf. H.-W. Kuhn, *Enderwartung und gegenwärtiges Heil,* 1966, esp. 34-43, 175-88. He concludes that ideas related to both future and present salvation can be found juxtaposed, and that the words "proleptic" *(propleptisch-eschatologisch),* as well as "now" *(jetzt)* and "not yet" *(noch nicht),* are appropriate ways to speak of this condition. *"Mit dem Leben in der Heilssphäre Gottes 'ist eigentlich alles weitere schon gegeben'"* (184, emphasis in original). P. R. Davies (1985, 52) also alludes to a combination "of anticipation and of realization" in eschatological teaching at Qumran.

69. Cf. M. A. Knibb, *The Qumran Community,* 1987, 234.

70. Talmon, 1986, 215-16, 222-23.

to materialize.[70] While it seems doubtful that the community, even at this later period, abandoned their sense of "realized eschatology," one can perhaps agree that the community held some kind of doctrine of delay (as cf. 1QpHab 7.6-14). But this does not appear to have developed into a timetabling attitude toward the future. The absence of deterministically oriented historical rehearsals or periodizations of the future in the scrolls would seem to suggest the opposite — namely, a hesitance to be too dogmatic about timing. It would seem rather that the community saw itself as living in an indefinable interim in which one eye was on the meaningful events of the past, which were still in effect, and the other eye was on the future consummation. This unique historical perspective helps to explain the occasional "confusion" of past, present, and future in the Qumran documents.

Such an ambiguity about time would accordingly once again throw into doubt the prevalent eschatological categorization of the scrolls. It is the community itself, not its eschatological teaching, that more frequently assumes center stage. To take one striking example, the Commentary 1QpHab, usually characterized as one of the most "eschatological" documents among the scrolls, consistently interprets even the most *inviting* and *provocative* (from an eschatological standpoint) passages in the book of Habakkuk, not by picking up on and adding further eschatological speculation, but by reflecting on the *history* of the *community* and their opponents. A good example of this is 2.1-10. This passage comments on Hab. 1:5, which contains the eschatologically provocative words: "I am doing a work in your days . . . ," but ll. 1-4 of the scroll start off by relating this not to the future but to the *past* experience of the community, while ll. 5-10 mention almost as an afterthought a secondary application to some indefinable future.

Other passages in the commentary also apply directly to the experiences of the community, betray a strongly *realized* view of eschatology, and are notably informed by the kind of soteriological dualism we have been investigating. This is true even in passages more clearly given over to eschatological concerns. In 5.1-5, for example, the commentator takes the words of judgment from Hab. 1:12-13, again not as an opportunity to describe the final events themselves but rather to describe the role of the community as instruments of vengeance in the final judgment: "The explanation of this word is that God will not destroy His people by the hand of the nations; but God will judge all the nations by the hand of His elect. And it is by the chastisement which the elect will dispense that all the wicked of His people will atone, because they have kept His commandments in their distress" (ll. 3-6). This passage, as analyzed earlier (ch. 2), indicates how the judgment of apostate Israel at the hand of the elect "atones" for the faithful and "for the land," and how the elect are (apparently on that basis) instruments of judgment for the nations.

It is arguably this kind of *community-centered realized eschatology,* not solely the events of the future, that gives *pešer* its distinctive quality. Accordingly the writer of the Habakkuk *pešer* seems particularly reluctant to make any judgment about the exact timing of the final events. On Hab. 2:1-2 the *pešer* comments: "God told Habakkuk to write down the things which will come to pass in the last generation, but *the consummation of time He made not known to him*" (7.1-2). The implication of the following lines is that this kind of knowledge *was* made known to the *moreh* — but what is related in the commentary is not the *timing* of the End at all, but the *circumstances* of the community and its opponents during the last days. Apparently "consummation" in l. 2 itself refers to the *quality* of this time, quite possibly intending to bring to mind the age in which the sect was now living.[71] It apparently does not function as a chronological marker. Again the emphasis is on the community rather than on eschatology.

While the scrolls contain no clear attempts to date or timetable the future, other familiar themes are abundantly represented in them. The notion of eschatological judgment for rebellious Israelites is, as already indicated, an important aspect of the teaching of the scrolls, and on the other side of things, there is certainly no lack of pronouncements regarding the vindication of the group either. Scenes of vindication become quite spectacular in the War Scroll, for example, which proclaims that God will "deliver the enemies of all the lands into the hand of the Poor, and by the hand of them that are bent in the dust wilt Thou humble the valiant of the peoples . . . to justify Thy judgment of truth in the midst of the sons of men and to make for Thyself an eternal name in the people whom [Thou hast redeemed]. . . ."[72] This passage suggests that through the holy war God's favor will not only rest on, but will be *shown* to rest on, the righteous. Another passage similarly tells how at the end of the war, after the wicked of the covenant and the nations have been destroyed, shall come "the time of salvation for the people of God, the hour of dominion for all the men of his lot and of final destruction for all the lot of Belial" (1:5) — clear references to the *yaḥad* and its vindication.[73] It requires little imagination to see that the unconscious function of the eschatological teaching in the War Scroll is to provide consolation for the righteous through this note of vindication (cf. esp.

---

71. Cf. Knibb, 1987, 234.

72. 1QM 11.13-15; cf. 17.6-8. Y. Yadin reconstructs the lacuna: "through Thy [holy] people . . ." (*The Scroll of the War of the Sons of Light against the Sons of Darkness,* 1962, 312), suggesting what is otherwise clear in the context of the passage, as well as in the passage itself: that the righteous are also instruments of judgment.

73. "People of God" here is yet another designation of the righteous, inasmuch as it is inscribed on the banner of the congregation in 3.12 (cf. Yadin, 1962, 258). The "dominion" alludes to that given unto the "people of the saints of the Most High" in Dan. 7:27.

17.6-8).[74] The aggressive posture of the scroll and its preoccupation with the triumph of the righteous troops suggest an unmitigated vindictiveness — although, in fairness to the Qumranites, the righteous community is reported to be doing quite a lot of suffering themselves during this war.

While there is no systematic presentation of a doctrine of restoration in the scrolls, there are many indications, in the form of allusions and related terms, that such a hope was entertained. After the war there will be a time of "righteousness" (1QM 1.8-9); the glory of Zion is envisaged (1QM 12.13-15; cf. 18.5-8); a fragment from Cave 1 refers to the time when "justice will be revealed like a sun which regulates the world . . . and knowledge will pervade the world" (1Q27 = 1QMysteries); CD 7.16 cites the Amos 9:11 prophecy about restoring the fallen booth of David; and 4QTanhumim (4Q176) promises a restoration for fallen Jerusalem employing a catena of Isaian texts, notably Isa. 40:1-5 (also 48:1-9; 49:13-17; 52:1-3; 54:4-10). Significantly 11QT refers to a time of repentance, but only *after* the apostates "fill up the measure of their guilt" (59.9). The frequent use of the term "the Many" *(rabbîm)* as a self-reference by the Qumran community may find its significance in this connection. This word would certainly be appropriate as a symbol of the belief that Israel would return *en masse* to the Lord, although this would be of quite curious significance, given the community's self-consciousness of being the chosen "few" out of Israel. Evidence suggests, rather, that the term was, at least originally, used in legal contexts to refer to the "majority" of the voting members of the *yaḥad*.[75] This would not rule out the possibility that the term was *later* applied to restoration hopes, however, or alluded to the idea of the community as the instruments of atonement in line with the "ransom" of the "many" in Isa. 53:11,[76] but explicit indications of this usage are wanting.

G. Jeremias finds a reference to restoration hopes in 1QH 2.13: "Thou

74. The importance of this war for the sect is adequately summarized by Schreiner: "Das ganze Leben der Gemeinde und ihrer einzelnen Mitglieder ist auf diesen eschatologischen Krieg ausgerichtet und von ihm her bestimmt" (1986, 43). For a similar function for the final war in *2 Baruch,* cf. T. W. Willett, *Eschatology in the Theodicies of 2 Baruch and 4 Ezra,* 1989, 118.

75. While the term can arguably be translated "the great ones," the occasional use of the abstract term "multitude" *(rōb)* to refer to the group suggests that the qualitative aspect is intended. Knibb points to the parallel phrase רוב אנשי היחד in 1QS 5.2-3, which refers to "the whole body of the full members of the community. In a similar way the Greek word *plēthos* (literally 'multitude') is used in Acts to refer to the Christian community; cp. e.g. Acts 15:30. . . . The idea underlying this figurative use of language is that the decisions of all the full members are as authoritative as the old sacred lot" (1987, 106).

76. For discussion and similar conclusions, cf. Ringgren, 1963, 211-12. *Jub.* 6:5, 9 commands Noah and his sons after the flood to become "many," although the connection of the two ideas is not apparent.

hast made of me a banner (נס *nēs*) for the elect of righteousness" — "In Judaism a consistent idea was associated with the word נס. On the basis of Is. 11:12; 49:22; 62:10 it was connected with the hope that God would in the end time gather and bring together again the dispersed members of the people of Israel. It was expected that God would raise a banner before the people to which the dispersed would be brought near."[77] If one accepts this connection,[78] the phrase would imply that the ministry of the *moreh* possessed implications for the anticipated restoration, although it does not seem to demand a messianic role for the Teacher — he is merely a signal or sign of the coming restoration. But notably, this passage also significantly qualifies the expectation, for it is only to the "elect of righteousness" that the *moreh* appears as a banner or standard. The strongly dualistic tone of the hymn, which was earlier examined as an example of the divisive nature of the teaching of the *moreh*, enhances this qualifying aspect.

Another passage that appears unambiguously to allude to the hoped-for restoration is quite fragmented (4QpPs37 3.10-13 *ad* Ps. 37:21-22), but can be reconstructed enough to grant some insight into the views of the group regarding this belief. It is worth quoting the passage in its entirety, reconstructing the lacunae:

> The interpretation (פשר *pešer*) of this concerns the Congregation of the Poor who [will possess][79] the inheritance of all [the land];[80] they will possess the lofty mountain of Isra[el], [and in] His holy place[81] they will delight. [But

77. "Mit dem Wort נס verband man im Spätjudentum eine feste Vorstellung. Auf Grund von Jes 11,12; 49,22; 62,10 war es verknüpft mit der Hoffnung, daß Gott in der Endzeit die verstreuten Glieder des Volkes Israel sammeln und wieder zusammenführen werde. Gott würde, so erwartete man, vor den Völkern ein Panier aufrichten, zu dem die Zerstreuen hinzugebracht würden" (G. Jeremias, *Der Lehrer der Gerechtigkeit*, 1963, 199).

78. Cf. also A. Dupont-Sommer, *The Essene Writings from Qumran*, 1961, 205 n. 3; *contra* S. Holm-Nielsen (*Hodayot*, 1960, 35), who calls the view "rash."

79. The scroll is torn and the edges badly disfigured at this point; J. Allegro reads ה[. . .]ם, a participial form, and there appears to be room for two to four consonants in the lacuna (cf. *DJD* V, 45, plate XVII). Dupont-Sommer (1961, 272) suggests "who *give* the inheritance" (√ נתן; hence ה[נתני]ם) following Ps. 37:21, although there is no indication elsewhere in the *pešer* that the interpreter chose to dwell on this first part of the text. Better, in the context of inheritance, is that of G. Vermes (*The Dead Sea Scrolls in English*, 1975, 245), "whom *shall possess*," or Knibb (1987, 252), "to whom will *belong* the inheritance" (both presumably √ ירש; hence ה[ירשי]ם).

80. התבל? cf. Lohse, ed., *Die Texte aus Qumran*, 1971, 274, 7.

81. Either the Temple mount (M. Burrows, *More Light on the Dead Sea Scrolls*, 1958, 402; Lohse, 1971, 277; Knibb, 1987, 252) or the (eschatological?) Temple itself (Vermes, 1975, 245).

those who are cursed by Him][82] will be cut off (כרת) — they are the ones who do violence against the [Covenant,[83] the wi]cked[84] of Israel, who will be cut off and destroyed for ever.

To "possess the inheritance of all the world" and "the lofty mountain of Israel" are patent restoration expressions,[85] the main point of the passage being that the sect will receive restoration benefits while the rest of Israel ("the ones who do violence against the Covenant, the wicked of Israel") will not. The latter will only experience the curses of the covenant. They will be "cut off" (√ כרת kārat) — an expression widely used in the Scriptures for excommunication from the covenant people (or eradication or even death, with a similar purpose; cf. Gen. 17:14; Exod. 12:15, 19; 30:33; Lev. 7:20-21; 17:4; Num. 15:30; etc.). It is evident that the words of the canonical Ps. 37:22 (according to the sectarian text), "His blessed will possess the Land (ארץ ereṣ), but those cursed by Him will be cut off," provided the opportunity for this commentator to express what otherwise must have been the widely current view of the Dead Sea sectarians: *the elect will experience restoration, but the apostates in Israel will be judged forever.* In this regard the commentary does not do all that much violence to its text, for even according to Psalm 37, those whom God blesses will receive the promised restoration (blessing and inheritance of "the Land" being promised to those in the covenant), and those whom God curses can expect to be "cut off" (since curse is fundamentally a recompense for those *breaking* the covenant). What could be termed the "covenantal dualism" of Psalm 37, therefore, has been adopted using more or less legitimate exegetical principles, although it has been thoroughly particularized under the influence of the exclusive theology of the interpreter. The Qumran covenanters are in the covenant, the rest are outside; therefore the community is the center of restoration and the others — sinful Israel ("the wicked of Israel") — are to be "destroyed for ever."

82. Following Lohse (1971, 276-77), who reads ו]מקול[לו; Knibb, 1987, 252. This reading picks up on the same verb in Psalm 37, and otherwise appears to suit the covenantal context of the language (blessings and curses).

83. Following Lohse (1971, 276-77), who reconstructs שעי[רית הב]עריצי; cf. also Knibb, 1987, 252. This would refer to the mass of unbelieving Israel according to 1QpHab 2.6 and 1QH 2.11, and not exclusively (cf. Knibb, 254) to former members of the community. The rendering "the violent ones of the nations and the wicked of Israel" would be equally intelligible within the context of the scrolls; cf. Dupont-Sommer, 1961, 272; Vermes, 1975, 245.

84. Clearly רשעי.

85. Possession of the land is a covenantal motif, obviously projected into the future here. For the "mountain of the Lord" in reference to the restoration, cf. Ezek. 20:40, esp. in the context of 20:40-44.

Whatever else may be said about the restoration theology of Qumran, therefore, one thing is abundantly clear from this passage, and entirely consistent with the judgment-of-Israel theme in the other passages from Qumran: *Restoration ideas do not cancel out judgment ideas.* The judgments pronounced against the rest of Israel, however austere they may appear to modern readers, are to be taken seriously as an essential part of the theology of Qumran. There is little room or reason for assuming a purely literary function for these texts. They must be considered constituent, even essential, expressions of Qumran theology.

The above-mentioned fragment from Cave 1 (1Q*Mysteries*) concurs with this double emphasis on judgment and restoration inasmuch as it makes the judgment of sinners (who ignored future as well as past "mysteries") a *requisite* for the arrival of the restoration:

> And for you this will be the sign that this is going to happen. When those born of sin are locked up, evil will disappear in front of justice as darkness disappears in front of light. As smoke disappears, and no longer exists, so will evil disappear for ever. And justice will be revealed like a sun which regulates the world. *And all those who curb the wonderful mysteries will no longer exist.*[86]

These passages strongly intimate that restoration is *limited* to the special group of the elect, perhaps to the *yaḥad* alone. Certainly this latter group played a central role in the restoration, but whether they believed themselves to *embody* the *totality* of the restoration is really a question bearing on the realized eschatology of the sect. Talmon's view that the community thought itself to be experiencing a kind of inaugurated restoration in their day has already been alluded to. And a passage like 1QH 11.13 may indicate that the "renewal," in the technical sense of the promised restoration (*ḥādaš*), was taking place at a personal level in the repentant members of the community: "Thou hast cleansed man of sin . . . that he may be *renewed (liḥiṯhadēš)* . . . and with them that know, in a common rejoicing" (ll. 10, 13-14). Given the decidedly *realized* nature of Qumran eschatology, one might be tempted to assume, even without the uncertain evidence of such a difficult passage, that the restoration doctrine was beginning to be spiritualized and applied exclusively to the sect (cf. "them that know").[87]

However, along with these hints that the Qumran community viewed it-

---

86. For the entire passage, cf. 1Q27 1, 1.2-7; cf. 4Q299-301; cited from F. García Martínez, *Qumran and Apocalyptic*, 1992, 399-400.

87. Even if, with Holm-Nielsen (1960, 127-28), it is impossible to interpret the passage of a new birth or new creation; the idea of restoration is removed significantly from the material realm and made a matter of the heart.

self at least to some extent as embodying the restoration in an exclusive way, another type of evidence suggests that a fuller restoration was expected for the future. Some of this evidence is admittedly conjectural. It is believed by some scholars, for example, that the addenda to 1QS (1QSa, "The Rule of the Congregation"; perhaps also 1QSb, "The Book of Blessings") were intended specifically for a future restoration period ("the messianic age").[88] The evidence for this includes: (1) the opening words of 1QSa: "And this is the rule for *all the Congregation of Israel* at the *end of days, when they shall join* . . ."; (2) the fact that a long process of training for every "native" Israelite, from a very early age (i.e., before conversion to the sect is possible?), appears to be assumed by 1QSa 1.6ff.;[89] and (3) the organization of the restored community under "chiefs of the Thousands," as well as, apparently, chiefs of hundreds, fifties, tens, and even of entire tribes (1.29–2.1; the text is broken), suggesting a much larger number than the sect ever composed in its known history. Even if, however, these columns from 1QSa allow an interpretation that relates them to a future gathering of *others* from Israel, it is crucial to note that this belief still does not entirely conflict with notions of judgment and exclusivity, inasmuch as *throughout the work the converts from Israel are said to join the community and to obey the ordinances taught by its members.* There is no such thing as a general restoration that does not have at its center the teaching and community organization already known by the sect. In the opening words of 1QSa one reads that the "Congregation of Israel" who *"join"* the community are to walk *"in obedience to the law of the sons of Zadok the priests and of the members of their Covenant* who have refused to walk in the way of the people . . ." (1.1-3). It appears from this passage that those who have avoided the apostasy (i.e., the sect) are given the prerogative of ruling over the whole people Israel during the restoration. If Israel wants their restoration, in other words, they must "join up";[90] they must accept the teachings as they are read to them by the community (1.4-5);[91] they must follow a program of instruction (1.7-8); they must fall in line with the

---

88. For discussion, cf. Knibb, 1987, 145, 157.

89. וזה הסרך לכול צבאות העדה לכול חאזרח בישראל. Dupont-Sommer: "for all the hosts of the Congregation, concerning every native in Israel" (1961, 105); Knibb: "for all the hosts of the congregation, for all who are native in Israel" (1987, 147). Both expressions in this line could refer to an entire restored Israel made up of those *presently* outside the community who will enter in later.

90. Accordingly Knibb comments on 1.6: "Implicit in these words is the claim that the community represents the true Israel, the ideal to which all Jews should follow" (1987, 149).

91. These verses may allude to a renewal of the covenant that takes place in perpetuity (cf. Knibb, 1987, 147). In any event, these verses strongly imply that *no one* can be part of the restoration without first joining the community and their covenant. Note the emphatic "all" (כול) repeated in ll. 4-5.

communal law already practiced by the sect (1.8ff.). In the light of such evidence, it is perhaps not too far off to view much of the legislative material of Qumran as intended originally for restoration circumstances. Such is the possible intention of parts, at least, of 1QS,[92] and this purpose has often been suggested for the extensive legislation in the Temple Scroll (which is also sometimes compared, in this connection, to the eschatological portion of Ezekiel 40–48).[93] It has even been suggested that the motivation for hiding the scrolls in Dead Sea caves was for the express purpose of preserving them for the future generation of the restoration, and this theory holds much conviction.[94] The point, in any case, is that such legislation, if it is intended for the future, is to be adhered to by any and all who want to experience the restoration blessings.

One can accordingly conclude that views of restoration were once again qualified and colored by the sect's own consciousness of composing the righteous in Israel. When this is recognized, other restoration passages are clarified, such as when the Damascus Document states that there will be no "survivor" or "remnant" remaining from those who "departed from the way" (2.5-7), but that the offspring of the righteous "survivors" will "fill the face of the world with their posterity" (ll. 11-12). The members of restored Israel, in other words, will come from the seed of the righteous only. The promise in Deut. 7:8 and 9:5 about Israel inheriting the nations in the future is repeated in 8.14-21, but the promise is clearly restricted to those who follow in the footsteps of the fathers by obeying the covenant of the fathers (cf. esp. ll. 16-19). CD may even presup-

92. Correspondingly we find words similar to 1QSa 1.1 in 1QS 9.3 in the midst of legislative material: "When these things come to pass in Israel according to all the appointed times. . . ."

93. Cf. esp. M. O. Wise, *A Critical Study of the Temple Scroll from Qumran Cave 11,* 1990a, 161-94; M. O. Wise, "The Teacher of Righteousness and the High Priest of the Intersacerdotium," 1990b, 587-613, 605-6, who holds that it contained a "law for the land" carefully edited to apply to the period of restoration. This law was continuous with Deuteronomy (esp. chs. 12–26; cf. 1990a, 162) and with the present teachings and practice of the sect; J. M. Allegro puts it this way: "To the Covenanters, the onset of the new order would mean a continuation of the pious existence they were then leading, for the whole idea of their present way of life was that it should be a rehearsal of the messianic age" (*The Dead Sea Scrolls,* 1964, 167).

94. H. J. Schonfield (*Secrets of the Dead Sea Scrolls,* 1957, 10-11, 150, 159-60) appeals to Jeremiah 32 for the idea that the scrolls were hidden in the caves at the shores of the Dead Sea for the express purpose of "sealing them up until the time of the End" (cf. 1QpHab 7.15 on 2:1-3). More widely accepted is the opinion that the scrolls were being hidden from the Roman legions (cf. recently Golb). However, the careful sealing and deliberate preservation of *at least some of* the scrolls suggest that the sectarians were looking sometime into the future, as this would hardly be necessary in the case of a short-term preservation.

pose that the restoration would be realized in a very gradual way through the natural regeneration of the sectarians (15.5-6) and through other converts (and proselytes) who join the community (15.7). If so, much can be read into this short passage (and other interpretations are no doubt possible); it would provide yet another indication of a group that believed in a *gradual* restoration — which would also seem to be required by Qumran's inaugurated eschatology.

REQUISITES FOR ISRAEL'S FUTURE SALVATION IN THE *TESTAMENTS OF THE TWELVE PATRIARCHS*

An analysis of the eschatology of the *Testaments* is complicated by the presence of two basically distinct categories of future revelations that have been united in a continuous narrative by their author(s). As pointed out earlier, each testament contains, besides true eschatological material, predictions that are future in their literary context only, and that refer *ex eventu* to the real author's *past*. This latter group of "future" passages are generally composed of apostasy "predictions" that form part of the historical rehearsals within the *Testaments*. They appear to be essentially Jewish in content, thus probably belonging to the original Jewish version(s) of the testaments. But these sections are not of immediate interest here.

The other group of future sayings is more properly eschatological. Since these sayings contain frequent Christian interpolations, however, they remain more suspect, and one must exercise caution when assuming the presence of authentic Jewish teaching in them. Perhaps the best way to proceed is to look first for any more-or-less obvious *Jewish* eschatological statements in the *Testaments* that can be identified. A few sayings appear to speak of a genuinely *future* (eschatological) apostasy (probably *TJud.* 22:1;[95] *TIss.* 6:1-2;[96] *TZeb.* 9:5-9;[97]

---

95. The passage contains the phrase "and conflicts will persist in Israel," after which comes the description of the restoration (vv. 2-3).

96. Vv. 1-2, concerning the apostasy of Issachar's sons, are related to the promise of restoration in vv. 3-4. The reference to "the last times" (ἐν ἐσχάτοις καιροῖς; cf. the usual ἐν ἐσχάταις ἡμέραις) also appears to refer to the apostasy of the real author's future. The reference, on the other hand, may be to the return from exile.

97. While the reference in v. 7 is to the exile (cf. H. W. Hollander and M. de Jonge, *The Testaments of the Twelve Patriarchs*, 1985, 272), v. 8 ("and after these things"; καὶ μετὰ ταῦτα) and v. 9 ("καὶ πάλιν (and again) . . . you will be rejected *until the time of the end*") refer to another (or continuing) future apostasy (cf. Hollander and de Jonge, 273). This is also confirmed by the idea of a future liberation from evil spirits: "He will liberate every captive of the sons of men from Beliar, and every spirit of error will be trampled down."

TGad 8:2), and it seems logical to conclude that they originated within the same context of intra-Jewish debate reflected in the other (*ex eventu* historical) apostasy sayings. Not much can be gathered from these sayings alone, but they perhaps provide important evidence of the degree to which the eschatology of the original Jewish work related to the matter of apostasy.

Another theme in the eschatological texts is the period of the restoration. Here it is rather difficult to dissect out original Jewish thought, given the amount of Christian interpolation. Nevertheless, the teaching itself is, in the main, actually quite consistent with the attitude toward the restoration already seen to be part of the Jewish teaching of the other writings.[98] It would accordingly be amiss not to use such texts, albeit cautiously, as evidence for a basically Jewish restoration theology that has been expanded in the light of Christian messianology. Further evidence that restoration doctrine had an original place in the Jewish testaments is that some of these references are found in the (Jewish) apostasy sections referred to above. When *TJud.* 22:2-3, for example, refers to the coming God ("the God of righteousness") — note: not the messiah as such — and to the kingdom *God* brings, one can recognize traditional *Jewish* perspectives. There is, significantly, no direct evidence of christological tampering in this passage.[99] This strongly suggests that the Jewish versions of the testaments spoke of a restoration, and that Christian embellishments were added to it. But this is far from assuming that all of the eschatological teaching followed Christian lines; indeed, these restoration sections seem to have possessed some importance in the original Jewish testaments.

Perhaps, therefore, de Jonge is *partly* correct when he suggests that the chief purpose of the *Testaments* is "to convince their readers that Israel will be saved if it really obeys God's commandments — as interpreted by Christians after the example of Jesus Christ — seriously and if they turn to the saviour of Is-

---

98. We can agree with the idea, as far as it goes, that the Christian circles responsible for the interpolations "were clearly genuinely concerned with the salvation of the Jews; they too, no doubt, were guided by the ideas expressed in this writing in their thinking about and their contacts with their Jewish brethren" (M. de Jonge, *Jewish Eschatology, Early Christian Christology, and the Testaments of the Twelve Patriarchs*, 1991, 211); thus, even if Christian in expression, these attitudes are universally Jewish.

99. The phrase "God of righteousness" hardly seems to demand an application to Jesus Christ (as Hollander and de Jonge, 1985, 224). The verses also refer to the reign of God being "terminated by men of alien race," which would again appear to be Jewish phraseology (Hollander and de Jonge, 223, refer it to the exile). The words "as well as all the nations" appear to be a Christian addition since they are not necessary to the thought of the passage; but on the basis of the idea itself, even this is not necessarily the case. Cf. also *TJud.* 23:5 with 25:1-5 (and note the contrast between this and the addition of all or parts of 24:1-6); *TGad* 8:2.

rael and the Gentiles,"[100] a statement that could be accepted as valid for the Christian recension of the *Testaments* only. A similar purpose may, however, have equally applied to the originally Jewish restoration sayings: they promise the restoration of Israel (not, of course, on the basis of obedience to Jesus Christ but) *on the basis of adherence to the community of Levi-Judah* — that is, to the beliefs of the group. This is nowhere more evident than in *TNaph.* 8:2-3:

> Command your children that they be in unity with Levi and Judah,
> for through Judah will salvation arise for Israel,
> and in him will Jacob be blessed.
> Through his kingly power God will appear . . .[101]
> to save the race of Israel.

Other passages promise that restoration will come through the agent of the deliverer-messiah from Levi and Judah (clearly part of the pre-Christian messianic conception) and imply that identity with the messiahs, and messianic teaching, of the Levi-Judah community will be a requisite for deliverance: "Tell these things to your children as well, so that they will honor Judah and Levi, because from them the Lord will raise up a Savior for Israel" (*TGad* 8:1). In a similar way, again within a quite Jewish context, the restoration is promised *on the condition that* the sons of Judah "return to the Lord in integrity of heart, penitent and living according to *all* the Lord's commands" (*TJud.* 23:5). As regards the essentially conditional nature of restoration, however, none of these sayings is as clear as *TBen.* 10:10-11: "You, therefore, my children, may your lot come to be with those who fear the Lord. Therefore, my children, *if* you live in holiness, in accord with the Lord's commands, you shall again dwell with me in hope; all Israel will be gathered to the Lord."

It would appear from such conditions, and from everything else discovered about the *Testaments* so far, that the corpus as a whole was originally intended either to win over the Jews who had strayed from the faith of the fathers or, if directed at readers within the group itself, to subtly condemn the others. In either case the social function of these eschatological sections was, appar-

---

100. De Jonge, 1991, 178-79.

101. The words deleted here ("dwelling among men on the earth") are quite possibly a Christian addition; the idea of God appearing, however, is entirely coherent with the restoration doctrine of the *Testaments* elsewhere (cf. *TJud.* 22:2; *TZeb.* 9:8-9), and the idea of God dwelling with men may itself be derived from Exod. 25:8; 29:45-46; Num. 5:3; 35:34; Deut. 12:29; 1 Kings 6:13; 8:27; 2 Chron. 6:18; Pss. 68:18; 132:14; Ezek. 43:7, 9; Zech. 2:10-11; 8:3; but esp. Ezek. 37:27 (cf. 2 Cor. 6:16; Rev. 21:3, which also cite or seem to allude to the biblical passages). *TBen.* 9:2 indicates that the restoration will include a new Temple, which is also significant here in view of the fact that many of these texts refer to God's dwelling among Israel *in the Temple.*

ently, to legitimize the beliefs of the group by making them *the sole require-ments for Israel's eventual salvation.*

One can accordingly summarize the eschatological teachings of the Jewish testaments, as well as these can be determined: (1) Israel will be guilty of apostasy as in the past; (2) those Israelites who remain faithful will be vindicated; (3) any hope for Israel's salvation depends on the rest of Israel accepting the point of view of the group responsible for the original Jewish testaments; (4) the function of eschatology once again would seem to be entirely related to these beliefs — namely, legitimizing the program of salvation of the group and at the same time outlining the requisites for Israel's salvation. Even accounting for the most obvious Christian additions, the amount of variation in eschatological teaching in the *Testaments* suggests, once again, that a systematic presentation was not the intention of the original authors or redactors.[102] Like the other writings also, a text like *TJud.* 22:2 may indicate that the author expected the End to come *immediately,* but this is less than certain.[103]

SEEKING ISRAEL'S PROMISED RESTORATION IN THE *PSALMS OF SOLOMON*

There is very little consistency in the view of the future in the *Psalms of Solomon,* and attempts to systematize their eschatological teaching have failed.[104] Part of the reason for diversity may again be that these sayings possess more of a literary than a theological purpose, intended to evoke emotions rather than teach doctrines.[105] Eschatological material is mostly found in Psalms 7, 8, 9, 11, 17, and 18. A few initial observations will be helpful in identifying the central concerns in the passages:

1. *Inaugurated eschatology.* Eschatological formulations are frequently

102. A. Hultgård delineates what he sees to be the order of eschatological events intended by the author (*L'eschatologie des Testaments des Douze Patriarches,* 1977, 1:265-66); but this is demonstrated by one or two texts only, while many other passages fail to include the same elements or to retain the same order. Hollander and de Jonge, in regard to the "expectations concerning the future," point to "the great variety within and the differences between the various types of passages, as well as their very uneven distribution over the testaments and the combinations of (elements of) the various types" (1985, 53). Hultgård also points to continued indefinite meanings for the expressions ἐν ἐσχάταις ἡμέραις and ἐν ἐσχάτοις καιροῖς (cf. באתרית הימים) found in the *Testaments* (1:85-86).

103. The words ἕως τοῦ ἐλθεῖν τὸ σωτήριον Ἰσραήλ, ἕως παρουσίας τοῦ θεοῦ τῆς δικαιοσύνης, although suggestive, hardly demand this. Cf. Hultgård, 1977, 1:145.

104. Cf. de Jonge, 1991, 4.

105. Cf. de Jonge, 1991, 4-5.

employed to speak of the recent *historical* events surrounding the sacking of Jerusalem by Pompey, as already noted. This would either imply that eschatological-sounding sayings are merely cases of borrowing of eschatological terminology in order to increase the drama or would indicate a strong consciousness of inaugurated eschatology. Since biblical promises serve as a catalyst for the hopes and pleas for intervention expressed during the recent difficulties, and since the impression is often given that the future is expected to emerge from the present, perhaps it is the latter. A sense of imminence accordingly results from what were certainly perceived to be extremely significant events. On the other hand, there is no attempt to date the End, only a rather nonspecific plea for the restoration to be brought about by God (e.g., 17:45 and 18:5).

2. *Apostasy as central presupposition.* Eschatological significance is given to the fact that the apostasy of the nation has reached a climax. God has already been moved to judge Israel's sin through his instrument Pompey, but this has only raised the anticipation of a still more severe and in some sense ultimate judgment, and warnings are projected toward the remaining apostates who, unmoved by the events of the past, continue in sin. This anticipated judgment will, of course, also include the Gentiles who have acted presumptuously in attacking the holy city. Contrary to what is usually perceived to be true in Judaism, however, the author does *not* hold the view that God will come when *righteousness* is at a *peak;* he rather warns that the divine intention is to intervene and judge the *sin* of the nation.[106] By this judgment the author's righteous community will also be vindicated.

3. *A conditional restoration.* The idea of a national deliverance and a complete restoration would appear on a superficial reading to be one of the outstanding features of the *Psalms.* But the idea is severely qualified, among other things, by the context of the psalms themselves. Although the relevant passages have already been subjected to initial consideration, the belief in restoration is important enough to give it more detailed attention by tracing the doctrine throughout the various texts and noting important characteristics or qualifications.

- In 7:8-10 the psalmist declares that God "will have compassion on the people Israel forever / and you will not reject them" (v. 8), and he looks forward to "the time of your support" when mercy will be shown to the "house of Jacob" as "promised" (v. 10). But he also writes of God's "discipline" and the "yoke" under which Israel presently suffers (v. 9).

---

106. This is another indication that our author could not have adopted a nationalistic view of things, for the sin of the nation, not its attempt to live righteously, is the focus of these psalms. Their message is set firmly "over against" the rest of Israel, and, as we have seen, the psalms *welcome* God's intervention in the judgment of sinners.

- In 8:27-34 the psalmist prays for mercy and compassion (v. 26) in bringing together the "the dispersed of Israel" (v. 28),[107] that God would not "neglect us" (v. 30), and that Israel would be blessed (v. 34). He recognizes that "we stiffened our necks,[108] but you are the one who disciplines us" (v. 29), and that Israel is presently and justly experiencing the "judgments" of God (v. 32). The passage becomes increasingly conditional and individualistic, however, as the psalmist prays that God might "be pleased with us and our children forever" (v. 33), and a distinction may be recognized between Israel as a whole and the elect within the nation when the psalmist relates that God's judgments come "by the mouth of the devout" (v. 34).[109]

- In 9:8-11 the psalmist prays again that God would be compassionate and show mercy to Israel "forevermore." However, the earlier verses of the psalm draw on the experience of the exile to demonstrate that one cannot hide from the judgments of God (vv. 1-3), and a highly individualistic view of righteousness is implied in the immediately preceding verses (vv. 4-7). Perhaps this explains the conditional phrase that creeps in with the restoration expressions in v. 10: "we hope in you *when we turn our souls toward you.*"[110] Restoration in these verses must, in any event, be seen in

---

107. Συνάγαγε τὴν διασποράν Ισραηλ, in comparison with συναγωγαὶ Ισραηλ in 10:7, suggests that groups of righteous could be found in the dispersion. Perhaps this relates to the view we have already seen regarding the relative righteousness of Israel *outside* of Jerusalem and Palestine. A possible reference in this verse to the "preserved of Israel" in Isa. 49:6 is particularly suggestive; cf. also Ps. 146:2 (EVV 147:2).

108. For "to stiffen the neck," cf. 2 Chron. 30:8; Neh. 9:16; Jer. 7:26; which also allude to the negative example of the fathers; cf. Deut. 10:16. Some relation to the "sins of the fathers" motif is likely here. The expression "be pleased with us and our children forever" may indicate a kind of reversal of this motif, another indication of a hope for restoration.

109. The expression "lest the gentiles devour us as if there were no redeemer (λυτρουμένου)" recalls the idea of the "kinsman redeemer" (גאל). The psalmist apparently thought of the Roman invasion as threatening the existence of the whole Israelite race. Perhaps the idea is that the *Psalms* community composes the remnant of Israel who would preserve the national hopes, should God grant them safety and deliverance. This idea also contains the implicit distinction between the elect and the rest of Israel.

110. The prepositional phrase (καὶ ἡμεῖς ἐλπιούμεν ἐπὶ σὲ ἐν ἐπιστροφῇ ψυχῆς ἡμῶν) is more emphatic than a simple participial phrase would be. Ἐπιστροφή is an important word. While it is used of "restoring" in the title of Psalm 7 (which refers to help God gives to the *Psalms* community!), it takes on a distinctively individual and spiritual sense here as an apparent parallel to ἐξηγορία in v. 6 of the present psalm: "He will cleanse from sins the soul in confessing, in *restoring*" (H. E. Ryle and M. R. James: "in acknowledgement" [*ΨΑΛΜΟΙ ΣΟΛΟΜΩΝΤΟΣ*, 1891, 92-93], perhaps from ἐξηγέομαι; the root, however, would seem to be ἐξεγείρω, "to arouse," "awaken," etc.). The connection with repentance is clear.

the context of the whole psalm, which is highly individualistic, and would appear to be conditional on the acceptance of the pious lifestyle. Here one witnesses an apparent struggling to harmonize the situation of apostasy with the hope for restoration.

- 10:5-8 contains a mixture of exclusivist and nationalistic statements. The psalmist declares, on the one hand, that "Israel shall praise the Lord's name in joy" (v. 5) and prays that "the Lord's salvation be upon the house of Israel / that they may be happy forever" (v. 8); on the other hand, "the *devout* shall give thanks in the assembly *(ekklēsia)* of the people, / and God will be merciful to the *poor* to the joy of Israel" (v. 6), and "the synagogues *(sunagōgai)* of Israel will glorify the Lord's name" (v. 7). While the exact significance of the words "assembly" and "synagogues" is not clear, the words "devout" and "poor" suggest that the author may see at least part of the fulfillment of restoration hopes taking place in his own community. This is further evidence for the view that the community has adopted the word "Israel" as a self-designation or in a representative sense, which would also significantly resolve other inconsistencies in the passage.

- The whole eleventh psalm is a joyful and moving psalm of proclamation promising the return of the dispersed to Jerusalem based on the mercy shown to Israel by God (vv. 1, 9). The psalmist is well aware that the conditions for restoration do not presently exist and accordingly prays that the Lord would "do what he has spoken about Israel and Jerusalem" (v. 8). Hardly a more straightforward presentation of belief in the gathering and restoration of Israel can be imagined, although the concepts and expression are largely borrowed from Scripture, and are unquestionably traditional, being heavily influenced by Isaiah 40–55.[111] It would appear nevertheless that the psalmist envisaged a widespread return, worthy of the colorful descriptions he borrows from the Bible.

- In 17:21-46 the psalmist concentrates on the reign of the Davidic king, and much of the language implies a period of restoration. As part of the function of the king to "judge"[112] Israel, he will root out "any person who knows wickedness" (v. 27); he will "purge Jerusalem" (v. 30); "there will be no unrighteousness among them in his days" (v. 32); "he will expose officials and drive out sinners" (v. 36); God will "raise him over the house of Israel / to discipline it" (v. 42). These statements all imply that the restoration time will be characterized by righteous living, and allusions to

111. De Jonge, 1991, 6.
112. In the sense here of wise leadership, or retribution (v. 26)? In view of the language of the following verses, it would appear to be as much the latter as the former.

correcting present wrongs are clearly intended. The blessings of this time are referred to as "the good fortune of Israel" (v. 44). The psalmist again prays that God would "dispatch his mercy to Israel" and deliver Israel "from the pollution of profane enemies" (v. 45).

• Finally in 18:5 the psalmist prays that God would "cleanse Israel for the day of mercy in blessing, / for the appointed day when his Messiah will reign." This prayer again reveals the contrast between the hoped-for blessing and the present unworthy state of the nation. Israel must first be "cleansed."

On the basis of some statements in these passages, it would be difficult to avoid the conclusion that their authors cherished an almost unqualified expectation of restoration. God will redeem Israel; he has simply promised to do so. We pointed out above the largely traditional language with which this doctrine is sometimes expressed, and the belief may have entered rather accidentally into the *Psalms* — steeped, as they are, in scriptural themes. In fairness to the independent value of the doctrine, however, the psalmist(s) betray(s) an impassioned commitment to Israel that could hardly have been fabricated for purely rhetorical reasons. At times the author so completely identifies with Israel that he speaks of the nation in the first person (cf. 7:9). This can only reflect a basically sincere sentiment. On the other hand, the tensions created by the juxtaposition of exclusive soteriology and restoration doctrine are as much in evidence here as in the other writings, and at times more so (cf. esp. 8:27-34; 9:8-11; and 10:5-8 and comments above). In short, one simply cannot ignore the rest of the theology of the *Psalms* — which has been considered in the preceding chapters — in favor of a single doctrine. A balance must be sought.

Perhaps a clue to how this tension is to be resolved is given in the final reference above (18:5), which is suggestively found near the end of the *Psalms*. Whether or not this verse has been deliberately placed at the end of the corpus, however, depends on one's theory of composition of the work. Recent theories do suggest a redactional or even compositional unity to the collection, and it is difficult to ignore the impression that the *Psalms* moves toward a climax in the final chapters where messianic and eschatological hopes are proffered. In any case, this verse does suggest a kind of resolution of the dialectic between restoration hopes and the present apostasy of Israel as it acknowledges the necessity of Israel's prior cleansing: "May God *cleanse Israel* for the day of mercy in blessing."[113] If there is any normative significance to this verse, the idea of a merciful cleansing may have been posited as part of the solution to the tension created

---

113. In the context of "discipline" (cf. v. 4), this cannot refer to a simple preparation, but to a wholesale change, in the hearts of Israelites.

by the disparity between the present state of Israel and that restoration ideal to which the psalmist so urgently aspired.

The view of the *Psalms* that restoration is conditional on prior cleansing, furthermore, seems to be linked with the need for repentance. It is only reasonable to expect that the author would demand from apostate Israel the same experience of repentance and concern for piety that he demanded from his own group. Perhaps repentance and a changed spiritual condition were believed to be part of the gift of restoration (cf. 7:8-10; 8:27-30; 18:5 and comments above), but 18:5 suggests that restoration is the *result* rather than the *cause* of this repentance and cleansing. It was earlier concluded that the mercy of God does not imply a unilateral forgiveness, but the strength to obey. It is reasonable to conclude that the act of "returning" is itself the indication of repentance, although such information is not provided by the *Psalms*.

Perhaps, on the other hand, the dialectic is by nature somewhat irresolvable, and one can only look for some indication of what the author believed to be the *primary* doctrine — just retribution or restoration. While there are no unambiguous statements regarding God's unilateral forgiveness and restoration, one does find (significantly in a restoration context) a statement emphasizing individual responsibility:

> The one who does what is right saves up life for himself with the Lord,
>> and the one who does what is wrong causes his own life to be
>>> destroyed;
>> *for the Lord's righteous judgments are according to the individual and*
>>> *the household.*[114]
> To whom will you be good, O God, except to those who call upon the
>> Lord?
>> He will cleanse from sins the soul in confessing, in *restoring.* (9:5-6b)

The expectation of Israel's restoration does not alleviate warnings of judgment in the *Psalms*. In the final analysis only mass conversion to the party of the pious can be thought to result in this blessing.

In short, the *Psalms* demonstrates an unequivocal commitment to other important doctrines besides restoration. These include: (1) the deservedness and certainty of judgment, (2) the necessity of choosing a righteous way and an escape from the impending crisis, and (3) the requisite that Israel submit to the view of the pious for restoration to occur (i.e., repent from their "stiffness of

---

114. Accordingly δικαιοσύναι refers to justice, in the sense of impartiality, according to Ryle and James (1891, 91): "God is just and distinguishes between man and man, between house and house." That "life" is a covenantal expression here is suggested by the mention of covenant in v. 10.

neck"; cf. 8:29). The result is that the recipients of the blessings of restoration will be a much *different* Israel from that represented by the Jerusalem sinners. Thus the common view that eschatology functions to assure the nation of its deliverance from all world powers and of its own domination of the world can be applied to the *Psalms* only with significant qualifications. De Jonge's view that the "aim and intention" of these restoration passages is concerned primarily with theocracy,[115] making the *Psalms* a kind of theodicy for the eventual reign of God, accordingly fails to take account of their more "sectarian" interests. The community behind the psalms was certainly *more* (although not exclusively) interested in their own vindication than in the survival of the traditional, national theocracy. Restoration has become a symbol for the hope that all Israel will accept the piety that they have accepted (cf. 9:10).

ESCHATOLOGICAL URGENCY IN 4 EZRA

Students of 4 Ezra are familiar with the problems of understanding the apparently inconsistent eschatology of this book. The view of earlier source and form critics like Gunkel, Box, Kabisch, and Keulers was that the author combined two major sources (or, at least, two conflicting thought forms) that were highly divergent in matters of eschatology, the one containing a particularistic nationalistic theology with its messianic eschatology, and the other a universalistic theology and a cosmic eschatology.[116] The combination of these divergent components by the author of 4 Ezra, it is believed, did not produce smooth or coherent results, but irresolvable inconsistencies. More recently, however, scholars have been stressing the redactional unity of this work.[117] Stone, for one, has investigated the source- and form-critical approaches and found them to be unsubstantiated: not only are the two kinds of eschatologies found side by

---

115. Cf. de Jonge, 1991, 12-13. De Jonge is correct in what he denies, namely, that "the aim and intention is not the setting free of the people or the destruction of internal and external enemies," but hardly in what he asserts: "it is concerned primarily with theocracy, the realization of God's rule over all peoples, groups and nations" (12). This, in our estimation, is far too nonpolemical for the *Psalms*. A phrase like "Truth and enduring values were to be fully realised" (13) is far too philosophical for our author, who may have embraced some forms of the Jewish wisdom tradition, but was certainly not as fully Hellenized in his philosophical expression as this phrase implies.

116. For analysis and critique, cf. M. E. Stone, *Features of the Eschatology of IV Ezra*, 1989, 14ff., 44ff.

117. Cf. M. E. Stone, "Coherence and Inconsistency in the Apocalypses," 1983, 229-43, 229-30, 235-36.

side but they are also at certain points so closely interwoven as to make the possibility of separate sources very unlikely.[118]

The question is also raised: What would motivate an author/editor to place two such differing eschatologies side by side, and with such illogical results, in the same book?[119] Or are these ideas only contradictory in a logical sense, while not contradictory in a more polemical context? It is certainly invalid to assume that universalistic elements necessarily contradict exclusive ones in the way the earlier scholars believed. Both ideas can be *a*-nationalistically oriented and may actually harmonize with one another — inasmuch as universalism implies the application of the same norms to Israel as are applied to the world. We have already noted this combination elsewhere. Or perhaps, if there really are two distinguishable strands of eschatology present in 4 Ezra, a more or less successful synthesis has taken place between traditional messianological eschatology and that form of eschatology embraced by the protest movement, which is more cosmic and less nationalistic. We have also witnessed this synthesis. There is, in any event, no need to posit any theory of sources to account for the various eschatological sayings in this book. The amount of diversity within the eschatological passages of 4 Ezra is not all that out of line with what is found in the other works. And this merely suggests, once again, that eschatology was not the chief concern in writing. Diversity and inconsistency would then be a by-product of an emotional response where logical consistency is not essential. The question of sources in the end becomes irrelevant.

In 4 Ezra even common eschatological *terms* are used inconsistently. Stone's doctoral thesis investigated a wide variety of eschatological motifs that were often not carefully harmonized,[120] and a later article uncovered a variety of applications of the word "End" (*finis* and synonyms) in 4 Ezra.[121] This latter article reveals that in some places "End" refers to the day of judgment and in others to the messianic kingdom, in some instances there is no clear meaning (although presumably in these places the word could be taken with one of these other referents in mind), while still other passages combine the two meanings (cf. 6:15, 25; 12:34).[122] According to Stone, this inconsistency does not represent contradic-

---

118. Cf. Stone, 1989, 14ff.; Stone, 1983, 235-36.

119. Stone, 1989, 46.

120. Stone, 1989, passim.

121. Stone, 1983, 230-34; cf. also Stone, 1989, 83-97.

122. When Stone attempts to find a root meaning that will tie together all the ideas associated with the "End," he can come up only with a very broad definition: "the [i.e., any] decisive point in the eschatological sequence" (1983, 239-41; a phrase first used in his 1965 thesis; cf. Stone, 1989, 91) — an idea that allows for great variation of meaning depending on the context. He does discern more than one type of eschatological teaching be-

tion so much as a kind of "imprecision" or "lack of logical systematization" born from a familiar use of terms in a social setting in which various applications were possible without consciously acknowledging, or even recognizing, any contradiction.[123] Inconsistency is therefore *inevitable* in a book like 4 Ezra, which is also Stone's answer to the source and form critics.[124] As with eschatological doctrine generally, therefore, the presence of eschatological terminology in a writing does not necessarily imply a clear-cut eschatological agenda. Social, rather than theological, reasons may well have inspired references to the future, and it is to this social context that one must look for clues to the coherence of such a presentation.[125] As for ideas and terms, these are formed within the diverse experiences and context of the community rather than in the independent mind of the author, and this gives to later readers who are divorced from that context an impression of inconsistency. Stone does not mean there was no underlying systematic concept of the final events in existence, so much as that no systematic *program* emerges or is presupposed by 4 Ezra, nor is the author concerned to formulate one. Eschatological terminology is *evocative,* not explicative, in 4 Ezra; it serves to *evoke* in the minds of the readers thoughts of the End so that the author can begin to set forth his *real* message, rather than to clarify or promote some specific eschatological question.[126]

Although Stone did not draw the conclusion,[127] such a lack of concern

---

hind the use of this term, however, but appropriately refers to these as "associational complexes" (1983, 241; a notion first used in his 1965 thesis; cf. Stone, 1989, 222), a description that implies that the two meanings of "End" were already joined subconsciously by the particular society that employed them.

123. Stone (1983, 242-43) aims at the same thing when he says that the inconsistencies were not problematic for, but were integral to, an expected level of incoherence for an ancient author. He appears to fall short of calling this type of treatment inconsistent, however, preferring to differentiate between the "systematic" nature of the author's treatment of *individual* statements and the "non-logical" approach to the subject as a whole (1989, 29).

124. Stone, 1989, 21. He refers to the attempts as "inappropriate."

125. In this respect Stone's comments are apposite when he remarks that the author of 4 Ezra "was *not sensitive to questions of precise consistency* between the explicit statements of the text, and coherence was given by views, assumptions, or other factors *lying outside the explicit statements of the text*" (1983, 242, emphasis added) — by which, apparently, Stone means not other concerns within 4 Ezra so much as the wider context for eschatological thought within the community — but the same thing could be said even within the confines of the message of the work itself.

126. Cf. Rowland, 1982, 134: "The burning question in both apocalypses [4 Ezra and *2 Baruch*] is not 'When will the end be?', but 'How can one make sense of the present and the promises of the past when history seems to contradict all that was originally sacrosanct?'"

127. Stone (1989, 226) in fact concludes that the author's interest "in the nature,

for systematization of eschatological beliefs might lead one to presume that the author would have been even less concerned with an exact timetabling of the final events. But how much is this borne out by the text itself? Stone maintains that the author held only a basic order of events: the "End" — the messianic age — the judgment.[128] But, in fact, this order is not entirely clear in many passages and occasionally seems to be inverted.[129] It is also much too general to refer to this basic outline as a "timetable." The most one can say is that an *expectation* of the final events helped shape the eschatological beliefs of this author, but even the one more or less consistent fact that the author seemed to have expected — that the end of the present age is to be followed immediately by the future age (6:7-10) — suggests little about the actual *timing* of the change.[130]

The only detailed descriptions of the author's expectations are in the form of *signs*, what are often referred to by scholars as the "messianic woes,"[131] again a rather curious designation since these signs are infrequently associated with any messiah, even in 4 Ezra.[132] Some of the passages appear, once again, to refer more to the author's *present*[133] than to the future, although a future type can also be

---

mechanics and time of the end" is "one of the most striking characteristics of the book." If this is so, and we would not even go this far, the author must have been largely unsuccessful in finding answers to these questions, or else he has settled for very vague solutions.

128. Stone, 1989, 86, etc.

129. Cf., e.g., 12:34, where the messianic age is said to precede the judgment *and* the "End"!

130. The common view that Jacob and Esau represent (eschatological) Israel and Rome (cf., e.g., Stone, 1989, 6, 52, 136) may read too much into the metaphor. Stone (49) does provide an interesting parallel from *Midrash Haggadol,* however, where Israel and Rome are represented by Jacob and Esau in a discussion about the turn of the ages. This raises the question of the validity of invoking such parallels, however, and differences between the two groups of writings may warn against oversimplistic comparison. Furthermore, there is the possibility that 4 Ezra has employed a conventional parallel in an unconventional way (or that *Midrash Haggadol* has!). In any event, the message is only that there will be no intervening period between the ages, and this by itself says little about the actual timing of the End.

131. Cf. 5:1-12; 6:16-28; 9:3; 13:29-30; cf. 4:52; 5:1, 13; 6:11, 20; 8:63; 9:1-2; 13:32; Stone, 1989, 100.

132. Explicitly only 13:32; perhaps implied in 9:1-2. Their association with a messianic figure is actually quite rare, and probably only coincidental with the belief that the suffering community was soon to see the messiah.

133. E.g., 5:1: "the days are coming when those who dwell on earth shall be seized with great terror, *and the way of truth shall be hidden, and the land shall be barren of faith.*" As noted above, the so-called "messianic woes" more often relate to the present sufferings of the righteous community (cf. also D. C. Allison, *The End of the Ages Has Come,* 1985, 11-13 — Allison's findings suggest that present woes refer to the suffering of the saints, while future woes center on the judgment of the wicked; cf. 8-17; in some texts the tribulation is even in the past; cf. 17-19; there is much diversity in this belief).

found.[134] Such a diversity of use would once again tend to downplay any eschatological purpose for the signs. Furthermore, even the clearly eschatological sign passages tell us very little about the *timing* of the End, as there is little indication of the significance of the sequence of the signs in the various passages. There is a general impression that the signs that lead to the End will follow closely on the signs presently experienced by the righteous,[135] but that these signs are intended to give a chronology of events is highly doubtful. Even the somewhat chronological statement of 9:1-2, "when you see that a certain *part* of the predicted signs are past, then you will know that it is the very time when the Most High is about to visit the world," hardly signifies a strict timetable.[136] The passage may in fact suggest that significant time elapses between this revelation to Ezra and the End, and it also appears deliberately ambiguous (note: "a certain part"). The signs unfold in such a way as to clarify, enlarge upon, or perhaps recapitulate the former ones, and the resulting repetition appears to be for the sake of literary effect rather than to delineate consecutive events. In fact, none of these lists of signs is suitable for the purpose of calculation.

One must conclude that a rather more pressing motivation inspired the signs. Since the lists of signs are a provocative and colorful form, they would have served particularly well to drive home the *urgency* of the writer's message, and since much more consistent features of the passages are their message of judgment and their forecast of suffering, it would make sense that the writer was using them to warn Israel of judgment and to console the righteous in their

---

134. Some judgment oracles are so vague and occasionally of such miraculous composition that one doubts whether the readers of the book would take these events to be signs that *they presently* witness. They appear to be meant for a relatively far-off period, and are associated with the present signs only through their literary context. E.g., 6:21: "Infants a year old shall speak with their voices [not so strange!], and women with child shall give birth to premature children at three or four months, and these shall live and dance [much more unusual, especially considering the times!]." 6:25-28 appears to refer to a restoration, although it is doubtful if this passage belongs to a signs passage *per se*.

135. Cf. esp. 5:1-3 with 5:4ff. Stone comments that the words "beyond what you yourself see" in 5:2 may hint that the woes have already begun (*Fourth Ezra*, 1990, 109-10; cf. 3:29, 33). "After the third period" in 5:4, on the other hand, seems to indicate a periodization of history, whether referring to the period following Daniel's three-and-one-half years (Box), or the beginning of the fourth period in a four-year schematization (cf. Stone, 110 n. 19; as would be suggested by allusions to the Daniel visions in chs. 11 and 13; but cf. 14:11-12), suggesting, in any event, the beginning of the final time. The use of the word "suddenly" in this verse seems to signal the End as well.

136. From the general language of the passage Ezra can hardly be expected to "calculate which [of the signs] have passed," as Stone suggests (1990, 294). For a view of these particular signs as alluding to the contemporary situation of the author, cf. Allison, 1985, 11-13; considered as a possibility also by Stone, 295. 9:4 suggests that the signs enumerated here are largely traditional.

sufferings. The listing of signs (especially when they give a semblance of order to the events — however vague) would have communicated particularly well the preordained nature and the divine purpose of suffering and/or judgment. As means of conveying eschatological teaching, however, they are limited in usefulness.

Similar conclusions must therefore be drawn about 4 Ezra 14:10-12, which appears on a superficial reading to calculate the time of the End. As vagueness was the rule in 5:50-55, however, vagueness would appear to be the rule here also.[137] In this passage a voice from a bush (14:1) reveals to Ezra that "the age is divided into twelve parts, and nine of its parts have already passed, as well as half of the tenth part; so two of its parts remain, besides half of the tenth part" (vv. 11-12) — that is, the world is nine-and-one-half parts out of twelve parts expired. This image strangely evokes the ten-tribes motif, and may be an indication that a purely symbolic level of meaning is intended by the use of such numbers.[138] Even assuming, for the sake of argument, that the numbers are intended literally, this still presents immense problems for attempts at calculation. The present time, to which this twelve-part scheme is oriented, would naturally be the time of Ezra (if it alludes to the "real" author's time, this would move the End even further into the future). On this understanding Beckwith has determined that the End comes at about A.D. 496.[139] This far-off date hardly suggests that either the dating itself or the imminent coming of the End composed a pressing concern for these readers from the late first, or early second, century.[140] The author, for whatever reason, appears satisfied to allow that

137. Cf. Stone, 1990, 153. For the view that the tribulations listed here refer to the author's time, cf. Allison, 1985, 11-13.

138. Cf. Stone, 1990, 421. Does the author suggest that nine-and-one-half tribes have been "cleansed" (i.e., judged), and that a remnant only remains from them, while the judgment upon the remaining two-and-one-half tribes is forthcoming (the community of 4 Ezra would then represent the remnant who will be preserved from these tribes as well)? Interestingly the Eth. has a tenfold vision — perhaps the translators were uncomfortable with the difficulties the twelvefold division made for predictions of the nearness of the End, unless they were bringing the teaching into conformity with the usual tenfold division, as cf. Apocalypse of Weeks; for other twelvefold divisions, cf. *2 Baruch* 53; *Apocalypse of Abraham* 29:2.

139. And P. F. Esler ("The Social Function of 4 Ezra," 1994, 117) calculates this date to be about A.D. 550!

140. R. T. Beckwith, "The Earliest Enoch Literature and Its Calendar," 1981, 537, employs the dating system of *Seder Olam Rabbah* as a guide in estimating the lengths represented here, since he accepts this writing as representative of attempts to date the age of the world according to the biblical history. The Rabbah sets the destruction of the Temple at A.M. 3338 which, when the mathematics are all worked out, sets the End for 4 Ezra, not in the near future of the author, but at A.M. 4253 (A.D. 496)! If, on the other hand, the Mes-

the final events will occur in some remote future time, and in this way also to remain safely ambiguous about the unfolding of events.

The conclusion to be reached from all this lack of precision is that eschatology functions primarily in relation to *other* concerns. This means that the usual questions put to eschatology (i.e., regarding the timing of the End, the order of events, the nature of the resurrection, etc.) were considerably less important to the original writers than they are to modern scholars. Stone recognizes this and leans toward a contextual solution to the function of eschatology and to the significance of the individual texts. The function of the eschatological statements in each passage depends, in other words, entirely on the specific question being asked by Ezra at the moment.[141] T. Willett has also approached the eschatologies of 4 Ezra and *2 Baruch* from the point of view of their function within those works. By function, however, Willett refers primarily to literary function rather than social function *per se*. This literary function is to provide the answer to theodicy.[142] Willett's study is illuminating for the way it discerns significance in God's future mercy as part of this solution to theodicy.[143] Perhaps even more significantly, Willett acknowledges that the recipients of mercy in 4 Ezra are the righteous alone, as we have also determined to be the case. Israel will be disappointed; they will not all have a place in the restoration.[144] We have already alluded to the fact that Israel must come to accept the faith of the righteous if they wish any part in the restoration. Passages like 6:25, "It shall be that *whoever remains* after all that I have foretold to you shall be saved and *shall see my salvation and the end of my world*," and 7:26-27, "the time will come, when the signs which I have foretold to you will come to pass; the city which now is not seen shall appear, and the land which now is hidden shall be disclosed. *And everyone who has been delivered* from the evils that I

---

siah's 400-year reign is included in this date, this would place the author's expectation for his coming at ca. A.D. 96, and this would have implications for the date of authorship. However, besides the fact that this date may have already passed by the time of writing, the author would hardly have included the "messianic age" within "the age" spoken of in v. 10. Again, according to Stone's analysis, the "End" generally precedes the coming of the messiah, which would also speak against including the 400 years into the twelve periods.

141. Stone, 1989, 29, 65, 87-88, 90, 224-25, etc. Stone allows a fair amount of importance to eschatology as the answer to the problems posed by Ezra (25).

142. Willett, 1989, 75, 120. In 4 Ezra it is that the promises of God will be fulfilled in the future; in *2 Baruch* it is that the retribution will happen in the future.

143. Willett, 1989, 68-71.

144. When Ezra protests that eschatology is *not* an adequate answer for the unrighteous — i.e., for those to whom God will not show mercy — God does acknowledge this complaint, but simply tells Ezra not to compare himself to the unrighteous (Willett, 1989, 70)! This is certainly an indication that no further comfort will be promised to the unrighteous since God has no word for them.

have foretold *shall see my wonders*," suggest that only the righteous will benefit from the messiah's coming.[145] There is, therefore, a typical amount of contradiction in the combination of restoration hopes with exclusive soteriology; nevertheless, they are both unmistakably and deliberately present, and perhaps held together in a not too unsuccessful tension. We once again witness a *qualified* restoration.

To better determine the function of eschatological teaching in 4 Ezra, let us first summarize some of the salient points of this teaching. Perhaps not surprisingly the same three basic elements are found here as in the other writings: (1) the judgment-of-Israel theme (6:18-19; 7:31-44[146]); (2) indications of a hope for vindication of the righteous (4:33-43;[147] 9:10-13;[148] 12:32-34[149]); and (3) indications of a doctrine of restoration (6:25-28; 7:26-28; 10:50, 55-56;[150] 12:34; 13:39-49). Complementing these three categories (and indeed forming part of them) are elements that are rather more characteristic of 4 Ezra but have not been lacking altogether in the other writings: (1) *the signs* that, as mentioned above, highlight the present *and* future *apostasy* and describe the judgments that result (5:1-

145. Cf. v. 28. 4 Ezra 12:34 refers to the messianic age (400 years), which would appear to be identical with the restoration period. It is perhaps significant that Israel is portrayed as being judged *before* this time (vv. 33-34), implying that the righteous alone experience this time of joy.

146. That Israel is also the focus of this judgment passage is evident in the imprecation of v. 37: "Look now, and understand whom you have denied, whom you have not served, whose *commandments you have despised!*" Cf. Stone, 1990, 222.

147. The travail motifs, like the cry for vindication by the "souls of the righteous in their chambers" ("How long are we to remain here?" v. 35; cf. "how long," v. 33), mark this passage off as being particularly concerned with the vindication ("reward," v. 35) of the righteous, perhaps related (but not identical here) to the similar metaphor of the righteous being like a woman in travail, awaiting their deliverance. This should, in our view, distract somewhat from the usual interpretation of the passage as relating to the deterministic doctrine of the repository of souls (cf. Stone, 1990, 99). While they are perhaps not unrelated ideas, one must see that the *purpose* of the repository is to explain the delay in the vindication of the *righteous*.

148. The vindication of the righteous is clearly portrayed here in terms of the forced confession of the ways of the righteous by the unrighteous after death ("these must in torment acknowledge it after death," v. 12). The judgment here also refers to Israelites; cf. "although they received my benefits" (v. 10) and Rom. 9:4-5. Stone: "In a striking image in Isa 1:3, Israel is accused of not recognizing God, who had done them benefits" (1990, 297).

149. The messiah renounces the wicked (clearly Israelites, v. 32) before he delivers the "remnant of my people." The "glory" (cf. כבוד) given to the saints in 7:42 seems to have played a role in the vindication theology of this author; "glory" here is associated with, and defends, the righteous (cf. Stone, 1990, 223).

150. 10:57 may imply that "few" will "see" the restored Jerusalem described in this passage.

13;[151] 6:21-24; 9:1-4[152]); and (2) passages that, more clearly than with the other writings, insist that the End is *near* (e.g., 4:26-50; 14:11-13). These warnings of imminence, like the signs with which they are often associated, are intended to intensify the sense of urgency of the message of 4 Ezra for the readers as well as for the opponents of the community. These components are entirely comprehensible if eschatology functions in 4 Ezra as consolation for the righteous and as a promise of the vindication of their faith in the future. The entire book, in fact, functions as a kind of eschatological theodicy that assures the suffering righteous of their vindication: the wicked from Israel and the nations — *all* who are opposed to the righteous community — will be judged, while the righteous will be ultimately victorious. The way embraced by the righteous will be seen to be the *right* way. This function was already seen to come into play in the eschatologically oriented motif of the viewing of the fates of righteous and wicked that is conspicuously present in this book.[153] Of considerable significance, in this regard, are the closing words of Ezra that come in his final address to his people: "after death the judgment will come, when we shall live again; and then the names of the righteous will become manifest, and the deeds of the ungodly will be disclosed" (14:35). The unique position of this statement at the end of the book signals the importance for this author's theodicy of eschatological vindication — vindication, not of all Israel, it should be emphasized, but of those deemed to be righteous by the Ezra community.

WARNING AND CONSOLATION
IN THE ESCHATOLOGY OF *2 BARUCH*

The similarity frequently noted to exist between 4 Ezra and *2 Baruch* applies to the eschatology of the two books and in particular to the literary and social functions of this eschatology. This fact is obvious from the observations of Willett:

> The answer Baruch receives to his complaint . . . points him to the
> eschaton. . . . Once again it is necessary to be clear to whom the passage [15:5-

---

151. It is apparent that vv. 1-3 refer to the present apostasy, to be distinguished from the unspecified future events of vv. 4ff., which are marked off by the literary device found in the words: "But if the Most High grants that you live . . ." (v. 4).

152. These verses particularly seem to speak of the *present* signs since they refer to "a certain part of the predicted signs": they include "earthquakes, tumult of peoples, intrigues of nations, wavering of leaders, confusion of princes" (v. 3).

153. Cf. 7:36-44, 78-99; ch. 5 above.

6] refers. Here it must be the Jewish nation, for it is they who have received the law, and the judgment upon the Jewish nation is Baruch's main concern. God defends his judgment upon the wicked Jews by making reference to the law. . . . The righteous, however, are to take no account of this world and the evils which they endure, but instead are to look to the world to come, which will be a crown with great glory (15:7-8). And so Baruch's complaints about the unfairness of the righteous suffering for the sins of the wicked are dismissed. The wicked deserve to be punished and the righteous are not to be concerned with this world but with the next. . . . The answers which he receives . . . *make a clear distinction between the fortunes of the wicked and those of the righteous, even within Israel.*[154]

The major eschatological components in the two books are the same: judgment of Israel (14:14; see also treatment above), vindication of the righteous (14:12-13; 15:7-8;[155] 51:7-13),[156] and a qualified restoration (6:9;[157] 32:4, 6;[158] 44:7;[159] chs. 73–74) — although the last of the three is significantly not developed and appears in its traditional form only. Only the righteous are said to be given special protection in this time (29:2; 32:1; 71:1). The messiah who arrives to judge the fourth world ruler will do so on behalf of the righteous community (40:2-3).[160] The nearness (20:1-2; 22:2-8; 23:7; 85:10), and signs (29:2–30:5; 70:2-10)[161] of the End, grant urgency to the message, but there is again no attempt to

154. Willett, 1989, 100-101, emphasis in original.

155. Cf. R. H. Charles, *The Apocalypse of Baruch translated from the Syriac*, 1896, 31-32, who explains this as referring to recompense for a life of suffering.

156. For the themes of retribution and vindication, cf. Willett, 1989, 118-19.

157. The restoration of Jerusalem is unqualified in this verse, but it is found in such a terse and traditional-sounding reference that it is impossible to determine the author's full view from it. Interestingly in 4:3 the destroyed Temple appears to be disowned in favor of the archetypical heavenly one. This may itself imply disregard for the present "earthly" Israel as well as her institutions.

158. A good example of where inconsistency in the author's eschatological thought has led Charles to posit interpolation (cf. 1896, 58). Against this theory, cf. P. Bogaert, *Apocalypse de Baruch*, 1969, 2:67.

159. The "consolation of Zion" is its restoration, according to Charles (1896, 70). A massive return of Israel on the basis of the faithfulness of the righteous may be implied in this verse, but the idea of "participating" (lit. "seeing") implies that the restoration is promised to the surviving remnant only.

160. Cf. Charles, 1896, 65. One MS of 32:1 also has the messiah doing the protecting. This is consistent with the view of the messiah throughout *2 Baruch*; cf. Willett, 1989, 103.

161. Although these passages both appear not to provide signs that precede the End so much as delineate the events of the End itself. The descriptions in 70:2-10 may be viewed as developing out of the present time of confusion experienced by the author and his community.

timetable events carefully. The signs are also said to give mixed signals (27:15;[162] cf. vv. 1-14), and while it is true that the wise (only) will understand, the time references are hardly exact or clear (28:1-2; "two parts: weeks of seven weeks"). Only God knows the time of the End (21:8); the End cannot come until "the number that has been appointed is completed" (23:5, but cf. v. 7). Again present evils appear to be a foretaste of worse evils in the End (32:5-6).[163] Elaborate descriptions of the fates of the righteous and the wicked, including a viewing-of-the-fates motif, are to be found in one passage (49:1–51:16).

The social function of eschatological sayings thus again appears to be to warn the apostate of their judgment and console the righteous with notions of their eventual vindication. It does all this while "justifying" God's actions in the form of its theodicy.[164] *2 Bar.* 14:12-14 conveniently provides a summary: "For the righteous justly have good hope for the end and go away from this habitation without fear because they possess with you a store of good works which is preserved in treasuries. Therefore, they leave this world without fear and are confident of the world which you have promised to them with an expectation full of joy. But woe to those of us who have also now been treated shamefully and who await evils at that time." As does 24:1: "For behold, the days are coming, and the books will be opened in which are written the sins of all those who have sinned, and moreover, also the treasuries in which are brought together the righteousness of all those who have proven themselves to be righteous." The future is significant for the way it puts things right — the judgment of the unrighteous and the reward of the righteous: "For that which will be in the future, that is what one will look for, and that which comes later, that is what we shall hope for. . . . For the coming world will be given to these [who 'have not withdrawn from mercy and . . . have preserved the truth of the Law,' v. 14], but the habitation of the many others will be in the fire" (44:11, 15; cf. vv. 12-14). Hardly a clearer indication of the consolatory function of eschatological pronouncements is to be found in these writings than what is offered to us in 54:4 (cf. 43:1): "You [Baruch] are the one who reveals to those who fear that which is prepared for them *so that you may comfort them.*"

---

162. Charles sees these verses as obscure, possibly corrupt (1896, *in loc.*); however, Klijn's translation (*OTP*, 1:610) suggests that they refer to the mixture of the different characteristics of the different times in the last days, obscuring the fact that the End is near. That a mixture of signs and seasons is implied tends to be confirmed by Zimmermann's helpful emendation of "minister" in v. 14 to "pass over" (cf. יַעַבְדוּ for יַעַבְרוּ; cited in Bogaert, 1969, 2:61).

163. While v. 5 of this passage refers to the fall of Jerusalem (Charles, 1896, 59), the following verse alludes to the "combat final, eschatologique, prélude au renouvellement des créatures" (according to Bogaert, 1969, 2:68).

164. Cf. Willett, 1989, 110.

This attempt to discern the real purpose and function — and thus also to a degree the significant content — of eschatology in these books contradicts many popular, and even scholarly, conceptions. Concerns about timing and the order of events do not preoccupy the minds of these writers, as is often assumed. This is evident in the wide variety of dates proffered as well as in the imprecision of the methods of dating. This lack of precision may be partly accounted for by difficulties these authors experienced in interpreting the book of Daniel, which in all probability formed the model, or at least the inspiration, for many of the eschatological passages.[165] Whatever the reason for the diversity, the events depicted are expected to come to fulfillment, depending on the specific book, within an extraordinarily wide margin of time extending from the second century B.C. to over a millennium later.[166] It has been suggested that expectations fluctuated depending on the level of unrest in the respective period,[167] but there is no evidence that such stresses contributed to a rise in *imminence* or to an inclination to set dates, as even in very turbulent periods the End was generally placed quite far off. In any case, one can only conclude that there was little consensus about the whole subject and, to judge from the lack of evidence that these groups were in open disagreement over dating (the teachings are not particularly polemical, in that sense), there appears to have been little concern to either proffer solutions or to establish a consensus. This is a significant clue to the unimportance of timetabling, since these groups were otherwise closely related theologically and seemed to have shared many common teachings. One is probably also witness to a reluctance, subconscious or otherwise, to make the schematization too "verifiable," as this might eventually prove fatal to the *legitimacy* of the revelation — which was clearly the more important concern. Besides the more limited matter of timetabling, there seems to

165. For the import of the book of Daniel in these writings and at this time, cf. Beckwith, "Daniel 9 and the Date of Messiah's Coming in Essene, Hellenistic, Pharisaic, Zealot and Early Christian Computation," 1981a, 521-42, 521-22. As for whether Daniel itself intends to submit precise details of dating, cf. Caird, 1980, 263.

166. Beckwith investigates some of the evidence in our books as well and concludes that dates for the messiah's coming range widely from 3 B.C. to A.D. 473 for pre-Christian Jewish writers and much later, of course, for Christian writings (cf. Beckwith, 1981a, 523-37, 539-40). L. L. Grabbe ("The End of the World in Early Jewish and Christian Calculations," 1982, 107-8) favors a somewhat earlier dating than the A.D. 2240 date associated with the *Seder Olam Rabbah* scheme and the belief in a six-millennium total age for the world.

167. Dates for the End in various ways reflected the zealot uprisings of 4 B.C. and A.D. 63-70, 115-17, and 132-35, according to Beckwith (1981a, 538-39). Dates were also postponed, not only from the failure of the messianic age to materialize, but also in way of *reaction* to the above-mentioned association of Essene-zealot tendencies and the timing of the End (which Beckwith largely traces to the Pharisees; 530-31, 537).

have been little systematization of eschatological beliefs on the whole. Many of the details of eschatological teaching conflict with one another.[168]

This imprecision and diversity tends to eliminate didactic, or systematizing, motivations for eschatological passages in these writings. Eschatology has not yet become a separate category of belief, or a separate item in a written creed, as it is today. The formulation and presentation of eschatological beliefs in these writings was significantly influenced by the social context, and this context we determined to be the highly motivating stimulus of perceived apostasy in Israel. Eschatology can be seen to function to offer consolation through vindication motifs, on the one hand, and warning through judgment themes, on the other. Its function to promote hope for vindication from enemies and oppressors has long been noted, but only *on a nationalistic basis* and on a *national scale.*[169] But the social influences also worked, perhaps at times even more vigorously, at the subnational level of society. Eschatological doctrine at this level reflected and even contributed to a deep-seated soteriological dualism,[170] a fact that itself demonstrates again the essentially nonnationalistic orientation of the movement. Worthy of notice and perhaps surprising in this eschatology is the presence of a restoration doctrine. This betrays a persistent hope for the eventual salvation of the nation. However, even this belief is dominated by a strict and exclusive soteriology usually resulting in a qualified understanding of restoration, which itself confirms the seriousness of the departure of this movement from more nationally oriented theologies.

168. Another good example of the variety in doctrine, which we have not taken the space to mention, is the many agents and means of judgment found in these writings (for which, cf. Volz, 1934, 93-97, who includes war, direct miraculous intervention in human affairs, the enemies of God's people as agents of God's vengeance, individual judgment in the afterlife, etc.).

169. Cf. Volz, 1934, 89-90, for example.

170. O. Plöger realized the importance of this intra-Jewish debate for early biblical apocalyptic passages when he concluded: "the result of these conflicts, which gradually increased, and of the conventicle-type breakaways, was the gradual transformation of the restoration eschatology . . . into the dualistic-apocalyptic form of eschatology" (*Theocracy and Eschatology,* 1968, 112).

CHAPTER TWELVE

"Destruction-Preservation Soteriology"

While preoccupation with the signs of the times and precise calculations of the time of the End were not the chief concerns of these groups, as has been popularly thought, the groups were nevertheless still very concerned about the tumultuous conditions of the days in which they lived, conditions that in their eyes were brought about by the judgment of God on the apostasy they perceived to be all around them. They were thus alarmed about the cataclysmic events they felt were going to take place, or were apparently *already* taking place, in which they also saw their own communities as participants (and not merely detached observers). They also seemed very aware that only *after* these experiences of judgment would the righteous be vindicated and the restoration begin. But several questions remain: What was the connection, in this view of things, between the reality of judgment and the hope of salvation? If Israel was presently in danger of judgment, how could any at all hope to be saved, either in the present or the future? Were any provisions made for an *effective* soteriology in this desperate situation of perceived apostasy in Israel? How, in other words, would the restoration begin, if Israel (and to an extent, the righteous) were in such a hopeless and helpless condition?

There is little doubt that our authors thought about such questions, and they did address them. (They are thus not simply *modern* questions foisted onto this literature.) While no available texts spell out the answers in a neat, systematic form — that would not be typical of the subdued, eclectic, and sometimes secretive nature of these writings — one can nevertheless discern a somewhat elusive but nevertheless *pervasive* underlying *"pattern of salvation"* in much of this literature that implicitly contains some answers. We will come to call this pattern of salvation "destruction-preservation soteriology" (D-P soteriology for short). This soteriology not only incorporates and explains many of the major motifs employed in this literature but tends to draw together and give meaning to many of the "loose ends" of the theologies of this movement. A good example is the way destruction-preservation soteriology tends to bring unity to the somewhat diverse *cosmological* beliefs of these groups. Scholars have for some time recognized the importance of cosmic thought in the context of a struggle between the righteous and the wicked,[1] something witnessed to be true in the investigation of covenantal and soteriological dualism above. By considering the very distinctive views on salvation held by these groups, one is able to place this and other very important pieces into the vast and intricate puzzle that the writings present to us.

PARADIGMS FOR SALVATION

One can understand this literature much better if it is viewed as a sincere attempt, emerging out of the historical circumstances of perceived apostasy, to grasp onto an effective salvation. Never before had this need been so pressing! These writings certainly did not originate the idea of a soteriology, but an increased attention to the need for salvation must have followed when these communities began to perceive the dangers facing Israel and, knowing themselves to be part of the nation, became threatened with the possibility of judgment along with the rest. They needed, therefore, to formulate and justify their view of salvation. The question of where to find a soteriology to build on was, however, perhaps not entirely straightforward. If the covenants once given to the fathers — the divinely authorized channels of blessing — were not a safeguard against judgment, then what possibility of salvation remained? The question thus became where to find, within the authoritative history of God's dealings with Israel (i.e., within biblical history), a *paradigm* or *paradigms* for salvation *that could again become effective when the covenants* (and their provisions for atonement) *became ineffective in maintaining Israel in her righteous status*. These groups found two such paradigms in the biblical *second deluge* and *new exodus* motifs.

1. Cf. H. G. May, "Cosmological Reference in the Qumran Doctrine of the Two Spirits and in Old Testament Imagery," 1963, 14.

The All-Important Flood Paradigm, Continued

The employment of flood motifs in the pneumatological teachings of these groups has already been noted (pp. 424-32). The flood narratives in some passages, however, appear to have nothing to do with pneumatology and to reflect little more than historical interest and a tendency to embellish tradition. The fact that such texts constantly relate the story to the present experience of Israel and to the soon-expected judgment, however, suggests that many of these traditions about the flood not only have pneumatological significance but also serve as a vitally important soteriological paradigm.[2] Indeed, the pneumatological and soteriological implications of this motif are not totally unrelated.

We can start with *1 En.* 6:1–16:3, the lengthiest of the treatments on the Noah theme. In our earlier investigation of the content of this and similar passages, we saw how they form, through the fallen Watchers thematic, part of the theoretical basis of a kind of *pneumatological dualism*. But there is more to the story, for in these passages the Noachic judgment scenes lead into descriptions of a second, and similar, judgment to take place sometime in the future. *1 Enoch* 10, for example, makes clear this correspondence between the first judgment and the second judgment in which the first appears either as a paradigm for the latter, or is seen to be completed in the latter. After the fall of the Watchers, God gives the angel Asuryal a message for Noah: "Tell him in my name 'Hide yourself!' and reveal to him the end of what is coming; for the earth and everything will be destroyed. And the Deluge is about to come upon all the earth; and all that is in it will be destroyed. And now instruct him in order that he may flee, and his seed will be preserved for all generations" (vv. 2-3). While these verses more or less clearly refer to the flood,[3] the following verses trail off into more of what appears to be a reference to the *future* judgment and restoration:

> *In those days* they will lead them into the bottom of the fire — and in torment — in the prison where they will be locked up forever. And at the time when they will burn and die, those who collaborated with them will be bound together with them from henceforth unto the end of all generations. And destroy all the souls of pleasure and the children of the Watchers, for they have

2. Lewis's study of the interpretation of Noah and the flood offers some interesting correspondences to our treatment, although soteriological paradigms based on Noah are not this author's chief interest; cf. J. P. Lewis, *A Study of the Interpretation of Noah and the Flood in Jewish and Christian Literature,* 1968, esp. 8-9, 102-3, 114-16, 167-69. He suggestively relates flood theology to New Testament and later Christian soteriology.

3. A changed orientation to the future, however, is perhaps already indicated by the statement of v. 3 that refers to Enoch's future "seed" and to the reference to the "end of what is coming."

done injustice to man. Destroy injustice from the face of the earth. And every iniquitous deed will end, and the plant of righteousness and truth will appear forever and he will plant joy. And then all the righteous ones will escape; and become the living ones until they multiply and become tens of hundreds; and all the days of their youth and the years of their retirement they will complete in peace. And in those days the whole earth will be worked in righteousness, all of her planted with trees, and will find blessing. (vv. 13-18)

That this passage conceals a reference to the author's future is confirmed by the fact that many other stock expressions for the restoration follow it (during which, incidentally, one sees yet another example of how the "the righteous ones" form the center and goal of the restoration). The only significant literary indication of this change of scene from past to future is the "in those days" of v. 13. This stock eschatological phrase also seems to indicate (although it is at best a hint) that the discussion is turning to *future* events. But the content of the whole passage reveals rather more unambiguously that a shift is intended, for there is posited a long period of time between what occurs in vv. 2-3 (the flood) and what will happen in vv. 13-18 (the second deluge). The verses between the two passages refer to a limited period of internment for the fallen angels (cf. esp. vv. 4, 9-10, 12), designated as "seventy generations" in one place (v. 12), although there appears also to be a further intermission between their sin and their incarceration in which they battle one another (vv. 9, 12). The total length of the period is not easily determined from these general allusions. If a generation is forty years, the total period would be a minimum of 2,800 years, and this might refer to the total time or a portion of the time between the flood and the second deluge, but there is no way to confirm this. It is evident, in any event, that a correspondence between the first and last judgments is intended in this book, even if it is concealed somewhat by the author's attempt to sustain the literary context of the first deluge.

A similar correspondence between past and future judgments can be discerned in the introduction to the Book of Watchers (chs. 1–5; esp. 1:1-9), where a correspondence between the first and last judgments also appears to be deliberately intended. The setting, including the placement of this introductory section immediately before the tale of the fall of the Watchers, implies that the literary context is the flood-judgment. But Enoch's parable, based on his vision in the first chapter, is clearly intended to refer to the *future* judgment: "I look not for this generation but for the *distant one that is coming*" (1:2). This future judgment is by fire, *not* water (v. 6). One would probably be safe therefore to assume that the judgment scene and the many embellishments and traditions inspired by the flood have now been largely applied to the *future* judgment. *As Noah experienced salvation from the first deluge, the readers will experience salvation from the second, fiery deluge.*

This book contains several indications of the correspondence between these two judgments, as the entire narrative sustains a close relationship between the experiences of the diluvian era and the author's present. As an example of this, one reads that following the sin of the angels, their giant offspring taught "the people" war, vain personal ornamentation, various sciences, incantations, astrology, and the lunar calendar,[4] with the result that "there were many wicked ones (or: 'there was much wickedness') and they committed adultery and erred, and all their conduct became corrupt" (8:1-4).[5] This passage implies that sin results from the activity of demonic beings, and that the knowledge the giants impart is a false wisdom. This is the same false wisdom referred to a little later when God pronounces the judgment of the Watchers and informs them that they do not have "all the mysteries" but only "the rejected mysteries" (16:3).[6] Since the knowledge that led to sin includes war, personal ornamentations, astrology, and the activities of the moon, it is certainly justifiable to also see here an allusion to the present sin of the Israelites who have accepted the "rejected mysteries," teachings that have their roots in demonic inspiration. The condition of fallen Israel *in the present* is accordingly being explained as the result of the inspiration of evil demons. The important thing here is *the correspondence between the deluge account and the future of Israel.*

Other parts of the Enochian corpus evidence the same correspondence. The Astronomical Book, for its part, may be entirely preoccupied with calendrical irregularities, and may rarely touch on matters of eschatology, but even here the Noachic typology plays an important part in the conceptualization of the coming events when it is announced that "the upright shall announce righteousness to the upright; and the righteous ones shall rejoice with the righteous ones and congratulate each other. But the sinners shall die together with the sinners; and the apostate shall *sink* together with the apostate. But those who do right shall not die on account of the deeds of the people; *it will gather* on account of the deeds of the evil ones" (81:7-9). We can assume from the language used that the judgment referred to is a future judgment, and it typically includes words of vindication for the righteous. As in the Book of Watchers, these verses suggestively apply flood language to future events.[7]

<hr>

4. As one can only understand "the course of the moon as well as the deception of man" in *1 En.* 8:3.

5. We take this statement to refer back to "the people" of v. 1, rather than giants, as it would appear that this is also the subject intended in v. 4: "And [they] cried and their voice reached unto heaven."

6. Isaac in *OTP*, 1:22, is probably justified in correcting the sg. "mystery" to the pl. "mysteries" since it is difficult to understand what the singular would refer to.

7. For evidence of this, cf. our prior treatment of the passage above. The words *yesaṭṭam*, "they will be flooded," "immersed," and *yetegābā'*, "it gathers" (according to the

1 Enoch Book 4 also contains what appears to be a deliberate intermingling of references to the first and last judgments, similar to that of the Book of Watchers. Enoch sees a vision, after which his grandfather Mahalalel exhorts him to pray for the survival of a remnant. In this prayer Enoch prays that *his* seed might be preserved (84:5-6), which, along with the dramatic context of the passage, suggests the first deluge. The prayer would then be simply for the coming of Noah. But *more* than this is suggested by 84:4, where Enoch refers to the sin of the angels and to the wrath that will rest on the world until the "great day of judgment." Since the final judgment of the angels would still be future during Enoch's time, and the language elsewhere in this passage elicits notions about a future judgment, the reader's attention is constantly drawn to this second judgment.[8] Enoch envisions the sky falling and the earth being swallowed up (83:3-4) and "destroyed" (83:5), details that go beyond descriptions of the flood. The vision itself is interpreted as the "*great* destruction" (83:7, 9).

Book 5 continues the correlation. While the flood judgment is again suggested by the dramatic context, especially by the fact that Enoch is addressing his own sons in the passage (91:5-11), the judgment Enoch describes sounds much more like the future judgment. One verse in particular suggests this: "They[9] shall be thrown into the judgment of fire, and perish in wrath and in the force of the *eternal judgment*" (91:9). That the resurrection and the advent of the messiah follow immediately (91:10-11)[10] also confirms that the main subject here is the *future* judgment. Similarly in the Apocalypse of Weeks, in the "second week" there is a revealing reference to "the *first* consummation" — that is, the flood (93:4). The expression used here suggests that there is yet to be a "second" consummation and that a pattern is being established in the first for the second. Thus, as in the first consummation "a certain man shall be saved" (Noah; 93:4), so also in the judgments of the ninth week "sinners shall depart from upon the whole earth, and be written off for eternal destruction;[11] and all

---

important *Tana*[9] witness), seem to allude to a floodlike judgment that is approaching. In the context of the Astronomical Book, the language of the first deluge is therefore being applied to the second.

8. Cf. S. Fujita, "The Metaphor of Plant in Jewish Literature of the Intertestamental Period," 1976, 37.

9. That these verses concern Israel's judgment is perhaps not immediately clear. The judgment shall be executed on the "earth" (v. 7), but this is directed against the "towers," which Charles takes as a reference to the Temple (cf. 89:50, 54, 56; but cf. M. Black, *The Book of Enoch or I Enoch*, 1985, 281). The expression "all which is (common) with the heathen" (v. 9) may refer to syncretistic practices.

10. In Black's reconstruction of the text the passage ends after v. 10b, but the subject to that point is the resurrection, which sustains the eschatological nature of the passage.

11. 4QEn[g] has "they will be cast into the Pit" (Eth. mistook ῥιφήσεται for γραφήσεται, according to Black, 1985, 294).

people [who remain!] shall direct their sight to the path of uprightness" (91:14). The pattern of the first judgment accordingly becomes the pattern for the second judgment. In fact, VanderKam detects a deliberate structuring of the entire Apocalypse of Weeks according to a chiastic pattern, which would also confirm this correspondence between the second week and the ninth week.[12] As the first consummation (temporarily) brought an end to evil and sin and the salvation of the righteous Noah, the final consummation will bring an (eternal) end to evil and sin and a time of unparalleled righteousness. Enoch accordingly instructs his readers on the "ways of righteousness" in the passage that follows (vv. 18-19) so that they may be among the righteous who survive in that time.

In the closing portions of the Enochian corpus, in the 106th chapter (cf. vv. 6-10; cf. also 1Q20 [= 1QapGn = *Genesis Apocryphon*] 2–5), are found some very peculiar remonstrations by Lamech over the wondrous birth of the child Noah, although this peculiarity is mitigated somewhat when one understands the significance of the passage. In these verses are found an unmistakable allusion to the event of the flood, about which Lamech comments that "a wondrous phenomenon may take place upon the earth *in his days*." And when Methuselah, Lamech's father, reports to Enoch the events that surrounded the miraculous birth of Noah, Enoch prophesies:

> The Lord will surely make new things upon the earth; and I have already seen this matter in a vision and made it known to you. For in the generation of Jared, my father, they transgressed the word of the Lord, the law of heaven. And behold, they commit sin and transgress the commandment; they have united themselves with women and commit sin together with them. . . . There shall be a great destruction upon the earth; and there shall be a deluge and a great destruction for one year. And this son who has been born unto you shall be left upon the earth; and his three sons shall be saved when they who are upon the earth are dead. And upon the earth they shall give birth to giants, not of the spirit but of the flesh. There shall be a great plague upon the earth, and the earth shall be washed clean from all the corruption. Now, make known to your son Lamech that the son who has been born is indeed righteous; and call his name Noah, for he shall be the remnant for you; and he and his sons shall be saved from the corruption which shall come upon the

---

12. J. C. VanderKam, "Studies in the Apocalypse of Weeks," 1984a, 518-21. Weeks one and ten correspond in their mention of the birth of Enoch and the judgment of the angels, each in the "seventh part" of their week (cf. 93:3 and 91:15). And weeks two and nine also correspond. "In them (and only in them) there occur world-wide judgments and destructions of sinful *humanity*" (519, emphasis in original). Thus the first judgment is the flood, and the second judgment, through this chiastic pattern, is deliberately correlated with that first judgment. The other weeks also fit into this broad chiastic pattern (cf. 519-20).

earth on account of all the sin and oppression that existed, and it will be fulfilled upon the earth, in his days. (106:13-18)

This description is clearly of the first deluge. The verses that follow (106:19;
107:1, and, if it belongs to the present section, 108:1ff.), on the other hand,
point clearly to a second, greater destruction, suggesting once again that the
flood has merely been used as a paradigm for the author's own generation:[13]

> *After that* there shall occur still greater oppression than that which was ful-
> filled upon the earth *the first time.* . . . Then I beheld the writing upon them
> [i.e., the heavenly tablets; cf. 106:19] that one generation shall be more
> wicked than the other, until a generation of righteous ones shall arise, wick-
> edness shall perish, sin shall disappear from upon the earth, and every good
> thing shall come upon her. (106:19–107:1)

Compare also ch. 108:

> Another Book of Enoch — which he wrote for his son Methuselah and *for those
> who will come after him, observing the law in the last days.* You who have ob-
> served the law shall wait patiently *in all the days until the time of those who work
> evil is completed, and the power of the wicked ones is ended. As for you, wait pa-
> tiently until sin passes away,* for the names of the sinners shall be blotted out
> from the Book of Life and the books of the Holy One; their seeds shall be de-
> stroyed forever and their spirits shall perish and die; they shall cry and lament
> in a place that is an invisible wilderness[14] and burn in the fire. (vv. 1-3)

Whether or not ch. 108 belonged originally to chs. 106–7, it is apparent that it
has also been placed here to further explicate the theme of the fiery judgment
already spoken of in 106:19 and 107:1 (and cf. 108:4-15 for another comparison of the fates of the wicked in a fiery judgment and of the righteous in eternal
bliss). There is therefore in every part of the book of Enoch a consistent correspondence between the flood and the coming judgment, between the first deluge and the second deluge.

For obvious reasons, Noah is not met as frequently in *Jubilees* as he is in the
Enochian writings. Nevertheless, this writing clearly reflects similar traditions

---

13. J. C. VanderKam, *Enoch and the Growth of an Apocalyptic Tradition*, 1984a, 515,
detects an *inclusio* between ch. 91 and 106:13–107:1 based on "their particular pattern for
Enoch's survey of the future: sin — flood — *greater* sin — judgment." If this is a valid observation, it confirms that the author was thinking of a correspondence between the first
water deluge and the final fire deluge.

14. Charles: "chaotic wilderness." The punishment includes a return to the chaos
that existed before creation.

about the flood (cf. 4:28; 5:1–6:22; 7:34). Here also the Noachic experience of the first destruction, particularly the associated judgment of the angels, is employed as a springboard for discussion of the second, future judgment.[15] In 5:10, for example, the children of the angels are said to have been interned in the depths of the earth "*until the day of great judgment* in order for judgment to be executed upon all of those who corrupted their ways and their deeds before the LORD."

More characteristic of *Jubilees* and significant, for the correspondence not only between the two judgments but between two events of *salvation* as well, is the grounding of the various blood laws and the Feast of Weeks in the Noah account (cf. 6:4-22 and discussion above). The Feast of Weeks, the paramount experience of covenantal renewal by Israel, is itself said to have been founded on the covenant made with Noah.[16] The implication is also drawn that every renewal of the covenant at the Feast of Weeks (properly celebrated, of course) brings about a new experience of salvation *similar* to that of Noah and his sons.[17] The importance of this typological salvation, not only for the regular celebration of the covenantal feast but also for the future judgment, is clear: those who benefit from God's saving provisions will, like Noah and his sons, find deliverance in the coming distress, while those who transgress the covenant (as understood by *Jubilees*, of course) will experience a similar judgment as Noah's generation, who are *also* said to have broken the eternal covenant (cf. 6:12-14, 17-19, 32-33). It may be, therefore, that the keeping of the feast was viewed, not only as a continual atonement, but in particular as protection from the future Noah-like judgment (cf. 6:17, 20-22).[18] Suggestive also of this Noachic typology, or pattern of salvation, is that, while the promise that a *flood* will never again destroy the world is recorded in *Jubilees* (6:4; cf. Gen. 9:11), this does not seem to preclude for the author the possibility of a future and final judgment by *fire* (cf. 36:10).[19] In *Jubilees*, there-

---

15. For Noah as a "type" of future history, cf. A. Jaubert, *La notion d'alliance dans le Judaïsme aux abords de l'ère chrétienne*, 1963, 106, who relates Noah's experience to the realization of a community of the repentant in the author's present and to the hope for a final salvation embodied within this movement of repentance.

16. Cf. Jaubert, 1963, 105, 8.

17. Jaubert appropriately comments: "Dans cette perspective, la fête des Semaines est comme la fête de délivrance du déluge . . . Noé et ses fils représentent l'humanité nouvelle sauvée des eaux" (1963, 105-6).

18. But more general acts of righteousness seem also to have been required — as Noah was "saved . . . from the water of the Flood," his testament exhorts his offspring to "do justice and righteousness" so that *likewise* their "honor may be lifted up" before God and they might be delivered from the second great destruction (7:34).

19. Gen. 8:21 might be interpreted to mean that a similar judgment will never occur; but the author interprets this to mean only that another *water* judgment will not occur, allowing for a fire judgment in the future. For the promise never to bring a flood again, cf. Gen. 9:11, 15; cf. also Sir. 44:18.

fore, there is a vital association between the judgment/salvation of Noah's time and the judgment/salvation that the author experiences in the present and/or anticipates for the future.

The scrolls are much less formally oriented to an explication of flood theology than either *1 Enoch* or *Jubilees,* but a couple revealing fragments from Cave 4, and many incidental references, imply that this group possessed a vitally important soteriology based on the flood.[20] One fragment, referred to by its editors as *Tanhumin,* contains a scathing Jerusalem critique in which Jerusalem's trouble is compared to that of Noah, employing the language of Isa. 54:9, which also draws this connection.[21] The other fragment (4Q252 = 4ApGen[a] = 4QGenesis Pesher[a]) is more reminiscent of the Noachic portions of *1 Enoch* in that it comprises a midrash of the flood and other stories from Genesis that have been suggestively called "salvation of the righteous stories," "escape and salvation stories," and "escape and rescue stories" by Eisenman and Wise.[22]

But other, less explicit passages in the scrolls also assume that the flood is a paradigm for judgment and salvation. Lengthy psalms in the Hymn Scroll describe the teacher's personal struggles not only in terms of a fiery "deluge" but also with a variety of images associated with suffering, distress, or afflictions of different kinds. One hymn (1QH 3.6ff.) seems to be especially inspired by Noachic theology,[23] as well as by several "tumult" motifs in the canonical psalms. The hymn opens with a startling marine image of a storm-tossed ship (l. 6), which has obvious relevance to a flood-based soteriology, and proceeds to speak of sufferings in terms of a fortified city and the travail associated with giving birth. Following this, in a passage investigated above, the hymn mixes the three metaphors:[24]

> And they made my soul like a ship in the depths of the sea, and like a fortified city before them that besiege it. And I was confused like the Woman about to bring forth at the time of her first child-bearing. For terrors and fearful pains

20. Jaubert recognizes "une typologie de déluge" (1963, 230).

21. We refer the reader to F. García Martínez, *Qumran and Apocalyptic,* 1992, 208, for this text (4Q176).

22. R. H. Eisenman and M. Wise, *The Dead Sea Scrolls Uncovered,* 1992, 80-81, although they may be reading too much into the Noah story, as it seems to us to be entirely dedicated to defending a 364-day year. The story of Lot and Gomorrah significantly mentions a "remnant."

23. Cf. Jaubert, 1963, 230-31.

24. For an interesting wordplay, note our earlier treatment of משבריה (p. 473n.98 above); cf. S. Holm-Nielsen, *Hodayot,* 1960, 54; M. Mansoor, *The Thanksgiving Hymns Translated and Annotated with an Introduction,* 1961, 113, for discussion. It is likely that the womb was viewed as a kind of watery world, facilitating the shift from marine to birth images.

have unfurled on its billows that She who is with child might bring into the world her first-born. For the children have reached as far as the billows of Death, and She who is big with the Man of distress is in her pains. For she shall give birth to a man-child in the billows of Death. (ll. 6-9)

A reference to the sufferings of the *moreh* (ll. 7-8) and of the *yaḥad* (ll. 8-12) has already been discerned in this passage. While a messianic reference is also being made, the *primary* concern of the passage is with suffering, not with the messiah *per se*. The hymnist continues this theme of suffering by developing the marine metaphor, applying it to his opponents:

And they shake the foundations of the rampart like a ship on the face of the waters, and the clouds roar in a noise of roaring. And they that live in the dust are, like them that sail the seas, terrified because of the roaring of the waters. And their wise men are for them like sailors in the deeps, for all their wisdom is destroyed[25] because of the roaring of the waters, because of the boiling of the deeps upon the fountains of the waters. And the waves are turbulent rearing into the air and the billows resound with the roaring of their voice. And Sheol and Abaddon open in the midst of their turbulence and all the arrows of the Pit fly out in their pursuit; they let their voice be heard in the Abyss. And the gates [of Sheol] open to all the works of the Asp, and the doors of the Pit close upon her who is big with Perversity, and the everlasting bars upon all the spirits of the Asp. (ll. 12-18)

Thus not only the community, but also its opponents, are viewed as being tossed about on the turbulent waves. It is to be assumed that the community will be saved from the tempest[26] while the ungodly drown in it and are taken to the Pit. References to the Pit, the Abyss, the gates of sheol, and particularly the "Asp" are reminders that this imagery is highly spiritualized, and the metaphorical quality of the entire passage might be noted. It would be going too far off to deny, however, that the imagery is meant to reflect real experience. The psalmist blamed these tumultuous experiences, whatever they may have been, on demons who will eventually devour the unrighteous and can only be subdued by God.[27]

The tumult metaphor continues in the same column, in what seems, however, to be the beginning of a new hymn.[28] Here the psalmist praises God

25. The word is probably "confused," from √ בעל, "to confuse" (Holm-Nielsen, 1960, 59).

26. Cf. 3.19ff.; often taken to be part of the next hymn; cf. discussion following. Holm-Nielsen finds a realized soteriology in this psalm (1960, 64).

27. For the likelihood that some of these references are to demons in the passage, cf. the treatment above, and cf. Holm-Nielsen, 1960, 59-60; Mansoor, 1961, 115-16.

28. Note the typical formula: "I give Thee thanks . . ."

for having redeemed his soul from the Pit (l. 19). He has risen from "Sheol of Abaddon."[29] He has been raised "to everlasting heights" and now walks on an even ("infinite") plain (l. 20). After expressing his wonder and awe at this salvation (ll. 20-24), he returns to an autobiographical account of his experiences:

> For I have stayed in the realm of wickedness and in the lot of the company of the wretched; and the soul of the poor one was an exceeding stranger in the midst of *the tumult* and overwhelming calamities accompanied my steps while all the traps of the Pit were opened and all the snares of wickedness spread out and the nets of the wretched *upon the face of the waters;* while all the arrows of the Pit[30] flew out straight to the target and shot out leaving no hope; while the cord (of destruction) beat upon the damned and the destiny of wrath upon the abandoned and the pouring out of fury upon the hypocrites, and while it was the time of wrath for all Belial. (ll. 24-28)

These words might be interpreted to mean that the author viewed his "preconversion" or "preenlightenment" as an experience of emptiness or "nothingness" in which he shared the life of the rest of the wicked. Perhaps, on the other hand, he is referring to a more recent time of persecution, as in the first passage. But all things considered, the psalm gives the impression that the entire *era* in which the hymn writer lived was, as it says, "the time of wrath for all Belial" (l. 28).[31] In this "time of wrath" all are caught together: the community, Israel, the whole world — all share in the same distress. This kind of thinking explains why expectations of judgment and salvation are brought together. They are not separate experiences — salvation arises *out of* judgment. For similar reasons the sufferings of the community are not entirely distinguishable from the judgments that had already begun to afflict the wicked. But what is noteworthy is that the psalmist suggests that while he has indeed been caught in the tumult and has suffered for it, the fortunes of the *unrighteous* through this distress will prove to be far worse than those of the *righteous*. Thus there is a

29. Metaphorical expressions for distress; cf. M. A. Knibb, *The Qumran Community,* 1987, 180.

30. As with the previous psalm, the Pit, and the demonic world as a whole, seem to be the origin of the distresses, if not also the destination of the wicked who are helplessly caught in them. For possible allusions to demons in expressions like "the nets of the wretched upon the face of the waters" and "arrows of the Pit," cf. Holm-Nielsen, 1960, 70; Knibb, 1987, 181.

31. The expression בליעל can, of course, be interpreted impersonally; cf. Holm-Nielsen: "the moment of anger upon all corruption" (1960, 71). In either case, however, the expression is best understood to mean that the tumult was caused by the forces of evil; cf. Knibb, 1987, 181. For the expression "Era [of evil?]," and "periods of Wrath," cf. 4Q266 (Eisenman and Wise, 1992, 219).

subtle, but essential, distinction: *the present is a time of testing for the righteous from which they would be saved, as well as the beginning of judgment for the wicked from which they would* not *be saved.*

The psalmist continues, using still more suggestive words:

> And the bonds of Death tightened leaving no escape, and the torrents of Belial overflowed all the high banks like a fire consuming all their shores, destroying from their channels every tree green and dry and whipping with whirlwinds of flame until the vanishing of all that drinks there. It devours all the foundations of pitch and the bases of the continent; the foundations of the mountains are prey to fire and the roots of flint become torrents of tar. It devours as far as the Great Abyss and the torrents of Belial pour into Abaddon and the recesses of the Abyss roar out amidst the roaring of swirling mud. And the earth cries out because of the calamity fallen on the world and all its recesses howl, and all that are on it are stricken with fear and stagger, the prey to great misfortune. For God bellows with His mighty roaring and His holy abode resounds with His glorious truth and the heavenly host lets its voice be heard. . . . and it shall not end until utter destruction, which shall be final, without anything like it. (ll. 28-36)

The highly symbolic and emotional rhetoric of this author defies attempts to find consistency of logic in this passage, but it is obvious that the same themes are evident here as before, including flood or tumult motifs. The present distress is a fight with Death. A variety of images of fire suggest a future judgment, however, and the last lines definitely tail off into a description of the final great assize.[32] Perhaps, as it seems, the author expected the *present* distress to continue, eventually to culminate in an incomparable *final* judgment by fire.[33] This apparent confusion of present experiences with future judgments probably indicates that the author gave to his soteriological paradigm both a *realized* and an *eschatological* interpretation.[34] If, as some suggest, the community actually is represented in the first-person references of this psalm,[35] the experience of sal-

---

32. It is difficult to decide where the present sufferings end and the final judgment begins in the psalm. This is partly due to the uncertainty in the verbal tenses in the passage. H. Ringgren suggests that the references to fire earlier in the hymn (cf. ll. 29-32) are metaphorical rather than literal, "an image of error's last gathering of strength before the decisive battle"; only at the very end of the hymn is the final judgment referred to (*The Faith of Qumran*, 1963, 157-58).

33. Cf. Knibb, 1987, 181.

34. Holm-Nielsen: "deliverance has already been realized in the midst of a world which is being destroyed by the wicked" (1960, 75).

35. Cf. Holm-Nielsen (1960, 75), who is willing to term it a "collective psalm of thanksgiving, providing that the term 'collective' is not too rigidly distinguished from the individual."

vation was already commonly shared by the *yaḥaḏ*. The final lines in particular seem to reflect an eschatological cosmic battle in which God is the Chief Contender: "For God bellows with His mighty roaring and His holy abode resounds with His glorious truth and the heavenly host lets its voice be heard. And the eternal foundations stagger and shake and the host of the Valiant of heaven brandishes its whip in the world" (ll. 34-36).[36] This kind of cosmic battle has a vital connection with the Noachic soteriological paradigm, but we will deal with this important matter more adequately below.

Other hymns from Qumran also allude to the present as a time of distress by using water imagery. Sometimes the end or goal of this distress is explicitly stated as the salvation of the elect. In 1QH 5.22 the psalmist declares that the community ("the poor of Grace") will "arise from the tumult together."[37] And in the sixth column we read that in spite of the "tumult of kingdoms," God would "soon raise up survivors among Thy people and a remnant in the midst of Thine inheritance" (ll. 7-8). Marine images, possibly derived from Jonah,[38] are again employed to speak of the psalmist's situation (mostly as being persecuted by Belial's party; cf. ll. 20-21): "And I, I was like a sailor on a ship. In the fury of the seas were their waves and all their billows roared against me; a wind of confusion and there was no breeze to restore the soul and no path to direct the way on the face of the waters. And the Abyss resounded to my groaning and my soul went down to the gates of Death" (ll. 22-24). Here again the source of the distress seems to be the Abyss, and the danger the psalmist faces appears to be that of sinking into the Pit, or death. But in spite of the dangers, he refers quite confidently to his salvation in the following verses:

> And I was like a man who entered a fortified city and sought refuge in a steep wall awaiting deliverance. And I leaned on Thy truth, O my God. For it is Thou who wilt set the foundation upon rock and the frame-work on the cord of righteousness and the plumb-line of truth to test the tried stones in order to build a stout building such as will not shake, and that none who enter there shall stagger. (ll. 25-27)

It is interesting, therefore, how water has become a symbol of judgment as well as of deliverance from judgment, as the righteous arise unharmed from its

36. The last lines Holm-Nielsen renders: "and the war of the heroes of heaven sweepeth across the world," referring to "angels who act as tools for God's righteous retribution in the eschatological war" (1960, 65, 73). The tenses and the context may suggest, however, that this judgment is thought to have already begun in the author's day.

37. An expression of salvation here, according to Holm-Nielsen (1960, 106).

38. Cf. Holm-Nielsen, 1960, 118; חרישית in 7.5 (which he takes as part of this hymn) is *hapax legomena* in the Hebrew Scriptures in Jon. 4:5.

dangers. (Here the psalmist is set on solid bedrock, as part of the elect "building" or temple, safe from the torrent and destruction.) It would appear that God not only saves *from* the distress, but in some way also *through* the dangerous situation of judgment, perhaps even *by means of* the judgment as it functions as a kind of "discipline" for the elect, or even as a kind of validation of their election. In any event, this soteriology "works" by combining God's action in judging and saving. Whether or not one should place this belief under the rubric of "Noachic soteriology," whether in fact the author's use of marine images was inspired at all by the traditions of Enoch and Noah, it is nevertheless evident that he applied similar salvation-from-danger motifs to his own situation as are evident in *1 Enoch* and *Jubilees*. Perhaps the author was more directly inspired by the canonical psalms with their "tumult" motifs — but these in turn may have their origins in the story of Noah and the flood. In any event, the writers of the scrolls often employed the images of turbulent, tumultuous waters, and the various marine and water motifs might well point to the flood as a more distant inspiration.

Water as an image of destruction and judgment makes its appearance in later writings also. The extended historical rehearsal in *2 Baruch* employs the water motif throughout (chs. 53–74; the "Vision of Dark and Light Waters"), and this motif may well go back to Noah traditions, as water is adopted from that story as an appropriate symbol of the several destructions that are brought on by the "black" periods in Israel's history (53:7, 9; cf. 36:4). In the climactic final destruction (i.e., deluge) by water *and* fire, it becomes particularly apparent that this judgment is modeled on that of Noah: "And it happened at the end of the cloud that, behold, it poured black water and it was much darker than all the water that had been before. *And fire was mingled with it*. And where that water descended, it brought about devastation and destruction" (53:7).[39] In the interpretation section (cf. 56:9-16) the correspondence becomes even more explicit. The flood belongs to the "*first* black waters," it says (56:16), implying that the following black waters bring floodlike experiences as well. Flood traditions bearing on the judgment of angels in this passage, reminiscent of the Book of Watchers, also connect the flood with the last judgment.[40] The twelfth period

---

39. R. H. Charles, *The Apocalypse of Baruch translated from the Syriac*, 1896, 88, takes this to refer to the "travail pains of the messiah"; the images, particularly fire, seem somewhat more destructive and final than that, however. Charles's view that the lightning in vv. 6 and 8 refers to the messiah is probably valid; that the cloud imagery was inspired by the association of the messiah with the cloud in Dan. 7:13, on the other hand, is a moot point.

40. The author relates that the sinning angels "were tormented in chains," perhaps alluding to their yet-future complete judgment, while "those living on earth perished together through the waters of the flood" (56:13, 15). Punishments of angels and humans were closely associated in the tradition, and were possibly even thought to occur concurrently during the first and second judgments.

of "bright waters" contains explicit flood motifs as well — although this time the more positive aspects of that event (68:1ff.). The familiar combination of the symbols of salvation and judgment is evident in connection with this twelfth period: while Baruch's people are "all together in *danger of* perishing," they will nevertheless "be saved." It is certainly significant that the lengthy water metaphor in *2 Baruch* includes references to the flood at its beginning and at its end, as well as, by implication, throughout the body of the vision. This suggests that the author was familiar with a soteriological pattern based on the flood, which he expressed in terms of his own very original water motif.

The parable in 4 Ezra about the narrow and wide places may well also point to the belief that salvation involves a passing through destructive (fiery *and* watery) paths. It states that the entrance to the heavenly city "is narrow and set in a precipitous place, so that there is fire on the right hand and deep water on the left; and there is only one path lying between them, that is, between the fire and the water, so that only one man can walk upon that path" (7:7-8). This is peculiar imagery, even for this highly symbolic passage. The use of water and fire images again appears to juxtapose two judgments or types of judgments — the Noachic "water" judgment, on the one hand, with the final "fiery" judgment, on the other. That the former "water" judgment was considered paradigmatic for the latter "fire" judgment would appear to be confirmed by the following interpretation section, in which it is conspicuously mentioned that sin brought the first judgment (v. 11) — that is, the flood. By saying that the entrances to this world (apparently an interchangeable symbol with the "path" that lies between the fire and water) were made "narrow and sorrowful and toilsome; they are few and evil, full of dangers and involved in great hardships" (v. 12), the writer may be hinting that the way to eternal life falls between two times, or types, of judgment.

Moses and Israel's Deliverance

Not all of the writings under investigation employ the flood for their chief soteriological paradigm. Nevertheless, a similar *pattern of salvation* can be discerned in other paradigms that do not seem, at first glance, to be as conducive to this pattern. In particular, certain interpretations or traditions of the story of Moses and the deliverance of Israel from Egypt are adopted as paradigms of salvation, notably those traditions that are developed into expectations of the "New" or "Second Exodus," a development not completely foreign to the prophetic literature and the canonical psalms. It is perhaps not totally surprising, however, that these writings actually exhibit a reticence toward the exodus motif. This reticence can be detected most conspicuously in the hymns or psalms of 1QH. While the biblical psalms that these hymns emulate frequently rehearse God's deliverance of Israel through the exodus, there is no mention of this deliverance in parallel passages in the *Hodayot*.[41] The apparent reason for this is that the exodus event possessed nationalistic overtones that these groups may have wished to avoid in favor of biblical teachings that referred to a remnant being saved. In other words, these groups had their reasons for preferring the Noah and flood account as their main model for salvation.

Even in texts where the exodus story is related, the preference for Noah shows through. Thus *Jubilees*, a book that centers on Moses, and even chs. 47–49, which rehearse the account of Moses' life, seems to deliberately employ *Noachic* language where it would not normally be found (particularly in the passage that narrates the hiding of Moses by his mother; 47:2-4). Indeed, the experience of Noah, in some places, seems to represent a typological experience that Moses was destined to repeat in his own life, and this is true even in interpretive details, such as when the angel informs Moses that his mother "hid you for three months. . . . And she made an *ark* for you" (47:3-4). The language used and events associated with the crossing of the Red Sea and with the institution of the Passover (48:13–49:6) also evoke Noachic images, probably because water featured so centrally in these stories, but also because the flood had become an interpretative key to the story.

It is evident from the way the story is told that the exodus event is also related for pneumatological purposes. One passage dwells on how Mastema attempted to prevent Moses from fulfilling his mission:

> Did he not desire to kill you with all of his might and save the Egyptians from your hand because he saw that you were sent to execute judgment and vengeance upon the Egyptians? . . . And Prince Mastema stood up before you and desired to make you fall into the hand of Pharaoh. And he aided the magicians of the Egyptians, and they stood up and acted before you. . . . Prince Mastema was not shamed until he had become strong and called to the Egyptians so that they might pursue after you with all the army of Egyptians. . . . (48:3, 9, 12; cf. vv. 15-19)

This passage makes it clear that the battle in which Moses found himself was a spiritual one. Accordingly God would deliver Moses, not so much from Pharaoh as from Mastema: "And I [God's angel] stood between the Egyptians and Israel, and we delivered Israel from his [Mastema's] hand and from the hand of his [Mastema's] people" (48:13; cf. vv. 4, 10-12). This kind of pneumatological thought recalls the role of the fallen Watchers in the flood traditions. In common with the Noachic paradigm also (and quite appropriate for exodus tradi-

41. Cf. Mansoor, 1961, 27.

tion) is that *water* is the instrument of redemption. Here salvation through water is understood as having cosmic significance: "And the LORD brought them out through the midst of the sea as through dry land. And all of the people whom he [Mastema] brought out to pursue after Israel the LORD our God threw into the middle of the sea *into the depths of the abyss beneath* the children of Israel" (48:13-14). That the Egyptians were not only drowned in a sea, but cast into "the depths of the abyss beneath the children of Israel," is in line with this spiritual perspective. The Abyss is elsewhere equated with Abaddon and death in *Jubilees,* and the combination of these motifs with the idea of a deliverance from water recalls the tumult passages in the Hymn Scroll. In a way reminiscent of these other passages, where water is both the instrument of judgment and of salvation, conspicuous reference is made here to the fact that the saved party goes through the water *along with* those who are judged. The water metaphor seems particularly important to the author (or his traditions) as a symbol for the *"locus" of salvation.*

Associated with this watery exodus-type deliverance in *Jubilees* is the institution of the Passover, and again there are many suggestive embellishments of the biblical account (cf. Exodus 12–13). Most noteworthy in this regard is that the celebration is given a spiritual interpretation: "You continued eating the Passover in Egypt and all of the *powers of Mastema* were sent to kill all of the firstborn in the land of Egypt . . . in every house where they saw the blood of a year-old lamb upon its doors . . . they would pass over so that all who were in the house might be saved" (49:2-3).[42] What is even more significant, this spiritual soteriology has seemingly influenced the Jubilaean understanding of the Passover *as it was celebrated in the author's time.* The celebration is thus presented as a spiritual victory, not only in Moses' day, but also in every faithful repetition and remembrance of the event that followed. This (along with the calendrical considerations explored above) would have made the timing of the feast in the author's day of *crucial* importance, since it carried spiritual implications. The passage that follows the "institution" passage above makes it clear how important it is that the rite be observed "in its time, on the fourteenth of the first month" (49:1).

---

42. R. H. Charles refers to this kind of reference as "another instance (cf. also ver. 17) where our author has followed the example of the Chronicler in 1 Chron. xxi.1, where he assigns to Satan the action that in 2 Sam. xxiv.1 is ascribed to Yahweh. The LXX and the Targums replace the divine name by the phrase 'an angel of the Lord'" (*The Book of Jubilees or Little Genesis, Translated from the Editor's Ethiopic Text,* 1902, 250). It is noteworthy that although this may explain the origin of the practice, it does not adequately explain this entire passage, which considerably enlarges on, and takes its cue from, Exod. 4:21-26. The author not only replaces references to Yahweh's acts with the agency of Mastema, as here, but also sees Mastema at work through the *entire* history recorded in *Jubilees.*

And you, *remember* this all of the days of your life and observe it from year to year all the days of your life, once per year on its day according to all of its law and you will *not delay one day from its day or from one month to another month.* For it is an eternal decree and engraved upon the heavenly tablets *for all of the children of Israel* that they might observe it in *each and every year . . . in all of their generations.* And there is no limit of days because it is ordained forever. (49:7-8)

The concern for timing is made even more emphatic by the fact that laws for observation of the proper dating of the feast are explicated in a lengthy section that follows the above passage (49:9-23) and that, along with more words about calendar and "sabbaths" (ch. 50), forms the significant conclusion to the book.

The entire picture can now be reconstructed: In the thought world of *Jubilees,* Mastema and his angels "make the rounds" on every successive Passover, just as they once did in Egypt, separating the righteous from the unrighteous. If Passover is not celebrated on the proper day, therefore, the angels, who would naturally follow the sectarian calendar, make their rounds on a day when Israel is not prepared. The protection for Israel provided in the rite is thus tragically forfeited. Those who *do* celebrate on the proper day, however, would find that Mastema "passes over" them (actually in *Jubilees* he is "bound"). This is confirmed in a preceding passage where it was said in regard to the first exodus that on the "fourteenth day . . . Prince Mastema was bound and shut up from coming after the children of Israel" (48:15; cf. v. 18: "on the fourteenth day we bound him"). As it was in the days of Moses, according to the strict logic of the *Jubilees,* so also, apparently, is it true on *each and every* fourteenth of the first month: Mastema is bound (or, if one prefers the traditional formulation, is ordered to "pass over" — i.e., to miss the Passover celebrants). The celebration of Passover *on this day* (according to the sectarian calendar) therefore was considered essential, in that it was believed that the celebrants of the feast could *only* acquire protection and salvation for themselves *on this day* — that is, on the day Mastema was bound. This attitude toward the Passover, which with the Day of Atonement is the main celebration of atonement, provides good reason to suspect that all of the atonement theology of *Jubilees* is understood *as if it involved a triumph over the powers of Mastema.* This atonement that involves spiritual triumph can, however, only be experienced on *Jubilees'* terms. It is no wonder that the rest of Israel was thought to be unable to experience this atonement, and that this was considered to have serious pneumatological implications.

The scrolls also show clear signs of a second-exodus soteriology. The Damascus Document refers to the time "when Israel was saved for the *first* time" (CD 5.19) and suggests that the sect (or an antecedent movement or group of some kind) ventured out into the wilderness for the very purpose of fulfilling the words of Isa. 40:3, a passage with clear exodus allusions (1QS 8.14; 9.19).[43] The experience of deliverance from Egypt apparently shaped the ideology of the final battle in the War Scroll as well. The exact nature of this final battle is a matter of debate, but its liturgical expression and miraculous descriptions give the impression that, whether the battle was to be fought on the earthly level or not, it was *certainly* also to be fought on the religious and spiritual level.[44]

The eleventh column of this work contains a victory hymn built around the refrain "Thine is the battle!" (1QM 11.1-7). In the light of such certainty of victory, the author describes the decisive battle in which God will "bring down the bands of Belial" (l. 8): "Thou wilt deal with them as with Pharaoh and as with the commanders of his chariots in the Sea of Reeds. And those whose spirit is broken Thou wilt cause to pass like a flaming torch in the straw, devouring the wicked and returning not until the destruction of the guilty. And Thou didst in former days announce in these words the time when Thou wouldst display the might of Thy hand against the Kittim" (ll. 9-11). Probably too much should not be taken from this passage, as many sources and traditions have contributed to its language. However, it at least corroborates the understanding that the final battle against the Kittim was conceptualized in terms of a new deliverance like that out of Egypt. That the community associated the bringing down of Belial in the final days with the victory over Egypt is also suggested by l. 11 ("Thou didst *in former days* announce in these words . . ."), which also suggests that a hermeneutical principle may even have been involved here in which the exodus was used as an instructive paradigm for a future battle.[45] This will be a spiritually decisive battle, as indicated by l. 8 in the quota-

43. N. Golb, *Who Wrote the Dead Sea Scrolls?* 1995, 73-74, maintains that Isa. 40:3 was interpreted metaphorically in 1QS and that the passages in question require no literal retreat to the wilderness. On the other hand, the exegetic methodology of the sect was hardly consistent, as we have seen; here the "expounding of the Torah" probably refers to the "making straight," not to the "in the desert" of Isa. 40:3, which was interpreted quite literally (cf. Mark 1:2-3 of John the Baptist). A trek to the wilderness is suggested also by the location of the Sons of Light as presupposed by the War Scroll, the escape-from-Jerusalem thematic in the scrolls, as well as the second-exodus motif itself.

44. The idea of a literal earthly battle has been argued by Eisenman. For critique of this view, cf. Ringgren (1963, 18-19), whose reasons for seeing the scroll as a "sort of apocalypse" and a battle operating on the religious plane are no more convincing. The theoretical language of the passage, particularly when borrowed from Scripture, does not preclude a literal battle. It is perhaps best to see a literal battle in which are involved to a high degree the powers resident in the heavens.

45. Although the word "Asshur" in l. 11 may suggest that the comparison is (also) with the destruction at the hands of Sennacherib (cf. Y. Yadin, *The Scroll of the War of the Sons of Light against the Sons of Darkness,* 1962, 312). Another reference may be found between cols. 13 and 14. The bottom and top of the War Scroll are mutilated, and the first

tion above.[46] The idea of the righteous being the instruments of vengeance is suggestively combined with that image of judgment of fire in this line.[47]

DESTRUCTION-PRESERVATION (D-P) SOTERIOLOGY

The Noah and Moses paradigms testify to a subtle but pervasive *"pattern of salvation"* that combines experiences of deliverance, salvation, or preservation (either of individuals or of the righteous remnant), on the one hand, with experiences of judgment, persecution, or calamities (natural or providential), on the other. That is to say, *salvation is experienced by means of, as well as in the midst of, danger and judgment.* It is appropriate, therefore, to call this soteriological pattern "destruction-preservation soteriology" (or, for convenience, D-P soteriology). Although this terminology has not been used before (as far as the present writer can ascertain), it adequately describes a soteriological pattern that not only established itself as a dominant one in Second Temple Judaism, but was to a certain degree anticipated by Hebrew thought and probably also by the beliefs of the entire Near Eastern world.[48] It is, of course, not surprising that such a soteriological pattern would emerge in late Second Temple Judaism, given the context of hardship in which the nation found itself and particularly the attitudes of the protest movement in its reaction to apostasy. But this

---

and last lines of each column are often undecipherable. It would appear, however, from the bottom of col. 13 and the top of 14, that the subject in 14 continues to be (as it is throughout the scroll) a description of the battle against the "sons of darkness" (13.16). At the top of the next scroll the words "like the fire of His Wrath against the idols of Egypt" survive. This theme is not continued, but may also evidence the importance of the exodus as a model for the final battle.

46. Interesting are the allusions in that line to Pharaoh (cf. Exod. 14:4; 17:8; cf. l. 9) or possibly Gog (Ezek. 39:13; cf. l. 16; Yadin, 1962, 311).

47. "Those whose spirit is broken" in l. 10 are the elect (cf. "Poor" in l. 9). For the idea that the elect will pass through the wicked like a flame devouring them, cf. Zech. 12:6 and John the Baptist's warning of the coming fire in Matt. 3:11-12 par. (it is interesting in this regard that Yadin chooses to translate "sheaf" for "straw" [1962, 312]). For fire burning the wicked, cf. also Isa. 9:18.

48. See below for discussion on the relevance of the findings of the "Myth and Ritual" school for this theology. Notable promoters of this view included S. H. Hooke (cf. Hooke, ed., *Myth, Ritual, and Kingship,* 1958, 1-21); A. R. Johnson, *Sacral Kingship in Ancient Israel,* 1955; A. R. Johnson, "Hebrew Conceptions of Kingship," 1958, 204-35; W. O. E. Oesterley, "Early Hebrew Festival Rituals," 1933a, 111-146; and G. Widengren, "Early Hebrew Myths and Their Interpretation," 1958, 149-203. Although the school blossomed several decades ago, and many corrections and qualifications of its findings have become necessary, its influence is still felt and appreciated.

soteriology may also have represented a synthesis of several ideas already found in the Hebrew Scriptures. One could name, among others: (1) holy-war and conquest motifs;[49] (2) Day-of-Yahweh theology;[50] (3) traditions reflecting upon the exodus[51] and the crossing of the Jordan;[52] (4) cosmic triumph motifs and other battle scenes in the heavens;[53] (5) references to a second deluge;[54] and of course (6) the implicit and explicit instances of remnant theology.

An important passage that may have played a role in the development of D-P soteriology is that well-known "apocalyptic" passage, Isaiah 24–27. In ch. 24 it is stated that the covenant has been broken (v. 5), and as a result a judgment upon the whole earth (land?) will mean that "few men are left" (v. 6).[55] Jerusalem specifically will be judged (vv. 10ff.). The passage goes on to speak of a new deluge:

> The windows of heaven are opened,
>   and the foundations of the earth [āreṣ, land?; here and below?] tremble.
> The earth is utterly broken,
>   the earth is rent asunder,
>   the earth is violently shaken.
> The earth staggers like a drunken man,
>   it sways like a hut. (vv. 18c-20a)[56]

This deluge is then associated with the punishment of the "host of heaven":

49. For the combination and use of holy-war and Day-of-Yahweh motifs in the War Scroll, cf. P. von der Osten-Sacken, *Gott und Belial,* 1969, 34-40. Particularly interesting is his view that the communion-with-angels doctrine at Qumran was derived from holy-war theology (222-23).

50. In the Ezekelian Day-of-Yahweh theology, the motifs of a cosmic battle are brought to bear on the final judgment of Egypt, particularly Pharaoh, who is described as a "dragon" in 32:2 (cf. May, 1963, 8).

51. Cf. Exod. 15:1-18; May, 1963, 8. A. R. Johnson (1958, 204-35, 222-23) gives credence to Mowinckel's association of exodus and triumph motifs. A good example of their combination is Isa. 51:9-11, where the exodus is also employed as a paradigm for the return from exile.

52. Cf., e.g., Ps. 74:13-15; Isa. 51:9-11; etc.

53. In Judg. 5:20 the stars play a role in the battles of Deborah. In Daniel the archangel Michael is said to take part in the final battle (Dan. 12:1). Other examples can be found.

54. Isa. 24:18ff.; cf. discussion below.

55. וְנִשְׁמוּ אֱנוֹשׁ מִזְעָר. The expression is reminiscent of the remnant doctrine in Isaiah.

56. To this can be compared the Noah passage, particularly Gen. 7:11, and the concentration in the following verses on the various effects upon the land (אֶרֶץ).

> On that day the LORD will punish
>> the host of heaven, in heaven,
>> and the kings of the earth, on the earth.
> They will be gathered together
>> as prisoners in a pit;
> they will be shut up in a prison,
>> and after many days they will be punished.
> Then the moon will be confounded,
>> and the sun ashamed. (vv. 21-23a)

This passage suggestively combines the judgment in the heavenlies (and on earth) with the idea of an internment in prison (of heavenly and earthly powers) for a period of time, after which another punishment will take place "after many days" (cf. the period of incarceration of the Watchers). Scriptures like this are frequently reflected in the passages investigated above. The first part of v. 23, for example, also reveals possible associations that could have been drawn at this time between aberrations in the heavenly bodies and calendrical irregularities.

The canonical psalms also feature in the background of the D-P soteriology of these writings. In Psalm 89 (cf. esp. 89:6-13, 20-38; EVV vv. 5-12, 19-37), to cite a prime example, it is proclaimed that the Lord dominates the heavenly places (vv. 6-9, 12; verse references that follow are to the Hebrew version) and thus rules over "the raging of the sea" (i.e, *Yām?;* v. 10), crushes *Rāhab* (v. 11) and scatters his enemies (v. 11). His "cosmic triumph" is to benefit the "servant David," who joins in the victory (vv. 21ff.) and also receives power over the "sea" and "rivers" (v. 26) and establishes a covenant with God his Father (vv. 27-30). Like Isaiah 24, this passage draws upon images of the sun and moon in their courses (v. 38; cf. Isa. 24:23). All of this language occurs within a context of apostasy in Israel, which appears to have been a chief concern of the ethically motivated psalmist (cf. vv. 31-35, 39-46).

Psalm 74 (cf. vv. 12-15) was doubtlessly also influential in the formulation of this soteriology. Here the strength of God is invoked on the basis of past experiences of his "working salvation in the *midst of the earth (beqereb hā-'āres)*" (v. 12). Whether "the midst of the earth" is to be understood terrestrially or cosmically is debatable, but an interpretation that gives *spiritual* significance to such divine battles corresponds well with the mythological language employed by these verses:

> Thou didst divide the sea by thy might;
>> thou didst break the heads of the dragons on the waters.
> Thou didst crush the heads of Leviathan,

> thou didst give him as food for the creatures of the wilderness.
> Thou didst cleave open springs and brooks;
> thou didst dry up ever-flowing streams. (vv. 13-15)[57]

The dividing of the sea appears to refer to the exodus, an appropriate context, as noted above, for speculations about the spiritual warfare that rages behind such events of deliverance.[58] Again the mention of luminaries in v. 16 suggests that this passage could have been used during the Second Temple period to address cosmic and calendrical themes.

It is clear even from these few passages that reflection on the exodus, as well as the flood, probably served as main building blocks upon which to erect full theologies of a cosmic battle in which God wins a major spiritual battle on behalf of the righteous. Other texts similarly speak of creation, or even of natural occurrences like thunderstorms, in such a way as to suggest that cosmic battles were believed to have inspired these events (cf. Ps. 18:8-16; EVV vv. 7-15).

Several decades ago all of these kinds of texts along with their distinctive concepts were thoroughly investigated by the "Myth and Ritual" school of comparative Near Eastern studies.[59] This school promoted the view that Israelite kingship ideas, and many of the practices of Israel's cult, consisted of or involved adaptations of Canaanite (and other) practices and beliefs.[60] Such theories were based on the view that the Jewish feasts originated among the rituals common to all Near Eastern peoples and that an "enthronement of Yahweh"

57. Oesterley (1933a, 129) takes the language here as evidence of a relationship with other ancient creation/combat myths.

58. Some scholars, however, have suggested that the passage is to be interpreted of a battle that took place at creation; cf. Oesterley (1933a, 129), who compares also Job 26:12-13; Ps. 89:9-11 (EVV vv. 8-10); and Isa. 51:9-10. On the other hand, Isa. 51:10 clearly uses this language of *the exodus* when it says that the Lord made "the depths of the sea a way / for the redeemed to pass over." Similarly we read in Ps. 106:9: "He rebuked the Red Sea and it became dry; / and he led them through the deep as through a desert," clearly referring to the exodus (see vv. 7-12). Perhaps much the same could be said of Hab. 3:8, cf. v. 5; or Nah. 1:4. A. R. Johnson (1958, 222 n. 2) shows how the term *"Rahab"* came to be used as a name for Egypt (as in Isa. 51:9; Ps. 87:4; and, somewhat less convincingly, Isa. 30:7). Ps. 104:7 appears to refer to creation, but the flood is clearly intended in v. 9.

59. This school has been associated with the names of scholars like Hooke, Johnson, Mowinckel, Oesterley, and Widengren, and has through such scholars penetrated Britain, Germany, and Scandinavia. See notes above for literature. On the origins of the school, cf. Hooke, 1958, 1-21; H. H. Rowley, "Ritual and the Hebrew Prophets," 1958, 236-60, 236-38; S. G. F. Brandon, "The Myth and Ritual Position Critically Considered," 1958, 261-91, 261-67.

60. For a good representative description, cf. A. R. Johnson, 1955, 61 and passim; A. R. Johnson, 1958, 220ff. The view is considered by Widengren, 1958, 172, 181, etc., and accepted.

was celebrated in Israel at the New Year in which the Davidic king participated as Yahweh's "co-regent."[61] Some scholars believe this involved a reenactment of the ritual death and resurrection (or rebirth) of the king, and perhaps even a reenactment of the death and resurrection of Yahweh that incorporated common Near Eastern notions about dying and rising gods.[62] This ritual was also thought to involve the reenactment of a primal combat that, in the Near Eastern parallels, took place between Marduk and Tiamat.[63] Ps. 68:25-28 (EVV vv. 24-27) is taken to be a key witness to the fact that an "enthronement of Yahweh" ritual was also celebrated in Israel. Not all of the details of this reconstructed ritual are agreed upon: that Israel celebrated anything corresponding to the rituals of adoption, the reenactment of the dying-rising god, or what is called the sacral marriage, for example, are details (albeit important ones) that have hardly enjoyed unanimous agreement.[64]

Whether there really was a common Near Eastern origin for these kinds of beliefs as they are found in the Hebrew Scriptures, however, or to what extent one can view the relationship as either outright synthesis or merely a borrowing of concepts,[65] is of little importance here. More important is the sheer number of passages brought to light by this school that *could* have been interpreted by later Judaism as implying:

1. a final cosmic battle in which God triumphs over, completely conquers, and even annihilates other gods and spiritual forces as Holy Warrior;[66]

61. Cf. A. R. Johnson, 1958, 225-26, for description. It is the existence of this New Year festival in Israel that is most violently debated; while there is no hard evidence for it, the theory relies rather precariously on the detail.

62. Cf. Widengren, 1958, 179-80, 191ff.

63. Cf. W. O. E. Oesterley, *II Esdras*, 1933, 128-29.

64. A. R. Johnson, e.g., rejects the notion that these practices were adopted by Israel (1958, 227-28).

65. For criticisms of extreme views of this school of thought (i.e., "patternism"), cf. Rowley, 1958, esp. 258-60; for even more penetrating critique of certain aspects, cf. Brandon, 1958, 267-89. This latter scholar's contrast of the fundamentally teleological Hebrew and Christian Weltanschauung and the cyclical one of the Myth and Ritual parallels reveals just one way in which the two differed in essence. Moreover, while borrowing (of a conceptual if not ideological type) may certainly have been possible for the ancient Hebrews, it is inconceivable that the later Christian soteriological parallels that he cites (cf. 279-84) represent anything but an inheritance from ancient Hebrew thought, probably by means of biblical exegesis at a much later period.

66. Often this takes the form of Yahweh's triumph over the gods of the Gentiles; cf. Pss. 82:1, 6-7; 89:7-14 (EVV vv. 6-13); Job 9:13; Nah. 1:14. For the view that the "dragon," "Leviathan" or "Rahab," the "Deep" *(Tehom)*, the Sea *(Ram)*, and the River *(Nahar)* actually refer by name to existing gods, cf. Widengren, 1958, 170-72. A. R. Johnson finds allu-

2. the importance of water as part of the cosmic battlefield in which the war takes place;[67]

3. the relevance, to this water imagery, of flood[68] and exodus paradigms;[69]

4. the role, particularly the suffering, or even death, of the Davidic or messianic king in this battle;[70]

---

sions to a god *Môt* (i.e., מות; 1955, 73-74, 77, 81) in the references to "Death" in the Psalms. Victory over "Death" is related in 6:20-24 (EVV vv. 19-23) and in Ps. 48:15 (EVV v. 14). Whether we can trace allusions to Near Eastern gods, or merely see a personification of death, *môt* represents one of the major spiritual foes against which Israel looks to God for victory.

67. Oesterley (1933, 137) and A. R. Johnson (1955, 52-53, 84) relate many of the biblical water motifs, such as the "River" of Pss. 72:8 and 46:5 (EVV v. 4); "Israel's Spring," which flows from the Temple (cf. Ps. 46:5; EVV v. 4); the "Sea" of Pss. 33:7; 46:5, 8-9 (EVV v. 4, 7-8); 68:27 (EVV v. 26); and the "bronze sea" of Solomon's Temple, to the mythical background that included a "cosmic sea" as the context for cosmic battles. Cf. also Pss. 24:1-2; 46:2-4 (EVV vv. 1-3); Daniel 7.

68. Flood motifs in the Psalms, for A. R. Johnson, relate to the primeval chaos of waters or the "cosmic sea," as, e.g., when Ps. 29:10 has Yahweh "enthroned over the flood (לַמַּבּוּל)." The entire scene this author also relates to the autumnal festival (i.e., Tabernacles, or "Booths"; 1955, 56-57). Oesterley (1933, 119-20) detects a borrowing of language from the Babylonian Flood account in Hab. 3:5, suggesting that the interplay of flood ideas may have been quite subtle. Widengren views Psalm 93, a "psalm of enthronement," in terms of the ritual of the New Year Festival (1958, 196-97). This psalm, which constantly makes reference to the "floods" (נְהָרוֹת), represents for this scholar the victory over the powers of chaos necessary for God to assume his throne high above the cosmos. Water libations are believed to be very important to this festival, according to Widengren, for the ancient belief that they bring rain. If the parallels are valid, one can see how ideas of creation, sustenance, and cosmic victory are united in this psalm.

69. Exod. 15:1-18, the ancient "Song of the Sea," widely acknowledged to be a very ancient passage, already refers to the exodus itself as a "flood," "deeps," and "mighty waters" (vv. 5, 8, 10). The soteriological implications of the exodus are also clear in the interpretation of the deed as a "purchase" (√ קנה, v. 16). Cf. also Ps. 74:12-15; Isa. 51:9-10. In this latter passage the exodus/D-P language appears to be employed as a paradigm for the return from exile (cf. v. 11).

70. Widengren (1958, 199) argues that "the so-called 'misery descriptions' in the royal psalms of lamentation reflect the mythical situation, when the god finds himself imprisoned in the nether world, surrounded by wild, demonic creatures." Cf. Ps. 18:5-7 (EVV vv. 4-6), where the Davidic king is saved (אִוָּשֵׁעַ) from death, sheol, and the "torrents of perdition" (וְנַחֲלֵי בְלִיַּעַל; a phrase familiar from the scrolls; and cf. "Belial"). Following a cosmic judgment theophany (vv. 8-16; EVV vv. 7-15), we read that the psalmist is delivered "out of many waters" (v. 17; EVV v. 16). According to A. R. Johnson (1955, 121), Ps. 110:1-4 recounts the "rebirth of the Messiah [i.e., the Davidic king]," which takes place with "his deliverance from the Underworld" (a significance not totally overlooked in the New Testament letter of Hebrews, which cites the psalm frequently). Cf. also Ps. 89:21-38 (EVV vv. 20-37).

5. the possible cultic associations of this cosmic battle, especially the relationship to the Passover, or to the Feast of Weeks;[71]
6. the relationship of such a cosmic battle to the making of covenants;[72]
7. the preservation of the righteous through danger or travail.[73]

The Myth and Ritual school has thus been of assistance in bringing the texts and their interrelationships to light.

However, this school dealt with the texts in their ancient (i.e., original) Near Eastern context, and we are concerned here with their much later interpretation during the late Second Temple period. This later interpretation departed in some important ways from the earlier significance of these passages, and some important distinctions need to be drawn. (1) While the texts are interpreted by the Myth and Ritual school as mostly referring to a *recurring ritual* celebrated annually at New Year,[74] it is obvious that these passages became more or less divorced from this cultic context and interpreted *eschatologically* at a later time (although many of the biblical texts that refer to a final cosmic battle are already incipiently eschatological).[75] (2) While these specifically ritual aspects of the "Myth and Ritual" texts are highly suggestive of aspects of D-P soteriology — most notably the possible associations with covenantal renewals — it would appear that *mostly* the *theology* of triumph persisted in the later manifestations of D-P soteriology, rather than the cultic aspects, although it should again be noted, on the one hand, that some of the canonical psalms have already spiritualized these ideas and, on the other, that some think that dramatic representations persisted in the Hebrew cult to a much later time.[76]

71. Cf. Oesterley, 1933, 119-20; A. R. Johnson, 1955, 56-57.

72. Psalm 93 relates, according to A. R. Johnson (1955, 58), to Yahweh's subjugation of the primal ocean, after which he created the world. This drama is connected throughout with the making of a covenant (59).

73. Cf. esp. Ps. 89:16-18.

74. Cf., e.g., Oesterley, 1933, 128; A. R. Johnson, 1958, 225-26.

75. For the view that the autumnal festival was eschatologically oriented from a very early time, cf. A. R. Johnson, 1958, 234-35. Daniel 7 is a particularly important example of where cosmic battle motifs appear in an explicitly eschatological context.

76. A. R. Johnson suggestively refers to the "ritual dramas" (elsewhere "mime") that occurred each year as a *māšāl* (parable), which he goes on to define as "an effective demonstration of Yahweh's ultimate will and purpose for Israel and the world"; the purpose of the drama was to portray salvation (1955, 92-93).

The Role of Water Rites in the Reparation of the Covenant

To say that the theology, rather than the cultic or ritual aspects of the "Myth and Ritual" texts, survived among later groups does not mean that this theology was not reapplied to new, and completely different, rites in Second Temple times. In fact, there would appear to be justification for treating certain water rites at this time in light of the water symbolism employed in the above texts, and especially in light of the D-P soteriological pattern emerging in the Second Temple period.[77] It is obvious from the examples of this pattern above that water was frequently incorporated as a symbol for the danger out of which the righteous are saved. How does this affect our understanding of water rites at Qumran (for example)?

One of the most conspicuous characteristics of the Dead Sea sect, as revealed by archaeology as well as by the writings of the group,[78] was their employment of water rites. The significance of these water rites is one of the thorniest and most hotly debated issues surrounding Dead Sea Scroll research, and space precludes any detailed interaction with the abundance of literature written on the subject.[79] But identifying a relationship between D-P motifs and water rituals would drastically improve on our presently limited knowledge of the rituals. Two of the three most explicit references to water rites at Qumran come in passages (1QS 3.4ff.; 5.13-14) that are part of longer sections providing instructions for the annual covenantal renewal celebration and entry into the community. This context has suggested to some scroll scholars that these particular water rites have special covenantal or initiatory significance, and are to be treated as distinctive from regular or daily ablutions that were practiced universally in Judaism for ritual cleansing or "purification." Other scholars vigorously reject this assumption. Our own preference — that these rites did have a special relationship to covenantal renewal — would render the rite not identical to, and possibly quite distinct from, the daily washings for which instruc-

---

77. We are not the first to propose a connection. A. R. Johnson alludes to the relation of baptism to more ancient water rituals. When the psalmist is saved "out of many waters" in Ps. 18:17 (EVV v. 16), he detects a reference to royal enthronement rituals that were "something like a baptismal scene" that took place in the Spring Gihon (1955, 110). The historical relationships between the earlier and later water rites, however, will probably remain uncertain.

78. While the religious purpose of the stone-hewn installations at Qumran is denied by Golb (1995, 20-21), E. P. Sanders (*Judaism: Practice and Belief, 63 BCE–66 CE*, 1992, 223-27) has marshaled the most convincing proofs of this purpose.

79. For literature on the particular questions associated with water rites and cleansing at Qumran, see B. E. Thiering, "Inner and Outer Cleansing at Qumran as a Background to New Testament Baptism," 1980, 266-77, 266-67 n. 1, and the literature in notes following.

tions are given in CD 10.10-13,[80] although one would be in a better position to argue this if one understood the rationale for a separate and unique water rite such as would be employed in an initiation or a covenantal renewal.

The problem seems to be that none of the texts in question is particularly clear about the significance of the water rite, since none was written with the purpose of making it clear. For example, the mention of water rites comes almost coincidentally in 1QS 3.4ff., which is really commenting on the unrepentant or recalcitrant Israelite who does not join the sect. It says of the stubborn one who "scorns to enter the ways of God" (and thus to enter the community; cf. 2.25-26): "He shall not be absolved by atonement, nor *purified by lustral waters*,[81] nor *sanctified by seas and rivers*, nor *cleansed by all the waters of washing*.[82] Unclean, unclean shall he be" (ll. 4-5). Following a short interlude insisting that any cleansing that takes place must take place, not through a ritual *per se*, but through the acceptance of the truth of the community and "by the Spirit of true counsel . . . by the Holy Spirit of the Community,"[83] the passage resumes the discussion, addressing the case of the *successful* candidate for membership in the *yaḥad*: "By his soul's humility towards all the precepts of God shall his flesh be cleansed when *sprinkled with lustral water* and *sanctified in flowing water*" (ll. 8-9).

In a similar way 1QS 5.13-14 also discusses those who are recalcitrant ("perverse men who walk in the way of wickedness," ll. 10-11), to whom will be left "no remnant" (l. 13). Then follows this direction: "Let not (the wicked) enter *the water* to touch the Purification of the holy, for a man is not pure unless he be converted from his malice" (ll. 13-14). It is possible that the much discussed "*Purification (ṭāhᵃrāh)* of the holy (lit. of the men of holiness)" mentioned in l. 13 is itself a term for the water rite, but, while nothing in our view

---

80. *Contra* Knibb (1987, 92), who, however, agrees that 1QS 3 refers to the ritual bath during the covenantal renewal; cf. also Thiering, 1980, 269-70. P. Wernberg-Møller (*The Manual of Discipline*, 1957, 60) interprets these as "atonement rituals in general," while A. R. C. Leaney (*The Rule of Qumran and Its Meaning*, 1966, 140) understands them of the specific purification belonging to the Day of Atonement.

81. Leaney: "waters for purification" (1966, 137; cf. Num. 19:9, 12-13, 20-21; 31:23; from נדה, "impurity," in the sense of waters that cleanse from impurity). The inclusion of such a direct reference would imply that if the water rite referred to was not itself a purification, its practice was related in some way to other purification rites.

82. Leaney (1966, 142) discerns a relationship here to the healing of Naaman in the Jordan (through use of רקצה in *Num. Rabbah* 14). If so, this suggests that the whole gamut of water rituals was being alluded to.

83. We cannot agree with Thiering (cf. 1980, 267ff.; repeated in "Qumran Initiation and New Testament Baptism," 1981a, 615-31, 615-16) that two separate rites are referred to here, an outward cleansing by water and an inward cleansing by the Spirit; nor that these rites were separated by up to two full years (cf. 1981a, 620)! Thiering typically asks much too much precision from what appears to be rather inexact language.

603

precludes the possibility, the majority of scholars have come to accept other, more conventional explanations for this "Purification."[84]

A third, and somewhat less explicit, reference to water rites comes in the concluding section of the much-discussed two-spirits passage. Here it is proclaimed that

> God will cleanse by His Truth all the works of every man, and will purify for Himself the fabric of every man, to banish all Spirit of perversity from his members, and purify him of all wicked deeds by the Spirit of holiness; and He will cause the Spirit of Truth *to gush forth upon him like lustral water.* . . . For God has chosen them for an everlasting Covenant. (1QS 4.20-21, 22)

The usefulness of this passage for our concerns is questionable. For one thing, it does not actually speak about water, but about "the Spirit of Truth," which, *like* lustral water, will "gush forth." This passage would also seem to refer, not to the present life of the community, but to a final event of (spiritual?) purification that ushers in or accompanies the restoration. On the other hand, much of the restoration-sounding language in Vermes' translation (which has been left unaltered) should probably be explained otherwise:[85] the experience of cleansing,

---

84. The more common interpretation is of the sanctified food or drink of the *yaḥad*, but it is perhaps illuminating that a probation period of two years is required before touching the "drink of the many," a restriction not mentioned in connection with the "Purification." Ringgren (1963, 218) dismisses the possibility of interpreting it of a water rite on the basis that the language of the line will not allow it, but this is hardly necessary. While the line is often interpreted, as Ringgren does, in a consecutive sense — i.e., the bath is necessary *before* touching the "Purification" — nothing prohibits taking it in an explanatory sense — i.e., the "perverse" man wishes to enter the water in order (in this same way) to come into contact with the "Purification" (i.e., believing that the water has purificatory power — which mistaken view of its power ll. 13-14 attempt to correct with the words "for a man is not pure unless he be converted from his malice"). Knibb (1987, 111) points to similarities between ll. 13-15 and 2.11-18; 2.25b–3.12, esp. 3.4b-6a, which would then suggest that an allusion is being made to the same covenantal ceremony (although not concluded by Knibb, who takes it to refer to "ritually clean articles and, particularly, to the ritually clean food of the community"; 111). A. Dupont-Sommer takes the "Purifications" to refer to daily baths (*The Essene Writings from Qumran*, 1961, 83 n. 1); cf. also Wernberg-Møller, 1957, 96. New evidence provided by Cave 4 MSS that prescribes separating an impure person from the "pure food" (4Q274) and makes mention of the "drink of the Many" (4Q279) is bound to reopen the question, as will 4Q512, which speaks of being purified and atoned for, apparently (depending on one's reconstruction) for the purpose of "*entering* the Purification," which would only suit a water rite.

85. An interpretative *crux* centers on the meaning of גבר and איש in l. 20, both of which Dupont-Sommer translates "every man." Vermes has argued that these terms are messianic, and that it is the messiah who is to be purified in these verses. This view has been rejected by Wernberg-Møller (1957, 86) and Leaney (1966, 157). Dupont-Sommer's

as with the "everlasting Covenant," probably reflects the present experience of the community. Furthermore, as was seen with passages cited from the third column above, the mention of the Spirit does not preclude a reference to a literal washing with water. In fact, all of these passages in their own way tend to spiritualize the language of ablutions. It is not really the water that cleanses, but God, through means of his Spirit, through entry into the community, and by means of its truth. But this in no way distracts from the fact that the community still practiced water rituals. In fact, this is clearly assumed by the passages, which would be incomprehensible otherwise.[86] It is likely that the idea of a spiritual cleansing merely gave meaning to and protected the inner significance of the water rite.[87] For these reasons this text can be taken, with due caution, to contribute something to the question.

But something else in each of these passages is worth noting. The descriptions of water in them evoke images of turbulent and massive bodies of water, not the calm stillness of small pools dug out of the rock like the receptacles used at Qumran. While "flowing water" in 1QS 3.9 suggests little more than the preference for running water over still water (a preference also characteristic of rabbinic discussions of purifications), expressions from the other texts reveal more. 1QS 3.9 speaks not only of "flowing" but of "sprinkled" water, and 1QS 4.21 speaks of God causing the Spirit of Truth to "gush forth" upon the celebrant, an expression that implies both a great deal of movement and a body of water greater than a cleansing receptacle, perhaps a large, rapid river or even a waterfall. A sizeable volume of water might also be implied in the statement that the recalcitrant one shall not be cleansed "by seas and rivers" (1QS 3.4-5).

---

paraphrase certainly removes any doubt about his rejection of the messianic interpretation, but falsely implies that *every* man will be cleansed. Besides the fact that the word "every" has been supplied, the phrase מבני איש, which he renders as "the (bodily) fabric (cf. מִבְּנֵי) of every man," may better be pointed מִבְּנֵי אִישׁ, "(some) from the sons of man," with Leaney (157-58) and Wernberg-Møller (27, 85), who explains that the passage alludes to Mal. 3:3, where the purifying of the "sons of Levi" is replaced by the purifying of "part of (lit. 'sons of') mankind" — namely, "the pious community" (85). Leaney also rejects the idea of all mankind being cleansed, since it is "a doctrine to which the scrolls are everywhere else completely opposed; although it might be argued that the elect would now represent mankind, all evil men and evil itself having been destroyed already, and that what is here being described is a new creation after that destruction" (158). Cf. also l. 22 — "the *just* will comprehend. . . ."

86. That water rites of some kind were practiced is the only conclusion to be drawn from the *miqva'ot* that are still visible on the site of Khirbet Qumran. Cf. Wernberg-Møller, 1957, 96. Golb's (1995, 20-21) denial of the religious function of these *miqva'ot* has been adequately anticipated by E. P. Sanders (1992, 223-27).

87. This would be the significance of the juxtaposition of outward and inward ideas of cleansing; *contra* Thiering, 1980, and 1981a, 615-31.

Of course, this kind of language, especially in the last text, might merely represent the use of the literary device of exaggeration, to emphasize the impossibility of cleansing the unrepentant. It is conceivable, on the other hand, that it actually envisions some aspect or convention of the practice of the water rite itself,[88] but what this aspect might be is quite indeterminable, and the author of 1QS hardly needs to have insisted that water rites could be performed only in large, moving bodies of water. (The sect may have used the nearby Jordan for some of their water rites and the pools only for the other daily ablutions, but this will unlikely ever be known for certain.) All in all, the significance of the language of turbulent, moving waters should probably be sought more in the *theology* than the actual practice of the rite. Can it be that these water rites evoked images of *perilous danger in the midst of turbulent expanses of water,* just as the language of the Hymn Scroll expressed the need for salvation from "turbulent waters"? If these water rites can be illuminated by the D-P soteriological pattern, in other words, this would mean that in their celebrations the community deliberately employed images of watery danger in their liturgical formulations and words of "invocation" and "institution" in order to evoke experiences of moving, turbulent, even expansive waters that symbolized their salvation — the flood, the exodus, and (appropriate for the location of the Qumran settlement) the crossing of the Jordan providing paradigms for salvation from Israel's history. Some, at least, of the sect's water rites, according to this understanding, evoked symbols of a unique experience of *salvation,* one that apparently went beyond regular cultic purifications. In fact, all of the water rites — both what we call purifications and initiation rites (if it is even valid to draw such a distinction) — may actually have been informed by this conceptuality.

To better explain how Qumran could understand their water rites "soteriologically," we should probably note that the rituals in 1QS cols. 3-5 are discussed in the context of the annual renewal of the covenant. The salvation offered in the water rite was thus probably related to the idea of *repairing the covenant.* A similar conclusion could have been reached from the close relationship of D-P metaphors to covenants already noticed in regard to *1 Enoch* and *Jubilees.* The fact that water rites had something important to do with covenants would also help, in turn, to confirm the suspicion mentioned above that a water rite formed a significant part of the order of the covenant renewal ceremony at Qumran.[89]

---

88. Wernberg-Møller (1957, 60) prefers "streams" for "seas" (ימים) for the very reason that the Qumranites did not perform water rites in "seas"!

89. K. Baltzer discerned a link between water rites and the reparation of the covenant. Seeking some evidence in the covenant renewal celebration for the element he calls

But what would be the *rationale* for renewing the covenant by means of water rites? Almost no hint of this is given in the major writings of the sect, but a suggestive reference to a "remembrance" of the covenant in 1Q34, l. 5, a fragmentary MS that seems to refer to the covenantal renewal, might carry the meaning of a *return* to the covenant.[90] This reference would probably go unnoticed except that the language of remembrance is often associated with the covenant in the Hebrew Scriptures (cf. Gen. 9:15-16; Lev. 26:42, 45; Deut. 8:18; Ps. 103:18; Jer. 14:21; Ezek. 16:60-61); and in Deut. 16:1-12; 26:1-11 the commandments for the Passover and first fruits clearly refer to the function of the feast as a "remembering" of the deliverance of Yahweh (for the exact word, cf. 16:4, 12; for the idea, cf. 26:3, 5-9).[91] Later rabbinical teaching similarly promotes the view that the covenant benefits related in the feast of Passover were to be appropriated by individuals when they *"reckoned themselves"* to be present at the crossing of the Red Sea with Moses and the children of Israel, who were apparently believed to have experienced salvation vicariously on behalf of all laterborn Israelites. In other words, *by remembering it they invoked its efficacy for themselves.*[92] Remembrance is associated with the feast in Jubilees (cf. 49:7 cited above); and 1QM 13.7-8 suggestively associates covenant, the preservation of a remnant, and a "remembrance."[93] It has been suggested that the *moreh ṣedeq* encouraged his followers to experience the covenant through the "remembrance," that is, the recalling, of the Sinai event. The attempt to appropriate the salvation provided in Israel's history similarly enabled the writer of *Jubilees* to

---

"mediation of forgiveness," Baltzer points to Ezek. 36:25-27, which speaks of Israel being sprinkled with clean water, perhaps pointing to a purification ceremony such as is referred to in 1QS 3.6-12 (*The Covenant Formulary in Old Testament, Jewish, and Early Christian Writings*, 1971, 50 n. 66). This would suggest, from another perspective, that the forgiveness of sins was mediated through the water rite, as part of the covenant renewal.

90. Cf. Jaubert, 1963, 217.

91. Cf. L. Hartman, *Asking for a Meaning*, 1979, 116-17.

92. Pesaḥim 10.5 ("In every generation a man must so regard himself as if he himself came forth from Egypt") is cited in this regard by J. Jeremias (*The Eucharistic Words of Jesus*, 1966, 58, cf. n. 10) in order to sustain his argument that "the special elements of the passover meal were interpreted to a large extent *in relationship to the present*" (emphasis in original). This same attitude may well be present in Deut. 5:3 (if it did not itself inspire the idea): "Not with our fathers did the LORD make this covenant, but with us, who are all of us here alive this day."

93. The relevant phrase reads זכר [ ] כה בקרבנו. Dupont-Sommer has "A reminder of Thy Grace is in the midst of us" (1961, 188); Yadin translates "remembrance of Thy [being] in our midst" (1962, 322; restoring כה[היות]; cf. Ps. 111:4; cf. "covenant" in v. 5). Except for the phrase "in all Thy glorious testimonies," which follows, this might imply a rather nontechnical remembrance. As it stands, however, it seems to allude to a rehearsal of God's acts especially at the exodus, also appropriate to a covenantal renewal, as we have seen.

make Noah's experience effective and valid for his own time through a Noachic connection in the Feast of Weeks. This kind of emerging "sacramental" thought in relation to the covenant (although the word "sacramental" represents a glaring anachronism) is quite appropriate to the view of history of these writers who attempted to bring the experiences of the past into the living reality of the present.[94] As part of the remembrance of the covenants of the past, therefore, our communities sought to "sacramentally" escape the Deluge with Noah, cross over the Red Sea with Moses,[95] or traverse the Jordan with Joshua.

The question remains: Were these water rites in any way unique among purifications, in the sense of being practiced as onetime intiatory rites? To the long-running debate over the existence of a separate, initiatory "baptism" among the scrolls community has now been added fresh evidence from the more recently published Cave 4 MSS that comes as close to a confirmation as we have hitherto possessed that water rites were used at Qumran with the character of initiatory or entrance celebrations. This is the fragment 4Q414, which Eisenman and Wise refer to as a "Baptismal Hymn" but qualify by noting that by baptism "the proponents of this literature did not necessarily mean anything different from traditional Jewish ritual immersion."[96] One wonders whether the qualification is not a little hasty, however, for some of the wording of this text (of which not much has survived) points to an *initial* water rite. Consider the words "those purified *for the appointed time*," which may well indicate the significance of this "baptism" in its relationship to the "era of apostasy" and the role of the water rite for plucking the repentant "out" of that age and into a new one.[97] This suggests a unique, onetime covenantal renewal experience — perhaps even "initiatory" in the sense of leaving the realm of sin and entering into the community of the repentant.[98] The words "you have abandoned" also seem to refer to some kind of initial repentance and abandonment of sin, such as would not characterize a repeated or annual renewal so much as an occasional and unique covenantal reparation ceremony. It would seem quite valid to refer to these kinds of rites as "baptisms," inasmuch as they exhibit similar features to the baptism of John and, to a certain extent, to later Christian baptism, al-

94. Cf. Jaubert, 1963, 217.

95. That entry into the covenant was understood as a second exodus and wilderness experience is suggested by 1QS 2.1-18.

96. Eisenman and Wise, 1992, 230; for text, cf. 231-33.

97. A renunciation of apostate Israel can be discerned in the fragmented line (reconstructed by García Martínez, 1992, 439-40): "his cloth[es] and in the water [. . .] [. . .] he will bless [. . .] Israel which [. . .] before from all [. . .] you have forsaken" (frag. 7, 2.1-5).

98. Entry into the community (1QS 1.16–2.18) as well as annual renewal of the covenant (2.19–3.12) combines repentance themes with the idea of changing dispensations (cf. 1.23-24; 2.19; 3.15; etc.).

though this aspect of the question deserves considerably more attention than we are able to give it here. For now, however, one can at least provisionally acknowledge that these groups practiced a water rite that called penitents *out from the midst of apostate Israel* and into a discipline that they understood to be the way of righteousness (a significance not unlike that of John's and perhaps even later Jewish Christian baptism).

Even if we have successfully identified a unique initiatory baptism at Qumran, it is still possible, of course, that all the water rituals practiced by the community — including more conventional purifications — projected and promoted the identical notion, reflective of the desperation felt by Qumran for the rest of Israel, that what was needed was a thorough and sincere and effective *repentance*. What little evidence is available intimates that the D-P pattern of salvation was applied by our groups not only to their unique or initiatory water rites, but to sacrifices and circumcision,[99] and logic suggests that this extends to other purifications as well. This possibility may in fact offer a solution to some of the confusion over the theology of purification vis-à-vis baptism at Qumran, and might partly explain why modern readers find it difficult to distinguish between the various types of purifications described in the scrolls, for if D-P soteriological thought pervaded the theology of all these water rites, it is probably true that the writers did not themselves think to draw distinctions, even if in practice distinctions were drawn in terms of function and mode.

The evidence for this explanation for the diversity of water rites at Qumran unfortunately remains somewhat ambiguous, however. A conclusion that can be drawn much more confidently is that not all Jews would have opted to relate their purification practices to the *apostasy of Israel* with the vigor that these groups did (although it is evident even in conventional Jewish lustrations that the idea of repentance from sin was intrinsic to the rite). D-P soteriology doubtless lent to all the water rites of our movement — whatever their exact function or application — their character as rites of exclusion and identity in disowning Israel's past to an extent not applicable, for obvious reasons, to other Jewish groups.

99. There are scattered bits of evidence that some schools in Judaism understood other cultic rites, such as sacrifice and circumcision, according to the similar ideas that (1) it was necessary to destroy in order to preserve, and (2) such acts grant protection from evil spirits. CD 16.4-6 might be taken to imply that circumcision does this: "And on the day on which a man undertakes to be converted to the Law of Moses, the Angel of Hostility will depart from him if he fulfils his promises. For this reason Abraham *circumcised* himself on the day on which he knew" (i.e., on the "proper" day according to the calendar); for this interpretation of circumcision, cf. Dupont-Sommer, 1961, 162 n. 2. *Jub.* 15:31-32 also promises protection from the evil spirits for Israel on the basis of circumcision. Elsewhere (1QS 5.5-6) Qumran reveals a spiritualized understanding of circumcision, which may have evolved from the idea.

The D-P Soteriology Applied to the Present Situation

The water rites at Qumran hint that the D-P pattern of salvation did not remain a source of theoretical reflection only (as one might conclude from the Watcher theodicy or the hymns of tumult at Qumran), but provided an important model for interpreting current events and God's act of salvation in the present. Theoretical reflection might be fine for those who huddle safe and secure in the confines of their small communities, but many remnant groups were compelled to suffer with all Israel under the circumstances of 167 B.C., 63 B.C., or A.D. 70, and therefore required a more "applied" theology. Even those who separated (like the scroll community) were no doubt aware of the need for God to work his salvation into the present situation. We have witnessed that groups like Qumran possessed a genuine concern for Israel. Their soteriology was accordingly not contemplative but based on experience: the pressure of the imminent danger forged pragmatic responses and expressions out of the raw materials of their more abstract theology. Of interest next, therefore, is how these groups applied the Noachic and exodus soteriological paradigms to themselves and their opponents *in their present situation*. How, in other words, did the soteriological pattern become an answer to the problem of Israel?

An Imminent Judgment

One factor in the situation of our groups that above all seems to have led to the development of the D-P pattern of salvation (as opposed to other patterns) was an awareness of the imminence of judgment. Even where an exact timetabling of future events was not undertaken, the time of judgment was nevertheless believed to have come upon Israel. This could mean either that judgment had already *begun* in the recent events and was *now* taking place, or that it was still future but nevertheless impending. As already noted, these authors were particularly interested in the implications of judgment for the rest of *Israel*, but they also knew that judgment (which they doubtless viewed, in this case, as "discipline") carried serious implications for the righteous as well since they were unavoidably caught up in the tumultuous events (cf. *1 En.* 1:7). Judgment, therefore, was understood to be God's instrument for both punishment and salvation — a paradox adequately portrayed through water, the symbol of chaos and danger to be overcome, and of the possibility of being either saved or drowned.

This sense of the imminence of judgment is often expressed through lists of signs, as noted above. While often categorized as "messianic travail" passages, these lists frequently reflect the *present* travail in which our communities found themselves. Often these lists include signs that are already taking place.

At other times the signs are believed to follow on the present circumstances. But there is nothing *necessarily* eschatological about them. They frequently appear to reflect biblical curses of the covenant for the wicked and covenantal blessing for the righteous,[100] things that might be realized anytime in history. This shows how mistaken has been the exegetical practice of viewing "signs of the times" as eschatological indicators rather than as what they really were — prophetic applications of covenantal thinking. And since soteriological thought is necessarily tied into covenantal thought, as one would expect in Judaism, the covenantal dualism incorporated in these signs matches closely the dual aspects of salvation implied in the signs, the division between the righteous and wicked through experiences of destruction, on one hand, and preservation, on the other. One of these sign passages from *1 Enoch* announces:

> For I know that the state of violence will intensify upon the earth; a great plague shall be executed upon the earth; all forms of oppression will be carried out; and everything shall be uprooted; and every arrow shall fly fast. Oppression shall recur once more and be carried out upon the earth; every form of oppression, injustice, and iniquity shall infect the world twofold. When sin, oppression, blasphemy, and injustice increase, crime, iniquity, and uncleanness shall be committed and increase. Then a great plague shall take place from heaven upon all these; the holy Lord shall emerge with wrath and plague in order that he may execute judgment upon the earth. (91:5-7)

This represents an attempt to describe, not only what is already happening in the author's world, but also how things will progressively become worse in the future. The citation ends with what appears to be a reference to the final judgment, or at least a future judgment, which is the author's way of saying that more judgment would evolve from the present distress. Following more detailed descriptions of this fiery judgment, however, the author goes on to assure his readers that the righteous will nevertheless survive: "Then the righteous one shall arise from his sleep, and the wise one shall arise" (v. 10ab). Thus in a paradoxical sort of way destruction of the wicked and preservation of the righteous are combined through a single experience of imminent judgment. Another passage from *1 Enoch* contains a warning to sinners. Here the judgment is presented in terms of a divine visitation. The sinners addressed are clearly known by the author, revealing that his own generation is in danger: "In those days, when he hurls out against you terror [wave, tempest][101] of fire, where shall you

---

100. Cf. M. E. Stone, *Fourth Ezra,* 1990, 108.

101. Black translates "a wave (tempest?) of blazing fire" (1985, 310). The Gk. has "the surge of the fire of your burning" (Isaac, *OTP,* 1:83). The image appears to characteristically combine fire and water motifs (cf. also Ps. 83:16; EVV v. 15; Amos 1:14).

flee, and where shall you find safety? When he flings his word against you, will you not faint and fear? . . . The children of the earth will seek to hide themselves from the presence of the Great Glory, trembling and confounded. You, sinners, you are accursed forever; there is no peace for you!" (102:1-3). Again, however, the righteous will be spared from the judgment and from the apostasy of the present time, and will be thoroughly vindicated: "But you, souls of the righteous, fear not; and be hopeful, you souls that died in righteousness! . . . indeed the time you happened to be in existence was a time of sinners, a time of curse and a time of plague . . ." (102:4-5).[102]

"Signs of the End" are quite common in 4 Ezra as well, and these also reveal an underlying D-P soteriology that is applied to both the present experiences and the future beliefs of the author. One of the lists of signs in 4 Ezra alludes to the present distresses[103] before it tails off into future predictions:

Now concerning the signs: Behold, the days are coming when those who dwell on earth shall be seized with great terror,[104] and the *way of truth shall be hidden, and the land shall be barren of faith. And unrighteousness shall be increased beyond what you yourself see, and beyond what you heard of formerly.* And the land which you now see ruling[105] shall be waste and untrodden, and men shall see it desolate. But if the Most High grants that you live,[106] you shall see it thrown into confusion *after the third period;*

and the sun shall suddenly shine forth at night,
and the moon during the day.
Blood shall drip from wood,
and the stone shall utter its voice;

102. There has been much corruption in this verse, and the Eth. MSS reveal attempts to smooth over the difficulties. Black's rendering: "But wait patiently for the day on which is the judgment of sinners, and for the day of cursing and punishment," might clarify (1985, 96, following R. H. Charles, *The Book of Enoch or 1 Enoch,* 1912, 255, who emends *konkemu xāṭe'ān,* "you became sinners," to *kʷennanē xāṭe'ān,* "the judgment of sinners"). The Gk. ("The days that you lived were days of sinners"; *OTP,* 1:83 n. *u*) generally supports the translation of Isaac offered above.

103. Cf. D. C. Allison, *The End of the Ages Has Come,* 1985, 11-13.

104. The fact that this fear is part of the covenantal curses (cf. Stone, 1990, 109; Lev. 26:16; Deut. 28:20) reveals that the author is still speaking of his present here, not the future. The phrases that follow confirm this.

105. Probably Rome (Stone, 1990, 110), which shall be overthrown. This indicates that the author is moving into the future at this point. "After the third period" (v. 4) suggests Daniel's fourfold historical vision in which Rome would be the fourth power to rule.

106. These words indicate that the subject matter turns at this point to the final events of judgment, which, however, certainly flow out of the present distress, since it is suggested that some (of the readers?) may still be alive.

the peoples shall be troubled,
and the stars shall fall. . . . (5:1-5; cf. vv. 6-12)

In this passage the salvation of the elect is not mentioned, but it is implied in the writing's distinctive doctrine of survival/survivors (on which see more below). The language of the passage has been influenced by Joel 3:1-5, which also portrays an event of judgment and salvation and speaks of the survivors. It is evident, in any event, that this is another example where the signs, or warnings of judgment, are related to the author's present (there is little reason to apply it to any other historical period than the Roman). The sense of anticipation that Joel's prophecy was soon to be fulfilled was no doubt ignited by memories of the recent sacking of Jerusalem, so that present troubles are again thought to lead to future judgments.

The D-P pattern of salvation had important implications for beliefs about judgment and salvation in the scrolls as well, as this pattern is reflected not only in the experiences of Israel in judgment but also in the vocation and sufferings of the saints themselves. Warnings of imminent "destruction" are brought to bear on the author's fellow Israelites (cf. 1QS 2.7-8; 4.12; 4Q177;[107] etc.), notably on Jerusalem (cf. esp. 4Q176; 4Q179). But the community also believed they were destined to suffer part of the judgment that was coming upon the nation, which they seem to have described collectively as their (and Israel's) "chastisement." This time of suffering for the righteous seems to have been associated with their vocation as instruments of judgment for Israel; both the suffering and the vocation were predestined and carefully orchestrated.[108] As a further indication of the close association of judgment and salvation, the *moreh* claims that it is his own teaching that has brought on the final upheavals. This is very conspicuous in 1QH 2.6-19, where his teaching divides the crowd, and while it brings judgment on the sinners and results in suffering for himself and his followers, it results in salvation for the latter alone:

> I have been a snare for sinners, but healing for all those that are converted from sin. . . . And I was exposed to the affronts of the wicked, an object of slander upon the lips of the violent; the mockers gnashed their teeth. . . . the assembly of the wicked raged against me and roared like storms upon the

107. This text, alternately called *4QCatena^a* (cf. also 4Q182), speaks of a destruction of Israel employing the words of Mic. 2:10-11: "a grievous destruction."

108. H, J. Schonfield (*Secrets of the Dead Sea Scrolls*, 1957, 2-3) has suggested that the "(Book of) *Hagu* (הגו)" (CD 9.2; 15.5; 17.5) is an "Atbash cipher" for צרף, "test," "purge," "refine." The book referred to would then be "The Book of Proof" or "Test Book," according to which the *moreh ṣedeq* would fulfill his ministry as "the Refiner" spoken of in Mal. 3:1-4. Schonfield also cites a commentary on Ps. 2:1-2 as referring to עת המצרף, "time of testing" (4).

seas when their billows rage throwing up slime and mud. But Thou hast made of me a banner for the elect of righteousness . . . to test [the men] of truth and to try them that love instruction . . . the men of deceit roared against me like the clamour of the roaring of great waters, and ruses of Belial were . . . their thoughts; *and they cast down towards the Pit the life of the man by whose mouth Thou hast established the teaching.* . . .

According to the War Scroll, the Sons of Light were even expected to suffer some measure of defeat in the war, something that was all in God's plan to perfect the righteous while simultaneously judging the others.[109] Unlike those upon whom the community would bring this judgment, however, they themselves would eventually experience salvation through the same battle. "This shall be the time of salvation for the people of God, the hour of dominion for all the men of his lot and of final destruction for all the lot of Belial" (1QM 1.5).

Perhaps the suffering, penitence, and submission of the elect to some aspects of the judgment were thought to take the place of, or at least obviate, the need for a more serious judgment. Those, on the other hand, who cave in to unrighteousness and pleasure during the "time of testing" would be victims of a much worse fate than the righteous. Accordingly the soteriology of this group reflects the D-P pattern of salvation in which they are saved *through* judgment, not *apart from* it. The community not only witnesses but takes part in the judgment by suffering, as well as having a role in inflicting that judgment. Typically, these things are not strictly relegated to the future, but have already begun in the present. The mixture of present and future can be seen in some of the tumult motifs in the hymns studied above (cf. esp. 1QH 3.6, 12ff., 28-36; 5.22). Does the following hymn, for example, refer to present or "final" experiences? "[Fire shall burn up] the foundations of the mountains and fire shall consume nethermost Sheol. But they that hope in Thy laws [Thou wilt deliver], [and bring aid] to them that serve Thee with faith" (1QH 17.13-14).[110] Apparently the author thought that he and his community would be around to view even greater judgments, but the important thing is that out of this judgment God would save the righteous.

---

109. Yadin explains that the periods of defeat intermingled with the periods of victory for the Sons of Light mentioned in the War Scroll (e.g., 1QM 16.13–17.9) are intended to portray that "war serves as a crucible in which God tests the members of the sect and causes Himself to be hallowed through their judgment" (1962, 12).

110. It is interesting, in this regard, how Holm-Nielsen suggests a liturgical *Sitz im Leben* for this psalm, in particular the annual feast of renewal (1960, 246). If so, this would further confirm our view that D-P soteriology lies behind the covenantal renewal celebration.

Purging the Heavens

The cosmological aspects of the Hebrew and ancient Near Eastern parallels to D-P soteriology have already been noted. As the similar theology is expressed in the Hebrew Scriptures, the Lord as divine Warrior has a "Day" in which he will once and for all conquer his demonic enemies. The writings of the movement of dissent adopt similar ideas and teach that God's spiritual foes will eventually be defeated. There is accordingly some justification for Becker's description of the soteriology of these writings as an interaction between the two spheres of *Heil* and *Unheil* — salvation implying the defeat of the latter sphere along with the sin and the spirits of darkness that dwelt in it.[111] This kind of dualistic cosmic soteriology is evident in the Book of Watchers where the Watchers are warned of their impending judgment. And in the final chapter of the Zoomorphic History all the spiritual foes of the righteous are assembled and their judgment is carried out:

> Then the Lord called those people, the seven first snow-white ones, and ordered them to bring before him from among the first stars that arose, and from among those stars whose sexual organs were like those of the horses [i.e., uncircumcised], as well as that first star which had fallen down earlier. And they brought them all before him. He spoke to the man who was writing in his presence . . . saying, "Take those seventy[112] shepherds to whom I had handed over the sheep, but who decided to kill many more than they were ordered." Behold I saw all of them bound; and they all stood before him. Then his judgment took place. First among the stars, they received their judgment and were found guilty, and they went to the place of condemnation; and they were thrown into an abyss, full of fire and flame and full of the pillar of fire. (*1 En.* 90:21-24)

Here the judgment is directed against the spiritual beings who rule over the world. The stars are the fallen angels, perhaps in particular those associated with calendrical irregularities.[113] The shepherds also seem to be more than merely earthly rulers, as is often thought, and are probably angelic beings, as has recently been convincingly argued by P. A. Tiller.[114] This implies the rather

111. J. Becker, *Das Heil Gottes,* 1964, 66-67 and passim; particularly interesting is his tracing of the incorporation of רשב-terminology into the spatial dualism of 1QS 10–11 (109-14).

112. Preferring this reading over the obviously erroneous "seven."

113. *1 En.* 102:2 states that "all the luminaries shall faint with great fear," apparently alluding to the fact that at this time the heavenly bodies — which are closely associated with spiritual beings or angels — shall be made to submit to judgment as well.

114. P. A. Tiller (*A Commentary on the Animal Apocalypse of I Enoch,* 1993, 7ff.,

shocking, but nonetheless entirely consistent, view that apostate Israel has been led about by demonic forces throughout history. (The older and quite contrasting view that the shepherds represent Gentile nations or kings hostile to Israel doubtlessly helped perpetuate the view that eschatology in books like this one was preoccupied with gaining liberation from Gentile overlords.) The way the shepherds receive their power by direct communication from God in 89:59-60 might suggest that they represent the angelic "heads" that inspire governments in power. This would also cohere with the symbolism of the vision where human beings generally symbolize angels rather than humans. The stars and the shepherds together experience a fiery judgment (90:25), and are joined by the blind sheep of Israel (vv. 26-27). This judgment is therefore presented as a purging of the heavenly realms. It is noteworthy that this purging results in a new era of blessing, vindication, and salvation for the righteous: "Then I saw all the sheep that had survived as well as all the animals upon the earth and the birds of heaven, falling down and worshiping those sheep, making petition to them and obeying them in every respect" (v. 30). It would appear that only when the score is settled in the heavenly places does a full salvation become possible on earth.

In the scrolls the descriptions of ultimate salvation are spiritualized and conceived in terms of a battle. In the two-spirits passage (1QS 4.15ff.), the final battle is colorfully portrayed together with various theological implications:

> God has allotted these (two Spirits) in equal parts *until the final end.* . . . But in His Mysteries of understanding and in His glorious Wisdom God has *set an end for the existence of Perversity;*[115] *and at the time of the Visitation He will destroy it for ever.* Then Truth shall arise in the world for ever; for the world has defiled itself in the ways of wickedness under the dominion of Perversity *until the time of final Judgment.* Then God will cleanse by His Truth all the works of every man, and will purify for Himself the bodily fabric of every man, *to banish all Spirit of perversity from his members,* and purify him of all

---

53ff.) expands on three "conclusive" reasons for accepting this identification, based on seven originally argued by Charles. They are: (1) humans always represent angels in the History, (2) they are associated with fallen angels in the judgment (90:24-25), and (3) the heavenly scribe of 89:61 is called "another" in association with the shepherds (90:14, 17, 22). The 70 shepherds probably relate to the 70 periods of exile taken from Jeremiah and Daniel; apparently these have been broken down into 12 from the Persian era (89:71) plus 23 again from the Persian era (90:1; perhaps those following Zerubbabel and Joshua or Ezra and Nehemiah in 89:72; here we find the accumulated total of 35 or 37, depending on the reading) plus 23 from the Greek era (90:5; total of 58) plus 12 "future" shepherds (90:22; total of 70 according to the probable reading). While the shepherds were angelic beings, this correlation suggests that they worked through pagan rulers.

115. L. 17 suggests that "Perversity" is a spiritual being.

wicked deeds by the Spirit of holiness; and He will cause the Spirit of Truth to gush forth upon him like lustral water. All *lying abominations shall come to an end, and defilement by the Spirit of defilement.* The just will comprehend the Knowledge of the Most High, and the perfect of way will have understanding of the wisdom of the Sons of Heaven. For God has chosen them for an everlasting Covenant and all the glory of the Man is theirs. *Perversity will exist no more:* shame upon all the works of deceit! *Till now the Spirits of truth and perversity battle in the hearts of every man . . .* For God has allotted these Spirits in equal parts *until the final end, the time of Renewal.* (1QS 4.16, 18-23, 25)

The italicized words highlight the temporal limitations placed on the dominion of the (evil) spirits: *now* they reign in the hearts of men; *then* the perverse spirit will be dealt the final blow of judgment. As with the "Asp" in 1QH 3.12, 18, much of the language of the passage is personified and spiritualized.[116] Both judgment and salvation are again represented here: the passage says the final visitation will be the occasion not only for the defeat of spiritual foes but also for the outpouring of the Spirit. The language of D-P soteriology accordingly pervades the passage. In this same section of the scroll the Spirit of Truth is said "to gush forth upon [the repentant] like lustral water," which seems to point to a Noachic, or at least a water, motif. In contrast to the defeat of spiritual foes, the "chosen" will survive, gaining great knowledge, etc. (ll. 22-23). The event is occasion, not only for judgment, but also for a salvation. Both are given deeply spiritual significance.

Although not usually considered a Qumran scroll *per se,* one passage in *Jubilees* seems to suggest a connection between restoration and spiritual conversion, possibly even implying that restoration will follow upon the reception of the Holy Spirit by Israel. If this holds true, it would also explain the nationalistic-sounding words of the prologue. Following the rather shocking indictment on Israel and her future, Moses prays for Israel's eventual blessing, "Create a pure heart and a holy spirit for them" (1:21), and God responds, "I shall create for them a holy spirit. . . . And I shall be a father to them, and they will be sons to me. And they will all be called 'sons of the living God.' And every angel and spirit will know and acknowledge that they are my sons and I am their father" (1:23-25). These verses indicate that the redeemed at the time of the restoration will be marked off by a renewed spiritual condition. That the blessing only occurs at the restoration is implied by

---

116. Leaney refers to the personification of "Truth" here (1966, 156), although this would seem to apply even more to "Perversity" (cf. also, perhaps, 1QH 3.18). He refers also to the *Fragment of the Book of Secrets* (1Q27 1.6-7), where "the same sort of personification of evil, righteousness and light appears . . . connected with a final *dénouement* on the stage of the universe" (156, emphasis in original).

the clear and direct allusions to Ezek. 36:26. The blessing of restoration also includes a "new" spirit somewhat in line with Jer. 31:33 (perhaps also Joel 2:28, which refers in this connection to "my [God's] spirit"). Other words in the passage inform us that restoration includes inner spiritual renewal ("I shall cut off the foreskin of their heart," v. 23) as well as moral cleansing that has the effect of granting constancy to the redeemed ("I shall purify them so that they will not turn away from following me from that day and forever," v. 23; cf. also v. 21, "a pure heart").

The Melchizedek Scroll (11Q13 = *11QMelchizedek*) is already well known for its usefulness in clarifying certain themes found in the New Testament, particularly the Hebrews epistle. It also contains one of the clearest examples of the D-P pattern of salvation. As can be seen from the following excerpt, this enigmatic work features the angelomorphic figure Melchizedek, who is probably identified with the messiah, although he seems at times to be more identified with God as a divine manifestation, perhaps deliberately reminiscent of the biblical "angel of the Lord." Perhaps even more striking about the subject matter of this text is that it centers on the events surrounding the restoration,[117] particularly the combined work of judgment and redemption performed by Melchizedek as divine agent. Restoration follows upon the storming and judgment of the spiritual world.

> And the day [of atonem]ent is the end of the tenth jubilee in which atonement will be made for all the sons of [God] and for the men of the lot of Melchizedek. [And on the heights] he will decla[re in their] favour according to their lots; for it is the time of the "year of grace" for Melchizedek, to exa[lt in the tri]al the holy ones of God through the rule of judgment, as is written about him in the songs of David, who said: "Elohim will stand up in the assem[bly of God,] in the midst of the gods he judges." And about him he said: "Above it return to the heights, God will judge the peoples." As for what he sa[id: "How long will yo]u judge unjustly and show partiality to the wicked? *Selah*." Its interpretation concerns Belial and the spirits of his lot who were rebels [all of them] turning aside from the commandments of God [to commit evil.] But, Melchizedek will carry out the vengeance of God's judges [on this day, and they shall be freed from the hands] of Belial and from the hands of all the sp[irits of his lot.] To his aid shall come all "the gods of [justice"; he] is the one [who will prevail on this day over] all the sons of God,

117. The presence of a messianic figure in this passage has typically preoccupied scholars, but it is evident that the purpose of this celebrated personage is to usher in the restoration; cf. one passage where Deut. 15:2 and Isa. 61:1 are interpreted of Melchizedek, who "will make them return . . . in the first week of the jubilee which follows the ni[ne] jubilees" (11Q13 2.3-7).

and he will pre[side over] this [assembly.] This is the day of [peace about which God] spoke [of old through the words of Isa]iah the prophet, who said: "How beautiful upon the mountains. . . ."[118]

The biblical language of restoration, the notion of a divine battle and decisive judgment in the heavenly realms, the inspiration of the opponents of the sect by Belial and their eventual demise together with their evil leader, the salvation of the elect and the reign of the divine priest Melchizedek over them — all are presented by this text. The vindication and glorification of the elect (along with their angelic counterparts?) appears to take place *simultaneously* with the judgment of the rest. All this again suggests the current notion of a decisive spiritual battle that will effectively bring unrighteousness to an end and usher in the age of the restoration.

The War Scroll seems to have been written for the very purpose of exposing a similar pattern of salvation and, in particular, to relate the events on earth to events in the spiritual realms. In fact, the scroll makes little sense apart from this pattern. Yigael Yadin, who was the first to carry out a detailed study of the War Scroll, took as the purpose of the scroll to provide answers to specific questions about the time and details of the final war, and particularly to enforce various laws for this battle that would ensure the final victory: "The fact that the angels fight on their side obliges the Sons of Light to conduct themselves in accordance with all the Biblical laws of purity of the camp. . . . This basic conception passes through the scroll like a purple thread. It determines its content, structure, and sequence."[119] This would appear to be more a perceptive summary of the scroll's contents than a discernment of its purpose. There is little reason to think that this writing, any more than the others we have investigated, was intended merely to convey information or teaching. (Yadin himself admits that many of the facts presented by the author were already "self-evident and known to his readers.")[120] As for the purpose of establishing safeguards for the purity of the camp, this is perhaps more likely, although many of the lengthy and detailed explanations of the plan of attack appear more to dwell upon the

---

118. 11Q13 2.7-16. Adapted from García Martínez, 1992, 139-40. Although the passage is fragmented toward the end, the translator has adequately anticipated the lacunae through attention to the content of the biblical passages contained in the excerpt. The exegetical methodology is reminiscent of the Talmuds, as well as the *pešer* methodology. The theology, in any event, is that of the same group that produced the other sectarian writings at Qumran.

119. Yadin, 1962, 5, cf. 4-6; cf. also P. R. Davies (*1QM, the War Scroll from Qumran*, 1977, 124), who sees it as a guide for the battle, which is believed to actually take place in Palestine in the future.

120. Yadin, 1962, 7.

certainty of victory in the predetermined war than upon the *halakah* required for the battle.[121] We accordingly prefer to see the purpose of the scroll as to assure the righteous of eventual victory by exposing the underlying spiritual forces and by dramatizing the way the battle leads up to a decisive victory for, and vindication of, the saints. More worthy of note than specific rules, in other words, is the way the tension and dualism of passages like 1QS 3.13-25, which describes the animosity that exists between the opposing forces of light and darkness, is resolved in this final war.[122] Evidence of a decisive spiritual battle involving a variety of heavenly beings is found in many passages (among which cf., esp., 1.10-14; 6.5-6; 7.6-7; 10.4-5; 11.1-17; 12.7-11; 13.14-15; 14.8-10, 15-16; 15.2-3, 13-14; 17.5-8; 18.1; 19.1; etc.), and this type of spiritual battle may be taken to characterize the entire work. The important introductory words of the War Scroll read:

> And on the day when the Kittim fall there shall be battle and rude slaughter before the God of Israel; for this is the day appointed by Him [i.e., the "Day of Yahweh"] from former times for the war of destruction of the sons of darkness. On this day shall approach for tremendous slaughter the congregation of the gods[123] and the assembly of men. On the Day of Misfortune[124] the sons of light and the lot of darkness shall battle together for the Power of God amid the tumult of a vast multitude and the cries of gods and men. (1.9-11)

The significance of some of the imagery used for this heavenly battle is uncertain, but the view of the author that the goal of this battle is the end of the domination of evil spiritual powers in the heavenlies is very clear (cf. also, esp., 1.10; 11.17(?); 13.15; 14.15; 15.3, 13-14; 18.1). In line with the D-P pattern of soteriology, however, this will not be an easy time for the elect: "it shall be a

---

121. We cannot, in any event, accept unreservedly the summary of Yadin that "DSW, like other scrolls which aim to provide the sect with a set of rules for its conduct in everyday life (i.e. DSD and CDC), was not essentially written for the purpose of consolation and description of the splendid future at the End of Days. *Its purpose was to supply an urgent and immediate need,* a guide for the problems of the long-predicted war, which according to the sect would take place in the near future" (1962, 15, emphasis in original).

122. Cf. Yadin, 1962, 242.

123. עדה אלים. Yadin translates "congregation of angels" (1962, 260); the term evokes the idea of the "divine council" found in the canonical psalms, but because they are judged in this passage, the reference is certainly to foreign gods — an idea also harmonious with the ancient Near Eastern background.

124. Perhaps equivalent to the "Day of Yahweh" (Dupont-Sommer, 1961, 171 n. 1), although Yadin notes that reading הווה as the Tetragrammaton "is precluded by the habit of the Scroll in avoiding it. (Other scrolls write it in Old Hebrew script)" (1962, 261).

time of distress for all the people redeemed by God" (ll. 11-12).[125] Their triumph is guaranteed, however, inasmuch as the battle is fought by God and his angels on their behalf (cf. also 6.5-6; 7.6-7; 10.4-5; 11.1-17; 12.7-9; 13.14; 19.1; etc.).

Other passages in the scrolls also associate the salvation of the righteous with overcoming spiritual foes (cf., e.g., CD 5.18-19; 1QH 12.11-18). In CD 16.4-6 this spiritual victory is associated with joining the community (a spiritual circumcision), which seems also to have been when the Holy Spirit was given to the new member. References to Abaddon and the Pit, which dominate in the hymns of tumult considered above (cf. 1QH 3.19-36), suggest that the real enemy to be overcome in the struggles of the psalmist are the spiritual foes of the community, not any visible foe *per se*. This is indicated moreover by the way the description of the present tumult of the author drifts into a description of a future judgment with cosmic implications —

> and the torrents of Belial pour into Abaddon and the recesses of the Abyss roar out amidst the roaring of swirling mud. And the earth cries out because of the calamity fallen on the world and all its recesses howl, and all that are on it are stricken with fear and stagger, the prey to great misfortune. For God bellows with His mighty roaring and His holy abode resounds with His glorious truth and the heavenly host lets its voice be heard. And the eternal foundations stagger and shake and the host of the Valiant of heaven brandishes its whip in the world; and it shall not end until utter destruction, which shall be final, without anything like it. (ll. 32-36)

A D-P pattern of soteriology seems, therefore, to have been particularly important in dealing with and interpreting the present situation of the Qumran community, inasmuch as a great deal of theological reflection, as well as liturgical formulation in the scrolls, presupposes such a pattern.

Salvation for the Remnant

Having recognized and spelled out this somewhat diverse but nevertheless everpresent D-P pattern of salvation, we can now better understand a significant group of motifs that pervade this literature. In mind here are terms like "survivors," "remnant," "those that are left/remain," "the preserved," "those who es-

---

125. The suffering of both Israel and the sect is a usual feature of these D-P motifs, which Yadin misunderstands: "The trouble here is not, as in [1QH and CD], restricted to the sect, but is that of all Israel: [1QM] does not discuss particular troubles of the sect" (1962, 261).

cape," etc., words that imply that only some from Israel will escape either some present danger or the judgments that are to come. Such terms effectively articulate the "preservation" part of "destruction-preservation" soteriology. *With such terms, and the concepts they entail, one reaches the summit of a-nationalistic thought in Judaism.*

One of the recurring themes of the Noachic theology of *1 Enoch*, as already noted, is warnings about a great judgment in Noah's time that will presage the great and final deluge. Scattered within these passages, fittingly enough, are references to the *preservation* of the righteous. Thus one reads not only that "the Deluge is about to come upon all the earth; and all that is in it will be *destroyed*" (10:2), but also: "instruct [Noah] in order that he may flee, and his seed will be *preserved* for all generations" (10:3). That both elements of this D-P (note *"destroyed" versus "preserved")* motif are intended to be paradigmatic for a final or future judgment[126] is apparent in 10:16-17, where the lessons of Noah are applied to the time of the real author: "*Destroy* injustice from the face of the earth. And every iniquitous deed will end, and the plant of righteousness and truth will appear forever and [it] will plant joy. And then all the righteous ones will *escape;* and become the living ones until they multiply and become tens of hundreds. . . ." Here the righteous are referred to as those who "escape" the judgment. The word "escape" has been significantly borrowed from biblical remnant traditions.

As with many other passages, it is implied that the restoration follows on the event of destruction and preservation (vv. 18-20). The idea of survivors, or of a remnant, however, is obviously not easily harmonized with hopes of restoration. Have these groups in some way synthesized views about a remnant and a restoration, or is the remnant of the present thought to be replaced by God with a fuller number of Israelites in the future? The same kind of synthesis would appear to be taking place in this passage as noted earlier (cf. ch. 11), where the righteous form the core of the restoration. It is the righteous seed that begins to multiply (10:17). The multitudes of the righteous who go on to populate the earth after the judgment accordingly descend from the *one* righteous plant. It is noteworthy that, unlike after the first deluge, the continuation of evil and the further reduction of the seed will not need to occur. Only righteousness will survive — "And the earth shall be *cleansed* from all pollution, and from all sin, and from all plague, and from all suffering; *and it shall not happen again that I shall send these upon the earth* from generation to generation and forever" (v. 22; cf. Gen. 8:21; 9:15).[127] It appears, therefore, that the

---

126. Something already alluded to in the opening of v. 2: "reveal to [Noah] the *end* [Gk. τέλος = סופה] of what is coming; for the earth and everything will be destroyed."

127. Gk. has οὐκέτι πέμψω (object supplied). Accordingly Black follows Eth. II MSS: "I shall not again send a *Deluge* upon it," explaining that the "translator of G (followed by

restoration and the remnant doctrines are both retained: there will be a restoration, but it will only be composed of the righteous remnant along with the multitudes of their offspring.

The idea of a surviving remnant also provides a helpful clue to the prayer of Enoch in chs. 83–84. Enoch receives a vision of judgment that relates rather more to a future judgment than to the flood, as already observed (83:3-5), but the entire passage is replete with what might be called D-P language, as the second judgment is modeled on the first. The cosmic nature of the second judgment is also obvious: the sky falls down upon the earth, which is then swallowed up into the Abyss (vv. 3-4). Enoch cries out in his dream, "The earth is being *destroyed*" (v. 5). Mahalalel's response and advice —

> How terrifying a thing have you seen, my son! You have seen in your dream a powerful vision — all the sins of the whole world as it was sinking into the abyss and being *destroyed with a great destruction*. Now, my son, rise and pray to the Lord of glory, for you are a man of faith, so that a *remnant shall remain* upon the earth and that the whole earth shall not be *blotted out*. My son, all the things upon the earth shall take place from heaven; and there will occur a *great destruction* upon the earth. (83:7-9)

The reference to the earth sinking into the Abyss suggests that the second destruction, not the first, is the primary reference in the vision. Enoch obediently prays:

> Now, O God, and Lord and Great King, I pray and beg so that you may *sustain* my prayer and *save* for me a generation that will *succeed* me in the earth; and do not *destroy all* the flesh of the people and *empty the earth* so that there shall be *eternal destruction*. *Do now destroy*, O my Lord, the flesh that has angered you *from upon the earth*, but *sustain* the flesh of righteousness and uprightness as a plant of eternal seed. (84:5-6)

Again, many of the concepts found in this passage, including notions like sustaining, preserving, destroying (all), emptying, removal "from upon the earth," etc., have been borrowed from biblical passages dealing with a remnant.[128]

Eth I) may have removed the reference to the deluge, in order to conform the text to his own later eschatology" (1985, 140-41). On the other hand, the Gk. also seems deliberately ambiguous — we are in any event witness to the struggles to justify a second-deluge theology with the statements of Gen. 8:21; 9:15. It would appear that our authors accept that a second deluge *by fire* is not precluded by those texts.

128. For discussion and bibliography, cf. M. A. Elliott, "Romans 9–11 and Jewish Remnant Theology," 1986, 48-67, 93-94; and esp. G. F. Hasel, *The Remnant*, 1972, passim, and "Remnant" in *IDB Suppl.* 735; G. Herntrich, "λεῖμμα, κτλ B. The 'Remnant' in the Old Testament," *TDNT,* 4:196-209.

Preservation motifs are equally evident in the Noachic portions of the final chapters of *1 Enoch:*

> There shall be a *great destruction upon the earth;* and there shall be a *deluge and a great destruction for one year.* And this son who has been born unto you *shall be left* upon the earth; and his three sons shall be *saved* when they who are upon the earth are dead. . . . There shall be a great plague upon the earth, and the earth shall be *washed clean from all the corruption.* Now, make known to your son Lamech that the son who has been born is indeed righteous; and call his name Noah, for he shall be *the remnant* for you; and he and his sons *shall be saved from the corruption which shall come upon the earth* on account of all the sin and oppression that existed, and it will be fulfilled upon the earth, in his days. *After that* there shall occur *still greater oppression* than that which was fulfilled upon the earth *the first time* . . . I have read in the heavenly tablets. (106:15-19)

The context for this story is the miraculous birth of Noah, but it is evident from the closing lines of the passage, which deliberately turn to the final time of judgment, and also from the fact that ch. 107 continues to dwell on this judgment, that the message applies to the second destruction. Again, therefore, the first deluge is intended to presage and serve as a warning of the coming judgment in the author's own time. The way both deluges are referred to as "oppressions" perhaps indicates that the suffering of God's elect under the hand of their oppressors is itself seen as a foretaste of God's judgment — that is, that the oppression is part and parcel of the judgment, and that the righteous are not totally exempt from the troubles that come upon the nation. This also brings the reader face-to-face with the time of the author. The remnant motifs of destruction, cleansing, survival, and salvation are thus related to the survival of a remnant in the author's time. As Noah and his sons were "left," so also shall the righteous be saved in the future judgment. (That "left" is a remnant term is obvious from its repeated use in association with "remnant" in the Scriptures.) The importance of the remnant concept in this passage is again obvious from the way it has influenced the interpretation of the name of Noah (usually derived from *nôaḥ,* "rest"): "call his name Noah, for he shall be the *remnant* for you."[129] The significance of the flood typology for the writer's own community

---

129. For a theology of "rest," cf. Heb. 4:1ff. As here, the idea of rest might be associated with remnant ideas if it is implicitly combined with the view that only a remnant would make it to the (spiritual?) Promised Land (i.e., God's "rest" promised in Deut. 12:9). With regard to the Noah typology in *1 Enoch,* Jaubert states, "La Reste représenté par Noé et ses fils sera sauvé dans une alliance nouvelle, tandis que le même déluge engloutira les pécheurs. Le caractère typologique du déluge est assez clair dans le livre d'*Henoch*" (1963, 262).

is accordingly caught up with the idea of a remnant: as there was a remnant in Noah's day, so there will be a remnant *after* the coming judgment. Here, then, is yet another reason why Noah and the flood provide such a useful paradigm for salvation for the author. The emphasis in this passage remains entirely on the survival of the remnant; the idea of the growth of the remnant into a fuller number (i.e., the restoration) is not touched upon.[130]

Jubilees also refers to the flood as a destruction (6:4) in which Noah and his sons are a remnant (those *"left,"* 7:26), and they are encouraged to become "many" (6:5, 9) — a significant word that could well be intended as a contrast with the "fewness" of those who are saved through the flood. Another indication that the word "remnant" here reflects a broader context of usage is the typical biblical employment of the term in this book as part of an expression for total annihilation: that is, in the form "(such a person) *will not have a remnant."* When Jacob is warned not to take a wife from any of "the seed of daughters of Canaan," an allusion is made to those who carelessly intermarry and give birth to mixed (i.e., foreign) offspring. To such as these the author applies some fearful language of destruction:

> do not take a wife from any of the seed of the daughters of Canaan,
> because *all of his seed is destined for uprooting from the earth;*
> because through the sin of Ham, Canaan sinned,
> and *all of his seed will be blotted out from the earth,*
> and *all his remnant,*
> and *there is none of his who will be saved.*
> And for all those who worship idols and for the hated ones. . . .
>
> (22:20-22a)

The final words, which tail off into an imprecation against idolaters and "the hated ones," serve as a warning to apostates.[131]

In typical contrast to this, however, the righteous Jacob is told that "the Most High God shall *protect you from destruction"* (v. 23) and "your seed and your name will *remain* in all the earth's generations" (v. 24). In this passage the remnant terminology of total annihilation is paralleled with the agricultural

---

130. These themes are somewhat less prominent in the Zoomorphic History, but certainly not lacking. The book speaks about "all the sheep that had survived" (90:30), referring to those who survive the future judgment. Notably, the use of the word "sheep" here probably implies some continuity with the sheep who "began to open their eyes and see, and cried aloud to the sheep" (90:6) — i.e., the righteous, particularly the writer's community. The message implied by the language of survival here is probably not much different from its use elsewhere in *1 Enoch.*

131. Cf. J. C. Endres (*Biblical Interpretation in the Book of Jubilees,* 1987, 44-45), who interprets 22:16-22 against the background of the dangers of assimilation.

seed motif: that the seed will be "uprooted" is equivalent to "no remnant will be left." In a similar way the judgment on the Philistines (24:17ff.) includes the quite standard words of judgment and again combines seed and remnant motifs:

> And no remnant will be left to them,
> nor one who escapes on the day of the wrath of judgment;
> because all of the Philistine seed is destined for destruction and uprooting and removal from the earth. (v. 30)

While Israelites are not so clearly addressed in this judgment oracle, the dramatic enlargement on the curse of the Philistines in vv. 31ff., which continues the language of judgment and emphasizes the totality of their annihilation, may well be intended to allude to intermarriage practices among Jews in Palestine in the author's day. The author seems particularly intent on contemporizing the curse in vv. 28-29, making the agents of the judgment of the Philistine offspring not only "sinners," "nations," and "Kittim," but also "the righteous people" who shall "uproot them from beneath the sky with judgment, because they will be enemies and foes to my sons in their generations upon the earth" (v. 29). The righteous are again instruments of judgment, this time against Gentiles, and perhaps against Israelite opponents who act like Philistines.

Note, however, that in *1 Enoch* and *Jubilees* remnant terminology (or the language of survival) is still closely associated with its context and expresses the idea of preservation from various kinds of judgment. This is in contrast to the much later theological use where the word "remnant" has assumed an independent meaning and is employed theologically, as an *election* term. This probably explains why the term was not used more frequently, or unambiguously, as a *title* by these groups, as one might otherwise expect. It is not that they did not consider themselves a "remnant"; in other words, it is merely that the word had not yet been wrested from its context in order to become a *terminus technicus.* Thus the protest of Sanders that these groups did not actually call themselves a remnant (which, by the way, is certainly not even correct, as far as it goes) is to look for the wrong kind of evidence: the word carries a different sense for theologians today than it did for these groups, where it merely referred to those who are spared in judgment. Accordingly one should not be surprised to find a certain indefiniteness in the use of the terminology.

This is a particularly important observation when it comes to the scrolls and to the well-known *crux interpretum* in the opening passage of the Damascus Document (CD 1.3-12). The controversy over this passage concerns whether the "remnant" in the phrase "He left a remnant to Israel" (ll. 4-5) refers to the historical group of exiles or the later community itself. As already observed, the word may well refer to a remnant spared during the exile, but it certainly also refers to the Qumran community (namely, to those who possessed and seem to have edited this portion of CD).[132] The community believed itself to represent the *continuation* of the former remnant, indeed, but they were not only the descendants of this remnant but were, in a sense, a *new remnant* who found themselves in need of surviving the present times of trouble, and who hoped to survive the future judgment as well. That the passage alludes to the *present* group of the righteous is confirmed by the fact that it is possible to discern here a typological interpretation of *exilic* history not unlike the extensive typology of the *exodus* and *wilderness* periods that are also explicated in CD.[133] All biblical history, in other words, is applied to the community. This rather introspective view of history is made possible by the fact that the main *focus* of the community, as G. Jeremias points out, was never on history for its own sake, so much as for the sake of the *yaḥad*.[134] All history is *history of the remnant, therefore, and the history of the remnant is the only truly significant history.*

When CD refers to the prehistory of the group in terms of a remnant drawn out from among those who "abandoned" God (ll. 3-4), therefore, it implicitly conceptualizes the existence of the *present* community in similar terms. This is obvious from the way the postexilic history presented in this passage runs immediately and subtly into the history of the sect, as well as from the significance of the phrase "a root of planting . . . from Israel and Aaron" (l. 7), which certainly alludes to this later group as the descendants of the "planting" at the time of the exile. A few lines later, it is stated quite explicitly that a remnant exists in *every age:* "in *all* these times [God] raised up for Himself men named with a name, in order to leave *survivors* upon the earth and to fill the face of the world with their *seed*" (2.11-12). Since the history of the *yaḥad* has just been recounted (1.8ff.), the words "in all these times" would naturally also include the time of the sect. Finally, that the *present yaḥad* has been implicitly designated as the "remnant" appears to be definitely confirmed when, speaking again of the exile, the writer reports that "because of those who clung to the commandments of God and *survived them as a remnant,* God established His Covenant with Israel for ever, revealing to them the *hidden things* in which *all* Israel had strayed: His holy Sabbaths and His glorious feasts, His testimony of

---

132. It is interesting in this regard that 4Q390 refers to a "remnant" that is spared from the apostasy, and although the whole passage is couched in terms reminiscent of the exile, the dating scheme used by the passage demands a reference to the Maccabean or post-Maccabean period.

133. Cf. G. Jeremias, *Der Lehrer der Gerechtigkeit,* 1963, 297-99.

134. G. Jeremias: "Die Gemeinde ist nur an ihrer eigene Geschichte interessiert" (1963, 155).

righteousness, and His ways of truth. . . ." (3.12-15). While again the allusion may partially be to the exilic survivors,[135] it is the present community that maintains the proper calendar and covenant, and it is to the present community that "the hidden things" have been revealed. In both passages, therefore, the main referent is to the present community, regardless of whether that community is explicitly *entitled* the "remnant" or whether the allusion is to be seen as rather more oblique. The important thing, furthermore, is that when it is said that God "delivered [Israel] up to the sword" (during the deportation, 1.4), and that he left a "remnant to Israel" (1.4-5), this shows that the author conceived of the possibility of "remnant" that was *not* equivalent to "Israel."

These passages are replete with other kinds of remnant terminology in association with D-P soteriological terminology: language like "He left a remnant to Israel and did not deliver them to *destruction*" (1.4-5) and "those who clung to the commandments of God . . . *survived them as a remnant*" (3.12-13). Here also God established his covenant "with Israel" (l. 13), by which is certainly meant that he established it with the remnant on Israel's behalf, or in their place, as the true "Israel." It is suggestive, in this regard, how the passage proceeds to speak of Israel as structured *around* the remnant community. God built for the remnant a "sure House *in* Israel such as did not exist from former times till now" (3.19-20). It is composed of

> priests and the Levites and the sons of Zadok who kept the charge of my sanctuary *while the children of Israel went astray from me.* . . . The priests are the converts of Israel who went out from the land of Judah; and the Levites are those who joined them. And the sons of Zadok are the chosen of Israel, the men named with a name who shall stand at the end of days. (3.21–4.4; Ezek. 44:15; the names of the sectarians, or at least of the priestly families, appear to have followed in what is now a lacuna after l. 6)

Israel's national identity is accordingly now defined by and wrapped up entirely with that of the remnant. This remnant fulfills Israel's destiny and receives its promises. That the entire passage may be part of a covenantal *rîb* pattern[136] also suggests a connection between the remnant, D-P soteriology, and the repair of the covenant.[137] It would follow from this also that the restoration would be composed of descendants (spiritual or otherwise) of this remnant, rather than from others in Israel.

Remnant motifs are employed in other D-P passages as well. In the

135. Knibb refers them to the "initial members of the movement" (1987, 32).
136. Cf. P. R. Davies, *The Damascus Covenant,* 1982, 66-67.
137. Davies (1982, 83) speaks of the three successive elements: destruction-remnant-covenant. This is preferable to S-E-R patterns, which are usually read into such texts.

hymns of tumult the writer justifies his reason for comfort and hope in the midst of confusion: "And I was comforted for the roaring of the crowd and for the tumult of kingdoms when they assemble, for I know Thou wilt soon raise up *survivors* among Thy people and a *remnant* in the midst of Thine inheritance, and that Thou hast purified them that they may be cleansed of all sin" (1QH 6.7-8). Here the "remnant" is either the community itself or those who will survive the final great upheaval — although this passage would appear to provide little basis for separating the two. The survivors[138] who first followed the teaching of the *moreh* are also those who will be preserved through the coming dangers of judgment. While unambiguous reference to a final great upheaval is not found in the *pešer* text known as *Florilegium,*[139] it nevertheless suggestively proclaims that a "remnant will remain," apparently referring to the "time of Belial" and "the time of trial," and significantly alluding to the strongly dualistic Daniel 12 in connection with these tumultuous times (1-3; 2.2). The remnant in the great final battle portrayed in the War Scroll is arguably more of an "eschatological remnant," but again no certain distinction between the "historical remnant" and the "eschatological remnant" can be drawn here — that is, those saved *before* the battle are probably the same as those saved *during* and *after* the battle. One notes that the elect will certainly not be removed from the scene of battle, or avoid all suffering (1.11-12), yet they shall be saved from slaughter (1.13-14). The elect are confident of their victory in battle (3.11), while the men of Belial's lot are "without any remnant" (4.2). There will be no "remnant" left to the nations either (14.5). The true "remnant," on the other hand, remains to praise the name of God (14.8-9), for they are redeemed and *preserved* at the end of the battle (14.10).[140] Belial's "spirits of destruction" will depart from them (14.10), and they will bless God that they are the "*remnant* and the *survivors* of Thy Covenant" (13.8),[141] whose very purpose of existence

138. מחיה. This word Holm-Nielsen translates "a lively few" (1960, 101), perhaps in order to distinguish it from other references to "survivors." The word, however, entails the idea of *preservation* of life, and is equated with a "remnant" and "survivors" in Gen. 45:5, 7, as here also.

139. 4Q174 = 4QFlor(ilegium) would appear to be, not a messianic proof text, as it is often interpreted to be, but more of a community *pešer,* since "the elect of Israel in the last days" forms its chief subject matter. This again shows, however, how interdependent were views on community and messiah.

140. Yadin detects in this passage allusions to Isa. 11:11, 16 and Jer. 31:7, which contain references to a "remnant" of Israel in eschatological contexts (1962, 327).

141. The phrase recalls Joseph's words in Gen. 45:5-7 (Yadin, 1962, 322). A similar expression can be found in 4Q390 in the context of apostasy: "they will forget Law and festival, sabbath and Covenant. They will . . . do what is evil in my eyes. . . . Yet I will *spare a remnant.*" This would appear to be yet another more or less direct reference to the *yaḥad* as a "remnant."

is to form a united testimony of God's faithfulness: "that they may recount Thy works of truth and the judgment of Thy marvellous lofty deeds" (13.9).

Finally we consider one moderately large and very illuminating fragment from Cave 4 that apparently combines in one text all the essential components of this soteriology: images of a deep, dark, watery pit from which a "refined" remnant is saved; the onset of a restoration and the reign, during this time, of the messiah,

> . . . from the well, and the dread of the precipice, and the anguish of the pit. And they shall be refined in them to be chosen of justice . . . on account of his pious ones; for the age of wickedness has expired and all unjustice will pass [away.] The time of justice has arrived, and the earth will be filled with the knowledge and the praise of God. In the da[ys . . .] the age of peace arrives, and the laws of truth, and the testimony of justice. . . . Every [creature?] will bless him, and every man will bow down before him, [and they will have] a single heart. . . . For the dominion <of justice> of goodness has arrived, and he will raise the throne of [. . .] and knowledge is exalted; intelligence, prudence, and success are proved by the deeds of [his] holiness. . . . (4Q215 2, 2.1-10)[142]

It is significant for comparative purposes that this presentation of the pre-existent messiah before whom "every man will bow down" is more than faintly reminiscent of a similar presentation in Phil. 2:3ff. The contexts are not at all dissimilar either: it can be argued that the experiences of ascension and descension in the Christ hymn reflect a type of D-P soteriology not totally foreign to the Cave 4 MS.

Recognizing the existence of this common soteriological pattern will make some of the "preservation" sayings in the *Psalms of Solomon* much clearer as well. While containing no theoretical presentation of the soteriology, the *Psalms* contain a variety of tumult motifs, mostly related to the recent destruction of Jerusalem, and in particular reflecting the sufferings of the author(s) and of the *Psalms* community. There are indications of the spiritualization of a final battle within the corpus (cf. 1:5; 2:25, 30; 7:4-5; 17:16-20; etc.), some of these passages applying such language to the recent plundering of Jerusalem (cf. 2:25-30; 17:16-20). While there is a certain amount of lamentation over this destruction of Jerusalem, other sayings imply the purposeful preservation of a remnant that takes form in the author's community:

> The right hand of the Lord covered me;
> the right hand of the Lord *spared* me.
> The arm of the Lord *saved us from the sword that passes through*,

142. Translation by García Martínez, 1992, 271.

from famine *and the sinners' death.*[143]
Wild animals attacked them viciously,
    they tore their flesh with their teeth,
    and crushed their bones with their molars.
The Lord *protected us* from meeting all these things. (13:1-4)

As for the occasion of this experience of salvation, the last line suggests the escape of the righteous from Jerusalem prior to the attack of Pompey. The escape was viewed as providential and interpreted as God's act of deliverance on behalf of the righteous. Thus once again salvation goes hand in hand with judgment. Lengthy descriptions of the judgment of the godless and sinners in this book are accordingly always interspersed with words of assurance regarding the escape of the righteous. The psalm continues:

nothing shall harm the righteous, of all these things. . . .
the Lord will spare his devout. . . .
For the life of the righteous goes on forever,
    but sinners shall be taken away *to destruction,*
and no memory of them will ever be found.
But the Lord's mercy is upon the devout,
    and his mercy is upon those who fear him. (vv. 6, 10, 11-12)

It is revealing how the author thus draws a sharp distinction between the fates of the respective groups through an experience of "tumult," resulting in a dualism similar to that of other D-P motifs: while the ungodly are destroyed (v. 6), the righteous are merely disciplined (vv. 7-10). Also suggestive of D-P soteriology is that the recent sacking of Jerusalem is referred to as the sinners' "destruction" (13:6, 11; 16:5) while the escape of the righteous is their "salvation" (cf. 13:2; 15:6; 16:4, 5; 17:17). Both groups were previously "marked" either for this salvation or destruction (15:6, 9), just as the Israelites had earlier been segregated from the Egyptians when the angel of death went about the camp (cf. Ezek. 9:4; Exod. 12:13) — a possible indication of the interpretation of the sacking of Jerusalem (= Egypt?) as part and parcel of a second-exodus typology. It would appear, therefore, that this entire period of history was treated as a D-P event in which the sinners were purged from Israel so that the righteous could be preserved and flourish. God "spared" these righteous ones (13:1, 10). They fled in order to escape (17:16-17) while others did not and, in the future, will not escape (15:8). Perhaps most interesting here is the way Jerusalem has become the implicit recipient of the "destruction" aspect of the "de-

---

143. Perhaps referring to pestilence (דבר; H. E. Ryle and M. R. James, *ΨΑΛΜΟΙ ΣΟΛΟΜΩΝΤΟΣ,* 1891, 108).

struction-preservation" typology. This is the first clear instance we have seen of where Jerusalem appears as the locus of both judgment/destruction and salvation/preservation in the *Psalms of Solomon.*[144]

4 Ezra and *2 Baruch* repeatedly employ the term "survivors," whose full significance can only be seen against the background of D-P soteriology. According to Stone, the "survivors" in 4 Ezra are those who "escape the Messianic woes" in some passages (6:25; 7:27; 9:8; 13:19), and those who "survive the great eschatological battle waged by the Messiah" in others (12:34; 13:26, 48-49).[145] Again one might doubt the wisdom of referring to the signs as "*messianic* woes" since they often allude to the present conditions experienced by Israel (and the group), but Stone's basic observation appears to be quite correct: some of these survival passages refer to surviving the *present* distresses in the period preceding the final events, while others refer to surviving a strictly *future* judgment. It is difficult to say how much time was thought to separate the two events, as even a passage like 4 Ezra 6:25: "It shall be that whoever remains after all that I have foretold to you shall be saved and shall see my salvation and the end of my world," might actually be addressed to the author's *contemporaries.* It could be argued, in fact, that this passage alludes to the destruction of Jerusalem that had taken place in the author's time (cf. "when the humiliation of Zion is complete," v. 19) and to the events that were expected to follow immediately. The possibility that this author, like the author(s) of the *Psalms of Solomon,* was alluding to this in his employment of D-P motifs suggests one of the ways he made sense of the recent sacking of Jerusalem and the destruction of the Temple — namely, as an event of salvation as well as destruction. The remnant then embodies whatever is left of the promise to Israel after this destruction, and will continue to do so after the judgment.

In still another type of reference, the remnant is the group belonging to the messiah who will be with and support the remnant/survivors: "he will deliver in mercy *the remnant of my people,* those who have been saved throughout my borders, and he will make them joyful *until the end comes,* the day of judgment" (12:34).[146] If this refers to a slightly different period from 6:25 (although

144. 4Q183 (= *4QHistorical Work*) speaks of God saving and setting some free, apparently in contrast to others who "defiled their temple." Although the context for this text is not at all clear, it may witness to a widespread expectation that Jerusalem is like a city of doom from which the righteous must escape.

145. Cf. M. E. Stone, *Features of the Eschatology of IV Ezra,* 1989, 103.

146. The view that only those in the holy land would be saved is shared by *2 Bar.* 29:1-2; 32:1; 40:2; 71:1. This would appear to locate these sects in Palestine. They seem to have rejected life in the Diaspora. It was probably believed that, as at the remarkable return of the *righteous* exiles, 14:39ff., God would arrange to have all of the saved safely located in the holy land.

it may also refer to the author's generation), this would again suggest that there is a "remnant" in every period. Presumably these survivors are the same individuals who live through the full four hundred years of the messianic kingdom: "And everyone who has been delivered from the evils that I have foretold shall see my wonders. For my son the Messiah shall be revealed *with those who are with him*, and *those who remain* shall rejoice four hundred years" (7:27-28). If this is an expression of the belief in the new *longevity* that will be granted to the righteous, who are expected to survive the entire four hundred years with the messiah, then it is possible to understand this as the same remnant as mentioned elsewhere. Perhaps, on the other hand, the author simply did not carefully distinguish between the individuals who form the remnants of the various periods — that is, he may be saying only that "there will be a remnant composed of righteous individuals *throughout* the messianic age."

Other passages tend to confirm that the messianic (restoration?) period will involve the salvation of a remnant only: "And it shall be that everyone who will be *saved* and will be able *to escape* on account of his works, or on account of the faith by which he has believed, *will survive the dangers* that have been predicted, and will see my *salvation* in my land and within my borders" (9:7-8). Accordingly both the remnant of the past and that of the future are saved by their works and by their faith.[147] They will survive and be saved, inheriting the possession promised to Israel from of old — "the land." Here, then, is a traditional formulation of the idea of restoration as a return to, and possession of, the land.[148] Perhaps by reason of the recent tragic circumstances in Israel, however, this author is relatively pessimistic about the restoration; it will consist only of those who survive the judgment.

The well-known few/many motif in 4 Ezra is best understood as yet another formulation of the belief in a remnant/survivors; its employment by the angel in defending the recent events in the providence of God suggests that the remnant idea formed a crucial part of 4 Ezra's theodicy, helping to explain the present as well as the future destruction of the unrighteous. There has always been, and always will be, a remnant — on this fact both Ezra and the angel fundamentally agree.[149]

147. Other passages contain suggestive references to survivors. In the final judgment two kinds of people will be present: those who "*do* survive" (13:16, 19) and those who "do *not* survive" (13:16, 17); the messiah "will direct *those who are left*" (13:26; cf. 13:48); they shall be "saved" (13:48); "when [the messiah] *destroys* the multitude of the nations that are gathered together, he will *defend* the people *who remain*" (13:49).

148. Cf. R. J. Coggins and M. A. Knibb, *The First and Second Books of Esdras*, 1979, 214; Stone, 1990, 296. For the use of "my land" in the suggestive context of apostasy, cf. Jer. 2:7.

149. Ezra speaks of what he "presently" believes to be the case about a remnant in

2 Baruch similarly refers to an eschatological remnant that will be "left" (29:4). The messiah will "protect the *rest of my people* who will be found in the place that I have chosen" (40:2). As with 4 Ezra, this remnant would appear to include in some way the community of the "real" author. The best evidence for this is that Baruch's words to the exilic community are probably intended for the later community, as observed above. The content of this address, as with the content of the "Epistle" of Baruch (chs. 78ff.), in other words, is as relevant to the situation of post–A.D. 70 as it was to the exilic community in Jeremiah's day. The author is accordingly addressing his own community when he has Baruch say: "Behold, I go to my fathers in accordance with the way of the whole earth. You, however, do not withdraw from the way of the Law, but guard and admonish the *people who are left* lest they withdraw from the commandments of the Mighty One" (44:2-3). The people complain at the prospect of Baruch leaving them leaderless: "Shall we truly be in darkness, and will there be no light anymore for *that people who are left?*" (46:2).[150] "People who are left" is a common biblical expression that can virtually be translated "remnant." Baruch's address in 77:2 expresses the same basic idea: "Hear, O children of Israel, behold how many are *left* from the twelve tribes of Israel." Both passages contain the view that not all Israel has been saved; only a few remain. It is clear that, as with 4 Ezra, the author's community felt themselves to be the remnant, even though in the literary context of the work the "historical" remnant of the exile is being addressed.

THE ULTIMATE GOAL — VINDICATION OF THE REMNANT BY THE REST OF ISRAEL

As has been noted, the D-P event, whether consisting of a present or future judgment or, as apparently in some cases, the destruction of Jerusalem, was be-

---

7:47-48, 136-40, and what he fears for the future, in 9:14-16. The angel likewise speaks of what is "presently" true in 7:51-59; 8:1-3, and refers to the future judgment in 7:60-61; 9:22. No particular time reference is given in 9:14-21, where the angel appears to refer to the predestined elect as well as to the historical preservation of a remnant. Remnant and few/many motifs are evident in the idea of the righteousness of Ezra and "the few like" him, in 8:62; 10:57; etc.

150. This does not merely refer to the law but to the special revelation belonging to the community, as noted above. P. Bogaert appears to ascribe an almost mystical sense to Baruch's role here: "Baruch n'enseignera plus la Loi . . . Baruch lui-même peut être la lumière" (*Apocalypse de Baruch*, 1969, 2:82; cf. 77:13-16). This would further confirm that we are speaking of a "corporate identity" appropriate for a "remnant" group.

lieved to be the catalyst that brought about, or at least the signal that heralded, the restoration.[151] With conspicuous consistency the remnant features largely in this restoration. Less consistently the idea is expressed that this event would provide a way for the "rest" of Israel to find repentance or salvation, even if formerly they behaved like stubborn apostates. Something like this appears to be intended by *Jub.* 50:5, a text that exhibits this strong restoration expectation: "And jubilees will pass until Israel is purified from all the sin of fornication, and defilement, and uncleanness, and sin and error. And they will dwell in confidence in all the land. And then it will not have any Satan or any evil one. And the land will be purified from that time and forever." This answers to the expectation expressed in the opening chapter of the book:

> And the LORD said to Moses, "I know their contrariness and their thoughts and their stubbornness. And they will not obey until they acknowledge their sin and the sins of their fathers. But after this they will return to me in all uprighteousness and with all of their heart and soul. And I shall cut off the foreskin of their heart and the foreskin of the heart of their descendants. And I shall create for them a holy spirit, and I shall purify them so that they will not turn away from following me from that day and forever." (1:22-23)

If this time of "purification" refers to a great event at the end of time in which Satan is defeated, then here again is expressed the idea that restoration only follows a combined act of judgment and salvation expected from the hand of God. However, this passage has been taken as evidence that the author expected a rather more *gradual* transformation, perhaps also expressing the view that God would bring his restoration blessings only in *response* to the repentance, "purity," and moral righteousness of Israel. If this is the case, then *Jubilees* evidences a somewhat different relationship between the restoration and the event of salvation, and perhaps one is to see this event of salvation, as noted earlier, taking place annually during the covenantal celebrations associated with the Feast of Weeks. *Jubilees'* answer to the problem of Israel would then center more on the proper celebration of the Festival of Weeks, which would purify and bring salvation to Israel, than on an external cataclysmic event of judgment. On the other hand, one can hardly miss the way that the "circumcision of the foreskin of the heart" in the above passage is given decisive and final consequence. This highly spiritualized expression is taken from Deut. 10:16 and 30:6,

---

151. We have already alluded to this order with regard to *1 En.* 106:19; 107:1-2; 1QH 12.13-18; 1QS 4.25; 1Q27 1, 1.2-7; 4Q215 2, 2.1-10; 4 Ezra 6:25-26; and *2 Baruch* 72–73 above. It is after the good angels "destroy injustice from the face of the earth" that the "righteous ones will *escape*" and the restoration blessings will begin in the Book of Watchers as well (*1 En.* 10:16-17).

the latter passage significantly from a restoration context. At the very least, the use of the expression here implies a distinctive period in which Israel would repent, followed by the restoration. It may therefore imply a decisive and final event of salvation rather than a lengthy process, and although the text is completely silent on this point, it has already been noted that circumcision could itself be understood according to a D-P pattern.[152] In any event, the author of *Jubilees* may well have envisioned the salvation of large parts, if not all, of Israel — unless, of course, by "Israel" he was referring only to the remnant (a possibility already considered).

This would seem to be a notable exception to the more predominant view that only a remnant would survive to see the blessings of the restoration (although even in such cases there is generally some ambiguity). This raises the question as to why these other authors held to any view of restoration at all, or what value they would see in nurturing any hopes related to ethnic, or national, Israel. It is possible, of course, that restoration was such a strongly held traditional belief, and so clearly expressed in the Hebrew Scriptures, that removing it completely from the theology of these groups would have been impossible. There is, however, another motivation that would make sense of the inclusion of the doctrine — sociologically as well as theologically speaking. The *continuation of Israel* in some form, even after judgment, *offered the opportunity to have vindicated the special teachings or "way" of the group.*

It is a feature of these writings, as determined in the review of their eschatology above, that Israel would eventually acknowledge that the righteous were correct all along, even openly honoring them (cf. *1 En.* 90:30). Since Israel was the larger unit (the larger society) over against which these groups defined themselves, since (the rest of) Israel was the group they argued with and protested against, and since Israel shared with these groups similar claims on a common "inheritance," it can be seen how a fuller restoration would grant to the "cause" of the remnant groups an especially satisfying, and ultimate, *vindication.* This motivation is already evident in the words of God to Moses in the prologue of *Jubilees* (1:25). When God creates a holy spirit for Israel, "*every angel and spirit will know and acknowledge* that *they are my sons* and I am their father." The Spirit is accordingly evidence to the heavenly beings that the community belongs to God, another important indication of the *validating* function of pneumatology in *Jubilees* — in this case, *the restoration and accompanying gift of the Spirit together confirm that the Jubilaean community has been on the right path all along.*

All of this means that history — history past and history still to come —

---

152. Cf. CD 16.4-6, which states that "on the day on which a man undertakes to be converted to the Law of Moses, *the Angel of Hostility will depart from him.* . . . For this reason Abraham *circumcised himself on the day on which he knew*" (i.e., about circumcision).

possessed a very practical importance for these groups, in contrast to some recent negative evaluations of apocalyptic historicism. They were not apocalyptic dreamers, in the traditional sense of transcending or ignoring history. Rather they hoped to be *vindicated* in and through their history and, even more importantly, vindicated by those Israelites whom they surpassed in their striving for righteousness. Christopher Rowland, in his consideration of transcendent eschatology in the apocalyptic literature, comments appropriately:

> A glance at the contents of the apocalypses reveals that other-worldly eschatology is by no means as typical as is often suggested. Indeed, when it is to be found, it is not usually at the expense of the vindication of God's ways *within the fabric of history.* The eschatology of the apocalypses may not have looked to God at work in history as the only means of final salvation, *but their authors expected a vindication of their righteousness within the world of men, not in some intangible existence beyond the sphere of history.*[153]

It would appear, therefore, that the restoration — in the particular way it was conceived by these groups — was to constitute this ultimate experience of vindication within history. This is an entirely plausible view of the function of this belief, given the overriding concern of this literature to *define, legitimize,* and *vindicate* the righteous. The faithful remnant of the present, having perceived an unprecedented degree of apostasy in the nation, and having voiced its protest against the present state of things in Israel, firmly believed that its message of protest and teachings about true righteousness would eventually be vindicated — not only by the Gentiles, but especially, even more significantly, by the "elect" nation itself as it honored the remnant and eventually joined their cause. In this way the nation Israel would finally fulfill her calling, and the pious in Israel would then be able to make sense of all the distress, persecution, and apostasy they were facing.

153. C. Rowland, *The Open Heaven,* 1982, 38, emphasis added.

CONCLUSION

Implications of the Theology
of the Movement of Dissent for
New Testament Study

The findings and contribution of this book can be summarized under four basic categories: theological, social, formal, and comparative.

THEOLOGICAL

After considering matters of prolegomena (ch. 1), this study began by observing how both Jewish and New Testament studies presupposed a "conventional view" of national election theology in Judaism (ch. 2). This assumption was then subjected to a reconsideration based on contrary evidence, including strong indications of a judgment-of-Israel theme, and of a limited, exclusive soteriology in some important writings from the period (chs. 3–4). This evidence placed in serious doubt earlier characterizations of pre-Christian Judaism. After recognizing and considering the importance of covenantal thought to an understanding of Judaism (ch. 6), we discovered that, far from evidencing an unconditional or unilateral covenantal theology, all indications pointed to a highly individualistic and conditional view of covenant. A kind of covenantal dualism, based on biblical dualistic covenantal formulations and expressed through a number of themes, such as the witness motif, or the viewing-of-fates motif, was uncovered. In the following chapter this dualism was discovered to be rooted in what is best termed soteriological dualism, the view that the world, and specifically Israel, is divided into righteous and unrighteous according to their experience of salvation (ch. 7). This dualism, expressed in a variety of literary forms and theological motifs (chs. 8, 9), appears to have been a (if not *the*) dominant theological influence in the beliefs (notably the pneumatology) and the literature of these groups.

This approach was confirmed through a consideration of the messianology (ch. 10) and the eschatology (ch. 11) of these writings. Messianology, in all its different manifestations, consistently produced a view of the messiah best characterized as a messiah-for-the-elect, not a nationalistic messiah. Two consistent elements in the eschatology of these writings were an expectation of judgment (for Israel as well as the nations) coupled with hopes for the vindication of the saved community. The exclusiveness of the groups was most clearly reflected, however, in their truncated view of restoration. Traditional views of restoration were everywhere qualified by the central role played at this time by the righteous community. It would appear that traditional views of restoration were largely transformed into the idea that some (or many) from Israel would repent and be transformed, accepting the teaching of the group, and in this way vindicating the group's beliefs. In ch. 12 it was found that the soteriology of the groups cohered with this theology: a time of outpouring of judgment on the wicked, and the sufferings of the righteous that accompanied this, would provide the occasion on which and *by* which God would save the "survivors." We termed this belief destruction-preservation soteriology because it expressed this dual aspect, and because the group believed that the righteous would be *preserved* as a "remnant" through the ordeal.

This leads to a couple of important conclusions: *the conventional nationalistic view of election theology is not accurately reflective of at least some important pre-Christian Jewish groups;* in contradistinction to past treatments, moreover, one must conclude from such evidence that a *Jewish theology of special election existed well in advance of the New Testament period.*

SOCIAL

In an attempt to confirm and understand these theological developments, an overview of the historical and social background of the writings was also undertaken (ch. 5). It was clearly seen how social and religious conditions provided limitless opportunity for the type of protest and dissent expressed in this literature. While our aim was not to classify these groups sociologically, we nevertheless concluded that our writings could best be understood as the literature of the decidedly *nonnationalistic* wing of a wider protest movement in late Second Temple Judaism. Largely as a result of their nonconformist position, perhaps also as a result of their aggressive rejection of "apostate Judaism," these groups were forced into a defensive position. Their response to this state of affairs was to reformulate their theology in corporate categories (centered on their own group identity), elevate certain "defining laws" to unprecedented importance, redirect their piety and worship in line with an in-group/out-group mentality (cf. the many blessings and curses), and even in some cases reorganize the cult. All these tendencies reflect attempts to *define* and *legitimize* the group in their claims to be the sole faithful members of the race of Israel.

FORMAL

Such sociological considerations possess importance for the adoption and employment of certain literary forms in these groups. Conventional forms like blessings and woes, revelations of the cosmos, and historical rehearsals and testaments (chs. 6 and 8) related well to the social background investigated in ch. 5. We determined how these functioned commensurate with the soteriological dualism and the corporate and elitist self-consciousness of our groups, to *warn, console, validate,* and *vindicate* the beliefs and posture of these groups. Such could also be said for many of the smaller motifs put into service of this theology: the important seed motif, along with other plant (especially tree) motifs (ch. 7), and the all-important remnant terminology (ch. 12). Through repeated use in this context, such terms apparently evolved into highly suggestive religious "symbols," possessing a world of meaning to the dissenting Israelite that, perhaps, would not be evident to an outsider.

COMPARATIVE

All of the above has importance for an approach to the New Testament — the underlying purpose of this study. This applies at the "macro-" level to the theologies of John, Jesus, and the New Testament writers, which can now be more *adequately* viewed against *pre-Christian* nonnationalistic Jewish "remnant" theology. It also applies at the "micro-" level, suggesting that motifs used in the New Testament relate to the soteriological dualism that held a determining influence over the theology of the movement investigated in this book. It is certainly possible that words like "seed" or "tree" (not to mention "kingdom") also possessed the attributes of religious *symbols* that, when used (especially in parables), would have evoked in the original hearers and readers a whole spectrum of meaning *not* evident to an outsider (cf. Mark 4:10ff., 34-35), and would have thus automatically signaled a soteriological dualistic, messiah-for-the-elect, *nuanced* restoration theology.

This is obviously not the place to pursue at any length or in any detail the many possible applications of our analysis for comparative purposes, since this work primarily concerns itself with the Jewish world. However, since its "focus" from the outset was on Judaism *in its relevance for the discipline of New Testament origins,* our task would be uncompleted, to say the least, if we did not close with at least a preliminary, if grossly inadequate, consideration of the implications of these findings for New Testament scholarship, details of which would necessarily form the subject matter of future studies.

New Directions in Comparative Research

Only a few of the most outstanding and representative issues that have had major influence on the history of New Testament scholarship, and continue to exert great influence today, can be considered briefly. Of interest here are questions like: To what extent are comparative studies based on the view that we have now shown to be outdated and inadequate? Are scholars aware of a discrepancy between the views of New Testament authors and this standard view of Judaism? Do they ever suggest that another view of election lies behind the ministry of Jesus and the New Testament faith? And, perhaps most importantly, do these facts demand a reconsideration of some of the facets of the study of New Testament origins?

The Ekklesia in the Ministry of Jesus

One best begins at an important point in early modern scholarship with the question of the *ekklesia* in Jesus' ministry, which, to a significant extent, is where the issues began to take form. Questions surrounding the origin and nature of the *ekklesia* in the ministry of Jesus set in motion a turbulent controversy in pre- and early postwar Germany and outside of Germany as well.[1]

---

1. Cf. R. Bultmann, "Die Frage nach der Echtheit von Mt. 16,17-19," 1941, 265-79, esp. 265-67, for the history of the debate in its heyday. More than a little influence of the war on this question can certainly be assumed, as such a discussion coheres well with the general tendency among German theologians in the postwar era to reassess questions of authority and election.

While this prewar context might appear to date the issue and make it somewhat irrelevant over fifty years later, the whole matter continues to have profound significance for more recent scholarship. In fact, it would not be too far off to refer to this issue as a foundational "kingpin" around which modern critical scholarship rotates.

To properly showcase the present issues, we will quickly review the history of the scholarship that has provided the suppositions that are operative at the present time. The prewar debate centered largely on Matt. 16:17-19, and somewhat less on Matt. 18:17, but, as can easily be seen, other considerations played a determinative role in the debate as well. Both exegetical and historical difficulties bear heavily on the two above-named passages. The following composed the main exegetical concerns: (1) the Matthean passages contain the only two references to an *ekklesia* in the Gospels, a statistic that seems to cast doubt on the authenticity of the passages;[2] (2) the language of the two passages on the whole does not compare favorably with sayings widely considered authentic;[3] (3) the message of 16:18 depends somewhat on a wordplay in Greek that is not readily conceivable in Aramaic;[4] (4) the meaning of ἐκκλησία (*ekklēsia*) is not identical in the two places,[5] resulting in still further doubt regarding the possibility of a single underlying Aramaic lexeme.[6] Of even more interest here, however, is the historical problem offered against the authenticity of the passages: *Could* Jesus have spoken of an *ekklesia* during his ministry at all?[7] This concern became particularly acute about the same time various eschatological approaches to the Gospel history denied that Jesus possessed any concern whatsoever for a *present* "earthly" community made up of his disciples.

In defense of the authenticity of the concept, on the other hand, a number of scholars appealed to the Jewish notion of a remnant or a "true Israel" in

2. Bultmann, 1941, 259.

3. Particularly expressions like σάρξ καὶ αἷμα, πύλαι ᾅδου, δέειν, and λύειν; Bultmann, 1941, 260.

4. Namely, the wordplay between Gk. *petra* and *petros* — a problem that is not formidable, however, in that the single Aramaic word could conceivably stand behind both. Cf. F. Kattenbusch, "Der Spruch über Petrus und die Kirche bei Matthäus," 1922, 96-131, 107. K. L. Schmidt ("Die Kirche des Urchristentums," 1927, 258-319, 288-90) argues for the suitability of the οἰκοδομεῖν metaphor in the face of contrary estimates.

5. Matt. 16:18 is thought to refer to a much more abstract and less well-defined idea than does 18:17.

6. K. L. Schmidt, *TDNT,* 3:519. The major options for lexicographical solutions are Heb. קָהָל or Aram. קְהָלָא (i.e., congregation, gathering, community; cf. Gk. οἰκοδομή) and Heb. כְּנֶסֶת or עֵדָה or Aram. כְּנִשְׁתָּא (i.e., synagogue; cf. Gk. συναγωγή). Kattenbusch opts for the former but gives an inner spiritual meaning to the idea (1922, 108-16).

7. For a summary of the problems, historical and exegetical, cf. Schmidt, *TDNT,* 3:320.

Jesus' ministry. Outstanding among these were, in Germany, F. Kattenbusch and K. L. Schmidt, and in Britain, R. N. Flew,[8] each of whom offered various lexicographical solutions for the passages. According to Kattenbusch, behind the Gk. ἐκκλησία *(ekklēsia)* stood the Heb. קָהָל *(qāhāl)*.[9] Schmidt, however, pointed to the Aramaic כְּנִשְׁתָּא *(kᵉnîštā')*, a word that Jesus could have used to refer at one and the same time to both the Jewish synagogue (cf. Matt. 18:17 for a local community) and the more abstract idea of the divine community (*as per* Matt. 16:18);[10] accordingly it would have been possible for Jesus to have used the one word to refer to both concepts.[11] Moreover, these scholars argued from things like the Lord's Supper that Jesus attempted to establish a new community,[12] and pointed to the self-designation "Son of man" as an indication that Jesus looked to Daniel 7 and understood his task to gather the "people of the saints of the Most High."[13] For Flew the idea of an elect people is also implied in the secrecy motif in the Gospels.[14]

As for the historical precedence of the *ekklesia,* the idea of a separate and exclusive synagogue (Schmidt: "Sonder-כְּנִשְׁתָּא") is found among other Jewish groups that claimed, like Jesus' disciples, to represent the true Israel.[15] Jesus'

---

8. Kattenbusch, 1922, 111; Schmidt, 1927, 280, 8; *TDNT,* 3:518-26, 34-36; R. N. Flew, *Jesus and His Church,* 1938, 25, 48-136. Cf. T. W. Manson (*The Teaching of Jesus,* 1935, 175-90), who places the idea of the church firmly within the Old Testament notion of the remnant. The idea of the *ekklesia* does not, of course, have to be considered equivalent to the remnant; the former idea is often seen only to be dependent in a general way upon the latter.

9. Kattenbusch, 1922, 116.

10. By analogy with third-century (or older) Syr. MSS — and presumably therefore with the (allegedly) closely related first-century Aram. — which employs *knewštā'* for both ἐκκλησία and συναγωγή (1927, 276-77; *TDNT,* 3:525). The use of ἐκκλησία is therefore primitive; later on ἐκκλησία became normative in the Gentile church, while συναγωγή was adopted among Jewish Christians (Schmidt, 1927, 271-72; *TDNT,* 3:516, 18). Cf. also G. Johnson, *The Doctrine of the Church in the New Testament,* 1943, 43.

11. Although Schmidt argues for the post-Easter provenance of Matt. 18:17 (1927, 296). The statistical problem of only two usages in the Gospels was also dismissed by these scholars, who pointed to the abundance of authentic terms used comparatively infrequently, and to the notion of *ekklesia* as discernible in other terms; cf. Schmidt, *TDNT,* 3:520-21; Flew, 1938, 125.

12. Schmidt, 1927, 293; *TDNT,* 3:521; Flew, 1938, 99.

13. Kattenbusch, 1922, 111-12; Schmidt, 1927, 294-95; *TDNT,* 3:520-21; cf. Manson, 1935, 227-34. While Flew (1938, 73, 75-80) denies the connection between Son of man and a people, he nevertheless attempts to substantiate the broader view, earlier held by Albert Schweitzer, that messianism generally implied the gathering of a people.

14. Flew, 1938, 88-89, cf. 130-32.

15. For the idea of Jesus' community as a counterpart to the synagogue, although not *itself* a synagogue, cf. Kattenbusch, 1922, 110-11, 114-15. Schmidt points to the

announcement of the eschatological kingdom of God, furthermore, could not be said to *preclude* the establishment of a church that itself possessed an eschatological self-consciousness.[16] For Schmidt, therefore, "The question whether Jesus gathered his disciples into an *ekklesia* must be affirmed." And Jesus' situation vis-à-vis Israel is fully comprehensible: "the attitude adopted by Jesus toward his people is illustrated by the fact that, on the one hand, he sought to win over the whole people — all Israel, but, on the other hand, by the fact that, after that attempt, he fell back upon his disciples as the remnant of Israel."[17]

In many circles, however, the exegetical and historical doubts regarding Matt. 16:18 and 18:17 won out over these arguments. And the Jewish idea of a remnant largely failed to overshadow the expectation by Judaism of an all-encompassing national deliverance. Important articles by Bultmann in 1941 and Kümmel in 1953 are representative of many others.[18] These scholars both adopt a basically eschatological approach to the question. With regard to Judaism they both agree that the universal belief was for a new people of God to be formed only *after* the eschatological event: *there would be no remnant or other preconstituted form* (Kümmel: *Vorausbildung*) *of the eschatological people of God prior to this time*.[19] Nor did the idea of a church assembled *between* the resurrection and parousia originate with Jesus' ministry,[20] as there exists no evidence

---

συναγωγὴ Ἀσιδαίων and συναγωγὴ γραμματέων of 1 Macc. 2:42 and 7:12, and to the CD covenant (for which he cites the Cairo MS), which refers to the community as עֵדָה and קָהָל as well as שְׁאֵרִית לְיִשְׂרָאֵל (the "remnant of Israel"; 1927, 279; *TDNT*, 3:526).

16. Schmidt, *TDNT*, 3:522-23.

17. "Die Frage, *ob* Jesus seine Jünger zur ἐκκλησία gemacht, muß bejaht werden"; "die Stellung Jesu zu seinem Volk ist einerseits damit gegeben, daß er versucht hat, das ganze Volk, ganz Israel zu gewinnen, und einerseits damit, daß er sich dann doch auf seine Jünger als den Rest Israels zurückgezogen hat" (Schmidt, 1927, 293, 6; author's translation).

18. Bultmann, 1941, passim; W. G. Kümmel, "Jesus und die Anfänge der Kirche," 1953, 1-27; cf. also A. Oepke, "Der Herrnspruch über die Kirche Mt 16,17-19 in der neuesten Forschung," 1948, 110-65, 134-65; N. A. Dahl, *Das Volk Gottes*, 1962, 145-46. According to Flew (1938, 23), Adolf Harnack first gave explicit expression to the objections against the foundation of the church by Jesus.

19. This is the view also of Johnson, 1943, 52. Cf. Bultmann, 1941, 270, 3, 5-6; Kümmel, 1953, 9. Notably Schmidt (1927, 286-88, 92-93) argues the very opposite from the same data — the *ekklesia* and the kingdom of God are both present entities! It is, however, very important to note, in order to set the discussion in context, that in its earliest forms the view arrived at by Kümmel depended on the infelicitous equation of "church" and "kingdom of God." Since the kingdom was eschatologically interpreted in this period, it was felt that the idea of the church must also be eschatologically understood. For rejection of the view, cf. also Flew, 1938, 15, 41-47.

20. *Contra* Flew, 1938, 41-47. It is obvious that here the prevailing notion of the parousia-delay heavily influenced the conclusions of these scholars.

that he had anything in view for the period following his resurrection. As Kümmel argues, his interest was solely in the *present* effects of his ministry among God's *entire* people.[21] God's kingdom in this present manifestation consisted of power, not an organized community.[22] From a somewhat different perspective Bultmann reached similar conclusions on this matter. He maintained that all messianic categories were read by the early church into Jesus' ministry; but even if one holds that Jesus did believe himself to be a messiah, Kattenbusch's connection of the messiah concept with a people is "eine phantastiche Konstruktion."[23] The language of Matt. 16:17-19 reflects the situation after Easter,[24] as do the Last Supper passages, which cannot therefore be used as evidence of the establishment of a church.[25] In fact, Jesus demonstrated his respect for existing Jewish institutions as a continuing member of his local synagogue.[26] One could not call Jesus' followers a "church";[27] they were not an "exclusive number" (Kümmel: *geschlossene Grösse*), but were still members of the historical people of God.[28] In sum, Jesus did not attempt to gather a people;[29] he neither planned for a remnant,[30] nor even implicitly created one — evidence to the contrary originates with the later church.[31]

Arguments against Jesus founding a "church" were not all exegetical and historical, however. As is evident in the above comments, theological reasons were also adduced. For some scholars the idea of "church" automatically implied a universalism and inclusion of Gentiles not applicable to Jesus' ministry.[32] For others, the *ekklesia* implied not only a community but a whole or-

---

21. Kümmel, 1953, 2, 8-9, 15.

22. Appeal to Jesus' understanding of Daniel 7 or to his employment of the Son of man terminology in support of the view that he gathered a group of elect is also invalid; cf. Bultmann, 1941, 273.

23. Kattenbusch, 1941, 276-77. This has been a significant point of investigation for us in the previous chapters. The Son of man is primarily an eschatological figure for Bultmann, thus confirming the idea of an eschatological people of God only (279).

24. Bultmann, 1941, 270-71, 279; Kümmel, 1953, 19-27.

25. *Contra* Kattenbusch. Bultmann also argues against this being the meaning of the institution in the first place (1941, 271-72).

26. Bultmann, 1941, 270.

27. Kümmel, 1953, 9.

28. Kümmel, 1953, 4-7.

29. Bultmann, 1941, 278; Johnson, 1943, 49-51, 7.

30. Oepke (1948, 140) adds to these arguments the observation that what Jesus rejected was the present Pharisaic "remnant." Cf. also J. Jeremias, "Der Gedanke des heiligen Restes im Spätjudentum und in der Verkündigung Jesu," 1949, 190. The argument seems to assume that if Jesus rejected one kind of remnant, he rejected all kinds of remnants.

31. Bultmann, 1941, 273-74; Dahl, 1962, 144-46.

32. E.g., Dahl, 1962, 145.

ganized cult,[33] or at least a developed Christology (i.e., *ecclesia triumphans*).[34] These approaches are obviously invalid because they introduced anachronistic assumptions and complicated unnecessarily the question at hand. There is no reason to assume that an *ekklesia* idea, if it existed in Jesus' ministry, must have included any of these developed theological notions. The fact that such invalid theological assumptions, as well as strictly critical and exegetical considerations, came into play in this discussion[35] did not go totally unnoticed. Oepke, in assessing the prejudices that entered into the debate, pointed to a growing alienation *(Entfremdung)* between contemporary theology and the established church at the time of these studies.[36] Nevertheless, discussion continued in major institutions and publications with the result that the momentum of Bultmann's and Kümmel's positions became somewhat normative. During this time, of course, the conventional view of Judaism, with its eschatological categories and its basic nationalistic thrust, was never challenged or superseded — in fact, all of these scholars in various ways subscribed to it. Hence, since the idea of a remnant could not be reconciled with the standard view of Judaism, the discussion continued to be dominated by theological rather than historical and exegetical considerations, and the opinion that Jesus sought to form a church began to be treated as naive and uncritical.[37] This attitude grew to the point that it produced the view that the notion of Jesus' *ekklesia, along with all the Gospel pericopes that assumed or depended upon the idea,* were later Christian constructs. Theories of discontinuity by which Gospel criticism judged the authenticity, or relevance, of a pericope by the presence in it of the "language of the church" discounted as important for an understanding of the ministry of Jesus passages that reflect any of this kind of "ecclesiology." The idea of a church, in short, seemed to

---

33. E.g., Johnson, 1943, 51.

34. Again, Johnson, 1943, 50, 56.

35. The entire debate would seem to suggest that while the exegetical difficulties of these passages are undeniably significant (they may not be insurmountable, however), exegetical difficulties in themselves are not the main concern here. It is the *historical* question that is crucial: Is it *conceivable* that Jesus intended, or otherwise created, a "church"? The Gospels as they stand would seem to support this possibility — all other theories depend on a critical reduction of the data. But for Bultmann and Kümmel this reduction became a necessity, for the environment of their discussion was predetermined by questions of eschatology, particularly that of the delay of the parousia, a concern receiving heightened attention at the time. According to the dictates of this nationalistic and eschatological view of Judaism, Jesus could have had nothing to do with a church.

36. Oepke, 1948, 163-64.

37. Cf. Bultmann's repeated references to the naive acceptance of the authenticity of Matt. 16:18 as well as the Lord's Supper and Son of man passages in regard to this question (1941, 268, 71-72, 75-76, etc.).

have been barred from respectable treatments of the ministry of Jesus once and for all.

The Jewish Quest for Jesus

It is perhaps of little surprise that even today there are very few references in scholarly publications to Jesus and his church; the words "church" and "historical Jesus," in fact, rarely appear in the same context. Given that this state of affairs became possible because of the flawed theological discussion of an early generation, it would seem that newer approaches to the question must try to reject that discussion and start afresh on better foundations. The negative results achieved by this process are so ingrained into the mood of critical thinking in biblical scholarship, however, that the tendency seems likely to continue. But the discussion cannot be carried out on purely theological grounds, especially when the exegetical justifications for it mentioned above remain ambiguous. *The most serious objection to the idea of Jesus forming a church remains the historical: Could Jesus really have adopted such an antinationalistic posture during his ministry?* To answer *this* question one necessarily looks to another field of study — (historical) Jesus research. In Jesus research the answer to the historical question "Could Jesus have called a church?" has persistently been expressed in the negative — no doubt largely because of the "exegetical" considerations of Bultmann et al. Perhaps again not surprisingly, although quite paradoxically, this prejudice against the idea of the church in Jesus' ministry has continued in studies of the historical Jesus even after the eschatological approaches of an earlier day were long abandoned. This is because the assumption, in the view of at least one perceptive scholar, had acquired the status of a "critical dogma."[38]

Jesus research, as is widely known, has entered a new stage in the last few decades, what has been called the "Jewish Quest" for the historical Jesus. After a century or more of Jesus research in which, for dogmatic and philosophical reasons, a wedge was driven between Jesus and his "Jewishness," many scholars are now reclaiming Jesus for Judaism — that is, attempting to set the historical Jesus in a credible relationship to his background and upbringing in Judaism[39]

---

38. For a survey of the main contributions that demonstrate this trend, cf. Oepke, 1948, 111-33. The denial that Jesus founded a church was soon referred to by Flew (1938, 25) as "a dogma of critical orthodoxy."

39. This trend is occasionally referred to as the "Third Quest" in studies by Christian scholars, or the "Jewish reclamation of Jesus" in those of Jewish scholars. For scholars who represent this school of thought, see notes below, and J. D. G. Dunn, *The Partings of the Ways between Christianity and Judaism and Their Significance for the Character of Christianity*, 1991, esp. comments on 16-17, 258-59, and passim.

— what must be seen as a promising return to historical foundations. This quest is not entirely new. Much earlier this century the Jewish scholar Joseph Klausner[40] anticipated the approach. Reflective of his time, however, Klausner held Jesus and Christianity to be in a fundamental *discontinuity* with Judaism, even if in some respects they originated in it. For Klausner Judaism in its highest form was thoroughly nationalistic; he even idealizes the national hopes of Judaism expressed in the Second Temple period.[41] At the outset of his ministry, Klausner's Jesus embraced this nationalistic vision, a fact this scholar uses to explain the wide appeal of his early ministry; but somewhat later Jesus departed fundamentally from Judaism when he abandoned the nationalistic basis of Jewish faith.[42]

Prejudices against Jesus calling a church have continued into this new stage of Jesus research, and even more recent attempts to consider Jesus in the light of Qumran and the Pseudepigrapha (Klausner and scores of others relied heavily on rabbinic literature) have brought few significant modifications to this basic position. Ben Meyer's *Aims of Jesus* (1979) certainly had the potential to do so. He revived the idea of the remnant, as earlier expressed in the *ekklesia* debate. He looked to the idea of restoration in Jewish expectation as embodied in the work of John the Baptist and Jesus,[43] but his major contribution centered on the remnant that naturally evolved from Jesus' attempts to bring restoration, and on Jesus' calling of that remnant.[44] Meyer's position, however, has not gained anything like overwhelming support, perhaps for the same reasons as the similar failure of the position with regard to the *ekklesia* debate. Meyer argues persuasively about the remnant doctrine, but fails to anticipate and deal with the underlying and highly influential "conventional view" of Judaism that still provides the chief barrier to such views being

40. J. Klausner, *Jesus of Nazareth,* 1925.

41. Klausner, 1925, 9-10, 135-228, 371, 6. Thus the work of the Maccabees is put forward as an example of the highest ideals of Judaism, while all opponents of that pure religion are held responsible for its misfortune (139, 169, 171-73, 187-92)!

42. Klausner, 1925, 142, 371-76.

43. B. F. Meyer, *The Aims of Jesus,* 1979, 116-17, 123, 139-73. Another exponent of the Jewish quest, Gerhard Lohfink, does not investigate the Jewish background for himself but assumes the doctrine of the restoration of Israel to be the central belief of Judaism at this time (*Jesus and Community,* 1984, 9), and one into which Jesus' ministry is seen to fit (xi, 10ff., 35-36, 71). Unlike Meyer, he does not envisage a period of time in which the righteous take the form of a remnant; Jesus intended to gather all Israel from the beginning of his ministry, and expected the final fruits of this gathering to appear imminently (25, 43-44). For "restorationists" like Lohfink the national salvation is the prominent presupposition to be taken from Judaism, and little or no consideration is given to alternate possibilities for either Jesus or Judaism.

44. Meyer, 1979, 117-22, 183, 196-97, 210-22.

widely accepted.[45] While Meyer gives summary evidence from the Hebrew Scriptures and from contemporary Judaism for the remnant belief, he deals mostly with collective and secondary scholarship on the Pharisees and Essenes rather than grappling with the primary texts.[46] Again he confronts old arguments against the doctrine;[47] but traditional views seem to be too well established for his general evidence and inferential argumentation, all of which have been previously offered with little consequence.

More recent studies within the "Jewish Quest" have almost abandoned the question of Jesus and a remnant, or Jesus and a church, altogether. For Geza Vermes Jesus is to be understood as a pious Galilean[48] who would naturally have come into conflict with other Jews, notably the Pharisees. But this conflict would have resembled "in-fightings of factions belonging to the same religious body, like that between Karaites and Rabbanites in the Middle Ages, or between the orthodox and progressive branches of Judaism in modern times," rather than a more serious division as would be implied by the doctrine of the remnant.[49] While Vermes denies that Jesus was a "nationalistic revolutionary," it is nevertheless clear that he presupposed a conventional view of Jewish election theology to which Jesus is most closely related.[50] In continuity with this basically nationalistic understanding of Jesus' Judaism, Vermes appeals to the frequently repeated[51] opinion that the most colorful

45. This, we would argue, is also the reason Manson's earlier attempt failed. Cf. Manson, 1935, 175-88.

46. Meyer, 1979, 225-40. It is interesting in light of our discussion above about the Pharisaic self-consciousness that scholars can be found who take the Pharisees as their starting point for a background in Judaism. L. Goppelt (*Jesus, Paul, and Judaism,* 1964), e.g., takes the particularism of the Pharisees, who tried to gather the "true Israel," as generally representative of Judaism (30, 52). Even here, however, the general appeal for the standard view of election shows through in his denial that Jesus shared this view of things.

47. Meyer, 1979, 120-22, 210-11.

48. G. Vermes, *Jesus and the World of Judaism,* 1983, 3-4.

49. Vermes, 1983, 11-12. This coheres with the understanding of "sectarianism" alluded to above.

50. Vermes paradoxically speaks of the "downright chauvinism" and "bias" of Jesus toward his Jewish nation but does not relate this to the attitudes of other Jews (1983, 50, 54-55). This is perhaps an understandable enough exaggeration (even if somewhat misdirected), given Vermes' objective to defend the Jewishness of Jesus.

51. The view is held by numerous form and redaction critics. Martin Albertz and Rudolf Bultmann coined the term *Streitgespräche* to speak of the "controversy form" which emerged due to the reaction of the early Christian community to the Jewish synagogue. Cf. also J. Hultgren, *Jesus and His Adversaries,* 1979, esp. 39, 162-64, 197-98. For recent redactionists who hold this view, cf. D. R. A. Hare, *The Theme of Jewish Persecution of Christians in Matthew's Gospel,* 1967, esp. 125-28, 147-48; J. L. Martyn, *History and Theology in the Fourth Gospel,* 1968; S. Sandmel, *Anti-Semitism in the New Testament?* 1978, pas-

encounters between Jesus and his opponents in the Gospel pericopes should be "post-dated and identified as exchanges between the leaders of the Jerusalem church, the 'Judaizing' circles of Palestinian Christianity, and their Pharisee opponents" (i.e., accredited to much later controversy between church and synagogue).[52] It is particularly revealing (and in continuity with much of what we have already witnessed) that Vermes postulates as three major differences between Jesus and later Christianity their views on law, the election of Israel, and his divinity. While Jesus adhered to conventional Jewish understandings, in other words, the early church altered his message in all three areas, and thereby effectively abandoned Jesus' Jewish roots. "Very many ages have passed since the simple Jewish person of the gospels stepped back and gave way to the rich and majestic figure of the church's Christ" — words that could have been spoken by practically any of the former Jesus researchers, "Jewish Quest" or not.[53]

E. P. Sanders has made significant contributions to the Jewish quest, as his book *Jesus and Judaism* (1985) applies to these questions the distinctly nationalistic view of Judaism explicated in his earlier work *Paul and Palestinian Judaism*. Sanders roots the ministry of Jesus in the idea of "restoration," by which he can salvage Jesus' ministry to all Israel out from the midst of later, exclusivistic

---

sim; R. Maddox, *The Purpose of Luke-Acts*, 1982, esp. 45-46, 54, 183-84; S. H. Brooks, *Matthew's Community*, 1987; J. T. Sanders, *The Jews in Luke-Acts*, 1987, esp. 20, 23, 49-50, 54, 63, etc.; for an overview, cf. K. H. Schelkle, *Israel im Neuen Testament*, 1985, esp. 13-20, 26-32, 40-42, 59. For a summary of the earlier foundational contributions of Wolfgang Trilling, M. J. Fiedler, and Ulrich Wilckens, cf. J. Rohde, *Rediscovering the Teaching of the Evangelists*, 1968, 74-91, 202-17.

52. Vermes, 1983, 31. Vermes compares the idea of Qumran as the "true Israel" with that of the later church as composed of twelve tribes (82-83, 117); however, he apparently only considers this a peripheral point of contact and does not attribute this idea to Jesus but credits it to later Christianity: "If the Scrolls exerted any influence on the New Testament . . . they will have done so not on Jesus himself, to whom the bulk of Qumran doctrine will have been alien, if not repugnant, but on Paul, John and other leaders of the new church. Their use . . . will reside in throwing light on Christianity of the apostolic age, and in showing, more clearly than ever before, negatively what Jesus was not, rather than what he was" (124).

53. Vermes, 1983, 57, cf. 54-57. On other merits, however, Vermes exhibits a distinctive tendency toward independence from this standard model. In his discussion on methodology for studying Judaism, he argues for a view that takes into account both the diversity and the interrelationship of types of Judaism. He offers a method that will trace beliefs through rabbinic material, the Pseudepigrapha, and even the New Testament, in order to arrive at "Jewish traditional teaching" (85, cf. 75-88). In spite of this laudable historicism, however, Vermes still reconstructs Judaism in large part upon the rabbinic texts (63, 68-69; although he cannot be said to ignore other Jewish groups altogether). For this reason his views do little to challenge common conceptions.

and extraneous judgment themes in the Gospels.[54] As a result of this process, Sanders concludes that the election theology of Jesus can be summed up, in harmony with the rest of Judaism, by the Tannaitic saying in Sanhedrin 10.1: "All Israelites have a share in the world to come." He repeats his view that not even the Pharisees or the Essenes attempted to gather a remnant.[55] While the remnant idea found a place among the prophets,

> in the post-biblical literature the theme of a threatened punishment which will leave only a remnant recedes. Remnant terminology, especially various terms designating the survivors as "poor" and "lowly," is often retained; but the emphasis is on reassembly, freedom from oppression and foreign domination. . . . In general terms it may be said that "Jewish eschatology" and "the restoration of Israel" are almost synonymous.[56]

Sanders concludes that Jesus in no way broke with classical election theology, or attempted to gather only a remnant. He agrees with those scholars who feel that Jesus' conflict with the Pharisees was largely read back into the Gospel story from a later time for polemical purposes. The overall result, according to Sanders, is that his views *contradict* past Jesus research that had the effect of accentuating Jesus' very un-Jewish, antinationalistic stance![57] But while Sanders has altered somewhat the approach of past treatments (and has contradicted a *few* studies like that of Meyer), he has more or less followed the majority view regarding the nationalistic approach to Judaism; his contribution has merely been to place Jesus in even closer harmony with it.

With Sanders one witnesses the tremendous influence of the conventional view of Judaism, which is now combined with another unwritten but pervasive policy in Gospel research: *when the New Testament appears to assume an unconventional understanding of election, it is the New Testament view that must be rationalized, rather than an alternative view sought in Judaism.* The conclusion of this short survey is therefore striking. For the most part even recent writers on Jesus and his ministry are acquainted only with a Judaism characterized by an intense nationalism, of which nationalistic election theology was an essential part — in other words, with "the conventional view" of Judaism.

---

54. See his conclusions about Jesus as a restorationist preacher; E. P. Sanders, *Jesus and Judaism,* 1985, 319, 340.

55. E. P. Sanders, 1985, 46, 96.

56. E. P. Sanders, 1985, 96-97. To this can be compared the view of W. D. Davies (*Paul and Rabbinic Judaism,* 1955, 78-85, 321-22) cited in ch. 1.

57. E. P. Sanders, 1985, 28-37, 96-97, 113, 291-92, 337-39. It is superfluous for us to add that this tendency is not at all clear, at least since the beginning of the critical period; Sanders appears to be referring to a prejudice long past.

Eschatological and Comparative Approaches
in New Testament Theology — Rudolf Bultmann

Interestingly, this tendency to accept without question conventional views of election theology is responsible for other influential trends in the history of New Testament study — namely, the widespread and persistent use of eschatological categories and non-Jewish comparative models for the understanding of the New Testament. This approach implicitly starts from the premise that the central importance of the Jewish writings, as regards comparison and contrast with the New Testament at least, lies not with their views on election or nationalism but with their eschatology. An allusion was made in the discussion about R. H. Charles above to the uniting of eschatological and nationalistic ideas in nearly all treatments of apocalyptic streams of Judaism. This combination of nationalism and eschatology also possesses implications for many major facets of New Testament study, at least in those treatments that allow in one way or another for the influence on the New Testament of the "apocalyptic" literature.

This preeminently applies to the systematic discipline of New Testament theology itself. Certainly one the most important factors in the wide dissemination of the eschatological approach for comparative purposes was the theological approach of Rudolf Bultmann, who presupposed a nationalistic orientation in Judaism, and accordingly drove a wedge between the nationalistic-eschatological theology of the Jewish world and the essentially nonnationalistic view of things found in the New Testament. Bultmann was consistent in his view of this nationalistic aspect of Judaism. He argued that even where Jewish hopes took on a cosmic form (namely, in apocalyptic), the nationalistic vision was maintained.[58] Conventional views of Judaism are accordingly evident throughout his writings. In *Das Urchristentum im Rahmen der antiken Religionen* (ET, *Primitive Christianity in Its Contemporary Setting*, 1956), Bultmann lays out his presuppositions about Judaism, although he incorporated them into the structure of his thought even before that, in his *Theologie des Neuen Testament* (ET, *Theology of the New Testament*, vol. 1, 1952). A few passages from the English version of *Urchristentum* demonstrate an understanding of Judaism heavily dominated by nationalistic presuppositions:

> In Judaism there was a lively hope that God would deliver the nation from its bondage and restore its former glory. . . . Its classical expression is to be found in the apocalyptic literature. (94)

---

58. Cf. R. Bultmann, *Primitive Christianity in Its Contemporary Setting*, 1956, 97, 101; cf. also R. Bultmann, *Theology of the New Testament*, 1952, 1:46-47, for other expressions of this nationalistic hope.

In its traditional form the hope of Israel was nationalistic in character. (95)

The Messiah would also be a warrior hero, who would destroy his enemies and restore Israel's sovereignty over the world. (96)

This presumption about nationalism strongly, if indirectly, influenced Bultmann's outlook on the New Testament — in two ways. First, since New Testament theology is explicitly nonnationalistic, he looked away from Judaism to gnostic and Hellenistic thought as background for many salient features of New Testament theology (dualism being a very important one).[59] Secondly, since Jesus rejected nationalistic exclusivity in favor of his own individualized message of salvation, Bultmann concluded that Jesus is to be strictly separated from the Jewish environment, which he transcended.[60] In fact, Jesus rejected every earthly interpretation of the kingdom.[61] Bultmann therefore articulated what had already become a common conception: in substance Jesus moved *beyond* Judaism.[62] In consequence of the impossibility Bultmann felt in harmonizing the national election theology of Judaism with the individualism (particularly the universalism) of Jesus, and with the corresponding demise of historical-based comparative approaches that it implied, opportunity was presented for the cultivation and dissemination of Bultmann's renowned existential/anthropological solution to the chief issues in New Testament theology. This approach, of course, proffered the advantage of a history-of-religions approach based on the universal quest for authentication that anthropology (applied by Bultmann using distinctly theological and existential language) posited as the driving force behind all religions. It is unnecessary to review how influential this existential solution has been among New Testament scholars, except to point out that many of those most influenced by it have long since lost sight of Bultmann's chief justification for applying the approach — namely, the belief that *in its very fundamentals the faith of Jesus cannot be reconciled with a nationalistic, eschatologically oriented Judaism.*

The Fourth Gospel

Gospel studies have naturally been influenced by these tendencies, both eschatological and nationalistic approaches to Judaism. We alluded to the general implications of this for Gospel studies above, but of special interest is how these

59. Cf. Bultmann, 1952, 1:172-75.
60. Cf. R. Bultmann, *Jesus and the Word,* 1935, 45.
61. Bultmann, 1935, 35-47.
62. For a survey of this view and critique, cf. E. P. Sanders, 1985, 28.

tendencies have affected the study of the Fourth Gospel in particular, which is noteworthy for various reasons, not least because of this Gospel's rather eclectic presentation of the ministry of Jesus and the difficulty it poses for discerning a helpful background for the Gospel in Judaism. The question that is again raised about this Gospel is whether the most important point of comparison lies with eschatology, since this has so far proved to be a most unfortunate and unproductive choice of approach. In spite of earlier attempts to relate John to its Jewish background,[63] it would seem that the world of the "de-eschatologized" Fourth Gospel so contrasts with standard views of eschatological Judaism that, in the end, scholars can find surprisingly little to compare.[64] Two major studies on John's Gospel in its relation to Judaism will illustrate this stalemate in Johannine studies.

It is unfortunately reflected first of all in the important studies of the Gospel of John by C. H. Dodd.[65] When Dodd disclaims firsthand knowledge of Jewish documents and acknowledges, in place of this, his debt to Moore, Strack and Billerbeck, Abrahams and Loewe,[66] it becomes obvious that he intends to work exclusively with a secondhand treatment of rabbinic writings — that is, with classical expressions of standard views of Judaism. It is no surprise, therefore, that Dodd finds relatively little in Judaism of real value for understanding the Fourth Gospel. In his chapter on rabbinic parallels he adopts the standard procedure of comparing basic motifs from Judaism with the same doctrines in John (Torah, messiah, and the name of God).[67] Other parallels come from Dodd's treatment of the Jew Philo;[68] but since Philo offers an example of what is generally known as "Hellenistic Judaism," points of comparison relate more to Greek than to Jewish thought.[69] The presence of Hellenistic thought and motifs in this Gospel is not to be contested: what we witness in Johannine scholarship, and in Dodd in particular, however, is a general inability to relate *Judaism* to this Gospel in a convincing way. Certainly this is yet another unfor-

---

63. For discussion and reaction to this approach, cf. H. M. Teeple, "Qumran and the Origin of the Fourth Gospel," 1960, 6-25. Unfortunately Teeple himself fell victim to a rather shallow approach to the Gospel. While looking no more deeply into the structure of Johannine thought than to a number of its separate and individual motifs, Teeple finally concludes that John is not a Jewish Gospel at all.

64. Particular impetus for the tendency can be traced to Martyn's (1968) treatment of historical questions in John. Martyn failed to consider whether the intense controversy in the Gospel could be related to any historical context within Judaism; the influence of his work has been incalculable.

65. C. H. Dodd, *The Interpretation of the Fourth Gospel*, 1953.

66. Dodd, 1953, 75.

67. Dodd, 1953, 75ff.

68. Dodd, 1953, 54-73.

69. Dodd, 1953, 54, 170-78, 263-85.

tunate symptom of the dominance of standard nationalistic views of Judaism in Gospel studies. In fairness to this particular scholar, however, Dodd was merely working with the tools scholars of Judaism have given him, and this is undoubtedly where the breakdown in the scholarly process has occurred.

A similar failure to root the Gospel in Judaism is evident in the works of C. K. Barrett, who paradoxically sets out with the specific intention to relate the Gospel to its Jewish backgrounds.[70] Barrett finds little more of real value for a comparative analysis than does Dodd. His approach provides another instance of the practice of picking up fragments of Jewish belief and presenting a short anthology for comparison (messianic terminology, legal questions, etc.).[71] This shortcoming was somewhat remedied in his later work, where he devotes a chapter to historical developments in Judaism;[72] but even here his discussion tends to center on Jewish and Christian relations rather than on Jewish theology. Furthermore, Barrett draws the rather speculative conclusion (in spite of overwhelming evidence for the lengthy continuing existence and production of these works in Judaism and Christianity alike) that "apocalyptic" was fading away in this period.[73] Barrett does take more interest in the significance of the apocalyptic literature than Dodd, but he finds no substantial comparisons here (other than certain trends in thought that he summarizes in one paragraph).[74] In a somewhat different context he announces that "as a whole Christianity became a non-Jewish organization"[75] — which actually serves quite well as a summary of what this scholar finds Jewish about John's Gospel. Barrett is satisfied to conclude that the milieu of John's community was largely gnostic (actually a mixture of gnosticism and Judaism that occurred within Christianity).[76] Hence the absence of traditional Jewish content leads him (not unlike Bultmann) to a significant dependency on gnostic thought. It is little wonder that the introductory section of his lengthy commentary on John's Gospel contains little more than two pages on the "Jewish background."[77]

The significance of these two important examples (among the many more that could have been cited from Synoptic and Johannine studies) is that they are *deliberate* attempts to deal with Jewish backgrounds — not all com-

70. Cf. C. K. Barrett, *The Gospel according to St. John*, 1955, 25-28; C. K. Barrett, *The Gospel of John and Judaism*, 1975, 40-76. Only the second work is cognizant of Dodd's 1953 monograph.
71. Cf. Barrett, 1955, 26-27.
72. Barrett, 1975, 40-58.
73. Barrett, 1975, 58.
74. Cf. Barrett, 1955, 26.
75. Barrett, 1975, 41.
76. Barrett, 1975, 55, 64-65.
77. Cf. Barrett, 1955, 25-28.

mentaries on the Fourth Gospel adopt such an explicit approach.[78] But if these more or less specialized studies betray a fragmenting view based on traditional treatments of Judaism (even if they fail to draw significant parallels from this comparison!), any deficient conclusions that result are not likely to be challenged by less specialized treatments, but are bound instead to be widely disseminated. Thus we find that even recent attempts to relate John's Gospel to Qumran have proven to be no more productive in this respect than the attempts of Dodd and Barrett.[79] Here the inadequacy of the conventional view of Judaism has made it unproductive and even costly to studies that attempt to relate Judaism to Johannine Christianity, for this view has neither invited significant comparison with the Fourth Gospel nor provided the tools for that task. One must seriously consider whether outdated views of Judaism are adequate for exegetical studies, let alone for the type of historical constructions so often undertaken by New Testament scholars interested in clarification and interpretation.

Pauline Studies

Pauline studies have not been exempt from the influence of this dominant trend in Jewish research. Recent studies either construct a fundamental divergence between Paul and Judaism (Sanders) or retreat into general comparisons based on eschatological themes (Beker). In the same important volume that Sanders explicates his highly nationalistic view of Judaism (discussed above), he also considers Paul's relationship to this view of Judaism. A distinct contrast results. Whereas Judaism's "pattern of religion" can be characterized as a "covenantal nomism," Paul's pattern of religion departs considerably from this — Sanders refers to it as "participationist eschatology."[80] This means, among other things, that Paul has an entirely different understanding of the "entry requirements" into the people of God than the nationalistic thought of Judaism: for Paul, one must be a Christian (i.e., mystically be "in Christ") to be saved.[81] His is an exclusive faith, based not on adherence to the law, but to Christ.[82] The conclusion to be drawn from this contrast between the "essence" of Paul and that of Judaism is that Paul departs from the nationalistic pattern of Judaism entirely: "*Paul in fact explicitly denies that the*

78. Notably that of Bultmann (*The Gospel of John*, 1971); Bultmann does not even discuss the question, but does offer a section on the relationship to gnosticism.

79. Barrett himself (1975, 56) largely dismisses the comparison as invalid.

80. E. P. Sanders, *Paul and Palestinian Judaism*, 1977, 549.

81. E. P. Sanders, 1977, 474-85.

82. E. P. Sanders, 1977, 474-82.

Jewish covenant can be effective for salvation, thus consciously denying the basis of Judaism. . . . In short, *this is what Paul finds wrong in Judaism: it is not Christianity.*"[83] Although Sanders does not settle the question of the origins of Paul's pattern of religion, it is clear that it cannot be understood according to Jewish belief. The contrast, inherent in Sanders's view, between the nationalistic soteriology in the Jewish world and Paul's mystical and individual soteriology prohibits this. Paul must have come to adopt this belief through his own experience of salvation, although the apostle nowhere attempts to justify this change of mind or the rejection of Jewish forms of covenantal nomism that it entailed. Rather, Paul's attitude is dogmatic: "since salvation is only in Christ, therefore all other ways toward salvation are wrong."[84] Any prospect of relating Paul to Judaism is accordingly abandoned in resignation to the influence Christ exercised over Paul's theology. Thus Sanders's view of Paul is strongly and consistently (if also indirectly and somewhat inversely) influenced by his nationalistic view of Judaism, and (vaguely reminiscent of treatments of Jesus mentioned above) the conclusion is again reached that Paul cannot be understood in a Jewish way.

J. Christiaan Beker's comparison between Paul and Judaism is entirely different, but it is a useful example of another direction in comparative analysis.[85] His work is based primarily on his views of "apocalyptic" forms of Judaism, fundamental to which is an intense eschatological expectation. As noted above, the eschatological approach is tolerant of conventional nationalistic views of Judaism. Beker, however, represents something of a move away from this association. He is even willing to allow that apocalyptic thought originated in remnant circles.[86] However, he places his major emphasis on the "symbolic structure" shared by Paul and the worldview of apocalyptic Judaism — that is, on the sociological aspects of the relationship — central to which was belief in the "imminent cosmic triumph of God," including the motifs of vindication, universalism, dualism, and imminence.[87] The "coherent centre" of Paul's thought is expressed in 1 Corinthians 15, which encapsulates the "apocalyptic world view" of Paul. Expressions of Pauline theology that appear to develop in other directions, notably those found in Galatians and Romans, are to be understood as "contingent" expressions of the gospel, and do not point to the

83. E. P. Sanders, 1977, 551-52; cf. 548-52, emphasis in original.

84. E. P. Sanders, 1977, 482.

85. Cf. J. C. Beker, *Paul the Apostle*, 1980; for the more popular and concise treatment, cf. J. C. Beker, *Paul's Apocalyptic Gospel*, 1982.

86. Cf. Beker, 1982, 22-23, 58.

87. Beker, 1980, 16-18, 135-52, 335-38, 362-67, passim; Beker, 1982, 30ff. Beker is followed in this characterization by R. P. Carlson, *Baptism and Apocalyptic in Paul*, 1984, passim. Beker also refers to this as "apocalyptic religious language" (1982, 57).

main aspects of Paul's thought, as has traditionally been assumed.[88] Beker draws some novel and interesting relationships between Paul and what he calls apocalyptic Judaism (notably the view that Paul's christological theology originated in the idea of the defeat of "apocalyptic powers"). It is unfortunate, however, that Beker does not challenge standard ideas about Judaism in election theology. This might have developed out of his consideration of "symbolic structures" and other implications of the linguistic compatibility of Paul and "apocalyptic." But the eschatological view of things dominates completely in Beker's work, and eventually the idea of election is swallowed up in an emphasis on universalism, which he discerns through a kind of existential christological reflection: "The first aspect of Paul's universalistic motif . . . is the rejection of any clitism, because the cross as God's universal indictment of humankind eliminates such a notion."[89] Although Beker's work, which is on the whole more sensitive to sociological factors, and even avoids certain pitfalls of previous studies of Paul, shows signs that advances in this area are possible and perhaps even imminent, it would nevertheless still seem that conventional views of Judaism prohibit any understanding of Paul that still recognizes his essential debt to Judaism.

The Book of Revelation

Preoccupation with eschatology in New Testament scholarship has thus in large part been occasioned by the tendency to view Judaism in a certain way (namely, as *nationalistic Judaism, conventionally understood*). Partly as a result of this importance granted to eschatology as an area of comparison with the New Testament, this concern has tended in turn to dominate in discussions of Judaism, resulting in a circularity that tends toward mutual confirmation and precludes objective analysis of either subject.

When one comes to the book of Revelation, the forces at work in biblical and Jewish scholarship seem to build to a climax — which is sadly inappropriate for the last book of the Christian Bible. The history of interpretation of Revelation has been misinformed by the same prejudices seen to be at work so far — namely, the dominance of eschatological priorities, on the one hand, and a tragic lack of understanding of the kinds of issues important to Judaism, on the other. The failure to successfully interpret Revelation is a well-known theme to students of the book. None of the four main interpretive approaches to the book, the so-called *futurist, historicist, idealist,* or *preterist* approaches, has pro-

88. Beker, 1980, 11-18, 23-108, and passim.
89. Beker, 1982, 36; cf. 335-37.

duced a satisfactory and consistent understanding of the Apocalypse. Even the approach that shows the most sensitivity to historical and contextual questions, namely, the *preterist* approach, has failed for its own reason — it has not known Judaism — and has correspondingly fallen back on philosophical abstracts. Elisabeth Schüssler Fiorenza has pointed to this failure:

> Although most exegetes have replaced the classical approaches to the inter-pretation of Rev. with the historical-critical approach, they still maintain a combination of the preterist or futurist interpretation, or insist that Rev. re-veals the course of salvation history or timeless historical principles.
>
> Contemporary scholars no longer dream of finding predictions for his-tory or for the future within Rev. They correctly reject, therefore, those inter-pretations maintaining that Rev. treats the history of the Church, or the world, and of the final times. However, they still retain . . . the basic approach and concern of these interpretations insofar as they attempt to show that his-tory is the main theme of Rev. and try to establish it as revelation for our time.[90]

Schüssler Fiorenza's insightful critique of past interpretation is, however, not followed up by a reevaluation of the comparative literature.

But her approach is nevertheless representative of a new direction in the comparative study of Revelation and is worthy of further comment. When she implies, in the above quote, that there is no history in Revelation, she not only confronts attempts to discern *later church history* from the prophecy but also disparages attempts to deal with historical thinking in the book altogether. This posture is at least partly motivated by her understanding of the place of history in books like *1 Enoch*. As a result of the dominating eschatological view she has of these writings, she opts for a rather unique brand of eschatological interpre-tation for Revelation as well, and for that reason makes few real advances on the interpretation of this book. Since in works like the Apocalypse of Weeks "the present and future are understood and deduced from the past"[91] (a summary with which we would not totally disagree), she opts for a kind of contempo-rary-eschatological approach for Revelation that understands it as a "prophecy for the present [i.e., for the community of the author] which receives its justifi-cation from the future, that is, from the coming of Christ (22:20)."[92] Accord-ingly Revelation concerns the present sufferings of the Christian community to whom it was written, but looks forward to their eventual salvation and the judgment of the oppressive Roman system that shall be secured by the coming

90. E. Schüssler Fiorenza, *The Book of Revelation*, 1985, 37.
91. Schüssler Fiorenza, 1985, 40.
92. Schüssler Fiorenza, 1985, 42.

of Christ, and addresses the community with that future event in mind. Unfortunately this scholar fails to discern the chronological contradiction in her own comparison, since if Revelation actually follows the Apocalypse of Weeks in its typological philosophy of history, it would require that Revelation throw light on the *present* by reflecting on Israel's *past,* just like the Apocalypse of Weeks, not that it throw light on the *present* by reflecting on the *future.* In other words, there has been a radical shift of the time line in Schüssler Fiorenza's treatment: while Revelation moves from *present to future* (or, should we say, from the future to the present), the time line for the Apocalypse of Weeks moves *from past to present.* This actually involves a *reversal* of the interpretive approach of the Apocalypse of Weeks, since the lesson is taken from the past in that book and from the future in Revelation. Except for this shortcoming, therefore, Schüssler Fiorenza has at least started to ask appropriate questions of the comparative literature, and has simultaneously pointed out infelicities in the interpretation of Revelation that practically demand a fresh approach.

While there is hardly space here to suggest such an approach, the conclusions reached in this book about the nature and function of the "apocalyptic writings" are obviously going to throw open again a whole series of comparative questions bearing on the interpretation of what for Christians has become the Apocalypse *par excellence:*

1. What is the *dominant purpose* of Revelation? Is it to offer an eschatological framework for the future? While there is little questioning that eschatology is featured in the book, to what point is the emphasis on fulfilled eschatology and to what point is it on the (real) future? And if there is a genuine kind of future, or prophetic eschatology, is this future considered distant, or near and pending? The comparative writings do contain both kinds of eschatology, one of fulfillment pertaining to significant events presently being experienced, as well as "true" future predictions (although often in the latter the future grows out of the present and is considered near to fulfillment). But perhaps more significant from the comparative literature is that, on a purely formal level, many of the future-sounding references — specifically, the "messianic travail" passages — relate more to the present than the future and are only superficially eschatological, or merely assume an eschatological *style* due to their "pseudepigraphic" literary setting, and this applies even to events that have happened (from the point of view of the real author) some distance in the past. What, then, are the implications of the fact that, even if the book of Revelation does not assume an exactly identical pseudepigraphic perspective (a still hotly debated question), the author nevertheless exhibits a similar *revelatory style* in his presentation? If so, does he do so in order to reveal the past or the present as well as the future (thus contradicting an emphasis on the future usually found in interpretations of the book)? In regard to the dominant purpose of the book

as well, it has long been recognized that it possesses social functions that are intrinsic to its purpose, most often some form of consolation (usually encouragement in the face of persecution), but one might consider what role such functions as warning, definition, identification, and signification might have played as well.

2. What *theological motifs possess dominating significance?* In the comparative literature it was demonstrated how soteriological dualism exercised a dominating influence on beliefs, motifs, and forms in ways that made this pattern of thought prevalent throughout the whole literature of a movement. Covenantal thought of a dualistic variety was also clearly influential on ideas and forms. The forms related to those dualisms — not to mention many individual motifs — recur with frequency in Revelation: historical rehearsals, revelations of the cosmos, blessings and woes, and judgment visions and oracles, to name a few. If a formal analysis of Revelation stands to gain more from a comparison with the literature of Second Temple Judaism than from other forms, or even if it more directly evokes the forms of the Hebrew Scriptures (and it is questionable what other choices are available), then to what extent the functional implications of these parallels (as we have understood them) come into play in Revelation must be treated as a serious question. A study of this book from a formal perspective, in other words, may seriously alter an appreciation for and interpretation of its message.

3. *What milieu should be sought for the book?* While centuries of Christian interpretation have found the significance of Revelation in its systematic judgment of the nations, largely in deference to a nationalistic understanding of Judaism, on the one hand, or a universalistic Christian theology, on the other, it must be asked whether the Jewish context of Revelation has ever been allowed a serious voice in interpretation. This would require that the Christian Apocalypse be read in light of themes and presuppositions of paramount significance to Jews living in the first century and, it should be added, to Christians who still considered themselves as belonging in some way to that society. The "re-Judaizing" of the interpretation of Revelation is occurring in scholarship, although with inconsistent results, but this process has never escaped centuries of interpretative history that have made Revelation into an exclusively "Christian" book. This concern applies with particular urgency to the existence of a central, if not the central, theme of Revelation — namely, the strong critique of Israel or Jerusalem that exists in it. Revelation might be interpreted as a Jerusalem prophecy, and glimpses of attempts to do this in the past have emerged, and perhaps would have prevailed, had it not been for the overpowering temptation to revert back to more utilitarian interpretations that rescue the book from first-century concerns in favor of contemporary application. The Vision of the Woman (ch. 12) and the New Jerusalem (ch. 21) evoke notions of the righteous

remnant in Jerusalem, and a score of terms and expressions relate back to exilic themes from the prophets — a recurring motif in the comparative writings — rather than to universalistic warnings of judgment. The judgment-of-Israel thematic can accordingly be found throughout the book, even in places where traditional lines of interpretation have found only oracles of judgment against the nations — although these also characteristically occur. If Jews and Jewish Christians alike were concerned about the eventual fate of the city that carried for them so much significance, and about the fulfillment of prophecy surrounding this city (cf., e.g., Isa. 65:17-25), it would make complete sense that an early Christian prophecy should be dedicated to this and related concerns. It almost goes without saying that these same questions could, and should, be applied to other eschatological passages in the New Testament, not least to the so-called Synoptic Apocalypse in Mark 13 and parallels.

A PAUSE FOR MISGIVINGS

Our startling conclusion is that conventional views of Judaism pose insurmountable difficulties for the comparative study of Judaism and the New Testament. In order to reduce these difficulties somewhat, comparative studies in the past have required that *the period between Jesus and the New Testament was a time of significant "de-Judaizing" or "Christianization" of doctrines previously held in a much different form in Judaism.* But if the New Testament faith is so radically different from this nationalistic Judaism (a fact we do not contest), this could imply, not that the early church (or in part Jesus himself)[93] in important points reformulated Judaism, but *alternatively,* that conventional nationalistic understandings of Judaism do *not* after all provide an adequate or complete basis for comparison. It may be, in that case, that *another kind of Judaism altogether* must be called upon if fruitful comparative analysis is to proceed into the future.

Similar concerns were expressed by Margaret Barker. Noting the sheer impossibility of Jesus creating his own entirely new symbolic context (what she calls a "mythology"), Barker comments:

93. The view that Jesus broke away from John and his message was a once-popular way of explaining the divergency. Cf. E. Käsemann, "The Beginnings of Christian Theology," 1969, 17-68, 40; E. Käsemann, "On the Topic of Primitive Christian Apocalyptic," 1969a, 99-133, 99; M. Goguel, *Jesus and the Origins of Christianity,* 1960, 1:260-79; W. G. Kümmel, *Promise and Fulfillment,* 1957, 88ff.; Dahl, 1963, 147-48; J. W. Bowman, *The Intention of Jesus,* 1945, 171-72, 176-77; E. J. Goodspeed, *A Life of Jesus,* 1950, 45-46, 48; E. P. Sanders, 1985, 92-93. These views are supported by Jeremias (1949, 190-94) and E. Stauffer (*Jesus and His Story,* 1960, 68-69).

It is unlikely that the events of the life and death of Jesus could have found expression at a very early date only in terms of a mythology alien to the setting in which the events occurred. Mythology and interpretation cannot arise simultaneously. Unless the pre-Easter and post-Easter followers of Jesus were two completely different sets of people, it should be possible to establish, within broad limits, the type of people who made the first interpretation of the death and resurrection. . . . The gospel sources make it abundantly clear what sort of people came to hear Jesus, and yet we still spend a great deal of time and energy upon the pursuit of parallels in the thinking of just that group by whom Jesus is known to have been rejected. . . . We have to find something appropriate for a group of Galileans, relevant to their needs and aspirations, but sufficiently coherent (and even recognizable) to draw the hostility of Jerusalem Judaism, as a threat to the Law. . . . Is it possible that amongst all those who were attempting to make sense of what they had seen there was none who operated within the same thought scheme as Jesus himself? Jesus and his first followers *must* have operated within the same thought-scheme, if the ministry was seen as a revelation and not as an irrelevance. . . .[94]

While the tendency to blame the gulf between Jesus and Judaism on Christian reformulation has dominated scholarship, perhaps the source of the problem lies with the choice of the type of Judaism employed for this comparison. In light of the analysis of the movement of dissent and remnant groups in this book, there can now be found suitable explanations *from Judaism* for many basic attitudes found in the New Testament — including that Israel, God's chosen people, is in danger of judgment and in this regard has been placed on a par with Gentiles; that the historical covenants are not unqualifiedly valid for all who consider themselves participants in them; that the normal rites of maintaining the covenant have become ineffective; that an individual soteriology *apart from* previous divine acts of deliverance on behalf of Israel has now become necessary. A reevaluation of these kinds of attitudes, previously seen to be inexplicable from the standpoint of the Jewish world, is demanded by the recent critique of "normative Judaism" and especially by the findings of this book.

94. M. Barker, *The Older Testament*, 1987, 4-5.

General Bibliography

Aalon, S.

[1967]   "St Luke's Gospel and the Last Chapters of I Enoch." *NTS* 13 (1967): 1-13.

Ackroyd, P. R.

[1970]   *Israel under Babylon and Persia.* New Clarendon Bible, Old Testament 4. Oxford: Oxford University Press, 1970.

Albright, W. F.

[1947]   *From the Stone Age to Christianity: Monotheism and the Historical Process.* 4th ed. Garden City: Doubleday, 1947.

Albright, W. F., and C. S. Mann

[1969]   "Qumran and the Essenes: Geography, Chronology, and Identification of the Sect." In *The Scrolls and Christianity,* edited by M. Black, 11-25. SPCK Theological Collections 11. London: SPCK, 1969.

Allegro, J. M.

[1964]   *The Dead Sea Scrolls: A Reappraisal.* 2nd ed. Harmondsworth: Penguin, 1964.

Allison, D. C.

[1985]   *The End of the Ages Has Come: An Early Interpretation of the Passion and Resurrection of Jesus.* Edinburgh: Clark, 1985.

Anderson, A. A.

[1962]   "The Use of 'Ruaḥ' in 1QS, 1QH and 1QM." *JJS* 7 (1962): 293-303.

Asheri, M.

[1980]   *Living Jewish: The Lore and Law of the Practicing Jew.* 2nd ed. New York: Dodd, Mead, 1980.

Aune, D. E.

[1993]   "Charismatic Exegesis in Early Judaism and Early Christianity." In *The Pseud-*

epigrapha and Early Biblical Interpretation, edited by J. H. Charlesworth and
C. A. Evans, 126-50. JSP(SS) 14. Studies in Scripture in Early Judaism and
Christianity 2. Sheffield: JSOT, 1993.

Baeck, L.

[1947]   *The Pharisees and Other Essays.* ET, New York: Schocken, 1947.

Bailey, L. R.

[1989]   *Noah: The Person and the Story in History and Tradition.* Columbia: University
of South Carolina Press, 1989.

Baltzer, K.

[1971]   *The Covenant Formulary in Old Testament, Jewish, and Early Christian Writings.* Translated by D. E. Green. Philadelphia: Fortress, 1971.

Bampfylde, G.

[1984]   "The Similitudes of Enoch: Historical Allusions." *JSJ* 15 (1984): 9-31.

Barker, M.

[1978]   "Slippery Words III. Apocalyptic." *ExT* 89 (1978): 324-29.

[1987]   *The Older Testament: The Survival of Themes from the Ancient Royal Cult in
Sectarian Judaism and Early Christianity.* London: SPCK, 1987.

[1989]   "The Temple Measurements and the Solar Calendar." In *Temple Scroll Studies:
Papers Presented at the International Symposium on the Temple Scroll, Manchester, December 1987,* edited by G. J. Brooke, 63-66. JSP(SS) 7. Sheffield: JSOT,
1989.

[1992]   *The Great Angel: A Study of Israel's Second God.* London: SPCK, 1992.

Baron, S. W.

[1952]   *A Social and Religious History of the Jews.* 2nd ed. 2 vols. New York: Columbia
University Press, 1952.

Barr, J.

[1975]   "Apocalyptic in Recent Scholarly Study." *BJRL* 58 (1975): 9-35.

Barrera, J. T.

[1994]   "The Authoritative Functions of Scriptural Works at Qumran." In *The Community of the Renewed Covenant: The Notre Dame Symposium on the Dead Sea
Scrolls,* edited by E. Elrich and J. VanderKam, 95-110. Christianity and Judaism
in Antiquity 10. Notre Dame: University of Notre Dame Press, 1994.

Barrera, J. T., and L. V. Montaner

[1992]   eds. *The Madrid Qumran Congress: Proceedings of the International Congress on
the Dead Sea Scrolls, Madrid 18-21 March, 1991.* 2 vols. Leiden: Brill, 1992.

Barrett, C. K.

[1955]   *The Gospel according to St. John: An Introduction with Commentary and Notes
on the Greek Text.* London: SPCK, 1955.

[1975]   *The Gospel of John and Judaism.* Translated by D. M. Smith. London: SPCK,
1975.

General Bibliography

Barth, M.
[1983]   *The People of God.* JSNT(SS) 5. Sheffield: JSOT, 1983.

Bartlett, J. R.
[1973]   *The First and Second Books of the Maccabees.* Cambridge: Cambridge University Press, 1973.

Basser, H.
[1985]   "The Development of the Pharisaic Idea of Law as a Sacred Cosmos." *JSJ* 16 (1985): 104-16.

Bauckham, R.
[1990]   "Early Jewish Visions of Hell." *JTS* 41 (1990): 355-85.
[1993]   "Resurrection as Giving Back the Dead: A Traditional Image of Resurrection in the Pseudepigrapha and the Apocalypse of John." In *The Pseudepigrapha and Early Biblical Interpretation,* edited by J. H. Charlesworth and C. A. Evans, 269-91. JSP(SS) 14. Studies in Scripture in Early Judaism and Christianity 2. Sheffield: JSOT, 1993.

Baumgarten, J. M.
[1982]   "Some Problems of the Jubilees Calendar in Current Research." *VT* 32 (1982): 485-89.
[1986]   "4Q503 (Daily Prayers) and the Lunar Calendar." *RQ* 3 (1986): 399-407.
[1987]   "The Laws of 'Orlah and First Fruits in the Light of Jubilees, the Qumran Writings, and Targum Ps. Jonathan." *JJS* 38 (1987): 195-202.
[1987a]   "The Calendars of the Book of Jubilees and the Temple Scroll." *VT* 37 (1987): 71-77.
[1991]   "Some Remarks on the Qumran Law and the Identification of the Community." In *Qumran Cave Four and MMT: Special Report,* edited by Z. J. Kapera, 115-17. Krakow: Enigma, 1991.
[1992]   "The Purification Rituals in *DJD* 7." In *The Dead Sea Scrolls: Forty Years of Research,* edited by D. Dimant and U. Rappaport, 199-209. Studies on the Texts of the Desert of Judah 10. Leiden: Brill, 1992.

Beale, G. K.
[1983]   "The Problem of the Man from the Sea in IV Ezra 13 and Its Relation to the Messianic Concept in John's Apocalypse." *NovT* 25 (1983): 182-88.

Beasley-Murray, G. R.
[1946]   "The Two Messiahs in the Testaments of the Twelve Patriarchs." *JTS* 47 (1946): 1-12.

Becker, J.
[1964]   *Das Heil Gottes. Heils- und Sündenbegriffe in den Qumrantexten und im Neuen Testament.* SUNT 3. Göttingen: Vandenhoeck & Ruprecht, 1964.

Beckwith, R. T.
[1980]   "The Significance of the Calendar for Interpreting Essene Chronology and Eschatology." *RQ* 10 (1980): 167-202.

[1981]   "The Earliest Enoch Literature and Its Calendar: Marks of Their Origin, Date and Motivation." *RQ* 10 (1981): 365-403.

[1981a]   "Daniel 9 and the Date of Messiah's Coming in Essene, Hellenistic, Pharisaic, Zealot and Early Christian Computation." *RQ* 10 (1981): 521-42.

[1982]   "The Pre-History and Relationships of the Pharisees, Sadducees and Essenes: A Tentative Reconstruction." *RQ* 11 (1982): 3-46.

Beker, J. C.

[1980]   *Paul the Apostle: The Triumph of God in Life and Thought.* Edinburgh: Clark, 1980.

[1982]   *Paul's Apocalyptic Gospel: The Coming Triumph of God.* Philadelphia: Fortress, 1982.

Bickermann, E.

[1979]   *The God of the Maccabees: Studies on the Meaning and Origin of the Maccabean Revolt.* Translated by H. R. Moering. Leiden: Brill, 1979.

Black, M.

[1961]   *The Scrolls and Christian Origins: Studies in the Jewish Background of the New Testament.* Edinburgh and London: Thomas Nelson and Sons, 1961.

[1969]   ed. *The Scrolls and Christianity.* SPCK Theological Collections 11. London: SPCK, 1969.

[1970]   ed. *"Apocalypsis Henochi Graece."* Edited by A.-M. Denis and M. de Jonge. *PVTG*, 3:19-44. Leiden: Brill, 1970.

[1976]   "The 'Parables' of Enoch (1 En 37–71) and the 'Son of Man.'" *ExT* 88 (1976): 5-8.

[1985]   *The Book of Enoch* or *I Enoch: A New English Edition with Commentary and Textual Notes.* Leiden: Brill, 1985.

[1992]   "The Messianism of the Parables of Enoch: Their Date and Contribution to Christological Origins." In *The Messiah: Developments in Earliest Judaism and Christianity,* edited by J. H. Charlesworth, 145-68. Minneapolis: Fortress, 1992.

Blenkinsopp, J.

[1988]   "Interpretation and the Tendency to Sectarianism: An Aspect of Second Temple History." In *Jewish and Christian Self-Definition,* vol. 2, *Aspects of Judaism in the Graeco-Roman Period,* edited by E. P. Sanders, 1-26. Philadelphia: Fortress, 1988.

[1990]   "A Jewish Sect of the Persian Period." *CBQ* 52 (1990): 5-20.

Blidstein, G. J.

[1991]   "The Import of Early Rabbinic Writings for an Understanding of Judaism in the Hellenistic-Roman Period." In *Jewish Civilization in the Hellenistic-Roman Period,* edited by S. Talmon, 64-72. JSOT(SS) 10. Sheffield: Sheffield Academic, 1991.

Bloch, J.

[1952]   *On the Apocalyptic in Judaism.* JQRNSMS 2. Philadelphia: Dropsie College for Hebrew and Cognate Learning, 1952.

Bogaert, P.

[1969] *Apocalypse de Baruch. Introduction, traduction du syriaque et commentaire.* 2 vols. Paris: Cerf, 1969.

Bonsirven, J.

[1964] *Palestinian Judaism in the Time of Jesus Christ.* Translated by W. Wolf. New York: Holt, Rinehart and Winston, 1964.

Bornkamm, G.

[1973] *Jesus of Nazareth.* Translated by I. McLuskey, F. McLuskey, and J. M. Robinson. Rev. ed. London: Hodder and Stoughton, 1973.

Borsch, F. H.

[1967] *The Son of Man in Myth and History.* Philadelphia: Westminster; London: SCM, 1967.

[1992] "Further Reflections on 'the Son of Man': The Origins and Development of the Title." In *The Messiah: Developments in Earliest Judaism and Christianity,* edited by J. H. Charlesworth, 130-44. Minneapolis: Fortress, 1992.

Bousset, D. W.

[1926] *Die Religion des Judentums im Späthellenistischen Zeitalter.* 3rd ed. Edited by H. Gressmann. Handbuch zum Neuen Testament 21. Tübingen: Mohr, 1926.

Bowman, J. W.

[1945] *The Intention of Jesus.* London: SCM, 1945.

Brandon, S. G. F.

[1951] *The Fall of Jerusalem and the Christian Church.* London: SPCK, 1951.

[1958] "The Myth and Ritual Position Critically Considered." In *Myth, Ritual, and Kingship: Essays on the Theory and Practice of Kingship in the Ancient Near East and in Israel,* edited by S. H. Hooke, 261-91. Oxford: Clarendon Press, 1958.

[1967] *Jesus and the Zealots: A Study of the Political Factor in Primitive Christianity.* Manchester: Manchester University Press, 1967.

Breech, J. E.

[1973] "These Fragments I Have Shored against My Ruins: The Form and Function of 4 Ezra." *JBL* 93 (1973): 267-74.

Brock, S.

[1990] "The Two Ways and the Palestinian Targum." In *A Tribute to Geza Vermes: Essays on Jewish and Christian Literature and History,* edited by P. R. Davies and R. T. White, 139-52. JSOT(SS) 100. Sheffield: Sheffield Academic, 1990.

Brooke, G. J.

[1981] "Qumran Pesher: Towards the Redefinition of a Genre." *RQ* 10 (1981): 483-503.

Brooks, S. H.

[1987] *Matthew's Community: The Evidence of His Special Sayings Material.* JSNT(SS) 16. Sheffield: JSOT, 1987.

Brown, R. E.

[1969]   "The Teacher of Righteousness and the Messiah(s)." In *The Scrolls and Christianity*, edited by M. Black, 37-44. SPCK Theological Collections 11. London: SPCK, 1969.

Brownlee, W. H.

[1964]   *The Meaning of the Qumran Scrolls for the Bible, with Special Attention to the Book of Isaiah*. New York: Oxford University Press, 1964.

[1979]   *The Midrash Pesher of Habakkuk*. SBLMS 24. Missoula: Scholars, 1979.

Bruce, F. F.

[1956]   *Second Thoughts on the Dead Sea Scrolls*. London: Paternoster Press, 1956.

[1960]   *Biblical Exegesis in the Qumran Texts*. London: Tyndale, 1960.

[1969]   "Recent Contributions to the Understanding of Hebrews." *ExT* 80 (1969): 260-64.

Buehler, W. W.

[1974]   *The Pre-Herodian Civil War and Social Debate: Jewish Society in the Period 76-40 B.C. and the Social Factors Contributing to the Rise of the Pharisees and the Sadducees*. Theologische Dissertationen 11. Basel: Friedrich Reinhardt Kommissionsverlag, 1974.

Bultmann, R.

[1935]   *Jesus and the Word*. Translated by L. P. Smith and E. Huntress. New York: Charles Scribner's Sons, 1935.

[1941]   "Die Frage nach der Echtheit von Mt. 16,17-19." *Theologische Blätter* 20 (1941): 265-79.

[1952]   *Theology of the New Testament*. Vol. 1. Translated by K. Grobel. London: SCM, 1952.

[1956]   *Primitive Christianity in Its Contemporary Setting*. Translated by R. H. Fuller. [*Das Urchristentum im Rahmen der antiken Religionen*.] Edinburgh: Clark, 1956.

[1971]   *The Gospel of John: A Commentary*. Translated by G. R. Beasley-Murray. [*Das Evangelium des Johannes*, 1964; rev. with additions, 1966.] Oxford: Basil Blackwell, 1971.

Burkitt, F. C.

[1914]   *Jewish and Christian Apocalypses*. London: Oxford University Press, 1914.

Burrows, M.

[1956]   *The Dead Sea Scrolls*. London: Secker & Warburg, 1956.

[1958]   *More Light on the Dead Sea Scrolls*. London: Secker & Warburg, 1958.

Caird, G. B.

[1965]   *Jesus and the Jewish Nation*. London: Athlone Press, 1965.

[1980]   *The Language and Imagery of the Bible*. Philadephia: Westminster, 1980.

Callaway, P. R.

[1990]   "Qumran Origins: From the *Doresh* to the *Moreh*." *RQ* 14 (1990): 637-50.

Campbell, J. C.
[1950]   "God's People and the Remnant." *SJT* 3 (1950): 78-85.

Caragounis, C. C.
[1986]   *The Son of Man: Vision and Interpretation.* WUNT 38. Tübingen: Mohr, 1986.

Carlson, R. P.
[1984]   *Baptism and Apocalyptic in Paul.* [Ph.D. diss., Union Theological Seminary, 1983.] Ann Arbor: University Microfilms International, 1984.

Carmignac, J.
[1969]   "La notion d'eschatologie dans la bible et à Qumran." *RQ* 7 (1969): 17-31.
[1979]   "Qu'est-ce que l'Apocalyptique? Son emploi à Qumrân." *RQ* 10 (1979): 3-33.

Casey, M.
[1976]   "The Corporate Interpretation of 'One Like a Son of Man' (Dan. VII 13) at the Time of Jesus." *NovT* 18 (1976): 167-80.
[1976a]   "The Use of the Term 'Son of Man' in the Similitudes of Enoch." *JSJ* 12 (1976): 11-29.
[1979]   *The Son of Man: The Interpretation and Influence of Daniel 7.* London: SPCK, 1979.

Charles, R. H.
[1895]   *maṣḥafa kufālē* [Eth.] or *The Ethiopic Version of the Hebrew Book of Jubilees Otherwise Known Among the Greeks as* Η ΛΕΠΤΗ ΓΕΝΕΣΙΣ. *Edited from four manuscripts.* Anecdota Oxoniensia 8. Oxford: Clarendon, 1895.
[1896]   *The Apocalypse of Baruch translated from the Syriac.* London: Adam and Charles Black, 1896.
[1902]   *The Book of Jubilees or Little Genesis, Translated from the Editor's Ethiopic Text.* London: Adam and Charles Black; Jerusalem: Makor Publishing, 1902.
[1908]   *The Greek Versions of the Testaments of the Twelve Patriarchs Edited from Nine MSS Together with the Variants of the Armenian and Slavonic Versions and Some Hebrew Fragments.* Oxford: Oxford University Press, 1908.
[1912]   *The Book of Enoch or 1 Enoch.* 2nd ed. Oxford: Clarendon Press; Jerusalem: Makor Press, 1912.
[1913]   *Eschatology: The Doctrine of a Future Life in Israel, Judaism, and Christianity.* 2nd ed. New York: Schocken, 1913.
[1913a]   ed. *Apocrypha and Pseudepigrapha of the Old Testament.* 2 vols. Oxford: Clarendon, 1913.
[1914]   *Religious Development between the Old and the New Testaments.* London: Williams and Norgate, 1914.

Charles, R. H., and W. O. E. Oesterley
[1917]   *The Apocalypse of Baruch.* London: SPCK, 1917.

Charlesworth, J. H.
[1969]   "A Critical Comparison of the Dualism in 1QS III,13–IV,26 and the 'Dualism' Contained in the Fourth Gospel." *NTS* 15 (1969): 389-418.

[1977]   "Jewish Astrology in the Talmud, Pseudepigrapha, the Dead Sea Scrolls, and
           Early Palestinian Synagogues." *HTR* 70 (1977): 183-200.

[1978]   "Rylands Syriac MS. 44 and a New Addition to the Pseudepigrapha: The Trea-
           tise of Shem, Discussed and Translated." *BJRL* 60 (1978): 376-403.

[1983]   ed. *The Old Testament Pseudepigrapha.* Vol. 1, *Apocalyptic Literature and Testa-
           ments.* Vol. 2, *Expansions of the "Old Testament" and Legends, Wisdom and
           Philosophical Literature, Prayers, Psalms, and Odes, Fragments of Lost Judeo-
           Hellenistic Works.* Garden City: Doubleday, 1983, 1985.

[1985]   *The Old Testament Pseudepigrapha and the New Testament: Prolegomena for the
           Study of Christian Origins.* SNTSMS 54. Cambridge: Cambridge University
           Press, 1985.

[1992]   ed. *The Messiah: Developments in Earliest Judaism and Christianity.* Minneapo-
           lis: Fortress, 1992.

[1992a]   ed. *Jesus and the Dead Sea Scrolls.* New York: Doubleday, 1992.

[1992b]   "From Messianology to Christology: Problems and Prospects." In *The Messiah:
           Developments in Earliest Judaism and Christianity,* edited by J. H. Charles-
           worth, 3-35. Minneapolis: Fortress, 1992.

[1992c]   "Jesus as 'Son' and the Righteous Teacher as 'Gardener.'" In *Jesus and the Dead
           Sea Scrolls,* edited by J. H. Charlesworth, 140-75. New York: Doubleday, 1992.

[1993]   "In the Crucible: The Pseudepigrapha as Biblical Interpretation." In *The Pseud-
           epigrapha and Early Biblical Interpretation,* edited by J. H. Charlesworth and
           C. A. Evans, 20-43. JSP(SS) 14. Studies in Scripture in Early Judaism and
           Christianity 2. Sheffield: JSOT, 1993.

Charlesworth, J. H., and C. A. Evans

[1993]   eds. *The Pseudepigrapha and Early Biblical Interpretation.* JSP(SS) 14. Studies
           in Scripture in Early Judaism and Christianity 2. Sheffield: JSOT, 1993,

Coggins, R. J., and M. A. Knibb

[1979]   *The First and Second Books of Esdras.* Cambridge Bible Commentary on the
           New English Bible. Cambridge: Cambridge University Press, 1979.

Cohen, S. J. D.

[1982]   "*Shekhinta ba-Galuta:* A Midrashic Response to Destruction and Persecution."
           JSJ 13 (1982): 147-59.

[1984]   "The Significance of Yavneh: Pharisees, Rabbis, and the End of Jewish Sectari-
           anism." *HUCA* 55 (1984): 27-53.

[1985]   "From *Nabi* to *Mal'ak* to 'Ancient Figure.'" *JJS* 36 (1985): 12-24.

[1986]   "The Political and Social History of the Jews in the Greco-Roman Antiquity:
           The State of the Question." In *Early Judaism and Its Modern Interpreters.* [*SBL
           The Bible and Its Modern Interpreters* 2], edited by R. A. Kraft and G. W. E.
           Nickelsburg. Philadelphia: Fortress; Atlanta: Scholars, 1986.

Cohn, N.

[1993]   *Cosmos, Chaos, and the World to Come: The Ancient Roots of Apocalyptic Faith.*
           New Haven: Yale University Press, 1933.

Collins, J. J.
[1973]   "The Date and Provenance of the Testament of Moses" and "Some Remaining Traditio-Historical Problems in the Testament of Moses." In *Studies on the Testament of Moses: Seminar Papers,* edited by G. W. E. Nickelsburg, 15-32, 38-43. SCS 4. Cambridge: SBL, 1973.
[1974]   "Apocalyptic Eschatology as the Transcendence of Death." *CBQ* 36 (1974): 21-43.
[1975]   "The Mythology of Holy War in Daniel and the Qumran War Scroll: A Point of Transition in Jewish Apocalyptic." *VT* 25 (1975): 596-612.
[1977]   "Cosmos and Salvation: Jewish Wisdom and Apocalyptic in the Hellenistic Age." *History of Religions* 17 (1977): 121-42.
[1979]   "Introduction: Towards the Morphology of a Genre." *Semeia* 14 (1979): 1-19.
[1979a] "The Jewish Apocalypses." *Semeia* 14 (1979): 21-59.
[1984]   *The Apocalyptic Imagination: An Introduction to the Jewish Matrix of Christianity.* New York: Crossroad, 1984.
[1984a] "Testaments." In CRINT II, 2, 325-55.
[1987]   "Prophecy and Fulfillment in the Qumran Scrolls." *Journal of the Evangelical Theological Society* 30 (1987): 267-78.
[1994]   "Teacher and Messiah? The One Who Will Teach Righteousness at the End of Days." In *The Community of the Renewed Covenant: The Notre Dame Symposium on the Dead Sea Scrolls,* edited by E. Elrich and J. VanderKam, 193-210. Christianity and Judaism in Antiquity 10. Notre Dame: University of Notre Dame Press, 1994.
[1995]   *The Scepter and the Star.* New York: Abingdon, 1995.

Collins, J. J., and G. W. E. Nickelsburg
[1980]   eds. *Ideal Figures in Ancient Judaism: Profiles and Paradigms.* Chico, Calif.: Scholars Press, 1980.

Comiskey, J. P.
[1965]   "A Remnant Will Return." *Bible Today* 1 (1965): 1210-15.

Coppens, J.
[1983]   *La relève apocalyptique du messianisme royal.* Vol. 2, *Le fils d'homme vétéro- et intertestamentaire.* Bibliotheca Ephemeridum Theologicarum Lovaniensium 61. Leuven: Leuven University Press, 1983.

Cotterell, P., and M. Turner
[1989]   *Linguistics and Biblical Interpretation.* Downers Grove, Ill.: InterVarsity Press, 1989.

Coughenour, R. A.
[1978]   "The Woe-Oracles in Ethiopic Enoch." *JSJ* 9 (1978): 192-97.

Crenshaw, J. L.
[1983]   *Theodicy in the Old Testament.* Philadelphia: Fortress, 1983.

Cullmann, O.

[1963]   *The Christology of the New Testament.* Translated by S. C. Guthrie and C. A. M. Hall. 2nd ed. London: SCM, 1963.

[1967]   *Salvation in History.* ET. New York: Harper & Row, 1967.

Dahl, N. A.

[1962]   *Das Volk Gottes. Eine Untersuchung zum Kirchenbewußtsein des Urchristentums.* 2nd ed. Darmstadt: Wissenschaftliche Buchgesellschaft, 1962.

Davenport, G. L.

[1971]   *The Eschatology of the Book of Jubilees.* Studia Post-Biblica 20. Leiden: Brill, 1971.

Davidson, M. J.

[1992]   *Angels at Qumran: A Comparative Study of 1 Enoch 1–36, 72–108 and Sectarian Writings from Qumran.* JSP(SS) 11. Sheffield: JSOT, 1992.

Davies, G. I.

[1978]   "Apocalyptic and Historiography." *JSOT* 5 (1978): 15-28.

Davies, P. R.

[1977]   *1QM, the War Scroll from Qumran: Its Structure and History.* Biblica et Orientalia 32. Rome: Biblical Institute Press, 1977.

[1982]   *The Damascus Covenant: An Interpretation of the "Damascus Document."* JSOT(SS) 25. Sheffield: JSOT, 1982.

[1983]   "Calendrical Change and Qumran Origins: An Assessment of VanderKam's Theory." *CBQ* 45 (1983): 80-89.

[1985]   "Eschatology at Qumran." *JBL* 104 (1985): 39-55.

[1990]   "Halakhah at Qumran." In *A Tribute to Geza Vermes: Essays on Jewish and Christian Literature and History,* edited by P. R. Davies and R. T. White, 37-50. JSOT(SS) 100. Sheffield: Sheffield Academic Press, 1990.

[1991]   "Sadducees in the Dead Sea Scrolls?" In *Qumran Cave Four and MMT: Special Report,* edited by Z. J. Kapera, 85-94. Krakow: Enigma, 1991.

[1992]   "Redaction and Sectarianism in the Qumran Scrolls." In *The Scriptures and the Scrolls: Studies in Honour of A. S. van der Woude on the Occasion of His Sixty-fifth Birthday,* edited by F. García Martínez, A. Hilhorst, and C. J. Labuschagne, 152-63. VT(S) 49. Leiden: Brill, 1992.

[1995]   "Who Can Join the 'Damascus Covenant'?" *JJS* 46 (1995): 134-42.

Davies, P. R., and R. T. White

[1990]   eds. *A Tribute to Geza Vermes: Essays on Jewish and Christian Literature and History.* JSOT(SS) 100. Sheffield: Sheffield Academic Press, 1990.

Davies, W. D.

[1952]   *Torah in the Messianic Age and/or the Age to Come.* JBL(MS) 7. Philadelphia: Society of Biblical Literature, 1952.

[1955]   *Paul and Rabbinic Judaism: Some Rabbinic Elements in Pauline Theology.* London: SPCK, 1948. 2nd ed., 1955.

[1962]   "Apocalyptic and Pharisaism." In *Christian Origins and Judaism*. London: Dartman, Longman and Todd, 1962.

[1964]   *The Setting of the Sermon on the Mount*. Cambridge: Cambridge University Press, 1974.

Dean-Otting, M.

[1984]   *Heavenly Journeys: A Study of the Motif in Hellenistic Jewish Literature*. Judentum und Umwelt 8. Frankfurt, Bern, and New York: Peter Lang, 1984.

Decock, P. B.

[1983]   "Holy Ones, Sons of God, and the Transcendent Future of the Righteous in 1 Enoch and the New Testament." *Neotest.* 17 (1983): 70-82.

Dedering, S.

[1973]   ed. "Apocalypse of Baruch." *Vetus Testamentum Syriace: The Old Testament in Syriac According to the Peshiṭta Version*. Leiden: E. J. Brill, 1973. IV, 3, i-iv, 1-50.

Denis, A.-M.

[1970]   ed. "Fragmenta Pseudepigraphorum Graeca." *PVTG*, 3:45-238. Leiden: Brill, 1970.

Dictionary of Sociology

[1944]   Westport, Conn.: Greenwood Press, 1944.

Dillmann, A.

[1866]   *Chrestomathia Aethiopica*. Leipzig: T. O. Weigel, 1866. Reprint, Berlin: Akademie-Verlag, 1950; Darmstadt, Wissenschaftliche Buchgesellschaft, 1967.

Dimant, D.

[1983]   "The Biography of Enoch and the Books of Enoch." *VT* 33 (1983): 14-29.

Dimant, D., and U. Rappaport

[1992]   eds. *The Dead Sea Scrolls: Forty Years of Research*. Studies on the Texts of the Desert of Judah 10. Leiden: Brill, 1992.

Dodd, C. H.

[1953]   *The Interpretation of the Fourth Gospel*. Cambridge: Cambridge University Press, 1953.

Donaldson, T. L.

[1981]   "Levitical Messianology in Late Judaism: Origins, Development and Decline." *JETS* 24 (1981): 196-97.

Doran, R.

[1989]   "The Non-Dating of Jubilees: Jub 34–38; 23:14-32 in Narrative Context." *JSJ* 20 (1989): 1-11.

[1990]   "Jason's Gymnasium." In *Of Scribes and Scrolls: Studies on the Hebrew Bible, Intertestamental Judaism, and Christian Origins Presented to John Strugnell on the Occasion of His Sixtieth Birthday*, edited by H. W. Attridge, J. J. Collins, and T. H. Tobin, 99-109. College Theology Society Resources in Religion 5. Lanham: University Press of America, 1990.

Driver, G. R.

[1965]   *The Judaean Scrolls: The Problem and a Solution.* Oxford: Basil Blackwell, 1965.

Duhaime, J. L.

[1977]   "L'instruction sur les deux esprits et les interpolations dualistes à Qumrân (1QS III,13–IV,26)." *RB* 4 (1977): 566-94.

[1987]   "Dualistic Reworking in the Scrolls from Qumran." *CBQ* 49 (1987): 32-56.

Dunn, J. D. G.

[1991]   *The Partings of the Ways between Christianity and Judaism and Their Significance for the Character of Christianity.* London: SCM, 1991.

Dupont-Sommer, A.

[1961]   *The Essene Writings from Qumran.* Translated by G. Vermes. London: Basil Blackwell, 1961.

Eisenman, R. H.

[1983]   *Maccabees, Zadokites, Christians, and Qumran: A New Hypothesis of Qumran Origins.* Leiden: Brill, 1983.

[1991]   "A Response to Schiffman on MMT." In *Qumran Cave Four and MMT: Special Report,* edited by Z. J. Kapera, 95-104. Krakow: Enigma, 1991.

Eisenman, R. H., and M. Wise

[1992]   *The Dead Sea Scrolls Uncovered.* Longmead, Shaftesbury: Element, 1992.

Elgvin, T.

[1985]   "The Qumran Covenant Festival and the Temple Scroll." *JJS* 36 (1985): 103-6.

Elliott, M. A.

[1986]   "Romans 9–11 and Jewish Remnant Theology." Th.M. thesis, University of Toronto, 1986.

[1992]   "Israel." In *Dictionary of Jesus and the Gospels,* edited by J. B. Green et al., 356-63. Downers Grove, Ill.: InterVarsity Press, 1992.

Elrich, E., and J. VanderKam

[1994]   eds. *The Community of the Renewed Covenant: The Notre Dame Symposium on the Dead Sea Scrolls.* Christianity and Judaism in Antiquity 10. Notre Dame: University of Notre Dame Press, 1994.

Encyclopedia of Sociology: New and Updated; The.

[1981]   Guilford, Conn.: DPG Reference Publishing, 1981.

Endres, J. C.

[1987]   *Biblical Interpretation in the Book of Jubilees.* CBQ(MS) 18. Washington: Catholic Biblical Association, 1987.

Enz, J. J.

[1976]   "Origin of the Dualism Expressed by 'Sons of Light' and 'Sons of Darkness.'" *BR* 21 (1976): 15-18.

Esler, P. F.

[1994]   "The Social Function of 4 Ezra." *JSNT* 53 (1994): 99-123.

Fairweather, W.
[1926]   *The Background of the Gospels: Judaism in the Period between the Old and New Testaments.* 4th ed. Edinburgh: Clark, 1926.

Farmer, W. R.
[1956]   *Maccabees, Zealots, and Josephus: An Inquiry into Jewish Nationalism in the Greco-Roman Period.* New York: Columbia University Press, 1956.

Ferrar, W. J.
[1917]   *The Assumption of Moses.* London: SPCK, 1917.

Finkel, A.
[1964]   *The Pharisees and the Teacher of Nazareth: A Study of Their Background, Their Halachic and Midrashic Teachings, the Similarities and Differences.* Leiden: Brill, 1964.

Finkelstein, L.
[1946]   *The Pharisees: The Sociological Background of Their Faith.* 2 vols. Philadelphia: Jewish Publication Society of America, 1938, 1940; 2nd ed. combined vol., 1946.

Fitzmyer, J. A.
[1971]   *The Genesis Apocryphon of Qumran Cave I: A Commentary.* 2nd ed. Rome: Biblical Institute Press, 1971.

Flew, R. N.
[1938]   *Jesus and His Church: A Study of the Idea of the Ecclesia in the New Testament.* London: Epworth, 1938.

Flusser, D.
[1988]   "The Hubris of the Antichrist in a Fragment from Qumran." Reprinted in *Judaism and the Origins of Christianity*, 207-13. Jerusalem: Magnes, 1988.

Förster, W.
[1964]   *Palestinian Judaism in New Testament Times.* Edinburgh and London: Oliver and Boyd, 1964.

Fröhlich, I.
[1986]   "Le genre littéraire des *pesharim* de Qumrân." *RQ* 12 (1986): 383-98.
[1990]   "The Symbolical Language of the Animal Apocalypse of Enoch (1 Enoch 85–90)." *RQ* 14 (1990): 629-36.

Fujita, S.
[1976]   "The Metaphor of Plant in Jewish Literature of the Intertestamental Period." *JSJ* 7 (1976): 30-45.

Fuller, R. H.
[1965]   *The Foundations of New Testament Christology.* London: Lutterworth, 1965.

Funk, R. W.
[1969]   ed. *Apocalypticism.* [= *JTC* 6.] New York: Herder and Herder, 1969.

Gager, J. G.

[1970]   "Functional Diversity in Paul's Use of End-Time Language." *JBL* 89 (1970): 325-37.

Gammie, J. G.

[1974]   "Spatial and Ethical Dualism in Jewish Wisdom and Apocalyptic Literature." *JBL* 93 (1974): 356-85.

García Martínez, F.

[1992]   *Qumran and Apocalyptic: Studies on the Aramaic Texts from Qumran.* Studies on the Texts of the Desert of Judah 9. Leiden: Brill, 1992.

[1994]   *The Dead Sea Scrolls Translated: The Qumran Texts in English.* Translated by W. G. E. Watson. Leiden: Brill, 1994.

García Martínez, F., and A. S. van der Woude

[1990]   "A 'Groningen' Hypothesis of Qumran Origins and Early History." *RQ* 14 (1990): 521-41.

Garnet, P.

[1977]   *Salvation and Atonement in the Qumran Scrolls.* WUNT 2. Tübingen: Mohr, 1977.

Gaster, T. H.

[1976]   *The Dead Sea Scriptures.* 3rd ed. Garden City: Doubleday, 1976.

Gerhardsson, B.

[1961]   *Memory and Manuscript: Oral Tradition and Written Transmission in Rabbinic Judaism and Early Christianity.* Lund: C. W. K. Gleerup, 1961.

Gewalt, D.

[1971]   "Neutestamentliche Exegese und Soziologie." *Evangelische Theologie* 31 (1971): 87-99.

Glasson, T. F.

[1976]   "The Son of Man Imagery: Enoch XIV and Daniel VII." *NTS* 23 (1976): 82-90.

[1981]   "What Is Apocalyptic?" *NTS* 27 (1981): 98-105.

Goguel, M.

[1932]   "Eschatologie et apocalyptique dans le christianisme primitif." *Revue de l'Histoire des Religions* 106 (1932): 381-424, 489-524.

[1960]   *Jesus and the Origins of Christianity.* Vol. 1, *Prolegomena to the Life of Jesus.* Translated by O. Wyon. [*La Vie de Jésus,* 1932, chs. 1-4.] New York: Harper & Brothers, 1960.

Golb, N.

[1980]   "The Problem of Origin and Identification of the Dead Sea Scrolls." *Proceedings of the American Philological Society* 124 (1980): 1-24.

[1987]   "Who Hid the Dead Sea Scrolls?" *BA* 28 (1987): 68-82.

[1995]   *Who Wrote the Dead Sea Scrolls? The Search for the Secret of Qumran.* New York: Scribner, 1995.

Goldenberg, R.
[1982]   "Early Rabbinic Explanations of the Destruction of Jerusalem." *JJS* 33 (1982): 517-25.

Goodenough, E. R.
[1958]   *Jewish Symbols in the Greco-Roman Period.* Vol. 7, *Pagan Symbols in Judaism.* Vol. 1. New York: Pantheon; Toronto: McClelland and Stewart, 1958.

Goodman, M.
[1994]   "E. P. Sanders' *Judaism: Practice and Belief, 63 BCE–66 CE.*" *SJT* 47 (1994): 89-95.

Goodspeed, E. J.
[1950]   *A Life of Jesus.* New York: Harper & Brothers, 1950.

Goppelt, L.
[1964]   *Jesus, Paul, and Judaism: An Introduction to New Testament Theology.* Translated by E. Schroeder. [*Christentum und Judentum im ersten und zweiten Jahrhundert, ein Aufriß der Urgeschichte der Kirche,* 1954.] New York: Thomas Nelson and Sons, 1964.

Goranson, S.
[1984]   "'Essenes': Etymology from עשה." *RQ* 11 (1984): 483-98.

Goshen-Gottstein, M. H.
[1970]   *A Syriac-English Glossary with Etymological Notes.* Wiesbaden: Otto Harrassowitz, 1970.

Goudoever, J. van.
[1988]   "Celebration of Torah." *Antonianum* 63 (1988): 458-84.

Gowan, D. E.
[1986]   *Bridge between the Testaments: A Reappraisal of Judaism from the Exile to the Birth of Christianity.* 3rd ed. Pittsburgh Theological Monograph Series 14. Allison Park, Pa.: Pickwick, 1986.

Grabbe, L. L.
[1982]   "The End of the World in Early Jewish and Christian Calculations." *RQ* 11 (1982): 107-8.

Grant, F. C.
[1959]   *Ancient Judaism and the New Testament.* New York: Macmillan, 1959.

Gray, J.
[1974]   "The Day of Yahweh in Cultic Experience and Eschatological Prospect." *Svensk Exegetisk Årsbok* 39 (1974): 5-37.

Greenfield, J. C., and M. E. Stone
[1977]   "The Enochic Pentateuch and the Date of the Similitudes." *HTR* 70 (1977): 51-65.
[1979]   "The Books of Enoch and the Traditions of Enoch." *Numen* 26 (1979): 89-103.

Gruenwald, I.

[1992]   "From Priesthood to Messianism: The Anti-Priestly Polemic and the Messianic
           Factor." In *Messiah and Christos: Studies in the Jewish Origins of Christianity,
           Presented to David Flusser on the Occasion of His Seventy-fifth Birthday*, edited
           by I. Gruenwald, S. Shaked, and G. G. Stroumsa, 75-93. Tübingen: J. C. B.
           Mohr (Paul Siebeck), 1992.

Gruenwald, I., S. Shaked, and G. G. Stroumsa

[1992]   eds. *Messiah and Christos: Studies in the Jewish Origins of Christianity, Pre-
           sented to David Flusser on the Occasion of His Seventy-fifth Birthday*. Tübingen:
           J. C. B. Mohr (Paul Siebeck), 1992.

Halpern-Amaru, B.

[1994]   *Rewriting the Bible: Land and Covenant in Post-Biblical Jewish Literature*. Valley
           Forge, Pa.: Trinity Press International, 1994.

Hann, R. R.

[1988]   "The Community of the Pious: The Social Setting of the Psalms of Solomon."
           Studies in Religion 17 (1988): 169-89.

Hanson, P. D.

[1963]   "Jewish Apocalyptic against Its Near Eastern Environment." *RB* 78 (1963): 31-
           58.

[1979]   *The Dawn of Apocalyptic: The Historical and Sociological Roots of Jewish Apoca-
           lyptic Eschatology*. Rev. ed. Philadelphia: Fortress, 1979.

Hare, D. R. A.

[1967]   *The Theme of Jewish Persecution of Christians in Matthew's Gospel*. SNTSMS 6.
           Cambridge: Cambridge University Press, 1967.

Harrington, D. J.

[1973]   "Interpreting Israel's History: The Testament of Moses as a Rewriting of Deut.
           31–34" and "Summary of Günther Reese, *Die Geschichte Israels in der
           Auffassung des frühen Judentums*, Ch. 3." In *Studies on the Testament of Moses:
           Seminar Papers*, edited by G. W. E. Nickelsburg, 59-68, 69-70. SCS 4. Cam-
           bridge: SBL, 1973.

Hartman, L.

[1966]   *Prophecy Interpreted: The Formation of Some Jewish Apocalyptic Texts and of the
           Eschatological Discourse, Mark 13 Par.* Translated by N. Tomkinson. Lund:
           C. W. K. Gleerup, 1966.

[1976]   "'Comfort of the Scriptures' — An Early Jewish Interpretation of Noah's Sal-
           vation." *Svensk Exegetisk Årsbok* 41–42 (1976-77): 87-96.

[1979]   *Asking for a Meaning, A Study of 1 Enoch 1–5*. Coniectanea Biblica, New Testa-
           ment Series 12. Lund: Gleerup, 1979.

[1983]   "Survey of the Problem of Apocalyptic Genre." In *AMWNE*, 329-43.

Hasel, G. F.

[1972]   *The Remnant: The History and Theology of the Remnant Idea from Genesis to*

Isaiah. Andrews University Monographs 5. Berrien Springs: Andrews University Press, 1972.

Healey, J. P.
[1990]   "The Maccabean Revolution." In *New Perspectives on Ancient Judaism,* vol. 5, *Society and Literature in Analysis,* edited by P. V. M. Flesher, 151-71. Lanham: University Press of America, 1990.

Heaton, E. W.
[1952]   "The Root *s'r* and the Doctrine of the Remnant." *JTS* 3 (1952): 27-39.

Helfgott, B. W.
[1954]   *The Doctrine of Election in Tannaitic Literature.* New York: King's Crown, 1954.

Hellholm, D.
[1983]   ed. *Apocalypticism in the Mediterranean World and the Near East.* Proceedings of the International Colloquium on Apocalypticism, Uppsala, 1979. Tübingen: Mohr, 1983.

Hengel, M.
[1961]   *Die Zeloten.* Leiden: Brill, 1961.
[1974]   *Judaism and Hellenism: Studies in Their Encounter in Palestine during the Early Hellenistic Period.* Translated by J. Bowden. 2 vols. Philadelphia: Fortress, 1974.
[1980]   *Jews, Greeks, and Barbarians: Aspects of the Hellenization of Judaism in the Pre-Christian Period.* Translated by John Bowden [1976]. Philadelphia: Fortress, 1980.

Hengel, M., and R. Deines
[1995]   "E. P. Sanders' 'Common Judaism,' Jesus, and the Pharisees." *JTS* 46 (1995): 1-70.

Hengel, M., J. H. Charlesworth, and D. Mendels
[1986]   "The Polemical Character of 'On Kingship' in the Temple Scroll: An Attempt at Dating 11QTemple." *JJS* 37 (1986): 28-38.

Herford, R. T.
[1924]   *The Pharisees.* London: George Allen and Unwin, 1924.
[1928]   *Judaism in the New Testament Period.* London: Lindsey, 1928.

Higgins, A. J. B.
[1967]   "The Priestly Messiah." *NTS* 13 (1967): 210-36.

Hill, D.
[1965]   "*Dikaioi* as a Quasi-Technical Term." *NTS* 11 (1965): 296-302.

Hill, M.
[1973]   *A Sociology of Religion.* London: Heinemann Educational Books, 1973.

Hillers, D. R.
[1969]   *Covenant: The History of a Biblical Idea.* Baltimore: John Hopkins University Press, 1969.

Himmelfarb, M.

[1983]   *Tours of Hell: An Apocalyptic Form in Jewish and Christian Literature.* Philadelphia: University of Pennsylvania Press, 1983.

Hindley, J. C.

[1968]   "Towards a Date for the Similitudes of Enoch: An Historical Approach." *NTS* 14 (1968): 551-65.

Hollander, H. W.

[1981]   *Joseph as an Ethical Model in the Testaments of the Twelve Patriarchs.* SVTP 6. Leiden: Brill, 1981.

Hollander, H. W., and M. de Jonge

[1985]   *The Testaments of the Twelve Patriarchs: A Commentary.* Leiden: Brill, 1985.

Holm-Nielsen, S.

[1960]   *Hodayot: Psalms from Qumran.* Acta Theologica Danica 2. Aarhus: Universitetsforlaget, 1960.

Hooke, S. H.

[1956]   "The Corner-Stone of Scripture." In *The Siege Perilous,* 235-49. London: SCM, 1956.

[1958]   ed. *Myth, Ritual, and Kingship: Essays on the Theory and Practice of Kingship in the Ancient Near East and in Israel.* Oxford: Clarendon Press, 1958.

Horbury, W.

[1985]   "The Messianic Associations of 'The Son of Man.'" *JTS* 36 (1985): 34-53.

Horgan, M. P.

[1979]   *Pesharim: Qumran Interpretations of Biblical Books.* CBQ(MS) 8. Washington: Catholic Biblical Association, 1979.

Horsley, R. A.

[1985]   "'Like One of the Prophets of Old': Two Types of Popular Prophets at the Time of Jesus." *CBQ* 47 (1985): 435-63.

[1986]   "Popular Prophetic Movements at the Time of Jesus: Their Principal Features and Social Origins." *JSNT* 26 (1986): 3-27.

Horsley, R. A., and J. S. Hanson

[1985]   *Bandits, Prophets, and Messiahs: Popular Movements in the Time of Jesus.* Minneapolis: Winston Press, 1985.

Hultgård, A.

[1977]   *L'eschatologie des Testaments des Douze Patriarches.* Acta Universitatis Uppsaliensis, Historia Religionum 6. 2 vols. Uppsala: Almqvist & Wiksell, 1977.

[1980]   "The Ideal 'Levite,' the Davidic Messiah, and the Saviour Priest in the Testaments of the Twelve Patriarchs." In *Ideal Figures in Ancient Judaism: Profiles and Paradigms,* edited by J. J. Collins and G. W. E. Nicklesburg, 93-110. Chico, Calif.: Scholars Press, 1980.

Hultgren, J.

[1979]   *Jesus and His Adversaries: The Form and Function of the Conflict Stories in the Synoptic Tradition.* Minneapolis: Augsburg, 1979.

Idinopulos, T. A.

[1991]   "Religious and National Factors in Israel's War with Rome." In *Jewish Civilization in the Hellenistic-Roman Period,* edited by S. Talmon, 50-63. JSOT(SS) 10. Sheffield: Sheffield Academic Press, 1991.

Ilan, T.

[1993]   "Queen Salamzion Alexandra and Judas Aristobulus I's Widow." *JSJ* 24 (1993): 181-90.

Isenberg, S. R.

[1974]   "Millenarism in Greco-Roman Palestine." *Religion* 4 (1974): 26-46.

Jagersma, H.

[1985]   *A History of Israel from Alexander the Great to Bar Kochba.* Translated by J. Bowden. Philadelphia: Fortress, 1985.

Jaubert, A.

[1963]   *La notion d'alliance dans le Judaïsme aux abords de l'ère chrétienne.* Patristica Sorbonensia 6. Paris: Éditions du Seuil, 1963.

[1965]   *The Date of the Last Supper.* Translated by I. Rafferty. New York: Abba House, 1965.

Jeremias, G.

[1963]   *Der Lehrer der Gerechtigkeit.* Göttingen: Vandenhoeck & Ruprecht, 1963.

Jeremias, J.

[1949]   "Der Gedanke des heiligen Restes im Spätjudentum und in der Verkündung Jesu." *ZNW* 42 (1949): 184-94.

[1958]   *Jesus' Promise to the Nations.* ET. London: SCM, 1958.

[1966]   *The Eucharistic Words of Jesus.* Translated by N. Perrin. London: SCM, 1966.

[1969]   *Jerusalem in the Time of Jesus: An Investigation into Economic and Social Conditions during the New Testament Period.* Translated by F. H. and C. H. Cave. [*Jerusalem zur Zeit Jesu,* 3rd ed., 1962, rev. 1967.] London: SCM, 1969.

Jervell, J.

[1971]   "Die offenbarte und die verborgene Tora. Zur Vorstellung über die neue Tora im Rabbinismus." *ST* 25 (1971): 90-108.

Jocz, J.

[1958]   *A Theology of Election: Israel and the Church.* London: SPCK, 1958.

[1968]   *The Covenant: A Theology of Human Destiny.* Grand Rapids: Eerdmans, 1968.

Johnson, A. R.

[1955]   *Sacral Kingship in Ancient Israel.* Cardiff: University of Wales Press, 1955.

[1958]   "Hebrew Conceptions of Kingship." In *Myth, Ritual, and Kingship: Essays on the Theory and Practice of Kingship in the Ancient Near East and in Israel,* edited by S. H. Hooke, 204-35. Oxford: Clarendon Press, 1958.

[1961]   *The One and the Many in the Israelite Conception of God.* 2nd ed. Cardiff: University of Wales Press, 1961.

Johnson, G.

[1943]   *The Doctrine of the Church in the New Testament.* Cambridge: Cambridge University Press, 1943.

[1960]   "'Spirit' and 'Holy Spirit' in the Qumran Literature." In *New Testament Sidelights: Essays in Honor of Alexander Converse Purdy,* edited by H. K. McArthur, 27-42. Hartford, Conn.: Hartford Seminary Foundation Press, 1960.

Jonge, M. de

[1975]   "Christian Influence in the Testaments of the Twelve Patriarchs." In *Studies on the Testaments of the Twelve Patriarchs,* 193-246. Leiden: Brill, 1975.

[1978]   ed. *The Testaments of the Twelve Patriarchs: A Critical Edition of the Greek Text.* PVTG 1/2. Leiden: Brill, 1978.

[1991]   *Jewish Eschatology, Early Christian Christology, and the Testaments of the Twelve Patriarchs: Collected Essays of Marinus de Jonge.* NovT(S) 63. Leiden: Brill, 1991.

[1991a]   "The Role of Intermediaries in God's Final Intervention in the Future according to the Qumran Scrolls." In de Jonge, *Jewish Eschatology, Early Christian Christology, and the Testaments of the Twelve Patriarchs: Collected Essays of Marinus de Jonge,* 28-47. NovT(S) 63. Leiden: Brill, 1991.

[1991b]   "The Expectation of the Future in the Psalms of Solomon." In de Jonge, *Jewish Eschatology, Early Christian Christology, and the Testaments of the Twelve Patriarchs: Collected Essays of Marinus de Jonge,* 3-27. NovT(S) 63. Leiden: Brill, 1991.

Kapera, Z. J.

[1991]   ed. *Qumran Cave Four and MMT: Special Report.* Krakow: Enigma, 1991.

Käsemann, E.

[1969]   "The Beginnings of Christian Theology." ET. ["Die Anfänge christlicher Theologie," *ZTK* 57 (1960): 162-85.] In *Apocalypticism,* edited by R. W. Funk, 17-68. *JTC* 6. New York: Herder and Herder, 1969.

[1969a]   "On the Topic of Primitive Christian Apocalyptic." ET ["Zum Thema der urchristlichen Apokalyptik," *ZTK* 59 (1962): 257-84.] In *Apocalypticism,* edited by R. W. Funk, 99-133. *JTC* 6. New York: Herder and Herder, 1969.

Kattenbusch, F.

[1922]   "Der Spruch über Petrus und die Kirche bei Matthäus." *TSK* 94 (1922): 96-131.

Kee, H. C.

[1977]   *Community of the New Age: Studies in Mark's Gospel.* London: SCM, 1977.

[1977a]   "The Ethical Dimensions of the Testaments of the XII as a Clue to Provenance." *NTS* 24 (1977-78): 259-70.

[1992]   "Membership in the Covenant People at Qumran and in the Teaching of Jesus." In *Jesus and the Dead Sea Scrolls,* edited by J. H. Charlesworth, 104-22. New York: Doubleday, 1992.

[1993]   "Appropriating the History of God's People: A Survey of Interpretations of the

History of Israel in the Pseudepigrapha, Apocrypha and the New Testament."
In *The Pseudepigrapha and Early Biblical Interpretation,* edited by J. H.
Charlesworth and C. A. Evans, 44-64. JSP(SS) 14. Studies in Scripture in Early
Judaism and Christianity 2. Sheffield: JSOT, 1993.

Kirschner, R.
[1985]   "Apocalyptic and Rabbinic Responses to the Destruction of 70." *HTR* 78
         (1985): 27-46.

Kister, M.
[1992]   "Some Aspects of Qumranic Halakhah." In *The Madrid Qumran Congress: Pro-
         ceedings of the International Congress on the Dead Sea Scrolls, Madrid 18-21
         March, 1991,* edited by J. T. Barrera and L. V. Montaner, 2:571-88. 2 vols.
         Leiden: Brill, 1992.

Klausner, J.
[1925]   *Jesus of Nazareth: His Life, Times, and Teaching.* Translated by H. Danby. Lon-
         don: George Allen & Unwin, 1925.

Klijn, A. F. J.
[1983]   ed. *Der lateinische Text der Apokalypse des Esra.* Texte und Untersuchungen zur
         Geschichte der altchristlichen Literatur 131. Berlin: Akademie, 1983.

Knibb, M. A.
[1978]   *The Ethiopic Book of Enoch: A New Edition in the Light of the Aramaic Dead Sea
         Fragments.* 2 vols. Oxford: Clarendon, 1978.
[1987]   *The Qumran Community.* CCWJCW 2. Cambridge: Cambridge University
         Press, 1987.
[1990]   "The Teacher of Righteousness — A Messianic Title?" In *A Tribute to Geza
         Vermes: Essays on Jewish and Christian Literature and History,* edited by P. R.
         Davies and R. T. White, 51-65. JSOT(SS) 100. Sheffield: Sheffield Academic
         Press, 1990.

Knowles, M. P.
[1989]   "Moses, the Law, and the Unity of IV Ezra." *NovT* 31 (1989): 257-74.

Koch, K.
[1969]   *The Growth of the Biblical Tradition: The Form-Critical Method.* Translated by
         S. M. Cupitt. New York: Charles Scribner's Sons, 1969.
[1972]   *The Rediscovery of Apocalyptic: A Polemical Work on a Neglected Area of Biblical
         Studies and Its Damaging Effects on Theology and Philosophy.* Translated by
         M. Kohl. [*Ratlos vor der Apokalyptik,* 1970.] Studies in Biblical Theology, 2nd
         ser., 22. London: SCM, 1972.

Köhler, K.
[1928]   *Jewish Theology.* Reprint, London: Lutterworth, 1928.

Kolenkow, A. B.
[1973]   "The Assumption of Moses as a Testament." In *Studies on the Testament of Mo-

ses: Seminar Papers, edited by G. W. E. Nickelsburg, 71-77. SCS 4. Cambridge: SBL, 1973.

[1974]   "What Is the Role of Testament in the Testament of Abraham?" *HTR* 67 (1974): 182-84.

Kraft, R. A.

[1972]   ed. *1972 Proceedings for the International Organization for Septuagint and Cognate Studies and the SBL Pseudepigrapha.* SCS 2. Missoula: SBL, 1972.

Kugler, R. A.

[1996]   *From Patriarch to Priest: The Levi-Priestly Tradition from "Aramaic Levi" to "Testament of Levi."* Atlanta: Scholars, 1996.

Kuhn, H.-W.

[1966]   *Enderwartung und gegenwärtiges Heil. Untersuchen zu den Gemeindeliedern von Qumran.* SUNT 4. Göttingen: Vandenhoeck & Ruprecht, 1966.

Kuhn, K. G.

[1950]   "Die in Palästina gefundenen hebräischen Texte und das Neue Testament." *ZTK* 47 (1950): 192-211.

[1957]   "New Light on Temptation, Sin, and Flesh in the New Testament." In *The Scrolls and the New Testament,* edited by K. Stendahl, 94-113. New York: Harper & Brothers, 1957.

[1957a]   "The Two Messiahs of Aaron and Israel." In *The Scrolls and the New Testament,* edited by K. Stendahl, 54-55. New York: Harper & Brothers, 1957.

[1960]   ed. *Konkordanz zu den Qumrantexten.* Göttingen: Vandenhoeck & Ruprecht, 1960.

Kümmel, W. G.

[1953]   "Jesus und die Anfänge der Kirche." *ST* 7 (1953): 1-27.

[1957]   *Promise and Fulfilment: The Eschatological Message of Jesus.* Translated by D. M. Barton. [*Verheißung und Erfüllung,* 3rd ed., 1956.] London: SCM, 1957.

Lacocque, A.

[1981]   "Apocalyptic Symbolism: A Ricoeurian Hermeneutical Approach." *BR* 26 (1981): 1-10.

Ladd, G. E.

[1957]   "Why Not Prophetic-Apocalyptic?" *JBL* 76 (1957): 192-200.

LaSor, W. S.

[1972]   *The Dead Sea Scrolls and the New Testament.* Grand Rapids: Eerdmans, 1972.

Laurin, R. B.

[1963]   "The Problem of Two Messiahs in the Qumran Scrolls." *RQ* 4 (1963): 39-52.

Leaney, A. R. C.

[1966]   *The Rule of Qumran and Its Meaning: Introduction, Translation, and Commentary.* London: SCM, 1966.

Lebram, J. C. H.
[1983]   "The Piety of the Jewish Apocalyptists." In *AMWNE,* 171-210.

Leemhuis, F., A. F. J. Klijn, and G. J. H. van Gelder
[1986]   eds., trans. *The Arabic Text of the Apocalypse of Baruch Edited and Translated with a Parallel Translation of the Syriac Text.* Leiden: Brill, 1986.

Leslau, W.
[1989]   *Concise Dictionary of Ge'ez (Classical Ethiopic).* Wiesbaden: Otto Harrassowitz, 1989.

Levine, B. A.
[1982]   "From the Aramaic Enoch Fragments: The Semantics of Cosmography." *JJS* 3 (1982): 311-26.

Lewis, J. P.
[1968]   *A Study of the Interpretation of Noah and the Flood in Jewish and Christian Literature.* Leiden: Brill, 1968.

Licht, J.
[1965]   "An Analysis of the Treatise on the Two Spirits in DSD." In *SH* IV: *Aspects of the Dead Sea Scrolls,* edited by C. Rabin and Y. Yadin, 88-99. 2nd ed. Jerusalem: Magnes Press, 1965.

Lightstone, J. N.
[1988]   *Society, the Sacred, and Scripture in Ancient Judaism: A Sociology of Knowledge.* Studies in Christianity and Judaism 3. Waterloo: Wilfred Laurier University Press, 1988.

Lindars, B.
[1976]   "A Bull, a Lamb and a Word: I Enoch XC.38." *NTS* 22 (1976): 483-86.

Loader, J. A.
[1983]   "The Model of the Priestly Blessing in 1QS." *JSJ* 14 (1983): 11-17.

Lohfink, G.
[1984]   *Jesus and Community: The Social Dimension of Christian Faith.* Translated by J. P. Galvin. [*Wie hat Jesus Gemeinde gewollt?* 1982.] Philadelphia: Fortress; New York: Paulist, 1984.

Lohse, E.
[1971]   ed. *Die Texte aus Qumran. Hebräisch und Deutsch.* 2nd ed. Munich: Kösel-Verlag, 1971.

Longenecker, B. W.
[1991]   *Eschatology and the Covenant: A Comparison of 4 Ezra and Romans 1–11.* JSNT(SS) 57. Sheffield: JSOT, 1991.

Longenecker, R. N.
[1970]   *The Christology of Early Jewish Christianity.* London: SCM, 1970.

Luck, U.

[1976]   "Das Weltverständnis in der jüdischen Apokalyptik dargestellt am äthiopischen henoch und am 4. Esra." *ZTK* 73 (1976): 283-305.

Maccoby, H.

[1988]   *Early Rabbinic Writings.* CCWJCW 3. Cambridge: Cambridge University Press, 1988.

Maddox, R.

[1982]   *The Purpose of Luke-Acts.* FRLANT 126. Göttingen: Vandenhoeck & Ruprecht, 1982.

Mann, M.

[1984]   ed. *The International Encyclopedia of Sociology.* New York: Macmillan, 1984.

Mannheim, K.

[1952]   *Essays on the Sociology of Knowledge.* Edited and translated by P. Kecskemeti. [Various articles published by Mannheim between 1923 and 1929.] London: Routledge and Kegan Paul, 1952.

Manson, T. W.

[1935]   *The Teaching of Jesus: Studies of Its Form and Content.* 2nd ed. Cambridge: University Press, 1935.

Mansoor, M.

[1961]   *The Thanksgiving Hymns Translated and Annotated with an Introduction.* Studies on the Texts of the Desert of Judah 3. Leiden: Brill, 1961.

Marmorstein, A.

[1950]   "The Unity of God in Rabbinic Literature." In *Studies in Jewish Theology,* edited by J. Rabbiniowitz and M. S. Lew, 72-105. Oxford: Oxford University Press, 1950.

Martyn, J. L.

[1968]   *History and Theology in the Fourth Gospel.* New York: Harper & Row, 1968.

May, H. G.

[1963]   "Cosmological Reference in the Qumran Doctrine of the Two Spirits and in Old Testament Imagery." *JBL* 82 (1963): 1-14.

McCready, W. O.

[1983]   "The Sectarian Status of Qumran: The Temple Scroll." *RQ* 11 (1983): 183-91.

Merrill, E. H.

[1975]   *Qumran and Predestination: A Theological Study of the Thanksgiving Hymns.* Leiden: Brill, 1975.

Meyer, B. F.

[1965]   "Jesus and the Remnant of Israel." *JBL* 84 (1965): 123-30.
[1979]   *The Aims of Jesus.* London: SCM, 1979.

Milgrom, J.

[1992] "First Day Ablutions in Qumran." In *The Madrid Qumran Congress: Proceedings of the International Congress on the Dead Sea Scrolls, Madrid 18-21 March, 1991*, edited by J. T. Barrera and L. V. Montaner, 2:561-70. 2 vols. Leiden: Brill, 1992.

Milik, J. T.

[1959] *Ten Years of Discovery in the Wilderness of Judaea.* Translated by J. Strugnell. London: SCM, 1959.

[1976] ed. *The Books of Enoch: Aramaic Fragments of Qumrân Cave 4.* Oxford: Clarendon, 1976.

Milikowsky, C.

[1982] "Again: *Damascus* in Damascus Document and in Rabbinic Literature." *RQ* 11 (1982): 97-106.

[1986] "Law at Qumran: A Critical Reaction to Lawrence H. Schiffman, *Sectarian Law in the Dead Sea Scrolls: Courts, Testimony, and the Penal Code.*" *RQ* 12 (1986): 237-49.

Millar, F.

[1978] "The Background to the Maccabean Revolution: Reflections on Martin Hengel's *Judaism and Hellenism.*" *JJS* 29 (1978): 1-21.

Miller, D. E.

[1979] "Sectarianism and Secularization: The Work of Bryan Wilson." *Religious Studies Review* 5 (1979): 161-74.

Minear, P. S.

[1956] *Jesus and His People.* London: United Society for Christian Literature, 1956.

Mitchell, G. D.

[1979] ed. *A New Dictionary of the Social Sciences.* New York: Aldine, 1979.

Modern Dictionary of Sociology, A

[1969] New York: Thomas Y. Crowell, 1969.

Moessner, D. P.

[1993] "Suffering, Intercession and Eschatological Atonement: An Uncommon Common View in the Testament of Moses and in Luke-Acts." In *The Pseudepigrapha and Early Biblical Interpretation*, edited by J. H. Charlesworth and C. A. Evans, 202-27. JSP(SS) 14. Studies in Scripture in Early Judaism and Christianity 2. Sheffield: JSOT, 1993.

Momigliano, A.

[1975] *Alien Wisdom: The Limits of Hellenization.* Cambridge: Cambridge University Press, 1975.

[1987] "A Note on Max Weber's Definition of Judaism as a Pariah-Religion." In *On Pagans, Jews, and Christians*, 231-37. Middletown, Conn.: Wesleyan University Press, 1987.

Montague, G. T.

[1976]   *The Holy Spirit: Growth of a Biblical Tradition. A Commentary on the Principal Texts of the Old and New Testaments.* New York: Paulist, 1976.

Montefiore, C. G.

[1914]   *Judaism and St. Paul: Two Essays.* London: Goschen, 1914.

Moore, G. F.

[1924]   "The Rise of Normative Judaism." *HTR* 17 (1924): 307-73.

[1927]   *Judaism in the First Centuries of the Christian Era: The Age of the Tannaim.* 3 vols. Cambridge: Harvard University Press, 1927.

Morgenstern, J.

[1955]   "The Calendar of the Book of Jubilees, Its Origin and Its Character." *VT* (1955): 34-76.

[1957]   "The Rest of Nations." *JSS* 2 (1957): 225-31.

Moule, C. F. D.

[1977]   *The Origins of Christology.* Cambridge: Cambridge University Press, 1977.

[1982]   *The Gospel according to Mark.* Corrected ed. Cambridge: Cambridge University Press, 1982.

Mowinckel, S.

[1956]   *He That Cometh.* Translated by G. W. Anderson. Oxford: Basil Blackwell, 1956.

Mowry, L.

[1962]   *The Dead Sea Scrolls and the Early Church.* Chicago: University of Chicago Press, 1962.

Muchowski, P.

[1991]   "Introductory Remarks on 4QMMT by Professor Sussman." In *Qumran Cave Four and MMT: Special Report,* edited by Z. J. Kapera, 69-73. Krakow: Enigma, 1991.

Müller, W. E., and H. D. Preuss

[1973]   *Die Vorstellung vom Rest im Alten Testament.* Neukirchen: Neukirchener Verlag, 1973.

Murphy, F. J.

[1985]   "2 Baruch and the Romans." *JBL* 104 (1985): 663-69.

Murphy, R. E.

[1958]   "*Yēṣer* in the Qumran Literature." *Biblica* 39 (1958): 334-44.

Myers, J. M.

[1974]   *I and II Esdras.* AB 42. Garden City: Doubleday, 1974.

Neugebauer, O.

[1985]   "The 'Astronomical' Chapters of the Ethiopic Book of Enoch (72–82)." In *The Book of Enoch or I Enoch: A New English Edition with Commentary and Textual Notes,* 386-419. Leiden: Brill, 1985.

Neusner, J.

[1972] "Judaism in a Time of Crisis: Four Responses to the Destruction of the Second Temple." *Judaism* 21 (1972): 313-27.

[1973] *From Politics to Piety: The Emergence of Pharisaic Judaism.* Englewood Cliffs, N.J.: Prentice-Hall, 1973.

[1975] *First Century Judaism in Crisis: Yohanan and the Renaissance of Torah.* New York: Abingdon, 1975.

[1984] *Judaism in the Beginning of Christianity.* Philadelphia: Fortress, 1984.

[1987] "'Israel': Judaism and Its Social Metaphors." *Journal of the American Academy of Religion* 55 (1987): 331-61.

[1988] *Wrong Ways and Right Ways in the Study of Formative Judaism: Critical Method and Literature, History, and the History of Religion.* Brown Judaic Studies 145. Atlanta: Scholars, 1988.

Newsom, C. A.

[1992] "4Q374: A Discourse on the Exodus/Conquest Tradition." In *The Dead Sea Scrolls: Forty Years of Research,* edited by D. Dimant and U. Rappaport, 40-52. Studies on the Texts of the Desert of Judah 10. Leiden: Brill, 1992.

Nickelsburg, G. W. E.

[1972] *Resurrection, Immortality, and Eternal Life in Intertestamental Judaism.* Cambridge: Harvard University Press, 1972.

[1973] ed. *Studies on the Testament of Moses: Seminar Papers.* SCS 4. Cambridge: SBL, 1973.

[1973a] "An Antiochan Date for the Testament of Moses." In *Studies on the Testament of Moses: Seminar Papers,* edited by G. W. E. Nickelsburg, 33-37. SCS 4. Cambridge: SBL, 1973.

[1977] "The Apocalyptic Message of 1 Enoch 92–105." *CBQ* (1977): 309-28.

[1979] "Riches, the Rich, and God's Judgment in 1 Enoch 92–105 and the Gospel according to Luke." *NTS* 25 (1979): 324-44.

[1981] "Enoch, Levi, and Peter: Recipients of Revelation in Upper Galilee." *JBL* 100 (1981): 575-600.

[1983] *Jewish Literature between the Bible and the Mishnah: A Historical and Literary Introduction.* Philadelphia: Fortress, 1983.

[1983a] "Social Aspects of Palestinian Jewish Apocalypticism." In *AMWNE,* 641-54.

[1992] "The Qumranic Transformation of a Cosmological and Eschatological Tradition (1QH 4:29-40)." In *The Madrid Qumran Congress: Proceedings of the International Congress on the Dead Sea Scrolls, Madrid 18-21 March, 1991,* edited by J. T. Barrera and L. V. Montaner, 2:649-59. 2 vols. Leiden: Brill, 1992.

Nickelsburg, G. W. E., and M. E. Stone

[1983] *Faith and Piety in Early Judaism, Texts and Documents.* Philadelphia: Fortress, 1983.

Nitzan, B.

[1995] "*4QBerakhot^{a-e} (4Q286-290):* A Covenantal Ceremony in the Light of Related Texts." *RQ* 16 (1995): 487-506.

Nöldeke, T.
[1904]   *Compendious Syriac Grammar.* Translated by J. A. Crichton. London: Williams and Norgate, 1904.

Obermann, J.
[1956]   "Calendaric Elements in the Dead Sea Scrolls." *JBL* 75 (1956): 285-97.

O'Dell, J.
[1961]   "The Religious Background of the Psalms of Solomon (Re-evaluated in the Light of the Qumran Texts)." *RQ* 3 (1961): 241-57.

Oepke, A.
[1948]   "Der Herrnspruch über die Kirche Mt 16,17-19 in der neuesten Forschung." *ST* 2 (1948-50): 110-65.

Oesterley, W. O. E.
[1933]   *II Esdras.* London: Methuen, 1933.
[1933a]   "Early Hebrew Festival Rituals." In *Myth and Ritual: Essays on the Myth and Ritual of the Hebrews in Relation to the Culture Pattern of the Ancient East,* edited by S. H. Hooke. London: Oxford University Press, 1933.
[1969]   ed. *Judaism and Christianity.* 3 vols. New York: KTAV, 1969.

Oesterley, W. O. E., and T. H. Robinson
[1930]   *Hebrew Religion: Its Origin and Development.* London: SPCK, 1930.

Olley, J. W.
[1987]   "'The Many': How Is Isa 53,12a to Be Understood?" *Biblica* 68 (1987): 330-56.

Olsson, T.
[1983]   "The Apocalyptic Activity: The Case of *Jamasp Namag.*" In *AMWNE,* 22-23.

Oppenheimer, A.
[1977]   *The Am Ha-Aretz: A Study in the Social History of the Jewish People in the Hellenistic-Roman Period.* Translated by I. H. Levine. Leiden: Brill, 1977.

Osten-Sacken, P. von der
[1969]   *Gott und Belial. Traditionsgeschichtliche Untersuchungen zum Dualismus in den Texten aus Qumran.* SUNT 6. Göttingen: Vandenhoeck & Ruprecht, 1969.

Paterson, J.
[1963]   "Remnant." In *Dictionary of the Bible,* edited by F. C. Grant and H. H. Rowley, 841-42. New York: Scribners, 1963.

Patten, P.
[1983]   "The Form and Function of Parable in Select Apocalyptic Literature and Their Significance for Parables in the Gospel of Mark." *NTS* 29 (1983): 246-58.

Pearlman, M.
[1973]   *The Maccabees.* London: Weidenfeld and Nicolson, 1973.

Perrin, N.

[1966]   "The Son of Man in Ancient Judaism and Primitive Christianity: A Suggestion." *BR* 11 (1966): 17-28.

Pfeiffer, C. F.

[1981]   *The Dead Sea Scrolls and the Bible.* Grand Rapids: Baker, 1981.

Pines, S.

[1992]   "Notes on the Twelve Tribes in Qumran, Early Christianity and Jewish Tradition." In *Messiah and Christos: Studies in the Jewish Origins of Christianity, Presented to David Flusser on the Occasion of His Seventy-fifth Birthday,* edited by I. Gruenwald, S. Shaked, and G. G. Stroumsa, 151-54. Tübingen: J. C. B. Mohr (Paul Siebeck), 1992.

Plöger, O.

[1968]   *Theocracy and Eschatology.* Translated by S. Rudman. Oxford: Basil Blackwell, 1968.

Porter, J. R.

[1965]   "The Legal Aspects of the Concept of 'Corporate Personality' in the Old Testament." *VT* 15 (1965): 361-80.

Pryke, J.

[1965]   "'Spirit' and 'Flesh' in the Qumran Documents and Some New Testament Texts." *RQ* 5 (1965): 345-60.

[1969]   "Eschatology in the Dead Sea Scrolls." In *The Scrolls and Christianity,* edited by M. Black, 45-57. SPCK Theological Collections 11. London: SPCK, 1969.

Rabin, C., and Y. Yadin

[1965]   eds. *SH* IV: *Aspects of the Dead Sea Scrolls,* 88-99. 2nd ed. Jerusalem: Magnes Press, 1965.

Rahlfs, A.

[1979]   ed. *Septuaginta.* 2nd ed. 2 vols. Stuttgart: Deutsche Bibelgesellschaft, 1979.

Reicke, B.

[1960]   "Official and Pietistic Elements of Jewish Apocalypticism." *JBL* 79 (1960): 137-50.

[1968]   *The New Testament Era: The World of the Bible from 500 B.C. to A.D. 100.* Translated by D. E. Green. [*Neutestamentliche Zeitgeschichte,* 1964.] Philadelphia: Fortress, 1968.

Reid, S. B.

[1989]   *Enoch and Daniel: A Form-Critical and Sociological Study of the Historical Apocalypses.* Bibal Monograph Series 2. Berkeley: Bibal, 1989.

Rhoads, D. M.

[1973]   "The Assumption of Moses and Jewish History: 4 B.C.–A.D. 48." In *Studies on the Testament of Moses: Seminar Papers,* edited by G. W. E. Nickelsburg, 53-58. SCS 4. Cambridge: SBL, 1973.

Richardson, G. P.
[1969]   *Israel in the Apostolic Church.* Cambridge: Cambridge University Press, 1969.

Ricoeur, P.
[1967]   *The Symbolism of Evil.* Translated by E. Buchanon. Religious Perspectives 17. New York: Harper & Row, 1967.

Riesner, R.
[1992]   "Jesus, the Primitive Community, and the Essene Quarter of Jerusalem." In *Jesus and the Dead Sea Scrolls,* edited by J. H. Charlesworth, 198-234. New York: Doubleday, 1992.

Ringgren, H.
[1961]   "The Branch and the Plantation in the *Hodayot.*" *BR* 6 (1961): 3-9.
[1963]   *The Faith of Qumran: Theology of the Dead Sea Scrolls.* Translated by E. T. Sander. Philadelphia: Fortress, 1963.

Robinson, H. W.
[1980]   *Corporate Personality in Ancient Israel.* 2nd ed. Philadelphia: Fortress, 1980; originally published, 1935.

Roehrs, W. R.
[1988]   "Divine Covenants: Their Structure and Function." *Concordia Journal* 14 (1988): 7-27.

Rogerson, J. W.
[1970]   "The Hebrew Conception of Corporate Personality: A Re-examination." *JTS* 21 (1970): 1-16.

Rohde, J.
[1968]   *Rediscovering the Teaching of the Evangelists.* Translated by D. M. Barton. London: SCM, 1968.

Rook, J. T.
[1981]   "A Twenty-eight-Day Month Tradition in the Book of Jubilees." *VT* 31 (1981): 83-87.

Roux, R. le
[1978]   "The 'Last Days' in Apocalyptic Perspective." *Neotest.* 12 (1978): 41-73.

Rowe, R. D.
[1982]   "Is Daniel's 'Son of Man' Messianic?" In *Christ the Lord: Studies in Christology Presented to Donald Guthrie,* edited by H. R. Rowdon, 71-96. Downers Grove, Ill.: InterVarsity Press, 1982.

Rowland, C.
[1982]   *The Open Heaven: A Study of Apocalyptic in Judaism and Early Christianity.* London: SPCK, 1982.
[1985]   *Christian Origins: An Account of the Setting and Character of the Most Important Messianic Sect of Judaism.* London: SPCK, 1985.

Rowley, H. H.

[1950]   *The Biblical Doctrine of Election.* London: Lutterworth, 1950.

[1958]   "Ritual and the Hebrew Prophets." In *Myth, Ritual, and Kingship: Essays on the Theory and Practice of Kingship in the Ancient Near East and in Israel,* edited by S. H. Hooke, 236-60. Oxford: Clarendon Press, 1958.

[1963]   *The Relevance of Apocalyptic.* 2nd ed. London: Lutterworth, 1963.

Ruppert, L.

[1972]   *Die leidende Gerechte. Eine motivgeschichtliche Untersuchung zum Alten Testament und zwischentestamentlichen Judentum.* Stuttgart: Katholischer Bibelwerk, 1972.

Russell, D. S.

[1960]   *Between the Testaments.* London: SCM, 1960.

[1964]   *The Method and Message of Jewish Apocalyptic, 200 B.C.–A.D. 100.* London: SCM, 1964.

[1986]   *From Early Judaism to Early Church.* London: SCM, 1986.

[1987]   *The Old Testament Pseudepigrapha: Patriarchs and Prophets in Early Judaism.* London: SCM, 1987.

[1994]   *Prophecy and the Apocalyptic Dream: Protest and Promise.* Peabody, Mass.: Hendrickson, 1994.

Ryle, H. E., and M. R. James

[1891]   *ΨΑΛΜΟΙ ΣΟΛΟΜΩΝΤΟΣ: Psalms of the Pharisees, Commonly Called the Psalms of Solomon.* Cambridge: Cambridge University Press, 1891.

Safrai, S., and M. Stern

[1974]   eds. *The Jewish People in the First Century: Historical Geography, Political History, Social, Cultural and Religious Life and Institutions.* Vol. 1. CRINT 1/1. Assen: Van Gorcum; Philadelphia: Fortress, 1974.

[1987]   *The Jewish People in the First Century: Historical Geography, Political History, Social, Cultural and Religious Life and Institutions.* Vol. 2. CRINT 1/2. Assen: Van Gorcum; Philadelphia: Fortress, 1987.

Sahlin, H.

[1983]   "Wie wurde ursprünglich die Benennung 'Der Menschensohn' verstanden?" *ST* (1983): 147-79.

Sanders, E. P.

[1973]   "Patterns of Religion in Paul and Rabbinic Judaism: A Holistic Method of Comparison." *HTR* 66 (1973): 455-78.

[1977]   *Paul and Palestinian Judaism: A Comparison of Patterns of Religion.* London: SCM, 1977.

[1985]   *Jesus and Judaism.* London: SCM, 1985.

[1992]   *Judaism: Practice and Belief, 63 BCE–66 CE.* London: SCM, 1992.

Sanders, J. A.

[1993]   "Introduction: Why the Pseudepigrapha?" In *The Pseudepigrapha and Early Biblical Interpretation,* edited by J. H. Charlesworth and C. A. Evans, 13-19.

JSP(SS) 14. Studies in Scripture in Early Judaism and Christianity 2. Sheffield: JSOT, 1993.

Sanders, J. T.
[1987]   *The Jews in Luke-Acts.* London: SCM, 1987.

Sandmel, S.
[1978]   *Anti-Semitism in the New Testament?* Philadelphia: Fortress, 1978.

Sayler, G. B.
[1984]   *Have the Promises Failed? A Literary Analysis of 2 Baruch.* SBL Dissertation Series 72. Chico, Calif.: Scholars Press, 1984.

Schechter, S.
[1909]   *Some Aspects of Rabbinic Theology.* New York: Macmillan, 1909.

Schelkle, K. H.
[1985]   *Israel im Neuen Testament.* Darmstadt: Wissenschaftliche Buchgesellschaft, 1985.

Schiffman, L. H.
[1981]   "Jewish Sectarianism in Second Temple Times." In *Great Schisms in Jewish History,* edited by R. Jospe and S. M. Wagner, 1-46. New York: KTAV, 1981.
[1983]   *Sectarian Law in the Dead Sea Scrolls: Courts, Testimony, and the Penal Code.* Brown Judaic Studies 33. Chico, Calif.: Scholars, 1983.
[1987]   "The Concept of the Messiah in Second Temple and Rabbinic Literature." *Review and Expositor* 84 (1987): 235-46.
[1987a]   "The Rabbinic Understanding of Covenant." *Review and Expositor* 84 (1987): 289-98.
[1991]   "4QMMT — Basic Sectarian Text." In *Qumran Cave Four and MMT: Special Report,* edited by Z. J. Kapera, 81-83. Krakow: Enigma, 1991.
[1992]   "Messianic Figures and Ideas in the Qumran Scrolls." In *The Messiah: Developments in Earliest Judaism and Christianity,* edited by J. H. Charlesworth, 116-29. Minneapolis: Fortress, 1992.
[1994]   *Reclaiming the Dead Sea Scrolls: The History of Judaism, the Background of Christianity, the Lost Library of Qumran.* Philadelphia: Jewish Publication Society, 1994.
[1994a]   "The Temple Scroll and the Nature of Its Law: The Status of the Question." In *The Community of the Renewed Covenant: The Notre Dame Symposium on the Dead Sea Scrolls,* edited by E. Elrich and J. VanderKam, 37-55. Christianity and Judaism in Antiquity 10. Notre Dame: University of Notre Dame Press, 1994.

Schmidt, J. M.
[1969]   *Die jüdische Apokalyptik. Die Geschichte ihrer Erforschung von den Anfängen bis zu den Textfunden von Qumran.* Neukirchen-Vluyn: Neukirchener Verlag des Erziehungsvereins, 1969.

Schmidt, K. L.
[1927]   "Die Kirche des Urchristentums." In *Festgabe für Adolf Deissmann zum 60. Geburtstag,* 258-319. Tübingen: J. C. B. Mohr (Paul Siebeck), 1927.

Schmithals, W.
[1975]   *The Apocalyptic Movement: Introduction and Interpretation.* Translated by J. E.
          Steely. [*Die Apokalyptik. Einführung und Deutung,* 1973.] Nashville: Abingdon,
          1975.

Schnabel, E. J.
[1985]   *Law and Wisdom from Ben Sira to Paul: A Tradition Historical Enquiry into the
          Relation of Law, Wisdom, and Ethics.* WUNT 2/16. Tübingen: Mohr, 1985.

Schoeps, H.-J.
[1950]   "Haggadisches zur Auserwählung Israels." In *Aus früchristlicher Zeit,* 184-211.
          Tübingen, 1950.

Schonfield, H. J.
[1957]   *Secrets of the Dead Sea Scrolls: Studies towards Their Solution.* New York: Barnes
          and Co., 1957.

Schreiner, J.
[1965]   "Geistbegabung in der Gemeinde von Qumran." *BZ* 9 (1965): 161-80.
[1986]   "Zur Eschatologie in der Zeit zwischen den Testamenten." In *Eschatologie in
          der Schrift und Patristik,* edited by B. Daley, 32-43. *Handbuch der Dogmen-
          geschichte,* 4/7a. Freiburg: Herder, 1986.

Schubert, K.
[1959]   *The Dead Sea Community: Its Origin and Teachings.* Translated by J. W.
          Doberstein. London: A. and C. Black, 1959.

Schüpphaus, J.
[1977]   *Die Psalmen Salomonis. Ein Zeugnis Jerusalemer Theologie und Frömmigkeit in
          der Mitte des vorchristlichen Jahrhunderts.* Leiden: Brill, 1977.

Schürer, E.
[1973]   *The History of the Jewish People in the Age of Jesus Christ (175 B.C.–A.D. 135).*
          Translated and revised by T. A. Burkill et al. Edited by G. Vermes, F. Millar, and
          M. Black. Vol. 1. Edinburgh: Clark, 1973.
[1979]   *The History of the Jewish People in the Age of Jesus Christ (175 B.C.–A.D. 135).*
          Translated and revised by T. A. Burkill et al. Edited by G. Vermes, F. Millar, and
          M. Black. Vol. 2. Edinburgh: Clark, 1979.

Schüssler Fiorenza, E.
[1985]   *The Book of Revelation: Justice and Judgment.* Philadelphia: Fortress, 1985.

Schwartz, D. R.
[1992]   "Law and Truth: On Qumran-Sadducean and Rabbinic Views of Law." In *The
          Dead Sea Scrolls: Forty Years of Research,* edited by D. Dimant and U. Rappa-
          port, 229-40. Studies on the Texts of the Desert of Judah 10. Leiden: Brill, 1992.

Schweizer, E.
[1980]   *The Holy Spirit.* Translated by R. H. Fuller and I. Fuller. Philadelphia: Fortress,
          1980.

Scott, J. J.

[1995]   *Customs and Controversies: Intertestamental Jewish Backgrounds of the New Testament.* Grand Rapids: Baker, 1995.

Segal, A. F.

[1987]   *The Other Judaisms of Late Antiquity.* Brown Judaic Series 27. Atlanta: Scholars Press, 1987.

[1987a]   "Dualism in Judaism, Christianity, and Gnosticism: A Definitive Issue." In Segal, *The Other Judaisms of Late Antiquity,* 1-40. Brown Judaic Series 27. Atlanta: Scholars Press, 1987.

[1987b]   "Covenant in Rabbinic Writings." In Segal, *The Other Judaisms of Late Antiquity,* 147-65. Brown Judaic Series 27. Atlanta: Scholars Press, 1987.

Seifrid, M. A.

[1992]   *Justification by Faith: The Origin and Development of a Central Pauline Theme.* NovT(S) 68. Leiden: Brill, 1992.

Sekki, A. E.

[1989]   *The Meaning of* RUAḤ *at Qumran.* SBL Dissertation Series 110. Atlanta: Scholars Press, 1989.

Shanks, H.

[1984]   "Synagogue Excavation Reveals Stunning Mosaic of Zodiac and Torah Ark." *BAR* 10, no. 3 (1984): 32-44.

Sigal, P.

[1988]   *Judaism: The Evolution of a Faith.* Grand Rapids: Eerdmans, 1988.

Simon, M.

[1967]   *Jewish Sects in the Time of Jesus.* Trans. J. H. Farley. Philadelphia: Fortress, 1967.

Sjöberg, E.

[1950]   "Wiedergeburt und Neuschöpfung im palästinischen Judentum." *ST* 4 (1950): 44-85.

[1955]   "Neuschöpfung in den Toten-Meer-Rollen." *ST* 9 (1955): 131-37.

Slingerland, H. D.

[1977]   *The Testaments of the Twelve Patriarchs: A Critical History of Research.* SBLMS 21. Missoula: Scholars, 1977.

[1986]   "The Nature of *Nomos* (Law) within the Testaments of the Twelve Patriarchs." *JBL* 105 (1986): 39-48.

Smith, M.

[1960]   "The Dead Sea Sect in Relation to Ancient Judaism." *NTS* 7 (1960-61): 347-60.

[1971]   *Palestinian Parties and Politics That Shaped the Old Testament.* New York: Columbia University Press, 1971.

[1983]   "On the History of ΑΠΟΚΑΛΥΠΤΩ and ΑΠΟΚΑΛΥΨΙΣ." In *AMWNE,* 9-19.

[1984]   "The Case of the Gilded Staircase: Did the Dead Sea Scroll Sect Worship the Sun?" *BAR* 10, no. 5 (1984): 50-55.

Sparks, H. F. D.
[1984]   ed. *The Apocryphal Old Testament.* Oxford: Clarendon, 1984.

Sperling, S. D.
[1989]   "Rethinking Covenant in Late Biblical Books." *Biblica* 70 (1989): 50-73.

Stauffer, E.
[1960]   *Jesus and His Story.* Translated by D. M. Barton. [*Jesus Gestalt und Geschichte.*]
          London: SCM, 1960.

Stegemann, H.
[1992]   "The Qumran Essenes — Local Members of the Main Jewish Union in Late
          Second Temple Times." In *The Madrid Qumran Congress: Proceedings of the In-
          ternational Congress on the Dead Sea Scrolls, Madrid 18-21 March, 1991,* edited
          by J. T. Barrera and L. V. Montaner, 1:83-166. 2 vols. Leiden: Brill, 1992.

Stendahl, K.
[1957]   ed. *The Scrolls and the New Testament.* New York: Harper & Brothers, 1957.

Steuernagel, C.
[1950]   "Die Strukturlinien der Entwicklung der jüdischen Eschatologie." In *Festschrift
          Alfred Bertholet,* edited by W. Baumgartner et al., 479-87. Tübingen: J. C. B.
          Mohr (Paul Siebeck), 1950.

Stewart, R. A.
[1961]   *Rabbinic Theology: An Introductory Study.* Edinburgh and London: Oliver and
          Boyd, 1961.

Stone, M. E.
[1968]   "The Concept of the Messiah in IV Ezra." In *Religions in Antiquity: Essays in
          Memory of Erwin Ramsdell Goodenough,* edited by J. Neusner, 295-312. Studies
          in the History of Religions 14. Leiden: Brill, 1968.
[1978]   "The Book of Enoch and Judaism in the Third Century B.C.E." *CBQ* 40 (1978):
          479-92.
[1981]   "Reactions to Destructions of the Second Temple: Theology, Perception, and
          Conversion." *JSJ* 12 (1981): 195-204.
[1983]   "Coherence and Inconsistency in the Apocalypses: The Case of 'the End' in
          4 Ezra." *JBL* 102 (1983): 229-43.
[1984]   ed. *Jewish Writings of the Second Temple Period: Apocrypha, Pseudepigrapha,
          Qumran Sectarian Writings, Philo, Josephus.* CRINT 2/2. Assen: Van Gorcum;
          Philadelphia: Fortress, 1984.
[1985]   "Three Transformations in Judaism: Scripture, History, and Redemption."
          Numen 32 (1985): 218-35.
[1988]   "Enoch, Aramaic Levi and Sectarian Origins." *JSJ* 19 (1988): 159-70.
[1989]   *Features of the Eschatology of IV Ezra.* Harvard Semitic Studies 35. Atlanta:
          Scholars, 1989.
[1990]   *Fourth Ezra: A Commentary on the Book of Fourth Ezra.* Hermeneia. Minneap-
          olis: Fortress, 1990.

Suter, D. W.

[1979]   *Tradition and Composition in the Parables of Enoch.* SBL Dissertation Series 47. Missoula: Scholars Press, 1979.

[1979a]   "Fallen Angel, Fallen Priest: The Problem of Family Purity in 1 Enoch 6–16." *HUCA* 50 (1979): 115-35.

Talmon, S.

[1965]   "The Calendar Reckoning of the Sect from the Judaean Desert." In *SH* IV: *Aspects of the Dead Sea Scrolls,* edited by C. Rabin and Y. Yadin, 162-99. 2nd ed. Jerusalem: Magnes Press, 1965.

[1986]   *King, Cult, and Calendar in Ancient Judaism: Collected Studies.* Jerusalem: Magnes Press, 1986.

[1987]   "The Emergence of Jewish Sectarianism in the Early Second Temple Period." In *Ancient Israelite Religion: Essays in Honor of Frank Moore Cross,* edited by P. D. Miller, Jr., P. D. Hanson, and S. D. McBride, 587-616. Philadelphia: Fortress, 1987.

[1991]   ed. *Jewish Civilization in the Hellenistic-Roman Period.* JSOT(SS) 10. Sheffield: Sheffield Academic, 1991.

[1991a]   "The Internal Diversification of Judaism in the Early Second Temple Period." In *Jewish Civilization in the Hellenistic-Roman Period,* edited by S. Talmon, 16-43. JSOT(SS) 10. Sheffield: Sheffield Academic, 1991.

[1992]   "The Concepts of *Māšiah* and Messianism in Early Judaism." In *The Messiah: Developments in Earliest Judaism and Christianity,* edited by J. H. Charlesworth, 79-115. Minneapolis: Fortress, 1992.

[1994]   "The Community of the Renewed Covenant: Between Judaism and Christianity." In *The Community of the Renewed Covenant: The Notre Dame Symposium on the Dead Sea Scrolls,* edited by E. Elrich and J. VanderKam, 3-24. Christianity and Judaism in Antiquity 10. Notre Dame: University of Notre Dame Press, 1994.

Tcherikover, V.

[1961]   *Hellenistic Civilization and the Jews.* Translated by S. Applebaum. Philadelphia: Jewish Publication Society of America, 1961.

Teeple, H. M.

[1960]   "Qumran and the Origin of the Fourth Gospel." *NovT* 4 (1960): 6-25.

Testuz, M.

[1960]   *Les idées religieuses du Livre des Jubilés.* Geneva: Librairie E. Droz; Paris: Librarie Minard, 1960.

Theissen, G.

[1978]   *The First Followers of Jesus: A Sociological Analysis of the Earliest Christianity.* Translated by J. Bowden. London: SCM, 1978.

Thiering, B. E.

[1980]   "Inner and Outer Cleansing at Qumran as a Background to New Testament Baptism." *NTS* 26 (1980): 266-77.

[1981]   *The Gospels and Qumran: A New Hypothesis.* Sydney: Theological Explorations, 1981.

[1981a]   "Qumran Initiation and New Testament Baptism." *NTS* 27 (1981): 615-31.

Thompson, A. L.
[1977]   *Responsibility for Evil in the Theodicy of IV Ezra: A Study Illustrating the Significance of Form and Structure for the Meaning of the Book.* Missoula: Scholars Press, 1977.

Tidball, D. J.
[1983]   *An Introduction to the Sociology of the New Testament.* Exeter: Paternoster Press, 1983.

Tiede, D. L.
[1973]   "The Figure of Moses in the Testament of Moses." In *Studies on the Testament of Moses: Seminar Papers,* edited by G. W. E. Nickelsburg, 86-92. SCS 4. Cambridge: SBL, 1973.

Tiller, P. A.
[1993]   *A Commentary on the Animal Apocalypse of I Enoch.* Atlanta: Scholars, 1993.

Trafton, J. L.
[n.d.]   *The Syriac Version of the Psalms of Solomon.* N.p., n.d.
[1985]   *The Syriac Version of the Psalms of Solomon: A Critical Evaluation.* SCS 11. Atlanta: Scholars, 1985.

Treves, M.
[1961]   "The Two Spirits of the Rule of the Community." *RQ* 3 (1961): 449-52.

Tromp, J.
[1993]   "The Sinners and the Lawless in Psalm of Solomon 17." *NovT* 35 (1993): 344-61.

Urbach, E. E.
[1975]   *The Sages — Their Concepts and Beliefs.* Translated by I. Abrahams. Jerusalem: Magnes, 1975, vol. 1, text; vol. 2, notes.

VanderKam, J. C.
[1977]   *Textual and Historical Studies in the Book of Jubilees.* Harvard Semitic Monographs 14. Missoula: Scholars Press, 1977.
[1981]   "2 Maccabees 6,7a and Calendrical Change in Jerusalem." *JSJ* 12 (1981): 52-74.
[1984]   *Enoch and the Growth of an Apocalyptic Tradition.* CBQ(MS) 16. Washington: Catholic Biblical Association of America, 1984.
[1984a]   "Studies in the Apocalypse of Weeks (1 Enoch 93:1-10; 91:11-17)." *CBQ* 46 (1984): 511-23.
[1991]   "The Qumran Residents: Essenes Not Sadducees!" In *Qumran Cave Four and MMT: Special Report,* edited by Z. J. Kapera, 105-8. Krakow: Enigma, 1991.
[1992]   "Righteous One, Messiah, Chosen One, and Son of Man in 1 Enoch 37–71." In *The Messiah: Developments in Earliest Judaism and Christianity,* edited by J. H. Charlesworth, 169-91. Minneapolis: Fortress, 1992.

[1993]   "Biblical Interpretation in 1 Enoch and Jubilees." In *The Pseudepigrapha and Early Biblical Interpretation*, edited by J. H. Charlesworth and C. A. Evans, 96-125. JSP(SS) 14. Studies in Scripture in Early Judaism and Christianity 2. Sheffield: JSOT, 1993.

[1994]   "Messianism in the Scrolls." In *The Community of the Renewed Covenant: The Notre Dame Symposium on the Dead Sea Scrolls*, edited by E. Elrich and J. VanderKam, 211-34. Christianity and Judaism in Antiquity 10. Notre Dame: University of Notre Dame Press, 1994.

[1994a]   "The Granddaughters and Grandsons of Noah." *RQ* 16 (1994): 457-61.

Vaux, R. de

[1978]   "Qumran, Khirbet-'Ein Feshkha." In *Encyclopedia of Archaeological Excavations in the Holy Land*, edited by M. Avi-Yonah and E. Stern, 4:978-86. 4 vols. Englewood Cliffs: Prentice-Hall, 1978.

Vawter, B.

[1960]   "Apocalyptic: Its Relation to Prophecy." *CBQ* 22 (1960): 33-46.

Vermes, G.

[1975]   *The Dead Sea Scrolls in English*. 2nd ed. Harmondsworth, U.K.: Penguin, 1975.

[1981]   "The Essenes and History." *JJS* 32 (1981): 18-31.

[1982]   "Jewish Literature and New Testament Exegesis." *JJS* 3 (1982): 361-76.

[1982a]   "Jewish Literature and New Testament Exegesis: Reflections of Methodology." *JJS* 33 (1982): 361-76.

[1983]   *Jesus and the World of Judaism*. London: SCM, 1983.

[1985]   "Methodology in the Study of Jewish Literature in the Graeco-Roman Period." *JJS* 36 (1985): 145-58.

Vetus Testamentum Syriace: The Old Testament in Syriac according to the Peshiṭta Version.

[1973]   Leiden: Brill, 1973.

Villiers, P. G. R. de

[1978]   "The Messiah and Messiahs in Jewish Apocalyptic." *Neotest.* 12 (1978): 75-110.

Volz, P.

[1934]   *Die Eschatologie der jüdischen Gemeinde im neutestamentlichen Zeitalter, nach den Quellen der rabbinischen, apokalyptischen und apokryphen Literatur*. Tübingen: Mohr, 1934.

Wacholder, B. Z.

[1983]   *The Dawn of Qumran: The Sectarian Torah and the Teacher of Righteousness*. Cincinnati: Hebrew Union College Press, 1983.

[1985]   "The Date of the Eschaton in the Book of Jubilees: A Commentary on Jub. 49:22–50:5, CD 1:1-10, and 16:2-3." *HUCA* 56 (1985): 87-101.

[1986]   "The 'Sealed' Torah versus the 'Revealed' Torah: An Exegesis of Damascus Covenant V,1-6 and Jeremiah 32,10-14." *RQ* 12 (1986): 351-68.

[1992]   "Ezekiel and Ezekielianism as Progenitors of Essenianism." In *The Dead Sea*

Scrolls: Forty Years of Research, edited by D. Dimant and U. Rappaport, 186-96. Studies on the Texts of the Desert of Judah 10. Leiden: Brill, 1992.

Weber, F.

[1897]   *Jüdische Theologie auf Grund des Talmud und verwandter Schriften gemein-faßlich dargestellt.* Edited by F. Delitzsch and G. Schnedermann. 2nd ed. Leipzig: Dörffling und Franke, 1897. Reprint, Hildesheim: Georg Olms Verlag, 1975.

Weber, M.

[1952]   *Ancient Judaism.* Edited and translated by H. H. Gerth and D. Martindale. [*Das antike Judentum,* 1919.] Glencoe, Ill.: Free Press, 1952.

[1963]   *The Sociology of Religion.* Translated by E. Fischoff. [*Religionssoziologie,* 1922.] Boston: Beacon Press, 1963.

Weise, M.

[1961]   *Kultzeiten und kultischer Bundesschluss in der "Ordensregel" vom Toten Meer.* Studia Post-Biblica 30. Leiden: Brill, 1961.

Wernberg-Møller, P.

[1957]   *The Manual of Discipline: Translated and Annotated with an Introduction.* Leiden: Brill, 1957.

[1961]   "A Reconsideration of the Two Spirits in the Rule of the Community (1QSerek III,13–IV,26)." *RQ* 3 (1961): 413-41.

Westermann, C.

[1968]   *Der Segen in der Bibel und im Handeln der Kirche.* Munich: Chr. Kaiser, 1968.

White, R. T.

[1990]   "The House of Peleg in the Dead Sea Scrolls." In *A Tribute to Geza Vermes: Essays on Jewish and Christian Literature and History,* edited by P. R. Davies and R. T. White, 67-98. JSOT(SS) 100. Sheffield: Sheffield Academic Press, 1990.

White, S. A.

[1987]   "A Comparison of the 'A' and 'B' Manuscripts of the Damascus Document." *RQ* 12 (1987): 537-53.

Widengren, G.

[1958]   "Early Hebrew Myths and Their Interpretation." In *Myth, Ritual, and Kingship: Essays on the Theory and Practice of Kingship in the Ancient Near East and in Israel,* edited by S. H. Hooke, 149-203. Oxford: Clarendon Press, 1958.

Wilcox, M.

[1969]   "Dualism, Gnosticism, and Other Elements in the Pre-Pauline Tradition." In *The Scrolls and Christianity,* edited by M. Black, 83-106. SPCK Theological Collections 11. London: SPCK, 1969.

Wilder, A. N.

[1931]   "The Nature of Jewish Eschatology." *JBL* 50 (1931): 201-6.

Willett, T. W.

[1989]   *Eschatology in the Theodicies of 2 Baruch and 4 Ezra*. JSP(SS) 4. Sheffield: JSOT, 1989.

Winter, P.

[1962]   "Psalms of Solomon." In *IDB*, 3:958-60.

Wise, M. O.

[1989]   "The Covenant of Temple Scroll XXIX,3-10." *RQ* 14 (1989): 49-60.

[1990a]   *A Critical Study of the Temple Scroll from Qumran Cave 11*. Oriental Institute Studies in Ancient Oriental Civilization 49. Chicago: University of Chicago Press, 1990.

[1990b]   "The Teacher of Righteousness and the High Priest of the Intersacerdotium: Two Approaches." *RQ* 14 (1990): 587-613.

Wright, N. T.

[1980]   "The Messiah and the People of God: A Study in Pauline Theology with Particular Reference to the Argument of the Epistle to the Romans." Ph.D. diss., Oxford, 1980.

Wright, R.

[1972]   "The Psalms of Solomon, the Pharisees, and the Essenes." In *1972 Proceedings for the International Organization for Septuagint and Cognate Studies and the SBL Pseudepigrapha*, edited by R. A. Kraft, 136-54. SCS 2. Missoula: SBL, 1972.

Yadin, Y.

[1962]   *The Scroll of the War of the Sons of Light against the Sons of Darkness*. Translated by B. Rabin and C. Rabin. [From Heb. ed., 1955.] Oxford: Oxford University Press, 1962.

[1984]   "The Temple Scroll — The Longest and Most Recently Discovered Dead Sea Scroll." *BAR* 10 (1984): 33-49.

[1985]   *The Temple Scroll: The Hidden Law of the Dead Sea Sect*. New York: Random House, 1985.

Young, B. H.

[1989]   *Jesus and His Jewish Parables: Rediscovering the Roots of Jesus' Teaching*. New York: Paulist Press, 1989.

Zeitlin, I. M.

[1988]   *Jesus and the Judaism of His Time*. Cambridge: Polity, 1988.

Zeitlin, S.

[1968]   *The Rise and Fall of the Judaean State: A Political, Social, and Religious History of the Second Commonwealth*, vol. 1. 2nd ed. Philadelphia: Jewish Publication Society, 1968.

[1969]   *The Rise and Fall of the Judaean State: A Political, Social, and Religious History of the Second Commonwealth*, vol. 2. 2nd ed. Philadelphia: Jewish Publication Society of America, 1969.

Zerbe, G.

[1993]   "'Pacifism' and 'Passive Resistance' in Apocalyptic Writings: A Critical Evaluation." In *The Pseudepigrapha and Early Biblical Interpretation,* edited by J. H. Charlesworth and C. A. Evans, 65-95. JSP(SS) 14. Studies in Scripture in Early Judaism and Christianity 2. Sheffield: JSOT, 1993.

Ziesler, J. A.

[1972]   *The Meaning of Righteousness in Paul: A Linguistic and Theological Enquiry.* SNTSMS 20. Cambridge: University Press, 1972.

Index of Subjects

Note: Passages containing particularly significant treatments appear in **bold** type.

Abraham, 181, 181n.202, 247, 318-19, 321, 322, 325, 331, 361n.17, 383n.81, 442

Abyss. *See under* Hell; Revelations of the cosmos

Agricultural motifs. *See under* Plant motifs

Alchimus, 222, 226

Alexander (the Great), 191, 208

Alexander Balas, 224

Alexander Jannaeus, 227-28

Alexandra. *See* Salome Alexandra

"All"-motif, 71, 79, 90, 91, 98, 116, 127, 129, 133, 142-43, 623; salvation of all Israel, 42, 53, 70, 86-87, 524-26, 532, 550, 550n.91, 622-23, 635-36

Angels, 328, 394, 397n.13, 405, 413-16, 619; Angel of Darkness, 401, 417; Angel of Truth, 409; communion of angels and humans, 333, 337, 339-40, 347, 398, 414-16, 418, 596n.49, 619; fallen or evil angels, 155-56, 399, 580; Prince of Light, 413; Watchers (theodicy), 426-32, 578, 580, 583, 589, 597, 615-16. *See also* Lot; Melchizedek

Antediluvian patriarchs (list of), 318-19, 318n.31, 437-42

Anthropological dualism. *See under* Dualism

Anthrōpos Theou (man of God), 466

Antichrist figures, 473-74, 477, 477n.108

Antigonus, 231

Antiochus IV ("Epiphanes"), **192-96**, 202, 214-15, 217-20, 223, 231, 310

Antiochus VII Sidetes, 226

Antipater, 231

Apocalyptic(ism), 3, 4-6, 13, 36-40, 197-98, 242, 310, 356, 377, 495, 502, 513, 517, 519n.11, 519n.12, 520n.13, 520n.14, 541-43, 573n.170, 576, 636-37, 653, 656, 658-59, 661

Apocalyptic forms, 265, 285, 292, 296, 329, 345, 349, ch. 8, 594n.44, 596-97

Apostasy/Breach of covenant, 55, 59, 60-65, 73, 79, 82-83, 85, **108-13**, 167, 173, 203, 213, 217, 220-21, 222n.114, 225n.121, 226, 232, 234, 235, 236-37, 263, 264, 265, 270, 271n.64, 272, 278, 282, 284, 288, 289, 292, 294n.127, 294n.129, 294n.130, 295, 303, 313n.19, 319-20n.33, 325n.44, 326n.48, 327,

Index of Modern Authors

compiled by K. Elliott

Index of Biblical and Extrabiblical Texts

compiled by K. Elliott